Introduction to

LEGAL STUDIES

FOURTH EDITION

edited by

Vincent Kazmierski
Jane Dickson-Gilmore
Betina Kuzmarov
Dawn Moore
Stephen Tasson

CANADIAN LEGAL STUDIES SERIES

Captus Press

Canadian Legal Studies Series
Introduction to Legal Studies, Fourth Edition

First Captus Press edition, 1990
Fourth edition, 2010

Captus Press Inc.
Units 14 & 15
1600 Steeles Avenue West
Concord, ON
L4K 4M2
Telephone: (416) 736–5537
Fax: (416) 736–5793
Email: Info@captus.com
Internet: http://www.captus.com

Library and Archives Canada Cataloguing in Publication

Introduction to legal Studies / edited by Vincent
Kazmierski ... [et al.]. — 4th ed.

(Canadian legal studies series)
Includes bibliographical references.
ISBN 978-1-55322-228-6

1. Law — Canada — Textbooks.   2. Sociological
jurisprudence — Canada — Textbooks. I. Kazmierski, Vincent
II. Series: Canadian legal studies series.

KE442.I57 2010   349.71   C2010–904061–9
KF385.A4I57 2010

Canada   *We acknowledge the financial support of the Government of Canada through the Book Publishing Industry Development Program (BPIDP) for our publishing activities.*

0 9 8 7 6 5 4 3 2 1
Printed and bound in Canada

Table of Contents

Preface xi

I

Law in Context

1 Social Context: Law in Social Life. 3

   (a) The Functions of Law
      Edward Adamson Hoebel 3

   (b) The Cheyenne Way
      Karl N. Llewellyn and E. Adamson Hoebel 6

   (c) Conflicts as Property
      Nils Christie. 8

2 Cultural Context: Legal Cultures in Canada 12

   (a) The Environment of Canada's Judicial System
      Peter H. Russell 12

   (b) By Reason of Authority or By Authority of Reason
      The Honourable Madame Justice Claire L'Heureux-Dubé 17

   (c) Societal Norms Offer a Frame of Reference
      Gérard Bouchard and Charles Taylor 22

   (d) Conceptions of History
      The Royal Commission on Aboriginal Peoples 27

3 Constitutional Context: Law, the State, and the Constitution 30

   (a) *Reference re Secession of Quebec* 30

   (b) *Roncarelli v. Duplessis* 34

   (c) *Reference re Firearms Act* (Can.) 40

4 Global Context: The Transnational Influence of Law 51

(a) Threat of NAFTA Case Kills Canada's MMT Ban
Shawn McCarthy 51

(b) Prosecuting Mass Rape: *Prosecutor v. Dragoljub Kunarac, Radomir Kovac
and Zoran Vukovic*
Doris Buss. 53

(c) *Baker v. Canada (Minister of Citizenship and Immigration)* 56

(d) Rethinking the Relationship Between International and Domestic Law
Armand de Mestral and Evan Fox-Decent 62

(e) *Abdelrazik v. Canada (Foreign Affairs)* 73

II

Looking at Law:
The Limits of Law and Legal Understanding

5 Law, Morality, and Justice 85

(a) Tragic Choices
Patrick J. Fitzgerald 85

(b) *R. v. Dudley & Stephens* 89

(c) Law and Morality
Lord Patrick Devlin. 92

(d) *R. v. Butler* 96

(e) *R. v. Latimer* 103

6 Law, Liberalism, and Critics 107

(a) *Christie v. York Corp.* 107

(b) *Delgamuukw v. B.C.* 111

(c) Women's Rights as Human Rights:
Toward a Re-Vision of Human Rights
Charlotte Bunch. 115

(d) Racially Based Jury Nullification:
Black Power in the Criminal Justice System
Paul Butler. 121

(e) Perpetuating the Cycle of Abuse: Feminist (Mis)use of
the Public/Private Dichotomy in the Case of Nixon v. Rape Relief
Ummni Khan. 130

(f) Toward a Political Economy of Law
Amy Bartholomew and Susan Boyd. 137

7 Connecting Law and Society. 141

(a) The New Legal Scholarship: Problems and Prospects
John Hagan. 141

(b) The Pedagogic Challenge
     Neil C. Sargent. 143
(c) How Does Law Matter in the Constitution of Legal Consciousness?
     David M. Engel 145

III

"Making Law":
Common Law and Legislation

8 Judicial Decisions and the Common Law 157
(a) Precedents, Statutes and Legal Reasoning
     F.L. Morton 157
(b) The Doctrine of Precedent
     Patrick Atiyah 160
(c) This Case System: Precedent
     Karl Llewellyn 162
(d) I Beg to Differ: Interdisciplinary Questions about
     Law, Language, and Dissent
     Marie-Claire Belleau and Rebecca Johnson 164

9 Interpreting Legislation 173
(a) *Re Rizzo & Rizzo Shoes Ltd.* 173
(b) *R. v. Mills* 179

IV

Law, the State, and Citizens

10 Citizenship: Who Belongs? Who Is Protected? 187
(a) *Henrietta Muir Edwards et al. v. Canada (A.G.)* 187
(b) Citizenship and Social Class
     T.H. Marshall 191
(c) Return of the Citizen: A Survey of Recent Work on Citizenship Theory
     Will Kymlicka and Wayne Norman 197
(d) The Exploitation of Vulnerability: Dimensions of Citizenship and
     Rightlessness in Canada's Security Certificate Legislation
     Christine Wilke and Paula Willis 203

11 Protecting Rights: Inside and Outside the Constitution 211
(a) The *Somerset* Case
     U.K. National Archive 211

(b) *Bliss v. Canada (Attorney General)* 213

(c) *Baker v. Canada (Minister of Citizenship and Immigration)* [Revisited] 217

(d) The Concept of Human Dignity
Pierre Elliott Trudeau 224

(e) The Legalisation of Politics in Advanced Capitalism:
The Canadian Charter of Rights and Freedoms
Harry J. Glasbeek and Michael Mandel 225

(f) Aboriginal Peoples and the Canadian Charter of Rights and Freedoms:
Contradictions and Challenges
Aki-Kwe/Mary Ellen Turpel 231

V

Law, Crime, and Social Order

12 What Is Crime? 243

(a) Law, State, and Class Struggle
Alan Hunt 243

(b) Theft of Time: Disciplining Through Science and Law
Laureen Snider 252

13 The Criminal Law Process 262

(a) The [Nova Scotia] Royal Commission on
the Donald Marshall, Jr., Prosecution
Royal Commission on the Donald Marshall, Jr., Prosecution 262

(b) Understanding Over-representation
Commission on Systemic Racism in the Ontario Criminal Justice System 264

(c) Crown Culture and Wrongful Convictions: A Beginning
Melvyn Green 270

(d) Is There a Place for the Victim in the Prosecution Process?
Patricia Clarke 276

(e) The Limits of Restorative Justice
Kathleen Daly 285

VI

Law, Economy, and Society

14 Regulating Relationships. 295

(a) Max Weber on Law and the Rise of Capitalism
David M. Trubek 295

(b) *Rudder v. Microsoft Corp.* 298

(c) *Donoghue v. Stevenson* 302

(d) *Childs v. Desormeaux* 305

(e) *Pettkus v. Becker* 310

15 Emerging Challenges for Legal Regulation 315

(a) Regulability of the Cyberspace
Lawrence Lessig 315

(b) Law, Cyberspace and the Role of Nation States
Michael Mac Neil 316

(c) The Strange Return of *Gyges' Ring*: An Introduction
Ian Kerr, Valerie Steeves, and Carole Lucock 319

VII

Dispute Resolution

16 Negotiating and Bargaining 327

(a) Non-Contractual Relationships in Business: A Preliminary Study
Stewart Macaulay 327

(b) Bargaining in the Shadow of the Law: The Case of Divorce
Robert H. Mnookin 332

17 Adjudication 341

(a) The Judge and the Adversary System
Neil Brooks 341

(b) 'Fight' Theory vs. 'Truth' Theory
Judge Jerome Frank 353

(c) Lawyer — Manufacturer — Painter
Franz Kafka 356

(d) Inquiry into Forensic Pathology in Ontario — Executive Summary
Honourable Stephen T. Goudge 361

18 Alternatives to Adjudication/Alternatives within Adjudication 367

(a) The Mediator and the Judge
Torstein Eckhoff 367

(b) Civil Justice Reform and Mandatory Civil Mediation in Saskatchewan:
Lessons from a Maturing Program
Julie Macfarlane and Michaela Keet 372

(c) Translating Justice and Therapy: *The Drug Treatment Court Networks*
Dawn Moore 384

(d) Collaborative Family Law and Gender Inequalities:
Balancing Risks and Opportunities
Wanda Wiegers & Michaela Keet 393

19 The Debate over Use of Settlement-based Dispute
Resolution Processes 402

   (a) Against Settlement
       Owen M. Fiss 402

   (b) For Reconciliation
       Andrew W. McThenia and Thomas L. Shaffer 407

   (c) Understanding the Critiques of Mediation:
       What Is All the Fuss About?
       Neil Sargent 410

VIII

Access to Justice

20 Access to Justice: Income Issues 415

   (a) Legal Services and the Poor
       R.J. Gathercole 415

   (b) Small Claims Courts: A Review
       Iain Ramsay 422

21 Access to Justice: Procedural Issues 426

   (a) The Challenges We Face
       Right Honourable Beverley McLachlin, P.C. 426

   (b) Civil Justice Reform — The Toronto Experience
       The Honourable Warren K. Winkler, Chief Justice of Ontario 429

   (c) Access to *Charter* Justice and the Rule of Law
       Carissima Mathen. 438

   (d) Legal Victory Still Leaves Rosa Becker Out in Cold
       William Marsden 443

IX

The Personnel of Law

22 Lawyers, Advocates, and Legal Practice 449

   (a) Legal Education as Training for Hierarchy
       Duncan Kennedy 449

   (b) Canadian Legal Ethics: Ready for the Twenty-First Century at Last
       Adam M. Dodek 453

   (c) Who is Afraid of the Big Bad Social Constructionists? Or Shedding Light
       on the Unpardonable Whiteness of the Canadian Legal Profession
       Charles C. Smith 456

(d) The Retention of Women in Private Practice Working Group Report
— Executive Summary
The Law Society of Upper Canada 462

(e) Specialization and the Legal Profession
Alvin Esau 465

(f) Styles of Legal Work
Edwin M. Schur 472

(g) Will the Law Society of Alberta Celebrate its Bicentenary?
Harry W. Arthurs 476

(h) Implementation of Paralegal Regulation in Ontario — Introduction
The Law Society of Upper Canada 482

23 Juries **488**

(a) Justice and the Jury
W. Neil Brooks and Anthony N. Doob 488

(b) *Morgentaler, Smoling and Scott* v. *The Queen* 493

(c) *R. v. Williams* 495

24 Judges **501**

(a) Embracing Change: How NJI Adapts to the Changing
Role of the Judge
Honourable Justice C. Adèle Kent 501

(b) The Meaning and Scope of Judicial Independence
Bora Laskin 503

(c) Antonio Lamer: Should Judges Hold Their Tongues?
Antonio Lamer 506

(d) Will Women Judges Really Make a Difference?
Justice Bertha Wilson 507

(e) *R. v. S. (R.D.)* 514

(f) Gavels, Microphones Don't Mix
The Globe and Mail Editorial 519

(g) *Re Conduct of Honourable Paul Cosgrove of
the Ontario Superior Court of Justice
Canadian Judicial Council.* 520

(h) Stupid Judge Tricks
Sandra Martin 528

25 Law Enforcement Personnel **531**

(a) Plural Policing: A Comparative Perspective — Canada
George S. Rigakos and Cherie Leung. 531

(b) Police Investigating Police — Executive Summary
Commission for Public Complaints Against the RCMP. 537

(c) *Doe v. Metropolitan Toronto (Municipality) Commissioners of Police* 545

X

Law and Social Transformation

26 The Charter of Rights and Social Change 553

   (a) Ardour in the Court
      Rainer Knopff and F.L. Morton 553

   (b) The Case for a Strong Court
      Judge Rosalie Abella 554

   (c) Screening Desire: Same-Sex-Marriage Documentaries, Citizenship,
      and the Law
      B.J. Wray 556

   (d) Beyond Self-congratulation: The *Charter* at 25 in
      an International Perspective
      Louise Arbour and Fannie Lafontaine 563

27 Critical Perspectives on the Role of Law
As an Agent of Change 572

   (a) In Memoriam: The Law Commission of Canada, 1997–2006
      Nathalie Des Rosiers 572

   (b) The Role of Law in Social Transformation:
      Is a Jurisprudence of Insurgency Possible?
      Stephen Brickey and Elizabeth Comack 579

   (c) Structure: The Mosaic of Dominion
      Samuel Bowles and Herbert Gintis. 587

   (d) Introduction: The Healing Dimension of Restorative Justice
      — A one-world body
      Dennis Sullivan and Larry Tifft 590

   (e) Postapartheid Justice: Can Cosmopolitanism and
      Nation-Building Be Reconciled?
      Rosemary Nagy 594

Preface

Introduction to Legal Studies has been designed as a course-book to support a full-year introductory course to the field of Legal Studies. Like its three predecessors, this fourth edition of the book is structured to reflect the diversity of approaches and perspectives employed within Legal Studies. At the same time, the course-book and the field of study are unified by an underlying theme that "law" cannot be understood simply as a set of formal rules, processes and institutions. Rather, law must be understood in its wider context, including the dynamic symbiosis that exists between the law, legal processes, and the political, cultural, social and economic forces that exist within society. Thus, any study of law must engage law critically, rather than accept without question its rules, processes and institutions as fixed or given. For this reason, most of the material in this reader engages in critical reflection on the role, operation and purpose of law, rather than providing descriptions or narrow explanations of the law. Readers may find that this course-book is usefully paired with a basic introductory text that outlines the pragmatic form and structure of the law, legal process, and system.

Many of the articles included in *Introduction to Legal Studies*, 4th ed. raise complex arguments that first-year university students may initially find difficult to fully appreciate. They are included to challenge students academically and conceptually, and to acquaint students with some of the broader debates in the field. It is our hope that the materials included in the course-book will encourage students to read and think more broadly and critically not only about what law is, but about its role and function in a wide range of societies.

This fourth edition of *Introduction to Legal Studies* builds upon the work of the many faculty members of the Department of Law at Carleton University who contributed to the previous editions. Previous editors who provided advice on the design of the current edition include Logan Atkinson, Neil Sargent, Peter Swan, and Barry Wright. Additional suggestions were also provided by Rueban Balasubramaniam, Lynn Campbell, Brettel Dawson, David Elliott, Sheryl Hamilton, Cheryl Picard, Rosemary Warskett, and Diana Young. The editors also wish to acknowledge the contributions of current faculty members who agreed to have their articles included in the course-book: Amy Bartholomew, Doris Buss, Alan Hunt, Ummni Khan, Michael MacNeil, Rosemary Nagy (adjunct professor), George Rigakos, Neil Sargent, and Christiane Wilke. Finally, the editors were greatly aided by research assistance provided by Gemma Rench and Alison Ronson. Our thanks to you all.

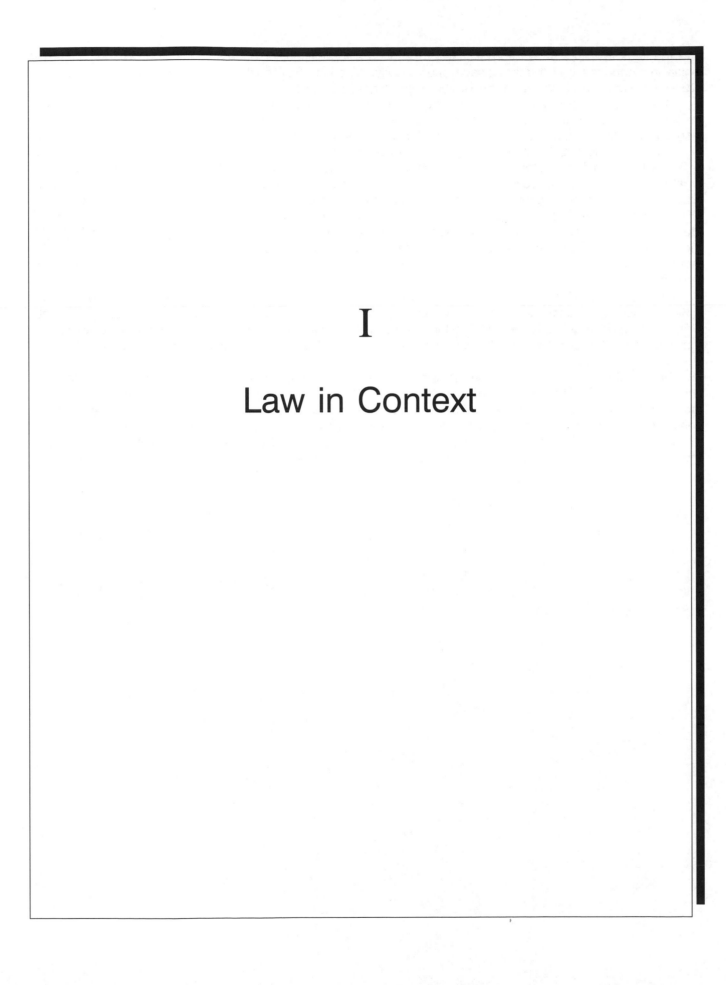

I

Law in Context

The readings in Part I have been selected to provide a foundation for understanding the broader context in which law operates both within Canada and globally. As such, they touch on both the role that law plays in organizing social behaviour and the way in which legal rules and institutions are themselves organized.

Chapter 1 includes readings that identify different social functions that law fulfills, including serving as a mechanism that facilitates social control, dispute resolution and social change. However, these readings also suggest that formal legal rules are not the only way in which these functions may be fulfilled, and that in some cases formal legal rules may inhibit desirable social interactions.

The readings in Chapter 2 outline a number of different legal cultures that have shaped the Canadian legal system. These legal cultures include the common law and civil law traditions imported from the United Kingdom and France, respectively. The readings explore the ways in which these legal traditions have shaped the Canadian legal system while also being influenced, shaped and modified by domestic political, ideological and social conditions. The excerpt from the Royal Commission on Aboriginal Peoples highlights the fact that aboriginal peoples had their own legal, cultural and political traditions prior to colonization — a fact that has often been ignored or dismissed by Canadian governments in their relationship with aboriginal peoples.

Chapter 3 includes excerpts from a number of important decisions of the Supreme Court of Canada, which identify the constitutional principles and rules that establish the framework for the Canadian state. This framework regulates the relationship between the different levels of government in Canada and between the different branches of government. It also regulates the relationship between the state and individuals and groups.

Finally, Chapter 4 includes a number of articles that explore the role of law within a global context. Understanding the global context of law requires familiarity with the operation of rules of international law, including the way in which formal treaties and covenants may impact the actions of states in the international arena. However, it also requires an understanding of how international law may impact the creation, interpretation and application of domestic legal rules. The readings in this final chapter explore and question the relationship between international and domestic legal rules and institutions.

1 Social Context: Law in Social Life

(a) The Functions of Law†

Edward Adamson Hoebel

Law performs certain functions essential to the maintenance of all but the most simple societies.

The first is to define relationships among the members of a society, to assert what activities are permitted and what are ruled out, so as to maintain at least minimal integration between the activities of individuals and groups within the society.

The second is derived from the necessity of taming naked force and directing force to the maintenance of order. It is the allocation of authority and the determination of who may exercise physical coercion as a socially recognized privilege-right, along with the selection of the most effective forms of physical sanction to achieve the social ends that the law serves.

The third is the disposition of trouble cases as they arise.

The fourth is to redefine relations between individuals and groups as the conditions of life change. It is to maintain adaptability.

Purposive definition of personal relations is the primary law-job. Other aspects of culture likewise work to this end, and, indeed, the law derives its working principles (jural postulates) from postulates previously developed in the nonlegal spheres of action. However, the law's important contribution to the basic organization of society as a whole is that the law specifically and explicitly defines relations. It sets the expectancies of man to man and group to group so that each knows the focus and the limitations of its demand-rights on others, its duties to others, its privilege-rights and powers as against others, and its immunities and liabilities to the contemplated or attempted acts of others. This is the "bare-bones job", as Karl Llewellyn likes to call it. It is the ordering of the fundamentals of living together.

No culture has a specific starting point in time; yet in the operation of the first function it is as though men were getting together and saying to each other. "Look here! Let's have a little organization here or we'll never get anywhere with this mess! Let's have a clear understanding of who's who, what we are to do, and how we are going to do it!" In its essence it is what the social-contract theorists recognized as the foundation of social order.

The second function of the law — the allocation of authority to exercise coercive physical force — is something almost peculiar to things legal.

Custom has regularity, and so does law. Custom defines relationships, and so does law. Custom is sanctioned, and so is law. But the sanctions of law may involve physical coercion. Law is distinguished from mere customs in that it endows certain selected individuals with the privilege-right of applying the sanction of physical coercion, if need be. The legal, let it be repeated, has teeth that can bite. But the biting, if it is to be legal and not mere gangsterism, can be done only by those persons to whom the law

† "The Functions of Law", reprinted by permission of the publisher from THE LAW OF PRIMITIVE MAN: A STUDY IN COMPARATIVE LEGAL DYNAMICS by E. Adamson Hoebel, pp. 275–284, 287. Cambridge, Mass.: Harvard University Press. Copyright © 1954 by the President and Fellows of Harvard College. Copyright c renewed 1982 by Edward Adamson Hoebel. [Notes and/of references omitted.]

has allocated the privilege-right for the affair at hand.

We have seen that in primitive law authority is a shifting, temporary thing. Authority to enforce a norm resides (for private wrongs) with the wronged individual and his immediate kinsmen — but only for the duration of time necessary to follow through the procedural steps that lead to redress or punishment of the culprit. In primitive law the tendency is to allocate authority to the party who is directly injured. This is done in part out of convenience, for it is easier to let the wronged party assume the responsibility of legal action. It is also done because the primitive kinship group, having a more vital sense of entity, is naturally charged with a heavier emotional effect. In any event, when the community qua community acknowledges the exercise of force by a wronged person or his kinship group as correct and proper in a given situation, and so restrains the wrongdoer from striking back, then law prevails and order triumphs over violence.

We have also found in our studies of primitive societies that in a limited number of situations authority is directly exercised by the community on its own behalf. It takes the form of lynch law in some instances where clear procedures have not been set up in advance, as in the Comanche treatment of excessive sorcery and Shoshone treatment of cannibalism. Lynch law among primitives, however, is not a backsliding from, or detouring around, established formal law as it is with us. It is a first fitful step toward the emergence of criminal law in a situation in which the exercise of legal power has not yet been refined and allocated to specific persons. It is a blunt crude tool wielded by the gang hand of an outraged public.

Yet lynch law is rare among primitives. Even the simplest of them have crystallized standards as to what constitutes criminal behaviour, and the exercise of public authority is delegated to official functionaries — the chieftain, the council of chiefs, and the council of elders.

Power may sometimes be personal, as is the power of the bully in the society of small boys, and as was to some extent the power of William the Conqueror. But personal tyranny is a rare thing among primitives. Brute force of the individual does not prevail. Chiefs must have followers. Followers always impose limitations on their leaders. Enduring power is always institutionalized power. It is *transpersonalized*. It resides in the office, in the social status, rather than in the man. The constitutional structures of the several tribes examined in this book have all

clearly revealed how political and legal authority are in each instance delimited and circumscribed.

This point is emphasized only to dispel any residue of the hoary political philosophies that assumed without basis in fact that primitive societies existed under the rule of fang and claw.

However, the personal still obtrudes. An "office" although culturally defined is, after all, exercised by an individual. And who that individual is at any moment certainly makes a difference. There is leeway in the exercise or non-exercise of power just as there are limits. A man may be skilled in finding the evidence and the truth in the cases he must judge and in formulating the norms to fit the case in hand — or he may be all thumbs. He may be one who thirsts for power and who will wield all he can while grasping for more. Or he may shrink from it. Power defined through allocation of legal authority is by its nature trans-personalized, yet by the nature of men it can never be wholly depersonalized. A Franklin Roosevelt is not a Warren Harding....

The third function of law calls for little additional comment.... Some trouble cases pose absolutely new problems for solution. In these cases the first and second functions may predominate. Yet this is not the situation in the instance of most legal clashes in which the problem is not the formulation of law to cover a new situation but rather the application of pre-existing law. These cases are disposed of in accordance with legal norms already set before the issue in question arises. The job is to clean the case up, to suppress or penalize the illegal behaviour and to bring the relations of the disputants back into balance, so that life may resume its normal course. This type of law-work has frequently been compared to work of the medical practitioner. It is family doctor stuff, essential to keeping the social body on its feet. In more homely terms, Llewellyn has called it, "garage-repair work on the general order of the group when that general order misses fire, or grinds gears, or even threatens a total breakdown." It is not ordinarily concerned with grand design, as is the first law-job. Nor is it concerned with redesign as is the fourth. It works to clean up all the little social messes (and the occasional big ones) that recurrently arise between the members of the society from day to day.

Most of the trouble cases do not, in a civilized society, of themselves loom large on the social scene, although in a small community even one can lead directly to a social explosion if not successfully cleaned up. Indeed, in a primitive society the individual case always holds the threat of a little civil war if procedure breaks down, for from its inception it sets kin group against kin group — and if it comes to fighting, the number of kinsmen who will be involved is almost always immediately enlarged. The fight may engulf a large part of the tribe in internecine throat-cutting. Relatively speaking, each run-of-the-mill trouble case in primitive law imposes a more pressing demand for settlement upon the legal system than is the case with us.

While system and integration are essential, flexibility and constant revision are no less so. Law is a dynamic process in which few solutions can be permanent. Hence, the fourth function of law: the redefinition of relations and the reorientation of expectancies.

Initiative with scope to work means new problems for the law. New inventions, new ideas, new behaviours keep creeping in. Especially do new behaviours creep in, nay, sweep in, when two unlike societies come newly into close contact. Then the law is called upon to decide what principles shall be applied to conflicts of claims rooted in disparate cultures. Do the new claims fit comfortably to the old postulates? Must the new realized ways of behaving be wholly rejected and legally suppressed because they are out of harmony with the old values? Or can they be modified here and altered there to gain legal acceptance? Or can the more difficult operations of altering or even junking old postulates to accommodate a new way be faced? Or can fictions be framed that can lull the mind into acceptance of the disparate new without the wrench of acknowledged junking of the old? What *is* that is wanted? The known and habitual, or the promise of the new and untested? Men may neglect to turn the law to the answer of such questions. But they do not for long. Trouble cases generated by the new keep marching in. And the fourth law-job presses for attention.

Recapitulation of just one Cheyenne case will throw the process into focus. The acquisition of horses greatly altered all Plains Indian cultures. One important Cheyenne basic postulate ran, "Except for land and tribal fetishes, all material goods are private property, but they should be generously shared with others." When it came to horses, this led some men to expect that they could freely borrow horses without even the courtesy of asking. For horse owners this got to the point of becoming a serious nuisance, as in the cases of Pawnee and Wolf Lies Down. Wolf Lies Down put his trouble case to the members of the Elk Soldier Society. They got his horse back for him with a handsome free-will offering of additional "damages" from the defendant to boot. The trouble case was neatly disposed of.

But the Elk Soldiers did not stop there. There was some preventive channeling of future behaviour to be done. Hence the "Now we shall make a new rule. There shall be no more borrowing of horses without asking. If any man takes another's goods without asking, we will go over and get them back for him. More than that, if the taker tries to keep them, we will give him a whipping." Here was the fourth function of law being performed. The lines for future conduct re horses were made clear.

Work under Function IV represents social planning brought into focus by the case of the instant and with an eye to the future.

The problem of reorienting conduct and redirecting it through the law when new issues emerge is always tied to the bare-bones demand of basic organization and the minimal maintenance of order and regularity. It may also shade over into work colored by a greater or lesser desire to achieve more than a minimum of smoothness in social relations. When this becomes an important aspect of law-work, a special aspect of law-ways activity may be recognized: the creation of techniques that efficiently and effectively solve the problems posed to all the other law-jobs so that the basic values of the society are realized through the law and not frustrated by it.

The doing of it has been called by Llewellyn "Juristic Method". It is the method not only of getting the law-jobs done but doing them with a sure touch for the net effect that results in smoothness in the doing and a harmonious wedding of what is aspired to by men and what is achieved through the law. It is the work not just of the craftsman but of the master craftsman....

. . . .

The very fact that the bulk of the substance and procedure of primitive law emerges through case action involving claim and counterclaim, pleading and counterpleading, tends to keep legal behaviour relatively close to the prevailing social values. Which way a new issue will go will depend not alone upon the facts but also upon the skill of the litigants in framing the issue and arguing the relevance of their respective positions to the prevailing social ideas of right conduct and group well-being — or upon persuasiveness in argument that a new orientation of values is in order to meet changed conditions, even though the tough man and his kinsman, though "wrong," may sometimes make his position stick with naked force. Thus, the wise claimant argues his case not in terms of "this is good for me" but rather by maintaining "this is what we all want and should do". If he is a primitive advocate, it is more likely than not that he will also insist, if he can, that this is the way it has been from time immemorial. But the past certainly has no inflexible grip on primitive law.

Fiction is one of the great devices of juristic method by means of which men fit new legal norms into old principles so as to reorient conduct without the need to junk long-standing postulates. Except for the universal practice of adoption, whereby outsiders are identified as *if* they are actually kinsmen, primitive men do not have to rely too heavily on the subterfuge of fiction to achieve legal change. Nevertheless, when the need is there many tribes have had recourse to its use.

An outstanding example may be found in adoptive marriage among the patrilineal groups of Indonesia. The important value for these people is to maintain the unbroken continuity of the paternal lineage. To do this, a family without sons adopts their daughter's husband as a "son" with the effect that her children remain within their clan and their inheritance will remain within their line. ...

. . . .

When the law-jobs get done, these norms inevitably become the common denominator of legal culture. But the functions of law, whatever the norms they may give rise to in any particular society, are what constitute the crucial universal elements of the law. Any one or half-hundred societies may select one rule of law and not another — the range is wide — but none can ignore the law-jobs. In the last analysis, that the law-jobs get done is more important than how they are done. Their minimal doing is an imperative of social existence. Their doing with juristic finesse is an achievement of high skill.

(b)   The Cheyenne Way†

Karl N. Llewellyn and E. Adamson Hoebel

A war party of eight Cheyennes, on its way south to take horses from the Kiowas, Comanches, or Apaches, was stopping at a large Arapaho camp. At the same time some Apaches came to visit Bull, an Arapaho leader. The Apaches told their host that the Kiowas and Comanches were seeking peace with the Arapahoes and Cheyennes. Bull took the opportunity to bring the eight Cheyennes together with the Apaches in his tipi; he filled his pipe and offered the smoke. The Cheyennes declined, Seven Bulls, the leader of the war party saying, "Friend, you know that we are not chiefs. We cannot smoke with these men, nor make peace with them. We have no authority; we can only carry the message. I have listened to what you say and tomorrow with my party I will start back [He has authority to call off his own raid.] to our Cheyenne village, and I will carry this word to the chiefs. It is for them to decide what must be done. We are young men and cannot say anything, but we will take your message back to the chiefs."

When Seven Bulls reached the Cheyenne camp with his companions, he told of the Kiowa-Comanche proposition. That night a crier went about the camp calling for the chiefs to convene the next day. The big double-sized chiefs' lodge was pitched and early the next morning the chiefs all gathered there. Seven Bulls and his companions were sent for to deliver their message officially. The proposal was then on the floor.

After the first speakers had sat down, it was evident that there was no ready agreement at hand within the Council, so the proposition was made and accepted that the Dog Soldier Society should be asked to render a decision to the Council on the question.

High Backed Wolf, who was the directing head chief of the Council, sent one of the door-servants to bring in White Antelope and Little Old Man, the bravest chiefs of the Dog Soldier Society. When these two had been greeted in the chiefs' lodge, High Backed Wolf told them about the order of business, describing to them

---

† From *The Cheyenne Way: Conflict and Case Law in Primitive Jurisprudence* by Karl N. Llewellyn & E. Adamson Hoebel, pp. 91–94, 127–28. Oklahoma: University of Oklahoma Press. Copyright © 1941 by the University of Oklahoma Press. All rights reserved.

the state of opinion in the Council. "Now, my friends," he concluded, "you go and assemble your Dog Soldiers. Tell them about this matter and talk it over among them. Let us know what you think of it. Tell us what you think is best to be done."

When the Dog Soldiers had assembled, White Antelope laid the problem before them. "The chiefs are leaving this matter to us," he told his followers, "because we are the strongest of the military groups. It is my own thought that our chiefs are in favor of making peace. What do you all think about it?"

Said another of the Dog Soldier chiefs, "I think it best to leave the decision to you two, White Antelope and Little Old Man. Whatever you say will please us all." All the Dogs agreed to this with one assent.

The two men accepted it and declared for peace. Leaving their troop, they went back to where the Council was waiting for them, to tell the Council that they would make peace with the enemies. The chiefs all stood up at this and gladly said, "Thank you, thank you, Dog Soldiers."[20]

The procedure which has just been described is a typical handling of an important situation in the Cheyenne manner. The proposition, the reader will realize, was no simple one. The Cheyenne had become dependent upon the horse, and any warrior's path to glory and wealth lay most easily and quickly in raids upon the rich horse herders of the south, these same Kiowas and Comanches. Acceptance of the proposal meant that the young men would be blocked in one of their main and favorite avenues of activity. Hostility with the Kiowas and Comanches had been unceasing for at least half a century. The alternative values to the Cheyennes are not clear to us, unless they lay in some scheme for trading horses, on which we lack information. The soldier interest in the case is obvious; no less obvious is the fact that it had the favorable aspect of coinciding with the interests of the whole Cheyenne tribe. In the light of this one understands the diplomatic reluctance of the Council of Forty-Four to reach a decision by themselves. So smooth a delegation of an important decision, inverting the pyramid without any bickering, yet with the machinery at all points for the sensing of opinion in widening representative groups, is an act of social beauty. From the Council to the Dog Men, from the Dog Men to their two most outstanding warriors, to a momentous decision binding on the entire tribe! Nevertheless, the Council at no time gave up its authority; the decision, be it noted, was reported for announcement back to the Council, which then discharged the Dog Soldiers

with thanks. This is also a superb face-producing, as well as face-saving, procedure. The actual announcement of the decision for peace was made to the camp at large by the head priest-chief himself.

Such interaction between the Council and the military societies was not unusual; rather, whenever there was an important problem of tribal policy (new policy in general or in particular) to be decided, it was the ordinary thing to see the chiefs' and the soldiers' messengers moving back and forth between the meeting lodges, sensing, reporting, and subtly influencing the state of both "expert" and "lay" opinion until the decision was accomplished. In this way, the legislative knot was cut without resort to dictatorship or friction.

But what happened when there was an irreconcilable opposition within the body politic? Then the governmental authority could act with force. It acted also with tact. It moved sometimes in involution. Power was present, form was not always achieved. Note, however, the Cheyenne drive for form, if repetition of situation makes it possible, if time serves, if dramatic urge finds — even for a sole occasion — an inventive voice. Seven Bulls was called on for an "official" presentation of a proposal the camp had buzzed with for a night. Little Wolf was "required" to be present. Compare the careful staging of Pawnee's rehabilitation. It is not too much to argue that *drama* is a vital *line* of reconciliation hit on by the Cheyennes, between their urge toward form (pattern, ritual) and their urge toward individualizing self-glorification. If this be sound, it suggests a relation between aesthetic balance and soundness of working institution, or of the individual's work in and with an institution, which deserves inquiry.

. . . .

While Wolf Lies Down was away, a friend took one of his horses to ride to war. This man had brought his bow and arrow and left them in the lodge of the horse's owner. When Wolf Lies Down returned, he knew by this token security who had his horse, so he said nothing.

A year passed without the horse's return, and then Wolf Lies Down invited the Elk Soldier chiefs to his lodge, because he was in their society. "There is this thing," he told them. "My friend borrowed my horse, leaving his bow and arrow; there they are yet. Now I want to know what to do. I want you to tell me the right thing. Will you go over and ask him his intentions?"

The borrower was in another camp well distant, yet the chiefs agreed. "We'll send a man to bring him in, get his word, or receive his presents," they promised.

The camp moved while the messenger was gone, but he knew of course where it would be on his return. The soldier returned with the borrower, who was leading two horses, "one spotted, one ear-tipped." He called for the four Elk chiefs on his arrival. The chiefs laid before him the story told by Wolf Lies Down.

"That is true," the man assented. "My friend is right. I left my bow and arrow here. I intended to return his horse, but I was gone longer than I expected. I have had good luck with that horse, though. I have treated it better than my own. However, when I got back to camp I found my folks there. Our camps were far apart and I just could not get away. I was waiting for his camp and mine to come together. Now, I always intended to do the right thing. I have brought two good horses with me. My friend can have his choice. In addition I give his own horse back, and further, I am leaving my bow and arrow."

Then up spoke Wolf Lies Down, "I am glad to hear my friend say these things. Now I feel better. I shall take one of those horses, but I am giving him that one he borrowed to keep. From now on we shall be bosom friends."

The chiefs declared, "Now we have settled this thing. Our man is a bosom friend of this man. Let it be that way among all of us. Our society and his shall be comrades. Whenever one of us has a present to give, we shall give it to a member of his soldier society.

"Now we shall make a new rule. There shall be no more borrowing of horses without asking. If any man takes another's goods without asking, we will go over and get them back for him. More than that, if the taker tries to keep them, we will give him a whipping."

Thus was a situation fraught with possible friction brought to an amicable close through the good offices of the chiefs of the society of an aggrieved member.

Far more important, however, was the crystallization of a new social policy, the formulation of a law making it a crime henceforth to borrow an owner's horse without his expressed permission. The old custom of free utilization of another's goods, providing one left an identifying "security," was apparently creating friction as it came to be applied to horses. What between good friends could develop into a tense situation — as evidenced here by the resort to soldier chiefs as spokesmen of inquiry — could become immediately and actively disruptive if the concept "friend" were loosely interpreted by a borrower, or the horse not cared for, or if the unnotified borrowing broke in upon the owner's plans, or one owner became the recipient of too many such evidences of friendship. Pawnee's case of horse "borrowing" and its punishment (CASE 2) shows the degree of social irresponsibility which the older practice, left unguarded, could engender. Black Wolf stated that the soldiers, and even the tribal chiefs, had been for some time talking about means of putting a stop to the practice. The Elk Soldier chiefs on this occasion took the opportunity to make the step. After declaring the case at hand settled, they moved into general policy. They did not mix the two. Note also, as a soldier society moves into the very unfamiliar matter of legislation, their sound technical attention to what they shall do, if....

(c)   Conflicts as Property†

Nils Christie

Abstract
Conflicts are seen as important elements in society. Highly industrialised societies do not have too much internal conflict, they have too little. We have to organise social systems so that conflicts are both nurtured and made visible, and also see to it that professionals do not monopolize the handling of them. Victims of crime have in particular lost their rights to participate. A court procedure that restores the participants' rights to their own conflicts is outlined.

† From The British Journal of Criminology, January 1977, vol. 17 at 1–5. Reproduced with permission of Oxford University Press. [Notes and/or references omitted.]

INTRODUCTION

Maybe we should not have any criminology. Maybe we should rather abolish institutes, not open them. Maybe the social consequences of criminology are more dubious than we like to think.

I think they are. And I think this relates to my topic. Conflicts as property. My suspicion is that criminology to some extent has amplified a process where conflicts have been taken away from the directly involved parties and thereby either disappeared or have become other people's property. In both cases a deplorable outcome. Conflicts ought to be used, not only left in erosion. And they ought to be used, and become useful, for those originally involved in the conflict. Conflicts *might* hurt individuals as well as social systems. That is what we learn in school. That is why we have officials. Without them, private vengeance and vendettas will blossom. We have learned this so solidly that we have lost track of the other side of the coin: our industrialised large-scale society is not one with too many internal conflicts. It is one with too little. Conflict might kill, but too little of it might paralyze. I will use this occasion to give a sketch of this situation. It can't be more than a sketch. This paper represents the beginning of the development of some ideas, not the polished end product.

ON HAPPENINGS AND NON-HAPPENINGS

Let us take our point of departure far away. Let us move to Tanzania. Let us approach our problem from the sunny hillside of the Arusha province. Here, inside a relatively large house in a very small village, a sort of happening took place. The house was overcrowded. Most grown-ups from the village and several from adjoining ones were there. It was a happy happening; fast talking, jokes, smiles, eager attention, not a sentence was to be lost. It was circus, it was drama. It was a court case.

The conflict this time was between a man and a woman. They had been engaged. He had invested a lot in the relationship through a long period, until she broke it off. Now he wanted it back. Gold and silver and money were easily decided on, but what about utilities already worn, and what about general expenses?

The outcome is of no interest in our context. But the framework for conflict solution is. Five elements ought to be particularly mentioned:

1. The parties, the former lovers, were in *the centre* of the room and in the centre of everyone's attention. They talked often and were eagerly listened to.

2. Close to them were relatives and friends who also took part. But they did not *take over*.

3. There was also participation from the general audience with short questions, information, or jokes.

4. The judges, three local party secretaries, were extremely inactive. They were obviously ignorant with regard to village matters. All the other people in the room were experts. They were experts on norms as well as actions. And they crystallized norms and clarified what had happened through participation in the procedure.

5. No reporters attended. They were all there.

My personal knowledge when it comes to British courts is limited indeed. I have some vague memories of juvenile courts, where I counted some 15 to 20 persons present, mostly social workers using the room for preparatory work or small conferences. A child or a young person must have attended, but except for the judge, or maybe it was the clerk, nobody seemed to pay any particular attention. The child or young person was most probably utterly confused as to who was who and for what, a fact confirmed in a small study by Peter Scott (1959). In the USA, Martha Baum (1968) has made similar observations. Recently, Bottoms and McClean (1976) have added another important observation: "There is one truth which is seldom revealed in the literature of the law or in studies of the administration of criminal justice. It is a truth which was made evident to all those involved in this research project as they sat through the cases which made up our sample. The truth is that, for the most part, the business of the criminal courts is dull, commonplace, ordinary and after a while downright tedious."

But let me keep quiet about your system, and instead concentrate on my own. And let me assure you: what goes on is no happening. It is all a negation of the Tanzanian case. What is striking in nearly all the Scandinavian cases is the greyness, the dullness, and the lack of any important audience. Courts are not central elements in the daily life of our citizens, but peripheral in four major ways:

1. They are situated in the administrative centre of the towns, outside the territories of ordinary people.

2. Within these centres they are often centralised within one or two large buildings of considerable complexity. Lawyers often complain that

9

they need months to find their way within these buildings. It does not demand much fantasy to imagine the situation of parties or public when they are trapped within these structures. A comparative study of court architecture might become equally relevant for the sociology of law as Oscar Newman's (1972) study of defensible space is for criminology. But even without any study, I feel it safe to say that both physical situation and architectural design are strong indicators that courts in Scandinavia belong to the administrators of law.

3. This impression is strengthened when you enter the courtroom itself — if you are lucky enough to find your way to it. Here again, the periphery of the parties is the striking observation. The parties are represented, and it is these representatives and the judge or judges who express the little activity that is activated within these rooms. Honoré Daumier's famous drawings from the courts are as representative for Scandinavia as they are for France.

   There are variations. In the small cities, or in the countryside, the courts are more easily reached than in the larger towns. And at the very lowest end of the court system — the so-called arbitration boards — the parties are sometimes less heavily represented through experts in law. But the symbol of the whole system is the Supreme Court where the directly involved parties do not even attend their own court cases.

4. I have not yet made any distinction between civil and criminal conflicts. But it was not by chance that the Tanzania case was a civil one. Full participation in your own conflict presupposes elements of civil law. The key element in a criminal proceeding is that the proceeding is converted from something between the concrete parties and into a conflict between one of the parties and the State. So, in a modern criminal trial, two important things have happened. First: the parties are being *represented*. Secondly: the one party that is represented by the State, namely the victim, is so thoroughly represented that she or he for most of the proceedings is pushed completely out of the arena, reduced to the triggerer-off of the whole thing. She or he is a sort of double loser. First vis-à-vis the offender, but secondly and often more cripplingly by being denied rights to full participation in what might have been one of the more important ritual encounters in life. The victim has lost its case to the State.

Professional Thieves

As we all know, there are many honourable as well as dishonourable reasons behind this development. The honourable ones have to do with the State's need for conflict reduction and certainly also its wishes for the protection of the victim. It is rather obvious. So is also the less honourable temptation for the State, or Emperor, or whoever is in power, to use the criminal case for personal gain. Offenders might pay for their sins. Authorities have back in time shown considerable willingness in representing the victim as receivers of the money or other property from the offender. Those days are gone. The crime control system is not run by profit. But they are also not gone. There are, in all banality, many interests at stake here, most of them related to professionalisation.

Lawyers are particularly good at stealing conflicts. They are trained for it. They are trained to prevent and solve conflicts. They are socialised into a sub-culture with a surprisingly high agreement concerning interpretation of norms, and regarding what sort of information can be accepted as relevant in each case. Many among us have, as laymen, experienced the sad moments of truth when our lawyers tell us that our best arguments in our fight against our neighbour are without any legal relevance whatsoever and that we for God's sake ought to keep quiet about them in court. Instead they pick out arguments we might find irrelevant or even wrong to use. My favourite example took place just after the war. One of my country's absolutely top defenders told with pride how he had just rescued a poor client. The client had collaborated with the Germans. The prosecutor claimed that the client had been one of the key people in the organisation of the Nazi movement. He had been one of the master-minds behind it all. The defender, however, saved his client. He saved him by pointing out to the jury how weak, how lacking in ability, how obviously deficient his client was, socially as well as organisationally. His client could simply not have been one of the organisers among the collaborators. He was without talents. And he won his case. His client got a very minor sentence as a very minor figure. The defender ended his story by telling me — with some indignation — that neither the accused, nor his wife, had ever thanked him, they had not even talked to him afterwards.

Conflicts become the property of lawyers. But lawyers don't hide that it is conflicts they handle. And the organisational framework of the courts underlines this point. The opposing parties, the judge, the ban against privileged communication within the court system, the lack of encouragement for specialisation — specialists cannot be internally controlled — it all underlines that this is an organisation for the handling of conflicts. *Treatment personnel* are in another position. They are more interested in *converting the image of the case from one of conflict into one of non-conflict*. The basic model of healers is not one of opposing parties, but one where one party has to be helped in the direction of one generally accepted goal: the preservation or restoration of health. They are not trained into a system where it is important that parties can control each other. There is, in the ideal case, nothing to control, because there is only one goal. Specialisation is encouraged. It increases the amount of available knowledge, and the loss of internal control is of no relevance. A conflict perspective creates unpleasant doubts with regard to the healer's suitability for the job. A non-conflict perspective is a precondition for defining crime as a legitimate target for treatment.

One way of reducing attention to the conflict is reduced attention given to the victim. Another is concentrated attention given to those attributes in the criminal's background which the healer is particularly trained to handle. Biological defects are per-

fect. So are also personality defects when they are established far back in time — far away from the recent conflict. And so are also the whole row of explanatory variables that criminology might offer. We have, in criminology, to a large extent functioned as an auxiliary science for the professionals within the crime control system. We have focused on the offender, made her or him into an object for study, manipulation and control. We have added to all those forces that have reduced the victim to a non-entity and the offender to a thing. And this critique is perhaps not only relevant for the old criminology, but also for the new criminology. While the old one explained crime from personal defects or social handicaps, the new criminology explains crime as the result of broad economic conflicts. The old criminology loses the conflicts, the new one converts them from interpersonal conflicts to class conflicts. And they are. They are class conflicts — also. But by stressing this, the conflicts are again taken away from the directly involved parties. So, as a preliminary statements: Criminal conflicts have either become *other people's property* — primarily the property of lawyers — or it has been in other people's interests to *define conflicts away*.

2 Cultural Context: Legal Cultures in Canada

(a) The Environment of Canada's Judicial System†

Peter H. Russell

SOCIAL AND ECONOMIC DEVELOPMENT

As an industrialized and urbanized society, Canada has experienced, to a relatively high degree, what the political sociologists refer to as "modernization." This modernization has been accompanied by increased complexity in Canadian law and increased professionalization of Canada's legal institutions. For the judicial system this has meant, among other things, an increased insistence on the possession of professional legal credentials by those adjudicating disputes about the law. Thus in Canada we have witnessed nearly a complete repudiation of the lay person as judge and a tendency to regard juries as technically too incompetent to be reliable fact-finders. Growing professionalism has also been felt, although in a much more delayed fashion, in the administration of Canadian courts, where there is increasing recognition of the merit of applying specialized administrative skills and the techniques of the computer age to managing court case flows.

But the effects of the modernization of Canadian society on its judicial system have been more pervasive and profound than a tendency to specialization. As industrialization and urbanization weaken traditional social bonds of family and community, basic social attitudes and relations are altered. We become a society of strangers relying increasingly, each of us, on formal positive law to define our rights and obligations; as a consequence, we turn increasingly to formal adjudication to settle our differences.[2] This transformation of social relations from those based on custom and informal sources of authority to a system depending much more on legally defined rights and duties tends to expand the role of adjudicative agencies. This can be seen in fields as far apart as family law and federalism: as squabbling spouses and government turn to positive law as a guide to good conduct, they resort increasingly to courts to adjudicate conflict. Another facet of the social alienation accompanying modernity is increased reliance on enforcement of the criminal law rather than more informal communal sanctions as a means of maintaining social order. This, too, places increased burdens on Canadian courts, not so much to adjudicate disputes (few criminal charges produce not guilty pleas and formal court adjudication) but to provide a judicial presence in the processing of those selected by the police for criminal prosecution.

Socio-economic development does not affect the business of courts in industrialized societies in a uniform way. The impact is considerably influenced by the litigiousness of a people — that is to say, their general propensity to settle disputes by pressing claims to formal adjudication rather than negotiating settlements more informally. A litigious tendency may be present in a society quite independently of its level of modernization.[3] Among modern industrialized countries, England, New Zealand, and the United States have much higher civil case loads per

---

† From *The Judiciary in Canada* (Whitby, Ontario: McGraw-Hill Ryerson Limited, 1987) at 31–39. [Notes and/or references omitted.] Reproduced by permission.

capita than Italy, Japan, or Spain.[4] The preference of the Japanese for mediation and conciliation over adjudication is reflected in the small size of their legal profession: 1 lawyer for each 10,000 of population compared with a ratio of 1 to 400 in the United States.[5] No systematic research has been done on the litigiousness of Canadians, but the fact that on a per capita basis the Canadian judiciary and legal profession are roughly comparable in size to their American counterparts suggests that Canada is one of the more litigious of the industrialized and urbanized countries, perhaps only slightly less so than the United States. Canadian patterns may have been brought closer to American ones by the rapid expansion of the legal profession and legal aid programs over the past decade or so.[6] These developments, while not necessarily altering the general disposition of Canadians to litigate, have made the option of taking disputes to court more available to people of limited means.

Increases in the number and complexity of laws, in the number of lawyers, and even in the litigiousness of the population, do not necessarily lead to a mushrooming of court business and expansion of the courts. Much depends on the relative attractiveness of judicial institutions as dispute-settling mechanisms and the availability of alternatives.[7] The evidence in Canada suggests that very little of the increased need for adjudicative services generated by social change and industrial development has been taken care of by the general jurisdiction trial courts (i.e., the superior, district, and county courts of the provinces), which at the time of Confederation were regarded as the most important of Canada's judicial institutions.[8] These provincial courts, staffed by federally appointed judges — the original linchpins of Canada's judicial system — have scarcely expanded at all. Whereas the number of judges serving at this level was 2.52 per 100,000 of population in 1867, by 1975 the ratio had actually declined to 2.23 per 100,000.[9] Some of this increased demand for adjudication, especially in the field of criminal justice, has been met by the provincially appointed judges in the so-called lower courts of the provinces, and a little, on the civil side, by the major federally established trial court, the Federal Court of Canada.[10] But probably a great deal more has been taken care of outside the formal court system through private arbitration and administrative tribunals. Improvements in the administration of courts may begin to reverse this trend by reducing some of the delay and inconvenience which in the past drove business away from the courts. Another factor working in the same direction is the Canadian version of what in the United States is

referred to as the "public law explosion."[11] On the one hand, the expanded use of the criminal sanction by the state; on the other hand, the expanded range of statutory and even constitutional rights that can be claimed by the individual or corporation against the state generate disputes which in our society must finally be settled by the courts.

POLITICAL BELIEFS AND IDEOLOGY

Here we encounter the second environmental influence on the judicial system: political beliefs and ideology. An increase in the degree of independence enjoyed by Canadian courts and their added capacity to serve as vehicles for challenging government has been closely related to a strengthening of support of liberalism in Canada's political culture. This growth in respect for liberal values — for the rights of individuals and the value of preventing excessive and illegal exercises of governmental authority — has not, to be sure, developed to the point of extinguishing strong conservative tendencies in Canada's political culture. Canada was founded by counter-revolutionaries suspicious of the excesses of American democracy.[12] The continued popularity of the national police force, the RCMP (despite the exposure of its infringements of the legal rights of Canadians and its intolerance of political dissent), as well as popular support for the invocation of the *War Measures Act* in the 1970 October crisis, point to the survival of this conservative strain. But liberal critics of these recent manifestations of Canadians' respect for authority and fear of disorder often fail to mark the liberalization of political attitudes that has been occurring in Canada.[13] Manifestations of moral outrage and the favourable treatment it receives in the popular media are, in themselves, an indication of this change.

A growing egalitarianism in Canadian society has fostered the extension of liberal values to all classes in society. This tendency has had important consequences for the functioning of the courts. Legal aid (the provision of publicly funded legal counsel to indigent persons) is, as we have noted, a leading example of this trend. Another is reform of the criminal justice system which has taken place over the last century.[14] The reduction of close ties between the criminal courts and the police, bail reform, and an upgrading of the qualifications of the judges who preside over the country's busiest criminal courts are part of this movement. These reforms are relatively modest; none goes as far as critics of the system might wish. But the direction of change is clearly liberal.

A further illustration of this liberalization of attitudes and its effect on the judicial system is the change which has taken place in the appeal system in criminal cases. Up until 1892 there was no right of appeal in criminal cases. When a right of appeal was included in the *Criminal Code*, it was typical of the mixture of values in Canadian society that not only was the accused given a right to appeal his conviction but the crown was also given a right to appeal the accused's acquittal, even if the verdict was rendered by a jury. The review of trial court decisions in criminal cases has become an increasingly important function of Canada's courts of appeal. We can get some idea of how much Canadian attitudes have changed by noting that in 1975 when the crown successfully appealed a jury's acquittal of Dr. Morgentaler, a Montreal physician who ran an abortion clinic, there was a sufficient public outcry to bring about an amendment of the *Criminal Code* removing the power of appeal courts to substitute a guilty verdict for an acquittal in a case heard by judge and jury.[15]

An egalitarian extension of legal rights has also affected the work of courts in non-criminal areas. New legal rights have been established for classes of persons whose bargaining position was relatively weak: for example, wives in relation to husbands, children in relation to parents, employees in relation to employers, students and professors in relation to university officials. The establishment of these rights means that disputes which might have been settled informally are now often litigated and go to court. Dispute settlement through informal negotiation becomes less acceptable when social and economic "underdogs" believe their interests will be better protected by claiming rights in court rather than counting on the benevolence of those in positions of power.

A similar reduction of trust in those exercising political authority has made Canadians more interested in the liberal notion of building checks and balances into their system of government. Canadians may continue to believe that the purpose of government is as much to provide for peace, order and good government as it is to protect the rights and liberties of the individual, but they have become increasingly apprehensive about the problems of controlling the governmental leviathan. Several generations of experience under big government have generated scepticism about the inherent good sense and self-restraint of those who govern. The nineteenth-century achievement of responsible government has proved to be no panacea for ensuring that government is accountable to the people. The decline of the legislature's significance in law-making and in its capacity for monitoring government operations has been evident for many years.[16] Cabinet government concentrates enormous power in the hands of a very few politicians and officials. There may be some dim recognition that the vitality of the division of powers and competition between federal and provincial governments in Canada by dispersing power enhances political liberty. Still, both provincial and federal governments are recognized as centres of power against whose arbitrary and unlawful activities citizens need further institutional protection.

Increasingly this liberal impulse looks to the judiciary for such protection. Where there is fear that government will abuse newly acquired powers, the judiciary is brought in to guard against this danger. A good example is the inclusion of a requirement for judicial warrants in the legislation that legalized electronic eavesdropping by the police.[17] More recently, in the debate over a federal *Access to Information Act*, distrust of the government forced the inclusion of a provision giving the courts, in most instances, the final word in deciding whether government refusals to provide information fall within statutory criteria.[18]

This tendency in the Canadian political system to rely on the judicial process as a means of preventing abuse of power and protecting rights may now be at a turning point. Canada's new constitutional *Charter of Rights and Freedoms* significantly expands expectations about the judiciary's capacity and inclination to check government. The apparent popularity of increasing the power of judges at the expense of the power of politicians and officials demonstrates the extent to which Canadians, at this point in their history, regard their judges as less tied to the interests of government; they are seen in a fundamental sense as being less political and more trustworthy than those holding executive and legislative positions. But, again, it is important to point out that this perception of the judiciary as the politically neutered branch of government may well be undermined by the political nature of the judiciary's responsibilities under the new Charter.

CANADA'S LEGAL CULTURE

The third and most direct of the environmental influences on the judicial system is a country's legal culture. The basic character of Canada's legal system, and hence of its judicial system, might be expected to reflect the legal cultures of the two European peoples, the English and the French, who founded Canada. But this expectation is not borne out by the facts. So dominant has the English common law system been that it is misleading to think of Canada's legal culture as fundamentally dualistic. This is especially true of its judicial system, which has been even more thoroughly anglicized than the substantive law. As far as the legal culture of Canada's original inhabitants is concerned, it was totally ignored and for all practical purposes obliterated by the European settlers.[19] Thus, in legal terms, Canada today belongs essentially to the common law world although, as with all the common law countries, there are some distinctive wrinkles stemming from the country's particular circumstances.

There is a strong element of legal dualism in Quebec's history. Soon after the British conquest of New France, through the *Quebec Act* of 1774, the laws of the French Canadians were made the basis of the colony's civil law, while its criminal law was to be British. Despite this original dualism, French civil law was subjected to powerful common law influences. The principal vehicle for this process of anglicization was the judicial system. British governors selected the judges and for the most part they chose persons whose legal knowledge, if it existed at all, was based process on English experience.[20] Most importantly, the appeal process was dominated by English Canadians and British judges. Consequently the judicial method in both civil and criminal law became the common law method, with its emphasis on judicial precedent. These common law techniques were so firmly embedded by the time a *Civil Code* was adopted in Quebec that English-style judicial precedents rather than French civilian doctrine became the dominant force in interpreting the code. The anglicization of Quebec's civil law system is a testament to the quiet way in which power can flow through a judicial system, especially one with a powerful appeals hierarchy.

An essential part of the Confederation settlement in 1867 was that Quebec, as the province in which the French Canadians could maintain a majority, would be able to preserve the distinctive language, religion, and laws of the French-Canadian people. Section 92(13) of the *British North America Act* gave all the provinces jurisdiction over "property and civil rights" — a concept that embraces most of the subjects included in Quebec's *Civil Code* and *Code of Procedure*.[21] Thus Quebec has retained legislative jurisdiction over those matters which are central to the French civil law tradition. On particular points of substantive law and civil procedure Quebec civil law differs from the laws of the common law provinces, although under the impact of secularization and modern commerce these differences have narrowed and may not be more significant than dif-

ferences that exist in some areas of statutory law among the common law provinces. Since Confederation the highest court of appeal, whose opinions interpreting Quebec's civil law bind Quebec judges, has been, first, an imperial court, the Judicial Committee of the Privy Council, and then the Supreme Court of Canada. Although Quebec judges have always been in a minority position on the latter court,[22] more often than not they have been the dominant influence on the panels hearing civil law cases from Quebec.

For our purposes here the most important point is that the judicial institutions of Quebec, despite any residue of French civil law and procedure that survives, bear the essential features of English common law courts. A lawyer from English-speaking Canada, or for that matter from virtually any other part of the English-speaking world, who wished to practise in Quebec, would not have to adapt to an alien judicial system. It is only in very recent years that Quebec court reformers have begun to look to continental French institutions for inspiration — for instance, to the idea of a career judiciary based on a special legal education for judges.[23] So far, this application of Quebec nationalism to judicial institutions has not borne fruit in any concrete changes.

Some of the features of the common law tradition that have important consequences for the role of the judiciary in Canada (for example, the use of juries and the adversary system) have already been mentioned and will be referred to later in the text. In this introductory discussion of judicial power there are two features of common law systems that deserve special emphasis: the central importance of the judges, and the power of the legal profession.

In any legal system based on the common law tradition, the judge has a preeminent position as compared with other legal functionaries. Common law is indeed judge-made law. On many subjects of contemporary legislative interest, common law rules are dwarfed in importance by statutes enacted by the legislature, by delegated legislation or regulations enacted by the executive, and in Canada by the written Constitution. Long ago common law judges accepted their subordination to Parliament as a sovereign law maker, and in Canada they must accept the Constitution of Canada as the highest source of law.[24] Even so, judicial decisions applying and interpreting regulations, statutes, and the Constitution, as we have already stressed, can have a tremendous influence on the policies that are actually effected and the rights that are actually established through these other sources of law. It is true that the difference between the legislative role of the judge in the common law system as compared with the civil law system has been exaggerated. Modern scholarship on civil law systems has revealed the important role that judicial interpretation and judicial opinions play in applying civil law codes, despite the civil law system's theoretical denial of their importance. Nevertheless the fact remains that it is the common law system that openly accepts the judicial opinion with all its potential for law development as an integral part of the system.

The pre-eminence of the judge in the common law system extends beyond the judge's law-making role. It is also manifest in the social and political status of the judge.[25] In continental Europe the legal scholar has a high, if not a higher, status than the judge. This is certainly not the case in Canada. The lustre of the judicial position in Canada is reflected in the practice, already commented upon, of assigning judges major extra-judicial responsibilities, notably on royal commissions and commissions of inquiry, on matters of great public interest. A symbolic indication of the high status of the judicial office in Canada is that the chief justice of the country's highest court, the Supreme Court of Canada, in the absence or incapacity of the governor general, represents the head of state.[26] Whether or not there is validity in the generalization that Canadian judges are self-restrained or uncreative in the exercise of their judicial powers, the high status accorded them in the Canadian legal and political systems continues to be a significant political resource for the Canadian judiciary.

The prestige and power of judges in the common law system is closely related to the strength of the legal profession. It might even be said that the pre-eminent position of the bench within common law legal systems largely derives from the pre-eminent position of the bar within common law societies. Going back to the roots of the common law judicial system in England, it was the ability of a small guild of private legal practitioners centred in the Inns of Court in London — first the sergeants, then the barristers — to monopolize appointments to the Royal Courts of Justice that was decisive in ensuring that the common law judiciary would not develop in the continental fashion as a career branch of government service.[27] Instead, judicial positions in the higher courts would be awarded to persons who had distinguished themselves in private legal practice. The bench in Canada, even at its lowest levels, is recruited almost exclusively from the bar. Thus, in studying the forces that shape the Canadian judiciary it is essential to take into account the nature of the Canadian legal profession.[28] Access to that profes-

sion, its education system, and the characteristics of private practice will have a great deal to do with determining what kinds of men and women become judges in Canada.

In Canada the bar is considerably less elitist than in England. Instead of the English division between a small group of barristers who plead cases in court and a great mass of solicitors advising clients and transacting legal business out of court, or France's four or five separate legal professions (advocates, avoues, notaries, and judges), Canada has a fused and unified legal profession. There are specializations within this profession, but all Canadian lawyers belong to a single profession. Further, the Canadian bar is not concentrated in a single metropolitan centre but is dispersed across the country; there are centres of professional activity in every Canadian province. Thus the professional pool from which Canadian judges are recruited is much larger and more diverse than the tiny coterie of London-based barristers from which English judges are drawn. As a social interest group, geographical dispersal is more than compensated for by professional unity. The Canadian bar's ability to assert itself as a unified profession has few parallels in other countries.

Some lawyers might object to the suggestion that they belong to a private interest group. Formally, as members of the bar, they are "officers of the court," and in that sense belong to a public institution. Nevertheless, the profession has emphasized the need to maintain its independence of government. It has insisted, successfully, on its own self-government, on controlling the standards of professional education and in most provinces, on keeping private legal practitioners, rather than salaried lawyers, as the mainstay of publicly funded legal aid programs. The rationale for this commitment to the profession's independence has been fundamentally ideological: recognition of the value in a liberal state under the rule of law of ensuring that individuals and groups have access to legal counsel not controlled by the government.

If the press can be referred to as the fourth estate, the legal profession as a private organization providing an essential public service might be thought of as a fifth estate in Canada. The power of this fifth estate is exercised through its professional activities and advocacy, and also through the participation of so many of its members at the highest levels of the political branches of government. The private practice of law provides exceptional opportunities for those who wish to take their chances in electoral competition. No other profession or occupational group has been so well represented in legislatures and cabinets at both the federal and provincial levels.[29] Among other things, the political prominence of the profession means that the views of professional lawyers are paramount in shaping policies with regard to judicial institutions and judicial reform. No major changes in the structure or functioning of Canada's courts can take place without the approval of leaders of the bar.

It would be a mistake, however, to think of the bar as an unchanging monolithic force. The winds of change which affect all other important social institutions are beginning to bring about significant changes in the size and shape of Canada's legal profession. The last decade has seen a major transformation. The ranks of the profession have expanded so that on a per capita basis it approximates the size of the American profession. The dominant position of males and the charter ethnic groups has declined.[30] Most significantly, the political diversity of the profession would appear to have increased with the formation of radical breakaway organizations outside of the professional establishment. In the long run, all of this is likely to have profoundly important effects on the social and political orientation of the Canadian judiciary.

(b)   By Reason of Authority or By Authority of Reason[†]

The Honourable Madame Justice Claire L'Heureux-Dubé

Chief Justice Anglin once remarked that decisions by courts in civil law jurisprudence were determined by authority of reason rather than by reason of authority.[1] However, in his last year on the bench, he also wrote: "In my opinion, the doctrine of *stare decisis* must equally apply in the determination of any case before this court, whatever may be the province of its origin."[2]

These apparently contradictory statements, made by a Supreme Court Justice trained in the common law,[3] reflect a historical reality which, for the past century, has been the object of great controversy among Quebec jurists and scholars. Specifically, the Supreme Court of Canada is a national court of last resort and the majority of its judges are trained in common law, with its emphasis on precedent. However, this same Court has power to review and reverse the Quebec Court of Appeal even in cases governed by civil law, though the civilian tradition favours the spirit and content of civil legislation as well as doctrine over strict adherence to judicial precedents. In Quebec, the conjunction of these factors has long seemed to be a contradiction in terms.[4]

Given the function and composition of the Supreme Court of Canada, was Quebec's civil law not effectively destined to be shaped by reason of authority rather than authority of reason? What have been the consequences for Quebec's civilian tradition and the authority it confers upon previously decided cases?

While I could not realistically hope to resolve these questions in a definitive and exhaustive manner, I do hope to provide perspectives on these questions while introducing the essential characteristics of Quebec's civilian tradition.

. . . .

Leaving aside for the moment the multiplicity of legal sources in Lower Canada prior to codification,[20] the unique nature of Quebec's system of private law can best be conveyed through an examination of the essential features of a civil code in the civilian legal system as a whole.

Although one author has remarked that "the characteristic features of a code are not easy to distil,"[21] every system of law has a primary organizing source, and so one can begin with a metaphor: the code is, first and foremost, the skeletal structure of the civilian legal system.[22] Non-codal legislation may be equal in authority, but it is the civil code which is the primary organizing source of law.[23] In that respect, Professor Brierley has compared the civil

† (1993) 27 U.B.C. L. Rev. 1 at 1–2, 6–18. [Notes and/or references omitted.] Reproduced with permission.

code's reservoir of concepts with the judicially-created English common law:

> ... [the Civil Code] has the status of a "common law" in its own right because of the scope of its regulation and the language in which it is expressed. It defines and sets out — it *constitutes* — the most fundamental categories and concepts that provide the *cadre* of Quebec legal thought in one of its main branches, the private law, and this mode of thought extends even beyond the private law to permeate other fields of legal regulation. The code in this regard has a role that is the functional equivalent of the accumulated work of the traditional (*i.e.*, judicially created) English common law in the shaping of private law concepts and relations. It provides, in this sphere, the first elements and the vocabulary of the law: what is a person (including a corporation), what is contract, inheritance, ownership, how property serves as security for debt and so on. In these respects, its language, whether English or French, acquires pre-eminent meaning. The Civil Code may even set the framework for the drawing of other large divisions of the law with which, however, it does not deal directly. It articulates therefore the basic concepts that are used and relied upon, or varied and extended, in other enactment that will moreover, when felicitously drafted, employ the same language and concepts.[24]

As the primary organizing source of law in private relations, the Civil Code enunciates its rules in a general fashion, in simple terms, and with an economy of words. The perfect example is Art. 1053 of the Quebec Civil Code, which reads:

> Art. 1053. Every person capable of discerning right from wrong is responsible for the damage caused by his fault to another, whether by positive act, imprudence, neglect or want of skill.

Although concepts such as "damage", "fault" and "another" will naturally have to be interpreted and adapted to a wide range of circumstances and factual situations, the general rule always remains the fundamental starting point in the civilian approach. In rendering a decision, the civilian judge is required to proceed by way of fundamental conceptual analysis. Because the law is deemed to be a coherent whole, civilian analysis is both systematic and rational. As Professors Smith and Kerby put it:

> In discovering the legislator's implied intention the civilian judge does not stop at adopting by *analogy* the rule laid down for some similar matter. He may formulate a rule by *deduction* from

a principle legislatively stated: this is how he arrived at the proportional allocation of blame in tort and it is what he does every time he adapts the law to new circumstances.[25]

Consistent with the basic premise that the law is complete, the civilian judge is obliged to decide every dispute. This fundamental obligation is expressed in Art. 11 of the Civil Code, which reads:

> 11. A judge cannot refuse to adjudicate under pretext of the silence, obscurity or insufficiency of the law.

Furthermore, in interpreting the rules in the Code, the civilian judge is to consider not only the letter, but equally the spirit of the law. Article 12 of the Quebec Civil Code states this principle and directs the judge to consider not only the language of the law, but also its purpose. It reads:

> 12. When a law is doubtful or ambiguous, it is to be interpreted so as to fulfil the intention of the legislature, and to attain the object for which it was passed.[26]

Beyond the language and the differing theoretical framework of a Code, the civilian tradition, in contrast to common law tradition, places a role of paramount importance on the doctrinal writings of legal scholars. The historical weight of *la doctrine* lies in its systematic and abstract articulation of the civil law.[27] Classical legal scholarship has played an important role by preceding, and allowing for, the codification movement of continental countries by way of its systematic and rational exposition of the private law; thus, scholarly opinion is traditionally viewed not simply as "writing *about* law," but is rather thought to be "fundamentally *constitutive* of law."[28] The great influence of academic writing is evidenced by Mignault J.'s description of the civilian adjudicative process. He observes:

> ... the civil law is a logical system, for from this it follows that the determination of controversies before the courts must proceed upon legal principles. The court is not bound to hunt up a case supporting the legal principle relied on, but it suffices that its decision conform to the dictates of reason as embodied in the maxims and principles of the civil law, or as taught by the jurists who have written on the law. The process whereby cases are decided, is the process of reasoning applied to the science of jurisprudence.[29]

This description, while illustrating the important function of civilian legal scholarship, also reveals the secondary role which is played by previously-decided cases. The classical function of the civilian judge is to interpret, not to create the law.[30] The natural flipside is that previously-decided cases are less important in the decision-making process and that the civilian judge is free to disregard precedent. The basic premise is inherent in the whole adjudicative process. As Planiol put it:

> Judicial interpretation is free in principle; each Court has the right of adopting the solution which seems to it the best and the most just: it is not bound either by decisions which it may have rendered previously in analogous cases, or by the decisions of another court though it be higher in rank.[31]

Therefore, through its conception of the judicial function, tradition civilian theory does not view judicial decisions as constituting, *per se*, binding sources of law.[32] This basic tenet of continental civil law tradition is illustrated in the French rule that a previous decision, even by a hierarchically superior court, is never binding;[33] the rationale being that in civil law, contrary to the common law, policy is for legislature, not for the courts. The courts interpret and apply the law. In common law, the courts determine policy as well.

It is against this background that one must consider the seemingly contradictory concepts of authority of reason and reason of authority. One can readily see that the language and theoretical framework of the Code, the traditional influence of legal scholarship and the restricted scope of previously-decided cases all point to a distinctive approach and a specific method of legal reasoning. The distinctive nature of the civilian legal system is not found too much in the solutions reached in particular cases. Rather, it is found in a reasoning process which favours a certain freedom and latitude in judicial interpretation. Thus, the very idea of a court of last resort laying down general principles through binding precedents seems, *a priori*, like the perfect antithesis of civilian theory.

When one considers the nature of the civilian legal system, and couples it with Lower Canada's reluctance concerning creation of the Supreme Court of Canada, one is forced to ask whether the Supreme Court's decisions in cases governed by the civil law were not effectively destined to be ignored within Quebec. What influence could a judicial hierarchy based on common law traditions possibly have on Quebec's civilian system?

As a starting point for the examination of these questions it is interesting to consider the early tendency of Quebec courts generally, and the Quebec Court of Appeal in particular, to ignore decisions of the Supreme Court of Canada in matters governed by the civil law. Although the principle of *stare decisis* was not expressly formulated by the Supreme Court of Canada until 1909,[34] Quebec courts demonstrated very early a reluctance to follow precedents laid down by Canada's court of last resort.[35] Despite Anglin C.J.'s statement that the principle of *stare decisis* also applied to cases governed by the civil law,[36] the Quebec Court of Appeal systematically contradicted certain Supreme Court of Canada decisions until the first half of this century.[37] Moreover, the authority of the Supreme Court of Canada in civil law matters suffered an additional setback as many Quebec scholars and practitioners severely criticized its judgments. Their main argument was that the integrity of civil law was at stake.[38]

Among the reasons put forward to explain this resistance, we find the Supreme Court's early tendency to unify certain aspects of Canadian private law.[39] In this regard, the case most frequently cited is *Canadian Pacific Railway v. Robinson*.[40] The issue was whether damages by way of *solatium doloris* could be claimed in an action under Art. 1056 of the Quebec Civil Code. The Supreme Court of Canada answered in the negative by referring to the English origin of Art. 1056. Taschereau J. wrote:

> It cannot have been intended by this legislation, that if a man was killed in Upper Canada, no *solatium* should be granted to his wife or legal representatives by way of damages, but that if he was killed in Lower Canada, such a *solatium* could be given. That in the present case, for instance, this plaintiff can get a *solatium* because her husband was killed in Lower Canada, whilst if he had been killed a few miles further west, in Upper Canada, none would be granted under the same statute....[41]

Justice Ritchie expressed a similar concern:

> I think it would be much to be regretted if we were compelled to hold that damages should be assessed by different rules in the different provinces through which the same railroad may run....[42]

This attempt to unify Canadian private law was criticized as ousting the civil law through a reasoning and interpretative process which was inspired by common law principles.[43] Further, the reasoning process in *Robinson* seemed to justify the application of common law principles to any civil law rules of English origin. By applying case law developed in common law jurisdictions, the Supreme Court of Canada risked importing principles without first addressing the question of whether these principles were even compatible with the recipient law. Although Quebec civil law embodies several rules of English origin in its Civil Code,[44] the reasoning of the Supreme Court was viewed as a threat to the integrity of the civil law. Under such conditions, it was feared that the interpretation of the Civil Code as a coherent and rational instrument would be hampered by the one-sided influence of the common law.[45]

The Supreme Court of Canada's early tendency towards unification of Canadian private law through reliance on common law judgments and authorities was, however, firmly halted by the influence of Mignault J. and his successors.[46] In the celebrated *Desrosiers*[47] decision in 1920, he argued forcefully against the use of common law precedents in civil law cases. In so doing, he distinguished the civil law from the common law on a systemic basis:

> ... With respect, it seems to me that it is time to react against the habit, in cases from the province of Quebec, of resorting to English common law precedents, on the ground that the Civil Code contains a rule which is in accordance with a rule of English law. On many points ... the Civil Code and the common law do have similar rules. However, the civil law is a complete system in itself and must be interpreted in accordance with its own rules. If, whenever the legal principles are the same, the courts can resort to English law in order to interpret French civil law, the monuments of French jurisprudence might equally be cited to throw light upon the rules of English law.[48]

The principle that each system of law should be administered through reference to authorities binding on that system alone has been reaffirmed very clearly by the Supreme Court of Canada ever since.[49] Illustrative of the Supreme Court of Canada's evolution on this question [is] Pigeon J.'s opinion in *Pantel v. Air Canada*.[50] Noting the English origin of Art. 1056 and recalling the Supreme Court's erroneous assumption in *Robinson, supra*, that the rule was to be interpreted following English authorities, Pigeon J. wrote:

> Art. 1056 C.C. must therefore be interpreted, not as reproducing a statute of English inspiration, but as a new provision forming part of a codification in which some fundamental principles are radically different from those of the common law, in terms of which *Lord Campbell's Act* was written.[51]

As mentioned earlier, the language and theoretical framework of a code, its internal coherence and its specific canons of interpretation are among the fundamental principles of civil law.[52] These basic tenets of civilian tradition were recently discussed, in the contexts of contempt of court and the compellability of parties to a civil action, in light of the *Code of Civil Procedure*.[53] The Quebec Court of Appeal's decision relied on common law precedents it considered binding. I have expressed a different view:

> There is nothing unusual about the fact that contempt of court is a concept borrowed from English law. Quebec private law includes a wealth of rules drawn from foreign sources. The common law principles cannot simply be applied to these rules, in my opinion, without first directly addressing the question of whether those principles are even compatible with the recipient law. Finally, such an approach seems particularly inappropriate where, as here, it is used in connection with provisions which form part of the general structure of a code [citations omitted].[54]

Since Mignault J., while upholding the reasoning and interpretative process inherent in each system of law, the Supreme Court of Canada has at the same time enhanced the authority of its decisions among Quebec judges, academics and practitioners. The scope of this *stare decisis* must then be considered against the background of two important factors.

First, in contrast to judges in France and other continental countries, Quebec judges administer a mixed system; private law matters are governed by the civil law, while public law matters are based on the foundation of the common law.[55] Beyond this strict duality in formal legal sources, the principles of judicial organization in Quebec private law itself are inspired from the common law.[56] As Jean-Louis Baudouin, now a judge of the Quebec Court of Appeal, explained, these organizational principles qualify one of the basic tenets of continental civil law tradition:

> In Quebec and Louisiana, the principle of the supremacy of legislation over other sources of law seems to be accepted as a premise. However, it would be futile to argue that this principle carries the same impact as it does in France, unless one forgets that both Quebec and Louisiana adopted the common-law procedure, most of the common-law rules of evidence, the common-law trial techniques, and, most important of all, the common-law respect and attitude towards the judiciary and the judicial function as a whole.[57]

This structural affinity with the common law judiciary could not but have an impact on the role played by previously-decided cases. Mignault J. himself recognized the impact of the hybrid character of Quebec's legal tradition on the role of judicial decisions:

> ... our civil law being French, our commercial law partly English and partly French, our procedure and mode of conducting trials a mixture of the two, and our criminal law entirely English — it is natural that, in so far as the authority of decided cases is concerned, we should be nearer to the English than to the French system.[58]

This Quebec legal tradition of mixed character has always tempered the theoretical freedom of the civilian judge to disregard precedent.[59] Some have even said that it is in greater danger of being mixed up. As the court of last resort in the judicial hierarchy, the Supreme Court of Canada itself is an integral part of this bi-systemic character of the Quebec legal tradition. This inevitably bears on the influence that the Court's decisions assume in the adjudicative process.

This being said, one cannot conclude that the doctrine of *stare decisis*, as understood and applied in common law jurisdictions, is the rationale of the present authority of the Supreme Court of Canada's decisions in cases governed by the civil law.[60] While precedent creates, to some degree, binding rules in common law jurisdictions, in the Quebec civil law system, precedent remains first and foremost a model.[61] Illustrative of this nuance is the Quebec Court of Appeal's position regarding its own precedents. It has always considered itself free to disregard a previous decision it later considers to be erroneous.[62] And so has the Supreme Court of Canada. As Laskin C.J. wrote in *Capital Cities Communications*, the Supreme Court of Canada "is not bound by judgments of the Privy Council any more than it is bound by its own judgments."[63] The authority which is given to the model cannot be separated from the model's respect for the content and spirit of codal legislation and the civilian tradition. It is in light of these constitutive elements that decisions of the Supreme Court of Canada in Quebec civil law may be thought to be "persuasive" in contrast to a strictly binding authority among Quebec courts. In reality, few, if any, today would dispute the authority of the Court's decisions in Quebec civil law.

In conclusion, the historical reluctance of Lower Canada concerning the Supreme Court of Canada should be seen against the background of the civilian tradition itself. Because this tradition reflects a distinctive approach and a specific method of legal reasoning, the authority of its decisions is indissociable from its endorsement of, and respect for, the basic tenets of the civil law. Through decisions which reflect these principles, the Court has affirmed its authority among Quebec judges and academics and has demonstrated that it could take up such a challenge. As Dickson C.J. recently said, before the International Academy of Comparative Law:

> The Supreme Court of Canada is fully conscious of its responsibility concerning the evolution of this dual heritage. Despite certain trends which at one time and particularly in certain areas, seemed to favour a policy of judicial unification of Canadian Private Law, it is now fully understood that each case before the Court must be dealt with according to and within the legal tradition from which it originated and in full respect for each of the two great legal traditions.[64]

This, of course, does not mean that comparative law has no place in Supreme Court of Canada decisions. While respecting two great legal traditions of the western world, it enjoys a privileged position. As political and economic systems seem to move irresistibly towards collaboration, cooperation and harmonization, a look at the forest may illuminate the trees. As my colleague Gonthier J. very aptly put it:

> Our two systems are legatees of the same foundation of Roman law, the subsequent evolution of each occurring at a time where communications were difficult. How much more simple, immediate and intimate are the communications and exchanges between societies of today, bringing new ideas, hopes and conceptions of law. Such an evolution is natural. We should not fear it as a menace to our identity. We need to remain conscious of the changes, and accept them as a necessary enrichment of the vitality of our law, of its capacity to respond to new demands, and to make a valuable contribution to the society of tomorrow, qualities which are, in short, the only true guarantees of the maintenance and integrity of the law.[65] [Translation]

These principles reflect nothing less, in my view, than reason itself.

(c) Societal Norms Offer a Frame of Reference†

Gérard Bouchard and Charles Taylor

One of the key sources of anxiety mentioned during our consultations concerns the putative absence of guidelines to handle adjustment requests. Aside from the legal guidelines indicated in section III, Québec society has nonetheless adopted over the years an array of norms and guidelines that underpin its "common public culture." It is thus wrong to believe that there are no guidelines governing harmonization practices. However, this does not mean, either, that some facets of the guidelines would not benefit from clarification. Our approach comprises two stages. First, we will examine the existing guidelines, then, in keeping with the wish expressed by many interveners, we will seek to clarify the integration model and the system of secularism that seem most appropriate to Québec society.

A. EXISTING GUIDELINES

1. Québec's liberal democracy

Let us begin by noting that Québec's political system is both democratic and liberal. It is democratic insofar as political power ultimately resides with the people, who [delegate] such power to representatives who exercise it in the people's name for a given period of time. Our democracy is thus representative, but it is also liberal in that individual rights and freedoms are deemed to be fundamental and are thus confirmed and protected by the State.

We often lose sight of the extent to which the legitimacy of our political system centres on the complementarity of these two facets, i.e. its democratic and liberal nature. This system is democratic since, as we noted earlier, the people are sovereign. All citizens, who are deemed to be equal, are the ultimate holders of political power. All of them may in principle participate in political debate and take advantage of the right to vote. Since individuals often disagree about political questions and vote for different parties, a democracy is quite rightly subject to the rule of the majority.

Québec's democratic system is also liberal since it protects rights and freedoms from possible abuse by the majority. For example, no one would want a government, even a properly elected one, to flout the basic rights of a group of citizens in the name of the majority's interests. It is precisely to offer additional protection of the rights and freedoms guaranteed to all individuals that such rights and freedoms are enshrined in a charter, which imposes limits on the government's action and manages relations between citizens.

We cannot examine in detail here the Québec and Canadian charters. Let us simply note that both charters spell out a series of rights and freedoms from which all citizens may benefit, e.g. the right to life and equality, freedom of conscience and religion, freedom of expression and association, political rights and legal guarantees. They also prohibit several forms of discrimination, including discrimination based on sex, ethnic origin and religion. Everyone must be able to exercise these rights and freedoms since all human beings are deemed to be equal in dignity. The Preamble of the Québec Charter states that "all human beings are equal in worth and dignity, and are entitled to equal protection of the law."

It is also important to point out that the exercising of these rights and freedoms is not absolute and must respect the rights of others and the collective interest. When two rights come into conflict, the courts do not seek to determine which of the two is superior to the other, i.e. to organize rights along hierarchical lines, but endeavour to hand down a decision in which the level of infringement of the two rights is "minimal." This approach stems from the principle whereby basic rights are equally important. They form, to some extent, the links in the same chain. For this reason, the 1948 *Universal Declaration of Human Rights* does not establish a hierarchy of basic rights.

---

† From [Québec] Commission on Accomodation Practices Related to Cultural Differences, *Building The Future: A Time for Reconciliation*, Abridged Report (Quebec: Commission de consultation sur les pratiques d'accommodement reliées aux différences culturelle, 2008) Section IV. Reproduced with permission of Government of Québec. [Notes and/or references omitted.]

2. French as the common public language

In Québec, French is the official language. The *Charter of the French language* (Bill 101), adopted in 1977, stipulates that French is "the language of Government and the Law, as well as the normal and everyday language of work, instruction, communication, commerce and business." Québec's language policy therefore seeks to promote French as the common public language. However, Bill 101 does not cover the language that Quebecers use in the home or in their private lives. In keeping with the liberal nature of Québec society, the government has undertaken to promote French in a spirit of respect toward the linguistic minorities that live in Québec.

Through the provisions in Chapter VIII of the *Charter of the French language* covering the language of instruction, Québec French-language schools attended by students of different origins have become a hub for integration and learning to live together. The French language is the main medium that allows Quebecers of all origins to interact, get to know each other, cooperate and participate in the development of Québec society.

3. Québec's integration policy

It is widely acknowledged that the key directions in Québec's integration policy were defined in the *Policy Statement on Immigration and Integration* adopted in 1990. The policy statement stipulated the components of a "moral contract" that established, in a spirit of reciprocity, the respective commitments of the host society and newcomers. In particular, the policy statement stipulates that Québec is:

- a society in which French is the common language of public life;
- a democratic society that expects and encourages everyone to participate and contribute;
- pluralistic and open to outside contributions, within the limitations imposed by respect for basic democratic values and the need for inter-community exchange.

It notes that immigration is essential to the development of Québec society. As for cultural diversity, it is perceived as an asset inasmuch as its expression is guided by the charters of human rights and freedoms and it is achieved in a spirit of interaction rather than a spirit of division. Immigrants are encouraged to learn French and contribute to Québec society's cultural, economic and political vitality.

In return, the government undertakes to facilitate their integration.

Successive governments may interpret differently any of these policy directions. However, we have noted that the principles of the civil pact formulated in the policy statement have not been fundamentally altered since 1990.

The factors that we have just examined, i.e. the liberal democratic system, the charters of human rights and freedoms, the *Charter of the French language*, and the *Policy Statement on Immigration and Integration*, have made it possible to establish in Québec in recent decades a relatively harmonious group climate. However, debate on reasonable accommodation has revealed that certain aspects of the "common public culture" would benefit from broader dissemination or clarification.

B. INTEGRATION AND INTERCULTURALISM: A MODEL TO BE CLARIFIED

Often mentioned in academic papers, interculturalism as an integration policy has never been fully, officially defined by the Québec government although its key components were formulated long ago. This shortcoming should be overcome, all the more so as the Canadian multiculturalism model does not appear to be well suited to conditions in Québec, for four reasons: *a)* anxiety over language is not an important factor in English Canada; *b)* minority insecurity is not found there; *c)* there is no longer a majority ethnic group in Canada (citizens of British origin account for 34% of the population, while citizens of French-Canadian origin make up a strong majority of the population in Québec, i.e. roughly 77%); *d)* it follows that in English Canada, there is less concern for the preservation of a founding cultural tradition than for national cohesion.

Generally speaking, it is in the interests of any community to maintain a minimum of cohesion. It is through such cohesion that a community can adopt common orientations, ensure participation by citizens in public debate, create the feeling of solidarity required for an egalitarian society to function smoothly, mobilize the population in the event of a crisis, and take advantage of the enrichment that stems from ethnocultural diversity. For a small nation such as Québec, constantly concerned about its future as a cultural minority, integration also represents a condition for its development, and perhaps, for its survival.

That is why the integrative dimension is a key component of Québec interculturalism. According to the descriptions provided in scientific documentation, interculturalism seeks to reconcile ethnocultural diversity with the continuity of the French-speaking core and the preservation of the social link. It thus affords security to Quebecers of French-Canadian origin and to ethnocultural minorities and protects the rights of all in keeping with the liberal tradition. By instituting French as the common public language, it establishes a framework in society for communication and exchanges. It has the virtue of being flexible and receptive to negotiation, adaptation and innovation.

The 11 proposals below allow us to define Québec interculturalism even more precisely.

1. Québec as a nation, as recognized by all Québec political parties and the federal government, is the operational framework for interculturalism.
2. In a spirit of reciprocity, interculturalism strongly emphasizes interaction, in particular intercommunity action, with a view to overcoming stereotypes and defusing fear or rejection of the Other, taking advantage of the enrichment that stems from diversity, and benefiting from social cohesion.
3. Members of the majority ethnocultural group, i.e. Quebecers of French-Canadian origin, like the members of ethnocultural minorities, accept that their culture will be transformed sooner or later through interaction.
4. Cultural, and, in particular, religious differences need not be confined to the private domain. The following logic underpins this choice: it is healthier to display our differences and get to know those of the Other than to deny or marginalize them.
5. The principle of multiple identities is recognized, as is the right to maintain an affiliation with one's ethnic group.
6. For those citizens who so wish, it is desirable for initial affiliations to survive, since ethnic groups of origin often act as mediators between their members and society as a whole. A general phenomenon arises in this regard: almost without exception, each citizen integrates into society through a milieu or an institution that serves as a link, e.g. the family, a profession, a community group, a church, an association, and so on.
7. Multilingualism is encouraged at the same time as French as the common public language. The

debate that opposes the language of identity and the common language (as a simple communication tool) is hardly promising. What is important, first and foremost, is the broadest possible dissemination of French, in whatever form.
8. To facilitate the integration of immigrants and their children, it is useful to provide them with the means to preserve their mother tongue, at least at the outset. This helps them to mitigate the shock of immigration by affording them a cultural anchor. It is also a means of preserving the enrichment that stems from cultural diversity.
9. Constant interaction between citizens of different origins leads to the development of a new identity and a new culture. This is what has been happening in Québec in recent decades without altering the cultural position of the majority group or infringing on the culture of minority groups.
10. Under a recent, highly promising orientation from the standpoint of pluralism, the groups present in Québec define themselves with reference to common, often universal, values stemming from their history rather than their ethnic traits. Québec is thus part of an international trend whereby societies choose to integrate diversity in light of shared values.
11. The civic and legal dimensions (and everything that concerns, in particular, non-discrimination) must be regarded as fundamental in interculturalism.

To summarize, we could say that Québec interculturalism *a*) institutes French as the common language of intercultural relations; *b*) cultivates a pluralistic orientation that is highly sensitive to the protection of rights; *c*) preserves the creative tension between diversity and the continuity of the French-speaking core and the social link; *d*) places special emphasis on integration; and *e*) advocates interaction.

As we noted earlier, we believe it would be useful for the Québec government to adopt an official text such as a statute, a policy statement or a declaration that broadly defines interculturalism. This text would thus constitute a key component of the social blueprint and would serve as a frame of reference for the elaboration of policies and programs. In addition to enhancing the coherence of the government's approach, it would offer all community interveners an official reference point.

C.   A SECULAR REGIME FOR QUÉBEC

During the public consultation held in the fall of 2007, Quebecers massively espoused the concept of secularism, one of the most frequently mentioned themes, but sometimes with highly different meanings. We will first seek to clarify the meaning of this concept then will describe the type of secularism that we believe is best suited to Québec.

An initial ambiguity: the distinction between what is public and private

The argument that "religion must remain in the private sphere" was often cited by the proponents of secularism. While at first sight it seems clear, this statement is not quite as clear as we may think. Indeed, "public" can be understood in at least two separate ways. According to the first meaning, what is public relates to the State and its common institutions, i.e. "public institutions." According to the second meaning, what is public is open or accessible to everyone, i.e. "places of public use," for example, a "garden open to the public."

The first meaning concurs with the secular principle of the neutrality of the State with respect to religion. According to this first meaning, it is therefore accurate to confirm that religion must be "private." However, it does not go without saying that secularism demands of religion that it be absent from public space in the broad sense. In point of fact, religions already occupy this space and, pursuant to the charters, religious groups and the faithful have the freedom to publicly display their beliefs.

Confusion arises when these two ways of understanding the distinction between what is public and private intersect. This is true, for example, when we ask whether students and teachers may display their religious affiliation in the school. If a public institution must be neutral, are the individuals who frequent it subject to this obligation of neutrality?

A second ambiguity: State neutrality

The notion of neutrality is also more complex that it may seem. Thus, it is widely acknowledged that the secular State must be neutral in respect of all religions. To this we must add that the State must not take sides as regards religion and non-religion. It must maintain its position of neutrality when faced with all deep-seated moral convictions, whether they are religious or secular.

However, the secular, democratic State is based on a political moral code and on certain principles that are not negotiable. This is true of democracy, human rights and the equality of all citizens. When these principles come into play, the State may not remain neutral. Ideally, all citizens must share these same principles and political moral code, although their deep-seated convictions may differ.

For example, everyone may agree on the idea that we must defend the right to life, although individuals may do so in light of markedly different justifications: a Christian may confirm that human beings are created in God's image, while a secular philosopher might claim that a human being as a rational subject possesses a dignity that no one must infringe. Other deep-seated reasons might similarly be cited. The secular State defends certain principles but it does so without taking sides in respect of the deep-seated reasons that citizens may cite to justify their adherence.

Open secularism

Liberal democracies, including Québec, all adhere to the principle of secularism, which can nonetheless be embodied in different systems. Which system is best suited to Québec society, bearing in mind its history and the very foundations of secularism? To answer this question, it is useful to distinguish the four principles that underpin secularism. Two of them define its final purpose:

1. the moral equality of persons; and
2. freedom of conscience and religion.

The other two principles are expressed in institutional structures that make it possible to achieve these purposes:

3. the separation of Church and State; and
4. the neutrality of the State with respect to religions and deep-seated secular convictions.

Any secular system achieves some form of balance between these four principles. Certain systems impose fairly strict limits on freedom of religious expression. France, which has just adopted restrictive legislation governing the wearing of religious signs in the schools, is deemed to have this type of system, although in reality it is much more flexible that its reputation suggests. This type of system defines State neutrality very broadly, which leads to the exclusion of certain forms of religious expression in the public sphere.

We do not think that this is the best type of system. Since freedom of conscience and religion is one of the purposes of secularism (second principle), the neutrality of the State (fourth principle) should be designed so as to foster, not hinder, its expression. If such was the case in France, it is perhaps because a certain conception of the neutrality of the State, sanctioned by a national tradition, was raised to the level of an ultimate purpose. Recent debate in France, where secularism has often been presented as an essential component of the Republic's identity, illustrates this shift. Certain French republicans believe that the mission of secular schools must be to emancipate students from religion. Others believe that cultural and religious identities only impede social integration, which should be based on citizenship that excludes any particularism.

There are three reasons why we believe that this type of restrictive secularism is not appropriate for Québec: *a*) it does not truly link institutional structures to the purposes of secularism; *b*) the attribution to the school of an emancipatory mission directed against religion is not compatible with the principle of State neutrality in respect of religion and non-religion; *c*) the integration process in a diversified society is achieved through exchanges between citizens, who thus learn to get to know each other (that is the philosophy of Québec interculturalism), not by relegating identities to the background.

Open secularism, which we are advocating, seeks to develop the final purposes of secularism (first and second principles) by defining institutional structures (third and fourth principles) in light of this objective. This is the path that Québec has followed historically, as witnessed by the Proulx report, which also promotes open secularism.[4] Our position, once again, is in keeping with the path that Québec has followed.

The wearing by government employees of religious signs

Must a regime based on open secularism allow government employees to wear religious signs? Does the neutrality of public institutions demand the prohibition of such signs? To answer these questions, we must consider the type of neutrality that it is to be expected of the public service. We naturally hope that public servants will perform their duties loyally and impartially. Would they relinquish these qualities simply because they wear a religious sign? We do not think so.

By prohibiting the wearing in the public service of any religious sign, we would prevent the faithful from certain religions from engaging in careers in the public service, which would contravene freedom of conscience and religion (second principle) and would largely complicate the task of building a public service that reflects Québec's population, which is

becoming increasingly diversified. This would also infringe the equality of citizens (first principle).

We do not believe that a general prohibition concerning the wearing by all government employees of religious signs is warranted. However, we acknowledge that certain duties may imply a duty of self-restraint. In the brief that it submitted to the Commission, the Bloc Québécois noted that certain functions "by their very nature embody the State and its essential neutrality." This is true, in particular, of judges, Crown prosecutors, police officers and the President of the National Assembly. Individuals who occupy these positions could be required to relinquish their right to display their religious affiliation in order to preserve the appearance of impartiality that their function requires.

Harmonization practices for religious reasons

In the course of our consultations, several interveners requested the adoption of legislation prohibiting any religious accommodation. This radical proposal cannot be adopted under a system based on open secularism, especially as it would require the amendment of the Québec *Charter of Human Rights and Freedoms*, which protects freedom of religion. Such an amendment would put Québec in an awkward position from the standpoint of the *Universal Declaration of Human Rights* and the numerous national charters based on it.

Furthermore, this proposal is incompatible with the principle of State neutrality. Since freedom of religion cannot be dissociated from freedom of conscience, the prohibition of religious accommodation would create inextricable legal problems. For example, let us consider the following case: a penitentiary offers a meat-based diet. Two inmates request a vegetarian meal, one because he is Hindu and the other (an atheist) because he believes it is immoral to kill animals for food. Should the first request be rejected under the pretence that it is motivated by religion and the second one accepted because it is not of a religious nature? How can we refuse requests related to freedom of religion without at the same time rejecting freedom of conscience? As we saw earlier, the neutrality of the State assumes that it does not take sides in favour of religion or non-religion.

According to another argument, the accommodation granted to the disabled should not be confused with religious accommodation because the disabled do not choose their disability, while a believer may decide to relinquish such and such a practice. This distinction, while it seems convincing, minimizes the fact that certain "religious choices" are actually experienced as non-optional. To infringe these choices of conscience would be tantamount to interfering with the individual's moral integrity and would entail relegating choices stemming from deep-seated convictions to the level of simple desires or whims. To no longer make a distinction between whims and deep-seated convictions, whether of a religious or a secular nature, would be to relinquish one of the most valuable established privileges of our civilization.

Religious heritage

Catholicism has left an indelible mark on Québec's history. Traces of it are all around us. Under the principle of the neutrality of the State, religious displays linked to the functioning of public institutions should be abandoned. Thus, we do not believe that the crucifix in the National Assembly and the prayers that precede municipal council meetings have their place in a secular State. In both instances, public institutions are associated with a single religious affiliation rather than addressing themselves to all citizens.

That being the case, it would be absurd to want to extend this rule of neutrality to all historic signs that no longer fulfil an obvious religious function, e.g. the cross on Mont-Royal or the crosses on old buildings converted to secular uses. The same is true of Québec toponymy, which is largely inspired by the calendar of the saints. Quebecers' common sense will surely prevail in this respect.

(d) Conceptions of History†

The Royal Commission on Aboriginal Peoples

2. AN HISTORICAL FRAMEWORK

> Some of the old people ... talk about the water ... and it is really nice to hear them talk about the whole cycle of water, where it all starts and where it all ends up.
>
> Chief Albert Saddleman
> Okanagan Band
> Kelowna, British Columbia, 16 June 1993

Aboriginal and non-Aboriginal people have had sustained contact in the part of North America that has become known as Canada for some 500 years, at least in some areas. To summarize and interpret the nature of so complex, fluid and interdependent a relationship ("where it all starts and where it all ends up") is a formidable assignment. This is especially the case when one considers the sheer diversity in the nature of the relationship in different areas of the country, populated by different Aboriginal peoples and settled at different periods by people of diverse non-Aboriginal origins.

In the Atlantic region, for instance, a sustained non-Aboriginal presence among the Mi'kmaq and Maliseet peoples has been a fact for nearly 500 years, but in most parts of the far north, Inuit have been in sustained contact with non-Aboriginal people only in recent times. In Quebec and southern and central Ontario, the relationship is of almost the same duration as that in the Atlantic region, while in northern Ontario and the Prairies, sustained contact and the development of formal treaty relationships has occurred only within the last 150 years. In parts of the Pacific coast, the nature of the relationship has yet to be formalized in treaties, even though interaction between Aboriginal and non-Aboriginal people has taken place for some 200 years.

In approaching the task of summarizing and interpreting the relationship between Aboriginal and non-Aboriginal people, the Commission has found it useful to divide its own account of the historical relationship into four stages.... The stages follow each other with some regularity, but they overlap and occur at different times in different regions.

---

† Source: *Report of the Royal Commission on Aboriginal Peoples: Looking Forward, Looking Back*, Vol. 1 (Ottawa: The Commission, © 1996) at 36–39 [ISBN 0-660-16413-2] Reproduced with the permission of the Minister of Public Works and Government Services, 2010, and Courtesy of the Privy Council Office. [Figure and notes and/or references omitted.]

2.1 Stage 1: Separate Worlds

In the period before 1500, Aboriginal and non-Aboriginal societies developed in isolation from each other. Differences in physical and social environments inevitably meant differences in culture and forms of social organization. On both sides of the Atlantic, however, national groups with long traditions of governing themselves emerged, organizing themselves into different social and political forms according to their traditions and the needs imposed by their environments.

In this first stage, the two societies — Aboriginal and non-Aboriginal — were physically separated by a wide ocean. From an Aboriginal philosophical perspective, the separation between the two distinct worlds could also be expressed as having been established by the acts of creation. Accordingly, the Creator gave each people its distinct place and role to perform in the harmonious operation of nature and in a manner and under circumstances appropriate to each people. Aboriginal creation stories are thus not only the repository of a people's distinct national history, but also an expression of the divine gift and caretaking responsibility given to each people by the Creator.

By the end of Stage 1 (see Chapter 4), the physical and cultural distance between Aboriginal and non-Aboriginal societies narrowed drastically as Europeans moved across the ocean and began to settle in North America.

2.2 Stage 2: Contact and Co-operation

The beginning of Stage 2 (see Chapter 5) was marked by increasingly regular contact between European and Aboriginal societies and by the need to establish the terms by which they would live together. It was a period when Aboriginal people provided assistance to the newcomers to help them survive in the unfamiliar environment; this stage also saw the establishment of trading and military alliances, as well as intermarriage and mutual cultural adaptation. This stage was also marked by incidents of conflict, by growth in the number of non-Aboriginal immigrants, and by the steep decline in Aboriginal populations following the ravages of diseases to which they had no natural immunity.

Although there were exceptions, there were many instances of mutual tolerance and respect during this long period. In these cases, social distance was maintained — that is, the social, cultural and political differences between the two societies were respected by and large. Each was regarded as distinct and autonomous, left to govern its own internal affairs but co-operating in areas of mutual interest and, occasionally and increasingly, linked in various trading relationships and other forms of nation-to-nation alliances.

2.3 Stage 3: Displacement and Assimilation

In Stage 3 (see Chapter 6), non-Aboriginal society was for the most part no longer willing to respect the distinctiveness of Aboriginal societies. Non-Aboriginal society made repeated attempts to recast Aboriginal people and their distinct forms of social organization so they would conform to the expectations of what had become the mainstream. In this period, interventions in Aboriginal societies reached their peak, taking the form of relocations, residential schools, the outlawing of Aboriginal cultural practices, and various other interventionist measures of the type found in the Indian Acts of the late 1800s and early 1900s.

These interventions did not succeed in undermining Aboriginal social values or their sense of distinctiveness, however. Neither did they change the determination of Aboriginal societies to conduct their relations with the dominant society in the manner Aboriginal people considered desirable and appropriate, in line with the parameters established in the initial contact period. (Hence the continuation of the horizontal line in dotted form in Figure 3.3.)

Non-Aboriginal society began to recognize the failure of these policies toward the end of this period, particularly after the federal government's ill-fated 1969 white paper, which would have ended the special constitutional, legal and political status of Aboriginal peoples within Confederation.

2.4 Stage 4: Negotiation and Renewal

This stage in the relationship between Aboriginal and non-Aboriginal societies, which takes us to the present day, is characterized by non-Aboriginal society's admission of the manifest failure of its interventionist and assimilationist approach. This acknowledgement is pushed by domestic and also by international forces. Campaigns by national Aboriginal social and political organizations, court decisions on Aboriginal rights, sympathetic public opinion, developments in international law, and the worldwide political mobilization of Indigenous peoples under the auspices of the United Nations have all played a role during this stage in the relationship.

As a result, non-Aboriginal society is haltingly beginning the search for change in the relationship.

A period of dialogue, consultation and negotiation ensues, in which a range of options, centring on the concept of full Aboriginal self-government and restoration of the original partnership of the contact and co-operation period, is considered. From the perspective of Aboriginal groups, the primary objective is to gain more control over their own affairs by reducing unilateral interventions by non-Aboriginal society and regaining a relationship of mutual recognition and respect for differences. However, Aboriginal people also appear to realize that, at the same time, they must take steps to re-establish their own societies and to heal wounds caused by the many years of dominance by non-Aboriginal people.

It is clear that any attempt to reduce so long and complex a history of interrelationship into four stages is necessarily a simplification of reality. It is as though we have taken many different river systems, each in a different part of the country, each viewed from many different vantages, and tried to channel them into one stream of characteristics that would be most typical of the river as it has flowed through Canada.

We have attempted to retain a sense of the diversity of the historical experience by presenting numerous snapshots or slices of history. Instead of providing a linear, chronological overview, we have chosen particular societies, particular events or particular turning points in history to illustrate each of the stages and to give the flavour of the historical experience in at least some of its complexity.

It is difficult to place each stage within a precise time frame. In part this is because of the considerable overlap between the stages. They flow easily and almost indiscernibly into each other, with the transition from one to the other becoming apparent only after the next stage is fully under way. Nor is the time frame for each period the same in all parts of the country; Aboriginal groups in eastern and central Canada generally experienced contact with non-Aboriginal societies earlier than groups in more northern or western locations.

Constitutional Context: Law, the State, and the Constitution

(a) *Reference re Secession of Quebec*†

[THE COURT:]

I. INTRODUCTION

[1] This Reference requires us to consider momentous questions that go to the heart of our system of constitutional government. The observation we made more than a decade ago in *Reference re Manitoba Language Rights*, [1985] 1 S.C.R. 721 (*Manitoba Language Rights Reference*), at p. 728, applies with equal force here: as in that case, the present one "combines legal and constitutional questions of the utmost subtlety and complexity with political questions of great sensitivity". In our view, it is not possible to answer the questions that have been put to us without a consideration of a number of underlying principles. An exploration of the meaning and nature of these underlying principles is not merely of academic interest. On the contrary, such an exploration is of immense utility. Only once those underlying principles have been examined and delineated may a considered response to the questions we are required to answer emerge.

· · · ·

III. REFERENCE QUESTIONS

A. Question 1

Under the Constitution of Canada, can the National Assembly, legislature or government of Quebec effect the secession of Quebec from Canada unilaterally?

(1) Introduction

[32] As we confirmed in *Reference re Objection by Quebec to a Resolution to Amend the Constitution*, [1982] 2 S.C.R. 793, at p. 806, "The *Constitution Act, 1982* is now in force. Its legality is neither challenged nor assailable." The "Constitution of Canada" certainly includes the constitutional texts enumerated in s. 52(2) of the *Constitution Act, 1982*. Although these texts have a primary place in determining constitutional rules, they are not exhaustive. The Constitution also "embraces unwritten, as well as written rules", as we recently observed in the *Provincial Judges Reference*, *supra*, at para. 92. Finally, as was said in the *Patriation Reference*, *supra*, at p. 874, the Constitution of Canada includes

> the global system of rules and principles which govern the exercise of constitutional authority in the whole and in every part of the Canadian state.

These supporting principles and rules, which include constitutional conventions and the workings of Parliament, are a necessary part of our Constitution because problems or situations may arise which are not expressly dealt with by the text of the Constitution. In order to endure over time, a constitution must contain a comprehensive set of rules and principles which are capable of providing an exhaustive legal framework for our system of government. Such principles and rules emerge from an understanding of the constitutional text itself, the historical context, and previous judicial interpretations of constitutional meaning. In our view, there are four fundamental

---

† [1998] 2 S.C.R. 217 at paras. 1, 32, 49, 51–52, 43, 59, 61, 63–64, 66, 68, 70, 72, 76–77, 79, 81, 82..

and organizing principles of the Constitution which are relevant to addressing the question before us (although this enumeration is by no means exhaustive): federalism; democracy; constitutionalism and the rule of law; and respect for minorities. The foundation and substance of these principles are addressed in the following paragraphs. We will then turn to their specific application to the first reference question before us.

.   .   .   .

(3) Analysis of the Constitutional Principles
(A) NATURE OF THE PRINCIPLES

[49] What are those underlying principles? Our Constitution is primarily a written one, the product of 131 years of evolution. Behind the written word is an historical lineage stretching back through the ages, which aids in the consideration of the underlying constitutional principles. These principles inform and sustain the constitutional text: they are the vital unstated assumptions upon which the text is based. The following discussion addresses the four foundational constitutional principles that are most germane for resolution of this Reference: federalism, democracy, constitutionalism and the rule of law, and respect for minority rights. These defining principles function in symbiosis. No single principle can be defined in isolation from the others, nor does any one principle trump or exclude the operation of any other.

.   .   .   .

[51] Although these underlying principles are not explicitly made part of the Constitution by any written provision, other than in some respects by the oblique reference in the preamble to the *Constitution Act, 1867*, it would be impossible to conceive of our constitutional structure without them. The principles dictate major elements of the architecture of the Constitution itself and are as such its lifeblood.

[52] The principles assist in the interpretation of the text and the delineation of spheres of jurisdiction, the scope of rights and obligations, and the role of our political institutions. Equally important, observance of and respect for these principles is essential to the ongoing process of constitutional development and evolution of our Constitution as a "living tree", to invoke the famous description in *Edwards v. Attorney-General for Canada*, [1930] A.C. 123 (P.C.), at p. 136. As this Court indicated in *New Brunswick Broadcasting Co. v. Nova Scotia (Speaker of the House of Assembly)*, [1993] 1 S.C.R. 319, Canadians have long recognized the existence and importance of unwritten constitutional principles in our system of government.

(B) FEDERALISM

.   .   .   .

[The Court discussed federalism in the context of Conferation earlier:]

[43] Federalism was a legal response to the underlying political and cultural realities that existed at Confederation and continue to exist today. At Confederation, political leaders told their respective communities that the Canadian union would be able to reconcile diversity with unity. It is pertinent, in the context of the present Reference, to mention the words of George-Etienne Cartier (cited in J. C. Bonenfant, "Les Canadiens francais et la naissance de la Confédération", [1952] C.H.A.R. 39, at p. 42):

> [TRANSLATION] When we are united, he said, we shall form a political nationality independent of the national origin or the religion of any individual. There are some who regretted that there was diversity of races and who expressed the hope that this distinctive character would disappear. The idea of unity of races is a utopia; it is an impossibility. A distinction of this nature will always exist, just as dissimilarity seems to be in the order of the physical, moral and political worlds. As to the objection based on this fact, that a large nation cannot be formed because Lower Canada is largely French and Catholic and Upper Canada is English and Protestant and the interior provinces are mixed, it constitutes, in my view, reasoning that is futile in the extreme.... In our own federation, we will have Catholics and Protestants, English, French, Irish and Scots and everyone, through his efforts and successes, will add to the prosperity and glory of the new confederation. We are of different races, not so that we can wage war on one another, but in order to work together for our well-being.

The federal–provincial division of powers was a legal recognition of the diversity that existed among the initial members of Confederation, and manifested a concern to accommodate that diversity within a single nation by granting significant powers to provincial governments. The *Constitution Act, 1867* was an act of nation-building. It was the first step in the transition from colonies separately dependent on the Imperial Parliament for their governance to a unified and independent political state in which different peoples could resolve their disagreements and work together toward common goals and a common interest. Federalism was the political mechanism by which diversity could be reconciled with unity.

. . . .

[59] The principle of federalism facilitates the pursuit of collective goals by cultural and linguistic minorities which form the majority within a particular province. This is the case in Quebec, where the majority of the population is French-speaking, and which possesses a distinct culture. This is not merely the result of chance. The social and demographic reality of Quebec explains the existence of the province of Quebec as a political unit and indeed, was one of the essential reasons for establishing a federal structure for the Canadian union in 1867. The experience of both Canada East and Canada West under the *Union Act, 1840* (U.K.), 3–4 Vict., c. 35, had not been satisfactory. The federal structure adopted at Confederation enabled French-speaking Canadians to form a numerical majority in the province of Quebec, and so exercise the considerable provincial powers conferred by the *Constitution Act, 1867* in such a way as to promote their language and culture. It also made provision for certain guaranteed representation within the federal Parliament itself.

. . . .

(C) DEMOCRACY

[61] Democracy is a fundamental value in our constitutional law and political culture. While it has both an institutional and an individual aspect, the democratic principle was also argued before us in the sense of the supremacy of the sovereign will of a people, in this case potentially to be expressed by Quebecers in support of unilateral secession. It is useful to explore in a summary way these different aspects of the democratic principle.

. . . .

[63] Democracy is commonly understood as being a political system of majority rule. It is essential to be clear what this means. The evolution of our democratic tradition can be traced back to the *Magna Carta* (1215) and before, through the long struggle for Parliamentary supremacy which culminated in the English *Bill of Rights* in 1688–89, the emergence of representative political institutions in the colonial era, the development of responsible government in the 19th century, and eventually, the achievement of Confederation itself in 1867. "[T]he Canadian tradi-

tion", the majority of this Court held in *Reference re Provincial Electoral Boundaries (Sask.)*, [1991] 2 S.C.R. 158, at p. 186, is "one of evolutionary democracy moving in uneven steps toward the goal of universal suffrage and more effective representation". Since Confederation, efforts to extend the franchise to those unjustly excluded from participation in our political system — such as women, minorities, and aboriginal peoples — have continued, with some success, to the present day.

[64] Democracy is not simply concerned with the process of government. On the contrary, as suggested in *Switzman v. Elbling, supra*, at p. 306, democracy is fundamentally connected to substantive goals, most importantly, the promotion of self-government. Democracy accommodates cultural and group identities: *Reference re Provincial Electoral Boundaries*, at p. 188. Put another way, a sovereign people exercises its right to self-government through the democratic process. In considering the scope and purpose of the *Charter*, the Court in *R. v. Oakes*, [1986] 1 S.C.R. 103, articulated some of the values inherent in the notion of democracy (at p. 136):

> The Court must be guided by the values and principles essential to a free and democratic society which I believe to embody, to name but a few, respect for the inherent dignity of the human person, commitment to social justice and equality, accommodation of a wide variety of beliefs, respect for cultural and group identity, and faith in social and political institutions which enhance the participation of individuals and groups in society.

. . . .

[66] It is, of course, true that democracy expresses the sovereign will of the people. Yet this expression, too, must be taken in the context of the other institutional values we have identified as pertinent to this Reference. The relationship between democracy and federalism means, for example, that in Canada there may be different and equally legitimate majorities in different provinces and territories and at the federal level. No one majority is more or less "legitimate" than the others as an expression of democratic opinion, although, of course, the consequences will vary with the subject matter. A federal system of government enables different provinces to pursue policies responsive to the particular concerns and interests of people in that province. At the same time, Canada as a whole is also a democratic community in which citizens construct and achieve goals on a national scale through a federal government acting within the

limits of its jurisdiction. The function of federalism is to enable citizens to participate concurrently in different collectivities and to pursue goals at both a provincial and a federal level.

. . . .

[68] Finally, we highlight that a functioning democracy requires a continuous process of discussion. The Constitution mandates government by democratic legislatures, and an executive accountable to them, "resting ultimately on public opinion reached by discussion and the interplay of ideas" (*Saumur v. City of Quebec, supra*, at p. 330). At both the federal and provincial level, by its very nature, the need to build majorities necessitates compromise, negotiation, and deliberation. No one has a monopoly on truth, and our system is predicated on the faith that in the marketplace of ideas, the best solutions to public problems will rise to the top. Inevitably, there will be dissenting voices. A democratic system of government is committed to considering those dissenting voices, and seeking to acknowledge and address those voices in the laws by which all in the community must live.

. . . .

(D) CONSTITUTIONALISM AND THE RULE OF LAW

[70] The principles of constitutionalism and the rule of law lie at the root of our system of government. The rule of law, as observed in *Roncarelli v. Duplessis*, [1959] S.C.R. 121, at p. 142, is "a fundamental postulate of our constitutional structure." As we noted in the *Patriation Reference, supra*, at pp. 805–6, "[t]he 'rule of law' is a highly textured expression, importing many things which are beyond the need of these reasons to explore but conveying, for example, a sense of orderliness, of subjection to known legal rules and of executive accountability to legal authority". At its most basic level, the rule of law vouchsafes to the citizens and residents of the country a stable, predictable and ordered society in which to conduct their affairs. It provides a shield for individuals from arbitrary state action.

. . . .

[72] The constitutionalism principle bears considerable similarity to the rule of law, although they are not identical. The essence of constitutionalism in Canada is embodied in s. 52(1) of the *Constitution Act, 1982*, which provides that "[t]he Constitution of Canada is the supreme law of Canada, and any law

that is inconsistent with the provisions of the Constitution is, to the extent of the inconsistency, of no force or effect." Simply put, the constitutionalism principle requires that all government action comply with the Constitution. The rule of law principle requires that all government action must comply with the law, including the Constitution. This Court has noted on several occasions that with the adoption of the *Charter*, the Canadian system of government was transformed to a significant extent from a system of Parliamentary supremacy to one of constitutional supremacy. The Constitution binds all governments, both federal and provincial, including the executive branch (*Operation Dismantle Inc. v. The Queen*, [1985] 1 S.C.R. 441, at p. 455). They may not transgress its provisions: indeed, their sole claim to exercise lawful authority rests in the powers allocated to them under the Constitution, and can come from no other source.

. . . .

[76] Canadians have never accepted that ours is a system of simple majority rule. Our principle of democracy, taken in conjunction with the other constitutional principles discussed here, is richer. Constitutional government is necessarily predicated on the idea that the political representatives of the people of a province have the capacity and the power to commit the province to be bound into the future by the constitutional rules being adopted. These rules are "binding" not in the sense of frustrating the will of a majority of a province, but as defining the majority which must be consulted in order to alter the fundamental balances of political power (including the spheres of autonomy guaranteed by the principle of federalism), individual rights, and minority rights in our society. Of course, those constitutional rules are themselves amenable to amendment, but only through a process of negotiation which ensures that there is an opportunity for the constitutionally defined rights of all the parties to be respected and reconciled.

[77] In this way, our belief in democracy may be harmonized with our belief in constitutionalism. Constitutional amendment often requires some form of substantial consensus precisely because the content of the underlying principles of our Constitution demand it. By requiring broad support in the form of an "enhanced majority" to achieve constitutional change, the Constitution ensures that minority interests must be addressed before proposed changes which would affect them may be enacted.

. . . .

(E) PROTECTION OF MINORITIES

[79] The fourth underlying constitutional principle we address here concerns the protection of minorities. There are a number of specific constitutional provisions protecting minority language, religion and education rights. Some of those provisions are, as we have recognized on a number of occasions, the product of historical compromises. As this Court observed in *Reference re Bill 30, An Act to Amend the Education Act (Ont.)* [1987] 1 S.C.R. 1148, at p. 1173, and in *Reference re Education Act (Que.)*, [1993] 2 S.C.R. 511, at pp. 529–30, the protection of minority religious education rights was a central consideration in the negotiations leading to Confederation. In the absence of such protection, it was felt that the minorities in what was then Canada East and Canada West would be submerged and assimilated. See also *Greater Montreal Protestant School Board v. Quebec (Attorney General)*, [1989] 1 S.C.R. 377, at pp. 401–2, and *Adler v. Ontario*, [1996] 3 S.C.R. 609. Similar concerns animated the provisions protecting minority language rights, as noted in *Société des Acadiens du Nouveau-Brunswick Inc. v. Association of Parents for Fairness in Education*, [1986] 1 S.C.R. 549, at p. 564.

. . . .

[81] The concern of our courts and governments to protect minorities has been prominent in recent years, particularly following the enactment of the *Charter*. Undoubtedly, one of the key considerations motivating the enactment of the *Charter*, and the process of constitutional judicial review that it entails, is the protection of minorities. However, it should not be forgotten that the protection of minority rights had a long history before the enactment of the *Charter*. Indeed, the protection of minority rights was clearly an essential consideration in the design of our constitutional structure even at the time of Confederation: *Senate Reference*, *supra*, at p. 71. Although Canada's record of upholding the rights of minorities is not a spotless one, that goal is one towards which Canadians have been striving since Confederation, and the process has not been without successes. The principle of protecting minority rights continues to exercise influence in the operation and interpretation of our Constitution.

[82] Consistent with this long tradition of respect for minorities, which is at least as old as Canada itself, the framers of the *Constitution Act, 1982* included in s. 35 explicit protection for existing aboriginal and treaty rights, and in s. 25, a non-derogation clause in favour of the rights of aboriginal peoples. The "promise" of s. 35, as it was termed in *R. v. Sparrow*, [1990] 1 S.C.R. 1075, at p. 1983, recognized not only the ancient occupation of land by aboriginal peoples, but their contribution to the building of Canada, and the special commitments made to them by successive governments. The protection of these rights, so recently and arduously achieved, whether looked at in their own right or as part of the larger concern with minorities, reflects an important underlying constitutional value.

(b) *Roncarelli v. Duplessis*†

[RAND J.:]

The material facts from which my conclusion is drawn are these. The appellant was the proprietor of a restaurant in a busy section of Montreal which in 1946 through its transmission to him from his father had been continuously licensed for the sale of liquor for approximately 34 years; he is of good education and repute and the restaurant was of a superior class. On December 4 of that year, while his application for annual renewal was before the Liquor Commission, the existing license was cancelled and his application for renewal rejected, to which was added a declaration by the respondent that no future license would ever issue to him. These primary facts took place in the following circumstances.

For some years the appellant had been an adherent of a rather militant Christian religious

---

† [1959] S.C.R. 121 at 131–34, 136–45.

sect known as the Witnesses of Jehovah. Their ideology condemns the established church institutions and stresses the absolute and exclusive personal relation of the individual to the Deity without human intermediation or intervention.

The first impact of their proselytizing zeal upon the Roman Catholic church and community in Quebec, as might be expected, produced a violent reaction. Meetings were forcibly broken up, property damaged, individuals ordered out of communities, in one case out of the province, and generally, within the cities and towns, bitter controversy aroused. The work of the Witnesses was carried on both by word of mouth and by the distribution of printed matter, the latter including two periodicals known as "The Watch Tower" and "Awake", sold at a small price.

In 1945 the provincial authorities began to take steps to bring an end to what was considered insulting and offensive to the religious beliefs and feelings of the Roman Catholic population. Large scale arrests were made of young men and women, by whom the publications mentioned were being held out for sale, under local by-laws requiring a licence for peddling any kind of wares. Altogether almost one thousand of such charges were laid. The penalty involved in Montreal, where most of the arrests took place, was a fine of $40, and as the Witnesses disputed liability, bail was in all cases resorted to.

The appellant, being a person of some means, was accepted by the Recorder's Court as bail without question, and up to November 12, 1946, he had gone security in about 380 cases, some of the accused being involved in repeated offences. Up to this time there had been no suggestion of impropriety; the security of the appellant was taken as so satisfactory that at times, to avoid delay when he was absent from the city, recognizances were signed by him in blank and kept ready for completion by the Court officials. The reason for the accumulation of charges was the doubt that they could be sustained in law. Apparently the legal officers of Montreal, acting in concert with those of the Province, had come to an agreement with the attorney for the Witnesses to have a test case proceeded with. Pending that, however, there was no stoppage of the sale of the tracts and this became the annoying circumstance that produced the volume of proceedings.

On or about November 12 it was decided to require bail in cash for Witnesses so arrested and the sum set ranged from $100 to $300. No such bail was furnished by the appellant; his connection with giving security ended with this change of practice; and in the result, all of the charges in relation to which he had become surety were dismissed.

At no time did he take any part in the distribution of the tracts: he was an adherent of the group but nothing more. It was shown that he had leased to another member premises in Sherbrooke which were used as a hall for carrying on religious meetings: but it is unnecessary to do more than mention that fact to reject it as having no bearing on the issues raised. Beyond the giving of bail and being an adherent, the appellant is free from any relation that could be tortured into a badge of character pertinent to his fitness or unfitness to hold a liquor licence.

The mounting resistance that stopped the surety bail sought other means of crushing the propagandist invasion and among the circumstances looked into was the situation of the appellant. Admittedly an adherent, he was enabling these protagonists to be at large to carry on their campaign of publishing what they believed to be the Christian truth as revealed by the Bible; he was also the holder of a liquor licence, a "privilege" granted by the Province, the profits from which, as it was seen by the authorities, he was using to promote the disturbance of settled beliefs and arouse community disaffection generally. Following discussions between the then Mr. Archambault, as the personality of the Liquor Commission, and the chief prosecuting officer in Montreal, the former, on or about November 21, telephoned to the respondent, advised him of those facts, and queried what should be done. Mr. Duplessis answered that the matter was serious and that the identity of the person furnishing bail and the liquor licensee should be put beyond doubt. A few days later, that identity being established through a private investigator, Mr. Archambault again communicated with the respondent and, as a result of what passed between them, the licence, as of December 4, 1946, was revoked.

In the meantime, about November 25, 1946, a blasting answer had come from the Witnesses. In an issue of one of the periodicals, under the heading "Quebec's Burning Hate", was a searing denunciation of what was alleged to be the savage persecution of Christian believers. Immediately instructions were sent out from the department of the Attorney-General ordering the confiscation of the issue and proceedings were taken against one Boucher charging him with publication of a seditious libel.

It is then wholly as a private citizen, an adherent of a religious group, holding a liquor licence and furnishing bail to arrested persons for no other purpose than to enable them to be released from detention pending the determination of the charges against them, and with no other relevant considerations to be taken into account, that he is involved in the issues of this controversy.

35

The complementary state of things is equally free from doubt. From the evidence of Mr. Duplessis and Mr. Archambault alone, it appears that the action taken by the latter as the general manager and sole member of the Commission was dictated by Mr. Duplessis as Attorney-General and Prime Minister of the province; that that step was taken as a means of bringing to a halt the activities of the Witnesses, to punish the appellant for the part he had played not only by revoking the existing licence but in declaring him barred from one "forever", and to warn others that they similarly would be stripped of provincial "privileges" if they persisted in any activity directly or indirectly related to the Witnesses and to the objectionable campaign. The respondent felt that action to be his duty, something which his conscience demanded of him; and as representing the provincial government his decision became automatically that of Mr. Archambault and the Commission. The following excerpts of evidence make this clear:

. . . .

LA COUR:

. . . .

D. Référant à l'article contenue dans la *Gazette* du 5 décembre, c'est-à-dire le jour suivant l'annulation du permis, vous trouvez là les mots en anglais :

In statement to the press yesterday, the Premier recalled that: "Two weeks ago, I pointed out that the Provincial Government had the firm intention to take the most rigorous and efficient measures possible to get rid of those who under the names of Witnesses of Jehovah, distribute circulars which in my opinion, are not only injurious for Quebec and its population, but which are of a very libellous and seditious character. The propaganda of the Witnesses of Jehovah cannot be tolerated and there are more than 400 of them now before the courts in Montreal, Quebec, Three Rivers and other centers."

"A certain Mr. Roncarelli has supplied bail for hundreds of witnesses of Jehovah. The sympathy which this man has shown for the Witnesses, in such an evident, repeated and audacious manner, is a provocation to public order, to the administration of justice and is definitely contrary to the aims of justice."

D. Je vous demande, monsieur le Premier Ministre, si ce sont les paroles presque exactes ou exactes que vous avez dites à la conférence de presse?

R. Que j'ai dit ici: "A certain Mr. Roncarelli has supplied bail for hundreds of witnesses of Jehovah. The Sympathy which this man has shown for the Witnesses, in such an evident, repeated and audacious manner, is a provocation to public order, to the administration of justice and is definitely contrary to the aims of justice." Je l'ai dit et je considère que c'est vrai.

...

M. ARCHAMBAULT:

D. Maintenant, ce jour-là où vous avez reçu une lettre, le 30 novembre 1946, avez-vous décidé, ce jour-là, d'enlever la licence?

R. Certainement, ce jour-là, j'avais appelé le Premier Ministre, en l'occurrence le procureur général, lui faisant part des constatations, c'est-à-dire des renseignements que je possédais, et de mon intention d'annuler le privilège, et le Premier Ministre m'a répondu de prendre mes précautions, de bien vérifier s'il s'agissait bien de la même personne, qu'il pouvait y avoir plusieurs Roncarelli, et [cetera]. Alors, quand j'ai eu la confirmation de Y3 à l'effet que c'était la même personne, j'ai rappelé le Premier Ministre pour l'assurer qu'il s'agissait bien de Frank Roncarelli, détenteur d'un permis de la Commission des Liqueurs; et, là, le Premier Ministre m'a autorisé, il m'a donné son consentement, son approbation, sa permission, et son ordre de procéder.

In these circumstances, when the *de facto* power of the Executive over its appointees at will to such a statutory public function is exercised deliberately and intentionally to destroy the vital business interests of a citizen, is there legal redress by him against the person so acting? This calls for an examination of the statutory provisions governing the issue, renewal and revocation of liquor licences and the scope of authority entrusted by law to the Attorney-General and the government in relation to the administration of the Act.

The liquor law is contained in R.S.Q. 1941, c. 255, entitled *An Act Respecting Alcoholic Liquor*. A Commission is created as a corporation, the only member of which is the general manager. By s. 5

The exercise of the functions, duties and powers of the Quebec Liquor Commission shall be vested in one person alone, named by the Lieutenant-Governor in Council, with the title of Manager. The remuneration of such person shall be determined by the Lieutenant-Governor in Council and be paid out of the revenues of the Liquor Commission. R.S. 1925, c. 37, s. 5; 1 Ed. VII (2), c. 14, es. 1 and 5; 1 Geo. VI, c. 22, es. 1 and 5.

The entire staff for carrying out the duties of the Commission are appointed by the general manager — here Mr. Archambault — who fixes salaries and assigns functions, the Lieutenant-Governor in Council reserving the right of approval of the salaries. Besides the general operation of buying and selling liquor throughout the province and doing all things necessary to that end, the Commission is authorized by s. 9 (e) to "grant, refuse or cancel permits for the sale of alcoholic liquors or other permits in regard thereto and to transfer the permit of any person deceased". By s. 12 suits against the general manager for acts done in the exercise of his duties require the authority of the Chief Justice of the province, and the Commission can be sued only with the consent of the Attorney-General. Every officer of the Commission is declared to be a public officer and by R.S.O. 1941, c. 10, s. 2, holds office during pleasure. By s. 19 the Commission shall pay over to the Provincial Treasurer any moneys which the latter considers available and by s. 20 the Commission is to account to the Provincial Treasurer for its receipts, disbursements, assets and liabilities. Sections 30 and 32 provide for the issue of permits to sell; they are to be granted to individuals only, in their own names; by s. 34 the Commission "may refuse to grant any permit"; subs. (2) provides for permits in special cases of municipalities where prohibition of sale is revoked in whole or part by by-law; subs. (3) restricts or refuses the grant of permits in certain cities the Council of which so requests; but it is provided that

> ... If the fyling of such by-law takes place after the Commission has granted a permit in such city or town, the Commission shall be unable to give effect to the request before the first of May next after the date of fyling.

Subsection (4) deals with a refusal to issue permits in small cities unless requested by a by-law, approved by a majority vote of the electors. By subs. (6) special power is given the Commission to grant permits to hotels in summer resorts for five months only notwithstanding that requests under subss. (2) and (4) are not made. Section 35 prescribes the expiration of every permit on April 30 of each year. Dealing with cancellation, the section provides that the "Commission may cancel any permit at its discretion". Besides

the loss of the privilege and without the necessity of legal proceedings, cancellation entails loss of fees paid to obtain it and confiscation of the liquor in the possession of the holder and the receptacles containing it. If the cancellation is not followed by prosecution for an offence under the Act, compensation is provided for certain items of the forfeiture. Subsection (5) requires the Commission to cancel any permit made use of on behalf of a person other than the holder; s. 36 requires cancellation in specified cases. The sale of liquor is, by s. 42, forbidden to various persons. Section 148 places upon the Attorney-General the duty of

1. Assuring the observance of this Act and of the Alcoholic Liquor [Possession] and Transportation Act (Chap. 256), and investigating, preventing and suppressing the infringements of such acts, in every way authorized thereby;
2. Conducting the suits or prosecutions for infringements of this Act or of the said Alcoholic Liquor Possession and Transportation Act. R.S. 1925, c. 37, s. 78a; 24 Geo. V, c. 17, s. 17.

The provisions of the statute, which may be supplemented by detailed regulations, furnish a code for the complete administration of the sale and distribution of alcoholic liquors directed by the Commission as a public service, for all legitimate purposes of the populace. It recognizes the association of wines and liquors as embellishments of food and its ritual and as an interest of the public. As put in Macbeth, the "sauce to meat is ceremony", and so we have restaurants, cafés, hotels and other places of serving food, specifically provided for in that association.

At the same time the issue of permits has a complementary interest in those so catering to the public. The continuance of the permit over the years, as in this case, not only recognizes its virtual [necessity] to a superior class restaurant but also its [identification] with the business carried on. The provisions for assignment of the permit are to this most pertinent and they were exemplified in the continuity of the business here. As its exercise continues, the economic life of the holder becomes progressively more deeply implicated with the privilege while at the same time his vocation becomes correspondingly dependent on it.

The field of licensed occupations and businesses of this nature is steadily becoming of greater concern to citizens generally. It is a matter of vital importance that a public administration that can refuse to allow a person to enter or continue a calling which, in the absence of regulation, would be free and legitimate, should be conducted with complete impartiality and integrity; and that the grounds for refusing or cancelling a permit should unquestionably be such and such only as are incompatible with the purposes envisaged by the statute: the duty of a Commission is to serve those purposes and those only. A decision to deny or cancel such a privilege lies within the "discretion" of the Commission; but that means that decision is to be based upon a weighing of considerations pertinent to the object of the administration.

In public regulation of this sort there is no such thing as absolute and untrammelled "discretion", that is that action can be taken on any ground or for any reason that can be suggested to the mind of the administrator; no legislative Act can, without express language, be taken to contemplate an unlimited arbitrary power exercisable for any purpose, however capricious or irrelevant, regardless of the nature or purpose of the statute. Fraud and corruption in the Commission may not be mentioned in such statutes but they are always implied as exceptions. "Discretion" necessarily implies good faith in discharging public duty; there is always a perspective within which a statute is intended to operate; and any clear departure from its lines or objects is just as objectionable as fraud or corruption. Could an applicant be refused a permit because he had been born in another province, or because of the colour of his hair? The ordinary language of the legislature cannot be so distorted.

To deny or revoke a permit because a citizen exercises an unchallengeable right totally irrelevant to the sale of liquor in a restaurant is equally beyond the scope of the discretion conferred. There was here not only revocation of the existing permit but a declaration of a future, definitive disqualification of the appellant to obtain one: it was to be "forever". This purports to divest his citizenship status of its incident of membership in the class of those of the public to whom such a privilege could be extended. Under the statutory language here, that is not competent to the Commission and a fortiori to the government or the respondent: *McGillivray v. Kimber*. There is here an administrative tribunal which, in certain respects, is to act in a judicial manner; and even on the view of the dissenting justices in *McGillivray*, there is liability: what could be more malicious than to punish this licensee for having done what he had an absolute right to do in a matter utterly irrelevant to the *Liquor Act*? Malice in the proper sense is simply acting for a reason and purpose knowingly foreign to the administration, to

which was added here the element of intentional punishment by what was virtually vocation outlawry.

It may be difficult if not impossible in cases generally to demonstrate a breach of this public duty in the illegal purpose served; there may be no means, even if proceedings against the Commission were permitted by the Attorney-General, as here they were refused, of compelling the Commission to justify a refusal or revocation or to give reasons for its action; on these questions I make no observation; but in the case before us that difficulty is not present: the reasons are openly avowed.

The act of the respondent through the instrumentality of the Commission brought about a breach of an implied public statutory duty toward the appellant; it was a gross abuse of legal power expressly intended to punish him for an act wholly irrelevant to the statute, a punishment which inflicted on him, as it was intended to do, the destruction of his economic life as a restaurant keeper within the province. Whatever may be the immunity of the Commission or its member from an action for damages, there is none in the respondent. He was under no duty in relation to the appellant and his act was an [intrusion] upon the functions of a statutory body. The injury done by him was a fault engaging liability within the principles of the underlying public law of Quebec: *Mostyn v. Fabrigas*, and under art. 1053 of the *Civil Code*. That, in the presence of expanding administrative regulation of economic activities, such a step and its consequences are to be suffered by the victim without recourse or remedy, that an administration according to law is to be superseded by action dictated by and according to the arbitrary likes, dislikes and irrelevant purposes of public officers acting beyond their duty, would signalize the beginning of disintegration of the rule of law as a fundamental postulate of our constitutional structure. An administration of licences on the highest level of fair and impartial treatment to all may be forced to follow the practice of "first come, first served", which makes the strictest observance of equal responsibility to all of even greater importance; at this stage of developing government it would be a danger of high consequence to tolerate such a departure from good faith in executing the legislative purpose. It should be added, however, that that principle is not, by this language, intended to be extended to ordinary governmental employment: with that we are not here concerned.

It was urged by Mr. Beaulieu that the respondent, as the incumbent of an office of state, so long as he was proceeding in "good faith", was free to act in a matter of this kind virtually as he pleased. The office of Attorney-General traditionally and by statute carries duties that relate to advising the Executive, including here, administrative bodies, enforcing the public law and directing the administration of justice. In any decision of the statutory body in this case, he had no part to play beyond giving advice on legal questions arising. In that role his action should have been limited to advice on the validity of a revocation for such a reason or purpose and what that advice should have been does not seem to me to admit of any doubt. To pass from this limited scope of action to that of bringing about a step by the Commission beyond the bounds prescribed by the legislature for its exclusive action converted what was done into his personal act.

"Good faith" in this context, applicable both to the respondent and the general manager, means carrying out the statute according to its intent and for its purpose; it means good faith in acting with a rational appreciation of that intent and purpose and not with an improper intent and for an alien purpose; it does not mean for the purposes of punishing a person for exercising an unchallengeable right; it does not mean arbitrarily and illegally attempting to divest a citizen of an incident of his civil status.

I mention, in order to make clear that it has not been overlooked, the decision of the House of Lords in *Allen v. Flood*, in which the principle was laid down that an act of an individual otherwise not actionable does not become so because of the motive or reason for doing it, even maliciously to injure, as distinguished from an act done by two or more persons. No contention was made in the present case based on agreed action by the respondent and Mr. Archambault. In *Allen v. Flood*, the actor was a labour leader and the victims non-union workmen who were lawfully dismissed by their employer to avoid a strike involving no breach of contract or law. Here the act done was in relation to a public administration affecting the rights of a citizen to enjoy a public privilege, and a duty implied by the statute toward the victim was violated. The existing permit was an interest for which the appellant was entitled to protection against any unauthorized interference, and the illegal destruction of which gave rise to a remedy for the damages suffered. In *Allen v. Flood* there were no such elements.

Nor is it necessary to examine the question whether on the basis of an improper revocation the appellant could have compelled the issue of a new permit or whether the purported revocation was a void act. The revocation was *de facto*, it was intended to end the privilege and to bring about the consequences that followed. As against the respondent, the appellant was entitled to treat the breach of duty as effecting a revocation and to elect for damages.

Mr. Scott argued further that even if the revocation were within the scope of discretion and not a breach of duty, the intervention of the respondent in so using the Commission was equally a fault. The proposition generalized is this: where, by a statute restricting the ordinary activities of citizens, a privilege is conferred by an administrative body, the continuance of that enjoyment is to be free from the influence of third persons on that body for the purpose only of injuring the privilege holder. It is the application to such a privilege of the proposition urged but rejected in *Allen v. Flood* in the case of a private employment. The grounds of distinction between the two cases have been pointed out; but for the reasons given consideration of this ground is unnecessary and I express no opinion for or against it.

A subsidiary defence was that notice of action had not been given as required by art. 88 C.C.P. This provides generally that, without such notice, no public officer or person fulfilling any public function or duty is liable in damages "by reason of any act done by him in the exercise of his functions". Was the act here, then, done by the respondent in the course of that exercise? The basis of the claim, as I have found it, is that the act was quite beyond the scope of any function or duty committed to him, so far so that it was one done exclusively in a private capacity, however much in fact the influence of public office and power may have carried over into it. It would be only through an assumption of a general overriding power of executive direction in statutory administrative matters that any colour of propriety in the act could be found. But such an assumption would be in direct conflict with fundamental postulates of our provincial as well as dominion government; and in the actual circumstances there is not a shadow of justification for it in the statutory language.

The damages suffered involved the vocation of the appellant within the province. Any attempt at a precise computation or estimate must assume probabilities in an area of uncertainty and risk. The situation is one which the Court should approach as a jury would, in a view of its broad features; and in the best consideration I can give to them, the damages should be fixed at the sum of $25,000 plus that allowed by the trial court.

I would therefore allow the appeals, set aside the judgment of the Court of Queen's Bench and restore the judgment at trial modified by increasing the damages to the sum of $33,123.53. The appellant should have his costs in the Court of Queen's Bench and in this Court.

(c) *Reference re Firearms Act* (Can.)†

† [2000] 1 S.C.R. 783 at paras. 1–61.

[THE COURT:]

I. INTRODUCTION

[1] In 1995, Parliament amended the *Criminal Code*, R.S.C., 1985, c. C-46, by enacting the *Firearms Act*, S.C. 1995, c. 39, commonly referred to as the gun control law, to require the holders of all firearms to obtain licences and register their guns. In 1996, the Province of Alberta challenged Parliament's power to pass the gun control law by a reference to the Alberta Court of Appeal. The Court of Appeal by a 3:2 majority upheld Parliament's power to pass the law. The Province of Alberta now appeals that decision to this Court.

[2] The issue before this Court is not whether gun control is good or bad, whether the law is fair or unfair to gun owners, or whether it will be effective or ineffective in reducing the harm caused by the misuse of firearms. The only issue is whether or not Parliament has the constitutional authority to enact the law.

[3] The answer to this question lies in the Canadian Constitution. The Constitution assigns some matters to Parliament and others to the provincial legislatures: *Constitution Act, 1867*. The federal government asserts that the gun control law falls under its criminal law power, s. 91(27), and under its general power to legislate for the "Peace, Order and good Government" of Canada. Alberta, on the other hand, says the law falls under its power over property and civil rights, s. 92(13). All agree that to resolve this dispute, the Court must first determine what the gun control law is really about — its "pith and substance" — and then ask which head or heads of power it most naturally falls within.

[4] We conclude that the gun control law comes within Parliament's jurisdiction over criminal law. The law in "pith and substance" is directed to enhancing public safety by controlling access to firearms through prohibitions and penalties. This brings it under the federal criminal law power. While the law has regulatory aspects, they are secondary to its primary criminal law purpose. The intrusion of the law into the provincial jurisdiction over property and civil rights is not so excessive as to upset the balance of federalism.

II. REFERENCE QUESTIONS

[5] The formal questions put to the Alberta Court of Appeal by the Alberta government in 1996 are attached in Appendix A. Simply put, the issue before us is whether or not the licensing and registration provisions in the *Firearms Act*, as they relate to ordinary firearms, were validly enacted by Parliament. The impugned provisions of the Act are attached in Appendix B.

III. LEGISLATION

[6] For many years, the *Criminal Code* has restricted access to firearms, mainly automatic weapons and handguns, by classifying some as prohibited and some as restricted. The *Firearms Act* amendments extended this regulation to all firearms, including rifles and shotguns. As a result, s. 84 of the *Criminal Code* now controls three classes of firearms: (1) prohibited firearms (generally automatic weapons); (2) restricted firearms (generally handguns); and (3) all other firearms (generally rifles and shotguns). The third class of guns is variously referred to as "ordinary firearms", "long guns", and "unrestricted firearms". We will refer to this class as "ordinary firearms".

[7] The reference questions focus on the validity of the licensing and registration provisions for ordinary firearms introduced by the *Firearms Act*. The licensing sections of the Act provide that a person must be licensed in order to possess a firearm. Eligibility for a licence reflects safety interests. An applicant with a criminal record involving drug offences or violence, or a history of mental illness, may be denied a licence. An applicant who seeks to acquire a firearm must pass a safety course which requires a basic understanding of firearm safety and the legal responsibilities of firearm ownership. The chief firearms officer, who issues licences, may conduct a background check on the applicant in order to determine eligibility, and may attach conditions to a licence. Once issued, a licence is valid for five years, but it

may be revoked for contravention of its conditions or for certain criminal convictions. A licence refusal or revocation may be appealed to a court.

[8] The registration provisions of the Act are more limited. A firearm cannot be registered unless the applicant is licensed to possess that type of firearm. Registration is generally done by reference to the serial number on the firearm. A registration certificate is valid as long as its holder owns the weapon. If ownership of a registered weapon is transferred, the new owner must register the weapon. In order to give gun owners time to register their weapons, people who owned ordinary firearms as of January 1, 1998 are deemed to hold registration certificates that are valid until January 1, 2003. Possession of an unregistered firearm of any type is an offence. All licences and registration certificates, along with imported, exported, lost and stolen guns, are recorded in the Canadian Firearms Registry, which is operated by a federal appointee.

IV. REASONS OF THE ALBERTA COURT OF APPEAL

[9] The Alberta Court of Appeal upheld the 1995 gun control law by a 3:2 majority: 1998 ABCA 306 (CanLII), (1998), 65 Alta. L.R. (3d) 1. The court wrote four judgments.

A. Majority

[10] Fraser C.J.A., in a comprehensive judgment, began by noting that guns may be regulated by both the federal and provincial governments for different purposes, and that the effectiveness of the law is irrelevant to its constitutional characterization. She found that Parliament's purpose in enacting the law was to enhance public safety. While guns preserve lives and serve as useful tools, they also wound and kill. The latter aspect of guns — their inherent dangerousness — is the focus of the impugned provisions of the Act. Parliament's aim was to reduce the misuse of guns in crime, including domestic violence, as well as to reduce suicides and accidents caused by the misuse of firearms. The licensing provisions, which require applicants to pass a safety course and undergo a criminal record check and background investigation, support this purpose. The registration system, by seeking to reduce smuggling, theft and illegal sales, also addresses misuse. The licensing and registration provisions are inextricably intertwined. While the provisions entail the regulation of property rights, this regulation is the means of the law, not its

end. On this basis, Fraser C.J.A. concluded that the Act is in pith and substance designed to protect public safety from the misuse of firearms.

[11] Fraser C.J.A. went on to the second step in the analysis: considering whether or not that pith and substance could be allocated to one of Parliament's heads of power under the *Constitution Act, 1867*. She held that the legislation falls under the criminal law power, s. 91(27), under either its "prevention" aspect or its "prohibition, penalty, and purpose" aspect. The law does not represent a "colourable" or improper intrusion into provincial jurisdiction.

[12] Berger and Hetherington JJ.A. wrote separate opinions agreeing with the Chief Justice. Hetherington J.A. held that any firearm, used improperly, is dangerous to human life and health. As a result, Parliament's purpose, in seeking to prevent crime and promote public safety by discouraging possession, is a valid criminal law purpose. The potential inefficacy of the law, highlighted by Alberta and the other provincial governments, is irrelevant unless it shows that Parliament had a different purpose — a colourable motive. Colourability has not been shown because the law genuinely attempts to improve firearms storage, reduce trafficking, and aid in tracking guns generally. While the law may affect property and civil rights, that does not prevent Parliament from enacting it. Hetherington J.A. concluded that the *Firearms Act* contains prohibitions accompanied by penal sanctions, enacted for criminal public purposes, and therefore it is a valid law under the test propounded by La Forest J. of this Court in *RJR-MacDonald Inc. v. Canada (Attorney General)*, 1995 CanLII 64 (S.C.C.), [1995] 3 S.C.R. 199, and *R. v. Hydro-Québec*, 1997 CanLII 318 (S.C.C.), [1997] 3 S.C.R. 213.

[13] Berger J.A. likewise noted that all guns are capable of causing death if misused. He held that Parliament's purpose in enacting the legislation was to ensure that firearms are only possessed by those qualified to use them. The licensing provisions identify those who are qualified. The registration system ensures that only qualified people can acquire firearms. As a prohibition backed by a penalty, for a public purpose, the law is a valid exercise of Parliament's criminal law power. The regulatory aspects of the law are merely the means to an end.

B. Minority

[14] Conrad J.A. dissented, Irving J.A. concurring. Conrad J.A. broadly defined the purpose of the law as regulating all aspects of the possession and use of firearms. While firearms and safety are subjects of

both federal and provincial concern, the criminal law power represents a "carve-out" from provincial jurisdiction. The regulation of ownership rather than use and the complexity of the regulations demonstrate that this legislation cannot be classified as valid criminal law. The *Criminal Code* generally prohibits acts, rather than regulating ownership. Possession itself is not dangerous; it is only misuse that is dangerous, and the law goes far beyond prohibiting misuse. This led Conrad J.A. to conclude that the *Firearms Act* represents a colourable intrusion into the provincial jurisdiction over property and civil rights, and is invalid as an exercise of Parliament's jurisdiction over criminal law or its peace, order and good government power. While she would have struck down the legislation entirely, she held that if the licensing scheme were deemed valid, the registration scheme could be severed from the licensing scheme.

V. ANALYSIS

[15] The issue before us is whether the licensing and registration provisions of the *Firearms Act* constitute a valid federal enactment pursuant to Parliament's jurisdiction over criminal law or its peace, order and good government power. In order to answer this question, we must engage in the division of powers analysis used so often by this Court, and most recently summarized in *Global Securities Corp. v. British Columbia (Securities Commission)*, 2000 SCC 21 (CanLII), [2000] 1 S.C.R. 494, 2000 SCC 21; see also *Whitbread v. Walley*, 1990 CanLII 33 (S.C.C.), [1990] 3 S.C.R. 1273, *R. v. Big M Drug Mart Ltd.*, 1985 CanLII 69 (S.C.C.), [1985] 1 S.C.R. 295, and *R. v. Morgentaler*, 1993 CanLII 74 (S.C.C.), [1993] 3 S.C.R. 463. There are two stages to this analysis. The first step is to determine the "pith and substance" or essential character of the law. The second step is to classify that essential character by reference to the heads of power under the *Constitution Act, 1867* in order to determine whether the law comes within the jurisdiction of the enacting government. If it does, then the law is valid.

A. Characterization: What Is the Pith and Substance of the Law?

[16] The first task is to determine the "pith and substance" of the legislation. To use the wording of ss. 91 and 92, what is the "matter" of the law? What is its true meaning or essential character, its core? To determine the pith and substance, two aspects of the law must be examined: the purpose of the enacting body, and the legal effect of the law.

[17] A law's purpose is often stated in the legislation, but it may also be ascertained by reference to extrinsic material such as Hansard and government publications: see *Morgentaler, supra*, at pp. 483–84. While such extrinsic material was at one time inadmissible to facilitate the determination of Parliament's purpose, it is now well accepted that the legislative history, Parliamentary debates, and similar material may be quite properly considered as long as it is relevant and reliable and is not assigned undue weight: see *Global Securities, supra*, at para. 25; *Rizzo & Rizzo Shoes Ltd. (Re)*, 1998 CanLII 837 (S.C.C.), [1998] 1 S.C.R. 27, at para. 35; and *Doré v. Verdun (City)*, 1997 CanLII 315 (S.C.C.), [1997] 2 S.C.R. 862, at para. 14. Purpose may also be ascertained by considering the "mischief" of the legislation — the problem which Parliament sought to remedy: see *Morgentaler, supra*, at pp. 483–84.

[18] Determining the legal effects of a law involves considering how the law will operate and how it will affect Canadians. The Attorney General of Alberta states that the law will not actually achieve its purpose. Where the legislative scheme is relevant to a criminal law purpose, he says, it will be ineffective (e.g., criminals will not register their guns); where it is effective it will not advance the fight against crime (e.g., burdening rural farmers with pointless red tape). These are concerns that were properly directed to and considered by Parliament. Within its constitutional sphere, Parliament is the judge of whether a measure is likely to achieve its intended purposes; efficaciousness is not relevant to the Court's division of powers analysis: *Morgentaler, supra*, at pp. 487–88, and *Reference re Anti-Inflation Act*, 1976 CanLII 16 (S.C.C.), [1976] 2 S.C.R. 373. Rather, the inquiry is directed to how the law sets out to achieve its purpose in order to better understand its "total meaning": W. R. Lederman, *Continuing Canadian Constitutional Dilemmas* (1981), at pp. 239–40. In some cases, the effects of the law may suggest a purpose other than that which is stated in the law: see *Morgentaler, supra*, at pp. 482–83; *Attorney-General for Alberta v. Attorney-General for Canada*, [1939] A.C. 117 (P.C.) (*Alberta Bank Taxation Reference*); and *Texada Mines Ltd. v. Attorney-General of British Columbia*, 1960 CanLII 43 (S.C.C.), [1960] S.C.R. 713; see generally P. W. Hogg, *Constitutional Law of Canada* (loose-leaf ed.), at pp. 15–14 to 15–16. In other words, a law may say that it intends to do one thing and actually do something else. Where the effects of the law diverge substantially from the stated aim, it is sometimes said to be "colourable".

[19] Against this background, we turn to the purpose of the *Firearms Act*. Section 4 states that the purpose of the Act is "to provide ... for the issuance of licences, registration certificates and authorizations under which persons may possess firearms" and "to authorize ... the manufacture of" and "transfer of" ordinary firearms. This is the language of property regulation. However, this regulatory language is directly tied to a purpose cast in the language of the criminal law. The licensing, registration and authorization provisions delineate the means by which people can own and transfer ordinary firearms "in circumstances that would otherwise constitute [a criminal] offence". Those who challenge the legislation point to the first part of the section and its regulatory focus. Those who seek to uphold the law point to the second part of the section and its criminal focus.

[20] The statements of the Honourable Allan Rock, Minister of Justice at the time, in his second-reading speech in the House of Commons, reveal that the federal government's purpose in proposing the law was to promote public safety. He stated: "The government suggests that the object of the regulation of firearms should be <u>the preservation of the safe, civilized and peaceful nature of Canada</u>" (*House of Commons Debates*, vol. 133, No. 154, 1st Sess., 35th Parl., February 16, 1995, at p. 9706 (emphasis added)). Mr. Rock went on to describe the contents of the bill in more detail (at p. 9707):

> First, tough measures to deal with the <u>criminal misuse of firearms</u>; second, specific <u>penalties to punish those who would smuggle illegal firearms</u>; and third, measures overall to provide a context in which the legitimate use of firearms can be carried on in a manner consistent with <u>public safety</u>. [Emphasis added.]
>
> (See also the judgment of Fraser C.J.A., at paras. 169–72.)

Later, the Minister referred to the problems of suicide, accidental shootings, and the use of guns in domestic violence, and detailed some of the shooting tragedies that had spurred public calls for gun control. Russell MacLellan, the Parliamentary Secretary of Justice at the time, underscored the government's concerns, noting that the Act pursues "three fundamental policies: the deterrence of the misuse of firearms, general controls on persons given access to firearms, and controls placed on specific types of firearms" ("Canada's firearms proposals" (1995), 37 *Can. J. Crim.* 163, at p. 163).

[21] Another way to determine the purpose of legislation is to look at the problems it is intended to address — the so-called "mischief" approach. The *Firearms Act* is aimed at a number of evils or "mischiefs". One is the illegal trade in guns, both within Canada and across the border with the United States: see *The Government's Action Plan on Firearms Control*, tabled in the House of Commons in 1994. Another is the link between guns and violent crime, suicide, and accidental deaths. In a paper commissioned by the Department of Justice in 1994, *The Impact of the Availability of Firearms on Violent Crime, Suicide, and Accidental Death: A Review of the Literature with Special Reference to the Canadian Situation*, Thomas Gabor found that all three causes of death may increase in jurisdictions where there are the fewest restrictions on guns. Whether or not one accepts Gabor's conclusions, his study indicates the problem which Parliament sought to address by enacting the legislation: the problem of the misuse of firearms and the threat it poses to public safety.

[22] Finally, there is a strong argument that the purpose of this legislation conforms with the historical public safety focus of all gun control laws. This reference challenges the licensing and registration provisions of the Act only as they relate to ordinary firearms. Alberta does not question the licensing and registration of restricted and prohibited weapons. It freely admits that the restrictions on those categories of weapons are constitutional. Indeed, Alberta would have difficulty alleging otherwise, as numerous courts have upheld the validity of different aspects of the federal gun control legislation that existed prior to the enactment of this Act: see *R. v. Schwartz*, 1988 CanLII 11 (S.C.C.), [1988] 2 S.C.R. 443; *McGuigan v. The Queen*, 1982 CanLII 41 (S.C.C.), [1982] 1 S.C.R. 284; and *Attorney General of Canada v. Pattison* (1981), 30 A.R. 83 (C.A.).

[23] More specifically, before the introduction of the *Firearms Act*, the registration of all restricted weapons was upheld by the British Columbia Court of Appeal in *Martinoff v. Dawson* reflex, (1990), 57 C.C.C. (3d) 482. Furthermore, the *Criminal Code* required anyone seeking to obtain <u>any kind</u> of firearm to apply for a firearms acquisition certificate. This requirement was upheld in *R. v. Northcott*, reflex, [1980] 5 W.W.R. 38 (B.C. Prov. Ct.). These cases upheld the previous gun control legislation on the basis that Parliament's purpose was to promote public safety. The *Firearms Act* extends that legislation in two respects: (1) it requires all guns to be registered, not just restricted and prohibited firearms; and (2) eventually all gun owners will be required to

be licensed, not just those who wish to acquire a firearm. These changes represent a continuation of Parliament's focus on safety concerns, and constitute a limited expansion of the pre-existing legislation. Given the general acceptance of the gun control legislation that has existed for the past hundred years, the constitutional validity of which has always been predicated on Parliament's concern for public safety, it is difficult to now impute a different purpose to Parliament. This supports the view that the law in pith and substance is about public safety.

[24] The effects of the scheme — how it impacts on the legal rights of Canadians — also support the conclusion that the 1995 gun control law is in pith and substance a public safety measure. The criteria for acquiring a licence are concerned with safety rather than the regulation of property. Criminal record checks and background investigations are designed to keep guns out of the hands of those incapable of using them safely. Safety courses ensure that gun owners are qualified. What the law does not require also shows that the operation of the scheme is limited to ensuring safety. For instance, the Act does not regulate the legitimate commercial market for guns. It makes no attempt to set labour standards or the price of weapons. There is no attempt to protect or regulate industries or businesses associated with guns (see *Pattison, supra*, at para. 22). Unlike provincial property registries, the registry established under the Act is not concerned with prior interests, and unlike some provincial motor vehicle schemes, the Act does not address insurance. In short, the effects of the law suggest that its essence is the promotion of public safety through the reduction of the misuse of firearms, and negate the proposition that Parliament was in fact attempting to achieve a different goal such as the total regulation of firearms production, trade, and ownership. We therefore conclude that, viewed from its purpose and effects, the *Firearms Act* is in "pith and substance" directed to public safety.

B. Classification: Does Parliament Have Jurisdiction to Enact the Law?

[25] Having assessed the pith and substance or matter of the law, the second step is to determine whether that matter comes within the jurisdiction of the enacting legislature. We must examine the heads of power under ss. 91 and 92 of the *Constitution Act, 1867* and determine what the matter is "in relation to". In this case, the question is whether the law falls under federal jurisdiction over criminal law or

its peace, order and good government power; or under provincial jurisdiction over property and civil rights. The presumption of constitutionality means that Alberta, as the party challenging the legislation, is required to show that the Act does not fall within the jurisdiction of Parliament: see *Nova Scotia Board of Censors v. McNeil*, 1978 CanLII 6 (S.C.C.), [1978] 2 S.C.R. 662.

[26] The determination of which head of power a particular law falls under is not an exact science. In a federal system, each level of government can expect to have its jurisdiction affected by the other to a certain degree. As Dickson C.J. stated in *General Motors of Canada Ltd. v. City National Leasing*, 1989 CanLII 133 (S.C.C.), [1989] 1 S.C.R. 641, at p. 669, "overlap of legislation is to be expected and accommodated in a federal state". Laws mainly in relation to the jurisdiction of one level of government may overflow into, or have "incidental effects" upon, the jurisdiction of the other level of government. It is a matter of balance and of federalism: no one level of government is isolated from the other, nor can it usurp the functions of the other.

[27] As a general rule, legislation may be classified as criminal law if it possesses three prerequisites: a valid criminal law purpose backed by a prohibition and a penalty: *RJR-MacDonald, supra*; *Hydro-Québec, supra*; and *Reference re Validity of Section 5(a) of the Dairy Industry Act*, 1948 CanLII 2 (S.C.C.), [1949] S.C.R. 1 (the "*Margarine Reference*"). The Attorney General of Canada argues that the 1995 gun control law meets these three requirements, and points to commentary on this legislation which supports its position: D. Gibson, "The *Firearms Reference* in the Alberta Court of Appeal" (1999), 37 *Alta. L. Rev.* 1071; D. M. Beatty, "Gun Control and Judicial Anarchy" (1999), 10 *Constitutional Forum* 45; A. C. Hutchinson and D. Schneiderman, "Smoking Guns: The Federal Government Confronts The Tobacco and Gun Lobbies" (1995), 7 *Constitutional Forum* 16; and Peter W. Hogg's testimony before the Standing Senate Committee on Legal and Constitutional Affairs, October 26, 1995.

[28] Before determining whether the three criminal law criteria are met by this legislation, some general observations on the criminal law power may be apposite. Criminal law, as this Court has stated in numerous cases, constitutes a broad area of federal jurisdiction: *RJR-MacDonald, supra*; *Hydro-Québec, supra*; and *Margarine Reference, supra*. The criminal law stands on its own as federal jurisdiction. Although it often overlaps with provincial jurisdiction

over property and civil rights, it is not "carved out" from provincial jurisdiction, contrary to the view of Conrad J.A. It also includes the law of criminal procedure, which regulates many aspects of criminal law enforcement, such as arrest, search and seizure of evidence, the regulation of electronic surveillance and the forfeiture of stolen property.

[29] Not only is the criminal law a "stand-alone" jurisdiction, it also finds its expression in a broad range of legislation. The *Criminal Code* is the quintessential federal enactment under its criminal jurisdiction, but it is not the only one. The *Food and Drugs Act*, the *Hazardous Products Act*, the *Lord's Day Act*, and the *Tobacco Products Control Act* have all been held to be valid exercises of the criminal law power: see *Standard Sausage Co. v. Lee*, [1933] 4 D.L.R. 501 (B.C.C.A.); *R. v. Cosman's Furniture (1972) Ltd.* (1976), 73 D.L.R. (3d) 312 (Man. C.A.); *Big M Drug Mart*, *supra* (legislation struck down on other grounds); and *RJR-MacDonald*, *supra* (legislation struck down on other grounds), respectively. Thus the fact that some of the provisions of the *Firearms Act* are not contained within the *Criminal Code* has no significance for the purposes of constitutional classification.

[30] Although the criminal law power is broad, it is not unlimited. Some of the parties before us expressed the fear that the criminal law power might be illegitimately used to invade the provincial domain and usurp provincial power. A properly restrained understanding of the criminal law power guards against this possibility.

[31] Within this context, we return to the three criteria that a law must satisfy in order to be classified as criminal. The first step is to consider whether the law has a valid criminal law purpose. Rand J. listed some examples of valid purposes in the *Margarine Reference* at p. 50: "Public peace, order, security, health, morality: these are the ordinary though not exclusive ends served by [criminal] law". Earlier, we concluded that the gun control law in pith and substance is directed at public safety. This brings it clearly within the criminal law purposes of protecting public peace, order, security and health.

[32] In determining whether the purpose of a law constitutes a valid criminal law purpose, courts look at whether laws of this type have traditionally been held to be criminal law: see *Morgentaler*, *supra*, at p. 491, and *RJR-MacDonald*, *supra*, at para. 204; see also *Scowby v. Glendinning*, 1986 CanLII 30 (S.C.C.), [1986] 2 S.C.R. 226, *Westendorp v. The Queen*, 1983 CanLII 1 (S.C.C.), [1983] 1 S.C.R. 43, and *R. v.*

Zelensky, 1978 CanLII 8 (S.C.C.), [1978] 2 S.C.R. 940. Courts have repeatedly held that gun control comes within the criminal law sphere. As Fraser C.J.A. demonstrated in her judgment, gun control has been a matter of criminal law since before the enactment of the *Criminal Code* in 1892, and has continued since that date (see also E. M. Davies, "The 1995 Firearms Act: Canada's Public Relations Response to the Myth of Violence" (2000), 6 *Appeal* 44, and M. L. Friedland, *A Century of Criminal Justice* (1984), at pp. 125 ff.).

[33] Gun control has traditionally been considered valid criminal law because guns are dangerous and pose a risk to public safety. Section 2 of the *Criminal Code* (as amended by s. 138(2) of the *Firearms Act*) defines a "firearm" as "a barrelled weapon from which any shot, bullet or other projectile can be discharged and that is capable of causing serious bodily injury or death to a person" (emphasis added). This demonstrates that Parliament views firearms as dangerous and regulates their possession and use on that ground. The law is limited to restrictions which are directed at safety purposes. As such, the regulation of guns as dangerous products is a valid purpose within the criminal law power: see *R. v. Felawka*, 1993 CanLII 36 (S.C.C.), [1993] 4 S.C.R. 199; *RJR-MacDonald*, *supra*; *R. v. Wetmore*, 1983 CanLII 29 (S.C.C.), [1983] 2 S.C.R. 284; and *Cosman's Furniture*, *supra*.

[34] The finding of a valid criminal law purpose does not end the inquiry, however. In order to be classified as a valid criminal law, that purpose must be connected to a prohibition backed by a penalty. The 1995 gun control law satisfies these requirements. Section 112 of the *Firearms Act* prohibits the possession of a firearm without a registration certificate. Section 91 of the *Criminal Code* (as amended by s. 139 of the *Firearms Act*) prohibits the possession of a firearm without a licence and a registration certificate. These prohibitions are backed by penalties: see s. 115 of the *Firearms Act* and s. 91 of the *Code*.

[35] It thus appears that the 1995 gun control law possesses all three criteria required for a criminal law. However, Alberta and the provinces raised a number of objections to this classification which must be considered.

(1) Regulation or Criminal Prohibition?

[36] The first objection is that the *Firearms Act* is essentially regulatory rather than criminal legislation because of the complexity of the law and the discre-

tion it grants to the chief firearms officer. These aspects of the law, the provinces argue, are the hallmarks of regulatory legislation, not the criminal law: see Hogg, *supra*, at pp. 18–25 and 18–26.

[37] Despite its initial appeal, this argument fails to advance Alberta's case. The fact that the Act is complex does not necessarily detract from its criminal nature. Other legislation, such as the *Food and Drugs Act*, R.S.C., 1985, c. F-27, and the *Canadian Environmental Protection Act*, R.S.C., 1985, c. 16 (4th Supp.), are legitimate exercises of the criminal law power, yet highly complex. Nor does the Act give the chief firearms officer or Registrar undue discretion. The offences are not defined by an administrative body, avoiding the difficulty identified in the dissenting judgment in *Hydro-Québec*, *supra*. They are clearly stated in the Act and the *Criminal Code*: no one shall possess a firearm without a proper licence and registration. While the Act provides for discretion to refuse to issue an authorization to carry or transport under s. 68 or a registration certificate under s. 69, that discretion is restricted by the Act. A licence shall be refused if the applicant is not eligible to hold one: s. 68. Eligibility to hold a licence is delineated in the rest of the Act: a person is ineligible to hold a licence if the person has been convicted of certain offences (s. 5(2)) or is subject to a prohibition order (s. 6); s. 7 requires the applicant to complete a safety course. Discretion regarding registration is also bounded by the Act. A refusal by the chief firearms officer or the Registrar must be for "good and sufficient reason": ss. 68 and 69; the refusal must be in writing with reasons given (s. 72). These provisions demonstrate that the Act does not give the chief firearms officer or the Registrar undue discretion. Furthermore, the chief firearms officer and the Registrar are explicitly subject to the supervision of the courts. Refusal or revocation of a licence or a registration certificate may be referred to a provincial court judge: s. 74. The courts will interpret the words "good and sufficient reason" in ss. 68 and 69 in line with the public safety purpose of the Act, ensuring that the exercise of discretion by the chief firearms officer and the Registrar is always wed to that purpose.

[38] Furthermore, the law's prohibitions and penalties are not regulatory in nature. They are not confined to ensuring compliance with the scheme, as was the case in *Boggs v. The Queen*, 1981 CanLII 39 (S.C.C.), [1981] 1 S.C.R. 49, but stand on their own, independently serving the purpose of public safety. Nor are the prohibitions and penalties directed to the object of revenue generation. Parliament's inten-

tion was not to regulate property, but to ensure that only those who prove themselves qualified to hold a licence are permitted to possess firearms of any sort.

[39] Alberta and the supporting interveners argued that the only way Parliament could address gun control would be to prohibit ordinary firearms outright. With respect, this suggestion is not supported by either logic or jurisprudence. First, the jurisprudence establishes that Parliament may use indirect means to achieve its ends. A direct and total prohibition is not required: see *Reference re ss. 193 and 195.1(1)(c) of the Criminal Code (Man.)*, 1990 CanLII 105 (S.C.C.), [1990] 1 S.C.R. 1123, and *RJR-MacDonald*, *supra*. Second, exemptions from a law do not preclude it from being prohibitive and therefore criminal in nature: see *R. v. Furtney*, 1991 CanLII 30 (S.C.C.), [1991] 3 S.C.R. 89, *Morgentaler v. The Queen*, 1975 CanLII 8 (S.C.C.), [1976] 1 S.C.R. 616, and *Lord's Day Alliance of Canada v. Attorney General of British Columbia*, 1959 CanLII 42 (S.C.C.), [1959] S.C.R. 497. Third, as noted above, the prohibition in this case is not merely designed to enforce a fee payment or regulatory scheme separate from the essential safety focus of the law: by way of contrast, see *Boggs*, *supra*. Finally, if prohibition is not required to make handgun control constitutional, which no one suggests, why should it be required for ordinary firearms?

[40] In a related argument, some provincial interveners contended that if the purpose of the legislation is to reduce misuse, then the legislation should deal with misuse directly. On this view, Parliament could prohibit the careless or intentional misuse of guns, as it has in ss. 85–87 of the *Criminal Code*, but could not prohibit people from owning guns if they present risks to public safety or regulate how people store their guns. Again, the answer is that Parliament may use indirect means to further the end of public safety. The risks associated with ordinary firearms are not confined to the intentional or reckless conduct that might be deterred by a prohibition on misuse. The Attorney General of Canada argued, for example, that the suicide rate is increased by the availability of guns. A person contemplating suicide may be more likely to actually commit suicide if a gun is available, it was argued; therefore Parliament has a right to prevent people at risk, for example due to mental illness, from owning a gun. A prohibition on misuse is unlikely to deter a potential suicide; a prohibition on gun ownership may do so. Other examples where a prohibition on misuse falls short are not hard to envisage. A prohibition on misuse is unlikely to prevent the death of a child who

plays with a gun; a prohibition on irresponsible ownership or careless storage may do so. Again, reducing availability may have a greater impact on whether a robber uses a gun than a law forbidding him to use it. Whether the 1995 gun law actually achieves these ends is not at issue before us; what is at issue is whether Parliament, in targeting these dangers, strayed outside its criminal law power. In our view, it did not.

(2) Property and Civil Rights or Criminal Law?

[41] Alberta's second major objection to classifying the 1995 gun control scheme as criminal law is that it is indistinguishable from existing provincial property regulation schemes such as automobile and land title registries.

[42] This argument overlooks the different purposes behind the federal restrictions on firearms and the provincial regulation of other forms of property. Guns are restricted because they are dangerous. While cars are also dangerous, provincial legislatures regulate the possession and use of automobiles not as dangerous products but rather as items of property and as an exercise of civil rights, pursuant to the provinces' s. 92(13) jurisdiction: *Canadian Indemnity Co. v. Attorney-General of British Columbia*, 1976 CanLII 195 (S.C.C.), [1977] 2 S.C.R. 504; *Validity of Section 92(4) of the Vehicles Act, 1957 (Sask.)*, 1958 CanLII 61 (S.C.C.), [1958] S.C.R. 608; *Provincial Secretary of Prince Edward Island v. Egan*, 1941 CanLII 1 (S.C.C.), [1941] S.C.R. 396.

[43] The argument that the federal gun control scheme is no different from the provincial regulation of motor vehicles ignores the fact that there are significant distinctions between the roles of guns and cars in Canadian society. Both firearms and automobiles can be used for socially approved purposes. Likewise, both may cause death and injury. Yet their primary uses are fundamentally different. Cars are used mainly as means of transportation. Danger to the public is ordinarily unintended and incidental to that use. Guns, by contrast, pose a pressing safety risk in many if not all of their functions. Firearms are often used as weapons in violent crime, including domestic violence; cars generally are not. Thus Parliament views guns as particularly dangerous and has sought to combat that danger by extending its licensing and registration scheme to all classes of firearms. Parliament did not enact the *Firearms Act* to regulate guns as items of property. The Act does not address insurance or permissible locations of use.

Rather, the Act addresses those aspects of gun control which relate to the dangerous nature of firearms and the need to reduce misuse.

[44] In a variation on the theme of property and civil rights, the opponents of the 1995 gun control law argue that ordinary guns, like rifles and shotguns, are common property, not dangerous property. Ordinary firearms are different, they argue, from the automatic weapons and handguns that Parliament has regulated in the past. Ordinary guns are used mainly for lawful purposes in hunting, trapping and ranching. Automatic weapons and handguns, by contrast, have few uses outside crime or war. The fact that Parliament has the right under the criminal law power to control automatic weapons and handguns does not, they argue, mean that Parliament has the right to regulate ordinary guns.

[45] The difficulty with this argument is that while ordinary guns are often used for lawful purposes, they are also used for crime and suicide, and cause accidental death and injury. Guns cannot be divided neatly into two categories — those that are dangerous and those that are not dangerous. All guns are capable of being used in crime. All guns are capable of killing and maiming. It follows that all guns pose a threat to public safety. As such, their control falls within the criminal law power.

[46] In a further variation on this argument, the provinces of Ontario and Saskatchewan submitted that even if the licensing provisions of the law were valid criminal legislation, the registration provisions are mainly provincial property legislation and should be severed and struck out. The argument is that the registration portions of the Act simply amount to regulation, with little connection to the public safety purpose advanced by the federal government to justify the Act as a whole. Conrad J.A. agreed with this argument, finding that although the Act "cleverly intertwines" the licensing and registration provisions through "clever packaging", the registration provisions could be severed from the gun control law. As proof, she pointed to the fact that the pre-existing firearms acquisition certificate scheme, governing prohibited and restricted arms, applied to ordinary firearms without being connected to a registration system.

[47] We are not persuaded that the registration provisions can be severed from the rest of the Act, nor that they fail to serve Parliament's purpose in promoting public safety. The licensing provisions require everyone who possesses a gun to be licensed. The registration provisions require all guns to be regis-

tered. The combination of the two parts of the scheme is intended to ensure that when a firearm is transferred from one person to another, the recipient is licensed. Absent a registration system, this would be impossible to ascertain. If a gun is found in the possession of an unlicensed person, the registration system permits the government to determine where the gun originated. With a registration scheme in place, licensed owners can be held responsible for the transfer of their weapons. The registration system is also part of the general scheme of the law in reducing misuse. If someone is found guilty of a crime involving violence, or is prohibited from possessing a weapon, the registration scheme is expected to assist the police in determining whether the offender actually owns any guns and in confiscating them. The registration scheme is also intended to reduce smuggling and the illegal trade in guns. These interconnections demonstrate that the registration and licensing portions of the *Firearms Act* are both tightly linked to Parliament's goal in promoting safety by reducing the misuse of any and all firearms. Both portions are integral and necessary to the operation of the scheme. The government is not prevented from improving the system because the pre-existing firearms acquisition certificate system was not connected to a registration system. Moreover, prior to this Act, the federal government had a registration system for handguns. It now seeks to extend it to all guns. Contrary to the suggestions of Conrad J.A., no improper purpose in including registration in the scheme has been demonstrated.

(3) Undue Intrusion into Provincial Powers?

[48] In a related argument, Alberta and the provincial interveners submit that this law inappropriately trenches on provincial powers and that upholding it as criminal law will upset the balance of federalism. In support of its submission, Alberta cites the work of D. M. Beatty, who suggests applying considerations of rationality and proportionality from the *Canadian Charter of Rights and Freedoms* s. 1 cases to questions of legislative competence: *Constitutional Law in Theory and Practice* (1995). It seems far from clear to us that it would be helpful to apply the technique of weighing benefits and detriments used in s. 1 jurisprudence to the quite different exercise of defining the scope of the powers set out in ss. 91 and 92 of the *Constitution Act, 1867*. This said, however, it is beyond debate that an appropriate balance must be maintained between the federal and provincial heads of power. A federal state depends for its very existence on a just and workable balance

between the central and provincial levels of government, as this Court affirmed in *Reference re Secession of Quebec*, 1998 CanLII 793 (S.C.C.), [1998] 2 S.C.R. 217; see also *General Motors of Canada Ltd. v. City National Leasing*, *supra*. The courts, critically aware of the need to maintain this balance, have not hesitated to strike down legislation that does not conform with the requirements of the criminal law: see *Boggs*, *supra*, and the *Margarine Reference*, *supra*. The question is not whether such a balance is necessary, but whether the 1995 gun control law upsets that balance.

[49] The argument that the 1995 gun control law upsets the balance of Confederation may be seen as an argument that, viewed in terms of its effects, the law does not in pith and substance relate to public safety under the federal criminal law power but rather to the provincial power over property and civil rights. Put simply, the issue is whether the law is mainly in relation to criminal law. If it is, incidental effects in the provincial sphere are constitutionally irrelevant: see, e.g., *Consortium Developments (Clearwater) Ltd. v. Sarnia (City)*, 1998 CanLII 762 (S.C.C.), [1998] 3 S.C.R. 3, and *Mitchell v. Peguis Indian Band*, 1990 CanLII 117 (S.C.C.), [1990] 2 S.C.R. 85. On the other hand, if the effects of the law, considered with its purpose, go so far as to establish that it is mainly a law in relation to property and civil rights, then the law is *ultra vires* the federal government. In summary, the question is whether the "provincial" effects are incidental, in which case they are constitutionally irrelevant, or whether they are so substantial that they show that the law is mainly, or "in pith and substance", the regulation of property and civil rights.

[50] In our view, Alberta and the provinces have not established that the effects of the law on provincial matters are more than incidental. First, the mere fact that guns are property does not suffice to show that a gun control law is in pith and substance a provincial matter. Exercises of the criminal law power often affect property and civil rights to some degree: *Attorney-General for British Columbia v. Attorney-General for Canada*, [1937] A.C. 368 (P.C.). Such effects are almost unavoidable, as many aspects of the criminal law deal with property and its ownership. The fact that such effects are common does not lessen the need to examine them. It does suggest, however, that we cannot draw sharp lines between criminal law and property and civil rights. Food, drugs and obscene materials are all items of property and are all legitimate subjects of criminal laws. In order to determine the proper classification of this law, then,

we must go beyond the simplistic proposition that guns are property and thus any federal regulation of firearms is *prima facie* unconstitutional.

[51] Second, the Act does not significantly hinder the ability of the provinces to regulate the property and civil rights aspects of guns. Most provinces already have regulations dealing with hunting, discharge within municipal boundaries, and other aspects of firearm use, and these are legitimate subjects of provincial regulation: see *R. v. Chiasson* reflex, (1982), 66 C.C.C. (2d) 195 (N.B.C.A.), aff'd 1984 CanLII 136 (S.C.C.), [1984] 1 S.C.R. 266. The Act does not affect these laws.

[52] Third, the most important jurisdictional effect of this law is its elimination of the ability of the provinces to <u>not</u> have any regulations on the ownership of ordinary firearms. The provinces argue that it is in their power to choose whether or not to have such a law. By taking over the field, the federal government has deprived the provinces of that choice. Assuming (without deciding) that the provincial legislatures would have the jurisdiction to enact a law in relation to the property aspects of ordinary firearms, this does not prevent Parliament from addressing the safety aspects of ordinary firearms. The double aspect doctrine permits both levels of government to legislate in one jurisdictional field for two different purposes: *Egan, supra.*

[53] Fourth, as discussed above, this law does not precipitate the federal government's entry into a new field. Gun control has been the subject of federal law since Confederation. This law does not allow the federal government to significantly expand its jurisdictional powers to the detriment of the provinces. There is no colourable intrusion into provincial jurisdiction, either in the sense that Parliament has an improper motive or that it is taking over provincial powers under the guise of the criminal law. While we are sensitive to the concern of the provincial governments that the federal jurisdiction over criminal law not be permitted such an unlimited scope that it erodes the constitutional balance of powers, we do not believe that this legislation poses such a threat.

(4) Is Moral Content Required?

[54] Yet another argument is that the ownership of guns is not criminal law because it is not immoral to own an ordinary firearm. There are two difficulties with this argument. The first is that while the ownership of ordinary firearms is not in itself regarded by most Canadians as immoral, the problems associated with the misuse of firearms are firmly grounded in morality. Firearms may be misused to take human life and to assist in other immoral acts, like theft and terrorism. Preventing such misuse can be seen as an attempt to curb immoral acts. Viewed thus, gun control is directed at a moral evil.

[55] The second difficulty with the argument is that the criminal law is not confined to prohibiting immoral acts: see *Proprietary Articles Trade Association v. Attorney-General for Canada*, [1931] A.C. 310 (P.C.). While most criminal conduct is also regarded as immoral, Parliament can use the criminal law to prohibit activities which have little relation to public morality. For instance, the criminal law has been used to prohibit certain restrictions on market competition: see *Attorney-General for British Columbia v. Attorney-General for Canada, supra.* Therefore, even if gun control did not involve morality, it could still fall under the federal criminal law power.

(5) Other Concerns

[56] We recognize the concerns of northern, rural and aboriginal Canadians who fear that this law does not address their particular needs. They argue that it discriminates against them and violates treaty rights, and express concerns about their ability to access the scheme, which may be administered from a great distance. These apprehensions are genuine, but they do not go to the question before us — Parliament's jurisdiction to enact this law. Whether a law could have been designed better or whether the federal government should have engaged in more consultation before enacting the law has no bearing on the division of powers analysis applied by this Court. If the law violates a treaty or a provision of the *Charter*, those affected can bring their claims to Parliament or the courts in a separate case. The reference questions, and hence this judgment, are restricted to the issue of the division of powers.

[57] We also appreciate the concern of those who oppose this Act on the basis that it may not be effective or it may be too expensive. Criminals will not register their guns, Alberta argued. The only real effect of the law, it is suggested, is to burden law-abiding farmers and hunters with red tape. These concerns were properly directed to and considered by Parliament; they cannot affect the Court's decision. The efficacy of a law, or lack thereof, is not relevant to Parliament's ability to enact it under the division of powers analysis. Furthermore, the federal government points out that it is not only career criminals who are capable of misusing guns. Domestic violence often involves people who have no prior

criminal record. Crimes are committed by first-time offenders. Finally, accidents and suicides occur in the homes of law-abiding people, and guns are stolen from their homes. By requiring everyone to register their guns, Parliament seeks to reduce misuse by everyone and curtail the ability of criminals to acquire firearms. Where criminals have acquired guns and used them in the commission of offences, the registration system seeks to make those guns more traceable. The cost of the program, another criticism of the law, is equally irrelevant to our constitutional analysis.

VI.   CONCLUSION

[58] We conclude that the impugned sections of the *Firearms Act* contain prohibitions and penalties in support of a valid criminal law purpose. The legislation is in relation to criminal law pursuant to s. 91(27) of the *Constitution Act, 1867* and hence *intra vires* Parliament. It is not regulatory legislation and it does not take the federal government so far into provincial territory that the balance of federalism is threatened or the jurisdictional powers of the provinces are unduly impaired.

[59] Having determined that the legislation constitutes a valid exercise of Parliament's jurisdiction over criminal law, it is unnecessary to consider whether the legislation can also be justified as an exercise of its peace, order and good government power.

[60] We would dismiss the appeal. The licensing and registration provisions in the *Firearms Act* do not constitute an infringement of the jurisdiction of the Legislature of Alberta with respect to the regulation of property and civil rights pursuant to s. 92(13) of the *Constitution Act, 1867*. The Act is a valid exer-

cise of Parliament's jurisdiction over criminal law pursuant to s. 91(27).

[61] The answers to the reference questions are as follows:

[Question 2:

(1) Do the licensing provisions, insofar as they relate to an ordinary firearm, constitute an infringement of the jurisdiction of the Legislature of Alberta with respect to the regulation of property and civil rights pursuant to subsection 92(13) of the *Constitution Act, 1867*?

(2) If the answer to the question posed in subsection (1) is "yes", are the licensing provisions *ultra vires* the Parliament of Canada insofar as they regulate the possession or ownership of an ordinary firearm?]

    (1) No.
    (2) No.

[Question 3:

(1) Do the registration provisions, as they relate to an ordinary firearm, constitute an infringement of the jurisdiction of the Legislature of Alberta with respect to the regulation of property and civil rights pursuant to subsection 92(13) of the *Constitution Act, 1867*?

(2) If the answer to the question posed in subsection (1) is "yes", are the registration provisions *ultra vires* the Parliament of Canada insofar as they require registration of an ordinary firearm?

    (1) No.
    (2) No.

4

Global Context:
The Transnational Influence of Law

(a) Threat of NAFTA Case Kills Canada's MMT Ban[†]

Shawn McCarthy

The Liberal government is beating an embarrassing retreat on its year-old ban of the gasoline additive MMT, despite new evidence that the manganese used in the octane enhancer can cause nervous-system problems.

Sources say government officials have reached a tentative deal with MMT-maker Ethyl Corp., of Richmond, Va., to avoid a potentially devastating legal challenge under the North American free-trade agreement.

Federal lawyers had warned the Liberal cabinet that Ethyl would be likely to win that NAFTA case, a ruling that could cost taxpayers hundreds of millions of dollars and hand a potent weapon to critics of the free-trade pact.

Sources said the negotiators for the two sides have agreed that Ottawa would drop its ban on MMT and pay the company an estimated $10-million for legal costs and lost profits. The government will also issue a statement to the effect that the manganese-based additive is neither an environmental nor a health risk.

In return, Ethyl would drop its NAFTA challenge and its claim for $250-million (U.S.) in damages.

However, Prime Minister Jean Chrétien must still approve the agreement.

The Liberal government legislated the ban on the cross-border sale of MMT last year, claiming the substance interferes with automobile emission controls and is therefore an environmental hazard. The legislation prohibited the importation or interprovincial sale of the additive.

The acrimonious debate pitted Ethyl and gasoline refiners, who wanted access to the inexpensive additive, against environmentalists and auto makers, who insisted the use of the substance ran counter to the goal of lower emissions.

Former environment ministers Sheila Copps and Sergio Marchi both argued that they couldn't ban MMT directly because Health Canada had found there was not sufficient evidence that it was toxic at low levels. So they resorted to the trade ban.

Federal lawyers had warned the government when the legislation was being debated that the importation ban would not likely withstand a NAFTA challenge. But Mr. Marchi, now International Trade Minister, has consistently vowed the government would defend its bill.

"We have a sovereign right to not only speak about alternate and cleaner fuels, but to do something about it." Mr. Marchi said last summer when he was named International Trade Minister.

Ethyl's NAFTA challenge has become a cause célèbre for critics of the trade deal, who see it as proof that such liberalizing agreements restrict governments' ability to pass the environmental and health legislation that might hurt corporate interests.

But the government's resolve to fight that challenge has crumbled.

---

† From *The [Toronto] Globe and Mail* (July 20, 1998) A1. Reproduced with permission from The Globe and Mail.

Senior ministers worry that the auto industry has failed to provide solid evidence that MMT does in fact interfere with emission-control hardware, undercutting Ottawa's case. As well, a panel ruled last month that the prohibition on interprovincial trade in MMT contravenes a four-year-old agreement on internal trade.

Still, the Liberals' reversal comes as new studies indicate the low-level exposure to manganese can cause memory impairment and tremors similar to those experienced by victims of Parkinson's Disease.

Elizabeth May, executive director of the Sierra Club of Canada, said the government should have prohibited the use of MMT because it was a health risk rather than relied on the indirect ban on trade.

"It should be banned because of its risk to public health. We are against MMT in gas for health and environmental grounds," she said.

Donna Mergler, a neurotoxicologist at the University of Quebec at Montreal, is conducting one study of 306 people in southwestern Quebec that correlates manganese blood levels with neurological problems.

Her work, which is supported by the U.S. Environmental Protection Agency, is not complete, but preliminary findings presented to a conference in Little Rock, Ark., last October suggested that even low levels of manganese in the blood can have health effects, particularly in children and the elderly.

"We know that in large concentrations, airborne manganese does pose a risk to human health," Ms. Mergler said in an interview. What we don't know is at what level does it not pose a risk.

"There remain a lot of questions about manganese and we should know a lot more about it before we use it."

Ethyl has responded with its own study in which 1,000 people in Toronto wore air-monitoring devices over a year. The Ethyl research done by Research Triangle Institute of North Carolina found that manganese levels in the air were mere fractions of the safe levels set by both Health Canada and the U.S. EPA.

(MMT has been used by Canadian refiners to boost octane since 1977, when lead was banned on the ground that it caused neurological problems in children. MMT is still used by Ontario refiners who had stockpiled it before the cross-border ban came into effect last year, though supplies are running out in other provinces.)

Ethyl says that only a small drop of MMT is added to a litre of gasoline and that only a small fraction of the manganese becomes airborne after combustion.

"The exposures are very, very low," said Ethyl vice-president Don Lynam. "They are far below levels set by Health Canada in its risk assessment."

However, critics question whether those levels, set by the Health Department in 1994, are appropriate in light of new evidence of low-level effects.

Meanwhile, the debate over MMT's impact on auto-emission controls continues.

Alain Perez, president of the Canadian Petroleum Products Institute, said the car makers have failed to prove their case and have used MMT as a scapegoat for their own inability to meet emission standards.

He noted that the U.S. environmental agency was forced to back off its ban of MMT in 1995 after a federal court found there was no basis for making the additive illegal.

If the Canadian ban was upheld, refiners say, they would be forced to spend up to $2-billion to retool their operations or use less efficient additives.

However, spokesmen for the auto industry insist that the manganese additive does do damage and will make it difficult for them to meet lower emission standards set by government.

Mark Nantais of the Canadian Motor Vehicle Manufacturers Association said 80 per cent of the manganese in MMT stays in the catalytic converter and "gums up the system."

While car makers are being pushed to improve controls on vehicle emissions, "nothing is happening on the fuel side," he said. "We can't get there from here with this poison in the gasoline. It's garbage in, garbage out."

(b)   Prosecuting Mass Rape: *Prosecutor v. Dragoljub Kunarac, Radomir Kovac and Zoran Vukovic*†

Doris Buss

INTRODUCTION

On February 22, 2001, the trial chamber of the International Tribunal for the former Yugoslavia (I.C.T.Y.)[1] delivered its decision in *Prosecutor v. Dragoljub Kunarac, Radomir Kovac and Zoran Vukovic*,[2] convicting the three male defendants of the rape, torture and enslavement of Muslim women in the municipality of Foca, Bosnia-Hercegovina. The decision is noteworthy in several respects. It is the first case solely to focus on the rape, torture and mistreatment of women during the armed conflict in Yugoslavia. It is the first case to prosecute successfully rape as a crime against humanity, and it is the first case to consider the phenomena of 'mass rape' in the context of Bosnia-Hercegovina.

For me personally, the decision is additionally important in light of my own scepticism about the I.C.T.Y.'s capacity to address rape and other wartime violence against women. In a 1998 article (Buss, 1998), I argued that the legal remit of the Tribunal reflected stereotypical constructions of women as 'victims', and left unchallenged discourses of war, militarism and nationalism that function to elide women's suffering with the suffering of the nation and, consequently, to marginalise women's experience of violence. Thus, as a long-awaited statement about how women's particular experiences during war are treated by the international community, *Kunarac* is an opportunity to take measure of the I.C.T.Y. and to consider if, in fact, it has lived 'up' to my low expectations.

In the following case comment, I aim to do three things. First, to provide an outline of the decision in *Kunarac*, exploring the significance of recognising rape as a crime against humanity. Second, I consider *Kunarac* in the context of earlier international developments in the area of rape and sexual violence, noting the several aspects of the decision which significantly advance international legal recognition of wartime violence against women. Third and finally, I evaluate *Kunarac* in light of my previous concerns about the I.C.T.Y. While concluding that the decision is important and contains a number of positive developments, I argue that there are aspects of the war crimes trial, as evidenced in *Kunarac*, which are still of concern for feminists seeking to secure greater international action on violence against women.

1.   THE DECISION

In April 1992, the city and [municipality] of Foca were overtaken by Serb forces. Muslims living in Foca and the surrounding area[] were attacked, expelled from the region, and/or[] detained, with women, children and some older men taken to detention centres at the local high school and sports hall. Prior to the war in Bosnia-Hercegovina,[3] fifty-two per cent of the 40,513 inhabitants of the Foca Municipality were Muslim. After the conflict, approximately ten Muslims remained.[4] For the Muslims detained in Foca, conditions were extreme. The facilities were unhygienic, little food was available, and the prisoners were subject to beatings,[5] and, in the case of women and girls, repeated rapes.[6]

It is this latter development that concerns the judgement in *Kunarac*. Serb soldiers routinely raped the women and girls kept at the local school and sports hall. The three defendants were involved, in different capacities, with those rapes as well as with the removal of a group of women and girls, most of them ranging in age from twelve to twenty, from these centres to local houses/apartments, where they were raped by the defendants and other soldiers. Some of these women were detained for several months and were subject to constant rapes, taken as the 'property' of the individual defendants, and made to do housework, cleaning, and cooking.[7] After a period of time, some of these women/girls, including a twelve-year-old, were then sold to other soldiers. The twelve-year-old girl was never seen again.[8]

The three defendants were charged under the Statute of the Yugoslav Tribunal with various crimi-

---

† (October 2002) 10:3/4 Feminist Legal Studies 91–99. Reproduced with kind permission from Springer Science + Business Media. [Notes and/or references omitted.]

nal offences. The Yugoslav Tribunal has authority, from the United Nations Security Council,[9] to prosecute violations of the laws of war, grave breaches of the Geneva Conventions, crimes against humanity, and genocide committed within the territory of the former Yugoslavia. The Tribunal's statute — its constituting document — outlines the types of acts considered 'criminal' for the purposes of the Tribunal. It was drafted to reflect only the most settled areas of international humanitarian law, and to include, to the extent that this allowed, provisions that would cover crimes committed under a policy of 'ethnic cleansing.' As such, it is a curious balancing act between a conservative and reactive reading of international humanitarian law, and an innovative document, seeking to open up a new era of international adjudication of war 'crimes'. The result is a complex set of rules that aims to elaborate and condemn systematic persecution of groups, within a juridical system focused on the individual acts of individual defendants against specific members of the 'civilian' population.

The result is that indictments, such as those in *Kunarac*, are lengthy and convoluted, referring to individual acts and patterns of activity, and laying charges under multiple headings. In the context of *Kunarac*, the defendants were charged with rape as a crime against humanity (Article 5 (g) of the I.C.T.Y. statute) and as a violation of the laws of war (Article 3), and rape as torture, constituting both a crime against humanity (Article 5 (h)) and a violation of the laws of war (Article 3). In addition, the defendants were charged with enslavement as a crime against humanity (Article 5 (c)) and with outrages upon personal dignity (Article 3). In most cases, the multiple charges of rape (as a crime against humanity and as a violation of the laws of war) and torture (also as a crime against humanity and as a violation of the laws of war) are made in respect of the same incident. The reasons for this relate to the ad-hoc development of humanitarian law, the details of which are too lengthy for this comment.[10] However, the multiple charges are significant because they constitute the recognition that wartime rape occurs in different contexts, for different reasons, with various impacts.

For example, rape is specifically referred to in the I.C.T.Y. statute as a crime against humanity; an offence committed as part of an attack against a civilian population. Crimes against humanity evolved out of the Nuremberg tribunal as a means to criminalise the actions of the Nazi regime against particular communities such as the Jews. A crime against humanity is an act, such as rape, which is part of a larger attack on a group of people. The attack on the community must be "widespread or systematic", and the accused must have knowledge "of the wider context in which his acts occur".[11] In the Yugoslav context, charges of crimes against humanity are directed at the 'ethnic cleansing' — the forced removal, by various means, of whole populations from specific regions — that resulted in widespread, outrageous violations of humanitarian law.[12]

In *Kunarac*, the Tribunal found that individual acts of rape committed against Muslim women by the accused amounted to crimes against humanity, and were part of a larger policy to terrorise Muslims, evict them from the area, and convert the region into a Serb stronghold. For example, the Tribunal noted that in addition to substantial evidence of a Serb policy to "gain supremacy over the Muslims in the region" (para. 579), the defendant Kunarac made clear that "the rapes against the Muslim women were one of the many ways in which the Serbs could assert their superiority and victory over the Muslims" (para. 583). After raping one Muslim woman, Kunarac "told her that she should enjoy being 'fucked by a Serb' ... [adding] that she would now carry a Serb baby and would not know who the father would be" (*ibid.*).

Rape was also charged as a violation of the laws of war under Article 3 of the Tribunal's statute.[13] Under this provision, rape does not have to constitute an act against a population but it does have to occur in the context of an armed conflict and there must be a close nexus between the rape and the armed conflict.[14] Thus, rape as a crime against humanity and as a crime of war relate not so much to two distinct acts as distinct motivations or contexts. In *Kunarac*, the Tribunal found the accused guilty of acts of rape as both crimes against humanity and violations of the laws of war.

Like rape, torture was alleged to constitute a violation of the laws of war and a crime against humanity. Torture, in this context, refers to rape as a "means of punishing, intimidating, coercing or humiliating the victim, or obtaining information, or confession, from the victim or a third person".[15] The Tribunal found the accused guilty of torture as a crime against humanity and as a violation of the laws of war. The three defendants were also found guilty of enslavement (a crime against humanity) and of outrages upon personal dignity (violations of the laws of war).

2. *KUNARAC* IN CONTEXT

The mass rape of Muslim women in the war in Bosnia-Hercegovina was a headline grabbing event, shocking the (largely complacent) Western world,[16] and mobilizing feminist activists.[17] The decision to include rape in the Tribunal's statute and in subsequent indictments was a hard-fought battle by feminists against an implacable international community. The extent of the resistance to action against wartime violence against women is remarkable. Despite the widespread publicity of mass rape of women during the Yugoslav conflict and the inclusion of rape as a crime within the reach of both the Yugoslav and Rwandan tribunals, prosecutors have not always been willing to include rape in the indictments. For example, the first case before the Rwandan Tribunal, *The Prosecutor v. Akayesu*,[18] did not include references to rape, and indeed, the human rights investigators in Rwanda overlooked and failed to pursue lines of inquiry about rape.[19] It was not until Judge Navanethem Pillay, the only woman on the bench hearing *Akayesu*, pursued her own line of questions, that it emerged rape had been a significant part of the campaign against Rwandan Tutsis.[20]

Thus, the decision in *Kunarac* is an important development and a hard-won victory in gaining international recognition of the different ways in which women are vulnerable during armed conflict. It also sends a clear signal that wartime violence against women is being taken seriously and acted upon, at least at the level of ad-hoc criminal prosecutions. Aspects of the decision in *Kunarac* are also promising, particularly in the area of the legal definition of rape and enslavement. The Tribunal held that the definition of rape, first outlined in the *Prosecutor v. Furundžija*,[21] did not sufficiently address the factors that might "render an act of sexual penetration *non-consensual*" (para. 438, emphasis in original). The *Kunarac* tribunal ruled that in considering coercion, force, and lack of consent, the test should be if a victim's "sexual autonomy" has been violated (para. 457). The language of sexual autonomy allows the Tribunal to consider a broad range of factors and conditions that might negate consent. This was particularly relevant in *Kunarac* where two of the defendants alleged that some of the sexual activity between them and individual Muslim women was consensual. The Tribunal, after considering the overall pattern of conduct of the accused, and the relative position of the victims, refused to accept that consent had been given.[22]

In finding two of the defendants guilty of enslavement, the Tribunal provides some indication of how the law in this area is developing. While directing its comments to the particular facts before it, the Tribunal adopted a broad definition of enslavement as "the exercise of any or all of the

powers attached to the right of ownership over a person" (para. 540). Factors suggesting enslavement include:

> the control of someone's movement, control of physical environment, psychological control, measures taken to prevent or deter escape, forces, threat of force or coercion, duration, assertion of exclusivity, subjection to cruel treatment and abuse, control of sexuality and forced labour (para. 543).

While there was evidence of trafficking in Muslim women, the Tribunal held that this was not a requirement of enslavement. According to Regan Ralph, Human Rights Watch, this will form "the basis to prosecute others who enslave women around the world."[23]

3. RETHINGING RAPE?

Having been a skeptic of the I.C.T.Y. process, has the decision in *Kunarac* changed my mind? In some respects, it has. *Kunarac* is an important outcome in an international environment unreceptive to acting on women's human rights abuses. In addition to the intransigence of the I.C.T.R., attempts to include specific 'gender' crimes in the newly drafted statute of the International Criminal Court[] resulted in lengthy debates, and a reluctance to recognise crimes such as 'forced pregnancy'.[24] Thus, although there have been substantial expressions of international support for combating violence against women, it is difficult to translate that commitment into action. *Kunarac* may go a long way in securing substantive action on violence against women.

Second, the jurisprudence coming out of the I.C.T.Y. and I.C.T.R., in the context of violence against women, appears progressive on many levels. Witnesses are entitled to protection and can retain their anonymity, no corroboration of a victim's testimony in a sexual assault case is required, the Tribunal has established a victim and witness protection unit, and the Tribunal's rules of procedure include a 'rape shield' provision, limiting evidence of victims' sexual history.[25]

Despite these important developments, I retain some scepticism about the I.C.T.Y. and its capability to meaningfully address violence against women. The Tribunal's willingness to adopt a broad, flexible and arguably progressive approach to rape and women's 'sexual autonomy' is laudable, but arguably not that surprising in the context of the war in Yugoslavia. Wartime rape, perhaps more than any other, closely approximates what is popularly perceived as 'real rape' — stranger rape. It is the 'ideal' of rape, where an innocent, helpless woman is at the mercy of a brutal stranger. In this context, issues of consent and competing narratives of women's sexuality that dominate rape trials in Western domestic legal systems[26] are more easily marginalised. The evidence of ethnic cleansing, the detention of Muslim women and girls, and the overwhelming evidence of Serb brutality provide a, perhaps unshakeable, foundation for finding that rape occurred on a mass scale. I am not suggesting by this that the Tribunal's findings were somehow inevitable. Indeed, it is likely that the Tribunal's willingness to take a progressive approach to sexual violence is the result of hard work by feminist activists. My concern is that these developments may leave unchallenged dominant assumptions and constructions of women's sexuality and their role — as 'victims' — in wartime. The more difficult question is if violence against women, which does not fit so easily within the mold of 'stranger rape'[,] can be acted upon within the limits of the war crimes trial.

The model of the war crimes trial, based on an adversarial system, can be a limiting environment within which to bring cases of sexual abuse. The [decisions] in *Kunarac* and other cases[] have an air of unreality about them. The decisions relate horrible experiences of abuse and suffering, at the same time as those experiences are measured against convoluted and sometimes archaic rules of evidence and relevance. In *Kunarac*, for example, the decision runs to over 300 pages and contains masses of evidence and testimony on the experience of women raped and abused while in detention. In evaluating this evidence, the Tribunal details individual acts of abuse, noting times, places, supporting evidence. On a number of indictments, the Tribunal rules that there is insufficient evidence, or the indictment has not been properly drawn, to sustain a conviction. The result is bizarre. After reading pages and pages of witness evidence about the existence of what are, in effect, 'rape camps', the Tribunal then dismisses individual charges of rape for lack of evidence. Arguably, within a strict reading of criminal evidence and international law, the Tribunal is 'right' in its conclusion, but the very process of analysis feels particularly ill suited to the task of accounting for, and reconciling the experiences of[,] these women. What lesson do we take away from a Tribunal that can, on the one hand, find evidence of rape camps, and yet find that individual women are not to be believed in their accounts of rape and violence at those same camps? In this respect, the Yugoslav Tribunal reproduces many of the same problematic aspects of 'the rape trial' found in Western domestic legal systems. Does this mean that feminists and others should not seek to use this system to prosecute rape and sexual violence? Certainly not. But it does raise additional questions about the war crimes tribunal as a mechanism of reconciliation and resolution in a post-conflict situation.

(c) *Baker v. Canada (Minister of Citizenship and Immigration)*†

[L'HEUREUX-DUBÉ J., Gonthier, McLachlin, Bastarache and Binnie JJ.:]

[1] Regulations made pursuant to s. 114(2) of the *Immigration Act*, R.S.C., 1985, c. I-2, empower the respondent Minister to facilitate the admission to Canada of a person where the Minister is satisfied, owing to humanitarian and compassionate considerations, that admission should be facilitated or an exemption from the regulations made under the Act should be granted. At the centre of this appeal is the approach to be taken by a court to judicial review of such decisions, both on procedural and substantive grounds. It also raises issues of reasonable apprehension of bias, the provision of written reasons as part of the duty of fairness, and the role of children's interests in reviewing decisions made pursuant to s. 114(2).

I.   FACTUAL BACKGROUND

[2] Mavis Baker is a citizen of Jamaica who entered Canada as a visitor in August of 1981 and has remained in Canada since then. She never received

---

† [1999] 2 S.C.R. 817 at paras. 1–7, 51, 63–81.

permanent resident status, but supported herself illegally as a live-in domestic worker for 11 years. She has had four children (who are all Canadian citizens) while living in Canada: Paul Brown, born in 1985, twins Patricia and Peter Robinson, born in 1989, and Desmond Robinson, born in 1992. After Desmond was born, Ms. Baker suffered from post-partum psychosis and was diagnosed with paranoid schizophrenia. She applied for welfare at that time. When she was first diagnosed with mental illness, two of her children were placed in the care of their natural father, and the other two were placed in foster care. The two who were in foster care are now again under her care, since her condition has improved.

[3] The appellant was ordered deported in December 1992, after it was determined that she had worked illegally in Canada and had overstayed her visitor's visa. In 1993, Ms. Baker applied for an exemption from the requirement to apply for permanent residence outside Canada, based upon humanitarian and compassionate considerations, pursuant to s. 114(2) of the *Immigration Act*. She had the assistance of counsel in filing this application, and included, among other documentation, submissions from her lawyer, a letter from her doctor, and a letter from a social worker with the Children's Aid Society. The documentation provided indicated that, although she was still experiencing psychiatric problems, she was making progress. It also stated that she might become ill again if she were forced to return to Jamaica, since treatment might not be available for her there. Ms. Baker's submissions also clearly indicated that she was the sole caregiver for two of her Canadian-born children, and that the other two depended on her for emotional support and were in regular contact with her. The documentation suggested that she too would suffer emotional hardship if she were separated from them.

[4] The response to this request was contained in a letter dated April 18, 1994 and signed by Immigration Officer M. Caden, stating that a decision had been made that there were insufficient humanitarian and compassionate grounds to warrant processing Ms. Baker's application for permanent residence within Canada. This letter contained no reasons for the decision.

[5] Upon request of the appellant's counsel, she was provided with the notes made by Immigration Officer G. Lorenz, which were used by Officer Caden when making his decision. After a summary of the history of the case, Lorenz's notes read as follows:

PC is unemployed — on Welfare. No income shown — no assets. Has four Cdn.-born children — four other children in Jamaica — HAS A TOTAL OF EIGHT CHILDREN

Says only two children are in her "direct custody". (No info on who has ghe [*sic*] other two). There is nothing for her in Jamaica — hasn't been there in a long time — no longer close to her children there — no jobs there — she has no skills other than as a domestic — children would suffer — can't take them with her and can't leave them with anyone here. Says has suffered from a mental disorder since '81 — is now an outpatient and is improving. If sent back will have a relapse.

Letter from Children's Aid — they say PC has been diagnosed as a paranoid schizophrenic. — children would suffer if returned

Letter of Aug. '93 from psychiatrist from Ont. Govm't. Says PC had post-partum psychosis and had a brief episode of psychosis in Jam. when was 25 yrs. old. Is now an out-patient and is doing relatively well — deportation would be an extremely stressful experience.

Lawyer says PS [*sic*] is sole caregiver and single parent of two Cdn born children. Pc's mental condition would suffer a setback if she is deported etc.

This case is a catastrophy [*sic*]. It is also an indictment of our "system" that the client came as a visitor in Aug. '81, was not ordered deported until Dec. '92 and in APRIL '94 IS STILL HERE!

The PC is a paranoid schizophrenic and on welfare. She has no qualifications other than as a domestic. She has FOUR CHILDREN IN JAMAICA AND ANOTHER FOUR BORN HERE. She will, of course, be a tremendous strain on our social welfare systems for (probably) the rest of her life. There are no H&C factors other than her FOUR CANADIAN-BORN CHILDREN. Do we let her stay because of that? I am of the opinion that Canada can no longer afford this type of generosity. However, because of the circumstances involved, there is a potential for adverse publicity. I recommend refusal but you may wish to clear this with someone at Region.

There is also a potential for violence — see charge of "assault with a weapon" [Capitalization in original.]

[6] Following the refusal of her application, Ms. Baker was served, on May 27, 1994, with a direction to report to Pearson Airport on June 17 for removal from Canada. Her deportation has been stayed pending the result of this appeal.

II. RELEVANT STATUTORY PROVISIONS AND PROVISIONS OF INTERNATIONAL TREATIES

[7] *Immigration Act*, R.S.C., 1985, c. I-2

82.1(1) An application for judicial review under the *Federal Court Act* with respect to any decision or order made, or any matter arising, under this Act or the rules or regulations thereunder may be commenced only with leave of a judge of the Federal Court — Trial Division.

83.(1) A judgment of the Federal Court — Trial Division on an application for judicial review with respect to any decision or order made, or any matter arising, under this Act or the rules or regulations thereunder may be appealed to the Federal Court of Appeal only if the Federal Court — Trial Division has at the time of rendering judgment certified that a serious question of general importance is involved and has stated that question.

114. ...

(2) The Governor in Council may, by regulation, authorize the Minister to exempt any person from any regulation made under subsection (1) or otherwise facilitate the admission of any person where the Minister is satisfied that the person should be exempted from that regulation or that the person's admission should be facilitated owing to the existence of compassionate or humanitarian considerations.

Immigration Regulations, 1978, SOR/78-172, as amended by SOR/93-44

2.1 The Minister is hereby authorized to exempt any person from any regulation made under subsection 114(1) of the Act or otherwise facilitate the admission to Canada of any person where the Minister is satisfied that the person should be exempted from that regulation or that the person's admission should be facilitated owing to the existence of compassionate or humanitarian considerations.

Convention on the Rights of the Child, Can. T.S. 1992 No. 3

Article 3

1. In all actions concerning children, whether undertaken by public or private social welfare institutions, courts of law, administrative authorities or legislative bodies, the best interests of the child shall be a primary consideration.

2. States Parties undertake to ensure the child such protection and care as is necessary for his or her well-being, taking into account the rights and duties of his or her parents, legal guardians, or other individuals legally responsible for him or her, and, to this end, shall take all appropriate legislative and administrative measures.

Article 9

1. States Parties shall ensure that a child shall not be separated from his or her parents against their will, except when competent authorities subject to judicial review determine, in accordance with applicable law and procedures, that such separation is necessary for the best interests of the child. Such determination may be necessary in a particular case such as one involving abuse or neglect of the child by the parents, or one where the parents are living separately and a decision must be made as to the child's place of residence.

2. In any proceedings pursuant to paragraph 1 of the present article, all interested parties shall be given an opportunity to participate in the proceedings and make their views known.

3. States Parties shall respect the right of the child who is separated from one or both parents to maintain personal relations and direct contact with both parents on a regular basis, except if it is contrary to the child's best interests.

4. Where such separation results from any action initiated by a State Party, such as the detention, imprisonment, exile, deportation or death (including death arising from any cause while the person is in the custody of the State) of one or both parents or of the child, that State Party shall, upon request, provide the parents, the child or, if appropriate, another member of the family with the essential information concerning the whereabouts of the absent member(s) of the family unless the provision of the information would be detrimental to the well-being of the child. States Parties shall further ensure that the submission of such a request shall of itself entail no adverse consequences for the person(s) concerned.

Article 12

1. States Parties shall assure to the child who is capable of forming his or her own views the right to express those views freely in all matters affecting the child, the views of the child being given due weight in accordance with the age and maturity of the child.

2. For this purpose, the child shall in particular be provided the opportunity to be heard in any judicial and administrative proceedings affecting the child, either directly, or through a representative or an appropriate body, in a manner consistent with the procedural rules of national law.

III. JUDGMENTS

.   .   .   .

(1) The Approach to Review of Discretionary Decision-Making

[51] As stated earlier, the legislation and Regulations delegate considerable discretion to the Minister in deciding whether an exemption should be granted based upon humanitarian and compassionate considerations. The Regulations state that "[t]he Minister is ... authorized to" grant an exemption or otherwise facilitate the admission to Canada of any person "where the Minister is satisfied that" this should be done "owing to the existence of compassionate or humanitarian considerations". This language signals an intention to leave considerable choice to the Minister on the question of whether to grant an H & C application.

.   .   .   .

(3) Was this Decision Unreasonable?

[63] I will next examine whether the decision in this case, and the immigration officer's interpretation of the scope of the discretion conferred upon him, were unreasonable in the sense contemplated in the judgment of Iacobucci J. in *Southam, supra*, at para. 56:

> An unreasonable decision is one that, in the main, is not supported by any reasons that can stand up to a somewhat probing examination. Accordingly, a court reviewing a conclusion on the reasonableness standard must look to see whether any reasons support it. The defect, if there is one, could presumably be in the evidentiary foundation itself or in the logical process by which conclusions are sought to be drawn from it.

In particular, the examination of this question should focus on the issues arising from the "serious question of general importance" stated by Simpson J.: the question of the approach to be taken to the interests of children when reviewing an H & C decision.

[64] The notes of Officer Lorenz, in relation to the consideration of "H & C factors", read as follows:

> The PC is a paranoid schizophrenic and on welfare. She has no qualifications other than as a domestic. She has FOUR CHILDREN IN JAMAICA AND ANOTHER FOUR BORN HERE. She will, of course, be a tremendous strain on our social welfare systems for (probably) the rest of her life. There are no H&C factors other than her FOUR CANADIAN-BORN CHILDREN. Do we let her stay because of

that? I am of the opinion that Canada can no longer afford this type of generosity.

[65] In my opinion, the approach taken to the children's interests shows that this decision was unreasonable in the sense contemplated in *Southam, supra*. The officer was completely dismissive of the interests of Ms. Baker's children. As I will outline in detail in the paragraphs that follow, I believe that the failure to give serious weight and consideration to the interests of the children constitutes an unreasonable exercise of the discretion conferred by the section, notwithstanding the important deference that should be given to the decision of the immigration officer. Professor Dyzenhaus has articulated the concept of "deference as respect" as follows:

> Deference as respect requires not submission but a respectful attention to the reasons offered or which could be offered in support of a decision.... (D. Dyzenhaus, "The Politics of Deference: Judicial Review and Democracy", in M. Taggart, ed., *The Province of Administrative Law* (1997), 279, at p. 286.)

The reasons of the immigration officer show that his decision was inconsistent with the values underlying the grant of discretion. They therefore cannot stand up to the somewhat probing examination required by the standard of reasonableness.

[66] The wording of s. 114(2) and of Regulation 2.1 requires that a decision-maker exercise the power based upon "compassionate or humanitarian considerations" (emphasis added). These words and their meaning must be central in determining whether an individual H & C decision was a reasonable exercise of the power conferred by Parliament. The legislation and regulations direct the Minister to determine whether the person's admission should be facilitated owing to the existence of such considerations. They show Parliament's intention that those exercising the discretion conferred by the statute act in a humanitarian and compassionate manner. This Court has found that it is necessary for the Minister to consider an H & C request when an application is made: *Jiminez-Perez, supra*. Similarly, when considering it, the request must be evaluated in a manner that is respectful of humanitarian and compassionate considerations.

[67] Determining whether the approach taken by the immigration officer was within the boundaries set out by the words of the statute and the values of administrative law requires a contextual approach, as is taken to statutory interpretation generally: see *R. v. Gladue*, 1999 CanLII 679 (S.C.C.), [1999] 1 S.C.R.

688; *Rizzo & Rizzo Shoes Ltd. (Re)*, 1998 CanLII 837 (S.C.C.), [1998] 1 S.C.R. 27, at paras. 20–23. In my opinion, a reasonable exercise of the power conferred by the section requires close attention to the interests and needs of children. Children's rights, and attention to their interests, are central humanitarian and compassionate values in Canadian society. Indications of children's interests as important considerations governing the manner in which H & C powers should be exercised may be found, for example, in the purposes of the Act, in international instruments, and in the guidelines for making H & C decisions published by the Minister herself.

(A) THE OBJECTIVES OF THE ACT

[68] The objectives of the Act include, in s. 3(*c*):

> to facilitate the reunion in Canada of Canadian citizens and permanent residents with their close relatives from abroad;

Although this provision speaks of Parliament's objective of reuniting citizens and permanent residents with their close relatives from abroad, it is consistent, in my opinion, with a large and liberal interpretation of the values underlying this legislation and its purposes to presume that Parliament also placed a high value on keeping citizens and permanent residents together with their close relatives who are already in Canada. The obligation to take seriously and place important weight on keeping children in contact with both parents, if possible, and maintaining connections between close family members is suggested by the objective articulated in s. 3(*c*).

(B) INTERNATIONAL LAW

[69] Another indicator of the importance of considering the interests of children when making a compassionate and humanitarian decision is the ratification by Canada of the *Convention on the Rights of the Child*, and the recognition of the importance of children's rights and the best interests of children in other international instruments ratified by Canada. International treaties and conventions are not part of Canadian law unless they have been implemented by statute: *Francis v. The Queen*, 1956 CanLII 79 (S.C.C.), [1956] S.C.R. 618, at p. 621; *Capital Cities Communications Inc. v. Canadian Radio-Television Commission*, 1977 CanLII 12 (S.C.C.), [1978] 2 S.C.R. 141, at pp. 172–73. I agree with the respondent and the Court of Appeal that the Convention has not been implemented by Parliament. Its provisions therefore have no direct application within Canadian law.

[70] Nevertheless, the values reflected in international human rights law may help inform the contextual approach to statutory interpretation and judicial review. As stated in R. Sullivan, *Driedger on the Construction of Statutes* (3rd ed. 1994), at p. 330:

> [T]he legislature is presumed to respect the values and principles enshrined in international law, both customary and conventional. These constitute a part of the legal context in which legislation is enacted and read. In so far as possible, therefore, interpretations that reflect these values and principles are preferred. [Emphasis added.]

The important role of international human rights law as an aid in interpreting domestic law has also been emphasized in other common law countries: see, for example, *Tavita v. Minister of Immigration*, [1994] 2 N.Z.L.R. 257 (C.A.), at p. 266; *Vishaka v. Rajasthan*, [1997] 3 L.R.C. 361 (S.C. India), at p. 367. It is also a critical influence on the interpretation of the scope of the rights included in the *Charter*: *Slaight Communications*, *supra*; *R. v. Keegstra*, 1990 CanLII 24 (S.C.C.), [1990] 3 S.C.R. 697.

[71] The values and principles of the Convention recognize the importance of being attentive to the rights and best interests of children when decisions are made that relate to and affect their future. In addition, the preamble, recalling the *Universal Declaration of Human Rights*, recognizes that "childhood is entitled to special care and assistance". A similar emphasis on the importance of placing considerable value on the protection of children and their needs and interests is also contained in other international instruments. The United Nations *Declaration of the Rights of the Child* (1959), in its preamble, states that the child "needs special safeguards and care". The principles of the Convention and other international instruments place special importance on protections for children and childhood, and on particular consideration of their interests, needs, and rights. They help show the values that are central in determining whether this decision was a reasonable exercise of the H & C power.

(C) THE MINISTERIAL GUIDELINES

[72] Third, the guidelines issued by the Minister to immigration officers recognize and reflect the values and approach discussed above and articulated in the Convention. As described above, immigration officers are expected to make the decision that a reasonable person would make, with special consideration of humanitarian values such as keeping connections between family members and avoiding hardship by sending people to places where they no longer

have connections. The guidelines show what the Minister considers a humanitarian and compassionate decision, and they are of great assistance to the Court in determining whether the reasons of Officer Lorenz are supportable. They emphasize that the decision-maker should be alert to possible humanitarian grounds, should consider the hardship that a negative decision would impose upon the claimant or close family members, and should consider as an important factor the connections between family members. The guidelines are a useful indicator of what constitutes a reasonable interpretation of the power conferred by the section, and the fact that this decision was contrary to their directives is of great help in assessing whether the decision was an unreasonable exercise of the H & C power.

[73] The above factors indicate that emphasis on the rights, interests, and needs of children and special attention to childhood are important values that should be considered in reasonably interpreting the "humanitarian" and "compassionate" considerations that guide the exercise of the discretion. I conclude that because the reasons for this decision do not indicate that it was made in a manner which was alive, attentive, or sensitive to the interests of Ms. Baker's children, and did not consider them as an important factor in making the decision, it was an unreasonable exercise of the power conferred by the legislation, and must, therefore, be overturned. In addition, the reasons for decision failed to give sufficient weight or consideration to the hardship that a return to Jamaica might cause Ms. Baker, given the fact that she had been in Canada for 12 years, was ill and might not be able to obtain treatment in Jamaica, and would necessarily be separated from at least some of her children.

[74] It follows that I disagree with the Federal Court of Appeal's holding in *Shah, supra,* at p. 239, that a s. 114(2) decision is "wholly a matter of judgment and discretion" (emphasis added). The wording of s. 114(2) and of the Regulations shows that the discretion granted is confined within certain boundaries. While I agree with the Court of Appeal that the Act gives the applicant no right to a particular outcome or to the application of a particular legal test, and that the doctrine of legitimate expectations does not mandate a result consistent with the wording of any international instruments, the decision must be made following an approach that respects humanitarian and compassionate values. Therefore, attentiveness and sensitivity to the importance of the rights of children, to their best interests, and to the hardship that may be caused to them by a negative decision is

essential for an H & C decision to be made in a reasonable manner. While deference should be given to immigration officers on s. 114(2) judicial review applications, decisions cannot stand when the manner in which the decision was made and the approach taken are in conflict with humanitarian and compassionate values. The Minister's guidelines themselves reflect this approach. However, the decision here was inconsistent with it.

[75] The certified question asks whether the best interests of children must be <u>a</u> primary consideration when assessing an applicant under s. 114(2) and the Regulations. The principles discussed above indicate that, for the exercise of the discretion to fall within the standard of reasonableness, the decision-maker should consider children's best interests as an important factor, give them substantial weight, and be alert, alive and sensitive to them. That is not to say that children's best interests must always outweigh other considerations, or that there will not be other reasons for denying an H & C claim even when children's interests are given this consideration. However, where the interests of children are minimized, in a manner inconsistent with Canada's humanitarian and compassionate tradition and the Minister's guidelines, the decision will be unreasonable.

E.   Conclusions and Disposition

[76] Therefore, both because there was a violation of the principles of procedural fairness owing to a reasonable apprehension of bias, and because the exercise of the H & C discretion was unreasonable, I would allow this appeal.

[77] The appellant requested that solicitor–client costs be awarded to her if she were successful in her appeal. The majority of this Court held as follows in *Young v. Young,* 1993 CanLII 34 (S.C.C.), [1993] 4 S.C.R. 3, at p. 134:

> Solicitor–client costs are generally awarded only where there has been reprehensible, scandalous or outrageous conduct on the part of one of the parties.

There has been no such conduct on the part of the Minister shown during this litigation, and I do not believe that this is one of the exceptional cases where solicitor–client costs should be awarded. I would allow the appeal, and set aside the decision of Officer Caden of April 18, 1994, with party-and-party costs throughout. The matter will be returned to the Minister for redetermination by a different immigration officer.

[IACOBUCCI J. and Cory J.:]

[78] I agree with L'Heureux-Dubé J.'s reasons and disposition of this appeal, except to the extent that my colleague addresses the effect of international law on the exercise of ministerial discretion pursuant to s. 114(2) of the *Immigration Act*, R.S.C., 1985, c. I-2. The certified question at issue in this appeal concerns whether federal immigration authorities must treat the best interests of the child as a primary consideration in assessing an application for humanitarian and compassionate consideration under s. 114(2) of the Act, given that the legislation does not implement the provisions contained in the *Convention on the Rights of the Child*, Can. T.S. 1992 No. 3, a multilateral convention to which Canada is party. In my opinion, the certified question should be answered in the negative.

[79] It is a matter of well-settled law that an international convention ratified by the executive branch of government is of no force or effect within the Canadian legal system until such time as its provisions have been incorporated into domestic law by way of implementing legislation: *Capital Cities Communications Inc. v. Canadian Radio-Television Commission*, 1977 CanLII 12 (S.C.C.), [1978] 2 S.C.R. 141. I do not agree with the approach adopted by my colleague, wherein reference is made to the underlying values of an unimplemented international treaty in the course of the contextual approach to statutory interpretation and administrative law, because such an approach is not in accordance with the Court's jurisprudence concerning the status of international law within the domestic legal system.

[80] In my view, one should proceed with caution in deciding matters of this nature, lest we adversely affect the balance maintained by our Parliamentary tradition, or inadvertently grant the executive the power to bind citizens without the necessity of involving the legislative branch. I do not share my colleague's confidence that the Court's precedent in *Capital Cities*, *supra*, survives intact following the adoption of a principle of law which permits reference to an unincorporated convention during the process of statutory interpretation. Instead, the result will be that the appellant is able to achieve indirectly what cannot be achieved directly, namely, to give force and effect within the domestic legal system to international obligations undertaken by the executive alone that have yet to be subject to the democratic will of Parliament.

[81] The primacy accorded to the rights of children in the Convention, assuming for the sake of argument that the factual circumstances of this appeal are included within the scope of the relevant provisions, is irrelevant unless and until such provisions are the subject of legislation enacted by Parliament. In answering the certified question in the negative, I am mindful that the result may well have been different had my colleague concluded that the appellant's claim fell within the ambit of rights protected by the *Canadian Charter of Rights and Freedoms*. Had this been the case, the Court would have had an opportunity to consider the application of the interpretive presumption, established by the Court's decision in *Slaight Communications Inc. v. Davidson*, 1989 CanLII 92 (S.C.C.), [1989] 1 S.C.R. 1038, and confirmed in subsequent jurisprudence, that administrative discretion involving *Charter* rights be exercised in accordance with similar international human rights norms.

(d) Rethinking the Relationship Between International and Domestic Law†

Armand de Mestral and Evan Fox-Decent

INTRODUCTION

In light of the increased significance of public international law since 1945, the proliferation of international treaties, and the basic obligation of all states to perform their international legal obligations in good faith, states have good reason to seek a measure of congruence between their domestic legal

---

† (2008) 53 McGill L.J. 573 at 575–602. This article first appeared in the McGill Law Journal. Reproduced with permission. [Notes and/or references omitted.]

orders and international law. This article argues that Canada has not yet struck the appropriate balance between domestic and international law. Canadian law views the two legal orders as fundamentally distinct and separate from one another. The result is that Canadian domestic law and its institutions have failed to articulate a persuasive account of the relationship between domestic and international law.

In this article we take stock of how this relationship is currently understood in Canada. We also make a series of recommendations that aim to recast the relationship between the two legal orders as a unity. The relationship between domestic and international law, properly understood, enables the two legal orders to complement one another as a unified and coherent set of legal rules and principles. This unity, we suggest, flows from the idea that all law, domestic and international alike, establishes norms and standards to which public bodies and private parties can be held publicly accountable. The unity of domestic and international law, in other words, follows from a shared and overarching commitment to public accountability.[1]

In Part I we provide background to the article's recommendations and outline several considerations relevant to the relationship between domestic and international law in Canada. We consider the impact of international law on Canadian domestic law and the worry that a democratic deficit attends international law-making. Part II analyzes those elements of the relationship between domestic and international law in Canada that pose concerns. In particular, we survey the approaches Canada has adopted to the domestic reception of customary and treaty law. Part III prescribes measures intended to contribute to the unity of domestic and international law. These measures relate to (1) parliamentary participation in treaty making, (2) implementation of international law in Canada, (3) the role of judges and administrative decision makers (e.g., tribunals, agencies, frontline decision makers, ministers), and (4) the role of provinces.

One of our main recommendations is that Canada should adopt a *Canada Treaties Act* in order to support the participation of legislators in the treaty-making process and to formalize the modes through which treaties may be implemented and received into Canada's domestic law. At the core of our argument is a new and generous approach to treaty implementation. Contrary to prevailing judicial opinion in Canada, we argue that treaties should be viewed as "implemented" — and therefore as capable of producing domestic legal effects — if Canadian law at the time of ratification provides sufficient discretionary or rule-making power to enable public decision makers to comply with Canada's international obligations.

I. BACKGROUND: CANADA AND THE CHALLENGE OF INTERNATIONAL LAW

Which institutions in Canada determine the relationship of domestic and international law? In the broadest sense all three branches of government — the executive, the judiciary, and the legislatures — are responsible for the current legal situation. Both the executive, charged with international relations, and the judiciary, charged with the interpretation of law, have been increasingly active throughout the twentieth century. For various reasons, the legislative branch has been largely absent from the making and interpretation of international law. This absence may be the source of much of the uncertainty that currently exists concerning the relationship between domestic and international law in Canada. Parliament and provincial legislatures have passed a host of laws giving effect to international rules, but they have seldom sought to be part of the making of the rules themselves. Instead, presumably with the willing concurrence of their respective governments, they prefer to leave it to the executive branch to negotiate treaties and conduct international affairs, on the assumption that the conduct of international relations is an executive function. But as we shall see below, the constitution of Canada is silent on the matter, the few laws dealing with foreign affairs provide little guidance, and domestic interpretation acts contain only a few provisions on the role of customary international law and treaty law. There is no general legislation governing interpretation of treaties or the place of international law in the domestic legal order.

The result of legislative inaction is that the courts have been left to deal with the relationship between international and domestic law without legislative guidance or even much assistance from the executive branch. This problem has been compounded by the often puzzling positions taken by officers of the various attorneys general at the federal and provincial levels in litigation before the courts. Winning the case by using any argument at hand sometimes seems to be more important than ensuring Canada's compliance with its international legal obligations. This tendency is especially unfortunate since Canada has clearly entered a period of history in which the courts are faced with an ever-increasing number of cases that raise issues of international law.

A. The Impact of International Law on Domestic Law-Making

Customary international law is a direct source of domestic legal rules unless a state takes explicit measures to ensure that a particular customary rule does not have the force of domestic law.[2] Failing any such step, the customary rule can be applied by courts in litigation between citizens. International customary law can also limit the exercise of public authority and may equally define the parameters within which a state may legitimately legislate. For example, it can define the limits of the jurisdiction of states over persons and territory.

Turning now to treaty law, international agreements frequently lead to the enactment of domestic legislation. International law may give rise to domestic law, for example, when UN specialized agencies, such as the International Civil Aviation Organization (ICAO), the International Maritime Organization (IMO), and the World Health Organization (WHO) adopt rules that bind their member states in accordance with their respective constitutional structures.[3] The same organizations sometimes adopt rules in the form of treaties that are negotiated in regular or special sessions.[4] They may range from the most general and comprehensive "law-making" treaties, such as the third *United Nations Convention on the Law of the Sea*,[5] or human rights treaties establishing rules for the protection of different categories of persons, such as the *Convention on the Rights of the Child*,[6] to much more specific treaties dealing, for example, with the regulation of the construction of ships, such as the *International Convention for the Safety of Life at Sea, 1979*,[7] or commercial matters, such as the *Convention on International Interests in Mobile Equipment*.[8] Moreover, virtually every type of intellectual property is now the object of an international convention that has given rise to implementing legislation.[9] International trade treaties — bilateral, regional or multilateral — have also required extensive legislative implementation in Canada.[10]

The domestic effects of treaty law-making do not end with implementation. An increasing number of treaties include provisions for compulsory dispute settlement. These proceedings can lead to rulings that require the losing state to change its legislation or reverse administrative decisions already taken.[11]

We estimate that roughly 40 per cent of federal statutes implement international rules in whole or in part. Examples include the *Canada Shipping Act, 2001*,[12] the *Aeronautics Act*,[13] the *Broadcasting Act*,[14] the *Special Import Measures Act*,[15] the *Special Economic Measures Act*,[16] the *Export and Import Permits Act*,[17] the *Customs Tariff*,[18] the *Customs Act*,[19] the *North American Free Trade Agreement Implementation Act*,[20] the *World Trade Organization Agreement Implementation Act*,[21] the *Oceans Act*,[22] and the *Remote Sensing Act*.[23] Other examples include the many double taxation acts,[24] as well as legislation concerning among other things Canada's membership in various international organizations,[25] international environmental protection,[26] the international protection of migratory species,[27] endangered species and wildlife,[28] heritage protection,[29] enforcement of chemical and biological weapons conventions,[30] enforcement of international humanitarian law,[31] enforcement of international human rights law,[32] and international arbitral procedure.[33]

This list represents an impressive body of law. The federal government, provincial governments, and even municipalities must enforce such legislation. Most of these statutes deal with both domestic and international issues, and it is frequently difficult to determine where one field stops and the other begins.

Given that international treaties play such an important role in the Canadian legislative process, it is important to understand where these treaties come from and the forces that have shaped them. If they condition the content of Canadian laws, it is important that Canada plays an appropriate part in their negotiation and drafting to ensure that they reflect Canadian values and protect Canadian interests.

B. The Democratic Principle

To be free and democratic, Canada must remain in control of its legislative processes at every level of government. No sovereign democracy can be subject to foreign control over the kind of laws it must adopt. Yet many issues have to be dealt with at the international level.

Canada is not alone in facing this dilemma: in different ways, all states must face it. The member states of the European Union must, in many respects, cope with an even greater dilemma than Canada. The majority of laws regulating business transactions in the twenty-seven member states are now made in Brussels. Some of these laws are automatically applicable in each member state, while others must be transposed into domestic law and applied by member states. Short of exiting the European Union, no choice is offered once these E.U. regulations and directives are adopted.[34]

This phenomenon is not limited to legislation in the economic sphere; it is now a daily fact of life for E.U.-member legislatures, governments, and courts.[35]

The issues of ensuring respect for domestic democracy and constitutional integrity vis-à-vis the E.U. legislative process have arisen in every member state. Problems have been most acute in those member states that possess a written constitution and a formal constitutional charter of rights. In Germany, a federal state governed by a complex constitutional document that includes a charter of rights, challenges have been made to E.U. laws or governing treaty amendments on the ground that they threaten constitutional protections of fundamental freedoms or central principles, such as democracy, in the *Basic Law* of Germany, the state's constitutional document.[36] The Federal Constitutional Court of Germany has on every occasion determined that legitimate bounds were not crossed by the ratification of the law or treaty in question.[37] However, the court has categorically affirmed its right to review E.U. treaty commitments in light of German constitutional principles and, if necessary, to declare that an E.U. measure must give way before the *Basic Law*.[38]

The E.U. example is perhaps unique, yet it contains lessons for all states. Interestingly, these lessons even apply to the European Union itself, the European Court of Justice having recently ruled that E.U. regulations pursuant to mandatory sanctions of the UN Security Council under chapter VII of the *Charter of the United Nations*[39] cannot violate fundamental human rights guaranteed by E.U. law.[40] The dilemmas of E.U. member states with respect to E.U. law can be resolved by political action and common policy making within the E.U. framework of supranational legislative processes. This type of resolution is virtually impossible at the international level: the international community does not possess the institutions necessary to reconcile the immense political differences that exist between the almost two hundred member states of the international community. Nonetheless, the degree of cooperation and interaction between states is increasing year by year. The result is an ever-growing body of treaty law that affects the domestic decisions of states.

Canada, like all other states, faces the dilemma of preserving its democracy and democratic legislative practices while accommodating the legitimate demands of international cooperation. In *Reference Re Secession of Quebec*,[41] the Supreme Court of Canada affirmed that "democracy expresses the sovereign will of the people" and that democratic institutions must allow for participation and accountability.[42] Nevertheless, the Court was quick to add that the significance of democracy is not exhausted by majority rule. Democratic institutions must rest on a legal foundation, and that foundation is supplied by one of the other organizing principles identified by the Court: the rule of law.[43] The domestic reception of international law must respect all these principles.

Our contention is that a concern for democracy and the rule of law supports a much more generous approach to the domestic effect of international law than the one currently taken by Canada's judiciary. A key aspect of the separation of international and domestic legal orders often stressed by Canadian courts is that treaties are made by the executive arm of government without parliamentary direction or participation. It is then argued that international law has scant legitimacy in the Canadian legal order unless it is formally implemented by a legislative act. We have argued elsewhere that this objection is unconvincing because domestic courts routinely impose duties, such as procedural fairness, on administrative decision makers without the prompt of statute.[44] That being said, a changed view of the place of treaties in the domestic legal order would be all the more appropriate if Parliament and the provincial legislatures were to signal their desire to enhance legislative involvement in the treaty-making process. But Canadian courts have been strongly influenced by the fact that treaties are made exclusively by the executive branch. It will thus not be a simple task to displace the view that treaties cannot have the force of law in the Canadian legal order without express legislative intervention.

This "dualist" approach to international law — one that conceives of international and domestic law as operating in separate domains, can be seen to be motivated by a desire to protect Canadians from the unlicensed intrusion of international law. The dualist approach allows the Canadian legal system to pick and choose the bits of international law it wishes to receive into its domestic law through legislative implementation. Dualism thus appeals to the populist democratic ideal of contemporary liberal democracies according to which law is to be made by popularly elected legislators.

Many other countries adopt a dualist position with respect to treaties. Few countries adopt an entirely "monist" approach, which affirms that treaties always have direct domestic effect merely upon ratification. Nonetheless, as we shall discuss below, there may be no developed country that continues to maintain as thoroughgoing a dualism as Canada.

How should Canada balance dualist and monist principles? We suggest that the approach to be followed is one that facilitates harmony between Canadian and international law by taking international law seriously when Canadian statutes are interpreted and applied. First of all, we argue that because customary international law is now clearly part of Canadian law, the rules of customary law should be enforceable by courts at the behest of individuals, unless the relevant legislature has expressly stated in its legislation that a particular customary rule is of no effect. Secondly, we propose that treaties, duly ratified and implemented by Canada, should be recognized as part of a common normative order that treats international law and domestic law as a unity. In other words, ratified and implemented treaties should be regarded as fully legitimate sources of law in Canada, and they should be treated as capable of producing legal effects in the Canadian legal system.

While the dualist approach admits that implemented treaties can produce domestic effects, we shall see that the dominant judicial understanding of implementation is deeply impoverished. Far more treaties deserve to be recognized as "implemented" than the courts currently acknowledge. We claim that all branches of government — Parliament, the provincial legislatures, the courts, and the different elements of the executive — can take a variety of steps to accomplish this objective. As outlined below, such steps relate to treaty adoption and legislative participation in the treaty process. But they also call for a more generous understanding of implementation by courts and administrative agencies. It should be acknowledged that Canadian domestic law is in most cases already consistent with international treaties at the time they are ratified. As a consequence, the search for explicit *ex post* implementing legislation as a threshold test for whether international law can have domestic effects is misguided.

II. THE CURRENT RELATIONSHIP BETWEEN DOMESTIC AND INTERNATIONAL LAW IN CANADA

International law requires each state to respect and fulfill its international obligations, but leaves to states a large degree of latitude as to how they will achieve this goal. Some countries, such as the Netherlands, are on the monist side of the spectrum: international law is assumed to have direct force of law in the domestic legal order.[45] Other states, such as the United States, have a hybrid system that makes considerable room for international law, while retaining several techniques requiring its positive implementation before it can have the force of law in the domestic system.[46] As noted above, Canada is at the dualist end of the spectrum. The Canadian position is somewhat surprising given Canada's historic commitment to the United Nations and to an interna-

tional legal system based on law rather than power.[47] One might reasonably expect to find Canada at the other end of the spectrum or at least in the middle. The fact that Canada continues to maintain an increasingly outmoded approach to the matter is the principal reason for this article.

A. Customary International Law in Canada

International customary law, unlike treaties, does not emanate from intergovernmental negotiations, although it is heavily influenced by the practice of states. Rather, it develops through the cumulative practice of states in accordance with what is perceived as a governing legal obligation (*opinio juris*). Historically, there has been considerable authority for the proposition that rules of customary international law have the force of law in Canada and that they may be invoked before the courts. As discussed at the end of this section, this view has been recently reaffirmed by the Supreme Court of Canada in *R. v. Hape*.[48]

Two theories exist with regard to how international law can be incorporated into domestic law. Adoption theory holds that international law is automatically part of domestic law, except in cases where it conflicts with domestic statutory laws or the common law. Transformation theory holds that international law can only become incorporated into domestic law when it has been integrated into domestic law by way of a legislative enactment.[49] Customary international law enters a legal system automatically by way of adoption.

The adoption approach means that customary international law is deemed to form part of the common law. As Gibran van Ert notes, "[t]he common law looks on customary international law as a facet of itself."[50] Thus, when a court is satisfied that a given proposition amounts to a rule of customary international law, it will apply it as a rule of common law. The adoption theory thus invites courts not only to render decisions that are consistent with international law, "but to adopt international custom as the rules upon which their adjudication is based."[51] As Ronald St. J. Macdonald observes in this regard, "customary rules of international law are adopted automatically into our law, amid a few caveats about sovereignty, and then directly applied unless they conflict with statute or some fundamental constitutional principle in which case legislation is required to enforce them."[52]

A conflict between customary international law and domestic legislation may arise if an international custom changes. A conflict may also be triggered by the "expansion of international custom beyond its former bounds and into spheres of law formerly reserved to domestic adjudication."[53] Nevertheless, incorporating international customary law into the common law does not depart from the principle of self-government because this process leaves the legislature with the authority to change or modify the common law through statutory action.[54] Similarly, a state that persistently objects to the emergence of an international custom cannot be bound by it.

Customary international law does pose special difficulties for those arguing for its adoption into the domestic legal framework.[55] The difficulty results from the fact that the use of customary international norms requires the party seeking their application to demonstrate the existence of "wide-sweeping objective and subjective evidence of the establishment of a custom."[56] This burden is often hard to discharge, as it can be daunting to determine what states believe as opposed to what they say.[57] Notwithstanding this difficulty, the rule holding that customary international law is genuinely part of domestic law appears to be firmly entrenched in Canada as well as in other democracies.

The rule was affirmed by eminent English jurists as early as the eighteenth century. In *Buvot v. Barbuit*, Lord Talbot stated that the law of nations to "its fullest extent was and formed Part of the law of England."[58] This dictum was reiterated in a case by Lord Mansfield.[59] Similarly, in *Heathfield v. Chilton*, Lord Mansfield affirmed that "the law of nations ... is part of the common law of England."[60] The unity of customary international law with the common law was also affirmed by Lord Langdale in *Charles Duke of Brunswick v. The King of Hanover*.[61]

Canadian jurisprudence suggests that customary international law is applicable in Canada so long as it does not conflict with existing Canadian law. The adoption doctrine was confirmed in early decisions such as *The Ship "North" v. R.*,[62] in which Justice Davies sanctioned the adoption approach taken by early English authorities. He declared that "[t]he right of hot pursuit ... being part of the law of nations was properly judicially taken notice of and acted upon by the learned judge ... "[63] A relatively recent example of this approach is provided by *Reference Re Newfoundland Continental Shelf*.[64] The Supreme Court of Canada unanimously identified a relevant rule of customary international law in determining whether Canada or Newfoundland had the right to seek and exploit natural resources of the continental shelf at the moment of Newfoundland's entry into Confederation. Unfortunately, as noted by

Van Ert, "[t]he [C]ourt's consideration of customary international law, while not inconsistent with [adoption], did not clearly invoke it."[65] Similarly, in the *Secession Reference*, while the Court took into account some aspects of international law with regard to state secession, "nowhere did it make clear that those parts of the law which were customary in nature enjoyed direct effect in Canadian law via the doctrine of [adoption]."[66]

Canadian courts could well rely on the interpretative authority of international customary law to address a wide range of human rights questions.[67] But in the context of customary law, it is difficult to fully agree with Justice La Forest's observation that human rights norms "are applied consistently, with an international vision and on the basis of international experience. Thus our courts — and many other national courts — are truly becoming international courts in many areas involving the rule of law."[68] Applications of international customary law by Canadian courts have been inconsistent and at times half-hearted. A recent Supreme Court of Canada decision failed to acknowledge the peremptory status of a *jus cogens* norm of customary international law — the kind of norm from which no derogation is possible.[69] In *Suresh v. Canada (Minister of Citizenship and Immigration)*, the Court considered the peremptory norm of security against torture, but would recognize only that the norm "cannot be easily derogated from."[70] In *114957 Canada Ltée (Spraytech, Société d'arrosage) v. Hudson (Town of)*, the majority hastily affirmed the precautionary principle's status as a rule of customary international law without even examining the requirements of state practice and *opinio juris*.[71]

This situation has led Stephen Toope to go as far as stating that "[w]e know for certain that we *do not* know whether customary international law forms part of the law of Canada."[72] As Van Ert has accurately remarked, "[t]he cases do not deny [adoption], but neither do they engage with customary international law as the doctrine — and the related doctrine of judicial notice — require."[73] As we shall see now, the *Hape* decision — the Court's most recent pronouncement on the issue at the time of writing — provides some salutary clarification.[74]

In *Hape*, Justice LeBel for the Court reaffirmed the rule that international customary law is part of the common law. It may thus be pleaded before the courts unless it is in direct conflict with the constitution or with a legislative act. Justice LeBel stated:

> In my view, following the common law tradition, it appears that the doctrine of adoption operates

in Canada such that prohibitive rules of customary international law should be incorporated into domestic law in the absence of conflicting legislation.[75]

Although the rules regarding the adoption of customary international law have been clarified by this decision, a number of questions still remain as to how the Supreme Court of Canada and lower courts will apply this holding. The dictum quoted above refers to prohibitive rules of customary international law. Many customary rules, however, empower states or confer rights to be exercised by their nationals, such as the rules governing navigation on the high seas.

Moreover, proof of custom is a thorny issue. How will the courts approach the issue of proof of a rule or custom? In particular, will the courts seek guidance from the minister of foreign affairs? Will the courts continue to be more comfortable with evidence from expert witnesses on matters that arguably should simply be pleaded as law? Many courts in recent years, when faced with pleadings based on customary international law, have allowed the parties to furnish expert evidence in writing and in testimony, which allows for cross-examination.[76] This approach to customary law is scarcely consonant with the idea that Canadian courts are dealing with part of the law of Canada. Justice LeBel has removed many ambiguities but only the future will tell where *Hape* will take the law.[77]

The approach in *Hape* is consistent with the approaches to customary international law adopted by courts in other jurisdictions, including the United Kingdom.[78] Also, the constitutions of a number of countries, notably South Africa,[79] Germany,[80] and the United States,[81] explicitly establish that customary international law is part of domestic law.

B. Treaty Law and Treaty Making in Canada

Contemporary international rule making is done largely by means of treaties to which states can commit themselves. Once the drafting stage has been completed and the text is formally adopted the treaty is subject to ratification, a process of formal acceptance by each state that takes place according to the state's domestic procedures and the ratification requirements established in the treaty. Through ratification the state indicates that it is both willing and able to fulfill its obligations under the treaty.

Having taken the decision to ratify, each state must consider how the provisions of the treaty will be respected. This process is generally called implementation. Implementation refers to a range of steps

that a state can take to ensure its compliance with the treaty. Many states, such as Canada, have adopted a wide variety of implementation methods, each tailored to the treaty in question and to the shape of domestic law. Some states must adopt new legislation when implementation requires a change in domestic law, while others give direct effect in their domestic law to the very words of the treaty and thus require no legislative intervention.

Since there is no international executive power, virtually all decisions concerning implementation depend upon the willingness of states to take appropriate measures, separately and in concert with others, to ensure that a treaty is put into operation. States must provide the means of administering a treaty and must ensure that their laws and public institutions are in a position to give full effect to the policies enshrined in the treaty. International organizations play an important coordinating role with respect to the implementation of a number of treaties, and a growing number of international organizations are empowered to inquire into the adequacy of domestic implementation.[82] But the state remains the primary vehicle through which treaty obligations are (or are not) fulfilled.

Some see state implementation as a source of weakness in the international legal system. But given the nature of the contemporary international order, it cannot, and arguably should not, be otherwise. States are closer to their populations than any international organization could be in the foreseeable future. Unless governments turn to tyranny and authoritarianism, states enjoy a far greater degree of legitimacy with their populations than international organizations. In the modern international order, enforcement of treaties by states ensures a vital degree of both efficacy and legitimacy.

1. How Does Canada Enter into Treaties?

Much scholarship has been devoted to the subject of Canadian treaty making and related diplomatic practice.[83] Internationally, treaty making is governed by the *Vienna Convention on the Law of Treaties*, adopted in 1969 and ratified by Canada in 1994.[84] Treaty making relating to the creation of new international organizations or under the aegis of the United Nations or other leading international organizations demands the most formal procedures.[85] Many major treaties are negotiated at international conferences specially convened for the purpose.[86] Some treaty negotiations are led by one or more like-minded states, which seek to promote a policy and then convene an international conference when the time is ripe for the conclusion of a treaty.[87]

In almost all cases, the individuals principally charged with treaty negotiation are diplomats or officials of government departments specially accredited for the purpose of negotiating a treaty. But governments recognize that the inclusion of a broad-based group of individuals in a negotiation is often of assistance in ensuring that negotiations yield positive results.[88] For example, in recent years, it has become common for major treaty-making conferences to be attended by large numbers of representatives of non-governmental organizations (NGOs).[89]

Until only last year there was no general official description of Canadian treaty-making practice, although a statement of treaty practice, prepared by the legal adviser of the Department of Foreign Affairs and International Trade (DFAIT), is published annually in the Canadian Yearbook of International Law.[90] But in 2008, the Treaty Section of the DFAIT published on its website a *Policy on Tabling of Treaties in Parliament*,[91] which closely follows the Ponsonby Rule, a U.K. procedure whereby treaties are laid before Parliament for at least twenty-one sitting days before ratification.[92] The policy puts flesh on the government of Canada's announcement on 25 January 2008 that it henceforth intends to table treaties in the House of Commons prior to ratification.[93] Nonetheless, the federal government still takes the position that it alone is authorized to negotiate and ratify international treaties. This principle is enshrined in the *Department of Foreign Affairs and International Trade Act*, which vests the conduct of foreign affairs, including the negotiation and ratification of treaties, in the minister and deputy minister of foreign affairs and international trade.[94]

Various departmental and interdepartmental committees consider and discuss the need for a treaty. The actual decision to initiate or participate in a treaty negotiation may be incremental or very formal. When officials determine that a formal decision is required, a policy on the matter is usually worked out by several federal interdepartmental committees, though it is possible that the policy can be developed by only one department. Regardless of how the underlying policy is developed, it must be approved by the federal cabinet. In most cases, the policy will be put to the appropriate committees of cabinet for approval. Some major decisions, involving significant treaties, are referred to the full cabinet for approval.

In short, the policy-formation process relating to treaty negotiation is entirely in the hands of the federal public service, subject to political direction from the federal cabinet and other elected members of the federal government. In formal terms, provincial, territorial, and First Nations governments are not part of this process. They can be invited to participate, but the invitation is entirely subject to the discretion of the federal government and public service.

Once a formal decision has been taken to initiate or participate in treaty negotiations, the method of negotiation must be established. Negotiations may be as simple as a summit-meeting decision signed by heads of state. Similarly, expeditious negotiations may take the form of a telephone call between officials in Ottawa and their counterparts elsewhere, followed by correspondence and ultimately the exchange of letters duly signed by the responsible ministers. At the opposite end of the spectrum might be a very complex negotiation on a matter of high political significance and public interest, as in the case of the 1988 *Free Trade Agreement Between the Government of Canada and the Government of the United States*.[95]

The typical negotiation is conducted by federal officials. In the event of a strong provincial interest, particularly if the subject matter falls within provincial jurisdiction, there is in almost all cases intergovernmental discussion between officials and possibly ministers. Yet, there is little uniformity of approach, nor is there a general framework, for federal–provincial consultations.[96] Public participation in treaty negotiation (or prior policy formation) is even more driven by political choice and ad hoc decision making. In some sectors, particularly those involving environmental issues and human rights issues, many NGOs clamour for attention and inclusion in the planning and negotiation of treaties.[97] Whether they succeed is left to the discretion of federal officials and those elected members of the federal government who direct them.

In other sectors, particularly those involving economic matters, commercial and industrial associations have developed a pattern of consultations with federal officials before and during negotiations.[98] But these situations seldom involve requests to participate in negotiations as such. These same groups are often consulted on the question of implementation. A similar pattern exists where the focus of treaty negotiations concerns health care, a profession, or a mode of transportation. Interested professional groups often have a fairly close relationship to the federal officials responsible for such treaty negotiations. There is little or no tradition of consultation with outside groups on issues that are predominately of international intergovernmental interest.

Many practitioners of international treaty making are skeptical of wide public participation in the treaty-making process. Their case, however, is much harder to make when it comes to the ratification of a treaty. Ratification is the decision by which Canada declares itself bound by international law and assumes the obligation to do everything necessary to ensure respect for its obligations under the treaty. Notwithstanding the new and laudable *Treaty-Tabling Policy*, the position of the Canadian government at the present time is that ratification is strictly an executive matter, regardless of how many Canadians might be affected and no matter what the division of legislative jurisdiction might be.[99] As a result, the federal government can commit Canada internationally, without any form of legislative consent, to treaty obligations requiring changes to both federal and provincial laws. Very serious consequences for Canadian federalism would ensue were it not for the fact that the federal government, out of prudence, does not actually ratify treaties requiring legislative changes until these changes have been adopted by Parliament or the provincial legislatures, or until it is confident that such changes as are necessary will be forthcoming.

It is important to emphasize that as a general rule, at both levels of government, law officers of the Crown have been careful to ensure that legislation is in place before authorizing ratification. And now, under the *Treaty-Tabling Policy*, the cabinet document seeking authorization to ratify a treaty must state the legislation or regulatory power under which Canada can perform its international obligations with respect to the treaty in question.[100] This responsibility is shared by both the DFAIT, which is ultimately charged with ratification, and the Department of Justice, which is charged with ensuring that adequate legislation and regulatory authority is in place.[101]

Such a careful consideration of domestic law can have the effect of delaying ratification for a considerable period. A particularly striking example of this delay was the ratification process surrounding the *International Convention on the Settlement of Investment Disputes Between States and Nationals of Other States*.[102] Signed in 1965 and quickly ratified by many states, the *ICSID* presented problems in Canada, as provincial governments insisted that arbitration, even over international investment, fell within the provincial powers over administration of justice. Rather than face both legal and political challenges, and despite considerable pressure from Canadian foreign investors, the federal government delayed signature until after 2006. Also, in the face of continued opposition from two provincial governments, it postponed ratification yet again, despite the fact that by that time, federal jurisdiction over international trade and

investment had been considerably strengthened, legislation had been adopted at the federal and provincial levels, and provincial governments supported the practice of international arbitration.[103] Despite the obvious frustrations that these delays may cause, the speed at which ratification occurs does ensure that only a very small number of treaties are ratified without adequate implementing legislation or regulatory authority, though some ratifications are delayed for strictly political reasons.[104]

2. Where Did the Canadian Approach Come From and What Is Currently Driving It?

A. SOURCES OF THE DUALIST APPROACH

The body of public law received from the United Kingdom as a result of British colonization of North America has been an influential factor in Canada's approach to treaties. This body of law vested the conduct of international relations and treaty making in the Crown.[105] It also established the principle that a treaty could not amend the positive law of the land unless the change received positive legislative endorsement.[106] As we have seen, however, U.K. public law did admit the principle that customary international law was part of the law of the land and could be enforced by the courts as domestic law.[107]

A further contributing factor has been the constitution of Canada and the division of powers between the provincial legislatures and Parliament. In *Canada (A.G.) v. Ontario (A.G.)*, which was decided in 1937 and remains the leading decision on treaty implementation in Canada, the Judicial Committee of the Privy Council, although asked to rule on both executive and legislative powers in respect of certain conventions, ruled only that legislative jurisdiction necessary to implement a treaty followed the normal division of powers and was not vested exclusively in Parliament.[108]

The result of *Labour Conventions* has been to establish a rule that the federal division of legislative powers requires treaties to be implemented in accordance with the federal principle. In so doing, the Privy Council refused to accept the proposition that there existed a "treaty power" beyond that created by section 132 of the *Constitution Act, 1867* concerning "Empire" treaties made for Canada by the United Kingdom.[109] Since no Empire treaties have been made since the time of these decisions, that power serves only to renew federal legislation in respect of such treaties as still remain.[110]

Canadian federalism raises the question of the role of the provincial crowns in international relations. An equally important issue is the capacity of the provincial legislatures to legislate in respect of treaty implementation covering matters within provincial jurisdiction. We discuss a number of the issues that complicate provincial participation in international affairs in Part III.E, below.

Also relevant in determining the role of the federal and provincial crowns in foreign affairs and treaty making is the unwritten law of the Royal Prerogative.[111] Apart from section 132 of the *Constitution Act, 1867*, and more recently section 11(g) of the *Canadian Charter of Rights and Freedoms*,[112] the constitution of Canada is silent on treaty making and the place of international law in the Canadian legal order.[113] Given the relative silence of the constitution on the matter, it is largely the exercise of the Royal Prerogative that sustains the federal government's claim to the exclusive exercise of the foreign-affairs power. Various federal and provincial laws governing interpretation of statutes or particular treaties, some of which we discuss below, apply to the exercise of the foreign-affairs and treaty powers.[114] But the origin of these powers traces back to the Royal Prerogative.

The Canadian approach to treaties and treaty making is thus an amalgam of history, principles of public law, case law, administrative practice, and legislative direction. Not surprisingly, it has generated significant scholarship in recent years.[115] The division of powers provides an answer to the question of whether the federal or provincial legislatures (or both) have jurisdiction to implement treaties. The issue of the relationship between treaties and Canada's domestic legal order, however, has largely been left to administrative practice, political debate at the occasional federal–provincial conference, and numerous judicial decisions that, in the main, affirm a strong commitment to dualism.[116] These decisions, and the dualist approach that underlies them, have played a leading role in determining the principles of public law applicable to treaty implementation, the status of treaties, and the interpretation of treaties.

B. LEGISLATIVE INTERPRETATION AND THE PRINCIPLE OF CONFORMITY

To some extent the commitment to dualism is tempered by the interpretive presumption of conformity that calls on administrative officials and courts to interpret domestic law in a manner that respects Canada's international legal obligations.[117] In *Baker v. Canada (Minister of Immigration)*, the Supreme Court of Canada reviewed a minister's refusal to exercise his discretionary authority to stay a deportation on humanitarian and compassionate grounds in the case

of a woman with Canadian-born dependent children.[118] In its analysis, the Court considered whether the *Convention on the Rights of the Child* could be used as an interpretative instrument in reviewing the exercise of the minister's discretion.[119] At issue was article 3 of the convention, which states that "[i]n all actions concerning children, whether undertaken by public or private social welfare institutions, courts of law, administrative authorities or legislative bodies, the best interests of the child shall be a primary consideration."[120] The convention had been ratified by Canada but, in the view of Justice L'Heureux-Dubé, had not yet been implemented and given effect under Canadian domestic law because no specific statute had been adopted whose purpose was implementation.[121] Nonetheless, the majority held that "the [concern for children's best interests] reflected in *international* human rights law may help inform the contextual approach to statutory interpretation and judicial review."[122]

In his remarkable book *Using International Law in Canadian Courts*, Gibran van Ert makes a powerful implicit case that many of the problems regarding the proper relationship of domestic and international law in Canada can be resolved by reference to the presumption of conformity.[123] In an earlier article, we have also noted the potential of the presumption of conformity to promote a more harmonious relationship between the two legal orders.[124] The presumption is further discussed at various points in this article. Nonetheless, we will argue below that legislative intervention and major policy changes to parliamentary practice are also desirable.

Since the adoption of the *Charter* the courts have been asked many times to determine the relevance of international human rights law to *Charter* interpretation, with the case law increasing almost exponentially.[125] In some decisions, however, the courts have put Canada in conflict with important ratified treaties or fundamental principles of public international law.[126]

The courts are thus dealing with arguments based on international treaty law on a routine basis. But they still lack clear guidance as to the approach they should adopt in different circumstances. Even the various interpretation acts have little to say to judges who are called upon to apply either treaties or laws based on treaties. The federal *Interpretation Act* states the following:

> 15(1) Definitions or rules of interpretation in an enactment apply to all the provisions of the enactment, including the provisions that contain those definitions or rules of interpretation.

(2) Where an enactment contains an interpretation section or provision, it shall be read and construed

    (a) as being applicable only if a contrary intention does not appear; and

    (b) as being applicable to all other enactments relating to the same subject-matter unless a contrary intention appears.[127]

This section has been judicially considered on a number of occasions[128] but does not appear to have had a major influence on the interpretation of treaties. Its greatest influence may be to suggest, by its very brevity, that treaties play a very small role in statutory interpretation and that they must give way to statutes. Even less guidance is provided with respect to the place of customary international law.[129] Similarly, many provincial interpretation acts contain limited guidance on the place of treaty law.[130]

c. Treaty Approval

No Canadian statute contains specific provisions on the approval of treaties except the *Loi sur le ministère des Relations internationales*.[131] This act, which was first adopted by the National Assembly of Quebec in 1988 and amended in 2002, gives the National Assembly an important role, along with the *ministre des relations internationales*, in the process of approval and implementation of treaties by the province of Quebec.[132] The law was adopted to regulate the process followed by Quebec in implementing treaties whose subject matter falls within provincial jurisdiction, and to clarify the role of the government of Quebec in the approval of all such treaties. While the government of Quebec has shown considerable interest in treaty approval, it has made less effort to clarify the status of rules of customary international law that fall within provincial jurisdiction. With the exception of possible implicit references in articles 2807 and 3155 to 3165 C.C.Q.,[133] the Civil Code of Quebec does not clarify the place of customary international law in the law of Quebec.

Some federal statutes contain indications of their relationship to treaties, as we discuss in Part III.C.1. But what is missing from federal implementing legislation is any sense of order or any governing principle. Each law appears to have been developed separately with very little regard to the development of a common approach to implementation.

One very striking absence from Canadian statutory texts is any reference to the *Vienna Convention*, although it is an important part of the *Treaty-Tabling Policy*.[134] The *Vienna Convention* is so widely adopted that many authorities have suggested that the convention is largely, if not entirely, declaratory of cus-

tomary international law. The convention sets out two fundamental rules. Article 26 lays down the principle that states are obligated to fulfill their treaty commitments in good faith.[135] Article 27 stipulates that states, having made a treaty commitment, cannot plead internal legal or constitutional difficulties in mitigation of their treaty obligations.[136] In other words, the *Vienna Convention* requires states to fulfill their obligations and brooks few excuses by states for the failure to do so. It reinforces the legal duty incumbent upon Canada when a treaty commitment is made and should be a powerful message to Canadian judges called upon to rule, directly or indirectly, on a matter involving a treaty ratified by Canada. Sadly, no Canadian law deals with these principles and this important source has seldom been cited by the courts. At best, it can be argued that the rules of the *Vienna Convention* reflect customary international law and are thus part of the domestic law of Canada. Legislative affirmation of this fact would be a powerful message to the judiciary and might well embolden the courts to give treaties greater weight when deciding cases.[137]

It is encouraging that the government recently announced that it intends to bring Parliament back into the treaty-approval process. On 25 January 2008, the federal government announced that henceforth all treaties between Canada and other states or entities would be tabled in the House of Commons.[138] As noted above, this policy has been further developed in the *Treaty-Tabling Policy*.[139] Under this new procedure the government is required to table "all instruments governed by public international law, between Canada and other states or international organizations ... " in the House of Commons.[140] It must also observe a waiting period of twenty-one sitting days from the date of the tabling before taking any action to make the treaty binding upon Canada. When treaties require legislative amendment, the government will be bound to delay consideration of any implementing legislation until this twenty-one sitting-day period has passed.[141]

This initiative is welcome and long overdue. It will give parliamentarians an opportunity to debate the content of treaties that they consider worthy of scrutiny. But such a debate will only take place in time allotted to the opposition parties and at their behest. A further restriction is that, when Parliament reconvenes, parliamentarians may have to choose to debate many treaties within the twenty-one sitting days that have accumulated over the period of the parliamentary recess. As well, the minister of foreign affairs and international trade and lead ministers may request from the prime minister an exemption from the necessity of tabling.[142]

Nonetheless, other features further strengthen the policy's value. The policy requires that each treaty be accompanied on tabling in the House of Commons by an Explanatory Memorandum setting out considerable information on the objectives and impact of the treaty, including a statement on the chosen means of implementation.[143] In addition, the policy is also accompanied by instructions to departments of government on the process of seeking authorization from cabinet to negotiate a treaty, and

it sets out the various stages of the participation of departments in the treaty-negotiation and approval process. It is in many respects a codification and will be of great utility to government departments and to the public in following the process.[144]

Yet, however well the new policy works, we suggest in Part III.B.3 that this initiative essentially reverts to the prevailing practice up to 1968, leaves unanswered many questions regarding the legal significance of parliamentary approval or disapproval, and comes much too late in the treaty-making process.

(e) *Abdelrazik v. Canada (Foreign Affairs)*[†]

[ZINN J.:]

[1] Mr. Abdelrazik lives in the Canadian Embassy in Khartoum, Sudan, his country of citizenship by birth, fearing possible detention and torture should he leave this sanctuary, all the while wanting but being unable to return to Canada, his country of citizenship by choice. He lives by himself with strangers while his immediate family, his young children, are in Montreal. He is as much a victim of international terrorism as the innocent persons whose lives have been taken by recent barbaric acts of terrorists.

[2] Mr. Abdelrazik says that the government of Canada has engaged in a course of conduct designed to thwart his return to Canada and in so doing has breached his right as a citizen of Canada pursuant to section 6 of the *Canadian Charter of Rights and Freedoms* (the Charter) to enter or return to Canada. He describes the actions taken by Canada and its failure to act as "procrastination, evasiveness, obfuscation and general bad faith."

[3] Canada challenges that characterization of its conduct. It says that the impediment to Mr. Abdelrazik's return is not of its making but is that of the United Nations Security Council 1267 Committee which has listed Mr. Abdelrazik as an associate of Al-Qaida, thus making him the subject of a global asset freeze, arms embargo and travel ban.

[4] There is a tension between the obligations of Canada as a member of the UN to implement and observe its resolutions, especially those that are designed to ensure security from international terrorism and the requirement that in so doing Canada conform to the rights and freedoms it guarantees to its citizens.

[5] In addition to the tension between Canada's international and national obligations, there is also a tension in this case between the roles of the executive and the judiciary. This is a positive tension; it results from the balancing necessary in a constitutional democracy that follows the rule of law. Lord Woolf[1] described this positive tension in the following manner:

> The tension ... is acceptable because it demonstrates that the courts are performing their role of ensuring that the actions of the Government of the day are being taken in accordance with the law. The tension is a necessary consequence of maintaining the balance of power between the legislature, the executive and the judiciary ...

[6] The rule of law provides that the Government and all who exercise power as a part of the Government are bound to exercise that power in compliance with existing laws. It is one of the "fundamental and organizing principles of the Constitution": *Reference re Secession of Québec*, 1998 CanLII 793 (S.C.C.), [1998] 2 S.C.R. 217 at para. 32. When

---

† [2009] F.C.J. No. 656, 2009 FC 580, at paras. 1–7, 45–57, 130–38, 148–69.

the Government takes actions that are not in accordance with the law, and its actions affect a citizen, then that citizen is entitled to an effective remedy. Mr. Abdelrazik seeks such an effective remedy. He seeks an Order of this Court directing Canada to repatriate him to Canada "by any safe means at its disposal." The respondents submit that no such remedy is required as there has been no violation of Mr. Abdelrazik's rights by Canada and they further submit that in requesting such an Order the applicant is asking this Court to improperly tread on the rights and powers of the executive.

[7] I find that Mr. Abdelrazik's Charter right to enter Canada has been breached by the respondents. I do not find that Canada has engaged in a course of conduct and inaction that amounts to "procrastination, evasiveness, obfuscation and general bad faith." I do find, however, there has been a course of conduct and individual acts that constitute a breach of Mr. Abdelrazik's rights which the respondents have failed to justify. I find that Mr. Abdelrazik is entitled to an appropriate remedy which, in the unique circumstances of his situation, requires that the Canadian government take immediate action so that Mr. Abdelrazik is returned to Canada. Furthermore, as a consequence of the facts found establishing the breach and the unique circumstances of Mr. Abdelrazik's circumstances, the remedy requires that this Court retain jurisdiction to ensure that Mr. Abdelrazik is returned to Canada.

. . . .

LEGAL BACKGROUND

. . . .

Canada's International Obligations

[45] Article 24 of the *Charter of the United Nations* (the UN Charter) confers "primary responsibility for the maintenance of international peace and security" on the Security Council. Pursuant to Article 41 of the UN Charter, the Security Council may decide on measures to be employed to give effect to its decisions and call upon member nations to apply them.

[46] Article 25 of the UN Charter provides that "Members of the UN agree to accept and carry out the decisions of the Security Council in accordance with the present Charter." Canada is a member of the UN and in furtherance of its obligations has enacted the *United Nations Act*, R.S.C. 1985, c. U-2 which provides that the Governor in Council may

make such orders and regulations as are "necessary or expedient" to effect decisions of the UN Security Council.

[47] In 1999, in response to the August 7, 1998 bombing of United States of America embassies in Nairobi, Kenya and Dar es Salaam, Tanzania, by Usama bin Laden and his associates, the UN Security Council passed Resolution 1267. Resolution 1267 was directed at the Taliban who were permitting their territory to be used by bin Laden and his associates. Section 4 of Resolution 1267 set out the measures the Security Council imposed on member nations. These were originally limited to a ban on Taliban aircraft landing or taking off from member states' territory, save for humanitarian purposes or for the performance of religious obligations such as the performance of the Hajj, and to a freeze on funds and financial resources of the Taliban. A Committee of all members of the Security Council (the 1267 Committee) was established to implement Resolution 1267 and report back to the Council.

[48] The sanctions set out in Resolution 1267 has been modified and strengthened by subsequent resolutions, including resolutions 1333 (2000), 1390 (2002), 1455 (2003), 1526 (2004), 1617 (2005), 1735 (2006) and 1822 (2008) so that the sanctions now apply to designated individuals and entities associated with Al-Qaida, Usama bin Laden and the Taliban wherever located. Specifically, by Resolution 1390 adopted January 16, 2002, these measures were expanded to address the Al-Qaida network and other associated terrorist groups as a response to the attacks on the United States of America on September 11, 2001. Notwithstanding these further Resolutions, the oversight group continues to be known as the 1267 Committee. The most recent Resolution, and that which presently applies to Mr. Abdelrazik as a consequence of being listed, is Resolution 1822, adopted June 30, 2008.

[49] As noted, Mr. Abdelrazik was listed by the 1267 Committee as being associated with Al-Qaida. Section 2 of Resolution 1822 defines "associated with" as including, but not being restricted to the following:

(a) participating in the financing, planning, facilitating, preparing, or perpetrating of acts or activities by, in conjunction with, under the name of, on behalf of, or in support of;

(b) supplying, selling or transferring arms and related materiel to;

(c) recruiting for; or

(d) otherwise supporting acts or activities of;

Al-Qaida, Usama bin Laden or the Taliban, or any cell, affiliate, splinter group or derivative thereof.

[50] A Study commissioned by the United Nations Office of Legal Affairs, summarizes the lack of legal procedures available to persons listed by the 1267 Committee.[3]

> Targeted individuals and entities are not informed prior to their being listed, and accordingly do not have an opportunity to prevent their inclusion in a list by demonstrating that such an inclusion is unjustified under the terms of the respective Security Council resolution(s). There exist different de-listing procedures under the various sanctions regimes, but in no case are individuals or entities allowed directly to petition the respective Security Council committee for de-listing. Individuals or entities are not granted a hearing by the Council or a committee. The de-listing procedures presently being in force place grcat cmphasis on the States particularly involved ("the original designating government" which proposed the listing, and "the petitioned government" to which a petition for de-listing was submitted by an individual or entity) resolving the matter by negotiation. Whether the respective committee, or the Security Council itself, grants a de-listing request is entirely within the committee's or the Council's discretion; no legal rules exist that would oblige the committee or the Council to grant a request if specific conditions are met.
>
> At the same time, no effective opportunity is provided for a listed individual or entity to challenge a listing before a national court or tribunal, as UN Member States are obliged, in accordance with Article 103 of the UN Charter, to comply with resolutions made by the Security Council under Chapter VII of the UN Charter. If, exceptionally, a domestic legal order allows an individual directly to take legal action against a Security Council resolution, the United Nations enjoys absolute immunity from every form of legal proceedings before national courts and authorities, as provided for in Article 105, paragraph 1, of the UN Charter, the General Convention on the Privileges and Immunities of the United Nations (General Assembly Resolution 1/ 22A of 13 February 1946) and other agreements.
>
> It has been argued by leading scholars of international law that the present situation amounts to a "denial of legal remedies" for the individuals and entities concerned, and is untenable under principles of international human rights law: "Everyone must be free to show that he or she has been justifiably placed under suspicion and that therefore [for instance] the freezing of his or her assets has no valid foundation."
> [footnotes and citations omitted]

[51] I add my name to those who view the 1267 Committee regime as a denial of basic legal remedies and as untenable under the principles of international human rights. There is nothing in the listing or de-listing procedure that recognizes the principles of natural justice or that provides for basic procedural fairness. Unlike the first Canadian security certificate scheme that was rejected by the Supreme Court in *Charkaoui v. Canada (Minister of Citizenship and Immigration)*, 2007 SCC 9 (CanLII), 2007 SCC 9; [2007] 1 S.C.R. 350, the 1267 Committee listing and de-listing processes do not even include a limited right to a hearing. It can hardly be said that the 1267 Committee process meets the requirement of independence and impartiality when, as appears may be the case involving Mr. Abdelrazik, the nation requesting the listing is one of the members of the body that decides whether to list or, equally as important, to de-list a person. The accuser is also the judge.

[52] The 1267 Committee process has been amended since its inception to include a requirement that a narrative summary of the reasons for listing be included on the web site of the Consolidated Listing. Notwithstanding that Resolution 1822 provides that such information is also to be provided for those, such as Mr. Abdelrazik, who were previously listed, there is not yet any such narrative provided as regards the rationale for the listing of Mr. Abdelrazik.

[53] Originally de-listing requests could only be made by the individual's home State. Again, there has been an amendment to allow a listed individual to make an application personally to the 1267 Committee or to do so through his home State. The *Guidelines of the Committee for the Conduct of Its Work* provide that a petitioner seeking de-listing "should provide justification for the de-listing request by describing the basis for this request, including by explaining why he/she <u>no longer meets</u> the criteria described in paragraph 2 of resolution 1617 (2005)..." (emphasis added). Those criteria are the four criteria set out above in paragraph 49. For a person such as Mr. Abdelrazik who asserts that he never met the criteria and was wrongly listed in the first instance, it is difficult to see how he can provide the requested justification, particularly when he has no information as to the basis for the initial listing. Section 7(g)(iii) of the Guidelines further provide that if the request for de-listing is a repeat request and if it does not contain any information additional to that provided in the first request, it is to be returned to the petitioner without consideration. It is difficult to see

what information any petitioner could provide to prove a negative, i.e. to prove that he or she is not associated with Al-Qaida. One cannot prove that fairies and goblins do not exist any more than Mr. Abdelrazik or any other person can prove that they are not an Al-Qaida associate. It is a fundamental principle of Canadian and international justice that the accused does not have the burden of proving his innocence, the accuser has the burden of proving guilt. In light of these shortcomings, it is disingenuous of the respondents to submit, as they did, that if he is wrongly listed the remedy is for Mr. Abdelrazik to apply to the 1267 Committee for de-listing and not to engage this Court. The 1267 Committee regime is, as I observed at the hearing, a situation for a listed person not unlike that of Josef K. in Kafka's *The Trial*, who awakens one morning and, for reasons never revealed to him or the reader, is arrested and prosecuted for an unspecified crime.

[54] The UN Security Council itself has recognized the extreme difficulty persons listed have to obtain de-listing. In the Security Council Report *Update Report, April 21, 2008, No. 4* respecting the 1267 Committee it is stated:

> It is far easier for a nation to place an individual or entity on the list than to take them off. For example, the US last year wanted to remove Abdul Hakim Monib, a former Taliban minister who switched sides and until recently served as the governor of Afghanistan's Uruzgan province, working with US and NATO troops. But Russia blocked it. In other cases, the US has prevented removal of names and entities it has submitted for <u>suspected</u> involvement with Al-Qaida. (emphasis added)

I pause to comment that it is frightening to learn that a citizen of this or any other country might find himself on the 1267 Committee list, based only on suspicion.

[55] There are three general consequences set out in section 1 of Resolution 1822 that flow from being listed by the 1267 Committee: an asset freeze, a travel ban and an arms embargo. Only the first two are relevant for our purposes.

[56] The asset freeze set out in paragraph 1(a) requires member nations to freeze the assets of listed persons and requires that member nations ensure that neither the funds of the listed persons "nor any other funds, financial assets or economic resources are made available, directly or indirectly, for such persons' benefit..." The respondents submit that this measure prevents Canada, or anyone within

Canada, from paying for transportation to Canada or providing such transportation for Mr. Abdelrazik. It was as a consequence of this measure that Canada sought an exemption from this restriction in order to provide Mr. Abdelrazik with the monthly loan it currently provides as well as the facilities it provides him in the Canadian Embassy in Khartoum.

[57] The travel ban set out in paragraph 1(b) requires member states to prevent the entry into or transit through their territories of listed individuals. There are three exceptions to the ban which the applicant submits would permit him to enter Canada. This submission will be considered in the Analysis section. The relevant provision reads as follows:

> 1(b) Prevent the entry into or transit through their territories of these individuals, provided that nothing in this paragraph shall oblige any State to deny entry or require the departure from its territories of its own nationals and this paragraph shall not apply where entry or transit is necessary for the fulfilment of a judicial process or the Committee determines on a case-by-case basis only that entry or transit is justified;

. . . .

ISSUES

Whether Canada Violated Mr. Abdelrazik's Right to Enter Canada

. . . .

The flight scheduled for April 3, 2009

[130] In March 2009, Mr. Abdelrazik managed to obtain and pay for a flight from Khartoum to Montreal with a stop over in Abu Dhabi. He had been repeatedly assured for years that an emergency passport would be provided in that eventuality. Notwithstanding the numerous assurances given by Canada over a period of almost 5 years, and repeated as recently as December 23, 2008, on April 3, 2009 just two hours before the flight was to leave, the Minister of Foreign Affairs refused to issue that emergency passport on the basis that he was of the opinion, pursuant to Section 10.1 of the *Canadian Passport Order*, "that such action is necessary for the national security of Canada or another country."

[131] The respondents make a number of submissions urging this Court not to consider or examine this refusal as part of the applicant's Charter challenge. With the greatest of respect for these respondents and their counsel, I find that none of these

submissions has merit. In light of the challenge the applicant has made asserting that his Charter rights have been violated, and in light of the evidence reviewed thus far, a failure of this Court to consider this refusal, in these circumstances, would bring the administration of justice into disrepute.

[132] The respondents firstly submit that because section 10.1 of the *Canadian Passport Order* has been found by the Federal Court of Appeal in *Canada (Attorney General) v. Kamel*, 2009 FCA 21 (CanLII), 2009 FCA 21, not to offend the Charter, it follows that decisions of the Minister made pursuant to the section likewise comply with the Charter. This submission is fundamentally contrary to the decision of the Supreme Court of Canada in *Eldridge v. British Columbia (Attorney General)*, 1997 CanLII 327 (S.C.C.), [1997] 3 S.C.R. 624. At paragraph 20 of that decision, the Court said that the *Canadian Charter* can apply in two ways — to the legislation or to decisions made under the legislation.

> First, legislation may be found to be unconstitutional on its face because it violates a *Charter* right and is not saved by s. 1. In such cases, the legislation will be invalid and the Court compelled to declare it of no force or effect pursuant to s. 52(1) of the *Constitution Act, 1982*. Secondly, the *Charter* may be infringed, not by the legislation itself, but by the actions of a delegated decision-maker in applying it. In such cases, the legislation remains valid, but a remedy for the unconstitutional action may be sought pursuant to s. 24(1) of the *Charter*.

This view has more recently been affirmed by that Court in *Multani v. Commission scolaire Marguerite Bourgeoys*, 2006 SCC 6 (CanLII), 2006 SCC 6.

[133] Therefore, although there is no doubt that section 10.1 of the *Canadian Passport Order* has been found to be constitutionally valid by the Federal Court of Appeal in *Kamel*, it does not follow that every refusal of the Minister made pursuant to that section must necessarily also be constitutionally valid. The issue before the Federal Court of Appeal in *Kamel* was limited to whether section 10.1 violated section 6 of the Charter and, if it did, whether it was justified under section 1. In his judgment, Justice Décary was careful to note: "I will not comment on other aspects of this case, and nothing in my reasons shall be interpreted as having an impact on the decision the Minister will eventually make after reconsidering Mr. Kamel's passport application." In other words, while the section is valid, the decision made under it may not be.

[134] As is implied in section 4(3) of the *Canadian Passport Order*, the issuance or refusal to issue a passport is a matter of royal prerogative. The Supreme Court of Canada in *Operation Dismantle Inc. v. The Queen et al.*, 1985 CanLII 74 (S.C.C.), [1985] 1 S.C.R. 441 held that where the Crown prerogative violates an individual's rights provided in the Charter, then the exercise of the prerogative can be reviewed by the Court.

[135] The Federal Court of Appeal in *Veffer v. Canada (Minister of Foreign Affairs)*, 2007 FCA 247 (CanLII), 2007 FCA 247; [2008] 1 F.C.R. 641 at paragraph 23 has also specifically confirmed that the exercise of the royal prerogative in the issuance of passports is subject to examination for compliance with the Charter.

> ... [T]here is no question that the Passport Canada policy is subject to Charter scrutiny, even though the issuance of passports is a royal prerogative. As stated by Justice Laskin in *Black v. Canada (Prime Minister)* 2001 CanLII 8537 (ON C.A.), (2001), 54 O.R. (3d) 215 (C.A.), at paragraph 46:
>
> > By s. 32(1)(*a*), the Charter applies to Parliament and the Government of Canada in respect of all matters within the authority of Parliament. The Crown prerogative lies within the authority of Parliament. Therefore, if an individual claims that the exercise of a prerogative power violates that individual's Charter rights, the court has a duty to decide the claim.

[136] The respondents submit that the validity of the Minister's decision of April 3, 2009 not to issue an emergency passport is not a matter that this Court may consider in the present application. It is argued that the proper course was for the applicant to file a judicial review application under section 18.1 of the *Federal Courts Act* challenging that decision. It is submitted that unless that course is taken, the Court does not have a proper evidentiary record before it on which to assess the validity of the decision.

[137] A similar submission was made by the Crown and rejected by this Court in *Khadr v. Canada (Attorney General)*, 2006 FC 727 (CanLII), [2007] 2 F.C.R. 218, 2006 FC 727. The Crown asked the Court not to decide the issue of whether the failure to issue a passport to Mr. Khadr was contrary to sections 6 and 7 of the Charter because of the inadequacy of the record. I adopt without reservation the following from paragraphs 57–59 of that decision of Justice Phelan:

The respondent's concern for the record is two-fold. Firstly, the respondent acknowledges that the applicant was not treated fairly because he did not have a chance to address the new grounds for denial of a passport — national security. This assumes that the Minister had the right to create this new ground outside the bounds of the *Canadian Passport Order*. Secondly, the respondent says that it has not put forward sufficient section 1 Charter evidence to demonstrate that any breach of a Charter right is justified.

The simple response to that is that the respondent cannot deprive the applicant of his rights to a proper determination because of the respondent's failure to put forward proper evidence. The applicant must take the record as it is — not the record it would like. So too, the respondent has to take the record it created — it does not get a second chance to create a further and better record.

With respect to section 1 evidence, the respondent gambled that the Charter arguments would be dismissed without the necessity of a section 1 analysis. Sometimes the gamble does not pay out.

[138] Justice Phelan ultimately determined that he would not decide the case on Charter grounds because, as stated in *Baker v. Canada (Minister of Citizenship and Immigration)*, 1999 CanLII 699 (S.C.C.), [1999] 2 S.C.R. 817, "courts should refrain from dealing with *Charter* issues raised in an application for judicial review where it is unnecessary to do so". In this case, the only claim raised by this applicant is his Charter claim; he has not raised the claim that the decision was procedurally unfair and contrary to the rules of natural justice. Accordingly, it is necessary in this case to determine the Charter issue raised with respect to the decision.

.   .   .   .

[148] In my view, the submission that the applicant had not been denied entry into Canada by the Government of Canada was not accurate when made 6 days after the Minister had denied the applicant an emergency passport. Whether or not the Etihad Airways flight scheduled for April 3, 2009 would breach the travel ban set out in the 1822 Resolution, there is no evidence before the Court that had Mr. Abdelrazik been in possession of an emergency passport issued by Canada that he would not have been on that flight and now in Canada. I find that the only reason that Mr. Abdelrazik is not in Canada now is because of the actions of the Minister on April 3, 2009.

[149] The respondents submit that the right to enter Canada as provided for in subsection 6(1) of the Charter does not entail positive obligations on Canada. Their submission, to paraphrase Justice L'Heureux-Dubé in *Haig v. Canada*, 1993 CanLII 58 (S.C.C.), [1993] 2 S.C.R. 995, is that the freedom to enter Canada contained in subsection 6(1) prohibits Canada from refusing a citizen's entry into the country (subject to section 1) but does not compel Canada to take positive steps such as the issuance of a passport or the provision of an airplane to effect travel to Canada.

[150] In *Gosselin v. Quebec (Attorney General)*, 2002 SCC 84 (CanLII), 2002 SCC 84; [2002] 4 S.C.R. 429, a case involving section 7 of the Charter, the Supreme Court acknowledged that one day the Charter may be interpreted to include positive obligations such that the failure to do the positive act will constitute a breach of the Charter. It was there stated:

> The question therefore is not whether s. 7 has ever been — or ever will be — recognized as creating positive rights. Rather, the question is whether the present circumstances warrant a novel application of s. 7 as the basis for a positive state obligation to guarantee adequate living standards.

[151] This Court and the Federal Court of Appeal in *Kamel* in the passage below noted the critical importance of a passport, not just to engage in travel, but for a citizen to enter Canada.[5] The fact that Mr. Abdelrazik had secured and paid for a flight for April 3, 2009 back to Canada but was prevented from flying only because he lacked the emergency passport previously promised by Canada, proves that importance.

> The appellant submits that subsection 6(1) of the Charter, which gives every Canadian citizen "the right to enter, remain in and leave Canada", does not impose a duty on the state to facilitate the international travel of Canadian citizens. The appellant also maintains that the respondent has not demonstrated that a passport is required to enter or leave Canada.
>
> At the hearing, we did not consider it useful to hear the respondent on this issue. In fact, we agree substantially with Justice Noël's remarks on this point. To determine that the refusal to issue a passport to a Canadian citizen does not infringe that citizen's right to enter or leave Canada would be to interpret the Charter in an unreal world. It is theoretically possible that a Canadian citizen can enter or leave Canada without a passport. In reality, however, there are very few countries that a Canadian citizen wish-

ing to leave Canada may enter without a passport and very few countries that allow a Canadian citizen to return to Canada without a passport (A.B., Vol. 7, p. 1406, Thomas Affidavit). The fact that there is almost nowhere a Canadian citizen can go without a passport and that there is almost nowhere from which he or she can re-enter Canada without a passport are, on their face, restrictions on a Canadian citizen's right to enter or leave Canada, which is, of course, sufficient to engage Charter protection. Subsection 6(1) establishes a concrete right that must be assessed in the light of present-day political reality. What is the meaning of a right that, in practice, cannot be exercised?

[152] I agree with the Court of Appeal. In my view, where a citizen is outside Canada, the Government of Canada has a positive obligation to issue an emergency passport to that citizen to permit him or her to enter Canada; otherwise, the right guaranteed by the Government of Canada in subsection 6(1) of the Charter is illusory. Where the Government refuses to issue that emergency passport, it is a *prima facie* breach of the citizen's Charter rights unless the Government justifies its refusal pursuant to section 1 of the Charter. As noted in *Cotroni*, the Supreme Court held that such interference must be justified as being required to meet a reasonable state purpose. In *Kamel* the Federal Court of Appeal held that section 10.1 of the *Canadian Passport Order* was a reasonable state purpose; however, the respondent must still establish that the decisions made under section 10.1 are "justified" on a case by case basis.

[153] I find that the applicant's Charter right as a citizen of Canada to enter Canada has been breached by the respondents in failing to issue him an emergency passport. In my view, it is not necessary to decide whether that breach was done in bad faith; a breach, whether made in bad faith or good faith remains a breach and absent justification under section 1 of the Charter, the aggrieved party is entitled to a remedy. Had it been necessary to determine whether the breach was done in bad faith, I would have had no hesitation making that finding on the basis of the record before me. As I have noted throughout, there is evidence that supports the applicant's contention that the Government of Canada made a determination in and around the time of the listing by the 1267 Committee that Mr. Abdelrazik would not be permitted to return to Canada. The only legal way to accomplish that objective was by order made pursuant to section 10.1 of the *Canadian Passport Order*. Rather than instituting that process then, Canada put forward a number of explanations

as to why he was not being provided with an emergency passport, only some of which were accurate: he is on a no-fly list and commercial air carriers will not board him; he has secured an itinerary but not paid for the flight; he is listed on the 1267 Committee list and cannot fly in the air space of Member States; and lastly, when he had managed to meet the last condition set by Canada that he have a paid ticket, the refusal is necessary for the national security of Canada or another country. This was an opinion the Minister was to make only after the process prescribed by his own department was followed, giving Mr. Abdelrazik an opportunity to know of and address concerns. Not only was that not done, the Minister waited until the very last minute before the flight was to depart to deny the emergency passport, and although the basis of the refusal is indicated, he provides no explanation of the basis on which that determination was reached, no explanation as to what had changed while Mr. Abdelrazik resided in the Canadian embassy that warranted this sudden finding, and nothing to indicate whether the decision was based on him being a danger to the national security of Canada or on being a danger to another country. Further, there was no explanation offered as to whether Mr. Abdelrazik posed a security risk if returned to Canada, or a greater security risk[] than he did in Sudan. In my view, denying a citizen his right to enter his own country requires, at a minimum, that such increased risk must be established to justify a determination made under section 10.1 of the *Canadian Passport Order*. If he poses no greater risk, what justification can there be for breaching the Charter by refusing him to return home; especially where, as here, the alternative is to effectively exile the citizen to live the remainder of his life in the Canadian Embassy abroad. In short, the only basis for the denial of the passport was that the Minister had reached this opinion; there has been nothing offered and no attempt made to justify that opinion.

[154] The respondents have provided no evidence to support a section 1 defence to the *prima facie* breach of the Charter from refusing to issue the emergency passport. They simply submitted to the Court that there had been no breach. Having found a breach, the burden then shifted to the respondents to justify that breach. In the absence of any evidence, it has not been justified. Notwithstanding this, I have considered whether the Minister's determination that Mr. Abdelrazik posed a danger to national security or to the security of another country constitutes a section 1 defence in itself and have concluded that it does not.

[155] As previously noted, the guidelines of Passport Canada provide that whenever a citizen may be denied passport privileges, there is a mechanism in place that provides the citizen with procedural fairness and natural justice. It is fair to assume that the minister put these processes in place in his Department in recognition of a citizen's Charter rights and the special relationship that exists between a citizen and his country. There is no suggestion that the Minister followed this process. In fact, the Minister appears to have made the decision to deny the emergency passport with no input from Passport Canada. He had many years to render such a decision after following the processes set by his own department, if there was any basis to support his opinion. He did not. There is nothing in the report of his decision to indicate that his decision is made based on recent information he has received. There is nothing to indicate the basis on which he reached his decision. Even if a decision such as his can be said to have been a decision prescribed by law as it is based on section 10.1 of the *Canadian Passport Order* the decision itself must also be shown to be justified as being required to meet a reasonable State purpose, as the Supreme Court stated in *Cotroni*. It is simply not sufficient for the Minister to say that he has reached this opinion and "trust me" — he must show more; he must establish that it was "required". While it is not the function of the judiciary to second guess or to substitute its opinion for that of the Minister, when no basis is provided for the opinion, the Court cannot find that the refusal was required and justified given the significant breach of the Charter that refusing a passport to a Canadian citizen entails. In this case, the refusal of the emergency passport effectively leaves Mr. Abdelrazik as a prisoner in a foreign land, consigned to live the remainder of his life in the Canadian Embassy or leave and risk detention and torture.

[156] I have found that Canada has engaged in a course of conduct and specific acts that constitute a breach of Mr. Abdelrazik's right to enter Canada. Specifically, I find:

(i) That CSIS was complicit in the detention of Mr. Abdelrazik by the Sudanese authorities in 2003;

(ii) That by mid 2004 Canadian authorities had determined that they would not take any active steps to assist Mr. Abdelrazik to return to Canada and, in spite of its numerous assurances to the contrary, would consider refusing him an emergency passport if that was required in order to ensure that he could not return to Canada;

(iii) That there is no impediment from the UN Resolution to Mr. Abdelrazik being repatriated to Canada — no permission of a foreign government is required to transit through its airspace — and the respondents' assertion to the contrary is a part of the conduct engaged in to ensure that Mr. Abdelrazik could not return to Canada; and

(iv) That Canada's denial of an emergency passport on April 3, 2009, after all of the pre-conditions for the issuance of an emergency passport previously set by Canada had been met, is a breach of his Charter right to enter Canada, and it has not been shown to be saved under section 1 of the Charter.

[157] Having found that the applicant's right as a citizen of Canada to enter this country has been breached by Canada, he is entitled to an effective remedy.

What is the effective remedy?

[158] I agree with the respondents that a Court should not go further than required when fashioning a remedy for a Charter breach: *Doucet-Boudreau v. Nova Scotia (Minister of Education)*, 2003 SCC 62 (CanLII), [2003] 3 S.C.R. 3. In this case, the applicant is entitled to be put back to the place he would have been but for the breach — in Montreal.

[159] In saying this, I am mindful of the international law principle that "reparation must, as far as possible, wipe-out all the consequences of the illegal act and re-establish the situation which would, in all probability, have existed if that act had not been committed," as it was put by the Permanent Court of International Arbitration in the *Chorzow Factory Case (Ger. v. Pol.)*, (1928) P.C.I.J., Sr. A, No.17, at 47 (September 13). To quote Chief Justice Dickson in the *Reference Re Public Service Employee Relations Act (Alta.)*, 1987 CanLII 88 (S.C.C.), [1987] 1 S.C.R. 313, at para. 57, "[t]he various sources of international human rights law — declarations, covenants, conventions, judicial and quasi-judicial decisions of international tribunals, customary norms — must, in my opinion, be relevant and persuasive sources for interpretation of the *Charter*'s provisions." Similarly, I am of the view that principles of international law are helpful where it is necessary to fashion a just and appropriate Charter remedy, as is the case here.

[160] Accordingly, at a minimum, the respondents are to be ordered to provide Mr. Abdelrazik with an emergency passport that will permit him to travel to and enter Canada. There is any number of ways available to him to return to Canada. He once secured an airline ticket and may be able to do so again. In the Court's view that would cure the breach and be the least intrusive on the role of the executive. If such travel is possible, and if funds or sufficient funds to pay for an air ticket are not available to the applicant from his April 3, 2009 unused ticket, then the respondents are to provide the airfare or additional airfare required because, but for the breach, he would not have to incur this expense.

[161] The applicant has asked that the respondents return him to Canada "by any safe means at its disposal." In my view, the manner of returning Mr. Abdelrazik, at this time, is best left to the respondents in consultation with the applicant, subject to the Court's oversight, and subject to it being done promptly.

[162] The respondents may submit that they are unable to provide any financial assistance to permit Mr. Abdelrazik to return to Canada as Resolution 1822 prohibits it. As noted, an exception to the travel ban and asset freeze is the fulfilment of a "judicial process".

[163] "Process" is defined in the *Canadian Oxford Dictionary* (2nd ed.) to mean "a course of action or proceeding". *Black's Law Dictionary* (8th ed.) states that "process" means "the proceedings in any action or prosecution". A judicial process means the same as a judicial proceeding. The Supreme Court of Canada in *Markevich v. Canada*, 2003 SCC 9 (CanLII), [2003] 1 S.C.R. 94, 2003 SCC 9 discussed the meaning of the word "proceeding" as found in the *Crown Liability and Proceedings Act*, R.S.C. 1985, c. C-50 and found it to have a broad meaning. Its observations are equally applicable here.

> Although the word "proceeding" is often used in the context of an action in court, its definition is more expansive. The Manitoba Court of Appeal stated in *Royce v. MacDonald (Municipality)* (1909), 12 W.L.R. 347, at p. 350, that the "word 'proceeding' has a very wide meaning, and includes steps or measures which are not in any way connected with actions or suits". In *Black's Law Dictionary* (6th ed. 1990), at p. 1204, the definition of "proceeding" includes, *inter alia*, "an act necessary to be done in order to obtain a given end; a prescribed mode of action for carrying into effect a legal right

[164] Accordingly, a judicial process, for the purposes of the exemption from the asset freeze and travel ban, encompasses more than the issuance of a summons to appear as a witness before a Court as was submitted by the respondents. It includes all steps in the judicial process, including the steps required by Order of the Court as a part of the completion of the suit or application. This view is supported by the French language version of Security Council Resolution 1617 which uses the phrase "le présent paragraphe ne s'applique pas lorsque l'entrée ou le transit est nécessaire pour l'aboutissement d'une procédure judiciaire". On a plain meaning reading "aboutissement" means "outcome, result".[6] Thus it would include, in my view, measures required to be taken in execution or the completion of a Court order.

[165] In this case, any such assistance provided by Canada is in fulfilment of this judicial process and is not a violation of the UN Resolution.

[166] It is further required, in the Court's opinion that the respondents, at Canada's expense, provide an escort from Foreign Affairs to accompany Mr. Abdelrazik on his flight from Khartoum to Montreal, unless he waives the requirement for an escort. In my view, this is required to ensure that Mr. Abdelrazik is not stopped or delayed in his return to Canada while in transit or when laying-over at a foreign airport. The escort is to use his very best efforts to ensure that Mr. Abdelrazik returns to Canada unimpeded. To use the words of Foreign Affairs earlier — this is their contribution to ensure that he does return to Canada.

[167] It is further required, in the Court's judgment that the Court satisfy itself that Mr. Abdelrazik has in fact returned to Canada. Accordingly, in fulfilment of this judicial process, the Court requires that Mr. Abdelrazik attend before it at the time and date specified in the Judgment.

[168] The Court reserves the right to oversee the implementation of this Judgment and reserves the right to issue further Orders as may be required to safely return Mr. Abdelrazik to Canada.

[169] As agreed upon by the parties, costs are reserved. The applicant shall provide his submissions on costs to the respondents and file a copy with the Court, not exceeding 15 pages, within 15 days of this Judgment. The respondents shall serve and file their reply submissions, not exceeding 15 pages within a further 15 days. The applicant shall have a further 10 days to reply, not exceeding 10 pages.

JUDGMENT

THIS COURT ORDERS AND ADJUDGES that:

1. This application is allowed;
2. The applicant's right to enter Canada has been breached contrary to subsection 6(1) of the Charter;
3. The respondents are directed to issue the applicant an emergency passport in order that he may return to and enter Canada;
4. The respondents, after consultation with the applicant, are to arrange transportation for the applicant from Khartoum to Montreal, Canada such that he arrives in Canada no later than 30 days from the date hereof;
5. Should such travel arrangements not be in place within 15 days of the date hereof, the parties shall advise the Court and an immediate hearing shall be held at which time the Court reserves the right to issue such further Orders as are deemed necessary in order to ensure the transportation to and safe arrival of the applicant in Canada within 30 days of this Judgment, or such longer period as this Court then finds to be necessary in the circumstances;
6. In fulfilment of this judicial process, the applicant is ordered to appear before me at 2:00 o'clock in the afternoon on Tuesday, July 7, 2009, at the Federal Court at 30 McGill Street, Montreal, Quebec, Canada or, at the option of the applicant on five days advance notice to the Court and respondents, at 90 Sparks Street Ottawa, Ontario, or at such other location as is subsequently fixed by the Court, subject to an extension of that date on application by either party and upon the Court being satisfied that through no fault of the respondents it is not possible or practicable for the applicant to appear at the date and time set; and
7. Costs are reserved.

II

Looking at Law:
The Limits of Law and
Legal Understanding

The readings in Part II invite readers into some of the seminal debates in legal studies and begin to sketch out some of the larger questions about the relationship between law and society and our understanding of the symbolic power of law. As such, the chapters in this section should begin to challenge the reader to recognize the ambiguity of legal approaches to social problems, highlight some of the dangers of narrow, unreflexive understandings of law, and hint at the potential limits of using law to address social problems.

Chapter 5 introduces some enduring questions about the relationship between law and morality. How does law address moral questions? Should law be used to address moral issues, and what consequences follow from this decision? Can law avoid being moral? The articles and cases in this chapter demonstrate the practical difficulties law often faces when confronted with what are traditionally understood as "moral" issues or dilemmas; from a classic tale of shipwreck and survival on the high seas to a contemporary case of "compassionate homicide". These readings also serve to highlight potential disconnects between the purpose of law and the aspiration of justice.

The articles in Chapter 6 challenge some of the foundational claims of classical political liberalism; most notably that the law offers a politically neutral framework to address social issues and maintain social order. What the articles and cases in this chapter demonstrate is that an overly narrow or rigid, formalized understanding of law and an unwavering belief in the law's "neutrality" may ultimately promote or reinforce the inequalities law aims to remedy. A number of the articles ask readers to consider the consequences of an uncritical faith in the law's guarantees of formal equality and the public/private divide that rests at the core of political liberalism. While all the authors in this chapter are critical of the myopia of law's traditional promise, each similarly points to the essential ambiguity of legal solution and offers insight into how we might rethink the practical use and symbolic promise of law.

Chapter 7 serves as an important introduction to the many challenges of articulating the complex relationship between law and society. It offers the reader some insight into transformations that have taken place in legal education and scholarship in recent years. All the articles outline how different scholars — lawyers and social scientists — have tried to understand the law and its relationship to other social processes. To this end, Neil Sargent draws attention to the difficulty of teaching critical interdisciplinary approaches to law and the limits of strictly empirical approaches to legal studies.

Each chapter in Part II highlights the importance of adopting broader approaches to the study of law: approaches willing to question the traditional assumptions and definitions of law, and approaches also willing to recognize the ambiguity and limits of legal solutions to complex social issues. These critical themes run throughout the rest of the book and are taken up again more explicitly in the final section on Law and Social Transformation.

(a) Tragic Choices†

Patrick J. Fitzgerald

"You can't win 'em all," we say to console ourselves when things go wrong. What if they go so wrong that winning is impossible? What if life really puts us on the spot and confronts us with a tragic choice? Let's look at the following examples.

A pilot named Marten Hartwell crashed in the Northwest Territories in the early 70's. He was the only survivor. To stay alive until he was rescued he had to eat. His only source of food was the dead body of his companion, a young nurse. What should he have done — become a cannibal or starved to death? He chose to live.

In another case, some years ago, an international expedition set out to climb Mount Everest. One of the team, a man called Harsh, slipped and fell. He came to rest suspended upside down over an icefield. To get to him his companions would have had to venture across the extremely dangerous ice; and when they reached him there was no guarantee that they could bring him back alive. What should they have done — risked their lives with little hope of saving Harsh, or let him die? They let him die.

There are even worse situations. Two mountaineers were climbing in the Alps, roped together. On an isolated peak, one slipped and fell. Unable to move, he lay dangling at the end of the rope. The other climber couldn't lift his companion back up, nor could he himself move on without cutting the rope. What should he have done — cut the rope and sent his companion to his death, or stayed where he was till both died of exposure? He cut the rope.

1. What would you have done in Hartwell's place?
2. Do you think the Everest climbers ought to have risked their lives to save Harsh?
3. If you had been the climber in the Alps, would you have cut the rope?
4. Which would you put first — self-preservation or the maintenance of another human life?
5. Do you think the law should have the answers to these questions?

THE ONLY WAY

Sometimes the law is forced to deal with these tragic choices, as it did in the following nineteenth century English case. The case concerned three shipwrecked sailors and a cabin boy. The story was a grisly one. The facts were not in dispute. The only question was: had the law been broken? To answer this, the judges had to decide what the law was. And their decision, given almost a hundred years ago in England, still contains the law for Canada today.

For over twenty days three sailors and a cabin boy had drifted in an open boat a thousand miles from land. Their only food was two tins of turnips and a turtle they had caught, their only drink the rain collected in their oilskin capes. When this gave out, they stayed seven days without food and five without water. They couldn't have lived many more days unless they took the only course remaining. That course, said one of them, Captain Dudley, was

---

† From *This Law of Ours* (Scarborough, ON: Prentice-Hall of Canada, 1977) at 40–47, 49. Reproduced with permission.

to sacrifice one life to save the rest — kill one for the other three to eat.

Which one? The captain, who proposed this course? The sailor, Stephens, who agreed with him? The other sailor, Brooks, who disagreed? Or the seventeen-year-old cabin boy, prostrate from famine and drinking seawater? Which one should be the sacrificial victim?

1. Even if there is only one course, would they be right to take it?
2. If so, who should be the victim?
3. And how should they decide on the victim?

The Agony and the Argument

"If no help comes," said Dudley and Stephens, "we'll have to sacrifice one to save the rest." Brooks knew they meant the boy and didn't agree.

"Let's do it this way," said the captain the next day; "let's all draw lots to see which one to kill." It was the twentieth day when he made this suggestion to Brooks and Stephens. He never made it to the boy himself. But Brooks would not agree and lots were never drawn.

"We have families," said Dudley and Stephens, "and the boy has no one dependent on him. Better to kill him to save the rest of us. If no help comes tomorrow, we'll have to kill the boy."

Next day no help came. No ship appeared. The captain motioned to Stephens and to Brooks that they had better kill the boy, who lay helpless at the bottom of the boat. He would have died anyway before the other three. Once again Brooks would have no part of it.

1. Three possibilities of setting the question emerge from what the captain said. What are they?
2. Which is the best?
3. Who should decide?

The Ultimate Solution

The captain, a religious man, offered a prayer. He asked forgiveness for them all. Then he and Stephens told the boy his time had come. They put a knife to his throat and killed him.

For four days afterwards the three men fed upon his body and his blood. Had they not done so, they would all have died. On the fourth day a passing ship picked them up. All three were in the lowest state of prostration. Their rescuers brought them home to England, where the law took over.

The authorities investigated the incident and then launched a murder prosecution against two of the survivors — Dudley and Stephens. Brooks was never charged, but was a witness at the trial.

The trial took place before a jury which gave a special verdict. Instead of pronouncing the defendants guilty or not guilty, they merely decided what had happened. They decided that Dudley and Stephens had killed the boy, and that they had had no other chance of survival. They left it to the judge to say whether this was murder or not.

1. Do you think the sailors were justified in killing the cabin boy?
2. Can you think of any circumstances where killing is justified?
3. Do you think the case should have come to trial at all?
4. Was it fair that Brooks wasn't charged?
5. Only very exceptionally does a jury refuse to say "guilty" or "not guilty." Why do you think they did so in this case?
6. If you had been on the jury, would you have wanted to refuse to give a verdict?

The Judges' Verdict

Was the act of Dudley and Stephens justified? The jury left it to the judges to determine. This is what the judges said:

There remains to be considered the real question in the case — whether killing under the circumstances set forth in the verdict be or be not murder.

Now except for the purpose of testing how far the conservation of a man's own life is in all cases and under all circumstances, an absolute, unqualified, and paramount duty, we exclude from our consideration all the incidents of war. We are dealing with a case of private homicide, not one imposed upon men in the service of their Sovereign and in the defence of the country. Now it is admitted that the deliberate killing of this unoffending and unresisting boy was clearly murder, unless the killing can be justified by some well-recognized excuse admitted by the law. It is further admitted that there was in this case no such excuse, unless the killing was justified by what has been called "necessity." But the temptation to the act which existed here was not what the law has ever called necessity. Nor is this to be regretted. Though law and morality are not the same, and many things may be immoral which are not necessarily illegal, yet the absolute divorce of law from morality would be of fatal consequence; and such divorce would follow if the temptation to murder in this case were to be held by law an absolute defense of it. It is not so. To preserve one's life is generally speaking a duty, but it may be the plainest and the highest duty to sacrifice it. War is full of instances in which it is a man's duty not to live, but to die. The duty, in case of shipwreck, of a captain to his crew, of the crew to the passengers, of soldiers to women and children, these duties impose on men the moral necessity, not of the preservation, but of the sacrifice of their lives for others, from which in no country, least of all, it is to be hoped, in England, will men ever shrink, as indeed they have not shrunk. It is not correct, therefore, to say that there is any absolute or unqualified necessity to preserve one's life.

It is not needful to point out the awful danger of admitting the principle which has been contended for. Who is to be the judge of this sort of necessity? By what measure is the comparative value of lives to be measured? Is it to be strength, or intellect, or what? It is plain that the principle leaves to him who is to profit by it to determine the necessity which will justify him in deliberately taking another's life to save his own. In this case the weakest, the youngest, the most unresisting, was chosen. Was it more necessary to kill him than one of the grown men? The answer must be "No."

It is not suggested that in this particular case the deeds were "devilish," but it is quite plain that such a principle once admitted might be made the legal cloak for unbridled passion and atrocious crime. There is no safe path for judges to tread but to ascertain the law to the best of their ability and to declare it according to their judgment; and if in any case the law appears to be too severe on individuals, to leave it to the Sovereign to exercise that prerogative of mercy which the Constitution has entrusted to the hands fittest to dispense it.

It must not be supposed that in refusing to admit temptation to be an excuse for crime it is forgotten how terrible that temptation was; how awful the suffering; how hard in such trials to keep the judgment straight and the conduct pure. We are often compelled to set up standards we cannot reach ourselves, and to lay down rules which we could not ourselves satisfy. But a man has no right to declare temptation to be an excuse, though he might himself have yielded to it, nor allow compassion for the criminal to change or weaken in any manner the legal definition of the crime. It is therefore our duty to declare that the prisoners' act in this case was wilful murder, that the facts as stated in the verdict are no legal justification of the homicide; and to say that in our unanimous opinion the prisoners are upon this special verdict guilty of murder.

(*R. v. Dudley & Stephens*, 1884)

1. What is the argument put forward by the defence?
2. Why did the judges say it wasn't necessary to kill the cabin boy? Do you agree with them?
3. What did the judges say would be the consequences of accepting the argument put forward by the defence? Do you agree?
4. Do you think it was easier for the judges than it was for the jury to decide whether Dudley and Stephens were guilty? If so, why?
5. What do you think the consequence would have been if the judges, like the jury, had been unable to decide?

The Sentence of the Court

What Dudley and Stephens did was murder, said the judges. And murder was a capital offence in England at that time. The Lord Chief Justice sentenced them as follows:

> The sentence of the court upon you is that you be taken from this place to a lawful prison and thence to a place of execution, and that you there suffer death by hanging; and that your body be afterwards buried within the precincts of the prison in which you shall have been confined before your execution. And may the Lord have mercy on your souls.
>
> (*R. v. Dudley & Stephens*, 1884)

1. Was the death penalty justified in this case?
2. Is it ever justified? Does this alter your views on the sanctity of human life?
3. If they had had to decide, do you think the jury would have decided any differently than the judges did?

The Punishment

Dudley and Stephens were sentenced to death, but they were given a reprieve: the *royal prerogative of mercy* was exercised in their favor and the death sentence was commuted to one of life imprisonment. But this was not the end of it. The authorities exercised their discretion and released the prisoners after six months.

1. Should there be a royal prerogative of mercy? Why or why not?
2. Should the government be able to alter the sentences passed by the judges?
3. Should the law fix the sentence the judges must pass (as it does in murder cases)? Why not leave sentencing to the judges' discretion?

87

4. Do you think it was their knowledge of the penalty for murder that prevented the jury from saying Dudley and Stephens were guilty? If so, do you think the jury should have allowed that knowledge to prevent them?

THE MORAL DILEMMA

Murder, says the law, is intentionally killing a person without lawful justification. This is common sense, because in general we believe it is wrong to kill. However, we think it is justified in exceptional cases. When is it justified? The difficulty of this question can be seen from the following example, well known to legal textbook writers.

Two sailors, X and Y, are shipwrecked. Neither can swim. X reaches a floating plank and climbs onto it. Y reaches the plank and tries to climb onto it. The plank will hold only one person, so X prevents Y from getting onto it and Y drowns.

1. Is this situation exceptional enough to make X's act morally justified?
2. Suppose Y had climbed onto the plank and pushed X off, would Y's act have been morally justified?
3. Suppose the survivor in 1 or 2 had been charged in front of Dudley's and Stephens's judges with murder. What verdict do you think would have been given?
4. Suppose Y climbed onto the plank and X remained on it, and they both drowned. Would each have been justified in staying on the plank?

JETTISONING THE CARGO

"Necessity knows no law," it is often said. In other words, you can't be held legally liable for an act you had to do. From this point of view Dudley and Stephens would not be guilty of the murder of the cabin boy because their act was one which was necessary for their survival. But the judges in their case rejected the defendants' plea of necessity. As a result, it has been said that there is no defence of necessity in common law.

This is not true. Necessity can be a good defence, as in the 1608 *Mouse's* case.

A ship carrying a cargo of goods was overtaken by a storm. The captain feared that it would sink and that all aboard would be drowned, because it was already dangerously low in the water. To stop it from sinking further he ordered the crew to throw the cargo overboard. This lightened the vessel and enabled her to keep afloat, survive the storm, and come to safety.

The captain, so the court held at this trial, was within his rights in throwing the cargo overboard. He had to sacrifice the cargo for the greater good of saving human life.

1. Suppose the cargo had been a human one. Would the captain's act have been justified?
2. Suppose the open boat with the three men and the cabin boy had been sinking. Would Captain Dudley have been entitled to throw one of the passengers overboard to save the rest? If so, which one? If not, can you think of any circumstances where a captain might be morally justified in throwing a passenger overboard?
3. Saving human life is obviously more important than saving cargo. In Dudley's and Stephens's case was it equally obvious that saving the lives of the three sailors was more important than saving the cabin boy's life?
4. In such a case do three lives have three times the importance of one life?
5. Because the cabin boy would have died before they were rescued, was it more important to save the sailors' lives?
6. Do you think Dudley and Stephens would have been well-advised to put forward such arguments? Would they have answered the judges' points?
7. What light does this case throw on the notion of necessity? What do we mean by saying it was necessary for the captain to throw the cargo overboard? What did Dudley mean by saying it was necessary to kill the cabin boy?
8. There is a well-known story about Oscar Wilde in which a beggar, trying to convince Wilde to give him some money, says, "Man must live." Wilde answers, "I don't see the necessity." What point is Wilde making? Strictly speaking, is anything ever really necessary?

· · · ·

ENEMIES IN WAR

· · · ·

During the Second World War a British bomber pilot was shot down over Germany and taken prisoner. He escaped and on his way through Germany to neutral territory, he carried on his own private war effort: each day he killed one German soldier.

Back in England, he resumed his flying duties and ended the war with high rank and honors.

1. Do you think such killings are justified?
2. Are there any moral limits to the right to kill the enemy in war?
3. If Dudley and Stephens had been survivors of a warship torpedoed by the enemy, and the boy a survivor of the enemy submarine, would they have been justified in killing him simply as an enemy?
4. Would they have been justified in killing him for food?

THE ROMAN SOLDIER'S WAY OUT

So far we've discussed the taking of other people's lives. What about taking one's own life? Suicide has often been seen as an honorable way out. The Roman solider, if defeated, preferred death to dishonor. Rather than surrender and allow himself to be captured he would fall upon his sword and kill himself. We see this in the story of Brutus.

(b) *R. v. Dudley & Stephens*†

Indictment for the murder of Richard Parker on the high seas within the jurisdiction of the Admiralty.

At the trial before Huddleston, B., at the Devon and Cornwall Winter Assizes, November 7, 1884, the jury at the suggestion of the learned judge, found the facts of the case in a special verdict which stated "that on July 5, 1884, the prisoners, Thomas Dudley and Edward Stephens, with one Brooks, all able-bodied English seamen, and the deceased also an English boy, between seventeen and eighteen years of age, the crew of an English yacht, a registered English vessel, were cast away in a storm on the high seas 1,600 miles from the Cape of Good Hope, and were compelled to put into an open boat belonging to the said yacht. That in this boat they had no supply of water and no supply of food, except two 1 lb. tins of turnips, and for three days they had nothing else to subsist upon. That on the fourth day they caught a small turtle, upon which they subsisted for a few days, and this was the only food they had up to the twentieth day when the act now in question was committed. That on the twelfth day the remains of the turtle were entirely consumed, and for the next eight days they had nothing to eat. That they had no fresh water, except such rain as they from time to time caught in their oilskin capes. That the boat was drifting on the ocean, and

was probably more than 1000 miles away from land. That on the eighteenth day, when they had been seven days without food and five without water, the prisoners spoke to Brooks as to what should be done if no succour came, and suggested that some one should be sacrificed to save the rest, but Brooks dissented, and the boy, to whom they were understood to refer, was not consulted. That on the 24th of July, the day before the act now in question, the prisoner Dudley proposed to Stephens and Brooks that lots should be cast who should be put to death to save the rest, but Brooks refused to consent, and it was not put to the boy, and in point of fact there was no drawing of lots. That on that day the prisoners spoke of their having families, and suggested it would be better to kill the boy that their lives should be saved, and Dudley proposed that if there was no vessel in sight by the morrow morning the boy should be killed. That next day, the 25th of July, no vessel appearing, Dudley told Brooks that he had better go and have a sleep, and made signs to Stephens and Brooks that the boy had better be killed. The prisoner Stephens agreed to the act, but Brooks dissented from it. That the boy was then lying at the bottom of the boat quite helpless, and extremely weakened by famine and by drinking sea water, and unable to make any resistance nor did he ever assent to his being killed. The prisoner Dudley offered a prayer asking forgiveness for them all if

† (1884), 14 Q.B.D. 273 at 273–75, 279–88.

either of them should be tempted to commit a rash act, and that their souls might be saved. That Dudley, with the assent of Stephens, went to the boy, and telling him that his time was come, put a knife into his throat and killed him then and there; that the three men fed upon the body and blood of the boy for four days; that on the fourth day after the act had been committed the boat was picked up by a passing vessel, and the prisoners were rescued, still alive, but in the lowest state of prostration. That they were carried to the port of Falmouth, and committed for trial at Exeter. That if the men had not fed upon the body of the boy they would probably not have survived to be so picked up and rescued, but would within the four days have died of famine. That the boy, being in a much weaker condition, was likely to have died before them. That at the time of the act in question there was no sail in sight, nor any reasonable prospect of relief. That under these circumstances there appeared to the prisoners every probability that unless they then fed or very soon fed upon the boy or one of themselves they would die of starvation. That there was no appreciable chance of saving life except by killing some one for the others to eat. That assuming any necessity to kill anybody, there was no greater necessity for killing the boy than any of the other three men. But whether upon the whole matter by the jurors found the killing of Richard Parker by Dudley and Stephens be felony and murder the jurors are ignorant, and pray the advice of the Court thereupon, and if upon the whole matter the Court shall be of opinion that the killing of Richard Parker be felony and murder, then the jurors say that Dudley and Stephens were each guilty of felony and murder as alleged in the indictment."

· · · ·

[LORD COLERIDGE C.J.:]

· · · ·

...From these facts, stated with the cold precision of a special verdict, it appears sufficiently that the prisoners were subject to terrible temptation, to sufferings which might break down the bodily power of the strongest man, and try the conscience of the best. Other details yet more harrowing, facts still more loathsome and appalling, were presented to the jury, and are to be found recorded in my learned Brother's notes. But nevertheless this is clear, that the prisoners put to death a weak and unoffending boy upon the chance of preserving their own lives by feeding upon his flesh and blood after he was killed,

and with the certainty of depriving *him* of any possible chance of survival. The verdict finds in terms that "if the men had not fed upon the body of the boy they would *probably* not have survived," and that "the boy being in a much weaker condition was *likely* to have died before them." They might possibly have been picked up next day by a passing ship; they might possibly not have been picked up at all; in either case it is obvious that the killing of the boy would have been an unnecessary and profitless act. It is found by the verdict that the boy was incapable of resistance, and, in fact, made none; and it is not even suggested that his death was due to any violence on his part attempted against, or even so much as feared by, those who killed him. Under these circumstances the jury say that they are ignorant whether those who killed him were guilty of murder, and have referred it to this Court to determine what is the legal consequence which follows from the facts which they have found.

· · · ·

There remains to be considered the real question in the case — whether killing under the circumstances set forth in the verdict be or be not murder. The contention that it could be anything else was, to the minds of us all, both new and strange, and we stopped the Attorney General in his negative argument in order that we might hear what could be said in support of a proposition which appeared to us to be at once dangerous, immoral, and opposed to all legal principle and analogy. All, no doubt, that can be said has been urged before us, and we are now to consider and determine what it amounts to. First it is said that it follows from various definitions of murder in books of authority, which definitions imply, if they do not state, the doctrine that in order to save your own life you may lawfully take away the life of another, when that other is neither attempting nor threatening yours, nor is guilty of any illegal act whatever towards you or any one else. But if these definitions be looked at they will not be found to sustain this contention. The earliest in point of date is the passage cited to us from Bracton, who lived in the reign of Henry III. ... But in the very passage as to necessity, on which reliance has been placed, it is clear that Bracton is speaking of necessity in the ordinary sense — the repelling by violence, violence justified so far as it was necessary for the object, any illegal violence used towards oneself....

It is, if possible, yet clearer that the doctrine contended for receives no support from the great authority of Lord Hale....

... For in the chapter in which he deals with the exemption created by compulsion or necessity he thus expresses himself: — "If a man be desperately assaulted and in peril of death, and cannot otherwise escape unless, to satisfy his assailant's fury, he will kill an innocent person then present, the fear and factual force will not acquit him of the crime and punishment of murder, if he commit the fact, for he ought rather to die himself than kill an innocent; but if he cannot otherwise save his own life the law permits him in his own defence to kill the assailant, for by the violence of the assault, and the offence committed upon him by the assailant himself, the law of nature, and necessity, hath made him his own protector *cum debito moderamino inculpatae tutelae."* (*Hale's Pleas of the Crown*, vol. 1, 51.)

But, further still, Lord Hale in the following chapter deals with the position asserted by the casuists, and sanctioned, as he says, by Grotius and Puffendorf, that in a case of extreme necessity, either of hunger or clothing; "theft is no theft, or at least not punishable as theft, as some even of our own lawyers have asserted the same." "But," says Lord Hale, "I take it that here in England, that rule, at least by the laws of England, is false; and therefore, if a person being under necessity for want of victuals or clothes, shall upon that account clandestinely and *anima furandi* steal another man's goods, it is felony, and a crime by the laws of England punishable with death." (*Hale, Please of the Crown*, i, 54). If, therefore, Lord Hale is clear — as he is — that extreme necessity of hunger does not justify larceny, what would he have said to the doctrine that it justified murder?

. . . .

Is there, then, any authority for the proposition which has been presented to us? Decided cases there are none. ... The American case cited by my Brother Stephen in his Digest, from Wharton on Homicide, in which it was decided, correctly indeed, that sailors had no right to throw passengers overboard to save themselves, but on the somewhat strange ground that the proper mode of determining who was to be sacrificed was to vote upon the subject by ballot, can hardly, as my Brother Stephen says, be an authority satisfactory to a court in this country....

The one real authority of former time is Lord Bacon, who, in his commentary on the maxim, "*necessitas inducit privilegium quoad jura privata*," lays down the law as follows: — "Necessity carrieth a privilege in itself. Necessity is of three sorts — necessity of conservation of life, necessity of obedience, and necessity of the act of God or of a stranger. First of conservation of life, if a man steal viands to satisfy his present hunger, this is no felony nor larceny. So if divers be in danger of drowning by the casting away of some boat or barge, and one of them get to some plank, or on the boat's side to keep himself above water, and another to save his life thrust him from it, whereby he is drowned, this is neither *se defendendo* nor by misadventure, but justifiable." On this it is to be observed that Lord Bacon's proposition that stealing to satisfy hunger is no larceny is hardly supported by Staundforde, whom he cites for it, and is expressly contradicted by Lord Hale in the passage already cited. And for the proposition as to the plank or boat, it is said to be derived from the canonists. At any rate he cites no authority for it, and it must stand upon his own. Lord Bacon was great even as a lawyer; but it is permissible to much smaller men, relying upon principle and on the authority of others, the equals and even the superiors of Lord Bacon as lawyers, to question the soundness of his dictum. There are many conceivable states of things in which it might possibly be true, but if Lord Bacon meant to lay down the broad proposition that a man may save his life by killing, if necessary, an innocent and unoffending neighbour, it certainly is not law at the present day.

. . . .

Now, except for the purpose of testing how far the conservation of a man's own life is in all cases and under all circumstances, an absolute, unqualified, and paramount duty, we exclude from our consideration all the incidents of war. We are dealing with a case of private homicide, not one imposed upon men in the service of their Sovereign and in the defence of their country. Now it is admitted that the deliberate killing of this unoffending and unresisting boy was clearly murder, unless the killing can be justified by some well-recognised excuse admitted by the law. It is further admitted that there was in this case no such excuse, unless the killing was justified by what has been called "necessity." But the temptation to the act which existed here was not what the law has ever called necessity. Nor is this to be regretted. Though law and morality are not the same, and many things may be immoral which are not necessarily illegal, yet the absolute divorce of law from morality would be of fatal consequence; and such divorce would follow if the temptation to murder in this case were to be held by law an absolute defence of it. It is not so. To preserve one's life is generally speaking a duty, but it may be the plainest and the highest duty to sacrifice it. War is full of instances in which it is a man's duty not to live, but to die. The duty in case of shipwreck, of a captain to his crew, of the crew to the passengers, of soldiers to women and children, as in the noble case of the *Birkenhead*; these duties impose on men the moral necessity, not of the preservation, but of the sacrifice of their lives for others, from which in no country, least of all, it is to be hoped, in England, will men ever shrink, as indeed, they have not shrunk. It is not correct, therefore, to say that there is any absolute or unqualified necessity to preserve one's life. "*Necesse est ut cam, no at vivam*," is a saying of a Roman officer quoted by Lord Bacon himself with high eulogy in the very chapter on necessity to which so much reference has been made. It would be a very easy and cheap display of commonplace learning to quote from Greek and Latin authors, from Horace, from Juvenal, from Cicero, from Euripides, passage after passage, in which the duty of dying for others has been laid down in glowing and emphatic language as resulting from the principles of heathen ethics; it is enough in a Christian country to remind ourselves of the Great Example whom we profess to follow. It is not needful to point out the awful danger of admitting the principle which has been contended for. Who is to be the judge of this sort of necessity? By what measure is the comparative value of lives to be measured? Is it to be strength, or intellect, or what? It is plain that the principle leaves to him who is to profit by it to determine the necessity which will justify him in deliberately taking another's life to save his own. In this case the weakest, the youngest, the most unresisting, was chosen. Was it more necessary to kill him than one of the grown men? The answer must be "No" —

So spake the Fiend, and with necessity,
The tyrant's plea, excused his devilish deeds.

It is not suggested that in this particular case the deeds were "devilish," but it is quite plain that such a principle once admitted might be made the legal cloak for unbridled passion and atrocious crime. There is no safe path for judges to tread but to ascertain the law to the best of their ability and to declare it according to their judgment; and if in any case the law appears to be too severe on individuals, to leave it to the Sovereign to exercise that prerogative of mercy which the Constitution has intrusted to the hands fittest to dispense it.

It must not be supposed that in refusing to admit temptation to be an excuse for crime it is forgotten how terrible the temptation was; how awful the suffering; how hard in such trials to keep the judgment straight and the conduct pure. We are often compelled to set up standards we cannot reach ourselves, and to lay down rules which we could not ourselves satisfy. But a man has no right to declare temptation to be an excuse, though he might himself have yielded to it, nor allow compassion for the criminal to change or weaken in any manner the legal definition of the crime. It is therefore our duty to declare that the prisoners' act in this case was wilful murder, that the facts as stated in the verdict are no legal justification of the homicide; and to say that in our unanimous opinion the prisoners are upon this special verdict guilty of murder.

The Court then proceeded to pass sentence of death upon the prisoners.

(c) Law and Morality†

Lord Patrick Devlin

The relationship between law and morals has recently, in England and in the United States and also in Canada, received quite a considerable degree of interest. Of course, if one wants to go back to the very beginning, one must begin with John Stuart Mill in 1859 and the publication of his essay *On Liberty*,

† (1964) 3 Manitoba Law School Journal 243 at 243, 248–54. [Notes and/or references omitted.] (Based on material in *The Enforcement of Morals*, published by Oxford University Press, 1965.) Reproduced with permission of Oxford University Press, Oxford, UK.

and his announcement of the famous principle which should govern, in his view, all law-making in relation to all subjects. That principle is, he said:

> ... the sole end for which mankind are warranted, individually or collectively, in interfering in the liberty of action of any of their number, is self-protection. That the only purpose for which power can be rightfully exercised over any member of a civilized community, against his will, is to prevent harm to others. His own good, either physical or moral, is not a sufficient warrant. He cannot rightfully be compelled to do or forbear because it will be better for him to do so, because it will make him happier, because in the opinions of others, to do so would be wise, or even right.[1]

This principle was attacked by Mr. Justice Stephen in the celebrated book, *Liberty, Equality, Fraternity*,[2] which he wrote in the 1870's. I think it is fair to say that the principle never got beyond academic discussion; nor had it ever been translated into practice. However, it was resurrected and translated into practice in 1957 in the report of the committee that was presided over by Sir John Wolfenden on the amendment of the laws on homosexuality and prostitution. There the principle was stated in this way:

> There must remain a realm of private morality and immorality which is, in brief and crude terms, not the law's business.

.　.　.　.　.

The attraction of the doctrine, for undoubtedly it is attractive, to me lies in this: that it seems to be a logical extension from freedom of religion. We have now achieved, not without a great struggle, the sort of society in which a man's religion is his own affair. Ought not his morals to be his own affair too? Is there any greater need, we may ask ourselves, for a common morality than there is for a common religion? However, there is a distinction. The ordinary free thinker has no religion. He can doubt the existence of God as he does the existence of the Devil, and if society can accommodate people who have no personal religion and yet reckon them as good citizens, as so many of them are, then there is no need for a common religion. But it is one thing to doubt the existence of God and the Devil and another thing to doubt the existence of good and evil. God and the Devil is what religion is about; good and evil is what morals are about. Whether good and evil are properly personified in God and the Devil is a theological question upon which the man of faith, and the free thinker, can

disagree, but there will be no disagreement, and can be no disagreement about whether good and evil exist.

Thus, while Mill, in common with most free thinkers, both of his century and of the present one, had no personal religion, and would deny the need for a common religion, he had a personal morality and he accepted the need for a common morality. Indeed, his opinion of what was virtuous did not substantially differ from that of his contemporaries, but no one, he felt, could be sure. In a free society, full scope must be given to individuality as one of the elements of well-being, and the individual must be free to question, to challenge, and to experiment. "The liberty of the individual", he wrote:

> must be thus far limited; he must not make himself a nuisance to other people. But if he refrains from molesting others in what concerns them, and merely acts according to his own inclination and judgment in things which concern himself, the same reasons which show that opinion should be free, prove also that he should be allowed, without molestation, to carry his opinions into practice at his own cost. That mankind is not infallible; that his truths, for the most part, are only half-truths; that unity of opinion, unless resulting from the fullest and freest comparison of opposite opinions, is not desirable, and diversity not an evil, but a good; until mankind is much more capable than at present of recognizing all sides of the truth, are principles applicable to men's modes of action, not less than to their opinions. As it is useful that while mankind is imperfect there should be different opinions, so it is that there should be different experiments of living; that free scope should be given to varieties of character, short of injury to others; and that the worth of different modes of life should be proved practically, when anyone thinks fit to try them.[11]

You see, it is with freedom of opinion and discussion that Mill is primarily concerned. Freedom of action follows naturally on that. Men must be allowed to do what they are allowed to talk about doing. Evidently, what Mill visualizes is a number of people doing things he himself would disapprove of but doing them earnestly and openly after thought and discussion in an endeavour to find a way of life best suited to them as individuals.

This seems to me on the whole to be an idealistic picture. It has happened to some extent, say in the last couple of generations in the growth of free love outside marriage. Although for many it is just the indulgence of the flesh, for some it is a serious decision to break the constraint of chastity outside marriage. But in the area of morals that is touched by the law I find it difficult to think of any other example of high-mindedness. A man does not, as a rule, commit bigamy because he wants to experiment with two wives instead of one. He does not, as a rule, lie with his daughter or sister because he thinks that an incestuous relationship can be a good one, but because he finds in it a way of satisfying his lust in the home. He does not keep a brothel so as to prove the value of promiscuity, but so as to make money. There must be some homosexuals who believe theirs to be a good way of life, but many more who would like to get free of it if only they could. And certainly no one in his senses can think that habitual drunkenness or drugging leads to any good at all. But Mill believed, you see, that diversity in morals and the removal of restraint on what was traditionally held to be immorality (and held by him to be immorality) would liberate men to prove what they thought to be good. He would have been the last man to have advocated the removal of restraint so as to permit self-indulgence. He conceived of old morality being replaced by a new and perhaps better morality. He would not have approved of those who did not care whether there is any morality at all, but he never really grappled with the fact that along the paths that depart from traditional morals, pimps leading the weak astray far outnumber spiritual explorers at the head of the strong.

But let me return to the distinction I was drawing between freedom of religion and freedom in morals. The abolition of established religion is a relatively recent development. It is a feature of modern thought. It came with the Reformation, which is comparatively late in the history of civilization. Before that it would have been thought that a society could not exist without a common religion. The pluralist society in which we now live was not achieved without the complete destruction of medieval thought, and it involved a change of civilization which was comparable with the triumphs of Christianity over paganism. Mill records how the Emperor Marcus Aurelius, whom he considered to be one of the greatest of world rulers — tender, enlightened and humane — persecuted Christianity because existing society, as he saw it, was held together by belief in and reverence of the received divinities. The struggle more recently between received religion and freedom of conscience was of the same order, and entailed as much suffering.

But the removal of religion from the structure of society does not mean that a society can exist without faith. There is faith in moral belief as well as in religious belief, and although it is less precise and less demanding, moral belief is not necessarily less intense. In our society we believe in the advance of man towards a goal, and this belief is the mainspring of our morals. We believe that at some time in the history of mankind, whether on a sudden by divine stroke, or imperceptibly in evolutionary millennia, there was extracted from the chaos of the primeval mind, concepts of justice, benevolence, mercy, continence and others, that we call virtues. The distinction between virtue and vice, between good and evil as it affects our actions, is what morals [are] about. A common religious faith means that there is common agreement about the end of man; a common moral faith means that there is common agreement about the way he should go. A band of travellers can go forward together without knowing what they will find at the end of the journey, but they cannot keep in company if they do not journey in the same direction.

Keeping in company is what society is about.

Diversity in moral belief and practice would be no more injurious to a society which had no common morality than the like diversity in religious matters is to a society without a common religion. However, as I have said, Mill and his disciples do not conceive of a society without a common morality. If they did, if they wanted a society in which morality is as free as religion, they would indeed be faint-hearted in what they preached. They could not then sensibly permit the law, as they do, to punish the corruption of youth or public acts of indecency. Where there is freedom of religion the conversion of a youth is not thought of as corruption. Men would have thought of it as that in the Middle Ages, just as we now think of the introduction of a youth to homosexual practices as corruption and not as conversion. Where there is true freedom of religion it would be thought intolerant to object to a religious ceremony in a public place on the ground that it was offensive to have brought to one's attention the exhibition of a faith which one thought false and pernicious. Why, then, do we object to the public exhibition of a false morality and call it indecency? If we thought that unrestricted indulgence in the sexual passions was as good a life as any other for those who liked it we should find nothing indecent in the practice of it either in public or in private. It would become no more indecent than kissing in public. Decency as an objective depends on the belief in continence as a virtue, a virtue which requires sexual activity to be kept within prescribed bounds.

These reflections show the gulf which separates the religious toleration we have achieved from the moral toleration that Mill wanted. The former is practicable, because while each man believes that his own religion, or the lack of it, is the truth or nearest to the truth, he looks upon the alternatives as lesser good and not as evil. What Mill demands is that we must tolerate what we know to be evil and what no one asserts to be good. He does not ask that in particular cases we should extend tolerance out of pity. He demands that we should cede it forever as a right. Because it is evil we can protect youth from corruption by it, but save for that we must allow it to spread unhindered by the law and infect the minds of those who are not strong enough to resist it. Why do ninety-nine of us have to grant this license to the other one? Because, the answer is, we are fallible; are all quite convinced that what we call vice is evil, but we may be mistaken. True it is that if the waters of toleration are poured upon the muck, bad men will wallow in the bog, but it may be (how can we tell otherwise?) that it is only in such a bog that seed may flourish that some day some good man may bring to fruit, and that otherwise the world would lose and be the poorer for it. That is the kernel of Mill's freedom; that is why we must not suppress vice. It is not because it is not evil; Mill thought that it was. It is not because legal suppression would be futile; some of Mill's followers advanced this argument, but he did not. Nor is it because Mill thought that virtue would be bound to triumph over vice without the aid of the law; in some cogent passages he refuted that argument. When all this is stripped away, the kernel of Mill is just this: that he beseeches us to think it possible that we may be mistaken. Because of this possibility he demands almost absolute freedom for the individual to go his own way, the only function of society being to provide for him an ordered framework within which he might experiment in thought, and in action, secure from physical harm.

There is here, I believe, a flaw. Even assuming that we accept Mill's ideal, it is unacceptable to the lawmaker as a basis for action because it fails to distinguish sufficiently between freedom of thought and freedom of action. It may be a good thing for the man to keep an open mind about all his beliefs so that he will never claim for them absolute certainty and never dismiss entirely from his mind the thought that he may be wrong. But where there is a call for action he must act on what he believes to be true. The lawyer, who in this respect stands somewhere midway between the philosopher and the man of action, requires to be satisfied beyond a reasonable doubt. If he is so satisfied, he would then think it right to punish a man for breach of the law while acknowledging the possibility that he may be mis-

taken. Is there any difference, so far as the freedom of the individual is concerned, between punishing a man for an act which admittedly he did, and which we believe, perhaps erroneously, to be wrong, he denying that it is wrong; and punishing him for an act that is admittedly wrong, and which we honestly but perhaps erroneously believe that he did, he denying that he did it? Suppose you prosecute a man for bigamy. His defence might be, "I honestly believed that my first wife was dead". If that defense is rejected, it is rejected because there is no reasonable doubt in the minds of the jury that he did not honestly believe it. And yet they must say, "We might be mistaken; we are not required to have absolute certainty, but we must act on what we reasonably believe to be true". Well, then, if his defence were simply that: "I admit I married a second time but I honestly believe that bigamy is a good thing", must we not act in the same way? We must say, "Well, we have no reasonable doubt that bigamy is a bad thing; we can't be certain, we may be mistaken, but we must act upon our belief". Philosophers, after all, may philosophize under the shadow of perpetual doubt, but the governors of society cannot do their duty if they are not permitted to act upon what they believe.

I might now usefully return to what Mill said about Marcus Aurelius. He cited him as an example of the fallibility of even the best and wisest of men. Marcus Aurelius thought Christianity wholly unbelievable, and could see in it only a force that would cause the society he governed to fall into pieces. Mill certainly did not regard Christianity as an unmixed blessing, but it might have been a different thing, he thought, if it had been adopted under Marcus Aurelius instead of under Constantine. So, Mill urged, unless a man flatters himself that he is wiser than Marcus Aurelius, let him abstain from that assumption of joint infallibility of himself and the multitude which the great man made with such unfortunate results. The example is a perfectly fair one on the point of fallibility. If we were to be confronted with the creed today which taught that constraint was the only vice and the unlimited indulgence of the appetites of all sorts the only virtue worth cultivating, we should look at it without any comprehension at all. But I dare say that our contempt would not be greater than that of Marcus Aurelius for Christianity, or that of a medieval philosopher for the notion that heresy was something to be tolerated. The example is also a fair one on the point I am making. What else, one may ask, did Mill expect Marcus Aurelius to do? It is idle to lament that he did not forestall Constantine in accepting

5. Law, Morality, and Justice

Christianity, for he could not accept what he disbelieved. In Mill's view, and probably in that of most of his disciples, Marcus Aurelius was right in rejecting the claims of Christianity. On this view the Emperor's mistake lay in his failure to realize that if he permitted the destruction of his society through the agency of a religion which he rightly concluded to be false, the successor civilization would be an improvement upon him. To put Mill's question again in another context, can any man, putting himself in the position of the great Emperor, flatter himself that he would have acted more wisely?

It is not feasible to require of any society that it should permit its own destruction by that which, whether rightly or wrongly, it honestly believes to be in error in case it may be mistaken. To admit that we are not infallible is not to admit that we are always wrong. What we believe to be evil may indeed be evil, and we cannot forever condemn ourselves to inactivity against evil because of the chance that we may by mistake destroy good.

For better or for worse, the lawmaker must act according to his lights, and he cannot, therefore, accept Mill's doctrine as practicable even if, as an ideal, he thought it desirable. But I must say that for my part I do not accept it even as an ideal. I accept it as an inspiration. What Mill taught about the value of freedom of inquiry and the dangers of intolerance has placed all free men forever in his debt. His admonitions were addressed to a society that was secure and strong and hidebound. Their repetition today is to a society much less solid. As a tract of the times, what Mill wrote was superb, but as dogma it has lost much of its appeal. I say dogma, for Mill's doctrine is just as dogmatic as any of those he repudiates. It is dogmatic to say that if only we were allowed to behave just as we liked so long as we did not injure each other the world would become a better place for all of us. There is no more evidence for this sort of utopia than there is evidence of the existence of heaven, and there is nothing to show that the one is any more easily attained than the other. We must not be bemused by words. If we are not entitled to call our society free unless we pursue freedom to an extremity that would make society intolerable for most of us, then let us stop short of the extreme and be content with some other name. The result may not be freedom unalloyed, but there are alloys which strengthen without corrupting.

(d) *R. v. Butler*†

[SOPINKA J., Lamer C.J., La Forest, Cory, McLachlin, Stevenson, and Iacobucci, JJ.:]

This appeal calls into question the constitutionality of the obscenity provisions of the Criminal Code, R.S.C., 1985, c. C-46, s. 163. They are attacked on the ground that they contravene s. 2(b) of the Canadian Charter of Rights and Freedoms. The case requires the Court to address one of the most difficult and controversial of contemporary issues, that of determining whether, and to what extent, Parliament may legitimately criminalize obscenity. I propose to begin with a review of the facts which gave rise to this appeal, as well of the proceedings in the lower courts.

1. FACTS AND PROCEEDINGS

In August 1987, the appellant, Donald Victor Butler, opened the Avenue Video Boutique located in Winnipeg, Manitoba. The shop sells and rents "hard core" videotapes and magazines as well as sexual paraphernalia. Outside the store is a sign which reads:

Avenue Video Boutique; a private members only adult video/visual club.

Notice: if sex oriented material offends you, please do not enter.

No admittance to persons under 18 years.

---

† [1992] 1 S.C.R. 452, 89 D.L.R. (4th) 449 at.

On August 21, 1987, the City of Winnipeg Police entered the appellant's store with a search warrant and seized all the inventory. The appellant was charged with 173 counts in the first indictment: three counts of selling obscene material contrary to s. 159(2)(a) of the Criminal Code, R.S.C. 1970, c. C-34 (now s. 163(2)(a)), 41 counts of possessing obscene material for the purpose of distribution contrary to s. 159(1)(a) (now s. 163(1)(a)) of the Criminal Code, 128 counts of possessing obscene material for the purpose of sale contrary to s. 159(2)(a) of the Criminal Code and one count of exposing obscene material to public view contrary to s. 159(2)(a) of the Criminal Code.

. . . .

The trial judge convicted the appellant on eight counts relating to eight films. Convictions were entered against the co-accused McCord with respect to two counts relating to two of the films. Fines of $1,000 per offence were imposed on the appellant. Acquittals were entered on the remaining charges.

The Crown appealed the 242 acquittals with respect to the appellant and the appellant cross-appealed the convictions. The majority of the Manitoba Court of Appeal allowed the appeal of the Crown and entered convictions for the appellant with respect to all of the counts, Twaddle and Helper JJ.A. dissenting.

. . . .

2.   RELEVANT LEGISLATION

Criminal Code, R.S.C., 1985, c. C-46

163.(1) Every one commits an offence who,
(a) makes, prints, publishes, distributes, circulates, or has in his possession for the purpose of publication, distribution or circulation any obscene written matter, picture, model, phonograph record or other thing whatever; or
(b) makes, prints, publishes, distributes, sells or has in his possession for the purpose of publication, distribution or circulation a crime comic.

(2) Every one commits an offence who knowingly, without lawful justification or excuse,
(a) sells, exposes to public view or has in his possession for such a purpose any obscene written matter, picture, model, phonograph record or other thing whatever;
(b) publicly exhibits a disgusting object or an indecent show;

(c) offers to sell, advertises or publishes an advertisement of, or has for sale or disposal, any means, instructions, medicine, drug or article intended or represented as a method of causing abortion or miscarriage; or
(d) advertises or publishes an advertisement of any means, instructions, medicine, drug or article intended or represented as a method for restoring sexual virility or curing venereal diseases or diseases of the generative organs.

(3) No person shall be convicted of an offence under this section if he establishes that the public good was served by the acts that are alleged to constitute the offence and that the acts alleged did not extend beyond what served the public good.

(4) For the purposes of this section, it is a question of law whether an act served the public good and whether there is evidence that the act alleged went beyond what served the public good, [but] it is a question of fact whether the acts did or did not extend beyond what served the public good.

(5) For the purposes of this section, the motives of an accused are irrelevant.

(6) Where an accused is charged with an offence under subsection (1), the fact that the accused was ignorant of the nature or presence of the matter, picture, model, phonograph record, crime comic or other thing by means of or in relation to which the offence was committed is not a defence to the charge.

(7) In this section, "crime comic" means a magazine, periodical or book that exclusively or substantially comprises matter depicting pictorially
(a) the commission of crimes, real or fictitious; or
(b) events connected with the commission of crimes, real or fictitious, whether occurring before or after the commission of the crime.

(8) For the purposes of this Act, any publication a dominant characteristic of which is the undue exploitation of sex, or of sex and any one or more of the following subjects, namely, crime, horror, cruelty and violence, shall be deemed to be obscene.

3.   ISSUES

The following constitutional questions are raised by this appeal:

1. Does s. 163 of the Criminal Code of Canada, R.S.C., 1985, c. C-46, violate s. 2(b) of the Canadian Charter of Rights and Freedoms?
2. If s. 163 of the Criminal Code of Canada, R.S.C., 1985, c. C-46, violates s. 2(b) of the Canadian Charter of Rights and Freedoms, can s. 163 of the Criminal Code of Canada be demonstrably justified under s. 1 of the Canadian Charter of Rights and Freedoms as a reasonable limit prescribed by law?

4. ANALYSIS

The constitutional questions, as stated, bring under scrutiny the entirety of s. 163. However, both lower courts as well as the parties have focused almost exclusively on the definition of obscenity found in s. 163(8). Other portions of the impugned provision, such as the reverse onus provision envisaged in s. 163(3) as well as the absolute liability offence created by s. 163(6), raise substantial Charter issues which should be left to be dealt with in proceedings specifically directed to these issues. In my view, in the circumstances, this appeal should be confined to the examination of the constitutional validity of s. 163(8) only.

.   .   .   .   .

(i) "Community Standard of Tolerance" Test

In Brodie, Judson J. accepted the view espoused notably by the Australian and New Zealand courts that obscenity is to be measured against "community standards". He cited, at pp. 705–6, the following passage in the judgment of Fullager J. in *R. v. Close*, [1948] V.L.R. 445, at p. 465:

> There does exist in any community at all times — however the standard may vary from time to time — a general instinctive sense of what is decent and what is indecent, of what is clean and what is dirty, and when the distinction has to be drawn, I do not know that today there is any better tribunal than a jury to draw it ... I am very far from attempting to lay down a model direction, but a judge might perhaps, in the case of a novel, say something like this: "It would not be true to say that any publication dealing with sexual relations is obscene. The relations of the sexes are, of course, legitimate matters for discussion everywhere ... There are certain standards of decency which prevail in the community, and you are really called upon to try this case because you are regarded as represent-

ing, and capable of justly applying, those standards. What is obscene is something which offends against those standards."

The community standards test has been the subject of extensive judicial analysis. It is the standards of the community as a whole which must be considered and not the standards of a small segment of that community such as the university community where a film was shown (*R. v. Goldberg*, [1971] 3 O.R. 323 (C.A.)) or a city where a picture was exposed (*R. v. Kiverago* (1973), 11 C.C.C. (2d) 463 (Ont. C.A.)). The standard to be applied is a national one (*R. v. Cameron* (1966), 58 D.L.R. (2d) 486 (Ont. C.A.); *R. v. Duthie Books Ltd.* (1966), 58 D.L.R. (2d) 274 (B.C.C.A.); *R. v. Ariadne Developments Ltd.* (1974), 19 C.C.C. (2d) 49 (N.S.S.C., App. Div.), at p. 59). With respect to expert evidence, it is not necessary and is not a fact which the Crown is obliged to prove as part of its case (*R. v. Sudbury News Service Ltd.* (1978), 18 O.R. (2d) 428 (C.A.); *R. v. Prairie Schooner News Ltd.* (1970), 75 W.W.R. 585 (Man. C.A.); *R. v. Great West News Ltd.*, [1970] 4 C.C.C. 307 (Man. C.A.)). In *R. v. Dominion News & Gifts (1962) Ltd.*, [1963] 2 C.C.C. 103 (Man. C.A.), Freedman J.A. (dissenting) emphasized that the community standards test must necessarily respond to changing mores (at pp. 116–17):

> Community standards must be contemporary. Times change, and ideas change with them. Compared to the Victorian era this is a liberal age in which we live. One manifestation of it is the relative freedom with which the whole question of sex is discussed. In books, magazines, movies, television, and sometimes even in parlour conversation, various aspects of sex are made the subject of comment, with a candour that in an earlier day would have been regarded as indecent and intolerable. We cannot and should not ignore these present-day attitudes when we face the question whether [the subject materials] are obscene according to our criminal law.

Our Court was called upon to elaborate the community standards test in *Towne Cinema Theatres Ltd. v. The Queen*, [1985] 1 S.C.R. 494. Dickson C.J. reviewed the case law and found (at pp. 508–9):

> The cases all emphasize that it is a standard of tolerance, not taste, that is relevant. What matters is not what Canadians think is right for themselves to see. What matters is what Canadians would not abide other Canadians seeing because it would be beyond the contemporary Canadian standard of tolerance to allow them to see it.

Since the standard is tolerance, I think the audience to which the allegedly obscene material is targeted must be relevant. The operative standards are those of the Canadian community as a whole, but since what matters is what other people may see, it is quite conceivable that the Canadian community would tolerate varying degrees of explicitness depending upon the audience and the circumstances. [Emphasis in original.]

Therefore, the community standards test is concerned not with what Canadians would not tolerate being exposed to themselves, but what they would not tolerate other Canadians being exposed to. The minority view was that the tolerance level will vary depending on the manner, time and place in which the material is presented as well as the audience to whom it is directed. The majority opinion on this point was expressed by Wilson J. in the following passage, at p. 521:

It is not, in my opinion, open to the courts under s. 159(8) of the Criminal Code to characterize a movie as obscene if shown to one constituency but not if shown to another.... In my view, a movie is either obscene under the Code based on a national community standard of tolerance or it is not. If it is not, it may still be the subject of provincial regulatory control.

(ii) "Degradation or Dehumanization" Test

There has been a growing recognition in recent cases that material which may be said to exploit sex in a "degrading or dehumanizing" manner will necessarily fail the community standards test....

. . . .

Among other things, degrading or dehumanizing materials place women (and sometimes men) in positions of subordination, servile submission or humiliation. They run against the principles of equality and dignity of all human beings. In the appreciation of whether material is degrading or dehumanizing, the appearance of consent is not necessarily determinative. Consent cannot save materials that otherwise contain degrading or dehumanizing scenes. Sometimes the very appearance of consent makes the depicted acts even more degrading or dehumanizing.

This type of material would, apparently, fail the community standards test not because it offends against morals but because it is perceived by public opinion to be harmful to society, particularly to women....

. . . .

(iv) The relationship of the tests to each other

. . . .

Pornography can be usefully divided into three categories: (1) explicit sex with violence, (2) explicit sex without violence but which subjects people to treatment that is degrading or dehumanizing, and (3) explicit sex without violence that is neither degrading nor dehumanizing. Violence in this context includes both actual physical violence and threats of physical violence. Relating these three categories to the terms of s. 163(8) of the Code, the first, explicit sex coupled with violence, is expressly mentioned. Sex coupled with crime, horror or cruelty will sometimes involve violence. Cruelty, for instance, will usually do so. But, even in the absence of violence, sex coupled with crime, horror or cruelty may fall within the second category. As for category (3), subject to the exception referred to below, it is not covered.

Some segments of society would consider that all three categories of pornography cause harm to society because they tend to undermine its moral fibre. Others would contend that none of the categories cause harm. Furthermore there is a range of opinion as to what is degrading or dehumanizing. See Pornography and Prostitution in Canada: Report of the Special Committee on Pornography and Prostitution (1985) (the Fraser Report), vol. 1, at p. 51. Because this is not a matter that is susceptible of proof in the traditional way and because we do not wish to leave it to the individual tastes of judges, we must have a norm that will serve as an arbiter in determining what amounts to an undue exploitation of sex. That arbiter is the community as a whole.

The courts must determine as best they can what the community would tolerate others being exposed to on the basis of the degree of harm that may flow from such exposure. Harm in this context means that it predisposes persons to act in an anti-social manner as, for example, the physical or mental mistreatment of women by men, or, what is perhaps debatable, the reverse. Anti-social conduct for this purpose is conduct which society formally recognizes as incompatible with its proper functioning. The stronger the inference of a risk of harm the lesser the likelihood of tolerance. The inference may be drawn from the material itself or from the material and other evidence. Similarly evidence as to the community standards is desirable but not essential.

In making this determination with respect to the three categories of pornography referred to above, the portrayal of sex coupled with violence will almost always constitute the undue exploitation of sex. Explicit sex which is degrading or dehumanizing may be undue if the risk of harm is substantial. Finally, explicit sex that is not violent and neither degrading nor dehumanizing is generally tolerated in our society and will not qualify as the undue exploitation of sex unless it employs children in its production.

If material is not obscene under this framework, it does not become so by reason of the person to whom it is or may be shown or exposed nor by reason of the place or manner in which it is shown. The availability of sexually explicit materials in theatres and other public places is subject to regulation by competent provincial legislation. Typically such legislation imposes restrictions on the material available to children. See *Nova Scotia Board of Censors* v. *McNeil*, [1978] 2 S.C.R. 662.

The foregoing deals with the interrelationship of the "community standards test" and "the degrading or dehumanizing" test. How does the "internal necessities" test fit into this scheme? The need to apply this test only arises if a work contains sexually explicit material that by itself would constitute the undue exploitation of sex. The portrayal of sex must then be viewed in context to determine whether that is the dominant theme of the work as a whole. Put another way, is undue exploitation of sex the main object of the work or is this portrayal of sex essential to a wider artistic, literary, or other similar purpose? Since the threshold determination must be made on the basis of community standards, that is, whether the sexually explicit aspect is undue, its impact when considered in context must be determined on the same basis. The court must determine whether the sexually explicit material when viewed in the context of the whole work would be tolerated by the community as a whole. Artistic expression rests at the heart of freedom of expression values and any doubt in this regard must be resolved in favour of freedom of expression.

. . . .

(a) Is s. 163 a Limit Prescribed by Law?

The appellant argues that the provision is so vague that it is impossible to apply it. Vagueness must be considered in relation to two issues in this appeal: (1) is the law so vague that it does not qualify as "a limit prescribed by law"; and (2) is it so imprecise that it is not a reasonable limit....

. . . .

Standards which escape precise technical definition, such as "undue", are an inevitable part of the law. The Criminal Code contains other such standards. Without commenting on their constitutional validity, I note that the terms "indecent", "immoral" or "scurrilous", found in ss. 167, 168, 173 and 175, are nowhere defined in the Code. It is within the role of the judiciary to attempt to interpret these terms. If such interpretation yields an intelligible standard, the threshold test for the application of s. 1 is met. In my opinion, the interpretation of s. 163(8) in prior judgments which I have reviewed, as supplemented by these reasons, provides an intelligible standard.

(b) Objective

The respondent argues that there are several pressing and substantial objectives which justify overriding the freedom to distribute obscene materials. Essentially, these objectives are the avoidance of harm resulting from antisocial attitudinal changes that exposure to obscene material causes and the public interest in maintaining a "decent society". On the other hand, the appellant argues that the objective of s. 163 is to have the state act as "moral custodian" in sexual matters and to impose subjective standards of morality.

. . . .

...To impose a certain standard of public and sexual morality, solely because it reflects the conventions of a given community, is inimical to the exercise and enjoyment of individual freedoms, which form the basis of our social contract. D. Dyzenhaus, "Obscenity and the Charter: Autonomy and Equality" (1991), 1 C.R. (4th) 367, at p. 370, refers to this as "legal moralism", of a majority deciding what values should inform individual lives and then coercively imposing those values on minorities. The prevention of "dirt for dirt's sake" is not a legitimate objective which would justify the violation of one of the most fundamental freedoms enshrined in the Charter.

On the other hand, I cannot agree with the suggestion of the appellant that Parliament does not have the right to legislate on the basis of some fundamental conception of morality for the purposes of safeguarding the values which are integral to a free and democratic society. As *Dyzenhaus, supra*, at p. 376, writes:

(d) R. v. Butler

Moral disapprobation is recognized as an appropriate response when it has its basis in Charter values.

As the respondent and many of the interveners have pointed out, much of the criminal law is based on moral conceptions of right and wrong and the mere fact that a law is grounded in morality does not automatically render it illegitimate. In this regard, criminalizing the proliferation of materials which undermine another basic Charter right may indeed be a legitimate objective.

In my view, however, the overriding objective of s. 163 is not moral disapprobation but the avoidance of harm to society. In Towne Cinema, Dickson C.J. stated, at p. 507:

> It is harm to society from undue exploitation that is aimed at by the section, not simply lapses in propriety or good taste.

The harm was described in the following way in the Report on Pornography by the Standing Committee on Justice and Legal Affairs (MacGuigan Report) (1978), at p. 18:4:

> The clear and unquestionable danger of this type of material is that it reinforces some unhealthy tendencies in Canadian society. The effect of this type of material is to reinforce male-female stereotypes to the detriment of both sexes. It attempts to make degradation, humiliation, victimization, and violence in human relationships appear normal and acceptable. A society which holds that egalitarianism, non-violence, consensualism, and mutuality are basic to any human interaction, whether sexual or other, is clearly justified in controlling and prohibiting any medium of depiction, description or advocacy which violates these principles.

. . . .

This Court has thus recognized that the harm caused by the proliferation of materials which seriously offend the values fundamental to our society is a substantial concern which justifies restricting the otherwise full exercise of the freedom of expression. In my view, the harm sought to be avoided in the case of the dissemination of obscene materials is similar. In the words of Nemetz C.J.B.C. in *R. v. Red Hot Video Ltd.* (1985), 45 C.R. (3d) 36 (B.C.C.A.), there is a growing concern that the exploitation of women and children, depicted in publications and films, can, in certain circumstances, lead to "abject and servile victimization" (at pp. 43–44). As Anderson J.A. also noted in that same case, if true equality between male and female persons is to be achieved, we cannot ignore the threat to equality resulting from exposure to audiences of certain types of violent and degrading material. Materials portraying women as a class as objects for sexual exploitation and abuse have a negative impact on "the individual's sense of self-worth and acceptance".

. . . .

... I would therefore conclude that the objective of avoiding the harm associated with the dissemination of pornography in this case is sufficiently pressing and substantial to warrant some restriction on full exercise of the right to freedom of expression. The analysis of whether the measure is proportional to the objective must, in my view, be undertaken in light of the conclusion that the objective of the impugned section is valid only in so far as it relates to the harm to society associated with obscene materials. Indeed, the section as interpreted in previous decisions and in these reasons is fully consistent with that objective. The objective of maintaining conventional standards of propriety, independently of any harm to society, is no longer justified in light of the values of individual liberty which underlie the Charter. This, then, being the objective of s. 163, which I have found to be pressing and substantial, I must now determine whether the section is rationally connected and proportional to this objective....

. . . .

The values which underlie the protection of freedom of expression relate to the search for truth, participation in the political process, and individual self-fulfilment. The Attorney General for Ontario argues that of these, only "individual self-fulfilment", and only in its most base aspect, that of physical arousal, is engaged by pornography. On the other hand, the civil liberties groups argue that pornography forces us to question conventional notions of sexuality and thereby launches us into an inherently political discourse. In their factum, the B.C. Civil Liberties Association adopts a passage from R. West, "The Feminist-Conservative Anti-Pornography Alliance and the 1986 Attorney General's Commission on Pornography Report" (1987), 4 Am. Bar Found. Res. Jo. 681, at p. 696:

> Good pornography has value because it validates women's will to pleasure. It celebrates female nature. It validates a range of female sexuality that is wider and truer than that legitimated by the non-pornographic culture. Pornography (when it is good) celebrates both female pleasure and male rationality.

101

A proper application of the test should not suppress what West refers to as "good pornography". The objective of the impugned provision is not to inhibit the celebration of human sexuality. However, it cannot be ignored that the realities of the pornography industry are far from the picture which the B.C. Civil Liberties Association would have us paint. Shannon J., in *R.* v. *Wagner, supra*, described the materials more accurately when he observed, at p. 331:

> Women, particularly, are deprived of unique human character or identity and are depicted as sexual playthings, hysterically and instantly responsive to male sexual demands. They worship male genitals and their own value depends upon the quality of their genitals and breasts.

In my view, the kind of expression which is sought to be advanced does not stand on an equal footing with other kinds of expression which directly engage the "core" of the freedom of expression values.

This conclusion is further buttressed by the fact that the targeted material is expression which is motivated, in the overwhelming majority of cases, by economic profit. This Court held in *Rocket* v. *Royal College of Dental Surgeons of Ontario*, [1990] 2 S.C.R. 232, at p. 247, that an economic motive for expression means that restrictions on the expression might "be easier to justify than other infringements".

. . . .

I am in agreement with Twaddle J.A. who expressed the view that Parliament was entitled to have a "reasoned apprehension of harm" resulting from the desensitization of individuals exposed to materials which depict violence, cruelty, and dehumanization in sexual relations.

Accordingly, I am of the view that there is a sufficiently rational link between the criminal sanction, which demonstrates our community's disapproval of the dissemination of materials which potentially victimize women and which restricts the negative influence which such materials have on changes in attitudes and behaviour, and the objective.

. . . .

There are several factors which contribute to the finding that the provision minimally impairs the freedom which is infringed.

First, the impugned provision does not proscribe sexually explicit erotica without violence that is not degrading or dehumanizing. It is designed to catch material that creates a risk of harm to society. It might be suggested that proof of actual harm should be required. It is apparent from what I have said above that it is sufficient in this regard for Parliament to have a reasonable basis for concluding that harm will result and this requirement does not demand actual proof of harm.

Second, materials which have scientific, artistic or literary merit are not captured by the provision. As discussed above, the court must be generous in its application of the "artistic defence". For example, in certain cases, materials such as photographs, prints, books and films which may undoubtedly be produced with some motive for economic profit, may nonetheless claim the protection of the Charter in so far as their defining characteristic is that of aesthetic expression, and thus represent the artist's attempt at individual fulfilment. The existence of an accompanying economic motive does not, of itself, deprive a work of significance as an example of individual artistic or self-fulfilment.

Third, in considering whether the provision minimally impairs the freedom in question, it is legitimate for the court to take into account Parliament's past abortive attempts to replace the definition with one that is more explicit. In Irwin Toy, our Court recognized that it is legitimate to take into account the fact that earlier laws and proposed alternatives were thought to be less effective than the legislation that is presently being challenged. The attempt to provide exhaustive instances of obscenity has been shown to be destined to fail (Bill C-54, 2nd Sess., 33rd Parl.). It seems that the only practicable alternative is to strive towards a more abstract definition of obscenity which is contextually sensitive and responsive to progress in the knowledge and understanding of the phenomenon to which the legislation is directed. In my view, the standard of "undue exploitation" is therefore appropriate. The intractable nature of the problem and the impossibility of precisely defining a notion which is inherently elusive makes the possibility of a more explicit provision remote. In this light, it is appropriate to question whether, and at what cost, greater legislative precision can be demanded.

Fourth, while the discussion in this appeal has been limited to the definition portion of s. 163, I would note that the impugned section, with the possible exception of subs. 1, which is not in issue here, has been held by this Court not to extend its reach to the private use or viewing of obscene materials....

(e) *R. v. Latimer*†

[TALLIS J.A. (Sherstobitoff J.A. concurring):]

INTRODUCTION

On November 16, 1994, following a jury trial for first degree murder, the appellant Robert Latimer was convicted of second degree murder for the killing of Tracy, his 12 year old daughter. The presiding judge imposed the mandatory sentence of life imprisonment without eligibility for parole for ten years.

Before dealing with the issues before this Court, we find it convenient to outline, in skeletal form, the circumstances giving rise to this indictment for murder.

BACKGROUND

In October 1993, Tracy, who was 12 years old, suffered from severe cerebral palsy — a permanent condition caused by brain damage at birth. She was quadriplegic. Her physical handicaps of palsy and quadriplegia were such that she was bedridden for most of the time. Except for some slight head and facial movements she was immobile. She was physically helpless and unable to care for herself. She was in continual pain.

In undisputed testimony at trial, her mother described Tracy's day-to-day condition in this way. Tracy had five or six seizures every day, notwithstanding attempts to control her condition with prescribed drugs. She was unable to sit up on her own and could not communicate with her parents and siblings except to laugh or cry.

In February 1990 Tracy underwent surgery for the purpose of balancing the muscles around her pelvis. In August 1992 she underwent further surgery to reduce the abnormal curvature in her back. This surgery was successful but problems then developed in her right hip which became dislocated. This caused considerable pain.

Her attending physicians scheduled further surgery for November 19, 1993 to deal with the dislocated hip and thereby reduce the consequent pain. The recovery period for such surgery was estimated to be approximately one year.

Tracy had to be "spoon fed" in order to eat. Taking food was so difficult for her that she could not consume a sufficient amount of nutrients. Although her weight loss was not characterized as life threatening, it was a matter of concern.

Speaking generally, the Latimer family provided constant care for their daughter Tracy. During the period July to October 1993 she was placed in a group home in North Battleford to provide respite for the family particularly while Mrs. Latimer was pregnant.

After Tracy returned home, Kathleen Johnson, a Social Services worker, learned that an application for permanent placement at the group home had been received from the Latimer family. On October 12, 1993 she spoke to the appellant by phone to ascertain more details of the family's application and wishes. During this discussion the appellant advised her that it was not an urgent matter. If there was any immediate opening at the home he was not sure if they wanted a placement.

While in the appellant's care on Sunday, October 24, 1993 Tracy passed away at her family farm home near Wilkie. Her father remained at home to care for her while her mother and the other three children attended church. When they returned from church at about 1:30 p.m., Mrs. Latimer prepared lunch. Then she went to get Tracy up for lunch but found that she was dead.

At approximately 2:00 p.m. on the same day the appellant spoke to Constable Hartle of the Wilkie detachment of the Royal Canadian Mounted Police and advised him that Tracy had passed away in her sleep. Constable Hartle and the local coroner, Dr. Bhairo, attended at the Latimer farm. The appellant again stated that Tracy had passed away in her sleep. While at the farm Dr. Bhairo examined Tracy's body for any apparent cause of death. He found no evidence of vomit or mucous to suggest suffocation. Under the circumstances Dr. Bhairo arranged for an autopsy.

During his conversation with Constable Hartle the appellant said that Tracy was in pain and that he put her to bed at about 12:30 p.m. He said that he never checked her again. He also told the officer that he wanted Tracy to be cremated. Mrs. Latimer

---

† (1995), 125 D.L.R. (4th) 203 at 208–11, 232–35. [Notes and/or references omitted.]

appeared shocked and shaken by such suggestion but after a private discussion with the appellant in their bedroom, she came out and advised the officer "Yes, we want her cremated." Tracy's body was removed by funeral home personnel.

Constable Hartle did not exclude homicide and conveyed his concern to the coroner. On October 25, 1993 Dr. Waghray, a pathologist, performed an autopsy. During this examination he found no pathological signs that would explain Tracy's death but he did find signs consistent with poisoning. Given these signs, samples of Tracy's blood were forwarded for analysis at the forensic laboratory in Regina. When examined this blood was found to be saturated with carbon monoxide.

Given this finding of death by carbon monoxide poisoning, members of the R.C.M.P. including Constable Hartle treated this matter as a homicide investigation.

On November 4, 1993 members of the R.C.M.P. arrived at the Latimer farm to execute a search warrant. They were accompanied by technicians from SaskPower for the purpose of checking the furnace and water heater in the house for any possible malfunction and consequent release of carbon monoxide. This possibility was excluded because no defects in the system were found.

With that, Sergeant Conlon and Corporal Lyons took the appellant into custody and returned to North Battleford for the purpose of interviewing him. During this interview the appellant admitted his role in causing Tracy's death. Following a *voir dire*, his written statement (P-25) was admitted in evidence before the jury. In this statement the appellant describes how he removed Tracy from her bed and placed her in the cab of a pickup truck in a shed. He then hooked the hose to the exhaust and placed the other end through the back window of the cab. After he left Tracy exposed to carbon monoxide in the cab for a significant period of time, he determined that she was dead and then placed her back in her bed at the house.

Later the same day the appellant returned to his farm with the two interviewing officers and on a "walk through" he pointed out the truck, hoses, rags and other equipment that he used in terminating Tracy's life. This partial re-enactment of events was videotaped at the farm.

At the conclusion of this stage of the investigation the appellant was formally charged with first degree murder.

. . . .

GROUND 4 — FAILURE TO INSTRUCT JURY ON DEFENCE OF NECESSITY

The learned trial judge withdrew the defence of necessity from the jury. This was made clear in the following passage of his instructions:[7]

> ... Mr. Brayford made the argument that if you find that Mr. Latimer committed culpable homicide you should, nevertheless, excuse him and find him not guilty because it was done out of necessity. He says medical science had done everything possible for Tracy but that it was incapable of relieving her excruciating pain. The only humane option was to see her put to sleep. Well, that may be an attractive argument and while the doctrine of necessity can sometimes operate to excuse criminal misconduct, I must tell you as a matter of law that the doctrine does not apply in this case. The defence of necessity exists only where the perpetrator's decision to break the law is inescapable and unavoidable and necessary to avert some imminent risk of peril. It arises only in cases where there is no option, no other choice. That was not the situation here. There was an option, albeit not a particularly happy one. The option was to persevere in the attempts to make Tracy comfortable in her life, however disagreeable and heartwrenching those attempts might have been.

The controlling authority with respect to this defence is *Perka v. The Queen*, 1984 CanLII 23 (S.C.C.), [1984] 2 S.C.R. 232. In *Perka* the Supreme Court recognized necessity as a possible "excuse" in criminal law but emphasized the limitations placed on such defence. This is clearly articulated in the following passages of the judgment of Dickson J. (as he then was) at pp. 248–252:

> Conceptualized as an "excuse", however, the residual defence of necessity is, in my view, much less open to criticism. It rests on a realistic assessment of human weakness, recognizing that a liberal and humane criminal law cannot hold people to the strict obedience of laws in emergency situations where normal human instincts, whether of self-preservation or of altruism, overwhelmingly impel disobedience. The objectivity of the criminal law is preserved; such acts are still wrongful, but in the circumstances they are excusable. Praise is indeed not bestowed, but pardon is, when one does a wrongful act under pressure which, in the words of Aristotle in the *Nicomachean Ethics, supra*, at p.49, "overstrains human nature and which no one could withstand".
>
> ...
>
> Relating necessity to the principle that the law ought not to punish involuntary acts leads to

a conceptualization of the defence that integrates it into the normal rules for criminal liability rather than constituting it as a *sui generis* exception and threatening to engulf large portions of the criminal law. Such a conceptualization accords with our traditional legal, moral and philosophic views as to what sorts of acts and what sorts of actors ought to be punished. In this formulation it is a defence which I do not hesitate to acknowledge and would not hesitate to apply to relevant facts capable of satisfying its necessary prerequisites.

c) *Limitations on the Defence*

If the defence of necessity is to form a valid and consistent part of our criminal law it must, as has been universally recognized, be strictly controlled and scrupulously limited to situations that correspond to its underlying rationale. That rationale, as I have indicated, is the recognition that it is inappropriate to punish actions which are normatively "involuntary". The appropriate controls and limitations on the defence of necessity are, therefore, addressed to ensuring that the acts for which the benefit of the excuse of necessity is sought are truly "involuntary" in the requisite sense.

In *Morgentaler, supra*, I was of the view that any defence of necessity was restricted to instances of non-compliance "in urgent situations of clear and imminent peril when compliance with the law is demonstrably impossible". In my opinion this restriction focuses directly on the "involuntariness" of the purportedly necessitous behaviour by providing a number of tests for determining whether the wrongful act was truly the only realistic reaction open to the actor or whether he was in fact making what in fairness could be called a choice. If he was making a choice, then the wrongful act cannot have been involuntary in the relevant sense.

The requirement that the situation be urgent and the peril be imminent, tests whether it was indeed unavoidable for the actor to act at all. In LaFave & Scott, *Criminal Law* (1972), at p.388, one reads:

> It is sometimes said that the defense of necessity does not apply except in an emergency — when the threatened harm is immediate, the threatened disaster imminent. Perhaps this is but a way of saying that, until the time comes when the threatened harm is immediate, there are generally options open to the defendant to avoid the harm, other than the option of disobeying the literal terms of the law — the rescue ship may appear, the storm may pass; and so the defendant must wait until that hope of survival disappears.

At a minimum the situation must be so emergent and the peril must be so pressing that normal human instincts cry out for action and make a counsel of patience unreasonable.

The requirement that compliance with the law be "demonstrably impossible" takes this assessment one step further. Given that the accused had to act, could he nevertheless realistically have acted to avoid the peril or prevent the harm, without breaking the law? *Was there a legal way out?* I think this is what Bracton means when he lists "necessity" as a defence, providing the wrongful act was not "avoidable". The question to be asked is whether the agent had any real choice: could he have done otherwise? If there is a reasonable legal alternative to disobeying the law, then the decision to disobey becomes a voluntary one, impelled by some consideration beyond the dictates of "necessity" and human instincts.

The importance of this requirement that there be no reasonable legal alternative cannot be overstressed.

Even if the requirements for urgency and "no legal way out" are met, there is clearly a further consideration. There must be some way of assuring proportionality. No rational criminal justice system, no matter how humane or liberal, could excuse the infliction of a greater harm to allow the actor to avert a lesser evil. In such circumstances we expect the individual to bear the harm and refrain from acting illegally. If he cannot control himself we will not excuse him.

Applying these controlling principles to the jury instructions under review, we must reject this ground of appeal. The trial judge was correct in finding that there was no factual foundation for this defence. In this case the appellant's life was not in peril. He was concerned with Tracy's quality of life. The evidence clearly established the bleak future that faced this little girl. Although her scheduled surgery involved a long recovery period, there was the prospect of some pain alleviation.

This is not a case of withholding potentially life-prolonging treatment to a seriously disabled person. It deals with the deliberate decision to terminate another's life rather than continue with the scheduled medical treatment and care. In such circumstances it is no defence for a parent to say because of a severe handicap, a child's life has such diminished value that the child should not live any longer. It does not advance the interest of the state or society to treat such a child as a person of lesser status or dignity than others.

In dealing with this aspect of the case learned counsel for the Crown stressed that Tracy's medical condition was not unique. She pointed to the many families that are visited with a similar type of misfortune. Dr. Snyder testified that one in 1,000 births involve children with cerebral palsy and ten percent of that unfortunate group have severe cerebral palsy. Dr. Dzus, a specialist in orthopaedic surgery limiting her practice mainly to children, testified that in her work at the Kinsmen Children's Centre in Saskatoon, she attended to many children with multiple handicaps similar to Tracy.

Although the appellant did not testify at trial, his statement to the investigating officers indicates how he set about the termination of Tracy's life. There is no evidence that his act in terminating her life was "involuntary" within the test articulated in *Perka*.

Furthermore the evidence is clear that the appellant and his family did have an option. If they could no longer bear the burden of caring for Tracy, there was the real prospect of permanent placement in a group home.

Accordingly this ground of appeal must fail.

Law, Liberalism, and Critics

(a) *Christie v. York Corp.*†

[RINFRET J. Duff C.J. and Crocket and Kerwin JJ.:]

The appellant, who is a negro, entered a tavern owned and operated by the respondent, in the city of Montreal, and asked to be served a glass of beer; but the waiters refused him for the sole reason that they had been instructed not to serve coloured persons. He claimed the sum of $200 for the humiliation he suffered.

The respondent alleged that in giving such instructions to its employees and in so refusing to serve the appellant it was well within its rights; that its business is a private enterprise for gain; and that, in acting as it did, the respondent was merely protecting its business interests.

It appears from the evidence that, in refusing to sell beer to the appellant, the respondent's employees did so quietly, politely and without causing any scene or commotion whatever. If any notice was attracted to the appellant on the occasion in question, it arose out of the fact that the appellant persisted in demanding beer after he had been so refused and went to the length of calling the police, which was entirely unwarranted by the circumstances.

The learned trial judge awarded the appellant the sum of $25 and costs of the action as brought. The only ground of the judgment was that the rule whereby the respondent refused to serve negroes in its tavern was "illegal," according to sections 19 and 33 of the *Quebec Licence Act* (Ch. 25 of R.S.P.Q., 1925).

The Court of King's Bench, however, was of opinion that the sections relied on by the Superior Court did not apply; and considering that, as a general rule, in the absence of any specific law, a merchant or trader is free to carry on his business in the manner he conceives to be best for that business, that Court (Galipeault, J., dissenting) reversed the judgment of the Superior Court and dismissed the appellant's action with costs [(1938) Q.R. 65 K.B. 104.]. The appeal here is by special leave, pursuant to sec. 41 of the *Supreme Court Act* [[1939] S.C.R. 50.].

In considering this case, we ought to start from the proposition that the general principle of the law of Quebec is that of complete freedom of commerce. Any merchant is free to deal as he may choose with any individual member of the public. It is not a question of motives or reasons for deciding to deal or not to deal; he is free to do either. The only restriction to this general principle would be the existence of a specific law, or, in the carrying out of the principle, the adoption of a rule contrary to good morals or public order. ...

.   .   .   .

We will discuss later the effect of sec. 33 of the *Quebec Licence Act,* but for the moment it may be stated that, in this case, either under the law or upon the record, it cannot be argued that the rule adopted by the respondent in the conduct of its establishment was contrary to good morals or public order. Nor could it be said, as the law stood, that the sale of beer in the province of Quebec was either a monopoly or a privileged enterprise.

---

† [1940] S.C.R. 139.

The fact that a business cannot be conducted without a licence does not make the owner or the operator thereof a trader of a privileged class.

The license in this case is mainly for the purpose of raising revenue and also, to a certain extent, for allowing the Government to control the industry; but it does not prevent the operation of the tavern from being a private enterprise to be managed within the discretion of its proprietor.

The only point to be examined therefore is whether sec. 33 of the *Quebec Licence Act*, upon which the learned trial judge relied in maintaining the appellant's action, applies to the present case.

The view of the majority of the Court of King's Bench was that it did not; and we agree with that interpretation.

Section 33 reads:

> No licensee for a restaurant may refuse, without reasonable cause, to give food to travellers.

For the purpose of our decision, there are three words to be considered in that section: "restaurant," "food," and "travellers."

The word "restaurant" is defined in the Act (sec. 19-2):

> A "restaurant" is an establishment, provided with special space and accommodation, where, in consideration of payment, food (without lodging) is habitually furnished to travellers.

The word "traveller" is also defined in the same section as follows:

> A "traveller" is a person who, in consideration of a given price per day, or fraction of a day, on the American or European plan, or per meal, à table d'hôte or à la carte, is furnished by another person with food or lodging, or both.

With the aid of those two definitions in the Act, we think it must be decided that, in this case, the appellant was not a traveller who was asking to be furnished with food in a restaurant.

Perhaps, as stated by the learned trial judge, a glass of beer may, in certain cases, be considered as food. But we have no doubt that, in view of the definitions contained in the Act, the appellant was not a traveller asking for food in a restaurant within the meaning of the statute. In the Act respecting alcoholic liquor (ch. 37 of R.S.P.Q., 1925) we find the definition of the words "restaurant" and "traveller" in exactly the same terms as above. But, in addition, the words "meal" and "tavern" are also defined (Sec. 3, subs. 6 and 9).

Those definitions, so far as material here, are as follows:

> 6. The word "meal" means the consumption of food of a nature and quantity sufficient for the maintenance of the consumer, in one of the following places:
>
> ...
>
> (b) In the dining-room of a restaurant situated in a city or town, and equipped for the accommodation of fifty guests at one time, and which is not only licensed for the reception of travellers but where full meals are regularly served.
>
> 9. The word "tavern" means an establishment specially adapted for the sale by the glass and consumption on the premises of beer as hereinbefore defined, or, in a hotel or restaurant, the room specially adapted for such purpose.

It will be seen therefore that the appellant cannot be brought within the terms of sec. 33 of the *Quebec Licence Act*. He was not a traveller asking for a meal in a restaurant. According to the definitions, he was only a person asking for a glass of beer in a tavern.

As the case is not governed by any specific law or more particularly by sec. 33 of the *Quebec Licence Act*, it falls under the general principle of the freedom of commerce; and it must follow that, when refusing to serve the appellant, the respondent was strictly within its rights.

But perhaps it may be added that the Quebec statutes make a clear distinction between a hotel or a restaurant and a tavern. The Act (sec. 32) provides that "no licensee for a hotel may refuse without just cause to give lodging or food to travellers" and that (sec. 33) "No licensee for a restaurant may refuse without reasonable cause, to give food to travellers."

No similar provision is made for taverns; and, in our opinion, it would follow from the statute itself that the legislature designedly excluded tavern owners from the obligation imposed upon the hotel and restaurant owners.

For these reasons, the appeal ought to be dismissed with costs.

[DAVIS J. (dissenting):]

The appellant is a British subject residing in Verdun near the city of Montreal in the province of Quebec. He came from Jamaica and has been permanently resident in the said province for some twenty years. He is a coloured gentleman — his own words are "a negro" though counsel for the respondent, for what reason I do not know, told him during his examination for discovery that he wanted it on record that he is "not extraordinarily black." He appears to have a good position as a private chauffeur in Montreal. He was a season box subscriber to hockey matches held in the Forum in Montreal and in that building the respondent operates a beer tavern. Beer is sold by the glass for consumption on the premises. Food such as sandwiches is also served, being apparently purchased when required from nearby premises and resold to the customer. The appellant had often on prior occasions to the one in question, when attending the hockey matches dropped into the respondent's tavern and bought beer by the glass there. On the particular evening on which the complaint out of which these proceedings arose occurred, the appellant with two friends — he describes one as a white man and the other as coloured — just before the hockey game went into the respondent's premises in the ordinary course. The appellant put down fifty cents on the table and asked the waiter for three steins of light beer. The waiter declined to fill the order, stating that he was instructed not to serve coloured people. The appellant and his two friends then spoke to the bartender and to the manager, both of whom stated that the reason for refusal was that the appellant was a coloured person. The appellant then telephoned for the police. He says he did this because he wanted the police there to witness the refusal that had been made. The manager repeated to the police the refusal he had previously made. The appellant and his two friends then left the premises of their own accord. The appellant says that this was to his humiliation in the presence of some seventy customers who were sitting around and had heard what occurred.

The appellant then brought this action against the respondent for damages for breach of contract and damages in tort. No objection was taken to the suit having been brought both on contract and in tort on the same set of facts and I assume that this form of action is permissible under the Quebec practice and procedure. The appellant recovered $25 damages and costs at the trial. This judgment was set aside and the action was dismissed with costs upon an appeal to the Court of King's Bench (Appeal Side), Galipeault J. dissenting [(1938) Q.R. 65 K.B. 104.].

The learned trial judge found that the appellant had been humiliated by the refusal and was entitled to be compensated upon the ground that the tavern was a restaurant within the meaning of the *Quebec Licence Act*, R.S.Q. 1925, ch. 25, sec. 19, and that as such the respondent was forbidden by sec. 33 to refuse the appellant. By sec. 19(2) a restaurant is defined as

an establishment, provided with special space and accommodation, where, in consideration of payment, food (without lodging) is habitually furnished to travellers.

By sec. 33,

no licensee for a restaurant may refuse, without reasonable cause, to give food to travellers.

The Court of King's Bench did not consider the above statute, which deals with various licences granted by the government under the Act, applicable to the facts of this case, and, I think rightly, dealt with the case of the tavern under another statute, the *Alcoholic Liquor Act*, R.S.Q. 1925, ch. 37, and the majority of the Court took the view that "chaque propriétaire est maître chez lui" on the doctrine of freedom of commerce — "la liberté du commerce et de l'industrie." Pratte, J. ad hoc agreed with the conclusion of the majority but upon the single ground that the respondent's refusal was made under circumstances such that it could not cause any damage to the appellant. Galipeault, J. dissented upon the ground that the conduct of the respondent towards the appellant was contrary to good morals and the public order — "contre les bonnes moeurs, contre l'ordre public," and considered that under the special legislation in Quebec governing the sale of liquor the respondent was not entitled to the "freedom of commerce" applicable to ordinary merchants and places like theatres, etc. Galipeault, J. would have affirmed the trial judgment.

This Court gave special leave to the appellant to appeal to this Court from the judgment of the Court of King's Bench upon the ground that the matter in controversy in the appeal will involve "matters by which rights in future of the parties may be affected" within the meaning of sec. 41 of the *Supreme Court Act* and also because the matter in controversy is of such general importance that leave to appeal ought to be granted [[1939] S.C.R. 50.].

The question in issue is a narrow one but I regard it as a very important one. That is, Has a tavern keeper in the province of Quebec under the special legislation there in force the right to refuse to sell beer to any one of the public? There is no suggestion that in this case there was any conduct of a disorderly nature or any reason to prompt the refusal to serve the beer to the appellant other than the fact that he was a coloured gentleman.

The province of Quebec in 1921 adopted the policy of complete control within the province of the sale of alcoholic liquors. (The *Alcoholic Liquor Act*, 11 Geo. V, Quebec Statutes 1921, ch. 24, now

R.S.Q. 1925, ch. 37.) The words "alcoholic liquor" in the statute expressly include beer (sec. 3(5)). The word "tavern" means an establishment specially adapted for the sale by the glass and consumption on the premises of beer or, in a hotel or restaurant, the room specially adapted for such purpose (sec. 3(9)). The sale and delivery in the province of alcoholic liquor, with the exception of beer, is forbidden expressly, except that it may be sold or delivered to or by the Quebec Liquor Commission set up by the statute or by any person authorized by it, or in any case provided for by the statute (sec. 22). The sale of beer is specifically dealt with by sec. 25, which provides that

> The sale or delivery of beer is forbidden in the province, unless such sale or delivery be made by the Commission or by a brewer or other person authorized by the Commission under this Act, and in the manner hereinafter set forth.

The Commission is given power by sec. 9d to control the possession, sale and delivery of alcoholic liquor in accordance with the provisions of the statute and by sec. 9e to grant permits for the sale of alcoholic liquor. By sec. 33 the Commission may determine the manner in which a tavern must be furnished and equipped in order to allow the exercise therein of the "privilege conferred by the permit." Beer may be sold by any person in charge of a grocery or of a store where beer only is sold, on condition that no quantity of less than one bottle be sold, that such beer be not consumed in such store, and that a permit therefor be granted him by the Commission, and that such permit be in force (sec. 30(4)). Now as to the sale of beer by the glass, sec. 30(5) provides as follows:

> Any person in charge of a tavern, but in a city or town only, may sell therein beer by the glass, — provided that it be consumed on the premises, and provided that a permit to that effect be granted him by the Commission ... and that such permit be in force.

Section 30 further provides that in every such case the beer must have been bought directly by the holder of the permit from a brewer who is also the holder of a permit. Section 42(3) fixes the days and hours during which any holder of a permit for the sale of beer in a tavern may sell. Then by sec. 43, certain named classes of persons are forbidden to be sold any alcoholic liquor:

1. Any person who has not reached the age of eighteen years;
2. any interdicted person;
3. any keeper or inmate of a disorderly house;
4. any person already convicted of drunkenness or of any offence caused by drunkenness;
5. Any person who habitually drinks alcoholic liquor to excess, and to whom the Commission has, after investigation, decided to prohibit the sale of such liquor upon application to the Commission by the husband, wife, father, mother, brother, sister, curator, employer or other person depending upon or in charge of such person, or by the curé, pastor, or mayor of the place.

But no sale to any of the persons mentioned in 2, 3, 4 or 5 above shall constitute an offence by the vendor unless the Commission has informed him, by registered letter, that it is forbidden to sell to such person. Sec. 46 provides that no beer shall be transported in the province except as therein defined.

By a separate statute, the *Alcoholic Liquor Possession and Transportation Act*, 11 Geo. V (1921), ch. 25, now R.S.Q. 1925, ch. 38, which Act is stated to apply to the whole province, no alcoholic liquor as defined in the *Alcoholic Liquor Act* (which includes beer) shall be kept, possessed or transported in the province except as therein set forth. Subsection 3 of sec. 3 excepts:

> in the residence of any person, for personal consumption and not for sale, provided it has been acquired by and delivered to such person, in his residence, previous to the 1st of May, 1921, or has been acquired by him, since such date, from the Quebec Liquor Commission.

It is plain, then, that the province of Quebec, like most of the other provinces in Canada, took complete control of the sale of liquor in its own province. The permit system enables the public to purchase from either government stores or specially licensed vendors. A glass of beer can only be bought in the province from a person who has been granted by the Government Commission a permit (sec. 33 refers to it as a "privilege") to sell to the public beer in the glass for consumption on the premises. The respondent was a person to whom a permit had been granted. The sole question in this appeal then is whether the respondent, having been given under the statute the special privilege of selling beer in the glass to the public, had the right to pick and choose those of the public to whom he would sell. In this case the refusal was on the ground of the colour of the person. It might well have been on account of the racial antecedents or the religious faith of the person. The statute itself has definitely laid down, by sec. 43, certain classes of persons to whom a licensee must not sell. The question is, Has the licensee the right to set up his own particular code, or is he bound, as the custodian of a government permit to sell to the public, to sell to anyone who is ready to pay the regular price? Disorderly conduct on the premises of course does not enter into our discussion because there is no suggestion of that in this case. One approach to the problem is the application of the doctrine of "freedom of commerce." It was held by the majority in the Court below, in effect, that the licensee is in no different position from a grocer or other merchant who can sell his goods to whom he likes. The opposite view was taken by Galipeault, J. on the ground that the licensee has what is in the nature of a quasi monopolistic right which involves a corresponding duty to sell to the public except in those cases prohibited by statute. Pratte J., ad hoc, did not take either view; his decision rests solely upon the ground that the respondent's refusal was made under circumstances such that it could not cause any damage to the appellant.

. . . .

The question is one of difficulty, as the divergence of judicial opinion in the courts below indicates. My own view is that having regard to the special legislation in Quebec establishing complete governmental control of the sale of beer in the province and particularly the statutory provision which prohibits anyone of the public from buying beer in the glass from anyone but a person granted the special privilege of selling the same, a holder of such a permit from the government to sell beer in the glass to the public has not the right of an ordinary trader to pick and choose those to whom he will sell.

In the changed and changing social and economic conditions, different principles must necessarily be applied to the new conditions. It is not a question of creating a new principle but of applying a different but existing principle of the law. The doctrine that any merchant is free to deal with the public as he chooses had a very definite place in the older economy and still applies to the case of an ordinary merchant, but when the State enters the field and takes exclusive control of the sale to the public of such a commodity as liquor, then the old doctrine of the freedom of the merchant to do as he likes has in my view no application to a person to whom the State has given a special privilege to sell to the public.

If there is to be exclusion on the ground of colour or of race or of religious faith or on any other ground not already specifically provided for by the statute, it is for the legislature itself, in my view, to impose such prohibitions under the exclusive system of governmental control of the sale of liquor to the public which it has seen fit to enact.

The appellant sued for $200. The learned trial judge awarded him $25 damages. I would allow the appeal, set aside the judgment appealed from and restore the judgment at the trial with costs here and below.

Appeal dismissed with costs.

(b) *Delgamuukw v. B.C.*†

(2) **Application of General Principles**

(a) *General Comments*

The general principle of appellate non-interference applies with particular force in this appeal. The trial was lengthy and very complex. There were 318 days of testimony. There were a large number of witnesses, lay and expert. The volume of evidence is enormous. To quote the trial judge at pp. 116–17:

> A total of 61 witnesses gave evidence at trial, many using translators from their native Gitksan or Wet'suwet'en language; "word spellers" to assist the official reporters were required for many witnesses; a further 15 witnesses gave their evidence on commission; 53 territorial affidavits were filed; 30 deponents were cross-examined out of court; there are 23,503 pages of transcript evidence at trial; 5898 pages of transcript of argument; 3,039 pages of commission evidence and 2,553 pages of cross-examination on affidavits (all evidence and oral arguments are conveniently preserved in hard copy and on diskettes); about 9,200 exhibits were filed at trial compris-

---

† [1997] 3 S.C.R. 1010 at 1070–79, per Lamer C.J.

ing, I estimate, well over 50,000 pages; the plaintiffs' draft outline of argument comprises 3,250 pages, the province's 1,975 pages, and Canada's over 1,000 pages; there are 5,977 pages of transcript of argument in hard copy and on diskettes. All parties filed some excerpts from the exhibits they referred to in argument. The province alone submitted 28 huge binders of such documents. At least 15 binders of reply argument were left with me during that stage of the trial.

The result was a judgment of over 400 pages in length.

It is not open to the appellants to challenge the trial judge's findings of fact merely because they disagree with them. I fear that a significant number of the appellants' objections fall into this category. Those objections are too numerous to list in their entirety. The bulk of these objections, at best, relate to alleged instances of misapprehension or oversight of material evidence by the trial judge. However, the respondents have established that, in most situations, there was *some* contradictory evidence that supported the trial judge's conclusion. The question, ultimately, was one of weight, and the appellants have failed to demonstrate that the trial judge erred in this respect.

One objection that I would like to mention specifically, albeit in passing, is the trial judge's refusal to accept the testimony of two anthropologists who were brought in as expert witnesses by the appellants. This aspect of the trial judge's reasons was hotly contested by the appellants in their written submissions. However, I need only reiterate what I have stated above, that findings of credibility, including the credibility of expert witnesses, are for the trial judge to make, and should warrant considerable deference from appellate courts.

On the other hand, the appellants have alleged that the trial judge made a number of serious errors relating to the treatment of the oral histories of the appellants. Those oral histories were expressed in three different forms: (i) the adaawk of the Gitksan, and the kungax of the Wet'suwet'en; (ii) the personal recollections of members of the appellant nations, and (iii) the territorial affidavits filed by the heads of the individual houses within each nation. The trial judge ruled on both the admissibility of, and the weight to be given to, these various forms of oral history without the benefit of my reasons in *Van der Peet*, as will become evident in the discussion that follows.

(b) Adaawk and Kungax

The adaawk and kungax of the Gitksan and Wet'suwet'en nations, respectively, are oral histories of a special kind. They were described by the trial judge, at p. 164, as a "sacred 'official' litany, or history, or recital of the most important laws, history, traditions and traditional territory of a House". The content of these special oral histories includes its physical representation totem poles, crests and blankets. The importance of the adaawk and kungax is underlined by the fact that they are "repeated, performed and authenticated at important feasts" (at p. 164). At those feasts, dissenters have the opportunity to object if they question any detail and, in this way, help ensure the authenticity of the adaawk and kungax. Although they serve largely the same role, the trial judge found that there are some differences in both the form and content of the adaawk and the kungax. For example, the latter is "in the nature of a song ... which is intended to represent the special authority and responsibilities of a chief...." However, these differences are not legally relevant for the purposes of the issue at hand.

It is apparent that the adaawk and kungax are of integral importance to the distinctive cultures of the appellant nations. At trial, they were relied on for two distinct purposes. First, the adaawk was relied on as a component of and, therefore, as proof of the existence of a system of land tenure law internal to the Gitksan, which covered the whole territory claimed by that appellant. In other words, it was offered as evidence of the Gitksan's historical use and occupation of that territory. For the Wet'suwet'en, the kungax was offered as proof of the central significance of the claimed lands to their distinctive culture. As I shall explain later in these reasons, both use and occupation, and the central significance of the lands occupied, are relevant to proof of aboriginal title.

The admissibility of the adaawk and kungax was the subject of a general decision of the trial judge handed down during the course of the trial regarding the admissibility of all oral histories (incorrectly indexed as *Uukw v. R.*, [1987] 6 W.W.R. 155 (B.C.S.C.)). Although the trial judge recognized that the evidence at issue was a form of hearsay, he ruled it admissible on the basis of the recognized exception that declarations made by deceased persons could be given in evidence by witnesses as proof of public or general rights: see Michael N. Howard, Peter Crane and Daniel A. Hochberg, *Phipson on Evidence* (14th ed. 1990), at p. 736. He affirmed that earlier ruling in his trial judgment, correctly in my view, by stating, at p. 180, that the adaawk and kungax were admissible "out of necessity as exceptions to the hearsay rule" because there was no other way to prove the history of the Gitksan and Wet'suwet'en nations.

The trial judge, however, went on to give these oral histories no independent weight at all. He held, at p. 180, that they were only admissible as "direct evidence of facts in issue ... in a few cases where they could constitute confirmatory proof of early presence in the territory". His central concern [was] that the adaawk and kungax could not serve "as evidence of detailed history, or land ownership, use or occupation". I disagree with some of the reasons he relied on in support of this conclusion.

Although he had earlier recognized, when making his ruling on admissibility, that it was impossible to make an easy distinction between the mythological and "real" aspects of these oral histories, he discounted the adaawk and kungax because they were not "literally true", confounded "what is fact and what is belief", "included some material which might be classified as mythology", and projected a "romantic view" of the history of the appellants. He also cast doubt on the authenticity of these special oral histories (at p. 181) because, *inter alia*, "the verifying group is so small that they cannot safely be regarded as expressing the reputation of even the Indian community, let alone the larger community whose opportunity to dispute territorial claims would be essential to weight". Finally, he questioned (at p. 181) the utility of the adaawk and kungax to demonstrate use and occupation because they were "seriously lacking in detail about the specific lands to which they are said to relate".

Although he framed his ruling on weight in terms of the specific oral histories before him, in my respectful opinion, the trial judge in reality based his decision on some general concerns with the use of oral histories as evidence in aboriginal rights cases. In summary, the trial judge gave no independent weight to these special oral histories because they did not accurately convey historical truth, because knowledge about those oral histories was confined to the communities whose histories they were and because those oral histories were insufficiently detailed. However, as I mentioned earlier, these are features, to a greater or lesser extent, of all oral histories, not just the adaawk and kungax. The implication of the trial judge's reasoning is that oral histories should never be given any independent weight and are only useful as confirmatory evidence in aboriginal rights litigation. I fear that if this reasoning were followed, the oral histories of aboriginal peoples would be consistently and systematically undervalued by the Canadian legal system, in contradiction of the express instruction to the contrary in Van der Peet that trial courts interpret the evidence of aboriginal peoples in light of the difficulties inherent in adjudicating aboriginal claims.

(c) Recollections of Aboriginal Life

The trial judge also erred when he discounted the "recollections of aboriginal life" offered by various members of the appellant nations. I take that term to be a reference to testimony about personal and family history that is not part of an adaawk or a kungax. That evidence consisted of the personal knowledge of the witnesses and declarations of witnesses' ancestors as to land use. This history had been adduced by the appellants in order to establish the requisite degree of use and occupation to make out a claim to ownership and, for the same reason as the adaawk and kungax, is material to the proof of aboriginal title.

The trial judge limited the uses to which the evidence could be put. He reasoned, at p. 177, that this evidence, at most, established "without question, that the plaintiff's immediate ancestors, for the past 100 years or so" had used land in the claimed territory for aboriginal purposes. However, the evidence was insufficiently precise to demonstrate that the more distant ancestors of the witnesses had engaged in specific enough land use "far enough back in time to permit the plaintiffs to succeed on issues such as internal boundaries". In the language of *Van der Peet*, the trial judge effectively held that this evidence did not demonstrate the requisite continuity between present occupation and past occupation in order to ground a claim for aboriginal title.

In my opinion, the trial judge expected too much of the oral history of the appellants, as expressed in the recollections of aboriginal life of members of the appellant nations. He expected that evidence to provide definitive and precise evidence of pre-contact aboriginal activities on the territory in question. However, as I held in *Van der Peer*, this will be almost an impossible burden to meet. Rather, if oral history cannot conclusively establish pre-sovereignty (after this decision) occupation of land, it may still be relevant to demonstrate that current occupation has its origins prior to sovereignty. This is exactly what the appellants sought to do.

(d) Territorial Affidavits

Finally, the trial judge also erred in his treatment of the territorial affidavits filed by the appellant chiefs. Those affidavits were declarations of the territorial holdings of each of the Gitksan and Wet'suwet'en houses and, at trial, were introduced for the purposes of establishing each House's owner-ship of its specific territory. Before this Court, the appellants tried to amalgamate these individual claims into collective claims on behalf of each nation and the relevance of the affidavits changed accord-ingly. I have already held that it is not open to the appellants to alter fundamentally the nature of their claim in this way on appeal. Nevertheless, the treat-ment of the affidavits is important because they will be relevant at a new trial to the existence and nature of the land tenure system within each nation and, therefore, material to the proof of title.

The affidavits rely heavily on the declarations of deceased persons of use or ownership of the lands, which are a form of oral history. But those declara-tions are a kind of hearsay and the appellants there-fore argued that the affidavits should be admitted through the reputation exception to the hearsay rule. Although he recognized, at p. 438, that the territorial affidavits were "the best evidence [the appellants] could adduce on this question of internal bound-aries", the trial judge held that this exception did not apply and refused to admit the declarations con-tained in the affidavits.

I am concerned by the specific reasons the trial judge gave for refusing to apply the reputation exception. He questioned the degree to which the declarations amounted to a reputation because they were largely confined to the appellants' communities. The trial judge asserted that neighbouring aboriginal groups whose territorial claims conflicted with those of the appellants, as well as non-aboriginals who potentially possessed a legal interest in the claimed territory, were unaware of the content of the alleged reputation at all. Furthermore, the trial judge rea-soned that since the subject-matter of the affidavits was disputed, its reliability was doubtful. Finally, the trial judge questioned, at p. 441, "the independence and objectivity" of the information contained in the affidavits, because the appellants and their ancestors (at p. 440) "have been actively discussing land claims for many years".

Although he regretted this finding, the trial judge felt bound to apply the rules of evidence because it did not appear to him (at p. 442) "that the Supreme Court of Canada has decided that the ordinary rules of evidence do not apply to this kind of case". The trial judge arrived at this conclusion, however, without the benefit of *Van der Peet*, where I held that the ordinary rules of evidence must be approached and adapted in light of the evidentiary difficulties inherent in adjudicating aboriginal claims.

Many of the reasons relied on by the trial judge for excluding the evidence contained in the territorial

affidavits are problematic because they run against this fundamental principle. The requirement that a reputation be known in the general community, for example, ignores the fact that oral histories, as noted by the Royal Commission on Aboriginal Peoples, generally relate to particular locations, and refer to particular families and communities and may, as a result, be unknown outside of that community, even to other aboriginal nations. Excluding the territorial affidavits because the claims to which they relate are disputed does not acknowledge that claims to aborig-inal rights, and aboriginal title in particular, are almost always disputed and contested. Indeed, if those claims were uncontroversial, there would be no need to bring them to the courts for resolution. Casting doubt on the reliability of the territorial affi-davits because land claims had been actively dis-cussed for many years also fails to take account of the special context surrounding aboriginal claims, in two ways. First, those claims have been discussed for so long because of British Columbia's persistent refusal to acknowledge the existence of aboriginal title in that province until relatively recently, largely as a direct result of the decision of this Court in *Calder*, supra. It would be perverse, to say the least, to use the refusal of the province to acknowledge the rights of its aboriginal inhabitants as a reason for excluding evidence which may prove the existence of those rights. Second, this rationale for exclusion places aboriginal claimants whose societies record their past through oral history in a grave dilemma. In order for the oral history of a community to amount to a form of reputation, and to be admis-sible in court, it must remain alive through the discussions of members of that community; those dis-cussions are the very basis of that reputation. But if those histories are discussed too much, and too close to the date of litigation, they may be discounted as being suspect, and may be held to be inadmissible. The net effect may be that a society with such an oral tradition would never be able to establish a his-torical claim through the use of oral history in court.

(e) Conclusion

The trial judge's treatment of the various kinds of oral histories did not satisfy the principles I laid down in *Van der Peet*. These errors are particularly worrisome because oral histories were of critical importance to the appellants' case. They used those histories in an attempt to establish their occupa-tion and use of the disputed territory, an essential requirement for aboriginal title. The trial judge, after refusing to admit, or giving no independent weight to these oral histories, reached the conclusion that the appellants had not demonstrated the requisite degree of occupation for "ownership". Had the trial judge assessed the oral histories correctly, his conclusions on these issues of fact might have been very different.

In the circumstances, the factual findings cannot stand. However, given the enormous complexity of the factual issues at hand, it would be impossible for the Court to do justice to the parties by sifting through the record itself and making new factual findings. A new trial is warranted, at which the evidence may be considered in light of the principles laid down in *Van der Peet* and elaborated upon here. In applying these principles, the new trial judge might well share some or all of the findings of fact of McEachern C.J.

(c) Women's Rights as Human Rights: Toward a Re-Vision of Human Rights†

Charlotte Bunch

Significant numbers of the world's population are routinely subject to torture, starvation, terrorism, humiliation, mutilation, and even murder simply because they are female. Crimes such as these against any group other than women would be recognized as a civil and political emergency as well as a gross violation of the victims' humanity. Yet, despite a clear record of deaths and demonstrable abuse, women's rights are not commonly classified as human rights. This is problematic both theoretically and practically, because it has grave consequences for the way society views and treats the fundamental issues of women's lives. This paper questions why women's rights and human rights are viewed as distinct, looks at the policy implications of this schism, and discusses different approaches to changing it.

Women's human rights are violated in a variety of ways. Of course, women sometimes suffer abuses such as political repression that are similar to abuses suffered by men. In these situations, female victims are often invisible, because the dominant image of the political actor in our world is male. However, many violations of women's human rights are distinctly connected to being female — that is, women are discriminated against and abused on the basis of gender. Women also experience sexual abuse in situations where their other human rights are being violated, as political prisoners or members of persecuted ethnic groups, for example. In this paper I address those abuses in which gender is a primary or related factor because gender-related abuse has been most neglected and offers the greatest challenge to the field of human rights today.

The concept of human rights is one of the few moral visions ascribed to internationally. Although its scope is not universally agreed upon, it strikes deep chords of response among many. Promotion of human rights is a widely accepted goal and thus provides a useful framework for seeking redress of gender abuse. Further it is one of the few concepts that speaks to the need for transnational activism and concern about the lives of people globally. The Universal Declaration of Human Rights,[1] adopted in 1948, symbolizes this world vision and defines human rights broadly. While not much is said about women, Article 2 entitles all to "the rights and freedoms set forth in this Declaration, without distinction of any kind, such as race, colour, sex, language, religion, political or other opinion, national or social origin, property, birth or other status." Eleanor Roosevelt and the Latin American women who fought for the inclusion of sex in the Declaration and for its passage clearly intended that it would address the problem of women's subordination.[2]

Since 1948 the world community has continuously debated varying interpretations of human rights in response to global developments. Little of this discussion, however, has addressed questions of gender, and only recently have significant challenges been made to a vision of human rights which

---

† (Nov. 1990) 12:4 Human Rights Quarterly 486 at 486–98. © 1990 The John Hopkins University Press. Reproduced with permission The John Hopkins University Press. [Notes and/or references omitted.]

excludes much of women's experiences. The concept of human rights, like all vibrant visions, is not static or the property of any one group; rather, its meaning expands as people reconceive of their needs and hopes in relation to it. In this spirit, feminists redefine human rights abuses to include the degradation and violation of women. The specific experiences of women must be added to traditional approaches to human rights in order to make women more visible and to transform the concept and practice of human rights in our culture so that it takes better account of women's lives.

In the next part of this article, I will explore both the importance and the difficulty of connecting women's rights to human rights, and then I will outline four basic approaches that have been used in the effort to make this connection.

1. BEYOND RHETORIC: POLITICAL IMPLICATIONS

Few governments exhibit more than token commitment to women's equality as a basic human right in domestic or foreign policy. No government determines its policies toward other countries on the basis of their treatment of women, even when some aid and trade decisions are said to be based on a country's human rights record. Among nongovernmental organizations, women are rarely a priority, and Human Rights Day programs on 10 December seldom include discussion of issues like violence against women or reproductive rights. When it is suggested that governments and human rights organizations should respond to women's rights as concerns that deserve such attention, a number of excuses are offered for why this cannot be done. The responses tend to follow one or more of these lines: (1) sex discrimination is too trivial, or not as important, or will come after larger issues of survival that require more serious attention; (2) abuse of women, while regrettable, is a cultural, private, or individual issue and not a political matter requiring state action; (3) while appropriate for other action, women's rights are not human rights per se; or (4) when the abuse of women is recognized, it is considered inevitable or so pervasive that any consideration of it is futile or will overwhelm other human rights questions. It is important to challenge these responses.

The narrow definition of human rights, recognized by many in the West as solely a matter of state violation of civil and political liberties, impedes consideration of women's rights. In the United States

the concept has been further limited by some who have used it as a weapon in the cold war almost exclusively to challenge human rights abuses perpetrated in communist countries. Even then, many abuses that affected women, such as forced pregnancy in Romania, were ignored.

Some important aspects of women's rights do fit into a civil liberties framework, but much of the abuse against women is part of a larger socioeconomic web that entraps women, making them vulnerable to abuses which cannot be delineated as exclusively political or solely caused by states. The inclusion of "second generation" or socioeconomic human rights to food, shelter, and work — which are clearly delineated as part of the Universal Declaration of Human Rights — is vital to addressing women's concerns fully. Further, the assumption that states are not responsible for most violations of women's rights ignores the fact that such abuses, although committed perhaps by private citizens, are often condoned or even sanctioned by states. I will return to the question of state responsibility after responding to other instances of resistance to women's rights as human rights.

The most insidious myth about women's rights is that they are trivial or secondary to the concerns of life and death. Nothing could be farther from the truth: sexism kills. There is increasing documentation of the many ways in which being female is life-threatening. The following are a few examples:

- Before birth: Amniocentesis is used for sex selection leading to the abortion of more female fetuses at rates as high as 99 percent in Bombay, India; in China and India, the two most populous nations, more males than females are born even though natural birth ratios would produce more females.[3]
- During childhood: The World Health Organization reports that in many countries, girls are fed less, breast fed for shorter periods of time, taken to doctors less frequently, and die or are physically and mentally maimed by malnutrition at higher rates than boys.[4]
- In adulthood: The denial of women's rights to control their bodies in reproduction threatens women's lives, especially where this is combined with poverty and poor health services. In Latin America, complications from illegal abortions are the leading cause of death for women between the ages of fifteen and thirty-nine.[5]

Sex discrimination kills women daily. When combined with race, class, and other forms of oppression, it constitutes a deadly denial of women's right to life and liberty on a large scale throughout the world. The most pervasive violation of females is violence against women in all its manifestations, from wife battery, incest, and rape, to dowry deaths,[6] genital mutilation,[7] and female sexual slavery. These abuses occur in every country and are found in the home and in the workplace, on streets, on campuses, and in prisons and refugee camps. They cross class, race, age, and national lines; and at the same time, the forms this violence takes often reinforce other oppressions such as racism, "able-bodyism," and imperialism. Case in point: in order to feed their families, poor women in brothels around US military bases in places like the Philippines bear the burden of sexual, racial, and national imperialism in repeated and often brutal violation of their bodies. Even a short review of random statistics reveals that the extent of violence against women globally is staggering:

- In the United States, battery is the leading cause of injury to adult women, and a rape is committed every six minutes.[8]
- In Peru, 70 percent of all crimes reported to police involve women who are beaten by their partners; and in Lima (a city of seven million people), 168,970 rapes were reported in 1987 alone.[9]
- In India, eight out of ten wives are victims of violence, either domestic battery, dowry-related abuse, or, among the least fortunate, murder.[10]
- In France, 95 percent of the victims of violence are women; 51 percent at the hands of a spouse or lover. Similar statistics from places as diverse as Bangladesh, Canada, Kenya, and Thailand demonstrate that more than 50 percent of female homicides were committed by family members.[11]

Where recorded, domestic battery figures range from 40 percent to 80 percent of women beaten, usually repeatedly, indicating that the home is the most dangerous place for women and frequently the site of cruelty and torture. As the Carol Stuart murder in Boston demonstrated, sexist and racist attitudes in the United States often cover up the real threat to women; a woman is murdered in Massachusetts by a husband or lover every 22 days.[12]

Such numbers do not reflect the full extent of the problem of violence against women, much of which remains hidden. Yet rather than receiving recognition as a major world conflict, this violence is accepted as normal or even dismissed as an individual or cultural matter. Georgina Ashworth notes that:

The greatest restriction of liberty, dignity and movement, and at the same time, direct violation of the person is the threat and realisation of violence.... However violence against the female sex, on a scale which far exceeds the list of Amnesty International victims, is tolerated publicly; indeed some acts of violation are not crimes in law, others are legitimized in custom or court opinion, and most are blamed on the victims themselves.[13]

Violence against women is a touchstone that illustrates the limited concept of human rights and highlights the political nature of the abuse of women. As Lori Heise states: "This is not random violence.... [T]he risk factor is being female."[14] Victims are chosen because of their gender. The message is domination: stay in your place or be afraid. Contrary to the argument that such violence is only personal or cultural, it is profoundly political. It results from the structural relationships of power, domination, and privilege between men and women in society. Violence against women is central to maintaining those political relations at home, at work, and in all public spheres.

Failure to see the oppression of women as political also results in the exclusion of sex discrimination and violence against women from the human rights agenda. Female subordination runs so deep that it is still viewed as inevitable or natural, rather than seen as a politically constructed reality maintained by patriarchal interests, ideology, and institutions. But I do not believe that male violation of women is inevitable or natural. Such a belief requires a narrow and pessimistic view of men. If violence and domination are understood as a politically constructed reality, it is possible to imagine deconstructing that system and building more just interactions between the sexes.

The physical territory of this political struggle over what constitutes women's human rights is women's bodies. The importance of control over women can be seen in the intensity of resistance to laws and social changes that put control of women's bodies in women's hands: reproductive rights, freedom of sexuality whether heterosexual or lesbian, laws that criminalize rape in marriage, etc. Denial of reproductive rights and homophobia are also political means of maintaining control over women and perpetuating sex roles and thus have human rights implications. The physical abuse of women is a reminder of this territorial domination and is sometimes accompanied by other forms of human rights abuse such as slavery (forced prostitution), sexual terrorism (rape), imprisonment (confinement to the home), and torture (systematic battery). Some cases are extreme, such as the women in Thailand who died in a brothel fire because they were chained to their beds. Most situations are more ordinary like denying women decent education or jobs which leaves them prey to abusive marriages, exploitative work, and prostitution.

This raises once again the question of the state's responsibility for protecting women's human rights. Feminists have shown how the distinction between private and public abuse is a dichotomy often used to justify female subordination in the home. Governments regulate many matters in the family and individual spheres. For example, human rights activists pressure states to prevent slavery or racial discrimination and segregation even when these are conducted by nongovernmental forces in private or proclaimed as cultural traditions as they have been in both the southern United States and in South Africa. The real questions are: (1) who decides what are legitimate human rights; and (2) when should the state become involved and for what purposes. Riane Eisler argues that:

> the issue is what types of private acts are and are not protected by the right to privacy and/or the principle of family autonomy. Even more specifically, the issue is whether violations of human rights within the family such as genital mutilation, wife beating, and other forms of violence designed to maintain patriarchal control should be within the purview of human rights theory and action.... [T]he underlying problem for human rights theory, as for most other fields of theory, is that the yardstick that has been developed for defining and measuring human rights has been based on the male as the norm.[15]

The human rights community must move beyond its male defined norms in order to respond to the brutal and systematic violation of women globally. This does not mean that every human rights group must alter the focus of its work. However it does require examining patriarchal biases and acknowledging the rights of women as human rights. Governments must seek to end the politically and culturally constructed war on women rather than continue to perpetuate it. Every state has the responsibility to intervene in the abuse of women's rights within its borders and to end its collusion with the forces that perpetrate such violations in other countries.

II. TOWARD ACTION: PRACTICAL APPROACHES

The classification of human rights is more than just a semantics problem because it has practical policy consequences. Human rights are still considered to be more important than women's rights. The distinction perpetuates the idea that the rights of women are of a lesser order than the "rights of man," and, as Eisler describes it, "serves to justify practices that do not accord women full and equal status."[16] In the United Nations, the Human Rights Commission has more power to hear and investigate cases than the Commission on the Status of Women, more staff and budget, and better mechanisms for implementing its findings. Thus it makes a difference in what can be done if a case is deemed a violation of women's rights and not of human rights.[17]

The determination of refugee status illustrates how the definition of human rights affects people's lives. The Dutch Refugee Association, in its pioneering efforts to convince other nations to recognize sexual persecution and violence against women as justifications for granting refugee status, found that some European governments would take sexual persecution into account as an aspect of other forms of political repression, but none would make it the grounds for refugee status per se.[18] The implications of such a distinction are clear when examining a situation like that of the Bangladeshi women, who having been raped during the Pakistan–Bangladesh war, subsequently faced death at the hands of male relatives to preserve "family honor." Western powers professed outrage but did not offer asylum to these victims of human rights abuse.

I have observed four basic approaches to linking women's rights to human rights. These approaches are presented separately here in order to identify each more clearly. In practice, these approaches often overlap, and while each raises questions about the others, I see them as complementary. These approaches can be applied to many issues, but I will illustrate them primarily in terms of how they address violence against women in order to show the implications of their differences on a concrete issue.

1. Women's Rights as Political and Civil Rights.

Taking women's specific needs into consideration as part of the already recognized "first generation" political and civil liberties is the first approach. This involves both raising the visibility of women who suffer general human rights violations as well as calling attention to particular abuses women encounter because they are female. Thus, issues of violence against women are raised when they connect to other forms of violation such as the sexual torture of women political prisoners in South America.[19]

Groups like the Women's Task Force of Amnesty International have taken this approach in pushing for Amnesty to launch a campaign on behalf of women political prisoners which would address the sexual abuse and rape of women in custody, their lack of maternal care in detention, and the resulting human rights abuse of their children.

Documenting the problems of women refugees and developing responsive policies are other illustrations of this approach. Women and children make up more than 80 percent of those in refugee camps, yet few refugee policies are specifically shaped to meet the needs of these vulnerable populations who face considerable sexual abuse. For example, in one camp where men were allocated the community's rations, some gave food to women and their children in exchange for sex. Revealing this abuse led to new policies that allocated food directly to the women.[20]

The political and civil rights approach is a useful starting point for many human rights groups; by considering women's experiences, these groups can expand their efforts in areas where they are already working. This approach also raises contradictions that reveal the limits of a narrow civil liberties view. One contradiction is to define rape as a human rights abuse only when it occurs in state custody but not on the streets or in the home. Another is to say that a violation of the right to free speech occurs when someone is jailed for defending gay rights, but not when someone is jailed or even tortured and killed for homosexuality. Thus while this approach of adding women and stirring them into existing first generation human rights categories is useful, it is not enough by itself.

2. Women's Rights as Socioeconomic Rights.

The second approach includes the particular plight of women with regard to "second generation" human rights such as the rights to food, shelter, health care, and employment. This is an approach favored by those who see the dominant Western human rights tradition and international law as too individualistic and identify women's oppression as primarily economic.

This tendency has its origins among socialists and labor activists who have long argued that political human rights are meaningless to many without economic rights as well. It focuses on the primacy of the need to end women's economic subordination as the key to other issues including women's vulnerability to violence. This particular focus has led to work on issues like women's right to organize as workers and opposition to violence in the workplace, especially in situations like the free trade zones which have targeted women as cheap, nonorganized labor. Another focus of this approach has been highlighting the feminization of poverty or what might better be called the increasing impoverishment of females. Poverty has not become strictly female, but females now comprise a higher percentage of the poor.

Looking at women's rights in the context of socioeconomic development is another example of this approach. Third world peoples have called for an understanding of socioeconomic development as a human rights issue. Within this demand, some have sought to integrate women's rights into development and have examined women's specific needs in relation to areas like land ownership or access to credit. Among those working on women in development, there is growing interest in violence against women as both a health and development issue. If violence is seen as having negative consequences for social productivity, it may get more attention. This type of narrow economic measure, however, should not determine whether such violence is seen as a human rights concern. Violence as a development issue is linked to the need to understand development not just as an economic issue but also as a question of empowerment and human growth.

One of the limitations of this second approach has been its tendency to reduce women's needs to the economic sphere which implies that women's rights will follow automatically with third world development, which may involve socialism. This has not proven to be the case. Many working from this approach are no longer trying to add women into either the Western capitalist or socialist development models, but rather seek a transformative development process that links women's political, economic, and cultural empowerment.

3. Women's Rights and the Law.

The creation of new legal mechanisms to counter sex discrimination characterizes the third approach to women's rights as human rights. These efforts seek to make existing legal and political institutions work for women and to expand the state's responsibility for the violation of women's human rights. National and local laws which address sex discrimination and violence against women are examples of this approach. These measures allow women to fight for their rights within the legal system. The primary international illustration is the Convention on the Elimination of All Forms of Discrimination Against Women.[21]

The Convention has been described as "essentially an international bill of rights for women and a framework for women's participation in the development process ... [which] spells out internationally accepted principles and standards for achieving equality between women and men."[22] Adopted by the UN General Assembly in 1979, the Convention has been ratified or acceded to by 104 countries as of January 1990. In theory these countries are obligated to pursue policies in accordance with it and to report on their compliance to the Committee on the Elimination of Discrimination Against Women (CEDAW). While the Convention addresses many issues of sex discrimination, one of its shortcomings is failure to directly address the question of violence against women. CEDAW passed a resolution at its eighth session in Vienna in 1989 expressing concern that this issue be on its agenda and instructing states to include in their periodic reports information about statistics, legislation, and support services in this area.[23] The Commonwealth Secretariat in its manual on the reporting process for the Convention also interprets the issue of violence against women as "clearly fundamental to the spirit of the Convention," especially in Article 5 which calls for the modification of social and cultural patterns, sex roles, and stereotyping that are based on the idea of the inferiority or the superiority of either sex.[24]

The Convention outlines a clear human rights agenda for women which, if accepted by governments, would mark an enormous step forward. It also carries the limitations of all such international documents in that there is little power to demand its implementation. Within the United Nations, it is not generally regarded as a convention with teeth, as illustrated by the difficulty that CEDAW has had in getting countries to report on compliance with its provisions. Further, it is still treated by governments and most non-governmental organizations as a document dealing with women's (read "secondary") rights, not human rights. Nevertheless, it is a useful statement of principles endorsed by the United Nations around which women can organize to achieve legal and political change in their regions.

4.   Feminist Transformation of Human Rights.

Transforming the human rights concept from a feminist perspective, so that it will take greater account of women's lives, is the fourth approach. This approach relates women's rights and human rights, looking first at the violations of women's lives and then asking how the human rights concept can change to be more responsive to women. For example, the GABRIELA women's coalition in the Philippines simply stated that "Women's Rights are Human Rights" in launching a campaign last year. As Ninotchka Rosca explained, coalition members saw that "human rights are not reducible to a question of legal and due process. ... In the case of women, human rights are affected by the entire society's traditional perception of what is proper or not proper for women."[25] Similarly, a panel at the 1990 International Women's Rights Action Watch conference asserted that "Violence Against Women is a Human Rights Issue." While work in the three previous approaches is often done from a feminist perspective, this last view is the most distinctly feminist with its woman-centered stance and its refusal to wait for permission from some authority to determine what is or is not a human rights issue.

This transformative approach can be taken toward any issue, but those working from this approach have tended to focus most on abuses that arise specifically out of gender, such as reproductive rights, female sexual slavery, violence against women, and "family crimes" like forced marriage, compulsory heterosexuality, and female mutilation. These are also the issues most often dismissed as not really human rights questions. This is therefore the most hotly contested area and requires that barriers be broken down between public and private, state and nongovernmental responsibilities.

Those working to transform the human rights vision from this perspective can draw on the work of others who have expanded the understanding of human rights previously. For example, two decades ago there was no concept of "disappearances" as a human rights abuse. However, the women of the Plaza de Mayo in Argentina did not wait for an official declaration but stood up to demand state accountability for these crimes. In so doing, they helped to create a context for expanding the concept of responsibility for deaths at the hands of paramilitary or right-wing death squads which, even if not carried out by the state, were allowed by it to happen. Another example is the developing concept that civil rights violations include "hate crimes," violence that is racially motivated or directed against homosexuals, Jews, or other minority groups. Many accept that states have an obligation to work to prevent such human rights abuses, and getting violence against women seen as a hate crime is being pursued by some.

The practical applications of transforming the human rights concept from feminist perspectives need to be explored further. The danger in pursuing

120

only this approach is the tendency to become iso-lated from and competitive with other human rights groups because they have been so reluctant to address gender violence and discrimination. Yet most women experience abuse on the grounds of sex, race, class, nation, age, sexual preference, and politics as interrelated, and little benefit comes from separating them as competing claims. The human rights com-munity need not abandon other issues but should incorporate gender perspectives into them and see how these expand the terms of their work. By recog-nizing issues like violence against women as human rights concerns, human rights scholars and activists do not have to take these up as their primary tasks. However, they do have to stop gate-keeping and guarding their prerogative to determine what is con-sidered a "legitimate" human rights issue.

As mentioned before, these four approaches are overlapping and many strategies for change involve elements of more than one. All of these approaches contain aspects of what is necessary to achieve women's rights. At a time when dualist ways of thinking and views of competing economic systems are in question, the creative task is to look for ways to connect these approaches and to see how we can go beyond exclusive views of what people need in their lives. In the words of an early feminist group, we need bread and roses, too. Women want food and liberty and the possibility of living lives of dignity free from domination and violence. In this struggle, the recognition of women's rights as human rights can play an important role.

(d) Racially Based Jury Nullification: Black Power in the Criminal Justice System†

Paul Butler

INTRODUCTION

I was a Special Assistant United States Attorney in the District of Columbia in 1990. I prosecuted peo-ple accused of misdemeanor crimes, mainly the drug and gun cases that overwhelm the local courts of most American cities.[3] As a federal prosecutor, I represented the United States of America and used that power to put people, mainly African-American men, in prison. I am also an African-American man. While at the U.S. Attorney's office, I made two dis-coveries that profoundly changed the way I viewed my work as a prosecutor and my responsibilities as a black person.

The first discovery occurred during a training session for new Assistants conducted by experienced prosecutors. We rookies were informed that we would lose many of our cases, despite having per-suaded a jury beyond a reasonable doubt that the defendant was guilty. We would lose because some

black jurors would refuse to convict black defendants who they knew were guilty.

The second discovery was related to the first, but was even more unsettling. It occurred during the trial of Marion Barry, then the second-term mayor of the District of Columbia. Barry was being prose-cuted by my office for drug possession and perjury. I learned, to my surprise, that some of my fellow African-American prosecutors hoped that the mayor would be acquitted, despite the fact that he was obviously guilty of at least one of the charges — he had smoked cocaine on FBI videotape.[4] These black prosecutors wanted their office to lose its case because they believed that the prosecution of Barry was racist.

Federal prosecutors in the nation's capital hear many rumors about prominent officials engaging in illegal conduct, including drug use. Some African-American prosecutors wondered why, of all those people, the government chose to "set up" the most

† (1995) 105 Yale L.J. 677 at 678–80, 690–701, 705–14, 725. Reproduced with permission of Paul Butler and The Yale Law Journal Com-pany, Inc. [Notes and/or references omitted.]

famous black politician in Washington, D.C.[5] They also asked themselves why, if crack is so dangerous, the FBI had allowed the mayor to smoke it. Some members of the predominantly black jury must have had similar concerns: They convicted the mayor of only one count of a fourteen-count indictment, despite the trial judge's assessment that he had "'never seen a stronger government case.'"[6] Some African-American prosecutors thought that the jury, in rendering its verdict, jabbed its black thumb in the face of a racist prosecution, and that idea made those prosecutors glad.

As such reactions suggest, lawyers and judges increasingly perceive that some African-American jurors vote to acquit black defendants for racial reasons,[7] a decision sometimes expressed as the juror's desire not to send yet another black man to jail.[8] This Essay examines the question of what role race should play in black jurors' decisions to acquit defendants in criminal cases. Specifically, I consider trials that include both African-American defendants and African-American jurors. I argue that the race of a black defendant is sometimes a legally and morally appropriate factor for jurors to consider in reaching a verdict of not guilty or for an individual juror to consider in refusing to vote for conviction.[9]

My thesis is that, for pragmatic and political reasons, the black community is better off when some nonviolent lawbreakers remain in the community rather than go to prison. The decision as to what kind of conduct by African-Americans ought to be punished is better made by African-Americans themselves, based on the costs and benefits to their community, than by the traditional criminal justice process, which is controlled by white lawmakers and white law enforcers. Legally, the doctrine of jury nullification gives the power to make this decision to African-American jurors who sit in judgment of African-American defendants. Considering the costs of law enforcement to the black community and the failure of white lawmakers to devise significant nonincarcerative responses to black antisocial conduct, it is the moral responsibility of black jurors to emancipate some guilty black outlaws.

· · · ·

My goal is the subversion of American criminal justice, at least as it now exists. Through jury nullification, I want to dismantle the master's house with the master's tools.[10] My intent, however, is not purely destructive; this project is also constructive, because I hope that the destruction of the status quo will not lead to anarchy, but rather to the imple-

mentation of certain noncriminal ways of addressing antisocial conduct. Criminal conduct among African-Americans is often a predictable reaction to oppression. Sometimes black crime is a symptom of internalized white supremacy; other times it is a reasonable response to the racial and economic subordination every African-American faces every day. Punishing black people for the fruits of racism is wrong if that punishment is premised on the idea that it is the black criminal's "just desert." Hence, the new paradigm of justice that I suggest in Part III rejects punishment for the sake of retribution and endorses it, with qualifications, for the ends of deterrence and incapacitation.

In a sense, this Essay simply may argue for the return of rehabilitation as the purpose of American criminal justice, but a rehabilitation that begins with the white-supremacist beliefs that poison the minds of us all—you, me, and the black criminal. I wish that black people had the power to end racial oppression right now. African-Americans can prevent the application of one particularly destructive instrument of white supremacy—American criminal justice—to some African-American people, and this they can do immediately. I hope that this Essay makes the case for why and how they should.[11]

· · · ·

II. "JUSTICE OUTSIDE THE FORMAL RULES OF LAW"[71]

Why would a black juror vote to let a guilty person go free? Assuming that the juror is a rational actor, she must believe that she and her community are, in some way, better off with the defendant out of prison than in prison. But how could any rational person believe that about a criminal? The following section describes racial critiques of the American criminal justice system. I then examine the evolution of the doctrine of jury nullification and argue that its practice by African-Americans is, in many cases, consistent with the Anglo-American tradition and, moreover, is legally and morally right.

A. The Criminal Law and African-Americans: Justice or "Just us"?[72]

Imagine a country in which more than half of the young male citizens are under the supervision of the criminal justice system, either awaiting trial, in prison, or on probation or parole.[73] Imagine a country in which two-thirds of the men can anticipate being arrested before they reach age thirty.[74] Imagine a country in which there are more young men in prison than in college.[75] Now give the citizens of the country the key to the prison. Should they use it?

Such a country bears some resemblance to a police state. When we criticize a police state, we think that the problem lies not with the citizens of the state, but rather with the form of government or law, or with the powerful elites and petty bureaucrats whose interests the state serves. Similarly, racial critics of American criminal justice locate the problem not so much with the black prisoners as with the state and its actors and beneficiaries. As evidence, they cite their own experiences and other people's stories,[76] African-American history, understanding gained from social science research on the power and pervasiveness of white supremacy, and ugly statistics like those in the preceding paragraph.

For analytical purposes, I will create a false dichotomy among racial critics by dividing them into two camps: liberal critics and radical critics. Those are not names that the critics have given themselves or that they would necessarily accept, and there would undoubtedly be disagreement within each camp and theoretical overlap between the camps. Nonetheless, for the purposes of a brief explication of racial critiques, my oversimplification may be useful.

1. The Liberal Critique

According to this critique, American criminal justice is racist because it is controlled primarily by white people, who are unable to escape the culture's dominant message of white supremacy, and who are therefore inevitably, even if unintentionally, prejudiced.[77] These white actors include legislators, police, prosecutors, judges, and jurors. They exercise their discretion to make and enforce the criminal law in a discriminatory fashion.[78] Sometimes the discrimination is overt, as in the case of Mark Fuhrman, the police officer in the O.J. Simpson case who, in interviews, used racist language and boasted of his own brutality,[79] and sometimes it is unintentional, as with a hypothetical white juror who invariably credits the testimony of a white witness over that of a black witness.

The problem with the liberal critique is that it does not adequately explain the extent of the difference between the incidence of black and white crime, especially violent crime. For example, in 1991, blacks constituted about fifty-five percent of the 18,096 people arrested for murder and non-negligent manslaughter in the United States (9924 people).[80] One explanation the liberal critique offers for this unfortunate statistic is that the police pursue black murder suspects more aggressively than they

do white murder suspects. In other words, but for discrimination, the percentage of blacks arrested for murder would be closer to their percentage of the population, roughly twelve percent.[81] The liberal critique would attribute some portion of the additional forty-three percent of non-negligent homicide arrestees (in 1991, approximately 7781 people[82]) to race prejudice. Ultimately, however, those assumptions strain credulity, not because many police officers are not racist, but because there is no evidence that there is a crisis of that magnitude in criminal justice. In fact, for all the faults of American law enforcement, catching the bad guys seems to be something it does rather well. The liberal critique fails to account convincingly for the incidence of black crime.

2. The Radical Critique

The radical critique does not discount the role of discrimination in accounting for some of the racial disparity in crime rates, but it also does not, in contrast to the liberal critique, attribute all or even most of the differential to police and prosecutor prejudice. The radical critique offers a more fundamental, structural explanation.

It suggests that criminal law is racist[83] because, like other American law, it is an instrument of white supremacy.[84] Law is made by white elites to protect their interests and, especially, to preserve the economic status quo, which benefits those elites at the expense of blacks, among others.[85] Due to discrimination and segregation, the majority of African-Americans receive few meaningful educational and employment opportunities and, accordingly, are unable to succeed, at least in the terms of the capitalist ideal.[86] Some property crimes committed by blacks may be understood as an inevitable result of the tension between the dominant societal message equating possession of material resources with success and happiness and the power of white supremacy to prevent most African-Americans from acquiring "enough" of those resources in a legal manner. "Black-on-black" violent crime, and even "victimless" crime like drug offenses, can be attributed to internalized racism, which causes some African-Americans to devalue black lives — either those of others or their own. The political process does not allow for the creation or implementation of effective "legal" solutions to this plight,[87] and the criminal law punishes predictable reactions to it.[88]

I am persuaded by the radical critique when I wonder about the roots of the ugly truth that blacks commit many crimes at substantially higher rates than whites. Most white Americans, especially liberals, would publicly offer an environmental, as opposed to genetic, explanation for this fact.[89] They would probably concede that racism, historical and current, plays a major role in creating an environment that breeds criminal conduct. From this premise, the radical critic deduces that but for the (racist) environment, the African-American criminal would not be a criminal. In other words, racism creates and sustains the criminal breeding ground, which produces the black criminal. Thus, when many African-Americans are locked up, it is because of a situation that white supremacy created.

Obviously, most blacks are not criminals, even if every black is exposed to racism. To the radical critics, however, the law-abiding conduct of the majority of African-Americans does not mean that racism does not create black criminals. Not everyone exposed to a virus will become sick, but that does not mean that the virus does not cause the illness of the people who do.

The radical racial critique of criminal justice is premised as much on the criminal law's *effect* as on its intent. The system is discriminatory, in part, because of the disparate impact law enforcement has on the black community.[90] This unjust effect is measured in terms of the costs to the black community of having so many African-Americans, particularly males, incarcerated or otherwise involved in the criminal justice system. These costs are social and economic, and include the perceived dearth of men "eligible" for marriage,[91] the large percentage of black children who live in female-headed households,[92] the lack of male "role models" for black children, especially boys,[93] the absence of wealth in the black community,[94] and the large unemployment rate among black men.[95]

3. Examples of Racism in Criminal Justice

Examples commonly cited by both liberal and radical critics as evidence of racism in criminal justice include: the Scottsboro case;[96] the history of the criminalization of drug use;[97] past and contemporary administration of the death penalty;[98] the use of imagery linking crime to race in the 1988 presidential campaign[99] and other political campaigns;[100] the beating of Rodney King and the acquittal of his police assailants;[101] disparities between punishments for white-collar crimes and punishments for other crimes;[102] more severe penalties for crack cocaine users than for powder cocaine users;[103] the Charles Murray and Susan Smith cases;[104] police corruption scandals in minority neighborhoods in New York and Philadelphia;[105] the O.J. Simpson case, including the extraordinary public and media fascination with it,[106]

the racist police officer who was the prosecution's star witness,[107] and the response of many white people to the jury's verdict of acquittal;[108] and, cited most frequently, the extraordinary rate of incarceration of African-American men.[109]

4. Law Enforcement Enthusiasts

Of course, the idea that the criminal justice system is racist and oppressive is not without dissent, and among the dissenters are some African-Americans. Randall Kennedy succinctly poses the counterargument:

> Although the administration of criminal justice has, at times, been used as an instrument of racial oppression, the principal problem facing African-Americans in the context of criminal justice today is not over-enforcement but under-enforcement of the laws. The most lethal danger facing African-Americans in their day-to-day lives is not white, racist officials of the state, but private, violent criminals (typically black) who attack those most vulnerable to them without regard to racial identity.[110]

According to these theorists, whom I will call law enforcement enthusiasts, the criminal law may have a disproportionate impact on the black community, but this is not a moral or racial issue because the disproportionate impact is the law's effect, not its intent. For law enforcement enthusiasts, intent is the most appropriate barometer of governmental racism.[111] Because law enforcement is a public good, it is in the best interest of the black community to have more, rather than less, of it. Allowing criminals to live unfettered in the community would harm, in particular, the black poor, who are disproportionately the victims of violent crime. Indeed, the logical conclusion of the enthusiasts' argument is that African-Americans would be better off with more, not fewer, black criminals behind bars.

To my mind, the enthusiasts embrace law enforcement too uncritically: They are blind to its opportunity costs. I agree that criminal law enforcement constitutes a public good for African-Americans when it serves the social protection goals that Professor Kennedy highlights. In other words, when locking up black men means that "violent criminals ... who attack those most vulnerable"[112] are off the streets, most people — including most law enforcement critics — would endorse the incarceration. But what about when locking up a black man has no or little net effect on public safety, when, for example, the crime with which he was charged is victimless?[113] Putting aside for a moment the legal implications, couldn't an analysis of the costs and benefits to the African-American community present an argument against incarceration? I argue "yes," in light of the substantial costs to the community of law enforcement. I accept that other reasonable people may disagree. But the law enforcement enthusiasts seldom acknowledge that racial critics even weigh the costs and benefits; their assumption seems to be that the racial critics are foolish or blinded by history or motivated by their own ethnocentrism.[114]

5. The Body Politic and the Racial Critiques

I suspect that many white people would agree with the racial critics' analysis, even if most whites would not support a solution involving the emancipation of black criminals. I write this Essay, however, out of concern for African-Americans and how they can use the power they have now to create change. The important practicability question is how many African-Americans embrace racial critiques of the criminal justice system and how many are law enforcement enthusiasts?

According to a recent *USA Today/CNN/Gallup* poll, sixty-six percent of blacks believe that the criminal justice system is racist and only thirty-two percent believe it is not racist.[115] Interestingly, other polls suggest that blacks also tend to be more worried about crime than whites;[116] this seems logical when one considers that blacks are more likely to be the victims of crime.[117] This enhanced concern, however, does not appear to translate into endorsement of tougher enforcement of traditional criminal law. For example, substantially fewer blacks than whites support the death penalty,[118] and many more blacks than whites were concerned with the potential racial consequences of the strict provisions of the Crime Bill of 1994.[119] While polls are not, perhaps, the most reliable means of measuring sentiment in the African-American community, the polls, along with significant evidence from popular culture,[120] suggest that a substantial portion of the African-American community sympathizes with racial critiques of the criminal justice system.

African-American jurors who endorse these critiques are in a unique position to act on their beliefs when they sit in judgment of a black defendant. As jurors, they have the power to convict the defendant or to set him free. May the responsible exercise of that power include voting to free a black defendant who the juror believes is guilty? The next section suggests that, based on legal doctrine concerning the

role of juries in general, and the role of black jurors in particular, the answer to this question is "yes."

B. Jury Nullification

When a jury disregards evidence presented at trial and acquits an otherwise guilty defendant, because the jury objects to the law that the defendant violated or to the application of the law to that defendant, it has practiced jury nullification. In this section, I describe the evolution of this doctrine and consider its applicability to African-Americans. I then examine Supreme Court cases that discuss the role of black people on juries. In light of judicial rulings in these areas, I argue that it is both lawful and morally right that black jurors consider race in reaching verdicts in criminal cases.

1. What Is Jury Nullification?

Jury nullification occurs when a jury acquits a defendant who it believes is guilty of the crime with which he is charged. In finding the defendant not guilty, the jury refuses to be bound by the facts of the case or the judge's instructions regarding the law. Instead, the jury votes its conscience. In the United States, the doctrine of jury nullification originally was based on the common law idea that the function of a jury was, broadly, to decide justice, which included judging the law as well as the facts.[121] If jurors believed that applying a law would lead to an unjust conviction, they were not compelled to convict someone who had broken that law.[122] Although most American courts now disapprove of a jury's deciding anything other than the "facts," the Double Jeopardy Clause of the Fifth Amendment prohibits appellate reversal of a jury's decision to acquit, regardless of the reason for the acquittal.[123] Thus, even when a trial judge thinks that a jury's acquittal directly contradicts the evidence, the jury's verdict must be accepted as final.[124] The jurors, in judging the law, function as an important and necessary check on government power.[125]

. . . .

C. The Moral Case for Jury Nullification by African-Americans

Any juror legally may vote for nullification in any case, but, certainly, jurors should not do so without some principled basis. The reason that some historical examples of nullification are viewed approvingly is that most of us now believe that the jurors in those cases did the morally right thing; it would have been unconscionable, for example, to punish those slaves who committed the crime of escaping to the North for their freedom. It is true that nullification later would be used as a means of racial subordination by some Southern jurors,[155] but that does not mean that nullification in the approved cases was wrong. It only means that those Southern jurors erred in their calculus of justice. I distinguish racially based nullification by African-Americans from recent right-wing proposals for jury nullification[156] on the ground that the former is sometimes morally right and the latter is not.

The question of how to assign the power of moral choice is a difficult one. Yet we should not allow that difficulty to obscure the fact that legal resolutions involve moral decisions, judgments of right and wrong. The fullness of time permits us to judge the fugitive slave case differently than the Southern pro-white-violence case. One day we will be able to distinguish between racially based nullification and that proposed by certain right-wing activist groups.[157] We should remember that the morality of the historically approved cases was not so clear when those brave jurors acted. After all, the fugitive slave law was enacted through the democratic process, and those jurors who disregarded it subverted the rule of law. Presumably, they were harshly criticized by those whose interests the slave law protected. Then, as now, it is difficult to see the picture when you are inside the frame.

In this section, I explain why African-Americans have the moral right to practice nullification in particular cases.[158] I do so by responding to the traditional moral critiques of jury nullification.

1. African-Americans and the "Betrayal" of Democracy

There is no question that jury nullification is subversive of the rule of law. It appears to be the antithesis of the view that courts apply settled, standing laws and do not "dispense justice in some ad hoc, case-by-case basis."[159] To borrow a phrase from the D.C. Circuit, jury nullification "betrays rather than furthers the assumptions of viable democracy."[160] Because the Double Jeopardy Clause makes this power part-and-parcel of the jury system, the issue becomes whether black jurors have any moral right to "betray democracy" in this sense. I believe that they do for two reasons that I borrow from the jurisprudence of legal realism and critical race theory: First, the idea of "the rule of law" is more mythological than real, and second, "democracy," as practiced in the United States, has betrayed African-Americans far more than they could ever

betray it. Explication of these theories has consumed legal scholars for years, and is well beyond the scope of this Essay. I describe the theories below not to persuade the reader of their rightness, but rather to make the case that a reasonable juror might hold such beliefs, and thus be morally justified in subverting democracy through nullification.

2. The Rule of Law as Myth

The idea that "any result can be derived from the preexisting legal doctrine" either in every case or many cases,[161] is a fundamental principle of legal realism (and, now, critical legal theory). The argument, in brief, is that law is indeterminate and incapable of neutral interpretation.[162] When judges "decide" cases, they "choose" legal principles to determine particular outcomes. Even if a judge wants to be neutral, she cannot, because, ultimately, she is vulnerable to an array of personal and cultural biases and influences; she is only human. In an implicit endorsement of the doctrine of jury nullification, legal realists also suggest that, even if neutrality were possible, it would not be desirable, because no general principle of law can lead to justice in every case.[163]

It is difficult for an African-American knowledgeable of the history of her people in the United States not to profess, at minimum, sympathy for legal realism.[164] Most blacks are aware of countless historical examples in which African-Americans were not afforded the benefit of the rule of law: Think, for example, of the existence of slavery in a republic purportedly dedicated to the proposition that all men are created equal, or the law's support of state-sponsored segregation even after the Fourteenth Amendment guaranteed blacks equal protection. That the rule of law ultimately corrected some of the large holes in the American fabric is evidence more of its malleability than of its virtue; the rule of law had, in the first instance, justified the holes.[165]

The Supreme Court's decisions in the major "race" cases of the last term underscore the continuing failure of the rule of law to protect African-Americans through consistent application. Dissenting in a school desegregation case,[166] four Justices stated that "[t]he Court's process of orderly adjudication has broken down in this case."[167] The dissent noted that the majority opinion "effectively ... overrule[d] a unanimous constitutional precedent of 20 years standing, which was not even addressed in argument, was mentioned merely in passing by one of the parties, and discussed by another of them only in a misleading way."[168] Similarly, in a voting rights case,[169] Justice Stevens, in dissent, described the majority opinion as a "law-changing decision."[170] And in an affirmative action case,[171] Justice Stevens began his dissent by declaring that, "[i]nstead of deciding this case in accordance with controlling precedent, the Court today delivers a disconcerting lecture about the evils of governmental racial classifications."[172] At the end of his dissent, Stevens argued that "the majority's concept of *stare decisis* ignores the force of binding precedent."[173]

If the rule of law is a myth, or at least is not applicable to African-Americans, the criticism that jury nullification undermines it loses force. The black juror is simply another actor in the system, using her power to fashion a particular outcome; the juror's act of nullification—like the act of the citizen who dials 911 to report Ricky but not Bob, or the police officer who arrests Lisa but not Mary, or the prosecutor who charges Kwame but not Brad, or the judge who finds that Nancy was illegally entrapped but Verna was not—exposes the indeterminacy of law, but does not create it.

3. The Moral Obligation to Disobey Unjust Laws

For the reader who is unwilling to concede the mythology of the rule of law, I offer another response to the concern about violating it. Assuming, for the purposes of argument, that the rule of law exists, there still is no moral obligation to follow an unjust law.[174] This principle is familiar to many African-Americans who practiced civil disobedience during the civil rights protests of the 1950s and 1960s. Indeed, Martin Luther King suggested that morality requires that unjust laws not be obeyed.[175] As I state above,[176] the difficulty of determining which laws are unjust should not obscure the need to make that determination.

Radical critics believe that the criminal law is unjust when applied to some antisocial conduct by African-Americans: The law uses punishment to treat social problems that are the result of racism and that should be addressed by other means such as medical care or the redistribution of wealth. Later, I suggest a utilitarian justification for why African-Americans should obey most criminal law: It protects them.[177] I concede, however, that this limitation is not *morally* required if one accepts the radical critique, which applies to all criminal law.

4. Democratic Domination

Related to the "undermining the law" critique is the charge that jury nullification is antidemocratic. The trial judge in the *Barry* case, for example, in remarks made after the conclusion of the trial, expressed this criticism of the jury's verdict: "'The jury is not a mini-democracy, or a mini-legislature.... They are not to go back and do right as they see fit. That's anarchy. They are supposed to follow the law.'"[178] A jury that nullifies "betrays rather than furthers the assumptions of viable democracy." In a sense, the argument suggests that the jurors are not playing fair: The citizenry made the rules, so the jurors, as citizens, ought to follow them.

What does "viable democracy" assume about the power of an unpopular minority group to make the laws that affect them? It assumes that the group has the power to influence legislation. The American majority-rule electoral system is premised on the hope that the majority will not tyrannize the minority, but rather represent the minority's interests. Indeed, in creating the Constitution, the Framers attempted to guard against the oppression of the minority by the majority.[179] Unfortunately, these attempts were expressed more in theory than in actual constitutional guarantees, a point made by some legal scholars, particularly critical race theorists.

The implication of the failure to protect blacks from the tyrannical majority is that the majority rule of whites over African-Americans is, morally speaking, illegitimate. Lani Guinier suggests that the moral legitimacy of majority rule hinges on two assumptions: 1) that majorities are not fixed; and 2) that minorities will be able to become members of some majorities.[180] Racial prejudice "to such a degree that the majority consistently excludes the minority, or refuses to inform itself about the relative merit of the minority's preferences," defeats both assumptions.[181] Similarly, Owen Fiss has given three reasons for the failure of blacks to prosper through American democracy: They are a numerical minority, they have low economic status, and, "as a 'discrete and insular' minority, they are the object of 'prejudice'—that is, the subject of fear, hatred, and distaste that make it particularly difficult for them to form coalitions with others (such as the white poor)."[182]

According to both theories, blacks are unable to achieve substantial progress through regular electoral politics.[183] Their only "democratic" route to success—coalition building with similarly situated groups—is blocked because other groups resist the stigma of the association. The stigma is powerful enough to prevent alignment with African-Americans even when a group—like low income whites—has similar interests.

In addition to individual white citizens, legislative bodies experience the Negrophobia described above. Professor Guinier defines such legislative racism as a pattern of actions [that] persistently disadvantag[es] a fixed, legislative minority and encompasses conscious exclusion as well as marginalization that results from "a lack of interracial empathy." It means that where a prejudiced majority rules, its representatives are American minority.[184]

Such racism excludes blacks from the governing legislative coalitions. A permanent, homogeneous majority emerges, which effectively marginalizes minority interests and "transform[s] majority rule into majority tyranny."[185] Derrick Bell calls this condition "democratic domination."[186]

Democratic domination undermines the basis of political stability, which depends on the inducement of "losers to continue to play the political game, to continue to work within the system rather than to try to overthrow it."[187] Resistance by minorities to the operation of majority rule may take several forms, including "overt compliance and secret rejection of the legitimacy of the political order."[188] I suggest that another form of this resistance is racially based jury nullification.

If African-Americans believe that democratic domination exists (and the 1994 congressional elections seem to provide compelling recent support for such a belief[189]), they should not back away from lawful self-help measures, like jury nullification, on the ground that the self-help is antidemocratic.[190] African-Americans are not a numerical majority in any of the fifty states, which are the primary sources of criminal law.[191] In addition, they are not even proportionally represented in the U.S. House of Representatives or in the Senate.[192] As a result, African-Americans wield little influence over criminal law, state or federal. African-Americans should embrace the antidemocratic nature of jury nullification because it provides them with the power to determine justice in a way that majority rule does not.

D. "[J]ustice must satisfy the appearance of justice":[193] The Symbolic Function of Black Jurors

A second distinction one might draw between the traditionally approved examples of jury nullification and its practice by contemporary African-Americans is that, in the case of the former, jurors refused to apply a particular law, e.g., a fugitive slave law, on the grounds that it was unfair, while in the case of the latter, jurors are not so much judging discrete statutes as they are refusing to apply those statutes to members of their own race. This application of

race consciousness by jurors may appear to be antithetical to the American ideal of equality under the law.

This critique, however, like the "betraying democracy" critique, begs the question of whether the ideal actually applies to African-Americans. As stated above, racial critics answer this question in the negative.[194] They, especially the liberal critics, argue that the criminal law is applied in a discriminatory fashion.[195] Furthermore, on several occasions, the Supreme Court has referred to the usefulness of black jurors to the rule of law in the United States.[196] In essence, black jurors symbolize the fairness and impartiality of the law. Here I examine this rhetoric and suggest that, if the presence of black jurors sends a political message, it is right that these jurors use their power to control or negate the meaning of that message.

As a result of the ugly history of discrimination against African-Americans in the criminal justice system,[197] the Supreme Court has had numerous opportunities to consider the significance of black jurors.[198] In so doing, the Court has suggested that these jurors perform a symbolic function, especially when they sit on cases involving African-American defendants,[199] and the Court has typically made these suggestions in the form of rhetoric about the social harm caused by the exclusion of blacks from jury service.[200] I will refer to this role of black jurors as the "legitimization function."

The legitimization function stems from every jury's political function of providing American citizens with "the security ... that they, as jurors actual or possible, being part of the judicial system of the country can prevent its arbitrary use or abuse."[201] In addition to, and perhaps more important than, seeking the truth, the purpose of the jury system is "to impress upon the criminal defendant and the community as a whole that a verdict of conviction or acquittal is given in accordance with the law by persons who are fair."[202] This purpose is consistent with the original purpose of the constitutional right to a jury trial, which was "to prevent oppression by the Government."[203]

When blacks are excluded from juries, beyond any harm done to the juror who suffers the discrimination or to the defendant, the social injury of the exclusion is that it "undermine[s] ... public confidence — as well [it] should."[204] Because the United States is both a democracy and a pluralist society, it is important that diverse groups appear to have a voice in the laws that govern them. Allowing black people to serve on juries strengthens "public respect for our criminal justice system and the rule of law.[205]

The Supreme Court has found that the legitimization function is particularly valuable in cases involving "race-related" crimes.[206] According to the Court, in these cases, "emotions in the affected community [are] inevitably ... heated and volatile."[207] The potential presence of black people on the jury in a "race-related" case calms the natives, which is especially important in this type of case because "[p]ublic confidence in the integrity of the criminal justice system is essential for preserving community peace."[208] The very fact that a black person can be on a jury is evidence that the criminal justice system is one in which black people should have confidence, and one that they should respect.

But what of the black juror who endorses racial critiques of American criminal justice? Such a person holds no "confidence in the integrity of the criminal justice system." If she is cognizant of the implicit message that the Supreme Court believes her presence sends, she might not want her presence to be the vehicle for that message. Let us assume that there is a black defendant who, the evidence suggests, is guilty of the crime with which he has been charged, and a black juror who thinks that there are too many black men in prison. The black juror has two choices: She can vote for conviction, thus sending another black man to prison and implicitly allowing her presence to support public confidence in the system that puts him there, or she can vote "not guilty," thereby acquitting the defendant, or at least causing a mistrial. In choosing the latter, the juror makes a decision not to be a passive symbol of support for a system for which she has no respect. Rather than signaling her displeasure with the system by breaching "community peace," the black juror invokes the political nature of her role in the criminal justice system and votes "no." In a sense, the black juror engages in an act of civil disobedience, except that her choice is better than civil disobedience because it is lawful.[209] Is the black juror's race-conscious act moral? Absolutely. It would be farcical for her to be the sole color-blind actor in the criminal process, especially when it is her blackness that advertises the system's fairness.[210]

At this point, every African-American should ask herself whether the operation of the criminal law in the United States advances the interests of black people. If it does not, the doctrine of jury nullification affords African-American jurors the opportunity to control the authority of the law over some African-American criminal defendants. In essence, black people can "opt out" of American criminal law.

How far should they go? Completely to anarchy? Or is there some place between here and there, safer than both? The next part describes such a place, and how to get there.

. . . .

CONCLUSION

This Essay's proposal raises other concerns, such as the problem of providing jurors with information relevant to their decision within the restrictive evidentiary confines of a trial. Some of these issues can be resolved through creative lawyering.[237] Other policy questions are not as easily answered, including the issue of how long (years, decades, centuries?) black jurors would need to pursue racially based jury nullification. I think this concern is related to the issue of the appropriate time span of other race-conscious remedies, including affirmative action. Perhaps, when policymakers acknowledge that race matters in criminal justice, the criminal law can benefit from the successes and failures of race consciousness in other areas of the law. I fear, however, that this day of acknowledgement will be long in coming. Until then, I expect that many black jurors will perceive the necessity of employing the self-help measures prescribed here.

I concede that the justice my proposal achieves is rough because it is as susceptible to human foibles as the jury system. I am sufficiently optimistic to hope that my proposal will be only an intermediate plan, a stopping point between the status quo and real justice. I hope that this Essay will encourage African-Americans to use responsibly the power they already have. To get criminal justice past the middle point, I hope that the Essay will facilitate a dialogue among all Americans in which the significance of race will not be dismissed or feared, but addressed. The most dangerous "forbidden" message is that it is better to ignore the truth than to face it.

(e) Perpetuating the Cycle of Abuse: Feminist (Mis)use of the Public/Private Dichotomy in the Case of Nixon v. Rape Relief†

Ummni Khan

OPENING REMARKS

The enshrined common law maxim, "a man's home is his castle",[1] has long stood for the principle of man's freedom and autonomy in private spaces. Though he must conform to legal codes and rules in public areas, man becomes the supreme ruler when nestled in his home. I use the words "man", "he", and "his" purposefully here, not as gender-neutral terms, but rather to foreshadow the feminist engagement with this legal principle. In this regard, feminist legal scholarship has argued that the notion of a man's home-cum-castle perpetuates a public/private dichotomy where men enjoy freedom and women suffer servitude in spaces designated as "private."

Tracing the public/private divide back to Aristotle,[2] feminists have argued that this ordering of society allowed "private" sites to become havens of legal impunity. For example, in the quintessential private space — the hallowed home — "man" (and here man operates metonymically for husband and father) can control, abuse, rape and exploit his wife and children without significant legal intervention, or with a mitigated punishment.[3] By analyzing family, criminal, employment, administrative and virtually every other aspect of law, feminists demonstrated that the carving off of certain spaces as "private" has often worked to the disadvantage of women and children. Harms and inequalities in these so-called private spaces were rendered invisible, irrelevant or inevitable. On this view, feminists posited that the separation of the public and the private in law was not an empirical observation of a natural division, but rather an ideological operation serving the status quo of patriarchy.

This article examines how the public/private divide was exploited to support the status quo, not of patriarchy, but of feminism, in the human rights case between Kimberly Nixon and Vancouver Rape Relief and Women's Shelter ("Rape Relief").[4] This high-profile case involved Kimberly Nixon, a transsexual woman[5] who filed a human rights complaint against Rape Relief, an all-woman collective that rejected Nixon as a potential peer counsellor. Rape Relief's refusal of Nixon was based on the claim that she was not born a woman, and therefore, had not been assigned the "historically subordinate status assigned to women", nor treated exclusively as a girl and woman. Based on this, Nixon did not qualify as a peer in Rape Relief's regard. A subsidiary justification offered by Rape Relief was that Nixon's appearance might cause discomfort to the clients who seek counselling and services from their organization.

The crux of my argument is that Rape Relief relied on a regressive understanding of law's proper role in regulating harmful behaviour, by capitalizing on the hegemonic concept of the public/private divide, in order to escape legal accountability for its members' discriminatory conduct. Further, Rape Relief's position on the contestability of Nixon's womanness, which was accepted by the appellate courts, relied on the larger implication of the public/private divide by re-entrenching that what matters for the law happens in the public sphere, and what does not matter for the law happens in the private and personal sphere. By framing the case as one centering on the autonomy interests of Rape Relief and the privacy interests of their clients, Rape Relief portrayed itself as the proverbial castle, with the women who run the organization as the ruling "queens." What will hopefully become evident throughout this paper is the irony of a purportedly feminist organization dichotomizing the public and the private spheres in order to discount the experiences and identities of one of the most marginalized subcategories of women: transsexual women.

As is obvious from the previous paragraph, I take it as a given that Kimberly Nixon is a woman. The purpose of this paper is not to advocate this viewpoint. Whether one subscribes to this position or not, I believe we need to be suspicious of the ways that Rape Relief exploited the governing assumptions of the public/private dichotomy in order to justify its

---

† (June, 2007) 23 W.R.L.S.I. 27 at 28–31, 32–45, 49–53. Reproduced with permission. [Notes and/or references omitted.]

behaviour. The arguments put forth by Rape Relief can be seen as highly problematic from a feminist perspective, even accepting its right to define who qualifies as a "woman" for the purposes of their volunteer program. As my title implies, I believe that Rape Relief's arguments could be understood as perpetuating a cycle of abuse: by deploying the public/private dichotomy as a cloaking and sanitizing measure, Rape Relief perpetuated the legitimacy of a legal principle that has consistently been used to the disadvantage of all women in society.

. . . .

The body of this article proceeds in two parts. The first part provides a background of the material facts of the case and its adjudicative progression. In the second part, I demonstrate how Rape Relief relied on the public/private divide to claim that Nixon's complaint was unjustified and should be dismissed. I explore five dimensions of the public/private dichotomy in play during the litigation of the human rights complaint. First, I examine Rape Relief's restrictive interpretation of the term "sex" as a prohibited ground of discrimination. Second, I critique their assertion that volunteering should not be considered an employment. Third, I deconstruct their rhetorical manipulation of their clients' privacy interests. Fourth, I turn to the reasoning of Justice Edwards of the British Columbia Supreme Court to examine how his concurrence with Rape Relief's position was built upon the problematic assumptions of the public/private dichotomy. Fifth, I deconstruct how the portrayal of Nixon's private identification as a girl and woman as materially irrelevant, [which] is premised on a privileging of the public sphere over the private sphere, as the space that demands judicial notice.

Ultimately, this paper takes issue with the hegemonic conception of the public/ private dichotomy perpetuated by Rape Relief, and how this worked against the interests of both non-transsexual women as well as transsexual and transgendered women.

PART I: BACKGROUND FACTS AND CASE HISTORY[10]

In August of 1995, Nixon responded to an advertisement from Rape Relief calling for volunteers who wished to be trained as peer counsellors for victims of male violence. Nixon herself had suffered male violence in multiple forms, including relationship violence, sexual assault, and street harassment. She had previously received counselling from Battered Women's Support Services (BWSS), an all-woman collective designed to assist women who have experienced violence and sexual assault. From this empowering experience, Nixon was inspired to give back to other women the kind of positive support she had received. Because BWSS had a policy against former clients volunteering immediately after having received counselling from them, Nixon turned to Rape Relief as an ideal venue to support women who, like her, had suffered from male violence.

Rape Relief has a pre-screening process for their training program, the goal of which is to ensure that potential volunteers adhere to the group's listed political beliefs, which are:

1. Violence is never a woman's fault;[11]
2. Women have the right to choose to have an abortion;
3. Women have the right to choose who their sexual partners are; and
4. Volunteers agree to work on an on-going basis on their existing prejudices, including racism.

At this pre-screening interview, Nixon accepted these four principles and was invited to begin her training at the next scheduled session, beginning the following week. At the first training session, Cormier, a facilitator for the workshop, visually identified Nixon as someone who may not belong. During a break, Cormier asked Nixon about her sex status.[12] When Nixon confirmed she was a transsexual woman, Cormier asked her to leave.

In response to this exclusion, Nixon filed a human rights complaint alleging that Rape Relief had discriminated against her by refusing her employment and by denying her a service on the basis of sex.[13] On judicial review, Rape Relief questioned the British Columbia Human Rights Tribunal decision to hear the case on the basis that the Tribunal lacked jurisdiction, primarily relying on the argument that freedom from discrimination on the basis of "sex" under the Code does not protect against discrimination based on transsexualism.[14] Rape Relief's challenge was unsuccessful and the complaint proceeded with a full evidentiary hearing in front of the Human Rights Tribunal in 2001. Tribunal member Heather MacNaughton found that Rape Relief breached the *Code* by discriminating against Nixon on the basis of sex, and held no statutory defences applied to its' members' conduct.

Rape Relief applied for judicial review of the Tribunal's decision. Justice Edwards of the British Columbia Supreme Court agreed that the Tribunal had erred and quashed the decision on the basis of two findings. First, he concluded that Rape Relief's refusal of transsexual women was allowed based on s. 41 of the *Code*, dubbed the "groups' rights exemption." This section provides a defence to a *prima facie* case of discrimination for a non-profit organization provided: its primary purpose is the promotion of an identifiable group of persons, characterized by sex (among other grounds); and the organization is granting a preference to members of that identifiable group of persons. Although he held this finding was dispositive of the case, Justice Edwards nevertheless applied the *Law* framework to the facts of the case. Using a mixed subjective–objective test, he concluded that Nixon did not satisfy the legal test for discrimination because she had failed to show an objective impact on her human dignity.

Though Nixon's appeal of this decision was unsuccessful, she was vindicated to a degree by the Court of Appeal's reasoning. Justice Saunders held that the *Law* framework was not applicable to the test for discrimination in the present case. Through this reasoning, it was established that Rape Relief had committed an act of *prima facie* discrimination. However, Justice Saunders agreed with Justice Edwards that Rape Relief's conduct was legally justified by the groups' rights exemption pursuant to s. 41 of the *Code*.

PART II: WORKING THE PUBLIC/PRIVATE DIVIDE TO ERASE THE HARMS OF GENDER ESSENTIALISM

A. Taking the Sex out of Transsexualism

As discussed above, Rape Relief first challenged Nixon's complaint by an application for judicial review, contesting the jurisdiction of the Human Rights Tribunal to hear the case. Rape Relief argued it was not the legislature's intention to "alter the ground 'sex' to encompass transsexualism or 'gender identity'".[15] Rape Relief submitted that sex discrimination refers exclusively to conduct that disadvantages a person based on their status as a man or a woman, or based on associations to a person's maleness or femaleness. It relied on earlier case law holding that the ground "sex" in human rights legislation did not include discrimination based on sexual orientation. Finally, Rape Relief argued that three previous decisions of the Tribunal, finding sex did include transsexualism, were wrongly decided.[16]

Had Rape Relief been successful in their argument to restrict the meaning of "sex" to address male and female inequality exclusively, transsexuals

and transgendered people would have faced serious barriers to access human rights protection in *any* kind of employment, service or housing relationship, not just women-only spaces. In consequence, transgendered and transsexual individuals would either have been completely excluded from protection from discrimination, or they would have been forced to self-construct as suffering from a disability.[17] Leaving transgendered and transsexual people with no protection would clearly be contrary to their human rights, as studies have shown that transgendered and transsexual people are acutely vulnerable to discrimination in all areas of life.[18] Though some transsexual persons have argued that discrimination has occurred on the basis of "disability" as well as "sex", other claimants object to what they perceive to be the medicalisation of their sex status.[19] In addition, this ground may not be available to transgendered claimants who have chosen not to undergo sex reassignment surgery. Though Rape Relief's main focus of concern regards women who were assigned the female sex at birth, I believe that as a feminist and justice seeking equality group, it betrayed its own principles. Rape Relief chose to pursue arguments that potentially had devastating repercussions on transgendered people, a group, which Rape Relief itself did not contest, is a minority group, is marginalized and is disadvantaged in Canadian society.

Beyond their harmful effects for transgendered people, Rape Relief's arguments further entrenched the public/private divide. In attempting to ground "sex" in a (bio)logical[20] discourse of female and male, Rape Relief needed to sever the connections of sexuality and gender from the category of sex. The logic of a public/private dichotomy lurks behind this reasoning and has the effect of rendering the private identifications of one's gender and/or one's sexual desires to be legally irrelevant. On Rape Relief's analysis, what counts for law is the public assignment and recognition of coherent sexed subjects without the gender imperatives that attach to one's sex.

This erasure of the gender components of sex is reflected in the rhetoric used by Rape Relief. According to the decision, Rape Relief submitted that "the issue is not what the term 'sex' might mean in the abstract, or in some other legislative or semantic context, but rather what it means in the context of the legal concept of sex discrimination."[21] In this argument, the use of the terms "abstract" and "semantic" work to dematerialize the issues of gender, implying that gender has less corporeality than sex, and that it primarily exists in the world of language and ideas, and not in the concrete world of "male" and "female". This concrete world is construed by Rape Relief as a "male dominated society" in which "sex discrimination" in law is meant to deal solely with issues of inequality between men and women. The inequality between transsexual women and non-transsexual women becomes an irrelevant issue within this binary thinking. Gender expression and identity are rendered epiphenomenal private choices and not public issues of inequality.

Discrimination based on sexual orientation is also deemed by Rape Relief to be outside of the scope of "sex." Relying on case law that predated the inclusion of sexual orientation as its own ground in human rights legislation, Rape Relief sought to demonstrate that these cases gave a restrictive meaning to "sex" that did not include sexual preference. By presenting these cases as part of their legal strategy to delimit "sex", Rape Relief further underscored the category of sex as something that is ontologically fixed, and not something that is policed through the regulation of sex roles. And yet, as Catharine MacKinnon argues, "[s]ame-sex discrimination is sex discrimination ... sex roles are socially enacted in part through sexual expression and sexual identity."[22] By citing jurisprudence that denies the [imbrications] of sexuality with sex, Rape Relief tacitly approved of the ways sexuality is coded as private within legal reasoning, and therefore outside of law's scrutiny.[23]

B. Disavowing the Dignity Issues in Volunteering

Rape Relief's second argument, concerning the nature of volunteering, also attempted to exploit the governing assumptions of the public/private divide. Rape Relief argued before the Tribunal that volunteering does not constitute "employment" under the *Code*, and that the Tribunal therefore lacked jurisdiction with regards to the complaint. In support of this proposition, Rape Relief submitted that performing paid work provides dignity in a way that volunteering does not, and that the denial of the opportunity to engage in paid work therefore harms dignity in a way that denial of the opportunity to volunteer does not. Rape Relief further argued that volunteering does not raise the same concerns regarding the power imbalance as are involved in paid relationships.

Rape Relief's strategy of bracketing volunteer work as work that does not implicate legally relevant dignity contributes to the patriarchal undervaluation of women's unpaid or underpaid work.[24] Although

men and women tend to volunteer about the same amount of time, there is a stark gender gap regarding the kinds of volunteer activities they perform and the significance it holds in their lives. According to a government sponsored research brief, men are more likely to occupy prestigious positions in the volunteer sector, such as serving on boards of directors, and women are more likely to be delivering hands-on services, such as care giving.[25] As such, men tend to have more supervisory roles, while women will have less power and less control over their volunteer work. Male volunteers are also more likely than women to have paid employment alongside their volunteer activity.[26] Women, who are systemically excluded from waged work, will often turn to volunteering to obtain skills and gain valuable experience in order to increase their chances of acquiring paid work.[27] For women, volunteering is also noted as a means to feel connected to the community and gain self-confidence.[28]

Had Rape Relief been successful in its bid to legally immunize volunteering from discrimination law, women — who have less power in their volunteer jobs and who rely on such work to upgrade skills, to connect with their community and to improve their self-esteem — would have been disproportionately affected. The non-profit volunteer-driven organization would become overdetermined as a private sphere that can escape accountability for harmful treatment because money is not exchanged.

Rape Relief's view that the dignity of work is inextricably tied to the value of money was reflected in its final argument that volunteering does not implicate the same power imbalance as paid work, presumably because being denied such work does not directly affect one's financial status. Yet, feminists have argued that the domestic sphere, where women continue to perform most of the unpaid work, involves stark power imbalances between parties that need to be addressed in law and economic policy.[29] In other words, feminists have argued that the fact that labour is unpaid, whether in the community or at home, should not indicate that such work is performed under fair or equal conditions.

In sum, Rape Relief's attempt to preclude Nixon's complaint by distinguishing volunteer work from paid work, premised on purported differential dignity and power issues, recalled the problematic ways the state has traditionally ignored the harms and inequality that occur when unremunerated work is performed, most often by women, in spaces designated as private.

C. Using the 'Best Interests of the Clients' Rhetoric to Justify Discrimination

Rape Relief argued before the Tribunal that even if *prima facie* discrimination was established, it was still not liable for a breach of the law because it was a *bona fide* occupational requirement that volunteers have lived their whole lives as girls and women. A substantial part of this alleged justification rested on the purported privacy and dignity interests of their clients. In [its] evidence, Rape Relief called on Edith Swain, a former client of the organization. Swain testified that she would not have confided her story to someone she believed was a man or had grown up as a man.

In [its] oral argument to the Tribunal, Rape Relief cited Supreme Court of Canada jurisprudence protecting the privacy of sexual assault victim records. Rape Relief then sought to draw an analogy between the privacy interests of those victims and the privacy interests of its clients. Rape Relief submitted:

> Women who have suffered male violence should be entitled to maintain the privacy of their stories and *to choose* to whom they tell their stories. Women like Ms. Swain cannot be honestly reassured that a transgendered person has lived as a woman.[30] [emphasis added]

Using Swain's discomfort as evidence, Rape Relief suggested that to accept a transgendered or transsexual woman as a volunteer would violate the right to privacy for victims of sexual assault.

The nexus, however, between a sexual assault victim's privacy interests and a transsexual woman counsellor is not elaborated upon. The mere fact that Swain would have felt uncomfortable with Nixon as a counsellor does not establish an invasion of privacy, and instead shows little more than the fact that Swain prefers certain types of women as counsellors over others. Interestingly, Rape Relief does not allow other types of stated client preferences to govern the choice of counsellor. For example, imagine a woman from a socially conservative background who requests a different counsellor because she is not comfortable disclosing sexual abuse to a woman who appears to be a lesbian. Rape Relief's policy is to refuse such requests, despite evidence from its own expert witness, Dr. Pacey, who testified under cross-examination that in her view, "the sexual orientation of a peer counselor could be an issue for a victim of sexual assault because the issues following a sexual assault sometimes differ for heterosexual and lesbian women."[31]

It is therefore clear that despite Rape Relief's claim that a woman's right to privacy entitles her "to choose" to whom she will confide with [regard] to her history of sexual abuse, the organization does not attempt to accommodate all such client requests, even if this may disturb or upset the client. Apparently, "privacy" interests are not at stake when a client suffers discomfort in the presence of a lesbian woman. Nixon, on the other hand, because of her transsexualism, is constructed as an invasive presence that would violate the privacy of clients who are not comfortable with transsexual women.

This perspective reflects a version of the public/private dichotomy, specifically the one that genders the public as male and the private as female.[32] Part of Rape Relief's semantic strategy was to emphasize Nixon's sex-designation at birth by continually referring to Nixon as a "male-to-female transsexual" and never as a transsexual woman. Counsel for Rape Relief sought to discursively bind Nixon to that temporal place of "maleness" in order to overdetermine her as "public" within a patriarchal framework. Thus, Rape Relief capitalizes on the underlying gendered nature of the public-man/private-woman dichotomy to couch an argument about client discomfort within the terms of a right to privacy.[33] The inconsistency in analysis — that discomfort with a transsexual counsellor violates one's right to privacy, while discomfort with a lesbian counsellor does not — is never addressed by Rape Relief.

Boyle maintained this strategy of using a client's discomfort with transsexualism in her academic article, arguing that a substantive approach to discrimination would take into consideration third party interests.[34] As part of her evidence, she cites a European Court of Human Rights decision, *X, Y, and Z v. United Kingdom*, which upheld a British law prohibiting a transsexual man from registering as the father of his partner's child, conceived through artificial insemination.[35] Boyle quotes the court, which stated, "'it is not clear that it [registration] would necessarily be to the advantage of the children' and 'might have undesirable or unforeseen ramifications for the children in Z's position.'"[36] Thus, Boyle borrowed rhetoric from the "best interest of the child" doctrine to forward the notion of the "best interest of the client".

Yet, feminists and other critical scholars have argued that the notion of "best interest of the child" is indeterminate and often manipulated by judges to justify their own prejudices or stereotypes.[37] For example, William Eskridge has argued that despite the fact that judges have replaced discourses of immorality with the discourse of best interests of the child, gay men and lesbians are still often disadvantaged because of homophobic conceptions of the capacities of gay and lesbian parents and assumptions regarding what a "healthy" and "normal" childhood should entail.[38]

Along the same lines, the majority decision-makers in *X, Y, and Z* cite no evidence in support of their suspicion that registration of the transsexual parent as father might "not be to the advantage" of the child, nor ever elaborate on their assertion that "undesirable or unforeseen ramifications" might flow from the registration.[39] Instead, the majority simply assumes that the mere fact of transsexuality is enough to justify the British government's decision to treat transsexual men differently from non-transsexual men where children are involved. In contrast to this perspective, the dissenting opinion of Judge Gotchev found that the best interest of the child standard would be best served by treating transsexual parents equally to non-transsexual parents, by drawing baseless distinctions between these groups, the British law violated the right of respect for one's private and family life.[40]

The same indeterminacy that plagues the "best interest of the child" analysis exists with respect to Rape Relief's arguments concerning the "best interest of the client". Based on evidence of merely one former client, who was already aware of Nixon's status as a transsexual, Boyle homogenizes and reifies Rape Relief's client base to support its anti-transsexual stance. She sets up false distinctions that inherently portray the use of transsexual women counsellors as being contrary to the best interests of sexual assault victims.

For example, Boyle argues, "[o]ne way of stating the issue is how to be attentive to the human rights of both [sic] transgendered persons, raped and beaten women seeking help from women-only space, and women with the life experience of being treated as women who want to combat male violence."[41] By framing the issue in this manner, Boyle suggests that the interests of transgendered women are necessarily in contradistinction to "raped and beaten" women and non-transgendered women. Yet, transgendered women could very well be the "raped and beaten" women that Boyle and Rape Relief seek to protect. Indeed, Nixon herself was a "raped and beaten" woman who sought services in a women-only space and Rape Relief members testified that the organization had, on at least two occasions, assisted transsexual or transgendered women.[42] Boyle's framework disavows the intersectional oppression that occurs

when transsexual or transgendered women suffer sexual abuse. These victims of male violence get erased and their possible interests are occluded from Rape Relief's analysis.

Further, even with non-transsexual women victims of male violence, Rape Relief and Boyle presented only inconclusive opinion evidence to support their argument that it was in the best interest of their clients not to have a transsexual woman counsellor. In this regard, expert witness Dr. Pacey hypothesized that a transsexual woman would not be appropriate as a peer counsellor. However, Dr. Pacey also testified that she had no experience with transgendered people in women's shelters or in peer counselling situations, either as members or as facilitators.[43] Under cross-examination, she further conceded that a transgendered woman may be an effective counsellor.[44] Edith Swain's evidence was similarly speculative, as she had never encountered a transsexual woman herself when seeking services and instead testified about how she would have felt had this situation occurred. By contrast, Nixon adduced uncontroverted evidence that she had been a successful counsellor at two women's shelters, BWSS and Peggy's Place.[45] Based on this evidence, it appears that the human rights and interests of Rape Relief's clients would have been best served by the organization enrolling Nixon into the volunteer training program, since she had already proven herself to be an effective counsellor for victims of male violence. In rushing to label Nixon as a volunteer who is contrary to its clients' best interests, Rape Relief ignored the direct evidence of her past accomplishments as a counsellor.

Boyle's "best interests of the client" framework also sets up an inherent antagonism between transsexual women and non-transsexual women — even though both groups of women may have as their goal the eradication of male violence. Indeed, many women-only organizations that advocate for the end of violence against women include both transsexual women and non-transsexual women.[46] Rather, the conflict of interest lies between transsexual women who seek inclusion, and non-transsexual women who seek to exclude transsexual women. Casting non-transsexual women's interests in the altruistic "best interests of the client" rhetoric obscures their self-interested desires of exclusion. Much like a parent who seeks exclusive custody of a child over her gay ex-spouse using the "best interest of the child" rhetoric to justify her own homophobia, Rape Relief sought to exclude Nixon partly using a "best (privacy) interest of the client" rhetoric to justify its own stereotypes and assumptions concerning the capacities of transsexual women.

. . . .

E. Transsexual Bodies that Do Not Matter

As was stated earlier, the Court of Appeal invalidated Justice Edwards' reasoning with [regard] to the applicability of the *Law* framework and found that Nixon had established a *prima facie* case of discrimination.[58] The Court of Appeal did find, however, that the exemption provision in s.41 of the *Code* was a valid defence for Rape Relief. It is not my purpose in this section to mount an argument against this finding, but instead to highlight how the hegemony of the public/ private divide was utilized in the Court's reasoning.

Justice Saunders, who wrote the main decision for the Court of Appeal, based her interpretation of s. 41 on the Supreme Court of Canada's reasoning in *Caldwell et al. v. Stuart et. al.*[59] In that case, the Court held that a Catholic school could legitimately refuse to rehire a Catholic teacher who had married a divorced man, contrary to the organization's own interpretation of church dogma. Relying on this reasoning, Justice Saunders determined that she need only inquire if Rape Relief's exclusionary practice was rationally connected to its work and done in good faith.

In the course of analyzing Rape Relief's arguments about *bona fide* occupational requirements, Tribunal member MacNaughton found that Rape Relief met both of these conditions; nevertheless the requirement that a volunteer counsellor must have been treated as female her whole life could not stand because it was not reasonably necessary.[60] Taking these findings, Justice Saunders concluded that for the purposes of a s. 41 exemption, so long as a rational connection and good faith were established, Rape Relief "... was entitled to exercise an internal preference in the group served, to prefer to train women who had never been treated as anything but female."[61] This assessment echoed Rape Relief's unwavering contention that Nixon did not fit their definition of "woman" because she did not have the life-long experience of having been treated exclusively as a girl and a woman.

This perspective imposes on Nixon a gender identity constituted by the public sphere, depoliticizing her personal experiences as a girl and a woman who has struggled against a patriarchal system that imposes and polices a rigid sex/ gender

binary. By accepting Rape Relief's assertion — that volunteers must have been treated by others as female for their entire lives — as rational and in good faith, Justice Saunders places paramount importance on how other people defined and treated Nixon. It should be recalled that in *Caldwell*, the appellant, Caldwell, was treated differently because it was perceived that she had contravened Catholic doctrine by marrying a divorced man in a civil ceremony. This was something she *did*. Nixon did not *do* anything to contravene Rape Relief's beliefs, and in fact had concurred with their list of stated political beliefs in her pre-interview with the organization. She was excluded simply because of the way others perceived and reacted to her, i.e. what *other* people did. This difference was immaterial in the eyes of the law, which found that the public sphere holds the trump card. It did not matter that Nixon had, her whole life, understood and treated herself as female. Ultimately, by rendering the public the final arbiter of Nixon's femaleness, the Court of Appeal reinscribed the public/private dichotomy by making Nixon's conviction from childhood that she was female irrelevant; something that does not matter.

When I say that the law accepted Rape Relief's contention that Nixon's self-identification as female does not matter, I want to exploit the overlapping double-meaning of "matter" as both physicality and as a subject of importance by recalling Judith Butler's useful reformulation of the materiality of the body in her book, *Bodies That Matter*.[62] Butler argues that the matter of bodies, and particularly the sex of the body, comes about through an effect of power, of coercive regulatory systems and of violent reiterative processes that materialize the sexed subject into intelligibility, as someone who matters in society. Rape Relief insists that Nixon's childhood, because she was iterated and reiterated as a boy, has thus now irrevocably made her into something other than a woman.

The rejection of Nixon from Rape Relief's "club-like sisterhood" continues this violent reiterative process by arguing that the truth of Kimberly Nixon lies in the gaze of others. Her own truth — that of a girl who was (mis)taken for a boy, who had to remain fearfully vigilant about hiding her true sex (knowing that publicly expressing herself would mean confronting violent opposition) and who sought assistance in order for her body to conform to her visceral sex identity — this truth does not matter. Nixon's ordeals — experiences of patriarchal oppression, including domestic violence, sexual assault and street harassment — these ordeals did not matter. By accepting Rape Relief's standards of womanhood for their volunteer program as rational and in good faith, Justice Saunders dematerializes both Ms. Nixon's own experiential truth and her life-long subordination under a patriarchal system. Once again, what matters for the law happens in public, what does not matter, happens in private.

CONCLUDING REMARKS

This paper has disclosed how the law and Rape Relief relied upon the governing principles of the public/private dichotomy in order to minimize, trivialize and neutralize the discriminatory nature of Rape Relief's policy against transsexual women volunteers. The fact that Rape Relief is a non-profit, equality-seeking feminist organization should not absolve or justify their complicity in naturalizing this divide. It is not only ironic, but also tragic, that a feminist organization exploited the public/private divide as part of its legal strategy to defend its policy, since this man-made divide has historically obscured the harms that women suffer in "private" spaces.

This is reflected in Rape Relief's arguments concerning the restrictive meaning of sex and the significance of volunteering that worked against the interests of all women. Indeed, arguments seeking to interpret the ground "sex" in a restrictive way have historically been used in attempts to deny legal recourse to women who suffered sexual harassment, who were victims of stalking, who suffered discrimination on the basis of pregnancy, who refused to

conform to stereotypes of femininity in the workplace, and who came out as lesbian or bisexual. Positioning volunteer work outside the scope of human rights protections would have left many women vulnerable to discrimination and harassment in an area that can be crucial to their livelihood, self-esteem, sense of community and future prospects. On a symbolic level, evacuating the dignity interests and disavowing the power imbalances present in many volunteer relationships would have continued the patriarchal tradition of devaluing the work that women do in spaces designated as "private".

Although Rape Relief failed in its attempt to restrict the scope of the "sex" and "employment" categories, its appropriation of the language of "privacy" rights found some support in the reviewing courts. Meanwhile, Nixon's struggle to be recognized and respected as the woman she has always known herself to be was construed as private business that did not ultimately matter to Rape Relief or for the proceeding. Thus, marginalized women like Kimberly Nixon, who suffer from the intersectional oppression of being female and transsexual, find themselves further isolated from the women's community and from social services. Ultimately, the case proceeded in a manner that further marginalized transgendered and transsexual people and furthered the inequality between non-transsexual women and transsexual women, while ignoring the history of prejudice and stigmatization continually faced by transsexual women in both public and private spaces and in both mainstream and feminist circles.[63]

(f)　Toward a Political Economy of Law†

Amy Bartholomew and Susan Boyd

Perhaps the most fundamental and problematic basis for the ideological aspect of law in organizing consent, legitimating oppressive social and material relations, and fragmenting collective endeavours emanates from the construction of "free" and "equal" subjects through juridical categories. Central premises of law in liberal democratic capitalism are that individuals are "free" in the economic realm, insofar as they may strike their own bargains and dispose of their labour and property "freely,"[118] and free from the juridical inequality and dependence present in pre-capitalist modes of production. The ideological importance of these premises is found in the way they may obscure and justify unequal and oppressive

† From "Toward a Political Economy of Law" in W. Clement and G. Williams, eds., *The New Canadian Political Economy* (Kingston: McGill-Queen's University Press, 1989) 212 at 229–33. Reproduced with permission of McGill-Queen's University Press. [Notes and/or references omitted.]

class, gender, and other relations. As many commentators note, "economic freedom" within capitalism is a particularly cramped notion of freedom. Moreover, as both Leo Panitch and Ellen Meiksins Wood have emphasized, because classes are constituted by the relations of production rather than directly by the state and law, the coercion that obtains within capitalist systems tends to be obscured.[119]

Formal juridical freedom and equality may thus obscure the fact that capitalist relations of production are neither free nor equal. By treating unequally situated individuals and groups as if they were equal at least some of the time, formal juridical equality also perpetuates unequal relations between classes, sexes, and races more directly. Rights are mediated by social, historical, political, and economic contexts which may be "invisible" to the law, a point illustrated by reference to struggles for formal equality rights. For instance, although obtaining the right to own property in the name of formal juridical equality with men was a significant victory for married women, other material and ideological constraints limited access by women to waged labour and the ability to acquire property in their own right. Similarly, capital and labour bargain collectively under conditions of structural inequality that include capital's greater material resources, greater "organizational and ideological resources," and "greater access to the state." Yet, in crucial respects, capital and labour are treated in collective bargaining law as if they meet on an equal footing.[120] Those who are "more equal" in reality are thereby favoured by the "neutrality" of law implicit in the concept of formal juridical equality, thus reinforcing the "net transfer" of power from those who do not own and control the means of production to those who do.[121]

Further, the discretion present in the law, operating against the backdrop of the presumed universal, neutral application of the law to "free and equal" individuals, simultaneously permits disparate and unequal treatment.[122] As Mandel points out, research into the invocation of criminal sanctions by courts demonstrates that "criminal law is applied in anything but an equal manner."[123] In labour law, the discretionary imposition of penalties by courts may be, and often is, particularly harsh when dealing with labour, as in the jailing of Jean-Claude Parrot in the last decade for refusing to order his workers back to work[124] and the recent jailing of Newfoundland labour leaders. The symbolic effects of such harsh example-setting should not be underestimated.

The juridical concepts of free and equal individuals are extended in capitalist democracies to the "interpellation" of people as free and equal citizens.

Individual citizenship rights tend to both disarticulate classes and to rearticulate individual citizenship interests as the "national interest." In one fell swoop, classes are thereby fractured at the political level insofar as liberal democracies typically represent citizens, rather than classes, in the state. And political parties tend — at least in Canadian liberal democracy — to represent and articulate the "national interest," while the "national interest" represents pre-eminently the interests of capital. Hence, while subordinate classes may be disorganized by the categories of "free and equal," the capitalist class is brought together and represented broadly as if its interests truly expressed the common good. Thus, despite the fact that the franchise constituted a genuine victory for subordinate classes, oppressed races, and women, the exclusiveness of this mode of representation — the absence of class representation mechanisms, workplace democracy, and the like — may curtail genuine participatory possibilities.[125]

Predicated on the core concepts of "free" and "equal" individuals, and contingent on historical resistances and struggles, is the constitution of state subjects as bearing other, predominantly individual-based civil liberties and rights in liberal democracies. The presumed atomizing consequences of these configurations are often commented on in the literature. However, the law does not only atomize. Vera Chouinard has provided an important corrective in the Canadian literature by arguing that historical and concrete class antagonisms and struggles may prey on systemic contradictions in particular conjunctures, thus creating possibilities for struggles to resist the logic of atomization. Chouinard indicates that concrete struggles may achieve both legal restrictions on the "degree and manner" of subjection to the logic of production and legal recognition as collectivities. She further argues that precisely to the extent that struggles achieve collectivized class-specific rights and recognition, class capacities may thereby be enhanced.[126]

It seems clear that political struggles often revolve around rights claims in liberal democracies partly because of the cultural and historical commitment to at least some rights in such societies. But the pre-eminence of formal juridical equality may facilitate the appropriation of rights discourse by any political group, progressive or otherwise. Jenson has argued, for example, that instead of the abortion issue being seen as a debate between women and men as groups divided by sex, women's "right" to choose abortion has been pitted against pro-life arguments for foetal rights, thereby obscuring the gendered nature of the issue: "In such a discourse, women disappear as a group and reappear as individuals with needs which can only be assessed against those of all other persons, including foetuses."[127] These sorts of struggles are implicitly, if not explicitly, premised on formal juridical equality — positing equality of "access" to the enormously important claim to "right."

The concepts of atomization, freedom, formal legal equality, individual civil liberties, and political and citizenship rights may currently constitute the most complex and pressing "'problem of legality' in historical materialism." The concepts of "free" and "equal" legal subjects do appear to fracture the subordinate classes, and the "centrality of a private isolated, autonomous, egoistic legal subject possessed above all of a freewill" *may* "enforce ... and legitimate ... oppressive class relations."[128] At the same time, insofar as the ideological role of law requires some kernel of truth to its claims, individual civil liberties may help protect us against at least the most direct and obvious state coercion and intrusions — a not unimportant point in the era of Thatcher, Reagan, and Vander Zalm. Moreover, citizenship and political rights, as limited as they are in Canada, are valuable and were bestowed on us by neither a beneficent nor a cunning state, but rather were won through struggle. And the importance to disadvantaged groups of legal instruments acquired through struggles for formal legal equality should not be underestimated.

Much work in political economy of law in Canada does not adequately address these important and complex contradictions and problems. Indeed, an unmitigated hostility is displayed toward individual rights, most especially in the work emanating from legally trained scholars.[129] Glasbeek and Mandel, for example, undervalue individual constitutional rights, while some work in administrative law also denigrates the importance of individual claims against the state.[130] These approaches fail to seriously investigate the admittedly problematic but potentially emancipatory status of the individual legal subject endowed with free will and deserving of respect. An unexplored assumption that notions of "autonomy" and "community" are necessarily antithetical also abounds in both the work of Glasbeek and Mandel and in the critical legal studies-inspired work of Hutchinson and Monahan. Hutchinson and Monahan claim, in fact, that "rights-based theories have corrosive implications for communal aspirations."[131]

The complexity of formal legal equality, the importance of civil and political rights against and within the capitalist state, and notions of individualism and citizenship must be explored much more

seriously in a developed political economy of law.[132] This task does not require us to concede significant ground to liberal approaches to law. It means simply refusing to throw the baby out with the bathwater. Ian Taylor has aptly criticized those who imply that we can simply take notice of the bourgeois form of law and then go home:

> The danger ... is that they frequently present law and legal institutions as an impenetrable and secure element in the apparatus of class domination, and that thereby they discourage the use of legal interventions as a useful move in political struggles. To say this is not, of course, to deny that one of the achievements of bourgeois law *is* to displace the *class* struggles that are constantly occurring in capitalist societies over commodities into disputes between *individual legal subjects* ... legal discourse is a mystification of the true character of social relations in a propertied, unequal society, but it is none the less an important (imperfect) instrument in the defence of the liberties of the classes and the sexes.[133]

We would add that the new political economy of law could do worse than to recall the work of some of the "old" political economists, including that of Macpherson and F.R. Scott in their defence of "liberties."[134] Finally, work such as Chouinard's, which begins to theorize how the construction of legal subjects and rights can be challenged, how class-specific, collective rights may be secured in particular capitalist conjunctures, and how collective constructions may enhance the potential for transformative politics, constitutes an important challenge for the new Canadian political economy. While the questions surrounding appropriate forms of socialist legality have not even been broached in the Canadian literature, commentators have begun to consider the nature of collective and "activist" rights and progressive rights strategies.[135] Even this work, however, is all too sparse and limited in Canada.

．．．．

Law, legal institutions, and rights represent both spaces and tensions, contradictions and possibilities, limitations and potential. We must, therefore, be cognizant of the ways in which law and legal institutions may contribute to the reconstitution and reproduction of existing relations of power. We must simultaneously begin to explore seriously what it means to say that law is embedded within struggle and is an arena of struggle itself; how and to what extent the discourse of rights and the forms of law may contribute to or detract from our struggles; how law, legal institutions, and rights may be used in strategic ways while minimizing the potentially demobilizing and integrative effects of participating within legal forms and legal arenas. If the new Canadian political economy meets these challenges, we will be that much better equipped to assess which strategies advance transformative and socialist politics.

Connecting Law and Society

(a) The New Legal Scholarship: Problems and Prospects†

John Hagan

DEFINING THE FIELD

Legal scholarship has changed dramatically in this century.[1] Early in this century, legal scholarship found form and coherence in a method of study and teaching often referred to as the doctrinal approach. This approach placed its emphasis on the determination of rules, principles and procedures through the detailed analysis of cases — a method that goes back at least as far as Langdell's reforms at the Harvard Law School.[2] There can be little debate as to the professional success of this approach to legal scholarship.[3] It provided a method for teaching and for the writing of legal treatises and law review articles that endures to this day.

Yet if there was a purity to this methodological emphasis on "law in the books", there was also an incompleteness that led others to call for research on the "law in action". Often known as the legal realist movement, and best documented in its emergence at the Yale Law School,[4] this approach to legal scholarship called attention to gaps between doctrine and practice. It is interesting to note that both the traditional doctrinal approach and legal realism were eager to claim the mantle of science.[5] In doing so, the doctrinal approach focused on recorded cases as its units for observation and analysis, while the realists moved beyond these official accounts to examine the way the law actually was applied and affected people's lives.[6] The realist's point was that the law often only affected social life indirectly and that doc-

trine frequently affected society in uncertain and unanticipated ways.[7]

Today, few scholars conceive of themselves as legal realists *per se*.[8] This is probably because there are now few legal scholars who see the "gap" between the law and the contexts in which it is applied as being as clear cut as the realists seemed once to imply. Rather, legal doctrine and the society out of which it grows are seen as intimately interconnected. That is, we now recognize that the meaning of legal rules resides not only in the internal relations of the principles and value they contain, but also in the ways rules are distributed, achieved and changed — through their career in the real world of claims, counter-claims, negotiations, arbitrations, etc.[9] In these and other ways (made explicit below), we have entered a world of post-doctrinal scholarship that now takes the law and the contexts in which it develops as the combined focus for research.

Two distinguishable streams of work characterize post-doctrinal legal scholarship. The first stream consists of what we will call normative interpretative legal studies, and is most provocatively represented by the critical legal studies movement in prominent American law schools.[10] This work is often historical and sometimes comparative in form, and is most frequently distinguished by the interpretative reanalysis of case law doctrine in the format of contextualized critiques. It is interesting to note that the case law base and library setting of much critical legal study marks a continuation of traditional doctrinal meth-

† (1986) 1 CJLS/RCDS 35 at 35–37. Notes omitted. Reproduced by permission of Canadian Journal of Law and Society/Revue Canadienne Droit et Societe. www.utpjournals.com.

ods.[11] However, the critical and contextualized form of this work makes it radically different from the older doctrinal approach.[12]

The second stream of post-doctrinal legal scholarship has taken on many names,[13] but here will be called empirical behavioral legal studies. These studies are not explicitly concerned with either the justification or criticism of case law doctrine, but instead strive to be value neutral. An explicit goal of this approach is to frame legal issues as empirical questions that can be answered without consideration of value preferences.[14] For example, "the gap problem" that so concerned the legal realists is not taken here as inherently good or bad, or as something to be reduced; rather, in empirical behavioral legal studies the gap is taken as something to be explained, as in Stewart Macaulay's classic study of non-contractual relations in business.[15] That is, the purpose is not to find the doctrinal principle that will reestablish legal order, thereby, for example, making all business relations contractual. The purpose instead is to make explicit the discontinuity between law and everyday practice and then to explain this discontinuity, so that what happens on each side of it can be better understood. The emphasis here is on causal and functional explanations, with the explanations made testable by the articulation of propositions that are predictive, and therefore assessable through comparisons of theoretically derived expectations with empirically generated observations. This work can be experimental as well as non-experimental, cross-sectional, longitudinal and comparative as well as historical and critical.

There is increasing reason to believe that the two streams of post-doctrinal scholarship we have described can be joined by a pragmatic tradition of empirical legal scholarship.[16] It is therefore worthwhile taking note of what this new legal scholarship offers, and of what the obstacles to this new tradition might be. We consider the possibilities first, and the obstacles second.[17]

In the most general terms, the new legal scholarship offers a more inclusive look at the interrelationships between law and the surrounding society. It does this first by shifting our attention outward and downward from "law at the top". This means moving our focus from the highly publicized and recognized importance of decisions made, for example, in appellate and trial courts, away from the professionals who "make" these cases, down to the law's users and consumers. Law at the bottom becomes as important and as interesting, and therefore as much in need of explanation, as law at the top. Among other things,

we begin to seek explanations of the movement of legal activity up and down this hierarchy.[18]

The downward thrust of the new legal scholarship extends attention simultaneously to less formal manifestations of law. Among the most central of these manifestations is the negotiated outcome. Bargaining is a pervasive feature of law more broadly conceived. Galanter writes that, "[t]he negotiated outcome in the shadow of the law turns out to be the master pattern of disputing ..."[19] What might otherwise be seen as adjudicative processes are now seen as negotiative ones, with authoritative decision makers now cast in the roles of arbitrators and mediators. Legal rules and principles surely still apply, but their role is less determinative, and now understood as less definitive.

The parties to the negotiated outcomes are also more broadly conceived, as are the settings in which they act. The actors in these larger social dramas include legally recognized authorities, users and consumers of law and their authorized and unauthorized agents, other interested parties, and the broader social audience that must be considered in shaping negotiated outcomes. These actors are seen and heard not only in more formal and heavily monitored legal settings, but in a plurality of other places. Private governments, semi-autonomous social and professional fields, indigenous law and other forms of regulation are related to law in ways that depend on one another for mutual effect. Governmental law is intimately interrelated with other kinds of law and social institutions in which regulators and regulatees conduct their everyday business. Law is seen here as plural, not singular.

The influence of law is also understood in symbolic as much as or more than in instrumental terms. Indeed, scarcity of legal resources requires that this must be so, for the cost of direct law enforcement sharply curtails the range over which the law can be applied. However, when law is conceived as symbolic information flows, apart from the direct and instrumental exercise of force, the broad impact of law, albeit indirect and often with unintended effects, is more easily grasped. For example, general deterrence, legal socialization and bargaining in the shadow of the law are all seen as broader manifestations of the law as it symbolically affects people's everyday lives.

In all of these ways, the new legal scholarship has dramatically increased what we know about the way law actually works — about plea bargaining, negotiated settlements, selective prosecution, litigants' strategies, the working routines of courts and judges; about the practice of law, client-lawyer relationships, the structure and politics of the bar; about legal education and the public consumption of law. Journals such as *Law & Society Review*, the *Journal of Legal Studies*, the *Journal of Law & Economics*, the *Journal of Legal Education*, *Law & Human Behaviour* and the *American Bar Association Research Journal* are alive with the emerging products of this work. An increasing number of monographs and texts are also available. All of this reflects an accumulation of empirical legal study that is impressive compared to the dearth of such material available less than a generation ago.

(b) The Pedagogic Challenge†

Neil C. Sargent

Roger Cotterrell (1986) points out that one of the defining characteristics of any discipline or knowledge-field lies in the fact that its intellectual frame of reference (its object of inquiry, the conceptual and methodological tools relied upon and the manner in which the autonomy of the field of inquiry is established) tends to be autonomous and self-validating. Consequently, one of the problems inherent in any attempt to challenge the intellectual hegemony of any discipline or paradigm lies in establishing the intellectual space from which to mount such a challenge.

Cotterrell's insight has particular relevance in relation to the difficulties inherent in developing an interdisciplinary approach to legal studies which is capable of challenging the dominant legal positivist tradition within legal education. This is because the intellectual hegemony of the legal positivist tradition is intimately connected with the professionalization of legal education and the institutional autonomy of the professional law school. This is no accident. The development of legal positivism as a closed form of knowledge-formation, with its own internal canons of enquiry, has played an important role in raising the status of law to that of a 'learned' profession (Arthurs, 1987). Moreover, the focus of legal positivism on the substantive content of legal texts and on internal conventions of reasoning and analysis reflects precisely those areas of knowledge and expertise over which legal professionals have traditionally exercised a monopoly.

The strength of this intellectual tradition lies in the way it colonizes the imagination of legal scholars. As such it imposes a powerful intellectual brake upon their research and teaching agendas, which is all the more insidious for being largely invisible. Legal positivism involves epistemological assumptions about the nature of law as an object of inquiry which reinforce the insularity of legal scholarship from the academic concerns of scholars in other disciplines. At its heart is a conceptualization of law as a normatively closed form of knowledge and system of inquiry which have few, if any, necessary reference points to the social, political or economic environment in which law operates (Cotterrell, 1986). Despite the recent burgeoning of critical perspectives on law which seek to challenge many of the tenets of the dominant positivist tradition, such as the Critical Legal Studies Movement, in one important respect little seems to have changed. The focus of enquiry of most contemporary legal scholarship remains defined by its concern with legal doctrine, notwithstanding the explicitly political agenda of much of the new critical scholarship. Moreover, the modes of inquiry relied upon even by critical legal scholars are still oriented around textual analysis and deconstruction, even if the claimed rationality and objectivity of traditional modes of legal interpretation have become increasingly contested with the new critical scholarship.

Consequently, there is still no obvious mandate for travel outside these conventional boundaries in search of empirical evidence about the impact of law in practice. Nor is there any need to investigate the role of legal institutions or legal actors other than as sources of authoritative texts for analysis or interpretation. In this respect, Supreme Court justices are necessarily more important as authors of legal texts

---

† November 1989, unpublished.

than trial court justices, notwithstanding the claims of the Legal Realists to the contrary. Similarly, the role of the court as a trier of fact and in processing disputes is less significant to most legal scholars than its role as a source of texts for interpretation and analysis.

By contrast, the assumption that legal texts can be read independently from their social, cultural, economic or political environment tends to be viewed by many social scientists with a considerable degree of skepticism, bordering at times on disbelief. Those issues which are of marginal concern to legal scholars in their search for authoritative texts are precisely the issues about the workings of the legal system, the behaviour of legal actors, the effectiveness of legal rules and decision-making processes, that are likely to be of interest to social science researchers. Consequently, the sources of data, the methods of enquiry and the conceptual frameworks utilised by social science researchers in their investigations of law are based on very different foundations than those which inform most conventional legal scholarship (Friedman, 1986; Hagan, 1986).

One of the major problems inherent in attempting to develop an interdisciplinary approach to legal studies which is able to draw from both these disciplinary traditions lies in the fact that they appear to be mutually exclusive of one another. This is borne out by the history of the law-and-society movement in the United States, which despite its promising beginnings and its relatively lengthy history, has largely failed to penetrate the mainstream of American legal scholarship (Friedman, 1986).

As a result, there is sometimes a tendency on the part of social science researchers to regard the disciplinary claims made by legal academics as something of a contradiction in terms. Legal scholarship tends to be dismissed by many social scientists on the grounds that it lacks theoretical or methodological coherence. The question is often asked whether there is anything sufficiently distinctive about law being treated as a separate disciplinary field (Friedman, 1986; Cotterrell, 1986). From this perspective, law is frequently seen as a proper object of inquiry only within the confines of another disciplinary tradition, such as sociology, political science, history, psychology or philosophy.

Why not then simply abandon the legal academics to their search for authoritative texts while the social scientists get on with the work of investigating the way in which law operates as a social phenomenon and impacts upon people's lives? The answer that I would give to this question is two-fold. First, that law is too important a social institution to be left only to lawyers. This implies that the language of law and content of legal doctrine should not be regarded as simply the dry, technical preserve of lawyers. Law plays a crucial ideological role in shaping popular understandings about the nature of power relations and the structure of social ordering within liberal democratic societies. Consequently, the entire terrain of law, which includes the role of legal education, the nature and form of legal reasoning, the hierarchical structure of legal authority, as well as the content of legal rules, needs to be studied as a complex social phenomenon that can only be fully understood through the use of social science concepts and methods of inquiry.

Closely related to this first point is a further observation concerning the limits of empirical enquiry as a means of understanding the social significance of law. Law as a social phenomenon is more than just a set of empirically observable relations or activities that can be examined according to well-established canons of enquiry to produce empirically-testable hypotheses about the behaviour or significance of law or legal institutions in practice. Here I clearly part company with many in the socio-legal studies movement in Britain and Australia and in the law-and-society movement in the United States and Canada. It follows from the point made above that legal discourse and doctrine must also become part of the province of social science enquiry, even if not readily amenable to empirical methods of investigation.

Given the significance of law as a source of contested meanings about the nature of social relations, a crucial question for investigation becomes what are the limits of law as an agency of social or political change? To what extent, for example, is the language of legal rights capable of redressing situations of substantive social, economic or political inequality? Or is the discourse of legal rights so closely wedded to liberal notions of abstract individualism and formal equality that it has the effect of channelling progressive political struggles into narrowly circumscribed legal issues? These are not questions which can be answered solely by reference to internal canons of interpretation and precedent, such as legal academics are used to. Rather, what is at issue are fundamental questions about the relationship between legal concepts and the structure of social, economic and political ordering within Canadian society.

What this translates to in practice is the need to insert questions of theory and method into the design of any legal studies curriculum in a way that is central to the pedagogic enterprise. This implies that conventional legal methods of inquiry are inadequate alone to generate meaningful hypotheses about the nature of law or the connection between legal relations and social relations. It also implies a significant degree of skepticism about the ability of empirical enquiry alone to produce any more meaningful responses to these questions unless explicitly informed by an awareness of wider theoretical issues.

Consequently, the prescription offered is for a legal studies approach which claims law as an appropriate field of inquiry, but which rejects any conception of law as a unitary mode of discourse that can be investigated by reliance on internal canons of inquiry alone. Rather, the focus should be on exploring the multi-faceted character of law as a complex social phenomenon, and the manner in which different theoretical and methodological perspectives give rise to different types of questions about the role and functions of law and the relationship between legal and social change (*cf.* Hunt, 1986; Boyd, 1989). Perhaps it should come as no great surprise that this also reflects the intellectual trajectory followed in the development of the Carleton law program.

(c) How Does Law Matter in the Constitution of Legal Consciousness?†

David M. Engel

I. INTRODUCTION

The interest of law and society scholars in "legal consciousness" is a relatively recent phenomenon. Although references to the term can be found in scholarship of the later 1970s and early 1980s, legal consciousness has emerged as a discrete topic of widespread research interest among sociolegal scholars only within the past eight to ten years. In this essay, I suggest that the subject of legal consciousness did not grow and bloom as a new species within the law and society field, but rather that it is an offshoot of earlier law and society research traditions. It is a concept, or a cluster of ideas, that now seems promising to a group of sociolegal scholars who have arrived at the topic of legal consciousness by way of research on legal needs, legal culture, dispute processing, and legal ideology. The restless search of these scholars is a story in itself. I will try to provide a sense of what it is they are looking for, why the earlier formulations ultimately proved too constraining, and why the concept of legal consciousness now seems promising. In doing so, I point to differing assumptions about how law matters in the constitution of legal consciousness and offer tentative suggestions for bringing greater clarity to this question.

In order to provide a focus for this discussion, I base my analysis primarily on six recent[1] and reasonably representative books and articles by widely read law and society scholars. Many other works and authors might have been chosen, of course, and some of these others are cited in the discussion that follows. The six works I have selected, however, provide a sense of the diversity as well as the commonality of interests within this emerging subfield as well as a range of assumptions about the ways in which law matters. Furthermore, all six share a quality that has come to define much of the most distinctive law and society research — a commitment to examine theoretical issues as they play themselves out in the lives and experiences of actual people. The six works are: John Comaroff and Jean Comaroff, *Ethnography and the Historical Imagination* (1992); Patricia Ewick and Susan S. Silbey, "Conformity, Contestation, and Resistance: An Account of Legal Consciousness" (1992); Carol J. Greenhouse, "Courting Difference: Issues of Interpretation and Comparison in the Study of Legal Ideologies" (1998); Sally Engle Merry, *Getting Justice and Getting Even: Legal Consciousness among Working-Class Americans* (1990); Austin Sarat, "'... The Law Is All Over': Power, Resistance, and the Legal Consciousness of the Welfare Poor" (1990); and Barbara

† From Bryant Garth and Austin Sarat (eds.), *How Does Law Matter?* (Evanston: Northwestern University. Press, 1998) at.109–11, 130–41. Reprinted with permission. [Notes and/or references omitted.]

Yngvesson, "Making Law at the Doorway: The Clerk, the Court, and the Construction of Community in a New England Town" (1988).[2]

The Comaroffs write about the "colonialization of consciousness" during historical encounters between British imperialists and South African peoples, a process that involved a transformation of both British and African worldviews. Ewick and Silbey illustrate a theory of legal consciousness with an early example from an ongoing study: Millie Simpson, a domestic housekeeper, loses and then wins in a criminal court where she was mistakenly charged for a vehicular offense committed by a teenager who took her car without permission. Greenhouse revisits "Hopewell," Georgia, in order to show how ideologies of law and court use as well as concepts of community and history are constructed around categories of difference (insider versus outsider, newcomer versus local, those prone to engage in conflict versus those able to control themselves, those who "belong" versus those who are rootless and without faith or commitment). Merry, who studied litigation and mediation among working-class New Englanders, examines transformations in the consciousness of those who go to court to assert their rights in family or neighbourhood conflicts only to find that such cases are viewed as "garbage" by clerks and judges, who try to channel them toward nonjudicial, "therapeutic" resolutions. Sarat explores the perceptions of welfare recipients who view themselves as caught in a vast web of legal rules dominating most aspects of their lives yet allowing some room for resistance and temporary, strategic victories. Yngvesson studies complaint hearings conducted by the court clerk in a district criminal court in Massachusetts and sketches the process by which this seemingly marginal actor in a seemingly peripheral judicial locale actually participates in important ways in the negotiation of concepts of community, of belonging, of appropriate behaviour, and of social order.

The discussion that follows is organized into four sections. First, I examine the concepts of legal consciousness that are presented in these six works. I focus in particular on whose consciousness the authors attempt to study and on what is meant by the term "legal consciousness." Second, I suggest that similar interests and concerns appeared in earlier research by law and society scholars working under such paradigms as legal needs, legal culture, dispute processing, and legal ideology. I ask why these earlier paradigms were ultimately considered inadequate by those who now focus on issues of legal consciousness. Third, drawing on these earlier research traditions as well as the six representative works on legal consciousness, I examine differing assumptions about the extent to which law matters. Finally, I offer my own suggestions about the study of legal consciousness and some ways in which insights gained from earlier law and society research might usefully be applied to this emerging subfield.

．．．．

4. HOW DOES LAW MATTER?

．．．．

A. Power and Resistance

The articles by Ewick and Silbey and by Sarat move their authors toward the end of the continuum that sees law as powerfully determinative of legal consciousness. Both articles explain why and how law plays a crucial constitutive role, yet both articles also suggest how individuals are able to contest the power of law and find some wiggle room in an otherwise predetermined set of meanings and practices.

Both articles cite and rely, in part, on the work of de Certeau (1984), who presents a model of "practice" and "resistance." Essentially, this model conceives of power as emanating outward from the sources of sociocultural production to shape the practices of everyday life. Such practices become givens of our day-to-day existence and are associated with particular ways of organizing time and space as well as shaping the norms and values that guide everyday behaviour. Thus, power is naturalized and disseminated broadly throughout most aspects of our lives, even when we are not aware that we are subject to its domination. Yet power is not totally determinative of all aspects of everyday life. Resistance to power is possible and frequently occurs in the form of "tactics." This term refers to the "art of the weak" (de Certeau 1984: 37) who attempt to "reappropriate the space organized by techniques of sociocultural production" (1984: xiv). Such reappropriations, however, always take place within the space organized by power:

> This space of a tactic is the space of the other. Thus it must play on and with a terrain imposed on it and organized by the law of a foreign power. ... It operates in isolated actions, blow by blow. It takes advantage of "opportunities" and depends on them, being without any base where it could stockpile its winnings, build up its own position, and plan raids. What it wins it cannot keep. (de Certeau 1984: 37)

De Certeau's model is clearly apparent in both of these articles, which associate law with the externalized sources of sociocultural production and concern themselves, in somewhat different ways, with the tactics of resistance of disempowered persons. Ewick and Silbey analyze the experiences of Millie Simpson, who attempts to plead not guilty to a false accusation that she left the scene of an accident and drove an uninsured vehicle. To her surprise, the judge finds her guilty and ignores her efforts to convey the fact that her car had been driven without permission by her son's friend. Ms. Simpson achieves a minor victory by retaining her driver's license when she was supposed to turn it in and by having the court sentence her to community service at a church where she already worked as a volunteer. Yet it is not until Simpson's employers, Bob and Carol Richards, put her in contact with a lawyer from the firm that worked for Bob's company that the case is reopened and she is acquitted.

Ewick and Silbey interpret the first phase of this case, in which Simpson is convicted and sentenced for a crime of which she is innocent, as an example of power and resistance. The "terrain" of the criminal justice system is organized entirely by external sources of power, and she is forced to fit herself — without much success — into the spaces and practices that the law creates:

> The rules, taxonomies and operating procedures of the court flattened and froze time into these separate occasions. The spatialized modes of knowledge abstracted the actors from their continuing interactions and arranged them in static impersonal roles, moments, and performances.... The human interaction that Millie believed was to be embodied in the paper was instead preempted by it. (1992: 744)

By her small arts of resistance — community service at her own church and retention of her driver's license — she merely "insinuated her life into the space of the law and, in doing so, reversed for a moment the trajectory of power," but this amounts only to "deflecting" power without actually "challenging" it (Ewick and Silbey 1992: 745, 746).

The involvement of the lawyer and the eventual reversal of her conviction is a more significant act of resistance in one sense: "Millie's contestation is now articulated explicitly within the discursive space of the law. It is a public engagement and official victory, rather than the private pleasures of her resistance" (Ewick and Silbey 1992: 746–47). Yet, in another sense, the formal legal victory only confirms her subordination to power. She has access to the

lawyer only because she is a poor African American woman working in a subordinate role as housekeeper for a wealthy white woman. She is able to escape subordination within the criminal justice system only by relying on her subordinate social position within the Richards' household. As Carol Richards herself observes, "To get justice, the poor black woman needs a rich white lady." And, as Ewick and Silbey add, "the story ends with Millie's reinscription in a system of domination from which the law provides no exit" (1992: 748).

Despite Simpson's "reinscription in a system of domination," Ewick and Silbey find significance in her acts of tactical resistance. Legal consciousness is shaped and transformed through the "shifting experiences and understandings of men and women as they move through legal institutions and other arrangements of power." Acts of resistance are "memorable" and important to those who experience them and help to forge identity "in the cracks of the law" (Ewick and Silbey 1992: 749).

Ewick and Silbey thus base their analysis on a model of power and resistance resembling that of de Certeau. Law is powerfully determinative of the terrain within which Simpson must operate, yet she finds room within that terrain to resist and ultimately to prevail. Her consciousness is not constituted entirely by law but by her act of resistance as well. Law, however, shapes the form of her resistance and requires her to acknowledge and depend upon her subordinate social status. Nonetheless, the authors suggest that even such small and temporary victories on the "terrain" of the "foreign power" (to borrow de Certeau's terms) can "prefigure more formidable and strategic challenges to power" (Ewick and Silbey 1992: 749) and thus, eventually, reshape the terrain and the consciousness of those who move upon it (see also Ewick 1992: 761).

Sarat's analysis is similar in its reliance on the model of power and resistance. For the welfare poor, whom he interviewed in legal services offices in two different middle-sized New England cities, the law is a "web-like enclosure in which they are 'caught.'" The law is experienced as a series of "they say(s)," and the "sayer" is the "embodied voice of law's bureaucratic guardians" (Sarat 1990: 345). In this analysis, as in Ewick and Silbey's, law organizes the terrain within which the disempowered are left to formulate acts of resistance: "The recognition that '... the law is all over' expresses, in spatial terms, the experience of power and domination; resistance involves efforts to avoid further 'spatialization' or establish unreachable spaces of personal identity and integrity" (Sarat 1990: 347).

147

Sarat finds that the welfare poor frequently do formulate acts of resistance, sometimes with the aid of legal services attorneys. The welfare poor, however, see no special significance in the fact that the attorneys possess expertise of a distinctively legal character. They perceive the attorney as functionally equivalent to the caseworker, in that either one can sometimes be helpful in "sending a message" to the welfare bureaucracy and creating "just a little space in which a self could claim recognition" (Sarat 1990: 364). Indeed, the primarily legal character of the welfare bureaucracy's rule structure is perceived as relatively unimportant by the welfare poor. They see the process as essentially political rather than legal, and recognize that the space within which they are "caught" is organized around personal power and "whom you know" rather than neutral legal principles administered by impartial and disinterested experts (Sarat 1990: 356).

Thus, when Sarat's interviewees try to oppose the welfare bureaucracy, they are as likely to invoke moral arguments as legal arguments couched in terms of rights violations. Whatever discourse they find expedient, however, the conversations "occur on law's terrain and depend on a vocabulary made available by law itself." Discourses of human need and of legal right both "reaffirm law's dominance even as they are used to challenge the decision of particular legal officials" (Sarat 1990: 374). Yet the tactics and the consciousness of the welfare poor have a distinctive quality. As a group, the welfare poor tend to encounter a formal legal structure more frequently than other groups in society. Consequently, they are less likely to incorporate into their legal consciousness an abstract view of law as lofty, dignified, and impartial. Their consciousness, instead, reflects their actual encounters with law in the grunge and personal politics of the welfare bureaucracy.

In Sarat's analysis, legal consciousness is "polyvocal, contingent and variable" (1990: 375). It is shaped by the distinctive experiences of particular groups who are differently situated in society and who encounter the law in different ways. Yet legal consciousness, for groups like the welfare poor, is always formed in the context of power and resistance. Their tactical challenges never "dislodge the power of law or the dominance of legal rules and practices" (Sarat 1990: 376). Equally important, their understandings of law and their legal consciousness, however shrewd and insightful they may be, never succeed in becoming a part of the structure or the practices in which the welfare poor are enmeshed:

[N]either their realism nor their sophistication guarantees the production of counterhegemonic views of law. Continuous, regular contact does not mean that the welfare poor are included, or can establish themselves, as full participants in the construction of legal meanings or in the practices through which power is exercised and domination maintained. (Sarat 1990: 377)

For Sarat and for Ewick and Silbey, law matters a great deal in the constitution of legal consciousness. Yet it does not matter in the simplistic sense that it inscribes its meanings and categories directly on the minds of persons like Millie Simpson or Sarat's welfare recipients. On the contrary, Sarat and Ewick and Silbey seem to suggest at times that legal consciousness is shaped as significantly by tactics of resistance as by the imposition of power. Even when relatively powerless persons adopt a counterhegemonic view of the world, however, they construct it around the cultural shapes and forms that law helps to create. Moreover, the authors stress that the legal consciousness of resistance is not empowering in any lasting way. Tactical victories are temporary, their effects short-lived. At most, as Ewick and Silbey suggest, they may prefigure a more broadly shared consciousness that, in the future, could transform the status quo and change the framework of meaning and practice through which power is currently exercised.

B. Communities of Meaning

The articles by Greenhouse and Yngvesson provide a different set of answers to the question, how does law matter in the constitutions of legal consciousness? As I have already noted, neither author uses the term "legal consciousness," but both explore the processes by which meanings are created and shared through social practices related to the law. In contrast to the power and resistance model adopted by Ewick and Silbey and by Sarat, both Greenhouse and Yngvesson present a model in which understandings of law and of community mutually constitute one another. Legal institutions, in particular the local courts of first instance in the towns studied by these two anthropologists, are among the sites where such meanings are constructed. Legal officials — lawyers, clerks, and judges — are important actors in this drama, but so are the litigants and the residents of the towns in which the courts are situated. The law is one agency for exercising social control, but others are found in local opinion and in the fabric of meaning local residents weave as they retell local histories and draw lines between those they perceive as insiders and outsiders. The relevant terrain is not predetermined by the law alone but is constituted by the continual struggles among local residents over their collective identity and the norms, practices, and social boundaries that should prevail in their imagined communities (to borrow a term from Anderson 1991).

Greenhouse explores the interplay between court and community in Hopewell by focusing first on the differing perspectives of the judge and the clerk of the Superior Court. The clerk is the descendant of a well-established family that has lived in Hopewell for many generations. He expresses concern about the rapid expansion of Hopewell's population and the unrestricted growth of the town caused by newcomers who have escaped from the nearby metropolis to live in the suburbs. He views the influx of newcomers as a negative social development that has produced negative consequences for the local court as well. Those he categorizes as outsiders are, in his view, quick to use the court, whereas those he considers insiders are not. The increase in litigation is thus "a signal of social fragmentation" (Greenhouse 1988: 693). The deterioration of social life is caused by people who reject the traditional Hopewell values of neighbourly harmony: "I think that people are being thrown together more now, and they are quicker to go to court. People with good neighbours don't need courts — people just don't *want* to get along now" (Greenhouse 1988: 694).

The perspective of the judge is somewhat different. Although he was born and raised in Hopewell, local residents say "he is not from here" because his parents were not Hopewell natives. Like the clerk, the judge expresses concern with the rise in litigation and interprets it as "a sign of social decline" (Greenhouse 1988: 696). Unlike the clerk, however, the judge does not locate this decline in the history of Hopewell as a community but in America as a whole. Throughout the country, people are more prone to litigate because relationships and exchanges have become more distant and impersonal, because people trust each other less than before, and because the pressures of work on two-income families produce less stable marriages and family relationships. From the judge's perspective, Hopewell and its court have changed because the town has become a part of the regional and national economy.

The judge, speaking for one segment of Hopewell's residents, views growth and development in generally positive terms, while regretting its inevitable negative side effects. The clerk, speaking for a different segment, identifies more closely with the town's imagined past and is disturbed by the values

and behavior of those he identifies as newcomers. His views are echoed by other longtime residents: "One woman says, 'They just came to take our money and make trouble.' Another woman refers to the people 'with dollar signs in their eyes'" (Greenhouse 1988: 696).

The Hopewell court is a site where differing perspectives are constituted and communicated and where struggles over the community itself are enacted. Greenhouse presents six short case studies and demonstrates how contending images of the community are associated with the litigants and their conflicts. She also suggests that both the judge and the clerk, as self-perceived "insiders," share certain perceptions of the cases despite their differing orientations toward social change, and that their shared perceptions draw on a "coherent set of representations" familiar to many in the town of Hopewell. These representations have four elements. First, the concept of community as a cultural category is based on "a fundamental distinction between a past predefined as harmonious and a future defined as perilous." Second, concerns about the future center on people who cannot handle conflict on their own, as contrasted with another category of people who can and who are always able to "get along." Third, approval is conferred on those who are able, through prayer and other forms of self-control, to prevent felt conflict from becoming overt. Fourth, the capacity for self-control is associated with "belonging" — to a community and to a family (Greenhouse 1988: 703, 704).

In Greenhouse's conception, these elements of what we are calling "legal consciousness" are shared by court officials and by a well-established group of longtime residents in the community. Contrary to the power and resistance model discussed above, Greenhouse assumes that the court does not determine these categories of meaning but that it becomes a conspicuous stage on which they are embodied and played out:

> The symbolic role of the court is relevant here, not as an agency can "do" anything about the encroachments of change, but as one that marks and measures those encroachments. If, as local people claim, newcomers in Hopewell are without the kinds of social ties that make other people prefer getting along, the court cannot change that situation in any fundamental way. The court reaffirms and sees reaffirmed the important distinctions out of which the local view is constructed. (Greenhouse 1988: 704)

The court thus "marks and measures" the perceived changes in Hopewell's imagined community and, in doing so, participates in a reaffirmation of the fundamental distinctions that constitute the local consciousness of an important segment of Hopewell's residents. Although this view of how law matters differs significantly from those of Ewick and Silbey and of Sarat, Greenhouse agrees with them that legal consciousness (not her term, of course) continually shifts and changes as these proceeds of symbolic reaffirmation unfold. In particular, she suggests that the very reaffirmation of an ethic of harmony is used by longtime residents to justify its opposite. That is, denunciation of the selfish individualism of the "newcomers" carries with it an acknowledgement that "oldtimers" need at times to act individualistically as a matter of self-defense:

> Insiders acknowledge the importance of being able to defend themselves against the newcomers, and so justify an individualistic and materialistic discourse even as they devalue it. Insiders, then, can live in two value systems simultaneously: one (ours) that emphasizes affective ties and cooperation, the other (theirs) that centers on competitive self-interest. (Greenhouse 1988: 705)

Thus, law matters not only in the sense that it provides a symbolically important stage where cultural categories and values can be reenacted but also in the sense that the reenactment leads to the continual transformation of consciousness in response to perceived social change.

Yngvesson's assumptions about how law matters resemble Greenhouse's in many ways. Like Greenhouse, she explores the ways in which locally contested meanings of community are enacted in the local court and projected back into the social context from which they emerge. Unlike Greenhouse, however, her emphasis is not on the conspicuous symbolism of the courtroom in "Riverside" but on a seemingly marginal process by which local citizens and policy apply to the court clerk's office for the issuance of criminal complaints. Yngvesson suggests that the clerk's role, while less potent symbolically than that of the trial judge, is significant because he stands at the boundary between the legal system and the society of which it is a part. Because of his unique position, the clerk has to operate with skill in legal matters (although he has no legal training) but also in matters that require an understanding of Riverside's culture and history. Attentive to the system of meanings shared by various local residents, the clerk distinguishes that which is worthy of legal handling from that which is "garbage." In so doing, he participates in the construction and reaffirmation of

a particular set of cultural categories that determine what the community is and who belongs to it.

Yngvesson, who observed complaint hearings in the clerk's office over an extended period of time, presents a series of case studies that demonstrate how concepts of both law and community are constructed in the interactions of the clerk and the disputants:

> By pulling the court into the most mundane areas of daily life, these hearings become forums for constructing the separateness of law while transforming the courthouse into an arena for "thinking the community," for constituting what the local community is and who is not of it, even as they involve the local community in defining the place of law. (Yngvesson 1988: 420)

The disputes become occasions for defining who is a "good neighbor," what lifestyles are undesirable, what neighborhoods are dangerous and disordered, what people are "brainless" and conflict-prone, how men, women, and children should behave toward one another, and how members of a community should conduct themselves during a time of perceived social change.

The complaint hearings, in Yngvesson's view, construct the law as well as the community. While the court is defined as an inappropriate site for "garbage cases," litigation is not in itself condemned. In appropriate circumstances, it is important to define some kinds of conflict as essentially legal in order to preserve the social order and protect time-honored concepts of "rights to property, privacy, and to live in peace." The clerk has to deploy two rather different "images of order and relationship to develop the meaning of events in a complaint and to argue for issuance or denial" (Yngvesson 1988: 444). One image centers on harmonious interactions among neighbors who care about one another; the other centers on the more individualistic imagery of rights.

Yngvesson, like Greenhouse, suggests that law matters in large part because of the symbolic centrality of the local court:

> Prominently placed at the cultural and political center of New England towns, the courthouse seems to stand guard. In Riverside, as elsewhere, it recalls a colonial republican tradition in which virtuous, public-spirited citizens keep watch, protecting the "community of visible saints" from corrupt forces within and beyond its boundaries. (Yngvesson 1988: 444)

In contrast to the studies by Ewick and Silbey and by Sarat, however, Yngvesson problematizes the concept of law and views the social construction of the legal as part of the same process as the social (and legal) construction of the community. Both aspects of this process require study; neither is taken as a given.

Thus, Yngvesson does not start with the assumption that law marks out a terrain that must be negotiated by the clerk and the disputants. Law is not simply imposed on the people Yngvesson studies. Instead, she views the legal and social terrain as mutually negotiated. The law has power, but its power is inseparable from the social context within which it functions and whose categories of meaning pervade the workings of legal institutions and actors. Yngvesson therefore poses a paradox: the clerk has power in both the legal and the social sense, yet the power is completely dependent on his ability to understand and reaffirm cultural meanings located in the community outside the courthouse:

> [W]hile he is the dominant figure in the hearings, his power is contingent, dependent not only on his authority as a legal official but also on his knowledge of, stature in, and connections to the local community, and his rhetorical skill in using these to define conflicts in particular ways. Paradoxically, then, the clerk is most powerful when he is most connected. (Yngvesson 1988: 444)

The paradox of legal power, although articulated in an especially compelling fashion in Yngvesson's work, reminds us of the line of law and society research stretching back to earlier concerns with legal culture. The law, a central symbol of power and social order, depends for its influence on the very culture it attempts to control.

C. Summary

I have explored a continuum of perspectives on the question of how law matters in the constitution of legal consciousness. At one end of the continuum, the power and resistance model sees law as significant because of its capacity to organize the categories, structures, meanings, and practices which less powerful people must then negotiate as they attempt to reclaim some portion of social space for their own. At the other end of the continuum, the communities of meaning model sees law as significant because of its symbolic centrality in the struggle among social groups to develop authoritative definitions of community, of social order and belonging, of appropriate behavior, and of law itself.

The two approaches are not mutually exclusive; they are points on a continuum rather than dichoto-mous alternatives. There is considerable overlap in the theoretical foundations of both approaches, and it is this overlap that defines the study of legal consciousness as a subfield distinct from the earlier law and society research traditions we have considered above. Yet, in their conclusions about how law matters, the two approaches are clearly distinguishable. In part, I would suggest, the difference can be understood in terms of a point made earlier in this essay: that legal consciousness can be understood either in terms of legal aptitude or competence or in terms of perceptions and images of the law. Writers who rely on the power and resistance approach tend to emphasize the first of these two possibilities: "law" is conceptualized primarily in terms of its substantive rules and procedures, and consciousness refers to knowledge and facility in using them. Writers who focus on communities of meaning, on the other hand, tend to emphasize the second possibility: "law" for them is conceptualized primarily in terms of its symbolic power, and their research focuses on the ideas people have about legal rules and institutions rather than the extent of people's familiarity with the rules and institutions themselves. In this sense, despite the many similarities and shared assumptions of all six studies, those that emphasize power and resistance have roots extending back to the legal needs research tradition (which was concerned with knowledge of rights), while those that emphasize communities of meaning have roots in research on legal culture (which was concerned with "values and attitudes" toward law and legal institutions).

5. CONCLUSION

Law and society studies of legal consciousness are as notable for their continuities with past law and society research traditions as they are for their engagement with critical, postmodern theory. I am not suggesting that these studies are no more than old wine in new bottles. I do think, however, that the assumptions and approaches brought to these studies can best be understood in terms of the decades of law and society research on which they build. The authors of all six studies that I have discussed had previously grounded their research in the law and society subfield of dispute processing. And, as suggested in the immediately preceding section of this essay, the two differing approaches to legal consciousness I have outlined reflect law and society perspectives reaching back to studies of legal needs and legal culture in the late 1960s. The connections between legal consciousness research and other related law and society research traditions is unmistakable.

Despite these important continuities with past law and society research, it strikes me that studies of legal consciousness have sometimes forgotten important lessons from the past. In the excitement of applying contemporary social theories to the subject matter of law and society research, we have sometimes failed to reinsert some of the very insights that represent the most distinctive achievements of law and society scholarship. In this concluding section, I provide three examples of lessons from the past that should, in my opinion, figure more significantly in the emerging subfield of legal consciousness.

(1) Different substantive areas of law are associated with different perceptions, understandings, and behaviors and must therefore be distinguished in research on legal consciousness.

Studies of legal consciousness tend to speak generically of "the law" as if its constitutive effects on consciousness operate in essentially the same way regardless of its substantive content. There is reason to be caution about such assumptions. The legal needs studies suggested that people behave and think quite differently about (for example) constitutional law or employment law than they do about wills and trusts or family law. In my own research in a Midwestern community (1984), I found that people attached fundamentally different meanings and significance to the law of personal injuries and to the law of contracts.

It would be interesting to know if law matters in different ways when issues of legal consciousness involve divorces or commercial transactions or housing as contrasted with criminal or welfare law. The question is not simply one of social class, although class certainly figures differently in these different fields of law. Different substantive areas of the law represent different kinds of social relationships and interactions and involve different kinds of legal actors, procedures, and institutions. Law may matter more for consciousness associated with some of them than for others. Yet none of the studies of legal consciousness considered in this essay attempted to make comparisons across different areas of substantive law. All tended to assume that one could generalize about the relationship between law and consciousness without differentiating between different kinds of law.

(2) Law in society is multicentered and assumes many different shapes. It is not necessarily an instrument of state power, and its connection with the state is a problem to be studied rather than a fact to be assumed.

Some studies of legal consciousness tend to assume that law is a projection of state power or otherwise emanates outward from the centers of sociocultural production associated with powered groups and interests in society. Yet law and society researches have consistently rejected simplistic, centralized conceptions of what law is and how it operates in society. Different groups have different kinds of law, and internal rule structures of groups interact in complex ways with laws of a more formal kind (Moore 1978; Macaulay 1987b). Even if one focuses on "official" law, one still finds a significant dependence on unofficial or customary rule structures to determine norms of reasonableness or fairness. In such instances, the relationship between state power and unofficial sources of rules and meanings located elsewhere in the society becomes a problem that requires study.

Studies of legal consciousness sometimes imply a more centralized, simplified, top-down conception of law than is justified when one considers the lessons of three decades of law and society research. Prior research teaches us to be sceptical of claims that official laws are highly effective in organizing social behavior or in controlling the production of social meaning. On the contrary, much of what we have learned points to the inefficiency and ineffectiveness of state law and calls attention to the making of law "from below." Perhaps earlier research was insufficiently sensitive to the more subtle and indirect effects of state law, but such effects must always be demonstrated rather than assumed.

(3) In some instances, official law directly touches and influences the lives of individuals, but more often law is mediated through social fields that filter its effects and merge official and unofficial systems of rules and meanings.

Law and society research has long emphasized the importance of intermediate-level structures associated with the activities of social groups that may have only indirect relationships to state law. Within such groups, state law may play some role, but its effects are uncertain because of the presence of other norms, procedures, and systems of meaning. In a recent article (1993), I have described an intermediate-level structure I call the "domain," and I suggest that from one domain to the next one finds significant variation in the construction of time and space, identity, norms, and concepts of community or belonging. Variations in domains produce radical differences in the effect of state laws designed to regulate behavior (in my article, I show extreme variations from one locality to the next in the impact of a sweeping federal civil rights law for children with disabilities in the public schools).

Studies of legal consciousness sometimes ignore the significance of these intermediate structures and assume that the effects of state law are uniformly distributed throughout society. In such characterizations, state law has a direct impact on individual lives. Yet law and society research has suggested that such direct contacts are not necessarily typical, and that researchers must often concern themselves with the ways in which state law is refracted as it passes through social fields (or domains) that provide the contexts within which individuals and groups carry on their lives.

These examples of lessons from earlier law and society research are intended as cautionary reminders. I am not suggesting that the six studies discussed in this essay necessarily ignore these lessons but that, as innovative works, they call our attention to new kinds of problems where earlier research findings may nonetheless prove very useful. The question of how law matters is an old one and will never be answered definitively. But as we adopt new strategies to address the question, we are likely to get closer to the truth if we bring to bear our most important and hard-won insights into the workings of law, culture, and society.

III

"Making Law":
Common Law and Legislation

Part III focuses on issues related to two formal processes of law-making in common law legal systems.

The articles in Chapter 8 discuss the basic elements of the process by which judges make common law rules through judicial decisions. These decisions become precedents that bind other judges. The excerpt from F.L. Morton's book provides a brief introduction to the distinctions between law-making through judicial precedents and law-making through legislation; it also introduces the critiques of judicial discretion raised by legal realists. Patrick Atiyah provides a more in-depth discussion of the way in which certain decisions become identified as precedents that must be followed according to the rule of *stare decisis* — which requires us to stand by the decided case. Karl Llewellyn revisits these basic elements of *stare decisis* by exploring the ways in which lawyers and judges may manipulate the interpretation of precedents to suit their interests. Llewellyn thus stresses the ambiguity and essential flexibility of the system of precedent. Finally, Marie Claire Belleau and Rebecca Johnson identify the powerful, authoritative nature of judicial decisions and explore both the important role of dissenting judgments and the ways that judges craft the language of their dissenting reasons.

Chapter 9 includes two case excerpts that highlight the Supreme Court of Canada's approach to interpreting legislation. *Re Rizzo & Rizzo Shoes Ltd.* is a leading Supreme Court decision on statutory interpretation, which outlines the court's modern approach to interpreting laws made by legislatures. *R. v. Mills* illustrates the Supreme Court's understanding of the relationship between the legislature and the judiciary and outlines many of the factors the Court considers when evaluating legislation that responds to judicial decisions.

As you read through this Part, ask yourself: in what ways might our view of the law-making process be shaped by the different theoretical approaches to understanding law discussed in Part II? In light of the important role of judicial decisions in the process of interpreting and making law, is the law ever static and knowable, or is it always evolving and uncertain? Is law-making by legislatures more desirable or legitimate than law-making by judges? If so, why? How do discretionary decisions by administrators or enforcement personnel shape the implementation of legal rules? Is this another form of law-making?

(a)   Precedents, Statutes and Legal Reasoning†

F.L. Morton

One of the most distinctive characteristics of the judicial process is its formalized method of reasoning. Because their authority flows from the public perception that they are "merely" applying pre-existing rules to resolve new disputes, judges are not permitted the broad prerogative enjoyed by the legislative and the executive branches. Unlike the latter, courts are not supposed to create new policies to deal with new problems. In their oral or written judgments, judges must explain where and how they derived the "rule" used to settle a case. There are three principal sources for these "rules": a written constitution, legislative statutes (including administrative regulations), and prior judicial decisions, known as precedents. Constitutional interpretation is the subject of the following two chapters. This chapter is concerned with the role of precedent and statutory interpretation in judicial reasoning.

Until the middle of the nineteenth century, most internal or domestic law in English-speaking societies was common law. Common law originated in the judicial recognition and enforcement of traditional usages and customs of the Anglo-Saxon and later Norman peoples in the British Isles. As these judicial decisions were made, they in turn became part of the common law. The common law in contemporary Canadian society consists of all previous judicial decisions by Canadian and British courts, as they are recorded in the case reports of these nations. The common law system is distinguished from the civil law system by its basis in precedent rather than legislative enactment. The civil law system originated in ancient Roman law, developed on the European continent, and was imported into Quebec by the French. It is based on a single, comprehensive code, enacted by the legislature.

The law of precedent, or *stare decisis*, is a self-imposed judicial rule that "like cases be decided alike." As Gordon Post explains, the law of precedent is essentially a formalization of the common sense use of past experience as a guide to present conduct. The value of judicial adherence to *stare decisis* is two-fold. First, continuity and certainty in the law is a prerequisite of civilized human activity. If there is no reasonable guarantee that what is valid law today will still be valid law tomorrow, personal, economic, and political intercourse would grind to a halt. In each of these spheres of human activity, present-day decisions and activities are predicated on expectations about the future. Ensuring a high degree of predictability and continuity between the present and the future is one of the primary purposes of a political regime. As the institutions charged with interpreting and adapting the laws over time, the courts are responsible for maintaining continuity and certainty. As Dicey said, "A law which was not certain would in reality be no law at all." Adherence to the rule of precedent — "deciding like cases alike" — is the mechanism that provides this certainty.

---

† From *Law, Politics and the Judicial Process in Canada* (Calgary: University of Calgary Press, 1984) at 185–89. Reproduced with permission. [Notes and/or references omitted.]

The rule of precedent also contributes to guaranteeing the "rule of law, not of men." One of the ideals of the Western tradition's conception of justice is that the laws be applied equally and impartially to all persons. This ideal precludes any *ad hoc* application of the laws, and demands instead that laws be applied uniformly, or that any deviation from the rule be justified on principle — that is, by another rule. The idiosyncrasies or personal preferences of a judge are not permissible grounds for judicial decisions. This would re-introduce the "rule of men" rather than the "rule of law." By minimizing the discretion or freedom of individual judges, *stare decisis* preserves the "rule of law."

It should be emphasized that *stare decisis* minimizes but does not eliminate the element of judicial discretion or creativity. While legal reasoning presents itself as a deductive process, the reality is a more subtle blend of both inductive and deductive reasoning. Legal reasoning is accurately described as "reasoning by example."[1] The judges are essentially asking, "Whether the present case resembles the plain case 'sufficiently' and in the 'relevant' aspects."[2] In determining what is "sufficient" and what is "relevant," the judge must ultimately make certain choices. Because of this element of choice, a judge is responsible for striking the balance between continuity and innovation. The central thrust of the theory of legal realism has been to emphasize this element of choice and judicial discretion, and the ensuing responsibility of the judge for his choice.

Weiler's analysis of the Supreme Court's responsibility for the development of tort law is based on this legal realist perspective. Weiler argues that judges can no longer claim that precedent "dictates" nonsensical or patently unfair legal conclusions. Judges must be critical in their use of precedent, and go beyond the surface "rule" to discover the animating "principle." The proper function of the common law judge, according to Weiler, is to derive specific rules from more general principles, as the situation demands. Since situations change, rules must change also. While the "cattle trespass" exemption to normal tort law responsibility may have been appropriate to the rural, agricultural society of eighteenth century England, it had become a dangerous anachronism in twentieth century Canada. Similarly in *Boucher v. The King*, the Court was faced with a conflict between the definition of "seditious libel" developed in nineteenth century, homogeneous, protestant Britain, and the norms of freedom of religion and speech in twentieth century, pluralistic Canada. Appeal court judges have a duty, says Weiler, to adapt the common law to the changing needs and circumstances of contemporary society.

Strict adherence to *stare decisis* is yet another aspect of the "adjudication of disputes" function of courts that poses problems for judicial policy-making. Refusal to disavow or change past decisions plays no constructive role in a policy-making institution, as the examples of legislative and executive practice make clear. While certainty and continuity are legal virtues, adaptability and innovation are more important in the policy-making process. The case for abandoning a strict adherence to precedent is especially strong in constitutional law. Not only is policy-impact more probable, but constitutional law lacks the flexibility of common law and statutes. If the courts make a "mistake" in the latter areas, it can be corrected by remedial legislation. But if the Supreme Court makes a constitutional decision with undesirable policy consequences, the only direct way to correct the damage is through formal constitutional amendment, an extremely cumbersome and difficult process.[3] Predictably, the U.S. Supreme Court was the first court of appeal in a common law nation to abandon *stare decisis* as an absolute requirement. The demotion of *stare decisis* from a binding rule to a guiding principle is another index of a court's evolution toward a greater policy-making role.

The recent advent of judicial realism in Canadian jurisprudence has brought with it a decline in the status of the rule of *stare decisis*. Long after the American Supreme Court had abandoned absolute adherence to precedent, the Canadian Supreme Court continued to perceive itself as bound to adhere not only to its own previous decisions but those of the British House of Lords as well. This latter restriction is attributable to the role of the Judicial Committee of the Privy Council as Canada's final court of appeal until 1949. Ten years after the abolition of that role, the Supreme Court declared its independence from British precedents as well. In 1966 the British House of Lords officially declared that, when appropriate, it would no longer follow its own prior decisions. However, the Supreme Court of Canada continued to profess strict adherence to its prior decisions until the 1970's. Under the leadership of Bora Laskin, the Canadian Supreme Court began to move in the same direction. In 1972, before his appointment as chief justice, Laskin had written that *stare decisis* was "no longer an article of faith in the Supreme Court of Canada, but it still remains a cogent principle."[4] Speaking as the new Chief Justice at the Centennial Symposium of the Supreme Court in 1975, Laskin repeated that *stare decisis* was no longer "an inexorable rule," but rather, simply an important element of the judicial process, a necessary consideration which should give pause to any but the most sober conclusion that a previous decision or line of authority is wrong and ought to be changed.[5]

Practising what he preached, Laskin led the Supreme Court to overturn three precedents during the next three years, including an old Privy Council decision dealing with the federal division of powers.[6] The abandoning of strict adherence to *stare decisis* is yet another indicator of the Supreme Court's institutional evolution toward more of a policy-making court.

The second principal source of law is legislative statutes. Beginning in the nineteenth century, legislatures in Great Britain, Canada, and the United States began to codify large portions of the common law. In large part this was a democratic reaction against the perceived elitism of the "judge-made" character of the common law. By reducing the confusing maze of common law precedent to clearly worded, legislative statutes, it was thought that the law would be made easier for "the people" to understand, and that the democratic authority of "government by consent" would be enhanced.

In 1892 the Canadian Parliament abolished all criminal offenses at common law, and replaced them with a comprehensive statute, the *Criminal Code*. In so doing, Parliament hoped to reap the alleged advantages of codification mentioned above, including restricting judicial discretion in the criminal law. Since crimes were now clearly and authoritatively defined, judges would simply apply the law as Parliament had written it. It would no longer be necessary to refer to a vast and confusing system of precedent to apply the criminal law, or so it was hoped.

In fact, precedent and *stare decisis* quickly found their way back into the criminal law. Perhaps, as Parker has suggested, it was (and still is) impossible for judges and lawyers trained in the common law tradition to properly construe a code of law.[7] More likely the common law "habit" simply compounds a more serious problem — the ultimate ambiguity of statutory terminology itself. Try as they might, legislators will never be able to draft statutes that anticipate and encompass all possible future situations. This is due in part to the inherent tension between the generality of words and the specificity of reality, and in part to human ignorance of the future. As new situations inevitably arise, the applicability of the original wording of statutes becomes increasingly questionable....

The preceding argument notwithstanding, judicial discretion in interpreting statutes, including the *Criminal Code*, is much more circumscribed than in interpreting the common law. As Weiler says, judges can develop new torts, but not new crimes, and there are sound reasons for preferring this arrangement. As issues of tort law are rarely the subject of partisan political controversy, an innovative court cannot be accused of usurping the legislative function. The controversies over capital punishment and abortion show that the same is not true of the criminal law. In the area of tort law, judicial expertise is very high, relative to other policy-making institutions. Finally, judicial initiatives in substantive criminal law would pose the threat of punishing innocent persons. No comparable problem of "due process" arises in tort law.

While codification and statutes clearly circumscribe the limits of judicial law-making, there is still the element of judicial "choice" and its accompanying responsibility. This is especially true of the *Criminal Code*, which authorizes the continued use of common law defenses such as *mens rea*. Once again, Weiler argues that judges should go beyond superficial resemblances of wording of facts and grasp the principles that animate this area of law. The examples used appear to be contradictory decisions concerning the availability of the *mens rea* defense. Weiler suggests that these can be reconciled by reference to the underlying competition between the "crime control" and "due process" principles of criminal law. Different judges could reasonably reach different conclusions in these two cases. The essential point from Weiler's perspective is not so much what a judge decides, but how he decides the case. A final appellate court should explicitly ground its decision in the underlying principles, and explain why the particular circumstances of this case dictated favouring one over the other. Failure to do so is a failure to live up to the standards of judicial craftsmanship that can reasonably be expected from a final appellate court in an age of legal realism.

(b) The Doctrine of Precedent†

Patrick Atiyah

There are, of course, rules about law-making by courts, rules laid down by the courts themselves. Not everything said by a judge makes law. In the first place, decisions on pure questions of fact clearly do not create precedents. The fact that X shot Y may make him guilty of murder but is of no relevance to another case in which Z is the accused. Even evaluative decisions, such as a decision that a certain piece of conduct constitutes negligence, are not regarded as decisions on points of law which can constitute precedents. To take a simple example, if a judge says that a defendant in a civil action was driving his car at 80 mph in a public street, and that he was therefore guilty of negligence, that is no precedent for holding that it is negligence for another driver in a subsequent case to have driven at the same speed (even on the same road). This is partly because (as is commonly said) evaluative decisions like this must depend on all the circumstances of the case, and so it is impossible to be sure that the relevant facts in the first decision were in all respects the same as in the second. But it also seems pretty clear that one reason why decisions of this kind are not treated as precedents is simply that the courts do not want to make their every decision suffocated under the weight of previous cases. If every case of this kind became a precedent, the volume of case law would become enormous, the argument of simple cases would become inordinately complicated, as each side would support its case with a mountainous pile of precedents, and judges would find it increasingly difficult to explain why and how decision Z was consistent with decisions A, B, C ... in favour of one side, and not inconsistent with decisions M, N, O ... in favour of the other side. So judicial decisions would inevitably appear inconsistent, and this is disliked by judges. Decisions on discretionary matters are also not decisions which can constitute precedents, although the guiding principles on which discretions are to be exercised are treated as questions of law.

The doctrine of precedent, then, is largely concerned with pure questions of law. A decision on a point of law constitutes a precedent which can in principle *bind* other courts to follow it. But before we can say that a decision constitutes a binding precedent two further qualifications need to be made. First, it must indeed be a *decision*, and not merely an *obiter dictum*, that is, a statement made by the way, an aside. In principle the distinction between the binding part of the decision (the *ratio decidendi*) and an *obiter dictum* is clear, but in practice it is not always easy to distinguish between them. Sometimes judges give several reasons for a decision: are they all binding, or is there one binding reason, the others being merely *dicta*? Or again, there may be several different judgements given in an appeal court, and the reasons given by all the judges may not wholly coincide, so what is the *ratio decidendi* then? In any event, the question of *ratio* or *dictum* may be less important than the weight of the remarks in their context, and the tribunal from which they emanate. Fully considered *dicta* in the House of Lords are usually treated as more weighty than the *ratio* of a judge at first instance in the High Court. So the whole distinction is more blurred than it might seem. Further, the distinction often does not matter at all. It does not matter basically when the second court agrees with the decision (or *dicta*) in the previous case, and would arrive at the same conclusion anyhow; it does not matter even when the second court might, if it were to go into the issue in depth, have doubts about the first decision (or *dicta*) but feel disinclined to reopen the issue for any one of a number of possible reasons. Nor does the distinction between *ratio* and *dicta* matter if the second court disagrees so strongly with what was said in the earlier case that it is not prepared to follow it, even if in theory some lawyers might regard the prior case as a binding precedent. Where this happens, the second court may 'distinguish' the first decision by finding some relevant fact to be decisive of the second case which was not present in the first. Every lawyer knows that fine distinctions are sometimes seized upon to justify departing from a prior decision with-

---

† From *Law and Modern Society* (London, U.K.: Oxford University Press, 1983) at 134–37. Reproduced with permission of Oxford University Press, Oxford, UK.

out an apparent breach with the rules of binding precedent.

The second qualification that needs to be made to the binding nature of the doctrine of precedent is that the strictly binding feature of the doctrine depends on the relative status of the courts concerned. Decisions of the House of Lords bind all lower courts, and are normally treated as binding by the House itself. Since 1966 the House has claimed the right to overrule previous decisions in exceptional cases, but it has so far been very sparing in its willingness to exercise this power. Decisions of the Court of Appeal bind lower courts, and also in principle bind the Court of Appeal itself. But there is much controversy on this and practice varies. Lord Denning, who as Master of the Rolls presides over the Court of Appeal, has frequently expressed his belief that that court ought to have the same freedom to depart from its own prior decisions as the House of Lords now claims; some of his colleagues appear to agree with him, but a majority do not. Furthermore, while most of those who agree with Lord Denning are generally prepared to accept the majority view that the Court of Appeal should remain bound by its own decisions, Lord Denning himself (and occasionally, it would seem, one or two others) are not. There are, in any event, a number of established exceptions to the rule that that court is bound by its own decisions, but their limits are somewhat ill-defined, so in practice it is really quite rare that the court must seriously face the question whether it is absolutely bound by one of its own decisions.

Decisions of Divisional Courts bind all lower courts, and even decisions of a single High Court judge are treated as binding on magistrates and tribunals, and generally by lawyers in the public service. Decisions of judges below the level of the High Court are not regarded as binding on anyone, and there is no systematic method of reporting such decisions.

The above account of the doctrine of precedent may well give a misleading impression of the importance of single binding decisions. Undoubtedly there are some situations where such decisions settle the law on a clear, simple point. In the interpretation of a statute, for instance, a simple ambiguity may be found which gives two alternative meanings to a section: the choice may be stark and straight-forward, even though the resolution of the ambiguity may be quite difficult. In such a case, a single decision may settle the issue, particularly if it is in the Court of Appeal or the House of Lords. But much more commonly, it is clusters of decisions which are important for the development of the law. Usually it is found

that areas of doubt and uncertainty in the law, as well as newly developing areas, give rise to more litigation than other areas: this occurs for the obvious reason that lawyers are unable to advise their clients with the same degree of confidence in these areas, and the prospects of successful appeals may well be higher in such cases. So it quite often happens that a whole series of new cases arises in a relatively short period of time. When this happens, it also often becomes clear that new vistas are opening up, and, perhaps, that new problems, hitherto unsuspected, have been thrown up. Such a cluster of cases may well trigger off academic writing, which in turn may influence counsel in arguing subsequent cases. After a while matters may settle down again, and a new bit of law is, as it were, digested by the law and lawyers. This sort of development does not necessarily raise serious issues about the binding force of particular precedents, though such a development is occasionally triggered off by a loosening-up of the effect of an earlier series of precedents.

One recent illustration of this process, of some general interest, concerns the liability of barristers and solicitors for negligence in handling their clients' affairs. Until the early 1960s the law was taken to be settled that (1) a solicitor was liable for negligence on the same footing as any other professional adviser, but (2) that a barrister was not so liable because a barrister did not have a direct contract with his client — the client being compelled to approach the barrister through the solicitor with whom he contracted. Then in 1964 the House of Lords decided the famous *Hedley Byrne* case [1964] AC 465 which had nothing at all to do with the liability of barristers or solicitors, but which recognized for the first time that liability for negligent professional advice might arise *in tort*, that is, even between parties not in a contractual relationship. Barristers, of course, were quick to appreciate that their own traditional immunities might now be called in question, and in two subsequent decisions the House of Lords has begun to explore this possibility. These two decisions have laid down a new framework of law, much of which remains to be filled in by later decisions. Barristers remain immune from negligence liability in respect of the actual conduct of a case in court and in respect of advisory work which is so closely connected with the conduct of the case that it is in effect preparatory work for the trial, but they are no longer immune in respect of purely advisory work. Further, although none of these cases has so far actually involved the liability of a solicitor, it is pretty clear from *dicta* in them, that a solicitor's liability will now be equated with a barrister's, and he will share the barrister's immunity in respect of the actual conduct of a case in court — and cases in lower courts often are handled by solicitors. What is now likely to happen is that there will be a number of cases defining somewhat more clearly the line between purely advisory work and preparation for actual litigation.

This series of cases (and I have omitted some of the less significant) illustrates the way in which the common law can still develop, step by step, almost as though it were an organic growth. We now have a number of judgments in several cases, each of which offers arguments and opinions in favour of this or that development. Hypothetical examples may also be given, some of the arguments in one judgment may be rebutted in another judgment, and so on. Then for a while, the issues may move into the public domain, particularly where, as in this case, there is a public interest in the legal rules being developed. There may be academic articles and notes, media discussion, perhaps anecdotal evidence of past injustices, and possibly even a parliamentary debate. All this may indirectly feed into the next round of developments, and so the process continues.

(c) This Case System: Precedent†

Karl Llewellyn

We turn first to what I may call the orthodox doctrine of precedent, with which, in its essence, you are already familiar. Every case lays down a rule, the rule of the case. The express ratio decidendi is prima facie the rule of the case, since it is the ground upon which the court chose to rest its decision. But a later court can reexamine the case and can invoke the canon that no judge has power to decide what is not before him, can, through examination of the facts or of the procedural issue, narrow the picture of what was actually before the court and can hold that the ruling made requires to be understood as thus restricted. In the extreme form this results in what is known as expressly "confining the case to its particular facts." This rule holds only of redheaded Walpoles in pale magenta Buick cars. And when you find this said of a past case you know that in effect it has been overruled. Only a convention, a somewhat absurd convention, prevents flat overruling in such instances. It seems to be felt as definitely improper to state that the court in a prior case was wrong, peculiarly so if that case was in the same court which is speaking now. It seems to be felt that this would undermine the dogma of the infallibility of courts. So lip service is done to that dogma, while the rule which the prior court laid down is disembowelled. The execution proceeds with due respect, with mandarin courtesy.

Now this orthodox view of the authority of precedent — which I shall call the *strict* view — is but *one of two views* which seem to me wholly contradictory to each other. It is in practice the dogma which is applied to *unwelcome* precedents. It is the recognized, legitimate, honorable technique for whittling precedents away, for making the lawyer, in his argument, and the court, in its decision, free of them. It is a surgeon's knife.

It is orthodox, I think, because it has been more discussed than is the other. Consider the situation. It is not easy thus to carve a case to pieces. It takes thought, it takes conscious thought, it takes analysis. There is no great art and no great difficulty in merely looking at a case, reading its language, and then applying some sentence which is there expressly stated. But there is difficulty in going underneath what is said, in making a keen reexamination of the case that stood before the court, in showing that the language used was quite beside the point, as the point is revealed under the lens of leisured microscopic refinement. Hence the technique of distinguishing cases has given rise to the closest of scrutiny. The technique of arguing for a distinction has become systematized. And when men start talking of authority, or of the doctrine of precedent, they turn naturally to that part of their minds which has been *consciously* devoted to the problem; they call up the

---

† From Karl Llewellyn, *The Bramble Bush: On Our Law and Its Study* (New York: Oceana Publications, Inc., 1960) at 66–69. Reproduced with permission of Oxford University Press, Oxford, UK.

cases, the analyses, the arguments, which have been made under such conditions. They put this together, and call this "*the* doctrine". I suspect there is still another reason for the orthodoxy. That is that only finer minds, minds with sharp mental scalpels, can do this work, and that it is the finer minds — the minds with a sharp cutting edge — which write about it and which thus set up the tradition of the books. To them it must seem that what blunt minds can do as well as they is poor; but that which they alone can do is good. They hit in this on a truth in part: you can pass with ease from this strict doctrine of precedent to the other. If you can handle this, then you can handle both. Not vice versa. The strict doctrine, then, is the technique to be learned. *But not to be mistaken for the whole.*

For when you turn to the actual operations of the courts, or, indeed, to the arguments of lawyers, you will find a totally different view of precedent at work beside this first one. That I shall call, to give it a name, the *loose view* of precedent. That is the view that a court has decided, and decided authoritatively, *any* point or all points on which it chose to rest a case, or on which it chose, after due argument, to pass. No matter how broad the statement, no matter how unnecessary on the facts or the procedural issues, if that was the rule the court laid down, then that the court has held. Indeed, this view carries over often into dicta, and even into dicta which are grandly obiter. In its extreme form this results in thinking and arguing exclusively from *language* that is found in past opinions, and in citing and working with that language wholly without reference to the facts of the case which called the language forth.

Now it is obvious that this is a device not for cutting past opinions away from judges' feet, but for using them as a springboard when they are found convenient. This is a device for *capitalizing welcome precedents*. And both the lawyers and the judges use it so. And judged by the *practice* of the most respected courts, as of the courts of ordinary stature, this doctrine of precedent is like the other, recognized, legitimate, honorable.

What I wish to sink deep into your minds about the doctrine of precedent, therefore, is that it is two-headed. It is Janus-faced. That it is not one doctrine, nor one line of doctrine, but two, and two which, *applied at the same time to the same precedent, are contradictory of each other*. That there is one doctrine for getting rid of precedents deemed troublesome and one doctrine for making use of precedents that seem helpful. That these two doctrines exist side by side. That the same lawyer in the same brief, the same judge in the same opinion, may be using the one doctrine, the technically strict one, to cut down half the older cases that he deals with, and using the other doctrine, the loose one, for building with the other half. Until you realize this you do not see how it is possible for law to change and to develop, and yet to stand on the past. You do not see how it is possible to avoid the past mistakes of courts, and yet to make use of every happy insight for which a judge in writing may have found expression. Indeed it seems to me that here we may have part of the answer to the problem as to whether precedent is not as bad as good — supporting a weak judge with the labors of strong predecessors, but binding a strong judge by the errors of the weak. For look again at this matter of the *difficulty* of the doctrine. The strict view — that view that cuts the past away — is *hard* to use. An ignorant, an unskilful judge will find it hard to use: the past will bind him. But the skilful judge — he whom we would make free — *is* thus made free. He has the knife in hand; and he can free himself.

Nor, until you see this double aspect of the doctrine-in-action, do you appreciate how little, in detail, you can predict *out of the rules alone*; how much you must turn, for purposes of prediction, to the reactions of the judges to the facts and to the life around them. Think again in this connection of an English court, all the judges unanimous upon the conclusion, all the judges in disagreement as to what rule the outcome should be rested on.

Applying this two-faced doctrine of precedent to your work in a case class you get, it seems to me, some such result as this: You read each case from the angle of its *maximum* value as a precedent, at least from the angle of its maximum value as a precedent *of the first water*. You will recall that I recommended taking down the ratio decidendi in substantially the court's own words. You see now what I had in mind. Contrariwise, you will also read each case for its *minimum* value as a precedent, to set against the maximum. In doing this you have your eyes out for the narrow issue in the case, the narrower the better. The first question is, how much can this case fairly be made to stand for by a later court to whom the precedent is welcome? You may well add — though this will be slightly flawed authority — the dicta which appear to have been well considered. The second question is, how much is there in this case that cannot be got around, even by a later court that wishes to avoid it?

You have now the tools for arguing from that case as counsel on *either* side of a new case. You turn them to the problem of prediction. Which view will this same court, on a later case on slightly different facts, take: will it choose the narrow or the loose? Which use will be made of this case by one of the other courts whose opinions are before you? Here you will call to your aid the matter of attitude that I have been discussing. Here you will use all that you know of individual judges, or of the trends in specific courts, or, indeed, of the trend in the line of business, or in the situation, or in the times at large — in anything which you may expect to become apparent and important to the court in later cases. But always and always, you will bear in mind that each precedent has not one value, but two, and that the two are wide apart, and that whichever value a later court assigns to it, such assignment will be respectable, traditionally sound, dogmatically correct. Above all, as you turn this information to your own training you will, I hope, come to see that in most doubtful cases the precedents *must* speak ambigu-

ously until the court has made up its mind whether each one of them is welcome or unwelcome. And that the job of persuasion which falls upon you will call, therefore, not only for providing a technical ladder to reach on authority the result that you contend for, but even more, if you are to have *your* use of the precedents made as *you* propose it, the job calls for you, on the facts, to persuade the court your case is sound.

People — and they are curiously many — who think that precedent produces or ever did produce a certainty that did not involve matters of judgment and of persuasion, or who think that what I have described involves improper equivocation by the courts or departure from the court — ways of some golden age — such people simply do not know our system of precedent in which they live.

(d) I Beg to Differ: Interdisciplinary Questions about Law, Language, and Dissent†

Marie-Claire Belleau and Rebecca Johnson

> The lawyer and judge live constantly at the edge of language, the edge of meaning, where the world can be, must be, imagined anew; to do this well is an enormous achievement; to do it badly, a disaster of real importance, not only for the lawyer or judge but for the social world of which they are a part, including the particular people whose lives they affect.
>
> *James Boyd White*[3]

INTRODUCTION

Stability. Change. Each is necessary, each is feared, and law is deeply implicated in both. Modern law, Fitzpatrick reminds us, is stretched between the demands of stable determination and responsive change.[2] There is a constant risk that the demand for equal application of law can blind law to the demands of particular justice, just as there is an equivalent risk that attention to the particular can

threaten to undermine the stability of law itself. Each time a new dispute comes before the court, a judge is require to ask whether it differs, and in what ways. Each story, as well as its outcome, must be articulated through language, with its nuance, promise, and instability. And so it is that the judge lives, as White suggest in the epigraph above, at the edge of language, at the edge of meaning, constantly charged with the tasks of both maintaining stability and of imagining anew.

In this paper, we consider the linking of law and language in the space of the judicial opinion. We are particularly interested in those insights about law and language that can be gained by focusing attention on the space of judicial dissent. In section 1, we offer some introductory remarks about language and the operations of force and persuasion in judicial decision making, turning our attention in section 2 to the specific practice of judicial dissent. In section 3,

---

† From Logan Atkinson and Diana Majury (eds.), *Law, Mystery and the Humanities: Collected Essays* (Toronto: University of Toronto Press Inc., 2008) at 145–61. Reproduced with permission of the publisher. [Notes and/or references omitted.]

we describe a category of dissenting practices that implicate what one might call a 'noetic' space of judgment, and consider how the resources of language might operate in this space. Finally, in section 4, we examine the deployment of language in majority and dissenting opinions, using *Mossop v. Canada* as an example. We suggest that there is much to be learned about dissent and judgment from taking an interdisciplinary approach that draws law and the humanities into closer dialogue.

1. PERSUASION AND FORCE IN THE SPACE OF JUDGMENT

> The power exerted by a legal regime consists less in the force that it can bring to bear against violators of its rules than in its capacity to persuade people that the world described in its images and categories is the only attainable world in which a sane person would want to live.
>
> Robert Gordon[1]

Judges, working in that space on the edge of meaning, are called upon not merely to settle the claims of particular litigants, but also to participate in the stabilization and/or reimagination of the world in which we live. Judgment always involves more than the resolution of a workplace dispute, the granting of joint custody, the sentencing of an accused to a term of imprisonment, the declaration that a category of business transactions is exempt from taxation, or an assessment of the damages to be paid by one neighbour to another. The judge must not only pronounce an outcome, but must also provide an explanation in language — must offer *reasons*.

In his or her reasons, the judge sketches out the dimensions of the legal and social worlds, articulates the social and legal standards against which behaviour will be measured. The judicial opinion tells us which harms are legally cognizable, and which are not; establishes codes of conduct, and zones of protection; decides which relationships will be fostered, and which denied legal recognition. These reasons give substance to a host of presumptions, maps, and blueprints about the world and its operations, about what it is to be an individual, about how individuals relate to each other and to the state.[4] Critical theorists, asked about the significance of judicial texts, might make the observation that this process is ideological at its core, and that judicial opinions are but another form of political discourse.[5]

Certainly, judicial discourse draws on the same resources of language used in other forms of political discourse that urge us to understand the world and

its occupants in certain ways. Judges (like politicians, teachers, artists, and scientists) necessarily rely upon 'culturally shaped processes of categorizing, storytelling and persuasion in going about their business.'[6] What language can lead us to 'know' about the world is a matter of some consequence, as knowledge is deeply implicated in power. Certainly, there are parallels in the construction of knowledge in the humanities, the arts, and the sciences. In all these forms of discourse, language plays a crucial role.

In producing a set of reasons, the judge uses these resources not simply to tell the reader 'what will be,' but also to *convince* the reader that the result is just, or inevitable, or necessary. As Robert Gordon so eloquently put it, a significant part of law's power lies in its capacity to persuade its readers that 'the world described in its images and categories is the only attainable world in which a sane person would want to live.'[7] The task of the judge is thus not simply to imagine the world anew, but also to share that imagination through language in a manner that draws readers to make common cause with the reasons, to willingly govern themselves in accordance with the dictates of the world there described. Law is most efficacious when it has the consent of the governed. Judges seek to persuade.

And yet, it is worth attending to Fried's reminder that, in the world of political discourses, the judicial opinion is unique: it is an *authoritative* explanation.[8] Supported by a majority of the court, a judicial opinion 'is not just power disciplined by reason; it is also reason disciplined by power.'[9] The language of law is backed up by the threat of force.[10] A judge does not merely describe the world that is, or indeed, a world that would be desirable. A judge has the power and ability to make that world real. Even those who are not persuaded — who do not believe in the images and categories described in judicial decisions — will be made subject to them; they are required to live as if those images and categories are real. Judicial opinion, in their pronouncements of social and legal knowledge, play a very real part in the maintenance (and disruption) of systems of power, with the accompanying race, gender, class, corporate, colonial, or imperializing inflections.

Up to this point, we have been speaking as if the judicial voice were 'singular,' but often it is not. Judges are not always of the same mind about the questions raised by the cases before them. Judges can and do disagree about the shape of the world as it exists, and about the ways that the world should be legally ordered. In struggles over meaning, judges, like the rest of us, sometimes find themselves in the space of dissent.

2. JUDGING IN THE SPACE OF DISSENT

'With the greatest respect, I cannot agree...'

'With respect, I must dissent in part...'

'I am unable to concur...'

'I must dissent from the judgment herein...'

'I must dissent to the judgment of the majority.'[11]

'Dissent' is the written (published) expression of judicial disagreement, in a context where an appellate court is not unanimous in the judgment. Where agreement breaks down, a case can produce multiple opinions: a majority opinion, plus one or more additional opinions expressing either 'dissent' or 'concurrence.' Narrowly defined, a 'dissenting opinion' is one in which the author disagrees with the result reached by the majority, and thus writes a set of reasons explaining the different reasoning and results. The 'concurring opinion' is a bit more nuanced. Though the word 'concur' means 'to agree,' a concurrence is a form of judicial disagreement. The judge who writes concurring reasons arrives at the same result as the majority, but finds it necessary to distance him- or herself from the majority's reasoning, or indeed, to provide a completely different rationale for the result. Agreeing with the result, but disagreeing with reasoning, the concurrence straddles the division between majority and dissent. It can be counted as a dissent when it comes to 'result,' but it can instead be counted as a dissent when it comes to 'reasoning.' In a context where the central issue is the shape of the 'reasons' given by a judge, the concurrence is best theorized as a form of dissent.

The published dissenting judicial opinion is not a feature of all legal regimes.[12] Neither has it been an unchanging feature where it has operated. The forms and manners and magnitude of judicial dissent have varied across time and location, with judges feeling, at various historical junctions, more or less pressure to speak with a unified voice.[13] Certainly, both in North America and abroad, there has been a history of debate about the value of judicial dissent: does it improve the system, or undermine the legitimacy and authority of a court?

Those who defend the tradition of dissent have drawn attention to at least three of its functions.[14] First, dissent is said to safeguard the integrity of the judicial institution. The possibility of dissent preserves and strengthens the tradition of judicial independence, fostering collegiality and enhancing coherence.[15] Because opinions can be expressed in dissent, the majority does not need to water down its view, or compromise on important principles in the interest of getting votes. A dissent forces the majority to more sharply justify their opinion and account for the implications of their decision, enhancing the coherence of the resulting opinions. Second, dissent sustains a robust ongoing legal dialogue across multiple constituencies. Dissenters may be speaking to their colleagues, but they may have different (or additional) audiences in mind: the parties themselves, future litigants, academics and other courts, legislatures, the public at large, and students of law. This dialogue is one that occurs across time, drawing connections both with the past and the future. Third, people emphasize dissent's 'prophetic' function. The dissent may provide a source of guidance for the resolution of similar issues in the future, may sow seeds of innovation which sometimes 'take root in the spirit of the law.'[16]

Like a majority opinion, a dissenting opinion seeks to persuade the reader to understand the world in a specific way. However, the dissenting opinion does not wield law's Solomonic sword of power.[17] A judicial opinion has the force of law (the ability to make its vision of law operational in the world) only where its author speaks for the majority of judges on the court. A dissenting opinion is, from this perspective, simply 'not law.' Some have gone as far as to suggest that a dissent is less an exercise of power than akin to a work of scholarship.[18] But this view provides an insufficient account of the authority that judicial dissent possesses, both for the majority judges who must respond to the dissenting text, and for the audiences that read the words of both.

The fact that the substance of the dissenting opinion is produced by a judge is a matter of some significance. Words of dissent are words uttered by a judge acting in the capacity of judge; those words remain enrobed with the authority of judicial office. This makes a dissenting opinion significantly different from other attempts to persuade or convince. A dissenter has the ability to force the majority to respond, to answer, to explain, to shift, or to accommodate. The words of a dissenting opinion are a direct challenge, and the majority may feel required to enter into dialogue. And even where a majority does not respond directly, the very fact of the dissent often means that the majority reasons must be written differently than they would have been in the absence of a dissent.

Indeed, dissents themselves often become part of the 'canon' of law.[19] Some dissents, with time, successfully bring about change in the law. A court may explicitly revisit a problem, expressly overturning the law and adopting what had formerly been a dissenting view.[20] But dissent may also bring about change in a more direct fashion. A dissent may fail to persuade the majority of the court, but encourage other lawmakers to act, and it may convince those with legislative power to propose changes in line with that suggested in a dissent. In the Canadian context, for example, Parliament introduced a set of legal reforms dealing with the disclosure of sexual assault victim's private records. Those reforms rejected the majority view expressed in *O'Connor*, adopting instead an approach like that which had been articulated by the dissent.[21] Legislators can make real that which is imagined in the space of dissent.

The relational nature of struggles over meaning is foregrounded in cases where judges disagree. In the face of disagreement, judges find themselves forced to attend even more closely to the ways in which they deploy all the persuasive resources of language. Though law self-presents as a world in which the heated passions are subjected to the rigour of cold rationality, legal reasoning has always involved appeals to both 'the rational' and 'the passionate' dimensions of human understanding. As Samuel Pillsbury notes, passion, though always present in law, may be more visible in dissenting than majority texts.[22] Though majority and dissenting opinions may have the same range of rhetorical moves available to them, the dissent, deprived of that element of force or violence provided by the legal authoritativeness of a majority opinion, may need to draw even deeper on the available tools of persuasion.

> The most enduring dissents ... seek to sow seeds for future harvest. These are the dissents that soar with passion and ring with rhetoric. These are the dissents that, at their best, straddle the worlds of literature and law.
> Justice William J. Brennan Jr[23]

In asking about the role of passion and persuasion in the space of dissent, one should note that dissent takes multiple forms.[24] Certainly, even a cursory scan of a single volume of the Supreme Court Reports leaves one struck by variances in the character, length, form, and seeming significance of different dissenting opinions. Some dissents read like novellas, while others consist of a terse, 'I disagree for the reasons given by the judge below.' Some are 'self-contained,' and can be read on their own with no reference to other opinions. Others are clear responses to majority reasons, and make sense only when being read in conjunction with those other opinions. Some dissents concern disputes over technical issues, while others involve policy choices, characterizations of facts, or conflicting values.

Though one might treat all dissent as equivalent for the purpose of certain statistical measures, there are contexts in which it is useful to distinguish between different kinds of dissent. In this discussion, we are interested in judicial dissents that draw deeply on the persuasive resources of language — those that seem most clearly to 'appeal to the future,' capture 'the brooding spirit,' or 'sow seeds for future harvest.'[25] Such dissents articulate an alternative vision of 'the real,' redescribe the facts, redraw the boundary between the legal and the social, and challenge how we think about law itself. We find it useful to think about such dissenting texts using Amsterdam and Bruner's concept of 'noetic space.'[26]

Noetic space is the term they use to describe the distinctive imaginative space maintained in every culture. It is the space linked to 'a distinctively human mental capacity that compels us to project our imaginations beyond the ordinary, the expectable, the legitimate — and to involve others in our imaginings.'[27] The term 'noetic space,' they note, comes from the Greek 'nous,' which includes not only the deliberations of the rational mind, but also its appetites and affections: its beliefs, desires, feelings, hopes, intentions.[28] Noetic space is a space of the mind, a space that integrates emotions and passions. Amsterdam and Bruner tell us that noetic space is specialized for testing the limits of the possible; as such, it is a pragmatic place that 'must honour the limits of lifelikeness — the limits beyond which [it] cannot go without losing the imaginative engagement of the audience.'[29] Noetic space is, they tell us, the space of literature, stories, and plays. We suggest that this is also an apt description of a body of judicial dissent. For judicial dissent is not simply a record of the judicial imaginary. Noetic dissent attempts to involve the legal reader in its imagination. This dissenting imagination does not only sketch out fantasy space, or utopic strivings. It is a purposefully pragmatic space. It attempts to persuade the reader that this alternative is within reach. The dissenter is less interested in documenting alternatives than in bringing the reader onboard. Successful interventions in noetic space say not simply 'things could be different,' but also encourage their listeners to (using the words of *Star Trek: The Next Generation's* Jean-Luc Picard) 'Make it so.'

Successful work in the noetic draws deeply on the tools of persuasion, attempting to convince its listeners at both the rational and the visceral levels. When interrogating a noetic text for emotion, one should press past a narrow understanding of what the language of 'emotion' looks like, and of the ways emotion can be made textually manifest.[30] It is not just a matter of attending to expressive language, or of focusing on 'hot' emotions like anger or outrage. One can also attend to 'colder' emotional states (like disgust or indifference); scrutinize less overtly expressive uses of language, including the structure of judgments, and textual silences;[31] understand something of the tonality of the texts produced in majority and dissenting space; explore the ways that the text weaves together reason and emotion; look closely at the intersection of law and language; consider multiple avenues of enquiry and methodological approaches.

In their work *Minding the Law*, Amsterdam and Bruner discuss some of the approaches one can take to judicial texts, approaches that help focus attention on the concrete processes of categorizing, storytelling, and persuasion that shape the resulting texts. They suggest watching for the kinds of categories and categorizing moves used. Categories, Amsterdam and Bruner remind us, are made in the mind, rather than found in the world; they are both 'indispensable instruments' and 'inevitable beguilers.'[32] Three of the most visible categories are 'natural theoretical,' 'human narrative,' and 'supernatural religious.'[33] Where the category of 'natural theoretical' is opening, authority comes from the ability to verify. Just as in the natural sciences, the production or existence of knowledge requires that evidence can be seen, witnessed, verified, or confirmed against some objective, abstract, or independent standard.[34] In the category of 'human narrative,' authority comes from verisimilitude: what matters most is the appearance of truth — the extent to which evidence before one conforms with what one expects in a society's stock stories.[35] For example, in the context of a woman charged with murdering her spouse, to what extent do her acts comport with dominant stories about 'battered wives' or 'vengeful and betrayed women'?[36] Where the category of 'supernatural religious' is functioning, authority is dependent on the ability to enlist belief as an act of faith. In this, theological and legal acts of faith are not dissimilar. Cases about 'the sanctity of life' (whether in the context of abortion, assisted suicide, or the patenting of the OncoMouse™) often deploy such acts of faith. But belief as a ground of authority is also visible in the routine sentencing practices of criminal law: one might ask, for example, why, knowing what we know (and don't know) about the relationship between incarceration and recidivism, we continue to use retribution in sentencing.[37]

All categories are put into place through scripts and narratives: stories that provide examples of canonical expectations, and stories that warn us about the threats that confront us when the traditional scripts are thrown off the rails. These stories help us know who the heroes and heroines are, where the threats lie, and what must be done to restore order and balance. In contrasting majority and dissenting judgments, one can often see the struggle to dictate the categories that will transform 'troubles' into 'issues,' and vice versa.[38] Does the dissenter accept the majority's categories, or attempt to shift the narratives, and identify different agents and threats to be avoided? And what rhetorical strategies are used to open up or shut down ways of thinking or understanding?

There are a number of rhetorical devices that judges can use to manage contestability in their opinions. Epistemological techniques can make the facts appear more or less certain. Phrases like 'evidence was presented' or 'nothing before the court indicates' are ways for the court to express epistemological angst or certainty. Ontological techniques of construction allow one to concretize and deconcretize; presuppose the world to be one way, or reify a given set of understandings; structure the possible and even the imaginable. Watch for metaphors of centrality or indispensability. When do courts rely on phrases like 'I am ineluctably led to conclude' or 'the inference is inescapable,' or tell us that the court 'is a prisoner of the case presented to them'?[39] Such techniques allow judges to foreground, conceal, and manage moments of choice.

Watch also for the ways texts make meaning through the deployment of symbols. Are judges evoking prototypes, or attempting to break through typesets? How does a text rely on ideas of 'the ordinary,' 'the normal,' 'the average,' 'the reasonable,' 'the typical'? What does the text tell us about 'the good mother,' 'the ordinary barroom brawl,' 'the average domestic dispute'? How does a text engage with or attempt to disengage coded meanings? Does a text encode new layers of meaning into old words, making those words do a different kind of political work?[40] How does the text draw on language's ability to capture, deploy, and convey passion and emotion? Here, the issue is not just the presence of 'hot' and 'cold' words, but of how texts express the facts, how stories get set up, how characters are (and are not) presented, how the stage is set to foreground an eventual outcome. Attend not only to the 'rich' texts — to those that soar with passion and ring with rhetoric — but also to those that feel flat, because 'flatness' is not necessarily a failure of judicial writing skill. Flatness of characters and of tone can press our affiliations in a variety of directions. By giving (and denying) personality to protagonists, the tonal character of a story can be made to shift. So, too, the moral centre and gravity of a story.

All the above techniques are presumably available to majority and dissenting judges. We are interested here in the ways the techniques are used in practice. Split decisions provide a fertile terrain for examining language, and the deployment of discourses of reason and emotion in law. Because majority and dissent are in dialogue with each other, one needs to attend to the ways in which the language chosen and tools deployed in one judgment are connected to the language chosen and tools deployed in the other.

4.   A CASE STUDY: *MOSSOP V. CANADA*

As an example, let us compare three opinions — majority, a dissent, and a concurrency — produced in a single case. The vehicle we will use is *Mossop v. Canada*,[41] an early case in a series of judgments concerning sexual orientation. In this case, Brian Mossop made an unsuccessful argument about the heteronormativity of law's definition of 'the family'. The point of the analysis here is not the legal resolution of the case; rather, it is attention to the tools of persuasion deployed in the three opinions.[42] The legal problem was straightforward: was Brian Mossop entitled to take a day of bereavement leave to attend the funeral of his (same-sex) partner's father? The terms of the collective agreement governing his employment stated that he could have bereavement leave in the event of a death of a family member. The definition of 'family' was fairly broad, including not only legally recognized 'in-laws' but also common-law spouses and their extended family members. However, same-sex couples were excluded from the definition of common-law spouses. In 1993, the Canadian Human Rights Act prohibited discrimination on the basis of a list of grounds: 'family status' was listed, but 'sexual orientation' was not. In denying bereavement leave to Mossop, was the employer discriminating against him on the basis of his 'family status' (prohibited) or on the basis of his 'sexual orientation' (not prohibited)? The majority of the court did not see the denial as based on his family status, and concluded that Mossop was not entitled to bereavement leave. The three judicial texts use quite different categorizing moves, narratives scripts, and rhetorical devices in addressing the problem.

The dissenting text of Madame Justice Claire L'Heureux-Dubé places Brian Mossop inside a narrative of 'family,' setting up the facts in a manner that emphasizes the ordinary dimensions of what are commonly seen as family issues. The opening of her text reads as follows: 'The complainant Mr. Mossop and his male companion Mr. Popert first met in 1974 and lived together from 1976 on in a jointly owned and maintained home. The two men shared day-to-day activities, maintained a sexual relationship, and were known to their friends and families as a homosexual couple. On June 3, 1985, Mr. Mossop attended the funeral of Mr. Popert's father.'[43] This paragraph is notable for its ordinariness. Indeed, it reads very much like the facts in any routine family law case involving separation and the division of property. The only difference seems to be that the two parties are both men. Compare that paragraph with the description of the facts in Chief Justice Antonio Lamer's majority reasons: 'In June 3, 1985, Mossop attended the funeral of the father of the man whom Mossop described as his lover. Mossop testified that the two men have known each other since 1974, and have resided together since 1976 in a jointly owned and maintained home. They share the day-to-day developments in their lives and maintain a sexual relationship. Each has made the other the beneficiary of his will. They are known to their friends and families as lovers.'[44] While both paragraphs mention the sexual relationship and the joint ownership of property, this second telling of the facts does so in a way that uses the terminology of sexuality rather than of companionship and family. The text does this by using the term 'lovers' twice in one paragraph. Significantly, one of these uses asserts that those most close to the men know them not as 'a couple' (the language used in the dissenting text), but as 'lovers.' Where a relationship is spoken of using the language of family or couple, the sexual dimension of the relationship is set in an authorized context, implying reciprocal obligations, responsibilities, and permanence. The term 'lover,' on the other hand, carries connotations of that which is unauthorized, illicit, or forbidden. It suggests elements of promiscuity, infidelity, and transience. In the terms used in formulation of the facts, Justice Lamer presses us away from legitimated narratives of 'family' and towards a narrative of individualized (with an edge of taboo) 'sexuality' — something perhaps to be tolerated, but not something to be confused with family.

There is a second set of moves visible in the above two articulations of the 'facts': rhetorical moves that make the facts appear more or less certain, that open up and close down the range of interpretive possibilities.[45] Note that the dissenting text provides a highly concrete description of the men. Consider the use of verbs in an indicative mode: the men 'met,' 'lived together,' 'shared,' 'maintained,' 'were known as.' In the majority formulation of the facts (one that will deny Brian Mossop's claim), things are not quite as solid. We are *not* told that Popert and Mossop *are* lovers. Rather, we are told that Mossop 'testified' that the two men had an intertwined life. Though the effect is subtle, this formulation inserts a bit of distance between the parties and the readers. Some rhetorical formulations suggest solidity, stability, reliability, and credibility. Words like 'described,' 'testified,' 'might,' 'alleged,' and other qualifying verbs introduce elements of uncertainty. The majority, using words like 'testified' and 'described as,' trigger the legal reader to ask questions about credibility. Such formulations, if not downgrading the credibility of any particular witness, nonetheless serve to introduce elements of uncertainty, reminding the reader that tales told are not always full descriptions of reality. Such approaches serve to de-emphasize the importance of any given account of the facts, drawing allegiances away from individual parties and towards (more abstract) legal principles, which are presented as being more reliable.

The concurring reasons of Mr Justice Gérard La Forest make another categorizing move altogether. Here, there is no description of the facts, and the male parties go nearly unnamed. A description of the men seems unimportant, since the opinion focuses on the jurisdictional dimensions of the legal problem: first, the standard judges should use before interfering with the decisions of administrative tribunals; and second, discerning the legislative intent behind the prohibition against 'family status' discrimination. Justice La Forest's reasons are built primarily on a narrative concerning the appropriate division of powers between judicial, administrative, and legislative functions. The 'threat' in this story is that judges might wrongly overstep the boundaries of their authority, either by failing to adequately police the behaviour of administrative tribunals, or by engaging in activist reinterpretation of language that does not accord with parliamentary will. The threat is of a court usurping legislative power.

With this different narrative foregrounded, Justice La Forest separates the 'human terms' from the 'legal terms' involved in the story. He disclaims judicial responsibility for the discrimination suffered by any particular party, placing that burden rather on the shoulders of Parliament. At the same time, the categorical and rhetorical moves that have been made affirm the placement of same-sex relationships

outside the protective scope of 'family.' Consider this passage: 'I recognize, however, that particularly in recent years the word [family] is loosely used to cover other relationships. The appellant here argues that "family status" should cover a relationship dependent on a same-sex living arrangement. While some may refer to such a relationship as a "family," I do not think it has yet reached that status in the ordinary use of language. Still less was it the case when the statute was enacted. In human terms, it is certainly arguable that bereavement leave should be granted to homosexual couples in a long-term relationship in the same way as it applies to heterosexual couples, but that is an issue for Parliament to address.'[46]

This passage works in complicated ways. First, the language used tends to disembody the case. Mossop is invoked here as 'the appellant,' but only for the purpose of identifying a legal argument. Though made in the name of 'the appellant,' the argument is concretely made through the body of a lawyer. The reader is not forced to grapple with the suffering of the parties before them. Mossop himself doesn't come into view except in the form of an abstract legal argument about statutory interpretation.

Note also that the language used by Justice La Forest to describe this 'abstract' legal argument anticipates the conclusion that family status does not apply. He states that the issue is whether family status 'should cover a relationship dependent on a same-sex living arrangement.' This is neither 'the couple' of Justice L'Heureux-Dubé's reasons nor 'the lovers' of Justice Lamer's. This is a much more vague 'relationship dependent on a same-sex living arrangement.' This terminology carries the air of something loose and unspecified, of uncertain meaning, perhaps vaguely contractual, maybe akin to arrangements between roommates, but certainly not a family. Consider also La Forest's comment that 'the word [family] is loosely used to cover other relationships.' The word 'loosely' does some important work here, helping to establish a boundary between 'real families' and 'other relationships.' The phrase 'loosely used' deprives these 'other relationships' of the dignity accorded to those having a legitimate claim to the imprimatur of the term 'family.' 'Such a relationship,' to use his language, is distinguishable from the real, is perhaps more akin to an approximation, a mock-up, or facsimile (perhaps even a forgery or a fake).

In invoking 'ordinary use of language' to counterpose 'family' and 'other relationships,' Justice La Forest also positions the implied reader (an ordinary user of language) as someone who is not familiar with or living in groupings, close and extended, where one knows of or has homosexual relationships. By invoking the 'human terms' as he does, by suggesting that bereavement leave should perhaps 'be granted to homosexual couples in a long-term relationship,' he also allows himself and the implied reader to position themselves as open-minded, free from prejudicial bias, while simultaneously denying Mossop's claim for equal treatment. Responsibility for the loss rests neither with the Court nor with the implied reader, but with Parliament.

In *Mossop*, the judges divided on strong ideological grounds. However, we do not believe that the language moves used in the case 'belong' to one side or the other, and would emphasize that neither dissent nor 'passion' is the exclusive provenance of 'progressive' or 'conservative' forces. Certainly, the shifts in the sexual orientation cases make this clear.[47] In the ten years following *Mossop*, the Court heard a number of sexual orientation cases. In them, one can see judicial opinions once expressed in dissent shifting to the majority and vice versa. One can also see that, with each new case, the forms of argument and the tools deployed shift back and forth, as the judges grapple with the different moves deemed necessary to persuade readers from within either majority or dissenting space.

For example, two years after *Mossop*, in a 5–4 split in *Egan and Nesbitt*, the majority again declined to grant benefits to same-sex partners.[48] Five of the nine judges concluded that the same-sex male partners had suffered discrimination through being denied access to pension plan benefits. The men, nonetheless, were unsuccessful, because one of those five judges believed that the denial of equality could be (at least temporarily) justified on the basis that Canadians were just getting used to acknowledging same-sex discrimination. Thus, five of the nine judges saw discrimination, but only four of the nine judges found the discrimination to be unjustified. Justice La Forest again wrote an opinion, one holding the day on the result, but in dissent on the question of discrimination. It is worth attending to the language he uses as he moves from majority to dissenting space.

In *Mossop*, Justice La Forest stepped lightly around the question of discrimination, focusing instead on legislative intent and ordinary meaning. In *Egan*, La Forest finds himself in dissent, against a majority who declare the restriction of benefits to opposite-sex couples to be discriminatory. Heteronormativity is no longer to be taken for granted, but must be justified. Justice La Forest takes up this challenge, saying: 'Marriage has from time immemo-

rial been firmly grounded in our legal tradition, one that is itself a reflection of long-standing philosophical and religious traditions. But its ultimate *raison d'être* transcends all of these and is firmly anchored in the biological and social realities that heterosexual couples have the unique ability to procreate, that most children are the product of these relationships, and that they are generally cared for and nurtured by those who live in that relationship. In this sense, marriage is by nature heterosexual. It would be possible to legally define marriage to include homosexual couples, but this would not change the biological and social realities that underlie the traditional marriage.'[49] In this passage, note that categories play an important role. Justice La Forest here draws on both the 'natural/theoretical' and the 'supernatural/religious' in his assertions that marriage is grounded both in a religious and biological higher reality. Recall also that in *Mossop* he suggested that Parliament was responsible for distinguishing between same- and opposite-sex couples. He also implied that 'human terms' might favour the extent of benefits across the sexual orientation divide. Here, however, note his statement that a change to legal definitions cannot alter a deeper reality. The persuasive move here appears to be directed at encouraging the reader to believe and accept something about the necessary heterosexual essence of marriage (if not family). It was not, however, necessary to articulate this vision of the natural/religious grounding of heterosexuality until its givenness was called into question. Here, Justice La Forest is making a passionate categorical argument in what has begun to become noetic space.

Indeed, by 2004, the Supreme Court was unanimous in upholding the constitutionality of the government's legislation making same-sex marriage a legal reality in Canada.[50] What was once articulated in noetic space had become a legal reality. The legal questions raised in the various cases along the path to that conclusion are not identical, and one should attend to those differences. But the cases offer a valuable site for exploring the kinds of shifts in language that one can see as majorities attempt to justify the state of the law that they produce, and as dissenters attempt to persuade readers, other judges, legislators, and the public that things can and should be otherwise. As various positions move from majority to dissent and back again, the cases make it possible to closely explore the deployment of language in majority and noetic space.

5.   CONCLUSION

> The statutes and conventions and authorities and orthodoxies of a culture are always in a dialectical relationship with contrarian myths, dissenting fictions, and (most important of all) the restless powers of the human imagination ... the dialectic between the canonical and imagined is not only inherent in human culture, but gives culture is dynamism and, in some unfathomable way, its unpredictability — its freedom.
>
> Anthony Amsterdam and Jerome Bruner[51]

The pull between the demands of stability and change is one constant in the life of law. Judges are called upon not only to specify the current balance, but also to persuade us that the balance is good, right, and necessary. The space of dissent plays an important role in maintaining a generative relationship between the canonical and the imagined. Noetic dissent is more than a mere failed majority, and what happens in that space is a matter of some significance. There are good reasons to extend the focus of legal enquiry beyond the substance of a dissent to include the language in which it is crafted. How is language practice implicated in the ability of some dissents to so powerfully occupy noetic space? Are there ways of asking about language and noetic space that might help us think in more complicated and nuanced ways about the processes of judging, and of the persuasive calls made by judges to different audiences? Might attention to language use in noetic space help us better grapple with some puzzles about dissent raised by empirical work on the Supreme Court?[52]

It seems clear enough that attempts to grapple with the power of law — in its authoritative and dissenting forms — require close attention to and understanding of the power of language. There are many puzzles to consider. What do dissenting judicial texts desire (or require) of us as readers? What questions do they ask? In what directions do they point? What courses of action do they suggest? How do they focus our attention in some places and not in others? How do judges use language to shore up or revolutionize specific understandings of legal concepts like 'the family,' 'the corporation,' or ['consent'?] How do judges set up the facts, describe the context, and elaborate the consequences? How do they characterize the parties, identify agents, describe the threats to be avoided, the choices to be confronted, and the prizes to be won? How do they articulate and disarticulate 'reality,' rending visible the voices and values that are muted or absent in the opposing reasons? And then, do judges do all this differently when writing in dissent than when writing for the majority? These are pressing questions to be explored, questions whose answers may be found at the intersection of law and language.

172

Interpreting Legislation

(a) *Re Rizzo & Rizzo Shoes Ltd.*[†]

[Iacobucci J. for the Court:]

[1] This is an appeal by the former employees of a now bankrupt employer from an order disallowing their claims for termination pay (including vacation pay thereon) and severance pay. The case turns on an issue of statutory interpretation. Specifically, the appeal decides whether, under the relevant legislation in effect at the time of the bankruptcy, employees are entitled to claim termination and severance payments where their employment has been terminated by reason of their employer's bankruptcy.

. . . .

2. RELEVANT STATUTORY PROVISIONS

[6] The relevant versions of the *Bankruptcy Act* (now the *Bankruptcy and Insolvency Act*) and the *Employment Standards Act* for the purposes of this appeal are R.S.C., 1985, c. B-3 (the *"BA"*), and R.S.O. 1980, c. 137, as amended to April 14, 1989 (the *"ESA"*) respectively.

Employment Standards Act, R.S.O. 1980, c. 137, as amended:

> 7. ...
>
> (5) Every contract of employment shall be deemed to include the following provision:
>
>> All severance pay and termination pay become payable and shall be paid by the employer to the employee in two weekly instalments beginning with the first full week following termination of employment and shall be allocated to such weeks accordingly. This provision does not apply to severance pay if the employee has elected to maintain a right of recall as provided in subsection 40a (7) of the *Employment Standards Act*.
>
> **40.**(1) No employer shall terminate the employment of an employee who has been employed for three months or more unless the employee gives,
> (a) one weeks notice in writing to the employee if his or her period of employment is less than one year;
> (b) two weeks notice in writing to the employee if his or her period of employment is one year or more but less than three years;
> (c) three weeks notice in writing to the employee if his or her period of employment is three years or more but less than four years;
> (d) four weeks notice in writing to the employee if his or her period of employment is four years or more but less than five years;
> (e) five weeks notice in writing to the employee if his or her period of employment is five years or more but less than six years;
> (f) six weeks notice in writing to the employee if his or her period of employment is six years or more but less than seven years;
> (g) seven weeks notice in writing to the employee if his or her period of employment is seven years or more but less than eight years;
> (h) eight weeks notice in writing to the employee if his or her period of employment is eight years or more, and such notice has expired.
>> ...
>
> (7) Where the employment of an employee is terminated contrary to this section,

---

† [1998] 1 S.C.R. 27 at paras. 1, 6, 17–43.

(a) the employer shall pay termination pay in an amount equal to the wages that the employee would have been entitled to receive at his regular rate for a regular non-overtime work week for the period of notice prescribed by subsection (1) or (2), and any wages to which he is entitled;

...

40*a* ...

(1a) Where,

(a) fifty or more employees have their employment terminated by an employer in a period of six months or less and the terminations are caused by the permanent discontinuance of all or part of the business of the employer at an establishment; or

(b) one or more employees have their employment terminated by an employer with a payroll of $2.5 million or more,

the employer shall pay severance pay to each employee whose employment has been terminated and who has been employed by the employer for five or more years.

Employment Standards Amendment Act, 1981, S.O. 1981, c. 22

2.(1) Part XII of the said Act is amended by adding thereto the following section:

...

(3) Section 40*a* of the said Act does not apply to an employer who became a bankrupt or an insolvent person within the meaning of the *Bankruptcy Act* (Canada) and whose assets have been distributed among his creditors or to an employer whose proposal within the meaning of the *Bankruptcy Act* (Canada) has been accepted by his creditors in the period from and including the 1st day of January, 1981, to and including the day immediately before the day this Act receives Royal Assent.

Bankruptcy Act, R.S.C., 1985, c. B-3

121.(1) All debts and liabilities, present or future, to which the bankrupt is subject at the date of the bankruptcy or to which he may become subject before his discharge by reason of any obligation incurred before the date of the bankruptcy shall be deemed to be claims provable in proceedings under this Act.

Interpretation Act, R.S.O. 1990, c. I.11

10. Every Act shall be deemed to be remedial, whether its immediate purport is to direct the doing of anything that the Legislature deems to be for the public good or to prevent or punish the doing of any thing that it deems to be contrary to the public good, and shall accordingly receive such fair, large and liberal construction and interpretation as will best ensure the attainment of the object of the Act according to its true intent, meaning and spirit.

...

17. The repeal or amendment of an Act shall be deemed not to be or to involve any declaration as to the previous state of the law.

. . . .

4.   ISSUES

[17] This appeal raises one issue: does the termination of employment caused by the bankruptcy of an employer give rise to a claim provable in bankruptcy for termination pay and severance pay in accordance with the provisions of the *ESA*?

5.   ANALYSIS

[18] The statutory obligation upon employers to provide both termination pay and severance pay is governed by ss. 40 and 40*a* of the *ESA*, respectively. The Court of Appeal noted that the plain language of those provisions suggests that termination pay and severance pay are payable only when the employer terminates the employment. For example, the opening words of s. 40(1) are: "No employer shall terminate the employment of an employee...." Similarly, s. 40*a*(1a) begins with the words, "Where ... fifty or more employees have their employment terminated by an employer...." Therefore, the question on which this appeal turns is whether, when bankruptcy occurs, the employment can be said to be terminated "by an employer".

[19] The Court of Appeal answered this question in the negative, holding that, where an employer is petitioned into bankruptcy by a creditor, the employment of its employees is not terminated "by an employer", but rather by operation of law. Thus, the Court of Appeal reasoned that, in the circumstances of the present case, the *ESA* termination pay and severance pay provisions were not applicable and no obligations arose. In answer, the appellants submit that the phrase "terminated by an employer" is best interpreted as reflecting a distinction between involuntary and voluntary termination of employment. It is their position that this language was intended to relieve employers of their obligation to pay termination and severance pay when employees leave their jobs voluntarily. However, the appellants maintain that where an employee's employment is involuntarily terminated by reason of their employer's bankruptcy, this constitutes termination "by an employer" for the

purpose of triggering entitlement to termination and severance pay under the *ESA*.

[20] At the heart of this conflict is an issue of statutory interpretation. Consistent with the findings of the Court of Appeal, the plain meaning of the words of the provisions here in question appears to restrict the obligation to pay termination and severance pay to those employers who have actively terminated the employment of their employees. At first blush, bankruptcy does not fit comfortably into this interpretation. However, with respect, I believe this analysis is incomplete.

[21] Although much has been written about the interpretation of legislation (see, e.g., Ruth Sullivan, *Statutory Interpretation* (1997); Ruth Sullivan, *Driedger on the Construction of Statutes* (3rd ed. 1994) (hereinafter "*Construction of Statutes*"); Pierre-André Côté, *The Interpretation of Legislation in Canada* (2nd ed. 1991)), Elmer Driedger in *Construction of Statutes* (2nd ed. 1983) best encapsulates the approach upon which I prefer to rely. He recognizes that statutory interpretation cannot be founded on the wording of the legislation alone. At p. 87 he states:

> Today there is only one principle or approach, namely, the words of an Act are to be read in their entire context and in their grammatical and ordinary sense harmoniously with the scheme of the Act, the object of the Act, and the intention of Parliament.

Recent cases which have cited the above passage with approval include: *R. v. Hydro-Québec*, [1997] 3 S.C.R. 213**; *Royal Bank of Canada v. Sparrow Electric Corp.*, [1997] 1 S.C.R. 411; *Verdun v. Toronto-Dominion Bank*, [1996] 3 S.C.R. 550; *Friesen v. Canada*, [1995] 3 S.C.R. 103.

[22] I also rely upon s. 10 of the *Interpretation Act*, R.S.O. 1980, c. 219, which provides that every Act "shall be deemed to be remedial" and directs that every Act shall "receive such fair, large and liberal construction and interpretation as will best ensure the attainment of the object of the Act according to its true intent, meaning and spirit".

[23] Although the Court of Appeal looked to the plain meaning of the specific provisions in question in the present case, with respect, I believe that the court did not pay sufficient attention to the scheme of the *ESA*, its object or the intention of the legislature; nor was the context of the words in issue appropriately recognized. I now turn to a discussion of these issues.

[24] In *Machtinger v. HOJ Industries Ltd.*, [1992] 1 S.C.R. 986, at p. 1002, the majority of this Court recognized the importance that our society accords to employment and the fundamental role that it has assumed in the life of the individual. The manner in which employment can be terminated was said to be equally important (see also *Wallace v. United Grain Growers Ltd.*, [1997] 3 S.C.R. 701). It was in this context that the majority in *Machtinger* described, at p. 1003, the object of the *ESA* as being the protection of "... the interests of employees by requiring employers to comply with certain minimum standards, including minimum periods of notice of termination". Accordingly, the majority concluded, at p. 1003, that, "... an interpretation of the Act which encourages employers to comply with the minimum requirements of the Act, and so extends its protections to as many employees as possible, is to be favoured over one that does not".

[25] The objects of the termination and severance pay provisions themselves are also broadly premised upon the need to protect employees. Section 40 of the *ESA* requires employers to give their employees reasonable notice of termination based upon length of service. One of the primary purposes of this notice period is to provide employees with an opportunity to take preparatory measures and seek alternative employment. It follows that s. 40(7)(a), which provides for termination pay in lieu of notice when an employer has failed to give the required statutory notice, is intended to "cushion" employees against the adverse effects of economic dislocation likely to follow from the absence of an opportunity to search for alternative employment. (Innis Christie, Geoffrey England and Brent Cotter, *Employment Law in Canada* (2nd ed. 1993), at pp. 572–81.)

[26] Similarly, s. 40*a*, which provides for severance pay, acts to compensate long-serving employees for their years of service and investment in the employer's business and for the special losses they suffer when their employment terminates. In *R. v. TNT Canada Inc.* (1996), 27 O.R. (3d) 546, Robins J.A. quoted with approval at pp. 556–57 from the words of D. D. Carter in the course of an employment standards determination in *Re Telegram Publishing Co. v. Zwelling* (1972), 1 L.A.C. (2d) 1 (Ont.), at p. 19, wherein he described the role of severance pay as follows:

> Severance pay recognizes that an employee does make an investment in his employer's business — the extent of this investment being directly related to the length of the employee's service. This investment is the seniority that the

employee builds up during his years of service.... Upon termination of the employment relationship, this investment of years of service is lost, and the employee must start to rebuild seniority at another place of work. The severance pay, based on length of service, is some compensation for this loss of investment.

[27] In my opinion, the consequences or effects which result from the Court of Appeal's interpretation of ss. 40 and 40*a* of the *ESA* are incompatible with both the object of the Act and with the object of the termination and severance pay provisions themselves. It is a well established principle of statutory interpretation that the legislature does not intend to produce absurd consequences. According to Côté, *supra*, an interpretation can be considered absurd if it leads to ridiculous or frivolous consequences, if it is extremely unreasonable or inequitable, if it is illogical or incoherent, or if it is incompatible with other provisions or with the object of the legislative enactment (at pp. 378–80). Sullivan echoes these comments noting that a label of absurdity can be attached to interpretations which defeat the purpose of a statute or render some aspect of it pointless or futile (Sullivan, *Construction of Statutes*, *supra*, at p. 88).

[28] The trial judge properly noted that, if the *ESA* termination and severance pay provisions do not apply in circumstances of bankruptcy, those employees "fortunate" enough to have been dismissed the day before a bankruptcy would be entitled to such payments, but those terminated on the day the bankruptcy becomes final would not be so entitled. In my view, the absurdity of this consequence is particularly evident in a unionized workplace where seniority is a factor in determining the order of lay-off. The more senior the employee, the larger the investment he or she has made in the employer and the greater the entitlement to termination and severance pay. However, it is the more senior personnel who are likely to be employed up until the time of the bankruptcy and who would thereby lose their entitlements to these payments.

[29] If the Court of Appeal's interpretation of the termination and severance pay provisions is correct, it would be acceptable to distinguish between employees merely on the basis of the timing of their dismissal. It seems to me that such a result would arbitrarily deprive some employees of a means to cope with the economic dislocation caused by unemployment. In this way the protections of the *ESA* would be limited rather than extended, thereby defeating the intended working of the legislation. In my opinion, this is an unreasonable result.

[30] In addition to the termination and severance pay provisions, both the appellants and the respondent relied upon various other sections of the *ESA* to advance their arguments regarding the intention of the legislature. In my view, although the majority of these sections offer little interpretive assistance, one transitional provision is particularly instructive. In 1981, s. 2(1) of the *ESAA* introduced s. 40*a*, the severance pay provision, to the *ESA*. Section 2(2) deemed that provision to come into force on January 1, 1981. Section 2(3), the transitional provision in question[,] provided as follows:

> **2.** ...
>
> (3) Section 40*a* of the said Act does not apply to an employer who became a bankrupt or an insolvent person within the meaning of the *Bankruptcy Act* (Canada) and whose assets have been distributed among his creditors or to an employer whose proposal within the meaning of the *Bankruptcy Act* (Canada) has been accepted by his creditors in the period from and including the 1st day of January, 1981, to and including the day immediately before the day this Act receives Royal Assent.

[31] The Court of Appeal found that it was neither necessary nor appropriate to determine the intention of the legislature in enacting this provisional subsection. Nevertheless, the court took the position that the intention of the legislature as evidenced by the introductory words of ss. 40 and 40*a* was clear, namely, that termination by reason of a bankruptcy will not trigger the severance and termination pay obligations of the *ESA*. The court held that this intention remained unchanged by the introduction of the transitional provision. With respect, I do not agree with either of these findings. Firstly, in my opinion, the use of legislative history as a tool for determining the intention of the legislature is an entirely appropriate exercise and one which has often been employed by this Court (see, e.g., *R. v. Vasil*, [1981] 1 S.C.R. 469, at p. 487; *Paul v. The Queen*, [1982] 1 S.C.R. 621, at pp. 635, 653 and 660). Secondly, I believe that the transitional provision indicates that the Legislature intended that termination and severance pay obligations should arise upon an employers' bankruptcy.

[32] In my view, by extending an exemption to employers who became bankrupt and lost control of their assets between the coming into force of the amendment and its receipt of royal assent, s. 2(3) necessarily implies that the severance pay obligation

does in fact extend to bankrupt employers. It seems to me that, if this were not the case, no readily apparent purpose would be served by this transitional provision.

[33] I find support for my conclusion in the decision of Saunders J. in *Royal Dressed Meats Inc., supra.* Having reviewed s. 2(3) of the *ESAA*, he commented as follows (at p. 89):

> ... any doubt about the intention of the Ontario Legislature has been put to rest, in my opinion, by the transitional provision which introduced severance payments into the E.S.A. ... it seems to me an inescapable inference that the legislature intended liability for severance payments to arise on a bankruptcy. That intention would, in my opinion, extend to termination payments which are similar in character.

[34] This interpretation is also consistent with statements made by the Minister of Labour at the time he introduced the 1981 amendments to the *ESA*. With regard to the new severance pay provision he stated:

> The circumstances surrounding a closure will govern the applicability of the severance pay legislation in some defined situations. For example, a bankrupt or insolvent firm will still be required to pay severance pay to employees to the extent that assets are available to satisfy their claims.
>
> ...
>
> ... the proposed severance pay measures will, as I indicated earlier, be retroactive to January 1 of this year. That retroactive provision, however, will not apply in those cases of bankruptcy and insolvency where the assets have already been distributed or where an agreement on a proposal to creditors has already been reached.
>
> (*Legislature of Ontario Debates*, 1st sess., 32nd Parl., June 4, 1981, at pp. 1236–37.)

Moreover, in the legislative debates regarding the proposed amendments the Minister stated:

> For purposes of retroactivity, severance pay will not apply to bankruptcies under the Bankruptcy Act where assets have been distributed. However, once this act receives royal assent, employees in bankruptcy closures will be covered by the severance pay provisions.
>
> (*Legislature of Ontario Debates*, 1st sess., 32nd Parl., June 16, 1981, at p. 1699.)

[35] Although the frailties of Hansard evidence are many, this Court has recognized that it can play a limited role in the interpretation of legislation. Writing for the Court in *R. v. Morgentaler*, [1993] 3 S.C.R. 463, at p. 484, Sopinka J. stated:

> ... until recently the courts have balked at admitting evidence of legislative debates and speeches.... The main criticism of such evidence has been that it cannot represent the "intent" of the legislature, an incorporeal body, but that is equally true of other forms of legislative history. Provided that the court remains mindful of the limited reliability and weight of Hansard evidence, it should be admitted as relevant to both the background and the purpose of legislation.

[36] Finally, with regard to the scheme of the legislation, since the *ESA* is a mechanism for providing minimum benefits and standards to protect the interests of employees, it can be characterized as benefits-conferring legislation. As such, according to several decisions of this Court, it ought to be interpreted in a broad and generous manner. Any doubt arising from difficulties of language should be resolved in favour of the claimant (see, e.g., *Abrahams v. Attorney General of Canada*, [1983] 1 S.C.R. 2, at p. 10; *Hills v. Canada (Attorney General)*, [1988] 1 S.C.R. 513, at p. 537). It seems to me that, by limiting its analysis to the plain meaning of ss. 40 and 40a of the *ESA*, the Court of Appeal adopted an overly restrictive approach that is inconsistent with the scheme of the Act.

[37] The Court of Appeal's reasons relied heavily upon the decision in *Malone Lynch, supra.* In *Malone Lynch*, Houlden J. held that s. 13, the group termination provision of the former *ESA*, R.S.O. 1970, c. 147, and the predecessor to s. 40 at issue in the present case, was not applicable where termination resulted from the bankruptcy of the employer. Section 13(2) of the *ESA* then in force provided that, if an employer wishes to terminate the employment of 50 or more employees, the employer must give notice of termination for the period prescribed in the regulations, "and until the expiry of such notice the terminations shall not take effect". Houlden J. reasoned that termination of employment through bankruptcy could not trigger the termination payment provision, as employees in this situation had not received the written notice required by the statute, and therefore could not be said to have been terminated in accordance with the Act.

[38] Two years after *Malone Lynch* was decided, the 1970 *ESA* termination pay provisions were amended by *The Employment Standards Act, 1974*, S.O. 1974, c. 112. As amended, s. 40(7) of the 1974 *ESA* eliminated the requirement that notice be given before termination can take effect. This provision makes it clear that termination pay is owing where an employer fails to give notice of termination and that

employment terminates irrespective of whether or not proper notice has been given. Therefore, in my opinion it is clear that the *Malone Lynch* decision turned on statutory provisions which are materially different from those applicable in the instant case. It seems to me that Houlden J.'s holding goes no further than to say that the provisions of the 1970 *ESA* have no application to a bankrupt employer. For this reason, I do not accept the *Malone Lynch* decision as persuasive authority for the Court of Appeal's findings. I note that the courts in *Royal Dressed Meats, supra*, and *British Columbia (Director of Employment Standards) v. Eland Distributors Ltd. (Trustee of)* (1996), 40 C.B.R. (3d) 25 (B.C.S.C.), declined to rely upon *Malone Lynch* based upon similar reasoning.

[39] The Court of Appeal also relied upon *Re Kemp Products Ltd., supra*, for the proposition that although the employment relationship will terminate upon an employer's bankruptcy, this does not constitute a "dismissal". I note that this case did not arise under the provisions of the *ESA*. Rather, it turned on the interpretation of the term "dismissal" in what the complainant alleged to be an employment contract. As such, I do not accept it as authoritative jurisprudence in the circumstances of this case. For the reasons discussed above, I also disagree with the Court of Appeal's reliance on *Mills-Hughes v. Raynor* (1988), 63 O.R. (2d) 343 (C.A.), which cited the decision in *Malone Lynch, supra*, with approval.

[40] As I see the matter, when the express words of ss. 40 and 40*a* of the *ESA* are examined in their entire context, there is ample support for the conclusion that the words "terminated by the employer" must be interpreted to include termination resulting from the bankruptcy of the employer. Using the broad and generous approach to interpretation appropriate for benefits-conferring legislation, I believe that these words can reasonably bear that construction (see *R. v. Z. (D.A.)*, [1992] 2 S.C.R. 1025). I also note that the intention of the Legislature as evidenced in s. 2(3) of the *ESAA*, clearly favours this interpretation. Further, in my opinion, to deny employees the right to claim *ESA* termination and severance pay where their termination has resulted from their employer's bankruptcy, would be inconsistent with the purpose of the termination and severance pay provisions and would undermine the object of the *ESA*, namely, to protect the interests of as many employees as possible.

[41] In my view, the impetus behind the termination of employment has no bearing upon the ability of the dismissed employee to cope with the sudden economic dislocation caused by unemployment. As all dismissed employees are equally in need of the protections provided by the *ESA*, any distinction between employees whose termination resulted from the bankruptcy of their employer and those who have been terminated for some other reason would be arbitrary and inequitable. Further, I believe that such an interpretation would defeat the true meaning, intent and spirit of the *ESA*. Therefore, I conclude that termination as a result of an employer's bankruptcy does give rise to an unsecured claim provable in bankruptcy pursuant to s. 121 of the *BA* for termination and severance pay in accordance with ss. 40 and 40*a* of the *ESA*. Because of this conclusion, I do not find it necessary to address the alternative finding of the trial judge as to the applicability of s. 7(5) of the *ESA*.

[42] I note that subsequent to the Rizzo bankruptcy, the termination and severance pay provisions of the *ESA* underwent another amendment. Sections 74(1) and 75(1) of the *Labour Relations and Employment Statute Law Amendment Act, 1995*, S.O. 1995, c. 1, amend those provisions so that they now expressly provide that where employment is terminated by operation of law as a result of the bankruptcy of the employer, the employer will be deemed to have terminated the employment. However, s. 17 of the *Interpretation Act* directs that, "[t]he repeal or amendment of an Act shall be deemed not to be or to involve any declaration as to the previous state of the law". As a result, I note that the subsequent change in the legislation has played no role in determining the present appeal.

6.   DISPOSITION AND COSTS

[43] I would allow the appeal and set aside paragraph 1 of the order of the Court of Appeal. In lieu thereof, I would substitute an order declaring that Rizzo's former employees are entitled to make claims for termination pay (including vacation pay due thereon) and severance pay as unsecured creditors. As to costs, the Ministry of Labour led no evidence regarding what effort it made in notifying or securing the consent of the Rizzo employees before it discontinued its application for leave to appeal to this Court on their behalf. In light of these circumstances, I would order that the costs in this Court be paid to the appellant by the Ministry on a party-and-party basis. I would not disturb the orders of the courts below with respect to costs.

(b) *R. v. Mills*†

[McLACHLIN AND IACOBUCCI JJ. and L'Heureux-Dubé, Gonthier, Major, Bastarache and Binnie JJ.:]

I. INTRODUCTION

[17] The question of when accused persons should have access to private records of complainants and witnesses in sexual assault trials is a vexed one. This Court addressed this issue in *R. v. O'Connor*, [1995] 4 S.C.R. 411. Following this decision, and a lengthy consultation process, Parliament reviewed the issue and drafted Bill C-46, (now S.C. 1997, c. 30) which came into force on May 12, 1997 and amended the *Criminal Code*, R.S.C., 1985, c. C-46. The issue in the present appeal is whether Bill C-46 is constitutional. The resolution of this appeal requires understanding how to define competing rights, avoiding the hierarchical approach rejected by this Court in *Dagenais v. Canadian Broadcasting Corp.*, [1994] 3 S.C.R. 835, at p. 877. On the one hand stands the accused's right to make full answer and defence. On the other hand stands the complainant's and witness's right to privacy. Neither right may be defined in such a way as to negate the other and both sets of rights are informed by the equality rights at play in this context. Underlying this question is the relationship between the courts and Parliament when Parliament alters a judicially created common law procedure that already embodies *Charter* standards.

II. SUMMARY

[18] This appeal presents an apparent conflict among the rights to full answer and defence, privacy, and equality, all of which are protected by the *Canadian Charter of Rights and Freedoms* (ss. 7 and 11(d), s. 8, and s. 15, respectively). The underlying issue is what is required by the "principles of fundamental justice" protected by s. 7. Bill C-46 reflects Parliament's effort at balancing these rights. Our task is to decide whether Parliament's balance is a constitutional one.

[19] As a preliminary matter, we conclude that this appeal is not premature. While it is true that the accused did not actually make an application for records under Bill C-46, this does not deprive the Court of a sufficient basis to decide the issues raised in the appeal.

[20] As noted above, this Court has previously addressed the issue of disclosure of third party records in sexual assault proceedings: see *O'Connor*, *supra*. However, it is important to keep in mind that the decision in *O'Connor* is not necessarily the last word on the subject. The law develops through dialogue between courts and legislatures: see *Vriend v. Alberta*, [1998] 1 S.C.R. 493. Against the backdrop of *O'Connor*, Parliament was free to craft its own solution to the problem consistent with the *Charter*.

[21] As this Court's decision in *Dagenais*, *supra*, makes clear, *Charter* rights must be examined in a contextual manner to resolve conflicts between them. Therefore, unlike s. 1 balancing, where societal interests are sometimes allowed to override *Charter* rights, under s. 7 rights must be defined so that they do not conflict with each other. The rights of full answer and defence, and privacy, must be defined in light of each other, and both must be defined in light of the equality provisions of s. 15.

[22] Turning to the legislation at issue in this appeal, we find it constitutional. It is undisputed that there are several important respects in which Bill C-46 differs from the regime set out in *O'Connor*. However, these differences are not fatal because Bill C-46 provides sufficient protection for all relevant *Charter* rights. There are, admittedly, several provisions in the Bill that are subject to differing interpretations. However, in such situations we will interpret the legislation in a constitutional manner where possible: see *Slaight Communications Inc. v. Davidson*, [1989] 1 S.C.R. 1038, at p. 1078. By so doing, we conclude that Bill C-46 is a constitutional response to the problem of production of records of complainants or witnesses in sexual assault proceedings.

. . . .

---

† [1999] 3 S.C.R. 668 at paras. 17–22, 43–60, 94, [1999] S.C.J. No. 68.

VI. ANALYSIS

. . . .

C. Background Considerations

(1) The O'Connor Regime and Bill C-46

[43] The respondent in this appeal and several interveners argued that the provisions of Bill C-46 are unconstitutional to the extent that they are inconsistent with the reasons of the majority of this Court in *O'Connor, supra*. Belzil J., for the court below, similarly held that Bill C-46 is unconstitutional because it alters the constitutional balance achieved in *O'Connor*. Before addressing these arguments, we will briefly review the production regimes at issue.

(A) THE *O'CONNOR* REGIME

[44] This Court's decision in *O'Connor* concerned the common law procedure to be followed by an accused seeking production of therapeutic records in the hands of third parties. As a preliminary matter, Lamer C.J. and Sopinka J., for the majority on the issue of production, also discussed the issue of disclosure of therapeutic records in the hands of the Crown. In their opinion, the Crown's obligation to disclose records in its possession or control, as established in *Stinchcombe, supra*, is unaltered by the confidential nature of therapeutic records where the records have been shared with the Crown or "confidentiality has been waived for the purpose of proceeding against the accused" (para. 9). Even if privileged, these records must be disclosed to the accused where "clearly relevant and important to the ability of the accused to raise a defence" (para. 11).

[45] In the context of ordering production of records that are in the hands of third parties, Lamer C.J. and Sopinka J. outlined a two-stage process. At the first stage, the issue is whether the document sought by the accused ought to be produced to the judge; at the second stage, the trial judge must balance the competing interests to decide whether to order production to the accused. At the first stage, the onus is on the accused to establish that the information in question is "<u>likely to be relevant</u>" (para. 19 (emphasis in original)). Unlike in the Crown disclosure context, where relevance is understood to mean "may be useful to the defence", the threshold of <u>likely relevance</u> in this context requires that the presiding judge be satisfied "that there is a reasonable possibility that the information is logically probative to <u>an issue at trial or the competence of a witness to testify</u>" (para. 22 (emphasis in original)). This shift in onus and the higher threshold, as compared to when records are in the possession of the Crown, was necessitated by the fact that the information in question is not part of the state's "case to meet", the state has not been given access to it, and third parties are under no obligation to assist the defence.

[46] Lamer C.J. and Sopinka J. held that the threshold of likely relevance at this first stage is not a significant or onerous burden. It is meant to prevent requests for production that are "speculative, fanciful, disruptive, unmeritorious, obstructive and time-consuming" (para. 24). Although Lamer C.J. and Sopinka J. disagreed with L'Heureux-Dubé J. that therapeutic records are rarely relevant to the accused, they declined to set out "categories of relevance" (para. 27).

[47] If the first stage is passed, the record is disclosed to the court and the application for production moves onto the second stage where the judge determines whether the record should be produced to the accused. At this second stage, Lamer C.J. and Sopinka J. require the trial judge to balance the competing interests in order to determine whether a non-production order would be a reasonable limit on the accused's ability to make full answer and defence. They list a series of factors that trial judges should consider in making this determination (at para. 31):

> (1) the extent to which the record is necessary for the accused to make full answer and defence; (2) the probative value of the record in question; (3) the nature and extent of the reasonable expectation of privacy vested in that record; (4) whether production of the record would be premised upon any discriminatory belief or bias; and (5) the potential prejudice to the complainant's dignity, privacy or security of the person that would be occasioned by production of the record in question.

Although L'Heureux-Dubé J., for the minority on this issue, outlined the same five factors as the majority, she also included two additional factors: the integrity of the trial process and the societal interest in reporting sexual crimes. Lamer C.J. and Sopinka J. held that the former is better dealt with when determining admissibility of the evidence and that the latter, while a relevant factor, was "not a paramount consideration" as there are many other avenues open to the trial judge to protect this interest than declining production (at paras. 32 and 33).

(B) BILL C-46

[48] On May 12, 1997, approximately 17 months after this Court released its decision in *O'Connor*, Bill C-46 came into force. Bill C-46 sets out a process to govern the production of the private records of complainants and witnesses in sexual assault trials in place of the common law regime this Court established in *O'Connor*. The preamble to the Bill indicates that Parliament was concerned about the incidence of sexual violence and abuse in Canadian society, its prevalence against women and children, and its "particularly disadvantageous impact on the equal participation of women and children in society and on the rights of women and children to security of the person, privacy and equal benefit of the law as guaranteed by sections 7, 8, 15 and 28 of the [*Charter*]". The preamble expressly declares that Parliament seeks to provide a framework of laws that are fair to and protect the rights of both accused persons and complainants.

[49] While the Bill retains the two-stage structure set out in *O'Connor*, there are significant differences between the two regimes. Many of these are uncontentious. In the following overview of the Bill, we expound on only the provisions brought under review in this appeal.

[50] Bill C-46 begins by defining the records to which it applies: "any form of record that contains personal information for which there is a reasonable expectation of privacy", excluding investigatory or prosecutorial records: s. 278.1. It goes on to define the types of offences that will trigger its application: s. 278.2(1). Generally, these are sexual assault and similar sexual offences. Section 278.2(1) states that an accused person charged with these offences cannot obtain the records relating to complainants or witnesses covered by s. 278.1, except in accordance with the process set out by the Bill.

[51] A third preliminary section, s. 278.2(2), states that the Bill applies to records in the possession or control of any person, including the Crown prosecutor, unless the complainant or witness "has expressly waived the application of [the Bill]". Absent waiver, documents in the possession of the prosecution are treated in the same manner as documents in the hands of a private individual or organization and therefore are subject to disclosure pursuant to the Bill's procedures.

[52] Yet another preliminary provision sets out "assertions" that are "not sufficient on their own" on an application for production to establish that a record is "likely relevant to an issue at trial or to the competence of a witness to testify": s. 278.3(4).

[53] This brings us to the heart of the Bill — the process established to govern the production of private records to an accused person in sexual offence proceedings. Like *O'Connor*, Parliament has set up a two-stage process: (1) disclosure to the judge; and (2) production to the accused. At the first stage, the accused must establish that the record sought is "likely relevant to an issue at trial or to the competence of a witness to testify" and that "the production of the record is necessary in the interests of justice" (s. 278.5(1)). Bill C-46 diverges from *O'Connor* by directing the trial judge to consider the salutary and deleterious effects of production to the court on the accused's right to full answer and defence and the complainant's or witness's right to privacy and equality. A series of factors is listed that the trial judge is directed to take into account in deciding whether the document should be produced to the court (s. 278.5(2)):

(a) the extent to which the record is necessary for the accused to make a full answer and defence;

(b) the probative value of the record;

(c) the nature and extent of the reasonable expectation of privacy with respect to the record;

(d) whether production of the record is based on a discriminatory belief or bias;

(e) the potential prejudice to the personal dignity and right to privacy of any person to whom the record relates;

(f) society's interest in encouraging the reporting of sexual offences;

(g) society's interest in encouraging the obtaining of treatment by complainants of sexual offences; and

(h) the effect of the determination on the integrity of the trial process.

[54] If the requirements of this first stage are met, the record will be ordered produced to the trial judge. At the second stage, the judge looks at the record in the absence of the parties (s. 278.6(1)), holds a hearing if necessary (s. 278.6(2)), and determines whether the record should be produced on the basis that it is "likely relevant to an issue at trial or to the competence of a witness to testify" and that its production is "necessary in the interests of justice" (s. 278.7). Again at this stage, the judge must consider the salutary and deleterious effects on the accused's right to make full answer and defence and on the right to privacy and equality of the complainant or witness, and is directed to "take into account"

the factors set out at s. 278.5(2): s. 278.7(2). When ordering production, the judge may impose conditions on production: s. 278.7(3).

[55] The respondent and several supporting interveners argue that Bill C-46 is unconstitutional to the extent that it establishes a regime for production that differs from or is inconsistent with that established by the majority in *O'Connor*. However, it does not follow from the fact that a law passed by Parliament differs from a regime envisaged by the Court in the absence of a statutory scheme, that Parliament's law is unconstitutional. Parliament may build on the Court's decision, and develop a different scheme as long as it remains constitutional. Just as Parliament must respect the Court's rulings, so the Court must respect Parliament's determination that the judicial scheme can be improved. To insist on slavish conformity would belie the mutual respect that underpins the relationship between the courts and legislature that is so essential to our constitutional democracy: *Vriend, supra*. We turn now to a brief discussion of that relationship.

(2) Relationship Between the Courts and the Legislature Generally

[56] A posture of respect towards Parliament was endorsed by this Court in *Slaight Communications*, *supra*, at p. 1078, where we held that if legislation is amenable to two interpretations, a court should choose the interpretation that upholds the legislation as constitutional. Thus courts must presume that Parliament intended to enact constitutional legislation and strive, where possible, to give effect to this intention.

[57] This Court has also discussed the relationship between the courts and the legislature in terms of a dialogue, and emphasized its importance to the democratic process. In *Vriend, supra*, at para. 139, Iacobucci J. stated:

> To my mind, a great value of judicial review and this dialogue among the branches is that each of the branches is made somewhat accountable to the other. The work of the legislature is reviewed by the courts and the work of the court in its decisions can be reacted to by the legislature in the passing of new legislation (or even overarching laws under s. 33 of the *Charter*). This dialogue between and accountability of each of the branches have the effect of enhancing the democratic process, not denying it.

See also P. W. Hogg and A. A. Bushell, "The *Charter* Dialogue Between Courts and Legislatures"

(1997), 35 *Osgoode Hall L.J.* 75. If the common law were to be taken as establishing the only possible constitutional regime, then we could not speak of a dialogue with the legislature. Such a situation could only undermine rather than enhance democracy. Legislative change and the development of the common law are different. As this Court noted in *R. v. Salituro*, [1991] 3 S.C.R. 654, at p. 666, the common law changes incrementally, "while complex changes to the law with uncertain ramifications should be left to the legislature". While this dialogue obviously is of a somewhat different nature when the common law rule involves interpretation of the *Charter*, as in *O'Connor*, it remains a dialogue nonetheless.

[58] Moreover, in this Court's recent decision *Reference re Secession of Quebec*, [1998] 2 S.C.R. 217, we affirmed the proposition that constitutionalism can facilitate democracy rather than undermine it, and that one way in which it does this is by ensuring that fundamental human rights and individual freedoms are given due regard and protection (at paras. 74–78). Courts do not hold a monopoly on the protection and promotion of rights and freedoms; Parliament also plays a role in this regard and is often able to act as a significant ally for vulnerable groups. This is especially important to recognize in the context of sexual violence. The history of the treatment of sexual assault complainants by our society and our legal system is an unfortunate one. Important change has occurred through legislation aimed at both recognizing the rights and interests of complainants in criminal proceedings, and debunking the stereotypes that have been so damaging to women and children, but the treatment of sexual assault complainants remains an ongoing problem. If constitutional democracy is meant to ensure that due regard is given to the voices of those vulnerable to being overlooked by the majority, then this court has an obligation to consider respectfully Parliament's attempt to respond to such voices.

[59] Parliament has enacted this legislation after a long consultation process that included a consideration of the constitutional standards outlined by this Court in *O'Connor*. While it is the role of the courts to specify such standards, there may be a range of permissible regimes that can meet these standards. It goes without saying that this range is not confined to the specific rule adopted by the Court pursuant to its competence in the common law. In the present case, Parliament decided that legislation was necessary in order to address the issue of third party records more comprehensively. As is evident from the language of the preamble to Bill C-46, Parlia-

ment also sought to recognize the prevalence of sexual violence against women and children and its disadvantageous impact on their rights, to encourage the reporting of incidents of sexual violence, to recognize the impact of the production of personal information on the efficacy of treatment, and to reconcile fairness to complainants with the rights of the accused. Many of these concerns involve policy decisions regarding criminal procedure and its relationship to the community at large. Parliament may also be understood to be recognizing "horizontal" equality concerns, where women's inequality results from the acts of other individuals and groups rather than the state, but which nonetheless may have many consequences for the criminal justice system. It is perfectly reasonable that these many concerns may lead to a procedure that is different from the common law position but that nonetheless meets the required constitutional standards.

[60] We cannot presume that the legislation is unconstitutional simply because it is different from the common law position. The question before us is not whether Parliament can amend the common law; it clearly can. The question before us is whether in doing so Parliament has nonetheless outlined a constitutionally acceptable procedure for the production of private records of complainants in sexual assault trials. This question is considered at length below, following the discussion of the constitutional rights at stake in this appeal.

IV

Law, the State, and Citizens

Part IV explores the ways in which law shapes and mediates the relationship between the state and the individuals and groups within it.

Chapter 10 considers the way in which law can be used to either extend or restrict the recognition of groups and individuals as citizens within a state. Here the term citizen is applied not just to those who qualify as formal citizens (who have the right to hold a passport and vote in national elections, for instance), but also to those accorded the fullest rights of participation within society. The excerpt from the famous Persons Case (*Henrietta Muir Edwards v. Canada (A.G.)*) provides an historical example of how the status and rights of an entire group may be affected by the decisions of a handful of judges and their preference for narrow or broad approaches to constitutional interpretation. In his influential essay "Citizenship and Social Class", T.H. Marshall claims that an expanded conception of citizenship is necessary to promote substantive equality and inclusion in democratic societies. He argues that modern citizenship requires civil, political, and social rights in order to integrate marginalized groups such as the working class that have been excluded from full participation due to a lack of resources. In recent years the adequacy of Marshall's ideal of citizenship has been challenged. In their article Kymlicka and Norman examine several critiques of Marshall, specifically, the New Right's contention that social rights create "passive citizens". While Kymlicka and Norman dismiss this, they argue that Marshall's goal of *universal citizenship* based on a single shared identity nevertheless fails to address issues of cultural and religious diversity in contemporary societies. They contend that his three types of rights do not go far enough in promoting inclusion and participation, so they propose a model of *differentiated citizenship* — grounded in new unique sets of "group rights" — that discards the requirement for a single shared identity but still fosters the inclusion and participation originally sought by Marshall.

Finally, Christiane Wilke and Paula Willis employ a multi-dimensional understanding of citizenship to analyze the Supreme Court of Canada decision in the *Charkaoui* case. Their article explores the ways in which the vulnerability of non-citizens in the face of governments focused on issues of state security may be exacerbated not just by their lack of formal citizenship, but also by their lack of belonging within the state more generally.

Chapter 11 considers a number of different ways in which rights may be protected through law — ranging from non-constitutional to constitutional rights protection — and raises questions about the effectiveness of law in protecting rights. First, the *Somerset Case* provides an historical example of both the potential and limits of the common law as a source of rights protection. In that case Justice Mansfield found that the British common law would not allow an American slave-owner to force his slave to leave England against his will. At the same time Justice Mansfield recognized that legislation could still legalize chattel slavery even if the common law would not. The limits of legislative rights protection are then illustrated by the Supreme Court of Canada's application of the *Canadian Bill of Rights* in *Bliss* v. *Canada*. The formalistic approach applied in *Bliss* is usefully contrasted with the more contemporary approach adopted in *Baker v. Canada*, where Justice L'Heureux-Dubé used administrative law principles (among others) to prevent the deportation of a mother with Canadian born children. The chapter then shifts to consider a series of debates concerning the utility of entrenching rights in a constitutional bill of rights, namely the *Canadian Charter of Rights and Freedoms*. Prime Minister Trudeau, one of the chief architects of the *Charter*, identifies the core liberal notion supporting constitutional entrenchment of the protection of individual rights constitutive of the dignity of human beings. Harry Glasbeek and Michael Mandel, by contrast, doubt whether the constitutional protection of rights is ever truly effective, arguing that judges have historically failed in their role as rights protectors. Furthermore, the two skeptics worry that the entrenchment of rights results in the legalization of politics, which may distance and depoliticize social issues and, ultimately, undermine popular struggles for reform. Finally, Aki-Kwe/Mary Ellen Turpel identifies the ways in which the conception of rights underlying the *Charter* conflicts with aboriginal culture and traditions. She goes on to advance an alternative approach: First Nations Human Rights and Responsibilities Laws.

As you read through the articles and cases in Part IV, ask yourself the following questions: What is the role of law in shaping the relationship between the state and citizens? What does full citizenship require? How do we choose who gets to participate fully within a political community? Which rights should be protected, and how best can they be protected? How should the culture, traditions, and rights of aboriginal peoples be recognized within or by the Canadian state? Can issues of accommodation and the recognition of cultural diversity within contemporary societies like Canada be addressed through rights?

Citizenship:
Who Belongs? Who Is Protected?

(a) *Henrietta Muir Edwards et al. v. Canada (A.G.)*[†]

[LORD SANKEY L.C.:]

By s. 24 of the *British North America Act, 1867*, it is provided that "The Governor General shall from time to time, in the Queen's name, by instrument under the Great Seal of Canada, summon qualified persons to the Senate; and, subject to the provisions of this Act, every person so summoned shall become and be a member of the Senate and a senator."

The question at issue in this appeal is whether the words "qualified persons" in that section include a woman, and consequently whether women are eligible to be summoned to and become members of the Senate of Canada.

Of the appellants, Henrietta Muir Edwards is the Vice-President for the Province of Alberta of the National Council of Women for Canada; Nellie L. McClung and Louise C. McKinney were for several years members of the Legislative Assembly of the said Province; Emily F. Murphy is a police magistrate in and for the said Province; and Irene Parlby is a member of the Legislative Assembly of the said Province and a member of the Executive Council thereof.

On August 29, 1927, the appellants petitioned the Governor General in Council to refer to the Supreme Court certain questions touching the powers of the Governor General to summon female persons to the Senate, and upon October 19, 1927, the Governor General in Council referred to the Supreme Court the aforesaid question. The case was heard before Anglin C.J., Duff, Mignault, Lamont, and Smith JJ., and upon April 24, 1928, the Court answered the question in the negative; the question being understood to be "Are women eligible for appointment to the Senate of Canada."

The Chief Justice, whose judgment was concurred in by Lamont and Smith JJ., and substantially by Mignault J., came to this conclusion upon broad lines mainly because of the common law disability of women to hold public office and from a consideration of various cases which [have] been decided under different statutes as to their right to vote for a member of Parliament.

Duff J., on the other hand, did not agree with this view. He came to the conclusion that women are not eligible for appointment to the Senate upon the narrower ground that upon a close examination of the *British North America Act 1867*, the word "persons" in s. 24 is restricted to members of the male sex. The result therefore of the decision was that the Supreme Court was unanimously of opinion that the word "persons" did not include female persons, and that women are not eligible to be summoned to the Senate.

Their Lordships are of opinion that the word "persons" in s. 24 does include women, and that women are eligible to be summoned to and become members of the Senate of Canada.

. . . .

The exclusion of women from all public offices is a relic of days more barbarous than ours, but it must be remembered that the necessity of the times often forced on man customs, which in later years were not necessary. Such exclusion is probably due to the fact that the deliberative assemblies of

---

[†] [1930] A.C. 124 (J.C.P.C.) at 126–31, 135–38, 140–143. [Notes and/or references omitted.]

the early tribes were attended by men under arms, and women did not bear arms. *"Nihil autem neque publicae neque privatae rei, nisi armati, agunt"*: Tac. Germ., c. 13. Yet the tribes did not despise the advice of women. *"Inessequin etiam sanctum et providum putant, nec aut consilia earum aspernantura ut responsa neglegunt"*: Germ., c. 8. The likelihood of attack rendered such a proceeding unavoidable, and after all what is necessary at any period is a question for the times upon which opinion grounded on experience may move one way or another in different circumstances. This exclusion of women found its way into the opinions of the Roman jurists, Ulpian (A.D. 211) laying it down. *"Feminae ab omnibus offiis civilibus vel publicis remotae sunt"*: Dig. 1.16.195. The barbarian tribes who settled in the Roman Empire, and were exposed to constant dangers, naturally preserved and continued the tradition.

In England no woman under the degree of a Queen or a Regent, married or unmarried, could take part in the government of the State. A woman was under a legal incapacity to be elected to serve in Parliament and even if a peeress in her own right she was not, nor is, entitled as an incident of peerage to receive a writ of summons to the House of Lords.

Various authorities are cited in the recent case of *Viscountess Rhondda's Claim*, where it was held that a woman was not entitled to sit in the House of Lords. Women were, moreover, subject to a legal incapacity to vote at the election of members of Parliament: Coke, 4 *Inst.*, p. 5; *Chorlton v. Lings*; or of town councillor: *Reg. v. Harrald*; or to be elected members of a County Council: *Beresford-Hope v. Sandhurst*. They were excluded by the common law from taking part in the administration of justice either as judges or as jurors, with the single exception of inquiries by a jury of matrons upon a suggestion of pregnancy: Coke, 2 *Inst.* 119, 3 Bl. Comm. 362. Other instances are referred to in the learned judgment of Willes J. in *Chorlton v. Lings*.

No doubt in the course of centuries there may be found cases of exceptional women and exceptional instances, but as Lord Esher M.R. said in *De Souza v. Cobden*: "By the common law of England women are not in general deemed capable of exercising public functions, though there are certain exceptional cases where a well recognised custom to the contrary has become established." An instance may be referred to in the case of women being entitled to act as churchwardens and as sextons, the latter being put upon the ground that a sexton's duty was in the nature of a private trust: *Olive v. Ingram*. Also of being appointed as overseer of the poor: *Rex v. Stubbs*. The tradition existed till quite modern

times: see *Bebb v. Law Society*, where it was held by the Court of Appeal that by inveterate usage women were under a disability by reason of their sex to become attorneys or solicitors.

The passing of *Lord Brougham's Act* in 1850 does not appear to have greatly affected the current of authority. Sect. 4 provided that in all acts words importing the masculine gender shall be deemed and taken to include female unless the contrary as to gender is expressly provided.

The application and purview of that *Act* came up for consideration in *Chorlton v. Lings*, where the Court of Common Pleas was required to construe a statute passed in 1861, which conferred the parliamentary franchise on every man possessing certain qualifications and registered as a voter. The chief question discussed was whether by virtue of *Lord Brougham's Act* the words "every man" included women. Bovill C.J., having regard to the subject-matter of the statute and its general scope and language and to the important and striking nature of the departure from the common law involved in extending the franchise to women, declined to accept the view that Parliament had made that change by using the term "man" and held that the word was intentionally used expressly to designate the male sex. Willes J. said: "It is not easy to conceive that the framer of that Act, when he used the word 'expressly,' meant to suggest that what is necessarily or properly implied by language is not expressed by such language."

Great reliance was placed by the respondents to this appeal upon that decision, but in our view it is clearly distinguishable. The case was decided on the language of the *Representation of the People Act, 1867*, which provided that "every man" with certain qualifications and "not subject to any legal incapacity" should be entitled to be registered as a voter. Legal incapacity was not defined by the Act, and consequently reference was necessary to the common law disabilities of women.

A similar result was reached in the case of *Nairn v. University of St. Andrews*, where it was held under s. 27 of the *Representation of the People (Scotland) Act, 1868*, which provided that every person whose name is for the time being on the register of the general council of such university shall, being of full age and not subject to any legal incapacity, be entitled to vote in the election of a member to serve in any future Parliament for such university, that the word "person" did not include women, but the Lord Chancellor, Lord Loreburn, referred to the position of women at common law, and pointed out that they were subject to a legal incapacity. Both in this case and in the case of the Viscountess Rhondda the various judgments emphasize the fact that the legislature in dealing with the matter cannot be taken to have departed from the usage of centuries, or to have employed loose and ambiguous words to carry out so momentous and fundamental a change.

The judgment of the Chief Justice in the Supreme Court of Canada refers to and relies upon these cases, but their Lordships think that there is great force in the view taken by Duff J. with regard to them, when he says that s. 24 of the *British North America Act, 1867*, must not be treated as an independent enactment. The Senate, he proceeds, is part of a parliamentary system, and in order to test the contention based upon this principle that women are excluded from participating in working the Senate or any other institution set up by the Act one is bound to consider the Act as a whole and its bearings on this subject of the exclusion of women from public office and place.

. . . .

The communities included within the Britannic system embrace countries and peoples in every stage of social, political and economic development and undergoing a continuous process of evolution. His Majesty the King in Council is the final Court of Appeal from all these communities, and this Board must take great care therefore not to interpret legislation meant to apply to one community by a rigid adherence to the customs and traditions of another. Canada had its difficulties both at home and with the mother country, but soon discovered that union was strength. Delegates from the three maritime Provinces met in Charlottetown on September 1, 1864, to discuss proposals for a maritime union. A delegation from the coalition government of that day proceeded to Charlottetown and placed before the maritime delegates their schemes for a union embracing the Canadian Provinces. As a result the Quebec conference assembled on October 10, continued in session till October 28, and framed a number of resolutions. These resolutions as revised by the delegates from the different Provinces in London in 1866 were based upon a consideration of the rights of others and expressed in a compromise which will remain a lasting monument to the political genius of Canadian statesmen. Upon those resolutions the *British North America Act of 1867* was framed and passed by the Imperial legislature. The Quebec resolutions dealing with the Legislative Council — namely, Nos. 6–24 — even if their Lordships are entitled to look at them, do not shed any light on the subject under discussion. They refer generally to the "members" of the Legislative Council.

The *British North America Act* planted in Canada a living tree capable of growth and expansion within its natural limits. The object of the Act was to grant a Constitution to Canada. "Like all written constitutions it has been subject to development through usage and convention": *Canadian Constitutional Studies*, Sir Robert Borden (1922), p. 55.

Their Lordships do not conceive it to be the duty of this Board — it is certainly not their desire — to cut down the provisions of the Act by a narrow and technical construction, but rather to give it a large and liberal interpretation so that the Dominion to a great extent, but within certain fixed limits, may be mistress in her own house, as the Provinces to a great extent, but within certain fixed limits, are mistresses in theirs. "The Privy Council, indeed, has laid down that Courts of law must treat the provisions of the *British North America Act* by the same methods of construction and exposition which they apply to other statutes. But there are statutes and *statutes*; and the strict construction deemed proper in the case, for example, of a penal or taxing statute or one passed to regulate the affairs of an English parish, would be often subversive of Parliament's real intent if applied to an Act passed to ensure the peace, order and good government of a British Colony": see Clement's *Canadian Constitution*, 3rd ed., p. 347.

The learned author of that treatise quotes from the argument of Mr. Mowat and Mr. Edward Blake before the Privy Council in *St. Catherine's Milling and Lumber Co. v. The Queen*: "That Act should be on all occasions interpreted in a large, liberal and comprehensive spirit, considering the magnitude of the subjects with which it purports to deal in very few words." With that their Lordships agree, but as was said by the Lord Chancellor in *Brophy v. Attorney-General of Manitoba*, the question is not what may be supposed to have been intended, but what has been said.

It must be remembered, too, that their Lordships are not here considering the question of the legislative competence either of the Dominion or its Provinces which arise under ss. 91 and 92 of the Act providing for the distribution of legislative powers and assigning to the Dominion and its Provinces their respective spheres of Government. Their Lordships are concerned with the interpretation of an Imperial Act, but an Imperial Act which creates a constitution for a new country. Nor are their Lordships deciding any question as to the rights of women but only a question as to their eligibility for a particular position. No one, either male or female, has a right to be summoned to the Senate. The real point at issue is whether the Governor General has a right to summon women to the Senate.

The Act consists of a number of separate heads.

The preamble states that the Provinces of Canada, Nova Scotia and New Brunswick have expressed their desire to be federally united into one Dominion under the Crown of the United Kingdom of Great Britain and Ireland with a constitution similar in principle to that of the United Kingdom.

. . . .

The word "person" as above mentioned, may include members of both sexes, and to those who ask why the word should include females the obvious answer is why should it not? In these circumstances the burden is upon those who deny that the word includes women to make out their case.

. . . .

Their Lordships do not think it possible to interpret the word "persons" by speculating whether the framer of the *British North America Act* purposely followed the system of Legislative Councils enacted in the *Acts of 1791* and *1840* rather than that which prevailed in the maritime Province for the model on which the Senate was to be formed, neither do they think that either of these sub-sections is sufficient to rebut the presumption that the word "persons" includes women. Looking at the sections which deal with the Senate as a whole (ss. 21–36) their Lordships are unable to say that there is anything in those sections themselves upon which the Court could come to a definite conclusion that women are to be excluded from the Senate.

So far with regard to the sections dealing especially with the Senate — are there any other sections in the Act which shed light upon the meaning of the word "persons"?

Their Lordships think that there are. For example, s. 41 refers to the qualifications and disqualifications of persons to be elected or to sit or vote as members of the House of Assembly or Legislative Assembly, and by a proviso it is said that until the Parliament of Canada otherwise provides at any election for a member of the House of Commons for the district of Algoma in addition to persons qualified by the law of the Province of Canada to vote every male British subject aged twenty-one or upwards being a householder shall have a vote. This section shows a distinction between "persons" and "males." If persons excluded females it would only

have been necessary to say every person who is a British subject aged twenty-one years or upwards shall have a vote.

Again in s. 84, referring to Ontario and Quebec, a similar proviso is found stating that every male British subject in contradistinction to "person" shall have a vote.

Again in s. 133 it is provided that either the English or the French language may be used by any person or in any pleadings in or issuing from any court of Canada established under this Act and in or from all of any of the courts of Quebec. The word "person" there must include females, as it can hardly have been supposed that a man might use either the English or the French language but a woman might not.

If Parliament had intended to limit the word "persons" in s. 24 to male persons it would surely have manifested such intention by an express limitation, as it has done in ss. 41 and 84. The fact that certain qualifications are set out in s. 23 is not an argument in favour of further limiting the class, but is an argument to the contrary, because it must be presumed that Parliament has set out in s. 23 all the qualifications deemed necessary for a senator, and it does not state that one of the qualifications is that he must be a member of the male sex.

. . . .

The history of these sections and their interpretation in Canada is not without interest and significance.

From confederation to date both the Dominion Parliament and the Provincial legislatures have interpreted the word "persons" in ss. 41 and 84 of the *British North America Act* as including female persons, and have legislated either for the inclusion or exclusion of women from the class of persons entitled to vote and to sit in the Parliament and Legislature respectively, and this interpretation has never been questioned.

From confederation up to 1916 women were excluded from the class of persons entitled to vote in both Federal and Provincial elections. From 1916 to 1922 various Dominion and Provincial Acts were passed to admit women to the franchise and to the right to sit as members in both Dominion and Provincial legislative bodies. At the present time women are entitled to vote and to be candidates:

1. At all Dominion elections on the same basis as men.

2. At all Provincial elections save in the Province of Quebec.

From the date of the enactment of the *Interpretation Acts* in the Province of Canada, Nova Scotia and New Brunswick prior to confederation and in the Dominion of Canada since confederation and until the franchise was extended, women have been excluded by express enactment from the right to vote.

Neither is it without interest to record that when upon May 20, 1867, the *Representation of the People Bill* came before a Committee of the House of Commons, John Stuart Mill moved an amendment to secure women's suffrage, and the amendment proposed was to leave out the word "man" in order to insert the word "person" instead thereof: see *Hansard*, 3rd series, vol. clxxxvii., col. 817.

A heavy burden lies on an appellant who seeks to set aside a unanimous judgment of the Supreme Court, and this Board will only set aside such a decision after convincing argument and anxious consideration, but having regard:

1. To the object of the Act — namely, to provide a constitution for Canada, a responsible and developing State;
2. That the word "person" is ambiguous, and may include members of either sex;
3. That there are sections in the Act above referred to which show that in some cases the word "person" must include females;
4. That in some sections the words "male persons" are expressly used when it is desired to confine the matter in issue to males;
5. To the provisions of the *Interpretation Act*;

their Lordships have come to the conclusion that the word "persons" in s. 24 includes members both of the male and female sex, and that, therefore, the question propounded by the Governor General should be answered in the affirmative, and that women are eligible to be summoned to and become members of the Senate of Canada, and they will humbly advise His Majesty accordingly.

(b) Citizenship and Social Class†

T.H. Marshall

The sociological hypothesis latent in Alfred Marshall's essay[1] postulates that there is a kind of basic human equality associated with the concept of full membership of a community — or, as I should say, of citizenship — which is not inconsistent with the inequalities which distinguish the various economic levels in the society. In other words, the inequality of the social class system may be acceptable provided the equality of citizenship is recognized. [...]

He recognizes only one definite right, the right of children to be educated, and in this case alone does he approve the use of compulsory powers by the state to achieve his object. He could hardly go further without imperilling his own criterion for distinguishing his system from socialism in any form — the preservation of the freedom of the competitive market. [...] His sociological hypothesis lies as near to the heart of our problem today as it did three-quarters of a century ago — in fact nearer. The basic human equality of membership [...] has been enriched with new substance and invested with a formidable array of rights. It has developed far beyond what he foresaw, or would have wished. It has been clearly identified with the status of citizenship. [...]

Is it still true that basic equality, when enriched in substance and embodied in the formal rights of citizenship, is consistent with the inequalities of social class? I shall suggest that our society today assumes that the two are still compatible: so much so that citizenship has itself become, in certain respects, the architect of legitimate social inequality. Is it still true that the basic equality can be created and preserved without invading the freedom of the competitive market? Obviously it is not true. Our

† From David Held et al. ((eds.), *States and Societies* (Oxford: Basil Blackwell in association with The Open University, 1985) at 248–60. Originally published in T.H. Marshall, *Citizenship and social class and other essays* (Cambridge: Cambridge University Press, 1950). Reproduced with the permission of Cambridge University Press. [Notes and/or references omitted.]

191

modern system is frankly a socialist system[2] not one whose authors are, as Marshall was, eager to distinguish it from socialism. But it is equally obvious that the market still functions — within limits. Here is another possible conflict of principles which demands examination. And thirdly, what is the effect of the marked shift of emphasis from duties to rights? Is this an inevitable feature of modern citizenship — inevitable and irreversible? [...]

I shall ask whether there appear to be limits beyond which the modern drive towards social equality cannot, or is unlikely to pass, and I shall be thinking, not of the economic cost (I leave that vital question to the economists), but of the limits inherent in the principles that inspire the drive. But the modern drive towards social equality is, I believe, the latest phase of an evolution of citizenship which has been in continuous progress for some 250 years. [...]

THE DEVELOPMENT OF CITIZENSHIP TO THE END OF THE NINETEENTH CENTURY

[...] I shall be running true to type as a sociologist if I begin by saying that I propose to divide citizenship into three parts. But the analysis is, in this case, dictated by history even more clearly than by logic. I shall call these three parts, or elements, civil, political and social. The civil element is composed of the rights necessary for individual freedom — liberty of the person, freedom of speech, thought and faith, the right to own property and to conclude valid contracts, and the right to justice. The last is of a different order from the others, because it is the right to defend and assert all one's rights on terms of equality with others and by due process of law. This shows us that the institutions most directly associated with civil rights are the courts of justice. By the political element I mean the right to participate in the exercise of political power, as a member of a body invested with political authority or as an elector of the members of such a body. The corresponding institutions are Parliament and councils of local government. By the social element I mean the whole range from the right to a modicum of economic welfare and security to the right to share to the full in the social heritage and to live the life of a civilized being according to the standards prevailing in the society. The institutions most closely connected with it are the educational system and the social services. [...]

By 1832 when political rights made their first infantile attempt to walk, civil rights had come to man's estate and bore, in most essentials, the appearance that they have today.[3] 'The specific work of the earlier Hanoverian epoch', writes Trevelyan, 'was the establishment of the rule of law; and that law, with all its grave faults, was at least a law of freedom. On that solid foundation all our subsequent reforms were built'. This eighteenth-century achievement, interrupted by the French Revolution and completed after it, was in large measure the work of the courts both in their daily practice and also in a series of famous cases in some of which they were fighting against Parliament in defence of individual liberty. The most celebrated actor in this drama was, I suppose, John Wilkes, and, although we may deplore the absence in him of those noble and saintly qualities which we should like to find in our national heroes, we cannot complain if the cause of liberty is sometimes championed by a libertine.

In the economic field the basic civil right is the right to work, that is to say the right to follow the occupation of one's choice in the place of one's choice, subject only to legitimate demands for preliminary technical training. This right had been denied by both statute and custom; on the one hand by the Elizabethan Statute of Artificers, which confined certain occupations to certain social classes, and on the other by local regulations reserving employment in a town to its own members and by the use of apprenticeship as an instrument of exclusion rather than of recruitment. The recognition of the right involved the formal acceptance of a fundamental change of attitude. The old assumption that local and group monopolies were in the public interest, because 'trade and traffic cannot be maintained or increased without order and government', was replaced by the new assumption that such restrictions were an offence against the liberty of the subject and a menace to the prosperity of the nation. [...]

By the beginning of the nineteenth century this principle of individual economic freedom was accepted as axiomatic. You are probably familiar with the passage quoted by the Webbs from the report of the Select Committee of 1811, which states that:

> no interference of the legislature with the freedom of trade, or with the perfect liberty of every individual to dispose of his time and of his labour in the way and on the terms which he may judge most conducive to his own interest, can take place without violating general principles of the first importance to the prosperity and happiness of the community.[4] [...]

The story of civil rights in their formative period is one of the gradual addition of new rights to a status that already existed and was held to appertain to all adult members of the community — or perhaps one should say to all male members, since the status of women, or at least of married women, was in some important respects peculiar. This democratic, or universal, character of the status arose naturally from the fact that it was essentially the status of freedom, and in seventeenth-century England all men were free. Servile status, or villeinage by blood, had lingered on as a patent anachronism in the days of Elizabeth, but vanished soon afterwards. This change from servile to free labour has been described by Professor Tawney as 'a high landmark in the development both of economic and political society', and as 'the final triumph of the common law' in regions from which it had been excluded for four centuries. Henceforth the English peasant 'is a member of a society in which there is, nominally at least, one law for all men'.[5] The liberty which his predecessors had won by fleeing into the free towns had become his by right. In the towns the terms 'freedom' and 'citizenship' were interchangeable. When freedom became universal, citizenship grew from a local into a national institution.

The story of political rights is different both in time and in character. The formative period began, as I have said, in the early nineteenth century, where the civil rights attached to the status of freedom had already acquired sufficient substance to justify us in speaking of a general status of citizenship. And, when it began, it consisted, not in the creation of new rights to enrich a status already enjoyed by all, but in the granting of old rights to new sections of the population. [...]

It is clear that, if we maintain that in the nineteenth century citizenship in the form of civil rights was universal, the political franchise was not one of the rights of citizenship. It was the privilege of a limited economic class, whose limits were extended by each successive Reform Act. [...]

It was, as we shall see, appropriate that nineteenth-century capitalist society should treat political rights as a secondary product of civil rights. It was equally appropriate that the twentieth century should abandon this position and attach political rights directly and independently to citizenship as such. This vital change of principle was put into effect when the Act of 1918, by adopting manhood suffrage, shifted the basis of political rights from economic substance to personal status. I say 'manhood' deliberately in order to emphasize the great significance of this reform quite apart from the second, and no less important, reform introduced

at the same time — namely the enfranchisement of women. [...]

The original source of social rights was membership of local communities and functional associations. This source was supplemented and progressively replaced by a *Poor Law* and a system of wage regulation which were nationally conceived and locally administered. [...]

As the pattern of the old order dissolved under the blows of a competitive economy, and the plan disintegrated, the Poor Law was left high and dry as an isolated survival from which the idea of social rights was gradually drained away. But at the very end of the eighteenth century there occurred a final struggle between the old and the new, between the planned (or patterned) society and the competitive economy. And in this battle citizenship was divided against itself; social rights sided with the old and civil with the new. [...]

In this brief episode of our history we see the *Poor Law* as the aggressive champion of the social rights of citizenship. In the succeeding phase we find the attacker driven back far behind his original position. By the Act of 1834 the *Poor Law* renounced all claim to trespass on the territory of the wages system, or to interfere with the forces of the free market. It offered relief only to those who, through age or sickness, were incapable of continuing the battle, and to those other weaklings who gave up the struggle, admitted defeat, and cried for mercy. The tentative move towards the concept of social security was reversed. But more than that, the minimal social rights that remained were detached from the status of citizenship. The *Poor Law* treated the claims of the poor, not as an integral part of the rights of the citizen, but as an alternative to them — as claims which could be met only if the claimants ceased to be citizens in any true sense of the word. For paupers forfeited in practice the civil right of personal liberty, by internment in the workhouse, and they forfeited by law any political rights they might possess. This disability of defranchisement remained in being until 1918, and the significance of its final removal has, perhaps, not been fully appreciated. The stigma which clung to poor relief expressed the deep feelings of a people who understood that those who accepted relief must cross the road that separated the community of citizens from the outcast company of the destitute.

The *Poor Law* is not an isolated example of this divorce of social rights from the status of citizenship. The early *Factory Acts* show the same tendency. Although in fact they led to an improvement of working conditions and a reduction of working hours to the benefit of all employed in the industries to which they applied, they meticulously refrained from giving this protection directly to the adult male — the citizen *par excellence*. And they did so out of respect for his status as a citizen, on the grounds that enforced protective measures curtailed the civil right to conclude a free contract of employment. Protection was confined to women and children, and champions of women's rights were quick to detect the implied insult. Women were protected because they were not citizens. If they wished to enjoy full and responsible citizenship, they must forgo protection. By the end of the nineteenth century such arguments had become obsolete, and the factory code had become one of the pillars in the edifice of social rights. [...]

By the end of the nineteenth century, elementary education was not only free, it was compulsory. This signal [*sic*] departure from *laissez faire* could, of course, be justified on the grounds that free choice is a right only for mature minds, that children are naturally subject to discipline, and that parents cannot be trusted to do what is in the best interests of their children. But the principle goes deeper than that. We have here a personal right combined with a public duty to exercise the right. Is the public duty imposed merely for the benefit of the individual — because children cannot fully appreciate their own interests and parents may be unfit to enlighten them? I hardly think that this can be an adequate explanation. It was increasingly recognized, as the nineteenth century wore on, that political democracy needed an educated electorate, and that scientific manufacture needed educated workers and technicians. The duty to improve and civilize oneself is therefore a social duty, and not merely a personal one, because the social health of a society depends upon the civilization of its members. And a community that enforces this duty has begun to realize that its culture is an organic unity and its civilization a national heritage. It follows that the growth of public elementary education during the nineteenth century was the first decisive step on the road to the reestablishment of the social rights of citizenship in the twentieth. [...]

THE IMPACT OF CITIZENSHIP ON SOCIAL CLASS

Citizenship is a status bestowed on those who are full members of a community. All who possess the status are equal with respect to the rights and duties with which the status is endowed. There is no uni-versal principle that determines what those rights and duties shall be, but societies in which citizenship is a developing institution create an image of an ideal citizenship against which achievement can be measured and towards which aspiration can be directed. The urge forward along the path thus plotted is an urge towards a fuller measure of equality, an enrichment of the stuff of which the status is made and an increase in the number of those on whom the status is bestowed. Social class, on the other hand, is a system of inequality. And it too, like citizenship, can be based on a set of ideals, beliefs and values. It is therefore reasonable to expect that the impact of citizenship on social class should take the form of a conflict between opposing principles. If I am right in my contention that citizenship has been a developing institution in England at least since the latter part of the seventeenth century, then it is clear that its growth coincides with the rise of capitalism, which is a system, not of equality, but of inequality. Here is something that needs explaining. How is it that these two opposing principles could grow and flourish side by side in the same soil? What made it possible for them to be reconciled with one another and to become, for a time at least, allies instead of antagonists? The question is a pertinent one, for it is clear that, in the twentieth century, citizenship and the capitalist class system have been at war....

It is true that class still functions. Social inequality is regarded as necessary and purposeful. It provides the incentive to effort and designs the distribution of power. But there is no overall pattern of inequality, in which an appropriate value is attached, *a priori*, to each social level. Inequality, therefore, though necessary, may become excessive. As Patrick Colquhoun said, in a much-quoted passage: 'Without a large proportion of poverty there could be no riches, since riches are the offspring of labour, while labour can result only from a state of poverty.... Poverty therefore is a most necessary and indispensable ingredient in society, without which nations and communities could not exist in a state of civilization.[6] [...]

The more you look on wealth as conclusive proof of merit, the more you incline to regard poverty as evidence of failure — but the penalty for failure may seem to be greater than the offence warrants. In such circumstances it is natural that the more unpleasant features of inequality should be treated, rather irresponsibly, as a nuisance, like the black smoke that used to pour unchecked from our factory chimneys. And so in time, as the social conscience stirs to life, class-abatement, like smoke-abatement, becomes a desirable aim to be pursued as far as is compatible with the continued efficiency of the social machine.

But class-abatement in this form was not an attack on the class system. On the contrary it aimed, often quite consciously, at making the class system less vulnerable to attack by alleviating its less defensible consequences. It raised the floor-level in the basement of the social edifice, and perhaps made it rather more hygienic than it was before. But it remained a basement, and the upper stories of the building were unaffected. [...]

There developed, in the latter part of the nineteenth century, a growing interest in equality as a principle of social justice and an appreciation of the fact that the formal recognition of an equal capacity for rights was not enough. In theory even the complete removal of all the barriers that separated civil rights from their remedies would not have interfered with the principles or the class structure of the capitalist system. It would, in fact, have created a situation which many supporters of the competitive market economy falsely assumed to be already in existence. But in practice the attitude of mind which inspired the efforts to remove these barriers grew out of a conception of equality which overstepped these narrow limits, the conception of equal social worth, not merely of equal natural rights. Thus although citizenship, even by the end of the nineteenth century, had done little to reduce social inequality, it had helped to guide progress into the path which led directly to the egalitarian policies of the twentieth century. [...]

This growing national consciousness, this awakening public opinion, and these first stirrings of a sense of community membership and common heritage did not have any material effect on class structure and social inequality for the simple and obvious reason that, even at the end of the nineteenth century, the mass of the working people did not wield effective political power. By that time the franchise was fairly wide, but those who had recently received the vote had not yet learned how to use it. The political rights of citizenship, unlike the civil rights, were full of potential danger to the capitalist system, although those who were cautiously extending them down the social scale probably did not realize quite how great the danger was. They could hardly be expected to foresee what vast changes could be brought about by the peaceful use of political power, without a violent and bloody revolution. The 'planned society' and the welfare state had not yet risen over the horizon or come within the view of the practical politician. The foundations of the market economy and the contractual system seemed strong enough to stand against any probable assault. In fact, there were some grounds for expecting that the working classes, as they became educated, would accept the basic principles of the system and be content to rely for their protection and progress on the civil rights of citizenship, which contained no obvious menace to competitive capitalism. Such a view was encouraged by the fact that one of the main achievements of political power in the later nineteenth century was the recognition of the right of collective bargaining. This meant that social progress was being sought by strengthening civil rights, not by creating social rights; through the use of contract in the open market, not through a minimum wage and social security.

But this interpretation underrates the significance of this extension of civil rights in the economic sphere. For civil rights were in origin intensely individual, and that is why they harmonized with the individualistic phase of capitalism. By the device of incorporation groups were enabled to act legally as individuals. This important development did not go unchallenged, and limited liability was widely denounced as an infringement of individual responsibility. But the position of trade unions was even more anomalous, because they did not seek or obtain incorporation. They can, therefore, exercise vital civil rights collectively on behalf of their members without formal collective responsibility, while the individual responsibility of the workers in relation to contract is largely unenforceable. These civil rights became, for the workers, an instrument for raising their social and economic status, that is to say, for establishing the claim that they, as citizens, were entitled to certain social rights. But the normal method of establishing social rights is by the exercise of political power, for social rights imply an absolute right to a certain standard of civilization which is conditional only on the discharge of the general duties of citizenship. Their content does not depend on the economic value of the individual claimant. There is therefore a significant difference between a genuine collective bargain through which economic forces in a free market seek to achieve equilibrium and the use of collective civil rights to assert basic claims to the elements of social justice. Thus the acceptance of collective bargaining was not simply a natural extension of civil rights; it represented the transfer of an important process from the political to the civil sphere of citizenship. But 'transfer' is, perhaps, a misleading term, for at the time when this happened the workers either did not possess, or had not yet learned to use, the political right of the franchise. Since then they have obtained and made full use of that right. Trade unionism has, therefore, created a secondary system of industrial citizenship parallel with and supplementary to the system of political citizenship. [...]

A new period opened at the end of the nineteenth century, conveniently marked by Booth's survey of Life and Labour of the People in London and the Royal Commission on the Aged Poor. It saw the first big advance in social rights, and this involved significant changes in the egalitarian principle as expressed in citizenship. But there were other forces at work as well. A rise of money incomes unevenly distributed over the social classes altered the economic distance which separated these classes from one another, diminishing the gap between skilled and unskilled labour and between skilled labour and non-manual workers, while the steady increase in small savings blurred the class distinction between the capitalist and the propertyless proletarian. Secondly, a system of direct taxation, ever more steeply graduated, compressed the whole scale of disposable incomes. Thirdly, mass production for the home market and a growing interest on the part of industry in the needs and tastes of the common people enabled the less well-to-do to enjoy a material civilization which differed less markedly in quality from that of the rich than it had ever done before. All this profoundly altered the setting in which the progress of citizenship took place. Social integration spread from the sphere of sentiment and patriotism into that of material enjoyment. The components of a civilized and cultured life, formerly the monopoly of the few, were brought progressively within reach of the many, who were encouraged thereby to stretch out their hands towards those that still eluded their grasp. The diminution of inequality strengthened the demand for its abolition, at least with regard to the essentials of social welfare.

These aspirations have in part been met by incorporating social rights in the status of citizenship and thus creating a universal right to real income which is not proportionate to the market value of the claimant. Class-abatement is still the aim of social rights, but it has acquired a new meaning. It is no longer merely an attempt to abate the obvious nuisance of destitution in the lowest ranks of society. It has assumed the guise of action modifying the whole pattern of social inequality. It is no longer content to raise the floor-level in the basement of the social edifice, leaving the superstructure as it was. It has begun to remodel the whole building, and it might even end by converting a skyscraper into a bungalow. It is therefore important to consider whether any such ultimate aim is implicit in

the nature of this development, or whether, as I put it at the outset, there are natural limits to the contemporary drive towards greater social and economic equality. [...]

The degree of equalization achieved [by the modern system of welfare benefits] depends on four things; whether the benefit is offered to all or to a limited class; whether it takes the form of money payment or service rendered; whether the minimum is high or low; and how the money to pay for the benefit is raised. Cash benefits subject to income limit and means test had a simple and obvious equalizing effect. They achieved class-abatement in the early and limited sense of the term. The aim was to ensure that all citizens should attain at least to the prescribed minimum, either by their own resources or with assistance if they could not do it without. The benefit was given only to those who needed it, and thus inequalities at the bottom of the scale were ironed out. The system operated in its simplest and most unadulterated form in the case of the *Poor Law* and old age pensions. But economic equalization might be accompanied by psychological class discrimination. The stigma which attached to the *Poor Law* made 'pauper' a derogatory term defining a class. 'Old age pensioner' may have had a little of the same flavour, but without the taint of shame. [...]

The extension of the social services is not primarily a means of equalizing incomes. In some cases it may, in others it may not. The question is relatively unimportant; it belongs to a different department of social policy. What matters is that there is a general enrichment of the concrete substance of civilized life, a general reduction of risk and insecurity, an equalization between the more and the less fortunate at all levels — between the healthy and the sick, the employed and the unemployed, the old and the active, the bachelor and the father of a large family. Equalization is not so much between classes as between individuals within a population which is now treated for this purpose as though it were one class. Equality of status is more important than equality of income. [...]

I said earlier that in the twentieth century citizenship and the capitalist class system have been at war. Perhaps the phrase is rather too strong, but it is quite clear that the former has imposed modifications on the latter. But we should not be justified in assuming that, although status is a principle that conflicts with contract, the stratified status system which is creeping into citizenship is an alien element in the economic world outside. Social rights in their modern form imply an invasion of contract by status, the subordination of market price to social justice, the replacement of the free bargain by the declaration of rights. But are these principles quite foreign to the practice of the market today, or are they there already, entrenched within the contract system itself? I think it is clear that they are. [...]

CONCLUSIONS

I have tried to show how citizenship, and other forces outside it, have been altering the pattern of social inequality.... We have to look, here, for the combined effects of three factors. First, the compression, at both ends, of the scale of income distribution. Second, the great extension of the area of common culture and common experience. And third, the enrichment of the universal status of citizenship, combined with the recognition and stabilization of certain status differences chiefly through the linked systems of education and occupation. [...]

I asked, at the beginning, whether there was any limit to the present drive towards social equality inherent in the principles governing the movement. My answer is that the preservation of economic inequalities has been made more difficult by the enrichment of the status of citizenship. There is less room for them, and there is more and more likelihood of their being challenged. But we are certainly proceeding at present on the assumption that the hypothesis is valid. And this assumption provides the answer to the second question. We are not aiming at absolute equality. There are limits inherent in the egalitarian movement. But the movement is a double one. It operates partly through citizenship and partly through the economic system. In both cases the aim is to remove inequalities which cannot be regarded as legitimate, but the standard of legitimacy is different. In the former it is the standard of social justice, in the latter it is social justice combined with economic necessity. It is possible, therefore, that the inequalities permitted by the two halves of the movement will not coincide. Class distinctions may survive which have no appropriate economic function, and economic differences which do not correspond with accepted class distinctions. [...]

(c) Return of the Citizen: A Survey of Recent Work on Citizenship Theory†

Will Kymlicka and Wayne Norman

INTRODUCTION

There has been an explosion of interest in the concept of citizenship among political theorists....

There are a number of reasons for this renewed interest in citizenship in the 1990s. At the level of theory it is a natural evolution in political discourse because the concept of citizenship seems to integrate the demands of justice and community membership — the central concepts of the political philosophy in the 1970s and 1980s, respectively. Citizenship is intimately linked to ideas of individual entitlement on the one hand and of attachment to a particular community on the other. Thus, it may help clarify what is really at stake in the debate between liberals and communitarians.

Interest in citizenship has also been sparked by a number of recent political events and trends throughout the world — increasing voter apathy and long-term welfare dependency in the United States, the resurgence of nationalist movements in Eastern Europe, the stresses created by an increasingly multicultural and multiracial population in Western Europe, the backlash against the welfare state in Thatcher's England, the failure of environmental policies that rely on voluntary citizen cooperation, and so forth.

† From Ronald Beiner (ed.), *Theorizing Citizenship* (Albany: State University of New York Press, 1995) at 283–91, 301–309. This article was originally published in the journal *Ethics*, vol. 104, #2 (1994): 351–81. Reproduced with permission of The University of Chicago Press. [Notes and/or references omitted.]

These events have made clear that the health and stability of a modern democracy depends, not only on the justice of its "basic structure" but also on the qualities and attitudes of its citizens,[1] for example, their sense of identity and how they view potentially competing forms of national, regional, ethnic, or religious identities; their ability to tolerate and work together with others who are different from themselves; their desire to participate in the political process in order to promote the public good and hold political authorities accountable; their willingness to show self-restraint and exercise personal responsibility in their economic demands and in personal choices which affect their health and the environment. Without citizens who possess these qualities, democracies become difficult to govern, even unstable.[2] ...

. . . .

THE POSTWAR ORTHODOXY

Before describing the new work on citizenship, it is necessary to outline quickly the view of citizenship that is implicit in much postwar political theory and that is defined almost entirely in terms of the possession of rights.

The most influential exposition of this postwar conception of citizenship-as-rights is T.H. Marshall's "Citizenship and Social Class," written in 1949.[4] According to Marshall, citizenship is essentially a matter of ensuring that everyone is treated as a full and equal member of society. And the way to ensure this sense of membership is through according people an increasing number of citizenship rights.

. . . .

For Marshall, the fullest expression of citizenship requires a liberal-democratic welfare state. By guaranteeing civil, political, and social rights to all, the welfare state ensures that every member of society feels like a full member of society, able to participate in and enjoy the common life of society. Where any of these rights are withheld or violated, people will be marginalized and unable to participate.

This is often called "passive" or "private" citizenship, because of its emphasis on passive entitlements and the absence of any obligation to participate in public life. It is still widely supported,[6] and with good reason: "the benefits of private citizenship are not to be sneezed at: they place certain basic human goods (security, prosperity, and freedom) within the grasp of nearly all, and that is

nothing less than a fantastic human achievement" (Macedo 1990, p. 39).

Nevertheless, this orthodox postwar conception of citizenship has come increasingly under attack in the past decade. For the purposes of this article, we can identify two sets of criticisms. The first set focuses on the need to supplement (or replace) the passive acceptance of citizenship responsibilities and virtues, including economic self-reliance, political participation, and even civility. These issues are discussed in section III.

The second set focuses on the need to revise the current definition of citizenship to accommodate the increasing social and cultural pluralism of modern societies. Can citizenship provide a common experience, identity and allegiance for the members of society? Is it enough simply to include historically excluded groups on an equal basis, or are special measures sometimes required? This issue is discussed in section IV.

THE RESPONSIBILITIES AND VIRTUES OF CITIZENSHIP

A. The New Right Critique of Social Citizenship and the Welfare State

The first, and most politically powerful, critique of the postwar orthodoxy came from the New Right's attack on the idea of "social right." These rights had always been resisted by the right, on the grounds that they were *(a)* inconsistent with the demands of (negative) freedom or (desert-based) justice, *(b)* economically inefficient, and *(c)* steps down "the road to serfdom." But in the public's eye, these arguments were seen as either implausible or, at any rate, as justifiably outweighed by considerations of social justice or by a citizenship-based welfare state such as Marshall's.

One of the revolutions in conservative thinking during the Thatcher/Reagan years was the willingness to engage the left in battle over the domain of social citizenship itself. Whereas Marshall had argued that social rights enable the disadvantaged to enter the mainstream of society and effectively exercise their civil and political rights, the New Right argues that the welfare state has promoted passivity among the poor, without actually improving their life chances, and created a culture of dependency. Far from being the solution, the welfare state has itself perpetuated the problem by reducing citizens to passive dependents who are under bureaucratic tutelage. According to Norman Barry, there is no evidence that welfare programs have in fact promoted more active citizenship (Barry 1990, pp. 43–53).

The New Right believes that the model of passive citizenship underestimated the extent to which fulfilling certain obligations is a precondition for being accepted as a full member of society. In particular, by failing to meet the obligation to support themselves, the long-term unemployed are a source of shame for society as well as themselves (Mead 1986, p. 240).[7] Failure to fulfill common obligations is as much of an obstacle to full membership as the lack of equal rights. In these circumstances, "to obligate the dependent as others are obligated is essential to equality, not opposed to it. An effective welfare [policy] must include recipients in the common obligations of citizens rather than exclude them" (Mead 1986, pp. 12–13).

According to the New Right, to ensure the social and cultural integration of the poor we must go "beyond entitlement," and focus instead on their responsibility to earn a living. Since the welfare state discourages people from becoming self-reliant, the safety net should be cut back and any remaining welfare benefits should have obligations tied to them. This is the idea behind one of the principal reforms of the welfare system in the 1980s: "workfare" programs, which require welfare recipients to work for their benefits, to reinforce the idea that citizens should be self-supporting.

This New Right vision of citizenship has not gone unchallenged. For example, the claim that the rise of an unemployed welfare-underclass is due to the availability of welfare ignores the impact of global economic restructuring, and sits uncomfortably with the fact that many of the most extensive welfare states (in Scandinavia, e.g.) have traditionally enjoyed among the lowest unemployment rates.

Moreover, critics charge, it is difficult to find any evidence that the New Right reforms of the 1980s have promoted responsible citizenship. These reforms aimed to extend the scope of markets in people's lives — through freer trade, deregulation, tax cuts, the weakening of trade unions, and the tightening of unemployment benefits — in part in order to teach people the virtues of initiative, self-reliance, and self-sufficiency (Mulgan 1991, p. 43).

Instead, however, many market deregulations arguably made possible an era of unprecedented greed and economic irresponsibility, as evidenced by the savings and loan and junk bond scandals in America (Mulgan 1991, p. 39). Also, cutting welfare benefits, far from getting the disadvantaged back on their feet, has expanded the underclass. Class inequalities have been exacerbated, and the working poor and unemployed have been effectively "disenfranchised," unable to participate in the new economy of the New Right (Fierlbeck 1991, p. 579; Hoover and Plant 1988, chap. 12).[8]

For many, therefore, the New Right program is most plausibly seen not as an alternative account of citizenship but as an assault on the very principle of citizenship. As Plant puts it, "Instead of accepting citizenship as a political and social status, modern Conservatives have sought to reassert the role of the market and have rejected the idea that citizenship confers a status independent of economic standing" (Plant 1991, p. 52; cf. Heater 1990, p. 303; King 1987, pp. 196–98).

B. Rethinking Social Citizenship

Given these difficulties with the New Right critique of welfare entitlements, most people on the left continue to defend the principle that full citizenship requires social rights. For the left, Marshall's argument that people can be full members and participants in the common life of society only if their basic needs are met "is as strong now ... as it ever was" (Ignatieff 1989, p. 72). However, many on the left accept that the existing institutions of the welfare state are unpopular, in part because they seem to promote passivity and dependence, and to "facilitate a privatist retreat from citizenship and a particular 'clientalization' of the citizen's role" (Habermas 1992, pp. 10–11; cf. King 1987, pp. 45–46).

How then should the state foster self-reliance and personal responsibility? The left has responded ambivalently to issues such as "workfare." On the one hand, the principle of personal responsibility and social obligation has always been at the heart of socialism (Mulgan 1991, p. 39). A duty to work is, after all, implicit in Marx's famous slogan, "From each according to his talents, to each according to his needs." Some people on the left, therefore, express qualified acceptance of workfare, if it "gives both responsibility and the power to use it" (Mulgan 1991, p. 46).

On the other hand, most people on the left remain uncomfortable with imposing obligations as a matter of public policy. They believe that the dependent are kept out of the mainstream of society because of a lack of opportunities, such as jobs, education, and training, not because of any desire to avoid work. Imposing obligations, therefore, is futile if genuine opportunities are absent, and unnecessary if those opportunities are present, since the vast majority of people on welfare would prefer not to be (King 1987, pp. 186–91; Fullinwider 1988, pp. 270–

78). Rather than impose an obligation to work, the left would try to achieve full employment through, for example, worker-training programs. So while the left accepts the general principle that citizenship involves both rights and responsibilities, it feels that rights to participate must, in a sense, precede the responsibilities — that is, it is only appropriate to demand fulfillment of the responsibilities after the rights to participate are secured.

A similar rejection of the New Right's view of citizenship can be found in recent feminist discussions of citizenship. Many feminists accept the importance of balancing rights and responsibilities — indeed, Carol Gilligan's findings suggest that women, in their everyday moral reasoning, prefer the language of responsibility to the language of rights (Gilligan 1982, p. 19). But feminists have grave doubts about the New Right rhetoric of economic self-sufficiency. Gender-neutral talk about "self-reliance" is often a code for the view that men should financially support the family, while women should look after the household and care for the elderly, the sick, and the young. This reinforces, rather than eliminates, the barriers to women's full participation in society.[9]

When the New Right talks about self-reliance, the boundaries of the "self" include the family — it is families that should be self-reliant. Hence, greater "self-reliance" is consistent with, and may even require, greater dependency within the family. Yet women's dependence on men within the family can be every bit as harmful as welfare dependency, since it allows men to exercise unequal power over decisions regarding sex, reproduction, consumption, leisure, and so on (King 1987, p. 47; Okin 1989, pp. 128–29).

Since perceptions of responsibility tend to fall unequally on women, many feminists share the left's view that rights to participate must, in a sense, precede responsibilities. Indeed, feminists wish to expand the list of social rights, in order to tackle structural barriers to women's full participation as citizens that the welfare state currently ignores, or even exacerbates, such as the unequal distribution of domestic responsibilities (Phillips 1991a, 1991b; Okin 1992). Given the difficulty of combining family and public responsibilities, equal citizenship for women is impossible until workplaces and career expectations are rearranged to allow more room for family responsibilities and until men accept their share of domestic responsibilities (Okin 1989, pp. 175–77).

However, if rights must precede responsibilities, it seems we are back to the old view of passive citizenship. Yet the left, as much as the right, accepts the need for change. The most popular proposal is to decentralize and democratize the welfare state, for example, by giving local welfare agencies more power and making them accountable to their clients (Pierson 1991, pp. 200–207). Hence, the now-familiar talk of "empowering" welfare recipients by supplementing welfare rights with democratic participatory rights in the administration of welfare programs.

This is the central theme of the contemporary left view of social citizenship.[10] Whether it will work to overcome welfare dependency is difficult to say. Service providers have often resisted attempts to increase their accountability (Rustin 1991, p. 231; Pierson 1991, pp. 206–207). Moreover there may be some tension between the goal of increasing democratic accountability to the local community and increasing accountability to clients (Plant 1990, p. 30). ...

. . . .

CITIZENSHIP, IDENTITY, AND DIFFERENCE

Citizenship is not just a certain status, defined by a set of rights and responsibilities. It is also an identity, an expression of one's membership in a political community. Marshall saw citizenship as a shared identity that would integrate previously excluded groups within British society and provide a source of national unity. He was particularly concerned to integrate the working classes, whose lack of education and economic resources excluded them from the "common culture" which should have been a "common possession and heritage" (Marshall 1965, pp. 101–102).[23]

It has become clear, however, that many groups — blacks, women, Aboriginal peoples, ethnic and religious minorities, gays and lesbians — still feel excluded from the "common culture," despite possessing the common rights of citizenship. Members of these groups feel excluded not only because of their socioeconomic status but also because of their sociocultural identity — their "difference."

An increasing number of theorists, whom we will call "cultural pluralists," argue that citizenship must take account of these differences. Cultural pluralists believe that the common rights of citizenship, originally defined by and for white men, cannot accommodate the special needs of minority groups. These groups can only be integrated into the common culture if we adopt what Iris Marion Young calls a conception of "differentiated citizenship" (Young 1989, p. 258).

On this view, members of certain groups would be incorporated into the political community not only as individuals but also through the group, and their rights would depend, in part, on their group membership. For example, some immigrant groups are demanding special rights or exemptions to accommodate their religious practices; historically disadvantaged groups, such as women or blacks, are demanding special representation in the political process; and many national minorities (Québécois, Kurds, Catalans) are seeking greater powers of self-government within the larger country, if not outright secession.

These demands for "differentiated citizenship" pose a serious challenge to the prevailing conception of citizenship. Many people regard the idea of group-differentiated citizenship as a contradiction in terms. On the orthodox view, citizenship is, by definition, a matter of treating people as individuals with equal rights under the law. This is what distinguishes democratic citizenship from feudal and other premodern views that determined people's political status by their religious, ethnic, or class membership. Hence "the organization of society on the basis of rights or claims that derive from group membership is sharply opposed to the concept of society based on citizenship" (Porter 1987, p. 128). The idea of differentiated citizenship, therefore, is a radical development in citizenship theory.

One of the most influential theorists of cultural pluralism is Iris Marion Young. According to Young, the attempt to create a universal conception of citizenship which transcends group differences is fundamentally unjust because it oppresses historically excluded groups: "In a society where some groups are privileged while others are oppressed, insisting that as citizens persons should leave behind their particular affiliations and experiences to adopt a general point of view serves only to reinforce the privilege; for the perspective and interests of the privileged will tend to dominate this unified public, marginalizing or silencing those of other groups" (Young 1989, p. 257).[24] Young gives two reasons why genuine equality requires affirming rather than ignoring group differences. First, culturally excluded groups are at a disadvantage in the political process, and "the solution lies at least in part in providing institutionalized means for the explicit recognition and representation of oppressed groups" (Young 1989, p. 259). These procedural measures would include public funds for advocacy groups, guaranteed representation in political bodies, and veto rights over specific policies that affect a group directly (Young 1989, pp. 261–62; 1990, pp. 183–91).

Second, culturally excluded groups often have distinctive needs which can only be met through group-differentiated policies. These include language rights for Hispanics, land rights for Aboriginal groups, and reproductive rights for women (Young 1990, pp. 175–83). Other policies which have been advocated by cultural pluralists include group libel laws for women or Muslims, publicly funded schools for certain religious minorities, and exemptions from laws that interfere with religious worship, such as Sunday closing, animal-slaughtering legislation for Jews and Muslims, or motorcycle helmet laws for Sikhs (Parekh 1990, p. 705; 1991, pp. 197–204; Modood 1992).

Much has been written regarding the justification for these rights and how they relate to broader theories of justice and democracy. Young herself defends them as a response to "oppression," of which she outlines five forms: exploitation, marginalization, powerlessness, cultural imperialism, and "random violence and harassment motivated by group hatred or fear" (Young 1989, p. 261). It would take us too far afield to consider these justifications or the various objections to them.[25] Instead, we will focus on the impact of these rights on citizenship identity.

Critics of differentiated citizenship worry that if groups are encouraged by the very terms of citizenship to turn inward and focus on their "difference" (whether racial, ethnic, religious, sexual, and so on), then "the hope of a larger fraternity of all Americans will have to be abandoned" (Glazer 1983, p. 227). Citizenship will cease to be "a device to cultivate a sense of community and a common sense of purpose" (Heater 1990, p. 295; Kristeva 1993, p. 7; Cairns 1993). Nothing will bind the various groups in society together and prevent the spread of mutual mistrust of conflict (Kukathas 1993, p. 156).

Critics also worry that differentiated citizenship would create a "politics of grievance." If, as Young implies, only oppressed groups are entitled to differentiated citizenship, this may encourage group leaders to devote their political energy to establishing a perception of disadvantage — rather than working to overcome it — in order to secure their claim to group rights.

These are serious concerns. In evaluating them, however, we need to distinguish three different kinds of groups and three different kinds of group rights, which both Young and her critics tend to run together: *(a)* special representation rights (for disadvantaged groups); *(b)* multicultural rights (for immigrant and religious groups); and *(c)* self-government rights (for national minorities). Each of these has very different implications for citizenship identity.

Special representation rights. — For many of the groups on Young's list, such as the poor, elderly, African-Americans, and gays, the demand for group rights takes the form of special representation within the political process of the larger society. Since Young views these rights as a response to conditions of oppression, they are most plausibly seen as a temporary measure on the way to a society where the need for special representation no longer exists. Society should seek to remove the oppression, thereby eliminating the need for these rights.

Self-government rights. — In some of Young's examples, such as the reservation system of the American Indians, the demand for group rights is not seen as a temporary measure, and it is misleading to say that group rights are a response to a form of oppression that we hope someday to eliminate. Aboriginal peoples and other national minorities like the Québécois or Scots claim permanent and inherent rights, grounded in a principle of self-determination. These groups are "cultures," "peoples," or "nations," in the sense of being historical communities, more or less institutionally complete, occupying a given homeland or territory, sharing a distinct language and history. These nations find themselves within the boundaries of a larger political community, but claim the right to govern themselves in certain key matters, in order to ensure the full and free development of their culture and the best interests of their people. What these national minorities want is not primarily better representation in the central government but, rather, the transfer of power and legislative jurisdictions from the central government to their own communities.

Multicultural rights. — The case of Hispanics and other immigrant groups in the United States is different again. Their demands include public support of bilingual education and ethnic studies in schools and exemptions from laws that disadvantage them, given their religious practices. These measures are intended to help immigrants express their cultural particularity and pride without its hampering their success in the economic and political institutions of the dominant society. Like self-government rights, these rights need not be temporary, because the cultural differences they promote are not something we hope to eliminate. But unlike self-government rights, multicultural rights are intended to promote integration into the larger society, not self-government.

. . . .

Would adopting one or more of these group rights undermine the integrative function of citizenship? A closer look at the distinction between the three kinds of rights suggests that such fears are often misplaced. The fact is that, generally speaking, the demand for both representation rights and multicultural rights is a demand for inclusion. Groups that feel excluded want to be included in the larger society, and the recognition and accommodation of their "difference" is intended to facilitate this.

. . . .

Self-government rights, however, do raise deep problems for traditional notions of citizenship identity. While both representation and multicultural rights take the larger political community for granted and seek greater inclusion in it, demands for self-government reflect a desire to weaken the bonds with the larger community and, indeed, question its very nature, authority, and permanence. If democracy is the rule of the people, group self-determination raises the question of who "the people" really are. National minorities claim that they are distinct peoples, with inherent rights of self-determination which were not relinquished by their (sometimes involuntary) federation with other nations within a larger country. Indeed, the retaining of certain powers is often explicitly spelled out in the treaties or constitutional agreements which specified the terms of federation.

Self-government rights, therefore, are the most complete case of differentiated citizenship, since they divide the people into separate "peoples," each with its own historic rights, territories, and powers of self-government, and each, therefore, with its own political community.

It seems unlikely that differentiated citizenship can serve an integrative function in this context. If citizenship is membership in a political community, then in creating overlapping political communities, self-government rights necessarily give rise to a sort of dual citizenship and to potential conflicts about which community citizens identify with most deeply (Vernon 1988). Moreover, there seems to be no natural stopping point to the demands for increasing self-government. If limited autonomy is granted, this may simply fuel the ambitions of nationalist leaders who will be satisfied with nothing short of their own undifferentiated nation-state. Democratic multination states are, it would seem, inherently unstable for this reason.

. . . .

What, then, is the source of unity in a multi-nation country? Rawls claims that the source of union in modern societies is a shared conception of justice: "Although a well-ordered society is divided and pluralistic ... public agreement on questions of political and social justice supports ties of civic friendship and secures the bonds of association" (Rawls 1980, p. 540). But the fact that two national groups share the same principles of justice does not necessarily give them any strong reason to join (or remain) together, rather than remaining (or splitting into) two separate countries. The fact that people in Norway and Sweden share the same principles of justice is no reason for them to regret the secession of Norway in 1905. Similarly, the fact that the anglophones and francophones in Canada share the same principles of justice is not a strong reason to remain together, since the Québécois rightly assume that their own national state could respect the same principles. A shared conception of justice throughout a political community does not necessarily generate a shared identity, let alone a shared citizenship identity that will supersede rival identities based on ethnicity (Nickel 1990; Norman 1993a).[33]

It seems clear, then, that this is one place where we really do need a theory of citizenship, not just a theory of democracy or justice. How can we construct a common identity in a country where people not only belong to separate political communities but also belong in different ways — that is, some are incorporated as individuals and others through membership in a group? Taylor calls this "deep diversity" and insists that it is "the only formula" on which a multination state can remain united (Taylor 1991). However, he admits that it is an open question what holds such a country together.[34]

Indeed, the great variance in historical, cultural, and political situations in multination states suggests that any generalized answer to this question will likely be overstated. It might be a mistake to suppose that one could develop a general theory about the role of either a common citizenship identity or a differentiated citizenship identity in promoting or hindering national unity (Taylor 1992b, pp. 65–66). Here, as with the other issues we have examined in this survey, it remains unclear what we can expect from a "theory of citizenship."

(d) The Exploitation of Vulnerability: Dimensions of Citizenship and Rightlessness in Canada's Security Certificate Legislation[†]

Christine Wilke and Paula Willis

. . . .

I. INTRODUCTION

That the majority on occasion must be checked when proceeding against a minority of its fellow citizens is inevitable and probably salutary; but that the majority must be checked in proceedings against hostile aliens by a judge, simply because he doesn't think deportation is a good idea, is intolerable.[1]

Non-citizens are often the first to be targeted by policies that are implemented in the name of national security: they easily appear to be "hostile aliens" about whom Rehnquist complained, as noted above. How are ideas of national security translated into policies that exclusively target non-citizens as security risks? And how do courts engage with the ideas of security, foreignness and risk on which these policies are based? This article examines the Canadian Supreme Court's *Charkaoui* decision's engagement with the politics of belonging, foreignness, and risk. *Charkaoui* invalidated portions of the security certificate mechanism that facilitated the long-term detention of non-nations deemed to pose a threat to

† (2008) 26 Windsor Y.B. Access Just. 25 at 25–31, 33, 37–40, 42–44, 50–51. Reproduced with permission. [Notes and/or references omitted.]

Canadian security.[2] This mechanism has parallels in the immigration legislation of other countries, notably the United Kingdom and the United States.[3] Since 2004, the highest courts in these countries have reviewed and partially challenged the legal framework underpinning the detention of non-citizens.[4] Some of these detentions, such as the ones complained about in *Charkaoui* and the British *Belmarsh* case,[5] have no clear end in sight. These cases raise the issue of indefinite detention: the application of immigration law mandates that the "strangers" who suddenly appear threatening to the body politic are detained to be sent home,[6] but they lack a home to which they can return without fear of torture or mistreatment. Indefinite detention arises at this intersection between immigration detention for the purpose of deportation and the presence of severe legal, moral or practical concerns about deportation.[7]

We examine the Canadian Supreme Court's *Charkaoui* decision on the security certificate procedure through the lens of citizenship and belonging and its opposites — statelessness and rightlessness. Our analysis of citizenship and rightlessness is based on a re-reading of Hannah Arendt's discussion of human rights in *The Origins of Totalitarianism*[8] through the lens of recent accounts that conceptualize citizenship and subordination as multidimensional and disaggregated practices and statuses. Which understandings of security and citizenship underpin these policies and the courts' responses to them? How do the legal challenges to such measures reconfigure the imaginations of rights, membership, and security? We argue that *Charkaoui* does not recognize but instead exploits the security certificate detainees' substantive rightlessness.

The security certificate process has the ostensible purpose of facilitating the speedy deportation of non-citizens deemed threats to Canadian security. As of February 2008, six persons are subject to security certificates: Mohamed Harkat, a refugee from Algeria; Hassan Almrei, a refugee from Syria; Mahmoud Jaballah and Mohammed Mahjoub, Egyptian citizens; Adil Charkaoui, a Moroccan citizen and permanent resident of Canada; and Manickavasagam Suresh, citizen of Sri Lanka.[9] The cases of Harkat, Charkaoui, Mahjoub, Jaballah, and Almrei have attracted special public attention since the certificates against them coincide with the wider post-9/11 securitization of Muslim men in North America and beyond. The "Security Certificate Five" are considered to be dangerous in Canada, but the *Charter* and human rights instruments halts their deportation due to the risk of torture in their countries of citizenship. Four of the

detainees have been released into supervised house arrest. Family members and communities have been enlisted in the control of the detainees. Hassan Almrei, who has no family in Canada, remains in detention.[10] We propose to interpret this regime of detention, supervised release and threat of deportation not as a specific human rights violation. Rather, we follow Hannah Arendt in conceptualizing the detainees' situation as a denial of the more fundamental "right to have rights" or the right to be treated as a person to whom the human rights envisioned in national constitutions and international law apply as a matter of right, not of discretion or charity.[11] While the detainees are not treated as non-persons without any rights whatsoever, the rights that they are granted appear as *grants* arising from the state's discretion and the commitment to the rule of law as procedural justice, not as rights inherent in the human status of the detainees.

In February 2007, the *Charkaoui* invalidated parts of the security certificate scheme but left the overall framework in place. In the media, the *Charkaoui* decision was hailed as "not just a ruling, [but] a statement"[12] in favour of reconciling competing legal values without jeopardizing security. Some commentators praised the Court for having "found a fair and pragmatic way to resolve the moral dilemma of the age of terror.[13] Yet in parliamentary committee hearings on a bill designed to render the partially invalidated legislation compatible with the *Charter*, a member of parliament cautioned against amendments that would grant detainees substantively more rights, remarking that "[t]he Supreme Court has upheld almost the entire security certificate regime, except for the part about the special advocate."[14] The complacent tone of the debate and Parliament's very moderate pace and scope of reforming the security certificate mechanism hint at serious limitations of *Charkaoui* as far as the rights of the detainees are concerned. Here, we scrutinize the decision for its theoretical underpinnings, its language, its silences, and its limits. We ask why certain non-citizens remain extremely vulnerable to harsh security measures and show how rightlessness persists alongside a robust commitment to human rights.

. . . .

II. DISPLACING INSECURITY: SECURITY CERTIFICATES IN CANADA

Security certificates are used when information surfaces indicating that a person who is lawfully present in Canada might nevertheless be "inadmissible".

Inadmissibility on security grounds is stipulated in section 34 of the *Immigration and Refugee Protection Act* (2002) [IRPA] as follows:

(1) A permanent resident or a foreign national is inadmissible on security grounds for:
(a) engaging in an act of espionage or an act of subversion against a democratic government, institution or process as they are understood in Canada;
(b) engaging in or instigating the subversion by force of any government;
(c) engaging in terrorism;
(d) being a danger to the security of Canada;
(e) engaging in acts of violence that would or might endanger the lives or safety of persons in Canada; or
(f) being a member of an organization that there are reasonable grounds to believe engages, has engaged or will engage in acts referred to in paragraph (a), (b) or (c).

Security certificates are issued by the Minister of Citizenship and Immigration and the Minister of Public Safety on the advice of the Canadian Security Intelligence Service [CSIS]. Upon the signature by the ministers, the certificate is automatically referred to a designated Federal Court judge who has to assess the "reasonableness" of the certificate.[17] The reasonableness test asks the Federal Court judge to decide whether there are "reasonable grounds to believe" that the evidence presented by the government establishes inadmissibility on security grounds. The designated judge merely needs "a *bona fide* belief in a serious possibility based on credible evidence," which is "more than a flimsy suspicion, but less than the civil test of balance of probabilities."[18] The threshold is much lower than the standard of proof beyond reasonable doubt required by criminal law.

Since 1991, twenty-eight security certificates have been issued, twenty of which were upheld.[19] Membership in a terrorist organization[20] has been the most common reason for the issuance of a security certificate. Yet, three suspected spies from Russia and two members of Yasser Arafat's secret security force were also deported under certificates.[21] Of the twenty-eight certificates, five have named women. The current detainees have been subjected to detention or subject to supervised house arrest since 2000, 2001, 2002, and 2003, respectively. They have been held on certificates for much longer than had been the custom prior to 9/11: in twelve out of the fifteen pre-9/11 cases, the persons named in the certificate were deported (occasionally to a third state) within two years; the large majority of them within one

year. Security certificates were designed to speed up the deportation of non-citizens who are inadmissible on security grounds, and they largely accomplished this goal prior to 9/11. In current practice, however, they facilitate indefinite detention instead of speedy removal. This shift in the practical application of pre-existing rules poses new moral and legal questions.

Under the old IRPA security certificate process, the Minister of Citizenship and Immigration may present *ex parte* evidence to the Federal Court judge *in camera* (in secret) if the disclosure of evidence to the individual, their legal counsel or the general public could jeopardize national security or the safety of any person. The designated judge reviews the file prepared by CSIS which may include evidence that would be inadmissible in criminal proceedings.[22] The judge provides a summary of the evidence to the individual named under a certificate to the extent that the information may be disclosed. Additionally, IRPA guarantees the 'opportunity to be heard' for the individual named to respond to the summary of evidence. Depending on the nature of such a summary, individuals named in a security certificate might be unaware of the evidence presented against them and thus in no position to counter it. This procedure has gained the IRPA security certificate process the nickname "secret trials" and caused considerable uneasiness for participants in the process, including some of the "designated judges".[23] The *Charkaoui* decision has invalidated this part of the IRPA as a violation of the "fundamental justice" guarantee contained in section 7 of the *Canadian Charter of Rights and Freedoms*,[24] but has suspended the effect of the invalidation until February 23, 2008. Parliament is tasked with devising a new procedure that gives more weight to the detainees' right to see and meet the case against them, and that provides for an "independent agent at the stage of judicial review"[25] to enable limited advocacy on behalf of the detainees. Drafts and committee deliberations indicate that Parliament intends to introduce the British special advocate system without, however, giving much weight to the criticisms of this system voiced by special advocates, British courts, and analysts.

How does the security certificate process facilitate potentially indefinite detention? The practical effects of the security certificate scheme result from the interaction between legislative framework, administrative practice, and political context. First, all non-residents and most permanent residents who are subject to a security certificate are detained. The detention review process before *Charkaoui* varied

205

depending on a person's residence status in Canada: if the individual named under the certificate is a permanent resident of Canada, she is entitled to a review of her case every six months until the certificate is either found reasonable or quashed. At each review, the person named in the certificate has the opportunity to present new evidence concerning the threat they pose to Canadian society. Under the old framework, non-resident foreign nations were only entitled to a review 120 days after the certificate has been found reasonable. In *Charkaoui*, the Supreme Court found this disparity of procedural rights according to immigration status unjustifiable and mandated that all persons subject to security certificates should have equal access to judicial review of the reasonableness of their detention.[26] Second, if a security certificate is upheld, the ruling immediately becomes a deportation order that is not subject to appeal. The final recourse is a Pre-Removal Risk Assessment [PRRA] which, if successful, classifies the individual as a "person in need of protection" and disallows deportation to the individual's country of origin[27]. This can be the case, for example, if the detainee would be at risk of torture in their country of citizenship. Under the *Convention against Torture*, states are not allowed to "expel, return ('refouler') or extradite a person to another State where there are substantial grounds for believing that he would be in danger of being subject to torture."[28] Since deportation is the only option envisioned in the security certificate mechanism for individuals deemed 'dangerous', but is disallowed by a different body of law, those caught between the regimes of security and immigration law and human rights are subsequently left in detention with no specific endpoint in sight.

. . . .

We now turn from the overview of the security certificate scheme to a contextual analysis of the social and legal vulnerabilities of the security certificate detainees that helps to see why certain people are more likely to be caught in a limbo between detention, supervised house arrest, and the threat of deportation to torture. The security certificate detainees belong to a population that is vulnerable along several axes: they are perceived as culturally foreign and even threatening to the country, they do not hold Canadian passports, and they have few other sources of rights and protection available to them. The confluence of these conditions fixes the specific status of these detainees in a particular zone of rightlessness. Attention to the multiple axes of rights

and membership claims helps us to position the detainees in relationship to, for example, Canadian citizens who were caught in the web of Canadian or U.S. anti-terrorism policies.

. . . .

IV. *CHARKAOUI*: DEALING IN RIGHTLESSNESS

The security certificate detainees largely lack the three dimensions of citizenship that would enable their rights claims to resonate with the Canadian public and the legal system. They are mostly perceived as foreign and threatening, outside of the realm of effective belonging. They are not Canadian citizens and therefore outside of the realm of full legal protection under Canadian laws. And they cannot rely on the protection of their countries of citizenship for any other rights claims. To the contrary, their formal citizenship becomes a liability because it raises the threat of deportation to torture. How does *Charkaoui* deal with these vulnerabilities? In the remainder of this article, we show that the *Charkaoui* ruling exploits each of these sources of rightlessness without fully acknowledging their effects on the status and experiences of the detainees. In short, *Charkaoui* presumes that the detainees effectively do not belong to the Canadian demos, it stresses the privileges of formal citizenship in order to counter allegations of discrimination against noncitizens, and it fails to recognize the detainees' lack of options for exit due to their lack of effective citizenship elsewhere.

A. Our Security, Their Insecurity: Effective Belonging

How does *Charkaoui* map the place of the detainees in relationship to the "imagined community"[65] of Canada? Although *Charkaoui* gestures towards the humanity and individuality of the security certificate detainees, the Court sees them as fundamentally alien to Canada. Not only do they not belong to the nation whose security is encompassed by the ubiquitous term "national security" — even worse, the detainees are deemed to threaten this, "our" security. They are positioned as clearly distinguishable from Canadian society, as irreducibly alien. The legal remedies suggested by the Court barely conceal this abyss.

Analyses of previous certificate decisions have noted that the Federal Courts have relied on "profiles" of terrorists based on travel patterns and ideology. Once a person is marched with a "profile", they have little room for disputing their designation as dangerous to Canadian security.[66] On a more fundamental level, the language of process, law, evidence and innocence obscures the nature of the accusations at the heart of the certificates: security certificates can be issued for people who are members of organizations that *might* engage in terrorism in the future.[67] Thus, the certificate is to a significant degree based on predictions of future conduct and on assessments of inner dispositions that might not have surfaced in material actions. But how is a person to prove that they will not engage in terrorism? Given the folk knowledge voiced in court rooms that terrorism is connected to certain Islamic fundamentalist ideologies that are acquired or nourished by visits to "the region", and that someone "hooked" on these ideologies will remain committed to them,[68] it is illusionary to expect someone who fits the terrorist profile to be able to prove that they are not dangerous. The speculative questions about a person's likely future associations, actions, and commitments have to be assessed by the Federal Court with the low standard of "reasonable grounds to believe" that favours the government's characterization of the case. The setup of the security certificate process encourages the translation of societal threat perceptions into legal exclusion orders.

In contemporary nation-states, the "imagined community" of the nation usually extends only to fellow citizens or nationals. The shape of the Canadian imagined community, expressed and shaped through institutionalized policies of multiculturalism and bilingualism, is elusive and widely debated.[69] What it means to be Canadian is rarely explicitly attributed to immutable characteristics such as ethnicity, common language or shared history. Canadian-ness is most often described in terms of commonality in beliefs (in diversity, tolerance and liberalism) underlined by the assumption of (at least) residency and family ties in Canada. These beliefs, in turn, are more readily attributed to some demographic groups and more easily disputed for other groups. The culturally dominant or "original citizens"[70] who derive their citizenship from ancestry and membership in a major cultural and language group have a firmer social standing than those who are relative "newcomers" and members of minority language and cultural groups. The Canadian *National Security Policy*, for example, begins by defining Canadian-ness by the moral (as opposed to legal or geographic) boundaries of the country. The "Canadian" of the *National Security Policy* is defined not by citizenship but through reference to Canadian values:

Canadians stand together in reaffirming that the use of violence to pursue political, religious or ideological goals is an affront to our values ... No one better appreciates the need to protect our society than those who chose this country as a place to build a better life or who fled the consequences of instability and intolerance in other parts of the world.[71]

Some immigrants, and [...] particularly those who "chose" Canada for themselves, are readily embraced in the Canadian demos. Yet, "somewhere between the people who 'chose' Canada and the homogenous 'Canadians' opposed to violence, is the insertion of some non-Canadian 'other' (in a legal or national sense)."[72] The "foreignness" of those whose alleged values do not fit the *National Security Policy's* vision of Canadian-ness is not given fact.[73] Rather, it is established through this policy and other government pronouncements. Foreignness, as Bonnie Honing puts it, is "a symbolic marker that the nation attaches to the people we want to disavow, deport, or detain because we experience them as a threat."[74] It is therefore not reducible to the lack of formal citizenship. In the context of terrorism threats, foreignness becomes an attribute of the threat as well as of persons associated with the threat.

In *Charkaoui*, the detainees' foreignness is presumed and affirmed from the opening paragraph on. The judgment situates itself by describing "a tension that lies at the heart of modern democratic governance":

> One of the most fundamental responsibilities of a government is to ensure the *security of its citizens*. This may require it to act on information that it cannot disclose and to *detain people who threaten national security*. Yet in a constitutional democracy, governments must act accountably and in conformity with the Constitution and the rights and liberties it guarantees.[75]

The government's mandate is to ensure the security of "its citizens" and to "detain people who threaten national security." These two groups presumably do not overlap: people who threaten national security are not part of the nation to be secured. The "citizens" are different from the "people who threaten national security" whom the government "may" be required to detain. "People who threaten national security" are implicitly associated with foreignness through contrasting them with "citizens". In framing the case as a balancing act between liberty and security, the Court slides towards balancing the citizens' security against the liberty (and security) of the detainees ("people who threaten national security"), keeping the desires and interests of these two groups strictly separated. *Charkaoui* does not contemplate, for example, that people who appear suspect share everyone else's vulnerability to acts of violence; or that "citizens" as well as non-citizens might see their personal security threatened by anti-terrorism policies. Such considerations could have helped to blur the line between the stipulated interests of the citizens and the "others".

. . . .

B. Citizens, Residents, Foreign Nationals: Formal Citizenship

Charkaoui engages with the formal meaning of citizenship by affirming that non-citizens suspected of being threats to national security are subject to a legal framework that citizens are never subject to: immigration law. By insisting that *Charkaoui* is an immigration matter, the Court evades arguments about the unequal treatment of citizens and non-citizens in terrorism-related matters. In addition, the Court asks Parliament to devise a new security certificate procedure. Yet democratic institutions are often complicit in establishing different sets of rights for citizens and non-citizens because only citizens' interests are systematically (though imperfectly) represented in such bodies.

Charkaoui highlights the distinction between citizens and non-citizens by disallowing comparisons between the treatment of citizen terrorism suspects and the non-citizen security certificate detainees. The treatment of the non-citizen terrorism suspects raises the question of discrimination since Canadian citizens, irrespective of their dangerousness or intention to engage in terrorism, cannot be detained unless as part of criminal proceedings against them. Discrimination, however, presumes that two groups of persons who share relevant characteristics are treated unequally on the basis of irrelevant traits. The Court found that the security certificate process does not constitute discrimination because the mobility and residence rights of s. 6 of the Charter "specifically allow ... for differential treatment of citizens and non-citizens in deportation matters: only citizens are accorded the right to enter, remain in and leave Canada."[88] The discrimination framework is unavailable as long as the case is treated as a deportation matter. The Court, relying on the *Suresh* exception that renders deportation never completely impossible, found that "the record on which we must rely does not establish that the detentions at issue have become unhinged from the state's purpose of deportation."[89] Indeed, the availability of an ongoing "effective review process that permits the judge to consider all matters relevant to the detention" ensures that detention will continue only as long as it is connected to deportation.[90] The procedural justice of ongoing review brings the detention closer to the principles of the rule of law and thereby normalizes it.[91] Yet it silences the underlying questions about the nature and effects of the detention that depend on the substantive rightlessness of the circumscribed group of non-citizens.

The Court raises two allegedly hypothetical constellations in which the security certificate detention scheme might be discriminatory: "[f]irst, detention may become indefinite as deportation is put off or becomes impossible, for example because there is no country to which the person can be deported."[92] This situation, however, is already present: the five men have been held for prolonged periods of time. In the case of Mahmoud Jaballah, deportation to Egypt was specifically prohibited by a Federal Court. It is not clear, then, how his continued detention and supervised release are meaningfully connected to the attempt to deport him, let alone deport him speedily. The indefinite character of this detention and surveillance is not seen by the courts.

The logic of *Charkaoui* hinges on the distinction between, on the one hand, "lengthy and indeterminate" detention, which is conceded for the cases at hand,[93] and, on the other hand, "indefinite detention", which is unconstitutional and allegedly not present in the current cases. *Charkaoui* affirms that "the IRPA ... does not authorize indefinite detention."[94] This statement is only plausible if "indefinite" is read to mean "endless", not if it means "lasting for an unknown or unstated length of time." The latter, however, is the *Oxford English Dictionary's* definition of "indefinite."[95] If the court had taken this definition of the term as its point of departure, it could have conceded that the combination of immigration legislation, administrative practice, and the protection against torture have created a constellation of indefinite immigration detention in Canada. By using a particular understanding of "indefinite" and insisting on the theoretical possibility of deportation even in the absence of strong evidence of governmental will or feasibility, *Charkaoui* upholds the fiction that security certificate detention is "lengthy"[96] but not "indefinite." These fine distinctions were lost on some commentators: a *Globe & Mail* editorial summarized *Charkaoui* as ruling that "the indefinite jailing of non-citizens suspected of being terrorists is legitimate, as long as their detention is subject to meaningful and regular review."[97] This is decidedly not what the Court intended to say, but the editorial might unwittingly have provided a perceptive account of the decision's effects.

The Court envisioned a second case in which, potentially, the detention would be unconstitutional: "the government could conceivably use the IRPA not for the purpose of deportation, but to detain the person on security grounds."[98] This scenario can also be seen as a description of the current situation. After all, security and immigration have become intertwined as policy matters in the post-9/11 period. The Court started the *Charkaoui* judgment with a meditation on the tension between security and liberty, not a discussion of immigration law. The deportations that are ostensibly sought are not very likely to materialize. Ultimately, none of the persons named by a security certificate who fit the "profile" of a transnational Islamic terrorist have been deported after 9/11. Detention on security grounds is at least a convenient side effect, if not the intended goal of the current administrative practice of issuing security certificates.

· · · ·

V. CONCLUSION

The *Charkaoui* ruling is an attempt to assimilate anti-terrorism policies to the rule of law. Yet the decision exploits rather than acknowledges the vulnerabilities of the people for whom being subject to security certificates means indefinite detention. The treatment of the non-citizens who are subject to security certificates does not hinge on their guilt or innocence as established in legal proceedings. Instead, security certificates are based on assessments of dangerousness. Dangerousness, in turn, is established on the basis of untested evidence and assumptions about future behaviour and associations. Persons who are subject to security certificates are judged according to what they *did*. Yet the security certificate process is often described in terms borrowed from criminal law in ways that suggest suspicions about specific individual culpability that are in fact absent in these cases. Even the criticism of "secret trials" fails to capture that the proceedings, however deficient they might be, do not adjudicate guilt or innocence and do not amount to trials at all. The conjunction of rightlessness and the irrelevance of legal innocence in this context leads us back to consider Arendt's observation on the treatment of stateless people in interwar Europe: "Jurists are so used to thinking of law in terms of punishment, which indeed always deprives us of certain rights, that they may find it even more difficult

than the layman to recognize that the deprivation of legality, *i.e.* of all rights, no longer has a connection with specific crimes."[129] The aspiration to being "judged by one's actions and opinions,"[130] in turn, can only be fulfilled if one belongs to a political community that recognizes one's distinctiveness and humanity, Arendt concluded. Security certificates do not adjudicate guilt or innocence in relationship to specific crimes, but a person's abstract dangerousness based on their "profile."

Security certificates exploit the rightlessness of some non-citizens by subjecting them to a process in which not their actions and opinions but their physical appearance, place of birth, and formal citizenship determine their fate. The Security Certificate Five are non-citizens of Canada who share additional vulnerabilities: they are perceived as alien and threatening to the national community, and their citizenships in Algeria, Morocco, Syria and Egypt operate as further liabilities rather than supplementary sources of rights. The Supreme Court's response to the detainees' claims adopted the language of constitutional rights rather than human rights. It addressed some concerns but upheld the fundamental distinction between citizens and non-citizens in the context of anti-terrorism policies.

Since the detainees' particular form of rightlessness results from a combination of their lack of formal citizenship, lack of effective belonging and the quality of their citizenships elsewhere, attempts to include them (and others) within the framework of ordinary legality need to pay attention to the intersecting sources of rightlessness. A proposal to follow the Law Lords' reasoning that citizens and non-citizens cannot be treated differently in anti-terrorism policies, for example, should take into account that the *Belmarsh* decision led to legislation that allows house arrest and extensive surveillance of citizens *and* non citizens who are seen as foreign and threatening to national security. This alternative route of normalized surveillance is no less exclusionary than the attempt to secure security on the backs of non-citizens. In the end, foreignness is not a natural attribute but a product of decisions about the shape of the nation whose security is to be protected; it is "not exhausted nor even finally defined by working papers, skin color, ethnicity, or citizenship. Indeed, it is not an empirical line at all; it is a symbolic one, used for political purposes."[131] As a result, the lines of foreignness drawn in national security policies and public rhetoric need to be challenged, not just redrawn. Finally, the threat of deportation despite the risk of torture holds the detainees hostage to their formal citizenships. The

Suresh exception that enables the continued detention fails to acknowledge that for some people who allegedly don't belong "here," there is no other place to go. Nurturing the mistaken and unethical hope of deporting all those who are deemed threats to Canadian security fails to recognize that for a number of them, Canada is the only home they have. They, too, should have the rights, meaning the right to belong "to a community willing and able to guarantee ... rights."[132] Respecting the detainees' right to have rights requires judging them by their actions.[133] The current regime, in contrast, judges them by their asserted dangerousness — a dangerousness that is first constructed and then invoked in order to balance "their" rights against "our" security from the threat they are seen to pose.

Protecting Rights: Inside and Outside the Constitution

(a) The *Somerset* Case†

U.K. National Archive

548. THE CASE OF JAMES SOMMERSETT, A NEGRO, ON A HABEAS CORPUS,* KING'S-BENCH: 12 GEORGE III. A.D. 1771–72.

Of this Case only a Statement of the Facts, and Mr. Hargrave's learned Argument were inserted in the former edition of this Work. I have here added the other Arguments, and the Judgment of the Court, from Lofft's Reports, in which is a Note of the Case under the name of Sommersett against Stewart.

On the 3d of December 1771, affidavits were made by Thomas Walklin, Elizabeth Cade, and John Marlow, that James Sommersett, a negro, was confined in irons on board a ship called the Ann and Mary, John Knowles commander, lying in the Thames, and bound for Jamaica; and lord Mansfield, on an application supported by these affidavits, allowed a write of Habeas Corpus, directed to Mr. Knowles, and requiring him to return the body of Sommersett before his lordship, with the cause of detainer.

Mr. Knowles on the 9th of December produced the body of Sommersett before lord Mansfield, and returned for cause of detainer, that Sommersett was the negro slave of Charles Steuart, esq. who had delivered Sommersett into Mr. Knowles's custody, in order to carry him to Jamaica, and there sell him as a slave. Affidavits were also made by Mr. Steuart and two other gentlemen, to prove that Mr. Steuart had purchased Sommersett as a slave in Virginia, and had afterwards brought him into England, where

he left his master's service; and that his refusing to return, was the occasion of his being carried on board Mr. Knowles's ship.

Lord *Mansfield* chusing to refer the matter to the determination of the court of King's-bench, Sommersett with sureties was bound in a recognizance for his appearance there on the second day of the next Hilary term; and his lordship allowed till that day for settling the form of the return to the Habeas Corpus. ...

. . . .

Lord Mansfield: The question is, if the owner had a right to detain the slave, for the sending of him over to be sold in Jamaica. In five or six cases of this nature, I have known it to be accommodated by agreement between the parties: on its first coming before me, I strongly recommended it here. But if the parties will have it decided, we must give our opinion. Compassion will not, on the one hand, nor inconvenience on the other, be to decide; but the law: in which the difficulty will be principally from the inconvenience on both sides. Contract for sale of a slave is good here; the sale is a matter to which the law properly and readily attaches, and will maintain the price according to the agreement. But here the person of the slave himself is immediately the object of enquiry; which makes a very material difference. The now question is, Whether any dominion, authority or coercion can be exercised in this country, on a slave according to the American

---

† From the U.K. National Archive website: <www.nationalarchives.gov.uk/pathways/blackhistory/rights/transcripts/somerset_case.htm>. Originally published in *Howell's State Trials*, vol. 20 (London: T.C. Hansard) at cols 1–6, 79–82.

laws? The difficulty of adopting the relation, without adopting it in all its consequences, is indeed extreme; and yet, many of those consequences are absolutely contrary to the municipal law of England. We have no authority to regulate the conditions in which law shall operate. On the other hand, should we think the coercive power cannot be exercised: it is now about 50 years since the opinion given by two of the greatest men of their own or any times, (since which no contract has been brought to trial, between the masters and slaves;) the service performed by the slaves without wages, is a clear indication they did not think themselves free by coming hither. The setting 14,000 or 15,000 men at once loose by a solemn opinion, is very disagreeable in the effects it threatens. There is a case in Hobart, (Coventry and Woodfall,) where a man had contracted to go as a mariner: but the now case will not come within that decision. Mr. Steuart advances no claims on contract; he rests his whole demand on a right to the negro as slave, and mentions the purpose of detainure to be the sending of him over to be sold in Jamaica. If the parties will have judgment, 'fiat justitia, ruat coelum;' let justice be done whatever be the consequence. *50l.* a-head may not be a high price; then a loss follows to the proprietors of above 700,000*l.* sterling. How would the law stand with respect to their settlement; their wages? How many actions for any slight coercion by the master? We cannot in any of these points direct the law; the law must rule us. In these particulars, it may be matter of weighty consideration, what provisions are made or set by law. Mr. Steuart may end the question, by discharging or giving freedom to the negro. I did think at first to put the matter to a more solemn way of argument: but if my brothers agree, there seems no occasion. I do not imagine, after the point has been discussed on both sides so extremely well, any new light could be thrown on the subject. If the parties chuse to refer it to the Common Pleas, they can give themselves that satisfaction whenever they think fit. An application to parliament, if the merchants think the question of great commercial concern, is the best, and perhaps the only method of settling the point for the future. The Court is greatly obliged to the gentlemen of the bar who have spoke on the subject; and by whose care and abilities so much has been effected, that the rule of decision will be reduced to a very easy compass. I cannot omit to express particular happiness in seeing young men, just called to the bar, have been able so much to profit by their reading. I think it is right the matter should stand over; and if we are called on for a

decision, proper notice shall be given. [The hearing was adjourned until June 22, 1771.]

Trinity Term, June 22, 1772.
Lord Mansfield: On the part of Sommersett, the case which we gave notice should be decided this day, the Court now proceeds to give its opinion. I shall recite the return to the writ of Habeas Corpus, as the ground of our determination; omitting only words of form. The captain of the ship on board of which the negro was taken, makes his return to the writ in terms signifying that there have been, and still are, slaves to a great number in Africa; and that the trade in them is authorized by the laws and opinions of Virginia and Jamaica; that they are goods and chattels; and, as such, saleable and sold. That James Sommersett is a negro of Africa, and long before the return of the king's writ was brought to be sold, and was sold to Charles Steuart, esq. then in Jamaica, and has not been manumitted since; that Mr. Steuart, having occasion to transact business, came over hither, with an intention to return; and brought Sommersett to attend and abide with him, and to carry him back as soon as the business should be transacted. That such intention has been, and still continues; and that the negro did remain till the time of his departure in the service of his master Mr. Steuart, and quitted it without his consent; and thereupon, before the return of the king's writ, the said Charles Steuart did commit the slave on board the Anne and Mary, to safe custody, to be kept till he should set sail, and then to be taken with him to Jamaica, and there sold as a slave. And this is the cause why he, captain Knowles, who was then and now is, commander of the above vessel, then and now lying in the river of Thames, did the said negro, committed to his custody, detain; and on which he now renders him to the orders of the Court. We pay all due attention to the opinion of sir Philip Yorke, and lord chancellor Talbot, whereby they pledged themselves to the British planters, for all the legal consequences of slaves coming over to this kingdom or being baptized, recognized by lord Hardwicke, sitting as chancellor on the 19th of October, 1749, that trover would lie: that a notion had prevailed, if a negro came over, or became a Christian, he was emancipated, but no ground in law: that he and lord Talbot, when attorney and solicitor-general, were of opinion, that no such claim for freedom was valid; that though the statute of tenures had abolished villeins regardant to a manor, yet he did not conceive but that a man might still become a villein in gross, by confessing himself such in open court. We are so well agreed, that we think there is no

occasion of having it argued (as I intimated an intention at first,) before all the judges, as is usual, for obvious reasons, on a return to Habeas Corpus. The only question before us is, whether the cause on the return is sufficient? If it is, the negro must be remanded; if it is not, he must be discharged. Accordingly, the return states, that the slave departed and refused to serve; whereupon he was kept, to be sold abroad. So high an act of dominion must be recognized by the law of the country where it is used. The power of a master over his slave has

been extremely different, in different countries. The state of slavery is of such a nature, that it is incapable of being introduced on any reasons, moral or political, but only by positive law, which preserves its force long after the reasons, occasion, and time itself from whence it was created, is erased from memory. It is so odious, that nothing can be suffered to support it, but positive law. Whatever inconveniences, therefore, may follow from the decision, I cannot say this case is allowed or approved by the law of England; and therefore the black must be discharged.

(b) *Bliss v. Canada (Attorney General)*†

[RITCHIE J. for the Court:]

This is an appeal brought with leave of the Federal Court of Appeal from a judgment of that Court which set aside the judgment rendered by Mr. Justice Collier sitting as an Umpire under the *Unemployment Insurance Act, 1971*, 1970-71-72 (Can.), c. 48 (hereinafter called the "Act"), whereby he had allowed an appeal from a decision of the Board of Referees and had thereby held that s. 46 of the Act was inoperative by reason of the provisions of s. 1(b) of the *Canadian Bill of Rights*. Notice of the question to be determined on this appeal was directed to be served on the Attorney General of Canada and the Attorneys General of the Provinces by order of Mr. Justice Martland in the terms following:

> Is section 46 of the Unemployment Insurance Act, S.C. 1971, as amended, rendered inoperative by the Canadian Bill of Rights, *R.S.C.* 1970, Appendix III, as amended?

The exclusive legislative authority of Parliament was extended by the *British North America Act, 1940*, 3-4 George VI, c. 36, which amended s. 91 of that Act by inserting therein Item 2A "Unemployment Insurance". In discharging the heavy financial burden involved in the exercise of the authority so conferred upon it, Parliament enacted the *Unemployment Insurance Act* by c. 44 of the Statutes of Canada 1940. In its original form which was maintained throughout a succession of confusing and sometimes obscure

amendments, that Act retained its essential character as a scheme for the insurance of those unemployed members of the work force who fulfil the qualifications therein specified.

Under the scheme embodied in the Act, the Government is cast in the role of an insurer and the individual unemployed members of the work force who have contributed by way of premiums and who have otherwise qualified to receive benefits are characterized as "beneficiaries". The Act is replete with references to the unemployed individuals who have fulfilled the statutory qualifications as "the insured" and the payments to which such persons are entitled, under the Act are throughout referred to as "benefits".

It was, in my view, necessary for the effective exercise of the authority conferred by s. 91(2A) of the *British North America Act* that Parliament should prescribe conditions of entitlement to the benefits for which the Act provides. The establishment of such conditions was an integral part of a legislative scheme enacted by Parliament for a valid federal purpose in the discharge of the constitutional authority entrusted to it under s. 91(2A) and the fact that this involved treating claimants who fulfil the conditions differently from those who do not, cannot, in my opinion, be said to invalidate such legislation.

The basic qualifications for the receipt of benefits are defined in s. 17 of the Act as follows:

> **17.**(2) An insured person qualifies to receive benefits under this Act if he

† [1979] 1 S.C.R. 183 at 186–194.

(a) has had eight or more weeks of insurable employment in his qualifying period, and

(b) has had an interruption of earnings from employment.

A considerable number of conditions of disentitlement are engrafted on this broad base, the most all encompassing of which is found in s. 25 which provides as follows:

> **25.** A claimant is not entitled to be paid benefit for any working day in an initial benefit period for which he fails to prove that he was either
> (a) capable of and available for work and unable to obtain suitable employment on that day, or
> (b) incapable of work by reason of any prescribed illness, injury or quarantine on that day.

Other restrictions on entitlement to benefits are enumerated in s. 16(1)(a) where the word "disentitled" is defined as follows:

> **16.**(a) "disentitled" means to be disentitled under sections 23, 25, 29, 33, 361 44, 45, 46 or 54 or under a regulation;

The section forming the subject of this appeal is s. 46 and I think that its meaning and purpose can best be appreciated by considering it in conjunction with s. 30. These two sections are concerned with the entitlement of women to benefits during a specified part of the period of pregnancy and childbirth and it must be remembered that prior to the 1971 revision of the Act there was no provision made for any benefits being payable to such women who were not capable of and available for work during that period although pregnancy and childbirth did not exclude a woman from entitlement to the regular benefits for so long as she continued to be capable of and available for work within the meaning of s. 25. The two sections read as follows:

> **30.**(1) Notwithstanding section 25 or 46 but subject to this section, benefits are payable to a major attachment claimant who proves her pregnancy, if she has had ten or more weeks of insurable employment in the twenty weeks that immediately precede the thirtieth week before her expected date of confinement; and for the purposes of this section, any weeks in respect of which the major attachment claimant has received benefits under this Act that immediately precede the thirtieth week before her expected date of confinement shall be deemed to be weeks of insurable employment.
>
> (2) Benefits under this section are payable for each week of unemployment in

> (a) the fifteen week period that begins eight weeks before the week in which her confinement is expected, or
> (b) the period that begins eight weeks before the week in which her confinement is expected and ends six weeks after the week in which her confinement occurs,
>
> whichever is the shorter, if such a week falls in her initial benefit period established pursuant to section 20 exclusive of any re-established period under section 32.
>
> (3) When benefits are payable to a claimant in respect of unemployment caused by pregnancy and any allowances, monies or other benefits are payable in respect of that pregnancy to the claimant under a provincial law, the benefits payable to the claimant under this Act shall be reduced or eliminated as prescribed.
>
> (4) For purposes of section 23, the provisions of section 25 do not apply to the two week period that immediately precedes the periods described in subsection (2).
>
> (5) If benefit is payable to a major attachment claimant under this section and earnings are received by that claimant for any period that falls in a week in the periods described in subsection (2), the provisions of subsection (2) of section 26 do not apply and all such earnings shall be deducted from the benefit paid for that week.

> **46.** Subject to section 30, a claimant is not entitled to receive benefit during the period that commences eight weeks before the week in which her confinement for pregnancy is expected and terminates six weeks after the week in which her confinement occurs.

These sections served to reverse the situation which previously existed so that pregnant women who can meet the conditions specified in s. 30(1) are entitled to the special benefits which that section provides during the period referred to in s. 30(2) that begins eight weeks before the confinement is expected and ends six weeks after the week in which it occurs. These benefits are payable irrespective of whether or not the claimant is capable of and available for work during that period.

Section 46, however, makes it plain that the extended benefits made available to all pregnant women under s. 30 are accompanied by a concomitant limitation of entitlement which excludes these women from any benefits under the Act during the period not exceeding 15 weeks that commences 8 weeks before her confinement is expected and terminates 6 weeks after the week in which it occurs unless she can comply with the condition of entitlement specified in s. 30(1). When these two sections are read together, as I think they must be, it will be seen that the governing condition of entitlement in respect of "unemployment caused by pregnancy" is the fulfilment of the condition established in s. 30(1) and that unless a claimant has had the "ten weeks of insurable employment" thereby required, she is entitled to no benefits during the period specified in s. 46.

The present appellant's "interruption of employment" occurred four days before the birth of her child and was therefore clearly "unemployment caused by pregnancy", but she had not fulfilled the conditions required by s. 30(1) when she applied for unemployment insurance six days later and this was the reason for her disentitlement.

The appellant's case, however, is that she is not claiming s. 30 pregnancy benefits at all but rather that she was capable of and available for work but unable to find suitable employment at the time of her application so that but for s. 46 she would have been entitled to the regular benefits enjoyed by all other capable and available claimants, and it is contended that in so far as that section disentitles her to the enjoyment of these benefits, it is to be declared inoperative as contravening s. 1(b) of the *Canadian Bill of Rights* in that it would constitute discrimination by reason of sex resulting in denial of equality before the law to the particular restricted class of which the appellant is a member. Section 1(b) of the *Bill of Rights* reads as follows:

> It is hereby recognized and declared that in Canada there have existed and shall continue to exist without discrimination by reason of race, national origin, colour, religion or sex the following human rights and fundamental freedoms, namely,
> (b) the right of the individual to equality before the law....

The *ratio decidendi* of the judgment rendered by Mr. Justice Collier sitting as the Umpire in this case appears to me to be contained in the following passage:

> I do not know the purpose of the legislators in injecting s. 46 into the 1971 legislation. It was suggested that, pre-1971, there was an assumption that women eight weeks before giving birth and for six weeks after, were, generally speaking, not capable of nor available for work; this, somehow, gave rise to administrative difficulties or abuses; section 46 was enacted to make it quite clear that, in the 14 week period, pregnant women and women who produced children, were, for the purpose of the statute not capable of nor available for work, and therefore not entitled to benefits. All that may be. Nevertheless, I am

driven to the inescapable conclusion that the impugned section, accidentally perhaps, authorizes discrimination by reason of sex, and as a consequence, abridges the right of equality of all claimants in respect of the Unemployment Insurance legislation.

As I have indicated, s. 30 and s. 46 constitute a complete code dealing exclusively with the entitlement *of* women to unemployment insurance benefits during the specified part of the period of pregnancy and childbirth; these provisions form an integral part of a legislative scheme enacted for valid federal objectives and they are concerned with conditions from which men are excluded. Any inequality between the sexes in this area is not created by legislation but by nature.

In this regard I am in accord with the reasoning contained in the following paragraph from the reasons for judgment of Mr. Justice Pratte in the Federal Court *of* Appeal:

> The question to be determined in this case is therefore, not whether the respondent had been the victim of discrimination by reason of sex but whether she has been deprived of "the right to equality before the law" declared by s. 1(b) of the *Canadian Bill of Rights*. Having said this, I wish to add that I cannot share the view held by the Umpire that the application of section 46 to the respondent constituted discrimination against her by reason of sex. Assuming the respondent to have been "discriminated against", it would not have been by reason of her sex. Section 46 applies to women, it has no application to women who are not pregnant, and it has no application, of course, to men. If section 46 treats unemployed pregnant women differently from other unemployed persons, be they male or female, it is, it seems to me, because they are pregnant and not because they are women.

It was contended, however, that the impugned section denied "equality before the law" for the period therein specified to pregnant and child-bearing women who failed to fulfil the conditions required by s. 30(1) because it denied them the benefits available to all other claimants both male and female, who had eight weeks of insurable employment and who were capable of and available for work.

The purpose and effect of s. 1 of the *Bill of Rights* was described by Laskin J., as he then was, in the course of his reasons for judgment rendered on behalf of the majority of the Court in *Curr v. The Queen*[2] where he said, in part, at p. 896:

> ... I do not read it as making the existence of any of the forms of prohibited discrimination a

sine qua non of its operation. Rather, the prohibited discrimination is an additional lever to which federal legislation must respond. Putting the matter another way, federal legislation which does not offend s. 1 in respect of any of the prohibited kinds of discrimination may nonetheless be offensive to s. 1 if it is violative of what is specified in any of the clauses *(a) to (f)* of s. 1. It is, *a fortiori*, offensive if there is discrimination by reason of race so as to deny equality before the law. That is what this Court decided in *Regina v. Drybones* ([1970] S.C.R. 282) and I need say no more on this point.

As I have indicated, s. 46 constitutes a limitation on the entitlement to benefits of a specific group of individuals and as such was part of a valid federal scheme. There is a wide difference between legislation which treats one section of the population more harshly than all others by reason of race as in the case of *Regina v. Drybones, supra*, and legislation providing additional benefits to one class of women, specifying the conditions which entitle a claimant to such benefits and defining a period during which no benefits are available. The one case involves the imposition of a penalty on a racial group to which other citizens are not subjected; the other involves a definition of the qualifications required for entitlement to benefits, and in my view the enforcement of the limitation provided by s. 46 does not involve denial of equality of treatment in the administration and enforcement of the law before the ordinary courts of the land as was the case in *Drybones*.

This latter test was applied in this Court when considering the meaning of equality before the law in *Attorney General of Canada. v. Lavell-Isaac v. Bédard*,[3] at pp. 1365 and 1366; and the same reasoning was adopted by Martland J. on behalf of the majority of the Court in *The Queen v. Burnshine*,[4] at pp. 703 and 704.

I agree with Mr. Justice Pratte that it is obvious that s. 46 did not have the effect of depriving the appellant of her right to "equality before the law" in the administration and enforcement thereof and that its validity cannot be challenged on this ground if the test which was approved in the last-mentioned cases is applied.

In the present case, however, Mr. Justice Pratte in the Court of Appeal, applied a somewhat different test saying:

> ... the right to equality before the law could be defined as the right of an individual to be treated as well by the legislation as others who, if only relevant facts were taken into consideration, would be judged to be in the same situation.

Mr. Justice Pratte concluded that where difference in treatment of individuals is based on a relevant distinction, the right to equality before the law would not be offended.

While agreeing that this constitutes a workable definition of equality before the law, the appellant's counsel contended that in treating pregnant and child-bearing women who failed to comply with s. 30(1) as a separate class, Parliament imposed a classification on women during the weeks specified in s. 46 which is "clearly irrelevant".

In the course of his reasons for judgment at first instance, Mr. Justice Collier made reference to a pre-1971 assumption "that women eight weeks before giving birth and for six weeks after, were, generally speaking, not capable of nor available for work", and in implementation of its apparent policy of encouraging women to take advantage of the pregnancy benefits provided by s. 30, Parliament has, by enacting s. 46, precluded those who did not or could not avail themselves of these benefits from being entitled to any insurance benefits at all during the period described in that section.

Whatever may be thought of the wisdom of this latter provision, there can, in my view, with all respect, be no doubt that the period mentioned in s. 46 is a relevant one for consideration in determining the conditions entitling pregnant women to benefits under a scheme of unemployment insurance enacted to achieve the valid federal objective of discharging the responsibility imposed on Parliament by s. 91(2A) of the *British North America Act*.

In this regard, the following passage which is also found in the reasons for judgment of the present Chief Justice in *Curr v. The Queen, supra*, although it is directed to the effect of the "due process" provision of s. 1(a) of the *Bill of Rights*, in my opinion applies with equal force in considering whether s. 1(b) renders the impugned section inoperative. He there said at p. 899:

> ... compelling reasons ought to be advanced to justify the Court in this case to employ a statutory (as contrasted with a constitutional) jurisdiction to deny operative effect to a substantive measure duly enacted by a Parliament constitutionally competent to do so, and exercising its powers in accordance with the tenets of responsible government, which underlie the discharge of legislative authority under the *British North America Act*.

In the case of *Prata v. Minister of Manpower and Immigration*,[5] Mr. Justice Martland, speaking for the Court, characterized the effect of the earlier decision of this Court in *The Queen v. Burnshine, supra*, as authority for the following proposition which he stated at p. 382 in the following terms:

> This Court has held that s. 1(b) of the *Canadian Bill of Rights* does not require that all federal statutes must apply to all individuals in the same manner. Legislation dealing with a particular class of people is valid if it is enacted for the purpose of achieving a valid federal objective. (*R. v. Burnshine*).

In the *Burnshine* case, Mr. Justice Martland, speaking for the majority of this Court, described the burden resting upon one who seeks to have legislation declared inoperative as offending section 1(b) of the *Bill of Rights* in the following language:

> In my opinion, in order to succeed in the present case, it would be necessary for the respondent, at least, to satisfy this Court that, in enacting s. 150, Parliament was not seeking to achieve a valid federal objective. This was not established or sought to be established.

These words are, in my opinion, directly applicable to the circumstances here disclosed.

To summarize all the above, I am of opinion that s. 46 forms an integral part of a valid scheme of legislation enacted by Parliament in discharge of its legislative authority under the *British North America Act*, and that the limitation on entitlement to benefits for which the section provides is to be read in light of the additional benefits provided by the scheme as a whole and specifically by the provisions of s. 30 of the Act. I am accordingly of the opinion that s. 46 of the *Unemployment Insurance Act* as amended was not rendered inoperative by the *Canadian Bill of Rights*, and I would answer the question as phrased in the notice served on the Attorney General of Canada and the Attorneys General of the Provinces in the negative.

For all these reasons, I would dismiss this appeal.

There will be no order as to costs.

Appeal dismissed.

(c) *Baker v. Canada (Minister of Citizenship and Immigration)* [Revisited]†

[L'HEUREUX-DUBÉ J., Gonthier, McLachlin, Bastarache and Binnie JJ.:]

[1] Regulations made pursuant to s. 114(2) of the *Immigration Act*, R.S.C., 1985, c. I-2, empower the respondent Minister to facilitate the admission to Canada of a person where the Minister is satisfied, owing to humanitarian and compassionate considerations, that admission should be facilitated or an exemption from the regulations made under the Act should be granted. At the centre of this appeal is the approach to be taken by a court to judicial review of such decisions, both on procedural and substantive grounds. It also raises issues of reasonable apprehension of bias, the provision of written reasons as part of the duty of fairness, and the role of children's interests in reviewing decisions made pursuant to s. 114(2).

. . . .

IV. ISSUES

[11] Because, in my view, the issues raised can be resolved under the principles of administrative law and statutory interpretation, I find it unnecessary to consider the various *Charter* issues raised by the appellant and the interveners who supported her position. The issues raised by this appeal are therefore as follows:

(1) What is the legal effect of a stated question under s. 83(1) of the *Immigration Act* on the scope of appellate review?
(2) Were the principles of procedural fairness violated in this case?

---

† [1999] 2 S.C.R. 817, [1999] S.C.J. No. 39, at paras 1, 11, 13–28, 30–40, 43–48, 76. See paras. 2–7, in Chapter 4(c), for a summary of the facts in the case.

(i) Were the participatory rights accorded consistent with the duty of procedural fairness?

(ii) Did the failure of Officer Caden to provide his own reasons violate the principles of procedural fairness?

(iii) Was there a reasonable apprehension of bias in the making of this decision?

(3) Was this discretion improperly exercised because of the approach taken to the interests of Ms. Baker's children?

I note that it is the third issue that raises directly the issues contained in the certified question of general importance stated by Simpson J.

V.   ANALYSIS

. . . .

B.   The Statutory Scheme and the Nature of the Decision

[13] Before examining the various grounds for judicial review, it is appropriate to discuss briefly the nature of the decision made under s. 114(2) of the *Immigration Act*, the role of this decision in the statutory scheme, and the guidelines given by the Minister to immigration officers in relation to it.

[14] Section 114(2) itself authorizes the Governor in Council to authorize the Minister to exempt a person from a regulation made under the Act, or to facilitate the admission to Canada of any person. The Minister's power to grant an exemption based on humanitarian and compassionate (H & C) considerations arises from s. 2.1 of the *Immigration Regulations*, which I reproduce for convenience:

> The Minister is hereby authorized to exempt any person from any regulation made under subsection 114(1) of the Act or otherwise facilitate the admission to Canada of any person where the Minister is satisfied that the person should be exempted from that regulation or that the person's admission should be facilitated owing to the existence of compassionate or humanitarian considerations.

For the purpose of clarity, I will refer throughout these reasons to decisions made pursuant to the combination of s. 114(2) of the Act and s. 2.1 of the Regulations as "H & C decisions".

[15] Applications for permanent residence must, as a general rule, be made from outside Canada, pursuant to s. 9(1) of the Act. One of the exceptions to this is when admission is facilitated owing to the existence of compassionate or humanitarian considerations. In law, pursuant to the Act and the Regulations, an H & C decision is made by the Minister, though in practice, this decision is dealt with in the name of the Minister by immigration officers: see, for example, *Minister of Employment and Immigration v. Jiminez-Perez*, [1984] 2 S.C.R. 565, at p. 569. In addition, while in law, the H & C decision is one that provides for an <u>exemption</u> from regulations or from the Act, in practice, it is one that, in cases like this one, determines whether a person who has been in Canada but does not have status can stay in the country or will be required to leave a place where he or she has become established. It is an important decision that affects in a fundamental manner the future of individuals' lives. In addition, it may also have an important impact on the lives of any Canadian children of the person whose humanitarian and compassionate application is being considered, since they may be separated from one of their parents and/or uprooted from their country of citizenship, where they have settled and have connections.

[16] Immigration officers who make H & C decisions are provided with a set of guidelines, contained in chapter 9 of the *Immigration Manual: Examination and Enforcement*. The guidelines constitute instructions to immigration officers about how to exercise the discretion delegated to them. These guidelines are also available to the public. A number of statements in the guidelines are relevant to Ms. Baker's application. Guideline 9.05 emphasizes that officers have a duty to decide which cases should be given a favourable recommendation, by carefully considering all aspects of the case, using their best judgment and asking themselves what a reasonable person would do in such a situation. It also states that although officers are not expected to "delve into areas which are not presented during examination or interviews, they should attempt to clarify possible humanitarian grounds and public policy considerations even if these are not well articulated".

[17] The guidelines also set out the bases upon which the discretion conferred by s. 114(2) and the Regulations should be exercised. Two different types of criteria that may lead to a positive s. 114(2) decision are outlined — public policy considerations and humanitarian and compassionate grounds. Immigration officers are instructed, under guideline 9.07, to assure themselves, first, whether a public policy consideration is present, and if there is none, whether humanitarian and compassionate circumstances exist. Public policy reasons include marriage to a Canadian

resident, the fact that the person has lived in Canada, has become established, and has become an "illegal de facto resident", and the fact that the person may be a long-term holder of employment authorization or has worked as a foreign domestic. Guideline 9.07 states that humanitarian and compassionate grounds will exist if "unusual, undeserved or disproportionate hardship would be caused to the person seeking consideration if he or she had to leave Canada". The guidelines also directly address situations involving family dependency, and emphasize that the requirement that a person leave Canada to apply from abroad may result in hardship for close family members of a Canadian resident, whether parents, children, or others who are close to the claimant, but not related by blood. They note that in such cases, the reasons why the person did not apply from abroad and the existence of family or other support in the person's home country should also be considered.

C. Procedural Fairness

[18] The first ground upon which the appellant challenges the decision made by Officer Caden is the allegation that she was not accorded procedural fairness. She suggests that the following procedures are required by the duty of fairness when parents have Canadian children and they make an H & C application: an oral interview before the decision-maker, notice to her children and the other parent of that interview, a right for the children and the other parent to make submissions at that interview, and notice to the other parent of the interview and of that person's right to have counsel present. She also alleges that procedural fairness requires the provision of reasons by the decision-maker, Officer Caden, and that the notes of Officer Lorenz give rise to a reasonable apprehension of bias.

[19] In addressing the fairness issues, I will consider first the principles relevant to the determination of the content of the duty of procedural fairness, and then address Ms. Baker's arguments that she was accorded insufficient participatory rights, that a duty to give reasons existed, and that there was a reasonable apprehension of bias.

[20] Both parties agree that a duty of procedural fairness applies to H & C decisions. The fact that a decision is administrative and affects "the rights, privileges or interests of an individual" is sufficient to trigger the application of the duty of fairness: *Cardinal v. Director of Kent Institution*, [1985] 2 S.C.R. 643, at p. 653. Clearly, the determination of

whether an applicant will be exempted from the requirements of the Act falls within this category, and it has been long recognized that the duty of fairness applies to H & C decisions: *Sobrie v. Canada (Minister of Employment and Immigration)* (1987), 3 Imm. L.R. (2d) 81 (F.C.T.D.), at p. 88; *Said v. Canada (Minister of Employment and Immigration)* (1992), 6 Admin. L.R. (2d) 23 (F.C.T.D.); *Shah v. Minister of Employment and Immigration* (1994), 170 N.R. 238 (F.C.A.).

(1) Factors Affecting the Content of the Duty of Fairness

[21] The existence of a duty of fairness, however, does not determine what requirements will be applicable in a given set of circumstances. As I wrote in *Knight v. Indian Head School Division No. 19*, [1990] 1 S.C.R. 653, at p. 682, "the concept of procedural fairness is eminently variable and its content is to be decided in the specific context of each case". All of the circumstances must be considered in order to determine the content of the duty of procedural fairness: *Knight*, at pp. 682–83; *Cardinal, supra*, at p. 654; *Old St. Boniface Residents Assn. Inc. v. Winnipeg (City)*, [1990] 3 S.C.R. 1170, *per* Sopinka J.

[22] Although the duty of fairness is flexible and variable, and depends on an appreciation of the context of the particular statute and the rights affected, it is helpful to review the criteria that should be used in determining what procedural rights the duty of fairness requires in a given set of circumstances. I emphasize that underlying all these factors is the notion that the purpose of the participatory rights contained within the duty of procedural fairness is to ensure that administrative decisions are made using a fair and open procedure, appropriate to the decision being made and its statutory, institutional, and social context, with an opportunity for those affected by the decision to put forward their views and evidence fully and have them considered by the decision-maker.

[23] Several factors have been recognized in the jurisprudence as relevant to determining what is required by the common law duty of procedural fairness in a given set of circumstances. One important consideration is the nature of the decision being made and the process followed in making it. In *Knight, supra*, at p. 683, it was held that "the closeness of the administrative process to the judicial process should indicate how much of those governing principles should be imported into the realm of administrative decision making". The more the pro-

cess provided for, the function of the tribunal, the nature of the decision-making body, and the determinations that must be made to reach a decision resemble judicial decision making, the more likely it is that procedural protections closer to the trial model will be required by the duty of fairness. See also *Old St. Boniface, supra*, at p. 1191; *Russell v. Duke of Norfolk*, [1949] 1 All E.R. 109 (C.A.), at p. 118; *Syndicat des employés de production du Québec et de l'Acadie v. Canada (Canadian Human Rights Commission)*, [1989] 2 S.C.R. 879, at p. 896, *per* Sopinka J.

[24] A second factor is the nature of the statutory scheme and the "terms of the statute pursuant to which the body operates": *Old St. Boniface, supra*, at p. 1191. The role of the particular decision within the statutory scheme and other surrounding indications in the statute help determine the content of the duty of fairness owed when a particular administrative decision is made. Greater procedural protections, for example, will be required when no appeal procedure is provided within the statute, or when the decision is determinative of the issue and further requests cannot be submitted: see D. J. M. Brown and J. M. Evans, *Judicial Review of Administrative Action in Canada* (loose-leaf), at pp. 7-66 to 7-67.

[25] A third factor in determining the nature and extent of the duty of fairness owed is the importance of the decision to the individual or individuals affected. The more important the decision is to the lives of those affected and the greater its impact on that person or those persons, the more stringent the procedural protections that will be mandated. This was expressed, for example, by Dickson J. (as he then was) in *Kane v. Board of Governors of the University of British Columbia*, [1980] 1 S.C.R. 1105, at p. 1113:

> A high standard of justice is required when the right to continue in one's profession or employment is at stake.... A disciplinary suspension can have grave and permanent consequences upon a professional career.

As Sedley J. (now Sedley L.J.) stated in *R. v. Higher Education Funding Council, ex parte Institute of Dental Surgery*, [1994] 1 All E.R. 651 (Q.B.), at p. 667:

> In the modern state the decisions of administrative bodies can have a more immediate and profound impact on people's lives than the decisions of courts, and public law has since *Ridge v. Baldwin* [1963] 2 All E.R. 66, [1964] A.C. 40 been alive to that fact. While the judicial character of a function may elevate the practical

requirements of fairness above what they would otherwise be, for example by requiring contentious evidence to be given and tested orally, what makes it "judicial" in this sense is principally the nature of the issue it has to determine, not the formal status of the deciding body.

The importance of a decision to the individuals affected, therefore, constitutes a significant factor affecting the content of the duty of procedural fairness.

[26] Fourth, the legitimate expectations of the person challenging the decision may also determine what procedures the duty of fairness requires in given circumstances. Our Court has held that, in Canada, this doctrine is part of the doctrine of fairness or natural justice, and that it does not create substantive rights: *Old St. Boniface, supra*, at p. 1204; *Reference re Canada Assistance Plan (B.C.)*, [1991] 2 S.C.R. 525, at p. 557. As applied in Canada, if a legitimate expectation is found to exist, this will affect the content of the duty of fairness owed to the individual or individuals affected by the decision. If the claimant has a legitimate expectation that a certain procedure will be followed, this procedure will be required by the duty of fairness: *Qi v. Canada (Minister of Citizenship and Immigration)* (1995), 33 Imm. L.R. (2d) 57 (F.C.T.D.); *Mercier-Néron v. Canada (Minister of National Health and Welfare)* (1995), 98 F.T.R. 36; *Bendahmane v. Canada (Minister of Employment and Immigration)*, [1989] 3 F.C. 16 (C.A.). Similarly, if a claimant has a legitimate expectation that a certain result will be reached in his or her case, fairness may require more extensive procedural rights than would otherwise be accorded: D. J. Mullan, *Administrative Law* (3rd ed. 1996), at pp. 214–15; D. Shapiro, "Legitimate Expectation and its Application to Canadian Immigration Law" (1992), 8 *J.L. & Social Pol'y* 282, at p. 297; *Canada (Attorney General) v. Human Rights Tribunal Panel (Canada)* (1994), 76 F.T.R. 1. Nevertheless, the doctrine of legitimate expectations cannot lead to substantive rights outside the procedural domain. This doctrine, as applied in Canada, is based on the principle that the "circumstances" affecting procedural fairness take into account the promises or regular practices of administrative decision-makers, and that it will generally be unfair for them to act in contravention of representations as to procedure, or to backtrack on substantive promises without according significant procedural rights.

[27] Fifth, the analysis of what procedures the duty of fairness requires should also take into account and respect the choices of procedure made by the

agency itself, particularly when the statute leaves to the decision-maker the ability to choose its own procedures, or when the agency has an expertise in determining what procedures are appropriate in the circumstances: Brown and Evans, *supra*, at pp. 7-66 to 7-70. While this, of course, is not determinative, important weight must be given to the choice of procedures made by the agency itself and its institutional constraints: *IWA v. Consolidated-Bathurst Packaging Ltd.*, [1990] 1 S.C.R. 282, *per* Gonthier J.

[28] I should note that this list of factors is not exhaustive. These principles all help a court determine whether the procedures that were followed respected the duty of fairness. Other factors may also be important, particularly when considering aspects of the duty of fairness unrelated to participatory rights. The values underlying the duty of procedural fairness relate to the principle that the individual or individuals affected should have the opportunity to present their case fully and fairly, and have decisions affecting their rights, interests, or privileges made using a fair, impartial, and open process, appropriate to the statutory, institutional, and social context of the decision.

. . . .

(3) Participatory Rights

[30] The next issue is whether, taking into account the other factors related to the determination of the content of the duty of fairness, the failure to accord an oral hearing and give notice to Ms. Baker or her children was inconsistent with the participatory rights required by the duty of fairness in these circumstances. At the heart of this analysis is whether, considering all the circumstances, those whose interests were affected had a meaningful opportunity to present their case fully and fairly. The procedure in this case consisted of a written application with supporting documentation, which was summarized by the junior officer (Lorenz), with a recommendation being made by that officer. The summary, recommendation, and material was then considered by the senior officer (Caden), who made the decision.

[31] Several of the factors described above enter into the determination of the type of participatory rights the duty of procedural fairness requires in the circumstances. First, an H & C decision is very different from a judicial decision, since it involves the exercise of considerable discretion and requires the consideration of multiple factors. Second, its role is also, within the statutory scheme, as an exception to

the general principles of Canadian immigration law. These factors militate in favour of more relaxed requirements under the duty of fairness. On the other hand, there is no appeal procedure, although judicial review may be applied for with leave of the Federal Court — Trial Division. In addition, considering the third factor, this is a decision that in practice has exceptional importance to the lives of those with an interest in its result — the claimant and his or her close family members — and this leads to the content of the duty of fairness being more extensive. Finally, applying the fifth factor described above, the statute accords considerable flexibility to the Minister to decide on the proper procedure, and immigration officers, as a matter of practice, do not conduct interviews in all cases. The institutional practices and choices made by the Minister are significant, though of course not determinative factors to be considered in the analysis. Thus, it can be seen that although some of the factors suggest stricter requirements under the duty of fairness, others suggest more relaxed requirements further from the judicial model.

[32] Balancing these factors, I disagree with the holding of the Federal Court of Appeal in *Shah*, *supra*, at p. 239, that the duty of fairness owed in these circumstances is simply "minimal". Rather, the circumstances require a full and fair consideration of the issues, and the claimant and others whose important interests are affected by the decision in a fundamental way must have a meaningful opportunity to present the various types of evidence relevant to their case and have it fully and fairly considered.

[33] However, it also cannot be said that an oral hearing is always necessary to ensure a fair hearing and consideration of the issues involved. The flexible nature of the duty of fairness recognizes that meaningful participation can occur in different ways in different situations. The Federal Court has held that procedural fairness does not require an oral hearing in these circumstances: see, for example, *Said*, *supra*, at p. 30.

[34] I agree that an oral hearing is not a general requirement for H & C decisions. An interview is not essential for the information relevant to an H & C application to be put before an immigration officer, so that the humanitarian and compassionate considerations presented may be considered in their entirety and in a fair manner. In this case, the appellant had the opportunity to put forward, in written form through her lawyer, information about her situation, her children and their emotional dependence on her, and documentation in support of

her application from a social worker at the Children's Aid Society and from her psychiatrist. These documents were before the decision-makers, and they contained the information relevant to making this decision. Taking all the factors relevant to determining the content of the duty of fairness into account, the lack of an oral hearing or notice of such a hearing did not, in my opinion, constitute a violation of the requirements of procedural fairness to which Ms. Baker was entitled in the circumstances, particularly given the fact that several of the factors point toward a more relaxed standard. The opportunity, which was accorded, for the appellant or her children to produce full and complete written documentation in relation to all aspects of her application satisfied the requirements of the participatory rights required by the duty of fairness in this case.

(4) The Provision of Reasons

[35] The appellant also submits that the duty of fairness, in these circumstances, requires that reasons be given by the decision-maker. She argues either that the notes of Officer Lorenz should be considered the reasons for the decision, or that it should be held that the failure of Officer Caden to give written reasons for his decision or a subsequent affidavit explaining them should be taken to be a breach of the principles of fairness.

[36] This issue has been addressed in several cases of judicial review of humanitarian and compassionate applications. The Federal Court of Appeal has held that reasons are unnecessary: *Shah, supra,* at pp. 239–40. It has also been held that the case history notes prepared by a subordinate officer are not to be considered the decision-maker's reasons: see *Tylo v. Minister of Employment and Immigration* (1995), 90 F.T.R. 157, at pp. 159–60. In *Gheorlan v. Canada (Secretary of State)* (1995), 26 Imm. L.R. (2d) 170 (F.C.T.D.), and *Chan v. Canada (Minister of Citizenship and Immigration)* (1994), 87 F.T.R. 62, it was held that the notes of the reviewing officer should not be taken to be the reasons for decision, but may help in determining whether a reviewable error exists. In *Marques v. Canada (Minister of Citizenship and Immigration) (No. 1)* (1995), 116 F.T.R. 241, an H & C decision was set aside because the decision-making officer failed to provide reasons or an affidavit explaining the reasons for his decision.

[37] More generally, the traditional position at common law has been that the duty of fairness does not require, as a general rule, that reasons be provided for administrative decisions: *Northwestern Utilities Ltd. v. City of Edmonton,* [1979] 1 S.C.R. 684; *Supermarchés Jean Labrecque Inc. v. Flamand,* [1987] 2 S.C.R. 219, at p. 233; *Public Service Board of New South Wales v. Osmond* (1986), 159 C.L.R. 656 (H.C.A.), at pp. 665–66.

[38] Courts and commentators have, however, often emphasized the usefulness of reasons in ensuring fair and transparent decision-making. Though *Northwestern Utilities* dealt with a statutory obligation to give reasons, Estey J. held as follows, at p. 706, referring to the desirability of a common law reasons requirement:

> This obligation is a salutary one. It reduces to a considerable degree the chances of arbitrary or capricious decisions, reinforces public confidence in the judgment and fairness of administrative tribunals, and affords parties to administrative proceedings an opportunity to assess the question of appeal....

The importance of reasons was recently reemphasized by this Court in *Reference re Remuneration of Judges of the Provincial Court of Prince Edward Island,* [1997] 3 S.C.R. 3, at paras. 180–81.

[39] Reasons, it has been argued, foster better decision making by ensuring that issues and reasoning are well articulated and, therefore, more carefully thought out. The process of writing reasons for decision by itself may be a guarantee of a better decision. Reasons also allow parties to see that the applicable issues have been carefully considered, and are invaluable if a decision is to be appealed, questioned, or considered on judicial review: R. A. Macdonald and D. Lametti, "Reasons for Decision in Administrative Law" (1990), 3 *C.J.A.L.P.* 123, at p. 146; *Williams v. Canada (Minister of Citizenship and Immigration),* [1997] 2 F.C. 646 (C.A.), at para. 38. Those affected may be more likely to feel they were treated fairly and appropriately if reasons are given: de Smith, Woolf, & Jowell, *Judicial Review of Administrative Action* (5th ed. 1995), at pp. 459–60. I agree that these are significant benefits of written reasons.

[40] Others have expressed concerns about the desirability of a written reasons requirement at common law. In *Osmond, supra,* Gibbs C.J. articulated, at p. 668, the concern that a reasons requirement may lead to an inappropriate burden being imposed on administrative decision-makers, that it may lead to increased cost and delay, and that it "might in some cases induce a lack of candour on the part of the administrative officers concerned". Macdonald and Lametti, *supra,* though they agree that fairness

should require the provision of reasons in certain circumstances, caution against a requirement of "archival" reasons associated with court judgments, and note that the special nature of agency decision-making in different contexts should be considered in evaluating reasons requirements. In my view, however, these concerns can be accommodated by ensuring that any reasons requirement under the duty of fairness leaves sufficient flexibility to decision-makers by accepting various types of written explanations for the decision as sufficient.

. . . .

[43] In my opinion, it is now appropriate to recognize that, in certain circumstances, the duty of procedural fairness will require the provision of a written explanation for a decision. The strong arguments demonstrating the advantages of written reasons suggest that, in cases such as this where the decision has important significance for the individual, when there is a statutory right of appeal, or in other circumstances, some form of reasons should be required. This requirement has been developing in the common law elsewhere. The circumstances of the case at bar, in my opinion, constitute one of the situations where reasons are necessary. The profound importance of an H & C decision to those affected, as with those at issue in *Orlowski*, *Cunningham*, and *Doody*, militates in favour of a requirement that reasons be provided. It would be unfair for a person subject to a decision such as this one which is so critical to their future not to be told why the result was reached.

[44] In my view, however, the reasons requirement was fulfilled in this case since the appellant was provided with the notes of Officer Lorenz. The notes were given to Ms. Baker when her counsel asked for reasons. Because of this, and because there is no other record of the reasons for making the decision, the notes of the subordinate reviewing officer should be taken, by inference, to be the reasons for decision. Accepting documents such as these notes as sufficient reasons is part of the flexibility that is necessary, as emphasized by Macdonald and Lametti, *supra*, when courts evaluate the requirements of the duty of fairness with recognition of the day-to-day realities of administrative agencies and the many ways in which the values underlying the principles of procedural fairness can be assured. It upholds the principle that individuals are entitled to fair procedures and open decision-making, but recognizes that in the administrative context, this transparency may take place in various ways. I conclude that the notes of Officer Lorenz satisfy the requirement for reasons under the duty of procedural fairness in this case, and they will be taken to be the reasons for decision.

(5) Reasonable Apprehension of Bias

[45] Procedural fairness also requires that decisions be made free from a reasonable apprehension of bias by an impartial decision-maker. The respondent argues that Simpson J. was correct to find that the notes of Officer Lorenz cannot be considered to give rise to a reasonable apprehension of bias because it was Officer Caden who was the actual decision-maker, who was simply reviewing the recommendation prepared by his subordinate. In my opinion, the duty to act fairly and therefore in a manner that does not give rise to a reasonable apprehension of bias applies to all immigration officers who play a significant role in the making of decisions, whether they are subordinate reviewing officers, or those who make the final decision. The subordinate officer plays an important part in the process, and if a person with such a central role does not act impartially, the decision itself cannot be said to have been made in an impartial manner. In addition, as discussed in the previous section, the notes of Officer Lorenz constitute the reasons for the decision, and if they give rise to a reasonable apprehension of bias, this taints the decision itself.

[46] The test for reasonable apprehension of bias was set out by de Grandpré J., writing in dissent, in *Committee for Justice and Liberty v. National Energy Board*, [1978] 1 S.C.R. 369, at p. 394:

> ... the apprehension of bias must be a reasonable one, held by reasonable and right minded persons, applying themselves to the question and obtaining thereon the required information ... [T]hat test is "what would an informed person, viewing the matter realistically and practically — and having thought the matter through — conclude. Would he think that it is more likely than not that [the decision-maker], whether consciously or unconsciously, would not decide fairly."

This expression of the test has often been endorsed by this Court, most recently in *R. v. S. (R.D.)*, [1997] 3 S.C.R. 484, at para. 11, *per* Major J.; at para. 31, *per* L'Heureux-Dubé and McLachlin JJ.; and at para. 111, *per* Cory J.

[47] It has been held that the standards for reasonable apprehension of bias may vary, like other aspects of procedural fairness, depending on the context and the type of function performed by the

administrative decision-maker involved: *Newfoundland Telephone Co. v. Newfoundland (Board of Commissioners of Public Utilities)*, [1992] 1 S.C.R. 623; *Old St. Boniface, supra*, at p. 1192. The context here is one where immigration officers must regularly make decisions that have great importance to the individuals affected by them, but are also often critical to the interests of Canada as a country. They are individualized, rather than decisions of a general nature. They also require special sensitivity. Canada is a nation made up largely of people whose families migrated here in recent centuries. Our history is one that shows the importance of immigration, and our society shows the benefits of having a diversity of people whose origins are in a multitude of places around the world. Because they necessarily relate to people of diverse backgrounds, from different cultures, races, and continents, immigration decisions demand sensitivity and understanding by those making them. They require a recognition of diversity, an understanding of others, and an openness to difference.

[48] In my opinion, the well-informed member of the community would perceive bias when reading Officer Lorenz's comments. His notes, and the manner in which they are written, do not disclose the existence of an open mind or a weighing of the particular circumstances of the case free from stereotypes. Most unfortunate is the fact that they seem to make a link between Ms. Baker's mental illness, her training as a domestic worker, the fact that she has several children, and the conclusion that she would therefore be a strain on our social welfare system for the rest of her life. In addition, the conclusion

drawn was contrary to the psychiatrist's letter, which stated that, with treatment, Ms. Baker could remain well and return to being a productive member of society. Whether they were intended in this manner or not, these statements give the impression that Officer Lorenz may have been drawing conclusions based not on the evidence before him, but on the fact that Ms. Baker was a single mother with several children, and had been diagnosed with a psychiatric illness. His use of capitals to highlight the number of Ms. Baker's children may also suggest to a reader that this was a reason to deny her status. Reading his comments, I do not believe that a reasonable and well-informed member of the community would conclude that he had approached this case with the impartiality appropriate to a decision made by an immigration officer. It would appear to a reasonable observer that his own frustration with the "system" interfered with his duty to consider impartially whether the appellant's admission should be facilitated owing to humanitarian or compassionate considerations. I conclude that the notes of Officer Lorenz demonstrate a reasonable apprehension of bias.

. . . .

E.   Conclusions and Disposition

[76] Therefore, both because there was a violation of the principles of procedural fairness owing to a reasonable apprehension of bias, and because the exercise of the H & C discretion was unreasonable, I would allow this appeal.

(d)   The Concept of Human Dignity†

Pierre Elliott Trudeau

The very adoption of a constitutional charter is in keeping with the purest liberalism, according to which all members of a civil society enjoy certain fundamental, inalienable rights and cannot be deprived of them by any collectivity (state or government) or on behalf of any collectivity (nation, ethnic group, religious group, or other). To use Maritain's phrase, they are "human personalities," they are

† From *The Essential Trudeau/Pierre Elliott Trudeau* edited by Ron Graham (Toronto: McClelland and Stewart, 1998) at 80. © by Pierre Elliott Trudeau. Used with the permission of the publisher.

beings of a moral order — that is, free and equal among themselves, each having absolute dignity and infinite value. As such, they transcend the accidents of place and time, and partake in the essence of universal Humanity. They are therefore not coercible by any ancestral tradition, being vassals neither of their race, nor to their religion, nor to their condition of birth, nor to their collective history.

(e)   The Legalisation of Politics in Advanced Capitalism: The Canadian Charter of Rights and Freedoms†

Harry J. Glasbeek and Michael Mandel

THE ENTRENCHMENT OF THE CHARTER AND THE EMERGENCE OF THE COURT

As recently as 1977, the leading Canadian constitutional law treatise stated that, despite the lack of entrenched guarantees,

> ...[i]t is a fact, however, that in Canada — as in the United Kingdom, Australia and New Zealand — civil liberties are better respected than in most other countries.[1]

This opinion was echoed by constitutional lawyers and civil libertarians up to and before that time.[2] While this does not prove that Canadians did have all the rights and freedoms they might have wanted, it does demonstrate that conventional wisdom sensed no serious lack of protection for individuals in Canada. Yet, a mere five years later, a *Charter of Rights and Freedoms* was entrenched in the Canadian *Constitution* to the applause of most of the same conventional wisdomeers.

The entrenchment is supposed to ensure that certain rights and freedoms will not be taken from individuals by acts of government. This is to be provided by giving the judiciary the power to disallow government action which infringes the rights and freedoms entrenched. Thus, the judiciary has been given a central role to play in Canadian sociopolitical affairs, beyond the role of umpire between the two levels of government. It has become a recognised participant. There had been no public demand for this change. Indeed, the process of constitutional rearrangement was remarkable for the lack of popular participation.[3] Given that the entrenchment of rights and freedoms was not a response to either a series of triggering events or to a palpable public demand, we may search for its origins in political economy.

.   .   .   .

This is of interest because the judiciary has always had implicit opportunities and, with the *Bill of Rights*, was given some encouragement to enforce human rights and freedoms in Canada well before the entrenchment of the *Charter*. The inhibition demonstrated by the courts raises two issues. First, why would it ever be thought useful to make that very judiciary, whose record on human rights and freedoms was anything but progressive, the dominant means of safe-guarding civil liberties? Second, why would an historically reluctant judiciary play a major role in the creation of this very situation, one in which it would be asked to play a role it had up to then abjured? ...

.   .   .   .

THE LEGALISATION OF POLITICS

The *Charter of Rights and Freedoms* grants to the judiciary a supervisory role over legislation and government activity in general. It constitutes a substantial step in a modern trend towards giving the judiciary a central role in Canadian politics. What view should socialists take of this development? Two possible criteria for appraisal suggest themselves, analogous to Wright's distinction between immedi-

† (1984) 2 *Socialist Studies* 84 at 84, 88, 95–101, 103–104, 106–109, 115. Reproduced with permission of Society for Socialist Studies. [Notes and/or references omitted.]

ate and fundamental interests of the working class.[58] While it is notorious that these interests may conflict, in that reform in the immediate interests of working people may indeed prolong the existence of capitalism, this is not always the case. Marx argued convincingly that legislative limitations on the hours of work were both in workers' immediate and fundamental interests.[59] Is the *Charter* such a "reform"? What, if anything, does it do for workers, either in the long or the short run? We want briefly to review a number of traditional approaches to *Bills of Rights* which can be adapted to this perspective, before coming to what we believe to be the main point.

The "Content" of Judicial Review

One approach is to analyse judicial review in terms of the "content" of court decisions. Are the courts likely to make more or less progressive decisions than legislatures? Are they likely to cause legislatures to make more or less progressive laws? One way of answering these questions is to look at the historical record. As we have seen, the Canadian Supreme Court's record under the *Canadian Bill of Rights* is one of deference to the federal Parliament. On the other hand, it might be argued that decisions concerning the *Bill of Rights* are not a good test because of the *Bill*'s "non-constitutional" nature. To this it could be said that the courts had power to give it much more reach than they did. Such arguments are inconclusive.

The long experience in the United States with an entrenched *Bill of Rights* provides a richer testing ground. But the record there is, at the very best, equivocal. Proponents of the *Charter* as a potentially progressive tool might cite the desegregation decisions, starting with *Brown* v. *Board of Education of Topeka* in 1954,[60] and the pro-abortion decision of *Roe* v. *Wade* in 1973.[61] On the other hand, the period of time which elapsed between these two cases seems to be the only really progressive one in the Supreme Court's entire 200 year history. Its most active period other than that one (that is to say, active in the enforcement of the *Bill of Rights* against legislation, as opposed to activism in respect of issues of federalism) was one in which it fought a vigorous rear-guard action on behalf of laissez-faire capitalism against the regulation of business between 1900 and 1937. The Court struck down hard-fought-for maximum hours, minimum wage, child labour and anti-trust legislation, and so on, until the confrontation with Roosevelt in 1937, after it had "cut the heart from the New Deal Program"[62]:

There is no way of estimating reliably the restraining effect of this cloud of negativisms on state legislators and congressmen who might otherwise have made haste more speedily along the road to the welfare state. No doubt the pace of social change was moderated; a respectable number of "excesses" were prevented; a respectable amount of money was saved for the businessmen; a good many labourers were left a little hungrier than they might have been if the Court had not been there to defend economic liberty.[63]

More recently, the Supreme Court of the United States has invalidated legislation limiting corporate spending in political campaigns as an infringement on "freedom of speech"[64] and local affirmative action programmes intended to benefit historically deprived racial minorities as an infringement of "equal protection of the law".[65] Then, there have been numerous instances throughout its history when the Supreme Court has merely sanctioned reactionary legislation. Famous examples include *Plessy* v. *Ferguson*,[66] which upheld legislation requiring blacks to ride in separate railway cars, the genesis of the "separate but equal doctrine" that stood for sixty years until *Brown*[67]; the *Korematsu* case[68] in 1945, sustaining removal of Japanese-Americans from their homes to internment camps without proof of anti-government activity by them; and, more recently, decisions sustaining legislation withholding medicare for abortions[69] even where medically necessary.[70] These are all examples of how weak a protector of even "bourgeois" liberty a judicially enforced *Bill of Rights* is. To suppose, on the basis of this record, that a court administering the *Charter* would be likely to launch an attack on the dominant relations of production, even without "property" enshrined therein (for now), would be naive. Moreover, there is nothing in the historical record to indicate that courts will protect those crucial political rights of criticism and dissent to which we are theoretically entitled, even under capitalism. During the prelude to the McCarthy period the *Bill of Rights* did not prevent the Supreme Court of the United States from upholding criminal convictions against Communists because they were Communists.[71] And when, during the same period, an otherwise qualified Canadian candidate was refused admission to the Bar on the sole ground that he was a Communist, none other than Judge C.H. O'Halloran, the Canadian advocate of an entrenched *Bill of Rights* mentioned earlier, approved of the action, notwithstanding the value he put on the principle (entrenched or not) of freedom of speech, thought or opinion:

Freedom of expression cannot be given to Communists to permit them to use it to destroy our constitutional liberties, by first poisoning the minds of the young, the impressionable, and the irresponsible.

...

[I]n Canada the accepted and non-technical use of the term "political opinions" is not related to the philosophies underlying different systems of Government, but is directed to adherence to or acceptance of the policies of a political party that upholds the constitution and is not subversive in its programme and tendencies.[72]

Nor did the freedom of speech clause in the American *Constitution* prevent the United States from denying the Marxist Ernest Mandel admission to the country for a speaking engagement, long after the McCarthy period had ended.[73]

Horrible though these decisions may seem, they are in no sense aberrations, though there are counter-examples in very different circumstances (besides cases like *Buckley*) where the courts have defended species of political freedom.[74]

The Enforceability of Judicial Decisions

There is also the problem of what one wins when one wins progressive court decisions, since they do not, after all, enforce themselves:

In 1955, the U.S. Supreme Court, in "Brown II", ordered that Topeka's schools racially desegregate "with all deliberate speed". Presently a federal district court judge is examining Topeka's schools to determine if they are in compliance with that original 1955 decision. Yet this remarkable fact should not surprise us, for in substantive areas as diverse as desegregation, school prayer, and criminal procedure, voluminous impact studies consistently informed us throughout this twenty-five year period of the difficulties encountered in implementing judicial decisions that mandate policy reform and social change.[75]

Enforcement depends on the alignment of real flesh-and-blood social forces, which are much more likely to be in favour of the overruled legislation than vice-versa. Indeed, more than one commentator has noticed that the abortion victories in the American courts in the seventies did more for the "pro-life" movement than for the pro-choice movement. While the legal victories "did not significantly move public opinion toward greater acceptance of abortion", they "triggered almost immediately a strong counterreaction, and the generation of a broad-based, well-organized right-to-life movement" which "gained political momentum throughout the 1970s

and now threatens to recriminalize abortion at the level of a constitutional amendment or a human life statute".[76] This may be too sanguine a view of the pro-life movement's chances of success. It may be as hard to *reverse* progressive decisions such as *Roe* v. *Wade* (not to mention reactionary decisions) as it is to *enforce* progressive decisions such as *Brown*. But the argument, that a preferable strategy would have consisted of ordinary political efforts to repeal abortion laws on a state by state basis, seems sound. At least this would have avoided confusing the abortion issue with the different one of democracy versus "government by judiciary" (of which more later).

The Forum of Judicial Review

Disappointment with the "content" of judicial review of legislation, and with the enforceability and impact of even successful litigation, has led some of its supporters to take a different tack altogether, one which emphasizes the political value of the litigation process itself, win or lose. ...

In other words, litigation provides a forum with special, mostly attention-getting, features for causes that are politically weak or unpopular, as progressive causes frequently are. Why should these features inhere in the judicial process and not in the legislative one? Why should the media pay more attention when interests or positions with minority support are advanced in court than when they are advanced out of court? Assuming that this is the case, we think that the answer has to do with the special nature of legal argument which seems to many to be capable of leading to a special sort of result. In legal argument, the ordinary indicia of political power (for example degree of mass support, wealth) are not supposed to count, and "reason" is supposed to prevail. So, win or lose, the judicial forum provides an opportunity to advance the superior reasoning supporting progressive causes, to challenge laws, to raise consciousness, etc., in a setting where one is likely to be listened to no matter how weak one's political support is. We think that this is an important point — for different reasons — and we return to it shortly. For now, we want to reiterate what we suggested in Part I in connection with the constitutional reference cases, namely that it is a specific kind of "reason" that prevails in court, specifically the kind in which numbers or, to be more precise, *classes* do not count. In other words, you cannot say anything you want in court. Argument must take a particular form. Furthermore, not anyone can speak in court. In most courts, particularly the ones in which these kinds of issues are decided, only lawyers do the actual debat-

227

ing. This may be why lawyers find this forum so appealing.[78] But the problem is not that it is lawyers who do the speaking; it is the language they speak.

Democracy and Judicial Review

. . . .

For all their faults, modern bourgeois legal systems, such as Canada's, do contain substantive and procedural legal rights in many realms of life which are not only of great value to workers, but which are the product of many years of working class struggle. Thus, many Marxists have greeted with approval E.P. Thompson's celebration of "the rule of law" as an "unqualified human good".[81] But the *rule of law* must be sharply distinguished from the *legalisation of politics*. The rule of law is a democratic ideal under which the judicial function is impartially to apply the law to the facts of each case. The ideal of the rule of law is most closely approached when laws are specific and leave little room for personal discretion. It is most democratic when there is popular participation in law making. But the rights in the *Charter* differ from the ordinary legal rights evoked by the notion of the rule of law in both of these respects. In the first place, most of them are entirely *abstract*. The *Charter* does not spell out with precision the nature of these rights. For example, instead of the right to strike in specified circumstances, the *Charter* enshrines "freedom of association" and the "right to liberty". Do these include the right to strike? If so, when? As the American legal philosopher, Ronald Dworkin, has pointed out, rights such as those in the *Charter*[] are "appeals to moral *concepts*", not "attempts to lay down particular *conceptions*".[82] They remain to be worked out. Worked out by whom, though? By the courts, of course. The government, on the other hand, has tried to give the impression that the rights in the *Charter* are as precise as can be, that indeed the *Charter* is meant to "clarify" as well as to "strengthen" them,[83] and that the judges have merely to apply them:

> Now, these rights *are* written into the *Constitution* so that you will know exactly where you stand.... The courts are there as an impartial referee to correct injustices in the event that you find that your constitutional rights are being denied.[84]

This is an attempt to conceal the basic democratic dilemma. Whereas without the *Charter*, the nature of rights can be, and is, largely worked out and made concrete by legislatures, with the *Charter*, a more or less substantial chunk of this job is handed over to the courts. The task is taken from people who must be elected on the basis of universal adult suffrage in constituencies all over the country, and who must face re-election on the basis of decisions they or their party have made, and handed over to a handful of lawyers appointed once and for all. Though these lawyers are appointed by the government of the day, their tenure typically outlasts that of their appointers and a relatively rigid hierarchy of judicial authority reposes the ultimate say in nine persons (to paraphrase Marx, nine "kings in the shape of irremovable inquisitors of legality"[85]), all appointed by the federal government. Not only are these people not responsible to any constituency, it is an offence even to criticise their decisions (disrespectfully at least), unless *they* should decide the contempt power is an infringement on "freedom of expression"![86]

. . . .

What is presented by the government as a strengthening of popular power[] turns out to be a restriction on the universal suffrage for which so many bloody struggles were fought over so many bitter years. (Viewed in this light, the absence of the holding of a referendum or the creation of a deliberative constituent assembly in the patriation process seems almost to have been a matter of principle!)

. . . .

Then there is the mystique surrounding the *Charter* itself, deliberately cultivated by such schemes as Ed Broadbent's to hang it "on the wall of every classroom in every school in every region of Canada",[90] which makes *Charter* interpretation a rather awesome process. So, a court administering the *Charter* is a force to be reckoned with by elected representatives. This means, in addition, that political activists must devote enormous resources to litigation which, besides promoting the direct extraction of surplus value in favour of the legal profession, is a drain on the reservoir of energy and material available for direct participation in the political process. The last several years have seen the energies of the Native peoples and the women's movement consumed in the process of constitution-making, the end-result of which is to entrench a series of concepts to be worked out by judges (mostly male and all non-native). Constitutionalism has reached such proportions that, in the case of aboriginal rights, the right to discuss the issues is being entrenched!

. . . .

The Legalisation of Political Discourse

We are concerned here with a change in discourse, not in the linguistic sense, but in the sense of the structure of discussion, the way in which political issues are categorised and dealt with and, most important, the way in which political decisions are justified. It is the *form of legitimation* which concerns us here. Naturally, a legalisation of political discourse involves a concomitant increment in the peculiar legalese spoken by lawyers, the acquisition of which comprises almost all of their training and which is largely incomprehensible to ordinary human beings. We are concerned that political debate will henceforth have to take this form and be that much more removed from ordinary language. But this is an effect, not the essence, of the phenomenon we seek to identify. Nor are we suggesting that the discourse peculiar to courts imposes significant restraints on them, which force them to come to results very different from those reached by politicians who use a different form of discourse. We accept what the so-called "legal realists" established long ago and what is demonstrated in every courtroom every day, namely that enormous "leeway" exists within judicial reasoning which enables judges to reach conclusions consistent with prevailing interests and values.[98]

Any alternative hypothesis requires (for example) that we believe that differences of judicial opinion such as those in *Re Resolution to Amend the Constitution* are based on profound stupidity on somebody's part (because neither majority nor dissent express any doubt about their positions) and that these differences are uninfluenced by consideration of the social impact of the decision. In other words, judges seem to be no more restrained by their rhetoric than politicians are by theirs. They too can, and do, choose between competing policies and interests, and they too legitimate such choices by reference to reasons which may not reflect their real thinking and motivation. In this they are like legislative politicians. Judges may occasionally support different interests or values than do legislators, reflecting their particular personal biases and the judiciary's separate institutional needs. That they do so is shown by those instances, mentioned earlier, when courts administering Bills of Rights have invalidated legislation. But the evidence also indicates that courts and legislatures generally agree. In other words, legal discourse legitimates decisions necessitated on other grounds, as do other forms of political discourse. Thus, the legalisation of political discourse is a change in the nature of legitimation, not in what is legitimated (though it may *signify* a change in what is legitimated, a point we will pursue later). We should now indicate what we mean by a legal form of discourse.

. . . .

The work of the Soviet legal scholar E.B. Pashukanis is of assistance here. In the 1920s Pashukanis attempted to develop a Marxist theory of law on the basis of the commodity form. His point of departure was the fully developed legal subject of jurisprudence which differed greatly from the zoological human being, in that the legal subject was private, isolated, autonomous, egoistic and possessed of a free will. "Idealist" and "dogmatic" jurisprudence "explained" these strange attributes as innate eternal qualities of human personality: "from this point of view, being a legal subject is a quality inherent in man as an animate being graced with a rational will".[112] And the legal powers of legal subjects were "explained" as emanations from these capacities. This, argued Pashukanis, was completely upside-down:

> In the logical system of judicial concepts, the contract is merely a form of legal transaction in the abstract, that is, merely one of the will's concrete means of expression which enable the subject to affect the legal sphere surrounding him. Historically speaking, and in real terms, the concept of the legal transaction arose in quite the opposite way, namely from the contract. Outside of the contract, the concepts of the subject and of will only exist, in the legal sense, as lifeless abstractions. These concepts first come to life in the contract. At the same time, the legal form too, in its purest and simplest form, acquires a material basis in the act of exchange.[113]

So, according to Pashukanis, it was the social practice of the contract that gave birth to all these innate qualities, which had no existence in the feudal world of serfdom and Guilds which lacked "any notion of a formal legal status common to all citizens"[114], especially one which included the freedom to contract. In fact, it was the requirements of capitalist exchange relations, especially in labour, first developed in practice and then in theory, that gave birth to the legal subject:

> After he has become slavishly dependent on economic relations, which arise behind his back in the shape of the law of value, the economically active subject — now as a legal subject — acquires, in compensation as it were, a rare gift: a will, juridically constituted, which makes him absolutely free and equal to other owners of commodities like himself.[115]

Anyone who doubts this should ask why the notion of free will demands that there be a total absence of all forms of coercion, *except those of history and class*. In other words, why is the concept of freedom so limited that a bargain entered into under *normal* economic pressure is nevertheless considered to be "free"? The answer is because it is precisely the real compulsions of class which are the essential preconditions for the unequal bargains between capitalist and worker being entered into [at] all. The notion of freedom is limited, that is determined, by its concrete role of legitimating the acute unfreedom of the status quo. According to Pashukanis, then, the juridical approach requires that class and history be denied and rendered irrelevant:

> The free and equal owners of commodities who meet in the market are free and equal only in the abstract relation of appropriation and alienation. In real life, they are bound by various ties of mutual dependence. Examples of this are the retailer and the wholesaler, the peasant and the landowner, the ruined debtor and his creditor, the proletarian and the capitalist. All these innumerable relationships of actual dependence form the real basis of state structure, whereas for the [juridical] theory of the state it is as if they did not exist.[116]

A good example of the juridical approach is the treatment of abortion by the Supreme Court of the United States. The decriminalisation of abortion in the United States was achieved, almost single-handedly, by the six judges of the majority in the 1973 decision of *Roe* v. *Wade*. In that case it was held that the Due Process clause of the *Bill of Rights* implicitly included "a freedom of personal choice in certain matters", including "the freedom of a woman to decide whether to terminate a pregnancy". Consequently, a Texas statute making abortion a crime (except where there was medical evidence that it was necessary to save the potential mother's life) was unconstitutional, as would be any statute preventing any abortion during the first trimester of pregnancy or preventing one during the second trimester, unless it could be shown that the mother's health would be adversely affected. We have already mentioned the reaction that this decision engendered. Whether or not this reaction influenced the subsequent decisions on the availability of financial assistance to indigents wanting abortions is neither here nor there. Nevertheless, various statutes were subsequently enacted by federal and state legislatures severely limiting the availability of "medicaid" funds for the abortions which had been legalised by the *Roe* v. *Wade* decision. In 1976, the Supreme Court upheld a Connecti-

cut regulation restricting such funds to abortions that were "medically necessary".[117] In 1980, it upheld the federal "Hyde Amendment" which restricted funding to abortions "where the life of the mother would be endangered if the fetus were carried to term" or "for the victims of rape or incest when such rape or incest has been reported promptly to a law enforcement agency or public health service".[118] The reasoning in *Harris* v. *McRae* is a classic illustration of the judicial approach which holds class entirely irrelevant and no obstacle to "freedom by choice". Here we find the fundamental and rigid distinction made by judicial reasoning between the public sphere of "Freedom, Equality, Property and Bentham"[119] and the private sphere of despotism and dependence:

> But, regardless of whether the freedom of a woman to choose to terminate her pregnancy for health reasons lies at the core or the periphery of the due process liberty recognized in *Wade*, it simply does not follow that a woman's freedom of choice carries with it a constitutional entitlement to the financial resources to avail herself of the full range of protected choices. The reason why was explained in *Maher*; although government may not place obstacles in the path of a woman's exercise of her freedom of choice, it need not remove those not of its own creation. Indigency falls in the latter category. The financial constraints that restrict an indigent woman's ability to enjoy the full range of constitutionally protected freedom of choice are the product not of government restrictions on access to abortions, but rather of her indigency. Although Congress has opted to subsidize medically necessary services generally, but not certain medically necessary abortions, the fact remains that the Hyde Amendment leaves an indigent woman with at least the same range of choice in deciding whether to obtain a medically necessary abortion as she would have had if Congress had chosen to subsidize no health care costs at all. We are thus not persuaded that the Hyde Amendment impinges on the constitutionally protected freedom of choice recognized in *Wade*.[120]

Another example of the quintessential judicial approach can be found in *Buckley* v. *Valeo*[121] where the Supreme court of the United States struck down a federal law imposing serious limitations on private campaign expenditures in the wake of the Watergate controversy. The court held that this was an infringement on freedom of speech, thereby denying the relevance of class to political influence or, in other words, denying that limitations of class (*viz.* lack of wealth) could adversely affect people's right to participate in politics.[122]

Yet another example of the "principled" approach characteristic of judicial reasoning is the famous decision of the Supreme Court of the United States in *Regents of the University of California* v. *Bakke*.[123] In this case, a California medical school's affirmative action programme, which gave preferential admission to members of historically disadvantaged minority groups (blacks, Chicanos, Asians, American Natives) who were also "economically and/or educationally disadvantaged", was ruled unconstitutional on the basis that it offended the Equal Protection clause. The decision embraces several classic elements including the preference of individual rights over collective interests and the requirement of individual blame as a justification for a deprivation ("a classification that imposes disadvantages upon persons like the respondent, who bear no responsibility for whatever harm the beneficiaries of the special admissions programme are thought to have suffered").[124] But the most significant aspect of the decision is its denial of the relevance of history. When the majority held that "[t]here is no principled basis for deciding which groups would merit 'heightened judicial solicitude' and which would not",[125] it was ignoring the historical and concrete fact of racism in the United States, as well as the fact that the specific clause under which it struck down the programme was supposed to have been enacted for the benefit of blacks. As the dissent pointed out, "during most of the past 200 years, the *Constitution* as interpreted by this Court did not prohibit the most ingenious and pervasive forms of discrimination against the Negro. Now, when a state acts to remedy the effects of that legacy of discrimination ... this same *Constitution* stands as a barrier".[126]

. . . .

No doubt, some of the concrete rights that might be comprehended by the abstract formulations in the *Charter of Rights and Freedoms* are rights that socialists should fight for. Others, however, are rights that we should fight against. As we noted earlier, given that the interest, points of view and strategic judgments of courts sometimes diverge from those of the legislators, and even from those of the bourgeoisie, victory in the courts is sometimes possible. But history tells us that there will be many more losses than victories. And, for judicial victories to become concrete gains, legitimacy must be accorded to the judicial process *in general*. Thus, each isolated victory legitimates the inevitably greater number of losses which will be suffered by the working class. We should not be seduced or forced to do our fighting in courts according to rules devised for capitalism's maintenance and survival. We should not do our fighting by *pleading*. We should not do our fighting in a form that presupposes that what rights we have [depend] on something other than what we have won by our struggles; that they fell from the sky to be interpreted by wise, rich men. But, most important, we should not do our fighting by denying the existence of class. To the contrary: it is at this moment that we should be doing our fighting on the basis of class. Collaboration in the legalisation of politics will prevent us from doing this.[145]

(f) Aboriginal Peoples and the Canadian Charter of Rights and Freedoms: Contradictions and Challenges†

Aki-Kwe/Mary Ellen Turpel

Whereas Canada is founded upon principles that recognize the supremacy of God and the rule of law ...

> Preamble to Part I, *Canadian Charter of Rights and Freedoms).*

Your religion was written upon tables of stone by the iron finger of your God so that you could not forget. The Red Aboriginal people could never comprehend nor remember it. Our religion is the traditions of our ancestors — the dreams

† From Elizabeth Comack and Stephen Brickey (eds.), *The Social Basis of Law*, 2d ed. (Halifax: Garamond Press, 1991) at 223–36. This article was originally published in (1989) 10:2 and 10:3 *Canadian Women Studies*. Reproduced by permission of Mary Ellen Turpel Lafond. [Notes and/or references omitted.]

of our old men, given them in solemn hours of night by the Great Spirit; and the visitations of our sachems: and it is written in the hearts of our people

> (Chief Seattle to the Governor of Washington Territory, 1854).

When anthropologists, government officials, and churchmen have argued that our ways have been lost to us, they are fulfilling one of their own tribal rituals — wish fulfilment.

> (Chief George Manuel, *The Fourth World*).

The contemporary world of aboriginal politics is inhabited by discussions about rights — the right to self-government, the right to title of land, the right to equality, the right to social services, and the right to practice spiritual beliefs. None of this is very new, nor is it surprising, given that non-aboriginal people have been writing on behalf of the "rights" of aboriginal people since the 16th century.

The earliest of these works were concerned primarily with how the colonial powers (Spain) should treat the "uncivilized" and savage peoples discovered in America (see, for instance de Las Casa, 1656 and de Victorio, 1917). Many would argue that there have been no real advances in "rights" for aboriginal people in America since the 16th century, but to seek advances in "rights" presupposes the acceptance of terminology. It strikes me that when aboriginal people discuss rights and borrow the rhetoric of human rights in contemporary struggle, we are using the paradigm of human rights, both nationally and internationally, as an instrument for the recognition of historic claims — and in many cases as the "only" resort. Is that really buying into the distinctly western and liberal vision of human rights concepts?

Underlying the use of human rights terminology is a plea for recognition of a different way of life, a different idea of community, of politics, of spirituality — ideas which have existed since time immemorial, but which have been cast as differences to be repressed and discouraged since colonization. In asking for recognition by another culture of the existence of your own, and for toleration of, and respect for, the practical difference that it brings with it, there seems to be something at stake which is larger than human rights, and certainly larger than the texts of particular documents which guarantee human rights, such as the *Canadian Charter of Rights and Freedoms*: a more basic request — the request to be recognized as peoples. I believe that from early colonization up to the present, no government or monarch has ever recognized aboriginal peoples as distinct peoples with cultures different from their own, in other words, as peoples whose ways of life should be tolerated and respected, even though certain customs may challenge the cultural assumptions of the newcomers.

I also believe that one reason for this, aside from the obvious one of the assertion of government power and the quest for economic dominance, is that aboriginal ways have been and still are presumed to be primitive, in the sense of "lesser" states of development. This presumption denies genuine differences by presuming that another culture is the same, just not quite as "civilized" yet. Hence, it is important for the colonial governments to take jurisdiction over aboriginal peoples in order to guide them to a more reasoned state where they can become just like them (it is not surprising that the church was usually the state's best ally).

No government has ever dealt with aboriginal peoples on an equal basis — without seeing us as means to an economic goal (settlement and development), as noble savages, the pagans without civilization, or as specimens for anthropological investigation and scientific collection.[1] Genuinely recognizing another people as another culture is more than recognizing rights of certain persons. It is not simply recognizing peoples of another colour, translated in European terms as "race," nor is it recognizing the presence of a minority because the minority is always defined by and in subordination to the majority. Placing the emphasis on race or minority (and consequently on rights) has the effect of covering over the differences at work to the majority's advantage. Aboriginal cultures are not simply different "races" — a difference explained in terms of biology (or colour): aboriginal cultures are the manifestations of a different human (collective) imagination.

To borrow the words of a non-aboriginal writer, [aboriginal] cultures "are oriented as wholes in different directions. They are travelling along different roads in pursuit of different ends, and these ends and these means in one society cannot be judged in terms of those of another society because essentially they are incommensurable ..." (Benedict, 1935). While it seems that, in the Canadian context, aboriginal peoples and non-aboriginal persons have some understanding and recognition of each other, it also seems that aboriginal peoples have been the ones who have had to suffer for tolerance (even by force and imprisonment).[2]

It is true that there have been treaties between aboriginal peoples and the British Crown. However, these do not amount, in my view, to a genuine recognition of diverse indigenous cultures; they were really Western-style (written in a highly legalistic form in most cases) methods to make way for progress, with "progress" defined according to the standards of the newcomers. After all, signing treaties was the British practice in almost all of the colonies, irrespective of cultural differences among those they "discovered" or "conquered." It is no wonder, then, that in studying the law of treaties, we quickly learn that, according to Anglo-Canadian legal standards, treaties (even before Confederation) are not seen as agreements between sovereign peoples or nations. When we inquire as to why treaties are not viewed as agreements between two (or more) sovereign peoples, we are generally led to the theory that aboriginal people (either at the time of treaty-making or now) were not sufficiently "civilized" and organized to qualify as "sovereign" peoples, or that they had already "lost" their sovereignty through some predestined and mysterious process (for example, by virtue of being "discovered").

Of course, there is no compelling reason, according to the doctrines and principles of international law, to view treaties between aboriginal peoples and the Crown as anything other than treaties between sovereigns, or *international* treaties. Nor does there seem to be any compelling reason for continuing to pretend that aboriginal peoples do not have distinct cultures, cultures which are deserving of recognition by the dominant (European) one which has been imposed in Canada. Why is it, then, that aboriginal peoples, and aboriginal claims, must be "fit-in" to the categories and concepts of a dominant culture, in some form of equivalence, in order to be acknowledged? There appears to be a contradiction at work in areas like human rights, that is, a contradiction between pretending, on the one hand to accept aboriginal peoples as distinct peoples and, on the other, of accepting something called aboriginal peoples' rights. This contradiction, which I explore briefly in the following pages, has led to a great deal of misunderstanding and has given the dominant culture (as represented by the government of Canada) plenty of scope in which to maneuvre, while avoiding a difference-based approach to aboriginal peoples as equals or as sovereigns.

"Aboriginal rights" is a category, primarily a category of law, in which most discussions about our historic claims and cultural differences are carried out in Canadian society. It is a category with severe limitations politically and legally — limitations which have been set, whether or not intentionally, by those who thought up the category — mostly non-aboriginal people. It is a realm in which discussions focusing on strange expressions like "title," "usufructory rights," "mere premises," "status," "ref-

erential incorporation," "extinguishment," and "existing" take on enormous significance, even though they do not seem to have anything to do with the everyday lives of aboriginal people. A frightening and frustrating thing about the centrality of these expressions is that they were thought up by the same non-aboriginal people that brought us the "rights" category; they seem incompatible with aboriginal ideas about land, family, social life, and spirituality. Yet, somehow, they are supposed to be helping us out, assisting in our struggle to continue to practice our cultures. Could it be that they just serve to limit the possibilities for genuine acknowledgement of the existence of aboriginal peoples as distinct cultures and political communities possessing the ability to live without external regulation and control?

I chose the first two quotations prefacing this article to illustrate the contradiction here. A *Charter* based on the supremacy of a foreign God and the (Anglo-American) rule of law just doesn't seem to be the kind of constitution that aboriginal peoples can get too excited about. Rather, it is the kind of constitution which we can get rather angry about because it has the effect of excluding aboriginal vision(s) and (diverse) views about the land and the society now called Canada. Clearly, as an historical document, it represents only one story of Canada — that is, the story of the colonialists. As a document held out to be the "supreme law of Canada" (according to Section 52 of the *Constitution Act*, 1982), it represents an act of ethnocentrism and domination, acknowledging at no point The Great Law of customary laws of the First Peoples of this territory (except unless through wish-fulfilment Section 35 is read in this way).[3]

Could aboriginal spirituality ever be represented by the likes of the preamble to the *Canadian Charter of Rights and Freedoms*? Do Chief Seattle's words render this impossible? Are we travelling along a different road, one which does not need formal written declarations to convince ourselves of what kinds of societies we are? Should we even try to do things this way? Who are we trying to please in doing so? Is it inevitable that aboriginal traditions and customs have to take the form of "rights" which are brought to courts, proven to exist, and then enforced? Is not the fundamental problem here the fact that everything has to be adjusted to fit the terms of the dominant system?

I view the problems of the aboriginal peoples — human rights area [—] as further evidence of the fact that the dominant culture has never recognized aboriginal peoples as distinct peoples and cultures. I suppose that the exclusion or repression of the "aboriginal fact" of Canada in the present *Constitution Act* in a strange way bolsters the idea that aboriginal peoples are sovereign and distinct (yet entrapped) nations. Unless there was a conscious strategy of "ignore them and they'll go away," one would presume more ink would have been spilt on setting out the nature of the relationship between the Crown and the First Peoples of Canada; or at least on mentioning it more directly than in two perfunctory sections in the *Constitution Act*.

Larger questions loom over all of these problems. What does it mean for aboriginal peoples to advance claims enveloped in the rhetoric of human rights? While there is no question that there are serious human problems in aboriginal communities which seem to warrant redress as "human rights" violations, are such claims too piecemeal? Is there a difference between having discrete "rights" incrementally recognized, and being recognized as a people? What alternatives to rights-based claims are available? In the very pragmatic-oriented work of human rights lawyers and activists in Canada — a discourse about litigation strategies and legal doctrines — there hardly seems to be an opportunity to stop and consider these kinds of questions about aboriginal rights and the *Canadian Charter of Rights and Freedoms*. I wonder to what extent those who support struggles for the recognition of aboriginal rights have really considered these issues?

Generally, we have never really had to address these problems during the first five years of the *Charter* because we were too preoccupied with negotiations to recognize (both within the *Charter* and within another specific section of the *Constitution Act*) the "right to self-government."[4] When these negotiations failed miserably at the final meeting of the First Ministers in 1987 — a failure which was something of a foregone conclusion given that the aboriginal peoples were never seen as equal parties in the negotiation process from the beginning (instead we were given special "observer" status) — people returned to the *Charter* and the vague provision on the aboriginal rights in section 35 of the *Constitution Act, 1982* to consider legal challenges and claims based upon these provisions. It is my belief that questions regarding *which* forums and laws are especially urgent now. Such questions can hardly be avoided any longer, especially in light of the fact that aboriginal peoples are turning more to the *Charter* for recognition of their rights *vis-à-vis* the Canadian Crown, and perhaps more disturbingly, turning to the *Charter* to fight out internal battles in communities.

I would like to explore some of the layers of contradiction or conflict which are raised in the context of aboriginal peoples' claims and the *Charter*, and describe briefly an effort to meet one aspect of these contradictions which has been made by aboriginal women through the Native Women's Association of Canada. The views put forward here are my own, many of which have been developed in the course of advising the Native Women's Association of Canada on human rights matters in recent years. I have been greatly influenced in these questions by situations facing the Association and its constituents, and by both my mixed education and ancestry.[5] I do not propose to consider in any detail traditional and customary practices of specific aboriginal peoples, both for reasons of the limits of space here and because I have reservations about the extent to which knowledge about these matters can be transmitted in such a medium.[6]

THE ORIGINS OF HUMAN RIGHTS

While it might seem obvious that human rights and the *Canadian Charter of Rights and Freedoms* are incompatible with aboriginal culture and traditions, it is helpful to trace the origin of the idea of human rights in the modern era in order to locate the differences here. The Anglo-American concept of rights was set out, for the most part, by two 17th century English political theorists, Thomas Hobbes (1651) and John Locke (1690). Locke is the more famous of the two on these matters. He developed a theory of "natural rights" — later "human" came to be substituted for "natural," after the recognition (post-Holocaust) that peoples are capable of barbaric actions in the name of what is "natural." Locke's theory of natural rights was based around his idea that every *man* (and emphasis should be on *man* because Locke is famous for his theory that society was naturally patriarchal) possesses a right to private property, or the right to own property. This right, he suggested, flowed from the fact that human beings are God's property ("God" as in the preamble to the *Canadian Charter*). He argued that people enter into "civil society" for the central, and negatively conceived, purpose of protecting their right to private property against random attack.

The idea of the absolute right to property, as an exclusive zone of ownership capable of being transmitted through the family (through males according to a doctrine called "primogenitor"), is the cornerstone of the idea of rights — the idea that there is a zone of absolute human right where the individual can do what he chooses: "The right is a loaded gun that the right holder may shoot at will in his corner of town" (Unger, 1986). It does not take much of a stretch of the imagination to see where slavery and the subordination of women found legitimacy in the Anglo-American tradition — with the absolute ownership of property, and autonomous domains, "naturally" rights will extend "even to another person's body" (Hobbes, 1651).

Although there is no pan-aboriginal culture of iron-clad system of beliefs, this notion of rights based on individual ownership is antithetical to the widely-shared understanding of creation and stewardship responsibilities of First Nations peoples for the land, or for Mother Earth. Moreover, to my knowledge, there are no notions among aboriginal Nations of living together for the purposes of protecting an individual interest in property. Aboriginal life has been set out in stories handed down through generations and in customary laws sometimes represented by wampum belts, sacred pipes, medicine bundles, and rock paintings. For example, the teachings of the Four Directions [are] that life is based on four principles: trust, kindness, sharing and strength. While these are responsibilities which each person owes to others, they represent the larger function of social life, that is, to honour and respect Mother Earth. There is no equivalent of "rights" here because there is no equivalent to the ownership of private property. The collective or communal bases of aboriginal life [do] not really have a parallel to individual rights; they are incommensurable. To try to explain to an Elder that, under Canadian law, there are carefully worked-over doctrines pertaining to who owns every inch of the country, the sky, the ocean, and even the moon, would provide disbelief and profound sadness.

THE STRUCTURE OF THE *CANADIAN CHARTER*

Nevertheless, the Canadian human rights system, having been distanced in time and space somewhat from its origin and conceptual basis in the theories about the right to individual ownership to property, seems little less foreign, especially since so much is said of aboriginal matters in the context of human rights. Some writers even argue that, in Canada, the *Charter* recognized certain collective rights, such as aboriginal rights, and not merely individual rights. However, my reading of the law leads me to believe that the individual property basis of human rights is revealed clearly in the text of the *Canadian Charter*, as well as in recent cases which have been decided under the *Charter*. The language of the *Charter*

refers to human rights enjoyed by "every citizen of Canada," "every individual," "any person," etc. The section of the *Charter* on enforcement applies to "[a]ny *one* whose rights or freedoms ... have been infringed," permitting them to apply to court for the order the court considers appropriate in the circumstances — almost always the singular subject.

The extent to which a human rights law set out in such individualist terms could ever either (i) be interpreted as including a collective understanding of rights, or (ii) lead to judges acknowledging that other peoples might not base their social relations on these individual "rights" notions, is highly questionable. There is nothing strong enough in the *Charter* to allow for either a collectivist idea of rights (or responsibilities), if such a theory is conceivable, or toleration of a community organized around collective values. When cases involving aboriginal peoples come before the courts, it is doubtful that different standards of legal analysis will be applied. Already the case law has taken a disturbing course from the viewpoint of aboriginal peoples.

With shades of private property notions in mind, the Supreme Court of Canada in the recent *Morgentaler* case on abortion suggested that "the rights guaranteed in the *Charter* erect around each individual, metaphorically speaking, an invisible fence over which the state will not be allowed to trespass. The role of the courts is to map out, piece by piece, the parameters of the fence."[7] In an earlier decision, one involving aboriginal persons, the Federal Court of Canada took the view that "in the absence of legal provisions to the contrary, the interests of individual persons will be deemed to have precedence over collective rights. In the absence of law to the contrary, this must be as true of Indian Canadians as of others."[8]

Even in the area of language rights — an area said to be a cornerstone of collective rights in the *Charter* — the Supreme Court of Canada in the recent case involving Québec's former *Bill 101* has indicated that this right is somehow both an individual and a collective one: "Language itself indicates a means by which a people may express its cultural identity. It is also the means by which the individual expresses his or her personal identity and sense of individuality."[9] How to go about reconciling these two aspects when they conflict is no easy task, and the Court gives little guidance here on its view of collective rights, except to say that the right to speak their language must be protected at law against the community's prohibition of it.

Even in the area of equality rights, as recognized in section 15 of the *Charter*, the text applies to "every individual." This provision has been interpreted by the courts not as a general recognition of the idea of equality (which, if read as "sameness," would be deeply disturbing to aboriginal people), but simply as a principle in relating to the application of given laws. In a recent equality case, the Supreme Court of Canada stated that section 15 "is not a general guarantee of equality, it does not provide for equality between individuals or groups within society in a general or abstract sense, nor does it impose on individuals or groups an obligation to accord equality treatment to others. *It is concerned with the application of the law.*"[10] The scope for aboriginal rights claims under section 15 is limited, even if such a course was seen as desirable by aboriginal leaders.

Moreover, we can begin to see the broader implications of these cases for aboriginal peoples or aboriginal claims. It is difficult to move in a certain direction as a people if individuals can challenge collective decisions based on infringement of their individual rights and if collective goals will not be understood or prioritized. Some people may view this as the triumph of democracy, but it makes the preservation of a different culture and the pursuit of collective political goals almost impossible.

In aboriginal communities where customary political and spiritual institutions are the guiding force (even alongside the imposed *Indian Act* system of Band Councils), such as the Haudenosaunee of the Iroquois Confederates, recourse to an individual-rights based law like the *Charter* could result in further weakening of the cultural identity of the community. This could take one of two forms: either a member of the community would challenge aboriginal laws based on individual rights protections in the *Charter* arguing that they have not been respected by their government (an internal challenge); or a non-aboriginal person could challenge the laws of an aboriginal government on the basis that they do not conform with *Charter* standards (an external challenge).

In the case of an external challenge, for example, on the basis of voting or candidacy rights where a non-aboriginal complainant argued that they could not vote or stand for elections in an aboriginal community because of cultural restrictions, the court would be given the authority to decide on an important part of the future of an aboriginal community. It would have to consider the protections of aboriginal rights in the *Charter* and weigh these against the individual right to vote recognized in section 3. Should Canadian courts (and non-aboriginal judges) have authority in these cases? Given the highly individualistic basis of the *Charter*, and of the history of

human rights, would the collective aboriginal right stand a chance? I doubt it. As the Assembly of First Nations argued before the Parliamentary Committee on Aboriginal Affairs in 1982:

> [as] Indian people we cannot afford to have individual rights override collective rights. Our societies have never been structured that way, unlike yours, and that is where the clash comes ... If you isolate the individual rights from the collective rights, then you are heading down another path that is even more discriminatory ... The *Canadian Charter of Rights* is in conflict with our philosophy and culture ...[11]

The other possible challenge, the internal challenge, where a member of an aboriginal community felt dissatisfied with a particular course of action the aboriginal government was taking and turned to the *Charter* for the recognition of a right, is equally if not more worrisome. This kind of challenge would be a dangerous opening for a Canadian court to rule on individual versus collective rights *vis-a-vis* aboriginal peoples; it would also break down community methods of dispute-resolution and restoration. Here, the example of the *Indian Civil Rights Act*[12] in the United States is instructive. This act, based on the idea that protections for the *American Bill of Rights* should be extended to aboriginal communities, along with the establishment of tribal courts which would have the same function as American courts generally, has been greatly criticized by aboriginal people as imposing alien ways of life. As two noted scholars suggest:

> In philosophical terms, it is much easier to describe the impact of the ... Act. Traditional Indian society understood itself as a complex of responsibilities and duties. The [Act] merely transposed this belief into a society based on rights against government and eliminated any sense of responsibility that people might have felt for one another. Granted that many of the customs that made duties and responsibilities a serious matter of individual action had eroded badly in the decades since the tribes had agreed to move to the reservations, the impact of the [Act] was to make these responsibilities impossible to perform because the Act inserted the trial court as an institution between the people and their responsibilities. People did not have to confront one another before their community and resolve their problems; they had only to file suit in tribal court (Deloria and Lytle, 1984).

The lessons of the *American Indian Civil Rights Act* and of the establishment of tribal courts are important ones in light of the *Charter*. If internal disputes are brought before Canadian courts, it will seriously undermine the aboriginal system of government based on responsibility (like the Four Directions) and interpose a system of individual-based rights. It also has the effect of encouraging people to go outside the community, and outside of custom, to settle disputes in formal courts — instead of having to deal with a problem within a community.

This might sound like a hard line to take, especially when one considers the extent to which customs and traditional methods of governance and dispute-resolution have been dislodged in aboriginal communities after more than a century of life under the *Indian Act*. The experience of gender-based discrimination was employed as a technique of assimilation up until the 1985 amendments to the *Indian Act* (many see the gender-based discriminatory provisions as having continuing effect despite the amendments), and scarred many aboriginal communities as male-dominated Band councils frequently sided against women and with the Canadian government in the belief that to do otherwise would undermine the Crown's responsibility for aboriginal peoples.

As a consequence, women were forced to go outside the community to resolve the injustices of gender discrimination, so cases were brought under the *Canadian Bill of Rights* and eventually under the *United Nations Covenant on Civil and Political Rights*. Changes were made to the *Indian Act*, but many of the after-effects of gender discrimination still plague aboriginal communities, including problems associated with women returning to communities and being able to take up residence, educate their children, share in social services, and receive per capita payments from resource exploitation on aboriginal lands.

Communities have been slow to address questions related to the aftermath of gender discrimination in the *Indian Act*, and the mechanisms available to resolve disputes according to customary practices are not necessarily available. This places a great deal of pressure on aboriginal communities, which could lead to cases being taken to Canadian courts pursuant to the *Charter* for recognition of rights against aboriginal governments. As a result of concern over what this could lead to, in light of the individual-based notions of rights under Canadian law, and in light of lessons derived from the United States experience with the *Indian Civil Rights Act*, aboriginal women have been working on projects to encourage the development of First Nations laws in areas like "citizenship" and human rights and responsibilities — laws based, as far as possible, on inherent First Nation jurisdiction and customary practices.

AN ALTERNATIVE APPROACH: FIRST NATIONS HUMAN RIGHTS AND RESPONSIBILITIES LAWS

The Native Women's Association of Canada has addressed questions relating to gender discrimination in the *Indian Act* and related problems in aboriginal communities since the late 1970s. In 1985, when amendments to the *Indian Act* aimed at eliminating gender discrimination were finally passed, the Native Women's Association took the position that, while aboriginal women could support the end of unfair bias against women, they could not simply support the Federal government's efforts to "improve" the *Indian Act* and the extension of legislative control over the lives of aboriginal peoples through its paternalistic provisions. Consequently, the Association turned its attention to the development of a "First Nation Citizenship Code," or a model law which would address the issues of membership or citizenship in a First Nation, but would base its principles and jurisdiction not on Canadian law, but on the inherent jurisdiction of First Nations to regulate citizenship as practices since time immemorial.

The model code was distributed to every aboriginal community in Canada with a letter encouraging communities to take a First Nations approach to citizenship (and not an *Indian Act* approach) and to set up local mechanisms based, as much as possible, on customary principles for settling disputes, so that problems regarding citizenship could be addressed in the community itself and not in the Canadian courts. As it became clear that citizenship was not the only area of concern in communities (although the issue of Indian status was by far the most divisive), it was evident that some other efforts would need to be expended to discourage internal challenges of aboriginal government actions getting into Canadian courts under the *Charter*. In 1986, the Native Women's Association of Canada began to consider the development of another model law, parallel to the Citizenship Code, which would be a First Nations human rights and responsibilities law.

It appears that this Code (which at the time of writing is still in the draft stages) will be based on the inherent jurisdiction of First Nations to make laws for their peoples. It will include a very loosely and generously worded part on human rights and responsibilities, corresponding to the four groups of rights and responsibilities which come from the teachings of the Four Directions. Hence, there are the following responsibilities and rights:

(i) *kindness* — social rights
(ii) *honesty* — political and civil rights

(iii) *sharing* — economic rights, and
(iv) *strength* — cultural rights.

For example, the responsibility and rights category of strength / cultural rights would include provisions on the right to pursue traditional occupations, the right to education in aboriginal languages, the right to customary marriage and adoptions, the right to participate in ceremonies according to laws and traditions of the Nation, and, most importantly, the recognition of the fundamental importance of Elders and spiritual leaders in the preservation of ancestral and customary law and in the health and well-being of the community as a whole.

The provisions on the model law developed by the Native Women's Association on dispute-resolution provide options for a particular community to consider creating a law which fits within its customs and aspirations. These include mediation, the establishment of a Human Rights Committee, and a Council of Elders. Also included are options for setting up methods to deal with conflicts on a regional basis (for example, an Iroquois or Ojibway council of Elders). It is hoped that the work of the Association will contribute to the development of community laws and less formal community solutions to reduce the possibilities that individual members of the First Nations communities will have to go outside their communities (to foreign courts) for redress of grievances. It appears that the development of community codes is the best available solution to the problems in communities and to the threat of the (further) imposition of a Western individualistic human rights system on aboriginal communities.

FUTURE CHALLENGES

The work of the Native Women's Association of Canada really only addresses the problem of internal challenges based on the *Charter* by members of First Nations communities. It does not attempt to deal with other areas of concern, such as external challenges or claims brought by non-aboriginal peoples pursuant to the *Charter*, calling into question the collective basis of aboriginal communities.[13] Even claims brought by aboriginal communities against the Federal Government based on provisions of the *Charter* seem to present a dangerous opportunity for the court to take a restrictive view of collective-based community goals. Any case which presents a Canadian court with the opportunity to balance or weigh an individual right against a collective understanding of community will be an opportunity to delimit the recognition of aboriginal peoples as distinct cultures.

This is something quite different from dealing on an equal footing with aboriginal peoples about historic claims and cultural differences which have to be addressed and settled. These cases permit the court to say, "Yes, we do have jurisdiction over you, and we will decide what is best for you under Canadian law." It is not that different from the imposed system of rule under the *Indian Act*, except in the *Charter* cases, the court can cloak its decision in the rhetoric of democratic freedom, emancipation, multiculturalism and human rights for "all Canadians." The only way to really consider the political and cultural differences between aboriginal peoples and the Canadian state is through discussions which are quasi-international, so that the respective "sovereignty" of the parties will be respected.

Aboriginal peoples have been trying to pursue this (international) course during the past decade. The United Nations has established a special Working Group on Indigenous Populations to consider the human rights violations (really historic claims under international law) of indigenous peoples from around the globe. During the past seven years, there have been six meetings of the Working Group, and recently efforts have been directed at the development of a United Nations [Declaration] on Indigenous Rights. Although aboriginal peoples have been participating quite actively in this process of development of a United Nations Declaration, once again, we are really on the outside of the United Nations system. Nevertheless, certain States which are part of the United Nations structure have been willing to advocate for the recognition of indigenous rights in a declaration.[14]

The matters dealt with in the proceedings of the Working Group and in the Draft Declaration can hardly be ignored, especially when one considers the extent to which they are present in all areas of the globe. As one noted international scholar has suggested, "[t]he peoples of entrapped nations are a sleeping giant in the workings of power politics" (Falk, 1987). A cornerstone of an eventual declaration would have to be, from the aboriginal perspective, a recognition and explicit extension of self-determination to indigenous peoples under international law. There are persuasive arguments that, even without a specific declaration, international law already recognizes the right of all peoples (including aboriginal peoples) to self-determination.

Self-determination is something different than self-government, although it could include the latter. Self-government (which has been the pinnacle of all human rights discussions in the Canadian context) implies that aboriginal peoples were not previously able to govern themselves because they were not at an advanced enough stage of civilization, but can now take on some responsibility for their own affairs.[15] Very few people make a distinction between self-government and self-determination. In a recent (1988) report by the Canadian Bar Association Special Committee on Native Justice, the idea of self-government is used throughout without any distinction as to its historical context or political implications. On this point, aboriginal women in Canada, through the voice of the Native Women's Association, have again made their position in support of self-determination over self-government quite clear.[16]

In the international context, the draft declaration on indigenous rights is silent on the issue of self-determination. It contains many disturbing provisions on lesser notions like "autonomy ... in local affairs" and the "right to exist." While these might seem progressive in some situations where the very life of aboriginal people is systematically threatened on a daily basis, the provisions do not go far enough in recognizing aboriginal people as distinct cultures and political entities, equally as capable of governing and making decisions as European sovereigns, except with different political and cultural goals.

A great deal more work will have to be done in the next few years to ensure that the text of the draft declaration is one which will recognize indigenous people as legitimate, though different, governments and cultures. The only way to do this, in international law, is through a recognition of self-determination. Realizing this goal will require broad-based support from international society, manifested in the work of non-government organizations, women's movements, and sympathetic States. The Canadian government and Canadian people could do much to assist the international process if the government would simply recognize aboriginal peoples as distinct peoples with different but equally legitimate cultures and ways of life. This cannot be done through Canadian courts and in the rhetoric of Canadian human rights — it has to be done through a joint aboriginal-Canadian discussion process where, unlike the series of discussions held on Canadian constitutional amendments, aboriginal peoples are equal participants in the process, along with the Prime Minister and perhaps Provincial Premiers.

In the meantime, aboriginal women will continue to do what can be done to ensure that aboriginal communities are governed by customary laws and practices, through the development of First Nations laws, and through the political and spiritual voice of the Native Women's Association of Canada as guided by its Elders and affiliated women's organizations.

V

Law, Crime, and Social Order

The readings in Part V explore and critique the way that law may be used as a broader mechanism of social control. In particular, they focus on the creation, enforcement and impact of criminal law; in so doing, they consider not only its legal rules, but also the actors and processes that constitute the criminal justice system.

The articles in Chapter 12 question the motivations behind the use of criminal law to prohibit some activities but not others. In particular, Alan Hunt explores the ways in which criminal law, like other forms of law, may be used as a tool of class domination. This domination occurs not just because law exercises coercive control over individuals, but also because it reinforces and legitimizes unequal social relationships through processes of "ideological domination". Laureen Snider's article critiques the trend to criminalize employees accused of "theft of time" amidst a corresponding trend to decriminalize anti-social or harmful activities of corporations. Together, these two articles challenge the reader to consider a number of questions. What is crime? What broader functions does criminal law play in society? How do we choose which behaviours or actors to discipline through criminal law? What "order" does criminal law maintain?

The reports and articles included in Chapter 13 focus on a range of problems that have been identified within the criminal law process itself. Among the problems discussed are the ways that both systemic issues and the decisions of individual actors in the system (such as police) can contribute to the overrepresentation of racial minorities in the criminal justice system (Commission on Systemic Racism in the Ontario Justice System), and sometimes the wrongful conviction of members of these groups (Royal Commission on the Donald Marshall Jr. Prosecution). The articles in this chapter also explore ways in which the criminal law system may be improved by providing for a more meaningful participation by victims of crime and by the adoption of restorative justice approaches. This is a critical shift in the way criminal law has traditionally understood the role of the victim. Patricia Clarke canvasses different ways in which the interests of victims may be promoted through the criminal justice process, including the creation of compensation regimes, victim impact statements and increasing communication between victims and prosecutors. Finally, Kathleen Daly considers the effectiveness of restorative justice initiatives within the context of youth criminal justice cases. She does so by identifying the limits of both criminal and restorative justice approaches within a framework that recognizes that justice itself is an ideal that we can never fully achieve.

What Is Crime?

(a) Law, State, and Class Struggle†

Alan Hunt

INTRODUCTION

This chapter sets out to examine the way in which law operates to maintain class domination. The argument that is developed shows that law should not simply be regarded as part of the coercive armoury of the state; but also must be understood as making a major contribution to what will be called "ideological domination." Ideological domination consists of those processes that produce and reaffirm the existing social order and thereby legitimize class domination. The processes involved in creating and reproducing ideological domination play a major part in ensuring the continuation of capitalist social relations.

There has been relatively little attention paid by Marxists to law. This absence of discussion has resulted in a tendency for the more obvious repressive characteristics to be stressed; and as a consequence the more pervasive contribution of law to the maintenance of capitalist society has not been sufficiently explored. The analysis of law in this wider context is of considerable political importance. Marxists are increasingly being forced to come to grips with the fact that modern capitalism has exhibited very considerable "staying power." In the period since the Second World War capitalism in Western Europe has shown what may be best described as relative stability; that is to suggest that despite the occurrence of very deep economic, social and political crises the capitalist social order in the major Western European states has survived substantially intact. This chapter examines the extent and the manner in which legal systems contribute to the perpetuation of capitalist systems.

STATE AND LAW

In class societies the economic and social dominance of an exploiting class does not sustain itself automatically. The exploiting class always strives to turn itself into a ruling class by means of an institutional structure, the state, which operates to sustain and to reproduce that position. While the state is a product of class antagonism it takes on the appearance of being an entity which stands above society and which embodies the interests of the community as a whole. This apparently *universal* quality is especially significant with reference to legal systems:

> Right, law, etc. are merely the symptom, the expression of *other* relations upon which State power rests.... These actual relations are in no way created by the State power; on the contrary they are the power creating it. The individuals who rule in these conditions, besides having to constitute their power in the form of the *State*, have to give their will, which is determined by these definite conditions, a universal expression as the will of the state, as law. (Marx/Engels 1968: 366)

The distinctive feature then of legal systems of class societies is the fact that they embody the material interests of the ruling class in a universal form,

---

† From *Explorations in Law and Society: Towards a Constitutive Theory of Law* (London: Routledge, 1993) at 17–35. Originally from (1976) 20 *Marxism Today* at 178–87. © New Statesman, 2000. Reproduced WITH permission. [Notes and/or references omitted.]

and thus present law as the embodiment of the interests of the community as a whole:

> In a modern state, law must not only correspond to the general economic condition and be its expression, but must also be an *internally coherent* expression which does not[,] owing to inner contradictions, reduce itself to nought. And in order to achieve this, the faithful reflection of economic conditions suffers increasingly. All the more so the more rarely it happens that a code of law is the blunt, unmitigated, unadulterated expression of domination of a class — this in itself would offend the "conception of right". (Engels 1890: 504)

This striving of "internal coherence," in which law comes to be seen as the embodiment of universal notions of "justice" and "right," needs to be explored. At the hands of bourgeois legal and political theorists it has been used to provide an ideological dogma, important in bourgeois political and legal theory, of the doctrine of the "separation of powers." The essence of this view is that the character of the democratic state is defined as one in which there exists a separation between the major components of the state. Specifically it is argued that not only is there, but also that there ought to be, a separation between the legislature, which makes the laws, and the judiciary, which apply those laws.

The doctrine of the separation of powers has played, and continues to play a central part in bourgeois theory of the law and the state. There has been a tendency of Marxists in seeking to expose the ideological character of this doctrine to react against it by asserting the identity of the state and law. Thus the legal system has been presented simply as the direct and totally subservient agent of the state. Such a position is too simple, but more importantly it obscures the real class character of the legal system as a mechanism whereby the existing form of class domination is perpetuated and reproduced.

We need to start by asking, how does it come about that a separation appears to exist between law and state? Engels provides a useful starting point:

> But once the state has become an independent power *vis-à-vis* society, it produces forthwith a further ideology. It is indeed among professional politicians, theorists of public law and jurists of private law that the connection with economic facts gets lost for fair [*sic*]. Since in each particular case the economic facts must assume the form of juristic motives in order to receive legal sanction; and since, in so doing, consideration of course has to be given to the whole legal system already in operation, the

juristic form is, in consequence, made everything and the economic content nothing. (Engels 1958: 396–97)

If these ideological functions are to be fulfilled they cannot operate exclusively as ideological forces, they must find some expression in the actual practice embodied within the legal system. As a consequence the legal system operates in a manner which cannot be explained exclusively by reference to the dictates of the state as a whole.

The doctrine of the separation of powers appeals to the independence of the judiciary. Yet this independence is clearly very restricted. Judicial appointments are made by the highest representatives of the political apparatus of the state.[1]

But what does need to be stressed is that even the relative degree of autonomy sets up stresses and contradictions within the state as a whole. Decisions by courts do not always please the holders of state power. The protracted struggle between the courts and Nixon throughout the "Watergate affair" is perhaps the most important recent example of such a tension in operation, in which the conflict between court and state contributed in no small measure to the downfall of Nixon.

But the tension between courts and state may also have advantages for the holders of state power. The institutional complexity of the English legal system allowed the government to brush the cobwebs off the Official solicitor whose intervention facilitated the release of the "Pentonville 5" in 1972 when faced with the prospect of a General Strike. Frequently it serves as a convenient smoke-screen behind which to hide; Roy Jenkins, as Home Secretary, consistently used the excuse of separation between government and courts to refuse to intervene and secure the release of the Shrewsbury pickets.

This discussion points toward the general conclusion that the relationship between the state and the legal system must always be a matter for concrete examination. While the general dependence of the law on the state as a whole is an important proposition within Marxist theory, this must not be treated as if it suggested a complete identity between law and state.

DOMINATION AND HEGEMONY

Domination is a universal feature of class society. It consists in the subjection of one or more classes to another class (or grouping of classes) in such a way that exploitative relations are perpetuated. But the form that domination takes varies with the form of the exploitative class relations; thus the domination of slave by slaveholder differs from the employer's domination of the factory worker. Domination must be viewed not as a single act but as a process that reproduces the conditions for exploitative social relations.

Domination can only be based for very short periods of time on direct physical coercion. Even the most barbarous and coercive systems do not rely exclusively upon coercive violence. Direct coercion will often play a major part in the establishment of a new system of class power, but, however much it continues to depend on physical repression, it will strive to promote other means of consolidating its domination.

An extremely fruitful approach to the discussion of domination is provided by the early leader of the Italian Communist Party, Antonio Gramsci, who made use of the concept of "hegemony." He used it to identify the processes that create

> the "spontaneous" consent given by the great mass of the population to the general direction imposed on social life by the dominant fundamental group (i.e., the ruling class). (Gramsci 1971: 12)

The vital characteristic of "hegemony" is that it is an active process; it is concerned not only with the *fact* of consent, but focuses on the creation and the mobilization of that consent. One major facet of the class struggle that takes place within capitalist societies is the continual struggle for influence over the ideas, perceptions, and values of members of the different classes. The maintenance of capitalism would be impossible unless the capitalist class was able to decisively influence the ideas, attitudes and consciousness of the working class.

It is important to stress that the ideological struggle is not simply concerned with the conflict between general theories of society. It is concerned with every aspect of the way in which people think about, react to, and interpret their position in class society.

COERCIVE AND IDEOLOGICAL DOMINATION

In examining the part that is played by law in the class struggle it is useful to distinguish between two different aspects. Law plays an important role in sustaining the domination of the ruling class because it operates both as a form of *coercive domination* and of *ideological domination*. It will also be necessary to stress that they are not simple alternatives. I hope to

show the way in which these two elements are closely bound together and as such contribute to the special effectiveness of law as a mechanism of social order.

Let us first consider the coercive character of law. The legal system is able to call upon the organized power of the state. This repression operates both through specific institutions, which range from the courts themselves to the prison system, probation service, etc. In addition it also operates more generally through the police system that operates with wide-ranging powers, sanctioned by law, but able to act with a very considerable degree of autonomy.

Legal coercion operates at a number of different levels. Of greatest importance is the application of coercion to protect the *general conditions* of the capitalist order. First and foremost coercion is applied to protect and reinforce the property relations of capitalist society. There exists an increasingly complex body of "offences against property" that are concerned with the defense of private property. First they are important in demarcating the "lawful" from the "unlawful"; they differentiate between the unlawful appropriation of property, the acts of the "criminals," and the lawful forms of appropriation that are the hallmark of the capitalist system. Just how close is the dividing line between lawful and unlawful appropriation has been clearly revealed by recent bribery and corruption cases. But second, it is not only the offender that is coerced, but all members of society because the coercion of the offender reinforces the values, attitudes, and behavior associated with the existence of private property. It is for this reason that it was stressed above that the coercive and ideological functions of law are closely related.

While the criminal law protects the property interests of the capitalist class it operates more generally to protect the "private property" of all members of society. Indeed it is important to recognise that the vast majority of "property offences" are committed, not against the property of the capitalist class, but rather against the property of noncapitalists. Property offences are usually directed against the privately owned consumption goods of working people.

Another way in which legal coercion is applied to defend the *general* conditions of capitalist society is with respect to "offences against the person." Again this area of the criminal law does not merely act against offences against members of the capitalist class. The significance of this type of legal coercion is that some level of general social order is a necessary precondition for the maintenance of its specifically capitalist content.

One of the most important manifestations of legal coercion is the application of law for the direct protection of the state itself. The state has at its disposal a veritable armory of measures that are ready to be invoked to defend the existing political order. These range from a number of traditional offences such as treason, treachery, and sedition (which have been invoked fairly infrequently in the recent past), through such legislation as the *Official Secrets Act* of 1911 and 1920 and the *Incitement to Disaffection Act* 1934, to the wide ranging emergency powers that the ruling class has gradually accumulated. *The Emergency Powers Acts* of 1920 and 1964 give very extensive powers to the civil and military authorities to intervene in the class struggle. These powers have been used on no less than eight occasions since the War; on four of these occasions by the Heath government against dockers, power supply workers, and the miners; Labour Governments have not shrunk from invoking them.

In the recent past Northern Ireland has been a fertile source of emergency regulations. *The Northern Ireland (Emergency Provisions) Act* 1973 and the *Prevention of Terrorism (Emergency Powers) Act* 1974 have aided the British government's struggle against the Irish people and their scope has been extended to the mainland.[2]

The ruling class also has at its disposal a wide range of legal devices that can be used against offences against public order. These range through riot, affray, unlawful assembly and breach of the peace. Of particular importance is the *Public Order Act* 1936, supposedly introduced to curb the Fascists, but used systematically against the Left. It is interesting to observe the skill of the police and courts in making use of "appropriate" legal mechanisms. A good example has been the recent resuscitation of the *Conspiracy and Protection of Property Act* 1875.

In protecting the existing political order the law does not only have at its disposal the wide ranging powers contained in the legislation discussed above. The general principles of criminal law offer not only ample scope, but also special advantage. It is often in the interest of the ruling class to seek to depoliticize the class struggle. One of the means that is frequently invoked is to charge the "political offender" with ordinary crimes. This can be achieved by using a charge that is incidental to the main social or political issue involved; the most favored police strategy being to invoke charges involving or implying violence. A very good example of this technique is to be seen in the trial of the Shrewsbury pickets. The use of such charges allows the political issues to be ignored while branding the defendants as "common criminals," a tactic favored by Roy Jenkins and Frank Chapple in their attacks on the Shrewsbury pickets.

A related prosecution strategy is to use blanket charges; much in favor in the recent past has been the use of conspiracy charges. These are not only significant in that they allow the prosecution to evade some of the restrictions with regard to the evidence and procedure that normally apply. But in addition, through the orchestration by the mass media, to create impressions of the existence of an unspecified "threat to law and order."

The legal order has at its disposal this powerful armoury of techniques of legal coercion that enable it to directly intervene in the class struggle to defend the interest of the existing order. This direct intervention in the class struggle stands out most sharply in the case of industrial and trade union laws.[3] The history of trade union law, from the *Combination Act* 1800 to the *Industrial Relations Act* 1971, is testimony to the attempt to provide a legal framework favorable to the interests of capital as opposed to those of labor. Yet it is also testimony to the extent of the resistance that over the period as a whole has not only forced tactical retreats, but has also witnessed significant advances in the legal positions of trade unions. I will return later to take up this question of law as an arena of class struggle.

What stands out in sharp relief is the extent to which the ruling class utilizes a legal framework for sustaining and buttressing their class interests. But a certain degree of care is needed in drawing conclusions from this common ground. The argument is frequently advanced that in periods of crisis the capitalist class resort to an increasingly repressive strategy and embark on major attacks on civil liberties. This type of analysis is very clearly presented in John Hostettler's article "Trends to Authoritarian Rule in Britain" (*Marxism Today*, Dec. 1973). This line of argument is sometimes presented in such a way that it obscures important contradictory dimensions, which if correctly considered throw much light on the specific role of law within capitalist society.

The lurch of legal authoritarianism is checked by an equally strong need on the part of the ruling class to maintain the legitimacy of their class rule. This contradiction is not an interaction between two equal forces that smoothly balance each other out; hence there are periods in which there are major shifts toward authoritarianism, but equally there are periods of movement toward more liberal and less coercive forms. The particular result at any point in time is a complex result of the level of class struggle itself.

There is a more general, and possibly more fundamental, political point that underlies this discussion that needs to be more fully discussed. Lenin was correct when he argued that

> bourgeois states are most varied in form, but their essence is the same; all these states, whatever their form in the final analysis are inevitably the dictatorship of the bourgeoisie. (CW 25: 413).

Yet there has been a tendency (which is present in Lenin as well as in others) to regard bourgeois democracy as simply a sham or fraud designed to conceal the class character of the rule of the bourgeoisie. Capitalism has been in existence long enough to demonstrate that its most persistent, stable and "successful" form has proved to be the *bourgeois democratic* political form. Thus for the bourgeoisie whatever pressures manifest themselves toward the "authoritarian solution" there is at the same time a profound concern to sustain the legitimacy of the capitalist order.

This analysis does not lead to the conclusion that the resort by the ruling class to fascism or to military coup is impossible. The tragic example of Chile is too urgent to allow such a naive conclusion. But this analysis does insist that the resort to fascism is not the automatic response of a capitalist class in crisis. We should have no illusions about the fact that the capitalist class has been prepared, in the final analysis, to abandon bourgeois democracy. But we should be equally insistent that the interests of the bourgeoisie have been best served where they have been able to sustain their class rule within the bourgeois democratic form and that the ruling class itself has an interest in the preservation of bourgeois democracy.

The legal order plays a central role within bourgeois democracy. Thus while the coercive role of the legal order has been emphasized in the first half of this article it is now necessary to draw attention to and to examine the contribution made by the legal system to sustaining the legitimacy of the bourgeois democratic order. In other words it is necessary to discuss law as a method of ideological domination.

LAW AS IDEOLOGICAL DOMINATION

Repressive and ideological domination are in no sense alternatives. On the contrary they are interdependent; they interact and reinforce each other. While the coercion of the criminal law is directed against those it punishes, its ideological effects are directed much wider. For example, the jailing of the Shrewsbury pickets was legal violence against the accused which was concerned with more than "deterring" others; it was an ideological offence against the strategy of the "flying picket" developed by the miners and applied so effectively by building workers.

Ideological domination describes those activities and processes whereby the assent to the existing social order is produced and mobilized. The notion of assent embraces both the idea of legitimacy as active assent and also acceptance as the passive form. The means by which assent is produced are ideological in that it involves the production and dissemination of ideas that affect social practice through the determination of the social consciousness of individuals, groups, and classes. This process is one of domination in that it involves two elements; first, a differential ability of groups and classes in society to produce, communicate, and disseminate ideas, and second, these ideas, directly or indirectly, have consequences for the maintenance of the existing social order.

Law is ideological in that it conveys or transmits a complex set of attitudes, values, and theories about aspects of society. Its ideological content forms part of the dominant ideology because these attitudes, values, etc. are ones that reinforce and legitimize the existing social order.

The most pervasive ideological effect of law is to be found in the fact that legal rules and their application give effect to existing social relations. The rules of law affirm the social and economic relations that exist within capitalist society. Thus the law of property is not only based on the inequality of property ownership but it reinforces it by allowing and facilitating the owners of property to make use of that property as capital. The complex of legal rules relating to mortgages, trusts, leases, etc. not only allows but also enables property to be used as capital. The law relating to contracts and commercial activity gives effect to the mechanisms of the market.

Similarly labor law facilitates the capitalist form of the relationship between labor and capital; it gives effect to the economic fact of the dependence of the majority on the sale of their labor power. It embodies the economic power of capital over labor by granting to the employer rights regarding not only the control of labor but also over hiring and firing of labor.

Rules of law impinge on almost every form of social relations. For example, family law, despite the reforms of the past decades, incorporates the fact of the dominant role of the husband over the wife, of the parents over the children. Likewise the law of landlord and tenant underlines the power of landlords over tenants in regard to the supply of housing. It is important to stress that the legal rules do not *create* the social relations that make up capitalist society. But by stating them as principles and by enforcing them the law operates not only to reinforce these relations but also to legitimize them in their existing form. This function is further advanced by the role of law in conferring authority upon officials such as the police, magistrates, etc.

The rules of law not only define social relations but confer rights and powers on certain categories of individuals. Thus, for example, landlord and tenant law not only incorporates the economic fact of the monopolization of housing by private interests, but it also legitimizes that economic power by granting rights to landlords to extract rent, to impose conditions, and to evict tenants. The legal system not only reinforces existing social and economic relations, but in addition it confers authority on dominant social interests.

One important aspect that should not be overlooked is the extent to which law operates to regulate the mutual interests of the bourgeoisie. It provides a mechanism for the resolution of disputes and conflicts that arise *between* capitalist interests:

> The administration of ... civil justice is concerned almost exclusively with conflicts over property and hence affects almost exclusively the possessing classes. (Marx 1958: II, 34)

Company law, for example, is concerned in the main with the respective interests of shareholders and directors. Much commercial law is likewise concerned with the interests of merchants, middlemen, and dealers.

The law regulating the interests of the propertied classes is detailed and complex, but it has a significant common core. The operation of capitalistic functions is facilitated where the law provides a degree of certainty and predictability. What bourgeois legal theory fails to recognize is that it is only that element of law that regulates the mutual interests of the bourgeoisie, and not the whole of law in a capitalist society that exhibits this quest for certainty.

It is necessary to consider more closely the nature of the correspondence between legal rules and the social relations to which they relate. Legal rules do not simply "reflect" social relations. The rules of law have an added ideological dimension. To explain this it is important to recall that a central feature of capitalist society is that its essential features are obscured or concealed by the very nature of the operation of the capitalist economy. Marx insisted on the need to distinguish between how things appear (the "appearance" or "phenomenal form") and how they really are ("real substratum" or "essence").

The "real" relations that exist find themselves expressed in legal rules in a distorted or truncated form because the law gives effect to only the appearance ("phenomenal form") of social relations. This theoretical point could be taken further by applying the argument developed by Marx in the famous section on "the fetishism of commodities" in *Capital* Vol. I in which he shows how our comprehension of commodities embodies not the real social relations of production which create them, but simply as things; and as a result what are relations between people come to be seen as relations between things.

So legal rules appear abstracted from social relations, and are therefore a "fetishistic" expression of social relations. Legal rules are further divorced from the social relations to which they refer because they (like the state itself) appear separated, independent of society; they seem to have an independent origin and life of their own. Thus as ideological forms of social relations legal rules are doubly removed from the real world.

Legal rules express the appearance of social relations:

> This phenomenal form, which makes the actual relations invisible ... forms the basis of all the juridical notions of both labourer and capitalist, of all the mystifications of the capitalist mode of production, of all its illusions as to liberty. (Marx 1961: I, 540)

Marx showed how our initial perception of the capitalist economy focuses on the process of circulation and exchange, and thus ignores the production process itself. It is significant to note that legal rules follow this pattern and reduce social relations to a system of exchanges. The key legal concept of bourgeois law is that of *contract*. All the most important relations within capitalist society are moulded into the form of contractual relations.

By treating social relations as "contracts" bourgeois law strips them of their most important characteristics. Perhaps the most important example is in the labor relationship between employers and workers. At law the labor relation is a contract between individual employer and individual employee; they are therefore presumed to bargain over the terms of the contract. This individualizing of the contract of employment by focusing on it as an individual exchange excludes the social character of the relation between capital and labor. It is incapable of embracing the increasingly collective determination of labor relations through negotiations between trade unions and employers' federations. English law has reduced itself to great confusion in attempting to preserve the "individual contract" while taking some note of the real "collective contract."

It is not only economic relations that are reduced to contractual form. A wide range of other social relations is similarly treated. Thus, for example, the social institution of marriage is enshrined in law as a contract within which the "parties" have obligations that derive from the contract, and the "breach" of which can result in the contract being terminated, i.e., in divorce. Yet by expressing the marriage relationship in contractual form the law inadvertently exposes something of the real economic basis on which the bourgeois marriage is based, founded on the economic dependence of women.

The principles of contract have been so pervasive that they have been developed into a contractual ideology which continues to have wider ranging influences. Contractual ideology leans heavily on the notions of freedom and equality. But the "freedom" and "equality" to which it refers is purely *formal*; that is individuals are regarded as free if there is no legal bar to them entering into a contract, and are therefore deemed to be equal. It is a notion of equality brilliantly captured by Anatole France:

> The law in its majestic impartiality forbids rich and poor alike to sleep under bridges, to beg in the streets and steal bread (1927: 91)

These formal notions of freedom and equality are characteristic of bourgeois legal and political theory. They do violence to social reality because they are incapable of grasping the real inequality and lack of freedom that results from the dependence of all workers on the sale of their labor.

This discussion has focused on the way in which the rules of law, far from being pure or independent creations, are but a distorted expression of the existing social relations which are thereby reinforced and legitimised. This ideological character of legal rules is extended by two further considerations.

One of the difficulties in penetrating the ideological form of bourgeois law stems from the fact that it operates by abstracting the cases that come before the courts from their social and class context. They are thereby reduced to the status of being pure *technical* issues, apparently divorced from any political or ideological overtones. If, for example, a householder inquires why it is that tax relief is granted on mortgage payments but not on rent, the law replies that it is not a question of relief on mortgage or rent, but on interest repayments. By focusing on a

technical distinction the law thereby obscures the social and economic reality.

Second, the law further depoliticizes social issues through the universal form of many legal rules. The fact that rules of criminal law protect the person and property of all members of society not only hides the fundamental class differences, but it also treats the capital of the employer and the personal belongings of the worker as if they were the same. The ideological significance is that it induces the view that all classes in society have a common interest in the protection of private property. Thereby the legal system is aided in fulfilling the ideological function of asserting the unity of interests of all classes. The ideology of the "rule of law" operates to assert and reinforce, and even seeks to celebrate, a social unity and cohesion in the face of the manifest class differentiation of capitalist society.

There is one further facet of the ideological character of law. It is directly ideological in the sense that the legal system propagates a range of views about the nature of the social and political system. This general ideological character of law is contained in what I will call "bourgeois legal ideology."

Bourgeois legal ideology is the fundamental component of the justification of the bourgeois democratic state; many of its elements directly enter into the consciousness of wide sections of the population. The central element of this ideology is the doctrine of "the rule of law." Its classic expression is to be found in Dicey:

> When we speak of the "rule of law" as a characteristic of our country we mean, not only that with us no man is above the law, but (what is a different thing) that every man, whatever be his rank or condition, is subject to the ordinary law of the realm.... With us every official, from the Prime Minister down to a constable ... is under the same responsibility for every act done without legal justification as any other citizen. (1967: 193)

The fundamental tenet is that both the ruled and the rulers are equally subject to a common system of the law. The "law" itself is thus viewed as something separate from the interests of classes. As such it plays a central role in the legitimation of the bourgeois democratic political order.

One particularly interesting feature of bourgeois legal ideology in the context of English law is the way in which it holds itself out as the protector of the individual against the incursions of the state. This antithesis between individual and state has a lengthy history in bourgeois legal thought. Its roots were in the historical alliance between the common law judges and the bourgeois interests against the absolutism of the Stuarts. It became more fully elaborated during the nineteenth century as the legal reflex of laissez-faire ideology. And in the twentieth century it has been used as the basis of antistate attitudes that characterize one element of the conservative reaction to the growth of the Welfare State.

In addition to explicit constitutional principles bourgeois legal ideology consists of a range of important background or implicit assumptions. The intention is only to roughly sketch some of these assumptions, but at the same time to argue that the more the "law and order" debate moves into the center of the political stage the more important it becomes to develop a systematic critique of bourgeois legal ideology.

Almost all discussion about law is based on the assumption that the existence of law is an inevitable or natural feature of social life. Hence law becomes identified with "civilization"; the absence of law is seen as synonymous with the absence of civilization. The classic expression of this assumption is the equation of the absence of law with anarchy; in its classical form in the political philosophy of Hobbes the absence of law implies a condition of "the war of all against all." The whole of society is presumed to have an interest in the existence of law, and is therefore closely connected with the "universalism" of law discussed above.

A closely associated assumption insists on the inherent rationality of law. The existence of rules of social life brought together or codified as law is presented as socially desirable in that it makes social life more certain and predictable. Social life is viewed as if it were a game or a sport in which it is essential that all the "players" adhere to the same rules; without this common set of rules social life would revert to anarchy. Such an attitude places stress on the desirability of rules *as such*, and hence leaves unquestioned the content of those rules and any questions concerning the social and economic interests that are embodied in the rules.

Flowing directly from the insistence on the naturalness and rationality of law is the insistence that adherence to law is natural, and as a corollary, that nonadherence to law is unnatural or deviant. The very existence of a state is treated as a sufficient condition to make obedience to law obligatory for all citizens. The assumption is made that the offender who violates the law is a deviant whose deviation stems from some pathological condition. While the nature of the pathology appealed to has varied, from the genetic inferiority of the "lower orders" to deficiencies in "socialization," the same assumption

of the naturalness of obedience to law persists. It is interesting to note that in the recent past this essentially conservative tradition has come under increasing attack from criminologists, and that radical theories of crime are being developed which draw upon Marxism (Taylor, Walton, and Young 1972).

These interrelated attitudes and assumptions about law are not usually expressed in a coherent form: they are a cluster of ideas, but they add up to an assertion of the "sanctity of law" that forms the heart of the pervasive and powerful "law and order" ideology. This ideology finds expression not only in the moralizing editorials of the *Times*, but also forms an important part of widespread and diffuse social attitudes. The essential substance of these views is that they appeal to the sanctity of law, elevated above social life itself, and thereby ignore the class content of law and its role in legitimising the existing forms of class domination.

There is one final aspect of the ideological character of law that needs to be mentioned. The most formal and systematic expression of legal ideology is provided by jurisprudence or legal theory. The history of jurisprudence consists in successive attempts to provide a justification for obedience to law. The central concern has been to provide a socially persuasive account of the legitimacy of the existing legal order, and through that of the social order itself. However, a very interesting development has occurred within jurisprudence which is worth noting. Increasingly a number of liberal academics have been afflicted with growing self-doubt and disillusionment with the whole edifice of law, and are increasingly aware of a very real decline in the legitimacy of the existing legal order (Rostow 1970; Wolff 1971).

The operation of law is, therefore, not confined to simply giving effect to the direct and immediate interests of the ruling class. It must be understood as having an ideological function of an extensive character. Within capitalist society the legal system not only provides substantial ideological underpinnings to the existing capitalist organization of society. It also provides a consistent and coherent legitimation of a multitude of key institutions and principles that are central to the smooth operation of a system of capitalist social relations.

It is this ability to integrate two critical functions, on the one hand to give practical effect to the interests of the dominant class, and, at the same time, to provide a justification or legitimation for these interests in terms of some higher and apparently universal interest of all classes that demonstrates the real power and influence of law in capitalist society.

LAW AND CLASS STRUGGLE

Our attention has been focused on the part that law plays in the process of reproducing capitalist social order. Yet law is not simply an instrument which can be wielded at will by an omnipotent ruling class. Precisely because it is an active element in the class struggle, it is at the same time affected by and involved in the class struggle. The law and the legal system form part of the context within which the class struggle takes place, and it is itself an arena in which that struggle occurs. To recognize that class struggle occurs *within* the legal system is not to suggest that the legal system is some neutral territory over which the class struggle wrestles for control. As a major component of the state law is necessarily part of the process through which the ruling class seeks to preserve its domination.

To argue that class struggle occurs within law is only the first step in examining the way in which class struggle makes itself evident within law. It has been argued above that law plays a central part in bourgeois democratic society, not only in theory but also in practice. The form taken by the class struggle has its boundaries broadly defined by the existing law. Thus, for example, trade union activity in Britain is pursued by forms of struggle that are recognized as being lawful. Some of the most important stages in the history of British trade unionism have been periods when struggle has occurred around attempts by the ruling class to narrow or restrict this lawful sphere of operations. The struggle against the *Industrial Relations Act* was a classic example of this type of struggle.

While law plays this important part of defining the parameters of class struggle, it also needs to be recognized that it does not necessarily stay confined within this framework. Indeed a change in this boundary or its breach will normally mark a critical phase in the class struggle. For example, a very important stage of the struggle against the *Industrial Relations Act* occurred in the months after it had been put on the statute book. The right-wing inside the Labour Movement argued that despite the objection they had to the Act it was now "law" and had to be accepted. The critical phase was the decisions made in the individual unions and within the TUC (Croydon and Blackpool Congresses 1971) as to whether they would "register" under the Act, and thus come within "the law," or whether to remain unregistered and to conduct trade union activity without the forms of protection that had been established since the beginning of the century.

Not only does law play an important part in defining the parameters of the class struggle, but many important stages in the class struggle take place around demands for legislative reforms. Marx himself gave considerable attention to one very important example of such struggles, the early *Factory Acts* (in particular the *Factories Regulation Act* of 1833). His chapter in *Capital* Volume I, on "The Working-Day" is a classic study of the interrelation and interaction of class forces in a struggle for legislative control of working hours.

> The creation of a normal working-day is, therefore, the product of a protracted civil war, more or less dissembled, between the capitalist class and the working-class. (1961: I, 231–302)

Elsewhere he summarized the significance of the victory underlying the Act in the following terms:

> it was the first time that in broad daylight the political economy of the middle class succumbed to the political economy of the working class. (1958: I, 383)

His analysis makes clear that the Factory Acts were not simply the direct result of class struggle between the capitalist and working classes. Two particular features of the analysis are worth drawing attention to. The first concerns the relationship between the state and the capitalist class. The advent of machinery and industrial production in the textile industry gives rise to a veritable orgy of exploitation in which the working-day is extended to such lengths that a real threat is posed to the survival of the work force. At this stage the state represents the collective interests of capital, as distinct from the interests of individual capitalists.

Second, he stresses the divisions between the various sections of the capitalist class. Not only is there the division between the landed and industrial capitalists, which led the Tories as representatives of landed capital, to support factory legislation. But more important are the divisions between the more advanced sections of industrial capital and the smaller, more traditional employers. The passage of the factory acts represented a victory not only for the working class, but also for the more advanced sections of capital, who triumphed over their less efficient rivals. The overall analysis therefore brings out with great sharpness the way in which the development of the productive forces, in association with the more or less conscious struggle of various classes, finds its expression in legislation.

In his discussion of factory legislation Marx showed clearly how each legislative victory was only partial; while each was a major practical and ideological victory, the employers, with the direct complicity of the magistrates and judges, impeded the effective enforcement of the provisions of the statutes.

CONCLUSION

In this chapter I have stressed the importance of law in capitalist society, and as a consequence argued that it is a question that requires a more thorough analysis by Marxists. While this chapter does not complete that task, it has sought to raise a number of questions, and to stress a number of areas for discussion. Some of these have been of a general nature that revolve around an assertion of law as an important agency in the maintenance of capitalist social relations. In particular I have argued the need to understand the significance of law as a system of ideological-coercive domination. It is through this emphasis on this combined process, rather than as two distinct or separate processes, that we can achieve a better understanding of the specific functioning of law within capitalist society, and is also of assistance in achieving a fuller theoretical treatment of the capitalist state.

The legal system within the bourgeois democratic state operates in such a way as to legitimize the class rule of the bourgeoisie. This legitimation involves not only the recognition and reinforcement of the social and economic relations of capitalism. It also encompasses the reification of law (through which law appears to be a power above and outside society) in which the social and political relations of capitalist society are presented as natural and universal. Law then operates to provide ideological reinforcement to those processes that make the reality of class and class power less visible.

The really difficult question is posed by the fact that bourgeois democratic society is not entirely a facade and a fraud. If it were its veils and deceits would have been stripped away long ago. Its strength and persistence result from the fact that in varying degrees it has successfully combined the continued social, political and economic dominance of the capitalist class with, at the same time, a significant level of involvement of the exploited classes sufficient to ensure a relatively high level of acceptance of, and even commitment to, the existing order.

Within the bourgeois democratic state law provides, alongside those aspects that reinforce the domination of the ruling class, an important set of rights, protections, and powers that in varying degrees incorporate certain class interests of the nonruling classes. The most obvious examples of these are such things as the right to vote, to form trade unions, to take strike action, etc.

It is important to recognize that most of these have been secured as the result of class struggle. But these facts should not lead us to view them simply as concessions wrung from the capitalist. Once granted they become woven into the fabric of bourgeois democracy. It should also be noted that we need to recognize that the range of legal rights that may be used to the advantage of the working class extends beyond the range of the more obvious "political" rights mentioned. The law confers rights and protections on all classes as "citizens" in bourgeois democracy. It is of course important to stress the inequality of their application and the inequality of access to legal redress. Yet this does not negate their political and ideological importance. Their very existence plays a significant part in securing the acceptance of, and allegiance to, the existing capitalist social order.

(b) Theft of Time: Disciplining Through Science and Law†

Laureen Snider

1. INTRODUCTION: THE SIGNIFICANCE OF CRIME CREATION

In America's one-sided class war, employers have taken to monitoring employees' workplace behav-

iour right down to the single computer keystroke or bathroom break.[1]

Time theft steals money as sure as someone picking your pocket. ... It is America's biggest crime, and until its victims — the owners and

---

† (2002) 40 Osgoode Hall L.J. 89–112 at paras. 1–34, 40–45. Reproduced with permission. [Notes and/or references omitted.]

managers of American industry — decide to do something about it, we'll continue to be stolen blind.[2]

[1] This commentary examines the genealogy of crime creation through an investigation into the discovery and management of a new type of crime against capital. Theft of time, defined as the misuse of the employer's time and property by an employee, is rooted in nineteenth century Taylorist discourses on time management and productivity. However, theft of time has come into its own in the twenty-first century workplace, spurred by a combination of ideological and technological developments. The purpose of this commentary is to begin to document and explain this phenomenon.

[2] My interest in this subject stems from earlier work on the disappearance, in statute and fact, of corporate crime. Creeds of neo-liberalism, rationalized by globalization, have persuaded governments throughout the industrialized world to repeal legislation aimed at controlling or censuring the anti-social acts of capital.[3] The most ardent evangelists of this point of view come out of the United States, not coincidentally the nation with the lion's share of world power and wealth. This commentary focuses on American practices and law because the United States sets the tone for countries around the globe. By persuasion, coercion, or example, and through its all-powerful media, market force, government, military, or theoretically international associations such as the World Bank or the World Trade Organization, what happens in the United States is pivotal. As Braithwaite[4] has explained, periphery apes centre. Thus, whether or not appropriate to their own history and culture, states throughout the world tend to reproduce ideas and structures embraced by the United States more quickly than ever with the advent of globalized communication systems.

[3] As neo-liberalism gained strength over the last two decades of the twentieth century, virtually every developed nation retreated from its historic obligation to assure the welfare of citizens by restraining and punishing corporations for antisocial policies and acts. It was argued that state laws that disciplined business [...] were expensive, unnecessary, inappropriate, and draconian. Corporations were to be viewed as complicated organisms run by well-intentioned, well-educated management teams. Harmful acts in which they might — accidentally, of course — engage were better handled by gentle persuasion or education rather than by arrest and prosecution. Market mechanisms such as competition and licencing were more efficient

and cost-effective than laws against corporate crime. Thus, pollution permits could replace laws against environmental crime; those who would fix or defraud markets would be automatically disciplined (at no cost!) by free trade and global competition, and voluntary compliance or self-regulation would deliver better worker protection than state law, enforced as it necessarily was by a bloated and bureaucratic government aligned with fat cat unions. In this discourse, government was always represented as fat or soft; business, in stark contrast, was lean, mean, and equipped to survive in the real world.

[4] Such arguments fit well with downsizing, deficit-cutting agendas in the nation state and with the newly discovered "need" to cut corporate taxes to allow business to compete in the highly touted "global" marketplace. Thus, laws against false advertising and hazardous products; laws stipulating minimum wage levels, maximum hours of work, or overtime pay; and laws setting standards and punishing businesses for poisoning the air or water, were systematically repealed, reformed or rendered inoperative by draconian budget and staff cuts. Through deregulation, decriminalization, and downsizing, corporate crime vanished, ideologically, politically, and legally.[5] However, at the same time that laws disciplining employers disappeared, laws disciplining employees were strengthened. The legal rights of employees, such as the right to resist sixty-hour work weeks, or refuse work in unsafe environments were eliminated, while new offences against employers were discovered and denounced. Theft of time, invented and brokered as a social problem by academics in business schools, organizational psychology, sociology, and criminology, is a quintessential example of this process.

[5] The links between knowledge, power, and discipline, usually credited to Foucault,[6] have often been noted. In the first instance, theft of time was made conceivable by ideas and languages developed in the early days of the Industrial Revolution, ideas that conceptualized time as a measurable commodity to which value could be assigned. Through the alliance of science and technology, timepieces (watches and clocks) were invented, making it possible for eighteenth century factory owners to begin paying workers by the hour. Such ways of thinking constitute the framework for punishing troublesome individuals by sentencing them to "do time" in specialist institutions (such as penitentiaries). Also, with factories replacing the home, shop, and pasture as the dominant sites of production, it became possible to conceive of time-motion studies, time-clocks, and other devices to

measure the link between productivity, time, and the costs of production. Efficiency, for example, is an inherently time-bound concept. Thus, technology, namely inventions pioneered by natural and applied science, in combination with the "science of man," which are the disciplines of social science, are components of a knowledge–power nexus that measures, knows, and disciplines people through their institutional, public, and private roles.

[6] New categories of knowledge are discursively constituted through social science, with each discipline putting forth a set of claims to "truth" over a particular area of human behaviour. These claims to truth are also claims to power, the power to define how people think and, therefore, how they act or "should" act. This agenda-setting power influences what kinds of behaviours come to be seen as "social problems," or what constitutes an "efficient" workplace or a "realistic" policy initiative. This power has important, tangible effects on peoples' life prospects, institutions, and on what people see as possible, necessary, and desirable in their own lives, both within and outside the workplace. Although the power to conceptualize reality is neither owned nor monopolized by any one discipline, institution, or class, nor blindly imposed on helpless subject populations, it is also not freely and equitably distributed across race, gender, and class boundaries. Although arguments about truth are actively debated, contested, and resisted within the academy and beyond, the playing field of ideas is not level but tilted. Truth claims are hierarchically ordered.[7] Thus, certain voices, certain ways of seeing and conceptualizing the world, are more powerful than others.

[7] In the industrialized, capitalist, democratic state, the loudest voices are those connected to key interests and, therefore, to privilege. The most persuasive, best publicized, and most assiduously promoted claims are those of first world-elites, claims which support, secure, or reinforce their own privilege. Only those in charge of the transnational corporation or the territory called the nation state can speak in its name or on its behalf. Additionally, the claims of elites are most likely to come fully clothed in the latest legitimizing concepts, such as modernity, efficiency, or prosperity. These claims will be fine-tuned to resonate with dominant cultural themes. In the increasingly corporate-driven university, key elites, particularly those that own and/or control institutions of economic and political power, direct the production of knowledge. Corporate elites, for example, influence which questions knowledge professionals will ask and structure how these ques-

tions will be defined, researched, and answered, by endowing chairs, sponsoring competitions, and funding private think tanks. Once knowledge is produced, elites who own and control mass media and generate mass culture through entertainment and sport are best positioned to publicize and popularize privilege-reinforcing claims.

[8] Eventually, through this process, some of these ideas and claims achieve the status of "fact." These ideas have been removed from the realm of political and contentious claims, that are open to disagreement and debate, and transformed into "common sense" assumptions or things that everyone just "knows." Thus, when the lead stories in print and television regularly feature experts claiming that the deficit is the major threat to Canada's prosperity in the twenty-first century, or that a massive brain drain of talented individuals caused by "excessive" tax rates is underway, or that "lax security" allows terrorists and criminals to enter Canada at will, these issues come to be seen as social problems and these receive national attention. This does not mean that there is no resistance, or that claims not supported by key elites never make the transition from knowledge claim to fact. Resistance is continuously generated and counter-hegemonic claims are sometimes heard. Ongoing battles over global warming, genetically modified foods, refugee rights, and sexual harassment are examples of elite-contested claims that have gained publicity and a measure of acceptance. Still, the process generally takes longer, claim-makers are held to a much higher standard of truth, and incessant vigilance is required to maintain any substantive consequences the claim may have (to secure law enforcement, for example). Elite-endorsed claims, experts, and studies, on the other hand, tend to be fast-tracked. These claims become front page news in mainstream or "reputable" publications, while opposing claims and experts are absent or marginalized, and portrayed as radicals or special interest groups spouting opinions rather than facts.

[9] Productivity, including the knowledge claims that constitute the concept of productivity, is a pivotal issue, vitally important to business elites because maximizing productivity is fundamental to profitability. Higher profit levels and share prices mean more prosperity, privilege, and power accrue to those who own, administer, and control corporations since these groups reap a disproportionate share of profits.[8] Therefore, it is not surprising that questions about productivity and its allied concept, efficiency, have been front and centre since the dawn of the Industrial Revolution, dominating research agendas

in many academic disciplines. While hundreds of studies have examined productivity from every possible perspective, particular attention has been focused on the basic human denominator, the worker. Thus, psychology typically concentrated on worker motivation, sociology on group relations and the working environment, including everything from early studies linking light levels and productivity to sexual harassment today, economics on identifying, conceptualizing, and managing efficiency. The study of the problematic-because-unproductive employee, then, is not new.

[10] However, linking productivity, or the lack thereof, to criminality is new. Transforming the unproductive employee into the criminal is significant. Not that law has ever been absent from the workplace; rather, employment and contract law have always focused on regularizing the employee–employer relationship.[9] Still, it is significant because calling something "criminal" is an ideological and moral claim. It categorizes a particular behaviour as an act that causes social harm, one that injures everyone in a geographically defined area. The act is no longer a private matter, nor a dispute to be settled by the parties directly involved. Furthermore, calling an act a crime is a claim for public resources, a summons that obligates the state to monitor and enforce. In the case of theft of time, the state is required to unleash its moral and legal power on behalf of employers, as the victims, to [rein] in or discipline employees, as the offenders or the criminals.

[11] The earliest explicit reference to theft of time, in sociological and criminological literatures, is in Hollinger and Clark's 1983 self-report study on occupational crime.[10] The authors administered questionnaires to a large sample of employees, mostly low and middle-level staff, in a broad range of business and government organizations. Subjects were asked whether or not they or their co-workers had participated in a list of on-the-job behaviours, from theft of money or goods, to faking illness or covering unauthorized absence. The authors coined the term "theft of time" to describe certain employee behaviours, such as coming back late from breaks, conducting personal business on the job, or loafing around while pretending to be working. They claimed that employee theft was widespread, a fact they attributed to job dissatisfaction, to perceived (not absolute) need, and to youth. Younger workers were more likely to offend, and they and the newly hired were more likely to be apprehended.

[12] The bulk of academic claim-making around theft of time, however, has come from other disciplines. Social scientists working in business schools, human or industrial relations, or private think-tanks and consulting firms, have been particularly active. With the advent of new technologies, communication systems, computers, and the Internet, the study of employee resistance and its causes and remedies has become an academic growth area. Particularly in applied and multidisciplinary fields, the study of time theft has come into its own.

II. TIGHTENING THE SCREWS ON EMPLOYEES: NAMING, BLAMING, AND SHAMING

[13] Crime creation is a process with several distinct parts. First, the offence must be isolated and named. Those making the claim must explain why the activity is bad and how it produces harm to society or to vulnerable members within society. Incidence is critical here; the behaviour is frequently presented in disease metaphor, for example, as "a raging epidemic" that is "out of control." Then, primary offenders and victims must be identified, categorized, classified, studied, and demographically and psychologically situated. Given the identification of modernity with the languages and methods of natural science, to be taken seriously, claims must be translated into numbers, then into statistical knowledge. A claim must be published in a "reputable" venue, then defended against counterclaims made by critics from the same and other disciplines or schools. Before the arrival of direct democracy in the form of victims' movements and the tabloid press, crime creation occurred almost entirely through the debates of socially authorized "experts" in various social sciences, especially criminology and law, as well as through the interactions of these experts with policymakers.

[14] As we shall see, the creation of theft of time follows the pattern outlined above, broadening and extending the concept of employee theft. Theft of employers' property by employees has long been recognized as a criminal offence in law. Criminologists have classified employee theft as a subspecies of white-collar crime, naming it occupational crime. Shoplifting, pilfering, computer crime, and expense account theft are typical examples of occupational crime.[11] Debates over classification and typology in white-collar crime have preoccupied criminologists for more than half a century,[12] but occupational crime is generally recognized as distinctive because

the typical victim is an organization, not an individual. It is an offence against business. This makes it very different, ideologically, politically, and economically, from organizational or corporate crime offences such as antitrust, dumping toxic waste, marketing fraudulent drugs, falsifying cotton dust levels, or asbestos fibre counts, which are offences by business that victimize the public, consumers, the environment, or employees.[13]

[15] In the 1980s and 1990s, social scientists from a variety of disciplines and institutional settings studying employee behaviour and efficiency began to isolate time theft and "specialists" in this area began to appear. A number of surveys and self-report studies on employees came up with lists describing "serious types of employee dishonesty."[14] A typical list situates and categorizes theft of time alongside "unauthorized long-distance phone calls, supplies or equipment theft, missing inventory, illicit electronic funds transfer and the selling of trade secrets."[15] When popularized through the business press — the original and most faithful vehicle of dissemination of such claims — the studies became news, producing headlines noting that: theft of time is "insidious" and constant, an ongoing threat to corporate profits; it delivers "A Severe Blow to the Nation's Productivity"; it is "An Abuse of Business"; it is "Canada's Biggest Crime."[16] More important, given the centrality of United States in the economic world, theft of time is "America's Biggest Crime: Time Theft — The Deliberate Waste, Abuse and Misappropriation of On-The-Job Time."[17]

[16] As the concept is popularized, it is, in academic parlance, "refined." New categories are discovered and investigated, old ones are extended. Theft of time soon includes: "idle chatter"; "hours spent on the phone with family and friends"; "counterproductive behaviour"; "holiday season shirking"; "arguing with customers"; "unauthorized long-distance calls"; "overstating time sheets"; "taking extended breaks, arriving at work late, leaving early, reading on company time" and even "over-associating with co-workers."[18] Description and categorization slide into censure. Labels, preferably eye-grabbing and pithy, are devised. Some of the most common include: "time bandits," "time thieves," "the organizationally impaired," and "loafers" who are constantly "goofing off."[19]

[17] Finally, and most significantly, since numbers carry a legitimacy that "mere" words do not, the claim was rendered in numerical form and statistically calibrated. As one claim-maker put it, "most of the companies were well aware of the problem [of time theft], but they never thought it was serious until we started to put some numbers to it."[20] The number of offenders and the economic cost of time theft were computed, then the yearly cost announced. Studies quantifying the vast amounts lost to "goof-off" employees have received maximum publicity and minimum critical scrutiny. Questions about the accuracy or reliability of these numbers, about sample size, techniques, and methodological assumptions, have seldom been asked. Had these questions been raised, the weakness of the claims would have been obvious to numerate audiences, since figures were typically generated by asking managers to estimate the number of employees they thought engaged in time theft, then converting lost time into lost dollar amounts. In many cases, the sample of managers was too small and the firms were too unrepresentative to persuade those versed in positivist or quantitative methodology. Still, at this stage in the process academic experts were not the primary target audience, and consequently, the scientific accuracy of the surveys was not a central issue.

[18] Therefore, we see a range of claims quantifying time theft, with the numbers escalating annually, faithfully reported in the business press. Time theft was deemed to cost $120 billion a year in 1982[21] and a mere $15 billion in Canada.[22] It rose to $137 billion the next year, then to $160 billion.[23] The escalation continued, with figures set at $161 billion, $170 billion, then at $200 billion.[24] By the end of the 1980s, theft of time had been constructed as both a fact and a serious social problem. A virtual epidemic of undisciplined, lazy, goof-off employees was loose in the North American workplace. These deviants, though not yet criminals, were sapping the nation's productivity (the implicit/explicit comparison group being the Asian, particularly the Japanese worker), making the corporation uncompetitive and draining away profits.

III. THE SOLUTIONS: DISCIPLINING THROUGH KNOWLEDGE, TECHNOLOGY, AND LAWA.

B. Disciplining Through Knowledge

[19] Once the offence is named, the cost of its consequences tallied, and minimally established as fact and problem, it is incumbent on claim makers to offer remedies. The solutions put forth change depending on the analytical model that is employed,

which in turn, varies by discipline. Experts who see employee ignorance as the primary cause of time theft recommend remedies based on educating employees. Those who attribute it to fraud or dishonesty, who constitute the venal, profit-maximizing employee, tend to favour intrusive technological surveillance combined with criminal penalties.

[20] Economic and political interests are not unimportant; those in the business of selling solutions usually advocate remedies that benefit their discipline, company, or consulting firm.[25] The underfunding of universities and the allied, constant pressure on academics to justify their existence through alliances with the private sector makes this a win–win situation. Professors can supplement their salaries by selling knowledge to the private sector and by doing so prove, to their employer and themselves, the legitimacy of their discipline, since marketability is the supreme arbiter of worth. Those outside the academy, the legions of freelance consultants in "the knowledge economy," are also able to secure a modest — or immodest — living by producing, selling, and promoting remedies. Addressing the problems of the rich and powerful tends to be rewarding.

[21] The initial task is usually to identify the problem group and to distinguish the culpable from the non-culpable employees. This requires the development of screening devices and tests to ferret out potential deviants since it is much more expensive to dismiss employees than it is not to hire them in the first place. Consequently, instruments such as the Preemployment Integrity Test, designed to predict "counterproductive employee behaviour," have been developed. The London House Personnel Selection Inventory (PSI), for example, identifies and weeds out problem employees. In a sample of ninety-five job applicants, the authors report that the PSI accurately predicted theft of time, theft of merchandise, and "poor job performance." Latent time thieves, it turns out, score high on character traits such as "general moral permissiveness."[26] Urine tests and compulsory DNA samples seem to represent the logical next step.

[22] However, since screening devices inevitably let some miscreants through, more is required. Employers must use knowledge to get inside the heads of employees, to persuade them to discipline and shame themselves. Experts who favour liberal remedies tell employers "to bring employees onside" to educate or persuade them that theft of time is wrong and that it constitutes a serious breach of the employer-employee contract. Responsible employers are advised to develop fair, consistently enforced time-use policies in order to inculcate a change in corporate attitude about time. This will purportedly improve morale which will, in turn, "increase productivity and recapture profits."[27] Along the same lines, employers are advised to design programs and activities to improve employee performance because, "most employees are ... unaware that their behaviour is inappropriate. ... [since] time-wasting habits ... reflect the way an employee has behaved all his [or her] life."[28] To underline the disciplinary message, employees should be provided with facts — numbers, of course — on the cost of "loafing." Also, employees should be asked to take "voluntary" tests, such as Sunoo's "How Many Hours Have You Wasted?" which aim to get employees to monitor their own on-the-job behaviour. Thus employees are asked to write down how many hours per week they spend "staring out the window, Christmas shopping, taking coffee breaks, smoking cigarettes, showing off your vacation photos, writing letters to Grandma, or surfing Penthouse's web site."[29] Interestingly, employees are seldom asked to record the number of hours they spend taking such tests. Less liberal solutions include keeping employees on edge through constant job insecurity and periodic downsizing. As one expert writes, "when people are afraid of losing their jobs they work harder and steal less time."[30] However, job insecurity is also identified as a double-edged sword, causing more time theft than it cures. One article in Personnel Journal,[31] a resource for human relations professionals, makes the point that employees are more likely to steal time by "loafing" if too many human relations professionals have been laid off.

B. Disciplining Through Technology

[23] Employee monitoring and surveillance, both covert and overt, have become the most common means of disciplining the work force, even though the intrusiveness, ubiquity and punitiveness of this practice varies widely depending on the sector and level of the employee. Technology supplements, rather than replaces, remedies devised by social science and law. In the name of productivity, the modern corporate employer has adopted computer-based technologies that make the scenarios of Orwell's 1984 look optimistic and the principles of Bentham's Panopticon look lax. In the quest for the "perfect," that is, maximally productive, employee, engineering and technological expertise from the natural and applied sciences have been combined with theories of human motivation and conformity generated by

257

the social sciences. Physical, sociological, and psychological resistance are enemies to be defeated. If human beings cannot yet be eliminated completely from the work process, which has historically been the ultimate goal, they must be rendered at least as efficient as machines.

[24] Consequently, businesses are ceaselessly on the lookout for slackers and thieves, for any and all forms of employee resistance. In the quest to achieve the compliant workforce and the docile subject, victory is never complete. Externally, employee protection laws and culturally generated attitudes of entitlement are a problem. Internally, every improvement, every change, can have unanticipated consequences, as employees constantly find ways to use technologies designed to maximize productivity to their own benefit, turning these technologies against the employer. The struggle to eliminate unauthorized uses of computer technology is a case in point.

[25] In the 1980s employers were primarily concerned that software, such as word processors, could be employed to further the private agendas of employees. "Is your Operator Secretly Writing Romances?" asks one article.[32] It remains difficult to distinguish, by visual surveillance alone, between workers doing legitimate computer-based tasks and those following their own agendas.[33] However the real subversive power of new technologies emerged with the development of cyberspace, electronic mail, the World Wide Web, and the internet. Businesses became obsessed by the time theft potential of internet surfing and electronic chat rooms, by employees' consulting "inappropriate" web sites or writing personal letters on office electronic mail systems. Added to time theft was the threat of lawsuits should employees visit pornographic web sites or use electronic mail systems to harass fellow employees. In a landmark 1995 U.S. decision, Chevron paid $2 million to settle a suit wherein one employee harassed another via corporate electronic mail. Still, access to these tools cannot be denied without compromising productivity; employees at a certain level of seniority need internet access and freedom of movement online to operate efficiently. Thus, law firms now urge companies to get employees to sign "voluntary" consent forms allowing the employer to intercept and monitor all electronic mail and internet activity.[34] With or without employee consent, 45 per cent of American companies now monitor all electronic communication.[35] Companies are also "cracking down on free Webmail," forbidding employees from subscribing to free services such as Hotmail and Yahoo.[36] The fact that employees think they are

getting away with something is sufficient reason to ban them from using these services, even though in reality, with surveillance, monitoring, and storage on magnetic tape of all electronic activity, nothing is unrecoverable once inscribed online. Relations of deference and authority are thereby reinforced alongside efficiency and productivity.

[26] Inappropriate internet use, however, is only an issue for middle and upper-level employees, still disproportionately male, middle-class, and white. At lower levels, in office, shop, and factory, internet access is a dream, on-the-job surveillance is constant, intense, and intrusive. Computer monitoring through automated time-and-attendance video display systems record employees' in-and-out times, compute hours worked, and individual and collective levels of productivity. The systems also generate lists of "job-costing alternatives," ways of improving efficiency by eliminating particular tasks and, subsequently, people.[37] Active badge or keycard systems must be swiped when employees arrive, leave, go to lunch or visit the washroom. In the electronic office, every keystroke is counted, every phone call recorded, and every "unproductive" moment assessed. Employee performance records, generated by measuring how long each employee takes to handle an order or complaint compared against the norms or targets produced by efficiency experts, are compiled every day, week, or month. Passive monitoring is supplemented by eavesdropping. In true Panopticon fashion, the employee never knows whether his or her supervisor is listening.

[27] The creation of what amounts to nationwide electronic sweatshops, while profitable for those employing the technology, has been disastrous for many employees. Some of the most common responses to surveillance have been studied, with experts paying particular attention to those that threaten productivity or increase costs.

[28] Overall, nervous breakdowns increase with the level of surveillance, while general health deteriorates. Fatigue or exhaustion, depression, apathy, stress, anxiety, pain in shoulders and wrists, stomach and back, indigestion, nausea, and sleep disturbances are common.[38] A workplace "syndrome" has been legitimized by the name "bathroom-break harassment," defined as the reluctance to take bathroom breaks for fear of losing one's job. The designation honours a United Airlines employee who was disciplined in 1996 for overly long bathroom breaks — a flight reservationist is allowed a total of twelve minutes to attend to personal needs over a seven and a

half hour shift. Indeed, there is no federally mandated right to rest periods at work in the United States. In fact, "employers often consider the time a worker spends urinating as 'stolen' time."[39]

[29] Old-fashioned spying techniques have not disappeared: informants or stooge employees are still planted inside firms to pose as employees and infiltrate work groups, gathering inside information on the personal lives, habits, and sins of co-workers. Covert surveillance is employed to deter "time or product theft" in a variety of sites. Occupations that historically enjoyed relative workplace autonomy, such as longshoremen, truck drivers and police officers, are particularly targeted.[40] Phone taps permit employers to eavesdrop on employees' telephone calls. "Snitch lines" — confidential, toll-free telephone lines — are set up to encourage employees to report, anonymously, on the time-wasting, time-stealing, drug-taking, or otherwise nefarious activities of co-workers.[41] Technological and aural surveillance is frequently supplemented by video surveillance to stamp out nonproductive, venal behaviour such as "fooling around" on the job or "horseplay."[42]

[30] Technological "creep" abounds as surveillance tools developed for other purposes in other institutional sites are imported into the workplace. Active badge systems, for example, originally designed to track the movements of convicted criminals on house arrest, are now common in factories and warehouses. Such systems let supervisors know the exact location of every employee beyond visual surveillance at any given time. "Currently, as many as 26 million workers in the United States are monitored in their jobs.... By the end of the decade, as many as 30 million people may be...."[43]

C. Disciplining Through Law

[31] Disciplining through criminal law is typically the last stage in the crime-creation process, a stage that more and more "social problems" eventually reach as the modern state becomes ever more dependent on coercion rather than consent.[44] In much of the developed world, theft of time, in and of itself, is still not a criminal offence. Theft of time is a legitimate reason for dismissal; employers can fire employees deemed guilty of theft of time for cause. Canadian law is typical, treating theft or "misuse" of time as analogous to theft of company property, although no specific law proscribes it.

[32] Case law is inconsistent. In Taylor v. Sears Canada Inc.,[45] the court upheld the firing of an employee for taking longer than authorized daytime

breaks who then claimed overtime when he did not finish his deliveries on time. However, the British Columbia Supreme Court rejected an employer's attempt to dismiss an employee for cause by claiming that this was analagous to theft from the employer.[46] On the other hand, the Canadian Charter of Rights and Freedoms[47] purportedly protects privacy rights, but its provisions on search and seizure only cover government, not private-sector employees. Quebec is the only province with comprehensive individual privacy legislation enshrined in Quebec's Charter of Human Rights and Freedoms.[48] Elsewhere, legislation is ad hoc and focused on the public sector.[49]

[33] The United States is the nation to watch because of its status as global business leader, its mammoth economic power and its worldwide ideological clout. At the present time, with the exception of privacy law, most of the relevant American case law is state-based rather than federal. In fact, the virtual absence of legal provisions protecting the employee from arbitrary actions by the employer or, on the positive side, establishing employees' rights, is striking. To achieve the "efficient," "productive" workforce, anything goes; the right of capital to act in the interests of profit maximization is uncontested. Setting limits on employers is seen as going against efficiency. The discursive privilege of capital in the United States is so strong at this time that its claims, goals, and needs easily trump rival claims. In the most basic way, capital — the employer class — defines meaning, and, consequently, practice and law in the workplace. Therefore, to employers, legislators and, often, employees, laws extending the rights of capital (the legitimate defenders of efficiency and productivity) make sense, while those restricting capital do not. Who could oppose efficiency? It becomes a non-choice, a classic no-brainer.[50]

[34] Thus, practical and economic reasons, not worker resistance or legislative reluctance, explain the scarcity of criminal laws against theft of time. North American employers are generally very familiar with the practical drawbacks of the criminal justice process. Literature on white-collar crime abounds with instructive case studies, showing that backlogged court dockets, year-long delays, and endless remands and minuscule sanctions are common.[51] The publicity attending criminal law is another disincentive. No corporation wants to be portrayed as unable to control its workforce or staffed by "thieves." However, if business assessments of the utility of criminal law change, there is every reason

to expect that, barring a major shift in the ideological, economic and political landscape and balance of power, legislation would follow.

. . . .

IV.   CONCLUSION

[40] It is ironic that theft of time has emerged as a social problem at a time when employers are increasingly stealing time from employees. Businesses routinely demand unpaid overtime, they expect white-collar employees to appear at corporate events, or oblige executives to donate evenings and weekends raising money for corporate charities. Employees who value their job and chances for promotion know enough to show up. In journalism and social service, many firms expect prospective employees to serve unpaid internships, or prove themselves as volunteers, sometimes for months or years, before being considered for paid employment or full-time jobs. Also, the average work week in North America is getting ever longer,[65] electronic mail demands instant response, and cell phones mean no employee is ever really out of reach, off limits, or off the job.

[41] While some salaried employees in managerial and professional positions put in ninety hour weeks and more, the wage worker may be even worse off. In the United States, under the 1938 Fair Labor Standards Act,[66] those classified as workers are not allowed to refuse overtime. While this time is compensated, it is often anything but voluntary. A lineman employed by Central Maine Power in 1999, for example, was killed when he grasped a 7200 volt cable without first putting on his insulating gloves. The man had worked two and a half days with a total of five hours off; every time he went home to bed, he was called back to work. Had he refused, he certainly would have been disciplined, and might have been fired. The coroner's inquest identified fatigue as a cause of death.[67] Firefighters in Connecticut took a different approach to lighten long hours of work. They launched a case challenging mandatory overtime as unconstitutional under the Thirteenth Amendment, the provision that bans slavery.[68] Ultimately, however, the firefighters lost.

[42] Theft of time by employers, on the other hand, is neither disciplined nor criminalized. Quite the reverse; in the fall of 2000, legislators in the United States introduced a bill to prevent information economy workers, including computer network analysts, database administrators, technology workers, sales personnel and the like, from demanding or receiving overtime pay. In the province of Ontario, the revised Employment Standards Act 2000,[69] which came into effect on September 4, 2001, extends, via the employees' agreement, the maximum work week from forty-eight to sixty hours. Also, overtime pay has been decreased by allowing employers to average it over a maximum four week period[70] and vacation days can now be assigned at the employers' convenience.[71] Although an employees' agreement is required for long hours of work and averaging overtime pay entitlements, few employees will say no to their employers. At the same time, unionized shops are forced to post instructions in every workplace telling employees how to dissolve unions.[72] However, there is no reciprocal provision for non-unionized workplaces to post instructions telling employees how to unionize. Like much similar legislation, the Employment Standards Act 2000 is justified as modern, necessary, and efficient, and seen as an Act that will allow Ontario employers to compete in the global economy.

[43] While the drive towards ever greater economies of production was predicted long ago by Karl Marx and other nineteenth-century theorists, the extent, speed, relentlessness, and success of this project was not. Disciplinary demands have been imperialistic, creeping up the job hierarchy from shop floor, to office, to the executive suite, and into every public and private institution and sector. Even senior management now faces demands for more disciplined, intensive performance, more transparency, and accountability. Nor was the unique role that social science disciplines would come to play foreseen. For many theorists of modernity, knowledge was a tool of enlightenment which would set workers free. Instead, disciplines have forged alliances with capital to produce technologies, assign meaning and attach particular practices to concepts of productivity and efficiency, thereby increasing expectation and performance demands. The knowledge claims of social science and law have penetrated deep into the psyche, changing habits of mind, thought, language, and culture in ways that transform the meaning of "exploitation" and "consent." The result is that, to a considerable extent, North American employees constitute their own domination. This does not make the domination any less real, nor does it mean that employees reap equal benefits from domination. The costs of higher productivity, including surveillance, less freedom of movement and thought, and escalating and unceasing demands for more physical and mental effort, are primarily borne by employees, the 80 to 90 per cent of the population that is depend-

ent on wages. The benefits of productivity, namely prestige and power, stock options, bonuses, private yachts, and jets, are disproportionately distributed among elites who sit atop corporate hierarchies in the developed world and, to a lesser degree, their counterparts in politics and academia.[73]

[44] Collective and positive resistance to the disciplinary spiral in the workplace has been surprisingly weak. As explored throughout this commentary, when progress and modernity are defined through concepts such as productivity and efficiency, allied with science and legitimized through law, resistance is difficult to conceptualize, let alone build. As noted above, the fact that disciplinary demands have not been confined to those at the bottom of the class, race, and gender hierarchy, although they are most intense and punitive there, and that material benefits have not gone exclusively to those at the top of corporate hierarchies, even though these elites have reaped a disproportionate share, has also produced widespread acquiescence, if not consent. Thus, resistance through law has been couched, primarily, in negative and individualistic terms, through legalizing the right to resist surveillance through privacy law, rather than, for example, formulating a charter of employee rights. The discourse of privacy leaves the primacy of private ownership unchallenged, never interrogating its status as a master claim, one that confers all power except that which can be wrestled away through special, exceptional claims, on employers. To those who cannot make ownership claims, it allocates a limited and almost indefensible space. If you are not wasting time or doing something you should not be doing, why do you object to urine tests, surveillance cameras, and time-monitoring devices? Are you in favour of malingering, theft, or inefficiency?

[45] The emergence of theft of time, as concept, practice, and law, is the latest development in an intense, four hundred-year-old struggle to transform the unruly feudal peasant into an efficient, profit-maximizing unit of production.[74] Theft of time is but the most recent example of the intensification of disciplinary demands in modern societies. The ultimate goal is to create an employee who will be resigned, if not content, because happy employees are more productive; intelligent (but only to a narrow, employer-prescribed end) untiring; compliant; loyal; respectful, and grateful for a job. At the end of the day, the happy employee will turn into the happy consumer, buying the products and services on offer and defining his or her identity through these goods. Through science, technology, and law this process has gone from strength to strength. To create alternative ways of seeing, acting, and doing, would require challenging all components in this disciplinary spiral.

The Criminal Law Process

(a) The [Nova Scotia] Royal Commission on the Donald Marshall, Jr., Prosecution†

Royal Commission on the Donald Marshall, Jr., Prosecution

FACTUAL FINDINGS

Introduction

We find:

- That the criminal justice system failed Donald Marshall, Jr. at virtually every turn from his arrest and conviction in 1971 up to — and even beyond — his acquittal by the Supreme Court of Nova Scotia (Appeal Division) in 1983.
- That this miscarriage of justice could have and should have been prevented if persons involved in the criminal justice system had carried out their duties in a professional and/or competent manner.
- That Marshall was not the author of his own misfortune.
- That the miscarriage of justice was real and not simply apparent.
- That the fact that Marshall was a Native was a factor in his wrongful conviction and imprisonment.

On May 28, 1971, four people came together in a brief, unplanned nighttime encounter in Wentworth Park in Sydney, Nova Scotia. One of them, a 17-year-old black youth named Sandford (Sandy) William Seale, was killed. Another, a 17-year-old Micmac Indian named Donald Marshal, Jr., was wrongfully convicted of his murder, and was sentenced to life imprisonment in November 1971.

Eleven years later, after Marshall's lawyer, Stephen Aronson, brought forward information suggesting Marshall did not commit the murder, the RCMP reinvestigated the case for a second time. After that investigation confirmed that Marshall did not kill Seale, he was released on parole and subsequently acquitted by the Supreme Court of Nova Scotia (Appeal Division) in May 1983. A third man, Roy Newman Ebsary, who was one of the four people who had come together in Wentworth Park that night, was charged with killing Seale and was convicted of manslaughter following three trials. He was sentenced to three years in prison. In 1986, the Court of Appeal reduced his sentence to one year. He died in 1988.

The events that took place in Wentworth Park in those few moments on that spring night in 1971 have spawned numerous official inquiries and proceedings, including three formal police investigations, two preliminary inquiries, four trials, three appeals to the Supreme Court of Nova Scotia (Appeal Division), a Reference to the Court of Appeal and two Royal Commissions, including this one. The cost in dollars has been tremendous. The toll in human anguish has been incalculable.

The principal task of this Royal Commission has been to determine why Donald Marshall, Jr. was wrongfully convicted and to make recommendations

---

† Nova Scotia, *Report of the Royal Commission on the Donald Marshall, Jr., Prosecution*: Findings and Recommendations, Vol. 1 (Halifax, N.S.: The Commission, 1989) at 15–18 (Chair: T. Alexander Hickman). Copyrighted by the Province of Nova Scotia. [Notes and/or references omitted.]

to ensure that such a miscarriage of justice does not happen again.

First, what did go wrong? Although we will examine in detail each of the relevant events of the Marshall case from its beginning on May 28, 1971, to our appointment on October 28, 1986, we can begin with the following general conclusions that flow from our consideration of all of the evidence.

The criminal justice system failed Donald Marshall, Jr. at virtually every turn, from his arrest and wrongful conviction in 1971 up to — and even beyond — his acquittal by the Court of Appeal in 1983. The tragedy of this failure is compounded by the evidence that this miscarriage of justice could have — and should have — been prevented, or at least corrected quickly, if those involved in the system had carried out their duties in a professional and/or competent manner.

If, for example, the Sergeant of Detectives of the Sydney City Police Department had not prematurely concluded — on the basis of no supporting evidence and in the face of compelling contradictory evidence — that Donald Marshall, Jr. was responsible for the death of Sandy Seale, Marshall would almost certainly never have been charged with the crime. If the Crown prosecutor had provided full disclosure to Marshall's lawyers of the conflicting statements provided by alleged eyewitnesses; if Marshall's lawyers had conducted a more thorough defence, including pressing for such disclosure and conducting their own investigations into the killing; if the judge in the case had not made critical errors in law; Marshall would almost certainly not have been convicted.

Even after he was convicted and sent to prison, however, there were numerous other occasions when this miscarriage of justice should have been discovered and rectified, but was not.

For example, when the Crown received evidence shortly after Marshall's conviction suggesting Roy Ebsary might have been involved in the killing, it did not disclose this information to Marshall's counsel. When the RCMP reinvestigated the murder as a result of that new evidence, it did so in such an entirely inadequate and unprofessional manner that it prevented his wrongful conviction from being discovered. During Marshall's appeal of his conviction, his lawyers failed to identify and argue critical errors of law which occurred during the trial. Similarly, the Court of Appeal failed to identify these errors.

When Marshall's wrongful conviction was finally discovered in the early 1980s, the Court of Appeal compounded the miscarriage of justice by describing Marshall as having contributed in large measure to his own conviction and by stating that any miscar- riage of justice in the case was more apparent than real.

This Commission has concluded that Donald Marshall, Jr. was not to blame for his own convic- tion and that the miscarriage of justice against him was real.

That is the inescapable, and inescapably distress- ing, conclusion we have reached after listening to 113 witnesses during 93 days of public hearings in Halifax and Sydney in 1987 and 1988 and after sift- ing through 176 exhibits submitted in evidence dur- ing those hearings.

But concluding that Donald Marshall, Jr. was the victim of a miscarriage of justice does not answer the complex question of why Marshall came to be wrongfully convicted and imprisoned in the first place. Was it because he was a Native? Was it because he was poor?

To answer those admittedly difficult questions, this Commission has looked not only at how the criminal justice system in Nova Scotia operated in the Marshall case, but it has also compared the han- dling of the Marshall case with the way in which the system dealt with cases involving powerful and prom- inent public officials. At the same time, we commis- sioned independent research studies to find out how Natives and Blacks are treated in the criminal justice system.

From all of that, the evidence is once again per- suasive and the conclusion inescapable that Donald Marshall, Jr. was convicted and sent to prison, in part at least, because he was a Native person. We will look at these issues in more detail in our section on visible minorities in the justice system later in this volume.

Having reached these conclusions, we take the next logical step in fulfilling our mandate and ask what can and should be done to make sure that the criminal justice system lives up to this promise of equal justice for all? That too is a question we will deal with later in this volume of our Report.

There are certain issues, however, that we will not be addressing in our Report. For example, this Royal Commission is not recommending that crimi- nal charges be laid against any specific individuals arising out of the findings of fact we will make. Although some counsel urged us to do so during their final arguments to the Royal Commission, it is our opinion that a decision on whether or not any charges should be laid is one that should be taken by the appropriate authorities after due consideration of all relevant factors. We agree with the senti- ments expressed by the Attorney General of Ontario when establishing the Grange Commission, sentiments which were concurred in by the Ontario Court of Appeal in *Re Nelles et al. and Grange et al.* (1984), 9 D.L.R. (4th) 79 at p. 84:

> The purpose of a public inquiry is not to attach criminal culpability. It is not a forum to put individuals on trial. The just and proper place to make and defend allegations of crime or civil liability is in a court of law.
>
> In this context, I am reminded of the remarks of an eminent Ontario jurist, Mr. Justice Riddell of the Ontario Court of Appeal, whose observations almost 50 years ago are equally applicable today.
>
> A Royal Commission is not for the purpose of trying a case or a charge against anyone, any person or any institution — but for the purpose of informing the people concerning the facts of the matter to be enquired into. The object of a Royal Commission is to determine facts, not try individuals or institutions, and this consideration is sufficient to guide the Commissioner in the performance of his duty.

The Court went on to say:

> A public inquiry is not the means by which investigations are carried out with respect to the commission of particular crimes.... Such an inquiry is a coercive procedure and is quite incompatible with our notion of justice in the investigation of a particular crime and the determination of actual or probable criminal or civil responsibility.

We share this view.

Further, we are not — as some have also urged us to do — specifically recommending that Donald Marshall, Jr. receive additional compensation. The Commission accepted that a settlement had been negotiated, and accordingly, heard no evidence on the amount of compensation that may have otherwise been appropriate. However, the Commission did examine the process by which compensation was ultimately negotiated and paid. We have concluded that the negotiations were strongly influenced by factors which, in our view, were either wrong or inappropriate, and that as a result the compensation process was so seriously flawed that the amount paid should be re-evaluated.

(b) Understanding Over-representation†

Commission on Systemic Racism in the Ontario Criminal Justice System

Why are black people over-represented among prison admissions? What explains the dramatic increase in the imprisonment of black women and men since 1986/87? Why is there such a large difference in imprisonment rates of black and white people for some offences and much smaller differences, or even under-representation of black people, for other offences?

A superficial answer might be that the data "prove" that black people are inherently criminal. This explanation does not fit the facts. Equally superficial — and equally unconvincing — is the conclusion that all white police officers, lawyers and judges are blatantly racist and deliberately criminalize black people.

Consider the superficial view that race determines criminal behaviour, and that racial inequality in prison admissions merely reflects black people's inherent criminality.

How could race cause people to commit criminal offences? Is the answer in biology — could a gene related to dark skin, curly hair and broad noses cause people to commit crimes? Would this gene lead black people to specialize in drug trafficking? Does a gene cause white people to drive after drinking alcohol? Does pale skin and straight hair, or a gene related to these characteristics, prevent people from obstructing justice?

Consider also the dramatic increase in prison admissions of black people. How could a biological

---

† From the *Report of the Commission on Systemic Racism in the Ontario Criminal Justice System* (Toronto: Queen's Printer, 1995) at 95–105. © Queen's Printer for Ontario. Reproduced with permission. [Notes and/or references omitted.]

link between race and crime explain this? Surely the genetic make-up of black Ontarians did not suddenly change during the late 1980s and early 1990s.

Most important, if biology causes criminality, why are only a small percentage of black Ontarians in conflict with the law? Even if each prison admission represented one individual (which is not the case), 96 percent of black people were not admitted to prison in 1992/93. If a "race gene" caused black people to commit crimes, then most of Ontario's black residents, and few or no white Ontarians, would be in jail.

Such questions are absurd, as is the belief that biology explains criminal behaviour. There is no such thing as a criminality gene, nor, more fundamentally, is there any scientific evidence of a race gene. As Stephen Jay Gould states:

> Intense studies ... have detected not a single "race gene" — that is a gene present in all members of one group and none of another. Frequencies vary, often considerably, among groups, but all human races are much of a muchness.... [T]he great preponderance of human variation occurs within groups, not in the differences between them....
>
> Human groups do vary strikingly in a few highly visible characteristics (skin colour, hair form) — and these external differences may fool us into thinking that overall divergence must be great. But we know now that our usual metaphor of superficiality — skin deep — is literally accurate.[19]

Clearly then, the dark skins and curly hair of black people do not cause criminal behaviour. Nor does some other genetic difference lead black people to commit crimes. Since biology is not destiny, the explanation of racial inequalities in prison admissions must lie elsewhere.

Some people who rightly reject biological explanations of criminal activity find cultural ones persuasive. Recognizing that racial appearance cannot determine behaviour, they may think, nonetheless, that culture does. Are cultural propensities to criminality, violence or lack of respect for law and authority the reasons for racial differentials in admissions to Ontario's prisons?

If all or some black cultures are inherently criminal, but white cultures are not, why are the vast majority of prison admissions people from white cultures? Why are most black people (like most white people) not in conflict with the law? If black culture causes criminality, what explains the relatively low proportions of black admissions in 1986/87 and the massive increase since then?

Finally, how do cultural explanations of criminality account for what John Pitts calls "one of the few things we know with any certainty about the relationship between race and crime" — the evidence, documented in many countries, that crime rates among immigrants are lower than among persons born in the country?[20] Crime rates among descendants of immigrants, however, tend to be the same as or higher than crime rates of the dominant culture.[21] If culture explains crime, why are members of the immigrant generation, who presumably have the allegedly criminal tendencies of an "alien" culture in its strongest form, less likely to commit offences than their children and grandchildren raised in the culture of the new society?

The answer, of course, is that cultural characteristics do not explain the evidence. As Pitts states,

> Crime rates are neither a simple product of the proclivities of individuals nor of the cultural penchant of particular ethnic groups but, rather, a product of the chances, choices and solutions available within the milieu they enter. The rise in crime rate among the second and subsequent generations of an immigrant group is a product of ... [the] process whereby people make an accommodation with, and establish ways of being within, a new social environment. In the process some "incoming" young people will adopt the strategies and behaviours of the established social group [where they live].[22]

Cultures may be real and enriching forces in people's lives, but they are not "timeless and inexorable determinants of behaviour."[23] They do not, in other words, dictate what people do. Culture cannot cause people to commit crimes or account for racial inequalities in prison admissions. Far from explaining anything, beliefs that some cultures are inherently violent, criminal, anti-social or disrespectful of law are stereotypes that racialize others. They promote constructions of races as real, different and unequal, and allow people to act as if such constructions were true.

Cultural characteristics of specific racialized groups or minority groups in general clearly cannot explain racial differentials in prison admissions. So how do we explain these differentials in Ontario prisons? In jurisdictions where disproportionate imprisonment of black people has been openly recognized for years, research suggests two general explanations, which may overlap. One explanation emphasizes the influence of social and economic inequality on behaviour; the other points to differential enforcement of the criminal law, including racial discrimination in the administration of justice.

SOCIAL AND ECONOMIC INEQUALITY

Some studies of differential imprisonment emphasize failures to integrate black and other racialized people into the wider society. They draw on evidence of disproportionately high rates of unemployment and dead-end jobs among racialized people, particularly young adults. They also cite poor housing conditions and lack of educational opportunities. These studies make the important point that social and economic opportunities are racialized. That is, members of racialized groups are much more likely than members of non-racialized groups to have limited opportunities. Since people with limited social and economic opportunities are most likely to be policed, prosecuted and punished as criminals,[24] racialized people are more likely than white people to be in conflict with the law. Thus they are over-represented at all stages of the criminal justice process, including prisons.

Three important elements of this explanation are worth emphasizing. First, those who adopt it may generally accept that racialized people are over-represented in prison populations, at least in part, because of greater participation in some criminal activities.[25] They do not accept, however, that biology or culture is the reason for higher rates of participation. Nor do they always see racism in the wider society as the only contributing factor.

According to this view, the social and economic conditions of people's lives are crucial to their participation in criminal activity. The criminality rate should be the same for racialized and non-racialized people where these conditions are the same. If, on the other hand, opportunities are unequally distributed, members of the socially disadvantaged groups are likely to commit a higher proportion of crimes than others. If a higher proportion of a particular racialized group has limited opportunities, compared with other groups, then the average crime rate for this group is likely to be higher.

Second, according to this approach sub-groups with similar life opportunities — in racialized and non-racialized communities alike — are likely to display similar levels of criminality. Young, unemployed white men living in areas of social stress and economic deprivation, for example, would be [as] likely to commit crimes as their young, male, unemployed black neighbours. Conversely, as Pitts noted of the British context, "...the amount of street crime perpetrated by 28-year-old, male, British Afro-Caribbean chartered accountants is the same as that perpetrated by 28-year-old, male, British Caucasian chartered accountants, namely 0.0 per cent."[26] The point is that any difference in street crime rates of British Afro-Caribbean men and British Caucasian men arises because fewer of the former have opportunities for economic advancement.

Finally, this viewpoint does not imply that lack of opportunities or social inequality causes individuals — whether white or racialized — to commit crimes. It does say, rather, that people with limited life-chances may be more likely to view some forms of criminal activity as more attractive or exciting than their other choices.[27] They may see crime as a means to acquire material goods otherwise unobtainable. They may fail to respect the rules of a society that excludes them from its benefits. They may feel they have much to gain and little to lose from criminal activity. Crime may make them feel powerful. It may add excitement to, or provide a means of escape from otherwise dreary lives. Crime, in short, may be a rational choice.

Experts who make these observations do not, of course, excuse or condone the actions of any individual who harms others. They recognize that crime is a serious social problem, hurting immediate victims and the families and friends of victims and perpetrators. They know that fear of crime may severely restrict people's lives. But since imprisonment does not appear to deter or in any other way significantly to reduce crime, it is important to develop strategies likely to work rather than to continue with those known to fail. More emphasis on or investment in crime prevention, as opposed to punishment, is their answer.

DIFFERENTIAL ENFORCEMENT

Other explanations of racialized patterns in prison admissions also stress social and economic conditions, but from a different perspective. These conditions are seen as explanations of who is caught, not who commits crimes.[28] Enforcement practices, rather than offending behaviours, are key.

People who hold this view argue that involvement in criminal activity is not limited to an identifiable group of anti-social and marginal individuals. Criminality is instead a widespread social phenomenon in which many ordinary and apparently respectable people participate. Drawing on studies of employers, employees, taxpayers, retailers and service suppliers, police officers, university students, youths and drug users, and women and children abused by men, these experts conclude that with regard to crime "everybody does it" at least occasionally.[29]

If criminal activity is indeed widespread among the population, the explanation for racial inequality in prison admissions cannot be attributed mainly to disproportionate involvement in crime. Studies in Canada and elsewhere consistently show, for example, that more than 90 percent of young men say they have committed criminal offences.[30] This indicates that variations in offending rates by race or economic class may be small. Variations in enforcement practices likely make the difference.

Law enforcement is not the only possible response to crime, nor is it always desirable. Many studies suggest that law enforcement is costly, blunt and not very effective in reducing crime.[31] Since law enforcement resources are finite, priorities must be established and variations in enforcement practices are inevitable. The critical question is what criteria are used to decide which offenders and which offences the criminal justice system should select.

Formal and informal selection criteria are used in law enforcement. Experts suggest that these criteria make black and other racialized people particularly vulnerable. They point, first, to poverty. Study after study shows that offences by those at the bottom of social and economic hierarchies are more likely to be policed, prosecuted and punished severely than offences committed by wealthier people.[32] The implication is clear: a society that allows racialization to influence people's economic opportunities is likely to produce racial inequality in its prison populations.

Even if criminal activity is widespread, patterns of offending behaviour differ according to the opportunities available. Those with access to other people's money through their employment or profession, for example, are much more likely to embezzle funds than to sell drugs on a street corner. They are also less likely to be caught. Crimes committed in the privacy of corporate offices tend to be more difficult to detect and prosecute than street crimes because of their low visibility, and because the law generally shelters these private spaces from state officials.

Enforcement practices clearly vary with the seriousness of offences committed, and also with factors such as whether and how offences are reported, ease of identification and apprehension, and likelihood of conviction. Racialization in the wider society may also influence law enforcement practices. The criminal justice system requires police officers, lawyers, justices of the peace and judges to make judgments about individuals and their behaviour. Though the law provides a general framework for these judgments, it seldom specifies fixed rules that dictate outcomes. Instead, the law sets out broad standards that allow considerable scope for interpretation of the standards, the individual and the (alleged) offence.

For example, when deciding if someone should be imprisoned before trial, judges or justices of the peace are expected to predict whether the accused, if released, will fail to appear for trial or is substantially likely to commit a criminal offence before the trial. Rarely does a judge or justice of the peace have much information about the accused relevant to such a prediction.* Consequently their decisions must draw more heavily on intuition and what lawyers responding to our survey describe as "empathy." This in turn increases subjectivity in decision-making. It creates conditions under which lack of familiarity with racialized communities may lead a decision-maker to rely subconsciously on stereotypes.

Because the processes leading to discretionary choices in the criminal justice system are subtle and complex, studies of racial discrimination in this system use an approach that is now well established in human rights law. They begin with evidence of adverse impact — such as our findings of racial disproportion in prison admissions — and investigate how far legitimate non-discriminatory factors explain the adverse impact. Racial inequalities that remain after these factors have been taken into account are then treated as evidence of racial discrimination that is tolerated by the criminal justice system.

Using this approach, studies in many jurisdictions have documented direct and indirect discrimination that results in over-representation of black or other racialized people in prisons.[33] Later in this Report we document the Commission's findings that racial discrimination in policing, bail hearings and sentencing decisions affects Ontario prison admissions. The remainder of this chapter presents a brief overview of the various stages where the exercise of discretionary authority may be susceptible to the introduction of racialization.

DECISIONS THAT PRODUCE IMPRISONMENT: AN OVERVIEW

The criminal justice process involves a great deal of interaction among different people with different roles. Decisions made at one stage affect those made later. It is essential to view the system as a whole. Imprisonment is always ordered by a particular judge or justice of the peace, but that decision results from the cumulative choices made by police officers, crown attorneys, defence counsel and probation officers.

Entry into the Criminal Justice Process

In general, accused persons are drawn into the criminal justice system in two ways. Reports of crime may come from victims or observers. In addition, accused persons may be identified by proactive policing.

Victims are an important source of information about violent offences and property crimes. Their decision about whether to report a crime is crucial. Surveys in Canada and elsewhere show that large proportions of individuals harmed by criminal offences do not report them to the police.[34]

These surveys raised the question of whether racialization influences people in selectively reporting offences. As yet, no Canadian data deal with this question, and evidence from other jurisdictions is mixed. Some studies indicate racial inequalities result from victim reporting;[35] others do not show such patterns.[36]

Offences may also be identified through planned and systematic police work. Police may seek evidence of specific offences or focus their attention on specific geographic areas or particular communities. Police may also initiate encounters, such as stopping vehicles and people on the street during routine patrols. Whether or not it is planned, such proactive policing is highly discretionary.

Much evidence from other jurisdictions indicates that this type of policing disproportionately pulls black people into the criminal justice system.[37] Officers working on "gut feelings" or popular stereotypes may stop black people more than others, and may question them more aggressively. Hostile encounters may not only uncover offences but also produce them.

Police Discretion to Charge

Once the police have information identifying a person with an alleged criminal offence, they must decide whether to charge the suspect. Police officers are not legally or professionally obligated to lay charges, even if they believe they have enough grounds (evidence) to meet the test. They may instead do nothing, simply caution suspects, or advise victims how to lay charges themselves.

The scope of police officers' discretion in laying charges is extremely broad. For example, an 18-year-old who shoves another and runs off with the other's baseball cap could be charged with robbery (punishable by up to life imprisonment), theft (two years), assault (five years) or possession of stolen property (two years). As an alternative to laying charges, the police could instead talk with the teenager, per-

haps in the presence of family members. This range of choices provides considerable scope for police officers' personal attitudes, perceptions and stereotypes to influence their decision. Even when an officer is acting with conscious fairness and objectivity, subtle influences may arise such as, in this example, whether the teenager comes from what the officer perceives to be a "good" or "stable" family. This assessment might lead to the conclusion that a black youth should be subjected to the criminal justice process, whereas a white youth could be dealt with adequately in the home.

Studies of the extent to which racialization influences police discretion over charging tend to concentrate on outcomes because police interpretations of alleged criminal incidents and their classification are not open to scrutiny. Formal records of officers' conclusions on whether and what to charge are available and may be studied, but the process by which officers arrive at these conclusions is not always obvious. Evidence from some jurisdictions, such as Britain, clearly shows that police discretion not to charge has racialized outcomes, at least with regard to youths. Canadian studies document class and other biases in police practices, particularly in their processing of Aboriginal people.[38]

Imprisonment before Trial

Once a charge is laid, the next critical set of decisions concern whether to hold accused persons in prison or to seek other controls on them during the period before trial. *Criminal Code* provisions suggest that once the accused have been processed by police and told of their duty to appear in court to answer the charges against them, the vast majority of accused persons should be set free.

However, a judge or justice of the peace may order imprisonment before trial if it is necessary to ensure that the accused person will attend court for trial. The accused may also be detained if it is necessary to protect the public. The decision to detain or free the accused takes into account the seriousness of the charges and accused's criminal record as well as criteria such as "ties to the community,"[39] employment status and mental health.

Racialization may influence police decisions about whether to release accused persons, and may affect the bail process through information the police supply to crown attorneys. Racialization may also be introduced through the criteria used to predict whether the accused will fail to appear at trial or is "substantially likely" to commit a criminal offence before trial. There is little Canadian research on imprisonment before trial. Some studies conducted in other jurisdictions have found evidence that racialization influences pre-trial release decisions;[40] others are inconclusive.[41] Chapter 5 reports our findings that racial inequalities do appear in the outcomes of bail decisions.

Processing Charges

Once charges have been laid, crown attorneys assume responsibility for how they are processed. Crown attorneys have a professional duty to scrutinize charges and decide whether some or all should be withdrawn because of lack of evidence or because prosecution would not be in the public interest. They may also engage in resolution discussions with defence counsel to see if charges can be disposed of without a contested trial. This may also be an important step for the exercise of crown discretion.

Since crown attorneys make these decisions mostly on the basis of written material rather than interaction with accused persons, there seems to be little scope for racialization to influence their choices. Nonetheless, research in other jurisdictions suggests that the possibility cannot be dismissed.[42] Much of the information available to crown attorneys is supplied by police officers who have met the accused and may have formed racialized judgments. For example, clues to accused persons' racial origin may be recorded on paper. Their names, countries of birth and physical descriptions are all normally included in the information available to crown attorneys. Moreover, some residential areas are identified with racialized communities, so that even an address may be taken to indicate the race of an accused. The exercise of crown discretion is discussed later in this Report (see chapters 5, 6 and 7).

Court Resolutions

Even if charges have been resolved through plea discussions, the accused person still appears in court. This appearance is a public announcement of the conviction and sentence. If the crown attorney and defence counsel have agreed on sentence before the court appearance, they present their agreement to the judge. Judges always have discretion to decide on an appropriate sentence, but they generally accept joint proposals. Consequently, in cases with a guilty plea, potential for racial inequality in sentencing may arise from the resolution discussions that led to the plea and from judges' responses to sentencing proposals.

An accused who contests the charge(s) appears in court for a trial at which verdicts and any punishment are determined. These are adversarial processes in which crown attorneys and defence lawyers compete to influence decision-makers (judges and juries). If there is any possibility that decision-makers may be swayed by racialization, one side or the other may use it (see Chapter 7).

This risk has been raised concerning jury trials of white police officers charged with shooting black persons.[43] It has also been addressed concerning jury trials of black and other racialized accused. In *R. v. Parks*, the Ontario Court of Appeal specifically acknowledged that anti-black racism may influence potential jurors in criminal trials.[44] Sentencing is highly discretionary. The *Criminal Code* sets out maximum sentences for each offence, but offers judges little further guidance about the appropriate penalty for a typical offender who commits a routine offence. Although appellate decisions provide a framework for sentencing, the trial judge retains a broad discretion to determine sentence.

Concerns about inconsistency in sentencing decisions in Canada and other jurisdictions are long-standing. Research has identified "extraordinary discrepancies in almost all aspects of sentencing"[45] and noted that "disparity between courts in sentencing practices ... is an established fact."[46] In this connection the prison admissions data presented earlier in this chapter raises the question of how far the disparity reflects racialization in the criminal justice system.

There are clearly strong and widespread perceptions that judges discriminate against accused people from racialized groups.* Evidence concerning sentencing practices in Canada and other jurisdictions is mixed. Many studies show racial inequalities in sentencing practices;[47] others do not or are inconclusive.[48] In Chapter 8 we report the Commission's findings that racial inequalities do appear in sentencing decisions.

CONCLUSION

There can be few more significant interventions by the public into the private than imprisoning someone ... the decision to imprison a person, to take away their capacity to act in private society and to subject them constantly and totally to the supervision of the state, stands therefore in need of particularly clear justification by law.[49]

Imprisonment is society's most vivid and extreme form of exclusion. The dramatic findings presented in this chapter show that black women, men and youth in Ontario disproportionately experience imprisonment, and that this massive inequality in Ontario prison admissions is a relatively recent occurrence. Ontario simply must not continue to admit black people to prisons at the current rates.†

These findings simply cannot be rationalized by suggesting that black people are inherently more criminal than others. Nor can they be rationalized as reflecting a criminal justice system consisting of officials who are driven by racial hatred.

However, racialization in Canadian society is a recognized fact both inside and outside the criminal justice system. Wherever broad discretion exists, racialization can influence decisions and produce racial inequality.

The criminal justice system operates through a series of highly discretionary decision-making stages. Discretion is exercised in subtle, complex and interactive ways, which leave considerable scope for racialization to influence practices and decisions, and for bias to be transmitted from one stage of the process to others.

In the remainder of this Report we document evidence of the influence of racialization on criminal justice practices, and evidence that this influence is tolerated — evidence of systemic racism. We also make recommendations for securing racial equality in the criminal justice system.

(c) Crown Culture and Wrongful Convictions: A Beginning†

Melvyn Green

A. INTRODUCTION

Wrongful murder convictions no longer shock the conscience of the legal community. Still, the occurrence of three such convictions in less than a decade in the Province of Newfoundland and Labrador was, by any measure, a disturbing development. Greg Parsons, one of the three wronged men, was convicted of the 1991 killing his mother. On appeal, a new trial was ordered. Parsons was later exonerated through DNA testing. The Crown's efforts to resolve the matter by way of a stay of proceedings was opposed by the defence. In the end, the Crown agreed to enter no evidence and Parsons was acquitted. Subsequently, another man confessed to and was convicted of the murder for which Parson was wrongly convicted. Randy Druken's fate was less fortunate. Like Parsons, the Court of Appeal reversed his 1995 conviction for murder and the new trial it ordered was never prosecuted. Unlike Parsons, the Crown entered a stay of proceedings. That stay has long dissolved, but the Province has steadfastly refused to recognize the widely-held and well-founded belief that Druken was factually innocent

of his girlfriend's demise. The third man, Ronald Dalton, was convicted in 1998 of killing his wife. It took eight years for the Court of Appeal to hear Dalton's appeal, and almost no time for the Court to order a new trial on the basis of fresh evidence demonstrating that there was no murder: the death was accidental. A jury agreed, acquitting Dalton at his second trial. The Province has thus far refused to recognize the acquittal as a finding of factual innocence.

The Province did strike a public inquiry, headed by the former Chief Justice of Canada, Antonio Lamer, to look into the events surrounding these three miscarriages of justice. In Dalton's case, the terms of reference restricted the inquiry to questions bearing on the appellate delay. The scope of inquiry in the other two cases was much broader, including all "practices or systemic issues" that may have contributed to these wrongful convictions. Police ineptitude undoubtedly played a part, as did a judicial failure to adequately protect against the risk of erroneous conviction. Prosecutorial conduct was also implicated and, in a rare departure for such inquiries, subject to modest institutional scrutiny.

† (2005) 29 Criminal Reports (6th) 262. Published by Carswell, a Thomson Reuters Business. Reproduced with permission. [Notes and/or references omitted.]

B. THE SYSTEMIC NATURE OF WRONGFUL CONVICTIONS

The phenomenon of wrongful convictions, and particularly the recent frequency of their disclosure in Canada, the United Kingdom and the USA, have discredited forever the suggestion that their occurrence is the aberrant product of a few maverick actors within an otherwise healthy criminal justice system. It is now roundly recognized that the causes of wrongful convictions are fundamentally systemic, and that the remedies, to prove effective, must be of the same order.

Wrongful convictions are best understood as the product of multiple system failures. Each presents its own constellation of factors that contribute to the miscarriage of justice. But there is a disheartening familiarity about them: in-custody informants, non-disclosure, mistaken identification, false confessions, "junk science", the mishandling of alibi witnesses and, of course, "tunnel vision".

Institutional elements also play a role. Indeed, the police, forensic facilities, trial and appellate courts and even provincial legal aid plans have all had their turn under the microscopes of social scientists and public inquiries. There are two conspicuous exceptions to this wide-ranging review: the defence bar and the office of the Crown prosecutor. This paper addresses the latter area of institutional neglect.[1]

Certainly, the conduct of individual Crown attorneys has been scrutinized — and, on occasion, found wanting — at several public inquiries into wrongful convictions. The risk that prosecutors, like the police, may succumb to "tunnel vision" has frequently been noted. And senior Crown attorneys have recently acknowledged, if only theoretically, that prosecutorial attitudes and practices may have a role in the genesis of wrongful convictions.[2] What is still missing is any critical analysis of the *institution* of "the prosecutor" — of those interdependent roles and functions that make up the Crown law office irrespective of the particular inhabitants of those roles at any given moment — and of how that institution contributes to the manufacture of wrongful convictions.

C. CROWN CULTURE

Individual prosecutors come and go. There are some things, however, about the very office of the Crown that both shape the behaviour of individual prosecutors and persist over time. It is at this level — elevated from the conduct of individual office holders — that one can speak of *systemic* factors that con-tributed to the occurrence of factually wrongful convictions. In the words of the *Morin Report*, these are factors "which transcend the particular case and speak generally to the administration of criminal justice."[3]

Social science research has long recognized the existence of a "police culture," a set of beliefs and attitudes that influence the thinking, loyalties and conduct of individual officers. Crown counsel are no more immune than the police to the laws of social dynamics. They too share a belief system that arises from their institutional mandate — in short, a "Crown culture." The phrase itself is neutral. That prosecutors share values and norms is of no necessary concern to the administration of justice. What is of concern is a Crown culture that places paramount value on winning, that confuses its functions with those of the police, and that stubbornly resists the prospect of factual error. It is this historical concentration of attitudes, practices and beliefs that gives rise to the tunnel vision, blinkered exercise of discretion and institutional tenacity that contributes to both wrongful convictions and their perpetuation.

While police culture has attracted considerable study, the culture of the Canadian prosecutor's office lies virtually unexplored. There have, of course, been learned studies of the powers and responsibilities of officers of the Crown.[4] There are ample policy manuals and much jurisprudence on the norms governing prosecutors' conduct. What is missing is a contemporary sociology of Crown law officers, a social anthropology of how legal norms and policy are translated into the conduct of everyday prosecutorial life and, *in particular*, the part these institutional and cultural features play in the creation and perseverance of factually wrongful convictions.[5]

D. THE POWER OF THE CROWN

This would all be of purely academic interest but for the central role of the Crown in any prosecution. As Wayne Gorman, then Director of Public Prosecutions (DPP) for Newfoundland and Labrador, observed, "[n]o other participant in the Canadian criminal trial process wields such immense power."[6] This power flows from the immense discretion exercised by the Crown at every stage of a prosecution. These decisions are critical to the life-cycle of most prosecutions and, where factually innocent persons are involved, crucial to both the occurrence and endurance of their wrongful convictions. As the Supreme Court noted in *R. v. Beare* (1988), 45 C.C.C. (3d) 57, 66 C.R. (3d) 97, at 76 [C.C.C.], "[prosecutorial] discretion is an essential feature of the criminal justice system." The exercise of this discretion is almost always institutionally informed.

E. THE CONTRIBUTION OF PUBLIC INQUIRIES

But for rare instances, Canadian wrongful convictions have been generally free of the conscious corruption and deliberate perversions of justice that characterize some notorious American and British cases. The role of the Crown in Canadian disasters of justice, like that of the police, appears more attributable to institutionally-rooted failings or defects than any conscious malice. Commissions of inquiry into Canadian wrongful homicide convictions have enjoyed broad mandates that expressly direct the Commission's attention to these systemic issues. Their published reports recognize, if subtly, that Crown culture may contribute to the genesis and perseverance of wrongful convictions. The recent report of the FPT and the paper "Convicting the Innocent" by Bruce MacFarlane, the Deputy Attorney General of Manitoba, reinforce this view.

The lessons learned through public inquiries are a particularly valuable resource. They help to identify systemic problems, provide a framework for their analysis, and craft recommendations for institutional reform. The issue of "disclosure" affords one obvious example. Every Canadian historical wrongful conviction is attributable, at least in part, to the Crown's failure to provide full disclosure to the defence. The patent non-disclosure in all these cases was not a product of coincidence. It did not just happen that the prosecuting counsel in each case was corrupt or incompetent. Material non-disclosure happened because adversarial advantage was more highly valued than was the risk of injustice and, as a result, disclosure was treated as a matter of tactical discretion. It took the Marshall Inquiry[7] — its reporting of the close nexus between non-disclosure and that terrible miscarriage of justice, and its recommendations for wholesale reform in this area of the law — to launch a national debate about full disclosure that, ultimately, found constitutional purchase in the Supreme Court's judgment in *R. v. Stinchcombe* (1991), 8 C.R. (4th) 277. Subsequent public inquiries — Morin in Ontario, Sophonow in Manitoba and, now, Milgaard in Saskatchewan — have revealed a similar practice of non-disclosure, and, thus, the same institutionally-ingrained, historical vulnerability to injustice. Non-disclosure, in short, was a system-wide problem rooted in the culture of the Crown prosecutor.

F. THE ROLE OF THE CROWN: THE NORMATIVE MODEL V. INSTITUTIONAL PRACTICE

Normative descriptions of the role of Crown counsel make clear the push-pull tension that defines the office. As set out in Justice Rand's oft-cited passage in the seminal case of *R. v. Boucher* (1954), 110 C.C.C. 263, 20 C.R. 1 (S.C.C.) at 270 [C.C.C.]:

> It cannot be over-emphasized that the purpose of criminal prosecution is not to obtain a conviction; it is to lay before a jury what the Crown considers to be credible evidence relevant to what is alleged to be a crime. Counsel have a duty to see that all available legal proof of the facts is presented; it should be done firmly and pressed to its legitimate strength but it also must be done fairly. The role of the prosecutor excludes any notion of winning or losing; his function is a matter of public duty than which in civil life there can be none charged with greater personal responsibility. It is to be efficiently performed with an ingrained sense of the dignity, the seriousness and the justness of judicial proceedings.[8]

This model of prosecutorial conduct — that of a quasi-minister of justice — contains inherent contradictions. It is also fundamentally at odds with the adversarial nature of the criminal justice system. As a guide to prosecutorial conduct, it requires a delicate balancing. In practice, the duty to pursue seemingly inconsistent goals too often, perhaps routinely, yields to a simpler *modus operandi*, one consonant with a more basic adversarialism. Gross misconduct and unfairness is kept in check, but the obligation to positively protect innocence is abandoned, left exclusively to "the defence." The first line of protection from wrongful convictions, that borne by the Crown, thus evaporates. Fairness replaces justice as a Crown normative imperative, and let the chips fall where they may. Inevitably, innocence suffers.

Doctrinal architecture aside, there are a number of institutional impediments to the fulfillment of the *Boucherian* ideal. A comprehensive inventory awaits further research. Nonetheless, any tentative typology of those cultural features of "the prosecutor" that contribute to the manufacture of wrongful convictions and the institutional resistance to their remedy must include the linkage of "winning" to career advancement, professional self-selection and adherence to a law enforcement ideology.

The first of these institutional concerns focuses on prosecutorial success as the essential measure of professional performance. Daniel S. Medwed, an

American legal scholar, has observed that the evaluation and career advancement of prosecutors in the United States is largely a product of their conviction rates, thus "placing a premium on 'winning' ... [and] encourag[ing] prosecutors to secure convictions in each and every trial, a dangerous concept considering oftentimes the strongest cases against defendants result in plea bargains and [only the] weaker ones go to trial."[9] While there are no parallel studies of Canadian prosecutors, it would be naïve to believe that trial performance, particularly in difficult or notorious cases, is not employed as a barometer of professional success. Further, once having secured a conviction, the individual prosecutor and his office may become vested in the integrity of the conviction. These two realities, says Medwed, "have arguably led to an organizational 'conviction psychology,' an environment where convictions are prized above all and the minister of justice concept becomes a myth."[10]

The prosecutorial environment may be less skewed in Canada, but the view that the performance of Crown counsel is assessed, at least in part, on the basis of courtroom success, and the notion that there exists an institutional investment in conviction maintenance, both seem sound propositions to anyone immersed in Canadian criminal practice. And both are inherently inimical with the model of the Crown as vigilant guardian of innocence.

A second class of institutional resistance to innocence-protection relates more to psychological or personal characteristics. These include certain self-selecting features of the prosecutorial personality: a commitment to public service and protection; personal morality; a "gung ho," "macho" or "crime fighter" persona — a personality profile familiar to any member of the Canadian criminal bar.

For many prosecutors there is, as well, an ideological identification with law enforcement. The interpersonal relations that accompany the work of a prosecutor reinforce these sentiments, including reliance on the police, the teamwork essential to any substantial prosecution and, naturally enough, sympathy for the victims of crime, particularly those most traumatized by their experiences. Further, a prosecutor's perspective is inevitably distorted by his or her professional circumstances. As S.Z. Fisher has observed, prosecutors are

> constantly exposed to victims, police officers, civilian witnesses, probation officers and others who can graphically establish that the defendant deserves punishment, and who have no reason to be concerned with competing values of justice. [Whereas] the prosecutor is normally isolated from those — the defendant his family and

friends, and often, his witnesses — who might arouse the prosecutor's empathy or stimulate concern for treating him fairly.[11]

These sets of factors have broad impact, whether conscious or otherwise, on the mindset, forensic orientation and decision-making of any North American prosecutor. They influence both the pre-trial and post-conviction assessment of a case. Having secured a hard-won conviction, there is little psychological or institutional incentive on the part of the prosecution team to question the sanctity of the verdict.

G. TUNNEL VISION AND THE CROWN DUTY TO PREVENT INJUSTICE

Tunnel vision is a large part of the problem. It filters out information inconsistent with the prosecution theory, or compels the Crown to strain to rationalize it in ways that often test both credulity and common sense. It leads to prosecutorial overreach and overzealousness. Wrongful conviction cases are particularly vulnerable to these prosecutorial sins. Unlike most homicide prosecutions, those involving persons ultimately recognized as factually innocent almost always rest on the most infirm of evidence: suspect confessions, inherently unreliable and self-interested informants, fleeting eye-witness identification of strangers, the thinnest of circumstantial evidence, uncertain motive and, often enough, plausible "other suspects." Once locked into their theory of the case, and faced with credible forensic challenges, it is hardly surprising that the police sometimes fall victim to the "noble cause corruption" that leads, by way of more benign examples, to such practices as "assisting" identifying witnesses and discouraging those prepared to support an alibi.

Crown counsel fall prey to similar temptations in order to shore-up a weak case. Too often, they uncritically inherit the police brief. Rather than exercising scepticism, they compensate for the evidentiary infirmities by pushing the limits, thereby risking a wrongful conviction. The prosecutions of Milgaard, Morin and Sophonow well illustrate the proposition that the weaker the case, the greater the incentive to overreach. Indeed, this is exactly what must be assiduously guarded against.

Increasingly, Canadian courts have recognized that the Crown is duty-bound to ask tough questions and to conduct its own investigations in cases involving inherently suspect evidence. In a cautionary guide to Crown counsel,[12] Robert Frater, a senior prosecutor with the federal Department of Justice, observed that this evolving jurisprudence[13] is a further attempt to bring home to the Crown one of the primary lessons of the Morin Commission: the Crown must be ever vigilant to guard against "tunnel vision" — whether our own or that of the police. The Crown may have to poke and prod the investigators, to ensure that they were not afflicted by tunnel vision. Hard questions must be asked, and firm measures taken to ensure the integrity of the administration of justice.

There appears to be little basis to conclude that Crown counsel applied these critical faculties to their prosecution of Greg Parsons and Randy Druken, the two most recent wrongful homicide convictions to be submitted to the retrospective scrutiny of a public inquiry. Instead, faced with a frail case, they strove to extend the goalposts of admissibility in Parsons and, in both prosecutions, tendered inherently unreliable evidence that had little value other than prejudice. These were institutional failings, the product of a Crown culture driven to compensate for the evidentiary frailties of its case by risking the fairness of the trial process and, thereby, inviting the wrongful convictions that followed.

H. POST-CONVICTION TUNNEL VISION

(a) The Crown Power to Stay Prosecutions

A similar overzealousness infected the Crown's approach at the post-conviction stages in Parsons and Druken. There appears to have been no immediate effort to independently re-assess the evidence or take seriously the early defence claims of factual innocence. The possibility that the juries' verdicts were founded on unreliable evidence and cumulative prejudice never appears to have been seriously considered at any pre-terminal stage of the appeal or re-trial proceedings.

One practice in the course of wrongful conviction prosecutions that has thus far escaped investigation at public inquiries is the use of the Crown power to stay proceedings.[14] This power serves various purposes, including (as in the cases reviewed at the Lamer Inquiry) the termination of criminal proceedings without conceding either factual innocence or prosecutorial error.

Three points need be made about the use of a prosecutorial stay. First, it is a peremptory power. But for manifest impropriety, its exercise is unreviewable by the courts. It is a residual Crown prerogative, an exercise of executive power that defies both judicial review and any other form of accountability. It is, arguably, both undemocratic and

contrary to post-*Charter* public understandings of the rule of law. It is the Crown saying, "I am the Crown. I can do what I want. I don't have to answer to anyone."

Second, as just suggested, the privilege of the stay is such that the Crown never has to say it's sorry — or, for that matter, anything at all. Subject to the rarely exercised power to revive within one year, a stay permanently terminates a prosecution. While some defendants undoubtedly welcome this resolution, others — in particular, those who have endured a false accusation — want something more: failing an apology, at least some meaningful words of explanation.[15] Typically, there are none. Some empty phrases might accompany the entry of a stay — the invocation of an "ongoing investigation," the earnest "after careful consideration," the ever-handy "public interest" — but rarely anything of substance. The Crown, in short, never has to publicly justify its use of the power to stay proceedings.

All of which relates to the third facet of a Crown stay: its grey-zone message. A stay, it is clear, is not an exoneration. There is no admission here of a misconceived or ill-executed prosecution. The defendant is left in a legal — and very public — limbo: no longer an accused but forever shrouded in a cloud of officially induced suspicion. This is a conscious and likely deliberate consequence of a Crown decision to enter a stay of proceedings in cases informed by claims of factual innocence. It preserves, if barely, the propriety of the initial prosecution while indelibly tarnishing the defendant. For the innocent accused, it is a resolution far closer to purgatory than redemption. Indeed, the public appreciation of the pejorative meaning of a Crown stay of prosecution was recently reinforced by the federal Minister of Justice. In explaining why he had referred the Steven Truscott case to the Ontario Court of Appeal rather than a trial court following his Department's review of Truscott's s. 696.1 application, the Minister observed that the latter remedy would, on account of the case's antiquity, likely result in the entry of a Crown stay of proceedings. If, the Minister continued, Truscott sought exoneration, his best hope rested in a referral to the Court of Appeal where justice — rather than the ambiguity flowing from the exercise of a Crown stay — would prevail.[16]

(b) Crown Resistance to Acknowledging Error

The entry of terminal stays is but one means by which the Crown contributes to the perpetuation of wrongful convictions. In Sophonow, the Attorney

General of Manitoba sought leave, unsuccessfully, to reverse the "technical" acquittal entered by the Court of Appeal and, thereby, conduct a fourth trial of a factually innocent man whose conviction the Court came within a hair's breath of describing as perverse. In Morin, the Ontario Attorney General persuaded the Court of Appeal, and then the Supreme Court of Canada, to set aside the accused's jury acquittal in a case in which it knew (but the appellate courts did not) that suppressed disclosure (respecting, for example, the defendant's window of opportunity, the unreliability of two jailhouse informants and the results of various forensic experiments) only buttressed the defence claim of innocence. In Milgaard, the Saskatchewan Attorney General resorted to a stay of proceedings rather than permit either a retrial or an acquittal; Milgaard was not publicly cleared until years later when DNA testing both excluded Milgaard and positively identified Larry Fisher, the now-obvious culprit who had been tunnel-visioned off the police and Crown radar screens. The post-conviction treatment of Parsons and Druken in Newfoundland and Labrador mirrored this cultural temperament.

Prosecutorial resistance to righting wrongful convictions is deeply ingrained. There is a profound reluctance to acknowledge even the possibility of error, and an equally profound reluctance to admit any responsibility for a miscarriage of justice once incontrovertibly exposed. This posture is an endemic form of institutional denial that inhibits the reforms necessary to eliminate further wrongful convictions.

I.   SUGGESTIONS FOR REFORM

(a) Acknowledging Error: Ethos and Practice

Students of wrongful convictions have learned that the most effective prophylactic is institutional reform: the acknowledgement by police and prosecuting authorities of their vulnerabilities, and the sincere resolve of these authorities to institute those measures necessary to identify and inoculate themselves against the risk of error. It is a matter of accountability and essential to public confidence. It is also the justice and fairness side of the *Boucher* injunction.

Acknowledgement of the risk of wrongful conviction means recognizing that there are unexposed miscarriages of justice, and that there is an institutional responsibility to identify and remedy them. As James Lockyer, the co-founder of AIDWYC, noted

in accepting the G. Arthur Martin award in Toronto in October, 2004:[17]

> Prosecutors then need to become far less reluctant to acknowledge that a wrongful conviction may have taken place. The adversarial system has its place, but the consequences of its use in cases which do not merit its use are profound, as wrongly convicted people have to wait years and years in agony and fear as they try to establish their innocence.

(b) Areas of Institutional Reform

Several remedial suggestions of a general nature commend themselves. They flow from the cultural and institutional impediments to wrongful conviction recognition and correction identified earlier in this paper. As put by Medwed[18], they are intended to "rehabilitate the ideal that prosecutors are obliged to do justice."

Education is a trite but effective starting point in any effort to liberate Crown counsel from a "conviction psychology." Training must be continuous. It must be anchored in the reality of wrongful convictions. It must encourage reflection. And it must enjoy the sanction and support of the most senior and respected members of the prosecution service. The FPT has lent its endorsement to Crown-directed education programs, recommending that, "Regular training for Crowns and police on the dangers and prevention of tunnel vision should be implemented."[19]

A blend of *incentives and disincentives* could also re-orient prosecuting counsel. Performance evaluations that rewarded prosecutors for identifying, and endeavouring to rectify, police misconduct would go some way to reducing the risk of miscarriages of justice, as would encouragement of post-conviction innocence-review initiatives. At the same time, prosecutorial misconduct that contributes to wrongful convictions should result in discipline proceedings and, where proven, public sanction. It is a constant source of discouragement that no Canadian prosecutor — or police officer or forensic scientist, for that matter — has ever been held accountable for his or her misdeeds (including continuing instances of material non-disclosure) in the course of a wrongful conviction prosecution.

Provincial Crown law offices should create special units to *investigate claims of* **factual** *innocence.* Their personnel should never include those who prosecuted the cases under review. These "innocence units" would inevitably generate an expertise in identifying sources of wrongful conviction and, in time, would develop a less adversarial relationship with defence counsel championing claims of miscarriage of justice. Thus far, only Manitoba, through the creation of a forensic committee that has been examining convictions founded, at least in part, on a now-discredited hair comparison methodology, has initiated such an agenda. These fledgling efforts warrant nation-wide support and replication.

Finally (if more radically), each province should consider *outsourcing* a portion of *the prosecution* caseload to private counsel. The result, as exemplified by the English criminal bar, would be a far less partisan or adversarial process than that which char-acterizes the Canadian public prosecutor model. It would also reduce the insularity and, on occasion, fortress mentality of the Crown. At minimum, counsel freed of any ideological commitment to obtaining or maintaining convictions would be introduced into the prosecutorial process. British Columbia is the only province where criminal "barristers" routinely practice on both sides of the prosecutorial divide. Perhaps coincidentally, it is also one of the very few provinces without a recognized case of wrongful homicide conviction.

(d) Is There a Place for the Victim in the Prosecution Process?†

Patricia Clarke

Victims of crime once were the central actors in bringing offenders to justice. Today they are neglected outsiders in a system which could not function without them, yet is not accountable to them, provides no role for them and does not necessarily serve them, for ours is "an adversary system in which the victim is not one of the adversaries" (Federal-Provincial Task Force, 1983:5).

Victims are organizing, in one of the significant developments in the justice system, to complain of their expulsion and to demand more participation. Sometimes they bypass the system entirely, either by systems of private justice or in extreme cases by becoming their own prosecutor, judge and executioner.

A number of jurisdictions have tried a number of ways over the past twenty years to answer the demands of victims, and in Canada a Federal-Provincial Task Force on Justice for Victims has made recommendations some of which have been embodied in proposed legislation. The question is no longer, the Task Force says, "whether the victim should participate in the (criminal justice) process or not. The question is rather the extent of that participation" (1983:7).

This paper will look at the current status of the victim in the prosecution process, the reasons for that status in the historic development of the process, and some reasons for the growth of the victims' rights movement. It will review proposals to change the victim's status but will argue that, as far as genuine participation is concerned, the proposed changes will be more cosmetic than real. That is because of the nature of the process, the nature of bureaucratic systems to resist change, and the aims and purposes of the criminal justice system. The exclusion of victims is not an accident or oversight which can be remedied by minor tinkering with a process whose purpose is to provide justice for victims. It is a necessary and inevitable fact of a process with a totally different purpose. If victims dare to find remedies for their victimization, they must find them outside the prosecution process.

EVOLUTION OF THE PROSECUTION PROCESS

Before there was a formal legal system, all wrongs were private wrongs. Victims and their families exacted the penalties. To temper and regulate such private justice, in Anglo-Saxon law there gradually

---

† (1987) 8 *Canadian Criminology Forum* at 31–42. Reproduced with permission. [Notes and/or references omitted.]

grew a system of restitution with fixed payments for various wrongs. At the same time there grew the notion that while some incidents were private disputes, which in the development of law became torts to be dealt with in civil courts, other acts threatened the fabric of society and destroyed "the King's peace". For such acts the offender made payment not only to the victim but also to the lord or the king. Holdsworth (1909:38) claims this was "the germ of the idea that wrong is not simply the affair of the injured individual — an idea which is the condition precedent to the growth of a criminal law".

Gradually as this idea developed, the victim lost control of the conflict and it became the property of the state. The focus shifted from a dispute between the offender and the victim, in which the offender was bound to make reparation to the person he had injured, to the relationship between the offender and society, in which the offender had injured society and must be punished by society. Common law developed to prevent victims from receiving reparations until they did all they could to bring the offender to justice and forbid victims to agree not to prosecute in order to get back their property. Individuals could not condone a crime against the state (Hudson and Galway, 1975:24).

The key to a criminal proceeding thus became, in essence, the exclusion of the victim as one of the parties. Full participation by the victim, Christie says (1977:3), presupposes elements of civil law.

Just as the state came to replace the victim as the injured party, so it gradually replaced the victim as the prosecuting party. Until the late 18th century, trials normally were conducted by the victim-prosecutor and the defendant (Beattie, 1986:13). By the 19th century Blackstone was able to state categorically that the sovereign "is therefore the proper person to prosecute for all public offences and breaches of the peace, being the person injured in the eye of the law" (Hagan, 1983:268).

In the evolution of the prosecution process, then, two important things have happened, according to Christie (1977:3), one, that both parties are being represented; and second, that the one represented by the state, the victim, "is so thoroughly represented that for the most part he has been pushed completely out of the arena". The victim is a double loser: his property may have been stolen by the offender, but "his conflict has been stolen by the state" (Christie, 1982:93). When the private conflicts become state property, they are made to serve "the ideological interests of state-subject authority relations and the organizational interests of the individual citizens" (Ericson and Baranek, 1982:4).

ROLE OF THE VICTIM IN THE PROSECUTION PROCESS

This transfer of the dispute between two persons into a dispute between one of them and the Crown means, according to Shearing and Stenning (1983:9), that victim neglect is not a "minor deficiency" in the justice system but arises from a "fundamental feature". The state owns the conflict and the roles left to victims are[] (1) to supply the system with raw material; (2) to give the evidence the system requires; and (3) to serve as a "ceremonial" or "symbolic" presence (Hagan, 1983:7) which legitimizes the mobilization of the law against the accused.

The fundamental policy objectives of the criminal justice system are based on a classical concept of society as a contract between a neutral arbitrating state and rational individuals. The state provides society and its members with a reasonable degree of security, and ensures just treatment for the accused (Griffiths et al., 1980:6). Punishments must be established if the sovereign is to "defend the public liberty, entrusted to his care, from the usurpation of individuals" (VOLD, 1979:24), and they must be fixed, known and in relation to the crime. These policy objectives ignore the victim as such, other than as a member of society. The second objective implies, far from participation by the victim, a moderation and rationality in the punishment the accused might otherwise receive from those who believe themselves wronged. The resulting court process may be seen as a sort of morality play where certain values are publicly affirmed, certain conduct publicly denounced, and certain persons identified, blamed and rejected as "criminals". "The process uses accused persons to help define the relationship between the individual and the state" (Ericson and Baranek, 1982:215). Victims and their needs simply are not part of the script.

As the process has evolved, the chief power left to victims is the power not to surrender their conflict to the state — not to report the victimization. More than half of victims appear to exercise this right (Task Force, 1983:14). Once the state takes over, they lose virtually all other power. They have no right to testify, although they may do so if they are called by the Crown and if theirs is the uncommon case which goes to trial. Approximately up to 70% of cases are settled by a guilty plea.[1] They have no right to express their views on bail or sentencing, though a judge or prosecutor is free to ask for them. They have no right to receive restitution, although they may in certain circumstances have a right to apply for it.[2]

In the prosecution, the Crown represents the interests of the community, which may or may not coincide with the interests of the victims. The Crown must consider, for example, priorities on police time and court time for investigating and prosecuting, availability of evidence, chances of a conviction, public attitudes toward the offence, desirability of plea negotiations, the protection of the community and the rehabilitation of the offender. The victim has no way to challenge these Crown decisions.

Not only does the Crown have to consider wider concerns than those of the victim, but it can be argued that to seem to represent the victim, or to press the victim's claim, might prejudice the Crown's function as an impartial presenter of all the evidence. Indeed, for the Crown to give any assistance or status to the alleged victim, which would not be given to any witness, might compromise the rights of the accused. Even to equate the complainant with a victim could prejudge facts to be proved, for instance in a sexual assault case where consent is an issue.

THE VICTIM MOVEMENT

Having been detached over the centuries from the prosecution process, some victims have organized to attempt to get back in. In the last few years such groups have mushroomed across North America. In Canada 28 groups claim 150 chapters in every province and 250,000 to 400,000 members (Toronto Star, 1984:1). Their numbers comprise an effective lobby, but are only a fraction of those eligible. Individual victims in Canada number at least 1.6 million a year.[3] Organizational victims may be even more numerous: in a study by Hagan (1983:35) they made up two-thirds of a random sample.

A number of factors appear to be involved in the birth and growth of victim groups. First, is "a widespread and apparently increasing fear of crime" of which Taylor (1983:93) says "countless research studies" have provided evidence. The fear, partly justified and partly promoted by the media, is expressed in purchases of burglar alarms and double-locks, in self-defence classes, in private security patrols and programmes such as Neighbourhood Watch, and in victim groups.

Second, is the law and order movement, which argues that the criminal justice system is "soft on criminals", thereby turning them loose to create more victims. It supports more "rights" for victims to balance what it claims are too many rights for "criminals".

Third, is the women's movement, which began with advocacy and assistance for rape victims and in

some jurisdictions achieved changes in statutes and rules of evidence which provided more rights for victim-witnesses.

Fourth, is the self-help movement, growing out of the protest movements of the 1960's, which leads people who don't trust big government or bureaucracy to form their own groups to represent themselves.

Fifth, is the general humanitarian impulse to help people in trouble (and earn political points) which in other fields has led to worker compensation programmes or the motorists' unsatisfied judgement fund.

Victim advocacy groups differ in their concerns and their goals. Some complain most about neglect, carelessness and insensitivity from police and the courts. They can't find out what is happening in their case, they can't understand what goes on in court and they are not notified when their case is coming up or when it is settled. These groups want more information, more support services, more "sensitivity".

Others complain that victims cannot get restitution for their losses, or even get back their stolen property promptly. According to a 1976 survey in Alameda County, California (Karmen, 1984:148), 30% of victims never got back the stolen property used as evidence, 42% never learned the outcome of their case, and 61% of those eligible for the state's crime compensation fund were not informed of its existence. These victims want more effective compensation schemes and help in applying to them.

Still others such as Mothers Against Drunk Driving want stiffer laws for specific offences. And some want an active role in the prosecution process. They ask to be acknowledged as a party to the proceedings, to be given access to the Crown case, to be supplied with reasons for every decision, even given a veto on plea negotiations and sentence submissions. Donald Sullivan, spokesman for a Canadian conference of victims' groups, says they want laws to give victims "a place in the courtroom" and rights in court "equal to those of the offender" (Toronto Star, 1985:2).

SOURCE OF RIGHTS FOR VICTIMS

A right has three key features (Task Force 1983:130). It is a legal recognition of interest, in this case the victim's interest in this court proceeding. A right for one party implies a responsibility or duty on another party. And it must be legally enforceable, so that one can secure either the right or damages.

At present the justice system is a balance (equal or not) of rights between prosecution and accused. If victims are to have more rights in the prosecution process, are they to come at the expense of the rights of police or the Crown or court officials? These have the greatest interest in encouraging the co-operation of victims, for as much as 87% of police workload — and consequently much of the court workload — comes from incidents reported by citizens (Griffiths et al., 1980:33). Clearly it is in the bureaucratic interests of the system to encourage a steady and increasing clientele. The more incidents that are reported, the higher the crime rate; and high crime rates are an effective argument for bigger budgets. Yet as we have seen, more than half of victimizations are not reported, and many victims "appear to feel that the system would only fail them or ignore them if they involved it" (Task Force, 1983:3).

Victims are essential not only to bringing in the cases but, as witnesses, to prosecuting them successfully. Treating victims in a "sensitive manner" will encourage their "constructive assistance", says a paper prepared for the Federal Department of Justice (Weiler and Desgagne, 1984:27). Or as Weigend (1983:93) puts it, "Happy victims make better witnesses" — a claim he says is unsubstantiated by any evidence except the "feelings" of the staff of victim/witness assistance programmes.

Sensitivity however does not confer power. It is not a right enforceable by law (Task Force 1983:131). It does not conflict with any of the prerogatives of the prosecution. None of the proposals of the Task Force on Justice for Victims involves any mandatory transfer of power from police or court to victims. They contain phrases such as "to be considered" or "where appropriate". Indeed, the Task Force says the key words in its proposals for victims are "concern, consideration and communication" and that these words sum up how the system can respond to the concerns of victims "without compromising its basic aims". (1983:152)

But the "basic aims", as we have seen, have no necessary connection with justice for victims. There is no transfer of power to victims in proposals which allow them to participate in their cases only at the discretion of judge or Crown. There is no transfer of power, either in the guidelines for fair treatment of victims set out by the Victim Committee of the American Bar Association and quoted with approval by the Task Force. (1983:152) They deal mainly with ways to improve communication between victims and decision-makers in the criminal justice system. Similarly, a case management programme in British

Columbia "improved convenience" for victims with no change in the "aims and purposes" of the system (Task Force, 1983:96).

If rights for victims are not to come from the prosecution, then they must come from the accused. If the victim of sexual assault, for instance, wins the right not to have evidence of sexual reputation considered, the accused loses the right to present that evidence. The transfer of rights is particularly evident in the California *Victims' Bill of Rights* of 1982 (Karmen, 1984:232–3), which limits the accused's opportunities for bail, restricts plea bargaining, restricts insanity defence, broadens standards for admissibility of evidence, and permits victims to press for greater penalties in sentencing, to appeal sentences they view as lenient and to argue against parole.

That is further than Canadians appear willing to go. The rhetoric is that the rights of the accused are inviolate, and the Task Force cautions that in focussing on the plight of the victim "we must not lose sight of the need to safeguard the accused" (1983:5). Perhaps it would be more realistic to say, with Ericson and Baranek (1982:233), that both accused and victim are dependents in the prosecution process and that neither has more "rights" than is expedient to allow and not "upset the operation of criminal control in the interests of the state".

PROPOSALS FOR CHANGE

It appears then that victims have almost no enforceable rights in the prosecution process. It also appears that they are excluded from any real rights in the process by its very nature as a conflict between the state and the accused. Within those limits, several ways have been suggested to recognize and recompense the victim.

One is financial reparation. Three of the 79 recommendations of the Task Force deal with this. A second is a "victim impact" statement, to be requested before sentencing, the subject of another Task Force recommendation. A third is a "victims' advocate" who attempts to influence the prosecution process. Two such experiments have been tried in the United States (McDonald, 1976:153). In one a lawyer was employed as a "victim advocate" to attempt to influence the process through out-of-court negotiations. In the other, a volunteer group of victim advocates attended court hearings en masse for a time, until they tired of it, and claimed fewer charges were dismissed or remanded when they were present. The second programme raises questions about fairness to the accused. As Griffiths says (1980:32), "The prototype of community involvement ... is the lynch mob." The first raises questions about who pays the advocate. If the victims pay, they may feel twice victimized. If the state pays, that may compromise its stance that the community, not the victim, is the injured party. In any case, such advocates have no standing in court since the victim is not one of the adversaries.

RESTITUTION AND COMPENSATION

The Task Force proposals on reparation would[] (1) amend s. 653 of the *Criminal Code* to require judges to consider restitution "in all appropriate cases" and to provide an opportunity for victims to make representations about their ascertainable losses; (2) empower the court to impose a jail term for wilful default on a restitution order; (3) amend s. 388 to raise its present limit on restitution for property damage from $50 to $500. Restitution as part of a probation order under s. 663 would continue unchanged.

"Whenever possible," the Task Force explains, "victims should be restored to the position they enjoyed prior to the victimization" (Task Force, 1983:35). The Law Reform Commission of Canada in its paper on Restitution and Compensation describes restitution as a "natural and just response" to the victim's plight which should be a "central consideration" in sentencing (Working Paper 5, 1974:6,8).

Yet such remedies for the victim already exist. Several sections of the *Criminal Code* make it possible for the court to order restitution.[4] These remedies appear to be seldom used. While Canadian data are lacking (Burns, 1980:29), the Task Force thinks judges are "reluctant" to use them (Task Force, 1983:54). It does not explain why judges would be less reluctant to use its new proposals.

Outside the criminal process, victims may apply to provincial crime injury compensation boards in all provinces except Prince Edward Island, or collect for property losses from private insurance, or file a civil suit both for property loss and for suffering and get judgement not only against the offender but, where negligence can be proved, against third parties.[5]

Restitution provisions in other jurisdictions appear to be an ineffective remedy for victims. In Britain, after passage of new restitution legislation in 1972, of those sent to custody and also given restitution orders only 12% paid the whole sum (Burns, 1980:15). In practice, said the British Advisory Council on the Penal System, a victim's prospects for restitution through a criminal court order "are remote" (Burns, 1980:15). After a study of United States res-

titution schemes, Burns found them of relatively little use to victims and concluded that their popularity reflected a conception of them as "potentially useful tools for rehabilitating the offender rather than as devices for restoring the victim" (Burns, 1980:12).

The compensation schemes outside the criminal process are not well used either. They are usually limited to victims of violent crime but are available regardless of whether an offender has been identified or convicted. In Ontario, one in 55 eligible victims actually seeks compensation (*Globe & Mail*, 1984:2). A study of the New York and New Jersey schemes showed that fewer than 1% of all victims of violent crime even applied to the boards, and only 35% of those who applied were compensated (Elias, 1983:219).

As for the possibility of civil suit, Allen Linden reported that 1.5% of victims surveyed collected anything by suit, although 74.2% of those studied suffered some economic loss (Linden, 1968:29).

Whether or not restitution is a "natural response", there appear to be a number of reasons why judges are reluctant to use the existing provisions and legislators are reluctant to impose more effective ones — reasons involving the nature of the criminal process, the objectives of sentencing, constitutional division of powers, and sometimes no doubt a combination of ignorance and inertia. Judge Cartwright of York County, in *Regina v. Kalloo* (Unreported; quoted in Moskoff, 1983:11), commented:

> those few Crown counsel who are even aware of the existence of this section (653) which allows the victim of an indictable offence to apply for an order to satisfy loss or damage to property caused in the commission of a crime are equally indifferent to its application.

He went on to suggest that if the Attorney General were paid by commission on completed restitution orders, "blood would be flowing from stones" all over Ontario (Moskoff, 1983:11).

The difficulty of getting blood from stones, however, is one reason restitution orders are seldom made, and civil suit is often useless as well. In making restitution a condition of probation under s. 663(2)(e), a judge is bound to consider an offender's ability to pay. (He is not so bound under s. 653.) Observation of the courts indicates that many offenders, particularly against property, have neither jobs nor assets.

A further reason for caution is the Supreme Court of Canada ruling in *R. v. Zelensky* ((1978), 2 C.R. (3d) 107 (S.C.C.)) that proceedings for restitution under s. 653 must not take on any character of a civil suit, and therefore the criminal court must not determine issues regarding the amount to be awarded. Restitution can be imposed, then, only when the amount is not in dispute, which Moskoff comments makes the section a "toothless tiger" (Moskoff, 1983:11). Burns comments that judges hesitate to order restitution under s. 663 as well, first because they fear using criminal law to enforce civil obligations, and second because they see it as suitable only for simple cases in which there is no dispute either over the amount involved or over the offender's ability to pay (Burns, 1980:25).

In addition, a restitution order once made is hard to enforce. Those made under s. 653 must be enforced by the victim as a civil judgement, if the offender has assets and can be located. Those made under s. 663(2)(e) are intended to be monitored by probation officers. If the probation officers notice that payments have not been made, and if they decide to charge the offender with failure to comply with probation, and if the offender can be located, they must prove the offender "wilfully" defaulted. If they succeed, the maximum penalty is a $500 fine and/or six months in jail. Note that the victim is not the complainant in the enforcement procedure.

The most serious problem with restitution involves the nature of the criminal process. Civil wrongs have grown in law to be those for which injured persons seek their own monetary compensation. Criminal wrongs have become a public relationship between offenders and the state with a public response applied through penal sanctions. The historical tie between the two remains in the *Criminal Code* provisions for restitution (s. 653 and s. 663) which the Law Reform Commission describes as carry-overs "grudgingly grafted onto penal law to save the victim the expense of a civil suit" (Working Paper 5, 1974:9). They enable the victim to circumvent civil procedure by obtaining a criminal judgement, enforceable as if it were civil, by a more expeditious and less expensive process. An example of the civil nature of s. 653 is that it comes into operation "on application" of the victim, not on the initiative of the court.

The *British North America Act* gives jurisdiction over criminal law and procedure to the federal parliament (1867: sect. 91(27)) but authority over property and civil rights to the provinces. This division, says Burns, means "an almost insurmountable obstacle to the establishment of efficient restitution systems in Canada" (1980:29).

Further, criminal courts are constituted to determine a person's criminal responsibility, not his/her civil liability. The two have different standards of proof and different rules of evidence. For example, examination for discovery is a civil procedure not available in the criminal court. An accused person would not have the same safeguards around challenging a victim's claim for damages in criminal court than would be available in civil court. For the criminal court to try to make such a determination raises the danger of infringing on the powers reserved to the civil court. Widespread use of restitution orders might encourage use of the criminal courts as a collection agency, and lead to threatening prosecution to collect a debt.

A further set of problems arises because the focus in sentencing is not on what is pleasing to the victim but on what is good for the offender and for society. Though the Law Reform Commission saw restitution as a "rational sanction" and the Zelensky decision accepted its "valid character" as part of the sentencing process, restitution cannot be argued in the criminal court on the basis that it would return the victim to wholeness or compensate for suffering. The only constitutional way to make the civil liability to the victim a valid part of the criminal sentence is to actively locate it within criminal law. The purpose which has been alleged is that it will deprive the offender of the fruits of crime, deter those who might hope to profit illegally, and facilitate the rehabilitation of the accused.

The Law Reform Commission argues that restitution[] "involves acceptance of the offender as a responsible person with the capacity to undertake constructive and socially approved acts.... To the extent that restitution works toward self-correction and prevents or at least discourages the offender's commitment to a life of crime, the community enjoys a measure of protection.... The offender too benefits.... He is treated as a responsible human being" (1974:7–8).

These desirable effects, Burns comments, are "entirely speculative" (1980:8). The momentum toward restitution as a sentence seems to him to depend on little more than "an intuitive sense of its rationality" (1980:7).

The Task Force, although it supports expanded restitution proposals, admits "there is little of the kind of 'hard' evidence which might allow us to decide conclusively whether the benefits of restitution outweigh its costs" (1983:92). To be fair, there is little hard evidence on whether any other sentencing dispositions work any better (Griffiths et al., 1980:233–34). The "safest conclusion", says Klein, is that restitution "as a correctional measure simply will not make any difference" (1978:400).

And finally, there are difficulties in implementing effective and just restitution schemes.

Crown attorneys will have discretion whether to recommend restitution, and judges will have discretion whether to order it. Can justice then be equal for offenders, or victims? The victims cannot "shop" for a judge who is known to make restitution orders.

Would the law fall unevenly on the person who steals $10 million and cannot possibly make restitution, and the person who steals $100 and can? If restitution is a correctional measure, imposed for the good of the offender, should it not then be imposed regardless of whether the victim has been paid for the loss by insurance?

Defence counsel often tell the court, in a bid for a more lenient sentence, that full or partial restitution has been made. If this does in fact result in leniency, does that mean that if a rich man and a poor man both break a window, and the rich man can afford to replace it, then he receives a less severe sentence than the poor man for the same offence?

What happens if there are several offenders? If one has no ability to pay, or reneges on payment, do the others pay more to make up the victim's total loss? Suppose there are multiple victims, and as part of plea negotiations some charges are dropped. Which victims are then to receive restitution?

Finally, if victims of crime are entitled to be restored to their original status, why not every victim? Why limit the recompense to those cases of property loss in which an offender can not only be identified, charged, convicted, and sentenced to make restitution but can actually pay damages?

Yet with all their flaws, restitution programmes (inside the criminal process) and compensation schemes (outside of it) have been legislated in many jurisdictions in the last 20 years. Though often underfunded, unadvertised and underused, obviously they have merits for lawmakers. For one, they enable governments faced with rising crime rates and rising public concern over crime to say, "Look what we're doing for the victims." Roger Meiners points out that large numbers of compensation programmes were established at least in part as a palliative for increasing crime and relatively inefficient restitution (Meiners, 1978:9–44). Voters are told that something will be done for them when and if they are victimized and few will find out otherwise. Elias claims compensation has:

> justified strengthened police forces, provided
> political advantages to its supporters, facilitated

social control of the population and yet substantially failed in providing most victims with assistance (1983:213).

A second purpose is to keep the victim from demanding a real role in the prosecution process. As Hagan says, such programmes open the possibility of bringing the victim back into the system without actually doing it, symbolically conveying a sense of concern while doing little to alter the actual origin of the concern (1983:60).

VICTIM IMPACT STATEMENTS

The other proposal of the Task Force, aside from restitution, to bring the victim back into the prosecution process was to amend the *Criminal Code* to "permit" the introduction of a victim impact statement "to be considered" at the time of sentencing (Task Force, 1983:157). Such a statement would presumably enable victims to tell the judge of their suffering and of any monetary loss as a result of the crime. Presumably they would then feel that somebody was paying attention to what happened to them.

At present nothing, except pressure of time, prevents a judge from asking to hear from a victim, or when ordering a pre-sentence report from asking that the victim be consulted. The intent of the Task Force proposal is to require the judge to request such a statement.

That proposal raises serious questions. To the degree that the statement dealt with monetary loss, it could be considered in assessing restitution as part of a sentence, subject to concerns already discussed about the purposes of sentencing and conflict with civil courts, particularly if the amount of the loss were in dispute. Questions arise whether the determination of loss would have to be based on receipts of appraisals, which might be difficult for some victims to produce; whether the statement would have to be sworn; whether it would be subject to contest by the accused, and if contested, whether the whole question would not then have to be referred to a civil court for adjudication.

To the degree that the statement dealt with pain or suffering, its usefulness would be questionable as long as the focus in sentencing is on the protection of society and the rehabilitation of the accused. A shut-in widow whose television set is stolen may suffer more from its loss than the wealthy bachelor who is seldom home, but that should weigh less with the judge than the characteristics of the offence, the previous record of the offender and the perceived need to deter such behaviour in the community. If the purpose of the sentence is to rehabilitate the offender, then its nature should be determined by presumed experts. If its purpose is deterrence, then it should be certain and predictable, not subject to modification by the victim. If the purpose is retribution, then the punishment must fit the crime rather than the victim (Karmen, 1984:155).

Then there is the problem of how the statement will be submitted. Ninety-eight percent of cases are concluded in the provincial courts (Griffiths et al., 1980:146) and about 70% of these without a trial (Griffiths et al., 1980:147). Dockets are crowded, hearings are rushed and pre-sentence reports are rare. If the victim is not present when the accused pleads guilty, how often will judges be willing to delay sentence to hear from the victim?

Perhaps too, it is only an assumption that many victims really want this input, or any input, into their cases. A Philadelphia judge, Lois Porer, who routinely offers victims a chance to speak on sentence, says they seldom do (Karmen, 1984:230). Since victim impact statements were legislated in Connecticut in 1981, only 3% of victims appear at sentence hearings (Karmen, 1984:231). When as an experiment victims were invited to take part in plea-bargaining sessions on their cases in Dade County, Florida, only a third attended. Those who were present generally spoke only in answer to questions, approved what the professionals suggested and were "passive and docile" (Heinz and Kerstetter, 1980:172).

RESISTANCE TO CHANGE

Having looked at the "rights" of the victim in the prosecution process and at proposals to give victims a larger role, it remains to ask: would these proposals, or any proposals, make any real difference in the conduct of the courts?

As we have seen, restitution is seldom ordered. Compensation schemes are seldom used. The majority of victims do not accept the limited opportunities to participate which are offered to them. It is not clear whether the last is because they don't care, or because they don't think it will make any difference, or because as the Dade County study suggests the system is not diligent in notifying them of opportunities (Heinz and Kerstetter, 1980:173).

One of the reasons advanced for helping victims is to encourage them to cooperate with the system in reporting more victimizations. In the United States, the percentage of incidents of violence which were reported to police went from 46% in 1973 to 47% in

1981, and of household burglaries from 47% in 1973 to 51% in 1981, despite the launching of numerous victim-assistance programmes during that period (Karmen, 1984:168).

After reviewing a decade of action and advocacy on behalf of victims in the United States, Weigend concluded it had generated "much rhetoric, more knowledge ... but little change" (1983:91).

Criminal justice systems are like any bureaucracy. They operate in their own interests. They are subject to what Karmen calls "goal displacement" (1984:169), which means that they substitute for the official goals of doing justice and serving the public, the unofficial goals of getting through the workload expeditiously, covering up mistakes and making themselves look as essential as possible so funding won't be cut. As King points out:

> Imagine for example the approach of the victim of a serious crime. He wishes to see the offender punished and deterred from further offences. Now compare that approach with that of a court administrator, whose major concern is the efficient running of the system, clearing the workload for the day and avoiding any unnecessary delays.... The one looks to the magistrate to revenge his loss ... and to compensate him, the victim, while another looks at his watch and wonders how long the case is going to last and whether the morning list will be completed by one o'clock (1981:13–14).

A place for victims in the prosecution process is limited to one that does not interfere with the smooth working of the system or the privileges and convenience of its principles.

Most reforms, as we have seen, seem to be intended to inform or assist or conciliate the victim, and these are worthy goals, but they involve no real rights or participation. Where the victim has been granted a role in the process, it appears to be subject to foot-dragging (the Dade County experiment), discretion (to be "considered" or to be applied "where appropriate") or co-opting.

The fate of reforms in the role of the victim is not surprising. Ericson and Baranek state:

> It is a common feature of bureaucratic organizations that rules intended to influence the action of agents are routinely absorbed by the agents to conform with their existing practices (1982:224).

Exciting reforms are "translated into mechanisms of convenience by control agents and relegated to their pragmatically appropriate place" (Ericson and Baranek, 1982:231).

CONCLUSION

If the public criminal justice process is impervious to change which would allow the victim any real participation, what then?

Organizational victims already bypass the public prosecution and set up their own system to deal with incidents which are classified not as "crime" (which by definition involves the public interest) but as "loss" (Shearing and Stenning, 1983:7). In these victim-oriented systems, run by and for victims, the priority is on restitution or compensation for the loss and prevention of future losses.

Then there are proposals, for example Christie's (1977, 1982), for similar decriminalization of offences against individuals. Christie argues that we "create crime by creating systems that ask for the word" (1982:74). He proposes to remove conflicts from the professionals and return them to the accused and the victims, and to set up quasi-civil procedures to assess compensation and penalties. Pointing out that "several less-industrialized countries" apply civil law where Europe applies criminal law (1982:92), he asks, "Could we imagine social systems where the parties by and large relied on civil solutions?" (1982:96).

Ericson and Baranek, discussing such proposals, are skeptical. Decriminalization may simply imply some other form of social control. Diversion programmes may lead to more cumbersome procedures and increase the number of persons subject to control (1982:228). They add, "All reform alternatives include an added role for some group of professionals" (1982:233).

It is also important to note that there is the vigilante, who tries his own case and administers his own justice, celebrated in the movies *Death Wish* and *Deadly Force* ("When the cops won't and the courts can't ... he will give you justice!" (Karmen, 1984:247)) and emulated by Bernhard Goetz of New York.

In Canada, at least, rates of reported crime are not escalating in a way that justifies the vigilante. But one of the arguments for compensating victims of crime rests on the assumption that they do not carry out their own justice. In Taylor's analysis (1983), a crucial function of the capitalist state is to maintain conditions under which production can flourish. One of these conditions is a "justice" system. There must be an overall sense in society of a free contract whereby the state protects the person and the property of its citizens, in exchange for those citizens subjugating themselves to the state.

The loss of liberty thereby involved is offset and made legitimate by the overall protection of the freedom of the citizen which is provided by a police force and a legal and penal system (1983:135). In other words, citizens give up the right to protect themselves and to pursue their own vengeance, and the state contracts to protect them and collects taxes from them to do so. Therefore, it can be argued that if the state fails in its side of the contract, it should compensate the victims.

Similar arguments for compensating crime victims can be raised on the basis of sociologist Emile Durkheim's theories that crime is normal, even necessary to a healthy society (Vold, 1979:204–208). Durkheim argued that society makes certain demands on its members, and fulfilling these demands is an important source of social solidarity. But the demands are constructed so that inevitably a certain identifiable group will not be able to fulfill them. This enables the rest to feel a sense of moral superiority which he says is the primary source of the social solidarity.

Durkheim informed us that it is not only inevitable that some will oppose the collective conscience, it is also healthy. Progressive social change comes about because some people dare to differ. Thus crime is the price society pays for the possibility of progress — all the more reason why society should compensate those few who are martyrs to its health.

What would we do if we were really serious about helping victims of crime? We would fund adequately and advertise widely a government-supported compensation fund. It would not be funded, as is often suggested, by convicted offenders, for that would imply that offenders are a distinct group and would hold all in that group, who happened to be caught, liable for the damage inflicted by some. Rather it might be funded like medical insurance (one might contribute to OHIP and to VICE — Victims Insurance (against) Criminal Enterprises), recognizing first, that there are more offenders than ever that are caught; second, that the definition of which acts are crimes and therefore which persons are offenders is made by society and changes from time to time; and third, that society has an obligation to those who suffer from one of its inevitable features. We would allow compensation both for material loss and for pain and suffering, and whether or not an offender has been identified. Yes, there would be cheating, just as people cheat now on claims for private insurance. But if private insurers live with that risk, surely a public scheme can.

(e)   The Limits of Restorative Justice†

Kathleen Daly

Restorative justice (RJ) is a set of ideals about jus-tice that assumes a generous, empathetic, supportive, and rational human spirit. It assumes that victims can be generous to those who have harmed them, that offenders can be apologetic and contrite for their behaviour, that their respective 'communities of care' can take an active role of support and assis-tance, and that a facilitator can guide rational dis-cussion and encourage consensual decision-making between parties with antagonistic interests. Any one of these elements may be missing and thus poten-tially weaken an RJ process. The ideals of RJ can also be in tension. For example, it may not be possi-ble to have equity or proportionality across RJ out-comes, when outcomes are supposed to be fashioned from the particular sensibilities of those in an RJ encounter.

Achieving justice — whether RJ or any other form — is a fraught and incomplete enterprise. This is because justice cannot be achieved, although it is important to reach for it. Rather, drawing from Derrida, justice is an 'experience of the impossible' (Pavlich 1996: 37), 'an ideal, an aspiration, which is supremely important and worth striving for constantly and tirelessly' (Hudson 2003: 192).

This chapter addresses a selected set of limits of RJ, those concerning its scope and its practices. My discussion is selective and limited. I do not consider the discursive limits of liberal legality as these are viewed through a postmodern lens (Arrigo 2004), nor do I consider related problems when nation states or communities cannot imagine particular offences or understand 'ultra-Others' (see Hudson 2003: 212–13). My focus instead is on the limits of current RJ prac-tices, when applied to youth justice cases in common law jurisdictions. There are other contexts where RJ can be applied, including adult criminal cases; non-criminal contexts (school disputes and conflicts, workplace disputes and conflicts, and child welfare); and responding to broader political conflict or as a form of transitional justice practice, among other potential sites (see Braithwaite 2002). I focus on RJ in youth justice cases because it currently has a

large body of empirical evidence. However, as RJ is increasingly being applied in adult cases and in dif-ferent contexts (pre- or post-sentence advice, for example, as is now the case in England and New Zealand), we might expect to see different kinds of limits emerging.

THE SCOPE OF RJ

Limit (1): there is no agreed-upon definition of RJ

There is robust discussion on what RJ is or should be, and there is no consensus on what prac-tices should be included within its reach. One axis of disagreement is whether RJ should be viewed as a process or an outcome (Crawford and Newburn 2003). A second is what kinds of practices are authentic forms of RJ, what kinds are not, and what is in between (McCold and Wachtel 2002; *Contempo-rary Justice Review* 2004). A third is whether RJ should be viewed principally as a set of justice val-ues, rather than a process or set of practices (com-pare, e.g. Braithwaite 2003 and Johnstone 2002, with von Hirsch *et al.* 2003), or whether it should include both (Roche 2003). Finally, there is debate on how RJ can or should articulate with established criminal justice (CJ).

A lack of agreement on definition means that RJ has not one but many identities and referents; and this can create theoretical, empirical, and policy confusion. Commentators, both advocates and critics, are often not talking about or imagining the same thing. Although the lack of a common understanding of RJ creates confusion, especially for those new to RJ, it reflects a diversity of interests and ideologies that people bring to the table when ideas of justice are discussed. A similar problem occurred with the rise of informal justice in the late 1970s. Informal justice could not be defined except by what it was not, i.e. it was not established forms of criminal justice (Abel 1982). An inability to define RJ, or jus-tice more generally, is not fatal. Indeed, it is a logi-

† From Dennis Sullivan and Larry Tifft (eds.), *Handbook of Restorative Justice* (Oxon, UK: Routledge, 2006), pp.134–45. Reproduced with permission of Taylor & Francis Books UK. [Notes and/or references omitted.]

cal and defensible position: there can be no 'fixed definition of justice' because justice has 'no unchanging nature' and 'it is beyond definition' (Hudson 2003: 201, characterizing the ideas of Lyotard and Derrida).

Gerry Johnstone (2004) suggests that the RJ advocates have too narrowly focused their efforts on promoting RJ by claiming its positive effects in reducing re-offending and increasing victim satisfaction. Instead of taking this instrumental and technical tack, Johnstone argues that we should see RJ as a set of ideas that challenge established CJ in fundamental ways. There is much to commend in having this more expansive vision of RJ as a long-term political project for changing the ways we think about 'crime,' 'being a victim,' 'responding to offenders,' among other categories nominated by Johnstone. However, I restrict my use of the term to a set of core elements in RJ practices. I do so not to limit the potential applicability of RJ to other domains or as a political project for social change but rather to conceptualize justice practices in concrete terms, not as aspirations or values. As RJ takes shape and evolves, it is important that we have images of the social interactions being proposed. I identify these core elements of RJ:

> It deals with the penalty (or post-penalty) not fact-finding phase of the criminal process.
>
> It normally involves a face-to-face meeting with an admitted offender and victim and their supporters, although it may also take indirect forms.
>
> It envisions a more active role for victim participation in justice decisions.
>
> It is an informal process that draws on the knowledge and active participation of lay persons (typically those most affected by an offence), but there are rules circumscribing the behavior of meeting members and limits on what they can decide in setting a penalty.
>
> It aims to hold offenders accountable for their behavior, while at the same time not stigmatizing them, and in this way it is hoped that there will be a reduction in future offending.
>
> It aims to assist victims in recovering from crime.

As we shall see, some (or all) of these elements may not be realized in RJ practices. For example, an RJ process aims to assist victims in recovering from crime, but this may be possible for some victims more than others. And although it is hoped that an RJ process will shift admitted offenders toward a law-abiding future, this too may occur for some, but not others. It should be emphasized that victims are not forced to meet an admitted offender in an RJ process. There can be other ways in which victims may engage an RJ process, including through the use of victim representatives or material brought into the meeting itself. In fact, some have proposed that victims have access to RJ processes when a suspect has not been caught for (or admitted to) an offence.

Limit (2): RJ deals with the penalty not fact-finding phase of the criminal process

There is some debate over whether RJ processes could be used in fact-finding, but virtually all the examples cited are of dispute resolution mechanisms in pre-modern societies, which rely on particular sets of 'meso-social structures' that are tied to kinship, geography, and political power (see discussion below by Bottoms 2003; see also Johnstone 2002). When we consider the typical forms of RJ practices, such as family group conferences (in New Zealand), family or community conferences (in Australia), police restorative cautioning schemes (in selected jurisdictions in England and North America), circles and sentencing circles (North America), or enhanced forms of victim offender mediation (North America and some European countries), we see that all are concerned with what a justice practice should be *after* a person has admitted committing an offence. RJ does not address whether a 'crime' occurred or not, or whether a suspect is 'guilty' of a crime or not. Rather, it focuses on 'what shall we do?' after a person admits that s/he has committed an offence.

Ultimately, as I shall argue, we should view this limit as a strength of RJ. The reason is that it bypasses the many disabling features of the adversarial process, both for those accused of crime and for victim complainants. Without a fact-finding or investigating mechanism, however, RJ cannot replace established CJ. To do so, it must have a method of adjudication, and currently it does not. However, RJ can make inroads into methods of penalty setting (in the context of court diversion or pre-sentence advice to judicial officers), and it may be effective in providing assurances of safety to individual victims and communities when offenders complete their sentences (in the context of post-sentence uses of RJ), but all of these activities occur only after a person has admitted committing an offence.

Several commentators point out that RJ differs from established CJ in that it is participatory and consensually based, not adversarial. However, this muddles things greatly. The reason that established CJ is adversarial is that its adjudication process rests on a fundamental right of those accused to say they did not commit an offence[2] and to defend themselves against the state's allegations of wrong-doing. There may well be better methods of adjudicating crime, and a troubling feature of established CJ is how long it takes for cases to be adjudicated and disposed; but surely, no one would wish to dispense with the right of citizens to defend themselves against the state's power to prosecute and punish alleged crime.

The focus of RJ on the penalty (or post-penalty) phase can be viewed as a strength. It enables us to be more imaginative in conceptualizing what is the 'right response' to offending behavior, and it opens up potential lines of communication and understanding between offenders, victims, and those close to them, when this is desirable (and it may not always be desirable). Communication and interaction are especially important elements because many victims want answers to questions: for example, about why *their* car was stolen, and not another person's car. They may be concerned about their security and seek reassurances from an offender not to victimize them again (although this may not stop an offender from victimizing others). There can be positive sources of connection between the supporters of offenders (say, a mother or father) and victims or their supporters. All of this is possible because RJ processes seek a conversational and dialogic approach to responding to crime. Decisions are not made by a distant magistrate or judge and an overworked duty solicitor and prosecutor with many files to process. In established CJ processes, research shows that in the courtroom, a defendant is typically mute and a victim is not present. State actors do all the work of handling and processing crime. The actual parties to a crime (the persons charged and victim-complainants) are bystanders or absent.

Some victim advocates who are critical of RJ think that it is 'outside' or not part of established CJ. Although a common perception, it is inaccurate. In all jurisdictions where RJ has been legislated in response to crime, it is very much 'inside' the established CJ process, as the police or courts make a decision about how to handle a case.

RJ IDEALS AND PRACTICES

There is a gap between the ideals or aspirations for RJ and actual practices. This gap should not surprise us because the ideals for RJ are set very high, and perhaps too high. Advocates have made astonishing claims for what RJ can achieve and what it

can do for victims, offenders, their family members, and communities. Thus, a gap arises, in part from inflated expectations for what RJ can achieve. There are deeper reasons for the gap, however.

First, as Bottoms (2003: 109) argues, the 'social mechanisms of RJ' rest on an assumption that 'adequate meso-social structures exist to support RJ-type approaches.' By 'meso-social structures,' Bottoms refers to ordered sets of relationships that are part of pre-modern societies (for example, residence, kinship, or lineage). These relationships embed elements of 'intra-societal power' and coercion, which make dispute settlement possible (see also Merry 1982). A second feature of relationships in pre-modern societies is that disputants are 'part of the same moral/social community.' They live in close proximity to one another or are related to one another, and typically wish to continue living in the community. These meso-social structures and 'thick' social ties, which are commonly associated with pre-modern (or *gemeinschaft*) societies,[3] are not present in modern urban contemporary societies. Thus, as Bottoms (2003: 110) suggests, 'a "blanket" delivery of RJ ... is always likely to achieve modest or patchy results in contemporary societies.'

Second, as I suggest elsewhere (Daly 2003: 200), gaps emerge because those participating in an RJ process may not know what is supposed to happen, how they are supposed to act, nor what an optimal result could be. Participants may have an idea of what 'their day in court' might be like, but they have little idea of what 'their day in an RJ conference' would be like. Moreover, effective participation requires a degree of moral maturity and empathetic concern that many people, and especially young people, may not possess. Finally, we know from the history of established CJ that organizational routines, administrative efficiency, and professional interests often trump justice ideals (Daly 2003: 232). RJ is no exception. It takes time and great effort to create the appropriate contexts for RJ processes to work effectively, including a facilitator's contacting and preparing participants, identifying who should be present, coordinating the right time for everyone, running the meeting, and following up after it is over.

Some commentators argue that it is more appropriate to compare 'what restorative justice has achieved and may still achieve with what conventional justice systems have to offer' (Morris 2002: 601). This is a valid and important point. We know that substantial gaps exist between the ideals and practices of established CJ. Thus, for example, it would be relevant to compare the effects of the court's sentencing practices on victims, offenders, and others with their participation in penalty discussions in RJ meetings. Although court-conference comparative research can be illuminating and helpful, there is also a value to observing and understanding what happens in an RJ process itself, including the variable degree to which the aims of RJ are achieved. When we do that, several limits of RJ are apparent. It is important to bear in mind that these limits are not necessarily peculiar to RJ; they may have their analogy in established CJ as well. I draw from my research on youth justice conference in South Australia (the South Australia Juvenile Justice [SAJJ] project, Daly 2000, 2001a, 2002, 2003, 2005; see Daly *et al.* 1998, Daly 2001b for SAJJ technical reports), along with other research, to elucidate these limits.

Limit (3): it is easier to achieve fairness than restorativeness in an RJ process

Studies of RJ in Australia, New Zealand, and England often examine whether the observer-researcher, offender, and victim perceive the process and outcome as fair. All published studies find high levels of perceived fairness, or procedural justice, in the process and outcome (see review in Daly 2001a for Australian and New Zealand research; see also Hoyle *et al.* 2002; Crawford and Newburn 2003). For example, to questions such as 'Were you treated fairly?' 'Were you treated with respect?' 'Did people listen to you?' among other questions, a very high percentage of participants (80 per cent or more) say that they were. In addition, studies show that offenders and victims are actively involved in fashioning the outcome, which is indicative that laypeople are exercising decision-making power. Overall, RJ practices in the jurisdictions studies definitely conform to the ideals of procedural justice.

Compared to these very high levels of procedural justice, there appears to be relatively less evidence of 'restorativeness.' The measures of restorativeness used in the SAJJ project include the degree to which the offender was remorseful, spontaneously apologized to the victim, and understood the impact of the crime on the victim; the degree to which victims understood the offender's situation; and the extent of positive movement between the offender, victim, or their supporters. Depending on the variable, restorativeness was present in 30 to 60 per cent of the youth justice conferences studied.[4] Thus, RJ conferences receive high marks for procedural fairness and victim and offender participation, but it may be more difficult for victims and offend-

ers to resolve their differences or to find common ground in an RJ meeting (Daly 2001a, 2003).

Why is fairness easier to achieve than restorativeness? Fairness is largely, although not exclusively, a measure of the behavior of the professional(s) (the facilitator and, depending on the jurisdiction, a police officer). As the professionals, they are polite, they listen, and they establish ground rules of respect for others and civility in the conference process. Whereas fairness is established in the relationship between the professionals and participants, restorativeness emerges in the relationships between a victim, an offender, and their supporters. Being polite is easier to do than saying you are sorry; listening to someone tell their story of victimization is easier to do when you are not the offender. Indeed, understanding or taking the perspective of the other may be easier when you are not the actual victim or the offender in the justice encounter.

Restorativeness requires a degree of empathic concern and perspective-taking; and as measured by psychologists' scales, these qualities are more frequently evinced for adults than adolescents. For example, from interviews with youthful offenders, the SAJJ project found that over half had not thought *at all* about what they would say to the victim. Most did not think in terms of what they might *offer victims*, but rather what they would be *made to do by others*. It is possible that many adolescents may not yet have the capacity to think empathetically, to take the role of the other (Frankenberger 2000); they may be expected to act as if they had the moral reasoning of adults when they do not (Van Voorhis 1985). And, at the same time, as we shall see in limits (4) and (5), victims may have high expectations for an offender's behavior in the conference process which cannot be realized, or victims' distress may be so great that the conference process can do little to aid in their recovery.

Limit (4): a 'sincere apology' is difficult to achieve

It is said that in the aftermath of crime, what victims want most is 'symbolic reparation, primarily an apology' (Strang 2002: 55, drawing from Marshall and Merry 1990). Perhaps for some offences and some victims this may be true, but I suspect that most victims want more than an apology. Fundamentally, victims want a sense of vindication for the wrong done to them and they want the offender to stop harming and hurting them or other people. A sincere apology may be a useful starting point,[5] but we might expect most victims to want more. In research on violent offences, for example, Cretney and Davis (1995: 178) suggest that a 'victim has an interest in punishment,' not just restitution or reparation, because punishment 'can reassure the victim that he or she has public recognition and support.'

Let us assume, for the sake of argument, that a sincere apology is what victims mainly desire. What are the elements of a sincere apology and how often might we expect this to occur in an RJ process?

Drawing from Tavuchis' work on the sociology of apology (1991) Bottoms (2003: 94–8) distils the 'experiential dynamics' of an 'ideal-typical apology':[6]

> In the fully-accomplished apology ... we have first a *call* for an apology from the person(s) who regard themselves as wronged, or from someone speaking on their behalf; then the *apology* itself; and finally an expression of *forgiveness* from the wronged to the wrongdoer.
>
> (p. 94, emphasis in original)

Bottoms then says that 'each of these moves' in the fully accomplished (or ideal-typical) apology 'can be emotionally fraught' such that 'the whole apologetic discourse is (on both sides) "a delicate and precarious transaction"' (quoting Tavuchis 1991: vii).

It is important to distinguish between two types of apologies: an 'ideal-typical apology,' where there is an expression of forgiveness from a victim to an offender, and a 'sincere apology,' where there is a mutual understanding between the parties that the offender is really sorry but there is no assumption of forgiveness. I make this distinction because we might expect a 'sincere apology' to occur in an RJ process but we should not expect a victim to forgive an offender. In fact, I wonder if Tavuchis' formulation may be unrealistic in the context of a victim's response to crime. Tavuchis analyzes a range of harmful or hurtful behavior, not just crime; and I suspect that forgiveness may arise more often in non-criminal than in criminal contexts.

There is surprisingly little research on the character of apologies in RJ processes. From the RISE project, we learn that conference victims rated the offender's apology as 'sincere' (41 per cent), and a further 36 per cent rated it 'somewhat sincere' (Strang 2002: 115; 2004). Hayes's (2004) summary of RISE observational and interview data on the apology process concludes that 'the ideal of reconciliation and repair was achieved in less than half of all cases.'

The SAJJ project explored the apology process in detail (see Daly 2003: 224–5). When we asked

the youth why they decided to say sorry to victims, 27 per cent said they did not feel sorry but thought they'd get off more easily, 39 per cent said to make their family feel better, and a similar per cent said they felt pushed into it. However, when asked what was the *main reason* for saying sorry, most (61 per cent) said they really were sorry. When we asked victims about the apology process, most believed that the youth's motives for apologizing were insincere. To the item, 'The youth wasn't sorry, but thought they would get off more easily if they said sorry,' 36 per cent of victims said 'Yes, definitely,' and another 36 per cent said 'Yes, a little.' A slim majority of victims believed that the youth said sorry either to get off more easily (30 per cent) or because they were pushed into it (25 per cent). Just 27 per cent of victims believed that the main reason that they youth apologized was because s/he really was sorry.[7]

This mismatch of perception between victims and offenders was explored further, by drawing on conference observations, interview material, and police incident reports to make inferences about the apology process for all eighty-nine conferences in the SAJJ sample (Daly 2005). The results reinforce the findings above: they reveal that communication failure and mixed signals are present when apologies are made and received. Such communication gaps are overlaid by the variable degree to which offenders are in fact sorry for what they have done. In 34 per cent of cases, the offenders and victims agreed (or were in partial agreement) that the offender was sorry,[8] and in 27 per cent, the offenders and victims definitely agreed that the offender was not sorry. For 30 per cent, there was a perceptual mismatch: the offenders were not sorry, but the victims thought they were (12 per cent); or the offenders were sorry, but the victims did not think so (18 per cent). For the remaining 9 per cent, it was not possible to determine. The findings show that a sincere apology may be difficult to achieve because offenders are not really sorry for what they have done, victims wish offenders would display more contrite behavior, and there are misreadings of what the other is saying.

Hayes (2004) proposes an added reason for why sincere apologies are difficult to achieve. He suggests that there are 'competing demands' placed on youthful offenders in the conference process: they are asked both to explain what happened (or provide an 'account') and to apologize for what they did. Hayes surmises that 'offenders' speech acts ... may drift from apologetic discourse to mitigating accounts and back again.' Victims may interpret what is said (and not said) as being insincere.

Limit (5): the conference process can help some victims recover from crime, but this is contingent on the degree of distress they experienced

One of the major aims of a RJ process is to assist victims in recovering from the disabling effects of crime. This central feature of RJ has not been explored in any systematic way. The SAJJ data offer insights on this complex process, and here I distil from a study of the impact of crime on victims for their likelihood of recovery a year later (see Daly 2005).

An important finding, although typically not discussed in the RJ literature, is that victims experience crime differently: some are only lightly touched, whereas others experience many disabling effects such as health problems, sleeplessness, loss of self-confidence, among others. To describe this variability, I created a measure of 'victim distress,' which was derived from a set of questions about the effects of crime.[9] Initially, I identified four categories of victims: no distress (28 per cent), low distress (12.5 per cent), moderate distress (36.5), and high distress (23 per cent). For ease of analysis, I then collapsed the four groups into two, combining the no/low distress (40.5 per cent) and the moderate/high distress (59.5 per cent), which, for convenience, I will refer to as the 'low' and 'high' distress victims, respectively.

Some important findings emerged. The high distress group was significantly more likely to be composed of female victims, personal crime victims (including those victimized in their occupational role or at their organizational workplace), violent offences, and victims and offenders who were family members or well known to each other. The offences most likely to cause victims distress were assaults on family members or teachers (89 per cent in the high distress group); adolescent punch-ups (76 per cent); and breaking into, stealing, or damaging personal property (75 per cent). By comparison, the offences least likely to cause victims distress were breaking into, stealing, or damaging organizational property (19 per cent) and stranger assault (33 per cent). Theft of bikes or cars was midway (55 per cent of victims were in the high distress group).

Victims' distress was significantly linked to their attitude toward offenders and their interest to find common ground during the conference. For example, while 43 per cent of high distress victims had negative attitudes toward the offender after the conference, this was the case for just 8 per cent of low distress victims. Most high distress victims said it was more important for them to be treated fairly (67 per cent) than to find common ground with the offender, whereas most low distress victims (71 per cent) said it was more important to find common ground. This is a key finding: what crime victims hope to achieve from an RJ process — that is, whether to seek mutual understanding with offenders (other-regarding victims) or to be treated well as individuals (self-regarding) — is related to the character and experience of the victimization. Organizational and stranger assault victims were most likely to be other-regarding — that is, to want to find common ground; personal property crime victims were least likely to be other-regarding; and adolescent, family, and teacher assault victims fell in between.

In general and in the context of youth justice, victims who are only lightly touched by a crime orient themselves more readily to restorative behaviors. Compared to high distress victims, it was easier for the low distress group to be other-regarding because the wrong had not affected them deeply. After a conference ended, the high distress victims were far more likely to remain angry and fearful of offenders, and to be negative toward them, than the low distress victims. This result anticipates findings on victim recovery a year later.

In 1999, the SAJJ researchers re-interviewed the victims and asked them, 'Which of the following two statements better describes how you're feeling about the incident today? Would you say that it is all behind you, you are fully recovered from it; or it is partly behind you, there are still some things that bother you, you are not fully recovered from it?' Two-thirds said that they had recovered from the offence and it was all behind them. Thus, most victims had recovered from the offence a year later, but which ones? And did the conference process assist in their recovery?

When comparing victim distress in 1998 with their recovery a year later, there were startling results. Whereas 63 per cent of the moderate, 78 per cent of the low, and 95 per cent of the no distress victims had recovered in 1999, 71 per cent of the high distress victims had *not* recovered. Thus, for the most highly distressed victims, an RJ process may be of little help in recovering from crime. In 1999, we also asked victims, 'Would you say that your ability to get the offence behind you was aided more by your participation in the justice process or things that only you could do for yourself?' Half (49 per cent) said their participation in the justice process, and 40 per cent, only things they could do for themselves; 11 per cent said both were of equal importance. The recovered victims were more likely to say participation in the justice process (72 per cent) than

290

the non-recovered victims (38 per cent). Likewise, the low distress victims were more likely to say participation in the justice process (77 per cent) than the high distress victims (49 per cent).

Non- (or partly) recovered victims held more negative views of the offender and how their case was handled compared to the recovered victims. They were significantly more likely to see the offender as a 'bad' person rather than a 'good' person who had done a bad thing, less satisfied by how their case was handled, and more likely to say they wished their case had gone to court. When asked what was the most important thing hindering their recovery, 74 per cent of the non- (or partly) recovered victims cited financial losses, injuries, and emotional harms arising from the offence.

These findings on victim distress and recovery pose significant challenges to the RJ field. They invite reflection on the variable effects of victimization for the ways in which victims orient themselves to a restorative process. For the high distress victims, it was harder to act restoratively at the conference, and it was more difficult to be generous to offenders. The effects of victimization did not end with the conference but continued to linger for a long time. A process like RJ, and indeed any legal process (such as court), may do little to assist victims who have been deeply affected by crime. Improving practices by conference facilitators may help at the edges but this too is unlikely to have a major impact. Victims who are affected negatively and deeply by crime need more than RJ (or court) to recover from their victimization.

Limit (6): we should expect modest results, not the nirvana story of RJ

The nirvana story of RJ is illustrated by Jim Consedine (1995: 9), who opens his book by excerpting from a 1993 New Zealand news story:

The families of two South Auckland boys, killed by a car, welcomed the accused driver yesterday with open arms and forgiveness. The young man, who gave himself up to the police yesterday morning, apologised to the families and was ceremonially reunited with the Tongan and Samoan communities at a special service last night.

The 20-year-old Samoan visited the Tongan families after his court appearance to apologise for the deaths of the two children ... The Tongan and Samoan communities ... later gathered at the Tongan Methodist Church in a service of reconciliation. The young man sat at the feast table flanked by the mothers of the dead boys.

Later, in discussing the case, Consedine sees it as

Ample evidence of the power that healing and forgiveness can play in our daily lives ... The grieving Tongan and Samoan communities simply embraced the young driver ... and forgave him. His deep shame, his fear, his sorrow, his alienation from the community was resolved.
(Consedine 1995: 162)

This nirvana story of RJ contains elements that are not likely to be present in most RJ encounters: it was composed of members of racial-ethnic minority groups, who were drawn together with a shared experience of church, and there appeared to be 'meso-social structures' and 'thick' social ties between the families and kin of the offender and victims. These *gemeinschaft* qualities are atypical in modern urban life, and thus we should expect 'modest and patchy results' (Bottoms 2003: 110) to be the norm, not the exception. Much depends on the capacities and orientations of offenders and victims to be empathetic or to understand the other's situation, and on the degree to which offenders are genuinely sorry for what they have done and can communicate their remorse effectively. It also depends on the character of the victimization itself and how deeply it affects victims. All of these elements are largely outside the control of facilitators or other professionals, who are in a position only to coordinate, guide, or encourage such processes. We must also recognize the limits of time and resources that can be put to RJ processes. Some propose, for example, that with better preparation, RJ conferences will go more smoothly and achieve intended results. This may well be true, but it sets up a policy question: does one put a lot of resources (including more time in preparation) in a fewer number of RJ encounters, or does one attempt to apply RJ as widely and broadly as possible? We should not assume that the nirvana story of RJ is typical, nor that it can be achieved often.[10] This sets up RJ to fail with unrealistic and too high expectations.

CONCLUSION

That there exist limits on what RJ can achieve should not be grounds for dispensing with it, nor for being disillusioned, once again, with a new justice idea. My reading of the evidence is that face-to-face encounters between victims and offenders and their supporters *is* a practice worth maintaining, and perhaps enlarging, although we cannot expect it to deliver strong stories of repair and goodwill most of the time.

In the penalty phase of the criminal process, both RJ and the established court process have limits. RJ is limited by the abilities and interests of offenders and victims to think and act in ways we may define as restorative. Established CJ is limited by the inability of formal legality to listen to the accounts of crime and their effects by those most directly involved. Legal professionals do the talking, and what is legally or administratively relevant takes precedence.

By recognizing the limits of both RJ and established CJ in the penalty (or post-penalty) phase of the criminal process, we more effectively grasp the nettle of justice as a promise, as something that may be partly but never fully realized. As such, we see that all justice practices, including RJ, are limited.

VI

Law, Economy, and Society

The readings in Part VI further explore the role of law in regulating particular types of relationships between individuals and groups in society, with a specific emphasis on economic relationships.

The articles and cases in Chapter 14 focus on the ways in which private law rules in contract, torts and family law may be used to shape relationships. Alex Trubek's article provides a summary of Max Weber's view that laws of contract were developed in order to provide certainty in the exchange relationships that emerged in early capitalist society. As demonstrated in the *Rudder v. Microsoft* decision, we continue to develop the basic rules of contract to define enforceable agreements in a modern economy. Regulation of capitalist relationships is only one of the many conjunctions that the law attempts to define and regulate. The classic case of *Donoghue v. Stevenson* included in this chapter was the first case to clearly define the legal duty of care that flows between individuals under the law of tort, while the *Childs v. Desormeaux* decision provides an example of how Canadian courts have approached the issue of that duty of care in more contemporary social contexts. Finally, the excerpt from the *Petkus v. Becker* case shows the way in which courts can creatively apply legal doctrines to enforce obligations within intimate personal relationships in an attempt to avoid inequalities that are sometimes reinforced by, or result from, the application of formal legal rules. Tragically, the *Petkus v. Becker* case is also an example of the limits of law and of how much may be lost in the translation of law into the practical, day-to-day relationships that define our lives (as will be explored in Chapter 21).

Chapter 15 moves on to consider the ways in which courts and legislatures are constantly challenged to adapt existing legal rules to an ever-changing society, and at times to develop new rules, to respond to technological innovations. Lawrence Lessig's article describes the broad challenges to legal regulation posed by the Internet. This is a theme taken up by Michael MacNeil in his analysis of the use of French law to prevent access to Yahoo! sites auctioning Nazi memorabilia. Drawing on Lessig, MacNeil notes that some of the architectural features of the Internet, and the increased concentration of private service providers, may actually facilitate legal regulation and allow for a diversity of legal approaches in different jurisdictions. Finally, Ian Kerr, Valerie Steeves and Carole Lucock discuss the ways in which both our conception of privacy and our ability to protect it are affected by new technologies and by our legal regimes. In their view, considerations of privacy must also include important related values of identity and anonymity, both of which are also mediated through technology and law.

As you read this section, consider again the choice we make in employing law to order, stabilize, or legitimize certain relationships or remedy social problems. Is law always the best option? How does law regulate in relation to other regulators of behaviour? As the articles in Chapter 15 highlight, the Internet is a critical case to consider: first, because social relationships are increasingly mediated by evolving technologies (e.g., facebook, twitter, etc.) and second, because — contrary to those who might still imagine the Internet as a new Wild West — behaviour on the Internet is still regulated. However, as all the authors underscore, traditional legal approaches are necessarily supplemented or, even, superseded by regulation through the very architecture of the Internet. What implications might follow from this?

(a)   Max Weber on Law and the Rise of Capitalism†

David M. Trubek

III.   LEGALISM AND CAPITALISM: A RECONSTRUCTION OF WEBER'S THEORY OF LAW IN ECONOMIC LIFE

We now have most of the elements needed to understand Weber's theory of the relationship between the rise of modern law and capitalism. We have examined his legal sociology, which identifies distinctive types of legal systems, and his political sociology, which shows that the structure of power determines to some degree the type of legal order that can exist. We have seen why Weber thought legalism developed in Europe. Now we must turn to his economic sociology, in which the dynamics of the market are developed. This analysis will show why capitalism and legalism are intimately related.

In his economic sociology, Weber stressed the importance for capitalist development of two aspects of law: (1) its relative degree of *calculability*, and (2) its capacity to develop *substantive* provisions — principally those relating to freedom of contract — necessary to the functioning of the market system.

The former reason was the more important of the two. Weber asserted that capitalism required a highly calculable normative order. His survey of types of law indicated that only modern, rational law, or logically formal rationality, could provide the necessary calculability. Legalism supported the development of capitalism by providing a stable and predictable atmosphere; capitalism encouraged legalism because the bourgeoisie were aware of their own need for this type of governmental structure.[38]

Legalism is the only way to provide the degree of certainty necessary for the operation of the capitalist system. Weber stated that capitalism "could not continue if its control of resources were not upheld by the legal compulsion of the state; if its formally 'legal' rights were not upheld by the threat of force."[39] He further specified that: "[T]he rationalization and systematization of the law in general and ... the increasing calculability of the functioning of the legal process in particular, constituted one of the most important conditions for the existence of ... capitalistic enterprise, which cannot do without legal security."[40]

Weber never worked out in detail a model of capitalist production which might explain why legal calculability was so important to capitalist development. I have developed such a model,[41] and I believe that underlying Weber's repeated emphasis on legal calculability is a vision similar to this latter-day ideal type.

The essence of the model is the conflict of egoistic wills, which is an inherent part of competitive capitalism. In pure market capitalism of the type idealized in micro-economics texts, each participant is driven to further his own interests at the expense of all other participants in the market. Theoretically, the profit motive is insatiable, and is unconstrained by any ethical or moral force. Thus, each actor is unconcerned with the ramifications of his actions on the economic well-being of others.

---

† (1972) Wisconsin L. Rev. 720 at 739–45, 748–50. [Notes and/or references omitted.] Copyright 1972 by The Board of Regents of the University of Wisconsin System. Reproduced with permission of the Wisconsin Law Review. [Notes and/or references omitted.]

At the same time, however, economic actors in this system are necessarily interdependent. No market participant can achieve his goals unless he secures power over the actions of others. It does little good, for example, for the owner of a textile plant to act egocentrically to further his interests if at the same time he cannot be sure that other actors will supply him with the necessary inputs for production and consume his product. If suppliers do not provide promised raw materials, if workers refuse to work, if customers fail to pay for goods delivered, all the ruthless, rational self-interest in the world will be of little value to the textile producer in his striving for profits.

Now if all the other actors were nice, cooperative fellows, our textile manufacturer might not have to worry. Others would play their roles in the scheme and he would come out all right. But this may not always happen because they are, by hypothesis, as selfish as he is. Thus, they, too, will do whatever leads to the highest profit; if this means failing to perform some agreement, so be it. And since one can assume that there will frequently be opportunities for other actors to better themselves at the expense of providing him with some service or product necessary to the success of his enterprise, our hypothetical businessman lives in a world of radical uncertainty.

Yet, as Weber constantly stressed, uncertainty of this type is seriously prejudicial to the smooth functioning of the modern economy. How can the capitalist economic actor in a world of similarly selfish profitseekers reduce the uncertainty that threatens to rob the capitalist system of its otherwise great productive power? What will permit the economic actor to predict with relative certainty how other actors will behave over time? What controls the tendency toward instability?

In order to answer these questions, Weber moved to the level of sociological analysis. The problem of the conflict between the self-interest of individuals and social stability — what Parsons calls "the Hobbesian problem of order"[42] — is one of the fundamental problems of sociology, and, to deal with it, Weber constructed his basic schemes of social action.[43] Weber recognized that predictable uniformities of social action can be "guaranteed" in various ways and that all of these methods of social control may influence economic activities. Actors may internalize normative standards, thus fulfilling social expectations "voluntarily." Or they may be subjected to some form of "external effect" if they deviate from expectations. These external guarantees may derive from some informal sanctioning system or

may involve organized coercion. Law is one form of organized coercion. All types of control may be involved in guaranteeing stable power over economic resources; factual control of this type, Weber observed, may be due to custom, to the play of interests, to convention, or to law.[44]

As I have indicated, however, Weber believed that the organized coercion of *law* was necessary in modern, capitalist economies. While internalization and conventional sanctions may be able to eliminate or resolve most conflict in simpler societies, it is incapable of serving this function in a way that satisfies the needs of the modern exchange economy. For this function, law, in the sense of organized coercion, was necessary. Weber stated:

> [T]hough it is not necessarily true of every economic system, certainly the modern economic order under modern conditions could not continue if its control of resources were not upheld by the legal compulsion of the state; that is, if its formally "legal" rights were not upheld by the threat of force.[45]

Why is coercion necessary in a market system? And why must this coercion take legal form? Finally, when we speak of *legal* coercion, do we mean state power, regardless of how it is exercised, or do we mean power governed by rules, or legalism? Weber gives no clear-cut answer to these questions. The discussion suggests answers but the issues are not fully developed. And the most crucial question, the interrelationship between the need for coercion and the model of legalism, is barely discussed at all. However, I think answers to the questions can be given which fit coherently with other aspects of his analysis.

Coercion is necessary because of the egoistic conflict I have identified above. While Weber never clearly identified this conflict, he himself was aware of it. Some principle of behavior other than short term self-interest is necessary for a market system. Tradition cannot function to constrain egoistic behavior because the market destroys the social and cultural bases of tradition. Similarly, the emerging market economy erodes the social groupings which could serve as the foci for enforcement of conventional standards. Indeed, the fact that the type of conflict I have described comes into existence is evidence of the decline of tradition and custom. Only law is left to fill the normative vacuum; legal coercion is essential because no other form is available.

A second reason why the necessary coercion must be legal is tied to the pace of economic activity and the type of rationalistic calculation characteristic of the market economy. It is not enough for the capitalist to have a general idea that someone else will more likely than not deliver more or less the performance agreed upon on or about the time stipulated. He must know exactly what and when, and he must be highly certain that the precise performance will be forthcoming. He wants to be able to predict with certainty that the other units will perform. But given the potential conflict between their self-interests and their obligations, he also wants to predict with certainty that coercion will be applied to the recalcitrant. The predictability of performance is intimately linked to the certainty that coercive instruments can be invoked in the event of nonperformance.

In this context, it becomes clear why a calculable legal system offers the most reliable way to combine coercion and predictability. Here the model of legalism and the model of capitalist dynamics merge. A system of government through rules seems inherently more predictable than any other method for structuring coercion. Convention is inherently too diffuse, and, like custom, was historically unavailable given the market-driven erosion of the groups and structures necessary for effective constraint of egoism. Like Balzac, Weber saw how the decline of family, guild, and Church unleashed unbridled egoism. Pure *power*, on the other hand, is available in the sense that the state is increasingly armed with coercive instruments. But untrammeled power is unpredictable; wielders of power, unconstrained by rules, will tend not to act in stable and predictable ways. Legalism offers the optimum combination of coercion and predictability.

It is here that the significance of legal autonomy can be seen. Autonomy is intimately linked to the problem of predictability. The autonomous legal system in a legalistic society is an institutional complex organized to apply coercion only in accordance with general rules through logical or purely cognitive processes. To the extent that it truly functions in the purely logical and, consequently, mechanical manner Weber presented, its results will be highly predictable. If it is constantly subject to interference by forces which seek to apply coercion for purposes inconsistent with the rules, it loses its predictable quality. Thus Weber observed that authoritarian rulers (and democratic despots) may refuse to be bound by formal rules since:

> They are all confronted by the inevitable conflict between an abstract formalism of legal certainty and their desire to realize substantive goals. Juridical formalism enables the legal system to operate like a technically rational machine. Thus

it guarantees to individuals and groups within the system a relative maximum of freedom, and greatly increases for them the possibility of predicting the legal consequences of their actions.[46]

Of course, the idea of legal autonomy is a much more complex one than this simplified model suggests. In Weber's work, the emergence of the autonomous legal order is correlated with other important phenomena. An autonomous legal order was essential if certain norms of a certain type were to emerge. Neither theocratic nor patrimonial rulers would allow the development of the substantive norms of economic autonomy contained in the idea of freedom of contract. Only an independent structure of normative order could guarantee these, and only a universal and supreme structure could guarantee that these norms would be adhered to. Thus the legal system had to be autonomous of other sources of normative order on the one hand, and of pure power on the other, and simultaneously control the adverse effects of both for capitalism. At least some areas of social life had to be freed of the bonds of kinship, religion, and other foci of traditional authority, and, at the same time, insulated from the arbitrary action of the state. This required that the state, as legal order, be strengthened, so that it superseded other sources of social control, and at the same time be limited, so that it did not encroach upon areas of economic action. The state was to provide a formal order, or facilitative framework within which free economic actors could operate.[47] Contained in the idea of an autonomous legal order are fundamental paradoxes of the 19th-century idea of the liberal state.[48]

. . . .

V. LEGALISM AND THE LEGITIMIZATION OF CLASS DOMINATION

Up to this point, "capitalism" has been presented as a vague abstraction. While Weber thought that capitalism was in some ways the most rational possible economic system,[60] he was no apologist for it. He could be scathingly critical of the moral effects of this system. These criticisms can be seen in several points; they emerge clearly in another part of the sociology of law where Weber takes up an issue raised by Marx: the role of legalism in legitimizing capitalist domination.

Legalism served more than purely economic functions under capitalism. Weber showed how the idea of an autonomous legal system dispensing formal justice legitimizes the political structure of capitalist society.

Legalism legitimizes the domination of workers by capitalists. The relationships between law, the state, and the market are complex. Legalism, while seeming to constrain the state, really strengthens it, and while the system guaranteed formal equality, it also legitimized class domination. Legalism strengthens the state by apparently constraining it, for the commitment to a system of rules increases the legitimacy of the modern state and thus its authority or effective power. And as the liberal state grows stronger, it reduces the hold of other forces on the development of the market. This strengthens the position of those who control property, since market organization increases the effective power of those individuals and organizations that control economic resources. "[B]y virtue of the principle of formal legal equality ... the propertied classes ... obtain a sort of factual 'autonomy'...," Weber observed.[61]

He believed that these effects of legalism stem from the fundamental antinomy between formal and material criteria of justice, and the negative aspects of purely formal administration of justice under modern conditions. Formal justice is advantageous to those with economic power; not only is it calculable but, by stressing formal as opposed to substantive criteria for decisionmaking, it discourages the use of the law as an instrument of social justice. In a passage reminiscent of Anatole France's famous quip that the law forbids both rich and poor to sleep under the bridges of Paris, Weber observed:

> Formal justice guarantees the maximum freedom for the interested parties to represent their formal legal interests. But because of the unequal distribution of economic power, *which the system of formal justice legalizes*, this very freedom must time and again produce consequences which are contrary to ... religious ethics or ... political expediency.[62]

Formal justice not only is repugnant to authoritarian powers and arbitrary rulers; it also is opposed to democratic interests. Formal justice, necessarily abstract, cannot consider the ethical issues raised by such interests; such abstention, however, reduces the possibility of realizing substantive policies advocated by popular groups.[63] Thus, certain democratic values and types of social justice could only be achieved at the cost of sacrificing strict legalism.[64] Weber also pointed out that formal legalism could stultify legal creativity, and that legal autonomy could lead to results opposed to both popular and capitalist values.

(b) *Rudder v. Microsoft Corp.*†

[WINKLER J.:]

[1] This is a motion by the defendant Microsoft for a permanent stay of this intended class proceeding. The motion is based on two alternative grounds, first that the parties have agreed to the exclusive jurisdiction, and venue, of the courts, in King County in the State of Washington in respect of any litigation between them, and secondly, that in any event, Ontario is not the appropriate forum for the conduct of this proceeding and that the service ex juris of the Statement of Claim ought to be set aside.

[2] The Microsoft Network ("MSN"), is an online service, providing, inter alia, information and services including Internet access to its members. The service is provided to members, around the world, from a "gateway" located in the State of Washington through computer connections most often made over standard telephone lines.

[3] The proposed representative plaintiffs in this action were subscriber members of MSN. Both are law school graduates, one of whom is admitted to the Bar in Ontario while the other worked as a legal researcher. They were associated with the law firm which originally represented the intended class. The plaintiffs claim under the Class Proceedings Act, 1992, S.O., C.6 on behalf of a Canada-wide class defined as:

---

† [1999] O.J. No. 3778 (Ont. Sup. Ct.).

All persons resident in Canada who subscribed for the provision of Internet access or information or services from or through MSN, The Microsoft Network, since September 1, 1995. This class is estimated to contain some 89,000 MSN members across Canada.

[4] The plaintiffs claim damages for breach of contract, breach of fiduciary duty, misappropriation and punitive damages in the total amount of $75,000,000.00 together with an accounting and injunctive relief. The plaintiffs allege that Microsoft has charged members of MSN and taken payment from their credit cards in breach of contract and that Microsoft has failed to provide reasonable or accurate information concerning accounts. The Statement of Claim was served on Microsoft at its offices in Redmond, Washington on January 5, 1998.

[5] The contract which the plaintiffs allege to have been breached is identified by MSN as a "Member Agreement". Potential members of MSN are required to electronically execute this agreement prior to receiving the services provided by the company. Each Member Agreement contains the following provision:

> 15.1 This Agreement is governed by the laws of the State of Washington, U.S.A., and you consent to the exclusive jurisdiction and venue of courts in King County, Washington, in all disputes arising out of or relating to your use of MSN or your MSN membership. The defendant relies on this clause in support of its assertion that the intended class proceeding should be permanently stayed.

[6] Although the plaintiffs rely on the contract as the basis for their causes of action, they submit that the court ought not to give credence to the "forum selection clause" contained within. It is stated in support of this contention that the representative plaintiffs read only portions of the Member Agreement and thus had no notice of the forum selection clause. Alternatively, the plaintiffs contend, in any event, that the Washington courts are not appropriate for the conduct of this lawsuit.

[7] I cannot accede to these submissions. In my view, the forum selection clause is dispositive and there is nothing in the factual record which persuades me that I should exercise my discretion so as to permit the plaintiffs to avoid the effect of the contractual provision. Accordingly, an order will go granting the relief sought by the defendant. My reasons follow.

ANALYSIS AND DISPOSITION

[8] Forum selection clauses are generally treated with a measure of deference by Canadian courts. Madam Justice Huddart, writing for the court in *Sarabia v. "Oceanic Mindoro"* (1996), 4 C.P.C. (4th) 11 (B.C.C.A.), leave to appeal denied [1997] S.C.C.A. No. 69, adopts the view that forum selection clauses should be treated the same as arbitration agreements. She states at 20:

> Since forum selection clauses are fundamentally similar to arbitration agreements, ... there is no reason for forum selection clauses not to be treated in a manner consistent with the deference shown to arbitration agreements. Such deference to forum selection clauses achieves greater international commercial certainty, shows respect for the agreements that the parties have signed, and is consistent with the principle of international comity. (Emphasis added.)

[9] Huddart J.A. further states at 21 that "a court is not bound to give effect to an exclusive jurisdiction clause" but that the choice of the parties should be respected unless "there is strong cause to override the agreement." The burden for a showing of a "strong cause" rests with the plaintiff and the threshold to be surpassed is beyond the mere "balance of convenience". The approach taken by Huddart J.A. is consistent with that adopted by courts in Ontario. (See *Holo-Deck Adventures Ltd. v. Orbotron Inc.* (1996), 8 C.P.C. (4th) 376 (Gen. Div.); *Mithras Management Ltd. v. New Visions Entertainment Corp.* (1992), 90 D.L.R. (4th) 726 (Ont. Gen. Div.)).

[10] The plaintiffs contend, first, that regardless of the deference to be shown to forum selection clauses, no effect should be given to the particular clause at issue in this case because it does not represent the true agreement of the parties. It is the plaintiffs submission that the form in which the Member Agreement is provided to potential members of MSN is such that it obscures the forum selection clause. Therefore, the plaintiffs argue, the clause should be treated as if it were the fine print in a contract which must be brought specifically to the attention of the party accepting the terms. Since there was no specific notice given, in the plaintiffs' view, the forum selection clause should be severed from the Agreement which they otherwise seek to enforce.

[11] The argument advanced by the plaintiffs relies heavily on the alleged deficiencies in the technological aspects of electronic formats for presenting the terms of agreements. In other words, the plaintiffs

contend that because only a portion of the Agreement was presented on the screen at one time, the terms of the Agreement which were not on the screen are essentially "fine print".

[12] I disagree. The Member Agreement is provided to potential members of MSN in a computer readable form through either individual computer disks or via the Internet at the MSN website. In this case, the plaintiff Rudder, whose affidavit was filed on the motion, received a computer disk as part of a promotion by MSN. The disk contained the operating software for MSN and included a multi-media sign up procedure for persons who wished to obtain the MSN service. As part of the sign-up routine, potential members of MSN were required to acknowledge their acceptance of the terms of the Member Agreement by clicking on an "I Agree" button presented on the computer screen at the same time as the terms of the Member Agreement were displayed.

[13] Rudder admitted in cross-examination on his affidavit that the entire agreement was readily viewable by using the scrolling function on the portion of the computer screen where the Membership Agreement was presented. Moreover, Rudder acknowledged that he "scanned" through part of the Agreement looking for "costs" that would be charged by MSN. He further admitted that once he had found the provisions relating to costs, he did not read the rest of the Agreement. An excerpt from the transcript of Rudder's cross-examination is illustrative:

> Q. 314. I will now take you down to another section. I am now looking at heading 15, which is entitled "General", and immediately underneath that is subsection 15.1. Now, do I take it, when you were scanning, you would have actually scanned past this, and you would have at least seen there was a heading that said "General"? Is that fair? Or did you not even scan all the way through?
>
> A. I did not go all the way down, I can honestly say. Once I found out what it would cost me, that is where I would stop.
>
> Q. 315. So, I take it that you did not read 15.1?
> A. No, I definitely did not read this, no.
>
> Q. 316. I now have 15.4 on the screen, and presumably you did not read that either?
> A. No, I did not.
>
> Q. 317. I take it, during the whole signup process that you did, you did the whole thing online on the computer ...
> A. Yes.

> Q. 318. ... using the disk? And we will come to the connection. You did not have any voice communication with MSN?
> A. No.
>
> Q. 319. Or with Microsoft Corporation?
> A. No.
>
> Q. 320. You did not have any written correspondence with them at the time of signup?
> A. No.
>
> Q. 321. All right. Now, I take it that, after doing the review of this that you did do, you clicked, "I agree"? Is that what you did?
> A. After I was satisfied with what it was going to cost me, I agreed. (Emphasis added.)

[14] I have viewed the Member Agreement as it was presented to Rudder during the sign up procedure. All of the terms of the Agreement are displayed in the same format. Although, there are certain terms of the Agreement displayed entirely in upper-case letters, there are no physical differences which make a particular term of the agreement more difficult to read than any other term. In other words, there is no fine print as that term would be defined in a written document. The terms are set out in plain language, absent words that are commonly referred to as "legalese". Admittedly, the entire Agreement cannot be displayed at once on the computer screen, but this is not materially different from a multi-page written document which requires a party to turn the pages. Furthermore, the structure of the sign-up procedure is such that the potential member is presented with the terms of membership twice during the process and must signify acceptance each time. Each time the potential member is provided with the option of disagreeing which terminates the process. The second time the terms are displayed occurs during the online portion of the process and at that time, the potential member is advised via a clear notice on the computer screen of the following:

> ... The membership agreement includes terms that govern how information about you and your membership may be used. To become a MSN Premier member, you must select "I Agree" to acknowledge your consent to the terms of the membership agreement. If you click "I Agree" without reading the membership agreement, you are still agreeing to be bound by all of the terms of the membership agreement, without limitation ....

[15] On cross-examination, Rudder admitted to having seen the screen containing the notice. In order to replicate the conditions, portions of the cross-examination were conducted while Rudder was being

led through an actual sign-up process including the online connection portion. While online, and after having been shown the notice posted above, Rudder responded to questioning as follows:

> Q. 372. All right. You see immediately below the printing that we have just read, a rectangular box that says, "MSN Premier Membership Rules"?
> A. Yes.
>
> Q. 373. And, below that, a larger white box that says, "Please click MSN Membership Rules and read the membership agreement"?
> A. Yes.
>
> Q. 374. Did you read the phrase that I just stated in the big white box?
> A. No. What I probably did ... I can't say for sure ... is I probably just went to "I Agree", and then "Next".
>
> Q. 375. Did you understand, when you clicked "I Agree" on this occasion, that [what] you were agreeing to was something that was going to govern your legal relationship surrounding your use of MSN?
> A. If you are asking me if I made a mental note, or if I had knowledge of that, no, I did not really pay attention to that. That is a common practice when I sign up on anything. Like I said, my main concern is what the costs are.

[16] It is plain and obvious that there is no factual foundation for the plaintiffs' assertion that any term of the Membership Agreement was analogous to "fine print" in a written contract. What is equally clear is that the plaintiffs seek to avoid the consequences of specific terms of their agreement while at the same time seeking to have others enforced. Neither the form of this contract nor its manner of presentation to potential members are so aberrant as to lead to such an anomalous result. To give effect to the plaintiffs' argument would, rather than advancing the goal of "commercial certainty", to adopt the words of Huddart J.A. in Sarabia, move this type of electronic transaction into the realm of commercial absurdity. It would lead to chaos in the marketplace, render ineffectual electronic commerce and undermine the integrity of any agreement entered into through this medium.

[17] On the present facts, the Membership Agreement must be afforded the sanctity that must be given to any agreement in writing. The position of selectivity advanced by the plaintiffs runs contrary to this stated approach, both in principle and on the evidence, and must be rejected. Moreover, given

that both of the representative plaintiffs are graduates of law schools and have a professed familiarity with Internet services, their position is particularly indefensible.

[18] Having found that the terms of the Member Agreement, including the forum selection clause, bind the plaintiffs, I turn to a consideration of whether it is appropriate to exercise my discretion to override the forum clause agreed to by the parties. In my view, the submissions made by the defendant are compelling. On the facts of this case, it would not be appropriate for this court to permit the plaintiff to continue this action in Ontario contrary to the forum selection clause.

[19] Simply put, I find that the plaintiffs have not met the burden of showing a "strong cause" as to why the forum selection clause should not be determinative. In Sarabia, Huddart J.A. referred to the English case, *"Eleftheria" (The) (Cargo Owners) v. "Eleftheria" (The)*, [1969] 2 All E.R. 641, as the decision most often followed in Canada in setting out the factors that a court will consider in determining whether it should exercise its discretion and refuse to enforce a forum selection clause in an agreement.

[20] The factors to consider may be paraphrased as follows:

1. in which jurisdiction is the evidence on issues of fact situated, and the effect of that on the convenience and expense of trial in either jurisdiction;
2. whether the law of the foreign country applies and its differences from the domestic law in any respect;
3. the strength of the jurisdictional connections of the parties;
4. whether the defendants desire to enforce the forum selection clause is genuine or merely an attempt to obtain a procedural advantage;
5. whether the plaintiffs will suffer prejudice by bringing their claim in a foreign court because they will be
   (a) deprived of security for the claim; or
   (b) be unable to enforce any judgment obtained; or
   (c) be faced with a time-bar not applicable in the domestic court; or
   (d) unlikely to receive a fair trial.

[21] When these factors are applied within the factual matrix of this case, it is apparent that the plaintiffs cannot meet the threshold of a "strong cause".

Most of the activities associated with the provision of services pursuant to the Member Agreements that are the subject of the allegations in the Statement of Claim are carried out in King County, Washington. This includes the business management of accounts of MSN members, member authentication, policy-making regarding member accounts, billing and customer service. All of the computers in which MSN content and information are contained are located in King County. The sheer size of the intended class means that there is a potential that voluminous amounts of billing statements and related information, which is most likely to be located in Washington, will be required as evidence. Furthermore, the MSN witnesses are located at the company's center of operations in King County.

[22] Since I have found that the forum selection clause applies in this case, by operation of that clause the choice of law agreed to by the parties is the law of the State of Washington. Regardless of whether this action [were] tried in Ontario or elsewhere, the law to be applied would remain the same.

[23] Microsoft has demonstrated substantial connection to the State of Washington, and in particular to King County. The plaintiffs, on the other hand, propose to represent a Canada-wide class whose connections to Ontario are not readily apparent on the evidence before the court. Class proceedings may be conducted under both the federal and state court systems in the State of Washington and while the test

for certification may be somewhat more advantageous to the plaintiffs in Ontario, it is not sufficiently so as to permit me to ignore the other factors which clearly favour the defendant in this case. Moreover, in the interests of international comity, and in the absence of any evidence to the contrary, there is nothing to suggest that the plaintiffs would not receive a fair trial in the State of Washington. Indeed, considering that the defendant is resident there, it would be more advantageous to the plaintiffs, in respect of enforcement, if a judgment were obtained from a court in that jurisdiction.

[24] I note in passing that this forum selection clause has been upheld on appeal in an intended class proceeding in the State of New Jersey. (*Caspi v. The Microsoft Network*, L.L.C., 732 A.2d 528 (N.J. App. 1999).

[25] In view of my disposition on the first point, it is unnecessary to deal with the forum non conveniens and service ex juris arguments.

[26] The defendant shall have the relief requested. The action brought by the plaintiffs in Ontario is permanently stayed. The defendant shall have its costs of this motion, which, by agreement of the parties will be fixed by the court and payable forthwith. Counsel may make brief written submissions with respect to costs within two weeks of the date of release of these reasons.

(c) *Donoghue v. Stevenson*

The defendant was the manufacturer of a well-known brand of ginger-beer which was sold in opaque bottles. The plaintiff consumed part of a bottle of the defendant's ginger-beer in which she found the remains of a decomposed snail. The bottle had been purchased by the plaintiff's friend at a railway café.

The defendants denied liability on the basis that as a manufacturer it owed no duty of care to the plaintiff consumer.

[LORD ATKIN:]

The sole question for determination in this case is legal: Do the averments made by the pursuer in her pleading, if true, disclose a cause of action? I need not re-state the particular facts. The question is whether the manufacturer of an article of drink sold by him to a distributor in circumstances which prevent the distributor or the ultimate purchaser or consumer from discovering by inspection any defect is under any legal duty to the ultimate purchaser or

---

† [1932] All E.R. 1 at 10–13, 20. (H.L.)

consumer to take reasonable care that the article is free from defect likely to cause injury to health. I do not think a more important problem has occupied your Lordships in your judicial capacity, important both because of its bearing on public health and because of the practical test which it applies to the system of law under which it arises. The case has to be determined in accordance with Scots law, but it has been a matter of agreement between the experienced counsel who argued this case, and it appears to be the basis of the judgments of the learned judges of the Court of Session, that for the purposes of determining this problem the laws of Scotland and the law of England are the same. I speak with little authority on this point, but my own research, such as it is, satisfies me that the principles of the law of Scotland on such a question as the present are identical with those of English law, and I discuss the issue on that footing. The law of both countries appears to be that in order to support an action for damages for negligence the complainant has to show that he has been injured by the breach of a duty owed to him in the circumstances by the defendant to take reasonable care to avoid such injury. In the present case we are not concerned with the breach of the duty; if a duty exists, that would be a question of fact which is sufficiently averred and for the present purposes must be assumed. We are solely concerned with the question whether as a matter of law in the circumstances alleged the defender owed any duty to the pursuer to take care.

It is remarkable how difficult it is to find in the English authorities statements of general application defining the relations between parties that give rise to the duty. The courts are concerned with the particular relations which come before them in actual litigation, and it is sufficient to say whether the duty exists in those circumstances. The result is that the courts have been engaged upon an elaborate classification of duties as they exist in respect of property, whether real or personal, with further divisions as to ownership, occupation or control, and distinctions based on the particular relations of the one side or the other, whether manufacturer, salesman or landlord, customer, tenant, stranger, and so on. In this way it can be ascertained at any time whether the law recognises a duty, but only where the case can be referred to some particular species which has been examined and classified. And yet the duty which is common to all the cases where liability is established must logically be based upon some element common to the cases where it is found to exist. To exist a complete logical definition of the general principle is probably to go beyond the function of the judge, for, the more general the definition, the more likely it is to omit essentials or introduce non-essentials. The attempt was made by Lord Esher in *Heaven v. Pender* in a definition to which I will later refer. As framed it was demonstrably too wide, though it appears to me, if properly limited, to be capable of affording a valuable practical guide.

At present I content myself with pointing out that in English law there must be and is some general conception of relations giving rise to a duty of care, of which the particular cases found in the books are but instances. The liability for negligence, whether you style it such or treat it as in other systems as a species of "culpa," is no doubt based upon a general public sentiment of moral wrong-doing for which the offender must pay. But acts or omissions which any moral code would censure cannot in a practical world be treated so as to give a right to every person injured by them to demand relief. In this way rules of law arise which limit the range of complainants and the extent of their remedy. The rule that you are to love your neighbour becomes in law: You must not injure your neighbour, and the lawyers' question: Who is my neighbour? receives a restricted reply. You must take reasonable care to avoid acts or omissions which you can reasonably foresee would be likely to injure your neighbour. Who then, in law, is my neighbour? The answer seems to be persons who are so closely and directly affected by my act that I ought reasonably to have them in contemplation as being so affected when I am directing my mind to the acts or omissions which are called in question. This appears to me to be the doctrine of *Heaven v. Pender* as laid down by Lord Esher when it is limited by the notion of proximity introduced by Lord Esher himself and A.L. Smith, L.J., in *Le Lievre and another v. Gould.* Lord Esher, M.R., says ([1893] 1 Q.B. at p. 497):

> That case established that, under certain circumstances, one man may owe a duty to another, even though there is no contract between them. If one man is near to another, or is near to the property of another, a duty lies upon him not to do that which may cause a personal injury to that other, or may injure his property.

So A.L. Smith, L.J., says ([1893] 1 Q.B. at p. 504):

> The decision of *Heaven v. Pender* was founded upon the principle that a duty to take due care did arise when the person or property of one was in such proximity to the person or property of another that, if due care was not taken damage might be done by the one to the other.

303

I think that this sufficiently states the truth if proximity be not confined to mere physical proximity, but be used, as I think it was intended, to extend to such close and direct relations that the act complained of directly affects a person whom the person alleged to be bound to take care would know would be directly affected by his careless act. That this is the sense in which nearness or "proximity" was intended by Lord Esher is obvious from his own illustration in *Heaven* v. *Pender* (11 Q.B.D. at p. 510) of the application of his doctrine to the sale of goods.

> This [*i.e.*, the rule he has just formulated] includes the case of goods, [etc.], supplied to be used immediately by a particular person or persons, or one of a class of persons, where it would be obvious to the person supplying, if he thought, that the goods would in all probability be used at once by such persons before a reasonable opportunity for discovering any defect which might exist, and where the thing supplied would be of such a nature that a neglect of ordinary care or skill as to its condition or the manner of supplying it would probably cause danger to the person or property of the person for whose use it was supplied, and who was about to use it. It would exclude a case in which the goods are supplied under circumstances in which it would be a chance by whom they would be used, or whether they would be used or not, or whether they would be used before there would probably be means of observing any defect, or where the goods would be of such a nature that a want of care or skill as to their condition or the manner of supplying them would not probably produce danger of injury to person or property.

I draw particular attention to the fact that Lord Esher emphasises the necessity of goods having to be "used immediately" and "used at once before a reasonable opportunity of inspection." This is obviously to exclude the possibility of goods having their condition altered by lapse of time, and to call attention to the proximate relationship, which may be too remote where inspection even by the person using, certainly by an intermediate person, may reasonably be interposed. With this necessary qualification of proximate relationship, as explained in *Le Lievre* v. *Gould*, I think the judgment of Lord Esher expresses the law of England. Without the qualification, I think that the majority of the court in *Heaven* v. *Pender* was justified in thinking that the principle was expressed in too general terms. There will, no doubt, arise cases where it will be difficult to determine whether the contemplated relationship is so

close that the duty arises. But in the class of case now before the court I cannot conceive any difficulty to arise. A manufacturer puts up an article of food in a container which he knows will be opened by the actual consumer. There can be no inspection by any purchaser and no reasonable preliminary inspection by the consumer. Negligently in the course of preparation he allows the contents to be mixed with poison. It is said that the law of England and Scotland is that the poisoned consumer has no remedy against the negligent manufacturer. If this were the result of the authorities, I should consider the result a grave defect in the law and so contrary to principle that I should hesitate long before following any decision to that effect which had not the authority of this House. I would point out that in the assumed state of the authorities not only would the consumer have no remedy against the manufacturer, he would have none against anyone else, for in the circumstances alleged there would be no evidence of negligence against anyone other than the manufacturer, and except in the case of a consumer who was also a purchaser no contract and no warranty of fitness, and in the case of the purchase of a specific article under its patent or trade name, which might well be the case in the purchase of some articles of food or drink, no warranty protecting even the purchaser-consumer. There are other instances than of articles of food and drink where goods are sold intended to be used immediately by the consumer, such as many forms of goods sold for cleaning purposes, when the same liability must exist. The doctrine supported by the decision below would not only deny a remedy to the consumer who was injured by consuming bottled beer or chocolates poisoned by the negligence of the manufacturer, but also to the user of what should be a harmless proprietary medicine, an ointment, a soap, a cleaning fluid or cleaning powder. I confine myself to articles of common household use, where everyone, including the manufacturer, knows that the articles will be used by persons other than the actual ultimate purchaser — namely, by members of his family and his servants, and, in some cases, his guests. I do not think so ill of our jurisprudence as to suppose that its principles are so remote from the ordinary needs of civilized society and the ordinary claims which it makes upon its members as to deny a legal remedy where there is so obviously a social wrong.

. . . .

If your Lordships accept the view that the appellant's pleading discloses a relevant cause of action, you will be affirming the proposition that by Scots and English law alike a manufacturer of products which he sells in such a form as to show that he intends them to reach the ultimate consumer in the form in which they left him, with no reasonable possibility of intermediate examination, and with the knowledge that the absence of reasonable care in the preparation or putting up of the products will result in injury to the consumer's life or property, owes a duty to the consumer to take that reasonable care.

It is a proposition that I venture to say no one in Scotland or England who was not a lawyer would for one moment doubt. It will be an advantage to make it clear that the law in this matter, as in most others, is in accordance with sound common sense. I think that this appeal should be allowed.

(d) *Childs v. Desormeaux*†

[McLACHLIN C.J. for the Court:]

1. INTRODUCTION

[1] A person hosts a party. Guests drink alcohol. An inebriated guest drives away and causes an accident in which another person is injured. Is the host liable to the person injured? I conclude that as a general rule, a social host does not owe a duty of care to a person injured by a guest who has consumed alcohol and that the courts below correctly dismissed the appellants' action.

2. FACTS

[2] This case arises from a tragic car accident in Ottawa in the early hours of January 1, 1999. At 1:30 a.m., after leaving a party hosted by Dwight Courrier and Julie Zimmerman, Desmond Desormeaux drove his vehicle into oncoming traffic and collided head-on with a vehicle driven by Patricia Hadden. One of the passengers in Ms. Hadden's car was killed and three others seriously injured, including Zoe Childs, who was then a teenager. Ms. Childs' spine was severed and she has since been paralyzed from the waist down. Mr. Desormeaux and the two passengers in his car were also injured.

[3] Mr. Desormeaux was impaired at the time of the accident. The trial judge found that he had probably consumed 12 beers at the party over two and a half hours, producing a blood-alcohol concentration of approximately 235 mg per 100 ml when he left the party and 225 mg per 100 ml at the time of the accident — concentrations well over the legal limit for driving of 80 mg per 100 ml. Mr. Desormeaux pleaded guilty to a series of criminal charges arising from these events and received a 10-year sentence.

[4] The party hosted by Dwight Courrier and Julie Zimmerman at their home was a "BYOB" (Bring Your Own Booze) event. The only alcohol served by the hosts was three-quarters of a bottle of champagne in small glasses at midnight. Mr. Desormeaux was known to his hosts to be a heavy drinker. The trial judge heard evidence that when Mr. Desormeaux walked to his car to leave, Mr. Courrier accompanied him and asked, "Are you okay, brother?" Mr. Desormeaux responded "No problem", got behind the wheel and drove away with two passengers.

[5] The trial judge found that a reasonable person in the position of Mr. Courrier and Ms. Zimmerman would have foreseen that Mr. Desormeaux might cause an accident and injure someone else. However, the *prima facie* duty of care this gave rise to was negatived, in his view, by policy considerations involving the social and legal consequences of imposing a duty of care on social hosts to third parties injured by their guests, government regulation of alcohol sale and use and the preferability of a legislative, rather than a judicial, solution. Accordingly, the trial judge dismissed the action ((2002), 217 D.L.R. (4th) 217).

[6] The Court of Appeal for Ontario dismissed Ms. Childs' appeal. In its view, the circumstances did not

---

† 2006 SCC 18, [2006] 1 S.C.R. 643 at paras. 1–11, 24–49.

disclose even a *prima facie* duty of care. Unless social hosts are actively implicated in creating the risk that gives rise to the accident, they cannot be found liable. Here, the social hosts "did not assume control over the supply or service of alcohol, nor did they serve alcohol to [Mr.] Desormeaux when he was visibly impaired" ((2004), 71 O.R. (3d) 195, at para. 75). Unlike commercial hosts, they were under no statutory duty to monitor the consumption of alcohol or to control the premises where alcohol was served, nor did anyone rely on them to do so. The court, *per* Weiler J.A., concluded (at para. 75):

> ... I cannot accept the proposition that by merely supplying the venue of a BYOB party, a host assumes legal responsibility to third party users of the road for monitoring the alcohol consumed by guests, ... It would not be just and fair in the circumstances to impose a duty of care.

[7] Ms. Childs appeals to this Court and asks that we reverse the courts below and conclude that Mr. Courrier and Ms. Zimmerman, as social hosts of the party where Mr. Desormeaux was drinking, are liable for the injuries she suffered.

[8] The central legal issue raised by this appeal is whether social hosts who invite guests to an event where alcohol is served owe a legal duty of care to third parties who may be injured by intoxicated guests. It is clear that commercial hosts, like bars or clubs, may be under such a duty. This is the first time, however, that this Court has considered the duty owed by social hosts to plaintiffs like Ms. Childs.

3. ANALYSIS

3.1 The General Test for a Duty of Care

[9] Before the decision of the House of Lords in *Donoghue v. Stevenson*, [1932] A.C. 562, the law governing tort liability for wrongs to others was a complex of categories derived from cases decided over the centuries. In *Donoghue v. Stevenson*, the House of Lords replaced the category approach with a principled approach. It recognized the existence of a "general conception of relations giving rise to a duty of care, of which the particular cases found in the books are but instances" (p. 580, *per* Lord Atkin). The general concept of a duty owed to those whom one might injure proved both powerful and practical. However, it brought with it a question — a question we wrestle with to this day. How do we define the persons to whom the duty is owed?

[10] Lord Atkin recognized this problem in *Donoghue v. Stevenson*. He accepted that negligence is based on a "general public sentiment of moral wrongdoing for which the offender must pay", but distinguished legal duties from moral obligation: "... acts or omissions which any moral code would censure cannot in a practical world be treated so as to give a right to every person injured by them to demand relief" (p. 580). My legal duty, he said, extends to my "neighbour". Legal neighbourhood is "restricted" to "persons who are so closely and directly affected by my act that I ought reasonably to have them in contemplation as being so affected when I am directing my mind to the acts or omissions which are called in question" (p. 580). This concept, sometimes referred to as proximity, remains the foundation of the modern law of negligence.

[11] In *Anns v. Merton London Borough Council*, [1978] A.C. 728 (H.L.), Lord Wilberforce proposed a two-part test for determining whether a duty of care arises. The first stage focuses on the relationship between the plaintiff and the defendant, and asks whether it is close or "proximate" enough to give rise to a duty of care (p. 742). The second stage asks whether there are countervailing policy considerations that negative the duty of care. The two-stage approach of *Anns* was adopted by this Court in *Kamloops (City of) v. Nielsen*, [1984] 2 S.C.R. 2, at pp. 10–11, and recast as follows:

(1) is there "a sufficiently close relationship between the parties" or "proximity" to justify imposition of a duty and, if so,

(2) are there policy considerations which ought to negative or limit the scope of the duty, the class of persons to whom it is owed or the damages to which breach may give rise?

. . . .

3.3 Stage One: A Prima Facie Duty?

[24] Applying the first stage of the *Anns* test requires, as noted above, an examination of the relationship between the parties to determine if it meets the requirement of sufficient proximity. The question is: What, if anything, links party hosts to third-party users of the highway?

[25] The law of negligence not only considers the plaintiff's loss, but explains why it is just and fair to impose the cost of that loss on the particular defendant before the court. The proximity requirement captures this two-sided face of negligence.

[26] I conclude that the necessary proximity has not been established and, consequently, that social hosts of parties where alcohol is served do not owe a duty of care to public users of highways. First, the injury to Ms. Childs was not reasonably foreseeable on the facts found by the trial judge. Second, even if foreseeability were established, no duty would arise because the wrong alleged is a failure to act or nonfeasance in circumstances where there was no positive duty to act.

3.3.1 Foreseeability

[27] Ms. Childs argues that the parties are linked by the foreseeability of physical harm due to the manner in which the party hosts exercised "control or influence over" the party at which Mr. Desormeaux was drinking.

[28] The question of foreseeability is complicated by ambiguity in the findings of the trial judge. The trial judge found that Mr. Desormeaux would be showing "obvious signs of impairment" (para. 73), but did not find that the hosts in the circumstances knew, or ought to have known, that Mr. Desormeaux was too drunk to drive. The risks of impaired driving, and their consequences for motorists and their passengers, are well known. However, if there is no finding that the hosts *knew*, or ought to have known, that the guest who was about to drive was impaired, how can it be said that they should have foreseen that allowing him to drive might result in injury to other motorists?

[29] Instead of finding that the hosts ought reasonably to have been aware that Mr. Desormeaux was too drunk to drive, the trial judge based his finding that the hosts should have foreseen injury to motorists on the road on problematic reasoning. He noted that the hosts knew that Mr. Desormeaux had gotten drunk in the past and then driven. He inferred from this that they should have foreseen that unless Mr. Desormeaux's drinking at the party was monitored, he would become drunk, get into his car and drive onto the highway. The problem with this reasoning is that a history of alcohol consumption and impaired driving does not make impaired driving, and the consequent risk to other motorists, reasonably foreseeable. The inferential chain from drinking and driving in the past to reasonable foreseeability that this will happen again is too weak to support the legal conclusion of reasonable foreseeability — even in the case of commercial hosts, liability has not been extended by such a frail hypothesis.

[30] Ms. Childs points to the findings relating to the considerable amount of alcohol Mr. Desormeaux had consumed and his high blood-alcohol rating, coupled with the fact that Mr. Courrier accompanied Mr. Desormeaux to his car before he drove away, and asks us to make the finding of knowledge of inebriation that the trial judge failed to make. The problem here is the absence of any evidence that Mr. Desormeaux displayed signs of intoxication during this brief encounter. Given the absence of evidence that the hosts in this case in fact knew of Mr. Desormeaux's intoxication and the fact that the experienced trial judge himself declined to make such a finding, it would not be proper for us to change the factual basis of this case by supplementing the facts on this critical point. I conclude that the injury was not reasonably foreseeable on the facts established in this case.

3.3.2 Failure to Act: Nonfeasance Versus Misfeasance

[31] Foreseeability is not the only hurdle Ms. Childs' argument for a duty of care must surmount. "Foreseeability does not of itself, and automatically, lead to the conclusion that there is a duty of care": G. H. L. Fridman, *The Law of Torts in Canada* (2nd ed. 2002), at p. 320. Foreseeability without more *may* establish a duty of care. This is usually the case, for example, where an *overt act of the defendant* has *directly caused foreseeable physical harm* to the plaintiff: see *Cooper*. However, where the conduct alleged against the defendant is a *failure to act*, foreseeability alone may not establish a duty of care. In the absence of an overt act on the part of the defendant, the nature of the relationship must be examined to determine whether there is a nexus between the parties. Although there is no doubt that an omission may be negligent, as a general principle, the common law is a jealous guardian of individual autonomy. Duties to take positive action in the face of risk or danger are not free-standing. Generally, the mere fact that a person faces danger, or has become a danger to others, does not itself impose any kind of duty on those in a position to become involved.

[32] In this case, we are concerned not with an overt act of the social hosts, but with their alleged failure to act. The case put against them is that they should have interfered with the autonomy of Mr. Desormeaux by preventing him from drinking and driving. It follows that foreseeability alone would not establish a duty of care in this case.

[33] The appellants' argument that Mr. Courrier and Ms. Zimmerman committed positive acts that created, or contributed to, the risk cannot be sustained. It is argued that they *facilitated* the consumption of alcohol by organizing a social event where alcohol was consumed on their premises. But this is not an act that creates risk to users of public roads. The real complaint is that having organized the party, the hosts permitted their guest to drink and then take the wheel of an automobile.

[34] A positive duty of care may exist if foreseeability of harm is present *and* if other aspects of the relationship between the plaintiff and the defendant establish a special link or proximity. Three such situations have been identified by the courts. They function not as strict legal categories, but rather to elucidate factors that can lead to positive duties to act. These factors, or features of the relationship, bring parties who would otherwise be legal strangers into proximity and impose positive duties on defendants that would not otherwise exist.

[35] The first situation where courts have imposed a positive duty to act is where a defendant intentionally attracts and invites third parties to an inherent and obvious risk that he or she has created or controls: *Hendricks v. The Queen*, [1970] S.C.R. 237; *Horsley v. MacLaren*, [1972] S.C.R. 441; *Arnold v. Teno*, [1978] 2 S.C.R. 287; and *Crocker v. Sundance Northwest Resorts Ltd.*, [1988] 1 S.C.R. 1186. For example, it has been held that a boat captain owes a duty to take reasonable care to rescue a passenger who falls overboard (*Horsley*)and that the operator of a dangerous inner-tube sliding competition owes a duty to exclude people who cannot safely participate (*Crocker*). These cases turn on the defendant's causal relationship to the origin of the risk of injury faced by the plaintiff or on steps taken to invite others to subject themselves to a risk under the defendant's control. If the defendant creates a risky situation and invites others into it, failure to act thereafter does not immunize the defendant from the consequences of its acts. These cases are akin to the positive and *continuing* duty of manufacturers or transferors of goods to warn of inherently dangerous products or dangerous uses of safe products: *Lambert v. Lastoplex Chemicals Co.*, [1972] S.C.R. 569; *Hollis v. Dow Corning Corp.*, [1995] 4 S.C.R. 634.

[36] The second situation where a positive duty of care has been held to exist concerns paternalistic relationships of supervision and control, such as those of parent–child or teacher–student: *Dziwenka v. The Queen in right of Alberta*, [1972] S.C.R. 419;

Bain v. Board of Education (Calgary) (1993), 146 A.R. 321 (Q.B.). The duty in these cases rests on the special vulnerability of the plaintiffs and the formal position of power of the defendants. The law recognizes that the autonomy of some persons may be permissibly violated or restricted, but, in turn, requires that those with power exercise it in light of special duties. In the words of Virtue J. in *Bain*, in the context of a teacher–student relationship, "[t]hat right of control carries with it a corresponding duty to take care for the safety of, and to properly supervise the student, whether he or she is a child, an adolescent or an adult" (para. 38).

[37] The third situation where a duty of care may include the need to take positive steps concerns defendants who either exercise a public function or engage in a commercial enterprise that includes implied responsibilities to the public at large: *Dunn v. Dominion Atlantic Railway Co.* (1920), 60 S.C.R. 310; *Jordan House Ltd. v. Menow*, [1974] S.C.R. 239; *Doe v. Metropolitan Toronto (Municipality) Commissioners of Police* (1998), 39 O.R. (3d) 487 (Gen. Div.). In these cases, the defendants offer a service to the general public that includes attendant responsibilities to act with special care to reduce risk. Where a defendant assumes a public role, or benefits from offering a service to the public at large, special duties arise. The duty of a commercial host who serves alcohol to guests to act to prevent foreseeable harm to third-party users of the highway falls into this category: *Stewart v. Pettie*.

[38] Running through all of these situations is the defendant's material implication in the creation of risk or his or her control of a risk to which others have been invited. The operator of a dangerous sporting competition creates or enhances the risk by inviting and enabling people to participate in an inherently risky activity. It follows that the operator must take special steps to protect against the risk materializing. In the example of the parent or teacher who has assumed control of a vulnerable person, the vulnerability of the person and its subjection to the control of the defendant creates a situation where the latter has an enhanced responsibility to safeguard against risk. The public provider of services undertakes a public service, and must do so in a way that appropriately minimizes associated risks to the public.

[39] Also running through the examples is a concern for the autonomy of the persons affected by the positive action proposed. The law does not impose a duty to eliminate risk. It accepts that competent

people have the right to engage in risky activities. Conversely, it permits third parties witnessing risk to decide not to become rescuers or otherwise intervene. It is only when these third parties have a special relationship to the person in danger or a material role in the creation or management of the risk that the law may impinge on autonomy. Thus, the operator of a risky sporting activity may be required to prevent a person who is unfit to perform a sport safely from participating or, when a risk materializes, to attempt a rescue. Similarly, the publican may be required to refuse to serve an inebriated patron who may drive, or a teacher be required to take positive action to protect a child who lacks the right or power to make decisions for itself. The autonomy of risk takers or putative rescuers is not absolutely protected, but, at common law, it is always respected.

[40] Finally, the theme of reasonable reliance unites examples in all three categories. A person who creates or invites others into a dangerous situation, like the high-risk sports operator, may reasonably expect that those taking up the invitation will rely on the operator to ensure that the risk is a reasonable one or to take appropriate rescue action if the risk materializes. Similarly, a teacher will understand that the child or the child's parents rely on the teacher to avoid and minimize risk. Finally, there is a reasonable expectation on the part of the public that a person providing public services, often under licence, will take reasonable precautions to reduce the risk of the activity, not merely to immediate clients, but to the general public.

[41] Does the situation of the social host who serves alcohol to guests fall within the three categories just discussed or represent an appropriate extension of them having regard to the factors of risk-control and reasonable preservation of autonomy that animate them? I conclude that it does not.

[42] The first category concerns defendants who have created or invited others to participate in highly risky activities. Holding a house party where alcohol is served is not such an activity. Risks may ensue, to be sure, from what guests choose to do or not do at the party. But hosting a party is a far cry from inviting participation in a high-risk sport or taking people out on a boating party. A party where alcohol is served is a common occurrence, not one associated with unusual risks demanding special precautions. The second category of paternalistic relationships of supervision or control is equally inapplicable. Party hosts do not enjoy a paternalistic relationship with

their guests, nor are their guests in a position of reduced autonomy that invites control. Finally, private social hosts are not acting in a public capacity and, hence, do not incur duties of a public nature.

[43] More broadly, do the themes that animate the cases imposing positive duties to act — risk enhancement and control, autonomy and reasonable reliance — suggest that the social hosts in this case owed a duty of care to third-party users of the highway, to take reasonable steps to prevent what happened? Again, the answer is that they do not.

[44] Holding a private party at which alcohol is served — the bare facts of this case — is insufficient to implicate the host in the creation of a risk sufficient to give rise to a duty of care to third parties who may be subsequently injured by the conduct of a guest. The host creates a place where people can meet, visit and imbibe alcohol, whether served on the premises or supplied by the guest. All this falls within accepted parameters of non-dangerous conduct. More is required to establish a danger or risk that requires positive action. It might be argued that a host who continues to serve alcohol to a visibly inebriated person knowing that he or she will be driving home has become implicated in the creation or enhancement of a risk sufficient to give rise to a *prima facie* duty of care to third parties, which would be subject to contrary policy considerations at the second stage of the *Anns* test. This position has been taken in some states in the U.S.A.: N.J. Stat. Ann. §§ 2A:15-5.5 to 2A:15-5.8 (West 2000). We need not decide that question here. Suffice it to say that hosting a party where alcohol is served, without more, does not suggest the creation or exacerbation of risk of the level required to impose a duty of care on the host to members of the public who may be affected by a guest's conduct.

[45] Nor does the autonomy of the individual support the case for a duty to take action to protect highway users in the case at bar. As discussed, the implication of a duty of care depends on the relationships involved. The relationship between social host and guest at a house party is part of this equation. A person who accepts an invitation to attend a private party does not park his autonomy at the door. The guest remains responsible for his or her conduct. Short of active implication in the creation or enhancement of the risk, a host is entitled to respect the autonomy of a guest. The consumption of alcohol, and the assumption of the risks of impaired judgment, is in almost all cases a personal choice and an inherently personal activity. Absent

the special considerations that may apply in the commercial context, when such a choice is made by an adult, there is no reason why others should be made to bear its costs. The conduct of a hostess who confiscated all guests' car keys and froze them in ice as people arrived at her party, releasing them only as she deemed appropriate, was cited to us as exemplary. This hostess was evidently prepared to make considerable incursions on the autonomy of her guests. The law of tort, however, has not yet gone so far.

[46] This brings us to the factor of reasonable reliance. There is no evidence that anyone relied on the hosts in this case to monitor guests' intake of alcohol or prevent intoxicated guests from driving. This represents an important distinction between the situation of a private host, as here, and a public host. The public host provides alcohol to members of the public, under a strict regulatory regime. It is reasonable to expect that the public provider will act to protect the public interest. There is public reliance that he will comply with the rules that prohibit serving too much alcohol to a patron and that if this should occur and the patron seeks to drive, that the public host will take reasonable steps to prevent the person from driving. The same cannot be said of the private social host, who neither undertakes nor is expected to monitor the conduct of guests on behalf of the public.

[47] I conclude that hosting a party at which alcohol is served does not, without more, establish the degree of proximity required to give rise to a duty of care on the hosts to third-party highway users who may be injured by an intoxicated guest. The injury here was not shown to be foreseeable on the facts as found by the trial judge. Even if it had been, this is at best a case of nonfeasance. No duty to monitor guests' drinking or to prevent them from driving can be imposed having regard to the relevant cases and legal principles. A social host at a party where alcohol is served is not under a duty of care to members of the public who may be injured by a guest's actions, unless the host's conduct implicates him or her in the creation or exacerbation of the risk. On the facts of this case, I agree with the Court of Appeal, at para. 75, *per* Weiler J.A.:

> The person sought to be held liable must be implicated in the creation of the risk.... The social hosts had no statutory duty to monitor the consumption of alcohol or to control the structure of the atmosphere in which alcohol was served. There is no evidence that anyone relied on them to do so.... I cannot accept the proposition that by merely supplying the venue of a BYOB party, a host assumes legal responsibility to third party users of the road for monitoring the alcohol consumed by guests, ... It would not be just and fair in the circumstances to impose a duty of care.

[48] Having concluded that a *prima facie* duty of care has not been established, I find it unnecessary to consider whether any duty would be negated by policy considerations at the second stage of the *Anns* test.

4. CONCLUSION

[49] I would dismiss the appeal with costs.

Appeal dismissed with costs.

(e) *Pettkus v. Becker*†

[DICKSON J., Laskin C.J. and Estey, McIntyre, Chouinard, and Lamer JJ. (Martland and Ritchie JJ concurring, with different reasons):]

The appellant, Lothar Pettkus, through toil and thrift, developed over the years a successful beekeeping business. He now owns two rural Ontario properties, where the business is conducted, and he has the proceeds from the sale, in 1974, of a third property, located in the Province of Quebec. It is not to his efforts alone, however, that success can be attributed. The respondent, Rosa Becker, through her labour and earnings, contributed substantially to

---

† [1980] 2 S.C.R. 834 at 839–40, 847–51, 852–53, 854.

the good fortune of the common enterprise. She lived with Mr. Pettkus from 1955 to 1974, save for a separation in 1972. They were never married. When the relationship sundered in late 1974, Miss Becker commenced this action, in which she sought a declaration of entitlement to a one-half interest in the lands and a share in the beekeeping business.

I THE FACTS

Mr. Pettkus and Miss Becker came to Canada from central Europe, separately, as immigrants, in 1954. He had $17 upon arrival. They met in Montreal in 1955. Shortly thereafter, Mr. Pettkus moved in with Miss Becker, on her invitation. She was thirty years old and he was twenty-five. He was earning $75 per week; she was earning $25 to $28 per week, later increased to $67 per week.

A short time after they began living together, Miss Becker expressed the desire that they be married. Mr. Pettkus replied that he might consider marriage after they knew each other better. Thereafter, the question of marriage was not raised, though within a few years Mr. Pettkus began to introduce Miss Becker as his wife and to claim her as such for income tax purposes.

From 1955 to 1960 both parties worked for others. Mr. Pettkus supplemented his income by repairing and restoring motor vehicles. Throughout the period Miss Becker paid the rent. She bought the food and clothing and looked after other living expenses. This enabled Mr. Pettkus to save his entire income, which he regularly deposited in a bank account in his name. There was no agreement at any time to share either monies or property placed in his name. The parties lived frugally. Due to their husbandry and parsimonious lifestyle, $12,000 had been saved by 1960 and deposited in Mr. Pettkus' bank account.

The two travelled to Western Canada in June 1960. Expenses were shared. One of the reasons for the trip was to locate a suitable farm at which to start a beekeeping business. They spent some time working at a beekeeper's farm.

They returned to Montreal, however, in the early autumn of 1960. Miss Becker continued to pay the apartment rent out of her income until October 1960. From then until May 1961, Mr. Pettkus paid rent and household expenses, Miss Becker being jobless. In April 1961, she fell sick and required hospitalization.

In April 1961, they decided to buy a farm at Franklin Centre, Quebec, for $5,000. The purchase money came out of the bank account of Mr. Pettkus.

Title was taken in his name. The floor and roof of the farmhouse were in need of repair. Miss Becker used her money to purchase flooring materials and she assisted in laying the floor and installing a bathroom.

For about six months during 1961 Miss Becker received unemployment insurance cheques, the proceeds of which were used to defray household expenses. Through two successive winters she lived in Montreal and earned approximately $100 per month as a babysitter. These earnings also went toward household expenses.

After purchasing the farm at Franklin Centre the parties established a beekeeping business. Both worked in the business, making frames for the hives, moving the bees to the orchards of neighbouring farmers in the spring, checking the hives during the summer, bringing in the frames for honey extraction during July and August, and the bees for winter storage in autumn. Receipts from sales of honey were handled by Mr. Pettkus; payments for purchases of bee hives and equipment were made from his bank account.

The physical participation by Miss Becker in the bee operation continued over a period of about fourteen years. She ran the extracting process. She also, for a time, raised a few chickens, pheasants and geese. In 1968, and later, the parties hired others to assist in moving the bees and bringing in the honey. Most of the honey was sold to wholesalers, though Miss Becker sold some from door to door.

In August 1971, with a view to expanding the business a vacant property was purchased in East Hawkesbury, Ontario, at a price of $1,300. The purchase monies were derived from the Franklin Centre honey operation. Funds to complete the purchase were withdrawn from the bank account of Mr. Pettkus. Title to the newly acquired property was taken in his name.

In 1973 a further property was purchased, in West Hawkesbury, Ontario, in the name of Mr. Pettkus. The price was $5,500. The purchase monies came from the Franklin Centre operation, together with a $1,900 contribution made by Miss Becker, to which I will again later refer. Nineteen seventy-three was a prosperous year, yielding some 65,000 pounds of honey, producing net revenue in excess of $30,000.

In the early 1970's the relationship between the parties began to deteriorate. In 1972 Miss Becker left Mr. Pettkus, allegedly because of mistreatment. She was away for three months. At her departure, Mr. Pettkus threw $3,000 on the floor. He told her to take the money, a 1966 Volkswagon, forty beehives containing bees, and "get lost". The beehives represented less than ten percent of the total number of hives then in the business.

Soon thereafter, Mr. Pettkus asked Miss Becker to return. In January, 1973, she agreed, on condition he see a marriage counselor, make a will in her favor and provide her with $500 per year so long as she stayed with him. It was also agreed that Mr. Pettkus would establish a joint bank account for household expenses, in which receipts from retail sales of honey would be deposited. Miss Becker returned; she brought back the car and $1,900 remaining out of the $3,000 she had earlier received. The $1,900 was deposited in Mr. Pettkus' account. She also brought the forty bee hives but the bees had died in the interim.

In February 1974 the parties moved into a house on the West Hawkesbury property, built in part by them and in part by contractors. The money needed for construction came from the honey business, with minimal purchases of materials by Miss Becker.

The relationship continued to deteriorate and on October 4, 1974 Miss Becker [again] left, this time permanently, after an incident in which she alleged that she had been beaten and otherwise abused. She took the car and approximately $2,600 in cash, from honey sales. Shortly thereafter the present action was launched.

At trial, Miss Becker was awarded forty beehives, without bees, together with $1,500, representing earnings from those hives for 1973 and 1974.

The Ontario Court of Appeal varied the judgment at trial by awarding Miss Becker a one-half interest in the lands owned by Mr. Pettkus and in the beekeeping business.

. . . .

III   CONSTRUCTIVE TRUST

The principle of unjust enrichment lies at the heart of the constructive trust. "Unjust enrichment" has played a role in Anglo-American legal writing for centuries. Lord Mansfield, in the case of *Moses v. Macferlan*[7] put the matter in these words: "... the gist of this kind of action is, that the defendant, upon the circumstances of the case, is *obliged by the ties of natural justice and equity to refund* the money". It would be undesirable, and indeed impossible, to attempt to define all the circumstances in which an unjust enrichment might arise. (See A.W. Scott, "Constructive Trusts", (1955), 71 L.Q.R. 39; Leonard Pollock, "Matrimonial Property and Trusts: The Situ-

ation from Murdoch to Rathwell", (1978), 16 Alberta Law Review 357). The great advantage of ancient principles of equity is their flexibility: the judiciary is thus able to shape these malleable principles so as to accommodate the changing needs and mores of society, in order to achieve justice. The constructive trust has proven to be a useful tool in the judicial armoury. See *Babrociak v. Babrociak*[8]; *Re Spears and Levy et al.*[9]; *Douglas v. Guaranty Trust Company of Canada*[10]; *Armstrong v. Armstrong.*[11]

How then does one approach the question of unjust enrichment in matrimonial causes? In *Rathwell* I ventured to suggest there are three requirements to be satisfied before an unjust enrichment can be said to exist: an enrichment, a corresponding deprivation and absence of any juristic reason for the enrichment. This approach, it seems to me, is supported by general principles of equity that have been fashioned by the courts for centuries, though, admittedly, not in the context of matrimonial property controversies.

The common law has never been willing to compensate a plaintiff on the sole basis that his actions have benefited another. Lord Halsbury scotched this heresy in the case of *The Ruabon Steamship Company, Limited v. London Assurance*[12] with these words: "... I cannot understand how it can be asserted that it is part of the common law that where one person gets some advantage from the act of another a right of contribution towards the expense from that act arises on behalf of the person who has done it." (p. 10) Lord Macnaghten, in the same case, put it this way: "there is no principle of law which requires that a person should contribute to an outlay merely because he has derived a material benefit from it". (p. 15) It is not enough for the court simply to determine that one spouse has benefited at the hands of another and then to require restitution. It must, in addition, be evident that the retention of the benefit would be "unjust" in the circumstances of the case.

Miss Becker supported Mr. Pettkus for 5 years. She then worked on the farm for about 14 years. The compelling inference from the facts is that she believed she had some interest in the farm and that that expectation was reasonable in the circumstances. Mr. Pettkus would seem to have recognized in Miss Becker some property interest, through the payment to her of compensation, however modest. There is no evidence to indicate that he ever informed her that all her work performed over the nineteen years was being performed on a gratuitous basis. He freely accepted the benefits conferred upon him through her financial support and her labour.

On these facts, the first two requirements laid down in *Rathwell* have clearly been satisfied: Mr. Pcttkus has had the benefit of nineteen years of unpaid labour, while Miss Becker has received little or nothing in return. As for the third requirement, I hold that where one person in a relationship tantamount to spousal prejudices herself in the reasonable expectation of receiving an interest in property and the other person in the relationship freely accepts benefits conferred by the first person in circumstances where he knows or ought to have known of that reasonable expectation, it would be unjust to allow the recipient of the benefit to retain it.

I conclude, consonant with the judgment of the Court of Appeal, that this is a case for the application of constructive trust. As Madam Justice Wilson noted, "the parties lived together as husband and wife, although unmarried for almost twenty years during which period she not only made possible the acquisition of their first property in Franklin Centre during the lean years, but worked side by side with him for fourteen years building up the beekeeping operation which was their main source of livelihood".

Madam Justice Wilson had no difficulty in finding that a constructive trust arose in favour of the respondent by virtue of "joint effort" and "teamwork", as a result of which Mr. Pettkus was able to acquire the Franklin Centre property, and subsequently the East Hawkesbury and West Hawkesbury properties. The Ontario Court of Appeal imposed the constructive trust in the interests of justice and, with respect, I would do the same.

IV THE "COMMON LAW" RELATIONSHIP

One question which must be addressed is whether a constructive trust can be established having regard to what is frequently, and euphemistically, referred to as a "common law" relationship. The purpose of constructive trust is to redress situations which would otherwise denote unjust enrichment. In principle, there is no reason not to apply the doctrine to common law relationships. It is worth noting that counsel for Mr. Pettkus, and I think correctly, did not, in this Court, raise the common law relationship in defence of the claim of Miss Becker, otherwise than by reference to *The Family Law Reform Act, 1978,* 1978 (Ont.) c. 2.

Courts in other jurisdictions have not regarded the absence of a marital bond as any problem. See *Cooke v. Head*[13]; *Eves v. Eves*[14]; *Spears v. Levy, supra*; and in the United States, *Marvin v. Marvin*[15] and a comment thereon (1977), 90 Harv. L.R. 1708. In *Marvin* the Supreme Court of California stated that constructive trust was available to give effect to the reasonable expectations of the parties, and to the notion that unmarried co-habitants intend to deal fairly with each other.

I see no basis for any distinction, in dividing property and assets, between marital relationships and those more informal relationships which subsist for a lengthy period. This was not an economic partnership nor a mere business relationship, nor a casual encounter. Mr. Pettkus and Miss Becker lived as man and wife for almost twenty years. Their lives and their economic well-being were fully integrated. The equitable principle on which the remedy of constructive trust rests is broad and general; its purpose is to prevent unjust enrichment in whatever circumstances it occurs.

In recent years, there has been much statutory reform in the area of family law and matrimonial property. Counsel for Mr. Pettkus correctly points out that *The Family Law Reform Act, 1978*, of Ontario, enacted after the present litigation was initiated, does not extend the presumption of equal sharing, which now applies between married persons, to common law spouses. The argument is made that the courts should not develop equitable remedies that are 'contrary to current legislative intent'. The rejoinder is that legislation was unnecessary to cover these facts, for a remedy was always available in equity for property division between unmarried individuals contributing to the acquisition of assets. The effect of the legislation is to divide 'family assets' equally, regardless of contribution, as a matter of course. The Court is not here creating a presumption of equal shares. There is a great difference between directing that there be equal shares for common law spouses, and awarding Miss Becker a share equivalent to the money or money's worth she contributed over some nineteen years. The fact there is no statutory regime directing equal division of assets acquired by common law spouses is no bar to the availability of an equitable remedy in the present circumstances.

. . . .

VII RESPECTIVE PROPORTIONS

Although equity is said to favour equality, as stated in *Rathwell* it is not every contribution which will entitle a spouse to a one-half interest in the property. The extent of the interest must be proportionate to the contribution, direct or indirect, of the claimant. Where the contributions are unequal, the shares will be unequal.

It could be argued that Mr. Pettkus contributed somewhat more to the material fortunes of the joint enterprise than Miss Becker but it must be recognized that each started with nothing; each worked continuously, unremittingly and sedulously in the joint effort. Physically, Miss Becker pulled her fair share of the load; weighing only 87 pounds, she assisted in moving hives weighing 80 pounds. Any difference in quality or quantum of contribution was small. The Ontario Court of Appeal in its discretion favoured an even division and I would not alter that disposition, other than to note that in any accounting regard should be had to the $2,600, and the car, which Miss Becker received on separation in 1974.

. . . .

I would dismiss the appeal with costs to the respondent.

Emerging Challenges for Legal Regulation

(a) Regulability of the Cyberspace†

Lawrence Lessig

GOVERNORS

A state — call it "Boral" — doesn't like gambling, even though some citizens like to gamble. But the state is the boss; the people have voted; the law is as it is. Gambling in the state of Boral is illegal.

Then comes the Internet. With the Net wired into their phones, some citizens of Boral decide that Internet gambling is the next "killer app." Someone sets up servers that provide access to online gambling. The state doesn't like this business; the businessmen are just illegal gamblers. Shut down your servers, the attorney general warns, or we will lock you up.

Wise even if dishonest, the gamblers agree to shut down their servers in the state of Boral. But they don't exit the gambling business. Instead, they rent space on a server in an "offshore haven." This offshore web server hums away, once again making gambling available on the Net.

And just as available to people in Boral. For here's the important point: given the architecture of the Internet (at least as it was), it doesn't matter where in real space the server is set up. Access doesn't depend on geography. Nor, depending on how clever the gambling sorts are, does access require that the user know anything about who owns or runs the real server. The user's access can be passed through anonymizing sites that make it practically impossible in the end to know what went where.

The Boral attorney general faces a difficult problem. She may have moved the gamblers out of her state, but she hasn't succeeded in reducing gambling on the Net. She once would have had a group of people she could punish, but now she has made them essentially free from punishment. The world for this attorney general has changed. By going online, the gamblers moved into a world where behavior, so the argument goes, is no longer regulable.

Regulable. I am told there is no such word, though lawyers apparently do not know that fact. By "regulable" I mean simply that a certain behavior is capable of regulation. The term is comparative, not absolute — in some place, at some time, a certain behavior will be more regulable than at another place and in another time. My claim about Boral is simply that the Net makes gambling less regulable there than it was before the Net.

. . . .

THEMES

. . . .

Regulability

Regulability means the capacity of a government to regulate behavior within its proper reach. In the context of the Internet, that means the ability of the government to regulate the behavior of its citizens (and perhaps others as well) on the Net. My second story, about gambling in Boral, was thus about regulability, or more specifically, about the

---

† From Lawrence Lessig, *Code and Other Laws of Cyberspace* (New York: Basic Books, 1999) at 14, 19–20. Copyright © 1999 Lawrence Lessig. Reproduced with permission of Basic Books, a member of Perseus Books Group.

changes in regulability that cyberspace brings. Before the Internet, it was relatively easy for the attorney general of Boral to control gambling within her jurisdiction; after the Internet, when the servers moved outside of Boral, regulation became much more difficult.

For the regulator, this story captures the problem that cyberspace presents generally. The architecture of cyberspace makes regulating behavior difficult, because those whose behavior you're trying to control could be located in any place (meaning outside of your place) on the Net. Who someone is, where he is, and whether law can be exercised over him there — all these are questions that government must answer if it is to impose its will. But these questions are made impossibly difficult by the architecture of the space — at least as it was.

The balance of part 1 is about this question of regulability. I ask whether "unregulability" is necessary. Can we imagine a more regulable cyberspace? And is this the cyberspace we are coming to know?

(b)   Law, Cyberspace and the Role of Nation States†

Michael Mac Neil

The development of the Internet and the growth of cyberspace pose new challenges for nation states seeking to regulate citizen conduct and to protect citizens from external threats. States typically apply legal rules and sanctions to regulate behaviour. Law is one of a number of tools used to both shape norms of conduct and to legitimize the imposition of coercive measures to induce compliance. The effectiveness of law as a tool rests in part on states' ability to employ legal institutions and policing mechanisms which operate directly on the individuals whose behaviour they are seeking to control. These direct effects depend on states having control over people or property within the political territory over which they assert their sovereignty. Johnson and Post[1] argue that there is a strong logical nexus between sovereignty, law, and territoriality, based on four factors. First, effective law making depends on exerting physical control over potential law violators. Second, there is a congruence between physical boundaries and the effects of particular behaviour. Third, democratic participation, enhancing the legitimacy of law, is facilitated by sovereignty within political boundaries. Fourth, boundaries serve to provide notice of the ambit of legal rules.

The question is whether the emergence of cyberspace fundamentally alters the ability of state sovereigns to exercise their authority to control behaviour. Johnson and Post contend that the old rules no longer apply, because cyberspace activity is untied from physical location. Individuals engage in social, political, and economic relations in cyberspace without regard to political boundaries. The technology and the architecture of the Internet facilitate global communication and global transactions, so that the behaviour of individuals is no longer easily subjected to physical control by a particular sovereign state, is no longer local in effect, and is no longer confined to a geographically based community. In the face of this, there are both practical and normative limitations on the ability and legitimacy of regulation of cyberspace activity by nation states. For Johnson and Post, the natural consequence is to develop both practical and normative models that rely on the unique features of cyberspace, allowing for a great deal more self-regulation within constantly reconfigured cyberspace communities from which exit is an easy option for those who do not accept the legitimacy of the rules being imposed in a particular community.

However, there is a considerable amount of evidence to belie the powerlessness of the nation state in the face of an emerging cyberspace. There may be less of a nexus between law and territory than Post and Johnson suppose. The emergence of international human rights norms, the development of

---

† A corrected version of original published in (2001) 2:1 McGill International Review 24–26. Reproduced with permission. [Notes and/or references omitted.]

cooperative international approaches to defining and enforcing acceptable rules of conduct, and some of the very features of cyberspace architecture which mark it as unique may also facilitate an ongoing role for nation states. It is on this last feature that I wish to concentrate.

There are a number of elements of Internet architecture which lead some to believe that there is likely to be a great deal more chaos or anarchy in cyberspace than exists in "real" space. The decentralized, non-hierarchical, global structure of the Internet appears, on the face of it, to enable individuals to easily route around state imposed restrictions on their conduct. However, recent trends towards concentration of ownership, combined with more sophisticated surveillance and monitoring techniques, may facilitate the ability of a single state to impose its will on activity which originates beyond its physical boundaries. The consequences for both our conceptions of governance and the future of cyberspace remain to be determined, but [it] is by no means certain that the emergence of cyberspace will lead to the decline of the nation state.

The recent decision[2] by a French court to apply French law prohibiting the display of Nazi memorabilia demonstrates these themes. In this case, several groups initiated an action against Yahoo, an American based web portal which also operates a companion portal, Yahoo France, specifically designed for French Internet users. Yahoo sponsors an auction web site, in which numerous Nazi artifacts were being made available for sale. The server hosting the auction site was located in the United States. The Yahoo France web site did not contain a direct link to the auction site, but there was nothing preventing a French user who originally connected to the Yahoo France site from browsing to the general Yahoo site and from thence to the auction site. The French court ordered Yahoo to implement measures which would prevent French users from gaining access to the auction site, with the threat of 100,000 franc per day fine in the event that Yahoo failed to implement appropriate measures. Is this merely an example of an ineffectual attempt by a national court to overreach the territorial boundaries within which its laws normally apply, or is it a sign of a wave of such actions which will entrench the power of nation states to protect their own culture and values from the libertarian imposition of individual choices?

It is probably too early to answer the preceding question, but there are a number of features of the case that deserve further reflection. First, it demonstrates that there continues to be a clash of values despite the forces which may otherwise be leading to considerable harmonization of laws. The choice of the French government (not alone on this score) to regulate forms of expression which may be considered hateful and thus harmful to minority groups stands in stark contrast to the claim made by Yahoo, that American law with its strong constitutional commitment to free speech should apply. If nation states can successfully regulate actions which are taking place outside their borders but which contravene the legal values which they have enacted to protect their citizens, the ability of cybercitizens to build communities governed by rules which do not defer to state laws and geographic boundaries is considerably attenuated.

Second, the case raises significant questions about how law can regulate. Earlier, I argued that the effectiveness of state-based regulation depends to a considerable extent on the ability of the nation state to impose coercive sanctions directly on those whose behaviour it seeks to control. However, cyberspace gives a great deal more scope for indirect action by law. Rather than seeking to directly regulate the behaviour of individuals who display Nazi memorabilia, the French court is seeking to apply law indirectly by taking advantage of the very architecture of cyberspace. Yahoo was ordered to develop filters which could be used to identify and deny access to French cyberspace browsers seeking to view the Yahoo auction site. In real space, a merchant may be able to control who is able to view its merchandise, e.g. by excluding minors, or by setting up shop in a trendy district. This succeeds in real space because the merchant is able to monitor and assess the clientele entering the store, or take advantage of geographic location to cater to a particular clientele. At first blush, it appears that such control is precluded by the architecture of cyberspace which enabled individuals to engage in cyberspace activity on an anonymous basis. However, the commercialization of the Internet has led to the development of ever more sophisticated monitoring tools, motivated in part by the desire to gather more accurate data about consumers and provide more targeted marketing schemes. That very same technology has the potential to enable nation states to erect virtual boundaries which emulate political-geographic boundaries. If major portals are able to identify who is seeking to view particular web pages, and if it is possible to selectively refuse "admittance" to the site on the basis of the geographical location of the browser, then the scope for control by nation states is considerably enhanced.

This enhancement, however, depends not only on the existence of monitoring and control technology, but also on the ability of the state to impose its will, by coercive sanctions, on those who control the communications routes of the Internet. This leads to a third point — the concentration of ownership and control, with a small number of large corporate actors who are actively engaged in a global enterprise, facilitates the ability of any one state to [significantly] impose its laws directly on those actors, and hence indirectly on all Internet users.

Lessig[3] writes about the ability of the state to regulate intermediaries — companies like Yahoo through whom cyberspace users must connect to the Internet. These intermediaries are more regulable because they are fewer, their interests are usually commercial and they are ordinarily pliant targets of regulation. On the face of it, the commercialization and privatization of provision of Internet services may appear antithetical to the ability of the state to govern cyberspace activity in the public interest.[4] The state is no longer directly involved as the provider of services nor is it typically the owner of the Internet infrastructure. These developments certainly make it more difficult for the government to directly achieve its goals, whether of expanding accessibility, fostering community, or monitoring cyberspace activity. Nevertheless, they may allow governments to employ law indirectly. This indirect regulation of intermediaries will be effective only if a nation state can actually impose their decisions on the intermediaries. That is becoming increasingly possible as a result of many of the giant global Internet service providers maintaining computer servers, offices and local sites in other countries, making them more vulnerable to enforcement action.[5] That is precisely what Yahoo has done in setting up Yahoo France, and it is Yahoo's French presence that makes the French court's threat of sanctions credible.

It would be imprudent to unduly stress the ability of [nation] states to harness the architectural features of the Internet to their own quest for maintaining control both over the actions of their own citizens and over content to which their citizens may be exposed. There is an inherent tension in the architecture of the Internet between its decentralizing features and the tendency towards centralization of power and control. Monitoring technology may not be sufficiently sophisticated to allow completely precise identification of browsers. Individuals can engage in a variety of actions, (e.g. use of encryption, anonymizers or long distance access), which makes it difficult to determine their geographic location, [let alone] their precise identity. Which of the trends towards decentralization or centralization will win out

remains to be seen, but certainly there is potential for individual nation states to exploit some features of cyberspace architecture in an attempt to continue using law as a tool for regulation of behaviour.

Having concluded that it may be possible for states to retain a measure of control over cyberspace activity through the indirect application of law to modify the code or architecture of cyberspace, I do not wish to be seen as endorsing this as a necessarily positive development. There are many problems with a future in which a multiplicity of states each attempt to regulate Internet code in a way to ensure that local values prevail. One of the positive boons of the Internet is the potential it [offers] for open communication, the facilitation of community development, and the promotion of democratic practices and human rights. If individual states can effectively build virtual borders that preclude or hamper these developments, much of the positive value of communicative freedom in cyberspace may be jeopardized.

Furthermore, not all states will be equal in their ability to shape cyberspace code and architecture. Because of the history of Internet development, much of the crucial architecture may be subject to greater control by the United States than by other countries. The domain name root servers for the Internet are housed in the United States, and continue to be under the control of the United States government. It is, for example, the United States which was able to play a dominant role in establishing the governing institutions for domain name policy, namely the Internet Corporation for Assigned Names and Numbers (ICANN). There is still considerable reluctance in the United States to accept that the Internet may have grown into something which is beyond the competence of the United States government to legitimately control and dominate.[6]

The Internet is a new technology hailed by some as revolutionary in a way that undermines the ability of sovereign states to maintain their sovereignty. However, the Internet is not the first technology to which sovereign states have responded in innovative ways to maintain their central role in the schemes of governance. The difficulties of employing law in traditional ways as a tool of governance of cyberspace activity undoubtedly [challenge] the state to develop new techniques and approaches to regulation. However, the challenges posed by cyberspace technology may be met with technologies which facilitate [government's] ability to engage in monitoring and to achieve indirectly that [] it may no longer be able to do directly.

(c)   The Strange Return of *Gyges' Ring*: An Introduction†

Ian Kerr, Valerie Steeves, and Carole Lucock

Book II of Plato's *Republic* tells the story of a Lydian shepherd who stumbles upon the ancient Ring of Gyges while minding his flock. Fiddling with the ring one day, the shepherd discovers its magical power to render him invisible. As the story goes, the protagonist uses his newly found power to gain secret access to the castle where he ultimately kills the king and overthrows the kingdom.

Fundamentally, the ring provides the shepherd with an unusual opportunity to move through the halls of power without being tied to his public identity or his personal history. It also provided Plato with a narrative device to address a classic question known to philosophers as the "immoralist's challenge": why be moral if one can act otherwise with impunity?

THE NETWORK SOCIETY

In a network society — where key social structures and activities are organized around electronically processed information networks — this question ceases to be the luxury of an ancient philosopher's thought experiments. With the establishment of a global telecommunications network, the immoralist's challenge is no longer premised on mythology. The advent of the World Wide Web in the 1990s enabled everyone with access to a computer and modem to become unknown, and in some cases invisible, in public spaces — to communicate, emote, act, and interact with *relative* anonymity. Indeed, this may even have granted users more power than did Gyges' Ring, because the impact of what one could say or do online was no longer limited by physical proximity or corporeality. The end-to-end architecture of the Web's Transmission Control Protocol, for example, facilitated unidentified, one-to-many interactions at a distance. As the now-famous cartoon framed the popular culture of the early 1990s, "On the Internet, nobody knows you're a dog."[1] Although this cartoon resonated deeply on various levels, at the level of architecture it reflected the simple fact that the Internet's original protocols did not require people to identify themselves, enabling them to play with their identities — to represent themselves however they wished.

In those heady days bookmarking the end of the previous millennium, the rather strange and abrupt advent of Gyges' Ring 2.0 was by no means an unwelcome event. Network technologies fostered new social interactions of various sorts and provided unprecedented opportunities for individuals to share their thoughts and ideas en masse. Among other things, the Internet permitted robust political speech in hostile environments, allowing its users to say and do things that they might never have dared to say or do in places where their identity was more rigidly constrained by the relationships of power that bracket their experience of freedom. Anonymous browsers and messaging applications promoted frank discussion by employees in oppressive workplaces and created similar opportunities for others stifled by various forms of social stigma. Likewise, new cryptographic techniques promised to preserve personal privacy by empowering individuals to make careful and informed decisions about how, when, and with whom they would share their thoughts or their personal information.

At the same time, many of these new information technologies created opportunities to disrupt and resist the legal framework that protects persons and property. Succumbing to the immoralist's challenge, there were those who exploited the network to defraud, defame, and harass; to destroy property; to distribute harmful or illegal content; and to undermine national security.

In parallel with both of these developments, we have witnessed the proliferation of various security measures in the public and private sectors designed to undermine the "ID-free" protocols of the original network. New methods of authentication, verification, and surveillance have increasingly allowed persons and things to be digitally or biometrically identified, tagged, tracked, and monitored in real time and in formats that can be captured, archived, and retrieved

† From Ian Kerr, Valerie Steeves and Carole Lucock (eds.), *Lessons from the Identity Trail: Anonymity, Privacy And Identity In A Networked Society* (New York: Oxford University Press, 2009) at xxiii–xxxi. Reproduced with permission of Oxford University Press, Oxford, UK. [Notes and/or references omitted.]

319

indefinitely. More recently, given the increasing popularity of social network sites and the pervasiveness of interactive media used to cultivate user-generated content, the ability of governments, not to mention the proliferating international data brokerage industries that feed them, to collect, use, and disclose personal information about everyone on the network is increasing logarithmically. This phenomenon is further exacerbated by corporate and government imperatives to create and maintain large-scale information infrastructures to generate profit and increase efficiencies.

In this new world of ubiquitous handheld recording devices, personal webcams, interconnected closed circuit television (CCTV) cameras, radio frequency identification (RFID) tags, smart cards, global satellite positioning systems, HTTP cookies, digital rights management systems, biometric scanners, and DNA sequencers, the space for private, unidentified, or unauthenticated activity is rapidly shrinking. Many worry that the regulatory responses to the real and perceived threats posed by Gyges' Ring have already profoundly challenged our fundamental commitments to privacy, autonomy, equality, security of the person, free speech, free movement, and free association. Add in the shifting emphasis in recent years toward public safety and national security, and network technologies appear to be evolving in a manner that is transforming the structures of our communications systems from architectures of freedom to architectures of control. Are we shifting away from the original design of the network, from spaces where anonymity and privacy were once the default position to spaces where nearly every human transaction is subject to tracking, monitoring, and the possibility of authentication and identification?

The ability or inability to maintain privacy, construct our own identities, control the use of our identifiers, decide for ourselves what is known about us, and, in some cases, disconnect our actions from our identifiers will ultimately have profound implications for individual and group behavior. It will affect the extent to which people, corporations, and governments choose to engage in global electronic commerce, social media, and other important features of the network society. It will affect the way that we think of ourselves, the way we choose to express ourselves, the way that we make moral decisions, and our willingness and ability to fully participate in political processes. Yet our current philosophical, social, and political understandings of the impact and importance of privacy, identity, and anonymity in a network society are simplistic and poorly developed, as is our understanding of the broader social impact of emerging network technologies on existing legal, ethical, regulatory, and social structures.

This book investigates these issues from a number of North American and European perspectives. Our joint examination is structured around three core organizing themes: (1) privacy, (2) identity, and (3) anonymity.

PRIVACY

The jurist Hyman Gross once described privacy as a concept "infected with pernicious ambiguities."[2] More recently, Canadian Supreme Court Justice Ian Binnie expressed a related worry, opining that "privacy is protean."[3] The judge's metaphor is rather telling when one recalls that Proteus was a shape-shifter who would transform in order to avoid answering questions about the future. Perhaps U.S. novelist Jonathan Franzen had something similar in mind when he characterized privacy as the "Cheshire cat of values."[4]

One wonders whether privacy will suffer the same fate as Lewis Carroll's enigmatic feline — all smile and no cat.

Certainly, that is what Larry Ellison seems to think. Ellison is the CEO of Oracle Corporation and the fourteenth richest person alive. In the aftermath of September 11, 2001, Ellison offered to donate to the U.S. Government software that would enable a national identification database, boldly stating in 2004 that "The privacy you're concerned about is largely an illusion. All you have to give up is your illusions, not any of your privacy."[5] As someone who understands the power of network databases to profile people right down to their skivvies (and not only to provide desirable recommendations for a better brand!), Ellison's view of the future of privacy is bleak. Indeed, many if not most contemporary discussions of privacy are about its erosion in the face of new and emerging technologies. Ellison was, in fact, merely reiterating a sentiment that had already been expressed some five years earlier by his counterpart at Sun Microsystems, Scott McNealy, who advised a group of journalists gathered to learn about Sun's data-sharing software: "You have zero privacy anyway. Get over it."[6]

To turn Hyman Gross's eloquent quotation on its head — the Ellison/McNealy conception of privacy is infected with ambiguous perniciousness. It disingenuously — or perhaps even malevolently — equivocates between two rather different notions of privacy in order to achieve a self-interested outcome: it starts with a *descriptive* account of privacy as the level of control an individual enjoys over her or his personal information and then draws a *prescriptive* conclusion that, because new technologies will undermine the possibility of personal control, we therefore ought *not* to expect any privacy.

Of course, the privacy that many of us expect is not contingent upon or conditioned by the existence or prevalence of any given technology. Privacy is a normative concept that reflects a deeply held set of values that predates and is not rendered irrelevant by the network society. To think otherwise is to commit what philosopher G. E. Moore called the "naturalistic fallacy,"[7] or as Lawrence Lessig has restyled it, the "is-ism":

> The mistake of confusing how something is with how it must be. There is certainly a way that cyberspace is. But how cyberspace is is not how cyberspace has to be. There is no single way that the net has to be; no single architecture that defines the nature of the net. The possible architectures of something that we would call "the net" are many, and the character of life within those different architectures are [sic] diverse.[8]

Although the "character of life" of privacy has, without question, become more diverse in light of technologies of both the privacy-diminishing and privacy-preserving variety, the approach adopted in this book is to understand privacy as a *normative* concept. In this approach, the existence of privacy rights will not simply depend on whether our current technological infrastructure has reshaped our privacy expectations in the descriptive sense. It is not a like-it-or-lump-it proposition. At the same time, it is recognized that the meaning, importance, impact, and implementation of privacy may need to evolve alongside the emergence of new technologies. How privacy ought to be understood — and fostered — in a network society certainly requires an appreciation of and reaction to new and emerging network technologies and their role in society.

Given that the currency of the network society is information, it is not totally surprising that privacy rights have more recently been recharacterized by courts as a kind of "informational self-determination."[9] Drawing on Alan Westin's classic definition of informational privacy as "the claim of individuals, groups, or institutions to determine for themselves when, how, and to what extent information about them is communicated to others,"[10] many jurisdictions have adopted fair information practice principles[11] as the basis for data protection regimes.[12] These principles and the laws that support them are not a panacea, as they have been developed and implemented on the basis of an unhappy compromise between those who view privacy as a fundamental human right and those who view it as an economic right.[13] From one perspective, these laws aim to protect privacy, autonomy, and dignity interests. From another, they are the lowest common denominator of fairness in the information trade. Among other things, it is thought that fair information practice principles have the potential to be technology neutral, meaning that they apply to any and all technologies so that privacy laws do not have to be rewritten each time a new privacy-implicating technology comes along. A number of chapters in this book challenge that view.

Our examination of privacy in Part I of this book begins with the very fulcrum of the fair information practice principles — the doctrine of consent. Consent is often seen as the legal proxy for autonomous choice and is therefore anchored in the traditional paradigm of the classical liberal individual, which is typically thought to provide privacy's safest harbor. As an act of ongoing agency, consent can also function as a gatekeeper for the collection, use, and disclosure of personal information. As several of our chapters demonstrate, however, consent can also be manipulated, and reliance on it can generate unintended consequences in and outside of privacy law. Consequently, we devote several chapters to interrogations of the extent to which the control/consent model is a sufficient safeguard for privacy in a network society.

Does privacy live on liberal individualism alone? Some of our chapters seek out ways of illuminating privacy in light of other cherished collective values such as equality and security. Although the usual temptation is to understand these values as being in conflict with privacy, our approach in this book casts privacy as complementary to and in some cases symbiotic with these other important social values. Privacy does not stand alone. It is nested in a number of social relationships and is itself related to other important concepts, such as identity and anonymity. We turn to those concepts in Parts II and III of the book.

IDENTITY

Although lofty judicial conceptions of privacy such as "informational self-determination" set important normative standards, the traditional notion of a pure, disembodied, and atomistic self, capable of making perfectly rational and isolated choices in order to assert complete control over personal information, is not a particularly helpful fiction in a network society. If a fiction there must be, one that is perhaps more worthy of consideration is the idea of identity as a theft of the self. Who we are in the world and how we are identified is, at best, a concession. Aspects of our identities are chosen, others assigned, and still others accidentally accrued. Sometimes they are concealed at our discretion, other times they are revealed against our will. Identity formation and disclosure are both complex social negotiations, and in the context of the network society, it is not usually the individual who holds the bargaining power.

Because the network society is to a large extent premised on mediated interaction, who we are (and who we say we are) is not a self-authenticating proposition in the same way that it might be if we were close kin or even if we were merely standing in physical proximity to one another. Although we can be relatively certain that it is *not* a canine on the other end of an IM chat, the identity of the entity at the other end of a transaction may be entirely ambiguous. Is it a business partner, an imposter, or an automated software bot?

The same could be true of someone seeking to cross an international border, order an expensive product online, or fly an airplane — assuming she or he is able to spoof the appropriate credentials or identifiers. As we saw in the extreme example of the shepherd in possession of Gyges' Ring, those who are able to obfuscate their identities sometimes take the opportunity to act with limited accountability. This is one of the reasons why network architects and social policymakers have become quite concerned with issues of identity and identification.

However, it is important to recognize that identification techniques can preserve or diminish privacy. Their basic function is to make at least some aspects of an unknown entity known by mapping it to a knowable attribute. An identification technique is more likely to be privacy preserving if it takes a minimalist approach with respect to those attributes that are to become known. For example, an automated highway toll system may need to authenticate certain attributes associated with a car or driver in order to appropriately debit an account for the cost of the toll. But to do so, it need not identify the car, the driver, the passengers, or for that matter the ultimate destination of the vehicle. Instead, anonymous digital credentials[14] could be assigned that would allow cryptographic tokens to be exchanged through a network in order to prove statements about them and their relationships with the relevant organization(s) without any need to identify the drivers or passengers themselves. Electronic voting systems can do the same thing.

In Part II of the book we explore these issues by investigating different philosophical notions of identity and discussing how those differences matter. We also address the role of identity and identification in achieving personal and public safety. We consider whether a focus on the protection of "heroic" cowboys who refuse to reveal their identities in defiance of orders to do so by law enforcement officers risks more harm than good, and whether unilateral decisions by the State to mandate control over the identities of heroic sexually assaulted women as a protective measure risk less good than harm. We examine the interaction of self and other in the construction of identity and demonstrate in several chapters why discussions of privacy and identity cannot easily be disentangled from broader discussions about power, gender, difference, and discrimination.

We also examine the ways in which identity formation and identification can be enabled or disabled by various technologies. A number of technologies that we discuss — data-mining, automation, ID cards, ubiquitous computing, biometrics, and human-implantable RFID — have potential narrowing effects, reducing who we are to how we can be counted, kept track of, or marketed to. Other technologies under investigation in this book — mix networks and data obfuscation technologies — can be tools for social resistance used to undermine identification and the collection of personal information, returning us to where our story began.

ANONYMITY

We end in Part III with a comparative investigation of the law's response to the renaissance of anonymity. Riffing on Andy Warhol's best known turn of phrase, an internationally (un)known British street artist living under the pseudonym "Banksy"[15] produced an installation with words on a retro-looking pink screen that say, "In the future, everyone will have their 15 minutes of anonymity."[16] Was this a comment on the erosion of privacy in light of future technology? Or was it a reflection of Banksy's own experience regarding the challenges of living life under a pseudonym in a network society? Whereas Warhol's "15 minutes of fame" recognized the fleeting nature of celebrity and public attention, Banksy's "15 minutes of anonymity" recognizes the long-lasting nature of information ubiquity and data retention.

Although privacy and anonymity are related concepts, it is important to realize that they are not the same thing. There are those who think that anonymity is the key to privacy. The intuition is that a privacy breach cannot occur unless the information collected, used, or disclosed about an individual is associated with that individual's identity. Many anonymizing technologies exploit this notion, allowing people to control their personal information by obfuscating their identities. Interestingly, the same basic thinking underlies most data protection regimes, which one way or another link privacy protection to an identifiable individual. According to this approach, it does not matter if we collect, use, or disclose information, attributes, or events about people so long as the information cannot be (easily) associated with them.

Although anonymity, in some cases, enables privacy, it certainly does not guarantee it. As Bruce Schneier has pointed out[17] and as any recovering alcoholic knows all too well, even if Alcoholics Anonymous does not require you to show ID or to use your real name, the meetings are anything but private. Anonymity in public is quite difficult to achieve. The fact that perceived anonymity in public became more easily achieved through the end-to-end architecture of the Net is part of what has made the Internet such a big deal, creating a renaissance in anonymity studies not to mention new markets for the emerging field of identity management. The AA example illustrates another crucial point about anonymity. Although there is a relationship between anonymity and invisibility, they are not the same thing. Though Gyges' Ring unhinged the link between the shepherd's identity and his actions, the magic of the ring[18] was not merely in enabling him to act anonymously (and therefore without accountability): the real magic was his ability to act invisibly. As some leading academics have recently come to realize, visibility and exposure are also important elements in any discussion of privacy, identity, and anonymity.[19] Indeed, many argue that the power of the Internet lies not in the ability to hide who we are,

but in freeing some of us to expose ourselves and to make ourselves visible on our own terms.

Given its potential ability to enhance privacy on one hand and to reduce accountability on the other, what is the proper scope of anonymity in a network society?

Although Part III of the book does not seek to answer this question directly, it does aim to erect signposts for developing appropriate policies by offering a comparative investigation of anonymity and the law in five European and North American jurisdictions. How the law regards anonymity, it turns out, is not a question reducible to discrete areas of practice. As we shall see, it is as broad ranging as the law itself.

Interestingly, despite significant differences in the five legal systems and their underlying values and attitudes regarding privacy and identity, there seems to be a substantial overlap in the way that these legal systems regard anonymity, which is not generally regarded as a right and certainly not as a foundational right. In the context of these five countries, it might even be said that the law's regard for anonymity is to some extent diminishing.

When one considers these emerging legal trends alongside the shifting technological landscape, it appears that the answer to our question posed at the outset is clear: the architecture of the network society seems to be shifting from one in which anonymity was the default to one where nearly every human transaction is subject to monitoring and the possibility of identity authentication. But what of the strange return of Gyges' Ring and the network society in which it reemerged? And what do we wish for the future of privacy, identity, and anonymity?

Let us begin the investigation.

VII

Dispute Resolution

The articles in Part VII consider the ways in which law may fulfill the function of dispute resolution (one of the four functions of law posited by Hoebel in Chapter 1). They also identify ways in which disputes may be resolved using alternatives to formal legal adjudication involving a trial before a judge.

The articles in Chapter 16 discuss how and why parties who may be entitled to rely on formal adjudication may choose to rely instead on informal negotiations to resolve their disputes. Stewart Macaulay discusses the incentives for businesses to avoid formal litigation in order to maintain long-term commercial relationships. Robert Mnookin similarly argues that divorce law, like contracts, should provide a formal framework for spouses to negotiate their own determinations of rights and responsibilities through a process he calls "private ordering", rather than having those determinations imposed by an external authority such as a judge. Both authors emphasize law's role in establishing informal norms of conduct that take place, as Mnookin says, "in the shadow of law" rather than within its formal frameworks. Does operating in the shadow of the law allow the parties to escape the tendency of actors in the formal legal process to "steal conflicts" as identified by Nils Christie in Chapter 1?

The articles in Chapter 17 then explore the key characteristics of formal adjudication in common law countries. Neil Brooks considers a series of problems with the adversarial nature of the system and suggests that judges may take a more active role in the trial process to mitigate some of those problems. Judge Jerome Frank, in turn, focuses on the ways that limited resources may undermine the ability of parties to mount an effective case. By contrast, the excerpt from Franz Kafka's *The Trial* raises concerns within the context of a fictionalized account of an inquisitorial justice system that has become bureaucratized to such an extent it has lost any aspiration to justice. Finally, the summary of the Inquiry into Forensic Pathology in Ontario provides an important reminder that human error and human failures may be aggravated through the adversarial nature of the courts and through unequal access to expertise inside and outside the courtroom. Such personal and systemic failures clearly jeopardize the capacity of even the modern Canadian trial process to provide justice.

Chapter 18 then explores alternatives to formal adjudication. These alternatives include the use of mediation and arbitration as alternatives to the trial-process, but also include the use of these alternatives within the context of ongoing litigation. In addition, the chapter includes articles on newer forms of litigation that try to reduce the negative impacts of traditional adversarial litigation. In particular, Dawn Moore's article discusses whether the multi-disciplinary approach adopted in drug courts can address issues of addiction more effectively than traditional criminal courts, while Wanda Wiegers and Michaela Keet discuss whether "collaborative lawyering" may allow for a less adversarial method of settling family law disputes.

Finally, Chapter 19 outlines some of the debates concerning the use of alternative dispute resolution processes. As you read the articles in Part VII, ask yourself: how effective are courts at resolving disputes? Can litigation and formal adjudication help resolve the problems at the root of legal conflicts? Do the alternatives to adjudication provide sufficient protection of vulnerable, less powerful parties? How do we balance between rights and interests, between healing processes and just results?

(a) Non-Contractual Relationships in Business: A Preliminary Study[†]

Stewart Macaulay

TENTATIVE FINDINGS

. . . .

The Adjustment of Exchange Relationships and the Settling of Disputes

While a significant amount of creating business exchanges is done on a fairly noncontractual basis, the creation of exchanges usually is far more contractual than the adjustment of such relationships and the settlement of disputes. Exchanges are adjusted when the obligations of one or both parties are modified by agreement during the life of the relationship. For example, the buyer may be allowed to cancel all or part of the goods he has ordered because he no longer needs them; the seller may be paid more than the usual contract price by the buyer because of unusual changed circumstances. Dispute settlement involves determining whether or not a party has performed as agreed and, if he has not, doing something about it. For example, a court may have to interpret the meaning of a contract, determine what the alleged defaulting party has done and determine what, if any, remedy the aggrieved party is entitled to. Or one party may assert that the other is in default, refuse to proceed with performing the contract and refuse to deal ever again with the alleged defaulter. If the alleged defaulter, who in fact may not be in default, takes no action, the dispute is then "settled."

Business exchanges in non-speculative areas are usually adjusted without dispute. Under the law of contracts, if B orders 1,000 widgets from S at $1.00 each, B must take all 1,000 widgets or be in breach of contract and liable to pay S his expenses up to the time of the breach plus his lost anticipated profit. Yet all ten of the purchasing agents asked about cancellation of orders once placed indicated that they expected to be able to cancel orders freely subject to only an obligation to pay for the seller's major expenses such as scrapped steel.[6] All 17 sales personnel asked reported that they often had to accept cancellation. One said, "You can't ask a man to eat paper [the firm's product] when he has no use for it." A lawyer with many large industrial clients said,

> Often businessmen do not feel they have "a contract" — rather they have "an order." They speak of "cancelling the order" rather than "breaching our contract." When I began practice I referred to order cancellations as breaches of contract, but my clients objected since they do not think of cancellation as wrong. Most clients, in heavy industry at least, believe that there is a right to cancel as part of the buyer-seller relationship. There is a widespread attitude that one can back out of any deal within some very vague limits. Lawyers are often surprised by this attitude.

Disputes are frequently settled without reference to the contract or potential or actual legal sanctions. There is a hesitancy to speak of legal rights or to

---

† (1963) 28:1 American Sociological Review 55 at 60–67. Reproduced with permission. [Notes and/or references omitted.]

threaten to sue in these negotiations. Even where the parties have a detailed and carefully planned agreement which indicates what is to happen if, say, the seller fails to deliver on time, often they will never refer to the agreement but will negotiate a solution when the problem arises apparently as if there had never been any original contract. One purchasing agent expressed a common business attitude when he said,

> if something comes up, you get the other man on the telephone and deal with the problem. You don't read legalistic contract clauses at each other if you ever want to do business again. One doesn't run to lawyers if he wants to stay in business because one must behave decently.

Or as one businessman put it, "You can settle any dispute if you keep the lawyers and accountants out of it. They just do not understand the give-and-take needed in business." All of the house counsel interviewed indicated that they are called into the dispute settlement process only after the businessmen have failed to settle matters in their own way. Two indicated that after being called in house counsel at first will only advise the purchasing agent, sales manager or other official involved; not even the house counsel's letterhead is used on communications with the other side until all hope for a peaceful resolution is gone.

Law suits for breach of contract appear to be rare. Only five of the 12 purchasing agents had ever been involved in even a negotiation concerning a contract dispute where both sides were represented by lawyers; only two of ten sales managers had ever gone this far. None had been involved in a case that went through trial. A law firm with more than 40 lawyers and a large commercial practice handles in a year only about six trials concerned with contract problems. Less than 10 per cent of the time of this office is devoted to any type of work related to contracts disputes. Corporations big enough to do business in more than one state tend to sue and be sued in the federal courts. Yet only 2,779 out of 58,293 civil actions filed in the United States District Courts in fiscal year 1961 involved private contracts.[7] During the same period only 3,447 of the 61,138 civil cases filed in the principal trial courts of New York State involved private contracts.[8] The same picture emerges from a review of appellate cases.[9] Mentschikoff has suggested that commercial cases are not brought to the courts either in periods of business prosperity (because buyers unjustifiably reject goods only when prices drop and they can get similar goods elsewhere at less than the contract

price) or in periods of deep depression (because people are unable to come to court or have insufficient assets to satisfy any judgment that might be obtained). Apparently, she adds, it is necessary to have "a kind of middle-sized depression" to bring large numbers of commercial cases to the courts. However, there is little evidence that in even "a kind of middle-sized depression" today's businessmen would use the courts to settle disputes.[10]

At times relatively contractual methods are used to make adjustments in ongoing transactions and to settle disputes. Demands of one side which are deemed unreasonable by the other occasionally are blocked by reference to the terms of the agreement between the parties. The legal position of the parties can influence negotiations even though legal rights or litigation are never mentioned in their discussions; it makes a difference if one is demanding what both concede to be a right or begging for a favour. Now and then a firm may threaten to turn matters over to its attorneys, threaten to sue, commence a suit or even litigate and carry an appeal to the highest court which will hear the matter. Thus, legal sanctions, while not an everyday affair, are not unknown in business.

One can conclude that while detailed planning and legal sanctions play a significant role in some exchanges between businesses, in many business exchanges their role is small.

TENTATIVE EXPLANATIONS

Two questions need to be answered: (A) How can business successfully operate exchange relationships with relatively so little attention to detailed planning or to legal sanctions, and (B) Why does business ever use contract in light of its success without it?

Why Are Relatively Non-Contractual Practices So Common?

In most situations contract is not needed.[11] Often its functions are served by other devices. Most problems are avoided without resort to detailed planning or legal sanctions because usually there is little room for honest misunderstandings or good faith differences of opinion about the nature and quality of a seller's performance. Although the parties fail to cover all foreseeable contingencies, they will exercise care to see that both understand the primary obligation on each side. Either products are standardized with an accepted description or specifications are written calling for production to certain tolerances or results. Those who write and read specifications are experienced professionals who will know the customs of their industry and those of the industries with which they deal. Consequently, these customs can fill gaps in the express agreements of the parties. Finally, most products can be tested to see if they are what was ordered; typically in the manufacturing industry we are not dealing with questions of taste or judgment where people can differ in good faith.

When defaults occur they are not likely to be disastrous because of techniques of risk avoidance or risk spreading. One can deal with firms of good reputation or he may be able to get some form of security to guarantee performance. One can insure against many breaches of contract where the risks justify the costs. Sellers set up reserves for bad debts on their books and can sell some of their accounts receivable. Buyers can place orders with two or more suppliers of the same item so that a default by one will not stop the buyer's assembly lines.

Moreover, contract and contract law are often thought unnecessary because there are many effective non-legal sanctions. Two norms are widely accepted. (1) Commitments are to be honored in almost all situations; one does not welsh on a deal. (2) One ought to produce a good product and stand behind it. Then, too, business units are organized to perform commitments, and internal sanctions will induce performance. For example, sales personnel must face angry customers when there has been a late or defective performance. The salesmen do not enjoy this and will put pressure on the production personnel responsible for the default. If the production personnel default too often, they will be fired. At all levels of the two business units personal relationships across the boundaries of the two organizations exert pressures for conformity to expectations. Salesmen often know purchasing agents well. The same two individuals occupying these roles may have dealt with each other from five to 25 years. Each has something to give the other. Salesmen have gossip about competitors, shortages and price increases to give purchasing agents who treat them well. Salesmen take purchasing agents to dinner, and they give purchasing agents Christmas gifts hoping to improve the chances of making a sale. The buyer's engineering staff may work with the seller's engineering staff to solve problems jointly. The seller's engineers may render great assistance, and the buyer's engineers may desire to return the favour by drafting specifications which only the seller can meet. The top executives of the two firms may know each other. They may sit together on government or trade committees. They may know each other socially and even belong to the same country club. The interrelationships may

be more formal. Sellers may hold stock in corporations which are important customers; buyers may hold stock in important suppliers. Both buyer and seller may share common directors on their boards. They may share a common financial institution which has financed both units.

The final type of non-legal sanction is the most obvious. Both business units involved in the exchange desire to continue successfully in business and will avoid conduct which might interfere with attaining this goal. One is concerned with both the reaction of the other party in the particular exchange and with his own general business reputation. Obviously, the buyer gains sanctions insofar as the seller wants the particular exchange to be completed. Buyers can withhold part or all of their payments until sellers have performed to their satisfaction. If a seller has a great deal of money tied up in his performance which he must recover quickly, he will go a long way to please the buyer in order to be paid. Moreover, buyers who are dissatisfied may cancel and cause sellers to lose the cost of what they have done up to cancellation. Furthermore, sellers hope for repeats for orders, and one gets few of these from unhappy customers. Some industrial buyers go so far as to formalize this sanction by issuing "report cards" rating the performance of each supplier. The supplier rating goes to the top management of the seller organization, and these men can apply internal sanctions to salesmen, production supervisors or product designers if there are too many "D's" or "F's" on the report card.

While it is generally assumed that the customer is always right, the seller may have some counterbalancing sanctions against the buyer. The seller may have obtained a large downpayment from the buyer which he will want to protect. The seller may have an exclusive process which the buyer needs. The seller may be one of the few firms which has the skill to make the item to the tolerances set by the buyer's engineers and within the time available. There are costs and delays involved in turning from a supplier one has dealt with in the past to a new supplier. Then, too, market conditions can change so that a buyer is faced with shortages of critical items. The most extreme example is the post World War II gray market conditions when sellers were rationing goods rather than selling them. Buyers must build up some reserve of good will with suppliers if they face the risk of such shortage and desire good treatment when they occur. Finally, there is reciprocity in buying and selling. A buyer cannot push a supplier too far if that supplier also buys significant quantities of the product made by the buyer.

Not only do the particular business units in a given exchange want to deal with each other again, they also want to deal with other business units in the future. And the way one behaves in a particular transaction, or a series of transactions, will colour his general business reputation. Blacklisting can be formal or informal. Buyers who fail to pay their bills on time risk a bad report in credit rating services such as Dun and Bradstreet. Sellers who do not satisfy their customers become the subject of discussion in the gossip exchanged by purchasing agents and salesmen, at meetings of purchasing agents' associations and trade associations, or even at country clubs or social gatherings where members of top management meet. The American male's habit of debating the merits of new cars carries over to industrial items. Obviously, a poor reputation does not help a firm make sales and may force it to offer great price discounts or added services to remain in business. Furthermore, the habits of unusually demanding buyers become known, and they tend to get no more than they can coerce out of suppliers who choose to deal with them. Thus, often contract is not needed as there are alternatives.

Not only are contract and contract law not needed in many situations, their use may have, or may be thought to have, undesirable consequences. Detailed negotiated contracts can get in the way of creating good exchange relationships between business units. If one side insists on a detailed plan, there will be delay while letters are exchanged as the parties try to agree on what should happen if a remote and unlikely contingency occurs. In some cases they may not be able to agree at all on such matters and as a result a sale may be lost to the seller and the buyer may have to search elsewhere for an acceptable supplier. Many businessmen would react by thinking that, had no one raised the series of remote and unlikely contingencies, all this wasted effort could have been avoided.

Even where agreement can be reached at the negotiation stage, carefully planned arrangements may create undesirable exchange relationships between business units. Some businessmen object that in such a carefully worked out relationship one gets performance only to the letter of the contract. Such planning indicates a lack of trust and blunts the demands of friendship, turning a cooperative venture into an antagonistic horse trade. Yet the greater danger perceived by some businessmen is that one would have to perform his side of the bargain to its letter and thus lose what is called "flexibility." Businessmen may welcome a measure of vagueness in the obligations they assume so that they may negotiate matters in light of the actual circumstances.

Adjustment of exchange relationships and dispute settlement by litigation or the threat of it also has many costs. The gain anticipated from using this form of coercion often fails to outweigh these costs, which are both monetary and non-monetary. Threatening to turn matters over to an attorney may cost no more money than postage or a telephone call; yet few are so skilled in making such a threat that it will not cost some deterioration of the relationship between the firms. One businessman said that customers had better not rely on legal rights or threaten to bring a breach of contract law suit against him since he "would not be treated like a criminal" and would fight back with every means available. Clearly actual litigation is even more costly than making threats. Lawyers demand substantial fees from larger business units. A firm's executives often will have to be transported and maintained in another city during the proceedings if, as often is the case, the trial must be held away from the home office. Top management does not travel by Greyhound and stay at the Y.M.C.A. Moreover, there will be the cost of diverting top management, engineers, and others in the organization from their normal activities. The firm may lose many days work from several key people. The non-monetary costs may be large too. A breach of contract law suit may settle a particular dispute, but such an action often results in a "divorce" ending the "marriage" between the two businesses, since a contract action is likely to carry charges with at least overtones of bad faith. Many executives, moreover, dislike the prospect of being cross-examined in public. Some executives may dislike losing control of a situation by turning the decision-making power over to lawyers. Finally, the law of contract damages may not provide an adequate remedy even if the firm wins the suit; one may get vindication but not much money.

Why Do Relatively Contractual Practices Ever Exist?

Although contract is not needed and actually may have negative consequences, businessmen do make some carefully planned contracts, negotiate settlements influenced by their legal rights and commence and defend some breach of contract law suits or arbitration proceedings. In view of the findings and explanation presented to this point, one may ask why. Exchanges are carefully planned when it is thought that planning and a potential legal sanction will have more advantages than disadvantages. Such a judgment may be reached when contract planning serves the internal needs of an organization involved in a business exchange. For example, a fairly detailed contract can serve as a communication device within a large corporation. While the corporation's sales manager and house counsel may work out all the provisions with the customer, its production manager will have to make the product. He must be told what to do and how to handle at least the most obvious contingencies. Moreover, the sales manager may want to remove certain issues from future negotiation by his subordinates. If he puts the matter in the written contract, he may be able to keep his salesmen from making concessions to the customer without first consulting the sales manager. Then the sales manager may be aided in his battles with his firm's financial or engineering departments if the contract calls for certain practices which the sales manager advocates but which the other departments resist. Now the corporation is obligated to a customer to do what the sales manager wants to do; how can the financial or engineering departments insist on anything else?

Also one tends to find a judgment that the gains of contract outweigh the costs where there is a likelihood that significant problems will arise. One factor leading to this conclusion is complexity of the agreed performance over a long period. Another factor is whether or not the degree of injury in case of default is thought to be potentially great. This factor cuts two ways. First, a buyer may want to commit a seller to a detailed and legally binding contract, where the consequence of a default by the seller would seriously injure the buyer. For example, the airlines are subject to law suits from the survivors of passengers and to great adverse publicity as a result of crashes. One would expect the airlines to bargain for carefully defined and legally enforceable obligations on the part of the airframe manufacturers when they purchase aircraft. Second, a seller may want to limit his liability for a buyer's damages by a provision in their contract. For example, a manufacturer of air conditioning may deal with motels in the South and Southwest. If this equipment fails in the hot summer months, a motel may lose a great deal of business. The manufacturer may wish to avoid any liability for this type of injury to his customers and may want a contract with a clear disclaimer clause.

Similarly, one uses or threatens to use legal sanctions to settle disputes when other devices will not work and when the gains are thought to outweigh the costs. For example, perhaps the most common type of business contracts case fought all the way through the appellate courts today is an action

for an alleged wrongful termination of a dealer's franchise by a manufacturer. Since the franchise has been terminated, factors such as personal relationships and the desire for future business will have little effect; the cancellation of the franchise indicates they have already failed to maintain the relationship. Nor will a complaining dealer worry about creating a hostile relationship between himself and the manufacturer. Often the dealer has suffered a great financial loss both as to his investment in building and equipment and as to his anticipated future profits. A cancelled automobile dealer's lease on his showroom and shop will continue to run, and his tools for servicing, say, Plymouths cannot be used to service other makes of cars. Moreover, he will have no more new Plymouths to sell. Today there is some chance of winning a law suit for terminating a franchise in bad faith in many states and in the federal courts. Thus, often the dealer chooses to risk the cost of a lawyer's fee because of the chance that he may recover some compensation for his losses.

An "irrational" factor may exert some influence on the decision to use legal sanctions. The man who controls a firm may feel that he or his organization has been made to appear foolish or has been the victim of fraud or bad faith. The law suit may be seen as a vehicle "to get even" although the potential gains, as viewed by an objective observer, are outweighed by the potential costs.

The decision whether or not to use contract — whether the gain exceeds the costs — will be made by the person within the business unit with the power to make it, and it tends to make a difference who he is. People in a sales department oppose contract. Contractual negotiations are just one more hurdle in the way of a sale. Holding a customer to the letter of a contract is bad for "customer relations." Suing a customer who is not bankrupt and might order again is poor strategy. Purchasing agents and their buyers are less hostile to contracts but regard attention devoted to such matters as a waste of time. In contrast, the financial control department — the treasurer, controller or auditor — leans toward more contractual dealings. Contract is viewed by these people as an organizing tool to control operations in a large organization. It tends to define precisely and to minimize the risks to which the firm is exposed. Outside lawyers — those with many clients — may share this enthusiasm for a more contractual method of dealing. These lawyers are concerned with preventive law — avoiding any possible legal difficulty. They see many unstable and unsuccessful exchange transactions, and so they are aware of, and perhaps overly concerned with, all of the things which can go wrong.

Moreover, their job of settling disputes with legal sanctions is much easier if their client has not been overly casual about transaction planning. The inside lawyer, or house counsel, is harder to classify. He is likely to have some sympathy with a more contractual method of dealing. He shares the outside lawyer's "craft urge" to see exchange transactions neat and tidy from a legal standpoint. Since he is more concerned with avoiding and settling disputes than selling goods, he is likely to be less willing to rely on a man's word as the sole sanction than is a salesman. Yet the house counsel is more a part of the organization and more aware of its goals and subject to its internal sanctions. If the potential risks are not too great, he may hesitate to suggest a more contractual procedure to the sales department. He must sell his services to the operating departments, and he must hoard what power he has, expending it on only what he sees as significant issues.

The power to decide that a more contractual method of creating relationships and settling disputes shall be used will be held by different people at different times in different organizations. In most firms the sales department and the purchasing department have a great deal of power to resist contractual procedures or to ignore them if they are formally adopted and to handle disputes their own way. Yet in larger organizations the treasurer and the controller have increasing power to demand both systems and compliance. Occasionally, the house counsel must arbitrate the conflicting positions of these departments; in giving "legal advice" he may make the business judgment necessary regarding the use of contract. At times he may ask for an opinion from an outside law firm to reinforce his own position with the outside firm's prestige.

Obviously, there are other significant variables which influence the degree that contract is used. One is the relative bargaining power or skill of the two business units. Even if the controller of a small supplier succeeds within the firm and creates a contractual system of dealing, there will be no contract if the firm's large customer prefers not to be bound to anything. Firms that supply General Motors deal as General Motors wants to do business, for the most part. Yet bargaining power is not size or share of the market alone. Even a General Motors may need a particular supplier, at least temporarily. Furthermore, bargaining power may shift as an exchange relationship is first created and then continues. Even a giant firm can find itself bound to a small supplier once production of an essential item begins for there may not be time to turn to another supplier. Also, all of the factors discussed in this paper can be viewed as *components* of bargaining power — for example, the personal relationship between the presidents of the buyer and the seller firms may give a sales manager great power over a purchasing agent who has been instructed to give the seller "every consideration." Another variable relevant to the use of contract is the influence of third parties. The federal government, or a lender of money, may insist that a contract be made in a particular transaction or may influence the decision to assert one's legal rights under a contract.

Contract, then, often plays an important role in business, but other factors are significant. To understand the functions of contract the whole system of conducting exchanges must be explored fully. More types of business communities must be studied, contract litigation must be analyzed to see why the non-legal sanctions fail to prevent the use of legal sanctions and all of the variables suggested in this paper must be classified more systematically.

(b) Bargaining in the Shadow of the Law: The Case of Divorce†

Robert H. Mnookin

I wish to suggest a new way of thinking about the role of law at the time of divorce. It is concerned primarily with the impact of the legal system on negotiations and bargaining that occurs *outside* of

† (1979) 32 Current Legal Problems 65 at 65–70, 93–95, 96–102. Reproduced with permission of Sweet & Maxwell Limited. [Notes and/or references omitted.]

court. Rather than regard order as imposed from above, I see the primary function of contemporary divorce law as providing a framework for divorcing couples themselves to determine their respective rights and responsibilities after dissolution. This process, by which parties to a marriage are empowered to create their own legally enforceable commitments, I shall call *"private ordering."*[2]

Available evidence concerning how divorce proceedings actually work suggests that a re-examination from the perspective of private ordering is long overdue. "Typically the parties do not go to court at all until they have worked matters out and are ready for the rubber stamp."[3] Both in the United States and England the overwhelming majority of divorcing couples resolve or settle the distributional questions concerning marital property, alimony, child support, and custody without bringing any contested issue to the court for adjudication.[4]

This new perspective and the use of the term "private ordering" [are] not meant to suggest an absence of important social interests in how this process works, or in the fairness of the outcomes. The implicit policy questions are ones of emphasis and degree: to what extent should law permit and encourage divorcing couples to work out their own arrangements? Within what limits should parties be empowered to make their own law that they bring into existence by their agreement? What procedural or substantive safeguards are necessary because of various social interests? Nor is this new perspective meant to imply that the law and the legal system are unimportant. For divorcing spouses and their children, family law is inescapably relevant. The legal system affects *when* a divorce may occur; *how* a divorce must be procured; and *what happens* as a consequence of divorce. The primary purpose of this paper is to develop a framework for thinking about how the legal rules and procedures used in court for adjudicating disputes affect the bargaining process that occurs between divorcing couples *outside* the courtroom.

Before setting out together, let me provide you with a road map of where we are going. Our first stop involves an examination of the degree to which the law today authorises private ordering at the time of divorce. In other words, to what extent can a divorcing couple create their own legally enforceable commitments? In this context, I will also explain why I think the legal system should provide divorcing couples broad power through agreement to resolve the various questions that arise.

Secondly, against this background, I present a simple bargaining model to suggest how the legal system affects negotiations between spouses and their representatives at the time of divorce.

Finally, I will apply this framework to several issues that have dominated much of the academic discussion concerning family law during recent years:

1. The advantages and disadvantages of discretion conferring legal standards for child custody;
2. Goldstein, Freud and Solnit's proposed standard for visitation;
3. The role of lawyers in the divorce process; and
4. The role of courts in "undisputed" divorces.

Let us now turn to the question of the extent to which the law today sanctions private ordering. At the outset it is important to recall that a legal system might allow varying degrees of private ordering upon the dissolution of marriage. Until the no-fault revolution, the law concerning divorce did reflect a highly regulatory model that attempted to restrict private ordering. Couples had no formal power to end their marriage by mutual agreement. Divorce was granted only after an official inquiry by a judge, who had to determine whether there were "appropriate grounds," which were themselves very narrowly defined in terms of marital offences. If a divorce were granted, the State asserted broad power to impose distributional consequences, and to have continuing regulatory jurisdiction over the children and their relationship to their parents. Doctrines such as collusion, connivance and condonation were meant to curtail the degree to which parties themselves could through agreement bring about a divorce; and the procedural requirements reflected the view, in R.M. Jackson's words, that both the petitioner and the respondent were "suspicious characters."[5] Obviously, the marital offence regime — even at its most restrictive — could not entirely eliminate collusion. Some divorcing spouses worked things out for themselves and then (with the help of their lawyers) staged a carefully rehearsed and jointly produced play for the court.[6] Nonetheless, the legal system was structured to minimise private ordering.

Dramatic changes in divorce law during the past decade now permit a substantial degree of private ordering. The "no fault revolution" has made the fundamental decision of whether there shall be divorce largely a matter of private concern. Parties to a marriage can now explicitly create circumstances that will allow divorce. Indeed, the reality is that agreement between spouses is not even necessary — either spouse can unilaterally create the grounds for dissolution simply by separation for a sufficient period of time.[7]

What about the parties' power to decide for themselves the consequences of divorce? Here the presence of children makes an important difference. Where the divorcing couple has no children, the law both in England and the United States largely recognises the power of the parties upon separation or divorce to make their own arrangements concerning marital property and alimony.[8] A spousal agreement may be subject to some sort of judicial proceeding — or submission to a Registrar — but on both sides of the Atlantic the official review appears to be largely perfunctory.[9] In some American states, a couple may if they choose make their agreement binding and final — i.e., not subject to later modification by a court after the divorce.[10] In England, strictly speaking, this probably is not possible.[11] Nonetheless, English courts are very slow after a divorce is granted to modify an agreement intended to be binding or an order issued with the consent of the parties.[12]

Where there are minor children, existing law imposes substantial doctrinal constraints. For those allocational decisions that directly affect children — that is, child support, custody and visitation — parents lack the formal power "to make their own law." The court, exercising the state's *parens patrine* power, is said to have responsibility to determine who should have custody and on what conditions. Private agreements concerning these matters are possible, and common, but these agreements cannot bind the court which is said to have an independent responsibility for determining what arrangements best serve the child's welfare.[13] Thus, the court has the power to reject a parental agreement, and order some other level of child support or some other custodial arrangement, if that is thought more desirable.[14] Moreover, even if the parties' initial agreement is accepted by the court, the parties entirely lack the power to provide for finality. A court may at any time during the child's minority reopen and modify the initial decree in light of any subsequent change in circumstances.[15] The parties entirely lack the power to deprive the court of this jurisdiction.

These limitations on parental power reflect a variety of policy concerns. They may acknowledge the fact that the child, although profoundly affected by the bargain, is not normally a meaningful participant in the negotiating process. A parental agreement concerning custody, visitation or support may not reflect the child's interests but instead the interests of the parents.[16] A parent eager to escape an unhappy marriage may agree to custodial arrangements and levels of support that are less advantageous to the child than some feasible alternative. Judicial scrutiny and continual supervision of the ele-

ments of the separation agreement concerning the child might therefore be seen as a safeguard of the child's interests.

Available evidence concerning how the legal system in fact processes undisputed divorce cases involving minor children suggests that in fact parents have very broad powers to make their own deals. Typically separation agreements are rubber stamped even in cases involving children. A study of custody here in England suggests, for example, that courts rarely set aside an arrangement acceptable to the parents. Anecdotal evidence in America suggests that the same is true in the U.S.

That the legal system in fact gives parents broad discretion is less than surprising when one considers a number of factors. First, getting information is difficult when there is no dispute. There are usually very limited resources for a thorough or an independent investigation of the family's circumstances. Secondly, the applicable legal standards are extremely vague and give registrars or judges very little guidance as to what circumstances justify overriding a parental decision.[17] Finally, there are obvious limitations on a court's practical power to control parental behaviour once they leave the courtroom. For all these reasons, it is not surprising that most courts behave as if their function in the divorce process is dispute settlement. Where there is no dispute, busy judges or registrars are typically quite willing to rubber stamp a private agreement, thus conserving resources for disputed cases.

Before proceeding, I should make clear the reasons I think law should give divorcing spouses broad powers to make their own agreement. When a couple can resolve distributional consequences of divorce without resort to court for adjudication, there are obvious and substantial savings. The cost of litigation, both private and public, is minimised. The pain of an adversarial proceeding is avoided. Recent findings from psychological studies suggest the desirability from a child's perspective in having parents agree on custodial arrangements. Moreover, through a negotiated agreement the parties can often avoid the risks and uncertainties of litigation which sometimes involve all or nothing consequences. Given the substantial delays that often characterise contested judicial proceedings, an agreement can often provide significant time-savings for the parties, thus allowing the spouses to proceed with their lives. Finally, a solution agreed to by the parties seems more likely to be consistent with their own preferences and accepted by them over time than a result that is simply imposed by a court.

For divorces where there are no minor children, divorcing couples should have very broad powers to make their own arrangements; significant limitations are inconsistent with the premises of no fault divorce. After all, who can better evaluate the comparative advantages of alternative arrangements than the parties themselves? In John Stuart Mill's words, each spouse "is the person most interested in his own well-being ... with respect to his own feelings and circumstances, the most ordinary man or woman has means of knowledge immeasurably surpassing those that can be possessed by anyone else."[18] Courts should not, of course, enforce agreements that reflect fraud or overreaching. Nor do I wish to minimise the importance of appropriate standards for alimony and marital property for, in ways that I will describe shortly, these standards very much affect negotiated outcomes. Nonetheless, against a backdrop of fair standards, parties should be encouraged to settle for themselves these economic issues. The state should provide an efficient and fair mechanism for enforcing such agreements, and for settling disputes when the parties are unable to agree.

Where there are minor children, the state obviously has broader interests than simply dispute settlement. The state also has a responsibility for *child protection*. To acknowledge this responsibility, however, is not to define its limits. Indeed the critical questions concern the proper scope of the child protection function at the time of divorce, and the mechanisms that best achieve this goal.

For reasons I have spelled out at length elsewhere,[19] the actual determination of what is in fact in a child's best interest is ordinarily quite indeterminate: it requires predictions beyond the capacity of the behavioural sciences. It also involves the imposition of values about which there appears to be little consensus in our societies today. Thus the fundamental question is: who decides on behalf of the child? To what extent should the child's parents be given the freedom to decide between themselves how responsibility for their children is to be allocated following divorce? I believe divorcing parents should be given considerable freedom to decide custody matters — subject only to the same minimum standards for child protection that the State imposes on *all* families with respect to neglect and abuse. A negotiated resolution is desirable from the child's perspective for several reasons. Since a child's social and psychological relationships with *both* parents ordinarily continue after the divorce, a process that leads to agreement between the parents is preferable to one that necessarily has a winner and a loser. A child's future relationship with each of his parents may be better maintained and his existing relationship less damaged by a negotiated settlement than by one imposed by a court after an adversarial proceeding. Moreover, the parents will know more about the child than the judge, since they have better access to information about the child's circumstances and desires. Indeed, given the basic indeterminacy of anyone knowing what is best for the child, having a privately negotiated solution by those who will be responsible for care after the divorce seems much more likely to match the parents' capacities and desires with the child's needs. These advantages suggest that courts should not second-guess parental agreements unless judicial intervention is required by the strict child-protection standard implicit in neglect laws.

If parents have the authority to decide, there can be no doubt that some parents will make mistakes. But so do judges. Parents (not the state) are primarily responsible for their children after divorce. Part of this responsibility involves attempting, themselves, to agree upon some allocation of responsibilities in the future. This is not to suggest that the State does not have an important responsibility to inform parents concerning the child's needs during and after divorce; nor does it mean that the State does not have an important interest in facilitating parental agreement. Nevertheless, the law in action (which acknowledges substantial parental power) strikes me as preferable to existing doctrine (which imposes substantial restrictions on parental power to decide for themselves).

Everyone may not share these premises concerning the desirability of private ordering. But no matter what one's thinking on these questions, the fact that most divorcing couples do not bring disputes to court for adjudication suggests the appropriateness of analysing how the legal system affects the bargaining behaviour of divorcing couples.

．．．．

An Evaluation of the Lawyer's Role

If one accepts the proposition that the primary function of the legal system should be to facilitate private ordering and dispute resolution, then several important questions come into sharp focus. To what extent does the participation of lawyers facilitate dispute resolution? Are there alternative procedures (in which lawyers play a lesser role) that are less costly and more fair? Many observers are very critical of the way some lawyers behave in divorce negotiations. Lawyers may "heat up" the process, make negotiations more adversarial and painful than they would otherwise be, and make it more difficult and costly for the spouses to reach agreement. Indeed, it may well be that lawyers more than lay people are prepared to adopt negotiating strategies involving threats, and the strategic misrepresentation of their client's true preferences in order to reach a more favourable settlement for the client. Ivan Illich has recently suggested that a broad range of illnesses are in fact "iatrogenic,"[33] i.e., induced and created by medical treatment and the health industry. The same charge might be laid on the legal profession. The participation of lawyers in the divorce process may on balance lead to more disputes and higher costs without improving the fairness of the outcomes.

There are also arguments that lawyers facilitate dispute settlement. The participation of lawyers may make negotiations more rational, may minimise the number of disputes, may increase the opportunities for resolution out of court, and may insure that the outcomes reflect the applicable legal norms. Professor Eisenberg has suggested how a pair of lawyers — each acting for his client — may make the process of negotiation in dispute settlement very much like adjudication, i.e., a process where "rules, precedents, and reasoned elaboration — may be expanded to determine outcome ..."[34] Where each spouse has a lawyer, the lawyers

> are likely to find themselves allied with each other as well as with the disputants, because of their relative emotional detachment, their interest in resolving the dispute, and, in some cases, their shared professional values. Each therefore tends to take on a Janus-like role, facing the other as an advocate of that which is reasonable in the other's position.... Because a lawyer is both a personal advisor and a technical expert, each actor-disputant is likely to accept a settlement his lawyer recommends. Because of their training and the fact that typically they become involved only when formal litigation is contemplated, lawyers are likely to negotiate on the basis of *legal* principles, rules, and precedents. When these two elements are combined, the result is that paired legal affiliates typically function as a coupled unit which is strikingly similar to a formal adjudicative unit in terms of both input and output. Indeed, in terms of sheer number of dispute-settlements effected, the most significant legal dispute-settlement institution is typically not the bench, but the bar.[35]

The perspective of private ordering exposes these various roles and raises the obvious question: what in fact do lawyers do in the process? Lawyers may serve various functions, and yet we know very

little about how in fact lawyers behave. Obviously, lawyers are not of all one piece. Their styles differ. Some lawyers may prefer (and be more effective at) certain roles. Some lawyers are known within the profession as negotiators who strive to find middle ground acceptable to both sides; others are fighters, who love the courtroom battle. Research could usefully explore how much specialisation there is, and the extent to which clients (when they are choosing a lawyer at the time of divorce) have any notion at all of their lawyers' skills or tastes for these various roles. More generally, systematic empirical research might illustrate how often (and in what circumstances) lawyers facilitate dispute settlement at the time of divorce, and how often (and in what circumstances) they hurt.

This framework also suggests how timely it is to re-examine the question of why the legal profession should have a monopoly with respect to these roles, and the extent to which it does in fact have such a monopoly. How well are lawyers trained to perform these various roles? Other professionals or paraprofessionals might serve some of these functions as well as lawyers at a substantially lower cost. This is most obviously the case where there is no dispute, and the attorney's role is essentially that of "clerk." A recent study in Connecticut suggests that in most uncontested divorces, clients believe their lawyer did no more than fill out the necessary forms (a complaint, a claim for a hearing, and a decree) and made an appearance at a *pro forma* hearing. Moreover, the same study suggests that because the forms and procedures are complicated, do-it-yourself "divorce dissolution kits" (without additional lay assistance) pose rather little threat to the monopoly of the organised bar.[36] Most people lack the time, confidence, or ability to navigate through the legal shoals themselves — even where they have no dispute with their spouse. This suggests that procedural reform aimed at simplifying the procedure for uncontested divorce could substantially reduce transaction costs in many cases.

· · · ·

THE ROLE OF COURTS

Let us consider the role of courts in the divorce process from the perspective of private ordering. Obviously, the judicial system provides a mechanism for dispute settlement through adjudication where the parties have not been able to agree. But courts also play a role in a much larger number of cases than those where the dispute is adjudicated. Because each party knows the other can invoke the court's power to settle their differences, the presence of the judiciary exerts considerable pressure towards settlement. Indeed, anecdotal evidence suggests that courts often put pressure on the parties in disputed cases "to settle their own differences" through private negotiations, thus avoiding the need for adjudication.

One striking feature of the present day system, however, is the requirement that undisputed cases pass through court. With a narrow exception recently enacted in California, every American state requires a judicial proceeding to secure a divorce in all cases. From a historical perspective, this requirement is not surprising: it represented a regulatory mechanism to ensure that divorces were only granted in narrowly defined circumstances. Before the no-fault revolution, dispute settlement was not the primary function of divorce proceedings.

The no-fault revolution has now empowered either spouse unilaterally to create the circumstances for divorce. The state no longer purports to have an interest preventing re-marriage where either spouse wants to dissolve an earlier marriage. Ironically, however, the shell of the same administrative and regulatory mechanisms has been preserved. Indeed, this analysis suggests a policy question of substantial importance: where there is no dispute between the divorcing spouses concerning the allocation implications of their divorce, why should a judicial proceeding be required? Absent a dispute, why should a court have any role? Why require a costly legal transaction in court when the questions can be resolved by negotiations?

It would not be difficult to imagine the elimination of a judicial proceeding in undisputed divorce cases. Getting married obviously does not require judicial proceedings. Why should getting a divorce?[42] The requirement of a judicial proceeding probably imposes significant transaction costs, both public and private. Because even uncontested divorces must go through court, parties may end up hiring a lawyer, even where the lawyer's function is basically that of a clerk. An appearance by a lawyer in court takes time — time for which the parties are charged. Moreover a judicial proceeding requires the use of judicial resources as well as the time of the parties themselves. Some countries have largely eliminated the requirement that undisputed divorces go through court; it certainly seems timely to examine the justifications for the requirement, and to ask whether there might not be alternatives that are preferable which cost less.

While the analysis that follows is necessarily preliminary, it is useful to identify and examine four arguments in defence of a judicial proceeding, in uncontested divorce cases.

Ceremonial Function

A judicial proceeding might be thought to serve a ceremonial function that re-confirms, both for the divorcing parties and the general public, the seriousness with which the state takes marriage and divorce. Rituals are important, and the court proceeding can be seen as a socially imposed divorce ritual. But as a ritual, the court proceeding for uncontested divorces[] seems peculiar. The marriage ceremony itself is, after all, extremely simple, and does not require lawyers and a judge. Moreover, in most states, the parties themselves are not usually required to appear in court in order to procure a divorce. Their lawyers, instead, can appear for them. If the ritual were for the benefit of the parties, presumably their presence would be required. In all events, one can ask how well the existing requirement serves the ceremonial function? Is the purpose of the requirement ceremonial? Or is it more like a civil fine, imposed on a divorcing couple; a fine payable not to the treasury but to the divorce bar?

Review Ensures Fair Outcomes: Fairness between the Spouses

The requirement of judicial approval of postmarital agreements might be justified on the ground that the state has an interest in ensuring that the results of the bargaining process are fair, as between the spouses. A judicial proceeding might protect people from their own ignorance, and might also be thought to prevent unfair results arising from unequal bargaining capacity between the spouses. These arguments have a plausible air, but the reality of the present day system might suggest that they mean very little in practice. Courts typically rubber stamp an agreement reached between the parties. Moreover, there are reasons to doubt that the requirement of judicial review is very often necessary for these purposes. There may well be cases where one spouse (presumably the husband) is highly sophisticated in business matters, while the other spouse (the wife) is an innocent lamb being led to the slaughter. But typically married couples generally have similar educational and cultural backgrounds. Moreover, most individuals perceive very well their own financial interests and needs at the time of divorce.

If there are systematic biases in the process, a more appropriate safeguard would be to change the *substantive standards* concerning who gets what. For example, if it is thought that husbands systematically provide their wives with an insufficient share of the family's assets, or with inadequate alimony, after marriages of long duration where the wife has not worked, the *legal standards* can be changed to provide greater claims for the wife. Moreover, procedural mechanisms can then be developed that require review and a hearing only in those cases where the spousal agreement falls outside the norm (e.g., where marital property was divided very unequally, or where alimony claims were being waived). In practice today, I suspect judges or registrars attempt to identify such cases for intensive examination. At the present time, however, cases falling within the normal range must also pass through a judicial proceeding, with its attendant costs. A system where the state defines reasonable norms, and then permits couples to reach agreement outside the norms provided there were additional procedural safeguards, would seem both more effective and less costly.

Effect on Out-of-Court Settlements

It might be thought that the requirement that undisputed cases go to court[] improves the private settlement process outside of court. Knowing that they will have to display their agreement to a judge, the parties (and their attorneys) may deal with each other in a fairer way and be more likely to reach an agreement reflecting the appropriate social norms. Behavioural scientists have suggested that the presence of an "audience" can affect bargaining.[43] With respect to out-of-court negotiations, the judge represents both an "actual" audience and "abstract" audience. He is an actual audience in that parties know that eventually they may have to explain their agreement to a judge. This may mitigate extreme claims. The judge also represents an abstract audience as well, which symbolically represents the social interests in the child and various notions of honour, reputation, and history.

It is extremely difficult to evaluate this argument, and to know how the requirement of judicial proceedings in undisputed cases affects negotiations in such cases. A requirement that disputed cases alone would go before a court might be sufficient to bring the "audience" benefits to the process of negotiation. Moreover, it is possible that the requirement of judicial approval makes dispute settlement more not less difficult. For one thing, the requirement probably means that lawyers are more often involved in the process than would otherwise be the case. As earlier noted, it at least seems an open question whether having lawyers in the process facilitates dispute resolution in those case where the parties might otherwise reach agreement anyway. Moreover, there is always the possibility that in the occasional case where the judge does upset the agreement reached by the parties, the eventual outcome may on balance be no more desirable (or even less desirable) than would otherwise be the case.

Child Protection

Where a divorcing couple has minor children, the state has an important interest in child protection. The requirement of court review of private agreements relating to custody or child support might be justified on this ground. For one thing, from the child's perspective, the quality of negotiated agreements may be improved. Some parents might otherwise engage in divorce bargaining on the basis of preferences that reflected narrowly selfish interests, rather than concern for the child. The review requirement might serve as an important reminder to the parents of the social concern for their children, and may somehow constrain otherwise selfish behaviour. Even a selfish spouse may be more concerned about his reputation as a parent if there is some sort of public process. Especially in cases where there are children, the judge may represent an important "audience" whose unseen presence affects bargaining behaviour. Finally, although most parental agreements are approved after only superficial examination by the judge, some agreements are in fact disapproved: to the extent courts succeed in identifying arrangements that are disadvantageous to a child in a particular case and in imposing some better alternative, the child's welfare is obviously improved.

A variety of arguments can be made on the other side, however. For one thing, what evidence we have suggests that in operation courts rarely overturn parental agreements. Given the resources that are devoted to this task there is little reason to believe that the process today in fact operates as much of a safeguard where there is no parental dispute. Moreover, the process itself probably imposes not insubstantial transaction costs — both public (in terms of traditional resources expended) and private (in terms of the cost to the parties, the legal fees and time). These extra transaction costs might otherwise enure (at least in part) to the benefit of the children.

There are also reasons to think that, in the vast majority of cases, this review may well be unnecessary. For one thing, the custodial spouse will typically perceive very clearly the economic consequences for the child of any support arrangement that he or she agrees to. There is after all, considerable joint consumption between the custodial parent and the child. Moreover, child support payments (like alimony and the earnings of the custodial spouse) typically go into a single economic pot that supports both the custodial parent and the child. In other words, the economic interests of the child and the economic interests of the custodial parent substantially coincide.

A second safeguard — banal as it sounds — is that most parents care deeply for their children. No court proceeding can of course require parents to love their children, and prevent selfish calculation by a divorcing parent. Nevertheless, to the extent that divorcing parents do love their children there is every reason to think that they will in fact themselves be very concerned with making arrangements that are beneficial to the child. Perhaps there are good reasons not to trust parents with child-rearing responsibilities on or after divorce. That was certainly the implicit attitude during the heyday of the marital offence regime. But is it really appropriate today? Indeed, it is interesting to compare the review requirements imposed by law if the child's family is disrupted by divorce with the review requirements imposed if the family is disrupted by the death of one of the parents. American law permits a parent to disinherit his minor children. A decedent cannot, however, disinherit his spouse and in effect present day law trusts the surviving parent with child-rearing responsibility in the light of existing economic resources. With respect to any inheritance of any surviving spouse, there is no supervision imposed by operation of law on how he or she spends the inheritance, and there is no examination of what portion is spent on the child. Instead, the surviving parent is trusted to look after the child, subject of course to the minimum limitations imposed by the child neglect laws which apply to all parents.

The review requirement may, ironically, send an inappropriate set of signals to parents at the time of divorce: it may suggest to them that because of the divorce they are no longer trusted to be adequate parents, and that the state will now assume special responsibility for their children. Indeed, court review might conceivably induce more selfish behaviour on the part of parents who take the attitude that it is the court's job, not their own responsibility, to be concerned with the interests of their children. In fact, the state does not and cannot assume a broad role for child-rearing responsibility after divorce.

CONCLUSION

Viewing the process of dissolution from the perspective of private ordering does not make previously intractable family law problems disappear. If anything, the world seems even more complex, for analysis involves the examination of the effects of alternative rules and procedures on informal and formal bargaining outside of court about which we have little understanding. There is little existing theory to inform the enquiry. There now exists no bargaining theory that can yield accurate predictions of the expected outcomes, assuming different legal rules where rational self-interested parties are negotiating over money issues. Where there are minor children involved, the parents are not simply bargaining over money; they also must be necessarily concerned with allocating child-rearing responsibilities in the future. We have tried to suggest how the variability of parental preferences with respect to custody makes the task of analysing bargaining especially difficult. Furthermore, rational bargaining may be in short supply when a family is in the process of breaking up. Some divorcing spouses seem motivated by spite or envy, more than a careful assessment of self-interest in the light of available alternatives. Where bargaining is motivated by emotional drives, the assessment of the effects of alternative legal rules seems even more speculative. Finally, it must sadly be reported that there has been little empirical work which has involved the systematic observation of how the process of private ordering in fact works today.

Given the absence of powerful theory or systematic data, this essay makes no claims at being definitive. It instead has suggested a theoretical perspective that permits a broader analysis of the probable consequences of family law rules and procedures. It also more sharply exposes a set of questions of enormous social importance. If one accepts the proposition that disputes settlement should be the primary goal of the legal system, the analysis does not imply that the state should simply withdraw all resources from the process, and leave it to the divorcing spouses to work things out on their own, unassisted by any professional help. Instead, this inquiry should underline the desirability of learning more about how alternative procedural mechanisms might facilitate dispute resolution during a typically difficult and painful time in the lives of parents and children alike.

The perspective certainly has implications far broader than family law. In a wide variety of contexts, individuals bargain in the shadow of the law. Few automobile accident claims are ever tried; most are settled out of court. Criminal prosecutions are typically resolved by a plea bargain, not an adjudication of guilt. Most administrative proceedings result in consent agreements not trials. In each of these contexts, the preferences of the parties, the entitlements created by law, transaction costs, and attitudes towards risk, will presumably substantially affect the negotiated outcomes. Indeed, I hope this essay will stimulate and encourage further work by others in a variety of contexts. Theoretical and empirical research concerning how people bargain in the shadow of law should provide us with a richer understanding of how the legal system affects behaviour, and allow a better appraisal of the consequences of reform proposals.

(a) The Judge and the Adversary System†

Neil Brooks

THE ROLE OF THE JUDGE IN THE ADVERSARY SYSTEM

A thorough discussion of this subject would require an examination of the judge's role at each stage of the litigation process: at the pre-trial investigative stage;[1] at the pre-trial procedural stages;[2] at the trial; at the sentencing hearing;[3] and at the hearing to determine law and policy.[4] While the same principles may be applicable to each stage, the discussion in this paper will focus on the role of the trial judge in the conduct of the trial. The trial has a first claim on our attention since it is at this stage of the litigation process that all aspects of the adversary system bear most directly on the judge's role. Moreover, restricting the discussion in this way will permit, in the time available, a more detailed development of the central theoretical themes of the subject.[5]

In determining the precise role that he will assume in discharging his responsibilities at trial, a judge will undoubtedly consider a wide range of factors: the peculiarities of his own temperament and abilities, the significance of the particular case to the parties and to the public,[6] the complexity of the factual and legal issues raised by the case, and the effectiveness of the parties or their counsel in presenting the case. However, whatever other factors a judge might consider in defining the precise nature of the role he will play, the fact that he is an arbiter in an adjudicative proceeding that is adversarial in nature necessarily prescribes for him the parameters of his involvement in the proceeding. In this paper I

will develop this theme by speculating about the justifications which have been or might be advanced supporting the adversary system, and then exploring the limitations that these justifications impose on the judge's role in conducting a judicial trial.

. . . .

Definition of "Adversary System"

The greatest impediment to clear thinking about the judge's role in the adversary system is the variety of meanings that are often assigned to the concept of the adversary system. Therefore, before examining the premises underlying the adversary system let me make clear the sense in which that concept is used in this paper by distinguishing it from various senses in which it is often misleadingly used.

The term is being used in this paper to refer generally to a procedural system in which the parties and not the judge have the primary responsibility for defining the issues in dispute and for carrying the dispute forward through the system. Thus, it should not be confused with what might more accurately be referred to as the adjudicative process. Adjudication is a method of settling disputes that is commonly contrasted with other methods of dispute resolution such as mediation, negotiation and conciliation. Used in this context, it refers characteristically to a means of resolving disputes in which some general principle or rule of law is applied to the facts that gave rise to the dispute and in which the parties involved are

---

† From Allen Linden, ed., *The Canadian Judiciary* (Toronto: Osgoode Hall Law School, 1976) at 89–118. Reproduced with permission. [Notes and/or references omitted.]

able to participate by presenting proofs and reasoned argument.[9]

Professor Lon Fuller, who in a series of essays clarified the tasks for which adjudication because of its institutional framework was well-suited as a means of social ordering,[10] argued that an adversary presentation is essential to adjudication.[11] He postulated that the fundamental characteristic of adjudication is the opportunity it provides for the affected parties to participate in the decision-making by presenting proofs and arguments. He concluded that only the adversary system is capable of affording this requisite degree of participation. Whether or not these two concepts need to be so closely wed,[12] it remains useful in analysing the judge's role to distinguish between them.

. . . .

[I]t is sometimes argued that the adversary system is deficient because it presents an all-or-nothing proposition — there are always winners and losers — and, as a consequence, the total satisfaction of the parties is often reduced.[16] This is particularly the case in areas such as family law, labour law, or criminal law where the parties are part of a close social or economic relationship. Again the adversary system is here a victim because of its close association with adjudication. The attempt at the outset to adjudicate this kind of claim is more properly criticized.[17]

. . . .

The adversary system, as that term is used by many proceduralists and as it will be used in this paper, embodies two distinct principles.[24] The issues resolved by these two principles raise the two most basic questions that confront any adjudicative procedural system. The first issue is what should the respective functions of the parties and the judge be with reference to the initiation and content of the adjudication. The adversary system rests on the principle of party-autonomy. That is to say, that the parties have the right to pursue or dispose of their legal rights and remedies as they wish. The second issue is what should the respective functions of the parties and the judge be with reference to the progress of a dispute through the procedural system once initiated and defined. The adversary system rests on the principle of party-prosecution. This principle holds that the parties have the primary responsibility to choose without interference from the judge the manner in which they will go forward with their case and the proofs they will present for the judge's consideration in adjudicating the dispute.

Party-Autonomy

In defining the judge's role in the conduct of the trial it is, of course, the principle of party-prosecution that requires careful analysis. However, to place that examination in perspective, the principle of party-autonomy must be briefly examined. The principle of party-autonomy has two aspects. First, it limits the judge's function to disputes which have been presented to him. A judge plays a role only when a conflict has arisen between two or more parties, and at least one of them seeks the assistance of the judge in resolving the dispute. John Chipman Gray, in defining a judge, summarized this principle: "A judge of an organized body is a man appointed by that body to determine duties and the corresponding rights upon the application of persons claiming those rights."[25] The authors of a casebook on civil procedure described the principle more prosaically: "Courts ought not to function as self-propelled vehicles of justice and right like King Arthur's knights in Good Humor trucks."[26] Lon Fuller quotes a socialist critic of bourgeois law who caricatured this premise of the adversary system by asserting that courts in such a system "are like defective clocks; they have to be shaken to set them going". Fuller noted that, "[h]e of course added the point that the shaking costs money".[27]

The second aspect of party-autonomy is that the parties have the sole responsibility for defining the dispute that they would like adjudicated. Thus, if the parties want the judge to decide one dispute, he will not insist on resolving another even though he perceives the other issue to be the real cause of the conflict between the parties.

Both aspects of party-autonomy are subject to qualifications. While the judge cannot initiate proceedings, he can prevent the parties from initiating certain proceedings. The courts have an important social function to perform by resolving disputes. Thus the judge can prevent parties from using the litigation process to resolve hypothetical or moot problems. He can judicially notice all facts that he considers beyond reasonable dispute and thus prevent the parties from consuming the time of the court by presenting evidence on clear factual issues. He can also prevent misuses of the process by a judicial screening of cases, he can give judgment on the pleadings or give a summary judgment. Indeed he is assisted in controlling the use of the court's process by counsel for the parties. Lawyers have a professional responsibility to ensure the claims and defences they put forward have merit and are related to a real conflict.

In criminal cases, the judge's role in controlling the issues disputed is even greater than his responsibility in civil cases.[28] While the judge cannot control the criminal cases to reach his docket, nor find the accused guilty of a crime he is not charged with, nor insist that the Crown amend the indictment to add charges, he does not permit the accused or the Crown complete autonomy in defining the issues contested. For instance, he can prevent the Crown from initiating the case if he concludes that the Crown is abusing the process. There is also an increasing recognition of the judge's responsibility to examine the factual basis of a plea of guilty. In the United States a Presidential Commission has recently recommended that the guilty plea be abolished entirely because, among other things, it leaves too much of the public interest to the parties.[29]

The limits of the principle of party-autonomy can, of course, only be defined by reference to the reasons why it is regarded as being an essential principle of the Anglo-American procedural system. Two justifications sometimes put forward fail to appreciate that party-autonomy is only a principle which defines the respective roles of the parties and the judge. In civil cases, it has been said that the principle of party-autonomy — that the judge only operates when the parties present him with a dispute to resolve — rests on the judgment that "the social interest in securing general observance of the rules of private law is sufficiently served by leaving their enforcement to the self-interest of the parties more or less directly affected".[30] However, while this reason might explain why the state need not become involved in the enforcement of the civil law, it does not go directly to the issue of the roles of the parties and the judge in initiating actions. In many areas where there is an important public interest in the enforcement of the civil law, as in the enforcement of the criminal law, the state, through an administrative agency, might initiate actions enforcing the law.[31] And yet, since it is not the judge who initiates such actions, the principle of party-autonomy would be satisfied.

Others have suggested that the principle of party-autonomy reflects a political ideology. Thurman Arnold asserted, "...the civil trial dramatizes the moral beauty of the noninterference of government in private affairs.... The whole ideology, and procedural organization of the civil trial is designed to insulate the court and the government from taking the initiative in enforcing or even protecting the civil rights of individuals".[32] Thurman Arnold was at the time decrying the resistance to the New Deal and exploring its causes. He went on, "[t]his role of the civil trial as a symbol of individual freedom

from active interference by the government makes it a most important factor in preserving conservative traditions in the face of new legislation". While party-autonomy may reflect a *laissez-faire* philosophy, Arnold's point goes to the role of the government generally in the enforcement of the civil law.[33]

. . . .

Party-Prosecution

The second major premise of the adversary system, as that term is used by most proceduralists, is the principle of party-prosecution. This principle holds that the parties have the right and the responsibility to choose the manner in which they will go forward with their case and the proof they will present to support it. The judge's role is to passively evaluate the merits of the case as and when it is presented to him.

In the remainder of this paper I will explore the reasons why the principle of party-prosecution is adhered to at trial, and offer some general comments on the parameters that these reasons place upon the judge's intervention in the conduct of the case. The conclusion that I reach is that viewed in this way the adversary system does not impose as severe restraints on the judge's intervention as is often assumed, and that in appropriate cases the judge should, if he deems it necessary, play a much larger role in the conduct of the case. My argument will be a plea for more judicial activism in controlling the conduct of the trial.

The principle of party-prosecution at trial rests, in the main, upon two broad empirical assumptions. Firstly, that the legitimacy of adjudication as a means of social ordering is enhanced if it is conducted according to an adversarial presentation. Secondly, that more accurate fact-finding is likely to result if parties motivated by self-interest are given the responsibilities of investigating facts and presenting arguments, and if the decision-maker remains passive.

The Adversary System Increases the Acceptability of Adjudication

Every means of social ordering used by the state must be acceptable not only to those immediately affected by its particular sanctions but also to all those governed by the state. This need for legitimacy is particularly paramount in a free society with respect to adjudication since a judge's decision might be perceived, in some sense at least, to be undemocratic.

343

Legitimacy or acceptability is a derivative value. That is to say, a decision-making process will be acceptable to the extent that it meets all the criteria that people expect of that decision-making process. With respect to adjudication these expectations undoubtedly include such considerations as expediency, finality, inexpensiveness, and the protection of privacy and other social values. To the extent that the adversary system furthers these values it will render the adjudicative process more acceptable than would some other procedural device for finding the facts. But aside from these considerations, which are necessary attributes of any acceptable adjudicative proceeding, it is often argued that the adversary system has unique characteristics which render it in judicial trials a more acceptable procedure in our society than other methods of fact-finding. The reasons for the acceptability of the adversary system, if indeed it is more acceptable than other methods of fact-finding, must rest ultimately upon complex questions of political theory and psychology. I can only be suggestive here, in part repeating what others have speculated. Four reasons might be given as to why the adversary system is a more acceptable method of fact-finding in judicial trials than any other method.

Relationship to the Prevalent Political and Economic Theory

The adversary system yields greater satisfaction to the litigants and others because it is a procedure that is consistent with the prevalent social and political ideology of western society. An assertion made in the editorial page of a bar association journal illustrates this argument: "If you believe in the Anglo-Saxon common law tradition, that the individual is the important unit of our society, and the state exists to serve him, then it seems that the adversary system is preferable. If you hold a corporate view of society, that is to say, that the community is the important unit, and that the citizen must be primarily considered as a part of the corporate unit, then it seems you should champion the inquisitorial system...."[36]

Jerome Frank is well known for linking the adversary system with economic theory. In his writings he repeatedly associated it with classic, *laissez-faire*, economic theory and unbridled individualism.[37] Surprisingly, however, only recently has scholarship emerged in the English language which attempts to seriously study the influence of political and economic theory on judicial procedure. Naively, perhaps, the assumption has been made that procedure is value-free. Scholars who have turned their attention to this question in recent years seem to agree that at least at a very general and theoretical level there are connections between ideology and procedural choices.[38] The connection may not be direct, nor empirically demonstrable.[39] However, at least arguably, the adversary system can be seen as reflecting the political and economic ideology of classic English liberalism in three ways: by its emphasis upon self-interest and individual initiative; by its apparent distrust of the state; and, by the significance it attaches to the participation of the parties.

The adversary system legitimizes, indeed necessitates, a self-interested role for the parties. Thus one of its premises would appear to be consistent with the premise of the capitalist system of economic organization that if each individual strives to promote his self-interest an optimum allocation of resources will result. As Professors Neef and Nagel note, "...at the base of the adversary proceeding we encounter the old *laissez-faire* notion that each party will (or indeed can) bring out all the evidence favorable to his own side, and that if the accused is innocent (if his is the best case) he can act to 'outproduce' the presentation made by his competitors".[40] With this competitive individualism at its base, if the party with the better case — that is the case that is correct on the facts — were to lose, that result would be satisfactory in an adversary system because he, not the system, would be the author of his defeat. Initiative is rightly rewarded, laziness or ignorance penalized. This justification for the adversary system is illustrated in a statement made in a commentary on the Japan *Code of Civil Procedure* that was enacted after World War II when Japan adopted the adversary system.

> [S]ince civil litigation is essentially a dispute concerning private rights, as a matter of course, the responsibility and duty to present proof rests with the parties; it is neither the responsibility nor the duty of the court.... When the necessary facts to maintain the allegation of a party cannot be proven, the disadvantage should be borne by such party, and it is sufficient grounds for the court to issue him an unfavorable determination. The disadvantage is a consequence invited by the party himself, over and beyond which the court should neither assist a party on one side nor interfere.[41]

If this is one of the justifications for the adversary system then not many people today would likely perceive [...] it as placing very serious constraints on the judge's intervention in the trial. *Laissez-faire* theory is no longer taken as being determinative in the economic and social fields. It would be incongruous if its basic postulate was still the premise used to define the respective roles of the parties and the judge in a judicial trial.[42]

A basic socialist value is a strong emphasis on collectivism. The interests of the state and the individual are assumed to coincide, state power is not distrusted. On the other hand, liberal political philosophy is premised on a distrust of the state and public officials. The adversary system can thus be viewed in a liberal state as a means of decentralizing power, and as an attempt to prevent abuses of political power.[43] This view finds some support in the fact that the genesis of at least some rules of procedure and evidence can also be explained on the basis of a felt concern to decentralize power. Professor Friedman in his recent text, a *History of American Law*, notes that the law of evidence "... was founded in a world of mistrust and suspicion of institutions; it liked nothing better than constant checks and balances...".[44] This concern in an adversary system to decentralize power was illustrated during the period of Jacksonian democracy in the United States when a serious effort was initiated to take many rights from the judge including not only the right to comment upon the evidence but also the right to summarize the evidence to the jury.[45]

. . . .

Finally, the adversary system can be seen as being consistent with our prevalent political philosophy because it affords the parties the opportunity to participate in the making of decisions that affect their interests. Both psychological and theoretical literature in political philosophy support the view that the most acceptable type of decision in a democracy is personal choice. However, since it is clearly impossible to realize personal choice in many situations the best alternative is a system that assures to those affected by the decision some participation in the decisional process.[46] A procedural system in which the judge assumes the primary responsibility for eliciting the proof, but permits the parties to assist in the proof-taking, would provide the parties a measure of participation in the decision-making process. However, Fuller argues that the adversary system "heightens the significance of ... participation" and thus "lifts adjudication toward its optimum expression".[47] For this reason, he concludes that the adversary system is an essential characteristic of the adjudicative process.[48]

The extent to which the judge's intervention in the trial, either in clarifying evidence or in calling for new evidence, impairs the parties' sense of participation is obviously an extremely complex question that cannot be explored in any detail here.[49] In some instances, however, it might clearly be a consideration that leads the judge to the conclusion that he should not intervene. But in other situations his intervention in the form of asking questions might actually increase the meaningfulness of the parties' participation. Everyone has different cognitive needs and if the judge makes these needs known to the parties then it will make their participation more meaningful — obviously their participation will be meaningless unless the judge's understanding of the case is the meaning that they are attempting to convey to him.[50] Also, even if the judge were to call additional proof, so long as he gives the parties the opportunity to test such proof and call rebutting proof their participation in the decision-making process would appear to remain meaningful.

Cathartic Effect

Particularly in civil suits the adversary system might be a more acceptable procedure for fact-finding than the inquisitorial system because it satisfies the psychology of the litigants by legitimizing a courtroom duel which is a sublimation of more direct forms of hostile aggression. It has been suggested that there are psychological benefits in the "battle atmosphere" of adversary litigation.[51] Charles Curtis in his book *It's Your Law* summarized this argument. He said:

> The law takes the position that we ought to be satisfied if the parties are; and it believes that the best way to get this done is to encourage them to fight it out, and dissolve their differences in dissention. We are still a combative people not yet so civilized and sophisticated as to forget that combat is one way to justice.[52]

The use of the adversary system to satisfy the primeval competitive urges of the litigants might be suggested by its genealogy. The ancestry of the trial is of course the blood feud, trial by battle and individual or class acts of revenge.[53] The justification for the adversary system is also apparent in the frequent analogy of the judicial trial to a sporting event.[54] It leads lawyers to talk of tactics and strategy and to refer to the judge as an umpire. This view of the adversary process is most clearly perceived if the trial is regarded as a "game", using that word in the sense that it is used by game theorists. The "sporting theory of justice" describes the rules of the game. There has been a social disturbance and the game is played only to gain some relief or satisfaction.[55]

The adversary system viewed as part of a game perhaps explains the system's acceptance of the result when a party loses on a technicality, even if his loss was due to a violation of one of the technical rules of evidence of procedure which regulate the game.[55] If Justice is equated to the satisfaction of the litigants then the adversary system, which is directly responsible for this satisfaction, becomes an end in itself. The true facts of the case are less important than how well the parties play the game. Reasoning from this premise, Charles Curtis concluded:

> Justice is something larger and more intimate than truth. Truth is only one of the ingredients of justice. Its whole is the satisfaction of those concerned.... The administration of justice is no more designed to elicit truth than the scientific approach is designed to extract justice from the atom.[57]

If this justification for the adversary system is correct then the judge's role in the trial would be a limited one. However, the basic premise of the argument is disputable. As one author posed the question: "Is the battle atmosphere of trial proceedings truly cathartic, in the sense of relieving tensions and aggressions that would otherwise find more destructive outlets, or does it instill an aggressive approach to problems that is incompatible with the need to compromise and co-operate in the vast majority of interpersonal contacts?"[58] Unfortunately, no serious effort has been made to resolve this question by asking the ultimate consumers of the system — the litigants. Basing a judgement on common experience, however, most people would probably agree with Professor Garlan who wrote at the height of the legal realist movement, referring to the jurisprudential theory of what he called "sporting fairness":

> The game has become too brutal, too destructive of human life, too exhaustive to those who win, and too fatal for those who lose. Living begins to look more like a struggle, than a game. The participant's sense of humor and sense of balance are worn, and the sporting morale is breaking up into a fighting morale. The sides are too unequal for successful competition, and, in the eyes of the defeated, the game looks more like exploitation than competition.[59]

While we know very little about the psychology of litigants, I suspect that most of them do not view social conflicts as social events. They come to court expecting justice, and unless the rules of substantive law are perverse, that means they expect their dispute to be resolved according to the law.[60] A theory about the judge's role that begins by assuming that rules of evidence and procedure are simply rules of competition is therefore deficient.[61]

Role of Counsel

A third aspect of the adversary system that might render it more acceptable than the inquisitorial system is the role played by counsel. It has been hypothesized that "[i]f parties perceive their adversary attorneys as having interests convergent with their own, they may begin to experience the comforting strength of belonging to a coalition the total purpose of which is to gain a favorable verdict at the expense of the opposing party".[62] Also the lawyer will be a person who, in some sense, shares in the litigant's defeat. Certain institutional characteristics of the adversary system might encourage this coalition and the apparent identity of interest between the adversary lawyer and his client. However, assuming this to be true, intervention in the trial proceedings by the trial judge is unlikely to destroy in any way this coalition or this sense of shared purpose.

Appearance of Impartiality

Finally, the adversary system might be more acceptable than an inquisitorial system because it gives the tribunal the appearance of impartiality.[63] Proponents of the Anglo-American procedural system attach great importance to the appearance of impartiality.[64] While its importance cannot be denied,[65] the intelligent control of the conduct of the trial need not leave a judge open to the charge of partiality. The possible appearance of impartiality is a matter a judge should consider when intervening, and to that extent it limits his intervention. For instance, if a judge calls a witness he must ensure that the parties have an opportunity to test the testimony of the witness and to call rebutting evidence or he might be open to the charge that he is shaping the record. If a witness is evasive in answering questions the judge must ensure that he does not appear hostile towards the witness.[66] However, if the judge intervenes in a fair and dispassionate manner this consideration should not seriously impair his ability to intervene when he thinks it is necessary.

The Adversary System Increases the Accuracy of Fact-Finding

A second justification given for the adversary system is that it is a better fact-finding mechanism than the inquisitorial system. That is to say, given all the interests that must be balanced in a procedural system more accurate factual judgments about past events are likely to be achieved using the adversary system than using some other system. This justification rests, in turn, upon two premises. The first premise is that the adversary system will result in a more thorough investigation of the facts than the inquisitorial system. The second premise is that under the adversarial system the trier of fact is more likely to reach the correct decision because during the proceedings he will not acquire a bias towards one conclusion or the other. He will be able to remain completely disinterested in the outcome until all the proof has been elicited and the arguments made. In order to define the role of the judge in the adversary system these two premises must be explored in detail.

Parties Motivated by Self-Interest Are Likely to Be Most Diligent in Presenting and Critically Evaluating All the Evidence

The first premise of this justification for the adversary system is that in an adversary proceeding the judge will, when he makes his decision, be more informed as to the facts than a similarly situated judge in an inquisitorial system. This is so, it is argued, because parties who are given a free hand in pursuing their perceived self-interest are more likely than an official motivated only by official duty to transmit to the judge all evidence favorable to their case and to critically test all unfavourable evidence presented to him.[67] Empirical studies have attempted to test whether this premise is correct.[68] However, for purposes of defining the judge's role in the adversary system the premise must be accepted as true.

The parties do not have complete control over the presentation and testing of proof and this premise of the adversary system does not require them to have such control. Control is given to the parties to promote accurate fact-finding and to further achieve this end the parties are constrained in the conduct of their case by rules of procedure and evidence. The need for these rules arises because if this premise of the adversary system is to achieve its objective a number of factors must be present in the litigation of particular disputes. The rules are intended, in part, to ensure that these factors are present. If these factors are not present in a particular case the adversary system will not achieve its goal of accurate fact-finding; or if it is to achieve this end in their absence the judge may have to regulate his conduct accordingly. Thus the judge, in defining his role must be sensitive to the presence or absence of these factors. For purposes of clarity I will discuss these factors as assumptions of the premise that the adversary system is an accurate fact-finding mechanism because parties motivated by self-interest will present and critically test all relevant evidence.

ASSUMPTION 1: THE PARTIES ARE INITIALLY MOTIVATED

The first assumption that this premise of the adversary system makes is that the parties are initially motivated to seek out all the evidence favorable to their case. This obviously depends upon both parties being equally interested in the outcome of the case, that is, equally interested in pursuing their respective rights and remedies and in opposing the rights of the other party.[69] If this is not the case, if one of the parties is not motivated to oppose the other party's case, the requisite factual investigation and presentation of proof will not take place. By way of illustration, one area where the parties may not be sufficiently interested in defending their legal rights, and in which, therefore, the adversary system breaks down, is in the area of divorce. A divorce cannot be granted under the *Divorce Act* unless the judge is satisfied that there has been no condonation or connivance on the part of the petitioner.[70] But since both parties in a particular case may want to be divorced, neither will be motivated to bring such evidence forward. In England, in recognition of the lack of motivation on the part of the parties in a divorce case, and of the state's interest in ensuring that divorces are only granted where the law authorizes them, an officer called the Queen's Proctor has been appointed.[71] His duty is to intervene in divorce cases and ferret out facts that might suggest a collusive divorce. In Canada, while a Queen's Proctor has been officially appointed in some provinces, he is seldom called upon to discharge his duties. However, section 9 of the *Divorce Act* would appear on a literal reading to require the judge to embark on his own investigation of the possibility of condonation or connivance in the undefended divorce cases.[72]

ASSUMPTION 2: THE PARTIES WILL SUSTAIN THEIR MOTIVATION

A second assumption of this premise of the adversary system is that throughout the proceedings both parties will sustain their motivation to present all the evidence. A number of rules of evidence have been developed to encourage parties to diligently pursue all the evidence favorable to their side; at least these rules can, in part, be understood by reference to this need. The privilege against self-incrimination, for instance, is sometimes justified on this basis. By denying the police the right to compel the accused to incriminate himself the rule forces them to seek more reliable evidence.[73] In the same way rules requiring the corroboration of certain witnesses who are generally assumed to be unreliable might be justified on the basis that they compel the Crown to search for additional independent evidence. It is interesting to note that these rules apply in the main against the prosecution in criminal cases — they encourage the police to seek additional evidence. Perhaps this is so because there is a fear that, at least in some cases, the prosecution motivated only by official duty, may not otherwise display the diligence in pursuing evidence that the adversary system demands.

A further rule of evidence that has the effect of encouraging the parties to independently investigate all evidence in their favour is the solicitor-client privilege — at least that part of it that the Americans call the work product rule. This rule, in general, prevents one lawyer or litigant from demanding disclosure, particularly before trial, of the other litigant's trial briefs, witness statements and related materials prepared or collected for use in the litigation. If a litigant could compel such disclosure there would be a great temptation for each litigant to rely on the other to do the investigations and to gather the necessary information. Eventually, litigants would become more and more reluctant to make an independent effort to collect information and to prepare arguments for trial. Thus, the rule contributes to the efficiency of the adversary scheme of litigation. Professor Maguire observed, "so long as we depend upon thorough advanced preparation by opposing trial counsel to accumulate the necessary information about law, fact and evidence, we must not let the drones sponge upon the busy bees. Otherwise it would not be long before all lawyers become drones".[74]

As well as forming the basis of a number of rules of evidence and procedure this assumption of party-prosecution has a more direct implication in defining the judge's role. In a system that relies on party prosecution the judge cannot intervene to such an extent in the trial that the parties begin to rely upon him to search out the facts favourable to their case and thus become less diligent themselves in seeking out the facts. There is some evidence that this attitude on the part of litigants results when the court assumes a large responsibility for proof-taking. At least it is a concern that has been expressed in countries in which the judge assumes such a role.[75] For example, in Japan, when the adversarial system was adopted in 1948 the commentators on the new *Code of Civil Procedure* noted that, "[e]xcessive interference by the Court dampens the zeal of the parties and instead — it being entirely impossible under the present trial system for the court completely to gather all evidence *ex officio* — produces a result which is accidental in nature. This is the reason why we thoroughly follow the doctrine of party presenta-

tion under the new constitution, in which the freedom and responsibility of the individual is made a fundamental principle."[76]

In some cases a judge might justifiably be unwilling to intervene to correct an oversight or to call further proof in order to discipline a prosecutor in a criminal case for the inefficient presentation of a case. However, within the framework of the present Anglo-American trial increased intervention by the judge would likely have little impact on the parties' presentation of their case. The stakes in most cases are too high to risk leaving important proof-taking to the judge's initiative. Even if increased judicial intervention did not have the effect in some cases of weakening the parties' presentation of proof, there is the further question of "whether in the long run this is outweighed by benefits, such as helping the party represented by an ineffective lawyer".[77]

ASSUMPTION 3: THE PARTIES HAVE EQUAL CAPACITY, SKILL AND RESOURCES

Party-prosecution, as a principle of the adversary system, rests on a third assumption: that each party has the ability, skill, and resources to search out the evidence favorable to his case and to present it to the court. Do the parties always have the capacity or ability to obtain access to all facts favourable to their case? The adversary system encourages parties to assume a self-interested role. While casting the parties into this role [...] ensures that they will be diligent in presenting evidence favorable to their cause, it also legitimizes or at least would appear to sanction their suppressing evidence that is unfavorable to their case. This temptation laid before the parties is regarded by many as the greatest obstacle to accurate fact-finding in the adversary system. Professor Brett argued that because "...neither of the rival theorists ... [is] bound to put forward all the data in his possession — indeed ... each ... [regards] it as proper to suppress any 'inconvenient' or inconsistent observations of whose existence he ... [knows,] 'the adversary system' must be regarded as basically unscientific in approach, and unsound".[78] He further asserted that Macaulay's justification of the adversary system that "we obtain the fairest decision when two men argue, as unfairly as possible, on opposite sides, for then it is certain that no important consideration will altogether escape notice", confuses an incentive to obtain contradictory evidence with the capacity or ability to obtain it.[79] Jerome Frank also noted, in supporting his contention that the "fight" theory of litigation does not coincide with the "truth" theory, that "frequently the partisanship of the opposing lawyers blocks the uncovering of vital evidence or leads to a presentation of vital testimony in a way that distorts it".[80] There is little a judge in any system can do to prevent the parties from suppressing or falsifying evidence.[81] A number of rules of evidence and procedure, however, attempt to provide both parties with access to as much evidence as possible. While these rules do not bear directly on the judge's role they are important in increasing our understanding of the adversary system and thus at least indirectly the judge's role in it.

First, rules of pre-trial discovery assist the parties in obtaining evidence. In civil cases, these rules generally permit a party to question the other prior to the trial about his knowledge of the facts in the case.[82] It has been argued that pre-trial discovery is inconsistent with the adversary system. However, this argument confuses means with ends. If one begins the analysis by looking at the reasons for the adversary system, the better view would appear to be that of Professor Goldstein who concluded the discovery "has as its object the harnessing of the full creative potential of the adversary process, bringing each party to trial as aware of what he must meet as his finances and his lawyer's energy and intelligence permit".[83]

Another device used both by the common law and by the legislatures to overcome the danger that the parties will suppress evidence and thus render the adversary system self-defeating is the presumption. While presumptions are sometimes created for reasons of social policy, or in order to expedite proof-taking, many presumptions operate against the party who has the superior access to the proof with respect to a particular fact. Thus it forces him to come forward with evidence that his opponent would have difficulty obtaining.[84] A simple illustration is the presumption that arises if a bailor proves that he delivered property to a bailee in good condition and that the property was returned to him in a damaged condition. Because the bailor is not likely to have access to evidence relating to the bailee's negligence the damage will be presumed, at common law, to have been caused by the negligence of the bailee. Thus the bailee will have to come forward with sufficient evidence to prove that the damage was not caused by his negligence.[85] In another situation a higher than normal standard of proof is placed on a party because he has control over the proof. The prosecutor must prove beyond a reasonable doubt that a confession is voluntary before the confession is admissible in evidence. At least one justification for imposing this high standard of proof is that the accused's adversary, the prosecution, has the ability, to some extent, to control the proof that relates to

the voluntariness of a confession. The police can usually take statements under circumstances in which there can be no doubt as to their voluntariness. The accused, if the burden were placed on him to prove involuntariness, would likely be able to produce only his own testimony as proof. If the burden on the Crown were to prove voluntariness only on the balance of probability, the confession would usually be admitted since the issue would resolve itself into the question of who is likely to be more credible, the police or the accused.[86]

To assist a party in gaining access to all the evidence favorable to his case an adverse inference is drawn against a party who fails to disclose to the court evidence which is within his power to produce.[87] This inference rests on the assumption that an "honest and fearless claimant" will produce all the evidence favorable to his case and over which he has control. Therefore if he fails to produce evidence over which he has control, it can be inferred that the evidence is unfavourable to his cause.[88] As well as drawing an adverse inference against a party who fails to produce evidence over which he has control, conduct by a party which renders it difficult or impossible for the other party to produce certain evidence will be regarded by the court as an admission of guilt or liability against that party. "Spoliation" admissions might include such things as the destruction or concealment of relevant documents or objects, intimidation, or the fabrication of evidence.[89]

Finally, to ensure that the party's strong sense of self-interest and stake in the trial [do] not result in the degeneration of the trial into fraud and deceit, interposed between the litigant and the process is a lawyer; a person who will, to a large extent, conduct the proceedings and who has a responsibility not only to the litigant, his client, but also to the process. While the exact nature of the lawyer's responsibility to the process is the subject of dispute, there is agreement that he has a responsibility in most cases to protect the process from evidence he knows to be falsified.[90]

For this assumption of the adversary system to be operative both parties must also have equal resources to investigate and collect facts favorable to their case, and both must be of equal skill in presenting these facts and in testing the facts presented that are unfavorable to their case. If the adversaries do not have equal representation — if for instance the accused in a criminal trial is unable to avail himself of effective counsel — this premise, upon which the adversary system rests, will be impaired. But even when both parties are represented by counsel, the quality of the representation will obviously seldom be equal. What is the role of the judge if one party is not represented or if his representation is inadequate? In such a situation the adversary system will fail to achieve its objective. The judge should not hesitate to intervene. Whatever dangers arise when a judge intervenes in such a situation, they are outweighed by the serious danger that is present if he does not intervene. Professor Fleming James noted that[91] "[a]nything that the law of procedure or the judge's role can do to equalize opportunity and to put a faulty presentation on the right track so that disputes are more likely to be settled on their merits, will in the long run bolster up rather than destroy the adversary system, and will increase the moral force of the decisions." Judge Breitel, in an article on judicial ethics, describes how, when he first went to the bench, he tried to be detached and disciplined in his conduct of the case — which he believed to reflect the ideal role of a judge in the adversary process. After several months, however, and after seeing numerous cases where the lawyers were not equal or were unequal to their task, he began, he says, "to feel revulsion and pangs of conscience". He concluded, "[p]assivity and silence in such a situation ceased to be an acceptable role. Indeed, it made the function and responsibility of being an umpire judge a distortion, an intolerable distortion of the whole process of the administration of justice".[92] Canadian case authorities would appear to support the proposition that when the parties' representation is unequal, the judge has a responsibility to intervene to a greater extent than he otherwise would.[93]

In many inquisitorial systems one of the principal justifications given for increasing the authority of the judge is the need to equalize the parties. The major innovation of the Austrian *Code of Civil Procedure* of 1895, which has had a great influence upon the legislation of many other European countries, was "...its emphasis on a more active role for the judge in both expediting the proceedings and of promoting the social aim of effective quality of the parties".[94] Socialist scholars have contended that there is a reluctance in bourgeois jurisprudence to give the judge a stronger role precisely so that the weaker party can be manoeuvred by the system into a disadvantaged position.[95]

A final aspect of this assumption of the adversary system is the necessity that both parties have the resources to carry out a thorough investigation of the facts. This, of course, is seldom the case. Jerome Frank suggested that in all cases there should be some kind of government intervention to help an impecunious litigant obtain evidence.[96] In criminal cases the state's facilities for investigation are obvi-

ously far superior to those of the ordinary defendant. It might be possible to reduce this disparity by providing legal aid programs with the resources necessary to locate and investigate evidence favorable to the accused. A more efficient remedy, since it does not involve the costly duplication of investigative efforts, would be to place the results of government investigations in the hands of the defence. In the United States a rule of procedure that will have this result is emerging.[97] Clearly if we do not wish to be accused of continuing to tolerate a system whose operations negate the reason for having it we will have to continue to move in this direction.

In some areas the adversary system might have to be completely abandoned because the potential parties are not likely to have sufficient resources to pursue their remedies. Where one spouse has been deserted, for instance, we assume that he or she will bring an action for maintenance. But because of the lack of resources this remedy is seldom pursued. The adversary system is simply not an adequate means of protecting civil rights in this area. Judicial intervention obviously cannot overcome this problem, and resort may be needed to administrative investigative bodies.[98]

ASSUMPTION 4: THE PARTIES WILL BE GIVEN THE OPPORTUNITY TO TEST ADVERSE EVIDENCE

Party-prosecution assumes that each party will have the opportunity and the ability to thoroughly test the evidence unfavorable to his case. It assumes, also, that this testing of adverse evidence must be done by an adversary cross-examination as opposed to a dispassionate inquisitorial examination. Opinions on the utility of cross-examination are sharply divided.[99] However, a judge presiding over an adversary proceeding must, to some extent at least, assume its efficacy. Numerous rules of evidence, the hearsay rule, the best evidence rule, and the opinion evidence rule, attempt to ensure that the parties will be given the opportunity to confront and cross-examine as effectively as possible the evidence that is introduced against them.[100] But whatever the value of cross-examination in revealing and in testing evidence, it can present grave dangers to the process. In some cases it will have the effect of misleading the trier of fact. Cross-examination, even with the best of intentions on the part of the cross-examiner, may make reliable testimony look debatable, and clear information look confused.[101] Witnesses on the witness stand, in a strange setting, compelled to give their testimony in an unnatural manner, and under the threat of a rigorous cross-examination, can very easily be led to say things that do not accurately represent their recollections. But more seriously, counsel might well use techniques in questioning a witness by which he deliberately attempts to force the witness to narrate his testimony in a way that gives a misleading impression as to his honest recollections.

Cross-examination has other costs of equal or greater significance, costs in terms of human dignity. Cross-examination sometimes results in the total humiliation and destruction of a witness without any corresponding benefits. But I have introduced here a value extrinsic to the adversary system, and I wish to discuss the judge's role only in terms of the assumptions of that system. The point is that if cross-examination is to achieve its purpose in the adversary system, the judge must ensure that it is not used as an instrument to distort and obscure testimony. That is not abandoning his role in the adversary system, it is assuming the responsibility of his role. Eliciting the testimony of children is an area, for instance, where there might be a need for strong intervention by the judge, perhaps to the point where all the questions directed to the child are asked through the judge. Harsh and critical cross-examination techniques can confuse the child to the point where he is unable to give intelligible answers.[102]

The judge is also in a dilemma when cross-examination has proved to be ineffective, or when counsel declines to cross-examine a witness about whose perception of the event described, for instance, the judge is in serious doubt. Should he ask questions, the answer to which he feels might assist him in evaluating the witness's perception? The answer would appear obvious. While certain dangers arise when the judge asks questions, these dangers are overridden by the fact that if the questions are not asked, the adversary system will have failed to achieve its objective.

ASSUMPTION 5: ALL INTERESTS AFFECTED ARE REPRESENTED

Finally, the principle of party-prosecution assumes that all interests affected by the adjudication are represented by the parties. The adversary system depends upon the parties to bring forward the information upon which the judge will rely in reaching his decision. In reaching a decision the judge must reconcile all the competing interests affected by his decision. If he does not receive information about some of these interests because they are interests of no immediate concern to the parties before him the adversary system will be a defective method of fact-finding for that decision. The importance of this assumption can be illustrated by reference to two

areas. In a custody proceeding the adversaries are commonly seen to be the parents of the child, both of whom will supply the court with information as to why they should take custody of the child. Both will obviously be arguing in their own perceived best interest. However, the real issue in the case is the best interest of the child. In such a situation it is possible that facts relevant to the real issue in the case will not be presented to the judge by the parties and if he is to reach a decision based on all relevant information, he will have to intervene in the fact-finding.[103]

Another area in which the adversaries will not represent all the interests might be described broadly, if not with some circularity, as being the area of public interest law, such as environmental, consumer protection law. Again, in these areas, the wise judge might well call upon the intervention of third parties to represent those interests not represented by the immediate parties to the particular dispute. At the appellant level this is commonly done by means of asking for or inviting *amicus curiae* factums. Justice Thurgood Marshall of the United States Supreme Court recently called upon the organized bar to finance public interest law on the grounds that the practice of public interest law is a vital function of the adversary system since that system presupposes representation of all interests affected.[104]

The Adversary System Counteracts Bias in Decision-Making

The second reason often given as to why the adversary system leads to more accurate fact-finding than an inquisitorial system is that the adversary system permits the judge to remain unbiased as between the parties throughout the proceedings.[105] Bias is a word used in a wide variety of senses, many of which shade into each other.[106] In this context, where important consequences are being drawn from the concept, it is particularly important to be clear about its meaning.

Bias in this context does not mean, as it commonly means in other contexts, a preconceived point of view about issues of law or policy, a personal prejudice against certain types of parties, or bias in the sense of being personally interested in the outcome of the case. No fact-finding mechanism can remove these types of biases. It refers to a bias or prejudgment that is acquired by a decision-maker because of the mechanism of fact-finding used. If the judge takes an active part in proof-taking, it could be argued that he might acquire a bias towards one party or the other for one of the following reasons:

1. If the judge questions a witness and the witness is evasive, disrespectful, hostile, or in some way does not live up to the expectations of the judge, the judge may become antagonistic towards the witness and therefore tend to discredit his testimony.

2. If the judge in proof-taking is responsible for having some important evidence revealed, he may tend to give too much weight to that evidence, either because he is overly impressed with the skilful manner in which the evidence was presented, or because it is important to him that his intervention is seen to have served a useful purpose.

3. The judge may, in his investigation, become so concerned about a detail of the case that the balance of the evidence will escape his careful attention. This is perhaps the kind of consideration that judges are concerned about when they assert that their ability to evaluate the credibility of a witness is impaired if they themselves become too involved in examining a witness. That is to say, as an investigator preoccupied with his own line of thought, the judge may unconsciously fail to explore important points, may amass so much detail that obvious truths are obscured, or may not carefully observe all of the diverse matters, such as demeanor evidence, that he should take into consideration in evaluating the probative value of testimonial proof.

4. A fourth source of bias that is not present in the adversary system, but which one might argue is present in the inquisitorial system, is the bias that is acquired when the judge is presented with a file of the evidence before the case is heard by him. In an inquisitorial system the judge will of course have had to study the documents contained in the file with some care if he is to be effective in carrying out the proof-taking at trial. There is an obvious danger that the information supplied in the file will bias the judge towards one side or the other. As Glanville Williams noted, "Our reaction to the French system is that it creates a danger that the point of view of the prosecution will communicate itself to the judge before the case has been heard."[107]

5. Finally, it has been contended that the adversary system is an unbiasing fact-finding technique because it counteracts what psychologists call decision-maker bias. Decision-maker bias is acquired when a decision-maker himself investigates the facts upon which he is to rest his judgement.[108] It arises because of the need when one begins to investigate facts to form certain tentative hypotheses about the reality that one is called upon to reconstruct. More or less imperceptively, these preconceptions influence the course of the investigation. As well, facts which confirm the original hypothesis will make a strong imprint upon the mind, while facts that run counter to it are received with diverted attention. This bias, which arises from the process of fact-finding, is avoided in the adversary system, it is argued. It is avoided because, in the adversary system, the judge, since he is not responsible for the investigation, is able to avoid any judgment of the case until he has heard all the evidence.

While all of these kinds of bias may be present in an adversary proceeding, none of them should limit to any great extent, within the framework of our present trial, the judge's intelligent intervention in the case. A recognition of their presence should permit the judge to conduct the proceedings in a fashion that minimizes the dangers that might arise.

Conclusion

I suggested at the outset of this paper that the role of the judge, at least the limits of his intervention in the conduct of the trial, must be established by a careful reference to the premises of the adversary system. However, in some sense, that is only a starting point in defining his role. The adversary system is not a moral axiom. We do [not] maintain it for its own sake, and the values that we seek by use of the adversary system — the acceptability of the process, and accuracy in fact-finding — are only two of the process values that must be pursued in any system of adjudication. As well as these values, any procedural system designed to resolve disputes must strike a balance among many other process values such as finality, expedition, administrative efficiency, and the protection of the dignity of the participants. Interests extrinsic to the process must also be considered, for instance, the protection of important relationships, the control of governmental power, and the protection of the innocent in criminal cases. This is not the place to expand on these interests and their implications, I merely mention them, and the fact that they must be considered by the judge in defining his role in particular situations, in order to place the discussion in this paper in its larger context.

I do not intend to explore the specific instances where a judge might be called upon to intervene in a trial. However, I will make reference to one such instance to illustrate how the premises of the adversary system could form the guidelines upon which the judge relies in defining the extent of his intervention. If a judge decided that a person, whom neither party had called, could perhaps give relevant testimony, the following dangers, in terms of the adversary system, might arise if he called that person as a witness himself: it could weaken the motivating force of the parties in calling all evidence favorable to their case, they might become careless about calling evidence knowing that if they do not call the evidence the judge will, or they might not call a witness hoping that the judge will and thus give a witness favorable to them the appearance of objectivity; it might bias the trier of fact in favour of that witness's testimony, the judge might acquire a commitment to the witness's credibility because of his interest in making his efforts appear worthwhile, the jury might give a witness called by the judge undue weight because of the witness's apparent objectivity; it could give the judge the appearance of partiality, if the witness gives testimony adverse to the accused, for instance, the judge, who called the witness, might appear to be biased against the accused; it could render the judge's ultimate decision less acceptable to the parties, if they view his intervention as an unjustified intrusion in their private fight; or, it could lead to inaccurate fact-finding if the judge called the witness at a time which made it difficult for one of the parties to lead evidence rebutting the testimony, or at a time when it had the effect of weakening the persuasive force of one of the parties' case. As well as these considerations, when the judge calls a witness a number of purely pragmatic procedural considerations arise: who can examine, cross-examine and impeach the witness; if the judge questions the witness, how do the parties effectively object to any improper questions or other procedural errors; and, how does the judge, who

does not likely have any detailed or even perhaps general knowledge about the proof in the case until it unfolds before him, know that his intervention is not going to simply waste time.

While I do not have time to explore each of these dangers, and others that might rise in specific contexts, in detail, it should be clear that they provide the judge a wide latitude in which to call witnesses in appropriate cases. A similar analysis could be done for each specific instance where a judge might intervene in a trial. Giving due considerations to the dangers that might be present in specific instances, if the judge thinks in a particular case it would be helpful, I see no reason why he should hesitate, for instance, to call his own witnesses, to question witnesses both to clarify and to develop additional evidence, to invite witnesses to give a narrative account of their testimony, to invite perhaps three or four witnesses to be sworn and take their evidence in a conference-room style, to intervene to protect witnesses from harassment and confusing questions, or to advise the parties in the presentation of their case so that they do not commit procedural errors.

In conclusion, there is undoubtedly considerable experience and knowledge of human nature captured in the adversary system. What I have attempted to do is re-examine the assumptions of the adversary system and review the judge's role in light of these assumptions. My conclusion is that the adversary system imposes on the judge as well as the parties an important and active role in the conduct of the trial.[109] The adversary system is not an end in itself; it is a procedural device which we have adopted in the pursuit of more ultimate process values. The judge has responsibility not only to arrive at a decision but also to ensure that these process values are attained.

(b) 'Fight' Theory vs. 'Truth' Theory†

Judge Jerome Frank

There is one most serious handicap in litigation that has received little attention:[8] With the ablest lawyer in the world, a man may lose a suit he ought to win, if he has not the funds to pay for an investigation,

† From Frank Jerome, *Courts on Trial: Myth and Reality in American Justice* (Ewing, N.J.: Princeton University Press, 1949) at 94–99. © 1949 Princeton University Press, 1977 renewed PUP. Reproduced with permission of Princeton University Press. [Notes and/or references omitted.]

before trial, of evidence necessary to sustain his case. I refer to evidence not in the files of the other party and therefore not obtainable by "discovery" procedure. What I mean is this: In order to prove his claim, or to defend against one, a man may need to hire detectives to scour the country — even sometimes foreign countries — in order to locate witnesses who alone may know of events that occurred years ago, or to unearth letters or other papers which may be in distant places. Or, again, he may need the services of an engineer, or a chemist, or an expert accountant, to make an extensive — and therefore expensive — investigation. Without the evidence which such an investigation would reveal, a man is often bound to be defeated. His winning or losing may therefore depend on his pocketbook. He is out of luck if his pocketbook is not well-lined with money. For neither his lawyer nor any legal-aid institution will supply the needed sums. For want of money, expendable for such purposes, many a suit has been lost, many a meritorious claim or defense has never even been asserted.

Let me illustrate. Fisher, in his recent excellent book, *The Art of Investigation*, writes: "The percentage of witnesses who cannot be found if enough effort is exerted is infinitesimal. A famous investigator once said that the man who could not be found is the man at the bottom of the sea, and even then he must be at the bottom at its points of greatest depth. Anyone alive can be found if enough effort is put forth." That statement may be exaggerated. But you get the point: Suppose there is one man, John Brown, who alone could testify to a crucial event — such as that Sam Jones was in New York City on June 12, 1948. Brown is missing. He may be in China, India or Peru. If he can be found, and if he testifies, the plaintiff will win his suit; otherwise he will lose it. If the plaintiff can afford to pay enough to investigators to scour the world for the missing witness, he may be located. If the plaintiff is a man of means, he will hire such investigators. But if he has little money, he can't do so — and will lose his case which may involve all his worldly goods.

That is not true justice, democratic justice. This defect in our judicial system makes a mockery of "equality before the law," which should be one of the first principles of a democracy. That equality, in such instances, depends on a person's financial condition. The tragedy of such a situation is etched in irony when a man's impoverished condition has resulted from a wrong done him by another whom he cannot successfully sue to redress the wrong. Many of our state constitutions contain a provision that "every person ought to obtain justice freely and

without being obliged to purchase it." But, as things stand, this is too often a provision in words only. For the advantage in litigation is necessarily on the side of the party that can "purchase justice" by hiring private assistance in obtaining evidence when his adversary cannot. Unless we contrive some method to solve the problem I have posed, we must acknowledge that, in a very real sense, frequently we are "selling justice," denying it to many under-income persons. It should shock us that judicial justice is thus often an upper-bracket privilege. Here we have legal *laissez-faire* at its worst.

That brings me to a point which the fighting theory obscures. A court's decision is not a mere private affair. It culminates in a court order which is one of the most solemn of governmental acts. Not only is a court an agency of government, but remember that its order, if not voluntarily obeyed, will bring into action the police, the sheriff, even the army. What a court orders, then, is no light matter. The court represents the government, organized society, in action.

Such an order a court is not supposed to make unless there exist some facts which bring into operation a legal rule. Now any government officer, other than a judge, if authorized to do an act for the government only if certain facts exist, will be considered irresponsible if he so acts without a governmental investigation. For instance, if an official is empowered to pay money to a veteran suffering from some specified ailment, the official, if he does his duty, will not rely solely on the applicant's statement that he has such an ailment. The government officer insists on a governmental check-up of the evidence. Do courts so conduct themselves?

In criminal cases they seem to, after a fashion. In such cases, there is some recognition that so important a governmental act as a court decision against a defendant should not occur without someone, on behalf of the government itself, seeing to it that the decision is justified by the actual facts so far as they can be discovered with reasonable diligence. For, in theory at least, usually before a criminal action is begun, an official investigation has been conducted which reveals data sufficient to warrant bringing the defendant to trial. In some jurisdictions, indigent defendants *charged* with crime are represented by a publicly-paid official, a Public Defender — a highly important reform which should everywhere be adopted. And the responsibility of government for mistakes of fact in criminal cases, resulting in erroneous court judgments, is recognized in those jurisdictions in which the government compensates an innocent convicted person if it is subsequently shown that he was convicted through such a mistake.

In civil cases (non-criminal cases), on the whole a strikingly different attitude prevails. Although, no less than in a criminal suit, a court's order is a grave governmental act, yet, in civil cases, the government usually accepts no similar responsibilities, even in theory. Such a suit is still in the ancient tradition of "self help." The court usually relies almost entirely on such evidence as one or the other of the private parties to the suit is (a) able to, and (b) chooses to, offer. Lack of skill or diligence of the lawyer for one of those parties, or that party's want of enough funds to finance a pre-trial investigation necessary to obtain evidence, may have the result, as I explained, that crucial available evidence is not offered in court. No government official has the duty to discover, and bring to court, evidence, no matter how important, not offered by the parties.

In short, the theory is that, in most civil suits, the government, through its courts, should make orders which the government will enforce, although those court-orders may not be justified by the actual facts, and although, by reasonable diligence, the government, had it investigated, might have discovered evidence — at variance with the evidence presented — coming closer to the actual facts.

Yet the consequence of a court decision in a civil suit, based upon the court's mistaken view of the actual facts, may be as grave as a criminal judgment which convicts an innocent person. If, because of such an erroneous decision, a man loses his job or his savings and becomes utterly impoverished, he may be in almost as serious a plight as if he had been jailed. His poverty may make him a public charge. It may lead to the delinquency of his children, who may thus become criminals and go to jail. Yet in no jurisdiction is a man compensated by the government for serious injury to him caused by a judgment against him in a non-criminal case, even if later it is shown that the judgment was founded upon perjured or mistaken testimony.

I suggest that there is something fundamentally wrong in our legal system in this respect. If a man's pocket is picked, the government brings a criminal suit, and accepts responsibility for its prosecution. If a man loses his life's savings through a breach of a contract, the government accepts no such responsibility. Shouldn't the government perhaps assume some of the burden of enforcing what we call "private rights"?

Some few moves have been made in the right direction. In an English divorce court, an official, the King's Proctor, brings forward evidence, bearing on possible collusion, not offered by either contestant; some American states provide that the public prosecutor shall do likewise in divorce actions. In our own Domestic Relations Courts, government officers procure and present most of the evidence. Lawyers for any of the parties may cross-examine any witness, may offer additional evidence, and may argue about the applicable legal rules. The advantages of the adversary method are fully preserved, but the fighting spirit is much diminished. Under the *Chandler Act*, enacted in 1938, in certain types of cases relating to corporate reorganization, the SEC, at large public expense, uses its expert staff to obtain and present to the court evidence which usually no private party could afford to procure; the judge and the private parties may treat this evidence like any other evidence, and the parties may introduce further supplementary or conflicting evidence.

Many of our administrative agencies have large and efficient staffs to conduct investigations in order to ferret out evidence put before those agencies in their own administrative proceedings. I know, from personal experience, that not much evidence escapes an agency like the SEC.[9] Mr. Justice Jackson has said: "Such a tribunal is not as dependent as the ordinary court upon the arguments of skilled counsel to get at the truth. Skilled advocacy is neither so necessary to keep such a body informed nor is stupid or clever advocacy so apt to blur the merits of a controversy."

I do not suggest that courts, like such administrative bodies, conduct their own investigations through their own employees. I do suggest that we should consider whether it is not feasible to provide impartial government officials — who are not court employees, and who act on their own initiative — to dig up, and present to the courts, significant evidence which one or the other of the parties may overlook or be unable to procure. No court would be bound to accept that evidence as true. Nor would any of the parties be precluded from trying to show the unreliability of such evidence (by cross-examination or otherwise) or from introducing additional evidence. Trials would still remain adversary. As I concede that to use that device in all civil cases would lead to many complications, I do not urge that it be at once generally adopted. But I think experiments along those lines should now be made.

This proposal resembles somewhat the procedures long used in criminal cases on the European continent. Critics may oppose it on that ground, saying that we should not take over ideas from countries which have been less democratic than ours. To any such argument, Woodrow Wilson gave the answer: "But why should we not use such parts of foreign contrivances as we want if they may be in any way serviceable? We are in no danger of using them in a foreign way. We borrowed rice, but we do not eat it with chopsticks."

It will also be said that any such proposal is absurdly radical. Yet something of the sort was endorsed by President Taft, by no means a radical. More than thirty years ago he said: "Of all the questions ... before the American people I regard no one as more important than this, the improvement of the administration of justice. We must make it so that the poor man will have as nearly as possible an opportunity in litigating as the rich man, and under present conditions, ashamed as we may be of it, this is not the fact."[10] Moreover, we now have public-utility commissions which, on behalf of private persons, bring rate-suits against utility companies. With that in mind, Willoughby wrote a book, published in 1927 by the conservative Brookings Institution, in which he proposed the appointment of a "public prosecutor of civil actions." If a complaint were made to the prosecutor, he would first try to settle the matter or to have the parties agree to submit the dispute to arbitration. Only if these efforts failed would he bring suit. No one would be obliged to retain prosecutor; his employment would be optional; and, if any action were brought on a person's behalf by the prosecutor, that person would be at liberty to retain a private lawyer to assist in the preparation for, and conduct of, the trial. That idea, I think, merits public discussion and consideration. Were it adopted, it should perhaps be supplemented to include a practice now adopted, in some states, by the Public Defender in criminal actions: That official is authorized to expend public funds to seek out and procure what he regards as essential evidence.

Statutes in some jurisdictions authorize the trial judge to call as a witness an expert selected by the judge. Judges might sometimes avail themselves of that power to help indigent or under-income litigants. But I believe that none of those statutes, as they now read, provides for payment by the government to judge-called experts in non-criminal suits. Moreover, those statutes will not meet the difficulties of a prospective litigant when making up his mind whether to bring or defend a suit. Nor do they permit expenditures for detectives and other investigators not regarded as "experts." Nevertheless, this expedient might be expanded so as partially to solve the problem I have presented.

None of these proposals, if adopted, would usher in the millennium. Official evidence gatherers, or public prosecutors of civil actions, will make mistakes, or become excessively partisan. The trial process is, and always will be, human, therefore fallible. It can never be a completely scientific investigation for the discovery of the true facts.

(c) Lawyer — Manufacturer — Painter†

Franz Kafka

One winter morning — snow was falling outside the window in a foggy dimness — K. was sitting in his office, already exhausted in spite of the early hour. To save his face before his subordinates at least, he had given his clerk instructions to admit no one, on the plea that he was occupied with an important piece of work. But instead of working he twisted in his chair, idly rearranged the things lying on his writing-table, and then, without being aware of it, let his out-stretched arm rest on the table and went on sitting motionless with bowed head.

The thought of his case never left him now. He had often considered whether it would not be better to draw up a written defense and hand it in to the Court. In this defense he would give a short account of his life, and when he came to an event of any importance explain for what reasons he had acted as he did, intimate whether he approved or condemned his way of action in retrospect, and adduce grounds for the condemnation or approval. The advantages of such a written defense, as compared with the mere advocacy of a lawyer who himself was not impecca-

---

† From *The Trial*, Definitive Edition, by Frank Kafka, translated by Willa and Edwin Muir (N.Y.: Schocken Books, 1988) at 113–26. translation copyright 1937, 1956, renewed 1965, 1984 by Alfred A. Knopf, a division of Random House, Inc. Copyright © 1925, 1935, 1946, renewed 1952, 1963, 1974 by Schocken Books, Inc. Used by permission of Schocken Books, a division of Random House, Inc.

ble, were undoubted. K. had no idea what the lawyer was doing about the case; at any rate it did not amount to much, it was more than a month since Huld had sent for him, and at none of the previous consultations had K. formed the impression that the man could do much for him. To begin with, he had hardly cross-questioned him at all. And there were so many questions to put. To ask questions was surely the main thing. K. felt that he could draw up all the necessary questions himself. But the lawyer, instead of asking questions, either did all the talking or sat quite dumb opposite him, bent slightly forward over his writing-table, probably because of his hardness of hearing, stroking a strand of hair in the middle of his beard and gazing at the carpet, perhaps at the very spot where K. had lain with Leni. Now and then he would give K. some empty admonitions such as people hand out to children. Admonitions as useless as they were wearisome, for which K. did not intend to pay a penny at the final reckoning. After the lawyer thought he had humbled him sufficiently, he usually set himself to encourage him slightly again. He had already, so he would relate, won many similar cases either outright or partially. Cases which, though in reality not quite so difficult, perhaps, as this one, had been outwardly still more hopeless. He had a list of these cases in a drawer of his desk — at this he tapped one of them — but he regretted he couldn't show it, as it was a matter of official secrecy. Nevertheless the vast experience he had gained through all these cases would now redound to K.'s benefit. He had started on K.'s case at once, of course, and the first plea was almost ready for presentation. That was very important, for the first impression made by the Defense often determined the whole course of subsequent proceedings. Though, unfortunately, it was his duty to warn K., it sometimes happened that the first pleas were not read by the Court at all. They simply filed them among the other papers and pointed out that for the time being the observation and interrogation of the accused were more important than any formal petition. If the petitioner pressed them, they generally added that before the verdict was pronounced all the material accumulated, including, of course, every document relating to the case, the first plea as well, would be carefully examined. But unluckily even that was not quite true in most cases, the first plea was often mislaid or lost altogether and, even if it were kept intact till the end, was hardly ever read; that was of course, the lawyer admitted, merely a rumor. It was all very regrettable, but not wholly without justification. K. must remember that the proceedings were not public; they could certainly, if the Court considered it necessary, become public, but the Law did not prescribe that they must be made public. Naturally, therefore, the legal records of the case, and above all the actual charge-sheets, were inaccessible to the accused and his counsel, [and] consequently one did not know in general, or at least did not know with any precision, what charges to meet in the first plea; accordingly it could be only by pure chance that it contained really relevant matter. One could draw up genuinely effective and convincing pleas only later on, when the separate charges and the evidence on which they were based emerged more definitely or could be guessed at from the interrogations. In such circumstances the Defense was naturally in a very ticklish and difficult position. Yet that, too, was intentional. For the Defense was not actually countenanced by the Law, but only tolerated, and there were differences of opinion even on that point, whether the Law could be interpreted to admit such tolerance at all. Strictly speaking, therefore, none of the counsels for the Defense was recognized by the Court, all who appeared before the Court as counsels being in reality merely in the position of pettifogging lawyers. That naturally had a very humiliating effect on the whole profession, and the next time K. visited the Law Court offices he should take a look at the lawyers' room, just for the sake of having seen it once in his life. He would probably be horrified by the kind of people he found assembled there. The very room, itself small and cramped, showed the contempt in which the Court held them. It was lit only by a small skylight, which was so high up that if you wanted to look out, you had to get some colleague to hoist you on his back, and even then the smoke from the chimney close by choked you and blackened your face. To give only one more example of the state the place was in — there had been for more than a year now a hole in the floor, not so big that you could fall through the floor, but big enough to let a man's leg slip through. The lawyers' room was in the very top attic, so that if you stumbled through the hole your leg hung down into the lower attic, into the very corridor where the clients had to wait. It wasn't saying too much if the lawyers called these conditions scandalous. Complaints to the authorities had not the slightest effect, and it was strictly forbidden for the lawyers to make any structural repairs or alterations at their own expense. Still, there was some justification for this attitude on the part of the authorities. They wanted to eliminate defending counsel as much as possible; the whole onus of the Defense must be laid on the accused himself. A reasonable enough point of view, yet nothing could be more erroneous than to deduce from this that accused persons had no need of defending counsel when appearing before this Court. On the contrary, in no other Court was legal assistance so necessary. For the proceedings were not only kept secret from the general public, but from the accused as well. Of course only so far as this was possible, but it had proved possible to a very great extent. For even the accused had no access to the Court records, and to guess from the course of an interrogation what documents the Court had up its sleeve was very difficult, particularly for an accused person, who was himself implicated and had all sorts of worries to distract him. Now here was where defending counsel stepped in. Generally speaking, he was not allowed to be present during the examination, consequently he had to cross-question the accused immediately after an interrogation, if possible at the very door of the Court of Inquiry, and piece together from the usually confused reports he got anything that might be of use for the Defense. But even that was not the most important thing, for one could not elicit very much in that way, though of course here as elsewhere a capable man could elicit more than others. The most important thing was counsel's personal connection with officials of the Court; in that lay the chief value of the Defense. Now K. must have discovered from experience that the very lowest grade of the Court organization was by no means perfect and contained venal and corrupt elements, whereby to some extent a breach was made in the water-tight system of justice. This was where most of the petty lawyers tried to push their way in, by bribing and listening to gossip, in fact there had actually been cases of purloining documents, at least in former times. It was not to be gainsaid that these methods could achieve for the moment surprisingly favourable results for the accused, on which the petty lawyers prided themselves, spreading them out as a lure for new clients, but they had no effect on the further progress of the case, or only a bad effect. Nothing was of any real value but respectable personal connections with the higher officials, that was to say higher officials of subordinate rank, naturally. Only through these could the course of the proceedings be influenced, imperceptibly at first, perhaps, but more and more strongly as the case went on. Of course very few lawyers had such connections, and here K.'s choice had been a very fortunate one. Perhaps only one or two other lawyers could boast of the same connections as Dr. Huld. These did not worry their heads about the mob in the lawyers' room and had nothing whatever to do with them. But their relations with the Court officials were all the more intimate. It was not even necessary that Dr. Huld should always attend the Court, wait in the Anteroom of the Examining Magistrates till they chose to appear, and be dependent on their moods for earning perhaps a delusive success or not even that. No, as K. had himself seen, the officials, and very high ones among them, visited Dr. Huld of their own accord, voluntarily providing information with great frankness or at least in broad enough hints, discussing the next turn of the various cases; more, even sometimes letting themselves be persuaded to a new point of view. Certainly one should not rely too much on their readiness to be persuaded, for definitely as they might declare themselves for a new standpoint favourable to the Defense, they might well go straight to their offices and issue a statement in the directly contrary sense, a verdict far more severe on the accused than the original intention which they claimed to have renounced completely. Against that, of course, there was no remedy, for what they said to you in private was simply said to you in private and could not be followed up in public, even if the Defense were not obliged for other reasons to do its utmost to retain the favor of these gentlemen. On the other hand it had also to be considered that these gentlemen were not moved by mere human benevolence or friendly feeling in paying visits to defending counsel — only to experienced counsel, of course; they were in a certain sense actually dependent on the Defense. They could not help feeling the disadvantages of a judiciary system which insisted on secrecy from the start. Their remoteness kept the officials from being in touch with the populace; for the average case they were excellently equipped, such a case proceeded almost mechanically and only needed a push now and then; yet confronted with quite simple cases, or particularly difficult cases, they were often utterly at a loss, they did not have any right understanding of human relations, since they were confined day and night to the workings of their judicial system, whereas in such cases a knowledge of human nature itself was indispensable. Then it was that they came to the lawyers for advice, with a servant behind them carrying the papers that were usually kept so secret. In that window over there many a gentleman one would never have expected to encounter had sat gazing out hopelessly into the street, while the lawyer at his desk examined his papers in order to give him good advice. And it was on such occasions as these that one could perceive how seriously these gentlemen took their vocation and how deeply they were plunged into despair when they came upon obstacles which the nature of things kept them from overcoming. In other ways, too, their position was not easy, and one must not do them an injustice by regarding it as easy. The ranks of officials in this judiciary system mounted endlessly, so that not even the initiated could survey the hierarchy as a whole. And the proceedings of the Courts were generally kept secret from subordinate officials, consequently they could hardly ever quite follow in their further progress the cases on which they had worked; any particular case thus appeared in their circle of jurisdiction often without their knowing whence it came, and passed from it they knew not whither. Thus the knowledge derived from a study of the various single stages of the case, the final verdict and the reasons for that verdict lay beyond the reach of these officials. They were forced to restrict themselves to that stage of the case which was prescribed for them by the Law, and as for what followed, in other words the results of their own work, they generally knew less about it than the Defense, which as a rule remained in touch with the accused almost to the end of the case. So in that respect, too, they could learn much that was worth knowing from the Defense. Should it surprise K., then, keeping all this in mind, to find that the officials lived in a state of irritability which sometimes expressed itself in offensive ways when they dealt with their clients? That was the universal experience. All the officials were in a constant state of irritation, even when they appeared calm. Naturally the petty lawyers were most liable to suffer from it. The following story, for example, was current, and it had all the appearance of truth. An old official, a well-meaning, quiet man, had a difficult case in hand which had been greatly complicated by the lawyer's petitions, and he had studied it continuously for a whole day and night — the officials were really more conscientious than anyone else. Well, toward morning, after twenty-four hours of work with probably very little result, he went to the entrance door, hid himself behind it, and flung down the stairs every lawyer who tried to enter. The lawyers gathered down below on the landing and took counsel what they should do; on the one hand they had no real claim to be admitted and consequently could hardly take any legal action against the official, and also, as already mentioned, they had to guard against antagonizing the body of officials. But on the other hand every day they spent away from the Court was a day lost to them, and so a great deal depended on their getting in. At last they all agreed that the best thing to do was to tire out the old gentleman. One lawyer after another was sent rushing upstairs to offer the greatest possible show of passive resistance and let himself be thrown down again into the arms of his colleagues. That lasted for about an hour, then the old gentleman — who was exhausted in any case by his work overnight — really grew tired and went back to his office. The lawyers down below would not believe it at first and sent one of their number up to peep behind the door and assure himself that the place was actually vacant. Only then were they able to enter, and probably they did not dare even to grumble. For although the pettiest lawyer might be to some extent capable of analyzing the state of things in the Court, it never occurred to the lawyers that they should suggest or insist on any improvements in the system, while — and this was very characteristic — almost every accused man, even quite simple people among them, discovered from the earliest stages a passion for suggesting reforms which often wasted time and energy that could have been better employed in other directions. The only sensible thing was to adapt oneself to existing conditions. Even if it were possible to alter a detail for the better here or there — but it was simple madness to think of it — any benefit arising from that would profit clients in the future only, while one's own interests would be immeasurably injured by attracting the attention of the ever-vengeful officials. Anything rather than that! One must lie low, no matter how much it went against the grain, and try to understand that this great organization remained, so to speak, in a state of delicate balance, and that if someone took it upon himself to alter the disposition of things around him, he ran the risk of losing his footing and falling to destruction, while the organization would simply right itself by some compensating reaction in another part of its machinery — since everything interlocked — and remain unchanged, unless, indeed, which was very probable, it became still more rigid, more vigilant, severer, and more ruthless. One must really leave the lawyers to do their work, instead of interfering with them. Reproaches were not of much use, particularly when the offender was unable to perceive the full scope of the grounds for them; all the same, he must say that K. had very greatly damaged his case by his discourtesy to the Chief Clerk of the Court. That influential man could already almost be eliminated from the list of those who might be got to do something for K. He now ignored clearly on purpose even the slightest reference to the case. In many ways the functionaries were like children. Often they could be so deeply offended by the merest trifle — unfortunately, K.'s behavior could not be classed as a trifle — that they would stop speaking even to old friends, give them the cold shoulder, and work against them in all imaginable ways. But then, suddenly, in the most surprising fashion and without any particular reason, they would be moved to laughter by some small jest which you only dared to make because you felt you had nothing to lose, and then they were your friends again. In fact it was both easy and difficult to handle them, you could hardly lay down any fixed principles for dealing with them. Sometimes you felt astonished to think that one single ordinary lifetime sufficed to gather all the knowledge needed for a fair degree of success in such a profession. There were dark hours, of course, such as came to everybody, in which you thought you had achieved nothing at all, in which it seemed to you that only the cases predestined from the start to succeed came to a good end, which they would have reached in any event without your help, while every one of the others was doomed to fail in spite of all your maneuvers, all your exertions, all the illusory little victories on which you plumed yourself. That was a frame of mind, of course, in which nothing at all seemed certain, and so you could not positively deny when questioned that your intervention might have sidetracked some cases which would have run quite well on the right lines had they been left alone. A desperate kind of self-assurance, to be sure, yet it was the only kind available at such times. These moods — for of course they were only moods, nothing more — afflicted lawyers more especially when a case which they had conducted satisfactorily to the desired point was suddenly taken out of their hands. That was beyond all doubt the worst thing that could happen to a lawyer. Not that a client ever dismissed his lawyer from a case, such a thing was not done, an accused man, once having briefed a lawyer, must stick to him whatever happened. For how could he keep going by himself, once he had called in someone to help him? So that never happened, but it did sometimes happen that the case took a turn where the lawyer could no longer follow it. The case and the accused and everything were simply withdrawn from the lawyer; then even the best connections with officials could no longer achieve any result, for even they knew nothing. The case had simply reached the stage where further assistance was ruled out, it was being conducted in remote, inaccessible Courts, where even the accused was beyond the reach of a lawyer. Then you might come home some day and find on your table all the countless pleas relating to the case, which you had drawn up with such pains and such high hopes; they had been returned to you because in the new stage of the trial they were not admitted as relevant; they were mere waste paper. It did not follow that the case was lost, by no means, at least there was no decisive evidence for such as assumption; you simply knew nothing more about the case and would never know anything more about it. Now, very luckily, such occurrences were exceptional, and even if K.'s case

were a case of that nature, it still had a long way to go before reaching that stage. For the time being, there were abundant opportunities for legal labor, and K. might rest assured that they would be exploited to the utmost. The first plea, as before mentioned, was not yet handed in, but there was no hurry; far more important were the preliminary consultations with the relevant officials, and they had already taken place. With varying success, as must be frankly admitted. It would be better for the time being not to divulge details which might have a bad influence on K. by elating or depressing him unduly, yet this much could be asserted, that certain officials had expressed themselves very graciously and had also shown great readiness to help, while others had expressed themselves less favorably, but in spite of that had by no means refused their collaboration. The result on the whole was therefore very gratifying, though one must not seek to draw any definite conclusion from that, since all preliminary negotiations began in the same way and only in the course of further developments did it appear whether they had real value or not. At any rate nothing was yet lost, and if they could manage to win over the Chief Clerk of the Court in spite of all that had happened — various moves had already been initiated toward that end — then, to use a surgeon's expression, this could be regarded as a clean wound and one could await further developments with an easy mind.

In such and similar harangues K.'s lawyer was inexhaustible. He reiterated them every time K. called on him. Progress had always been made, but the nature of the progress could never be divulged. The lawyer was always working away at the first plea, but it had never reached a conclusion, which at the next visit turned out to be an advantage, since the last few days would have been very inauspicious for handing it in, a fact which no one could have foreseen. If K., as sometimes happened, wearied out by the lawyer's volubility, remarked that, even taking into account all the difficulties, the case seemed to be getting on very slowly, he was met with the retort that it was not getting on slowly at all, although they would have been much further on by now had K. come to the lawyer in time. Unfortunately he had neglected to do so and that omission was likely to keep him at a disadvantage, and not merely a temporal disadvantage, either.

The one welcome interruption to these visits was Leni, who always so arranged things that she brought in the lawyer's tea while K. was present. She would stand behind K.'s chair, apparently looking on, while the lawyer stooped with a kind of miserly greed over his cup and poured out and sipped his tea, but all the time she was letting K. surreptitiously hold her hand. There was total silence. The lawyer sipped, K. squeezed Leni's hand, and sometimes Leni ventured to caress his hair. "Are you still here?" the lawyer would ask, after he had finished. "I wanted to take the tea tray away," Leni would answer, there would follow a last handclasp, the lawyer would wipe his mouth and begin again with new energy to harangue K.

Was the lawyer seeking to comfort him or to drive him to despair? K. could not tell, but he soon held it for an established fact that his defense was not in good hands. It might be all true, of course, what the lawyer said, though his attempts to magnify his own importance were transparent enough and it was likely that he had never till now conducted such an important case as he imagined K.'s to be. But his continual bragging of his personal connections with the officials was suspicious. Was it so certain that he was exploiting these connections entirely for K.'s benefit? The lawyer never forgot to mention that these officials were subordinate officials, therefore officials in a very dependent position, for whose advancement certain turns in the various cases might in all probability be of some importance. Could they possibly employ the lawyer to bring about such turns in the case, turns which were bound, of course, to be unfavorable to the accused? Perhaps they did not always do that, it was hardly likely, there must be occasions on which they arranged that the lawyer should score a point or two as a reward for his services, since it was to their own interest for him to keep up his professional reputation. But if that were really the position, into which category were they likely to put K.'s case, which, as the lawyer maintained, was a very difficult, therefore important case, and had roused great interest in the Court from the very beginning? There could not be very much doubt what they would do. A clue was already provided by the fact that the first plea had not yet been handed in, though the case had lasted for months, and that according to the lawyer all the proceedings were still in their early stages, words which were obviously well calculated to lull the accused and keep him in a helpless state, in order suddenly to overwhelm him with the verdict or at least with the announcement that the preliminary examination had been concluded in his disfavor and the case handed over to higher authorities.

It was absolutely necessary for K. to intervene personally. In states of intense exhaustion, such as he experienced this winter morning, when all these thoughts kept running at random through his head, he was particularly incapable of resisting this conviction. The contempt which he had one left for the case no longer obtained. Had he stood alone in the world he could easily have ridiculed the whole affair, though it was also certain that in that event it could never have arisen at all. But now his uncle had dragged him to this lawyer, family considerations had come in; his position was no longer quite independent of the course the case took, he himself, with a certain inexplicable complacence, had imprudently mentioned it to some of his acquaintances, others had come to learn of it in ways unknown to him, his relations with Fräulein Bürstner seemed to fluctuate with the case itself — in short, he hardly had the choice now to accept the trial or reject it, he was in the middle of it and must fend for himself. To give in to fatigue would be dangerous.

(d) Inquiry into Forensic Pathology in Ontario — Executive Summary†

Honourable Stephen T. Goudge

THE DEATH OF A CHILD AND THE CRIMINAL JUSTICE SYSTEM

The sudden, unexpected death of a child is a devastating event for parents, for family, and for the entire community. If something suggests that a criminal act may have been involved, the devastation takes on a further tragic dimension. This reality lies at the core of the work of this Inquiry.

For the parents, the loss is shattering. Children are not supposed to die unexpectedly, and certainly not before their parents. If a suspicion arises that a parent killed the child, the death is only the beginning of the nightmare. The parent is immediately subjected to an intensive police investigation that inevitably stands in the way of any grieving process. If a charge is laid, it is very likely to be a serious one, with the parent removed from the home and often held without bail. The child protection authorities will likely seize the surviving children, remove them from the home, and place them in care. Emotions in the community will often run high. Each new trauma builds on the ones before.

For the surviving children, the impact is profound as well. They are often very young themselves, yet must cope with the sudden inexplicable loss of a sibling. If one of their parents is suspected, the children will likely be removed from their home and family, sometimes for years or even permanently. The same fate may befall children born later to the parents. They must live with the horror that the parent they love is suspected of killing a brother or sister.

For the extended families, there is also much pain. The child's death is their loss too. Some family members will be prepared to sacrifice everything to defend their loved one against any criminal charge. Others may be convinced of the suspected parent's guilt. Splits can emerge that remain painful for years, if not forever.

If the person suspected is not a parent but the child's caregiver, such as a babysitter, there can be similar trauma. Babysitters are often young people themselves. The shock of being suspected of killing a child in their care is profound. The families of young suspects will also likely exhaust all the family's resources to come to their defence. A suspected caregiver who is charged faces the same lost freedom and the same community stigma as a suspected parent.

For the community itself, the death of a child in criminally suspicious circumstances is deeply disturbing. Children are the community's most precious and most defenceless asset. The sense of outrage and the urgent need to understand what happened are overwhelming.

Thus, the tragedy of a child who dies unexpectedly in suspicious circumstances has many victims. It becomes vital for society to deal with the tragedy in a way that is right and just, and that allows all those affected to come to terms with it. The criminal justice system is central to this task. It must seek to determine whether there is truth to the suspicion that the child was killed and, if so, by whom. Despite the complex and difficult challenges of investigating and adjudicating pediatric death cases, the criminal justice system must do so correctly and fairly, often in a highly charged emotional atmosphere.

The consequences of failure in these circumstances are extraordinarily high. For the parent or caregiver who is wrongly convicted, it almost certainly means time, perhaps years, unnecessarily suffered in jail, a shattered family, and the stigma of being labelled a child killer. Even if the criminal justice system stops short of conviction, family resources, both financial and emotional, are often exhausted in the struggle. And in either case, there may be a killer who goes unpunished. For the community at large, failure in such traumatic circumstances comes at a huge cost to the public's faith in the criminal justice system — a faith that is essential if the justice system is to play the role required of it by society.

The cases we examined at the Inquiry demonstrate how vital the role of the forensic pathologist can be in the success or failure of the criminal justice system in coping with the sudden, unexpected death of an infant in criminally suspicious circumstances. The suspected parent or caregiver will often have been the only person in contact with the child in the hours preceding death. There may be little additional evidence. But if the forensic pathologist determines the cause of the child's death, that opinion may be enough to play a decisive role in whether someone is charged and convicted. In these circumstances, the criminal justice system must be able to rely confidently on the opinion if it is to deliver a just outcome. The fate of the person suspected, the family, the surviving children, and the peace of mind of the community all depend on it.

The far-reaching human consequences of flawed forensic pathology provided the context for our work from the very beginning. Before the hearings began, I had the benefit of meeting with individuals who were directly affected by the events that precipitated the Inquiry. They spoke poignantly about the pain of losing a child, and the added stress and shame that follow when the loss becomes the subject of criminal proceedings. The central role that flawed pediatric forensic pathology played in these cases was unmistakeable.

One tragic case involved William Mullins-Johnson, who was convicted of the first-degree murder of his niece Valin, in large measure because of the pathology evidence of Dr. Charles Smith. Dr. Smith's opinion was that the little girl had been strangled and sexually assaulted while Mr. Mullins-Johnson was babysitting her. This opinion was ultimately determined to be wrong. Mr. Mullins-Johnson has been found to have been wrongly convicted and was acquitted, but only after spending more than 12 years in prison.

During his testimony at the Inquiry, Dr. Smith was invited by Mr. Mullins-Johnson's lawyer to apologize. Mr. Mullins-Johnson was pointed out to him in the audience. Struggling with emotion, Dr. Smith offered his apology. Mr. Mullins-Johnson's spontaneous and deeply moving response is an eloquent testament to the human cost of failed pathology where a child dies in suspicious circumstances. This was their exchange:

DR. CHARLES SMITH: Could you stand, sir?

(BRIEF PAUSE)

DR. CHARLES SMITH: Sir, I don't expect that you would forgive me, but I do want to make it — I'm sorry. I do want to make it very clear to you that I am profoundly sorry for the role that I played in the ultimate decision that affected you. I am sorry.

MR. WILLIAM MULLINS-JOHNSON: For my healing, I'll forgive you but I'll never forget what you did to me. You put me in an environment where I could have been killed any day for something that never happened. You destroyed my family, my brother's relationship with me and my niece that's still left and my nephew that's still living. They hate me because of what you did to me. I'll never forget that but for my own healing I must forgive you.

This Inquiry was given two tasks. The first is to determine what went so badly wrong in the practice and oversight of pediatric forensic pathology in Ontario, especially as it relates to the criminal justice system. This task is addressed in Volume 2. It is my report on the systemic review and assessment of the practice and oversight of pediatric forensic pathology in Ontario from 1981 to 2001. It chronicles the systemic failings that occurred as they affected the criminal justice system.

My second task is to make recommendations to restore and enhance the public confidence in pediatric forensic pathology. That is the subject of Volume 3. My recommendations attempt to ensure that pediatric forensic pathology appropriately supports society's interest in protecting children from harm and bringing those who do harm children before the courts to be dealt with according to the law. If implemented, my recommendations will, I hope, also ensure that no one has to endure the horror of being charged criminally or having a family pulled apart or being wrongfully convicted because of flawed forensic pathology.

GROWING CONCERNS AND THE ESTABLISHMENT OF THE COMMISSION

From 1981 to 2005, Dr. Smith worked as a pediatric pathologist at Toronto's world-renowned Hospital for Sick Children (SickKids). Although he had no formal training or certification in forensic pathology, as the 1980s came to an end he started to become involved in pediatric cases that engaged the criminal justice system. Then, in 1992, he was appointed director of the newly established Ontario Pediatric Forensic Pathology Unit (OPFPU) at SickKids. He soon came to dominate pediatric forensic pathology in Ontario. He worked at the best children's hospital in Canada. His experience seemed unequalled, and his manner brooked no disagreement. He was widely seen as the expert to go to for the most difficult criminally suspicious pediatric deaths. In many of these cases his view of the cause of death was the critical opinion, and figured prominently in the outcome.

Over the course of the 1990s, Dr. Smith's reputation grew. But public concerns about his professional competence did as well. As early as 1991, a year before Dr. Smith's appointment as director, a trial judge acquitted a girl who, as a 12-year-old babysitter, had been charged with manslaughter in the death of 16-month-old Amber. His reasons for judgment strongly criticized Dr. Smith, the Crown's central witness, for both his methodology and his conclusions. The case is a cautionary tale of the devastating impact that flawed forensic pathology and irresponsible expert testimony can have on the lives of both those whose children die in suspicious circumstances and those accused of having caused the death. It was also a harbinger of things to come.

Over the decade, this judgment was followed by other warning signals about Dr. Smith's competence and professionalism. Unfortunately, throughout the 1990s, these signs were largely ignored by those tasked with the oversight of Dr. Smith and his work. Ultimately, 14 years after the first warning signal had sounded, the growing concerns could no longer go unrecognized. They culminated in what is now known as the Chief Coroner's Review. In 2005, Dr. Barry McLellan, who had recently become the Chief Coroner for Ontario, called a full review into the work of Dr. Smith in criminally suspicious cases and homicides in the 1990s.

He announced that, to maintain public confidence, five highly respected forensic pathologists external to the Office of the Chief Coroner for Ontario (OCCO) would conduct a formal review of all the criminally suspicious cases since 1991 in which Dr. Smith had conducted the autopsy or provided a consultation opinion. The purpose of the review was to ensure that the conclusions reached by Dr. Smith were reasonably supported on the materials available.

Each of the five reviewers has formal training and certification in forensic pathology, and all are eminently qualified for the task asked of them. I am satisfied that the five forensic pathologists are among the very best in the world. The OCCO was extremely fortunate to obtain their services.

The results of the Chief Coroner's Review may be summarized as follows:

1. In all but one of the 45 cases examined, the reviewers agreed that Dr. Smith had conducted the important examinations that were indicated.
2. In nine of the 45 cases, the reviewers did not agree with significant facts that appeared in either Dr. Smith's report or his testimony.
3. In 20 of the 45 cases, the reviewers took issue with Dr. Smith's opinion in either his report or his testimony, or both.[1] In 12 of those 20 cases, there had been findings of guilt by the courts.[2]

The results of the Review, released on April 19, 2007, constituted the last and most serious blow to public faith in pediatric forensic pathology and the central role it must play in criminal proceedings involving child deaths. Six days later, by an Order in Council signed on April 25, 2007, the Province of Ontario established this Commission.

The Order in Council required the Commission to conduct a systemic review and assessment of the way in which pediatric forensic pathology was practised and overseen in Ontario, particularly as it relates to the criminal justice system from 1981 to 2001, the years in which Dr. Smith was involved. It was also to consider any changes made since 2001. The purpose of the review was to provide the basis for the Commission to make recommendations to restore and enhance public confidence in pediatric forensic pathology in Ontario and its future use in investigations and criminal proceedings.

The Order in Council directed me to the cases examined by the Chief Coroner's Review, particularly the 20 in which the reviewers had serious concerns about Dr. Smith's work. The purpose was not to examine every aspect of these cases, but to determine what they reveal about what can and did go wrong in the practice and oversight of pediatric forensic pathology in those years, to enable recommendations about the future to be made.

Like many public inquiries, this Inquiry was called in the aftermath of a loss of public confidence in an essential public service. The public was understandably shocked by the results of the Chief Coroner's Review. In many of the 20 cases, parents or caregivers were charged with criminal offences that bear a significant social stigma. Some of those charged were convicted and incarcerated. In some of the cases, siblings of the deceased children were removed from the care of their parents. In Valin's case, the Court of Appeal for Ontario has determined that a miscarriage of justice occurred. An examination of the practice and oversight exemplified in these cases is essential if the systemic review is to achieve the purpose intended for it in the Order in Council — namely, to provide the basis for recommendations to restore the public confidence lost as a result of what happened in these cases. The Inquiry was required to address the legitimate questions about what went wrong with the practice and oversight of pediatric forensic pathology in order to fulfill that purpose and to ensure, so far as possible, that what went wrong does not happen again.

THE SCIENCE OF FORENSIC PATHOLOGY

The purpose of forensic pathology is to assist the state to find out why its citizens die. The medical dimension of forensic pathology involves the study of disease and injury in a deceased person, using the basic principles and methodologies of pathology to determine, if possible, the cause of death, and to address the timing of injuries or other medical issues that help explain the death. Its legal dimension is to assist the state's legal systems, most importantly, the criminal justice system, to understand how the death occurred by explaining the relevant pathology.

Forensic pathology typically involves the performance of a post-mortem examination, also called an autopsy, which entails the dissection of the body, an examination of organs and tissues, and ancillary investigations including X-rays, laboratory examinations, and toxicology testing. Forensic pathologists do more than just perform the post-mortem examination, however. They are called on to meet with other members of the death investigation team to discuss their work. And they must be able to communicate their findings effectively to various participants in the criminal justice system, including police, prosecutors, defence counsel, and the court. In summary, the forensic pathologist focuses on interpreting the post-mortem findings to assist in the end point of the death investigation required by the state, which may include a criminal trial, an inquest, or a coroner's finding of cause and manner of death made without an inquest.

Pediatric forensic pathology encompasses the subset of cases within forensic pathology that involves the deaths of infants, children, and adolescents. Although training and experience in pediatric pathology can add great value to the forensic investigation of a pediatric death, forensic pathology remains the core discipline for death investigations in pediatric forensic cases.

The distinctiveness of forensic pathology can be seen by comparing it to clinical pathology. Although the fundamental scientific principles of pathology apply equally to forensic pathology and to clinical pathology, their analytical frameworks are very different. The clinical pathologist focuses on providing diagnostically useful advice to a clinician to assist in the medical management of a patient. The forensic pathologist, in contrast, focuses on providing diagnostically useful conclusions for the death investigation team and the judicial process.

It follows that, although every forensic pathologist needs to be a competent clinical pathologist, the opposite is not true. Many competent clinical pathologists will never have an interest in forensic work and will never need to obtain the requisite knowledge and expertise in forensic work. A forensic pathologist, however, must be trained in, and develop an aptitude for, the requirements of the legal process. This requires an emphasis in the conduct of the post-mortem examination on identifying forensically significant findings such as injury, collecting potentially relevant evidence, and maintaining its continuity, none of which arise in clinical pathology. It requires that post-mortem documentation serve the needs of the participants in the justice system, including the coroner, police, Crown, defence, and court — another dimension that does not arise in clinical pathology. And it is essential that forensic pathologists be able to testify fairly, objectively, and in language that clearly communicates their findings. Few medical practitioners have, or require, any detailed understanding of the legal system and the legal investigative method. Becoming proficient in these areas is thus one of the features distinguishing forensic pathologists from their clinical counterparts.

The criminal justice system values finality. However, forensic pathology is an evolving science in which controversies exist, and where findings and opinions often require interpretation. This tension underlies much of the discussion in Volume 3. Moreover, the evolution of scientific knowledge will often be accompanied by controversy — as pathologists debate whether the existing scientific knowledge permits certain opinions to be reasonably formed, and whether new scientific knowledge casts doubt on previously expressed opinions or, at the very least, modifies the levels of confidence with which those opinions can reasonably be expressed.

The reliability of forensic pathology opinions matters a great deal to the criminal justice system. In cases in which there are important issues of pathology, as often occurs in pediatric death cases, flawed pathology can lead to tragic outcomes. The cases we examined at this Inquiry provide graphic evidence of that reality. Flawed pathology can result in a parent, family member, or caregiver being wrongly entangled in the criminal justice system, and wrongfully convicted and incarcerated, as happened to Mr. Mullins-Johnson in Valin's case.

It is equally tragic, however, if flawed pathology steers the criminal justice system away from the true perpetrator, as happened in Jenna's case. In that case, the erroneous pathology failed to focus the criminal investigation on Jenna's babysitter. Instead, Brenda Waudby, Jenna's mother, became the focus of the investigation. As a result, the babysitter, who was the one responsible for Jenna's death, escaped detection for many years.

In either situation, whether the flawed pathology plays a part in a wrongful conviction or in allowing a criminal to escape detection, justice is not served and public confidence in the legal system is diminished. As we will see, both the science and the criminal justice system have important roles to play in ensuring against either possibility.

THE PRACTICE OF PEDIATRIC FORENSIC PATHOLOGY

My review clearly demonstrates the kinds of serious failures that occurred in the practice of pediatric forensic pathology in Ontario from 1981 to 2001. It must be remembered, however, that what was happening with pediatric forensic pathology reflects in very large measure what was happening with forensic pathology generally. The practices used, the oversight mechanisms available, and the short-comings were common to both. In this sense, pediatric forensic pathology is a subset of forensic pathology.

Moreover, these serious failures took place within a setting larger than the individual pathologists. As I later describe, the senior officials who oversaw the death investigation system must also be held responsible for the tragic events about which I heard.

I have necessarily drawn heavily on the evidence I heard about the work of Dr. Smith in the criminally suspicious cases that were the subject of the Chief Coroner's Review. The evidence provides little basis, however, on which firm conclusions can be drawn about his work in hospital pathology or his work for the OCCO in cases that were not criminally suspicious.

This focus on Dr. Smith's work in criminally suspicious cases reflects the reality that the errors he made were a primary cause of the significant loss of public confidence in the use of forensic pathology in pediatric criminal cases which made the review necessary. I have not attempted to determine the frequency with which these kinds of errors were made, or the extent to which flawed practices were followed by Dr. Smith or by others in those years. That was not my task. What is important is to determine the ways in which the practice of pediatric forensic pathology could and did go badly wrong, so that the problems thus revealed can be addressed and, to the extent possible, prevented from happening again.

Although much of what we heard dealt with Dr. Smith, the evidence also showed that, in a number of instances, other pathologists were involved as well. Some made the same errors he did. Many, and in some instances most, followed some of the same practices. In all these instances, however, the serious errors that were made, whether by Dr. Smith or others, exemplify grave systemic problems with the practice of pediatric forensic pathology in Ontario at that time. These troubling problems were not confined to Dr. Smith. Without correction of these systemic failings, these errors could well occur again. They were not merely the isolated acts of a single pathologist which could be fixed by his removal.

My review thus identifies a wide range of failings in the practice of pediatric forensic pathology in Ontario from 1981 to 2001. These failings provide the basis for devising systemic changes to the practices used by pathologists particularly in criminally suspicious pediatric cases. The recommendations I make in Volume 3 respond directly to these findings and will, I hope, ensure that pediatric forensic pathology can properly serve the criminal justice system in the future.

I turn, then, to the various aspects of Dr. Smith's work that I found wanting and that demonstrate systemic failings in the practice of pediatric forensic pathology from 1981 to 2001.

18 Alternatives to Adjudication/Alternatives within Adjudication

(a) The Mediator and the Judge†

Torstein Eckhoff

Mediation consists of influencing the parties to come to agreement by appealing to their own interest. The mediator may make use of various means to attain this goal. He may work on the parties' ideas of what serves them best, for instance, in such a way that he gets them to consider their common interests as more essential than they did previously, or their competing interests as less essential. He may also look for possibilities of resolution which the parties themselves have not discovered and try to convince them that both will be well served with his suggestion. The very fact that a suggestion is proposed by an impartial third party may also, in certain cases, be sufficient for the parties to accept it (*cf.* Schelling, 1960, pp. 62, 63, 71 and 143 ff.). The mediator also has the possibility of using promises or threats. He may, for instance, promise the parties help or support in the future if they become reconciled or he may threaten to ally himself with one of them if the other does not give in. A mediator does not necessarily have to go in for compromise solutions, but for many reasons he will, as a rule, do so. The compromise is often the way of least resistance for one who shall get the parties to agree to an arrangement. As pointed out by Aubert (1963, p. 39) it may also contribute to the mediator's own prestige that he promotes intermediate solutions. Therewith he appears as the moderate and reasonable person with ability to see the problem from different angles — in contrast to the parties who will easily be suspected of having been onesided and quarrelsome since they have not managed to resolve the conflict on their own.

In order that both parties should have confidence in the mediator and be willing to co-operate with him and listen to his advice, it is important that they consider him impartial. This gives him an extra reason to follow the line of compromise (Aubert, 1963, p. 39, and Eckhoff, 1965, pp. 13–14). For, by giving both parties some support, he shows that the interests of one lie as close to his heart as those of the other. Regard for impartiality carries with it the consequence that the mediator sometimes must display caution in pressing the parties too hard. That the mediator, for instance, makes a threat to one of the parties to ally himself with the opponent unless compliance is forthcoming, may be an effective means of exerting pressure, but will easily endanger confidence in his impartiality. This can reduce his possibilities for getting the conflict resolved if threats do not work and it can weaken his future prestige as a mediator.

The conditions for a mediator are best in cases where both parties are interested in having the conflict resolved. The stronger this common interest is, the greater reason they have for bringing the conflict before a third party, and the more motivated they will be for co-operating actively with him in finding a solution, and for adjusting their demands in such a way that solution can be reached.

If the parties, or one of them, is, to begin with, not motivated for having the conflict resolved, or in any case not motivated to agree to any compromise, such motives must be *created* in him, for instance with the help of threats or sanctions. Cases may occur where the parties (or the unwilling one of them), may have a mediator forced upon them, and under pressure of persuasion from him or from the environment agree to an arrangement. But mediation under such circumstances presents difficulties, among other reasons, because it demands a balancing between the regard for impartiality and the regard for exertion of sufficient pressure. If the conditions for resolving the conflict by a judgement or administrative decision exist these will, as a rule, be more effective procedures than mediation in the cases described here.

That normative factors are considered relevant for the solution[] can in certain cases be helpful during mediation. By referring to a norm (e.g., concerning what is right and wrong) the mediator may get the parties to renounce unreasonable demands so that their points of view approach each other. Even if the parties do not feel bound by the norms, it is conceivable that others consider it important that they be followed and that the mediator can therefore argue that a party will be exposed to disapproval if he does not accommodate.

The norms will be of special support for the mediator if the parties are generally in agreement on their content and are willing to submit to them, so that the reason that there is a conflict at all can be traced back to the fact that the norms do not cover all aspects of the difference. The remainder which is not covered will then have the features of a fairly pure conflict of interests where the norms have brought the points of departure nearer one another than they would otherwise have been.

If, however, the parties consider the norms as giving answers to the questions being disputed, but disagree on what the answers are, the possibilities for mediation will, as a rule, be weakened. In the first place, the probability that the conflict will at all be made the object of mediation is reduced, among other reasons, because bringing it before a judge will often be possible and more likely in these cases. Secondly, mediation which has been begun may be made difficult because of the parties' disagreement concerning the norms or the relevant facts. This is the more true the more inflexibly the opinions are opposed to each other and the more value-laden they are. The parties' resistance to compromising on questions of rights or truth makes itself felt also when the mediator appears in the arena. Perhaps the presence of a third party will make the parties even more set on asserting their rights than they otherwise

would have been. The mediator can try to 'de-ideologize' the dispute by arguing that it is not always wise to 'stand on one's right' and that one should not 'push things to extremes', but go the 'golden middle road'.[1] Sometimes he succeeds in this and manages to concentrate attention on the interest-aspects, so that the usual mediation arguments will have an effect. But it may also go the other way. The mediator lets himself be influenced by the parties to see the normative aspects as the most important, and ends up by judging instead of mediating. And even if he does not go so far, his opinions concerning norms and facts may inhibit his eagerness to mediate. In any case, it may be distasteful for him to work for a compromise if he has made up his mind that one of the parties is completely right and the other wrong.

Hoebel's survey (1954) of conflict-resolution in various primitive cultures confirms the impression that conditions are, generally speaking, less favourable for mediation than for other forms of conflict-resolution when the conflicts are characterized by disagreements about normative factors. Most of the third party institutions he describes have more in common with what I in this article call judgemental and administrative activity than with mediation. The only example in Hoebel's book of the development of a pure mediation institution for the resolution of disputes[,] which have a strongly normative element, is found among the Ifugao-people in the northern part of Luzon in the Philippines. This is an agricultural people without any kind of state-form but with well developed rules governing property rights, sale, mortgage, social status (which is conditional on how much one owns), family relations, violation of rights, etc. Conflicts concerning these relations occur often. If the parties do not manage to solve them on their own they are regularly left to a mediator, who is called a *mokalun*. This is not a permanent office that belongs to certain persons but a task to which the person is appointed for the particular case. In practice the *mokalun* is always a person of high rank and generally someone who has won esteem as a head-hunter. He is chosen by the plaintiff, but is regarded as an impartial intermediary, not as a representative for a party. The parties are obligated to keep peace so long as mediation is in progress and they may not have any direct contact with each other during this period. The *mokalun* visits them alternately. He brings offers of conciliation and replies to these offers, and he tries, with the help of persuasion, and also generally with threats, to push through a conciliation. If he attains this he will receive good pay and increased prestige. If the mediation is not successful the conflict will remain unresolved and will perhaps result in homicide and blood feuds, for the *mokalun* has no authority to make decisions which are binding on the parties.

It is easy to point to features in the Ifugao culture which can have favoured the growth of such a method of conflict-resolution. On the one hand, there has obviously been a strong need to avoid open struggle within the local society, among other reasons, because the people were resident farmers who had put generations of work into terraces and irrigation works. On the other hand, there was no political leadership and no organized restraining power, and the conditions were therefore not favourable for conflict-resolution by judgement or coercive power. Nevertheless, it is noteworthy that the mediation arrangement functioned so well as it did, considering that it was applied to conflicts where divergent opinions of right and wrong were pitted against each other. It is natural to make a comparison with our present international conflicts, where the conditions are parallel to the extent that the danger for combat actions and the absence of other kinds of third party institutions create a strong need for mediation, but where the mediation institutions so far developed have been far less effective.

The *judge* is distinguished from the mediator in that his activity is related to the level of norms rather than to the level of interests. His task is not to try to reconcile the parties but to reach a decision about which of them is right. This leads to several important differences between the two methods of conflict-resolution. The mediator should preferably look forward, toward the consequences which may follow from the various alternative solutions, and he must work on the parties to get them to accept a solution. The judge, on the other hand, looks back to the events which have taken place (e.g., agreements which the parties have entered into, violations which one has inflicted on the other, etc.) and to the norms concerning acquisition of rights, responsibilities, etc. which are connected with these events. When he has taken his standpoint on this basis, his task is finished. The judge, therefore, does not have to be an adaptable negotiator with ability to convince and to find constructive solutions, as the mediator preferably should be. But he must be able to speak with authority on the existing questions of norms and facts in order to be an effective resolver of conflicts.

The possibility for judging in a dispute presupposes that the norms are considered relevant to the solution. The norms may be more or less structures.

They may consist in a formal set of rules (e.g., a judicial system, the by-laws of an organization or the rules of a game), in customs or only in vague notions of what is right and just. The normative frame of reference in which a decision is placed does not have to be the same — and does not even have to exist — for all those who have something to do with the conflict. What one person perceives as a judgement another may perceive as an arbitrary command. If, however, *none* of those involved (the parties, the third party, the environment) applies normative considerations to the relationship because all consider it a pure conflict of interests, decision by judgement is excluded.

A decision may be a 'judgement' (in the sense in which the term is used here) even if the parties do not comply with it. But the greater the possibility that a judgement will be lived up to, the more suitable judgement will be as a method for conflict-resolution, and the better reason will the person who desires a solution have for preferring that procedure. It is therefore of significance to map out the factors which promote and hinder compliance to judgements.

The parties' interests in the outcome play an important role in this connexion. If the main thing for them is to have the dispute settled, and it is of secondary importance what the content of the solution is, it will require very little for them to comply with the judgement. If, on the other hand, there are strong and competing interests connected with the outcome, so that submission to the judgement implies a great sacrifice for one or both of the parties, the question of compliance is more precarious.

That one party (voluntarily or by force) submits to a judgement in spite of the sacrifice it means for him[] may be due in part to norms and in part to the authority of the judge. There may be many reasons for the parties' respect for those *norms* on which the judge bases his decision; for instance, they may be internalized, or one fears gods' or people's punishment if one violates them, or one finds it profitable in the long run to follow them (e.g., because it creates confidence in one's business activities if one gains a reputation for law-abidance or because it makes the game more fun if the rules are followed). If the parties are sufficiently motivated to comply with the norms and give exhaustive answers to the question under dispute, then relatively modest demands are made on the judge's authority. If he is regarded as having knowledge of the norms and as having ability to find the facts, this will be sufficient to assure that his judgements are respected. Sometimes this is a simple assignment which many can fulfill. We may, for instance, take the case of two

369

chess players who have not yet completely learned the rules of the game and who disagree as to whether it is permissible to castle in the present position. They ask a more experienced player who is present and comply without question to his decision because they consider it obvious that the rules should be followed and know that he is acquainted with them. But there are also cases where insight into norms, and perhaps also ability to clarify the factual relations in the matter, presuppose special expertise which only a few have. The kind of expertise required varies with the nature of the normative ideas. It may be, for instance, that contact with supernatural powers is considered to provide special prerequisites for finding out what is true and right, or it may be life-experience or professional studies. Monopolizing of insight may be a natural consequence of the fact that a norm system is large and cannot be taken in at a glance, but there are also many examples of systematic endeavours on the part of experts to prevent intruders from acquiring their knowledge.

If the parties are not sufficiently strongly motivated to comply with the norms which regulate their mutual rights and duties, or if they do not regard these as giving exhaustive answers to the matter of dispute, the judgement must appear as something more than a conveyance of information in order to command respect. The parties must, in one way or another, be bound or forced to adhere to it. One condition which may contribute to this is that, in addition to the primary norms which define the parties' mutual rights and obligations, there is also a set of secondary norms of adjudication which single out the judge as the proper person to settle the dispute and which possibly also impose upon the parties the duty to abide by his decision. That the judge is in this way equipped with *authority* is in many cases sufficient reason for the parties to consider themselves bound to live up to his decisions. But the establishment of authority often presupposes power, and even if the authority-relationship is established, it may sometimes be necessary to press through a decision by force. The power can reside with the judge, with someone he represents (e.g., the state) or with others who are interested in the decision being respected (e.g., the winning party or his relatives or friends). And it can have various bases: physical or military strength, control of resources on which the parties are dependent, powers of sorcery, etc. How *much* power is necessary depends partly on what other factors promote and hinder compliance, and partly upon the relative strength of the enforcing authority and the disobedient party.

That the parties and others have confidence in the judge's impartiality promotes compliance [with] judgements. It strengthens the belief that the decisions he makes are right and it facilitates enforcement by making the application of force more legitimate. As mentioned before, it is also important for the mediator to appear impartial, but the manner of showing impartiality is different for the two kinds of third parties.[2] To a certain extent the judge can display that he gives equal consideration to both parties, for instance, by giving both the same possibilities for arguing and for presenting evidence. But he cannot, like the mediator, systematically endeavour to reach compromises, because the norms sometimes demand decision in favour of one of the parties. If he finds that one party is completely right he must judge in his favour, and the outcome of the case will not in itself be a testimony to his giving equal consideration to both.

But the judge has other possibilities for appearing impartial. Sometimes his person gives sufficient guarantee. He is, for instance, because of his high rank, his contact with supernatural powers or his recognized wisdom and strength of character regarded as infallible, or at least freed from suspicion of partisanship. The privilege of the judge to assume a retired position during the proceedings and not to engage in argumentation with the parties makes it easier to ascribe such qualities to him than to the mediator. Another significant factor is that there are, as a rule, small possibilities for checking the rightness of a judgement because this presupposes knowledge of both the system of norms and the facts of the particular case. To maintain a belief that certain persons are infallible can, nevertheless, present difficulties, especially in cultures characterized by democratization and secularization. To reduce or conceal the human factor in decision-making will therefore often be better suited to strengthening confidence in the decisions. Letting the judge appear as a 'mouthpiece of the law', who cannot himself exert any influence worth mentioning on the outcome of the cases, tends to remove the fear that his own interests, prejudices, sympathies and antipathies may have impact on his rulings.

Tendencies to overestimate the influence of the norms and underestimate the influence of the judge may also have other functions than strengthening confidence in the judge's impartiality. Firstly, these tendencies contribute to the transmission of authority from the norm system to the individual decisions. Secondly, the conditions are favourable for a gradual and often almost unnoticeable development of a norm system through court practice, so that the resistance to change is reduced. And thirdly, the judge will be less exposed to criticism and self-reproach when he (both in his own and others' eyes) avoids appearing as personally responsible for his decisions. This is important because it might otherwise involve great strain to make decisions in disputes where the parties' contentions are strongly opposed to each other, where there are perhaps great interests at stake for both, and where it may be extremely doubtful who is right (*cf.* Eckhoff, and Jacobsen, 1960, especially pp. 37 ff.). It is therefore not surprising that many techniques have been used in the various judicial systems for the purpose of eliminating, limiting or concealing the influence of the judge. The use of ordeals and drawing of lots in the administration of justice (*cf.* Eckhoff, 1965, pp. 16–17; and Wedberg, 1935) may be mentioned as examples of this, and the same is true for the technique of judicial argumentation which gives the decisions the appearance of being the products of knowledge and logic, and not of evaluation and choice.

Judicial activity and formation of norms serve to support each other mutually. On the one hand, the judge is dependent on normative premises on which he can base his decisions. The greater the relevance attributed to them, and the stronger the ideological anchoring of the norm system, the more favourable are the conditions for conflict-resolution by judgement. On the other hand, the activity of judges can contribute to the spreading of knowledge about norms, to their increased recognition and authority, and to a gradual extension of the norm system to cover new types of conflict situations.

The activity of judging is in these respects quite different from the activity of mediating. As mentioned before, the task of the mediator becomes more difficult the more emphasis the parties place on the normative aspects of the conflict (presupposing that there is disagreement about these, as there usually will be in conflict situations). The mediator, therefore, must try to 'de-ideologize' the conflict, for instance, by stressing that interests are more important than the question of who is right and who is wrong, or by arguing that one ought to be reasonable and willing to compromise. The use of mediation in certain types of disputes may tend to create or reinforce the norm that willingness to compromise is the proper behaviour in conflict situations, and thereby to reduce the significance of such norms as judges base their decisions on.

The contrasts between the two types of third-party intervention make it difficult to combine the role of the judge and the role of the mediator in a satisfactory way. Indeed it does happen that a third party first tries to mediate between the parties and if that does not succeed, passes judgement.[3] Also the reverse is conceivable: that a third party first passes judgement and then proceeds to mediate when he sees that the judgement will not be respected. But in both cases attempts to use one method may place hindrances in the way of the other. By mediating one may weaken the normative basis for a later judgement and perhaps also undermine confidence in one's impartiality as a judge; and by judging first one will easily reduce the willingness to compromise of the party who was supported in the judgement, and will be met with suspicion of partiality by the other.

When the establishment of new third-party institutions is sought, for instance, by a legislator who is looking for new ways of settling labour conflicts, or by those who are working for the peaceful adjustment of international conflicts, there may be a dilemma about which way to go. Should one go in for building up the norm system, and for strengthening the normative engagement with the aim of having as many conflicts as possible decided by judgement? Or ought one rather [to] rely on 'de-ideologization' and mediation? In considering such questions it is important not to let oneself be led by superficial analogies but to take account of all the relevant factors. Regarding international conflicts, for instance, one must consider that there is no superior instance which is powerful enough to force a powerful state to obedience. This has the consequence that courts can hardly be effective organs for the resolution of conflicts where substantial interests are at stake. Mediation also presents difficulties, among other reasons because the parties often place great emphasis on the moral and legal aspects of the conflict, and have strongly divergent opinions concerning both norms and (perhaps especially) the relevant facts. But there is good reason to believe that the difficulties in mediation are, after all, easier to overcome and that endeavours should therefore go in the direction of reducing the normative engagement.

(b) Civil Justice Reform and Mandatory Civil Mediation in Saskatchewan: Lessons from a Maturing Program†

Julie Macfarlane and Michaela Keet

I. INTRODUCTION

[1] Court-connected mediation is becoming an increasingly familiar process in Canada, a model of dispute resolution that litigants and lawyers encounter regularly in different venues across the country. Ten years ago, only Ontario and Saskatchewan were innovating in this area. While Ontario's Superior Court mandatory mediation program has received widespread attention as it progressed from Practice Directions to an established rule of civil procedure,[1] Saskatchewan's equally ambitious civil justice reform has gone relatively unnoticed. Moreover, the Saskatchewan program is unique in its focus on broadening access to justice and quality outcomes, in a province that has never suffered from the type of court backlog that has driven reforms elsewhere. After ten years of experience, combined with an extensive earlier history of farm debt mediation, the Saskatchewan Queen's Bench program offers an excellent window into an evolved court-connected mediation model — and a chance to look deeper into the incremental development of civil justice reform.

[2] Ten years ago, the Saskatchewan legislation proposing mandatory mediation in the Queen's Bench was met with an outburst of rhetoric on all sides. Program administrators and their political leaders described the proposed mandatory mediation program as a response to problems in the civil justice system. During the second reading of the Bill, Justice Minister Robert Mitchell set the stage with the following statement:

> In the best of all possible worlds, justice would be done efficiently, inexpensively and with minimal emotional pain to those involved. But until legal reforms take place ... you're entering a less than perfect world that will require caution, stamina and bravery to survive.[2]

"The challenge," he continued, "is fundamental — the justice system's failure to serve the needs of our citizens."[3] He went on to identify "two major failings" as "the high cost and delay associated with traditional adversarial litigation," and the fact that "the formal adversarial basis of litigation is simply not suited to resolving certain types of disputes," including disputes that carry a "heavy emotional overtone."[4]

[3] The Saskatchewan Bar was less convinced. Lawyers saw the imposition of mediation as removing their control from the litigation and resolution process, and carrying the suggestion that they were failing in their role as advocates. They responded, in defense, that the new program added additional expense and delay to litigation and that "the interests of litigants ... are better served by the advice of counsel than by the compulsory mediation provisions recently introduced."[5] The polarization of the debate surrounding mandatory mediation continued through the program's early years.

[4] The original concerns of the Saskatchewan Bar regarding mandatory civil case mediation were unsurprising and mirrored reservations expressed in other Bars over the introduction of these types of initiative. Court-connected mediation programs are embedded within a process that is inherently adversarial. The interaction of those programs with the litigation process — and the norms, behaviors and expectations that support it — produces a complex and often tense interplay of opposing cultures of conflict and conflict resolution.[6] Mandatory mediation introduced a process that was new to most lawyers and clients and concepts that challenge traditional expectations of dispute resolution between adversaries. Mediators invite collaborative discussion at a time when most lawyers and their clients are preparing for battle. The process of mediation shifts the focus away from the law to the parties' underlying interests and, in its tone, differs fundamentally from the steps of a lawsuit that come before and after.[7]

[5] The passage of ten years, however, has produced dramatic change in the shape and size of resistance

---

† (2005) 42 Alta. L. Rev. (Special Issue: Civil Justice and Civil Justice Reform) 677–709 at paras. 1–18, 28–78. Reproduced with permission. [Notes and/or references omitted.]

to mandatory mediation, a change noticeable in both the process and the outcome of the Saskatchewan program's recent evaluation.[8] Representatives of the Government, Bar, Bench and the professional mediation association came together to work in an Advisory Committee, which provided both input and legitimacy to the independent evaluation. Lawyers, judges, clients and mediators committed themselves to conversations in focus groups and in interviews about the pros and cons of their experiences with mandatory mediation. The evaluation concluded that the central issue in this debate is no longer whether there should be some form of mediation requirement in Saskatchewan, but how the program can be enhanced and improved for lawyers and clients alike. The evaluation pinpointed a number of lessons from experience that suggested modifications in the systems design and provided useful signposts for other, less evolved court-connected programs.

[6] Program evaluation in this setting has tended to focus on quantitative, efficiency-related characteristics including settlement rates, impact on court dockets and comparative costs of the processes for clients.[9] A focus on efficiencies reflects the primary objective of most court-based and institutional mediation programs: saving resources expended on protracted litigation. However the concerns that have tended to drive programs in other parts of Canada have played a secondary role in Saskatchewan. Instead, a concern for the quality of people's encounters with the civil justice system figures prominently in the original objectives for the Saskatchewan program. Mediation here is said to be about broadening the parameters of the dispute, returning control to the parties and paying respect to relationships. The Saskatchewan program envisioned a greater role for litigants in the resolution of their own disputes, an objective that emerged from the Department of Justice's broader Core Strategy on Dispute Resolution:

> Behind this Core Strategy lies a recognition of a growing expectation by people throughout the world for greater input into the resolution of their own disputes and greater control over solutions that affect them. No longer are people completely satisfied with decisions that are imposed on them by a third party. People are seeking solutions that they have created themselves.[10]

Quantitative research methods by their very nature cannot capture the details and nuances of such experiences. An evaluation of how successful the Saskatchewan program has been in enriching the experience of participatory justice in the court system called for the adoption of a qualitative approach to data collection and analysis. This is described in further detail below.

[7] The ultimate impact of mandatory mediation in Saskatchewan was expected to be both systemic and cultural, affecting how litigants understand the civil justice process and their role and responsibilities within it, and how lawyer–advocates participate in consensus-based problem-solving processes. Some of the indices of cultural change can be gleaned from earlier studies.[11] They include how seriously lawyers prepare for mediation; how and how much information is exchanged in advance of mediation; the seniority and experience of the lawyer sent to represent a client in mediation; expanding expectations of client participation in negotiation discussions; the willingness of counsel to accept a range of mediator expertise including non-lawyer mediators; the parallel use made of private voluntary mediation; and generally, the recognition of the need for new and different skills and knowledge in order to maximize the effectiveness of mediation. Indices that appear to reflect growing maturity among clients with the mediation process include recognition of the range of uses and benefits (including but not limited to settlement) of an early face-to-face meeting with the other side, rising expectations that their lawyers take mediation seriously and prepare thoroughly, and rising expectations of the mediator. Many of these issues and characteristics surfaced in the Saskatchewan evaluation.

[8] The nature of the program's original goals, coupled with the depth of experience and expertise generated before and through the program's operation, presented researchers with an opportunity to move beyond quantitative questions over settlement rates and timing to the next level of inquiry about the impact of court-connected mediation. The evaluation shows that over the program's ten year history, some of its ambitious goals for cultural and systemic change are being realized. The process of litigation has been altered in some significant ways, for both lawyers and clients. The evaluation report also reveals barriers that continue to affect the experience of lawyers, clients and mediators in negative ways. The Department of Justice has incorporated several changes in response to the evaluation and is poised to move forward in relation to others. In the following discussion, we will provide an overview of the evaluation and will identify some significant results tied to the perspectives of lawyers and clients. As one of Canada's first court-connected mediation programs to enter a stage of maturation, the Saskatche-

wan program offers a rich learning opportunity in the evolving process of civil reform.

II. EVALUATING THE SASKATCHEWAN PROGRAM

A. Program Structure

[9] Mediation programs in the civil court structure are rarely complex. Most variations turn on the "mandatory/voluntary" question: to what extent the parties must opt in or can opt out of the mediation requirement. In Saskatchewan, all civil cases filed in the Queen's Bench must proceed to a mediation unless an exemption is formally granted (the so-called "opt out" model also used in Ontario).[12] Programs also vary somewhat in the procedural requirements that accompany the mediation session. Ontario's program, for example, requires that the parties exchange a statement of issues in advance of the mediation. In this respect, the Saskatchewan program is not prescriptive. Aside from the requirement to attend the mediation session, the program operates within a minimal framework of procedural rules, something seen as increasingly important in maintaining the program's flexibility.

[10] Another notable variable between programs is how the costs of mediation are covered. The Ontario program provides a roster of "approved" mediators with whom the parties privately contract at a fixed tariff.[13] In Saskatchewan, mediators are assigned by the Department of Justice from a pool of staff and contract mediators — all experienced mediators with a variety of professional backgrounds, only some of whom are lawyers. Because the pool of Justice mediators is small, mediators work together on a regular basis and have a cohesive commitment to an interest-based approach.[14] For the initial session, the cost of the mediation is borne by the Department of Justice, with the parties only covering the cost of an increased filing fee.[15] The cost of any subsequent sessions is shared by the parties themselves.

[11] First introduced in 1994 in the form of a pilot project in Regina and Swift Current, Saskatchewan's mandatory mediation program has since been expanded to Saskatoon and Prince Albert and applies to 80 percent of all (non-family) civil cases in the Court of Queen's Bench.[16] As soon as a case enters the system, the parties must attend a mediation session; the requirement to attend is invoked "after the close of pleadings" and is subject to few exceptions.[17] The requirement to attend applies to litigants themselves, although in most cases they will be accompanied by counsel.

[12] The mediation session begins with two individual caucuses, each roughly one half-hour in length, and, in the vast majority of cases, proceeds to a joint session immediately following the caucuses. This first session may last up to three hours in total, leaving parties the option to continue at that time, or later, by agreement with the mediator.

[13] As is the case with standard steps in the litigation process, the program operates with enforcement mechanisms. The mediator will file a Certificate of Completion at the end of the mediation.[18] A party may request a Certificate of Non-Attendance if another party fails to attend.[19] The mediation session must be completed "before taking any further step in the action or matter"[20] and is avoided at the peril of the non-complying party. In response to the Certificate of Non-Attendance, the court may either order the party to attend mediation, order another mediation with specific terms or, under certain conditions, strike the pleadings of the party that failed to attend.[21]

[14] When the program was first introduced, the initial session was described as "mediation orientation." Mediators concentrated on informing the parties and their counsel about the option to mediate and helping them explore its feasibility in their particular case.[22] After a short time in operation (and perhaps once a critical mass of lawyers had heard the presentations), the sessions evolved into full mediations.[23] Mediators began more quickly to wade into the cases themselves, at first with the quiet and sometimes reluctant cooperation of clients and lawyers. Such "working sessions" are now the norm. Unlike some U.S. jurisdictions,[24] the legislation does not require that the parties negotiate or participate in the sessions in good faith. While concern over good faith participation lingers (see the discussion below), lawyers, mediators and clients have for the most part been motivated by the desire to use their time effectively, to move the case forward, exploring settlement wherever possible — a motivation that demonstrates the increasing acceptance of early mediation in Saskatchewan.

B. Historical Context

[15] While the structure of the program outlined above appears deceptively uncomplicated, it disguises a complex interplay of tension and opportunity. Ten years ago the concept of mandating a process whose success had, until that point, been attributed to its

voluntary nature[] was both ambitious and controversial. The history of mandatory mediation in Saskatchewan in fact begins years earlier, as a response to the agricultural crisis in the mid-1980s.[25] Administrators and policy makers hoped to mitigate the impact of the farm crisis by inserting mandatory mediation into foreclosure litigation, requiring lenders to attend mediation with landowners before proceeding with a foreclosure action. The program was a creative solution that increased the potential for lenders to receive money while farmers retained their land.[26] Where farmers could not keep their land, the process allowed them to negotiate the transition in a way that was more humane and respectful, and to emerge with their dignity intact. The farm debt program was an important part of the evolution of a mediation culture in Saskatchewan, which also included a family mediation program and a successful pre-trial settlement program.[27]

[16] The farm program has been considered extremely successful, achieving settlement rates in the range of 70–80 percent.[28] The volume of mediations generated by the farm program also enabled the Mediation Services branch (now the Dispute Resolution Office) of Saskatchewan Justice to develop a depth of expertise in mediation and a rapport with lawyers and with individual and institutional clients.[29] Meanwhile, the Branch was gaining experience with mediations in other areas, many of those also involving issues around land use (for example, expropriations and surface rights disputes).[30] In fee-for-service matters, where the parties voluntarily contract into mediations with a Justice mediator, the Branch was achieving a significant rate of full or partial resolutions — over 50 percent.[31]

[17] The Branch's cumulative experience, along with other examples of successful settlement-oriented processes in the province, led them to envision change on a larger scale. The "made in Saskatchewan" approach is clear in the following statement by the then Assistant Deputy Minister in the Department of Justice:

> Saskatchewan intends to remain on the leading edge of innovation in the area of dispute resolution, as it has traditionally been in the areas of health care, public insurance and public administration.[32]

The Department's growing experience with mediation was accompanied by shifts in the outside climate. Initiatives were beginning in the federal public service, recognizing the importance of government leadership in promoting collaborative approaches.[33]

Other external factors also played their part. The unregulated state of the mediation profession was starting to cause some discomfort for practitioners and for the government, and a program based on a qualified, supervised group of government mediators was one way to deal with these legitimate quality control questions.[34] Ontario was proceeding with its own court-connected dispute resolution program at roughly the same time.[35] Public opinion, as revealed through the press, and the perspective of some practicing lawyers, reveals a shifting consciousness, a readiness to accept the shortcomings of litigation and consider alternatives.[36]

[18] All of these factors combined to help crack open the window for the Justice Department to proceed with its ambitious goals.

. . . .

III. FEEDBACK FROM LAWYERS

A. Changing Views: Acceptance of Mediation

[28] Ten years into the program's operation, lawyers are expressing surprisingly consistent opinions about mandatory civil mediation. Although many identified reservations about design issues (and a few focused on the absence of widespread consultation at the time that legislation was passed), most lawyers share a positive view of the program. Furthermore, they see its objectives — the faster and more satisfactory reaching of settlement in some civil matters — as fully achievable.

[29] The benefits of mediation as described by Saskatchewan lawyers are highly consistent with the results of work conducted elsewhere.[43] Many lawyers we questioned spoke about the value of a structured face-to-face meeting that provides an opportunity to meet the other side and evaluate their credibility, as well the credibility of one's own client.[44] Some counsel also talked about the usefulness of mediation to address and defuse intense emotional issues.[45] A number acknowledged the difficulty of predicting whether a mediation meeting would be useful, a difficulty that could lead to both positive and negative results. Even in circumstances that did not seem conducive to mediation, lawyers have been surprised with what could be gained through early intervention.

[30] Most lawyers, including those who were more negative about mediation, acknowledged a significant shift in the attitude of the Saskatchewan Bar towards mediation in the last ten years. In addition to identi-

fying a cultural change within the Bar in the degree of openness and receptivity towards mediation and mandatory mediation (one respondent describing himself as originally "dragged into this kicking and screaming"), a number of lawyers gave us personal accounts of what was sometimes described as their "conversion." These lawyers all described their initial reactions to the introduction of mandatory mediation as highly skeptical and/or critical, and spoke of becoming gradually convinced of its real worth in at least a significant number of cases. Even those who were more personally cautious — broadly supportive but not entirely convinced — described a significant shift of attitudes among members of the Bar. As one lawyer put it, "mediation is no longer a dirty word."

[31] Most respondents were more interested in discussing how the program could be enhanced, not whether it should be maintained. The consensus that emerged from the evaluation was that the program is reaching its goals in many individual cases, but not in others. The reasons given for the failure or inappropriateness of mediation in these cases often refer to the behaviour of other lawyers; for example, the failure of the other side to adequately prepare, to take the mediation process seriously and a general absence of "good faith." These issues, and the design modifications proceeding from the evaluation, are discussed further below. In addition, the need to broaden the mediator's role in some cases — and in particular a desire to see greater pro-activity on the part of the mediator — was articulated by a number of lawyers and clients. This conclusion could have significant and general implications for the training of mediators in mandatory mediation programs, and is discussed in a separate section below.

B. Being Prepared: Pre-Mediation Information Exchange

[32] Since mediation in Saskatchewan, like Ontario, generally takes place prior to discovery, what information is exchanged before mediation has a significant impact on the usefulness of a mediation session at this stage. The present Saskatchewan program does not impose any explicit requirements of documentary or other exchange between the parties before coming to mediation. One of the principal reservations expressed about the program by lawyers and clients alike is the lack of information upon which to base substantive negotiations. This informational gap may arise from the nature of the file. In some medical malpractice cases, for example, damages may be difficult to assess at an early stage.

However in other cases, adequate information exists, but is simply not made available to the other side in a manner that facilitates settlement discussions.

[33] This problem is characteristic of frequently voiced concerns about a small minority of lawyers, who attend mediation but resist any serious negotiations. Lawyers often framed concerns in terms of an absence of "good faith" — that some of their colleagues were entering the mediation process unwilling to disclose relevant information or to search genuinely for a solution. A number of lawyers indicated, with high levels of frustration, that they have prepared conscientiously for mediation with their client only to be confronted by a lawyer on the other side who was not willing to bargain openly or in good faith. In other jurisdictions using mandatory mediation, some counsel have developed a practice of exchanging affidavits of documents before mediation and ensuring that information is furnished to the other side on their request.[46] Some Saskatchewan counsel, especially in smaller centers, told us that they have routinely asked the other side for documents in advance of mediation — a piecemeal solution to a widespread problem.

[34] Other jurisdictions have tried various strategies to address a similar issue of lack of preparedness. Some have required the parties to file pre-mediation submissions (for example, Ontario[47]), requirements that sometimes raise confidentiality concerns and often result in only minimal compliance.[48] Good faith rules[49] are highly controversial, and neither option found favour among our Saskatchewan respondents. Despite the level of complaints about the practice of not preparing or not committing to the process, lawyers were extremely reluctant to consider a rule that would penalize this type of behaviour.

[35] The evaluation concluded that a formal requirement to exchange information in advance of mediation would benefit all the users of the Saskatchewan program. The evaluation recommended the introduction of a new rule of civil procedure that would require that before proceeding to mediation, all parties file their statement of documents with the Court (sometimes described as the affidavit of documents). Such a modification would result in a slight adjustment to the stage at which mediation takes place, facilitating a further exchange of information between the parties that would occur naturally as the litigation process proceeds.[50] In their response to the evaluation, the Department of Justice has determined that rather than impose an obligation to exchange a statement as to documents, the program manager

will be given new powers to delay or adjourn mediation (at the request of one party) until this or other relevant information has been exchanged.[51]

[36] Complaints about lack of preparedness may simply mask a deeper problem. Some members of the Bar continue to regard mediation as a necessary hurdle to be jumped through rather than a constructive settlement opportunity. What is interesting about the data collected from the Saskatchewan Bar is the number of times that lawyers expressed themselves to be fully supportive of mediation, but complained that "the other side" was often less committed. This may or may not be the case, but it suggests that it is now normative to express support for mediation and to "blame" the other side (and in particular their lack of preparedness) for any failures. Predictably, few (if any) lawyers identified themselves as "inadequately prepared," and the risk revealed in such responses is that the inadequacies of the other side will be seen as an acceptable "excuse" for not using mediation constructively. However, the discourse may in fact indicate the achievement of maturity in the program, with the emphasis shifting from a debate over the legitimacy of mediation to a debate over who is doing it most effectively.

IV.   FEEDBACK FROM CLIENTS

A.   Collateral Benefits: The Value of a Face-to-face Meeting

[37] Clients we interviewed[] consistently identified classic benefits of mediation: the process's potential to humanize the dispute, enabling them to see the other party as a person and the process's ability to defuse emotion. Many tied these benefits to the opportunity to sit and discuss matters with the other party, face-to-face:

> "David," a corporate client involved in a contract dispute, said that he was able to gain more information than he would have in any other process, because the discussion was not constrained by the law. Mediation helped the parties reach an agreement, although the resolution was not finalized for two or three months after the session. He assigned importance to being able to speak honestly, without fear of legal repercussions: "It helped me to offload where I couldn't before"; "I felt I had something to say and to contribute to the process."

The message communicated by the following client was repeated often in client focus groups and interviews:

> It all started over hurt feelings. But then the lawyers got involved and it escalated. This was the first time we could sit down, face-to-face, and talk about it. That in itself was worth it.

[38] For some, it was the first time that the parties had actually met. A large institutional client in a commercial contract dispute appreciated that "we finally got to put a face to the voice and meet the people we were dealing with." For some clients, this chance to talk face-to-face left them feeling better about the dispute. An individual we questioned, involved in a debt collection with a large organizational plaintiff, described his experience as follows:

> [The process] gave me a chance to express my complaints.... I felt quite at ease, and was able to express what I wanted to express, and the [other party] was able to express their concerns. We were both listening and talking. It had a good feeling in that respect.

[39] In another matter, a client involved in a dispute with family members reflected that "there was a very good discussion ... we could see both points of view ... it was so good to sit face-to-face and just talk."

[40] Some clients, like David above, described themselves as having a significant role in the process and making a meaningful contribution. A significant number of institutional and individual clients valued the chance to explain their perspective. For example, a representative from a large corporation said that "it's an opportunity for [us] to make our philosophies and policies known." Others described the value of the information they gained from listening to the other side, leading them to change or broaden their perspectives on the dispute. One client, a representative of a large institutional defendant, expressed relief that he was finally able to see what the real issues were and to understand "where the other party was coming from." Importantly, most clients separated collateral benefits from the outcome of the session; many they described having made these types of gains regardless of whether the matter was settled that day.

[41] That is not to say that such positive experiences were universal. One plaintiff, whose complaints included physical and emotional abuse by the defendant, emphasized that telling her story again was both difficult and unproductive. Some clients indicated that they did not see any collateral benefits emerging from the process at all, with the sole result being delay, and held out little hope for the success

of mediation in other cases.[52] Overall, however, clients focused on the advantages of an early meeting with the other parties in an attempt to settle their dispute.

B. The Lawyer's Role: Lawyers Shaping Their Clients' Experiences

[42] That a face-to-face meeting can be valuable, and can generate collateral benefits for clients, is not a surprising conclusion. These kinds of benefits were arguably the very target of program designers in the Saskatchewan case. The more complex — and less openly anticipated — results of the evaluation are those that speak to the lawyer–client relationship and the lawyer's role. A large number of the clients we talked with spoke positively about mediation and its potential, but went on to express disappointment or even frustration with the influence of lawyers on the process. Some described the process as having been thwarted by other factors (such as the position taken by the other side or lack of information). However, over half of the clients complained of the actions or omissions of the lawyers, either their own or counsel for the other side. Whether lawyers deserve to carry this degree of responsibility for the process's outcomes is questionable; what is abundantly clear, however, is the extent to which lawyers shape the mediation experience from their clients' point of view:

> "Robert," a representative of an institutional defendant, recalls his first few experiences with the mandatory mediation program. His early experiences were largely frustrating, which he now attributes to the influence of the organization's lawyer, who had instructed him not to speak during the sessions. Once the organization changed lawyers, Robert's experience in mandatory mediation opened up. He now goes into sessions expecting to gain an understanding about "what the other side is really thinking," and comfortable that "if it's a legitimate case, I can say sorry."[53]

> "Mary," another representative of a large institutional client, describes lawyers' attitudes as being largely determinative of the effectiveness, and outcome, of mediation. Mary's organization has consciously chosen to work with a lawyer who supports the mediation sessions, and indicates that "we're as open as the plaintiff's lawyer is going to be ... we're led by how open they are." She has appeared as the representative for the defendant on roughly ten cases of an almost identical nature, and indicates that what has made the difference in result is not the facts of the case, but the attitudes of the lawyers.[54]

[43] Lawyers are most commonly described as bringing an adversarial approach into the mediation room, "shutting down" open information exchange or being reluctant to negotiate. The frustration experienced by some was expressed by one client as follows: "if I could have sat down with the other person, and no lawyer, we would have settled." Some clients described how their lawyers created an atmosphere that was about "winning and losing"; conducting, in effect, an examination for discovery; taking over the session; and sometimes instructing their client to keep quiet and leave the talking to counsel.[55] One frustrated client, who had wanted to use mediation at the very least to narrow the issues in dispute, summarized the dynamic he experienced as follows:

> I find the litigators in the room are wary of [using the session] for fear of showing their hand. That becomes a barrier to moving anywhere in the mediation process.

[44] Almost 50 percent of clients told us that they felt ill-prepared for their mediation session. Many went into their mediations not knowing, or confused about, what to expect. Several said that their preparation was limited to a short conversation with their lawyer in the car on the way to the session, meeting their lawyer fifteen minutes in advance of the session or receiving a letter that told them only where to be and when to be there. Very few remembered receiving the literature that has been developed by the Dispute Resolution Office for the preparation of clients.

[45] Not only do clients notice when they are not adequately prepared by their lawyers, but they also have ideas about what adequate preparation might mean. They want more information exchange between the parties, both in advance and during the session. They want to be "supported" but not "shut down" by their lawyers. They want preparation that includes:

- The basics of the mediation, what to expect generally from the process;
- Information about the principles of confidentiality and "without prejudice";
- What paperwork to bring to mediation;
- Some information about negotiation strategy, the idea of give and take;
- Guidance on the appropriate division of roles between lawyer and client — what is valuable for clients to say as distinct from lawyers, and some written material on the client's role and how the client can prepare; and

• Discussion of the different purposes of mediation; for example, when the goal should be gaining a better understanding of what the issues are rather than striving for settlement.

[46] One might be tempted to conclude from the above summary that clients would prefer to proceed with mediation alone, leaving their lawyers out of the process. The opposite message came through. Clients who described success stories in mediation were also likely to attribute their success in part to the presence of their lawyers.[56] Lawyers may be more likely to judge the likelihood of success in mediation based on the character of the dispute. For clients, however, the single most influential factor is the approach taken by the lawyers. Despite increasing numbers of applicants, lawyers remain the primary agents of disputing in civil justice processes.[57] The results of the evaluation are a timely reminder of the significance of their impact on the process.

V. FEEDBACK ABOUT THE MEDIATOR'S ROLE: THE CALL FOR PRO-ACTIVITY

[47] It is interesting to note that the mediators in the Saskatchewan program, unlike mandatory mediation programs elsewhere in North America, are generally non-lawyers. Roughly half of the program mediators are veterans of the farm debt program, and a number are also experienced family mediators. However, there is a broad acceptance of non-lawyer mediators by the Saskatchewan Bar and there are some important lessons for other jurisdictions in the expectations Saskatchewan lawyers have of the mediator's role. While it is common for court-connected mediation programs to adopt a facilitative, non-evaluative approach to resolution, in the Saskatchewan Queens Bench this admonition seems to have greater authenticity than other programs given that fact that few mediators have legal training.[58] The present cadre of Justice mediators are very cohesive in their commitment not to give any opinion on the legal merits of the case. As one mediator expressed this to us, "I see my role in these files as being to facilitate, to assist people in their communications, to poke, prod, give gentle nudges, to try to move people forward."

[48] Lawyers who participated in the study fully appreciated that most mediators were not qualified to provide a legal assessment, and few viewed this as a problem or a disadvantage. Most lawyers appear to accept mediation as a purely facilitative process, thus clearly distinguishing it from the later pre-trial con-

ference process. A number of lawyers commented that given the timing and nature of pre-trials in the Queen's Bench, it made more sense to make mediation a distinctive and earlier process. There was no suggestion that the mediator should act as a judge; in fact, there were many examples in the interviews we conducted of lawyers distinguishing the role of a judge from the role of a mediator. The judicial function was seen as quite different from that of a mediator. For example:

> Some clients won't settle unless a judge tells them that they're liable.
>
> The pre-trial judge provides evaluation — it is sometimes important for the client to hear what judge says about their case. Members of the judiciary who were interviewed also stressed the need to offer two distinctive processes to encourage settlement — one a facilitative mediation, and the second, a more evaluative process as the action proceeds closer to trial.

[49] Compared with jurisdictions where mediators are almost always lawyers,[59] Saskatchewan presents a striking example of a culture that has become attuned to the benefits of an early, purely facilitative mediation model. There appeared to be relatively little objection to this approach among participants in the evaluation. Indeed, many lawyers and their clients expressed their appreciation of the skill and experience of the Queen's Bench program mediators. This stands in sharp contrast to lawyers elsewhere, who are sometimes completely dismissive of non-lawyer mediators.[60]

[50] The preference for a facilitative approach was not unanimous among the lawyers interviewed. Some lawyers would prefer a more evaluative approach in mediation generally, and others could see some types of cases in which an evaluation would be more useful than a purely facilitative approach. While these comments came from a small minority, taken with other suggestions about mediator role, they suggest that more might be done to provide counsel with choices over mediators (style, expertise, etc.). In our final recommendations for the Saskatchewan program, we proposed that lawyers be provided with a choice among the available cadre of mediators, in order to fit the mediator to the particular case. Although program managers have not implemented a formal selection system, they continue to accommodate lawyers' preferences on an informal basis.

[51] The other striking response, offered consistently by both lawyers and clients, reflects a desire for a more interventionist style (while stopping short of

379

evaluation) on the part of the mediator. A significant number of remarks from both lawyers and clients suggest that program users want the mediators to take a more proactive role in working for settlement in the session. Where settlement is not an option, many lawyers and clients indicated an interest in having mediators help to "manage" the file, for example, by assisting to set a future timetable for steps in negotiation or litigation, instead of simply releasing the parties at the end of the session.

[52] Among lawyers in particular, the call for pro-activity tended to be linked to the complaint that the "other side" was not taking the mediation seriously. Lawyers spoke often of the need for mediators to "lean on" the parties and their lawyers more, to "get their hands dirty" and "make us talk." Other consistent comments included the need for mediators to stand up to counsel who are unwilling either to stay in the session or to bargain in good faith; hold counsel to account where they are unwilling to exchange information in the session (and have not done it in advance); prevent counsel from dictating the tone of the meeting; require counsel to answer questions and to justify their positions; and generally work harder to keep the parties at the table. These comments clearly point to a desire for a mediation that keeps the parties focused and working on settlement, even where there is initial resistance. Many lawyers preferred a strong-armed approach (where needed), and still saw it as distinct from an evaluative function. These respondents believed that a facilitative mediator will be most effective where she is proactive and, sometimes, quite directive.

[53] For the most part, clients were very complimentary about mediators.[61] Most described an atmosphere that felt comfortable and attributed that to the work of the mediator. At no point were concerns about mediator neutrality raised. Where there were complaints, they were consistent with those offered by lawyers: that the mediator was too hands-off, not "active" enough or did not "take control." The most common view was that it is the mediator's responsibility to "push back" against the lawyers and to exercise their persuasive powers to keep the negotiation moving forward. The clients' desire for mediators to be more proactive in this way is clearly linked to their frustration with the lawyers.[62]

[54] Just as frequently, the clients we talked with expressed a desire to have mediators be more proactive following the mediation sessions:

> "Kerry," a personal injury client, felt positive about mediation, and about the fact that she did

much of the talking in the session. However, she would have liked more to happen in the period of time following the session: "So I got to tell my story, so what? I've told my story a million times." It was important for her to see progress after the session, and this did not happen.[63]

[55] Clients are not as accustomed as their lawyers to the sometimes slow pace of the litigation process. Many that we talked to were frustrated in that they seemed to make some progress in the mediation session, but that things fell apart after the session, or sat dormant for a period of time. Many saw it as the mediator's role to continue to facilitate the file's progress after the initial session, issuing a clear invitation for mediators to do more follow-up work.

[56] These comments suggest an important, although perhaps slight, shift in the conception of the mediator's role in mandatory court-connected programs. There has been a tendency — at least in mediation training — to conflate a facilitative approach with a hands-off, non-directive style of mediation. Equally widespread is the assumption that evaluative approaches to mediation are characterized by some pressure and arm-twisting by the mediator. This evaluation shows a program moving beyond stereotyped assumptions and acknowledging that some combination of characteristics is required. Its responses affirm that the ultimate focus (facilitating an open discussion) can be achieved through a variety of styles (from hands-off to hands-on) — a mediator can use an interest-based approach, keeping the parties centered on achieving a better understanding of each other's concerns and goals (rather than making assessments of the strength of each position), and do so in a way that employs directive techniques — reality-testing, confronting, caucusing and otherwise re-framing or influencing the direction of the discussion and the parties' commitment to the process.

[57] Another layer of complexity in images of the mediator's role also emerged from the study. The comments of lawyers and clients, described above, indicate that a need for pro-activity might arise at different stages in the mediation. The mediator may be called to use her persuasive powers to influence how the parties and their counsel are interacting with each other — to influence the development of the negotiating relationship among them. This might involve, for example, encouraging the parties and counsel to negotiate openly and in good faith, wherever possible — an opportunity that generally arises in the heart of the session. On the other hand (and usually at the inception or closure of the mediation), the mediator may be called to be proactive in an

administrative capacity: designing and managing the procedural elements of mediation to maximize the process's potential. Perhaps due to the absence of formal procedural rules surrounding the sessions, clients and lawyers often expect some process management from the mediator, including arranging for the exchange of information in advance; ensuring that parties with decision-making power and the proper authority attend; scheduling a second session where appropriate; ensuring that undertakings made during a session are completed; and taking responsibility for any other necessary follow-up work after the initial session has wrapped up. Both dimensions of mediator pro-activity — the development of a good negotiating relationship and a type of managerial leadership role — are linked: each supports and sustains the other.

[58] These comments have important implications for the training of mediators not only in Saskatchewan but also elsewhere. The Dispute Resolution Office has picked up on both forms of pro-activity in its post-evaluation changes. Mediators are being encouraged to be stronger about keeping people in the room and working towards settlement. They are also being encouraged to do more front-end work, for example, contacting lawyers ahead of time to discuss the file and prepare for the session.[64]

VI. CHARACTERISTICS OF A MATURING PROGRAM

[59] Refining and strengthening the Saskatchewan program's commitment to participatory justice — whether in the degree of pro-activity of its mediators or the level of genuine engagement by participating counsel — is a matter for training and long-term future debate and development. Areas of procedural weakness identified in the evaluation report have already been addressed in amendments to the legislation, passed in June 2004.[65] In making adjustments to the program, program managers have seized on two key conclusions in the Learning from Experience Report:[66] that something more needs to be done to encourage information exchange in advance of the mediation session, and that there needs to be more flexibility in process design to respond to procedural needs in individual cases. Amendments to the primary legislation now give the Director flexibility to postpone the mediation session until after the parties have exchanged documents (or documentary lists), or until any other time, and also clarify the court's ability to refer a case to mediation at any time later in the litigation process. They maintain an emphasis

on early sessions, but invite rearrangement of the process where it is likely that a more productive mediation will occur at a different stage.

[60] The evaluation revealed the need for program modifications, but not wholesale change. The Saskatchewan program has reached a "settling point" in its evolution, having passed clearly through the early stages, where building legitimacy was the primary concern. Although the program cannot be static (it must continue to be responsive to changing context and to evolve accordingly), it has reached an important point of maturation. It is currently influenced by three forces that, in light of the program's early controversies, are especially significant. We offer these observations as characteristics of a maturing mandatory civil mediation program: the preference for flexibility, an alignment of goals and extending the overall legitimacy of mediation and its place in the local legal culture.

A.   A Preference for Flexibility

[61] With the layers of procedural rules that surround litigation, it would be tempting to move a court-annexed mediation program in the same direction. In Saskatchewan, however, program managers have decided to do the opposite, minimizing the procedural complexities and requirements of mandatory mediation. The original choice may have been a strategic one, designed to minimize the intrusion of the program from the perspective of lawyers. Striving for simplicity also meant however that the program inevitably took a "one-size-fits-all" approach. As the program matures, in the wake of the evaluation, there has been a renewed commitment to flexibility that will leave room for the professionals involved (mediators, administrators, lawyers and judges) to exercise their judgment on a case-by-case basis.

[62] Until now, one of the program's areas of weakness has been the failure of parties to exchange any information in advance of the session. Instead of inserting a requirement that parties disclose positions or documents before mediation, program managers have committed to encouraging mediators to do more "upfront" work on files (contacting lawyers in particular), and clarified administrators' ability to defer mediation until some later point in the litigation process, where appropriate and justifiable (for example, after examinations for discovery). Additionally, the "certificate of completion" and accompanying "certificate of non-attendance"[67] has been changed to a "certificate of compliance,"[68] which increases flexibility in the determination of who must attend the media-

tion session. Previously, all litigants had to attend the session, unless exempted by either the Director or the court. This new wording allows the mediator to determine, on a case-by-case basis, who should be attending in order to comply with the program's intent. So, for example, in a case where a number of individuals have been sued in their capacity as representatives of an organization (members of a board, for example) it may be more important to have a representative of the organization than to require that board members attend individually.[69] Both of these changes are minor adjustments and to an extent simply confirm informal practices that already existed. As the program passes through these stages of its development, however, a continued commitment to flexibility is strengthened in these and other ways.

[63] What is significant about a commitment to maintaining and even enhancing flexibility is that it invites — indeed requires — the professional players to invest some trust in each other. Underneath the desire for flexibility is a vision of a mediation program that is offered on a [large scale] and is accessible to all, but is still capable of responding to the particular procedural needs of individual cases: identifying who should be at the table and what information is needed in order that the session can be productive, engaging the lawyers and their clients in a meaningful discussion regardless of whether they have yet initiated settlement discussions and shifting to case management when more steps in the litigation process are inevitable. Program managers need to invest some trust in the judgment of lawyers who ask for a mediation session to be deferred; equally, lawyers need to trust mediators and program managers who suggest that discoveries, and post-discovery negotiations, are not always or necessarily the most effective or efficient way to reach settlement in a particular case. Mediators and lawyers need to trust each other as they discuss files in preparation for upcoming sessions.

[64] In the early years, trust was absent and flexibility was not a message that would carry the program forward. Some rigidity in the program structure was required in order to get lawyers and litigants accustomed to the option of mediation. Even now, Saskatchewan lawyers generally agree that the mediation program should not be completely flexible (for example, there was a clear view against substituting an opt in program[70]). Over the ten years of the program, with some accompanying cultural and attitudinal shifts, professionals involved are begin-

ning to consider themselves team players more than adversaries.

[65] The program's longstanding commitment to a facilitative and non-legalistic mediation process may have been the ultimate factor in developing trust. Non-lawyer mediators, using an interest-based style for mediation sessions, re-framed the negotiation process, focusing on client concerns and overall objectives rather than arguing and evaluating legal positions or strategizing on litigation process. This was the lawyer's area of expertise and it now appears clear the Saskatchewan mediators neither wished to nor were expected to go there. Facilitative mediators have their sights trained on the potential benefits — uncovering hidden obstacles to a resolution and bringing all parties and their counsel "to the same page" in understanding what it will take to satisfy clients on both sides of the dispute. While mediators may have different techniques at their disposal (see discussion of mediator pro-activity above), the only way to achieve such an open discussion is with willing engagement of the lawyers. The program's commitment to a facilitative mediation process, relatively free of procedural rules, guaranteed this dynamic: that in order for the process to be successful, lawyers and mediators would have to work together, case by case. The program required the development of relationships between lawyers and mediators, and ultimately, the building of trust. What was perhaps the program's greatest challenge — inserting a non-legalistic and quasi-informal step into the litigation process — became a foundation for growth.

[66] At this juncture, now that working relationships among lawyers, mediators and program managers are beginning to settle, the Saskatchewan program can easily sustain adjustments that continue to emphasize the exercise of discretion and flexibility.

B. Goal Alignment

[67] As the program has matured, views on all sides — originally polarized — have begun to merge. Common ground among the various perspectives is easier to locate. Not only have lawyers and clients generally accepted that mediation has a place in the resolution of civil disputes (a conclusion that obviously propelled mediators and program managers), but mediators have begun to define their jobs in a way that matches the multi-dimensional, pro-active role envisioned by clients and lawyers, and described above.

[68] Interviews with mediators conducted during the course of the evaluation revealed an emerging com-

plexity (perhaps a dichotomy) in terms of how they conceptualized their roles. One group was more likely to describe the mediator's role as classically hands-off: to help the parties understand each other, to respond to resistance softly, by building rapport, asking questions and using gentle prods. The other group was more likely to describe the mediator's role in a way that invites more force and direction: to get the parties and their lawyers working, believing that keeping them in the room is necessary to reach mediation's educative and transformative function. Each reveals differing levels of comfort with mediator pro-activity. The second perspective may be regarded as somewhat inconsistent with a "classic" facilitative style, and also with the program's original commitment to a "hands-off" educative environment. Despite this, interviews revealed it to be a view that was [as predominant as, or more predominant than,] the first among program mediators — suggesting that experienced mediators, along with lawyers and clients, now see a need for strong pro-activity in many cases.

[69] Mediators in this second group tend to worry less about their credibility with lawyers and the legal community, feeling comfortable with the relationship building they had already done. Not surprisingly, their views on the mediator's role were much more closely aligned with the views expressed by both lawyers and clients. Once again, this speaks to the shift that can occur when a program reaches a certain level of maturity, and the process agents (mediators and lawyers alike) gain some history with each other. Time and experience may move the professional players closer together in terms of their expectations of each other and the process.

C. Extending Legitimacy

[70] Like any innovation, and especially those that impact social relationships and benefits, the success of mandatory civil mediation depends to a large extent on its ability to become regarded as legitimate (credible, effective, worthwhile) in the eyes of its users, both lawyers and clients. The Saskatchewan evaluation confirmed what other studies of court-connected mediation have shown — that with increasing exposure to mediation and experience with the process, more positive attitudes emerge among both lawyers and clients and that these same positive attitudes tend to beget better results[71] — which might include more serious preparations, more effective negotiations with better use of the expertise of both third party and lawyers, and better all round outcomes both substantively and in terms of procedural satisfaction.

[71] Saskatchewan also offered a chance to speculate a little further on some of the phases or stages of legitimacy as they emerge over time as a program matures and experience deepens. We concentrate here in particular on the attitudes towards the legitimacy of mediation among lawyers, as they still appear to play the primary role in determining client attitudes.[72] We suggest that it may be helpful to conceptualize deepening legitimacy in three possible phases or stages.

[72] In stage one, as a new mandatory mediation program is introduced, generally, there is widespread skepticism. The introduction of a new procedural step is regarded as implicitly critical of what lawyers and courts have done to this point. Civil justice reform may be politically motivated (perhaps to save money) and this adds to the skepticism. A common attitude among lawyers at this stage is not to take the innovation especially seriously, and sometimes to find ways to assimilate mediation into more familiar and established practices (for example by using mediation as a positional negotiation absent vital information). This attitude is frequently communicated to clients, who see mediation as a waste of their time and money.

[73] In stage two, which we suggest will emerge once most lawyers and institutional clients have had multiple experiences of mediation (that is, the stage mediation has reached in Saskatchewan), counsel's attitude towards the legitimacy of mediation becomes more complex and turns on some important distinctions. Most lawyers will now feel that they need to explain their position on mediation with more depth than previously, when they could get away with being fairly dismissive. Generally attitudes become much more positive. In Saskatchewan very few of the lawyers with whom we spoke (only 13 percent) did not begin or end their descriptions of their mediation experiences with some acknowledgement of the unique benefits of mediation — indicating the growing legitimacy of mediation and showing clearly a movement away from phase one, above. At this stage it is important for lawyers to associate themselves with some degree of positive attitude towards mediation.[73]

[74] However support for mediation is by no means unequivocal. At least two distinct sets of equivocations are apparent from our Saskatchewan data. Around half of the Saskatchewan lawyers whom we interviewed for this evaluation assert that while they are now personally convinced that mediation is an excellent process, its potential is often diminished by

the approach of other lawyers who do not take it seriously — who have not "seen the light" as they have. In blaming "the other guy" for problems with the mediation process these lawyers were far from unambiguously committing to its use — rather they were providing a rationale for why they might not always take it very seriously themselves. They are, however, also recognizing that the answer to some of the problems they identify with mediation may lie within the legal community itself.

[75] A second group (roughly 50 percent) defined the barriers to the realization of full potential for mandatory mediation as wholly external or structural. This group blames faulty system design (for example, lack of adequate screening processes or the timing of mediation), mediators (as we have seen some are characterized as insufficiently proactive) or program managers (sometimes seen as overly bureaucractic and inflexible) for their disappointments with mediation. These lawyers are saying that mediation is a good innovation and that they like it, but it is destined to fail because of reasons that have nothing to do with the role of the Bar.

[76] In stage three, the ambivalence and blaming has been replaced by a widespread desire among lawyers to ensure their expertise in mediation processes, with a range of new skills and knowledge becoming important to their continued professional development. It may be that stage three legitimacy is reached faster in smaller communities where the legal culture (or "community of practice"[74]) is more cohesive with stronger prevailing norms and a relatively homogeneous client base. In Saskatchewan, this

stage appeared to have been reached in one such smaller community. Our discussions with Prince Albert lawyers were characterized by a seriousness and commitment to mediation from senior down to junior lawyers, with an emphasis on describing positive enhancements (for example, conventions over advance exchange of documents) rather than complaining about process spoilers, either external or internal.

[77] The extent of mediation legitimacy appears to be directly tied to the consciousness and rationalizations of lawyers. The Saskatchewan program reflects at least a stage two, or in some cases a stage three, level of legitimacy.

[78] As court-connected mandatory mediation continues to play a role in civil justice reform across Canada, we need to find reliable means of evaluating not only the achievement of primary program goals — such as settlement rates and client satisfaction — but also the impact of the local cultural context, historical factors and the nature of any systemic changes including the consciousness of lawyers. The Saskatchewan evaluation provided an opportunity to look deeper into these broader and perhaps more complex factors in "successful" civil justice reform. Mandatory mediation programs in the general civil court structure are only just coming of age, offering new opportunities to define and assess the characteristics of maturing programs. The indices of maturity that are appearing in Saskatchewan are important signposts, with the potential to guide future design and development decisions across the country.

(c) Translating Justice and Therapy: *The Drug Treatment Court Networks*†

Dawn Moore

INTRODUCTION

The judge calls the drug treatment court (DTC) to attention. He is addressing a specific client but makes it clear he wants the entire court to listen. He

proceeds to reiterate the goals of the treatment court, concluding that 'the purpose of this court is to cure addiction, the closer he (the client) or anyone is brought to cure the better'. The promotional video

† (2007) 47 Brit. J. Criminol. 42 at 42–45, 47–51, 53–57. Reproduced with permission of Oxford University Press. [Notes and/or references omitted.]

produced in 1999 for this same court (Toronto Drug Treatment Court) illuminates this goal. Both the judge and the Crown attorney explain that the mandate of this court is to 'close the revolving door on crime' by treating drug addicts. Drug treatment courts are meant to cure those who come before them through the direct supervision of the court and, quite literally, within the walls of the courtroom. The project formalizes and amplifies extant crossovers between law and therapy in order to translate the courtroom into a curative realm. This paper maps these crossovers by looking at the circulation of disciplinary knowledges and actors. Borrowing analytic tools from Actor Network Theory (Latour 1987; Law 1999), I show how the DTCs are legal spaces deliberately set up for knowledge exchanges. These exchanges are effected by the uncoupling of psy and legal knowledges from their respective actors. Through a series of translations, knowledges circulate in the court and both the therapeutic and legal actors realign themselves, their goals and interests, to ally with the broader goal of curing the offender.

Drug treatment courts are part of a broader phenomenon born out of a theoretical movement called therapeutic jurisprudence (TJ). Coined by David Wexler and Bruce Winnick (1996: xvii), TJ is:

> ... the study of the role of law as a therapeutic agent. It is an interdisciplinary enterprise designed to produce scholarship that is particularly useful for law reform. Therapeutic Jurisprudence proposes the exploration of ways in which, consistent with principles of justice, the knowledge, theories and insights of the mental health and related disciplines can help shape the development of the law.

> The notion of TJ emerged from the observed need to provide extra support to individuals in conflict with the law who also have mental health problems. The movement rapidly expanded to encompass all kinds of issues, including drug use, domestic violence, labour conflicts, youth crime and sex offenses. The expansion of the ideal of TJ is so profound that a search on any university data base of the terms 'Therapeutic Jurisprudence' reveals hundreds of hits.[1]

TJ, as it is written about in the fecund literature, is not limited solely to advocating for the establishing of special courts organized around addressing therapeutic issues. Instead, TJ is applied to all kinds of legal practices in which a crossover between law and therapy is possible. The most definitive text on TJ, Wexler and Winnick's (1996) edited collection, *Law in a Therapeutic Key*, features debates on long-standing legal doctrine, including the insanity defense

(Perlin 1996), the tort doctrine of standard of care[2] (Shuman 1996) and the court's *in loco parenti* responsibility to underage participants (as either litigants, victims or accused) (Shiff and Wexler 1996). Those aspects of TJ that do centre on the courtroom, however, offer accounts of courtroom dynamics and reforms to legal processes that mandate the interplay of legal and psy knowledges. Courts focusing on issues of mental health, family violence and drugs all work through formal crossovers between law and treatment. The DTC arm of TJ enjoys giddy popularity throughout the United States and is expanding globally. The first DTC opened in Miami in 1989 (Goldkamp *et al.* 2001). Now, there are over 600 DTCs in the United States, and more operating and slated to begin operations in Australia, Great Britain, Guam, the Cayman Islands, Puerto Rico and Scotland (Anderson 2001; Belenko 1999). Through the application of TJ, the DTCs bring together therapeutic and legal actors in the courtroom, reorienting them around the unified goal of curing the offender.

The interplay between law and other forms of knowledge is not innovative. Law, as both an epistemology and a discipline, has never been pure. This is what the law and society project and the legal realist movement have been teaching us for the better part of a century (Tomlins 2000). Noting the ways in which the social seeps into legal arenas, legal philosophers such as Pound (1921) were quick to point out that law is not only driven by legal knowledges or processes. Instead, social factors (including knowledges) are firmly fixed within law. In the earlier realist tradition, the project tended toward normativity and positivism with an eye to reimagining the juridical project as deeply sociological. More recent incantations gesture toward the descriptive and genealogical, looking at the role of law in society and society in law (see Ewick *et al.* 1999).

Psy disciplines, actors, knowledges and practices (coming from psychiatry, psychology and social work), in particular, are stock features of Western penal systems (Arrigo 2002). Prisoners and probationers are actuarially assessed and managed through psychologically based risk-prediction tools and offered cognitive–behavioural programming to target criminogenic factors (see Andrews and Bonta 1998; Mair 2004). The advent of the conditional sentence in Canada introduced psy interventions into the courtroom by way of allowing judges to place treatment orders on offenders as part of sentencing (Chiodo 2002; Fisher *et al.* 2002). In the broader realm of addictions, Canadian law continues to be used as a means to force people into treatment (Fisher *et al.* 2002).

Social scientists and socio-legal scholars have been quick to interrogate these developments. Some of the best work here arises out of concerns about the application of psy interventions to women in conflict with the law, revealing the gendered and discriminatory nature of these initiatives (Hannah-Moffat 2001; Kendall 2000; 2005). Other work lays open these programmes as culturally insensitive and empirically ineffective (Shaw and Hannah-Moffat 2004; Doob and Webster 2004). The rise of psy interventions, although often held up as an indicator of the humanization of punishment, is also arguably a punitive wolf in a benevolent sheep's clothing, with the potential for exerting and justifying extensive and harsh punishments (Moore and Hannah-Moffat 2005). The DTCs have not escaped this criticism. A growing body of scholars (Anderson 2001; Fisher *et al.* 2002; Nolan 2001) raise doubts about the effectiveness of these initiatives and share concerns with those writing in the realm of punishment about the humaneness of forced or legally supervised treatment. We know, then, that even as they are commonplace, these intersections between law and psy are cause for concern. The extant literature focuses on the outcomes of these initiatives. I am interested in their processes. Specifically, I focus on the kinetics of legal and psy knowledges and actors within the DTCs.

This paper maps out the knowledge exchanges between law and psy in the two operating Canadian DTCs (Toronto and Vancouver). From 2003 to 2006, I conducted courtroom observations in both courts. During this time, I also conducted interviews with key practitioners in both settings (judges, lawyers, therapists, court advocates and liaisons). Exploring movements of knowledge is important because ways of knowing are also ways of governing (Foucault 1980). Thus, exploring knowledge exchanges has something to tell us about practices of rule. The DTCs are likely spaces in which to conduct such a study because the knowledge crossovers in these courts are so explicit and the actors involved define their own work as markedly different from the work done in traditional criminal courts. At the opening of the Ottawa Drug Treatment Court, Deputy Attorney General for Ontario, Murray Segal,[3] makes this point quite plain in stating that the DTCs 'sit outside the traditional punitive paradigm ... by embracing multidisciplinary, interdisciplinary and collaborative work'. The courts mandate a collective enterprise, drawing on the same actors and the same set of knowledges, marking their uniqueness through

the particular collection of knowledges and actors found in these courts.

Taking my cue from Latour's (1987) work on the Actor-Network and Rose's (1998) study of psy knowledges, I show how expert knowledges are freed from expert actors. This uncoupling allows for the translation of the goals and interests of legal and therapeutic actors involved in the court. Translations influence the ways in which both justice and therapy are imagined in these settings. These developments have concerning implications for questions of due process and the ethical treatment of court clients as they explicitly erase fundamental protections against abuse of power in the realms of both therapy and justice (Boldt 2002). These erasures are allowable, even desirable, in the assuredly benevolent quest to cure the offender.

I begin with an overview of the ways in which knowledges are theorized with an eye to legal settings. Through this, I explain why some Actor Network Theory tools are useful in developing an understanding of the knowledge dynamics of the DTCs. I then offer a descriptive map of the knowledge exchanges in the courtrooms, drawing on court observations. Here I pay careful attention to the ways in which court actors affect translations of their actions such that legal actions like sanctioning serve therapeutic purposes and therapeutic acts such as assessing an individual's motivations become justifications for legal decisions. From here, I consider the role of the 'team' structure of the court as a primary means of facilitating the translations that occur. Within this team structure, I am also interested in how the team members themselves reorient their own personal goals and interests to align with the broader goals of the DTC. These translations have particular implications for the legal notion of due process on the one hand and the therapeutic ethic of care on the other. In the final section of this paper, I explore how actors redefine these notions as part of participating in the DTC network.

. . . .

TREATMENT COURTS IN CANADA

The first DTC opened in Toronto in 1997, the second in Vancouver in 2001. In 2006 four more courts opened in Edmonton, Ottawa, Regina and Winnipeg. The Toronto and Vancouver courts function similarly, although there are notable differences between the two. Both courts are mandated to deal with people convicted of non-violent crimes for which they would otherwise receive custodial sentences. Accused persons wanting to apply to the court programmes must undergo an assessment to show that they have an addiction of at least three months' duration to either heroin, crystal methamphetamine or crack/cocaine. Potential 'clients' are also evaluated for violent histories, mental health issues and levels of motivation to actively engage in an addiction treatment programme. Once accepted to the programme, successful court clients cascade down through levels of supervision as indicated by frequency of court appearances and participation in treatment. Through their time in the programme, clients are placed on a special bail[5] specific to the treatment courts. They also must sign a waiver acknowledging that sentencing will be delayed and quitting a number of other rights and protections (they must agree to participate in a random urine screen programme, have their therapeutic experiences discussed in open court and accept their inability to fully participate in legal processes, described in more detail below). Clients considered to be of higher risk must enter a guilty plea to be admitted to the court programme. Those who successfully complete the programme are guaranteed non-custodial sentence. The courts follow a system of sanctions and rewards. The sanctioning systems in the two courts are quite different and discussed independently below. In both courts, clients are rewarded for consistent attendance and showing progress in their treatment (as defined by periods of abstinence or decreased drug use). Rewards include easing up on bail restrictions, decreasing court appearances and praise from the judge and the court.

The differences between the courts are as considerable as their similarities. Most primary here is the location of the courts in the different cultures of drug use from which they emerge. Vancouver boasts one of the largest and most visible drug-using populations in the world. The acuity of Vancouver's drug scene indicates that responses to drug use there are tailored to fit the surroundings. Vancouver is the first Canadian city to host a safe injection site, needle exchange programme and harm-reduction hotel. The drug scene in Vancouver has a huge influence on policing in the downtown core, rendering the area a de facto decriminalized zone for small-scale drug possession and sex trade work. At least one marijuana café operates in the Downtown Eastside without much reported police intervention.

The Vancouver DTC (VDTC) is shaped to fit the contours of its surroundings. The court itself is located in the heart of the Downtown Eastside, placing court clients in the thick of the drug trade on a regular basis. The court programme tempers this by offering a 'one stop shopping' day treatment centre for court clients deliberately located outside of the Hastings and Main neighbourhood. Clients are either encouraged or mandated (depending on their status in the court) to attend the treatment centre daily, especially at the start of their participation in the programme. The centre offers addiction-related programming, social programmes, individual therapy, a methadone clinic and a breakfast and lunch programme. Clients also have access to a physician, nurse, housing and child custody support services through the centre. The court and some treatment centre programmes are gender-segregated — an initiative which attempts to alleviate the gendered exploitation and victimization often faced by street-involved women. Largely because of *de facto* decriminalization, the court does not, for the most part, deal with simple possession charges. Instead, almost all the clients in the court are facing possession for the purpose of trafficking charges or property offences. Sanctions in the VDTC are typically placed on clients who fail to appear either in court or at the treatment centre. The sanctions most commonly used in this court include issuing a warrant unique to the VDTC that mandates treatment centre attendance, placing clients in custody or altering bail conditions such that clients are mandated to attend a residential treatment facility. Finally, the VDTC does not demand total abstinence from all substances in order to graduate. Clients need only test negative for six months for the three mandated substances.

The drug scene in Toronto lacks the truculence of Vancouver, although, as a large urban centre, Toronto hosts a considerable amount of drug trafficking and use. Crack, cocaine, crystal methamphetamine and, to a lesser extent, opiates are all common in the city. The scene in Toronto is geographically dispersed, lacking the dramatic, palpable concentration found in Vancouver. The city has a needle exchange programme, methadone clinics and, alongside Vancouver and Montreal, is one of the sites for the current prescription heroin trials. The Toronto DTC (TDTC) does not have gender-specific programming or a comprehensive treatment centre (although the Centre for Addiction and Mental Health — part of a downtown hospital — does serve as a hub for the treatment programme). Abstinence is a requirement for graduation in Toronto and the court tends to take a harder line in general on drug use. In the Toronto court, there are two kinds of sanctions available: community service orders (CSOs), through which the individual is mandated to perform a set number of hours of community service (ranging from working at a homeless shelter to tearing posters off of phone poles), and bail revocation, referred to in this court as 'therapeutic remand'. CSOs are given far more often than therapeutic remands. These orders are assigned to clients who miss treatment groups and urine analyses, and do not 'process' relapses well.

EXCHANGING KNOWLEDGES

The positioning of actors in the courts is instructive. In Vancouver, a liaison from the treatment team holds a permanent position in the witness box and several other treatment team members are present in the courtroom, moving back and forth across the Bar. In Toronto, a probation officer and two therapists sit along side the duty counsel at the Bar. The presence of treatment people in a courtroom is not particularly curious; certainly, therapists, psychologists and psychiatrists are called into court on a regular basis to provide testimony, report on assessments and offer support to victims. The DTC treatment people are not, however, invited into the courts as witnesses or to offer court support. Instead, flagging the oddity of these courts, treatment people participate directly in legal processes. In this venue, legal knowledges and actors do not serve as filters for other kinds of expert knowledges (Jasanoff 1995). Instead, legal knowledges share space with clinical (mainly psy) knowledges and experts.

In both treatment courts, each of the clients has to go before the judge to report in. On one occasion in the Toronto court, a man is called up who has been on methadone maintenance for a few weeks. When the judge asks him whether he has any drug use to report, he admits that he has been using heroin fairly regularly for the last week. The judge thanks him for his honesty, as he always does, and asks the man why he used. The man responds that he was craving heroin and had been unable to overcome those cravings. The judge refuses to accept this response, relying on clinical knowledge to justify his position. The judge says, 'Look, the whole purpose of methadone is to stop you from having cravings. That's why you're on methadone is so you don't feel that need to use the heroin anymore. That's how methadone works.' The judge goes on to explain that the court encourages heroin users to get on methadone so that they can stabilize their lives, learn and practise coping mechanisms. 'And,' he concludes, 'it's dangerous to mix methadone and heroin.' Here, the judge takes up clinical knowledge in considering the pharmacological properties and clinical purposes of methadone as well as the psychological

techniques of addressing and attempting to remedy drug addiction (in talking about cravings and coping mechanisms).

The judges in both courts not only engage in clinical–medical assessments, but also take up psychological treatment knowledges in dealing with clients. After listening to a client named Paulo[6] explain his reasons for wanting to be admitted to the VDTC, the judge offers an assessment of his level of motivation to actually change his drug-using behaviours. The judge says:

> I think you are very sincere about wanting to get treatment and wanting to get clean but I am not convinced by your plan so far. I want you to go to develop a tight plan that will get you into a recovery house.[7] Come back and show me you've done this and that will show me your commitment.

Here, the judge is referring to the body of knowledge around addiction recovery on which the court programme is based. Motivation-based psychology holds that before you can expect someone to change a set of behaviours, s/he has to be motivated to change those behaviours (Prochaska et al., 1988). Programming can start to foster those motivations by using external forces such as the sanction and reward system followed by the court. At a point, as the theory goes, the individual begins to internalize motivations and programming no longer needs to rely on external incentives to get an individual to want to change.

The judge's ability to bring her own psy knowledge into the courtroom does not merely serve the purpose of lectures directed at clients. It also justifies legal actions against clients. If a client shows a pattern of absence from or late arrival to the treatment centre, the judge typically reads this behaviour as a sign of the client's waning motivation to participate in the programme (and, ultimately, to become drug-free). In the Vancouver court, on reaching this diagnosis, the judge often offers the remedy of adding the client's name to the warrant list, thus making attendance at the treatment centre part of her bail conditions and giving police reason to arrest her if she does not attend the treatment centre. The judge's rationale for placing a client on the warrant list draws on therapeutic principles. For example, in responding to Carrie's admission that she is having a hard time getting to the treatment centre, the judge suggests that perhaps being added to the warrant list would help Carrie with this problem. When Carrie agrees, the judge confirms the decision by saying 'I'll give you that motivating factor then'.

In the treatment court, the notion of punishment is translated into the therapeutic goal of motivation. Increasing surveillance and the possibility of arrest and incarceration are decidedly punitive, akin to sanctioning through heightened probation conditions. Here, however, the punitive act is translated into a therapeutic one. Exercising a warrant in the DTC becomes the therapeutic application of external motivating forces described above. The act itself remains unaltered but its purpose is modified by rationalizing it through therapeutic rather than legal knowledges. This is similar to Hannah-Moffat's (2005) conclusions about risk assessments in prisons. Hannah-Moffat shows how, in the name of rehabilitation, prisoners are rated higher-risk and placed under amplified security. While the results (increased security) are clearly punitive, the risk/need assessment is justified, in part, through the therapeutic desire to meet women's needs.

Crowns and duty counsel also use clinical knowledges. This is made most clear when an individual is facing expulsion from the programme. Lying to the judge, breaching bail conditions, dealing drugs to other programme participants and having new criminal charges are all grounds for expulsion from either DTC. Clients can also be ejected from the programmes if they consistently show a lack of motivation to change their drug-using behaviours. While ejection does not arise that often, when it does happen, it is typically on the grounds of lacking motivation. For example, Karen — a client in the TDTC — faced ejection. Karen was consistently using heroin. The Crown takes her repeated use as evidence of her low motivation. The Crown's submission claims '[Karen] has shown poor quality and quantity of effort in her own recovery and clearly doesn't want to be here'. The duty counsel submits that Karen can complete her recovery and should be able to remain in the programme. Karen, she argues, simply needs time in detox to sort herself out. Again, engaging in translation, the Crown is not concerned with legal issues such as Karen's threat to public safety or criminal culpability. Karen's failure to comply with directions set out by a criminal court is not evidence of her dangerousness or blameworthiness. Instead, her actions speak to her status as a viable recipient of addiction treatment. Ejecting Karen from the programme is not presented as a punitive measure but rather as the clinical best practice for a therapeutically non-responsive client.

The treatment team plays a significant role in the court and also participates in knowledge exchanges and translations. Often, their role is supportive, offering comments to the judge on a client's progress, and on-the-spot counselling for those in crisis in the court. But treatment team members use legal knowledges and participate in legal actions as well. Frequently, treatment providers are positioned to make recommendations and, in some cases, legal decisions regarding clients. The most typical here is to see treatment team members advising the court on sanctions against clients.

An exchange around a client shows not only how treatment uses legal knowledges, but also how therapeutic knowledge is taken up by the legal actors. This passage comes from my research notes on the TDTC.

Sam is next to be called before the judge. I have never seen Sam fail to report drug use in the court and today is no different. Sam is new to the programme so his continued drug use has always been excused and he has typically been commended for being forthright about having used. Today, though, Sam also admits that he missed a treatment group and a drug screen. A member of the treatment team stands immediately to speak. She indicates that the treatment team is concerned about Sam's missing a group and that his case management officer has recommended that he do four hours of community service in order to make up for the group. She adds that the treatment team feels that it is very important for Sam to learn how important it is to attend groups. The Crown is next to speak and argues that in fact Sam's continued use coupled with his failure to attend groups calls into question Sam's motivation to be in the programme. The Crown calls for a revocation of Sam's bail in order to have him think about his motivation. The defence argues that it is still early days for Sam and that he has been up-front with the court about his use as well as his failure to attend groups. The judge decides to revoke Sam's bail, taking the [Crown's] position that Sam needs to show greater motivation and that perhaps having a strong external motivation like being placed in custody will help him to commit to the programme. Sam is taken into custody and led away.

Here, a therapeutic actor takes up the legal practice of sanctioning, not directly to achieve therapeutic ends but rather to serve a deterrent function of encouraging both Sam as well as the other court participants not to miss groups. On the other hand, the Crown takes up a therapeutic discourse about Sam's levels of motivation to voice his concerns, not about Sam's status as a law breaker, but rather about Sam's level of commitment to change his substance-using habits. Just as therapeutic actions and knowledges need not be altered in order to be marshalled by legal actors, punitiveness can translate into therapeutic practice without need of removing itself from even the most literal place of punishment — a prison.

. . . .

TRANSLATING ACTORS

. . . .

The DTC, then, is not only a venue with the purpose of curing addiction. Through the exchange of knowledges and the realignment of goals, the DTC is also a locale in which social justice is created, public safety protected, access to social services facilitated and punishment carried out effectively. In helping legal actors and institutions to redefine their goals and see their interests represented in different ways and in liberating knowledges from their perceived bonds to disciplines and disciplinary actors, the DTC network takes both law and psy from their imagined positions as pure disciplines and makes them utterly impure through varying relationships to diverse actors, interests and goals.

But what does this overt sullying of law and therapy mean for each of these disciplines? We have a society which holds out for the promises of due process on the one hand and ethical therapy on the other (even if no one knows what those terms mean and we are hard pressed to find pure examples of the application of these principles). These principles are meant to shield vulnerable people from huge power imbalances and potential for abuse and exploitation inherent to the practices of both therapy and law (Banks 2003; Roach *et al.* 2004). The goals of actors working under each of these paradigms are realigned through the network such that they fit with the network's goal of curing addiction while still being able to maintain pre-existing individual and organizational goals. In these shifts, it is clear the mythology of the purity of the discipline vanishes. This being the case, how do the actors within these networks understand this realignment vis-à-vis the principles of their respective disciplines? I want to explore this question with respect to law's promise of procedural fairness and psy's ethic of caring for clients.

PROCEDURAL FAIRNESS

Boldt (2002) argues that the adversarial mode of decision making favoured in the common law system runs counterintuitive to therapeutic practices. The adversarial system is based on the premise that fairness is ensured by having opposing 'sides' in a hearing and appointing someone to act only on behalf and in the interest of the client. One of the goals of structuring in this opposition is to offer procedural protections and assurances of fairness to those who come before the law. In Canadian criminal law, the adversarial system is meant to enshrine notions of procedural fairness — rules that are supposed to protect the most vulnerable from the overarching power of the law. These protections are laid out in the codes of professional conduct for most Bar Associations (cf. Law Society of Upper Canada 2000). Boldt suggests that when therapeutic ends are injected into the adversarial system, the principles of fairness are compromised to serve the emergent therapeutic goals.

These compromises are apparent in the DTCs. Clients enrolled in the DTCs are asked to sign a waiver giving up the right to [plead] not guilty, the right to a swift and determinate sentence (which in most cases would amount to less time in custody than the time that clients are expected to participate in the DTC programme) and the right to confidentiality (from both attorney and therapist). Clients also give up, through their agreement to participate in the urine screen, protections against unreasonable search and seizure. Clients must participate in a random drug-screening programme in which they have to produce a urine sample for testing at least once a week.

The actors within the DTC are aware that these aspects of the programme compromise legal protections. However, the importance of safeguards (and their subsequent promise of justice) is eclipsed through the broader court goal of curing addiction. The duty counsel for the Toronto court speaks to this issue:

> You know, it's probably the biggest thing that comes up is the whole issue are you acting in your client's best interest? If you're acting in a program where you're representing the clients but you're also part of this whole realm then how do you balance that? ... But I don't actually see it as a problem because basically what I say to people is that my role hasn't changed.... When it comes down to it, I'm not going to do what the team wants me to do. I'm going to talk to my client and I'm going to do what the client wants me to.[13]

Here, the duty counsel privileges the interests of her client over those of the court. Earlier on in this same interview, however, she defines her own notion of the client's best interest as getting the client into the programme and keeping her there. This definition is closely aligned with the interests of the court (to get an individual to stop using drugs) and assumes that all people in conflict with the law who also use drugs are best served through efforts to arrest their drug use.

Justice Bentley (2000), penning an early description of the TDTC programme, argues that the DTC is structured to make the role of defence counsel near irrelevant. He (2000: 268) writes that 'unless the judge is considering a revocation of bail or expulsion from the program, defence counsel does not attend court and duty counsel contributes simply as a member of the team'. The constitution of the duty counsel as 'simply a member of the team' indicates a formal breakdown of the traditional adversarial roles taken by Crown and defence. Here, the defence counsel's goal of working solely in the interest and on behalf of her client is translated through team membership. The defence counsel now works as part of a larger whole within the network rather than (as is the intent in the adversarial system) an independent representative of the accused. Importantly, the defence counsel does not understand her own translation that way. Her role as client advocate has not changed in her eyes. She still works in the best interest of her client. It is those best interests that are translated. Thus, the best possible outcome in the DTC is to have the client become drug-free — not to have the client be acquitted of criminal charges.

THE ETHIC OF CARE

The changes in goals and interests made through the DTC networks are not exclusive to the realm of law. Those involved in the DTC teams as psy actors are also engaged in a process of realignment. Traditionally, therapeutic initiatives work directly with and for the individual and have their own procedural safeguards and ethical best practices (see O'Donohue and Ferguson 2003; Samuels 2002). Paramount are guarantees of client confidentiality and the idea that the therapist (like the lawyer) works in the best interests and under the direction of the client.

The majority of therapists working in the DTCs are either psychologists or social workers, bound by Codes of Ethics set out by professional colleges and governing bodies.[14] Their locations within the DTCs effect a realignment of these therapeutic operatives. I show above that therapists often participate in making legal decisions about their clients, including, from time to time, recommending sanctions. Like the lawyers involved in the court, the therapists are also

keenly aware of the ways in which their participation in the DTC team indicates a shift in their professional practices.

One therapist observes that her role changed considerably since joining the DTC. She reasons that presenting a 'united front' to clients is vital to her ability to do her job well — a practice that she did not have to engage in before coming to the DTC. She explains that even if she disagrees with the way in which a client is handled in court, she will not directly advocate for her client in the courtroom.[15] Her practice, instead, is to take her dissatisfaction back to the DTC team for discussion. 'We make decisions as a team and only as a team,' she explains.[16] This therapist's phraseology is itself informative. United fronts are united fronts because there is an enemy whose presence warrants collective and strategic action in order to win (and thereby to ensure that the enemy loses) (Sontag 1978). In an interesting role reversal, the role of a therapist for this person changes from assistive to adversarial and the therapeutic process becomes akin to war, not care.

Another therapist recalls the first few times she watched a client of hers taken into custody based on her recommendation. She felt 'awful' but learned to accept this part of the client's therapy (spending up to five nights in a detention centre) and now has few reservations[17] about participating in the DTC process. The head of the treatment team in Vancouver maintains that 'the only time you should sanction is to engage people in treatment'.[18] She justifies this approach to dealing with drug addicts by saying that coercion must be used in addiction treatment programmes outside the court as well. She explains that people are always coerced on some level, whether the coercion comes from a partner who vows to leave, a child protection worker who threatens to take children away or a police officer who promises arrest if the user does not get help.

Involvement in the network has notable procedural effects for those involved. Consistently, narratives of the DTC practitioners, both therapeutic and legal, reveal rationalizations of their participation that allow them to change their practices while maintaining, according to their own account, their original goals. This is not to suggest, however, that the actions of any of these actors preceding their involvement with the DTC were necessarily any more closely aligned with maintaining the traditional goals of their respective disciplines. Promises of procedural fairness and ethical care do not themselves translate into guaranteed real actions or protections. If they did, we would have little need for appeals courts or disciplinary bodies set up to police professional conduct. And even if there were some absolute way of ensuring that these promises were carried out in the DTCs or indeed in any courtroom or therapist's office, there is good reason to resist normative claims that these promises somehow translate into 'fairness', 'ethical treatment' or 'justice', as these notions themselves are loaded with ambiguity. This flags the wide gap between formal and substantive equality (cf. Ontario 1995; Manfredi 2004).

CONCLUSION

In the DTCs, knowledges and goals are redefined and the boundaries surrounding knowledges are blurred. These courts are assembled networks in which therapeutic and legal knowledges are exchanged among the different personnel rendering the courts, at the same time and often in the same breath, spaces of both justice and therapy. Members of the network undergo processes of translation whereby their goals and interests shift. Translation, however, does not indicate the erasure of individual goals and interests which pre-exist DTC involvement. Rather, participation in the network allows the actors to maintain their old interests but redefine them so as to have them met through the technologies and practices of the DTC.

Latour (1993) claims 'we have never been modern'. The purity of disciplines and knowledges never existed. If we have never been modern, then neither law nor psy has ever been pure. A broader consideration of justice bears this out. Law and psy are well met in other facets of the criminal justice system. In actuality, the criminal law routinely blends knowledges as a matter of codification (think of how important mental capacity is to a criminal proceeding) (Sarat et al. 2003). The same court house that hosts the TDTC is also home to courts designed specifically to address mental health, family violence and Aboriginal peoples in conflict with the law. The growing movement of collaborative family law in Canada sees lawyers trained by psychologists and social workers to assist in assuaging family conflicts.

I emphasize the point of contamination here to caution against the possibility of hailing fictional juxtapositions to the treatment courts that come in the form of 'pure' therapy or 'pure' law. That is, I want to avoid concluding that the arrangement of expert actors and knowledges in the DTC is somehow unique as compared to what we might call 'traditional' assemblies of law and psy in which each discipline is imagined to be bounded and untainted. The DTCs might be best understood not as revolutions in the practices of either law or therapy, but as markers of a more explicit turn toward abandoning the suggestion of purity and formalizing governing practice that rely on the convergence of expertise and expert actors and, with these, the broader project of modernity. Beyond these rather tentative attempts to predict the future, the DTCs also give us a handy window on the present. Because the intersections between law and psy are so clear in this space, the courts lend themselves to attempts to further understand these interactions as governing strategies.

Through translation in the DTCs, cure and control become synonymous. This stylized murkiness re-imagines justice. The courts are recruited in the progressive project of curing addiction. In the face of the, at times, dark and ugly side of habitual drug use, the frustratingly apparent futility of imprisonment, the disasters of the war on drugs and the reality that decriminalization is a far distant possibility (Bourgeoise 2003; Erickson and Smart 1988; Marez 2004; Mauer 1999), it is hard to argue against an initiative that directs people out of the penal system, offers them rarified social services and health care and attempts to rid them of what, in actuality, can be a debilitating problem. Still, despite their very real and apparent appeal, DTCs maintain the same old practices of justice and punishment, only now they are known by different names. Detention translates into therapy, a warrant is now an incentive and appearance in a criminal court a chance to process a drug-use relapse. Translating these practices into a network with a broader curative goal does not erase their punitive, disciplinary intentions or effects. This does not make the treatment courts inherently good or bad. Instead, it reveals the rather complicated assemblages of power/knowledge through which they are formed.

(d) Collaborative Family Law and Gender Inequalities: Balancing Risks and Opportunities†

Wanda Wiegers & Michaela Keet

[1] The vast majority of family law disputes in Canada are settled rather than adjudicated.[1] Restricted legal aid coverage, high litigation costs, and mounting institutional pressures[2] combine to render settlement the most viable option for most family law clients.[3] In negotiating these settlements, the stakes are high since agreements negotiated with legal counsel are difficult to overturn and are likely to affect clients in profound ways long into the future.[4] Against this backdrop, lawyers and clients continue to search for more effective ways to enhance the settlement process. Dissatisfied with both litigation and mediation, many lawyers have recently turned to Collaborative Law (CL) as their process of choice.[5]

[2] In this article, we examine whether and how the distinctive features of CL affect the impact and salience of gender inequalities in the negotiation of family law disputes. First developed by lawyers in the United States, the emergence of CL has been described as a "paradigm shift" in legal practice.[6] One of the key distinguishing features of CL is the role lawyers play in the settlement process. CL seeks to realize the benefits of client participation and interest-based negotiation through the active involvement of lawyers as both facilitators and advocates. Unlike in traditional negotiation or litigation, CL lawyers commit to a set of transparent values that emphasizes the importance of the emotional and participatory needs of their clients, the possibility of creative outcomes, and the interdependence of the parties.[7] In another departure from most settlement processes, CL requires that both lawyers and clients work together in open four-way sessions toward the resolution of their dispute.

[3] The CL process is also typically structured according to rules of engagement and disengagement that are set out in agreements entered into by both clients and their lawyers. The content of these agreements varies between provinces and/or regions, but generally these agreements require open disclosure of all material information within the four-way session and demand that lawyers cease representing their clients if the process fails to generate a settlement. To date, the CL process, in both Canada and the United States, has been restricted largely to the family law area.[8]

[4] The impact of CL on gendered inequalities in bargaining power in family disputes has, as of yet, been largely unexplored. In an earlier article, we documented the results of a small-scale qualitative study that examined the experience of eight clients and twelve lawyers in CL.[9] We explored variables affecting client engagement inside the process and identified gendered power imbalances as one factor that led to varying, and often problematic, results. Given the same sample size of this study, our results could not be generalized to the client population at large. In the present article, we undertake a more comprehensive analysis of CL's potential to alleviate gendered differences in bargaining power between family law clients. We focus specifically on gender inequalities and draw to a greater extent on our lawyer interviews[10] to shed further light on the role of the lawyer in CL and on the effect of various procedural norms or constraints unique to the CL process. We also draw more broadly on the academic literature in the dispute resolution field, to the extent that this literature provides a critical lens into the potential risks and dangers of CL for the client population as a whole.

[5] The results of our qualitative study are consistent with established correlations between gender inequalities and well-recognized sources of unequal bargaining power in the context of separation.[11] Much higher rates of spousal abuse have been reported in past or previous relationships than in subsisting ones.[12] In intimate relationships generally, women are more likely than men to experience repeated incidents and more serious forms of physical violence[13] — including a higher risk of lethal violence after separation[14] — and are more likely to confront a climate of coercive control.[15]

---

† (2008) 46 Osgoode Hall L.J. 733–72 at paras. 1–27, 32–36, 29–51, 54–56, 64–67. Reproduced with permission. [Notes and/or references omitted.]

[6] Women's disproportionate responsibility for childcare[16] and lower earning potential also function as sources of power imbalance. Women are more likely to have both a stronger preference for custody and a greater need for support than men. Economically, women are more likely than men to have lower and often untested earning power[17] and less access to income-generating assets of the marriage. They may also have less accurate information regarding assets and future earning potential, and be more concerned about the cost of prolonged negotiation and litigation.[18]

[7] Gender role socialization further suggests that women might perceive themselves, or be perceived by others, as having less credibility or status in asserting their needs or interests,[19] might tend to prefer co-operation to conflict or strategic negotiation, and might compromise their claims to obtain better interpersonal relations in the longer run.[20] Finally, men are more likely than women to benefit from the difficulty of reliably predicting or quantifying legal entitlements in the area of family or divorce law.[21] These sources of power imbalance can render women in heterosexual relationships particularly vulnerable to settlement pressures and may not be fully offset or muted by other individualized variables.[22]

[8] There are inevitable limits on the extent to which any dispute resolution process can address inequalities in bargaining power that are rooted in social structures and relations external to the bargaining process. In the private dispute resolution context, critics worry that processes such as mediation will both obscure inequitable outcomes[23] and legitimize them as a product of voluntary consent.[24] Adjudication, however, can similarly reinforce social inequalities. Adjudication can provide a public record, provide a check on the quality of legal representation, and has the potential to generate new substantive norms, but it is also highly constrained in its ability to address poverty and inequality.[25] Not only is litigation dependent on the resources of the disputants, but many judges also remain insensitive to the impact of systemic inequalities[26] and to a host of process-based shortcomings that plague female litigants. These limitations include litigation's tendency to escalate hostilities and delay a resolution, clients' lack of control or understanding of the proceedings, high financial costs, and use of the process to harass and control.[27]

[9] No dispute resolution method will provide a panacea, but processes may well differ in their potential to mitigate the impact of inequalities and offer other benefits to clients. Advocates of CL have argued that

the more extensive involvement of lawyers, among other features, has the potential to deal more effectively with vulnerable clients than current forms of either litigation or family mediation.[28] We agree that CL's potential in managing gender inequalities flows largely from the integration of lawyers in the process because counsel can facilitate the provision of more thorough legal advice and more individualized negotiating support. This potential, however, will not be fully realized unless lawyers demonstrate high levels of sensitivity to imbalances, utilize effective screening strategies, provide timely and specific legal advice, and work at achieving deeper and more effective client–lawyer communication. In particular, we raise serious concerns regarding the risks arising from the use of the standard disqualification provision (DP), which heightens the importance of building adequate screening into the process.

[10] Given the limitations in current research on the specific impact of CL, the analysis we provide is by necessity speculative or exploratory in nature and is limited to the variables we identify. In Part I, we examine the common goals and background norms of mediation and CL, and provide a summary of the extensive literature on gender imbalances in the context of mediation. In Part II, the potential risks we identify are evaluated in light of the unique structural features of the CL process.

I. EVIDENCE OF OUTCOMES AND BACKGROUND NORMS

[11] Although CL agreements vary across communities of practice, the background norms and goals of CL closely mirror those of family mediation.[29] Both processes follow the basic stages of an interest-based model: identifying issues, exploring interests, generating options, and reaching agreement.[30] Both CL and family mediation strive to return ownership of the problem — and the solution — to the clients and, through future-oriented, co-operative frameworks, seek to avoid strategic positional bargaining, improve communication, and facilitate emotional healing.[31] Proponents of both processes claim similar benefits: psychological empowerment, emotional healing, durable agreements, and, in the best of cases, personal transformation.[32]

[12] Researchers have had more opportunity to evaluate the outcomes of mediation given its long-established use in the family law field; yet, even in this context, alleged benefits have not been conclusively established or universally acknowledged. Connie Beck

and Bruce Sales, for example, question the extent to which existing studies of mediation use sound methodologies[33] and point out that, when separated by gender, the results of empirical studies of satisfaction rates are mixed.[34] Empirical assessments of substantive outcomes are sparse, likely due to the difficulty of controlling for all salient variables — and again the results are mixed.[35] Research also overlooks the effect of mediation on distinctive groups of women, such as racialized women or homosexual women.[36]

[13] Drawing on the largest longitudinal study of mediation conducted in Canada, Desmond Ellis and Noreen Stuckless found that women in a voluntary, publicly-funded mediation sample were more likely to be satisfied with child support alone, but women in the lawyer negotiation sample, funded through legal aid tariffs, more often obtained sole legal custody.[37] They also found that differences in income, or the experience of abuse, did not significantly correlate with outcomes, which considered access, custody or property division, and levels of child support among wives in both samples.[38] It is important to note that couples with "power imbalances great enough to adversely influence the bargaining capacity of the partners" were screened out of the mediation sample at intake and that abusive behavior was consistently monitored by trained mediators throughout the process.[39] Ellis and Stuckless also did not assess the impact of either process on spousal support. It is unclear with what specificity they examined property division because the economic differences between parties did not appear to have been great in either sample. In a subsequent article, Desmond Ellis and Laurie Wight note that available evidence "strongly suggests" that "[economic] resources ought to be included in a theory of interpersonal power in divorce mediation."[40]

[14] In its findings on the question of custody, the Ellis and Stuckless study is consistent with others that suggest a tendency among mediators to favour joint custody or shared parenting.[41] Critics have complained that this tendency reflects a bias on the part of mediators who present their primary concerns as emotional healing, equal participation, and minimal conflict, and are insensitive both to the impact of the primary care role performed disproportionately by women and to issues of abuse.[42] In 1988, Martha Fineman argued that the use of family mediation and the growing influence of social workers and psychologists had precipitated a shift in substantive norms toward shared parenting and had dramatically reallocated power between mothers and fathers.[43] While this emphasis on contact and joint custody

has since become increasingly evident in all legal modes of dispute resolution, including lawyer-to-lawyer negotiations, pre-trial conferences, and adjudicated outcomes, it is likely intensified through the collaborative frame of mediation.

[15] Early research into CL has shown high settlement rates[44] but has also raised red flags about a similar "harmony agenda"[45] that is linked to a specific conception of what "healthy family transitions" entail.[46] Prominent CL authors, such as Nancy Cameron and Pauline Tesler, emphasize the importance of deescalating conflict and acrimony for the sake of the children, promote the importance of contact with each parent through the restructuring of the post-divorce family, and portray the adversarial system largely as a catalyst for increased hostilities.[47] Within such a normative vision, the parties' interests are focused on maintaining a good relationship between parents, promoting future co-operation, and settling promptly without protracted debate.[48]

[16] In some respects, CL goes further than mediation to de-emphasize adversarial tendencies and defuse conflict. In addition to the DP, which intensifies the commitment to settlement, CL requires a more overt commitment to the concept of teamwork: "the lawyers and clients work together as a team of equals, all pulling together on the same side of the problem."[49] The commitment of each party's lawyer to these ideals has the potential to reinforce the collaborative framework to a greater extent than typically occurs in mediation.

[17] This "harmony agenda" can also affect women differently than men. On the one hand, CL's value orientation may strongly validate negotiation behaviour or an "ethic of care" that, some argue, is more common to women, both as clients and lawyers.[50] To the extent that they do prefer collaborative negotiation, CL might provide some comfort to women and simultaneously influence or put pressure on men to adopt a more co-operative, conciliatory style.[51] Ultimately, the magnitude of this benefit depends on how successful the CL process is in encouraging men to abandon strategic, adversarial bargaining. While CL's formalized collaborative approach may be more successful in this respect than mediation, if unsuccessful, the process may simply induce a false sense of security in women. As Trina Grillo indicates in relation to mediation: "[i]f she is easily persuaded to be co-operative, but her partner is not, she can only lose."[52]

[18] The emphasis on familial welfare can also pressure weaker parties, typically mothers, to abandon

legitimate claims to reduce conflict and obtain closure.[53] The emphasis on harmony may be particularly problematic for victims in abusive relationships since it can compound an abused spouse's reluctance or impaired ability to communicate.[54] Linda Neilson's New Brunswick study[55] found evidence that both mediators and lawyers failed to recognize abuse and pressured clients to accept generic settlements. Case studies of mediation in England also suggest that allegations of violence, even if identified through screening instruments, can often be sidelined, marginalized, and eventually discounted.[56] In her study of CL, Julie Macfarlane notes one instance where a client could not admit, in the joint four-way meeting, that she was afraid to go home that night because the parties were cohabiting.[57]

[19] As is common in mediation, the Collaborative Law Contract in Saskatchewan specifies that "unnecessary discussions of past events are to be avoided."[58] This exclusive orientation toward the future can suppress not only the disclosure of past domestic violence or abuse,[59] but also the expression of negative feelings that may be necessary for empowerment or healing.[60] Although collaborative strategies typically acknowledge emotions, critics argue that they can discourage the expression of anger, which, in the context of abuse or violence, can silence a spouse who should otherwise be speaking out.[61] Tesler, a leading proponent of CL, suggests that lawyers should help clients avoid their "shadow states," which are described as "the temporary upwelling(s) of intense and primitive emotions such as fear, rage, grief, or shame."[62] In an effort to preserve the ideal of the "higher self," CL lawyers may thus inadvertently suppress their clients' anger and other intense emotions that can legitimately arise from abuse.

[20] Given these substantive and co-operative norms, CL can be expected to generate concerns regarding gender-based power imbalances that are similar to those cited in the mediation context. The question, to be examined in the next part of this article, is how effectively the unique procedural framework of CL can address or moderate the impact of such power imbalances.

II. STRUCTURAL FEATURES OF COLLABORATIVE LAW

A. Entrenchment of Lawyers into the Process

[21] In family mediation, clients typically consult lawyers only on a periodic basis, outside sessions or after a tentative agreement has been reached.[63] In CL, by contrast, the lawyers of each client are actively involved and jointly part of the process from the outset. One of the principal arguments advanced by scholars,[64] lawyers,[65] and clients[66] who favour CL is that the ongoing involvement of lawyers can effectively address power imbalances. In the mediation context, Jane Murphy and Robert Rubinson similarly argue that legal advocates can act as "power enhancers and equalizers," as "they can speak on behalf of clients, evaluate proposed solutions in light of applicable legal norms and the specific experiences of the client, and, if necessary, suggest opting out of the mediation itself if it is not serving the interests of the client."[67]

[22] It is not entirely clear why family mediation has developed without the continuous presence of legal advocates. The emphasis on therapeutic intervention in the divorce context[68] and the lack of a functional role for lawyers inside the mediation process may have had some impact.[69] From a practical standpoint, family mediators may not have encouraged lawyer participation since lawyers who lack significant training in dispute resolution and have not internalized co-operative norms can critically undermine the possibility of collaboration. Perhaps one of the most influential factors weighing against lawyer participation has been the cost to clients.

[23] CL can also increase costs relative to the cost of a single mediator. William Schwab's survey in the United States produced a profile for CL clients that was largely "white, middle-aged, well-educated and affluent."[70] Surveys conducted by collaborative organizations also suggest that CL is significantly more costly than mediation.[71] These studies, however, do not indicate whether the costs of legal advice have been factored into the mediation tab, nor do they control for factors such as degrees of conflict or complexity.

[24] The recruitment of lawyers into the heart of the dispute resolution process in CL would appear to increase protection for vulnerable clients. However, a number of assumptions underlie this conclusion: that lawyers can effectively determine whether and how clients ought to participate in collaborative processes, that lawyer involvement increases the client's access to legal information, and that lawyers can provide clients with the right balance of self-determination and negotiation support. The following discussion explores the extent to which these assumptions are likely to be true in the CL context.

1. Screening for Power Imbalances and Abuse

[25] Despite the development of protocols and screening tools, there are still no clear criteria among mediators for determining "what a power difference is and when it is occurring."[72] Mediation literature addresses power differentials caused by abuse and individual incapacity but does not adequately acknowledge inequalities arising from socialized gender roles, differences in earning power, and contributions to domestic labour that affect the bargaining process.[73] Mediators largely agree that allegations of domestic violence require "special treatment"[74] and support the screening out of cases involving systematic patterns of control — physical, emotional, or economic abuse — particularly where women victims are fearful or abusive partners seek to hide, deny, or minimize abuse.[75] Although academic discussion suggests that mediators have a fairly high level of consciousness of domestic violence, empirical research suggests that mediators in practice often fail to screen for it.[76] Critics argue that mediators underestimate the frequency and impact of power imbalances and rely too heavily on "quick-fix power balancing techniques."[77]

[26] Available research suggests that lawyers are not necessarily more conscious of unequal power or more prepared to deal with screening than mediators. Neilson's extensive research of case law, court files, and interview data in New Brunswick in 2001 revealed that evidence of abuse was siphoned off continuously throughout the legal process, possibly because lawyers either failed to detect abuse or underestimated or discounted its existence.[78]

[27] In the CL literature, issues of power and abuse are only beginning to be acknowledged. Collaborative Family Law includes only a few paragraphs on power issues;[79] Collaborative Practice: Deepening the Dialogue devotes more attention to these issues but acknowledges that the comments offer only a "starting point."[80] Basic CL training sessions may also pay little attention to screening issues, providing no template or systematic screening checklist and no training on how to conduct a screening interview.[81]

. . . .

[32] The task of screening for domestic violence or emotional abuse — whether in mediation or in CL — is inherently difficult and requires specialized knowledge of the nature and dynamics of spousal abuse and its long-term effects on children and victims. Women may raise allegations in indirect and tentative ways, often to test whether it is safe to provide more extensive disclosure.[97] Lesbian, immigrant, and Aboriginal women are less apt to report violence to authorities for fear of child protection proceedings, deportation, or loss of status in their communities, and these fears may inhibit disclosure even in more private negotiations.[98] After establishing a basis for trust, lawyers need to screen using specific questions while also paying attention to behavioural cues, such as unexplained injuries, absences from work, unusual fear, and avoidance of conflict.[99] Faced with ambiguity, lawyers, like mediators, may tend too often to reformulate the victim's story to conform to the presumptions of equality that underpin collaborative processes.[100]

[33] The potential for abuse or violence to remain hidden suggests that lawyers require specific training not only to identify its existence, but also to assess the type of violence and the magnitude of risks clients may face.[101] Standard screening protocols should be used to help lawyers recognize the continuum of abuse and respond in different ways, such as by declining to proceed, recommending against the process, or proceeding with safety or other supportive measures clearly in place. Abusive spouses may contest allegations of abuse, and they may be highly skilled in presenting themselves. To identify spousal abuse and distinguish it from claims of mutual abuse, a lawyer must examine the history of the relationship and consider both the context in which the violence or abuse occurs and its consequences. Third party verification of claims and counter-claims may also need to be explored.[102]

[34] Relationships involving a history of escalating acts or threats of harm against spouses or children (or threats of, or attempted suicide), along with a pattern of domination, control, or obsessive jealousy can particularly pose a serious risk to the well-being of victims and children, and to the possibility of an agreement that meets the parties' needs.[103] In such circumstances, conventional advocacy, rather than CL or mediation, could result in more ready access to restraining or protective orders, less direct exposure to the abusive party, and less risk that the victim's substantive claims will be devalued.

[35] Assumptions that power imbalances can be easily managed, even through the joint action of lawyers, belies the complexity of these issues. While screening is essential for mediation, it is even more important in CL, given the heightened costs of terminating the process and the inevitability of face-to-face encounters through the use of four-way meetings.[104]

2. Ambiguity Over the Influence of Legal Norms

[36] To the extent that legal entitlements provide a defence against the impact of power imbalances, the ongoing presence of lawyers in the CL process could render legal advice more accessible and help to ensure that a client's legal entitlements are respected. Studies to date, however, find significant variations between CL lawyers in how much legal advice they give, when they give it, and how specific it is to the client's situation.[105] These differences in practice reflect differences in the weight lawyers themselves place on legal entitlements relative to the "interests" identified by clients in the negotiation process. As with mediation, CL acknowledges that both parties' interests can be fully met outside the bounds of legal norms.[106] Indeed, proponents of CL argue that legal positions easily get in the way of creative problem solving. Instead, clients should feel "free to compromise and substitute their own standards of acceptability and reasonableness for the legal standard,"[107] and lawyers should avoid "premature advice-giving [that] may put a chill on the negotiations."[108]

. . . .

[39] Unfortunately, our lawyer and client interviews suggest that some CL lawyers are divesting themselves of the protective role advocated by Murphy and Robinson in mediation.[114] This is problematic because less powerful clients may be losing access to legal standards that have evolved over time precisely to protect their interests. These standards are especially significant in family cases, given the social devaluation of women's domestic labour and the prevalence of abuse. In this context, legal norms remain an important benchmark against which a client can assess her interests.

3. *Traditional Advocacy and Emotional Support*

[40] In its emphasis on client self-determination and control as a central norm of the process,[115] CL calls for a reformulation of the lawyer–client relationship and a redefinition of lawyer advocacy. In line with this objective, CL agreements typically provide that each client is expected to assert his or her own interests, and lawyers attempt to avoid reinforcing feelings of dependency or treating the client as simply a passive recipient of terms or entitlements. However, feedback from our study suggests that vulnerable clients may still depend heavily on their lawyers as a source of emotional support.[116] Clients who complained of abuse in their relationships

objected to their lawyers' "hands-off" approach; they felt they needed an advocate to "back [them] up,"[117] to respond to harassment and put-downs, and to help them "stand up to"[118] their spouse. CL lawyers must therefore navigate not only a tension between "zealous advocacy" and "peace-making,"[119] but also a tension between client autonomy and protective support and representation.

[41] Are lawyers adequately equipped to fulfill these complex expectations given the emotional intensity of such negotiations, the manipulative dynamics of long-standing abusive relationships, and the limits of conventional legal training?[120] For economically privileged clients, many of these concerns may be mitigated by the involvement of other counsellors, such as mental health professionals who work separately with clients; however, this Cadillac version of CL is not widely accessible.

[42] Managing these issues requires intensive lawyer–client communication such as open, ongoing feedback from the client to the lawyer through initial screening and preparatory interviews. Relative to a single mediator, CL lawyers are in a position to provide more individualized negotiating support. Lawyers can also try to work as a team in order to challenge rather than reinforce power imbalances between the parties.[121] While engaging the efforts of both lawyers is a creative and no doubt helpful response, there are also limits to this strategy. In the context of longstanding abusive relationships, these strategies may simply be unable to alter the dynamics.[122] Lawyers for an abusive spouse can only go so far to contain the abuse because of their professional duty to represent their individual client. Without adequate support, professional teamwork can leave the abused client feeling isolated, unprotected, or abandoned.[123] These limitations again underline the importance of careful screening.

[43] In summary, the integration of lawyers into CL can provide a number of significant potential benefits for clients through the integration of legal advice, the opportunity to develop deeper, more supportive solicitor–client relationships, and the opportunity to work jointly with other counsel to facilitate and preserve respectful communication on the part of both parties. However, as with screening, these potential benefits are also subject to limitations, such as insensitivity to the existence of power differentials and their implications for the bargaining process, formal rules discouraging lawyers from providing legal advice at appropriate stages of the process, and limited skill sets in dealing with problems of abuse.

B. Disclosure, Good Faith Bargaining, and Limits on Communication

[44] In addition to the extent to which it integrates lawyers into the problem-solving process, CL differs from mediation in its allegiance to particular rules of engagement — its "choreography."[124] Both mediation and CL agreements include a range of commitments that require the parties to negotiate with openness, co-operation, integrity, and in good faith. Since lawyers are signatories to the CL agreement and are, relative to mediation, more actively involved in the process, these commitments can come to life in a more meaningful way in CL. Whereas the mediation process is flexible and is designed in accordance with the guidance and preferences of the mediator,[125] the CL process imposes unique procedural norms and limitations on communications between lawyers and clients.

[45] First, CL lawyers are active participants in the commitments to full disclosure of all relevant information and rectification of any mistakes,[126] and they must typically withdraw from the process if they know such commitments are not being fulfilled.[127] In mediation, only the parties themselves agree to disclosure and lawyers are not usually witness to the exchange of information. Through the lawyers' contractual commitments and their ability to monitor disclosure, the promise of openness can be enforced more consistently in CL than in mediation.

[46] Nonetheless, CL lawyers, like mediators, must ultimately depend on their clients' veracity and good faith and on assumptions that may be ill-founded.[128] While any settlement may be explicitly premised on full disclosure, redress for the failure to disclose will also generally require court action. Clients may request that statements making full and final disclosure be sworn; however, not all lawyers use or recommend sworn statements.[129] Whether such assumptions of honesty are warranted is questionable and, in part, depends on whether lawyers have adequately screened for basic levels of trust, prior levels of financial disclosure, and the particular dynamics of the parties' relationship.

[47] The CL process imposes additional constraints through the inclusion of a DP that prohibits lawyers from acting for their clients in any contested court proceeding.[130] Unless clients specifically agree in advance to formal discovery procedures, they give up their right to access formal discovery procedures during CL. As well, where a client takes "unfair advantage" of the process by non-disclosure or bad faith bargaining to the knowledge of his or her lawyer, the lawyer must withdraw, bringing the CL process to an end.[131] In effect, the party acting in bad faith is able to force the discharge of the other party's lawyer, increasing the costs for that party.[132]

[48] The requirement that information exchange and negotiation occur primarily in four-way open sessions with both lawyers and clients[133] can also be of mixed benefit to clients affected by power imbalances. Four-way meetings are intended to help achieve openness and transparency, and avoid the strategic positioning or tactical maneuvering that can accompany traditional advocacy. Collaborative law proponents believe that these goals are more easily achieved if "all important conversations are ... experienced directly by each participant."[134] Lawyers and clients are encouraged to debrief between CL sessions,[135] but according to some agreements, full discussion of the substantive issues and exchange of information about the law should occur only in the four-way and not in private lawyer–client meetings.[136] These explicit constraints represent a significant change from both lawyer-led negotiations, where most communication would occur in two-way meetings between the lawyer and client and be subject to solicitor–client privilege, with follow up negotiation between the two lawyers — and from family mediation, where most mediators would ask the parties to seek information about their legal rights and obligations outside of the sessions.

[49] This emphasis on four-way communication can negatively affect spouses in abusive situations by discouraging lawyers from caucusing separately with their clients and fully discussing the matters in dispute. Private dialogue between lawyer and client may often be necessary to effectively manage the process, to ensure that the client fully understands his or her legal position, and to support his or her participation in the process. Providing information or advice privately is not per se being adversarial or positional. Where there are power imbalances and, particularly, patterns of control and abuse, open disclosure of concerns to the other party can in some circumstances impede the recovery process, undermine the client's coping strategies, or even put her in danger. While separate caucusing with the client may produce tension, under abusive or unequal conditions it may in fact work to advance the goals of openness and transparency. In our exploratory study, the four clients dealing with abuse or power imbalances all indicated a need for more intensive management and support beyond the four-way meetings.[137]

[50] Thus, while the CL structure may encourage more open and transparent communication between

the parties, it can also disadvantage parties in unequal or abusive relationships. An undue emphasis on the four-way model as a primary mode of negotiation can restrict access to the verification tools of the discovery process, and restrict the advice and independent support for vulnerable clients. Where an abusive party bargains in bad faith or does not fully disclose, the DP will operate to penalize the innocent spouse through the loss of his or her counsel.

C. Disqualification Provision (DP)

[51] The DP is the key distinguishing feature in CL, and many lawyers[138] view it as essential.[139] Most CL agreements require the parties not to threaten or commence court action during the process and to compromise if necessary to reach a settlement. The DP further provides that contracting lawyers are disqualified from representing their clients in any contested court proceeding involving the parties.[140] This clause is broad enough to be triggered by a number of events leading to court action, including the failure to reach an agreement; the need for a restraining order to protect a client; the reliance on formal discovery methods in order to obtain full disclosure; or the need for an order to prohibit the disposition of family property, to compel enforcement after reaching a settlement, or to vary the terms of the initial agreement.[141]

. . . .

[54] There is significant academic controversy in the United States as to whether the DP is consistent with ethical rules of professional conduct.[148] Nine state ethics committees have considered collaborative agreements in relation to their professional codes of conduct and all but one have upheld their use.[149] Three states have passed statutes authorizing the use of CL. Although DPs might be seen as analogous to agreements allowing for the withdrawal of one's lawyer — and which are enforceable in Canada[150] — there is a key difference in that the loss of one's lawyer under the DP can be triggered by the conduct of either party, and not only the lawyer's own client. Some writers have argued that parties might be better served by a different process, especially where the parties' economic resources and the merits of their legal positions differ significantly.[151] An alternative process is Co-operative Law, which includes a Co-operative Agreement that incorporates the co-operative norms of CL but excludes the DP.[152] According to Hilary Linton, in circumstances of financial and legal inequality, the DP will unfairly

compromise the power of the party with the superior legal claim and deny a legitimate source of leverage.[153]

[55] Although the DP is gender neutral in form, it is likely to have a disparate impact on female clients and place them at greater risk of relative disadvantage. Since women are most often the claimants in family disputes, legal entitlements are more apt to operate as a source of power for them.[154] Upon separation, it is women who more often lack access to an adequate income stream or marital assets or who may have superior claims to custody through their disproportionate role as primary caregivers.[155] To the extent that the DP raises the financial and emotional costs of litigation, it can increase the pressure to accept agreements that meet neither womens' identified interests nor their legal entitlements.

[56] Because both parties must share the eventual cost of litigation, the risk of being undermined in this way is most significant where trust is lacking, economic resources are unequal, and clients are affected by abusive and controlling dynamics. By increasing the cost of litigation as an alternative, the DP affords one more lever for manipulation and control.[156] Unequal, abusive, and controlling dynamics can also have a far more negative emotional impact where clients have high expectations and are encouraged to engage, from the outset, in co-operative rather than adversarial negotiation.[157]

. . . .

III. CONCLUSION

[64] Access to justice has been identified as a key concern in family law.[173] The future significance of collaborative family law for women will depend on the extent to which it addresses existing barriers to access to justice, including its accessibility and cost-effectiveness, and its response to underlying inequalities in the bargaining process. The intense involvement of legal advocates in CL provides an opportunity not only to enhance the problem-solving experience for women in the family law system but also to contribute, through a resocialization of lawyers, to more lasting systemic change. CL has given lawyers, both male and female, permission to talk about negative aspects of the image of the litigious lawyer.[174] Although many such accounts still rely on "simplistic dichotomous images" and a "generic horror story,"[175] the obvious passion, commitment, and "ethic of care"[176] that many CL lawyers bring to their work highlight what may be too often missing

in the adversarial system. In this sense, the turn to CL from mediation is more than an appropriation of similar rhetoric or a power grab in a professional turf war.

[65] CL could ultimately do more than mediation to change the legal culture.[177] Although mediation has been institutionalized to a greater degree and extended to other areas of law, its impact has been limited by the peripheral and uncertain role lawyers have played in its development. The excitement that many lawyers have for CL likely flows precisely from the discovery of a "functional role model" within an alternative dispute resolution process — accompanied by a new, still rule-oriented, procedural structure and ethical framework. The fact that many lawyers practising CL continue to include litigation in their family practice also suggests that rather than polarizing the practice of family law, the co-operative norms and values of CL may "spill over" into traditional negotiations and litigation.

[66] CL may also have a unique capacity to raise lawyers' sensitivity to power differentials through the organizational structures the movement has spawned among practising lawyers. Whereas mediation practice groups and policy debates tend to exclude lawyers who are not also professional mediators, CL can draw on professional associations and community groups that have formed across the country to provide information to the public as well as training and support for lawyers.[178] Through training and collective discussion, these groups have the potential to increase sensitivities and work through new approaches.

[67] Under current social conditions, the fundamental conflict of interest between the men and women who ultimately finance the provision of CL will inevitably limit the extent of this influence. Gendered inequalities are also difficult issues for a movement still struggling for legitimacy in a conservative profession to confront, particularly in times of political reaction and resistance to feminist discourse and initiatives.[179] However, heightened attention to the existence of gendered power differentials, the exploration of variations in the "meaning of co-operation" by screening clients into different processes,[180] timely and specific legal advice, and deeper and more effective lawyer–client communication could provide meaningful ways of improving the experience of female clients in the family law justice system. While not a radical challenge to systemic inequality, the adoption of such measures could at least mitigate the damage that can otherwise result when power differentials are obscured for the sake of family harmony.

19 — The Debate over Use of Settlement-based Dispute Resolution Processes

(a) Against Settlement†

Owen M. Fiss

In a recent report to the Harvard Overseers, Derek Bok called for a new direction in legal education.[1] He decried "the familiar tilt in the law curriculum toward preparing students for legal combat," and asked instead that law schools train their students "for the gentler arts of reconciliation and accommodation."[2] He sought to turn our attention from the courts to "new voluntary mechanisms"[3] for resolving disputes. In doing so, Bok echoed themes that have long been associated with the Chief Justice,[4] and that have become a rallying point for the organized bar and the source of a new movement in the law. This movement is the subject of a new professional journal,[5] a newly formed section of the American Association of Law Schools, and several well-funded institutes. It has even received its own acronym — ADR (Alternative Dispute Resolution).

The movement promises to reduce the amount of litigation initiated, and accordingly the bulk of its proposals are devoted to negotiation and mediation prior to suit. But the interest in the so-called "gentler arts" has not been so confined. It extends to ongoing litigation as well, and the advocates of ADR have sought new ways to facilitate and perhaps even pressure parties into settling pending cases. Just last year, Rule 16 of the Federal Rules of Civil Procedure was amended to strengthen the hand of the trial judge in brokering settlements: The "facilitation of settlement" became an explicit purpose of pretrial conferences, and participants were officially invited, if that is the proper word, to consider "the possibility of settlement or the use of extrajudicial procedures to resolve the dispute."[5] Now the Advisory Committee on Civil Rules is proposing to amend Rule 68 to sharpen the incentives for settlement: Under this amendment, a party who rejects a settlement offer and then receives a judgment less favorable than that offer must pay the attorney's fees of the other party.[7] This amendment would effect a major change in the traditional American rule, under which each party pays his or her own attorney's fees.[8] It would also be at odds with a number of statutes that seek to facilitate certain types of civil litigation by providing attorney's fees to plaintiffs if they win, without imposing liability for the attorney's fees of their adversaries if they lose.[9]

The advocates of ADR are led to support such measures and to exalt the idea of settlement more generally because they view adjudication as a process to resolve disputes. They act as though courts arose to resolve quarrels between neighbors who had reached an impasse and turned to a stranger for help.[10] Courts are seen as an institutionalization of the stranger and adjudication is viewed as the process by which the stranger exercises power. The very fact that the neighbors have turned to someone else to resolve their dispute signifies a breakdown in their social relations; the advocates of ADR acknowledge this, but nonetheless hope that the neighbors will be able to reach agreement before the stranger renders judgment. Settlement is that agreement. It is a truce more than a true reconciliation, but it seems preferable to judgment because it rests on the consent of both parties and avoids the cost of a lengthy trial.

---

† (1984) 93 Yale L. J. 1073 at 1073–78, 1082–90. Reproduced with permission. [Notes and/or references omitted.]

In my view, however, this account of adjudication and the case for settlement rest on questionable premises. I do not believe that settlement as a generic practice is preferable to judgment or should be institutionalized on a wholesale and indiscriminate basis. It should be treated instead as a highly problematic technique for streamlining dockets. Settlement is for me the civil analogue of plea bargaining: Consent is often coerced; the bargain may be struck by someone without authority; the absence of a trial and judgment renders subsequent judicial involvement troublesome; and although dockets are trimmed, justice may not be done. Like plea bargaining, settlement is a capitulation to the conditions of mass society and should be neither encouraged nor praised.

THE IMBALANCE OF POWER

By viewing the lawsuit as a quarrel between two neighbors, the dispute-resolution story that underlies ADR implicitly asks us to assume a rough equality between the contending parties. It treats settlement as the anticipation of the outcome of trial and assumes that the terms of settlement are simply a product of the parties' predictions of that outcome.[11] In truth, however, settlement is also a function of the resources available to each party to finance the litigation, and those resources are frequently distributed unequally. Many lawsuits do not involve a property dispute between two neighbors, or between AT&T and the government (to update the story), but rather concern a struggle between a member of a racial minority and a municipal police department over alleged brutality, or a claim by a worker against a large corporation over work-related injuries. In these cases, the distribution of financial resources, or the ability of one party to pass along its costs, will invariably infect the bargaining process and the settlement will be at odds with a conception of justice that seeks to make the wealth of the parties irrelevant.

The disparities in resources between the parties can influence the settlement in three ways. First, the poorer party may be less able to amass and analyze the information needed to predict the outcome of the litigation, and thus be disadvantaged in the bargaining process. Second, he may need the damages he seeks immediately and thus be induced to settle as a way of accelerating payment, even though he realizes he would get less now than he might if he awaited judgment. All plaintiffs want their damages immediately, but an indigent plaintiff may be exploited by a rich defendant because his need is so great that the defendant can force him to accept

a sum that is less than the ordinary present value of the judgment. Third, the poorer party might be forced to settle because he does not have the resources to finance the litigation, to cover either his own projected expenses, such as his lawyer's time, or the expenses his opponent can impose through the manipulation of procedural mechanisms such as discovery. It might seem that settlement benefits the plaintiff by allowing him to avoid the costs of litigation, but this is not so. The defendant can anticipate the plaintiff's costs if the case were to be tried fully and decrease his offer by that amount. The indigent plaintiff is a victim of the costs of litigation even if he settles.[12]

There are exceptions. Seemingly rich defendants may sometimes be subject to financial pressures that make them as anxious to settle as indigent plaintiffs. But I doubt that these circumstances occur with any great frequency. I also doubt that institutional arrangements such as contingent fees or the provision of legal services to the poor will in fact equalize resources between contending parties: The contingent fee does not equalize resources; it only makes an indigent plaintiff vulnerable to the willingness of the private bar to invest in his case. In effect, the ability to exploit the plaintiff's lack of resources has been transferred from rich defendants to lawyers who insist upon a hefty slice of the plaintiff's recovery as their fee. These lawyers, moreover, will only work for contingent fees in certain kinds of cases, such as personal-injury suits. And the contingent fee is of no avail when the defendant is the disadvantaged party. Governmental subsidies for legal services have a broader potential, but in the civil domain the battle for these subsidies was hard-fought, and they are in fact extremely limited, especially when it comes to cases that seek systemic reform of government practices.[13]

Of course, imbalances of power can distort judgment as well: Resources influence the quality of presentation, which in turn has an important bearing on who wins and the terms of victory. We count, however, on the guiding presence of the judge, who can employ a number of measures to lessen the impact of distributional inequalities. He can, for example, supplement the parties' presentations by asking questions, calling his own witnesses, and inviting other persons and institutions to participate as amici.[14] These measures are likely to make only a small contribution toward moderating the influence of distributional inequalities, but should not be ignored for that reason. Not even these small steps are possible with settlement. There is, moreover, a critical difference between a process like settlement, which is based on bargaining and accepts inequalities of wealth as an integral and legitimate component of the process, and a process like judgment, which knowingly struggles against those inequalities. Judgment aspires to an autonomy from distributional inequalities, and it gathers much of its appeal from this aspiration.

. . . .

THE LACK OF A FOUNDATION FOR CONTINUING JUDICIAL INVOLVEMENT

The dispute-resolution story trivializes the remedial dimensions of lawsuits and mistakenly assumes judgment to be the end of the process. It supposes that the judge's duty is to declare which neighbor is right and which wrong, and that this declaration will end the judge's involvement (save in that most exceptional situation where it is also necessary for him to issue a writ directing the sheriff to execute the declaration). Under these assumptions, settlement appears as an almost perfect substitute for judgment, for it too can declare the parties' rights. Often, however, judgment is not the end of a lawsuit but only the beginning. The involvement of the court may continue almost indefinitely. In these cases, settlement cannot provide an adequate basis for that necessary continuing involvement, and thus is no substitute for judgment.

The parties may sometimes be locked in combat with one another and view the lawsuit as only one phase in a long continuing struggle. The entry of judgment will then not end the struggle, but rather change its terms and the balance of power. One of the parties will invariably return to the court and again ask for its assistance, not so much because conditions have changed, but because the conditions that preceded the lawsuit have unfortunately not changed. This often occurs in domestic-relations cases, where the divorce decree represents only the opening salvo in an endless series of skirmishes over custody and support.[26]

The structural reform cases that play such a prominent role on the federal docket provide another occasion for continuing judicial involvement. In these cases, courts seek to safeguard public values by restructuring large-scale bureaucratic organizations.[27] The task is enormous, and our knowledge of how to restructure on-going bureaucratic organizations is limited. As a consequence, courts must oversee and manage the remedial process for a long time — maybe forever. This, I fear, is true of most school desegregation cases, some of which have been pending for twenty or thirty years.[28] It is also true of antitrust cases that seek divestiture or reorganization of an industry.[29]

The drive for settlement knows no bounds and can result in a consent decree even in the kinds of cases I have just mentioned, that is, even when a court finds itself embroiled in a continuing struggle between the parties or must reform a bureaucratic organization. The parties may be ignorant of the difficulties ahead or optimistic about the future, or they may simply believe that they can get more favorable terms through a bargained-for agreement. Soon, however, the inevitable happens: One party returns to court and asks the judge to modify the decree, either to make it more effective or less stringent. But the judge is at a loss: He has no basis for assessing the request. He cannot, to use Cardozo's somewhat melodramatic formula, easily decide whether the "dangers, once substantial, have become attenuated to a shadow,"[30] because, by definition, he never knew the dangers.

The allure of settlement in large part derives from the fact that it avoids the need for a trial. Settlement must thus occur before the trial is complete and the judge has entered findings of fact and conclusions of law. As a consequence, the judge confronted with a request for modification of a consent decree must retrospectively reconstruct the situation as it existed at the time the decree was entered, and decide whether conditions today have sufficiently changed to warrant a modification in that decree. In the Meat Packers litigation, for example, where a consent decree governed the industry for almost half a century, the judge confronted with a request for modification in 1960 had to reconstruct the "danger" that had existed at the time of the entry of the decree in 1920 in order to determine whether the danger had in fact become a "shadow."[31] Such an inquiry borders on the absurd, and is likely to dissipate whatever savings in judicial resources the initial settlement may have produced.

Settlement also impedes vigorous enforcement, which sometimes requires use of the contempt power. As a formal matter, contempt is available to punish violations of a consent decree.[32] But courts hesitate to use that power to enforce decrees that rest solely on consent, especially when enforcement is aimed at high public officials, as became evident in the Willowbrook deinstitutionalization case[33] and the recent Chicago desegregation case.[34] Courts do not see a mere bargain between the parties as a sufficient foundation for the exercise of their coercive powers.

Sometimes the agreement between the parties extends beyond the terms of the decree and includes stipulated "findings of fact" and "conclusions of law," but even then an adequate foundation for a strong use of the judicial power is lacking. Given the underlying purpose of settlement — to avoid trial — the so-called "findings" and "conclusions" are necessarily the products of a bargain between the parties rather than of a trial and an independent judicial judgment. Of course, a plaintiff is free to drop a lawsuit altogether (provided that the interests of certain other persons are not compromised), and a defendant can offer something in return, but that bargained-for arrangement more closely resembles a contract than an injunction. It raises a question which has already been answered whenever an injunction is issued, namely, whether the judicial power should be used to enforce it. Even assuming that the consent is freely given and authoritative, the bargain is at best contractual and does not contain the kind of enforcement commitment already embodied in a decree that is the product of a trial and the judgment of a court.

JUSTICE RATHER THAN PEACE

The dispute-resolution story makes settlement appear as a perfect substitute for judgment, as we just saw, by trivializing the remedial dimensions of a lawsuit, and also by reducing the social function of the lawsuit to one of resolving private disputes: In that story, settlement appears to achieve exactly the same purpose as judgment — peace between the parties — but at considerably less expense to society. The two quarrelling neighbors turn to a court in order to resolve their dispute, and society makes courts available because it wants to aid in the achievement of their private ends or to secure the peace.

In my view, however, the purpose of adjudication should be understood in broader terms. Adjudication uses public resources, and employs not strangers chosen by the parties but public officials chosen by a process in which the public participates. These officials, like members of the legislative and executive branches, possess a power that has been defined and conferred by public law, not by private agreement. Their job is not to maximize the ends of private parties, nor simply to secure the peace, but to explicate and give force to the values embodied in authoritative texts such as the Constitution and statutes: to interpret those values and to bring reality into accord with them. This duty is not discharged when the parties settle.

In our political system, courts are reactive institutions. They do not search out interpretive occasions, but instead wait for others to bring matters to their attention. They also rely for the most part on others to investigate and present the law and facts. A settlement will thereby deprive a court of the occasion, and perhaps even the ability, to render an interpretation. A court cannot proceed (or not proceed very far) in the face of a settlement. To be against settlement is not to urge that parties be "forced" to litigate, since that would interfere with their autonomy and distort the adjudicative process; the parties will be inclined to make the court believe that their bargain is justice. To be against settlement is only to suggest that when the parties settle, society gets less than what appears, and for a price it does not know it is paying. Parties might settle while leaving justice undone. The settlement of a school suit might secure the peace, but not racial equality. Although the parties are prepared to live under the terms they bargained for, and although such peaceful coexistence may be a necessary precondition of justice,[35] and itself a state of affairs to be valued, it is not justice itself. To settle for something means to accept less than some ideal.

I recognize that judges often announce settlements not with a sense of frustration or disappointment, as my account of adjudication might suggest, but with a sigh of relief. But this sigh should be seen for precisely what it is: It is not a recognition that a job is done, nor an acknowledgment that a job need not be done because justice has been secured. It is instead based on another sentiment altogether, namely, that another case has been "moved along," which is true whether or not justice has been done or even needs to be done. Or the sigh might be based on the fact that the agony of judgment has been avoided.

There is, of course, sometimes a value to avoidance, not just to the judge, who is thereby relieved of the need to make or enforce a hard decision, but also to society, which sometimes thrives by masking its basic contradictions. But will settlement result in avoidance when it is most appropriate? Other familiar avoidance devices, such as certiorari,[36] at least promise a devotion to public ends, but settlement is controlled by the litigants, and is subject to their private motivations and all the vagaries of the bargaining process. There are also dangers to avoidance, and these may well outweigh any imagined benefits. Partisans of ADR — Chief Justice Berger, or even President Bok — may begin with a certain satisfaction with the status quo. But when one sees injustices that cry out for correction — as Congress

405

did when it endorsed the concept of the private attorney general[37] and as the Court of another era did when it sought to enhance access to the courts[38] — the value of avoidance diminishes and the agony of judgment becomes a necessity. Someone has to confront the betrayal of our deepest ideals and be prepared to turn the world upside down to bring those ideals to fruition.

THE REAL DIVIDE

To all this, one can readily imagine a simple response by way of confession and avoidance: We are not talking about *those* lawsuits. Advocates of ADR might insist that my account of adjudication, in contrast to the one implied by the dispute-resolution story, focuses on a rather narrow category of lawsuits. They could argue that while settlement may have only the most limited appeal with respect to those cases, I have not spoken to the "typical" cases. My response is twofold.

First, even as a purely quantitative matter, I doubt that the number of cases I am referring to is trivial. My universe includes those cases in which there are significant distributional inequalities; those in which it is difficult to generate authoritative consent because organizations or social groups are parties or because the power to settle is vested in autonomous agents; those in which the court must continue to supervise the parties after judgment; and those in which justice needs to be done, or to put it more modestly, where there is a genuine social need for an authoritative interpretation of law. I imagine that the number of cases that satisfy one of these four criteria is considerable; in contrast to the kind of case portrayed in the dispute-resolution story, they probably dominate the docket of a modern court system.

Second, it demands a certain kind of myopia to be concerned only with the number of cases, as though all cases are equal simply because the clerk of the court assigns each a single docket number. All cases are not equal. The Los Angeles desegregation case,[39] to take one example, is not equal to the allegedly more typical suit involving a property dispute or an automobile accident. The desegregation suit consumes more resources, affects more people, and provokes far greater challenges to the judicial power. The settlement movement must introduce a qualitative perspective; it must speak to these more "significant" cases, and demonstrate the propriety of settling them. Otherwise it will soon be seen as an irrelevance, dealing with trivia rather than responding

to the very conditions that give the movement its greatest sway and saliency.

Nor would sorting cases into "two tracks," one for settlement, and another for judgment, avoid my objections. Settling automobile cases and leaving discrimination or antitrust cases for judgment might remove a large number of cases from the dockets, but the dockets will nevertheless remain burdened with the cases that consume the most judicial resources and represent the most controversial exercises of the judicial power. A "two track" strategy would drain the argument for settlement of much of its appeal. I also doubt whether the "two track" strategy can be sensibly implemented. It is impossible to formulate adequate criteria for prospectively sorting cases. The problems of settlement are not tied to the subject matter of the suit, but instead stem from factors that are harder to identify, such as the wealth of the parties, the likely post-judgment history of the suit, or the need for an authoritative interpretation of law. The authors of the amendment to Rule 68 make a gesture toward a "two track" strategy by exempting class actions and shareholder derivative suits, and by allowing the judge to refrain from awarding attorney's fees when it is "unjustified under all of the circumstances."[40] But these gestures are cramped and ill-conceived, and are likely to increase the workload of the courts by giving rise to yet another set of issues to litigate.[41] It is, moreover, hard to see how these problems can be avoided. Many of the factors that lead a society to bring social relationships that otherwise seem wholly private (e.g., marriage) within the jurisdiction of a court, such as imbalances of power or the interests of third parties, are also likely to make settlement problematic. Settlement is a poor substitute for judgement; it is an even poorer substitute for the withdrawal of jurisdiction.

For these reasons, I remain highly skeptical of a "two track" strategy, and would resist it. But the more important point to note is that the draftsmen of Rule 68 are the exception. There is no hint of a "two track" strategy in Rule 16. In fact, most ADR advocates make no effort to distinguish between different types of cases or to suggest that "the gentler arts of reconciliation and accommodation" might be particularly appropriate for one type of case but not for another. They lump all cases together. This suggests that what divides me from the partisans of ADR is not that we are concerned with different universes of cases [and] that Derek Bok, for example, focuses on boundary quarrels while I see only desegregation suits. I suspect instead that what divides us is much deeper and stems from our understanding of the purpose of the civil law suit and its place in society. It is a difference in outlook.

Someone like Bok sees adjudication in essentially private terms: The purpose of lawsuits and the civil courts is to resolve disputes, and the amount of litigation we encounter is evidence of the needlessly combative and quarrelsome character of Americans. Or as Bok put it, using a more diplomatic idiom: "At bottom, ours is a society built on individualism, competition, and success."[42] I, on the other hand, see adjudication in more public terms: Civil litigation is an institutional arrangement for using state power to bring a recalcitrant reality closer to our chosen ideas. We turn to the courts because we need to, not because of some quirk in our personalities. We train our students in the tougher arts so that they may help secure all that the law promises, not because

we want them to become gladiators or because we take a special pleasure in combat.

To conceive of the civil lawsuit in public terms as America does might be unique. I am willing to assume that no other country — including Japan, Bok's new paragon[43] — has a case like *Brown v. Board of Education*[44] in which the judicial power is used to eradicate the caste structure. I am willing to assume that no other country conceives of law and uses law in quite the way we do. But this should be a source of pride rather than shame. What is unique is not the problem, that we live short of our ideals, but that we alone among the nations of the world seem willing to do something about it. Adjudication American-style is not a reflection of our combativeness but rather a tribute to our inventiveness and perhaps even more to our commitment.

(b)   For Reconciliation†

Andrew W. McThenia and Thomas L. Shaffer

Professor Owen Fiss, in his recent comment, *Against Settlement*,[1] weighs in against the Alternative Dispute Resolution (ADR) movement. He brings to the discussion his often stated preference for adjudication, which he views as "a tribute to our inventiveness,"[2] to be encouraged because it is a forum for the articulation of important public values. Fiss argues that the entire movement for alternatives to litigation is misplaced. He understands that the movement's claim to legitimacy turns on the inefficiency of the legal system and on popular dissatisfaction with law as a means for maintaining order,[3] and he challenges this claim.

Fiss attacks a straw man. In our view, the models he has created for argument in other circumstances[4] have become mechanisms of self-deception not only for him but for most of those who write about alternatives to litigation. His understanding that the plea of ADR advocates is based on efficiency reduces the entire question to one of procedures. Fiss's argument rests on the faith that justice — and he uses the word — is usually something people get from the government. He comes close to

arguing that the branch of government that resolves disputes, the courts, is the principal source of justice in fragmented modern American society.[5]

Fiss's view that the claims of ADR advocates arise from a popular dissatisfaction with law reduces the issue to one of order.[6] As his first stated understanding reduces justice to statism, this understanding reduces justice (or, if you like, peace) to a tolerably minimum level of violence in the community. In our view, an appropriate engagement of the Fiss attack on ADR must go all the way back to these two characterizations in his argument against ADR and in favor of court-dominated dispute resolution. We are not willing to let him frame the issue.

Certain themes recur in the ADR literature. Many advocates of ADR make efficiency-based claims. And a plea for ending the so-called litigation explosion, and for returning to law and order, runs through the rules-of-procedure branch of the ADR literature.[7] But the movement, if it is even appropriate to call it a single movement, is too varied for Fiss's description. Rather than focusing on the substance of claims made for ADR, Fiss has created a

---

† (1985) 94 Yale L.J. 1660. Reproduced with permission. [Notes and/or references omitted.]

view of the function of courts that he can comfortably oppose.

In an earlier and provocative article, Fiss called for both a recognition and an affirmation of the expanded role of courts in modern America.[8] He urged an explicit recognition that "[a]djudication is the social process by which judges give meaning to our public values."[9] Further, he argued that a new form of adjudication, "structural reform," be celebrated as "a central — maybe the central — mode of constitutional adjudication."[10] To develop his thesis and to meet Professor Lon Fuller's arguments on the limits of adjudication,[11] Fiss resorted to modelling. He contrasted his preferred view of adjudication, "structural reform," with what he described as a "traditional" model of adjudication. Although it is not clear whether he understood the *substance* of the two types of adjudication to be fundamentally different,[12] he clearly viewed the *form* of structural reform litigation as "breathtakingly different"[13] from the "dispute resolution" or "traditional" model of adjudication.

While Fiss was initially content to construct contrasting models of adjudication simply in order to accentuate his position and argue against Fuller's, he has in more recent writings asserted that one of these models, that of traditional dispute resolution, has a life of its own, a life that has "long dominated the literature and our thinking."[14] In fact, Fiss's later positive description of structural reform continues to flower, while his negative description of traditional adjudication has become abstract and lifeless. Fiss's response to the imperfections of life that lay bare the difficulties with his model of structural reform has been, it seems to us, to provide a shrill description of traditional judicial dispute resolution.[15]

Fiss's description of traditional dispute resolution is a story of two neighbors "in a state of nature" who each claim a single piece of property and who, when they cannot agree, turn to "a stranger" to resolve their dispute.[16] He asserts that traditional dispute resolution depicts a sociologically impoverished universe,[17] operates in a state of nature where there are no public values or goals[18] except a supposed "natural harmony" of the status quo,[19] and calls on the exercise of power by a stranger.[20] That was never Fuller's position. Nor do we find much support in the literature or in reality for such a view of traditional adjudication. If there ever was such a world we expect it was "nasty, brutish and short." However, we don't really believe that traditional adjudication ever bore much resemblance to that story. Yet this is the view of the world that Fiss attributes to

the advocates of ADR; his attack on ADR is premised on that notion.[21]

Models are, of course, human creations. The good ones contain elements of the creator's perception of the world and of the reality he seeks to perceive.[22] They are designed to invite conversation and to appeal to the reader in a search for understanding. They are abstractions; but to be effective, they must have some connection either with the creator's view of reality or with what he wants the world to be like. Fiss's model of structural reform is, in this way, an effective model.[23] While it may not depict the world that many of us observe, it does reflect his view of the world he wishes he could find. It reflects, we suspect, more his hope than his actual belief. We honor that. The model is rich. It leads to conversation and debate.

But Fiss's model of traditional dispute resolution is flat; it is only an abstraction, and is therefore also a caricature. It has no relation to the world as it is; it does not appeal to the reader as a convincing way to understand adjudication or its alternatives. It does not permit one to express hope in alternatives to adjudication.

In any event, after setting up his "state of nature" model of dispute resolution, Fiss attributes that view of the world to the advocates of ADR. He understands pleas to consider alternatives to current means of resolving disputes as turning on the inefficiency of traditional adjudication (his negative model), and popular dissatisfaction with it. He equates the ADR movement with those who urge settlement more than judgment and who seek a "truce more than a true reconciliation."[24] He argues that settlement is "a capitulation to the conditions of mass society," a capitulation that "should be neither encouraged nor praised."[25] He assumes that the ADR movement is one that wants peace at any price and treats settlement as "the anticipation of the outcome of trial,"[26] that is, trial in his stranger-judge, negative model of adjudication.

Fiss is against settlement because he views the matters that come before courts in America, and that are inappropriate for ADR, as including cases in which: (1) there are distributional inequities; (2) securing authoritative consent or settlement is difficult; (3) continued supervision following judgment is necessary; and (4) there is a genuine need for an authoritative interpretation of law.[27] Fiss characterizes disputes in this limited way — as arguments between two neighbors, one of whom has vastly superior bargaining power over the other. It is then easy for him to prefer litigation to settlement, because litigation is a way to equalize bargaining power.

The soundest and deepest part of the ADR movement does not rest on Fiss's two-neighbors model. It rests on values — of religion, community, and work place — that are more vigorous than Fiss thinks. In many, in fact most, of the cultural traditions that argue for ADR, settlement is neither an avoidance mechanism nor a truce. Settlement is a process of reconciliation in which the anger of broken relationships is to be confronted rather than avoided, and in which healing demands not a truce but confrontation. Instead of "trivializing the remedial process,"[28] settlement exalts that process. Instead of "reducing the social function ... to one of resolving private disputes,"[29] settlement calls on substantive community values. Settlement is sometimes a beginning, and is sometimes a postscript, but it is not the essence of the enterprise of dispute resolution. The essence of the enterprise is more like the structural injunction, about which Fiss has written so eloquently, than like an alternative to the resolution-by-stranger described by his negative model.[30]

The "real divide"[31] between us and Fiss may not be our differing views of the sorts of cases that now wind their way into American courts, but, more fundamentally, it may be our different views of justice. Fiss comes close to equating justice with law. He includes among the cases unsuited for settlement "those in which justice needs to be done, or to put it more modestly, where there is a genuine social need for an authoritative interpretation of law."[32] We do not believe that law and justice are synonymous. We see the deepest and soundest of ADR arguments as in agreement with us: Justice is not usually something people get from the government. And courts (which are not, in any case, strangers) are not the only or even the most important places that dispense justice.[33]

Many advocates of ADR can well be taken to have asked about the law's response to disputes, and alternatives to that response, not in order to reform the law but in order to locate alternative views of what a dispute is. Such alternatives would likely advance or assume understandings of justice (or, if you like, peace) that are also radically different from justice as something lawyers *administer*, or peace as the absence of violence. They assume not that justice is something people get from the government but that it is something people give to one another. These advocates seek an understanding of justice in the way Socrates and Thrasymachus did in the *Republic*: Justice is not the will of the stronger; it is not efficiency in government; it is not the reduction of violence; Justice is what we discover — you and I, Socrates said — when we walk together, listen together, and even love one another, in our curiosity about what justice is and where justice comes from.

Most of us who have gone to college know something about Socrates. Many more of us who grew up in the United States know something about Moses and Jesus. It is from Torah and Gospel, more than from Plato, that we are most likely to be able to sketch out radical alternatives to the law's response to disputes. As a matter of fact, our religious culture contains both a theoretical basis for these alternatives and a way to apply theory to disputes.

In the Hebraic tradition (as in the Islamic), scripture is normative. Judaism, for example, does not merely seek to follow Torah; it loves Torah, it finds life in Torah, it celebrates Torah as one might celebrate the presence of a lover, or of a loving parent, or of a community that nourishes peace — commitment to common well being, and even a feeling of being well. (Salvation is not too strong a word for it.) Justice is the way one defines a righteous life; justice does involve according other persons their due but, more radically, in the Hebraic view, it involves loving them. Such a justice is the product of piety, to be sure, but not piety alone; it is the product of study, of reason, and of attending to the wise and learning from them how to be virtuous.[34] *Quare fidem intellectum.*[35]

The Christian side of the Hebraic tradition has, or should have, all of this. It also has a unique procedure established in St. Matthew's Gospel — a *system* backed up by stern condemnation of Christians who turn from the Gospel and seek instead the law's response to disputes. In this system — as well as Judaism[36] — the religious community claims authority to resolve disputes and even to coerce obedience. The procedure involves, first, conversation; if that fails, it involves mediation; if mediation fails, it involves airing the dispute before representatives of the community. If the dispute goes so far as judgment, the system — as is also the case in Judaism — permits pressure: "[I]f he refuses to listen to the community, treat him like a pagan or a tax collector. I tell you solemnly, whatever you bind on earth shall be considered bound in heaven; whatever you loose on earth shall be considered loosed in heaven."[37]

Thus, the procedure gives priority to restoring the relationship. Hebraic theology puts primary emphasis on relationships, a priority that is political and even ontological, as well as ethical, and therefore legal.[38] And so, most radically, the religious tradition seeks not *resolution* (which connotes the sort of doctrinal integrity in the law that seems to us to be Fiss's highest priority) but *reconciliation* of brother to brother, sister to sister, sister to brother, child to parent, neighbor to neighbor, buyer to seller, defendant to plaintiff, *and judge to both*. (The Judge is also an I and a Thou.) This view of what a dispute is, and of what third parties seek when they intervene in disputes between others, provides an existing, traditional, common alternative to the law's response. The fact seems to be that this alternative has both a vigorous modern history and a studiable contemporary vitality (Jerrold Auerbach[39] to the contrary notwithstanding).

Contemporary manifestations of the Hebraic tradition claim adherence to a moral authority that is more important than the government.[40] The Torah is the wisdom of God, the Gospel is the good news that promises a peace the world cannot give. From one perspective, theology makes such religious views of dispute and resolution seem peripheral. That impression is deceptive, though: In the aggregate these views of what a dispute is are consistent with one another and, as such, consistent with the moral commitments of most people in America. The numbers of people in this country who might find them so is not declining; it is increasing. "In the aggregate" is an appropriate consideration, as one assays radical alternatives to the law's response to disputes, because there is substantial commonality among the practitioners of this radical Hebraic alternative. Religious systems of reconciliation rest on a substantively common theology and on a substantively common argument that, contrary to the implications of Fiss's view of justice, the government is not as important as it thinks it is.

Professor David Trubek ends a recent and pessimistic essay on alternative dispute resolution[41] with a paradox: "[N]o one," he says, "really seems to believe in law any more."[42] The "elites" who complain of a litigation explosion — Chief Justice Warren Burger and others "who champion alternatives"[43] — "question the law's efficacy."[44] But so do those who criticize the law as political and oppressive, most notably scholars in the Critical Legal Studies movement. The elites exalt an informalism they don't believe in, Trubek says; and the radicals exalt a formalist they distrust. Apparently the new legal-process school — or at least one of its eloquent spokesmen, Owen Fiss — still believes in law. Fiss's writing on structural reform is powerful. It may not reflect the way the world actually is, but it is a statement of hope. And that is important in an age of nihilism. But we suspect those who believe in law and in nothing else; we hope Fiss is not among them. Informalism of the Chief Justice's formulation[45] may deserve distrust. But informalism has some contemporary manifestations — many of them resting on the most ancient and deepest of our traditions — that deserve trust and even celebration. These manifestations too are statements of hope. Suggestions for alternatives to litigation need to be critically examined — no doubt many of them are hollow. What they do not need, and what the legal community does not need, is an argument that reduces these alternatives to a caricature.

(c) Understanding the Critiques of Mediation: What Is All the Fuss About?†

Neil Sargent

The essential claim I am making in this paper is that it is difficult, if not impossible, to discuss the topic of 'critical perspectives on mediation' in any coherent way as if there is a comprehensive set of critiques of mediation which can be talked about in the same breath, or listed in one extended paragraph. Instead, I argue that there is a range of critiques of media-

tion which start from very different theoretical positions, which view the role and functioning of the formal justice system from quite different perspectives, and which have very different implications for the development of mediation theory and practice.

On the one hand, there is a strong liberal consensus critique of mediation which critiques the

---

† Unpublished. [Notes and/or references omitted.]

advocates of mediation for their supposed emphasis on the quantity of justice over the quality of justice. Within this liberal consensus critique, mediation and other forms of Alternative Dispute Resolution, or ADR, are often described as offering, at best, a commitment to 'second class justice'.[1] It may be, according to even some of the liberal critics of mediation and ADR, that there is a place for mediation and informal justice in relation to some types of disputes for which mediation might be appropriate. But, according to this liberal critique, we must never lose sight of the fact that the formal justice system, with its commitment to the rule of law, the requirements of due process, and the adversarial trial process, provides the only true measure of justice within the liberal, democratic state.[2]

It is worth observing that even many advocates for an increased role for mediation and other ADR initiatives articulate their support for this position in terms which are not inconsistent with this liberal critique of mediation.[3] In other words, the liberal critique always insists that a clear hierarchy of the forms of justice be drawn, with mediation and other ADR initiatives being seen as supplements to the existing formal justice system, but never as a substitute or alternative to the formal justice system. In consequence, here the language of mediation existing "in the shadow of the law", as Mnookin and Kornhauser put it, is very clearly articulated.[4]

In addition to the liberal consensus critique of settlement and mediation there is an equally strong contingent of critics of mediation who frame their critique of mediation and informal justice from within a conflict perspective which differs radically from the liberal consensus critique in its view of the ideological function of law within liberal democracy. Rather than viewing the formal justice system as a reflection of a shared liberal democratic value system, the conflict perspective begins from the assumption that conflict, rather than consensus, characterizes the structured inequalities of social, economic and political relations within capitalist societies. Consequently, here the emphasis of the critique of mediation is not so much the liberal consensus view of the inadequate promise of mediation as it is with what a conflict theorist might refer to as the false promise of mediation.

Thus, critics such as Richard Abel and Laura Nader have pointed to the insidious nature of the state sponsored community justice movement, which seems to provide a means of empowerment for communities which have been traditionally marginalized by the formal justice system. They warn that the promise of increased community control over the

forms of justice is a trojan horse, by means of which the liberal state seeks to gain entrance within the walls of those very communities which are capable of providing sites of resistance to capitalist liberal hegemony, precisely because they have been so marginalized. Community justice models, which provide a means by which such communities will effectively police themselves according to standards and values established outside their own milieu, offer a very powerful mechanism of informal social control to the liberal state, which is all the more effective because it is voluntary, and thus avoids the social, economic and political costs of more direct, coercive forms of social control.

A primary concern in much of this literature is that the ideology of mediation and informal justice operate to neutralize social conflict by privatizing and individualizing conflict and making it appear that all conflicts can be resolved through consensual processes such as mediation, rather than through more confrontational forms of political action. Nader argues that the 'harmony ideology' associated with mediation and other forms of alternative dispute resolution functions to suppress legitimate social conflict.[7] According to Nader, the theory of harmony justice which undergirds the alternative dispute resolution movement views conflict as "dysfunctional and threatening to the social order".[8] For Nader, however, social conflict is rational and to be expected in a society in which access to economic, legal and political power is unevenly distributed. Indeed, social conflict may be a way to expose inequalities and make claims to social justice.[9] In this context, Nader views official expressions of state support for harmony justice models with suspicion, as part of a legitimizing ideology which is aimed at defusing and depoliticizing forms of societal conflict which otherwise have the potential to challenge the status quo.[10]

In some respects it seems as if the conflict critique of community mediation and harmony ideology provides an inverted mirror image of the liberal consensus critique of mediation and ADR. Different sides of the same coin, neither critique seems to recognize mediation as a form of justice having any identity, any history, or any integrity in its own right. Thus, conflict theorists like Auerbach and Harrington also tend to see the informal justice system as existing 'in the shadow of the law'.[11] But here that shadow is a more ominous presence. The formal legal system retains all of its power and authority, while the informal justice system looks after the minor dispute processing; all the while reinforcing, rather than challenging, the legitimacy of the existing set of power relations within capitalist society.

411

Alongside the liberal and conflict critiques of mediation there is also a significant camp of feminist critics of mediation, who raise the question whether mediation (and by implication other forms of alternative dispute resolution) is capable of addressing imbalances of power between the participants in mediation. The focus of much of this feminist critique of mediation has been directed to the particular context of divorce mediation;[12] although there has also been a significant degree of concern expressed in the feminist literature over attempts to promote mediation as an alternative to formal criminal proceedings in the context of violence against women.[13]

In its concern with the family as a site of oppression against women, the feminist critique of mediation differs from both of the preceding liberal and conflict positions. And yet, at the same time, the feminist critique of mediation also has affinities with each of the above critiques. Thus, many feminist commentators have pointed to the lack of due process safeguards for women in mediation; as well as to a risk that women's hard won substantive legal rights in the area of family property and support entitlements may be sacrificed within the mediation process in the interest of reaching a 'consensual' mediated agreement between participants who are often in very unequal bargaining positions.[14] In this sense, the feminist critique of divorce mediation bears more than a passing resemblance to the liberal critique of settlement as an inadequate alternative to the formal justice system, one that is less concerned with protecting the legal rights and procedural interests of the participants than is the adversarial trial process.

At the same time, feminist critics have also pointed to the ideological dimensions of the divorce mediation movement in suppressing and depoliticizing conflicts over systemic gender inequalities within 'the family'. Thus, Pickett argues that the 'familial ideology' of divorce mediation constructs the 'private' emotional nature of family disputes as being illfitted to the adversarial forum of the court system; thereby succeeding in transforming feminist struggles over the legal norms governing property and custody entitlements on family breakdown into individualized

disputes which are suited to therapeutic treatment by divorce mediators.[15] In this context, Pickett's critique of the ideological function of divorce mediation in legitimizing the existing 'gendered' structure of power relations within the nuclear family bears an obvious relation to many conflict theorists' critique of 'harmony justice'. Divorce mediation is presented as a trojan horse which women accept at their peril.

In conclusion, two themes seem to emerge out of this brief discussion of the critiques of mediation. We could categorize them as emphasizing on the one hand, the inadequate promise of mediation, and on the other the false promise of mediation. Both themes are concerned with the problem of power. However, they appear to address the problem of power in very different ways. The liberal critique of mediation assumes that the procedural requirements of due process within the formal justice system provide an appropriate (and sufficient) mechanism for redressing imbalances of power between litigants. Indeed, within the liberal conception of justice, law occupies a privileged institutional position as a protector of the interests of the weak against those of the strong.

However, seen from a conflict perspective, (and from many feminists' perspective) the liberal ideal of justice is just that, an ideal, which operates to legitimize the unequal structure of class, gender and race relations within capitalist and patriarchal society. From this critical perspective, mediation also functions to legitimize the status quo, rather than to pose any real challenge to it. However, in some respects mediation is seen as being even more ideologically 'dangerous' than the formal justice system, because it appears to hold out the promise of individual 'empowerment' to those who feel disempowered by the formal justice system. As a result, many conflict and feminist critics of mediation are forced into the position of becoming reluctant defenders of the formal justice system as the 'least worst alternative' available for pursuing claims to social justice. It is one of the ironies of this field of study that from a certain distance it is hard to tell the liberal and the conflict and the feminist critics of mediation apart.

VIII

Access to Justice

The readings in Part VIII explore issues concerning access to justice from a number of different perspectives.

Chapter 20 includes articles that highlight two traditional approaches to increasing access to justice for persons living in poverty. R.J. Gathercole discusses the benefits and detriments of two models of providing legal aid services, while Iain Ramsay examines whether small claims courts are effective and efficient mechanisms for providing access to justice for individuals with lower incomes. Are these methods of improving access to justice effective? Are they sufficient?

The articles in Chapter 21 consider other impediments to access to justice that are more closely tied to procedural aspects of the legal system. Chief Justice McLachlin of the Supreme Court of Canada discusses the challenges posed by the high cost of litigation, long trials, delays in the justice system, and endemic social problems. Her comments are important because they emphasize that issues of access are not only faced by low-income Canadians but, increasingly, by the middle-class as well, whose options she says "are grim". Justice Winkler's article describes the specific, sometimes unsuccessful, measures implemented to limit delays within the Ontario justice system. The Ontario example highlights the fact that sometimes well-intentioned procedural reforms actually exacerbate existing problems. For her part, Carissima Mathen identifies additional impediments to access to justice that arise when individuals and groups are prevented from raising *Charter* issues due to changes in rules of "standing" and the retraction of government support for initiatives like the Court Challenges Program, which funds test case litigation. Finally, William Marsden's report on the tragic story of Rosa Becker (recall the *Petkus v. Becker* decision from Chapter 14) provides a chilling reminder that success in court does not always translate to financial or personal victory outside the court. Sometimes, when you "win" you still lose.

As you read these articles, ask yourself: what does access to justice really mean? Can access to justice be defined by economic or chronological measures alone, or does it require some form of substantive measure of the quality of the result in addition to the affordability and efficiency of the process? In the context of questions about whether law can or should be used for social transformation, can we still ask this question without acknowledging that access to justice is, for most Canadians, an ideal more than the reality?

(a)   Legal Services and the Poor†

R.J. Gathercole

Justice is open to all — like the Ritz Hotel.[1]

Making legal services accessible to the poor[2] is an issue that has long confronted the legal profession, although significant developments in legal aid have taken place only in the last two decades.[3] There had been relatively little discussion of whether the poor really are in dire need of lawyers' services; rather lawyers assume that the poor, like the rest of society, need these services almost as much as food, clothing, shelter and medical attention.

Nor have lawyers been modest about what legal services — as provided by lawyers[4] — can accomplish for the poor. Reginald Heber Smith in his classic work, *Justice and the Poor*, published in 1919 and generally regarded as the motivating force of the American legal aid movement, wrote "In vast tracts of the civil law and in all of the criminal law related to the more severe crimes, equality in the administration of justice can be had only by supplying attorneys to the poor."[5] If more legal aid offices were opened and existing staff increased, "that part of the denial of justice which is traceable solely to the inability of the poor to employ counsel will be completely overcome."[6]

Forty-six years later, E. Clinton Bamberger Jr., a young Baltimore attorney who attended an A.B.A. conference to learn about the new neighbourhood legal offices being established in the United States and found himself recruited as the first Director of Legal Services in the Office of Economic Opportu-nity (O.E.O.) — the central office of the "War on Poverty"[7] — went even further than Smith.

> We cannot be content with the creation of systems rendering free legal assistance to all the people who need it but cannot afford a lawyer's advice. Our responsibility is to marshal the forces of law and the strength of lawyers to combat the causes and effects of poverty. Lawyers must uncover the legal causes of poverty, remodel the systems which generate the cycle of poverty, and design new social, legal and political tools and vehicles to move poor people from deprivation, depression and despair to opportunity, hope and ambition.[8]

These high expectations of what lawyers could accomplish for the poor were not restricted to the United States. In a 1971 study prepared for the National Council of Welfare, a leading Canadian legal aid activist wrote:[9]

> At the lowest level of abstraction, a legal services programme can at least assist in mitigating the surface attributes of poverty. As a service provided to the poor at no cost, it has a redistributive effect. The nature of the day-to-day legal care provided would lessen at least the effect of poverty. Illegal evictions, consumer fraud, and abuses of official discretion, all wrongs to which the poor are particularly vulnerable, could be vigilantly monitored and often remedied. As well, efforts directed at law reform might succeed in gaining even more widespread relief.

---

† From Robert G. Evans and Michael J. Trebilcock (eds.), *Lawyers and the Consumer Interest: Regulating the Market for Legal Services* (Toronto: Butterworth & Co. (Canada) Ltd., 1982) 407 at 407–18, 423, 426–29. Reproduced with permission. [Notes and/or references omitted.]

...

The lawyer's business is to assist his client in analysing alternatives. He is expected to be partial, to act as the advocate of those with interests to pursue. This work, carried on in a way which encouraged the participation of the individual and the group in the work involved in the pursuit of grievances could offer the poor an opportunity to come to grips, perhaps for the first time, with problems heretofore beyond reach.

...

At first, through their lawyers, but later with progressively less and less assistance, the poor could make articulate and knowledgeable inputs into decision-making processes which affect their lives. This new access to the levers of policy-making might be an important first step in the efforts of the poor to gain some control of their own lives. The degree to which this control can be achieved is the degree to which a legal services programme can contribute to the alteration of the structure of poverty in this country.

It is almost 15 years since these goals of the legal aid movement were articulated. During that time virtually every Canadian province that did not already have one[] has developed a legal aid program to provide at least the services envisioned by Smith.[10] A Legal Services Corporation has been established in the United States as an outgrowth of the legal services work started in the O.E.O.[11] and the United Kingdom has made some significant, if somewhat overdue improvements in its legal aid services.[12] Nevertheless, the poor in each of these countries are at best only marginally better off for all of these efforts and even the relatively limited goals articulated by Reginald Heber Smith 60 years ago have not been achieved. It is doubtful that they will be in the foreseeable future.

What went wrong? Although the leaders of the legal aid movement in Canada, and elsewhere, were motivated by the best intentions and a genuine desire to help alleviate the problems of the poor, they did not and perhaps could not fully understand their problems. Contrary to their expectations, the fundamental problems of the poor are not susceptible to traditional legal solutions. They are not the traditional middle class legal problems that lawyers are familiar with. As Bernard Veney, Executive Director of the National Clients' Council in the United States put it:[13]

The problems of low-income people are different from the problems of other people; and their cases must be handled differently. Most attorneys in private practice do not have, as a matter of

routine, the skills necessary to practice law for poor people ... low-income people have lives of constant crisis. What may be a casual matter for someone who has options is a life and death matter for a low-income person because one of the characteristics of poverty is the *absolute lack of options*. That lack of options may mean that to meet one crisis, people do something that is going to cause another crisis further down the line.

So it is not enough just to handle the legal matter that is there on the surface. Unless you are skilled at recognizing this problem, and skilled at recognizing what the possible remedies are, skilled enough to resolve the initial crisis but also take care of the longer-range crisis, you haven't done anything for low-income people.

Most legal aid programs, even if not so designed originally, have tended to develop according to the interests and priorities of lawyers providing the services rather than those of their clients. Legal services are traditionally provided on a one-to-one, private enterprise basis. The legal profession is generally identified with, and identifies itself with the *status quo*. Lawyers cannot accept the fact that the problems of the poor can only be solved through a fundamental restructuring of traditional institutions, not by suing someone in a court of law. While the motivations ascribed by one observer to the early development of legal aid in the United Kingdom (that "[it] was produced to justify ideologically the operations of the legal system, which was primarily concerned with property interests, by giving the appearance of making equal access to the legal system available to the lower classes")[14] may not be applicable to recent developments in legal aid, the fact remains that the legal profession remains identified in the minds of the poor with the source of their problems rather than with the solution. An equally important consideration is that governments have consistently underfunded legal services, partly because the poor are not a powerful political constituency[15] but also because government departments and agencies are prime targets of legal aid lawyers. Both of these factors will be discussed more fully later. First, a brief history of the development of legal aid is necessary.

JUDICARE VERSUS LEGAL SERVICES

Civil legal aid has generally followed one of the two models — Judicare or legal services.[16] The Judicare model utilizes members of the private bar as the prime deliverers of legal services. They are paid on a fee-for-service basis, usually in accordance with a specified tariff. The administrative responsibility for most Judicare plans is assigned to the legal profession. The underlying philosophy of Judicare is to provide the poor with access to the same services as are available to the rest of society. Judicare plans tend to concentrate on providing legal assistance for serious criminal offences and for civil actions in superior courts. For example, 41% of the Ontario legal aid budget in 1978 was spent on criminal offences and 27% on divorce and other civil matters.[17] There were only 184 small claims and 578 review board cases out of a total of more than 24,000 civil cases.[18] There were insufficient welfare, landlord-tenant, or unemployment insurance cases to justify a separate heading in the annual report.[19] Judicare's emphasis on litigation stresses a "problem solving" rather than "problem preventing" approach. The emphasis is on ensuring that the poor are accorded their "day in court" rather than on substantive reform of existing laws and institutions.

The legal services model did not become a significant alternative to Judicare until the 1960s and early 1970s. This model stresses the use of full-time salaried lawyers and non-legal personnel operating from offices located in low-income communities, generally of the "storefront" variety. Emphasis is placed on providing legal services in areas of prime concern to the poor — welfare, housing, unemployment insurance, workers' compensation, small claims, domestic disputes — providing assistance to groups and organizations in the community, education programs and law reform activities such as lobbying and test case litigation.

The stated philosophy of the legal services movement is that the goal of legal aid should be nothing less than the eradication of poverty.[20] Poverty is a question of power — or, more particularly, lack of it — and the role of the lawyer is to assist the poor person to gain the power to change the institutions, both private and public, which contribute to his poverty and control his life. Case-by-case legal services must be provided but only within this overall framework. In jurisdictions that have adopted the legal services model, administration of legal aid is generally the responsibility of an independent board or commission rather than the legal profession.

For years proponents of the two models carried on a sometimes heated debate over their respective merits.[21] Questions of cost-effectiveness, the efficacy of professional control and whether lawyers had any role to play in social change were argued at great length. Generally, the traditional bar and most politicians tended to support the development of Judicare, professional administrative control and limitations on

law reform and lobbying activities by legal aid lawyers.[22] Legal services lawyers criticized Judicare for its adherence to traditional legal solutions and its failure to deal with the "real" problems of the poor.

However, it became apparent that neither approach had all the answers and both had important strengths and weaknesses. As a result, most jurisdictions have developed mixed civil legal aid systems, albeit with the emphasis on one of the two models.

. . . .

Canada, as it often does, has borrowed extensively from both the United States and the United Kingdom. Legal aid in Canada falls within provincial constitutional jurisdiction as part of the administration of justice, although the federal government does provide financial assistance to the provinces for legal aid in criminal matters based on a negotiated formula which can vary from province to province. All provinces, with the exception of Prince Edward Island and New Brunswick, have well-developed legal aid programs. Most have a mixed Judicare and legal services system. Quebec, Saskatchewan and Nova Scotia have adopted legal services as the basic model with a limited Judicare component. The other provinces have adopted the Judicare model.

Both the Manitoba and British Columbia plans have a legal services component. Ontario has a fairly extensive network of legal services offices (approximately 40 throughout the province as of September 1980).[49] They initially developed outside the Ontario Legal Aid Plan, are not referred to in the *Legal Aid Act*[50] and have, at best, only the grudging support of the Law Society of Upper Canada.[51] Funding of these offices is now provided for by regulation, amounting to $4.75 million for the 1980–81 fiscal year,[52] and they now are part of the Ontario Legal Aid Plan under the general supervision of the Clinical Funding Committee which allocates their funding and closely monitors their operations. For example, it is empowered by regulation to require a clinic to employ a solicitor and to train personnel to an approved standard.[53]

The Ontario Legal Aid Plan arose from the report of a joint committee of the Law Society and the government of Ontario released in March 1965.[54] This report drew heavily on the English experience in recommending a Judicare plan to be operated by the Law Society and made no reference at all to the American experience. On the other hand, the Quebec Plan, established in 1972[55] and the Saskatchewan Plan, established in 1974[56] adopted the American legal services model which by then was well established. Service under both plans is provided primarily by full-time salaried lawyers. However, the Quebec plan has a more significant Judicare component,[57] and is less community based than the Saskatchewan plan. The boards of directors of the Quebec offices (or "bureaux") are appointed by the Commission de Services Juridiques which administers the plan while boards of the Saskatchewan clinics are elected by the communities for which they operate. The Saskatchewan Plan also has a specific mandate to undertake law reform and related activities.[58] Other provinces have drawn from the Ontario, Quebec and Saskatchewan plans for inspiration depending upon the political views of each provincial government and its susceptibility to the pressures of the provincial bar.

The legal services offices established in Ontario, British Columbia and Manitoba[] also imitated the American experience. The first such office in Ontario, Parkdale Community Legal Services, located in a low income area of Toronto, was one of four such offices funded by the federal Department of Health and Welfare on the basis of a study which strongly supported the American approach.[59] Parkdale also received funding from the Council for Legal Education in Professional Responsibility, a branch of the Ford Foundation, which also funded a number of legal services offices in the United States affiliated with law schools as Parkdale was with Osgoode Hall Law School of York University.

The early development of legal aid in Canada produced some tension between the proponents of Judicare and the supporters of the legal services movement. This was particularly true in Ontario, where Judicare was well established and the Law Society was particularly powerful. After a decade or more of relatively peaceful co-existence, however, the clear consensus is that both models are needed. The traditional bar has overcome its initial paranoia about legal services offices, in part because the fundamental social changes that they feared and legal services lawyers hoped for have not materialized, and in part because legal services offices have created work for private lawyers, both through direct referral and through bringing legal action against their clients. Legal services lawyers, on the other hand, have come to accept that the private bar has a role to play in legal aid, both because of its special expertise and its ability to take cases where legal services lawyers might have conflicts of interest.

THE INADEQUACIES OF LEGAL AID

"Comprehensive" legal aid plans have existed for a decade or more, but the fact remains that the poor still have, at best, only limited access to legal services. One main reason is that legal aid is funded from public monies and governments have failed to provide more than minimal funding. This is partly because the poor do not constitute an effective political constituency, but also because the most effective legal aid programs are continually engaged in fighting government agencies. Accordingly, politicians react with, at best, grudging support and, at worst, outright hostility.

. . . .

A recent Canadian example is the decision of the Saskatchewan government in June 1978 to require the legal services offices in that province to cease their practice of referring criminal cases to private lawyers under the Judicare component of the Saskatchewan plan, while concentrating themselves on the provision of the civil legal aid. The legal services lawyers felt that the demands for services could best be met by utilizing the experience of the private bar in criminal matters and developing their own expertise in civil matters, such as housing and welfare. The government, however, stated that budgetary restraints were necessary and money could be saved if the offices did the criminal work themselves because using private lawyers cost more. This, of course, meant that legal services lawyers would be spending most of their time on criminal matters and would have to neglect what they considered to be the more important civil cases. It was not clear whether the government was motivated solely by financial concerns or whether it wanted to limit the effectiveness of legal services offices. After the Saskatoon Legal Assistance Clinic threatened to close rather than comply with the government's directive, the government backed down and agreed to conduct a review of the province's legal aid system.[66] However, the government appears to have succeeded in the end. The 1979–80 *Annual Report* of the Saskatchewan Community Legal Services Commission showed that the number of criminal cases completed by the private bar in the fiscal year dropped to 505 from 2,562 the previous fiscal year. Private bar civil cases also were reduced from 281 to 120.[67]

Governments continue to refuse to fund legal aid adequately. In 1977 Clinton Bamberger claimed that it would cost $500 million to provide basic minimum legal services to the poor in the United States.

This represented 5 lawyers for every 10,000 poor people, compared to the ratio in the general population of 14 lawyers for every 10,000 persons.[68] This year, after years of inflation the Legal Services Corporation budget is still under $300 million, with no chance of any increase in the next few years.[69]

In Canada the situation is no better. In Ontario, legal aid is funded through the Ministry of the Attorney General. The Ministry's entire budget represents less than 1% of the provincial budget ($165.5 million out of $17.1 billion in 1980–81).[70] The legal aid component is $43.3 million or about 26% of that total,[71] but a portion of that amount (about $8 million)[72] is received from the federal government as a contribution towards the provision of criminal legal aid. In other words 1/4 of 1% of the provincial budget is allocated to legal aid. The legal aid expenditure in Quebec ($32 million in the 1978–79 fiscal year)[73] has not increased significantly in the past few years. New Brunswick continues to refuse to establish a civil legal aid program mainly for financial reasons.[74] Similar situations exist in other provinces.

Even with adequate funding however, there are inherent weaknesses in existing legal aid programs which result in seriously inadequate access of the poor to legal services. The main weakness is the emphasis on individual case service. This results in a curative rather than a preventive approach to legal problems. It also means that available legal aid resources cannot begin to cope with the potential caseload let alone undertake effective law reform, lobbying or other group-oriented activities.

The emphasis on case-by-case service of both Judicare and legal services plans results from different factors. The Judicare approach is predicated on this type of service delivery. The legal profession is organized on a free enterprise, single lawyer, single client basis and Judicare seeks to apply this approach in delivering legal services to the poor. Legal services offices, however, have to some extent been forced to emphasize individual cases by funding agencies. While lawyers' training and interests and client demand are also important factors, the requirements of funding agencies that individual services be stressed is the predominant reason for the "caseload crisis" faced by most legal services offices. The evaluation of a legal services office is based on its caseload. This is easier to measure than more nebulous factors such as acceptance in the community, long-term interests of clients and law reform. It is also easier to persuade politicians that public money is being properly used if something concrete,

e.g., a thousand cases handled, has resulted from the expenditure.

There are other inadequacies in both legal aid models which have to be considered. Judicare suffers from the underlying assumption that all the poor need is access to the same services that lawyers traditionally provide. Not only does this ignore the specific legal problems of the poor, most of which are substantively different than those of the middle class, but reliance on the private bar also creates particular problems. Most law offices are physically and psychologically inaccessible to the poor. They are located some distance from most poor communities and are designed to appeal to traditional clients. Most poor people find this a completely foreign environment, adding to the pressures of dealing with lawyers. The poor person also identifies the private bar with the "other side" — landlords, finance companies, government agencies — that represent the source of his problem.

The private lawyer lacks expertise in the legal problems of the poor. The intricacies of social welfare legislation, for example, are not easily grasped by handling one or two such cases a year. Conflicts of interest can and do arise between the poor and other existing or potential clients of the lawyer (for example in landlord-tenant and debtor-creditor cases). There is an inability to identify patterns and to organize strategies to deal with underlying problems. Most Judicare plans lack effective research components resulting in a great deal of duplication of effort, as individual lawyers continue to re-invent the wheel. The Ontario Legal Aid plan, in existence for some 13 years, has only recently created a research facility and then only because it was one of the conditions imposed by the provincial Attorney General for his support of a tariff increase.[75]

The method of payment — fee for service, usually in accordance with an established tariff — also limits the coverage which can be provided by Judicare. It is not acceptable politically or economically to expend $500 of public funds in an attempt to recover $50 in unpaid welfare benefits, to sue for $200 in Small Claims Court or to force a landlord to effect small but necessary repairs or to cease harassing tenants. Legal aid assistance is therefore given only in very special cases. In Ontario, for example, clients are entitled to legal aid services for indictable criminal matters and for civil cases brought in the "higher" courts.[76] In other civil cases the test is whether a person of modest means would retain a lawyer in the circumstances. Given the present level of legal fees, the answer is usually negative. The result is that Judicare plans tend to concentrate on providing services for serious criminal cases, traditional civil lawsuits (e.g., motor vehicle accidents, collections) and divorce and other family matters. The Ontario Legal Aid Plan, a representative Judicare plan, shows a very high proportion of certificates granted for these types of cases.[77] In his oft-quoted article "Practicing law for Poor People,"[78] Stephen Wexler pointed out that "poor people are not just like rich people without money. Poor people do not have legal problems like those of private plaintiffs and defendants in law school casebooks."[79] Judicare plans are premised on the opposite assumption and limit themselves to providing services for those "casebook" problems.

Outside of the United States, most legal services programs came into being because of the deficiencies of Judicare and were specifically tailored to deal with the particular problems of the poor. The salaried lawyers employed in these offices were expected to — and did — develop an expertise in these areas.[80] In jurisdictions where legal services were the basic delivery model, such as the United States and Quebec, provision was made for a substantial research component to assist lawyers in the field and to identify particular problem areas which might require collective action. Emphasis was also supposed to be placed on law reform activities, both judicial and legislative.

However, as noted above, the emphasis in legal services programs as in their Judicare counterparts has been on the provision of individual case services. Although the type of case emphasized has been somewhat different than in Judicare programs, the fact remains that the essential service provided is the same — problem-solving on a one-to-one basis rather than preventive services on a collective basis as was the hope of many of the early proponents of the legal services movement.[81]

. . . .

If the legal profession as presently structured, even if supplemented by trained non-legal personnel, cannot adequately deal with the problems of the poor, what is the answer? The assumption is that increased access to lawyers and traditional legal services will benefit the poor. In fact that is not the case. The poor need services which will assist them in dealing effectively with their problems; this cannot be done on a case-by-case basis. While there is, and will continue to be, a huge demand for individual case service, the resources do not presently exist to fill that demand and alternative approaches must be considered.

. . . .

Community organization must also be a priority. An effective tenants' organization prepared to utilize techniques such as rent strikes is more effective in enforcing a landlord's repair obligations than any number of individual court cases, particularly given the problems of enforcement. The welfare bureaucracy is more likely to respond to the immediate pressure of an organized welfare group than to the strictures of a court. When a welfare cheque is not forthcoming on time, this type of pressure, unlike a time-consuming application to a court, can bring quick results. In 1972 Stephen Wexler argued that only effective community organizing could give the poor power to effect change.[115] The passage of time has only proven the validity of this argument.

New methods of dispute resolution are also required. Traditional methods are slow, costly and ineffective. Too much emphasis is placed on due process rather than on effective decision-making. Procedures need to be streamlined and simplified so that individuals can effectively represent themselves. More emphasis should be placed on providing official assistance to persons appearing before tribunals. This would reduce the need for lawyers and allow more effective participation by the individuals concerned.[116]

These changes would have serious ramifications for the legal profession. Lawyers are not necessarily the most effective lobbyists and they are certainly not trained to be organizers. They are trained to provide specific services to individual clients. This means that the lawyer's role in providing services to the poor is limited. Most bar associations and professional governing bodies have opposed any developments along these lines, suggesting that the profession could not operate effectively in the type of service system.

The provision of legal services to the poor should be the responsibility of persons, both lawyers and non-lawyers, specifically trained for that purpose. How should they be trained? There is no scope in this chapter for a discussion of the problems in legal education but there is no doubt that law schools have a dismal record of training lawyers to serve the poor. Law school curricula emphasize traditional legal subjects, with the special legal problems of the poor being dealt with in one or two courses with such titles as "Poverty Law" and "Law and the Poor", a phenomenon that caused Wexler to remark that "[these courses] serve a useful function by making it crystal clear that the remainder of the curriculum deals with law and the rich; they do little, however, to change the law schools' treatment of legal problems, or their perception of the proper roles and concerns of a lawyer."[117] The calendar of the People's Law School of Los Angeles, California, a law school whose aim is "the development and training of lawyers dedicated to the struggle for social change in the communities of oppressed peoples",[118] puts it more graphically:[119]

> In the past, traditional legal institutions have mass-produced lawyers whose concept of lawyering consisted of joining an elite organization dedicated to maintaining the national socio-economic *status quo*, as well as the lawyer's superior position in it, by serving the rich or acting as legal functionaries of the state.... Existing law schools, at their worst, destroy the development of socially-conscious students, and at their best allow only a limited development of skills by a highly motivated and often select group. Traditional legal education almost uniformly teaches the skills which are required to serve the establishment; the non-establishment student, if not an outcast, is nevertheless segregated with a small group concerned with what are institutionally considered the marginal interests of society: the areas of poverty, civil rights, labour and criminal law.

Specially trained people are needed to serve the interests of the poor. If the law schools are not prepared to meet this challenge, other institutions will, and the law schools will be limited to providing training to a limited portion of the legal services community.

In any legal aid system it is crucial that the poor have some control over the nature of the services to be provided. Most legal services plans recognize this and provide for representation of the client community on the board of directors of each legal services clinic. Invariably, however, client representation is limited to one-half or less. Sometimes express provision is made for lawyers and legal staff to form a majority of the board of directors; sometimes the client representation is specifically restricted, but, in either case, the poor are allowed only to participate in, but not control, the decision-making process. Given lawyers' ability and propensity to control meetings, it is unlikely that lawyers' influence would be seriously diminished even if non-lawyers had a majority on any board.

· · · · ·

Codes of Professional Conduct also support lawyer control. A lawyer is responsible for the conduct of any case he undertakes; he must take instructions from his individual client. Any attempt by outsiders, such as boards of directors, to interfere in a case must be resisted. Additionally, a lawyer is under a duty of confidentiality. He cannot disclose details of any case to outsiders without the express consent of the client or in other very limited circumstances. Therefore any attempt by a client-controlled board of directors to determine what cases should or should not be undertaken by lawyers in its employ, or how a particular case should be handled (e.g., whether it should be settled in the interest of the individual client or carried through to litigation in the hope of obtaining a favourable decision which might benefit a broader community) must, under the present Codes, be resisted by a lawyer. Meaningful client input into the determination of the services to be provided and the manner of their provision seems possible by non-legal personnel not subject to the same professional constraints. This is not to say that these constraints are necessarily wrong in every case; only that they do militate against effective client control of legal services.

In the final analysis, whether the poor are to receive effective services from the legal profession either through the provision of traditional services by the established bar or through a more sophisticated and responsive model, depends on whether governments and the people they represent are prepared to make that commitment. Even if the legal profession were to change fundamentally its outlook on legal aid and itself make a profound commitment to providing adequate services to the poor (an admittedly unlikely development) this would not be enough. To date, few, if any, governments or societies have shown any such inclination. There are too many vested interests to overcome. Governments, the economically and politically powerful, and the legal profession, have no immediate interest in alleviating the plight of the poor. Until we are prepared to accept that fundamental changes are required, we will continue to provide, always grudgingly, inadequate legal assistance. The underlying problems will continue to be ignored. The poor, it seems, will always be with us and justice will continue to be identified with the Ritz Hotel.

(b)   Small Claims Courts: A Review†

Iain Ramsay

INTRODUCTION

Small claims courts are often regarded as important symbols for the justice system. Dubbed "The People's Court" by the media, many writers argue that since this is the court most often encountered by the ordinary person,[1] it is an important symbol for the legitimacy of the justice system.[2]

Several objectives have been hitched to the star of small claims court reform throughout their history. The idea of access to justice[3] — in the 1900s for the wage earner and tradesperson — in the 1970s for the consumer — is often associated with this court. But the court has also been conceived as a laboratory for testing new ideas in dispute settlement, such as mediation and arbitration, providing an alternative to the adversary system of the higher courts.[4] Small Claims Courts have been one focus for the intellectual and political movement of alternative dispute resolution. Within this framework, it has been argued that these courts might contribute to "solving problems" rather than merely "deciding" disputes, becoming a positive force within communities. The court has also been viewed as providing a channel for diverting claims from higher courts, hopefully providing a partial solution to the perceived problems of caseloads in higher courts. The greatest continuity in the role of small claims courts in Canada has however been its role as a low-cost cog in the process of debt collection by business against individuals.

It is clear that there are a variety of objectives which may be attributed to the court: dispute settlement[;] social problem solving[;] effective debt enforcement[;] acccss to justice. These differing objectives may lead to different prescriptions for reform and make it difficult to make simple judgments about success or failure in relation to these courts.

An important modern perspective on these courts has been to view them as part of the "Access to Justice" movement.[5] The institution of small claims courts is one response to the "problem" of the small claim, which has often been conceptualized as that of achieving a forum for the vindication of the rights and resolving the dispute of the ordinary individual where the costs (economic, psychological, legal costs) of the existing system of litigation are prohibitive. Cappelletti and Garth argue that the characteristics of such a forum should be "speed, relative informality, an active decision maker and the possibility of litigating effectively without attorneys".[6] The introduction of small claims courts represents institutional change to make individualized legal justice more accessible to the ordinary individual. But it should be recognized at the outset that the small claims "problem" may be addressed in many ways. Substantive rule changes or public enforcement may reduce or prevent the occurrence of disputes: self-help remedies may reduce the need for third party intervention: developing party capability (e.g. through class actions, public substitute actions) may be a further alternative. Moreover, small claims courts now compete with a variety of other private and quasi-public redress mechanisms in the area of consumption activity. A rational approach to policy cannot view the court in isolation from these mechanisms.

Canada presents a number of models of small claims courts. Most of these courts grew out of earlier Small Debt Court and it was only in the 1970s that a significant effort was made to rethink the role of these courts. The Ontario model presents a court which is essentially a modified version of the higher courts. There are no restrictions on business filings, or corporate claims, lawyers and agents may appear for the parties, the rules of evidence are relaxed and there are restrictions on costs. Quebec, following US precedents, was the first jurisdiction to enact a specific small claims court and remains the only Canadian jurisdiction where the court meets almost all the reform ideals outlined by Cappelletti and Garth. Under the *Loi favorisant l'accès à la justice* of 1971 lawyers were barred from the court, business corporations could not use the court,[7] judges may mediate as well as adjudicate, are empowered to use

---

the procedure most appropriate to the case and the court provides a conciliation service to litigants. The rules envisage an active role for the judge and there is no appeal. The court currently has a jurisdiction of $3000.

. . . .

3. EXISTING SMALL CLAIMS COURT PROCESS

. . . .

(b) Jurisdiction of Small Claims Court

Since 1993 the Small Claims Court has jurisdiction in any action for the payment of money or recovery of property where the value does not exceed $6000. This limit is established by regulations made under s. 53(1)(c) of the *Courts of Justice Act*. There is no restriction on who may bring an action and both corporations and individuals may file claims in the court. The broad terms of its jurisdiction will cover many actions in contract and tort including defamation, wrongful dismissal, consumer and business claims.[42]

It is important, however, to note those situations where the court does not have jurisdiction. Landlord/ Tenant issues in relation to eviction and repairs are addressed elsewhere, issues of discrimination are under the jurisdiction of the Ontario Human Rights Commission, employment standards are addressed by the Employment Standards tribunal, issues of social security by the Social Assistance Review Board. Unionized employees will take grievances concerning employment to arbitration rather than the courts. Complaints concerning government agencies may be channelled to the Ombudsman who received approximately 31,000 complaints in 1994–95. Many issues associated with the welfare state have bypassed the courts as the primary adjudicator and administrative tribunals may be a more significant dispute settlement mechanism than the courts for the average individual. This obvious but important point is sometimes overlooked in evaluating the small claims court. In addition, many of these tribunals may be more "legalized" than the small claims court and it might be useful to compare the small claims courts process with tribunals rather than the higher courts.

. . . .

(d) Fees

There is a fee of $35 for filing and $20 for serving a small claim under $1000, $50.00 and $20 for claims over $1000, and no fee for filing a defense. The court carries out service of the documents unless the plaintiff is represented by a solicitor. The court serves the claim on behalf of the plaintiff.

(e) Process: Pre-Trial: Adjudication

If a claim is defended then in many areas of Ontario there will be a pre-trial hearing, which is heard before a referee (a court employee), a part-time judge or a judge. If there is a trial then the vast majority of trials will be before deputy judges. These are not full-time judges but lawyers appointed by the regional senior judge with the approval of the Attorney General.[43] There are approximately 380 of these judges who sit approximately one day each month. They may be appointed for up to a three year, renewable, term. They are paid a per diem rate of $235. There are no province-wide guidelines or criteria for appointment, no measures to train or evaluate their performance and no guidelines on conflicts of interest.

(f) Costs

Costs are limited generally to 15 percent of the amount claimed.[44] There are limited possibilities for night sittings for cases under $500 in Toronto which could reduce litigants costs through lost wages. The court may provide and pay for a court interpreter for a French language trial. For other languages the parties have to bring their own interpreter.

(g) Enforcement of Judgments

Judgments obtained in the small claims court may be enforced by the small claims court bailiff. The most common means of enforcement is the use of garnishment orders, but seizure of personal property is used in a minority of cases. Where a judgment remains unpaid creditors may request an examination hearing of the debtor concerning the reason for non-payment and the debtor's ability to satisfy the judgment. This is an increasingly common form of enforcement activity.

. . . .

4. SOCIAL SCIENCE EVIDENCE AND SMALL CLAIMS COURTS

. . . .

(a) Type of Case Brought before the Small Claims Court

The majority of actions in small claims courts are debt actions brought by businesses against individuals. In those courts where corporations may not sue, such as Quebec, it would appear that debt collection by unincorporated businesses and professionals continues to represent the majority of cases.[51] There are also significant numbers of cases between businesses.[52] Apart from debt claims, the balance of the caseload consists of landlord actions for arrears of rent, consumer claims, tort actions, and employment actions.

Many studies of the 60s and 70s indicated that consumer claims, defined as individuals bringing a consumer claim against a business, made up a small percentage of the total claims filed with the court, perhaps at most 10% of disputed cases.[53] It became almost a part of conventional wisdom to view the small claims courts as a court "colonized" by business repeat-players suing individuals for debt.[54] The court appeared to have failed in its promise to provide consumers and other individuals with an accessible forum for redress, seemingly confirming the McRuer Commission's conclusion that it functioned as a "statutory collection system".

Vidmar challenged these findings in a study of the small claims court in Middlesex County drawing data from cases in 1980.[55] His study is the only major published study of an Ontario Small Claims court [Hildebrandt *et al* is described as an exploratory study]. His data indicated that of the total number of claims filed (Sample size 2079) 25% never proceeded beyond filing a statement of claim, 54% resulted in a default judgment and 21% of cases were contested. Of the default judgment cases, 75% were by a business against a consumer and 16% a business against a business. Of disputed cases, 22% were a business versus an individual, 11% a consumer versus a business, 27% a business versus a business and 12% an individual versus an individual. The median amount claimed in the default case was $279.

Vidmar argued that previous research had underestimated the number of consumer cases because they had only counted as consumer cases those situations where a consumer appeared as plaintiff. When cases where a consumer defended by withholding payment are added, consumer cases comprised 33% of all disputed cases. In addition, he introduced the concept of "partial liability". He argued that a typical situation was where a consumer withholds payment for renovations because of dissatisfaction with some aspect of performance. The consumer is willing to

pay a percentage of the bill but not the total bill. At trial the plaintiff might not recover the total amount, possibly the amount which the consumer was willing to pay. Judgment will be recorded for the plaintiff, therefore inviting coding as "plaintiff win", but the plaintiff may have lost, if her claim was for $900, and the defendant had been willing to pay $600 and judgment was given for $600. The judgment would be a vindication of the rights of the defendant consumer.

Vidmar drew a picture of the typical consumer case:

> Consider some cases where the consumer was the defendant. A service station claimed for car repairs; the defendant argued that she had been overcharged on labor ... A real estate firm claimed for a brokerage fee, but the consumer said the plaintiff had failed to provide the service ... a tile company sued for an unpaid account, but the defendant asserted that the work was inferior and that in addition the final account exceeded the original estimate ... Consider cases where the consumer was plaintiff ... The plaintiff's boat was destroyed when wind blew down the defendant [bailee's] shed ... A consumer had a new roof installed and paid upon completion, but when it rained the roof leaked; the roofer asserted that the water damage had occurred before repairs were made ... the underlying nature of the disputes was similar.[56]

He concluded that in disputed cases individuals seemed to succeed as often as [businesses] whether as plaintiffs or defendants,[57] business plaintiffs in disputed cases tended to be [small businesses] and although businesses were more likely to be repeat players and be represented by lawyers, there was no association between these factors and dispute outcomes.

Vidmar's study underlines a distinction which may be drawn between the two major businesses of the court; debt-collection resulting in default judgment and disputed cases before the court. Unfortunately, his study did not investigate in any detail the default judgment cases, or the demographic characteristics of those using the court. Having noted that limitation, his analysis does provide us with some pause before drawing a blanket conclusion that the small claims court is solely a tool for the "haves".

(b) Demographic Profile of Users

Studies of small claims courts have tended to focus on the demographics and experiences of plaintiffs. Existing studies in Canada, the US, and elsewhere indicate that it is middle income, better educated, male, individuals who bring cases as plaintiffs in small claims courts.[58] Studies of the court have often obtained small and unreliable samples of defendants, or simply neglected to study defendants, in particular those who were involved in default actions.[59] This is of policy significance since defendants and default defendants are also users of the court and by finding out more about their circumstances and their reasons for default we might learn about the role of the court process in the process of debt collection.

In order to gain some insight into the demographics of default judgment defendants we can turn to studies which have looked at the court process as part of a study of debt collection. These provide some data to fill the gaps in the court studies. The profile of an individual taken to judgment for debt [indicates] that the majority are in blue-collar occupations, have lower than average incomes, have less post-secondary education than the general population and rent rather than own.[60] Most have been unable to pay the debt because of a change in life circumstances such as unemployment or the loss of a partner's income.

It might be hypothesized that there are class differences between differing "users" of the court.

The majority of those involved in disputed cases may be drawn more from the ranks of the middle class. Those who are defendants in default judgment cases may however be drawn more from the working class and those in more precarious economic positions in our society. This latter category may overlap with issues of gender and race, given that statistical data indicate the precarious position of single parent families headed by women and the likelihood that lower income and new immigrant groups are often the targets of fraudulent selling practices. This hypothesis gains strength from the consultations carried out for the Civil Justice Review. There was a significant distinction between differing groups' perception of satisfaction with the small claims court. Business groups and middle class consumer groups thought that the existing court system was satisfactory, while poverty groups indicated that courts were intimidating for their clients and that reforms such as full time inquisitorial judges and a duty counsel would make small claims more effective for the poor. Minority groups were concerned about language barriers, [judges'] lack of knowledge of the problems faced by minority groups and a general lack of confidence of minority groups in the civil justice system.

(a)   The Challenges We Face†

Right Honourable Beverley McLachlin, P.C.

Mr. President, distinguished guests, thank you for that welcome. I am delighted to be here again to address the Empire Club. More than a quarter century ago, a Canadian Justice Minister, Pierre Elliott Trudeau, challenged Canadians to build "the just society". In the ensuing years, thousands of Canadians have worked to establish their visions of a just society. The centrepiece of Prime Minister Trudeau's vision of the just society was the *Charter of Rights and Freedoms*, adopted in 1982, and whose 25th anniversary we will celebrate on April 17, 2007. Whatever our political persuasion or our particular conception of justice, there can be no doubt that Canadians today expect a just society. They expect just laws and practices. And they expect justice in their courts. Today, I would like to share with you my perspective on justice in our courts and the challenges we face in assuring Canadian men, women and children a just and efficacious justice process. Let me begin by asserting that Canada has a strong and healthy justice system. Indeed, our courts and justice system are looked to by many countries as exemplary. We have well-appointed courtrooms, presided over by highly qualified judges. Our judges are independent and deliver impartial justice, free of fear and favour. The Canadian Judicial Council, which I head, recently issued an information note on the judicial appointments process in which it affirmed these long-standing principles on which our justice system is based. Canadians can have confidence that judges are committed to rendering judg-

ment in accordance with the law and based on the evidence. Corruption and partisanship are non-issues. In all these things, we are fortunate indeed. Yet, like every other human institutional endeavour, justice is an ongoing process. It is never done, never fully achieved. Each decade, each year, each month, indeed each day, brings new challenges. Canadian society is changing more rapidly than ever before. So is the technology by which we manage these changes. Thus it should not come as a surprise that Canada's justice system, in 2007, faces challenges. Some represent familiar problems with which we have yet to come to grips. Others arise from new developments, and require new answers. In my comments today I will touch on four such challenges:

- the challenge of access to justice,
- the challenge of long trials,
- the challenge of delays in the justice system, and
- the challenge of dealing with deeply rooted, endemic social problems.

THE CHALLENGE OF ACCESS TO JUSTICE

The most advanced justice system in the world is a failure if it does not provide justice to the people it is meant to serve. Access to justice is therefore critical. Unfortunately, many Canadian men and women find themselves unable, mainly for financial reasons, to access the Canadian justice system. Some of them

---

† Remarks presented at the Empire Club of Canada, Toronto, March 8, 2007. Source: http://www.scc-csc.gc.ca/court-cour/ju/spe-dis/bm07-03-08-eng.asp. Reproduced with the permission of the Supreme Court of Canada, 2010. [Notes and/or references omitted.]

decide to become their own lawyers. Our courtrooms today are filled with litigants who are not represented by counsel, trying to navigate the sometimes complex demands of law and procedure. Others simply give up. Recently, the Chief Justice of Ontario stated that access to justice is the most important issue facing the legal system.[1]

The Canadian legal system is sometimes said to be open to two groups — the wealthy and corporations at one end of the spectrum, and those charged with serious crimes at the other. The first have access to the courts and justice because they have deep pockets and can afford them. The second have access because, by and large, and with some notable deficiencies, legal aid is available to the poor who face serious charges that may lead to imprisonment. To the second group should be added people involved in serious family problems, where the welfare of children is at stake; in such cases the Supreme Court has ruled that legal aid may be a constitutional requirement.[2]

It is obvious that these two groups leave out many Canadians. Hard hit are average middle-class Canadians. They have some income. They may have a few assets, perhaps a modest home. This makes them ineligible for legal aid. But at the same time, they quite reasonably may be unwilling to put a second mortgage on the house or gamble with their child's college education or their retirement savings to pursue justice in the courts. Their options are grim: use up the family assets in litigation; become their own lawyers; or give up. The result may be injustice. A person injured by the wrongful act of another may decide not to pursue compensation. A parent seeking custody of or access to the children of a broken relationship may decide he or she cannot afford to carry on the struggle — sometimes to the detriment not only of the parent but the children. When couples split up, assets that should go to the care of the children are used up in litigation; the family's financial resources are dissipated. Such outcomes can only with great difficulty be called "just". To add to this, unrepresented litigants — or self-represented litigants as they are sometimes called — impose a burden on courts and work their own special forms of injustice. Trials and motions in court are conducted on the adversary system, under which each party presents its case and the judge acts as impartial decider. An unrepresented litigant may not know how to present his or her case. Putting the facts and the law before the court may be an insurmountable hurdle. The trial judge may try to assist, but this raises the possibility that the judge may be seen as "helping", or partial to, one of the

parties. The proceedings adjourn or stretch out, adding to the public cost of running the court. In some courts, more than 44 per cent of cases involve a self-represented litigant.[3] Different, sometimes desperate, responses to the phenomenon of the self-represented litigant have emerged. Self-help clinics are set up. Legal services may be "unbundled", allowing people to hire lawyers for some of the work and do the rest themselves. The Associate Chief Justice of the British Columbia Provincial Court is quoted as saying this is "absurd", not unlike allowing a medical patient to administer their own anaesthetic.[4]

It is not only the unrepresented litigants who are prejudiced. Lawyers on the other side may find the difficulty of their task greatly increased, driving up the costs to their clients. Judges are stressed and burned out, putting further pressures on the justice system. And so it goes.

The bar and the bench are attempting to improve the situation. Some modest progress is being made. Lawyers are organizing themselves to give free, or *pro bono*, service to needy clients. Clinics have been set up by governments, NGOs and legal groups to help self-represented litigants. Rule changes to permit contingency fees — the lawyer is paid out of the proceeds of the litigation, if any — and class actions provide ways for people of modest means to litigate some tort and consumer actions. Thought is being given to coverage for legal services within specified limits as an endorsement to home insurance policies. Justice groups are working to simplify procedures and thus reduce costs or assist the unrepresented litigant.

All this is good. Yet much more needs to be done if access to justice is to become a reality for ordinary Canadians.

THE CHALLENGE OF LONG TRIALS

A second challenge is the challenge of long trials, an increasingly urgent problem both in civil and criminal litigation. Not too many years ago, it was not uncommon for murder trials to be over in five to seven days. Now, they last five to seven months. Some go on for years.[5] The length of civil trials is also increasing. For example, in 1996, the average length of a trial at the Vancouver Law Courts was 12.9 hours. Six years later, the average length of a trial had doubled, to 25.7 hours.[6] This trend is consistent with developments in other jurisdictions throughout Canada.

There are a number of reasons why trials seem to have taken on a life of their own. On the criminal side, the *Canadian Charter of Rights and Free-*

doms has had a significant impact on the criminal trial process. *Charter* pre-trial motions regularly last two to three times longer than the trial itself.[7] Changes in the law of evidence have also increased litigation and lengthened trials.[8]

On the civil side, there are also a number of reasons why trials have become longer. Although Canadian rules of procedure impose limits on examinations for discovery, some argue that they are still too broad, allowing parties to canvass issues that are not relevant and material to the issues in the litigation. This results in longer, and more expensive discoveries, and a larger volume of evidence being placed before the trier of fact at trial. The expanded use of expert witnesses has also lengthened trials.

Efforts at reform are underway. On the criminal side, a recent report by the Ontario Superior Court of Justice makes a number of recommendations to improve the efficacy and effectiveness of judicial pre-trial conferences with a view to improving the efficiency of criminal trials.[9] The Ontario government recently launched a process to suggest reforms to the province's civil justice system.[10] A similar review is underway in British Columbia.[11]

THE CHALLENGE OF DELAYS IN THE JUSTICE SYSTEM

A third and related challenge is the problem of delays in the processing of cases. Here again, the problem afflicts both criminal and civil cases. On the criminal side, delays in proceedings may result in serious cases being stayed, since the *Charter* guarantees a trial within a reasonable time. Delays may also result in lengthy periods of incarceration for the accused person prior to trial. Even where the accused is out on bail, the stress of the ongoing proceedings and the upcoming, ever-deferred trial may be considerable. Witnesses are less likely to be reliable when testifying to events that transpired many months, or even years, before trial. Not only is there an erosion of the witnesses' memories with the passage of time, but there is an increased risk that a witness may not be available to testify through ordinary occurrences of sickness or death. As the delay increases, swift, predictable justice, which is the most powerful deterrent of crime, vanishes. The personal and social costs are incalculable. On the civil side, different but similar problems arise. Whether the litigation has to do with a business dispute or a family matter, people need prompt resolution so they can get on with their lives. Often, they cannot wait for years for an answer. When delay becomes too

great, the courts are no longer an option. People look for other alternatives. Or they simply give up on justice.

Courts have been promoting various forms of out-of-court mediation and arbitration as a more effective way of achieving settlement and dealing with many civil cases. This is good. But the fact is, some cases should go to court. They raise legal issues that should be considered by the courts for the good of the litigants and the development of the law.

I do not want to give the impression that all is bleak. Ten years ago, in Ontario, civil appeals were taking two to three years from the date of perfection to be heard. Criminal appeals were not much better. They were being heard one and a half to two years from the date of perfection.[12] Today, the time required for bringing appeals on for hearing has been greatly reduced.

In a recent speech, Ontario Court of Appeal Justice Michael Moldaver noted that the solution to delays in the justice system was not to hire more judges, but for the court to take control of the process from the litigants and put it back in the hands of the judges. This is what happened in Ontario. Within a space of 18 months, the backlog was gone. Civil appeals in Ontario are now being heard within nine to 12 months of perfection. Criminal appeals are being heard within six to nine months.

THE CHALLENGE PRESENTED BY ENDEMIC SOCIAL PROBLEMS

The final justice challenge I wish to discuss is the challenge presented by intractable, endemic social problems, including drug addiction and mental illness.

A few years ago, I found myself at a dinner at government house. Next to me sat the chief of one of Toronto's downtown precincts. I asked him what his biggest problem was. I thought he would say the *Charter* and "all those judges who pronounce on rights". But he surprised me. "Mental illness", was his reply. He then told me a sad story, one I have heard throughout the country in the years since. Every night, his jails would fill up with minor offenders or persons who had created a nuisance — not because they are criminals, but because they are mentally ill. They would be kept overnight or for a few days, only to be released — the cycle inevitably to repeat itself.

Such people are not true criminals, not real wrong-doers in the traditional sense of those words. They become involved with the law because they are mentally ill, addicted or both. Today, a growing awareness of the extent and nature of mental illness and addiction is helping sensitize the public and those involved in the justice system. This sensitization and knowledge is leading to new, more appropriate responses to the problem.

One response has been the development of specialized courts — such as mental health courts and drug courts. As Brian Lennox, Chief Justice of the Ontario Court of Justice, said recently at the opening of the Mental Health Court in Ottawa:

> The Ottawa Mental Health Court is an example of a progressive movement within criminal justice systems in North America and elsewhere in the world to create "problem-solving courts". These courts, with collaborative interdisciplinary teams of professionals and community agencies, attempt to identify and to deal with some of the underlying factors contributing to criminal activity, which have often not been very well-addressed by the conventional criminal justice process. The goal is to satisfy the traditional criminal law function of protection of the public by addressing in individual cases the real rather than the apparent causes that lead to conflict with the law.

Mental health courts have opened in Ontario, New Brunswick and Newfoundland.[13] Many other jurisdictions, including British Columbia, Manitoba, Nunavut and Yukon, are in various stages of developing these courts. These courts can do much to alleviate the problems.

Other problem-solving courts within the Ontario Court of Justice include drug treatment courts and *Gladue* courts, the latter dealing with aboriginal offenders. Such courts are also being used in other Canadian jurisdictions.

This is just the beginning. I could go on. The point is this. In a variety of ways, throughout Canada we are adapting our criminal law court procedures to better meet the realities of endemic social problems and better serve the public.

CONCLUSION

I have shared with you four challenges faced by Canada's justice system in 2007 — challenges close to my heart, and that of justice workers, including judges, throughout Canada. I have also described the efforts which are being made to alleviate the problems and ultimately, with luck, perhaps solve them.

Let me close on this note. Nothing is more important than justice and the just society. It is essential to [the] flourishing of men, women and children and to maintaining social stability and security. You need only open your newspaper to the international section to read about countries where the rule of law does not prevail, where the justice system is failing or non-existent.

In this country, we realize that without justice, we have no rights, no peace, no prosperity. We realize that, once lost, justice is difficult to reinstate. We in Canada are the inheritors of a good justice system, one that is the envy of the world. Let us face our challenges squarely and thus ensure that our justice system remains strong and effective.

(b)   Civil Justice Reform — The Toronto Experience†

The Honourable Warren K. Winkler, Chief Justice of Ontario

[1] I am very pleased that the University of Ottawa is holding a series of lectures on the important topic of civil procedure, and flattered that the members of the Faculty of Law were so kind as to both name the series in my honour and invite me to deliver the first of the lectures.[1]

[2] J'aimerais remercier sincèrement le Vice-récteur Feldthusen, le Doyen intérimaire Gervais et la Professeure Bailey pour avoir organisé cette conférence.

[3] I propose to make a few comments today about procedural reforms that were introduced almost

† (2007–2008) 39 Ottawa L. Rev. 99–113. (The Warren Winkler Lectures on Civil Justice Reform, delivered at the University of Ottawa's Faculty of Law on September 12, 2007.) Reproduced with permission. [Notes and/or references omitted.]

three years ago for civil cases in the Superior Court of Justice in the Toronto Region, but before I do so, I would like to say a few words on a more general level about the importance of civil justice reform.

[4] Civil litigation in this province is too expensive and too slow, with the result that many people in Ontario may be denied access to justice. In a recent article in the Toronto Star entitled "Access to justice a 'basic right,'"² it was reported that the cost of taking a routine civil case through to a three-day trial in Ontario is about $60,000. This is more than the average Canadian family earns in a year, which means, of course, that the average Canadian family may not be able to afford a simple civil suit, especially if they lose at the end of trial.

[5] None of this is news. Charles Dickens' criticisms of the legal system in Bleak House, which focused in a most pointed way on the costs and delays of civil proceedings, were published almost two centuries ago, and yet they still ring true today. In Ontario as well as across the country, it has been widely acknowledged within the profession for years that there are significant flaws with our civil justice system. Moreover, clients can be short-sighted, lawyers can give bad advice and judges can become too easily frustrated. Even where reasonable clients find themselves in the hands of good lawyers, who appear before the most able judges, lawsuits can take on very nasty lives of their own.

[6] It may be that some of the problems are, at least to a degree, intractable. However, we must also keep in mind that many of the very same processes that drive up costs provide us with assurances that the system is fundamentally fair. We could eliminate all manner of pleadings, oral and documentary discovery, and move each and every case directly to a 15 minute trial, similar to those seen on popular television, but few would argue that the resulting costs savings would justify the damage done to the process. Without meaning to suggest that we could not do better in terms of reducing costs and delay, we should recognize that a just and fair legal system will, by definition, have very real costs associated with it.

[7] Lawyers should, and do, donate their time pro bono for worthy causes and needy clients, and I commend the members of the profession who engage in this form of public service. It is not realistic, however, to expect that charity will, by itself, provide meaningful access to justice for all those who need it. Similarly, it is not realistic to think that we will

have universally available legal aid for civil cases any time soon.

[8] I therefore wish to preface my comments with a simple proposition: If one accepts that there will necessarily be costs associated with any justice system worthy of the name, and that funding sources — apart from the clients themselves — are necessarily limited, one would wish to ensure that careful consideration is given to the true cost implications of any proposed reforms, in very practical terms. I will return to this theme at the conclusion of my remarks today.

[9] We should remember that our system does manage to provide meaningful redress for many ordinary Ontarians, in spite of the costs associated with it. Many apparently vulnerable individuals, such as tort victims, wrongfully dismissed employees and others, are routinely able to obtain legal remedies on a cost effective basis. The legislative changes that explicitly allowed lawyers to charge contingency fees³ has opened the doors of the justice system for many plaintiffs who would otherwise never be able to afford to hire a lawyer, without generating the flood of frivolous cases anticipated by those who opposed permitting such fee arrangements. Similarly, class action legislation⁴ in Ontario has allowed plaintiffs who would not ordinarily be able to afford to bring an action to do just that.

[10] Once again, I am not suggesting that the system is perfect; there are many types of cases that are not amenable to contingency fee arrangements or class actions, and even when they are, they are not always fair to the client. My point is merely that it is wrong to think about our civil justice system as a complete failure. Given that the settlement rate for civil lawsuits in Ontario is over 96%, it distorts our analysis somewhat if we focus too closely on the cost associated with the 3% or 4% of cases that go all the way through trial.

[11] We cannot design a process that will make perfect justice available for everyone, at no cost. I am confident, however, that the legal community in Ontario (in which I include not only the bench and bar, but also academic institutions and the government) can achieve a system in which an increasing number of ordinary people can achieve a fair result when resolving their civil disputes, in a cost effective manner. As I have said, in working towards this goal, we should focus not only on the present system's short-comings but also on its successes. For the simple fact is that our justice system is the envy of

the world and a model for every free and democratic society.

[12] I turn now to the situation that presented itself in the Toronto Region of the Superior Court in the spring of 2004. I think it is fair to say that the changes to the civil justice system in the Toronto Region of the Superior Court, which were implemented in late 2004, were successful in dealing with the problems that confronted us. My hope is that there are lessons to be learned from the approach which was taken to address the very significant challenges we faced at the time.

[13] The adage that "necessity is the mother of invention" is entirely apt in describing the reforms. By mid-2004, dates for routine motions were being set more than six months out. Long trials (that is, those projected to last more than ten days) were being scheduled more than three years into the future and the waiting times for shorter trials were increasing to over a year. As a consequence of the delays in getting cases on to trial, the number of interlocutory motions was increasing exponentially. In June of that year, it emerged that the Court had not managed to reach some 38 long trials that were to have started that spring on fixed trial dates, because there were no judges to hear the cases. The simplified procedure for claims under $50,000 (a then recent innovation intended to provide affordable, accessible and timely justice for smaller cases) was generating involved, multi-day trials, thereby defeating its very purpose and using up valuable judicial resources in the process. Any sensible observer of the justice system in the Region knew that the end was in sight when the staff at the case management masters office, the nerve centre for civil case management, literally "took the phone off the hook," signifying that the system was hopelessly backlogged.

[14] It was apparent that if a solution was not found and implemented immediately, and the backlog haemorrhaging was not staunched, the Toronto civil lists would implode come September 2004.

[15] The Toronto Region of the Superior Court is the largest civil trial court in Canada. It is composed of more than one hundred judges and masters, who are supported in their work by over five hundred court services employees.

[16] Toronto is the commercial and financial engine of the country, as the home to many head offices, insurance companies, banks, manufacturing concerns and as the primary centre of the Canadian securities industry. The ability to attract and retain business depends in part on access to fair and timely dispute resolution. A properly functioning civil justice system in Toronto is integral to the success of Ontario's economy.

[17] On an individual level, the people of Canada's largest city also require a dynamic and responsive justice system. They are entitled to expect that their legal rights and civil liberties will not be compromised simply because the legal system is too busy to deal with them.

[18] It was unimaginable and unacceptable that the civil justice system could "melt down" for the beginning of a new court year. In order for the Court to meet its obligations as an important part of the economic infrastructure and as one of the province's most important public institutions, a solution had to be found quickly, without alarming Ontarians or sending a wave of panic through business circles.

[19] Although the seriousness and magnitude of the problems were known by those involved, it was another matter to ascertain the root causes of the problems, so that viable solutions could be developed. The problems had to be viewed through the lens of three fundamental principles: Access to justice, judicial economy and proportionality. More to the point, once answers were forthcoming, the solutions had to be capable of speedy implementation.

[20] I had only recently been appointed as the Regional Senior Justice for Toronto, and I began by consulting with as many people as I could in an effort to pinpoint the causes of the problems. Work began in earnest over the July 1st weekend. A small team, comprised of a handful of judges, civil servants and leading lawyers, was put together. It became clear at the outset that the case management system was going to need major surgery. Full case management had been introduced in Toronto only three years previously, with the enactment of Rule 77 of the Rules of Civil Procedure.[5] A great deal of hard work and planning had gone into the introduction of Rule 77, and any major changes were going to require close communication with a number of stakeholders, in order to ensure their support, such as chief justices, the Toronto Region judiciary and masters, bar organizations, mediators and courts services staff.

[21] It also appeared at the outset that the aggressive timeline which was needed to prevent a full-blown crisis made it impossible to effect the solutions by way of amendment to the Rules of Civil Procedure. A decision was taken to introduce the

most urgently needed changes by means of a Practice Direction, in which such changes could be mandated and made effective almost immediately. We set a deadline of December 31, 2004 for identifying the causes of the problems, designing the solutions, and drafting, publishing and implementing the Practice Direction. As events unfolded, it was ultimately possible to enact a new rule on an expedited basis. Rule 78 was enacted to codify some of the reforms and on January 1, 2005, sweeping changes were introduced in the civil justice system in the Toronto Region, for the second time in less than four years.

[22] We now have more than two years of experience with this new regime, and while there is unquestionably a great deal of work that remains to be done, the Practice Direction[6] and Rule 78 are widely seen to have brought about vast improvements for those who use, and work in, the civil justice system.

[23] As I mentioned a moment ago, Rule 77 came into effect for all civil cases in Toronto in 2001. In an attempt to address the costs, delays, and backlogs that plagued the system, and thereby acted as barriers to justice, Rule 77 of the Rules of Civil Procedure had been designed so that virtually all of the civil cases would be aggressively and intensively managed by the courts (i.e., "universal case management"). Rule 77 had previously been implemented in Ottawa and Windsor and was generally viewed as a success in those jurisdictions. In the months leading up to its implementation in Toronto, there was great optimism that it would bring meaningful improvements there as well.

[24] As I also mentioned before, however, it was apparent by mid-2004 that the civil justice system in Toronto was lurching towards a crisis, which many judges and lawyers believed had been brought about, at least in part, by the ambitious package of reforms symbolized by Rule 77. We had to figure out what had gone wrong.

[25] As you know, there are a variety of steps which occur in a civil action before the case is actually heard by a trial judge, such as the exchange of pleadings, disclosure of documents, examinations for discovery and pre-trial conferences. Prior to the introduction of case management, the pace and the way in which these steps occurred were determined almost entirely by the parties and their counsel, sometimes with considerable inefficiency and at great cost. In an effort to address this problem, under case management, the courts were given an immediate supervisory role over the progress of cases moving through the system. The various steps prior to trial were to be determined by pre-fixed timetables, and case management judges and masters were to be assigned to individual cases to assist the parties in moving matters along, or in settling or narrowing issues.

[26] The theory was that with early and active intervention by the court, proceedings would become streamlined and judicial resources would be focused where they were needed most. Cases would either settle earlier, or if they were not going to settle, would be brought on for trial more quickly and more efficiently.

[27] Under the Rules of Civil Procedure, case-managed actions began with "early mandatory mediation" at the very outset of the lawsuit. Mediation is an informal process in which a neutral third party helps participants reach their own agreement for resolving their dispute. Unlike a judge or arbitrator, the mediator has no authority to impose a solution. Rather, the mediator's role is to serve as a neutral facilitator, to try to bring the parties to a mutually agreeable compromise. He or she is ordinarily selected by mutual agreement between the parties, as someone in whom they all have confidence. Significantly, for our purposes, mediators are in private practice and are outside the court system, and thus are paid by the parties.

[28] The case management rules prescribed extremely short deadlines for conducting the mediation.[7] However, in practice the parties would frequently not communicate or cooperate in scheduling the mediation session, or could not agree on a mediator, or did not agree about what steps, if any, could or should be taken in advance of the mediation. In serious casualty cases, parties could be required to attend mediation before the plaintiff's injuries had stabilized. The rule was deliberately designed so that the mediation would take place before one party could compel the other to provide any type of disclosure, such as providing copies of their documents or names of witnesses. In cases with multiple defendants, the mediation deadline sometimes expired before all the parties had been served, and thus were even aware of the lawsuit.

[29] As stated, a failure to agree to conduct the mediation within the time limits set out in the rule resulted in court staff assigning a mediator to the case, who was randomly selected from a roster of whichever mediators happened to be available. He or she was ordinarily unknown to the parties and their lawyers, would usually not have any expertise in the

subject of the dispute and would be left with the unenviable task of bringing the reluctant parties to the table. Not surprisingly, the vast majority of these forced early mediations did not result in settlement.

[30] The upshot of all of this was that the mediation became an unavoidable, costly and useless obstacle in the path of the party who wanted to move the lawsuit forward (normally the plaintiff). There were countless case conferences in which judges and masters were asked to extend deadlines or otherwise assist parties in cancelling or delaying the mediations. A body of law developed, as a result of contested motions, about the circumstances in which a mandatory mediation could be deferred, or whether parties could proceed to mediation with a mediator of their choice when they had missed the deadline and the court office had already randomly assigned a stranger from the roster.

[31] Another important feature of case management was the establishment of timetables for the completion of the steps required to advance the proceeding. Under Rule 77, timetables had to be filed within 30 days after the mandatory mediation session if it had not resulted in a settlement of the lawsuit. Thereafter, case conferences were convened, in which judges and masters were asked to fix or vary timetables, where parties could not, or would not, agree on deadlines, or where they later failed to live up to them. Once again, these case conferences ate up costs and slowed cases down, since the booking dates for case conferences stretched further and further into the future because of the backlog of cases.

[32] Time does not permit me to elaborate today about a number of the other aspects of Rule 77, but I would like to mention one final example. As part of the philosophy of case management, trial dates were fixed regardless of whether or not any of the parties had set the action down for trial. As I mentioned a few moments ago, fewer than four percent of the civil cases that are started in Ontario actually go all the way through to trial. Most are either not defended at all, or settle at some stage before trial. Ordinarily, a trial date is assigned only if the case has not settled and one of the parties indicates that he or she is ready for trial and does not want to take any further pre-trial steps (e.g. discoveries). Because the vast majority of cases settle before this happens, trial dates are ordinarily only given out in a small number of cases.

[33] Under Rule 77, a trial date was assigned for every single lawsuit in the system at trial scheduling court (a court that sat regularly simply to set trial

dates), even though the majority of the cases were not ready for trial (although they were supposed to be), and would probably never go to trial in any event. It did not take long for the trial schedules to fill up for months and then years into the future, and the waiting times for trial dates mushroomed. As soon as lawyers noticed this, they attempted to secure trial dates years down the road for cases that were not ready to proceed, on the assumption that they would be ready for trial by the time they were reached. Needless to say, as often as not, when the trial dates were reached, the parties were still not ready to go, and before long, the trial lists were in shambles.

[34] As some lawyers described the process, it was "hurry up and wait" which meant that cases were pushed through on tight timetables, only to languish waiting for trial dates that were three years away, mainly because the ballooned trial list was laden with cases that were not ready for trial. One side effect of this was there were many motions that would not have been brought if trial dates were available on a timely basis.

[35] Notwithstanding its early success in Ottawa and Windsor, universal case management was not workable in Toronto. This was largely due to the volume of cases and relative lack of resources. The bulk of the case management work fell to a handful of case management masters and court administrators, but notwithstanding their Herculean efforts, it soon became apparent that they could not micromanage the almost 20,000 cases filed every year in the Toronto Region, to the extent mandated by Rule 77.

[36] In addition to the problems faced by the Court, the litigants bore the cost of the numerous procedural steps that were added to the civil justice process. As I have said, the various case conferences, filings and mandatory mediations referred to above usually did very little to move the case along, while clients were paying their lawyers for what were frequently premature or unproductive steps.

[37] What I have euphemistically called the "challenges" that we faced in 2004 were not caused solely by Rule 77. The simplified procedure cases that I spoke about before and long trials (those projected to last more than ten days) were also presenting us with great "challenges."

[38] More than 25 percent of the cases commenced each year in Toronto are filed under the simplified procedure available for cases involving less than $50,000. Unfortunately, the provisions of this rule

that were designed to keep the pre-trial steps as simple and inexpensive as possible, were making the trials themselves extremely complicated. Because the parties had not had any discoveries before trial, counsel often conducted one during the trial, which consumed excessive amounts of time. More generally, there was a lack of proportionality and trials involving $20,000 or $30,000 were dragging on for four or five days. The judges blamed the lawyers and the lawyers blamed the judges, but no one seemed to be able to stop it.

[39] At the other end of the spectrum, long trials also created their own set of "challenges." Many different types of cases are projected as "long" trials; however, it is important to bear in mind that a significant proportion (approximately two-thirds) are large casualty cases, where plaintiffs are attempting to obtain compensation for serious personal injuries. As I mentioned at the outset, 38 long-trial dates were missed in the spring of 2004. When these cases were adjourned to the fall, it produced a domino effect, since all the long trials that were supposed to start in the fall had to be put off.

[40] As the number of long trials that were not being reached on their appointed dates increased, the settlement rate decreased. When word got around that the Court would be forced to adjourn a fixed trial date, settlement rates took a free fall. This compounded the backlog and brings me to a very important point that applies not just to long trials, but to all cases: Real trial dates lead to settlements.

[41] I begin with the proposition that responsible counsel do not settle their cases until they have considered the issues involved, assessed the strengths and weaknesses of their case and investigated the facts, including facts that may initially be within the exclusive knowledge of the opposite party. I hasten to add that all of this should be proportionate to the amounts of money involved and the seriousness of the issues, and as cost-effective as possible.

[42] My next proposition is that, subject only to investigating the matter in a proportionate and cost-effective way, responsible lawyers settle their cases as early in the life of the file as they can. Unfortunately, for a variety of reasons, the parties will not simultaneously arrive at the moment when they are all ready to settle if left to their own devices.

[43] It is for this reason that I say that real trial dates settle cases. What I mean by this is that the intense preparation that ordinarily takes place immediately before a trial, and the parties' collective real-ization that they are going to have a result imposed on them by a court if they do not sort the dispute out themselves, leads all parties to focus very attentively on settlement, and to do so at the same time. This is a good thing: There should be a point of reckoning when the parties can make an informed decision about whether or not they wish to settle or proceed to trial. When the trial lists fell apart and the parties knew that their case was not likely to be reached for trial (or that the Court would happily adjourn the case if it was), the day of reckoning — the necessary catalyst for settlement — never arrived. The settlements of the more intractable cases, which ordinarily take place on the very eve of trial, stopped occurring. The long trial list worked on a fine balance and was judicially staffed based on a known settlement rate for cases. When the settlement rate fell off, there were not enough judges for the cases scheduled to start.

[44] In short, by mid-2004, costs and delays had ballooned for litigants in Toronto. The court system was overburdened with unproductive work tying up valuable resources. While the simplified procedure had proven to be popular, it was not achieving its goal of making civil justice more affordable. Because parties could not get their cases heard, especially if their trial was expected to be lengthy, cases that would ordinarily have been settling were languishing in the system.

[45] Through the summer and early fall of 2004 there were extensive consultations with lawyers, judges, masters and court administrators both inside and outside Toronto. A number of key themes emerged. First, the volume of cases in Toronto had made it impossible to transfer the successes and flexible practices from Ottawa and Windsor to the unique challenges present in the Toronto Region. Successful case management requires a degree of flexibility that cannot be achieved when the court is dealing with vast numbers of cases. Universal case management had to be reworked to apply resources to the cases that "needed" case management. The court-overseen timetabling requirements were unachievable and vast court resources were being eaten up arranging and rearranging lawyers' schedules. The escalation of case conferences was imposing considerable and unnecessary costs on the parties, and draining court resources. The work required of the masters had to be reduced to fit the available personnel. Second, imposing mediation at the very outset of each and every case, before the parties and their counsel were properly informed, was proving to be costly and unproductive. Third, the delays in get-

ting cases on to trial were unacceptable and were creating [their] own host of problems. Fourth, simplified procedures were not working and were tying up critical resources. Finally, Toronto was known as the "motions capital of the world" because [of] the many motions generated by the problems set out above.

[46] I do want to say what, in my view, did not cause the problem. Court staff, judges and in particular the case management masters were more dedicated and diligent than anyone had a right to expect. They were given an impossible task, and worked under what ultimately proved to be impossible circumstances. Similarly, I do not accept the assertion, advanced in some quarters, that Toronto lawyers are to blame, and that the members of the bar in Toronto work less cooperatively and civilly than lawyers elsewhere in the province. As someone who grew up in Alberta, I can certainly understand that anything that has to do with Toronto is a useful whipping post, but in my experience the negative stereotype about the Toronto Bar has no basis in fact.

[47] Finally, I emphasize that the drafter of Rule 77 had shown great insight about addressing problems in the civil justice system. For the reasons I have already stated, it makes perfect sense for parties to know that real, fixed, trial dates — what I called their day of reckoning — await them. It is reasonable to insist that parties attempt to resolve their case by mediation before they consume the significant public and private resources involved in the conduct of a trial. Moreover, it is in the parties' and the public's interest for the Court to assume some control over pending cases, to ensure that they are not languishing because of inattentive lawyers, or because the case has taken on a nasty life of its own. The theories behind Rule 77 were unassailable, but procedure needed to accommodate the reality of dealing with 20,000 new cases every year.

[48] In countless meetings through September and October, the ad hoc committee turned its attention to the detailed work of figuring out the solutions, which would form the basis of the Practice Direction and later, Rule 78. It soon became clear that it was critically important to ensure that the various individual reforms we were considering could work together as a whole. Further, while the reforms had to set out the basic procedure for the effective management of all of the many cases in the system, it was equally important that there should be a degree of flexibility, in recognition of the fact that the issues, problems and personalities involved in each piece of litigation are different.

[49] After a great deal of coffee and debate, the Practice Direction was finalized and approved by Chief Justice Smith in November 2004, and came into effect on December 31, 2004. Rule 78 came into force shortly thereafter.

[50] Case management was not eliminated. Rather, there was to be "case management as necessary, but not necessarily case management." The reform was to eliminate "universal case management" in Toronto. The goal was to provide "effective, flexible and targeted case management," by only case managing the cases that truly required court intervention. The intention was that there would be a reduction in the number of unnecessary attendances by counsel and thus reduced costs to parties. At the same time, court resources would be freed up to address more substantive issues.

[51] Specifically, case management could be obtained on motion in complex multi-party actions, or where one or more parties were guilty of chronic obstruction. Apart from this, the parties were to be left to run their own lawsuits. Lawsuits were returned to the lawyers to manage and flexibility was to be the touchstone in cases that were to be case managed by the Court.

[52] The other notable aspects of the reforms included discontinuing trial scheduling court, and returning to a system where trial dates would only be given out after one of the parties signified that he or she was ready to proceed to trial. Steps were taken to ensure that trials actually proceeded on their fixed date, and a strict "no adjournment" policy was put in place. The jurisdiction of case management masters was expanded, in order that they could preside at pre-trials in cases involving less than $50,000.

[53] The notion that the parties would run their own cases was subject to an important caveat: Parties or counsel would have to attend Status Hearings if their case appeared to be languishing, and in particular, if the case was not set down for trial within two years of being issued. The procedures governing Status Hearings, which were first introduced in the early 1980s, were modified so that counsel could avoid attending if they took concrete steps to move their action forward after the court office advised them that their delay had not gone unnoticed, and so that case management masters could preside in place of judges.

[54] Further, in an attempt to make pre-trials more meaningful, the requirements as to the information

that had to be included in pre-trial briefs was greatly enhanced, so that both the parties and judges would be better prepared to focus on the case at the pre-trial. It was felt that this would increase the rates of settlements which could be achieved at pre-trials, and make trial management more effective in those cases that could not be settled.

[55] The way we dealt with mandatory mediation was as important as any other single reform. There was considerable pressure by the Bar to eliminate mandatory mediation altogether as a costly and ineffective unnecessary step. This was rejected. Instead, the members of the ad hoc committee were uniformly of the view that the right approach was to insist that the parties engage in mediation at some point before trial, but to extend the timelines so that mediation would occur when it was most likely to be effective. A recommendation of the mediation community was adopted expanding mandatory mediation to include simplified procedure cases, which had been excluded under the former rules. The only expandable resource available to the court system was the outside mediation community and the decision was to capitalize on this valuable resource, not reject it!

[56] The essence is that mediation continues to be mandatory, but the parties should control the timing of such an important event to the extent that this is possible. To ensure that parties do not bypass the step, trial dates are not provided until mediation has been conducted, or at least booked. Mediators know that mediation is about "timing, timing and timing," and the reform in Rules 24.1 and 78 recognizes this truism. Mediation must now, in the words of the practice direction, be conducted "at the earliest stage at which it is likely to be effective," and in any event within 90 days after the case is set down for trial at the latest.[8] In wrongful dismissal and simplified procedure cases, the mediation must take place at the very front end of the lawsuit.

[57] As a further reform, I introduced what is known colloquially as "designated hitter" mediations, which are conducted by handpicked judges with expertise both as mediators and in the area of law involved in the dispute. This is done immediately prior to trial. There are, therefore, three mediations under the present regime: Mandatory mediation, a pre-trial conference and a DH mediation immediately before trial.

[58] The overarching theory of these and the other reforms introduced by Rule 78 and the Practice Direction was to reduce the number of appearances and formal litigation steps as much as possible, and to maximize the effectiveness of those steps that were taken. As stated, the underlying principles are access to justice in the form of shortened delays and reduced costs, the most efficient use of judicial resources, and proportionality and tailor-made case management where needed. Mediation became the centrepiece. Arrangements are underway to conduct a formal study of the results of the reforms over the next several months.

[59] It is nonetheless not too early to declare at least partial victory.

[60] We already know that although the number of civil cases in the system continues to grow, the waiting times for motion dates and trial dates are down. In some cases, such as masters' motions and trials under ten days, the reductions are especially dramatic. Dates for trials under ten days are now available within less than one month in cases of five days or less and available within five months for trials of six to ten days. These cases formerly had a 24-month waiting period. Even for long trials, the waiting time has been reduced from approximately three years to just over 12 months.

[61] Because case management masters have been relieved of the chore of conducting unnecessary case conferences for scheduling matters in routine cases, their time has been freed up to deal with more important practice motions, on a more timely basis, to conduct pre-trials in simplified procedure cases and to conduct Status Hearings. This in turn has freed up more judges to conduct trials, which shortens the waiting times, which leads to earlier negotiated settlements before costs spin out of control. Notably, although early dates are available, there has been a marked reduction in the nature of two-thirds fewer court "events" (which can mean anything from a motion or case conference, to a pre-trial or trial) for each case before trial.

[62] Altogether, the reforms led to a number of changes that improved the court system. Trial scheduling court has been disbanded, removing this time consuming step. Masters have been re-deployed to perform important pre-trials and motions.

[63] Since the timelines have been extended, the success rate for mandatory mediations has almost doubled. Further, it is said that the number of pre-trials in simplified procedure cases has been reduced to about one-third the former number, reflecting the wisdom in extending mediation to those cases. The shortened waiting time for trials has resulted in

fewer motions. The bottom line is that as a result of the changes taken globally, more judges have been freed up to handle estates, family and criminal matters which had been suffering from lack of judicial resources, and delays on those lists have been reduced.

[64] Lest anyone think that I am being immodest in declaring at least partial victory, let me repeat what I said before. The reforms were borne of necessity and were the culmination of a great deal of input from a wide variety of people. They were designed by a working group that included representatives of mediators, bar groups, masters, the judiciary and government court administrators. They were implemented by the assiduous efforts of the court staff, masters and judges of the Superior Court in the Toronto Region. Equally important, the members of the Bar rose to the challenge and, with the assistance of the Law Society of Upper Canada's Continuing Legal Education programmes, are working with the re-designed practices and procedures.

[65] In spite of the work that has gone into these reforms, and although the Bench and Bar have achieved substantial success in Toronto, litigation is nevertheless still beyond the financial means of the average person in Ontario. If we are committed to the rule of law and access to justice, we must redouble our efforts to address cost and delay. When the formal review of the Rule 78 reforms has been completed, I am hopeful that there will be valuable lessons to assist in our continuing effort to introduce constructive reforms to the civil justice system in Ontario.

[66] In the meantime, and in concluding my remarks today, I would like to offer some preliminary observations of what those lessons might be.

[67] First of all, I would begin with the proposition that every step that is added to a proceeding must be presumed to be an impediment to justice, unless the benefits of the proposed added step are empirically demonstrable. Recall[] that the average Canadian family cannot afford unnecessary and costly steps to their already expensive lawsuit.

[68] Early mandatory mediation, detailed mandatory timetables and numerous case conferences may be justifiable on a theoretical basis, but each and every one of these steps costs money, and if the added steps are not in fact moving cases towards resolution, they will drain away resources that litigants could otherwise use on steps that would have greater value in the long run. It was the litigants of modest means

— those intended to be the primary beneficiaries of Rule 77 — whose counsel argued most vociferously for the reforms.

[69] It is imperative that when adopting any added procedure, the approach ought to be to add more steps only when they can be justified after rigorous scrutiny of the likely practical results. We must strive to find a balance where we "touch" each file as few times as possible, but make each "touch" of the file as productive as possible in moving the case forward. This should be done with a view to reducing the costs that the parties must bear for multiple attendances and with a view to reducing the depletion of judicial resources. Under the reforms, the "events" on average have been reduced by more than half.

[70] Secondly, I suggest that we remain ever mindful that procedure should be the servant of substantive justice, and not vice versa. There is the temptation because of our training as judges and lawyers to become focused on procedural points to the exclusion of the substantive rights of parties. At the risk of stating the obvious, process is not an end in itself. If a procedural code or provision is ornate and intricate, the chances are that it will be expensive and cumbersome to administer for both lawyers and courts and that it will thus detract from substantive justice. Keep it simple.

[71] Thirdly, I suggest that mediation has become an integral part of our justice system. This is a good thing, but we must also keep this broad generalization in perspective. For one thing, not every type of case is amenable to mediation. Not every party wants a mediated resolution to his or her dispute. A wasted mediation is an added cost to the litigants and may have other serious negative effects on the case. Even in those cases that are ripe for mediation, the terms of any negotiated settlement will be dictated by the parties' knowledge of what the non-mediated result might look like. Obviously, a party with a strong case on the merits can expect to negotiate a more favourable result than a party with a weak case, which is as it should be.

[72] Quite apart from the merits of a party's case, however, the "non-mediated" result which will drive settlement discussions also refers to process. Parties, and in particular vulnerable parties, will approach negotiations very differently, depending on whether or not a trial is affordable and available without unreasonable delay. There is a risk that the negotiations that take place during mediations, and the terms of any settlement, will become badly lopsided if costs and delays become a disproportionate factor

in the mediation dynamic. No party should be forced to accept an unfair settlement at mediation simply because the opponent will be able to grind him or her down and drag a case out so that it takes on Dickensian proportions.

[73] In conclusion, nothing is more effective in the court system than a "day of reckoning" — the prospect of an early and "real" trial date. The very least, and at the same time the most constructive thing that our trial courts can provide to assist parties in resolving their disputes is to ensure that a judge is available to try the case if it cannot be settled, and that a trial date is available within as short a time as possible after the case is ready for trial. In short, a

fair and just system of justice requires a courtroom, a judge and a non-adjournment policy which, in turn, will produce settlements and be less costly to the litigants.

[74] My job today has been easy. I have spoken only in general terms about access to justice, judicial economy and proportionality, all of which are complex and difficult subjects. Let's hope that the speakers who come after me in this series can contribute to the rigorous debate that is needed to build the civil justice system we would all like to see and strive to create.

[75] Thank you. Merci pour votre attention aujourd'hui.

(c) Access to *Charter* Justice and the Rule of Law†

Carissima Mathen

1. INTRODUCTION

The difficulties experienced by most people in gaining access to the courts are generally acknowledged to be at crisis levels.[1] Numerous judges have expressed frustration at the continuing problems.[2] These difficulties are multiplied in constitutional cases. Ideally, courts would recognize that how people get to court is integrally connected to a properly functioning legal system. For the most part, this has not been the case. The current situation is dire, providing little assurance of essential review of laws and government action. This contributes to an overall deficit in state accountability.

This article argues that it is vital to ensure that (a) there is some mechanism by which the constitutionality of law and actions can be judged and (b) people have access to legal services. A society which fails in these tasks is little better than a society unbound by constitutional limits — and at risk of losing a key determinant of the rule of law.

The article first discusses developments in the law of standing and funding for litigation. The fact that constitutional litigation vindicates fundamental legal and political values warrants a generous approach to both issues. It is through these mecha-

nisms that we ensure that the legal system promotes and protects such things as the equal protection and benefit of the law, the achievement of social justice and fundamental rights. I conclude by returning more specifically to the rule of law and its implications for access to justice through a discussion of the Supreme Court of Canada's decision in *Christie v. British Columbia (Attorney General)*.[3]

2. STANDING

The standing issue most relevant in *Charter* cases is the ability to litigate in the public interest,[4] a role ordinarily confined to Attorneys General.[5] This role was confirmed in *Alliance for Marriage and Family v. A.A., B.B., C.C. and D.D.*,[6] a 2007 Supreme Court of Canada decision. A.A. *et al.* sought a declaration under Ontario's *Children's Law Reform Act*[7] to recognize as a third parent the lesbian partner of D.D.'s biological mother. The Alliance for Marriage and Family intervened against the applicants. After the Ontario Court of Appeal granted the application under its *parens patriae* jurisdiction and the Attorney General of Ontario (which had not participated in that court)[8] declined to pursue an appeal to the

† (2008–2009) 25 N.J.C.L. 191 at 191–93, 197–204. Published by Carswell, a Thomson Reuters Business. [Notes and/or references omitted.]

Supreme Court of Canada, the Alliance sought to appeal under Rule 18(5).[9] Dismissing the motion, Justice LeBel held that the Alliance was attempting to "substitute itself for the Attorney General in order to bring important legal questions relating to the development and application of the law before this Court".[10] He ruled that it is not open to a private litigant to "revive litigation in which it ha[s] no personal interest", noting that the Court's "flexibility" had "limits".[11]

Notwithstanding the Court's reasoning, the likelihood that an Attorney General will challenge laws enacted or relied upon by his or her government is remote. Thus, public interest standing retains great importance. As the Court has noted elsewhere, such litigation can ensure that "ordinary citizens have access to the justice system when they seek to resolve matters of consequence to the community as a whole".[12]

The framework for public interest standing is found in a quartet of cases decided in the 1970s and 1980s.[13] Three criteria are key: (a) there must be a serious issue raised as to the invalidity of the legislation; (b) the litigant must have a genuine interest in the legislation's validity; and (c) there must be no other reasonable or effective manner to bring the issue before the Court.[14]

The *Charter* posed the potential for enormous growth in the Supreme Court's docket including cases initiated by public interest litigants. In an early challenge to aspects of the immigration process, the Court limited the scope of such cases.[15] Though the Court recognized that the test for public interest standing should not be so limited as to render certain areas of the law immune from *Charter* challenge,[16] it was concerned at the prospect of a deluge of "marginal or redundant suits" initiated by well-meaning but misguided public organizations.[17] The Court therefore declined to expand the criteria mentioned above, ruling that the provisions at issue could be challenged by putative immigrants and refugees making a public interest challenge unnecessary.[18]

The most stringent criterion in the standing test is that there must be no other effective means for the issue to come before a court. This factor can be a particularly difficult hurdle in immigration cases. An applicant may be deported or (in cases with greater public appeal) the government may grant individual requests thereby removing the need for a hearing. The continued obstacles to meaningful challenges to immigration law emerged most recently in litigation of the Canadian Council for Refugees (CCR) against the *Safe Third Country Agreement* (STCA). Under the SCTA, refugee claimants entering Canada through U.S. land ports are returned to that country.[19] CCR argued that, in designating the United States as a "safe third country", the Governor in Council exceeded its authority under the *Immigration Act* and violated refugee claimants' *Charter* rights. While CCR was successful in the Federal Court, it lost in the Federal Court of Appeal, *inter alia*, on the basis that it did not have standing to argue the *Charter* issues. The Court noted that a similar claim could be brought by a refugee claimant presenting at a Canadian port of entry. It did not matter that such a lawsuit was extremely unlikely to occur; so long as a hypothetical plaintiff was identified, it would be inappropriate to grant standing to a public interest litigant. The Supreme Court of Canada refused leave to appeal.[20]

. . . .

3.   FUNDING

If standing is the heart of much public law litigation, funding is the lifeblood. It is also under tremendous strain. The lack of a stable source of funding for litigation leads to an *ad hoc* approach to rights advocacy, placing incredible pressure on individual lawyers and groups. It tends to inhibit the development of comprehensive litigation strategies, collaboration and compromise among like-minded interest groups. A lack of funding means that, for the vast majority of people, their ability to seek redress for wrongs done is illusory.

The federal government's decision in 2006 to cancel the Court Challenges Program (CCP), which provided modest funding for a narrow range of *Charter* cases,[40] removed one of the very few stable sources of funding in Canada for constitutional litigation. Though it was limited in scope, the program — perhaps more than any other post-*Charter* initiative — encapsulated the particular nature of the rights project in Canada. It embodied the belief that the protection and promotion of rights is a collective project, not a battle between state and citizen. The program recognized, in a modest but profoundly symbolic way, that we are all part of a rights-respecting culture and that constitutional limits on the state require independent, proactive and effective enforcement.

The program did not just fund litigation; it supported research and analysis on a host of issues important to marginalized communities. Providing opportunities for organizations to develop analytical and strategic approaches to rights advocacy, the CCP showed how the *Charter* and, indeed, constitutionalism itself not only sets limits on state power, but also channels and directs that power in positive ways. It demonstrated that constitutionalism can be a tool to enable the state to do more, not simply an obstacle to be manoeuvred around.

When terminating the program, the government said that it did not make sense to subsidize lawyers to challenge the government's own laws.[41] This statement reveals an impoverished view of rights: an obsession with safeguarding the state's power to enact laws, with minimal or no consideration for the boundaries that properly confine it.

One area that illustrates the challenge facing would-be public interest litigants is interim costs. A court may order the government to pay legal costs in advance if the interests of justice require it or if the case is exceptionally important. In *British Columbia (Minister of Forests) v. Okanagan Indian Band*,[42] four Bands claimed the right to log on Crown lands by virtue of Aboriginal title. After the Minister of Forests served the Bands with stop-work orders and commenced proceedings against them, the Bands brought a constitutional challenge to the *Forest Practices Code of British Columbia Act*.[43] In responding to an attempt by the Crown to have the issue remitted for trial, the Bands argued that such action was appropriate only if the Court made an interim costs award. A six–three majority of the Supreme Court upheld the provincial appellate court's decision that interim costs were justified. The trial judge actually supported an interim costs award, but had wrongly permitted that conclusion to be overtaken by irrelevant considerations. The majority noted that the judge found the case to be one of great public importance, raising novel and significant issues the resolution of which was very much in the interests of justice, even going so far as to urge the federal and provincial governments to provide funding.[44] The majority endorsed this view that resolving the issues would be "a major step towards settling the many unresolved problems in the Crown–aboriginal relationship in that province".[45] The circumstances were "special, even extreme".[46]

The following factors would favour (though not mandate) interim costs: (a) the plaintiff's impecuniousness together with an unlikelihood that the case otherwise would proceed; (b) a *prima facie* meritorious claim; and (c) unresolved issues of public importance that transcend the individual interests of the particular litigant.[47] The *Okanagan* factors suggest that allowing a particular case to lapse because of a lack of funds is not in the interests of justice. The Court also specifically acknowledged the role of public interest litigation (indeed, of public law cases in general), noting that society is not served when fiscal concerns deter ordinary citizens from bringing forward constitutional cases. The notion of "public interest" that underlies all constitutional litigation was thus identified as a relevant consideration when making an interim costs award.[48]

A markedly different result occurred in 2007, when a majority of the Court refused to uphold an interim costs award to the Little Sisters Bookstore in its ongoing battle with Canada Customs.[49] When analyzing this decision, one must recall that previous litigation[50] had established systemic discrimination against this bookstore, which served the lesbian and gay community, and had at least suggested bad faith on the state's part (for example, its failure to remove discriminatory criteria[51] from an operations manual after it would have been aware of the inappropriateness).[52] In 2000, the Supreme Court accepted that discrimination had occurred, but declined to impose a direct remedy because the government claimed that the offending aspects of the inspection regime had since been fixed:

> A more structured s. 24(1) remedy might well be helpful but it would serve the interests of none of the parties for this Court to issue a formal declaratory order based on six-year-old evidence supplemented by conflicting oral submissions and speculation on the current state of affairs. The views of the Court on the merits of the appellants' complaints as the situation stood at the end of 1994 are recorded in these reasons ... These findings should provide the appellants with a solid platform from which to launch any further action in the Supreme Court of British Columbia should they consider that further action is necessary.[53]

Believing that it continued to be the subject of disproportionate seizures of its materials, the Little Sisters bookstore launched a new action. Having already spent hundreds of thousands of dollars, the bookstore sought interim costs in the B.C. Supreme Court.[54] That Court separated the case into three parts: a challenge to specific findings of obscenity, a systemic claim against the customs regime and a constitutional question concerning the correct application of obscenity law to gay and lesbian materials. The Court awarded interim costs for the first and second arguments but not for the third. The Court of Appeal set the order aside.

A majority of the Supreme Court of Canada affirmed the Court of Appeal's decision.[55] Essentially the case was reduced to a fact-based dispute over individual publications. The Court simply rejected the claim that *Little Sisters* was about anything more than one bookstore's mistreatment at the hands of Canada Customs. No broader public interest was recognized.

Advance costs are contentious and do not enjoy unqualified support in the legal community.[56] But, if they are to remain a viable choice, it is challenging to think of a *Charter* case in which they would be more justified than *Little Sisters*. Indeed, the strongest advocate for the bookstore was Justice Binnie who, as author of the Court's 2000 decision, declined to award the bookstore a more structured remedy. Dissenting strongly from the majority in the 2007 decision, he wrote:

> I differ from my colleagues about what is truly at stake in this appeal and this leads to our disagreement about the appropriate outcome. In my view, *Little Sisters No. 1* provides more than "important context" [as my colleagues describe it. The ramifications of that decision go to the heart and soul of the appellant's present application.... This case is not the beginning of a litigation journey. It is 12 years into it ...
>
> The present application for advance costs comes before us precisely because the appellant says that the Minister's assurances proved empty in practice, that the systemic abuses established in the earlier litigation have continued, and that (in its view) Canada Customs has shown itself to be unwilling to administer the Customs legislation fairly and without discrimination. Of course there are two sides to the story. Although for good reason the majority declined to strike down the legislation, it was never doubted that Customs has been given a difficult job to do by Parliament, and that solutions to entrenched problems would take time to put in place. The question of public importance is this: was the Minister as good as his word when his counsel assured the Court that the appropriate reforms had been implemented?[57]

For Justice Binnie, *Little Sisters 2* was an appropriate case for interim costs because to rule otherwise risked rendering the state beyond judicial scrutiny when it could well be operating in disregard of constitutional norms. While the state could vigorously contest such a claim, he suggested that the broader public interest was better served by having the claim ensue — even if paid for by the state — than by allowing the exigencies of protracted litigation to put such action out of reach.

So, while the precedent set by *Okanagan* remains, *Little Sisters 2* does not bode well for the scope of discretionary mechanisms to promote access to justice.

A distinct yet related disappointment emerges in *British Columbia (A.G.) v. Christie*,[58] discussed below.

4. *CHRISTIE*: THE FRAGILITY OF THE RULE OF LAW

Earning no more than $30,000 annually, Dugald Christie ran a law practice in B.C. serving only low-income families ineligible for legal aid. Under the *Social Service Tax Amendment Act (No 2), 1993*,[59] legal services are subject to a 7% tax. Due to his clients' precarious finances, Christie could not pay the tax owed on those services and had to close his practice. He claimed that the Act was contrary to the rule of law because the legislation, by burdening access to legal counsel, undermined citizens' access to the courts[60] and interfered with citizens' effective use of the courts even if it did not prevent formal access to them.[61] The B.C. Supreme Court agreed that the Act violated indigent citizens' right to access to justice.[62] A majority of the B.C. Court of Appeal dismissed the appeal.[63]

The Supreme Court allowed the government's appeal.[64] Though the Court acknowledged the existence of a constitutional right to access the courts, such a right is not absolute[65] since the *Constitution Act, 1867* grants provincial legislatures "the power to pass laws in relation to the administration of justice".[66] Furthermore, though the Court agreed that the rule of law *might* support a right to assistance of counsel in certain situations, it rejected the idea that it could entail such a right in every case implicating a person's rights and obligations.[67]

In support of his argument that a 7% tax on legal services on its face presents a hurdle for indigent litigants, Christie adduced affidavit evidence. It appears, though, that the Court really wanted to see evidence in favour of the very different argument that such a tax would make the difference between access and lack of access. In the context of this case, such a burden was extremely onerous. The additional evidence that could support this claim would have to show that a sufficient number of lawyers in British Columbia would not and do not lower their fees to accommodate those people who would retain them but for the tax alone; that legal aid does not address the "access deficit" caused by the tax; and that the deficit is not resolved through some other social mechanism.

The success of the case presented depended on the Court's receptiveness to arguments concerning unwritten constitutional principles and to the notion that the rule of law entails a wider right to counsel than that contained in s. 7 of the *Charter*. In previous cases, though, the Court has made it clear that the rule of law imposes few substantive limits on legislative power. In *British Columbia v. Imperial Tobacco Canada Ltd.*,[68] it said that the rule of law embodies three principles: the preclusion of arbitrary exercises of power, the creation and maintenance of an actual order of positive laws, and the expectation that the state–individual relationship will be regulated by law. The conception is highly formalistic, a conclusion supported by the Court's musing in *Imperial Tobacco* that it was "difficult to conceive of how the rule of law could be used as a basis for invalidating legislation ... based on its content".[69]

The first principle articulated in *Imperial Tobacco* might have assisted Christie. If the rule of law first and foremost precludes the "influence of arbitrary power", it is reasonable to ask whether the existing legislative framework — which arguably permits indigent defendants to access the courts only if they happen to find a lawyer willing to provide representation for free or at a substantial discount — truly achieves that goal. Every legal aid system in Canada operates on the assumption that lawyers will "do the right thing" and represent a number of clients on at least a discounted basis. In British Columbia, 97% of the lawyers providing legal aid services in 2005–6 were private, as opposed to staff, lawyers.[70] This means they were under no formal legal obligation to take on legal aid cases.[71] Legal professionals can take pride in the fact that they already do much to help those in need. But the current approach to access to justice institutionalizes a relationship in which lawyers can exercise arbitrary power over lower-class Canadians (even if they exercise it compassionately). Viewed in that light, there may be something to the claim that the existing legislative framework for providing legal representation offends even a deeply formalistic understanding of the rule of law.

Christie raises issues about how unwritten constitutional principles fit alongside written ones. In *Imperial Tobacco*, the Court suggested that where written constitutional provisions protect a value in a certain context and to a certain degree it would hesitate to infer that the rule of law protects that value in other contexts to a greater degree. Thus, inasmuch as s. 11(g) of the *Charter* bars criminal legislation with retroactive application, the rule of law cannot be understood as barring all retroactive legislation.[72] In *Christie*, the Court applied that reasoning. Section 10(b) of the *Charter* protects the right to counsel upon arrest or detention. Section 7 protects the right to counsel in s. 10(b) scenarios as well as

state-initiated court proceedings where life, liberty and security of the person are implicated and counsel is necessary for a fair trial. Given the content of these sections, the Court reasoned, the rule of law cannot protect a *general* right to counsel without defeating the *Charter*'s plain meaning.[73]

Now, s. 7 of the *Charter* has been interpreted as both including and *extending* the legal rights enumerated in ss. 8–14.[74] The mere fact that s. 10(b) expressly limits the right to counsel to situations of arrest or detention has not prevented the Supreme Court from finding that s. 7 implicitly guarantees a right to counsel in other contexts, for example, where lack of counsel would put the accused at an unfair risk of suffering a deprivation of security of the person.[75] Yet that understanding of s. 7 appears to make s. 10(b) "redundant" — to defeat the plain meaning of the *Charter*'s text — just as surely as a broad right to counsel read into the rule of law. Put starkly, by interpreting s. 7 in such a way that it effectively swallows s. 10(b), the Court implicitly accepted the possibility that some "larger" constitutional principle — like the rule of law — could swallow s. 7. In *Christie*, it shrank from the consequences of applying that principle to a situation involving socio-economic rights.

The Court's use of *Charter* provisions when interpreting the rule of law illustrates how the *Charter* does not function just as a sword to be used by claimants against the state, but as a shield capable of insulating the state from some constitutional claims. Insofar as the express terms of the *Charter* are used to delimit the scope of rule-of-law challenges, it emerges as a tool by which the Supreme Court can declare certain questions, at least inasmuch as they are framed as *legal* questions, foreclosed by the political decision to protect certain rights in certain terms, to the exclusion of protecting other rights through other terms.

The formalistic understanding of the rule of law articulated in *Christie* is disconcerting. To say that the rule of law does not require legislation to have any particular content is to reinforce the idea that our entrenched civil rights are simply contingent. On the formalist view, the rule of law is fundamentally apolitical and, therefore, has nothing to say about the sort of laws or constitutions a given country should have. A depoliticized understanding of the rule of law may protect judges, as it did in the early days of the *Charter* when the Court was careful to emphasize that it was politicians, and not judges, that made legislation subject to constitutional scrutiny. But it does little to protect anyone else. Those left exposed, those who experience first-hand the gross deficiencies in access to justice that have become endemic in this country, will also experience first-hand just how little work the rule of law does.

5. CONCLUSION

These are not easy times for would-be *Charter* litigants. Recent failures by organizations seeking to mount systemic challenges to laws and policies that detrimentally affect the most downtrodden in our society reflect a failure of judicial imagination. This failure is an odd contrast with the positively lax approach to standing taken in *Chaoulli*, a case that articulates classic liberal principles by which the state is rendered less able to deal effectively with pressing social needs. It is hard, at times, to avoid cynicism.

The question of how to fund such challenges is a vexed one. Interim costs remains largely untested in the area of public litigation. However, any approach should be principled and consistent. The differing results in *Okanagan* and *Little Sisters* appear arbitrary.

The state is at the heart of the issues of both funding and standing. The state's limits in acting as guardian of the public interest is apparent when one recognizes that the traditional guardian of that interest — the Attorney General — is institutionally reluctant to challenge laws. Requiring the state to fund some litigation against itself, at times, may be necessary in order to uphold the fundamental values on which our legal system depends. If the government is unwilling to set aside funds for this purpose, and the courts continue to be wary of interim costs, private wealth and fundraising will quickly become the only game in town (supplemented somewhat by *pro bono* litigation). The losers will include not only the most downtrodden who cannot command attention at glittering charity events, but they will also include everyone whose need for the government to do no harm is buttressed by no more than state benevolence and the (occasional, weak) threat of political accountability.

(d) Legal Victory Still Leaves Rosa Becker Out in Cold†

William Marsden

Money was the operative word, but revenge was what Rosa Becker really wanted.

Revenge for being tossed out on her fanny by her common-law husband Lothar Pettkus, who showed his appreciation for their 18 years by throwing $3,000 on the floor and suggesting she "get lost."

Rosa thought: That's no way to say goodbye. Not after 18 years (during which she literally cleaned and tied his shoes and ran their business).

So, in 1974, she sued for half of all Pettkus's property, and her revenge turned into one of the most celebrated palimony cases in Canadian history.

In 1980, all nine judges of the Supreme Court of Canada awarded her half of a bee farm the couple built up and half-interest in three properties — setting a legal precedent that the late Chief Bora Laskin believed would settle the matrimonial-property issue.

Her victory was front-page news. Editorials applauded. Her lawyer, Gerald Langlois, predicted a $150,000 settlement for the beekeeping business and other properties. Then the excitement died — and now only law books remember Rosa Becker.

She still has not got her revenge.

Eleven years after she launched her suit and five years after the Supreme Court ruled, she has not received one cent from Lothar Pettkus.

Alone in a 9-room farmhouse in Franklin Centre near Ormstown, where she is paid $3,000 a year plus room and board to clean and cook for a dairy farmer and his farmhand, Becker, 58, reflects on Canadian justice:

"It's weird. I don't understand it."

Lothar Pettkus is 52, 5-foot-11, 200 lbs., strong. He likes hunting moose, is an excellent shot, keeps German shepherds, has thin blond hair, blue eyes.

† From *Montreal Gazette* (February 16, 1985) at B5. Reproduced with permission of The Gazette, a division of Canwest Publishing Inc.

By his calculation, Rosa Becker has lied 460 times to the Supreme Court of Canada in 1980 and 68 times to the Supreme Court of Ontario during a 1982 trial to divide up the property. He's trying to persuade the Ontario ombudsman to investigate his allegations.

"She was lying so badly that she had the (Supreme Court of Canada) judges convinced that this is the truth and it's definitely not the truth," Pettkus says.

(Judge K.A. Flannigan of the Ontario Supreme Court told Lothar Pettkus at a hearing in 1982: "It's the truth because the court found it to be true." But that hasn't stopped Lothar Pettkus.)

Convinced that the courts have been tricked by Rosa and her lawyer and their "lies," he decided that he cannot become a party to the Supreme Court ruling.

"A person who is perjuring herself with her lawyer — I should be party to a criminal act?" he asks rhetorically.

"I am just an innocent citizen sitting back and watching what the law is doing to people like me."

He might prove that, while you can't fight city hall, you sure can fight the Supreme Court of Canada.

Every move Rosa Becker makes, he thwarts, Becker's lawyer Langlois said.

He has exhausted seven lawyers and wielded every available weapon in the justice system to counter the Supreme Court ruling, he said.

Since the Supreme Court judgment, there have been 21 motions, judgments, affidavits, appeals and court orders issued concerning this case and the division of property — and still no money for Rosa Becker.

Court appearances are catfights, with Pettkus at times attempting to retry the case.

At a 1982 hearing into the division of property, Pettkus, between lawyers, represented himself and was questioning Becker about rent received from a West Hawkesbury, Ont., property they owned:

Rosa Becker: In the beginning it was $80 and then it gone up to $100.

Lothar Pettkus: Your honour, that's not true. At the beginning it was $40 and she says April the 14th, this year, that she paid $80. What was the truth now? Tell your honour the truth.

Becker: It was never $40. It was always $80 and then $100 but never $40.

Pettkus: You don't know if it's $80, you don't know if it was $40 and you don't know if it's $100, because you're so confused you can't answer the question proper.

Becker: Can you blame me for being confused after eight years with you in court?

Q: You took me to court.

A: No. I had no choice.

Q: Establish what was paid for in 1980. When you left...

A: I don't care anymore. You want it, shove it, shove it. I'm sick and tired. (Witness leaves courtroom.)

Rosa Becker, small, missing some front teeth, remembers when she first met Lothar Pettkus 30 years ago in the spring of 1955.

It was at a German Club dancehall near the Windsor Hotel. She was 28. He was 22. She earned $28 a week in a lace factory. He earned $75 a week as a garage mechanic.

She thought his tall brushcut made his face "look a mile long." They moved in together. He saved his money. They spent hers.

"Things happen in life that you can't explain and that's one of those things," she said without malice.

He said he "fell into her trap" and stayed for almost 20 years.

In 1960, they bought a 125-acre farm for $5,000, which he paid for out of his savings.

In 1971 and 1973, they purchased properties in East and West Hawkesbury in Ontario, where they moved their beekeeping business.

By that time, they were making as much as $30,000 profit a year. She played a major part in every aspect of the business. Everything was in his name.

But Judge Omer H. Chartrand of the Ontario District Court ruled that Rosa Becker's contribution was in the form of "risk capital invested in the hope of seducing a younger defendant into marriage."

He awarded her 40 empty beehives (which without bees are worthless) and $1,200.

The Court of Appeals ruled in 1978 that Chartrand had undervalued Becker's contributions. It gave her half the assets, valued as of 1974 when the two broke up. The Supreme Court agreed and implied that Chartrand's reference to risk capital "lacked gallantry."

The task then was to evaluate the assets as of 1974, apply interest and give Becker her share.

That process, which normally might take a year, is still not over.

Court judgments so far would put Becker's total claim on Pettkus at about $95,000.

In November 1983, Pettkus offered Becker a deal. He would pay her $46,408.90 if she would allow the Hawkesbury properties to be transferred to Pettkus's wife Monique.

Becker refused because she realized this would leave Pettkus without assets and make it impossible for her to receive the balance owing.

Eric Williams, Pettkus's latest lawyer, points to this offer as an example of Pettkus's willingness to settle. "I'll bet you 99 to one she doesn't get better than that offer," he said, adding that Pettkus has always been willing to settle the matter fairly.

Langlois said he attempted to freeze Lothar Pettkus's bank accounts but found only $12. Pettkus said his wife owns everything now.

Indeed, Monique Pettkus is claiming half her husband's interest in the beekeeping business and the East Hawkesbury property where she and Pettkus live with about 550 beehives. This claim will be fought out in court Feb. 21.

When Langlois tried last fall to seize the beehives, Pettkus's wife went to court and appealed the seizure, claiming that the hives are hers. That trial will be heard in March.

When the bees were seized by the court in November, Pettkus refused to feed them. By the time a court order could be obtained demanding that he feed and maintain the hives (valued at $50 each), most of the bees were dead, Monique told *The Gazette*. Without the bees, the business is worthless.

The only cash available is the $69,000 received from the sale last fall of the two Hawkesbury properties. The money is being held by the court.

By this June, Becker's half with interest will total $32,785.10. But all of that will go to pay her legal fees, which Langlois estimates total about $35,000. She also has to pay half the sheriff, appraisal and real-estate broker fees of about $10,000.

There's a good chance she will get all the $69,000, said Langlois. But it will take a fight, perhaps another year.

"That's the tragedy of this whole thing," Langlois said. "He (Pettkus) is ready to pay whatever amount to whatever lawyers it takes and it's clear that he doesn't intend to pay anything to Rosa Becker.

"She has been given the benefit of these judgments but the law has afforded protection to Pettkus on the realization of the funds."

Williams argues that Becker is trying to get blood out of a stone. "No matter how you cut it, the man is not rich."

Rosa Becker has visions. Ghosts tell her things.

They tell her her lawyer is conspiring with Lothar Pettkus.

"They (the visions) are always true and I know that makes Gerry Langlois uneasy about me," she said.

In 1983, she asked the Law Society of Upper Canada to investigate Langlois. They did and found "absolutely no evidence of professional misconduct."

She has also asked Chief Justice Brian Dickson of the Supreme Court of Canada to intervene on her behalf. He has refused.

"I can understand Rosa's frustration," Langlois said. He knows about her visions.

In December, he sent Rosa Becker a letter suggesting that he withdraw from the file since she has lost confidence in him.

Meanwhile, he is preparing her next court appearance and his bill.

And she's thinking she might take her case to the World Court. Still seeking revenge.

Last month, the Supreme Court of Canada decided that the entire question of division of matrimonial property needed another look. It decided to hear an appeal from Mary Sorochan, 69, of Two Hills, Alberta.

"After 40 years of common-law marriage, she received nothing from her estranged husband, who argued that he owned their 190-hectare farm before she came on the scene.

She wants recognition for her help in maintaining the farm.

IX

The Personnel of Law

Part IX includes articles that discuss several important actors in our legal system: lawyers and paralegals, judges and juries, and law enforcement personnel. It goes beyond simply outlining the roles played by the different actors in the legal system to explore the ways in which these actors are educated and trained and how they are regulated and disciplined. Many of the articles and reports in Part IX also critically assess how these actors perform their roles in the legal system.

The articles in Chapter 22 critically assess a number of issues relevant to the training, work, and regulation of lawyers and paralegals. These issues include the education of lawyers, the establishment and teaching of ethical principles and standards of practice, the ways in which the business of practising law has changed over time, and the role of law societies in regulating both the legal profession and, in some cases, paralegals. The important issue of the lack of adequate representation of women and racial minorities within the legal profession is also discussed in the chapter.

Chapter 23 addresses the role of the jury in contemporary legal systems. Neil Brooks and Anthony Doob outline a number of roles for the jury within modern trials and discuss the role of jury nullification. The excerpt from the *Morgentaler* decision further discusses the role of the jury as "a safety-valve" within the Canadian justice system, and the limits of jury nullification in the Canadian context. The excerpt from *R. v. Williams* outlines the Supreme Court of Canada's guidelines for addressing concerns of bias within jury pools in Canada. Readers should note the link to Paul Butler's article in Chapter 6 where he makes the controversial case for what he calls "racially-based jury nullification".

Chapter 24 addresses the role of judges in the Canadian legal system. It includes articles that discuss the role of the National Judicial Institute in training judges, the restraints on judges imposed by the principle of judicial independence, and the ways in which personal identity and experience may influence judging. The chapter also considers the process for disciplining judges, and in extreme cases, dismissing judges for unacceptable conduct.

Finally, Chapter 26 provides a brief survey of issues relevant to policing in Canada. George Rigakos and Cherie Leung canvass the different forms of policing and police organizations in Canada. The RCMP Complaints Commission report identifies the need to ensure arm's length investigation of allegations of police misconduct, and the excerpt from the *Jane Doe* case identifies the very real consequences that arise when police fail to fulfill their roles with the necessary care.

As you read Part IX, ask yourself: how do we ensure that the actors in the legal system are performing their roles adequately? Do certain actors have too much power within the system? How do we ensure that all groups in society are appropriately represented among the various actors in the legal system?

22   Lawyers, Advocates, and Legal Practice

(a)   Legal Education as Training for Hierarchy†

Duncan Kennedy

Law schools are intensely political places despite the fact that they seem intellectually unpretentious, barren of theoretical ambition or practical vision of what social life might be. The trade-school mentality, the endless attention to trees at the expense of forests, the alternating grimness and chumminess of focus on the limited task at hand, all these are only a part of what is going on. The other part is ideological training for willing service in the hierarchies of the corporate welfare state.

To say that law school is ideological is to say that what teachers teach along with basic skills is wrong, is nonsense about what law is and how it works; that the message about the nature of legal competence, and its distribution among students, is wrong, is nonsense; that the ideas about the possibilities of life as a lawyer that students pick up from legal education are wrong, are nonsense. But all this is nonsense with a tilt; it is biased and motivated rather than random error. What it says is that it is natural, efficient, and fair for law firms, the bar as a whole, and the society the bar services to be organized in their actual patterns of hierarchy and domination.

Because students believe what they are told, explicitly and implicitly, about the world they are entering, they behave in ways that fulfill the prophecies the system makes about them and about that world. This is the linkback that completes the system: students do more than accept the way things are, and ideology does more than damp opposition.

Students act affirmatively within the channels cut for them, cutting them deeper, giving the whole a patina of consent, and weaving complicity into everyone's life story.

. . . .

THE FORMAL CURRICULUM: LEGAL RULES AND LEGAL REASONING

The intellectual core of the ideology is the distinction between law and policy. Teachers convince students that legal reasoning exists, and is different from policy analysis, by bullying them into accepting as valid in particular cases arguments about legal correctness that are circular, question-begging, incoherent, or so vague as to be meaningless. Sometimes these are just arguments from authority, with the validity of the authoritative premise put outside discussion by professorial fiat. Sometimes they are policy arguments (e.g., security of transaction, business certainty) that are treated in a particular situation as though they were rules that everyone accepts but that will be ignored in the next case when they would suggest that the decision was wrong. Sometimes they are exercises in doctrinal logic that wouldn't stand up for a minute in a discussion between equals (e.g., the small print in a form contract represents the "will of the parties").

Within a given subfield, the teacher is likely to treat cases in three different ways. There are the cases that present and justify the basic rules and

---

basic ideas of the field. These are treated as cursory exercises in legal logic. Then there are cases that are anomalous — "outdated" or "wrongly decided" because they don't follow the supposed inner logic of the area. There won't be many of these, but they are important because their treatment persuades students that the technique of legal reasoning is at least minimally independent of the results reached by particular judges and is therefore capable of criticizing as well as legitimating. Finally, there will be an equally small number of peripheral or "cutting-edge" cases the teacher sees as raising policy issues about growth or change in the law. Whereas in discussing the first two kinds of cases the teacher behaves in an authoritarian way supposedly based on his objective knowledge of the technique of legal reasoning, here everything is different. Because we are dealing with "value judgments" that have "political" overtones, the discussion will be much more freewheeling. Rather than every student comment being right or wrong, all student comments get pluralist acceptance, and the teacher will reveal himself to be mildly liberal or conservative rather than merely a legal technician.

The curriculum as a whole has a rather similar structure. It is not really a random assortment of tubs on their own bottoms, a forest of tubs. First, there are contracts, torts, property, criminal law, and civil procedure. The rules in these courses are the ground rules of late-nineteenth-century laissez-faire capitalism. Teachers teach them as though they had an inner logic, as an exercise in legal reasoning, with policy (e.g., commercial certainty in the contracts course) playing a relatively minor role. Then there are second- and third-year courses that expound the moderate reformist program of the New Deal and the administrative structure of the modern regulatory state (with passing reference to the racial egalitarianism of the Warren Court). These courses are more policy oriented than first-year courses, and also much more ad hoc.

Liberal teachers teach students that limited interference with the market makes sense and is as authoritatively grounded in statutes as the ground rules of laissez-faire are grounded in natural law. But each problem is discrete, enormously complicated, and understood in a way that guarantees the practical impotence of the reform program. Conservative teachers teach that much of the reform program is irrational or counter-productive or both, and would have been rolled back long ago were it not for "politics." Finally, there are peripheral subjects, like legal philosophy or legal history, legal process, clinical legal education. These are presented as not

truly relevant to the "hard"[,] objective, serious, rigorous analytic core of law; they are a kind of playground or finishing school for learning the social art of self-presentation as a lawyer.

It would be an extraordinary first-year student who could, on his own, develop a theoretically critical attitude toward this system. Entering students just don't know enough to figure out where the teacher is fudging, misrepresenting, or otherwise distorting legal thinking and legal reality. To make matters worse, the most common kind of liberal thinking the student is likely to bring with her is likely to hinder rather than assist in the struggle to maintain some intellectual autonomy from the experience. Most liberal students believe that the liberal program can be reduced to guaranteeing people their rights and to bringing about the triumph of human rights over mere property rights. In this picture, the trouble with the legal system is that it fails to put the state behind the rights of the oppressed, or that the system fails to enforce the rights formally recognized. If one thinks about law this way, one is inescapably dependent on the very techniques of legal reasoning that are being marshalled in defense of the status quo.

This wouldn't be so bad if the problem with legal education were that the teachers *misused* rights reasoning to restrict the range of the rights of the oppressed. But the problem is much deeper than that. Rights discourse is internally inconsistent, vacuous, or circular. Legal thought can generate equally plausible rights justifications for almost any result. Moreover, the discourse of rights imposes constraints on those who use it that make it difficult for it to function effectively as a tool of radical transformation. Rights are by their nature "formal," meaning that they secure to individuals legal protection for as well as from arbitrariness — to speak of rights is precisely *not* to speak of justice between social classes, races, or sexes. Rights discourse, moreover, presupposes or takes for granted that the world is and should be divided between a state sector that enforces rights and a private world of "civil society" in which individuals pursue their diverse goals. This framework is, in itself, a part of the problem rather than of the solution. It makes it difficult even to conceptualize radical proposals such as, for example, decentralized democratic worker control of factories.

Because it is incoherent and manipulable, traditionally individualist, and willfully blind to the realities of *substantive* inequality, rights discourse is a trap. As long as one stays within it, one can produce good pieces of argument about the occasional case on the periphery where everyone recognizes value judgments have to be made. But one is without guidance in deciding what to do about fundamental questions and fated to the gradual loss of confidence in the convincingness of what one has to say in favor of the very results one believes in most passionately.

Left liberal rights analysis submerges the student in legal rhetoric but, because of its inherent vacuousness, can provide no more than an emotional stance against the legal order. It fails liberal students because it offers no base for the mastery of ambivalence. What is needed is to think about law in a way that will allow one to enter into it, to criticize it without utterly rejecting it, and to manipulate it without self-abandonment to *their* system of thinking and doing.

. . . .

INCAPACITATION FOR ALTERNATIVE PRACTICE

Law schools channel their students into jobs in the hierarchy of the bar according to their own standing in the hierarchy of schools. Students confronted with the choice of what to do after they graduate experience themselves as largely helpless: they have no "real" alternative to taking a job in one of the firms that customarily hire from their school. Partly, faculties generate this sense of student helplessness by propagating myths about the character of the different kinds of practice. They extol the forms that are accessible to their students; they subtly denigrate or express envy about the jobs that will be beyond their students' reach; they dismiss as ethically and socially suspect the jobs their students won't have to take.

As for any form of work outside the established system — for example, legal services for the poor and neighborhood law practice — they convey to students that, although morally exalted, the work is hopelessly dull and unchallenging, and that the possibilities of reaching a standard of living appropriate to a lawyer are slim or nonexistent. These messages are just nonsense — the rationalizations of law teachers who long upward, fear status degradation, and above all hate the idea of risk. Legal services practice, for example, is far more intellectually stimulating and demanding, even with a high caseload, than most of what corporate lawyers do. It is also more fun.

Beyond this dimension of professional mythology, law schools act in more concrete ways to guarantee that their students will fit themselves into their appropriate niches in the existing system of practice. First, the actual content of what is taught in a given school will incapacitate students from any other form

of practice than that allotted graduates of that institution. This looks superficially like a rational adaptation to the needs of the market, but it is in fact almost entirely unnecessary. Law schools teach so little, and that so incompetently, that they cannot, as now constituted, prepare students for more than one career at the bar. But the reason for this is that they embed skills training in mystificatory nonsense and devote most of their teaching time to transmitting masses of ill-digested rules. A more rational system would emphasize the way to learn law rather than rules, and skills rather than answers. Student capacities would be more equal as a result, but students would also be radically more flexible in what they could do in practice.

A second incapacitating device is the teaching of doctrine in isolation from practice skills. Students who have no practice skills tend to exaggerate how difficult it is to acquire them. There is a distinct lawyers' mystique of the irrelevance of the "theoretical" material learned in school, and of the crucial importance of abilities that cannot be known or developed until one is out in the "real world" and "in the trenches." Students have little alternative to getting training in this dimension of things after law school. It therefore seems hopelessly impractical to think about setting up your own law firm, and only a little less impractical to go to a small or political or unconventional firm rather than to one of those that offer the standard package of postgraduate education. Law schools are wholly responsible for this situation. They could quite easily revamp their curricula so that any student who wanted it would have a meaningful choice between independence and servility.

A third form of incapacitation is more subtle. Law school, as an extension of the educational system as a whole, teaches students that they are weak, lazy, incompetent, and insecure. And it also teaches them that if they are willing to accept extreme dependency and vulnerability for a probationary term, large institutions will (probably) take care of them almost no matter what. The terms of the bargain are relatively clear. The institution will set limited, defined tasks and specify minimum requirements in their performance. The student/associate has no other responsibilities than performance of those tasks. The institution takes care of all the contingencies of life, both within the law (supervision and backup from other firm members; firm resources and prestige to bail you out if you make a mistake) and in private life (firms offer money but also long-term job security and delicious benefits packages aimed to reduce risks of disaster).

451

In exchange, you renounce any claim to control your work setting or the actual content of what you do, and agree to show the appropriate form of deference to those above and condescension to those below.

By comparison, the alternatives are risky. Law school does not train you to run a small law business, to realistically assess the outcome of a complex process involving many different actors, or to enjoy the feeling of independence and moral integrity that comes of creating your own job to serve your own goals. It tries to persuade you that you are barely competent to perform the much more limited roles it allows you, and strongly suggests that it is more prudent to kiss the lash than to strike out on your own.

. . . .

For committed liberal students, there is another possibility, which might be called the denunciatory mode. One can take law school work seriously as time serving and do it coldly in that spirit, hate one's fellow students for their surrenders, and focus one's hopes on "not being a lawyer" or on a fantasy of an unproblematically leftist legal job on graduation. This response is hard from the very beginning. If you reject what teachers and the student culture tell you about what the first-year curriculum means and how to enter into learning it, you are adrift as to how to go about becoming minimally competent. You have to develop a theory on your own of what is valid skills training and what is merely indoctrination, and your ambivalent desire to be successful in spite of all is likely to sabotage your independence. As graduation approaches, it becomes clearer that there are precious few unambiguously virtuous law jobs even to apply for, and your situation begins to look more like everyone else's, though perhaps more extreme. Most (by no means all) students who begin with denunciation end by settling for some version of the bargain of public against private life.

I am a good deal more confident about the patterns that I have just described than about the attitudes toward hierarchy that go along with them. My own position in the system of class, sex, and race (as an upper-middle-class white male) and my rank in the professional hierarchy (as a Harvard professor) give me an interest in the perception that hierarchy is both omnipresent and enormously important, even while I am busy condemning it. And there is a problem of imagination that goes beyond that of interest. It is hard for me to know whether I even understand the attitudes toward hierarchy of women and blacks, for example, or of children of working-class parents, or of solo practitioners eking out a

living from residential real-estate closings. Members of those groups sometimes suggest that the particularity of their experience of oppression simply cannot be grasped by outsiders, but sometimes that the failure to grasp it is a personal responsibility rather than inevitable. Often it seems to me that all people have at least analogous experiences of the oppressive reality of hierarchy, even those who seem most favored by the system — that the collar feels the same when you get to the end of the rope, whether the rope is ten feet long or fifty. On the other hand, it seems clear that hierarchy creates distances that are never bridged.

It is not uncommon for a person to answer a description of the hierarchy of law firms with a flat denial that the bar is really ranked. Lawyers of lower-middle-class background tend to have far more direct political power in the state governments than "elite" lawyers, even under Republican administrations. Furthermore, every lawyer knows of instances of real friendship, seemingly outside and beyond the distinctions that are supposed to be so important, and can cite examples of lower-middle-class lawyers in upper-middle-class law firms, and vice versa. There are many lawyers who seem to defy hierarchical classification, and law firms and law schools that do likewise, so that one can argue that the hierarchy claim that everyone and everything is ranked breaks down the minute you try to give concrete examples. I have been told often enough that I *may* be right about the pervasiveness of ranking, but that the speaker has never noticed it himself, himself treats all lawyers in the same way, regardless of their class or professional standing, and has never, except in an occasional very bizarre case, found lawyers violating the egalitarian norm.

When the person making these claims is a rich corporate lawyer who was my prep school classmate, I tend to interpret them as a willful denial of the way he is treated and treats others. When the person speaking is someone I perceive as less favored by the system (say, a woman of lower-middle-class origin who went to Brooklyn Law School and now works for a small, struggling downtown law firm), it is harder to know how to react. Maybe I'm just wrong about what it's like out there. Maybe my preoccupation with the horrors of hierarchy is just a way to wring the last ironic drop of pleasure from my own hierarchical superiority. But I don't interpret it that way. The denial of hierarchy is false consciousness. The problem is not whether hierarchy is there, but how to understand it, and what its implications are for political action.

(b)   Canadian Legal Ethics: Ready for the Twenty-First Century at Last†

Adam M. Dodek

I.   WHAT IS CANADIAN LEGAL ETHICS AND WHY DOES IT MATTER?

. . . .

Given the evolving nature of legal ethics, "Canadian legal ethics" could mean several different things. A strong positivist strain permeates legal ethics in Canada, which views the field as simply encompassing the ethical rules of lawyering, contained for the most part in the CBA's *Code of Professional Conduct*[12] (and its provincial counterparts) as well as in traditional areas of law, such as tort, contract, and agency, among others. While the issues in the codes of conduct provide excellent fodder for analysis and debate, legal ethics consists of much more than "the law governing lawyers."[13] To begin with, the prominence or the relevance of such codes is itself a hotly contested issue in legal ethics, Canadian and otherwise.[14] In addition, many of the codes are silent on some of the most interesting and most debated issues in Canadian legal ethics: lawyers' duties respecting physical evidence of a crime, sex with clients, and corporate fraud, among others. Legal ethics is concerned not only with the positivist inquiry of what is, but very much with the normative inquiry of what ought to be.[15]

Legal ethics consists of "macro-ethics" as well as "micro-ethics." Macro-ethical inquiries address systemic issues within the legal system and the legal profession, such as access to justice, public interest, diversity within the profession, and independence of the bar. Micro-ethics focuses on the ethical issues that confront individuals within the legal system. Micro-ethics — issues such as conflicts of interest, confidentiality, and client perjury — occupy most of the ethical space in discussions about legal ethics, but the macro-ethical issues go to the heart of the legitimacy of the legal profession and the legal system. In addition, legal ethics should be concerned about all of the actors in the legal system: lawyers, judges, clients, self-represented litigants, witnesses, jurors, court administrators, and the media, as well as those outside the formal boundaries of the profession who also provide legal services, such as notaries, immigration consultants, Aboriginal caseworkers, and — dare I suggest — paralegals.[16]

Canadian legal ethics must also attempt to situate ethical issues within a distinctly *Canadian* context.[17] A Canadian scholarship of legal ethics must further seek to identify and articulate uniquely Canadian aspects of our legal system and the practice of lawyering in our country. These distinctions may be structural (such as the impact of federalism, articling, discipline by law societies, and a unitary legal profession, among others) as well as normative or cultural (such as the values of multiculturalism and diversity,[18] or the ethic of "zealous representation.")[19]

One theme of this article is that there are multiple accounts of legal ethics in Canada and that significant disparities exist between them. A public account of Canadian legal ethics emphasizes the issues that the public sees, mostly through reporting in the popular press. The legal profession's account of legal ethics is reflected by the activities of law societies and legal associations, most notably through codes of conduct and discipline, but also through other activities such as task forces, public advocacy, and litigation. Sociological accounts examine what is actually happening within the profession and historical accounts analyze what has happened in the past. We can also conceive of the body of collected academic work on Canadian legal ethics as the scholarly account of the subject. As will be apparent throughout this article, significant gaps exist between the different accounts. In this article, I focus on the accounts of the public and the legal profession and compare their contents to the developing scholarly account of Canadian legal ethics.

. . . .

---

† (2008) 46 Osgoode L.J. 1 at 5–8, 9–20. Reproduced with permission. [Notes and/or references omitted.]

II. A BRIEF HISTORY OF CANADIAN LEGAL ETHICS IN THE FIRST DECADE OF THE TWENTY-FIRST CENTURY

Until recently, the Canadian legal academy was not particularly interested in legal ethics. Hutchinson attributes this to the lack of a defining Canadian cultural moment like Watergate "in which lawyers were placed under national scrutiny and obliged to reconsider the legitimacy of their professional practices and norms of conduct."[20] While Hutchinson is correct that there has been no "lawyergate" in Canada to capture the public imagination, the last few years have seen numerous ethical scandals that, cumulatively, seemed capable of exerting some pressure on the legal profession. In this Part, I outline a brief history of Canadian legal ethics in the first decade of this century. For the most part, this history draws heavily on the public account of Canadian legal ethics, but also includes elements from the legal profession's account. The purpose of this section is to discuss examples of lawyers' poor ethical behaviour to which the public has been recently exposed and the legal profession's responses, or lack thereof in some cases, to these and other issues.

For Canadian legal ethics it has been an eventful and challenging decade. The twenty-first century began with the trial of Ken Murray, the lawyer originally retained to defend Canada's notorious murderer, Paul Bernardo. Murray was acquitted, barely, of obstruction of justice in connection with the infamous Bernardo/Homolka videotapes.[21] The Law Society of Upper Canada (LSUC) began a disciplinary investigation into Murray's conduct, but abandoned it in favour of enacting a rule of professional conduct on the issue of lawyers' duties respecting physical evidence of a crime. After releasing a draft rule, the LSUC shelved this project as well. The Murray case thus ended in three negatives: no conviction against Murray, no disciplinary action by the LSUC, and no action by the LSUC to address the issue.[22]

The next big ethical scandal involved law students, rather than lawyers. In 2001, thirty students at the University of Toronto Law School ("U of T" or "Toronto") were caught up in allegations of misrepresenting their grades to prospective summer employers, and twenty-four received sanctions ranging from reprimands to one-year suspensions. The U of T "fake grades scandal" also became an international *cause célèbre* in academic freedom circles because of allegations against a U of T law professor.[23] As might be expected, one of the students sought judicial review and succeeded in having the Dean's decision against her quashed on jurisdictional grounds.[24] Three years later, another cheating scandal erupted in Toronto, this time at the LSUC's Bar Admission Course. However, while the U of T "fake grades scandal" dragged on for over a year, the Bar Admission Course cheating scandal ended abruptly after a few weeks. When the LSUC made an allegedly secret decision to abandon the investigation,[25] the scandal continued to fester.[26] In between the two Toronto student scandals, the President of the Law Society of British Columbia resigned in 2003, after a conviction for impaired driving, and was subsequently suspended from practice.[27] He would not be the last law society head during the decade forced to resign amidst ethical improprieties.

Lawyers' conduct in the courtroom and in the bedroom dominated ethical discussions at the beginning of this century. Midway through the decade, the CBA embarked on another revision to its Code of Conduct, which had not been overhauled since 1987. The revised CBA Code, based on amendments in 2004 and 2006, is notable mostly for what it did not address, rather than for any ethical boldness. The CBA ducked the Ken Murray problem, took a very modest approach to the issue of dealing with corporate fraud, and rejected a proposed amendment to restrict sexual relations between lawyers and clients,[28] an issue that would resurface sooner rather than later. In 2007, the former Treasurer of the LSUC received a two-month suspension for conflict of interest arising out of a sexual relationship with a client who is now suing him and his law firm.[29] Concerned also with lawyers' misbehaviour in the courtroom, the decade saw the rise of the civility and professionalism movement. Precipitated by the conduct of counsel in several cases,[30] Ontario's Advocate's Society formed a Civility Committee, which produced a Code of Civility[31] that the CBA included as an appendix in its revised Code. Similar concerns motivated the Nova Scotia Barristers' Society to establish a Task Force on Civility.[32] Meanwhile, in British Columbia, solicitor Martin Wirick perpetrated the largest legal fraud in Canadian history, an estimated $50 million, triggering the largest audit and investigation ever undertaken by the Law Society of British Columbia and sending shockwaves throughout the legal profession, as well as the real estate and business communities.[33]

As class action lawsuits began proliferating across the country, the role of lawyers came under scrutiny, especially with regard to fees. Whether it was the $56 million in fees for the settlement of the tainted blood scandal before a single victim was paid, or the $100 million that Regina's Tony Merchant hoped to obtain as part of the record estimated $1.9 billion settlement of residential schools abuse claims, public perception that lawyers put their own interests ahead of those of their clients ran high.[34] Along these lines, concerns about lawyers taking advantage of vulnerable clients led the CBA, the Law Society of Yukon, and the LSUC to each establish guidelines for lawyers acting in Aboriginal residential school abuse cases.[35]

In the courts, the Supreme Court of Canada continued where it left off in *Martin v. Gray* (1990),[36] issuing two decisions, *Neil* (2002)[37] and *Strother* (2007),[38] which helped keep conflict of interest at the top of the legal profession's ethical priority list.[39] On the regulatory front, the Court held that provincial law societies could not prohibit non-lawyers from appearing as counsel before the Immigration and Refugee Board,[40] but that law societies do have the power to regulate Crown prosecutors.[41] In a leading case, the Ontario Court of Appeal held that the Ontario Securities Commission (OSC) could regulate the conduct of lawyers appearing before it.[42] The Supreme Court held that law societies do not have a general duty of care to persons who are defrauded by their lawyers,[43] but also that law societies will not be immunized from liability by ignoring their statutory responsibilities to protect the public.[44] Along these lines, the Court vindicated the Law Society of New Brunswick for meting out the ultimate sanction of disbarment to a lawyer who misled his clients for five years.[45] The Court continued its strong interest in solicitor-client privilege that began in 1999,[46] deciding no fewer than eight cases since then,[47] and elevating that privilege to a constitutional right.[48] The bar across Canada, led by the Federation of Law Societies, exerted tremendous energy and resources to successfully challenge regulations that, among other things, would have required lawyers to report "suspicious transactions" involving $10,000 or more in cash.[49]

In the area of judicial ethics, the Court decided two cases regarding judicial discipline, one involving statements made by a judge in court,[50] and the other concerning attempts to remove a judge because of a later-discovered criminal conviction.[51] The Court dealt with two judicial disqualification cases, both of which arose under unique circumstances and both involving allegations of bias against members of the Court itself. First, in Wewaykum (2003), the losing litigant before the Court was unsuccessful in its attempt to vacate the decision based on the alleged reasonable apprehension of bias arising from Justice Binnie's involvement in the case while holding the position of Associate Deputy Minister of Justice.[52]

Second, in *Mugesera* (2005), lawyer Guy Bertrand made accusations that a Jewish conspiracy had tainted the impartiality of the Court, which the Court found was an "unqualified and abusive attack on the integrity of the Judges of this Court."[53] Bertrand was later formally reprimanded by the Barreau du Quebec.[54]

Over the decade, access to justice was increasingly recognized as an important issue by the courts, the profession, and the media. The Court recognized a doctrine of advance costs but then significantly narrowed it.[55] It unanimously and unceremoniously rejected the constitutional claim for state-funded legal counsel in civil cases,[56] and it forced a representative plaintiff to pay costs likely totaling over one million dollars in an unsuccessful class proceeding.[57] The Court's treatment of access to justice issues was at odds with an increasingly strong *cri de coeur* being heard both within the profession[58] and in the press.[59] The Chief Justice of Canada and other justices and leaders of the bar frequently lament barriers to access to justice for Canadians, but have offered little in the way of solutions. One bright note has been the rise of institutionalized pro bono initiatives, through Pro Bono Law Ontario, Pro Bono Law of British Columbia, and now Pro Bono Law Alberta. Over the decade, the plight of self-represented litigants has increasingly caught the attention of Canada's judges, lawyers, policy-makers, and to some extent, the press.[60]

The years 2006 and 2007 might well be considered the legal profession's *anni horribiles* from the perspective of Canadian legal ethics. With British Columbia still reeling from the Wirick fraud, the Treasurer of the LSUC in Ontario resigned in January 2006 and was ultimately disciplined and suspended for two months in connection with a sexual relationship with a client.[61] In August 2006, legal heavyweight Peter Shoniker pled guilty to money laundering and was sentenced to fifteen months of incarceration.[62] In the spring of 2007, lawyers from Torys LLP were frequently in the news in relation to advice that they gave Conrad Black and other members of Hollinger Inc. regarding non-compete agreements at the center of the Black trial in Chicago. In a deal struck between Torys and the prosecution, the Torys lawyers — not subject to the jurisdiction of the American courts — agreed to testify by recorded videotape in Toronto, with resulting negative press coverage of the lawyers and the law firm.[63] Not to be missed, of course, was the fact that two of the defendants in the Black trial were lawyers: Mark Kipnis and Peter Atkinson (a member of the Ontario bar and a former Torys partner). Rarely mentioned was the fact that Conrad Black is a law graduate (Laval), although not a member of the bar.

In July, lawyers were featured on the cover of *Maclean's* under the headline "Lawyers Are Rats" with titles above various lawyers reading, "I Pad My Bills," "I'm Dishonest," "I sleep with my clients," and "I take bribes" among other things.[64] The cover accompanied an interview with Philip Slayton, ethics columnist for Canadian Lawyer and former law professor, law dean, Bay Street lawyer, and author of *Lawyers Gone Bad: Money, Sex and Madness in Canada's Legal Profession.*[65] The sensationalism of *Maclean's* succeeded in provoking a rash of responses from the organized bar as well as from its individual members.[66] It was likely responsible for temporarily catapulting Slayton's anecdotal collection of lawyer malfeasance onto the bestseller list where it quietly retreated after having wrought havoc on the legal profession for two months.

The year ended with a collective sigh of relief from the legal profession with the Competition Bureau of Canada's report on self-regulated professions, including law.[67] The legal profession had been anxiously awaiting this report, looking over its shoulder at the changes precipitated by similar reports in the United Kingdom and the European Union.[68] On 11 December 2007, the Commissioner released her report amidst minimal fanfare and negligible public interest.[69] While the follow-up remains uncertain, law societies will be able to make small changes in response to the Competition Bureau's report without upsetting the apple cart.

Thus ended the Canadian legal profession's two-year *anni horribiles*, with a whimper not a bang. Somewhat surprisingly, these events appear not to have had much impact on the level of public trust towards lawyers in Canada, which actually went up in 2006 and again in 2007 after a decrease for several years in a row. In 2007, 54 per cent of Canadians said that they trust lawyers, the same level as in 2002. This is a much lower level of trust than that received by perennial favourites — firefighters (97 per cent) and nurses (94 per cent) — but far ahead of politicians (15 per cent) and used car salespersons (12 per cent).[70] While the decade was full of ethical lows and challenges for the Canadian legal profession, Hutchinson's point, first made in 1999, that there has not been a single defining cultural moment for lawyering in Canada, is still the case. Despite the absence of a "lawyergate" that succeeded in capturing the public imagination and spurring an agenda for reform, many of the events described above did have an impact within the profession and the legal academy. Importantly, these events helped stimulate some of the initiatives described in Parts III and IV below, and certainly provided both motivation and opportunities for the scholarship described in the following parts.[71]

(c) Who is Afraid of the Big Bad Social Constructionists? Or Shedding Light on the Unpardonable Whiteness of the Canadian Legal Profession†

Charles C. Smith

I. INTRODUCTION

In 2005, I was asked to participate in a session entitled, "The Implications of 'Bleached-Out' Professionalism for Racialized Lawyers and Communities," which was one of the former Chief Justice of Ontario's forums to discuss contemporary issues within the legal profession.[1] At the time, I remarked that the title of this forum is one of those metaphors that seems easy to grasp. Most of us are aware of efforts within the legal profession, including law schools, law firms, the courts, and so forth, to diversify their representation so that it is more inclusive of the racialized and cultural makeup of the broader society. The record of positive intention has been and continues to be articulated repeatedly in

† (2008) 45 Alta. L. Rev. 55 at 55–66, 72–73. (Special Issue: Law Society of Alberta 100th Anniversary Conference "Canadian Lawyers in the 21st Century"). Reproduced with permission. [Notes and/or references omitted.]

studies, reports, policies and programs that are written, developed, and implemented by law schools, law societies, legal associations, and law firms. Since the 1993 report of the Task Force on Gender Equality in the Legal Profession, chaired by Bertha Wilson J. (as she then was),[2] a considerable number of these reports and studies have been published.[3]

Over the past eight years I have had the benefit of working in three legal associations on these issues. I have also provided advice and services to several law firms and legal associations. Through all of this, I have gained considerable insight into the challenges related to this topic. This experience has enabled me to research this matter and to develop policies and programs for the Law Society of Upper Canada (LSUC), the Canadian Bar Association (CBA) and, very recently, the Indigenous Bar Association (IBA) where I support their efforts to form a national secretariat to identify, challenge, and eliminate hate and racism in Canada.[4]

It is for these reasons that I questioned the topic of this session. There are two notions which are at issue here. One is that "Bleached-Out Professionalism" suggests eradicating stains or foreign elements in order to return to or "create" a more homogenous, uniform construction. And this is exactly where the second contentious issue emerges. I shall phrase it in the form of a question: Assuming that "bleaching" renders its objects white, when was the legal profession not bleached?[5] Was there ever really a need to "bleach" it? Or would it not be more important to talk about "unbleaching" the profession, particularly now given the challenges faced by Aboriginal peoples and subordinate racialized groups who enter it?

Looking at the faulty metaphor conjures up the great difficulty the legal profession has in talking about race and racism in society generally, and within its ranks in particular. Rather than talk about race and racism directly, problematic metaphors are used. Given the rather undramatic increase in the numbers of Aboriginal lawyers and lawyers from subordinate racialized groups, one would think this issue would be named directly. However, it appears that there is a lack of commitment by the legal profession to produce concrete results aimed at ensuring that the profession reflects the makeup of the Canadian population. For example, a recent article entitled "Reducing the Democratic Deficit: Representation, Diversity and the Canadian Judiciary, or Towards a 'Triple P' Judiciary,"[6] points out the challenges in increasing the racial diversity of the bench. One of the key challenges the authors encountered in doing their research was that there was no infor-

mation at the federal level about the racialized composition of the bench and that the same finding held true for most provinces and territories.[7] Further, neither law societies nor the CBA have canvassed their members to assess their representation based on race or Aboriginal status.

On a related point, Alan J.C. King, Wendy K. Warren, and Sharon R. Miklas note in their recent study of "accessibility" in five Ontario law schools that "[a]dmissions policies that target groups with unique characteristics are not necessarily intended to produce a student body that mirrors the Canadian population."[8] As well, the former Governor General of Canada recently commented on the difficulties in increasing the racial diversity of the legal profession,[9] and the Law Society of British Columbia (LSBC) produced a report on discriminatory barriers faced by Aboriginal law students and lawyers.[10]

In this regard, the legal profession, which may pride itself on being "different" because of its adherence to the rule of law and democratic principle, is really not unlike other professions or the Canadian society at large. Or as Troy Duster wrote in his submission to the Association of American Law Schools (AALS):

> Professions and the institutions which serve them tend to view themselves as having unique traditions, values, skills and missions — even callings. While to some degree this is true, from the perspective of students of higher education, there are strong patterns or parallel trends and forces for a wide range of academic disciplines and professional schools. These parallel experiences and subsequent institutional and organizational dilemmas are particularly salient when we look to the changes that are occurring and have occurred over the last twenty years in institutions of higher education around the shifting demographic composition of undergraduate and graduate student bodies. The experiences of other institutions — both educational and corporate — as they have confronted contested terrain around issues of gender, race, and ethnicity, can help clarify the strategies for addressing these areas of conflict or contest within schools of law.[11]

Evidence indicates the same dilemmas across the legal profession. Finally, one other underlying but critical issue is that the construction of a "bleached" or overwhelmingly white profession requires us to consider the agents behind the bleaching/whiteness. In other words, who is "bleaching" the legal profession? Or keeping it white? Why? How is this being done? And what must be done to change this?

The above discussion is the reason for the title and focus of this article. Given the number of studies, reports, policies, task forces, programs, and so forth, one might expect that the legal profession would be much further along in addressing issues of its racialized composition. One might expect more significant numbers of Aboriginal peoples and individuals from subordinate racialized groups to be studying and practising law, or results that were at least similar to other elite professions, such as medicine, engineering, and the professoriate. Unfortunately, this is not the case. The legal profession, for all its attention to issues of race, lags well behind these other professional fields and so, once again, we are gathered to discuss this fact.

My contention with this subject forms the basis of this article, and in discussing the legal profession, I also contend that it is essential to look at the pathways to it, which requires some discussion on the importance of education and, in particular, legal education.

II. WHITENESS AND THE LEGAL PROFESSION IN CANADA

Discursive analysis on the education of non-dominant groups and its influence on professional attainment has been emerging over the course of a considerable period of time, particularly that concerning legal education and entry into the practice of law. These matters do not exist in isolation, but rather form part of a social context in which relations between dominant and non-dominant groups are situated, especially in terms of race. This issue has been explored by Aboriginal thinkers and critical race theorists.[12] Many of these authors contend that this relationship is symbiotic and based on an inequitable sharing of resources and power. In particular, Aboriginal peoples and peoples from subordinate racialized groups describe the power imbalance dominating their lives as a centrifugal force placing the pressures of assimilation squarely before them or blocking their access into society's elite professions. Further, as Cornel West notes, these prevailing forces, which are particularly influenced by the regime of law and legal education, have shaped and continue to shape social policy, institutional practices, and community interactions.[13]

In this context, discrimination in education and professional occupations is mirrored and reinforced by discrimination in society through statutes, social policy, institutional practices, or individual and community actions. Such statutes and practices are con-

doned as acceptable within the social mores of their times and, as such, impact on the abilities of non-dominant groups to participate in and benefit from the study and practice of law. In examining the whiteness of the legal profession, it is essential to look at the pathways to the practice of law. This means looking at access to a legal education and to those institutions which enable individuals to consider and pursue a legal education and legal practice. In this context, the history of racial discrimination in Canadian educational systems is inescapable.

For example, based on statutes adopted in 1850, such as *The Common Schools Act*[14] in Ontario, separate schools for black children "continued until 1891 in Chatham, 1893 in Sandwich, 1907 in Harrow, 1917 in Amherstburg, and 1965 in North Colchester and Essex counties."[15] Based on statutes dating back to 1833, black children were barred from attending the only public school in Halifax County until 1940, and in 1959, school buses still only stopped in white sections of Hammonds Plains.[16] In 1960, there were seven formal black school districts and three additional exclusively black schools in Nova Scotia.[17] The repeal of the Ontario and Nova Scotia statutes authorizing racial segregation in education did not occur until the mid-1960s. Further, the *Indian Act*[18] had extremely restrictive provisions regarding the education of Aboriginal peoples.

In terms of legal education, W. Wesley Pue summarizes the racist values that contributed to the establishment of common law legal education in Canada. In detailing the history of its development, he writes:

> The period from roughly 1910 to 1920 was important in laying new cultural foundations for modern common law legal education. It produced a melding of persuasive new ideas developed and tested in the USA with longstanding British middle class traditions regarding practical knowledge, honour and authority. For a variety of reasons English Canada's dominant cultural ethos was receptive to influences of both sorts. The conjuncture of industrialisation and westward expansion dominated English Canadian imperial visions.... Challenged by a world of ideas which held no traditions sacrosanct, English élites ... were freed and forced to reconsider their own futures. This reappraisal included fundamental questions about which sorts of institutional arrangements were best suited to the peculiar position of this new, northern, British, and free people.[19]

In this context, Pue describes efforts by the Law Society of Manitoba to stop the development of proprietary schools which:

Judging by U.S.A. experience ... would also almost certainly have opened the door to legal careers for much larger numbers of young men (and women?) of working class or minority ethnic background. This prospect would not have been viewed with equanimity by Manitoba's Anglo élite, who were embedded in a culture which was fiercely pro-British and hierarchical, nativist, even xenophobic.[20]

Pue also notes "the most vigourous proponents of what might be called a 'cultural' agenda in legal education were prominent, energetic, busy, successful practising lawyers. All were either born into the Anglo élite or thoroughly integrated into it. All were active in matters of law society governance or in the activities of bar associations,"[21] and further, that "the cultural assumptions of individuals in that period must be assessed if we are to make any sense of the history of common law legal education in Canada. If we are to understand at all, we have to begin to understand the intellectual climate of the élite, British, Protestant world in which these men lived."[22]

Mirroring Pue's comments, Christopher Moore provides a sense of what the legal profession looked like in the nineteenth and early twentieth centuries. He notes that "[t]he vast majority of nineteenth century Ontario lawyers were English, Scots, or Irish in origin and Protestant in religion, and they tended to take in students of their own class and kind. ... Throughout the nineteenth century, successful families from outside the Anglo-Protestant mainstream were occasionally able to find articling positions for sons inclined to the law."[23]

It was not until 1855 that Robert Sutherland was called to the Bar in Ontario, becoming the first black Canadian lawyer.[24] This was followed by Delos Rogest Davis in 1885.[25] Davis's call to the Bar was not a simple passage but, rather, required a special act of the Ontario Legislature against which the LSUC protested.[26] While information on other black students called to the practice of law is difficult to ascertain, it appears certain that the effects of discrimination in education, combined with racism in society generally, limited the number of black students who entered law school and, further, those who did enter faced barriers in undertaking legal education, particularly in attracting articling positions.[27]

Chinese, Japanese, South Asian, and Aboriginal peoples were prohibited from becoming members of the LSBC until 1947, and until 1948 for people of Japanese descent.[28] Further, until it was amended in 1951, the *Indian Act* required Aboriginal peoples to relinquish their status if they were to pursue higher education.[29] This prevented many Aboriginal peoples from entering university and considering a legal education.

The prevailing presence of social and statutory barriers made it barely possible, and in some cases impossible, for particular groups to receive a legal education in Canada and to enter into legal practice. These barriers have resulted in some communities having few successes in legal education and are a matter of grave concern in terms of efforts to promote equity and diversity in legal education and the legal profession.

III. CONTEMPORARY CHALLENGES AND THE UNPARDONABLE WHITENESS OF BEING

Michael Ornstein has conducted two studies of the demographic makeup of the legal profession.[30] While focusing particularly on Ontario, his research provides insights into the personal characteristics of lawyers across Canada. In both of these studies, Ornstein confirms that the legal profession is predominantly white.[31] This view is also supported by reports by the CBA and the LSBC.[32] Ornstein points out that individuals from subordinate racialized groups and Aboriginal peoples tend to choose professions other than law for their careers. In some cases, the differences are quite significant. For example, in 2001, 3.1 percent of Ontario lawyers were South Asian compared with 9.6 percent of physicians, 7.0 percent of engineers, 4.2 percent of university professors; and 2.1 percent of Ontario lawyers were Chinese compared with 7.7 percent of physicians, 9.6 percent of engineers, and 4.7 percent of university professors.[33] While there is no data examining career choices within these communities, these results are a clear indication of the strong differences in this matter. Ornstein further notes that subordinate racialized groups comprise 25.9 percent of physicians, 27.3 percent of engineers, 15.2 percent of professors, 11.2 percent of high-level managers, and 15.7 percent of middle managers compared to 9.2 percent of lawyers.[34]

The racialized composition of the legal profession has been an issue for some time. Both statistical and anecdotal accounts have been written on this subject and, to date, numerous legal associations have been formed within subordinate racialized communities and amongst Aboriginal lawyers to provide opportunities for them to come together, nurture each other, and support each other's social, cultural, educational, and professional growth and development.[35]

The legal profession is not alone in this dilemma. The experience of Aboriginal lawyers and those from subordinate racialized groups is not much different than that of individuals from these communities working within other professions. For example, in a recent submission to the United Nations International Committee on the Elimination of All Forms of Racial Discrimination, the African Canadian Legal Clinic summarized a number of common issues besetting peoples of African descent and other subordinate racialized groups in terms of equality in employment.[36] This submission describes the numerous reports identifying challenges and barriers to equal employment and provides sociological data identifying the wage and position differential between groups based on race. In presenting this data, the report suggests that such differences are evident even when individuals from subordinate racialized groups have higher educational credentials than their white counterparts.[37]

When it comes to the practice of law, while there may be nuances that are different from other professional fields, clear and compelling explorations demonstrating the commonality of this issue with those of other employment sectors have been addressed in a number of articles.[38] Further, law societies, the CBA, law schools, and law firms have undertaken various initiatives to address this challenge.[39] Unfortunately, the pace of change appears to be very slow and this is particularly a concern in terms of the racial composition of Canada's largest and most prestigious law firms. For example, Michael St. Patrick Baxter suggests, "[h]ere is the reality. Based on the 1997 *Canadian Law List*, there are about 23 Bay Street firms in Toronto. These 23 firms represent a total of about 3,117 lawyers. Of these 3,117 Bay Street lawyers, about 20 are black. This represents six-tenths of 1 percent of the Toronto Bay Street lawyers."[40] This has happened for several reasons: (1) because of the absence of a critical mass of Aboriginal lawyers or lawyers from subordinate racialized groups being within these law firms; (2) large law firms work in ways that are both alien and alienating to individuals from these communities; and (3) the impact of the discriminatory treatment, individual and systemic, that numerous individuals say they have experienced when working in these firms.[41]

As has been noted elsewhere, law schools are "the gatekeepers of legal education.... Ultimately the ethos of the profession is determined by the selection process at law school. In order to ensure that our legal system continues to fulfill its important role in Canadian society it is important that the best can-

didates be chosen."[42] This concern has been quite a focal point in terms of studying the issue of access to legal education and the implications of the deregulation of tuition fees on Aboriginal peoples and individuals from subordinate racialized communities, particularly in terms of the increasing costs of legal education and the potential barriers this may present to these communities. For example, two Ontario law schools approved significant increases to their tuition fees, marking a rise from approximately CDN$2,451 in 1995 to $16,000 for 2003–04 at the University of Toronto, and from $3,228 in 1997 to approximately $8,961 in 2003 at Queen's University.[43] Further, the University of Toronto intends to increase tuition fees until they total $22,000, and Queen's University has projected to increase its fees to $12,856 by 2005.[44]

Concerns regarding the impact of tuition fees on individuals from historically subordinate communities have been addressed by a number of organizations. For example:

- Statistics Canada data indicates that 38.7 percent of youth aged 18–21 years from wealthy families attended university compared to 18.8 percent of youth from poorer families.
- In the report by the Canadian Centre for Policy Alternatives entitled *Missing Pieces V: An Alternative Guide to Canadian Post-Secondary Education*, it is suggested that higher tuition fees result in lower participation rates and that "[r]esearchers at the University of Guelph found that 40% fewer students from low-income families were attending University after tuition fees rose."[45]
- The Canadian Association of University Teachers suggests that, if current trends continue, access to post-secondary education will be increasingly divided along income lines.
- Recent census data indicates that Aboriginal peoples and individuals from subordinate racialized groups tend to fall below the Low-Income Cut Off (LICO) more so than others. The result of this is lowered earnings, leaving these groups less able to support the educational advancement of their children.[46]

The potential impact of increasing law school tuition fees has been explored by the University of Toronto.[47] As the basis for increasing its law school tuition fees to CDN$22,000, the University initiated a study to demonstrate that there would be little, if any, negative impact. This study was completed by the University's Provost and released to its Committee on Academic Policy and Programs of the Governing Council. The points noted immediately above are critical to examining the University of Toronto

Provost's study on accessibility. However, the Provost's study "ignores the well-known history of disparate outcomes in legal practice, including articling, for specific groups and appears to operate on the assumption that once in law school all are equal. This masks deeply entrenched societal and systemic inequalities and evades a critical point on the likely deleterious impact that increasing tuition fees will have."[48]

In terms of first-year students from families with low incomes, the report indicates that in 2002–2003, 17.3 percent of students came from families in the low-income area of less than $60,000, compared to 33 percent of students with family incomes above $90,000, and 33.5 percent of students who did not report their family income.[49] Given that individuals from this latter group do not seek financial assistance, it is likely safe to assume that these individuals are financially well off. As such, this indicates that over 66 percent of students in the Faculty of Law came from families with incomes above $90,000 per year as compared to 17 percent with incomes less than $60,000 per year.[50]

This data supports the concerns expressed earlier, specifically that 38.7 percent of youth aged 18–21 from wealthy families attend university, compared to 18.8 percent of youth from poorer families and, further, that if such trends in increasing tuition fees continue, post-secondary education will be increasingly divided along class lines. Given the intersections between race and family incomes, these divisions will likely be along the lines of race as well.

Following this study, all five law schools in Ontario have examined the issue of accessibility in legal education and the implications/impact of deregulation of tuition fees. There are some startling indicators from this research, including that:

- Aboriginal students comprise 1.3 percent of law school students but make up 3.6 percent of the Ontario population and their numbers have decreased in law school;[51]
- The number of students of African descent have decreased in law school;[52]
- African-Canadian students are nearly twice as likely as their cohorts to leave law school with an accumulated debt of over CDN$70,000 and South Asian students have significant numbers with similar debt loads;[53]
- Choosing a specialization in law affects student course selection and most students prefer civil litigation and commercial law, which are the more financially lucrative areas of practice. This tendency has particular relevance to student interest

in human rights and social justice studies, which has declined from 11 percent to 5.6 percent from first- to third-year students, with only 1.2 percent of recent graduates practising in these areas.[54] Some of the comments of these students are worth noting. For example:

> With the rising tuition costs, it will be very difficult for other black students like myself to have access to a legal education or to finish the legal education they have already commenced. I am one of five black law students in a class of 180 and I see the numbers going down in the future years because of the high expense incurred to go to law school and the few avenues available which provide financial assistance. (Year 3, Female)[55]
>
> ...
>
> If tuition costs keep going up, First Nations people will not be able to pursue professional careers. As it is now, most Bands will not allow its members to apply to U of T due to high cost. Raising costs will inhibit First Nations People's career choices. (Year 1, Female)[56]

Beyond the direct impact of increasing tuition fees, it is useful to once again review Ornstein's data on the significant earning differential between lawyers based on race. His research indicates that:

- White lawyers between the ages of 25–29 earn approximately CDN$4,000 more per year than lawyers from subordinate racialized groups ($52,000 versus $48,000). This gap increases to approximately $14,000 for lawyers between the ages of 35–39 ($85,000 versus $71,000), and to $39,000 for lawyers between the ages of 40–44 ($97,000 versus $58,000);[57]
- Wage differentials between white lawyers and those from subordinate racialized communities are quite dramatic in the peak earning years of 50–54, with whites earning $70,000 more.[58]

As the CBA article on the University of Toronto study suggests:

> It is essential to highlight these points.... It is rather unusual to approach a study on accessibility and to decontextualize the fundamental issues affecting students, particularly their personal characteristics and how individuals from specific social groups have succeeded in the practice of law. By omitting reference to this information, the Provost study ignores the well-known history of disparate outcomes in legal practice, including articling, for specific groups and appears to operate on the assumption that once in law school all are equal. This masks deeply entrenched societal and systemic inequali-

ties and evades a critical point on the likely deleterious impact that increasing tuition fees will
have.[59]

The same might be said of King, Warren, and
Miklas's study. Reviewing the earlier comments
regarding students who graduate with higher debt
loads and limited practice opportunities (Aboriginal
peoples, South Asian, and African-Canadians), it is
likely that increasing tuition fees will pose significant barriers to their entry and success in the practice of law.

. . . .

V.   CONCLUSION

While there has been some increase in the racial
diversity of law school students and members of the
legal profession, this diversity needs to be increased
dramatically in order to develop a critical mass
of Aboriginal lawyers and lawyers from subordinate
racialized groups so that the legal profession will be
at the same level of other professions and begin to
reflect the makeup of the population.

To achieve this goal, law schools and law firms
must demonstrate clear and unequivocal leadership
that is measurable and that has specific timelines.
The importance of this matter is underscored when

considering the social significance of attaining a legal
education, a point which is well articulated in the
University of Windsor study on law school admissions criteria:

> By necessity, the nature, quality, and effective-
> ness of the legal system is greatly dependent
> on the types of individuals who receive a formal
> legal education. As lawyers, judges, educators,
> administrators, and legislators, legally trained
> persons control or materially affect the majority
> of decision-making and law-enactment processes
> in society. Law school graduates continue to
> develop careers in many non-traditional occupa-
> tions requiring legal expertise; this broadens the
> profession's sphere of influence. Thus, the legal
> system, intended for the benefit of all members
> of society, reflects in some measure the cultural,
> social, and economic views of the legally trained.
> To the extent that the legally trained influence
> the organs of government, access to formal legal
> education can also be viewed as an important
> determinant of the political, social, and economic
> reality. Yet, legal education has traditionally
> been accessible only to majority social groups in
> Canada. Therefore, minority perspectives con-
> cerning our societal choices may have had only
> limited influence.[96]

This is what we have to change.

(d)   The Retention of Women in Private Practice Working Group Report — Executive Summary†

The Law Society of Upper Canada

I — OVERVIEW

1. Women have been entering the legal profession
   and private practice in record numbers for at
   least two decades. However, they have been
   leaving private practice in droves largely
   because the legal profession has not effectively
   adapted to this reality. This report discusses the
   differences between the legal careers of women
   and men and outlines business and social rea-

sons for developing strategies to retain women
in private practice. It also makes a series of
recommendations to promote the advancement
of women in the private practice of law.

2. Women's realities, which often include childbirth and taking on a significant share of the
   family responsibilities, impact on the choices
   they make in their professional lives. While
   neither the Law Society nor the profession gen-

---

† From *Final Report to Convocation — Retention of Women in Private Practice Working Group*, May 22, 2008. (Prepared by the Equity Initiatives Department.) Reproduced with permission of Law Society of Upper Canada. [Notes and/or references omitted.]

erally should, nor can, determine the roles women play in their own family relationships, the failure of the profession to adapt to what is not a neutral reality will inevitably affect the quality and competence of the legal services available to the public.

3. The departure of women from private practice means that the legal profession is losing a large component of its best and brightest in core areas of practice. Studies have shown the staggering cost of associate turnover, which is estimated at $315,000 for a four year associate. This cost is equally applicable to associate turnover of men and women, but women are more likely than men to leave their firms before joining the partnership. A shift in thinking is required both on the part of associates and on the part of the employers/firms. This shift would recognize the biological reality of an associate's child bearing years, for which some accommodation is required, the long term nature of a career in private practice and the economic realities of operating a law firm.

4. The legal profession should not assume that change will occur without conscious efforts to create a shift in the legal culture. Law firms have a legal responsibility to provide environments that allow women to advance without barriers based on gender. It is in the public interest for the providers of private legal services to reflect the make up of the society in which we live.

5. We also note that the responsibility to provide leadership in the retention and advancement of women in private practice does not only lie with law firms. Law societies and legal associations have a responsibility to the legal profession and to the public to act as catalysts to influence change and to empower women to take responsibility for their careers and progress.

6. Self-regulation of the legal profession is a privilege and relies on the assumption that the profession is in the best position to set standards and establish ethical rules of conduct for the bar and to regulate lawyers in the best interest of the public. Meeting the public interest requires lawyers to have a sense of professionalism, which includes a sense of integrity, honour, leadership, independence, pride, civility and collegiality.[1] A profession that is represen-

tative of the public, and one that provides equal opportunities to men and women serves to enhance the sense of professionalism of our legal profession.

7. In response to the realities outlined above, the Law Society created in 2005 the Retention of Women in Private Practice Working Group (the "Working Group") with a mandate to,
   a. identify best practices in law firms and in sole practice to enhance the retention of women;
   b. determine the role of the Law Society in addressing the issue of retention of women in private practice;
   c. design and implement strategies for medium and large law firms to retain women;
   d. develop strategies to respond to the socio-economic needs of women in small firms and sole practices including the viability of their practices as well as their unique child-care challenges; and
   e. take into account the needs of women from diverse communities.

8. In developing its recommendations, the Working Group considered findings of focus groups conducted with women and interviews conducted with Managing Partners. It also reviewed literature about challenges faced by women in the legal profession, more particularly private practice, and best practices in the legal profession in Ontario, in Canada and in foreign jurisdictions. The Working Group's recommendations aim at allowing women lawyers to make career choices related to their aspirations, may they decide to work as in-house counsel, as government lawyers, in private practice or to stay at home, without being hindered by barriers based on gender.

9. From March to May, 2008, the Law Society embarked on a province-wide consultation to seek the profession's comments on the report and proposed recommendations. The Law Society held meetings in Toronto, Ottawa, Sudbury, Oakville, Kingston, Windsor, Thunder Bay, Orillia, Ajax and London with lawyers, including law firm managing partners and presidents of legal associations. Approximately 900 lawyers and students attended the meetings and the Law Society received more than 55 written submissions.

10. The final consultation attracted a broad spectrum of lawyers, men and women, from all types of practice settings and firm sizes, the government, in-house counsel, articling and law students. Participants included associates, partners and managing partners of all levels of experience and practising in a wide range of areas.

11. Responses to the final consultation were overwhelmingly positive, with some lawyers indicating that they hope this is a first step toward further initiatives. An overview of the final consultation findings is presented in sections VII and VIII of this report. A Final Consultation Report is also available on-line at www.lsuc.on.ca.

II — RESEARCH FINDINGS

12. Studies have identified the following challenges in private practice:
    a. although men and women identify time spent with their family as the aspect of their lives that gives them the most satisfaction, maintaining demanding law careers often [conflicts] with family life and is the most common reason for leaving law practice;
    b. the most immediate issues for women in private practice appear to result from childbirth and parenting responsibilities;
    c. women are particularly affected by the unavailability of support and benefits such as part-time partnerships, part-time employment, predictable hours, job sharing and flexibility in hours;
    d. women in small firms or in sole practices face unique challenges in part because of the lack of income or benefits during leaves and lack of assistance to maintain the practice during absences;
    e. women from Aboriginal, Francophone and/ or equality-seeking communities are often more vulnerable and their experiences and perspectives should be taken into account when developing strategies to retain and advance women in private practice.

13. The Working Group reviewed best practices in Ontario and in other jurisdictions to develop its recommendations. The following conclusions can be drawn from this review:

    a. Similar findings are noted in other jurisdictions in Canada and in foreign jurisdictions.
    b. Barriers faced by women are systemic and will require organizational and cultural change, along with a focus on the issue if meaningful change is to occur.
    c. A number of initiatives designed to assist women would also benefit male lawyers.
    d. The experiences and realities of women in larger firms are significantly different than those of women in smaller environments, and therefore recommendations to address challenges faced by women in large and medium firms should be different than those designed to address the needs of women in small firms and sole practices.
    e. The recommendations and implementation should take into account the unique challenges faced by women lawyers who are members of Aboriginal, Francophone and/ or equality-seeking communities and their historic under-representation in the legal profession.
    f. In the context of large and medium firms, systemic cultural change is necessary and firms will require leadership and commitment from managing partners to implement practices such as the following:
        i. the collection and analysis of law firms' demographic data to assist in the development of strategies based on the firm's needs;
        ii. the adoption, acceptance and effective implementation of maternity/parental leaves and flexible work arrangements;
        iii. programs to assist women to become leaders, both inside and outside their firms, such as effective mentoring programs, gender-based networking opportunities and leadership skills development opportunities.
    g. Women in small firms and sole practices are particularly vulnerable because they do not have the financial or human resources to take leaves. The following initiatives would be beneficial:
        i. access to funding to cover some of the expenses of leaves of absences;
        ii. access to practice locums and guidelines to assist in retaining locum lawyers to maintain the practice while on leave;
        iii. access to networking opportunities.

(e)   Specialization and the Legal Profession†

Alvin Esau

INTRODUCTION

Pressures for Change

Lawyers have often reminded themselves of the need to be responsive to changing needs in fulfilling the self-regulating mandate of the legal profession to focus on the public interest.[1] This challenge appears to have become particularly urgent in our time as increasing pressures for change from both inside and outside the profession are converging around a number of often interrelated and difficult issues which have found their way to the top of the profession's agenda for consideration.

Informed Access to Legal Services

The increasing growth and complexity of the law in substance and range, coupled with the increasing demands made by people for participation, protection, and equal rights within the legal process has led to increasing demands for legal services.[2] We have witnessed in response a growing emphasis on legal aid plans aimed at providing essential legal services for those who cannot afford to pay for them. The provision of legal aid is still a very live issue for the legal profession due to such continuing problems as funding and the formulation of the most appropriate form of delivery system. However, the pressure for change appears to have shifted now to the legal needs of the majority of the population, namely the middle income groups.[3] There appears to be some evidence that the general public has difficulty knowing when a legal problem exists, or how to find a lawyer to help, and that a segment of the public fears the size of legal fees or has a general distrust or even fear of lawyers. A recent survey in the United States revealed that even though adult Americans experience an average of 3.3 "serious legal problems" during their lives, a third of the public has never used a lawyer and another 28.9% has used a lawyer only once.[4] This survey also revealed that 79.2% of all respondents agreed that "[a] lot of people do not go to lawyers because they have no way of knowing which lawyer is competent to handle their particular problem".[5] As well, the survey revealed that over 60% of the respondents, including both people who have used and those who have not used lawyers, thought that lawyers cost too much.[6]

That middle income groups in Canada have difficulty making informed choices about legal services and how much they cost, given traditional professional advertising rules, was recently documented in the *Canadian Consumer*.[7] From inside the profession, Stuart Thom, the Treasurer of the Law Society of Upper Canada, confirmed that the public needs more knowledge about the availability and kinds of the legal services:

> The large corporation or institution with sophisticated personnel in charge of its affairs usually has a well-established legal connection. The average man or woman who as a rule seeks legal assistance only occasionally and for some immediate specific reason such as buying a house, because of an accident, to get a divorce, is not so equipped. The questions the occasional clients have to ask and try to get answered are "How do I get in touch with a lawyer who will do the work I want done?", "How do I know he will be any good?", "How much will he charge me?". The legal profession hasn't done much, in fact it has done very little, to help people answer these questions.[8]

At the same time that these claims are made about unmet needs for legal services there appears to be a serious and growing problem finding articling positions and jobs for the increasing number of law school graduates. Thus pressure for change to provide better access to legal services is increased by the perception that a "job gap" should not exist when there is a "need gap" to fill.

Quality of Legal Services

Delay and neglect continue to be frequent complaints lodged against lawyers by their clients,[9] and there is a rise in the number of successful malpractice suits against lawyers.[10] Much of the pressure which has made the competency issue of such current concern, however, has come from within the

---

† (1979) 9 Man. L.J. 255 at 255–63, 265–73. Reproduced with permission. [Notes and/or references omitted.]

legal fraternity itself. For example, Chief Justice Warren Burger of the United States Supreme Court has expressed the opinion on several occasions that up to one-half of the attorneys practising before the courts are incompetent as trial advocates.[11] Professor Irving Younger, a former New York State Court judge, has stated:

> Perhaps half of the lawyers who tried cases before me showed an inadequate grasp of the law of evidence, the law of procedure, and trial technique. Some — perhaps 10% — were total strangers to those interesting subjects. The remaining 40% did not know enough about them to do a workmanlike job. Usually they stumbled through somehow — because the lawyer on the other side was just as bad, or the judge helped, or the jury managed to figure the case out despite the lawyer. This state of affairs is inexcusable.[12]

Chief Justice Irving Kaufman of the United States Court of Appeals has stated that many attorneys lack competency as well as integrity,[13] and one judge went so far as to say that only two percent of the lawyers appearing before him were competent.[14]

Whether or not incompetence has reached such a [crisis] proportion can certainly be debated with regard to trial skills,[15] and in non-trial aspects of lawyering as well,[16] but in this period of both rapid change and increased complexity within many areas of the law, the problem of what the profession's response to the incompetency problem should be[] is a current issue of utmost importance occupying a great deal of the profession's attention, not only in the United States but also in Canada.[17]

The Delivery and Cost of Legal Services

Related to the need for informed access to quality legal services[] is the issue involving the method of delivering these services and their cost.[18] The suitability of the traditional delivery system of the sole practitioner or small law firm has been challenged by demands for prepaid and group legal services plans,[19] by demands for special community legal clinics utilizing a high degree of standardization procedures and paraprofessional services,[20] and by "public interest" law firms.[21] Furthermore, demands for change in the method of delivering legal services are related to concurrent demands for change in the legal process such as legalization of certain conduct, no-fault laws, law reform proposals aimed at simplified and understandable legal forms and procedures, and the utilization of less formal mechanisms of dispute resolution.

. . . .

THE CONCEPT OF SPECIALIZATION

One of the most debated proposals aimed at responding to the challenge of providing more informed access to competently performed, efficiently delivered, reasonably priced legal services is the demand for some formal regulation of specialization within the legal profession. This paper will outline the developments on this front in the United States and Canada and raise some of the specific problems involved in the formal regulation of specialization. First, however, some comments on *de facto* specialization, and the assumed positive goals and possible negative effects of specialization must be presented as a background to understanding the developments taking place.

De Facto Specialization

Leaving aside for a moment the problems of defining what it means to be a "specialist", it is at least common knowledge within the legal profession that some lawyers only handle certain matters and not others, or spend most of their time on certain matters. It is also common knowledge in the profession that the growth of large law firms is often based on teamwork within the context of a high degree of individual specialization.

Generally, a poll of Wisconsin lawyers found that 55% of the respondents indicated that their practices were more than 50% in one given field.[28] A random survey of 125 Toronto lawyers in 1971 found that 72% were restricting their practice and that 58% of the lawyers were spending more than 70% of their time in one field of law or spending their full time in one or two fields.[29] On a provincial basis, the MacKinnon Committee in Ontario found that of 4,411 lawyers responding to a questionnaire in 1972, approximately 50% said they specialized rather than engaged in general practice.[30] According to a 1969 California survey, two out of three lawyers in that State considered themselves specialists, and four out of five lawyers called themselves specialists.[31] A 1975 Illinois State Bar Association survey found that 48% of the lawyers in that State said they engaged in specialized practice only, while 51% called themselves general practitioners who also had one or more specialties.[32]

While surveys may not help establish the actual amount of *de facto* specialization that exists, and until there is a consensus as to what the definition of "specialization" is, one can conclude at least that many lawyers do not hold themselves out as willing to help every potential client who happens to call. Thus, the issue is not whether specialization should exist in the profession, since it already does; but rather the issue is whether it should be encouraged and formally regulated and what the approach to that regulation should be.

There are undoubtedly many factors leading to the *de facto* narrowing of legal practice. Commonly noted is that with the increasing complexity of society, there is an increasing complexity in the law and an increasing difficulty in keeping up with legal developments in many areas. Some typical expressions in favor of narrowing practice are as follows:

> If a lawyer truly tries to be proficient in a great number of fields, he must necessarily spend a fantastic number of hours in understanding those fields before he can move forward in them. When he develops a particular subject as his field, he can much more expeditiously accomplish the work to his own benefit, as well as to the benefit of his client, so that his time is utilized in the most efficient manner.[33]
>
> Concentration of experience enables lawyers to provide better legal services in their speciality in less time with consequent savings to their clients.[34]
>
> New developments, procedures and problems in every field of practice are generated continuously by the courts, legislatures, administrative agencies and special bar groups. Many popular and active fields of legal practice did not even exist forty years ago. The volume of current material in the form of advance sheets, services, synopses, summaries, articles, journals and the like are so numerous and voluminous that no practitioner can possibly read it all. It is unrealistic to expect any modern lawyer to stay abreast of all the developments in all the areas of law or to be competent in all fields of general practice.
>
> Since most lawyers simply cannot maintain more than a nodding acquaintance with most areas of the law, we have witnessed the growth of an informal system of legal specialization.[35]
>
> Few practitioners today can hope, claim, or even pretend to be master of every field of the law—the day of the true general practitioner who handles every matter himself without referring to or consulting with others who have more particularized knowledge and experience is a thing of the past.[36]

The connection between competence and specialization, then, appears to be a leading factor in the development of *de facto* specialization. Competence, furthermore, is a dimension of professional ethics, and thus to some degree *de facto* narrowing of practice is encouraged by our Code of Professional Conduct.[37] Even the general practitioner may not be so "general" after all. Chapter II of the Code dealing with "Competency and Quality of Service" has the following rule:

> (a) The lawyer owes a duty to his client to be competent to perform the legal services which the lawyer undertakes on his behalf.
> (b) The lawyer should serve his client in a conscientious, diligent and efficient manner and he should provide a quality of service at least equal to that which lawyers generally would expect of a competent lawyer in a like situation.[38]

The commentary after the rule includes the following provision:

> It follows that the lawyer should not undertake a matter unless he honestly believes that he is competent to handle it or that he can become competent without undue delay, risk or expense to his client. If the lawyer proceeds on any other basis he is not being honest with his client. This is an ethical consideration and is to be distinguished from the standard of care which a court would invoke for purposes of determining negligence.[39]

If becoming competent in a matter without undue delay, risk, or expense is an increasingly difficult problem, then one may conclude that *de facto* specialization is not only a present reality but may well substantially increase in the future.

One factor, however, which may be pointing away from a substantial increase in *de facto* specialization is the greater number of lawyers who are not able to stay with the law firms they articled in or find jobs with established law firms and thus move immediately into setting up their own independent practices, alone or in association with lawyers in the same position. This growth of independent practice by very recently licensed lawyers may lead to a greater number of general practitioners, unable economically to restrict their practices to a few fields, at least for many years. How are the Code provisions noted above accepted by these lawyers who may have a considerable lack of confidence and experience in many areas of the law, but who must nevertheless gain experience and confidence by taking cases if their independent practices are going to survive? What reforms, if any, should be undertaken by the legal profession to be fair both to young lawyers caught in a "job squeeze" and to the public who deserve high quality legal services?

Aside from the difficulty of being "omnicompetent" as one factor leading to *de facto* specialization, a variety of other factors could be cited, including a lawyer's own special interests in certain fields; or a lawyer's innate aptitude, or lack thereof, in particular skills like advocacy or negotiation; or the lawyer's sensitivity to perceived economic, political, or moral status attributed to certain kinds of firm or being employed for the particular needs of a certain group or individual, in government or industry.

The Definitional Problem

Any movement from the existence of *de facto* specialization to some formal regulation of specialization, including the provision for advertising to the public of the availability of specialists, must first deal with the fact that no consensus appears to exist as to what "specialization" really means.

. . . .

... How one chooses to define specialization — as expertise or concentration, in specialized areas or in all areas — may depend on the goal to be accomplished by the regulatory scheme.

Assumed Positive Goals of Specialization

While the existence, and perhaps increase, of *de facto* specialization may by itself further certain sought-after goals, the formal regulation of specialization may both accelerate the movement toward these goals as well as add to or modify them. At this stage, however, one must still make assumptions and speculate about the effects of formal regulation schemes because sophisticated evaluations of existing formal regulation programs have not been completed.[45] The most recent report of the A.B.A. Committee on Specialization stated: "No data exists now, or will exist in the foreseeable future, which provides definitive answers to the access, quality and cost implications of specialization regulation."[46] Until we have more data on the effects of formal regulation we are left with a number of assumed effects which may be considered worthwhile if achieved by regulation. These assumed effects are related directly to the demands for change cited earlier.

Improved Quality of Legal Service

The A.B.A. Committee on Specialization formulated a list of possible "pros and cons" of specialization.[47] Of the sixteen items on the "pro" list, at least eight items related to the argument that specialization improves the quality of legal services:

1. The certified specialist will become more proficient in solving problems in his specialized field.
2. Other lawyers will become more proficient in solving legal problems.
3. The overall quality of legal services to the public will improve.

...

6. The quality of solutions to legal problems on an individual basis will improve.
7. Specialized services will be made available to the general practitioner.

...

14. Specialists will recognize a legal problem or solution overlooked by a general practitioner.
15. Law schools will be encouraged to offer in depth courses in the areas of specialization certification.
16. Because quality of legal work will be improved, there will be less load on court dockets.

How could a formal regulation scheme arguably lead to this effect of increased quality of service and competency of lawyers, individually and generally? As noted earlier,[49] incentives to narrow practice may help lawyers to keep up with developments in their chosen areas and help lawyers gain substantial experience in certain matters which should lead to increased skill and familiarity in handling them. The primary function of a formal regulation scheme should be to encourage greater numbers of lawyers to move from generalist practice and thus generally raise the level of competence in the profession.[50] With the advertising of the availability of specialized legal services, matters calling for special expertise will more likely be channelled away from nonspecialists to the specialists and thus these matters will be better handled and the overall quality of legal services will be higher than in the present situation where some of these matters would be handled by generalists wanting work. Setting high standards and testing for experience, skill, and knowledge as entrance requirements for the formal certification or recognition of specialists may serve to weed out those who do not deserve to be called specialists and generally encourage achievement to reach the standards set, all of which may serve to improve standards of legal practice.[51] Furthermore, periodic mandatory recertification requirements may serve to maintain high standards of competence over time.[52] The formal regulation of specialization may encourage development and utilization of specialized C.L.E. programs and special post-graduate university educational programs all of which would help lawyers become more competent and maintain such competency. The formal regulation of specialization may provide general practitioners with more knowledge about the availability of specialists than they now have, and thus, a greater number of referrals may result with a consequent rise in the general quality of legal service.[53]

These propositions about increased competency depend obviously on what form the scheme of regulation would take. As well, the effects of specialization on competency must be taken together with the effects of the many other factors bearing on the competency issue.

Informed Access to Legal Services

Professor Reed, commenting on the view that formal regulation of specialization coupled with informational advertising[] might increase informed rather than random access to legal services, noted that: "If I've got trouble with my head and I want to see a psychiatrist, I can find out who one is. I don't have to call some doctor and say, 'Do you know anything about psychiatry, Doctor?'"[54] Similarly, demands for the formal regulation of specialization in California arose originally, not out of a perceived competency problem, but out of the suggestion of a Committee on Group Legal Services which urged the certification of specialists as a possible alternative or adjunct to meeting the needs of the public for informed access to legal services.[55]

More informed access is accomplished through a formal regulation scheme providing some method whereby lawyers who meet certain standards can hold themselves out to the public as specialists in a certain field or fields of law. Again the achievement of this goal will depend on what form the specialization scheme takes, what fields of law are chosen, how many lawyers will meet the standards set or attempt to meet them and thus be able to participate in the program, how quickly the program can be implemented, and so forth.

The definitional problem of what it means to be a "specialist" may well depend on which goal is primarily pursued, increased access to legal services or increased quality.[56] Whether the focus is, or should be[,] primarily on access[] may depend on the policies adopted or lacking regarding other factors that aim at public knowledge of the availability and kind of legal services.

Efficient Delivery and Lower Cost of Legal Services

Another assumed positive goal of the regulation of specialization is that the specialist can spend much less time on matters because the substantial experience gained by concentration should lead to increased efficiency. Decreased costs should also result because the client would not have to pay for as many research hours and perhaps in some situations with high volume, the lawyer may even have standardized procedures and paralegal services, which will lower the cost for the client.[57] Of course, in all of this, the specialist, it is argued, will still be able to earn more than the generalist.[58]

Public Trust and Legal Ethics Improved

Clients generally may be more satisfied with results achieved when specialists are used, so the public image of the legal profession may improve.[59] The formulation of special standards of ethics and increased discussion of the special ethical problems encountered within certain areas of practice may lead to heightened sensitivity toward ethical dimensions of practice.

Controlled Advertising

While the formal regulation of specialization may *encourage* advertising to achieve the goal of informed access to legal services, the formal regulation of specialization may also serve to *control* advertising. If lawyers will be allowed to advertise fields of law in which they are willing to accept cases, then some formal regulation of specialization may serve to minimize the problem of misrepresentation to consumers of implied special expertise that results from such advertising in the absence of a specialization scheme.[60] The most recent report of the A.B.A. Committee on Specialization noted that the changes made in advertising policy have resulted in an increased demand for regulation of specialization as "One step toward increasing the accuracy of information which the public and the bar will have about the lawyers who have appropriate qualifications to help with particular problems."[61] Such regulation, of course, requires the formulation of generally accepted labels, definitions and quality standards if it is going to be successful in providing accurate information to the public. Specialization regulation might have the effect of allowing only those who are likely to be *able* to take problems in certain fields and not just *willing* to take them, to advertise such actual or implied competence.

Less "Unauthorized Practice"

The Alberta Law Society Committee reporting on specialization noted:

If the public does not have specialist legal assistance available, there is a likelihood it will turn to other professions and groups for assistance in some fields. An example given is that a great deal of the work in tax matters formerly done by the legal profession is now done by chartered accountants. Similarly, in real estate transactions the parties may not use a lawyer at all or, at any event only in a late stage of the transaction. The specialist doing a volume of such work as a routine, can offer superior service at a lower fee.[62]

Possible Negative Effects of Specialization

The formal regulation of specialization may be criticized without necessarily pointing to a list of possible negative effects that must be balanced against the assumed positive effects listed above. Rather the criticism can proceed by asserting that the positive effects cannot be attained by formal regulation anyway. For example, it may be argued that setting standards and testing for competency cannot achieve a measure of quality assurance because standards cannot be formulated that objectively measure competence in any case, and that furthermore, the cost to the consumer of legal services will rise with specialization, not fall.[63]

The criticism of formal regulation might proceed as well with the assertion that the need to examine possible positive and negative effects is unnecessary because there is no public demand for specialized legal services in the first place. Those groups in need of specialized service have the legal connections to serve them in the present situation, and the public simply needs competent generalists and more information about their services.[64] This, of course, begs the question again as to what the definition of a "specialist" should be.

If a critic, however, does accept that positive goals may be furthered by formal regulation, the argument may be made that the negative effects may outweigh the positive effects. What these negative effects are will depend on what form the regulation takes in the light of what priority of goals is emphasized and what concept of specialization is adopted.

Overspecialization Dangers

Beneath the surface of the pressures for change in the legal profession there appears to be a tension between two value clusters which might broadly be labelled "consumerism" and "humanism." While these two movements are certainly not opposing systems of thought, there are points of tension discernible between them. On one hand, the consumer movement appears to favor developments that provide legal services very much like the supply of goods in a supermarket. Standardization of forms and procedures, check-list interviews, pre-advertised fees, labelled services, and the like, are indicative of this consumer movement stressing efficiency, low cost, and accessibility. On the other hand, there is a movement, most visible in legal education, but also discernible from both within and without the profession, stressing the need for greater awareness and aptitude on the part of lawyers in handling the relational aspects of legal practice.[65] Legal educators stress the need to be sensitive to the whole person, to see the client as a person not simply as a problem, to have greater sensitivity to the interaction of nonlegal aspects with the legal aspects of a client's problems, to be sensitive to feelings in the interviewing and counselling process, and generally to concentrate on the lawyer-client relationship rather than on commercial dimensions of law practice. These humanistic values may be difficult to pursue within the delivery systems arising out of the consumer movement.

Perhaps a third force, partly related to humanism, might be labelled "traditionalism" which views many of the proposed changes in the legal profession with scepticism. Related to both the humanistic and traditionalistic forces are criticisms of the formal regulation of specialization focusing on a series of dangers brought about by over-specialization. The bad joke is told about the old doctor who was talking to the young doctor, who was just going into a specialty. The old doctor said, "I hear you are not going to be an ear, nose, and throat doctor like your daddy. You are just going to take the nose?" "Oh no," said the young man, "just the left nostril."[66] The legal profession has traditionally viewed itself as being the architect of democracy, a prime source of wise leadership at all levels of policy making, with the capacity for a broad vision applied to human problems. Thus, a mass movement toward narrow practice is feared by some lawyers. The following comments are indicative:

> In some ways, it seems that as we get better and better at more restricted assignments, we are valued less and less on matters of general importance.[67]

> A specialist loses touch with the many problems which present themselves in the general practice of law; specialists are generally ignorant of matters outside their specialty; a narrow and confined approach to overall problems tends to hasten the disintegration of a free society which needs generalists as well as specialists; and, the well-rounded lawyer can more easily see the

interrelated problems of a client and can thus better serve him.[68]

The principal and overriding defect of most certification/recognition proposals is their acceptance of the theory of *expertise*. That concept is delusive because technical experts tend to destroy the integrity of any discipline of which they are a part. In the legal profession, more likely than not, they will substitute the ways of the expert for the traditional qualities of the generalist lawyer: reflection, comprehension, discrimination, imagination, inspiration, wisdom, fortitude and tenacity.[69]

[S]pecialization, of necessity, tends to segmentize the law and, to some extent, emphasizes the mechanics of law as distinguished from a broad sense of justice acquired from familiarity with the legal problems of people of different walks of life in a variety of situations.[70]

While some specialization of the "specialist area" or "specialist problem" variety giving rise to a number of "lawyer's lawyers" might be acceptable to these critics, any movement in the direction of full scale encouragement of narrow practice is viewed as leading to a dehumanized, less creative, overly technical profession. As one commentator, speaking about the virtues of a country lawyer, expressed it, "He will sometimes sacrifice efficiency to solve individual problems individually."[71]

Is this just naive, romantic traditionalism or is there something here which must be taken seriously? After all, legal education continues to be based on a broad exposure to many doctrinal fields and some orientation to the "seamless web" view of law. Is it really true, however, that most general practitioners perform such a variety of work that their skill of legal analysis is particularly creative and that their understanding of legal principles is likely to be sharper than that of the lawyer concentrating on a few areas? Or is broad perspective more likely to result from a willingness to study with focused intensity the policies, practices, theories, and principles both legal and non-legal interacting on a particular area of practice? How can we have omnicompetent judges, however, if they are to be picked from a profession which will be largely specialized? Must we have a great number of specialized courts as well? Our perception of the importance of these questions may depend partly on how narrow or broad the recognized specialty fields will be. A formal regulation scheme which encourages very wide participation by formulating attainable standards, and allowing lawyers a number of specialty designations from many broadly defined fields, including perhaps even a catch-all "general practice" field, would hardly

mean a mass movement away from generalist practice, even if lawyers called themselves specialists. But, how meaningful would such a scheme be? Similarly, support for such a scheme might affect our perception of the importance of possible negative effects on those who choose to remain nonspecialists.

General Practitioners May Be Hurt

The formal regulation of specialization may accelerate the movement of business from the sole practitioners and small firms to the large law firms.[72] Even if specialists do not have a monopoly in their field, and lawyers are allowed to take on whatever they feel willing to do, in reality the market forces with formal regulation may result in an inability to practice in as broad a way as one might prefer.[73] It has been suggested that the regulation of specialization will tend inevitably to the next step of a monopoly. Professor Mindes writes:

> The desire of specialists to distinguish themselves from other less "professional" practitioners is the key to the internal processes that lead a group to want to separate itself from the rest and also to its subsequent course after separation is achieved.
>
> ...
>
> A distinctive identity increases the feeling of commonality with others in the specialty and increases the psychological, social, and professional distance from other members of the bar. Contacts within the group increase, and those with other lawyers decrease. A special language develops by stages, as do special techniques and attitudes. The in-group feeling of "we" against "they" grows, and this in turn leads to more isolation of the specialty group.[74]

Professor Mindes suggests the final step would be a monopoly by specialists of the right to practice in their area.

A formal regulation scheme may have the further effect of implying to the public that a nonspecialist is not special and therefore not competent or important, and so public confidence in the nonspecialist may fall. Furthermore, a traditional concept is that law is a "seamless web" and that problems may result from clients self-diagnosing which specialist is needed.[75] The validity and weight of some of these criticisms may depend on how generalists are related to the specialists in a formal regulation scheme.

The problem of possible negative effects on the nonspecialist is most often countered by the argument that formal regulation schemes include provisions relating to the referral of business from nonspecialist to specialist which protect the nonspecialist. "Anti-pirating" provisions could be formulated so

471

that the specialist would be prevented from providing services to the referred client beyond the confines of the referral.[76] The client would still "belong," as it were, to the generalist. This argument does not of course counter the argument that many clients will, or should, self-diagnose which lawyer they need, this being part of the goal of more informed access to legal services, which may lead to a movement of business from the generalist to the specialist.

The A.B.A. Committee on Specialization in 1969 suggested that formal regulation may, nevertheless, help rather than hinder the sole practitioner or small firm to compete with the large firm:

> The most frequently voiced objection to regulation of specialization presented to our committee was its supposed harmful effect upon the sole practitioner and the small partnership in rural areas. Everyone agrees that the big firm lawyer already has the benefits of specialized practice. It was argued that large law firms in general are not adversely affected by the failure of the bar to regulate specialization, because a large law firm usually has little difficulty in making the availability of the specialized services of its individual lawyers collectively known to its prospective clients, and that regulation would only encourage clients to leave general practitioners to go to those large conglomerates of legal specialists. The committee did not accept that

argument as we believe that experimentation may demonstrate that regulation of legal specialization tends to equate the sole practitioner and small law firm with the large firm in making specialized services available to their respective clients.

> Realistically, one of the principal reasons for the success of large law firms is that they have had no difficulty in communicating to the public that they offer specialized services, and that the collective abilities of their lawyers enable them to be specialists in every field of the law. Many lawyers argue that the official recognition of specialists would enable general practitioners more easily to obtain qualified specialists to assist them in situations where they may occasionally need such specialized legal services. Certainly, the committee believes that it would aid those lawyers in informing the public that specialized legal services can be made available by general practitioners as well as by large law firms. If experimentation does show that it enables the small practitioner more effectively to compete with the large law firms, regulated specialization may be the means whereby the ultimate survival of the independent sole practitioner is insured.[77]

That ever present ghost of definition haunts us again with the statement made above that "specialized legal services can be made available by general practitioners."

(f)   Styles of Legal Work[†]

Edwin M. Schur

Another avenue to an understanding of the law in action involves studying the organization and routine work patterns of the legal profession. As was mentioned earlier, some of the current sociological interest in the legal system developed out of research focused on the general analysis of occupations and professions. From this standpoint a broad array of sociological concepts may be applicable to analyzing the positions and work of the individuals who man the legal order — ranging from "professional self-image" to occupational "role set," from "recruitment" and "socialization" to colleague relationships

and possible "role conflicts." Similarly, at least for other than lone practitioners, organization theory may be relevant, with such concepts as "bureaucracy," organizational "commitment," and organizational "goals" coming into play.

It has been suggested, by at least one legal critic, that research along these lines may produce an overly narrow concentration on certain small-scale and mundane aspects of the realm of law. Thus, it is argued that law is much more than simply what lawyers do and further that the lawyer's role is, in some essential aspects, not at all like other occupational

---

† From Edwin M. Schur, *Law and Society: A Sociological View* (New York: Random House, 1968) at 163–71. Reproduced with permission. [Notes and/or references omitted.]

and professional roles. Hazard states that "the term 'lawyer' refers less to a social function than to a type of training, a type which in fact is shared by people doing a bewildering variety of tasks." The same writer also insists that for full understanding of legal work one must recognize that with respect to any important legal problem "there is a long, a rich and a demanding intellectual culture."[49] Certainly it is true, and most sociologists accept the fact, that lawyers operate in a great many different settings, that any conception of *the* lawyer (believed to apply to the entire profession) would be misleading. Likewise, sophisticated social analysts are aware of both the relevant heritage of legal philosophy and the significant technical formulations embodied in the legal system. Yet these factors do not vitiate an investigation of law as a profession. Such research represents one of a number of complementary, rather than mutually exclusive, approaches to the study of legal institutions. Nor is it an absolute prerequisite for such research that the sociologist have extensive training in the law. Clearly, some familiarity with legal substance and procedure will be of great help to the investigator. At the same time, it should be kept in mind that to require of the researcher lengthy formal and technical training in the discipline or occupational field to be investigated would greatly hamper sociological research in any number of fields, such as the sociology of science, of medicine, of religion, and indeed the social analysis of any occupation or profession. There is no greater need for specialized knowledge in studying the legal profession than in these other instances. Of course, a very good argument can be made for better communication and more cooperative interaction between sociologists and lawyers; cross-disciplinary team research will often provide a useful means of averting some of the problems just mentioned.

We have already seen that there is a very real social stratification within the legal profession, and that the lawyer's general standing and specific work patterns may be partly determined by his social background and type of legal education. The interplay between the numerous variables involved here is complex, but the overall relationship between recruitment and professional role is well summarized in the following statement: "Social background prescribes two major career contingencies: level of technical skill and access to clients."[50] Whereas all lawyers theoretically share a common body of technical knowledge and special skills, as well as a dual commitment to serve the client (in a personal and confidential relationship) and the public (as "servant of the court"), in practice there is an enormous amount of

variation not only in what particular types of lawyers do but also in how they relate to their clients and other individuals and agencies and in how they view their professional roles. If we examine actual work situations, a few dominant patterns emerge.

The Large Law Firm

The major law firms maintain a position of considerable power in modern American society. They wield a substantial influence in the business community and on public policy in general. Members of such firms tend to be held in high social esteem. Under these circumstances, it is probably not surprising that the large, well-established firms tend to recruit as new members individuals of relatively high socioeconomic status. Members of large firms are much more likely than are members of small firms or individual practitioners to be Protestant; to have fathers who were in business, managerial or professional positions; to have attended an Ivy League or other high-quality college; and to have attended (and done well at) one of the major, nationally known law schools or at least some other full-time, university-connected law school (as compared with nonuniversity-connected and night law schools).[51] In particular, a man who obtains top grades (and is on the "law review," the prestigeful and influential student-edited journal) at the top, nationally known schools (primarily Harvard, Yale, and Columbia) may be "ticketed for life as a first-class passenger on the escalator for talent." As David Riesman goes on to comment, there is a "self-confirming myth" in legal education, in which the law-review men get the top jobs, make the contacts, and gain the experience necessary for advancement, and hence attain a success that "proves" that the law-school marking system (which, in the first year, determines law-review membership) is an accurate indicator of talent. At an early point in their training, such men gain a high level of confidence and the conviction that they are destined for important jobs.[52]

This conviction is usually upheld through their work experience in the large firms. As one observer puts it, "What the Wall Street lawyers do in their professional capacity is nothing less than to provide prudential and technical assistance in the management of the private sector of the world economy."[53] Surveys reveal significant differences in work patterns and clientele between large-firm lawyers on the one hand and small-firm members and individual practitioners on the other. The former are more likely than the latter to serve business clients (mainly large corporations in the field of heavy industry and finance) and wealthy, Protestant, individual clients, to have an overwhelming concentration of work in the areas of business and probate law, to spend much less time in court, and to deal with federal and appellate courts (rather than local ones) when such contact does occur. There is also a pronounced pattern of higher income for lawyers in the larger firms.[54]

At the very top of the bar's status hierarchy, in the major New York firms described in Smigel's *The Wall Street Lawyer*, the lawyer deals almost exclusively with the corporate and financial problems of big business. Here too, the incoming lawyer gains membership in a substantial organization, which is impressive in its own right. He finds himself part of an establishment that may occupy three or four floors of a downtown office building and that may comprise as many as 50 to 150 lawyers and up to 250 nonprofessional staff. The firm is likely to have a long and renowned history, an atmosphere all its own, and an almost tangible aura of importance. Lawyers in the firm hold positions within a well-elaborated hierarchy — as reflected in the distribution of income and general prestige and in the allocation of status symbols, such as office space, secretaries, and so forth, and of professional tasks and responsibilities. Although the young lawyer's initial work may be of a segmental or highly specialized variety, not involving direct contact with clients and perhaps dealing with only one small facet of a broader matter, he is likely at once to be impressed by the wealth and power of the clients and the sizable nature of their business transactions. Nor is he dealt with as a mere underling. He has been hired for his demonstrated competence and his potential for leadership in the profession and in many respects he is treated as a colleague, albeit a junior one.[55]

Work in such a setting is not, of course, without its difficulties. Some lawyers feel that the firms engender too early and too great specialization; most of the large firms have separate departments, officially or unofficially, to deal with such areas of work as corporate law, tax law, litigation, and so on. Others find troublesome the very keen competition for advancement to full partnership. Then too, some lawyers may be concerned that the work in the impersonal, bureaucratic setting seems to have little relation to the ideal of the lawyer as a "free professional," as a free-wheeling and confidential advisor to trusting clients. A few of the lawyers may even be defensive about the close ties between Wall Street firms and big business and conscious of the fact that the bulk of their work contributes little to protecting the underdog, an important theme in popular conceptions of the lawyer's role. And notwithstanding the firms' attempts to maintain a spirit of collegueship, the fact that they are salaried employees who must in the last analysis take orders is disturbing to some. Finally, the pervasive pressures to conform — personally, socially, and even politically — may cause irritation.[56]

For most of its members most of the time, however, the large law firm provides good earnings, excellent experience, and satisfying work. The prospect of a partnership holds out the possibility of a really sizable income combined with enormous prestige and entrée to the inner circles of the corporate and financial worlds. And for those not destined to achieve partnership, or for those who may be dissatisfied with the firm for one reason or another, there is the possibility of using their positions in the large firm as a stepping stone to other favorable situations — in industry, government, teaching, or in somewhat smaller but still very successful law firms.

INDIVIDUAL PRACTICE

Sharply contrasting with the situation of the elite, large-firm lawyer, is that of the typical individual practitioner in a large city. As we have already seen, there are significant differences between lawyers in the two types of practice, both in social background and in the kinds of work they do and the success they achieve. The lone practitioner is likely to be the son of an immigrant, who has worked his way up; he is likely to have attended either a "proprietary" or a Catholic night law school and not to have completed college, which at one time was not always a requirement for admission to such law schools. At least at the lower levels of individual practice, he is earning a precarious living, and his clientele tends to be a transient one of lower-income individuals. His legal work involves mainly small-scale and routine business matters and litigation between individuals. His contact with agencies and courts (the latter being particularly frequent) tends to be at the local level. As Jerome Carlin points out in *Lawyers on Their Own*, an important study of individual practice in Chicago, these men constitute something like a "lower class" of the metropolitan bar. Their practice consists largely of "those residual matters (and clients) that the large firms have not pre-empted" — such as matters too inconsequential (financially or otherwise) for such firms to handle, and "the undesirable cases, the dirty work, those areas of practice that have associated with them an aura of influencing and fixing and that involve arrangements with clients and others that are felt by the large firms to be professionally damaging. The latter category includes local tax, municipal, personal injury, divorce, and criminal matters."[57]

Carlin distinguishes between upper-level and lower-level individual practitioners; the former may have a more stable and secure small-business clientele for whom they perform a wider range of less routine services. It is primarily the lower-level, solo practitioners who are bogged down in the dirty work of the law, whose financial circumstances are perilous, and for whom getting business represents a continuous battle.

At the outset, many lawyers trying to establish practices of their own are closely tied to the local neighbourhood, a situation that few find satisfactory. As a fairly successful neighbourhood practitioner told Carlin:

> People don't look at the neighbourhood lawyer as on the same professional level as the lawyer in the Loop — but on the same level as service people, real estate and insurance brokers, and similar types of nonprofessional categories. He's looked at more as a neighbourhood businessman rather than as a professional. Doctors don't have that problem; you don't consider Loop doctors to be on a completely different level.[58]

Going beyond the neighbourhood, the solo lawyer seeks contact with potential clients through membership in a range of communal organizations, which usually have an ethnic or religious basis. Politics is also seen as a useful means of extending one's clientele, as well as developing helpful court and other official contacts. But often these methods are insufficient, and it becomes necessary to rely on individuals who, for one reason or another may be in a position to channel legal business in his direction. As Carlin notes, such a "broker" (between lawyer and client) may be "another lawyer, an accountant, a real estate or insurance broker or agent, a building contractor, a doctor, a policeman, bondsman, precinct captain, garage mechanic, minister, undertaker, plant personnel director, foreman, etc."[59] Personal injury cases often are referred by a variety of individuals who may serve as "runners"; waitresses and bar girls may refer divorce matters, policemen criminal matters. At the same time, and especially in connection with wills, business, and real-estate matters, these lawyers face continuous and increasingly strong competition from nonlegal sources, such as banks, real-estate brokers, and accountants. These competitors often have the edge both in specialized skill and visibility; and as Carlin points out, the lawyer cannot today claim exclusive access to the agencies that process the matters in question.

Apart from the sheer difficulty of earning a decent living under these circumstances, the less successful of the individual practitioners experience a generalized and severe status dilemma. Whereas "law appeared to provide the easiest and cheapest avenue to professional status ... they find that access to the higher status positions is all but closed to them and that the positions they do manage to achieve are often marginal, their practice residual, and their foothold in the profession precarious."[60] Not only is much of their work relatively insignificant by the dominant standards of the profession, but they have very little contact (and virtually no sense of real colleagueship) with the more successful, large-firm lawyers. Individual practitioners rarely attain positions of leadership in the bar, and in fact they are not even as likely as large-firm lawyers to maintain membership in the leading professional associations, often finding it more valuable to be active in the smaller, ethnic bar associations. While solo lawyers can at least pride themselves on being their own boss, most seem to recognize that this independence is a very mixed blessing.[61]

Of course it must be kept in mind that the "Wall Street lawyer" and the lower-level individual practitioner represent the extreme points of a continuum along which legal practices vary. In between are numerous gradations involving membership in a variety of middle-sized and small firms, many of which are very successful and handle a considerable range of interesting legal work. Also, it should be noted that there certainly are some individuals who practice on their own and attain a high degree of success, both financially and in terms of professional standing. This attainment may occur particularly when a lawyer develops a reputation for great skill in a highly specialized field, such as patent law, literary property, civil liberties, or even matrimonial or criminal law. Indeed, all of the comments made thus far concerning stratification within the metropolitan bar must be recognized as reflecting statistical regularities only. They refer to large classes of individual instances, and to each generalization there are undoubtedly specific exceptions.

Furthermore, the major studies of legal practice have concentrated almost exclusively on lawyers in the largest metropolitan centers. As Carlin mentions, "In comparison with the highly stratified metropolitan bar, the smaller city bar has over the years remained a fairly homogeneous professional community." Attributing this homogeneity partly to the absence of huge "law factories," he noted that (in 1958) there were no firms with as many as fifteen lawyers in American cities of less than 200,000 population, and very few with more than five or six lawyers.[62] Similarly, there has been virtually no sociological analysis of the position and functions of the small-town lawyer. Legal practice in such a setting undoubtedly varies a good deal from that of the lone practitioner in the metropolis. It is quite possible that some lawyers in small towns may be able satisfactorily to combine the independence of individual practice with a considerable measure of financial success and professional and social standing within the local community.[63] Other varieties of legal work — including positions in government agencies, in prosecutor's and legal-aid offices, and as "house-counsel" on corporation staffs — also deserve further attention from researchers. Undoubtedly each type of legal practice has its peculiar recruitment and work patterns, compensations, drawbacks, strains, and dilemmas.

(g) Will the Law Society of Alberta Celebrate its Bicentenary?[†]

Harry W. Arthurs

I. INTRODUCTION: THE LINK BETWEEN PROFESSIONAL KNOWLEDGE AND PROFESSIONAL GOVERNANCE

The title of this essay, "Will the Law Society of Alberta Celebrate its Bicentenary?" is intended not as a prediction of impending doom, but rather as an acknowledgment that things change. Things change not only inside the legal profession, but also and especially outside it in society, in the economy, in our political system, and in our natural environment. Those external changes, I will argue, are the primary drivers of internal change. These drivers are so powerful that they are transforming not only legal processes and institutions, not only the profession's clientele and competitive environment, not only the technology and economics of practice, but the very essence of what makes law a profession.[1]

Professions are founded on two premises.[2] The first is that members of the profession know things other people do not. Some of those things they learn from books, others from experience, but always a core body of knowledge is supposedly shared by the members of the profession. Acquiring this body of knowledge is how one gains admission to the profession, and not having a credential which attests to possessing it disqualifies one from doing professional work.[3] The second premise is that their work requires that professionals be allowed to do things forbidden to other people, and vice versa. What can and cannot be done is sometimes laid down by law, sometimes inscribed in formal codes governing professional conduct, and sometimes embedded in cultural practices and traditions. This second premise explains why professions are licensed monopolies and why almost all are at least semi-autonomous and many self-regulating.[4]

Alas, both premises underpinning professionalism have less and less relevance to Canada's legal profession. Lawyers share knowledge less and less with other lawyers, and more and more with people in adjacent lines of work. And lawyers adhere less and less to common codes of conduct, live less and less within a common professional culture, behave more and more like other people, and enjoy dwindling, though still considerable, autonomy.

I am not going to debate whether the decline and fall of legal professionalism might be a good thing or a bad one. Rather I will explain how and why it is happening and sketch out the likely consequences. In each case, I will identify a development out there in the world and then try to show how that development has altered the bar's knowledge base and, ultimately, its political economy, culture, solidarity, autonomy, and governance structures.

II. THE EFFECT OF EXTERNAL CHANGE ON LEGAL ORGANIZATION AND PROFESSIONALISM

I will begin with demographic changes that have occurred since the Law Society of Alberta (LSA) was

† (2008) 45 Alta. L. Rev. 15–27 (Special Issue: Law Society of Alberta 100th Anniversary Conference "Canadian Lawyers in the 21st Century"). Reproduced with permission. [Notes and/or references omitted.]

founded 100 years ago. Canada's population has shifted westwards; it has moved from the countryside to the cities; affluence has increased along with economic inequality; immigration has declined as a percentage of the country's population, but increased in terms of the variety of countries, cultures, and creeds represented amongst our newest communities; the generational balance between young and old has tipped; and, of course, gender roles have been transformed.[5]

These demographic changes have fundamentally altered Canada's political economy and, inevitably, that of the profession as well.[6] Rural societies — like Alberta in 1907 — typically generated little investment capital, supported a short list of businesses, and developed fairly basic forms of social relations and social controls. But greater affluence brings more intense debates over the generation, protection, taxation, and redistribution of wealth; greater inequality and ethno-cultural diversity bring more intense concerns about human rights; urbanization brings greater possibilities for the specialization of economic functions and greater need for and the possibility of the provision of public goods and services; and shifts in the generational balance and in gender roles bring new social tensions and generate the need for new institutions to mediate those tensions.[7]

These demographic changes made possible and necessary the development of fields of legal practice that the founding fathers of the LSA would never have been able to imagine: taxation and consumer law, human rights and refugee law, land use and environmental law, labour law, intellectual property law, estate planning, and energy law. These new, specialized fields of practice are defined by new, specialized forms of knowledge. Obviously, that new knowledge is only distantly related to what lawyers knew in 1907.[8] Less obviously, it is almost equally different from what was taught in law schools as recently as, say, 1967 or 1987.[9] Moreover, specialists do not just become immersed in the new knowledge; they tend to abandon the old. Further, the key point: specialists do not simply read different texts and law reports and develop different skill sets and experiential knowledge; they tend also to serve different clienteles, to speak to them in different vernaculars, and to charge fees which are a different order of magnitude from those charged by other lawyers.[10] And finally, a point I will return to below, the trend to specialization in the legal profession has closely tracked the trend to stratification.

And now a paradox: while specialized knowledge is moving lawyers farther and farther away from most of their professional colleagues, it is moving

them closer and closer to their "relevant others." If you are an energy lawyer, you will want to walk the walk and talk the talk of the oil and gas industry; if you are a labour lawyer, your "relevant others" are Human Resources managers and union officials; and if you are a tax lawyer, you will be spending a lot of time with accountants. Good lawyering for specialists, then, tends to immerse them in adjacent bodies of non-legal knowledge.

Where do general practitioners fit into this picture? They too deploy specialized knowledge, both legal and non-legal, but its depth and breadth is determined by the modest needs and means of their clientele — typically middle- and working-class individuals, and small- or medium-sized businesses. These clients need wills and divorces; they need to incorporate companies and be helped through routine transactions; they need to collect debts and be defended in lower-level civil, criminal, and regulatory proceedings. But they usually do not need — and often cannot afford — the new legal knowledge dispensed by large law firms with their specialized departments. Consequently, compared to specialists, the knowledge base of general practitioners more closely resembles that of their predecessors in 1907.

These disparities in knowledge lead to stratification — to the establishment of a pecking order within the legal community.[11] By and large, specialists enjoy higher economic, social, and professional status than general practitioners.[12] There are exceptions: generalists still count for something in small towns, and they may still make their mark in the general legal community, if they are people of unusual character or talents. However, most general practitioners in large cities, like foxes and racoons, survive and prosper in their new habitat by living on the margins. Survival and prosperity usually involve two strategies. First, they must provide efficient legal services at modest prices: this is achieved by routinizing work, delegating it to lay employees, and keeping overheads low. Second, they must exploit their non-legal advantages, such as close affinity with particular client communities, their familiarity as "repeat players" with the bureaucracies of civic governments or lower courts, or their access to financing or other services desired by clients.[13]

So we have specialists, general practitioners, and a variety of lawyers in other settings such as legal clinics, government offices, and corporate law departments. Now come three key points. The first is that these different kinds of lawyers do not simply know different things and serve different clienteles: they work in different practice settings; they receive different psychic and financial rewards; they are shaped by different professional cultures; and they are subject to what amounts de facto to different professional norms and governance structures.[14]

The second point is that while lawyers do move from one elite firm to another, to boutique firms, or to positions as in-house corporate counsel, there is relatively little movement into elite firms from general practice. Those who begin practice in small firms providing routine services for ordinary people are likely to remain in such firms for the rest of their careers.[15]

The third point is that the lawyers who inhabit these different practice roles do not represent a demographic cross-section of the profession. The "typical" lawyer is no longer a white, male, Anglo-Saxon, middle-aged generalist practising in a suburb or small town. There is no longer a "typical" lawyer. With urbanization, immigration, and feminization, the legal profession has indeed become diverse. The problem is that some lawyers are more "diverse" than others. Women remain under-represented in the higher echelons of elite law firms and over-represented in legal clinics, government jobs, and the ranks of in-house counsel. Members of recent immigrant communities are likely to be found most often in small, general practices, or in specialties, like immigration law, which serve their own communities.[16]

To sum up, then, diversity in professional knowledge, experience, culture, and "success" is significantly determined, reinforced, and compounded by diversity in gender, religion, race, and ethnicity. That is what is meant by "stratification."

So far, I have tried to show how demographic change has transformed the economic context of legal practice, which in turn has radically altered — has in fact shattered — the knowledge base of the profession. The fragmentation of knowledge thus reinforces long-standing tendencies to stratification within the profession.

These developments — specialization, stratification, and the transformation of knowledge — are obviously going to have an effect on professional governance. To make a not very bold prediction: we will soon reach the point where a generic law degree will no longer suffice for admission to all kinds of practice; indeed, in some provinces, specialist credentials are already issued to those with practical experience and advanced knowledge of their field.[17] To make a slightly bolder prediction: law societies will have to formally acknowledge that real estate lawyers, those who act for large corporations in merger and acquisitions (M & A) transactions, and criminal lawyers in boutique firms, present quite different gover-

nance challenges in terms of enforcing fiduciary duties, requiring pro bono work, paying for malpractice insurance, or maintaining competence through mandatory continuing legal education. Law societies will also have to acknowledge that lawyers who work in large organizations, including large law firms, are usually subject to closer surveillance and sometimes held to higher performance standards by those organizations than by the law society itself. And to make the boldest prediction of all: law societies will ultimately have to acknowledge that the many new sub-professions of law are in any practical sense largely beyond their reach, and that they can best be regulated by bodies whose jurisdictions are defined by the new fault lines of an increasingly disparate and divided profession. Hence my first question: "Will the Law Society of Alberta Celebrate its Bicentenary?"

Now another development which also calls into question the longevity of existing forms of professional governance: the development of national and global markets for all goods and services, including legal services.[18] In 1907, Alberta lawyers would have acted almost exclusively for individuals and local businesses, except for a few who were lucky enough to be retained by the banks, railways, or the government. Today, however, many lawyers in Alberta represent giant national and trans-national companies, or local companies closely linked to them on the food chain.[19] These corporations operate on a scale larger than that of many states: they have complex legal needs; they can pay large fees to specialists to have those needs attended to; and they feel they are best served by lawyers who already have a good knowledge of their business rather than having to educate a new lawyer each time they need one. This logic explains the decline of solo practice and small partnerships that predominated [in] the legal profession from its inception in 1907 until the first wave of large metropolitan and regional firms emerged in the 1960s and 1970s, closely followed by national law firms beginning in the 1980s.[20]

The growth of national law firms, in turn, had a significant impact on provincial and local legal cultures, institutions, and governance arrangements. Because of their large and affluent client base, national law firms could afford to assemble teams of specialists; because of their large revenues, they could afford the most advanced information technology and professional management practices; and because of their contacts outside the province, they were able to acquire knowledge of national, foreign, and international law, which enabled them to corner the market on transactions and disputes requiring such expertise. These advantages allowed them, in effect, to transform the local market for legal services. Local law firms could not compete with them, and consequently, had either to merge with an existing national firm, reinvent themselves as national firms, discover a local niche based on unique local connections or information, or face long-term decline.

The advent of national law firms also raised issues of professional governance. Key members of the firm — often leaders or prospective leaders of the local bar — would migrate across provincial boundaries to wherever they were needed, and sometimes, carried on their practice in more than one province. Provincial law societies could no longer justify the exclusion from practice of these peripatetic but prominent practitioners.[21] Provincial and local bar associations suddenly had to contend with members whose professional contacts and concerns were no longer provincial or local. Local legal cultures, built around shared experiences and values, lost some of their capacity to shape professional behaviour, as key members moved away, or were increasingly influenced by experiences and values shared with their colleagues and counterparts in other jurisdictions.

Even the substance of local law was affected. Provincial law schools could no longer pretend to prepare people only for local practice; they had to design their curricula for graduates who would look for jobs in the new national and international markets for legal talent. Local academics understandably shifted their scholarly focus to issues with national or international salience.[22] Local legislators and regulators suddenly had to contend with lobbying and advocacy by lawyers whose imaginations were no longer dominated by local traditions and expectations, with lawyers who knew how things were done elsewhere, and with clients doing business worldwide, who often resented having to comply with idiosyncratic local regulatory regimes in fields such as securities, pensions, and employment standards.[23]

If I were to end my narrative here, I would have made a strong case that the development of national law firms has put into question the long-term survival of provincial law societies. At the very least I would have demonstrated the necessity of designing new national governance structures to complement, perhaps even eclipse, local governing bodies. However, there is another chapter to the story.

III. GLOBALIZATION AND THE ERODING LOGIC OF LOCAL PROFESSIONAL GOVERNANCE

Globalization has also begun to call into question the future of those very same national law firms or,

if not globalization in the broadest sense, then our increasing integration into a North American economic space dominated by the United States. This crucial development I have called "the hollowing out of corporate Canada."[24] Let me first define my terms, and then explain the significance of "hollowing out" for Canada's lawyers and Alberta's in particular. "Hollowing out" has two dimensions. First, significant Canadian corporations, especially in the energy and resource sectors, have been bought out by large firms based in the U.S.[25] Second, other large companies, especially in manufacturing, have been reorganized so that their well-established Canadian subsidiaries enjoy far less functional autonomy than they used to.[26] The result of these two developments is that there are fewer Canadian corporate head offices than previously, and that those which have survived often have less need for high-end legal services than they used to. Moreover, Canadian firms in the financial services sector, in commercial real estate, advertising, accounting, consulting, and other so-called "business services," also face a loss of clientele, and consequently a diminishing need for lawyers. And even when they do need lawyers — to apply for a trademark, say, or to float an initial public offering of equities — the value-added contributed by their Canadian lawyer has been diminished to the extent that Canadian securities and intellectual property legislation has been brought closely into line with that of the U.S.[27]

To be clear, I am neither attacking nor defending globalization in general, or continental economic integration under the *North American Free Trade Agreement Between the Government of Canada, the Government of Mexico, and the Government of the United States*[28] in particular. Rather, I am offering an hypothesis about the possible effects of our new political economy on the prospects of Canadian lawyers. If my hypothesis proves to be correct, law firms in Calgary, Edmonton, Toronto, and Montreal, which used to provide high-end legal services to important locally-based corporations, will have to start looking elsewhere for clients.

Where might they look? One place, of course, is to the new foreign-based corporations which increasingly dominate some sectors of the Canadian economy. In the short term, this tactic will prove successful. When companies are merged, acquired, or restructured, there is lots of one-off work for corporate, pension, real estate, and securities lawyers.[29] But over time, as the new corporate arrangements are set in place, Canadian lawyers will gradually be replaced on key files by lawyers retained in Chicago or Houston by global head offices located in those cities. Major Canadian law firms may then try to restore their client base by poaching clients from their direct competitors. This strategy again may succeed in the short-term, but in the long-term, as the number and the autonomy of surviving Canadian corporations continues to dwindle, there will be fewer and fewer clients left to poach. A third strategy for national law firms is to reinvent themselves as international firms,[30] or to become the Canadian affiliate of international firms based in New York or London.[31] This is an intriguing possibility, but so far, results have been rather disappointing. Canadian firms can only survive abroad if they can ride the coat-tails of Canadian corporate clients doing business in Shanghai, Frankfurt, or Bangalore. The problem is that not very many Canadian businesses are doing business in such exotic locales. Thus, while a few Canadian law firms have managed to gain a toe-hold in the U.S., and a few in the United Kingdom and Asia, they seem to have had difficulty in sustaining momentum.

Thus, the hollowing out of corporate Canada may turn out to be the hollowing out of legal Canada as well. This would be a severe disappointment for people who hoped that the emergence of national markets, corporations, and law firms might provide Canada with concentrations of wealth and talent, with economies of scale, and with the new thinking necessary to build a successful economy and a compassionate society. Ironically, however, the demise of corporate Canada and the disappearance of national law firms might leave us back where we began a century ago: with a profession devoted to the simple problems of local clients — not a bad thing in itself, but not a happy prospect for over-invested law firms and ambitious lawyers. If that is the trajectory of Canada's legal professions, it becomes more likely that governing bodies in 2107 will still be provincial. Whether they will also be parochial depends a great deal on the next and final theme I will explore.

IV. HYPHENATED PROFESSIONALISM: THE MOST FUNDAMENTAL CHALLENGE TO PROFESSIONAL GOVERNANCE

That theme involves what I will call "hyphenated professionalism." As I suggested earlier, professionalism involves two main aspects: a unique base of knowledge, and a regulated monopoly over the use of that knowledge. What happens, then, when lay people gain access to knowledge that formerly was exclusively possessed by professionals, and when lawyers lose or surrender their monopoly over the use of such knowledge?

De-professionalization is my first example.[32] Lay people today can acquire legal knowledge which they formerly would have had to buy from a lawyer. Bookstores sell self-help books and the internet has become an infinite font of legal wisdom. Service providers and paralegals incorporate companies, litigate traffic tickets, and represent would-be immigrants and injured workers before specialized tribunals. Law firms and law societies themselves legitimize de-professionalization, if they do not actively promote it, by delegating many legal functions to law clerks and, in Ontario at least, by undertaking to credentialize and regulate them.[33] The net effect is that the legal profession has gradually surrendered its monopoly over many of the tasks that it used to perform or control.

The causes of de-professionalization are pretty obvious: people are more educated than they used to be and have greater confidence in handling their own affairs; many legal procedures have been simplified and standardized to the point where they can be easily mastered by people who lack formal training in law; and information technology has made legal knowledge almost as accessible to lay people as it is to lawyers themselves. And there is one more reason: lawyers are unwilling or unable to deliver certain kinds of standard services at prices that most people can afford. Of course, de-professionalization is fraught with risks. Law clerks, legal agents, service providers, and especially individuals representing themselves can overlook complexities, make mistakes, and exacerbate disputes. On the other hand, they generally do not do so; and lawyers sometimes do.

De-professionalization, whatever its causes and consequences, raises difficult issues for law societies. How can they fight to protect a monopoly over knowledge which clients — the supposed beneficiaries of monopoly — are keen to access directly? How can they insist on the exclusive right of lawyers to deliver certain kinds of services when lawyers retained to deliver those services insist on delegating them to law clerks? And how can the provision of services no longer within the profession's monopoly be regulated to ensure that consumers are protected and unscrupulous service providers are banned from the market?

It would be rash to predict that the profession's monopoly over routine legal procedures and transactions will continue to erode to the point where there is no monopoly left at all. But in the past hundred years, things which were once the staples of legal practice have ceased to be, and the trend seems unlikely to abate.

Indeed, the trend seems likely to move up-market, which brings me to the second of my hyphens, multi-professionalism. As I have already suggested, many legal specialists work in close collaboration with experts in other disciplines. That collaboration is organized either through free-standing, multi-disciplinary practices or, in states which do not permit such practices, through large consulting firms. Indeed, several consulting firms employ so many lawyers that they rank amongst the largest law firms in the world.[34] Sometimes, too, law firms in Canada and elsewhere build up their own in-house consultancies, in which lawyers work alongside economists, planners, other professionals. And sometimes, members of several professions simply work together within the departmental structures of large business corporations.

There is a powerful logic to multi-professional or multi-disciplinary practice.[35] It enhances the likelihood that all relevant skills and knowledge will be mobilized to address the problem at hand; it reduces the likelihood that members of one profession will play a dominant role to the prejudice of another, and ultimately, of the client; it forces all professional participants to rethink the unexplored assumptions of their own discipline or profession in ways which can lead to useful innovation; and of course it can be, should be, more cost-effective for clients.

Professional governing bodies, however, have been reluctant to allow lawyers to participate in multi-disciplinary practices other than those clearly controlled by members of the bar.[36] The ostensible reason is that members of other professions cannot be held to the same high ethical standards as lawyers. While this reasoning is somewhat suspect as a veiled effort at market control, the Enron scandal and others involving the "big five" (or "four" or "three") international consulting firms certainly dampened enthusiasm for multi-professional practices in Canada and elsewhere.

The question is whether the advantages mentioned earlier will ultimately lead to a revival of their credibility and popularity. That is what is going to happen, I believe: multi-disciplinary practices are coming to Canada and the U.S., just as they have come to some European countries, and very recently, to England.[37] Law societies will therefore have to find a way to cope with the new reality that many lawyers will be collaborating more closely with colleagues in other professions than they do with fellow lawyers. Obviously, there are difficulties. At least in the short run, the governing body of each profession will have to restrict its regulatory activities to its own members. And in light of the different histories of the professions, each of the governing bodies is likely to have its own special view of how to regulate honesty, confidentiality, conflicts of interest, and especially, competence. However, sooner, rather than later, we are likely to find that regulation is being exercised by or under the supervision of an umbrella body whose mandate extends to all members of multi-professional or multi-disciplinary practices. In the long run, it seems quite possible that the boundaries amongst the professions will begin to dissolve.

This leads me to my third example of hyphenated professionalism: "post-professionalism."[38] The idea of post-professionalism is pretty simple, but its implications are far-reaching. Essentially, the argument runs, professional boundaries laid down in earlier times no longer have much meaning in the context of our post-industrial, knowledge-based economy. All information, all learning, and all skills relevant to the solution of a given problem should be mobilized for the purpose, and can be mobilized, thanks to new information technologies. However, unlike multi-professional firms, in which each member contributes from within the defined territory of his or her profession, post-professionalism envisages that individual practitioners will be able to do whatever they have the inclination and capacity to do. In a post-professional world, clusters of professions — broadly construed to include all knowledge-based occupations — will dissolve into each other. What post-professional practitioners will have in common is their general knowledge of a social, economic, or technical field, and the ability to recognize its problems, to find solutions, and to know when to seek help from someone with specialized knowledge.

This is not an entirely far-fetched scenario. In fact, it is a reasonably accurate description of the way many lawyers practice today: working far outside the boundaries of their formal legal knowledge; providing strategic advice based on their experience and specialized knowledge of other fields; assembling ad hoc teams of collaborators; and, as suggested earlier, seeing the "client" community as their relevant other, rather than the legal profession. It is also a description of the way in which many students are already pursuing their "legal" educations: taking advanced degrees in other disciplines before or after law school, taking courses in other faculties while studying law, or reading materials from other disciplines as part of their regular law courses.

So legal professionalism is being redefined by three hyphens and three prefixes: de-, multi-, and post-. In each case, a change in the nature, distribution, and deployment of knowledge is detaching lawyers from their familiar, historical roles as advice-givers and advocates who "own" a monopoly over a particular field of human endeavour because they "own" a monopoly over a particular kind of knowledge. Because law societies are mandated to police that monopoly, prevent its abuse, and ensure its use in the public interest, this represents a challenge to their very existence.

V.   CONCLUSION

I have tried to show how developments external to the legal profession are leading to internal changes which are likely to threaten its knowledge base, its monopoly, its governance structures, and perhaps its very existence. I have mentioned three specific examples of such developments: changing demography, globalization, and the dissolution of professional boundaries. I could have mentioned many more: climate change, technology, juridification, the privatization of law production, and new ideas about states and markets come immediately to mind. Thus the question confronting Canadian lawyers, and their governing bodies, is not simply whether, or even how, law societies will be affected by these transformative developments, it is whether they can survive them at all.

(h)   Implementation of Paralegal Regulation in Ontario — Introduction†

The Law Society of Upper Canada

OVERVIEW

The regulation of paralegals has been discussed and recommended in Ontario since the early 1990s. Many studies commissioned by government and by paralegals concluded that a regulatory system was essential to protect the public interest. The increasing number of individuals providing legal services without a licence, without rules, and often without insurance meant the public was increasingly at risk.

In August 1999 the Ontario Court of Appeal commented, in the case of *R. v. Romanowicz*:

> A person who decides to sell T-shirts on the sidewalk needs a licence and is subject to government regulation. That same person can, however, without any form of government regulation, represent a person in a complicated criminal case where that person may be sentenced to up to 18 months imprisonment. Unregulated representation by agents who are not required to have any particular training or ability in complex and difficult criminal proceedings where a person's liberty and livelihood are at stake invites miscarriages of justice.

There was, however, no consensus on the question of who should regulate paralegals. The 1990 Ianni Task Force recommended that paralegals be regulated within the Ministry of Consumer and Commercial Relations. In 2000, Justice Peter deCarteret Cory recommended a free-standing regulatory agency funded by the government. There were conflicting opinions also on the areas of practice for which paralegals should be licensed. There were calls to expand and recommendations to restrict the scope of practice.

There were concerns that the costs of creating a new government regulatory body would be significant and an unwanted burden to taxpayers. The time and money required to establish such a body also militated against it. The option of self-regulation by paralegals, although frequently discussed over the years, had not been achieved.

While regulation was not progressing, the presence of paralegals, particularly in traffic court and small claims court, and before administrative boards and tribunals, grew markedly. Most of these para-

---

† From The Law Society of Upper Canada, *Report to the Attorney General of Ontario on the Implementation of Paralegal Regulation in Ontario: Pursuant to subsection 63.01.1(2) of the Law Society Act*, January 2009. Reproduced with permission. [Notes and/or references omitted.]

legals were competent and ethical. But stories began to appear in the media about members of the public being victimized by unscrupulous individuals providing legal services. Without a regulatory program in place for paralegals, members of the public had no recourse when problems arose. When problems with a lawyer arise, the public can turn to The Law Society of Upper Canada to address their concerns.

Early in 2004, the Attorney General of Ontario asked The Law Society of Upper Canada (the Law Society) to consider taking on the responsibility for regulating paralegals in the province. The Law Society established a Task Force that undertook extensive consultations through much of that year, meeting with paralegal associations, lawyers, judges, legal associations, community and private colleges and the public. Members of the Task Force travelled to Ottawa, London, Thunder Bay, North Bay, Sudbury, Kitchener–Waterloo, Orangeville, Windsor, Kingston and Toronto to gather input. They were then faced with the task of transforming hours of comment into a succinct and representative report. In September of 2004, the Law Society adopted the Task Force Report with 22 recommendations outlining a regulatory framework and a scope of practice. The Law Society submitted the report to the government.

After reviewing the report, the government introduced Bill 14. Consideration of the Bill included 14 days of public hearings by the legislature's Standing Committee on Justice Policy. Bill 14 contained amendments to the Law Society Act, expanding the mandate of the Law Society to provide for the regulation of paralegals in the public interest. The Bill was given Third Reading and received Royal Assent on October 19, 2006.

MAKING PARALEGAL REGULATION A REALITY

With the passage of Bill 14, the Law Society had six months to put the fundamentals of an entirely new regulatory framework in place. Specifically, by May 1, 2007, the Law Society had to provide paralegal applicants with a registration process, application forms, insurance requirements and rules of professional conduct. Work also had to begin urgently on a licensing examination, and a fee structure. The administrative support necessary to accomplish all this drew heavily from every department in the Law Society.

At the beginning of the process no one knew how many paralegals were practising in Ontario. The Law Society and the paralegal associations estimated there might be between 750 and 1,000. No registry or database with contact information existed. No infrastructure was in place to contact paralegals, or to respond to their many inquiries about regulation.

From that starting point, the Law Society has built an entire regulatory system in two years, complete with educational standards, rules of professional conduct, a licensing process, insurance requirements, a public directory, a complaints and disciplinary process, and a compensation fund. This was accomplished by the Law Society without burdening taxpayers or the government.

THE PARALEGAL STANDING COMMITTEE

The Paralegal Standing Committee was the first part of the regulatory model to be implemented. This committee has five paralegal members, five lawyers and three lay members. The chair is a paralegal. The committee develops and recommends to Convocation the necessary policy for all aspects of licensing, accreditation, monitoring and discipline of paralegals. The individuals who made up the original committee were Chair Paul Dray, Vice-Chair William Simpson, Andrea Alexander, Marion Boyd, James Caskey, Anne Marie Doyle, Michelle Haigh, Abraham Feinstein, Thomas Heintzman, Brian Lawrie, Margaret Louter, Stephen Parker and Bonnie Warkentin.

The work of the committee, supported by Law Society staff, continues to be extensive. The deadlines are often compressed. The Committee reviews all aspects of paralegal regulation and takes forward recommendations to Convocation.

In the first six months of 2007, the committee met eight times. Its reports for those meetings total 563 pages. It worked through a daunting range of issues including:

- Grandparent and transitional applicant criteria
- Application process, forms and reference letters
- *Paralegal Rules of Conduct*
- Trust account rules
- Exemptions and licensing by-laws
- Licensing process
- Insurance requirements
- Budget and fee schedule
- Communications plans
- Professional corporations and business structures rules.

LICENSING PROCESS FOR GRANDPARENT AND TRANSITIONAL CANDIDATES

Paralegals with at least three years prior experience providing legal services were invited to apply under a 'grandparent' provision with a six-month window, beginning May 1, 2007. Transitional candidates were those with less than three years experience but with relevant education or training. The application forms and instruction guides for both grandparent and transitional candidates were created and posted on-line in time for the May 1, 2007 implementation date. This required considerable technical support to build the web pages that housed the application, develop the application into a downloadable, fill-able PDF and Word document, and create a tool to automatically generate a unique application ID number for each application downloaded.

Through the same period, a major focus for staff from the Professional Development and Competence Department was the establishment of paralegal competencies, the development of reference materials, and the formulation of the licensing examination questions. This work was without precedent. Again, the deadlines were tight. The licensing examinations had to be produced in English and French, validated and kept entirely secure. Staff prepared a complete study guide in hard copy and electronic format to help paralegals prepare for the licensing examination.

Looking beyond the grandparent and transitional candidates, the Law Society was also working throughout this period with public and private colleges and with the Ministry of Training, Colleges and Universities to establish a system of standards and accreditation for paralegal diploma courses. By the end of the review period, there were nine accredited colleges offering programs of study that will give paralegal students the opportunity to write the licensing examination.

Many of the grandparent and transitional applicants applied during the last week. Client Service Centre staff along with volunteers from other staff departments worked virtually around the clock to review and process more than 2,200 applications that arrived by the October 31, 2007 deadline. Those applicants who met all the criteria were permitted to practise as "paralegal candidates" and invited to write a licensing examination early in 2008.

Paralegals were able to write the examination in English or French in five locations across the province: Toronto, London, Ottawa, Sudbury and Thunder Bay. This meant that Law Society staff needed to find secure venues and competent invigilators in all those cities. The first sitting of the examination was on January 17, 2008. Two additional sittings were provided on February 27 and April 2 for those applicants who were unable to attend the January session or who needed a second chance to write the examination.

Successful applicants were notified by the Law Society and invited to complete the licensing process by submitting their annual fee and a registration package, subject to the 'good character' review discussed below. By May of 2008, the Law Society began issuing licences. At the end of October 2008, the 2,000th licence had been issued.

LEGAL AFFAIRS

The amendments to the *Law Society Act* contained in Bill 14 are extensive. One consequence has been the need to draft amendments to the Law Society's by-laws. This work, done by the Law Society's own legal department, has been a significant task, and continues to be so. Through the implementation of paralegal regulation, the Paralegal Standing Committee and Convocation have passed amendments to virtually every by-law of the Law Society. The revised by-laws must be translated into French and vetted carefully in both languages before being posted on the website.

PARALEGAL RULES OF CONDUCT

In a very compressed time period, Law Society staff from the Professional Regulation Department developed a complete set of rules to govern the conduct of paralegals. The rules are based on the existing *Rules of Professional Conduct* for lawyers and on principles found in the 2004 *Report of the Task Force on Paralegal Regulation*, as well as on comments from stakeholders. The rules are structured around obligations to various parties, including general duties, as well as duties to clients, tribunals, other licensees and to the Law Society. Other issues covered by the rules are conflicts of interest, confidentiality, advocacy, civility, and fees and retainers.

Of particular importance was the establishment of the rules on trust accounts — an important safeguard for client fees in the event a paralegal becomes incapacitated or is otherwise unable to provide paid-for services. Once fully phased in, by 2010, these rules will be the same as the rules governing lawyers' trust accounts.

Work was then required on the process for receiving and investigating consumer complaints about paralegals. This meant updating and adapting procedures, policies and case management to ensure the Law Society would be able to deal with complaints about paralegals in a timely, fair, transparent and effective manner. The Law Society also established a compensation fund to help clients who have suffered financial loss as a result of a paralegal's dishonesty.

GOOD CHARACTER REQUIREMENT

During the grandparent and transitional licensing process, some 400 applicants disclosed matters that required an investigation of their good character. More than half have now been approved for licensing.

A dedicated team of Law Society staff is continuing to process the remaining matters and conclude investigations as soon as possible. In some cases, the Law Society expects a formal, public hearing will be necessary to determine whether a paralegal licence should be granted or refused.

These applicants are permitted to continue practising as long as they meet the requirements of the application process, such as maintaining professional liability insurance and complying with the *Paralegal Rules of Conduct*, until a Hearing Panel determines that they are ineligible for a licence. The public directory on the website denotes these individuals as 'paralegal candidates' instead of licensees.

NEW PARALEGAL CANDIDATES

The next group of paralegals to be licensed are those who have been enrolled in a paralegal program of study ending in 2008. They were invited to write a licensing examination in August, with a second sitting in October 2008. There are about 300 of these candidates. Law Society staff prepared a complete licensing examination and study package for this group, just as for the grandparent candidates. Successful candidates will receive licences to practise before the end of the year, provided good character issues are not raised.

COMMUNICATING WITH PARALEGALS, LAWYERS, AND THE PUBLIC

The first communications priority in early 2007 was to reach paralegals who were already practising and those already enrolled in formal training to provide legal services — the 'grandparent' and 'transitional' applicants. No registry or database with contact information existed. The first formal communication between the Law Society and paralegal applicants was a teleconference held on April 24, 2007. More than 800 participants took part in the call. The licensing process for grandparent applicants was explained, as well as the rules for continuing to practise, before examinations were held and licences issued. An hour-and-a-half of questions and answers made up the second half of the teleconference.

After the teleconference the Law Society received over 200 queries by e-mail. Staff from Professional Regulation, Professional Development and Competence, Legal Affairs, Policy and the Client Service Centre met for two days to review and develop answers to the questions. A list of Questions and Answers was posted on the website. Over the following two months, the Client Service Centre received an additional 600 e-mail enquiries. The majority of these questions were answered within two days. Client Service Centre staff continue to receive queries on a daily basis and strive to maintain the same response time.

Electronic registration for the teleconference allowed the Law Society to build a distribution list for e-mail use. The Law Society created an electronic newsletter, *Paralegal Update*, specifically for paralegals, with monthly summaries of new developments in the growth of the regulatory system. Nine editions of *Paralegal Update* have been issued to date. A new section dedicated to paralegals was created on the Law Society's website. Professional notices, amendments to rules and by-laws, insurance requirements and other material continue to be provided to paralegals through these pages. They attract several thousand visits every month, including more than 48,000 in the first half of 2008. Representatives of the Law Society continue to meet with paralegal organizations and to attend seminars and conferences as another way to provide current information. A second teleconference for paralegals, held in 2008, covered issues related to business structures and the use of trust accounts.

The Law Society also needed to keep lawyers, the courts and the public informed of the development and implementation of paralegal regulation. Law Society publications, including the *Ontario Lawyers Gazette* and the *Ontario Reports*, as well as media releases, the website, e-mails and printed brochures were distributed. Many media interviews have been given on all aspects of paralegal regulation. Staff have appeared as guest speakers at conferences and meetings with various members of the legal community.

Since May 2007, the Law Society has maintained a public directory of licensed paralegals. The directory provides contact information and is searchable by name or postal code. It mirrors the public directory for lawyers.

OTHER OUTREACH ACTIVITIES

In building the regulatory model, the Law Society worked closely with other stakeholders in the legal system. This included establishing consultative roundtables with interested organizations and consulting with key contacts:

- Senior judges from all levels of court.
- Justices of the Peace and Deputy Small Claims Court Judges, before whom paralegals very often appear.
- Paralegal organizations including the Paralegal Society of Ontario, the Institute of Agents at Court (now the Licensed Paralegal Association of Ontario), the Paralegal Society of Canada and several other smaller groups and individual paralegals.
- College Advisory Group — this group, established by the Law Society, met several times to advise on the development of the requirements for the accredited college course and field placement.
- The Legal Organizations Group, including major legal organizations such as the Ontario Bar Association, The Advocates' Society and the County & District Law Presidents' Association, met several times.
- The Criminal Lawyers' Association and the Family Lawyers' Association also met with the Law Society several times.
- The Law Society organized advisory meetings with tribunals, to which a large number of the administrative tribunals in Ontario sent senior representatives. This was in addition to separate meetings with several of the larger tribunals, including:
  - The Financial Services Commission of Ontario (FSCO) — this tribunal had developed a form of paralegal regulation, the Register of Statutory Accident Benefit Representatives. The advice of the staff at FSCO was particularly helpful.
  - The Workplace Safety and Insurance Board (WSIB) — this board is one of the largest in Ontario in terms of paralegal activity and the Law Society continues to work closely with the WSIB on a range of issues.
  - The Workplace Safety and Insurance Appeals Tribunal, to which cases from WSIB may be appealed, also provided helpful advice.

- The Assessment Review Board met with the Law Society several times to discuss its perspective.

THE COST OF PARALEGAL REGULATION

The many studies undertaken prior to 2004 raised concerns about the costs of establishing a regulatory scheme for paralegals. A new regulatory body of this nature would normally be expected to incur significant new costs in overhead and development. The ability to use the existing Law Society infrastructure has enhanced the efficiency of the regulatory model. Paralegals pay a proportionate share of the services offered by the Law Society, including information technology, advisory services, human resources and policy development.

The licensing fee structure set out for paralegals and approved by Convocation in February 2007 was as follows:

Application fee	$500
Examination fee	$1,075
Additional materials	$150
Licensing fee	$125

The annual fee approved by Convocation was $845, which included a Compensation Fund levy of $145 and a capital levy of $75. Since licences were issued part way through 2008, paralegals were required to pay only a pro-rated portion of the annual fee for 2008.

The larger-than-expected number of applicants has assisted with the self-funding of the model. Taxpayers and lawyers have not borne the cost of paralegal regulation. The fee structure is designed to sustain this self-funding model.

OTHER PERSPECTIVES ON PARALEGAL REGULATION

The Law Society welcomed the newly licensed paralegals in a series of receptions held in their honour in May and June of 2008. Six receptions were held, in London, Ottawa, Thunder Bay, Sudbury, and two in Toronto. More than 900 paralegals attended. Their comments were overwhelmingly positive about the work of the Law Society in creating and implementing the regulatory system.

In a recent note to the Chief Executive Officer of the Law Society, the Attorney General commented on paralegal regulation: "The Law Society continues to face this challenge with great professionalism and you have made remarkable progress. The people of Ontario will not only have greater access to justice as a result of increased access to a greater selection of legal service providers, but they will also be better served by licensed and regulated professionals."

The President of the Paralegal Society of Ontario, Chris Surowiak, says: "Paralegal regulation has been a positive step in our profession. The Law Society has an open door for the Paralegal Society of Ontario, which makes it easier to address our concerns. Knowing that exemptions to licensing are being looked at is important to us as well."

LOOKING AHEAD

Implicit in the comments of both the Attorney General and the President of the Paralegal Society of Ontario is the positive acceptance of the regulatory work done to date by the Law Society. There is also an understanding that further development of the model will be required over time.

The Law Society's implementation of paralegal regulation will continue to attract the interest of other jurisdictions. Paralegals are not regulated anywhere else in North America. The increasing demands for access to justice and consumer protection are not limited to Ontario. What happens here, therefore, will be watched very closely.

Ontario now has more than 2,000 licensed paralegals providing legal services throughout the province. A year ago, there were none. The regulation of paralegals by the Law Society is precedent-setting. It is transforming the provision of legal services in the province by improving consumer protection and access to justice.

The process of achieving regulation has been open and efficient. The regulatory system is self-funding and has won the support of paralegals, lawyers, judges and the public.

(a)   Justice and the Jury†

W. Neil Brooks and Anthony N. Doob

The jury has been described as serving one of two separate functions. It can be seen as an institution designed to ensure the accuracy of fact finding in the adjudication of disputes, applying to the facts of the dispute the law as given by the judge; or it can be seen as an institution which has the right to construe or ignore a relevant rule of law in a case in which its application would not be in accord with the notions of justice and fairness prevailing in the community. After a short review of some of the views taken on each of these sides, we consider the kinds of extra-legal factors that appear to influence jury decisions.

An important function of the legal process is settling controversies by adjudicating competing claims. Characteristically, judicial dispute resolution involves the application of a relevant and fixed rule of law to the factual conflict situation that is found to exist between two contesting parties. To be an effective means of social ordering in a democratic society the application of rules of law must obviously result in decisions that are morally acceptable to the community at large. That is to say, the outcome of adjudication must correspond with shared notions of what is equitable and fair between the parties to the dispute, whether one party is the state and the other a private person, or whether both are private parties.

Rules of law, however, have another important function. They permit social intercourse by serving as guidelines on the basis of which people may plan their affairs, knowing the consequence of different

courses of action. To achieve this purpose, rules of law must be formulated at a level of generality that permits each rule to govern the consequence of recurrent factual situations. The necessity on the one hand for general fixed rules of law to regulate social action and the necessity on the other hand for rules that will result in the just resolution of all disputes poses a dilemma for the legal system. A general rule can be formulated that guides behavior and that results in the just resolution of most disputes controlled by it. However, a fact situation will inevitably arise in which, because of the particular equities between the parties to the dispute, a disposition of the case in accord with the relevant rule of law will result in an outcome that does not correspond with the community's notion of fairness, since a judge's decision in a particular case gives rise to a precedent that controls the disposition of all similar cases. Attempts by judges to interpret a general rule of law to reach a just decision in a case in which the equities between the parties are peculiar might cause injustices in future cases: "Hard cases make bad law" is a well known legal adage. A judicial institution that is capable, at least in theory, of resolving the tension between the need for general rules of law and the need to resolve each dispute equitably is the jury.

The proper role of the jury has been the subject of extended and often vigorous debate in legal and political literature. The jury may be seen and defended as fundamentally a political institution

---

† (1975) 31 *Journal of Social Issues* at 171–82. Copyright c1975 by W. Neil Brooks and Anthony N. Doob. Reproduced with permissions of Blackwell Publishing Ltd.. [Notes and/or references omitted.]

which has the right to construe or ignore a relevant rule of law in a case in which its application would not be in accord with the notions of justice and fairness prevailing in the community. This view has been advocated by a number of eminent legal scholars.

Wigmore, the great evidence scholar, urged that the jury's role was to supply "that flexibility of legal rules which is essential to justice and popular contentment" (1929, p. 170). Justice Holmes suggested:

> One reason why I believe in our practice of leaving questions of negligence to the jury is that jurors will introduce into their verdict a certain amount — a very large amount, so far as I have observed — of popular prejudice, and thus keep the administration of the law in accord with the wishes and feelings of the community. (1889, pp. 459–460)

Dean Pound noted that "Jury lawlessness is the great corrective of law in its actual administration" (1910, p. 36). As stated in a Columbia Law Review paper: "Respect for the law is increased when law operates with scrupulous firmness, but with the leaven of charity that is added when the jury acts as the conscience of the community" ("Trial by Jury," 1969, p. 471). The relative importance that is often placed on the jury's role in construing the law in a particular case is illustrated by a statement made in 1789 by Thomas Jefferson: "Were I called upon to decide whether the people had best be omitted in the legislative or judicial departments, I would say it is better to leave them out of the legislative. The execution of the laws is more important than the making of them" (cited in Howe, 1939). Indeed Lord Devlin went so far as to declare: "Each jury is a little parliament. The jury sense is the parliamentary sense" (1956, p. 114).

On the other hand, the jury may be viewed simply as an institution designed to ensure the accuracy of fact finding in the adjudication of disputes, its task being to apply to the facts of the dispute before it, as the jurors find them, the law as given to them by the judge in his instructions. If the general rule of law they are asked to apply appears to result in a harsh or unjust decision in the particular case, that is of no consequence to them in reaching their verdict. Indeed the United States Supreme Court in a case in 1895 (*Sparf & Hansen v. United States*) expressly held that the jury was bound to follow the judge's instructions on the law. The court reasoned that certainty and uniformity in the application of the law was more important than flexibility in individual cases.

Throughout history the legal system has been ambivalent about which of these two roles the jury should assume. When jury trials first emerged in England in the twelfth century, juries were required to apply the law to the facts of the dispute, of which they were assumed to have personal knowledge. If a jury returned a verdict that was found to be wrong they were subject to punishment (Thayer, 1898). However, by the seventeenth century the prevailing view appeared to be that the jury could consider in reaching their verdict the peculiar equities in the case before them. Lord Hale, discussing the function of the jury in 1665, stated, "It is the conscience of the jury that must pronounce the prisoner guilty or not guilty" (cited in Scheflin, 1972). Five years later the judges in Bushnell's Case (1670) held that there was no recourse against the jury for acquitting a person even though the judge or a subsequent jury concluded that the jury's decision was not decided according to the law. Even though it was taken as established that the jury was not accountable for its verdict, and that a verdict of acquittal by the jury was final, several American judges in the middle and late nineteenth century returned to the theoretical position that the jury's only role was to determine the propositions of fact in dispute. The jury, they argued, had no right to refuse to apply the strict letter of the law. These cases are discussed in Howe (1939), in the Yale Law Journal ("The Changing Role," 1964) and in Scheflin (1972). Within the past five years, however, there appears to have been a return to the common law position of the sixteenth century. The decisions in a number of cases, including several Supreme Court of United States decisions have assumed, and several judges have noted, that an important function of the jury is to consider the conscience of the community in reaching its verdict ("Trial by Jury," 1969).

In two states, Indiana and Maryland, the jury's right to nullify the law is given constitutional status, and juries in those states are instructed that they may ignore the strict application of the law. The state of Kansas was considering a constitutional amendment requiring that the following instruction be given to juries:

> It is difficult to draft legal statements that are so exact that they are right for all conceivable circumstances. Accordingly, you are entitled to act upon your conscientious feelings about what is a fair result in this case. (Scheflin, 1972, p. 206)

Whatever role the jury has in theory, in practice it is clear that the jury can ignore the strict application of the law and respond to the unique aspects of each case that comes before it. The jury deliberates in secrecy, they do not give reasons for their verdict, they are in no way accountable for their verdict, their decisions do not establish a precedent that is binding on future cases, and in criminal cases if the jury acquits the accused their decision is final. Indeed the jury's right to determine the facts gives them an almost unlimited discretion in returning whatever verdict they choose. As chief Justice Hughes (cited in Broeder, 1954) in 1931 remarked, "An unscrupulous administrator might be tempted to say, 'Let me find the facts for the people of my country and I care little who lays down the general principles'." Lord Devlin has observed, "I do not mean that they [the jury] often deliberately disregard the law. But if they think it is too stringent, they sometimes take a merciful view of the facts" (1959, p. 21). Indeed the jury's power to ignore the strict application of a relevant rule of law in itself has been construed as the right to do so in certain cases (Kadish and Kadish, 1971).

The jury's right to ignore the law may be supported as an effective means of protecting individuals from the oppressive or unjust use of governmental power. However, whether the rules controlling the jury should permit it wide latitude in deciding a particular case, or indeed if we should retain the jury, because of the need for the exercise of an equitable jurisdiction to mitigate rigid rules in particular cases, depends upon how the jury exercises that function. This empirical question is of overriding importance in the debate on the jury in general. Kalven, co-author of one of the most definitive studies done to date on the jury, has remarked, "Debate about the merits of the jury system should center far more on the value and propriety of the jury's sense of equity, of its modest war with the law, than on its sheer competence" (1964, p. 1702).

Those who oppose the jury on the ground that it is lawless contend that the jury exercises its "equitable" jurisdiction on the basis of prejudices and biases, such as race or physical attractiveness, that are not in accord with acceptable community notions of equity. They argue that jury verdicts result not only in a lack of uniformity in the law but also in malicious decisions and invidious discrimination (Frank, 1949). Those who support the jury and the exercise by it of an equitable jurisdiction, argue that the extra-legal factors that might influence it in reaching its verdict are factors that should be considered by a rational decision maker in reaching a just decision.

STUDIES OF JURY DECISION-MAKING

A few years ago if disputants over the jury were to join on this issue their supporting arguments could only be based on conjecture and isolated personal experiences. In 1954 Broeder observed with respect to the jury's law dispensing function that "we do not know how well it works; the verdict is a seal of secrecy which the law has thus far refused to open" (p. 412). Although the jury's deliberations are still shrouded in secrecy, the use of various methods of empirical research has yielded some data on the extra-legal variables that influence the jury's decision-making process. These studies permit us to draw some tentative conclusions about the basis upon which the jury exercises its equitable jurisdiction.

In the remainder of this paper we will review a few recent studies which illustrate the kinds of extra-legal factors that appear to influence jury decisions. Even this impressionistic review should reveal the direction in which the jury appears to exercise its equitable jurisdiction and thus enable us to draw a tentative conclusion about whether it is a useful social institution for imparting justice into one aspect of societal decision making. But more importantly, it will hopefully illustrate the importance of research on jury decision-making in studying the justice motive (Lerner, 1970; Mysliwiec, 1974).

Common experience suggests that the jury's verdict is likely to be influenced by the personal characteristics of the parties in the dispute, such as their physical attractiveness, character, and race. Empirical studies tend to confirm this commonsense judgment. Efran (1974) found that when subjects were asked to judge a student who was accused of cheating, physically attractive defendants were less likely to be seen as guilty than were unattractive defendants. In this case, attractiveness was manipulated by giving subjects a picture of the hypothetical defendant, one group receiving a photo of an attractive person, the other receiving a photo of an unattractive person. Efran found that students drawn from a similar population generally reported that they did not feel that the defendant's physical attractiveness should influence such decisions. This same bias in favor of physically attractive persons was reflected in a study done by Dion (1972). She found that a transgression by an unattractive child was seen by adults as more serious than was an identical transgression committed by an attractive child.

The attractiveness of a person's personality also affects decisions made by laymen about another's culpability. In a jury simulation experiment, Landy and Aronson (1969) found that on a charge of causing death by criminal negligence the jury recommended a shorter prison term for a defendant who was described as being happily married, regularly employed, and friendly with everyone than they did for a person described as being a janitor, a two-time divorcé, and an ex-convict. Although this was a study in which the simulated jurors were asked to give a judgment about sentencing, it seems likely that the jurors would also consider such facts in deciding on the guilt or innocence of the defendant. Indeed, in view of the danger that if the jury hears about the "bad" character of the accused they might be less careful about determining the certainty of his guilt before convicting, the law tries to keep this information from them. In no Anglo-American jurisdiction can evidence of the accused's bad character be led by the prosecution for the purpose of tending to prove that the accused committed the crime with which he is charged, even though it is sometimes undoubtedly relevant for that purpose.

In apparent conflict with the concern reflected by this rule is the rule whereby if an accused takes the witness stand in his own defense, evidence of his previous criminal convictions can be led by the prosecution. In such a situation, the judge must instruct the jury that this evidence of bad character can be used by them only in evaluating the accused's credibility as a witness. The jury must expressly be told not to infer from the criminal record that the accused is a bad person and therefore is more likely to have committed the crime with which he is charged. Simulations (Doob and Kirshenbaum, 1972; Hans, 1974) and correlational findings from reports of cases (Kalven and Zeisel, 1966) support the conclusion that such instruction is futile. An accused person with previous criminal convictions stands a much greater chance of being convicted of a crime than does a person with no such history.

Race is another personal characteristic that in some jurisdictions has clearly influenced juries in reaching their verdicts. Studies have demonstrated that it is a factor taken into account by the jury in the sentencing process (Bullock, 1961; Thornberry, 1973), and interviews with actual jurors reveal that it is a recurrent topic of conversation throughout their deliberations (Broeder, 1965a).

In criminal cases, the personal characteristics of the victim as well as the accused appear to influence the jury in reaching their verdict. Brooks, Doob, and Kirshenbaum (Note 1), in a jury simulation of a rape case, showed that jurors thought that it was less justified to convict a man of raping a woman who had a history of prostitution than it was to convict a man (on identical evidence) of raping a woman of chaste character. There was no evidence whatsoever that people thought that the defendant who was accused of raping the prostitute was less likely to have done it; rather it seemed that they simply felt that, given the amount of evidence that existed and the circumstances surrounding the rape, the person ought not to be convicted if the victim were "only" a prostitute. Similarly, Landy and Aronson (1969) found that people recommended longer sentences for someone who had been found guilty of killing (through criminal negligence) a "good" person than they did if the victim were a "bad" person.

The consequence of their decision, although in law irrelevant, is another factor which the jury considers in doing individual justice. In a criminal case, the consequence might be that the defendant will be incarcerated as a result of the decision or, in a few cases, could be executed. Vidmar (1972) and Hester and Smith (1973) have both shown that these consequences do indeed affect jury decision making. Where a jury sees that a consequence might be very severe, they seem less likely to come to a decision that might lead to such a severe result. Similarly, in civil actions the relative ability of the parties to absorb a financial loss is considered by the jury. In cases in which a simulated jury was told that the defendant had liability insurance, the average damages awarded rose considerably. Correspondingly, the jury takes into account any collateral benefits mitigating the loss (Kalven, 1958).

A study based on personal interviews with actual jurors about the deliberation in the jury room revealed that in a civil suit the plaintiff's family responsibilities influenced the jury both in finding liability and in awarding damages (Broeder, 1965b). The government of the province of Prince Edward Island, sensitive to the "deep pocket" philosophy sometimes adopted by jurors in doing individual justice, has recently moved to abolish the jury in civil suits where the government is the defendant (Charlottetown *Guardian*, 1973).

In criminal cases such as assault or various sexual offences, the victim though legally blameless may be partially responsible for the criminal act. The jury, however, is likely to consider the whole situation surrounding the particular crime in coming to a "just" (though not strictly legal) decision. Kalven and Zeisel (1966) found that in cases in which there was some degree of victim precipitation the jury was less likely to convict the accused or at least more likely to convict him of a lesser offense. In the past, a similar result was often revealed by juries in civil cases. Until recently, in many jurisdictions, if the plaintiff contributed to an accident to any degree, he was

491

completely barred from any recovery no matter how negligent the defendant had been in causing the damages. In such cases, rather than bar the plaintiff completely, the jury would take a "merciful view of the facts," and adjust the size of their verdict to correspond to the comparative negligence of the parties (Ulman, 1933).

Kalven and Zeisel (1966) also cite a number of cases where the jury seemed to acquit the defendant because he had suffered enough, even though he might technically be guilty. Thus, for example, it would seem that a jury is less likely to convict a man on a charge of causing death by criminal negligence when it was the defendant's wife who was killed (through his negligence) and the defendant himself was permanently and totally paralyzed in the accident.

Finally, in criminal cases, although only the accused is on trial, the jury in reaching a decision appears to consider whether the state "deserves" to win. If the police have used grossly unfair methods in obtaining evidence against the accused, or if the accused is being singled out for prosecution among many who appear to be equally guilty of the crime, the jury is less likely to convict (Kalven and Zeisel, 1966).

DISCRETION AND EXTRA-LEGAL FACTORS

The argument is often made that to ensure certainty and equal treatment there should be no discretion in the legal process. If injustices result from decisions in particular kinds of cases, then it is the rules of substantive law that should be changed. The rules should not be subverted by ignoring them or by applying them liberally. While many rules of law are in need of reform, it is doubtful whether any system in which fixed rules were applied rigidly, untempered by considerations of justice and fairness in individual cases, could maintain its legitimacy. Kalven has asserted that "we have a sense that many of the jury's most interesting deviations would be exceedingly hard to codify and incorporate by rule" (1964, p. 1071).

The legal system recognizes this need to take into account the peculiar facts of each case. Prosecutors have a broad and largely unreviewable discretion in deciding whether to prosecute a suspected offender. In exercising their discretion, they undoubtedly consider many of the factors reviewed above. Another place in the criminal justice system where most of this kind of information can legally affect the

court's decisions is in the sentencing of a convicted defendant. Indeed, many of the factors that are specifically excluded from the trial of an accused are to be taken into account in determining the proper disposition for a convicted person. Thus such factors as the defendant's criminal record, his standing in the community, his occupational status, etc., often form a critical part of the presentence report on which the judge bases his sentencing decision. The American Law Institute's Model Penal Code states:

> The presentence investigation shall include an analysis of the circumstances attending the commission of the crime, the defendant's history of delinquency or criminality, physical and mental condition, family status and background, economic status, education, occupation and personal habits and any other matters that the probation officer deems relevant or the Court directs to be included. (American Law Institute, 1962, p. 118)

In Canada, recent legislation has given further recognition to the fact that these extra-legal factors should be considered in "doing justice." Where the maximum penalty for a crime is imprisonment of ten years or less, the judge can avoid some of the effects of a guilty verdict by granting an absolute or conditional discharge. The effect of this is that even though the man has been found guilty of a crime, a conviction is not registered. The intent behind the legislation appears to be to encourage a judge to find the defendant guilty or not guilty on the basis of the relevant facts, and then allow himself to be influenced by the totality of the circumstances surrounding the case in his decision to grant or not grant a discharge. (For a more complete description see Greenspan, 1973).

THE JURY'S FUNCTION

The question of whether we should retain the jury because of its ability to dispense justice in individual cases thus depends on the answer to two distinct questions: (a) does the jury exercise discretion in ways that are considered to be just, and (b) in view of the other stages in the legal process where such discretion can be exercised by both the prosecutor and the judge, is there any need for the additional institution of the jury[?] With respect to the first question, it appears, for instance, that in a shoplifting case, if the defendant is a person of some stature and will lose his job if convicted, the jury is likely to find that he has learned his lesson and that the consequences are too serious to warrant conviction. If the prosecutor does not prosecute the ringleader of a gang, but instead calls him as a witness against his underlings, the jury is likely to protest that this is unfair and acquit the accused. If the accused was seriously injured in an accident in which his beloved wife was killed because of his criminal negligence, the jury is likely to find that he has suffered enough. But law dispensing by the jury appears to cut both ways. The fact that minority groups have historically been unfairly subjected to jury lawlessness cannot be doubted. Furthermore, many people would argue that the fact that the accused is a nice fellow, a good looking woman, a cripple, or employed, or that his or her victim is insufferable, should not affect the disposition of the case.

It would appear, not surprisingly, that the jury injects into the legal process notions of fairness that are shared by the average person. However, they are not able to rise above the prejudices and biases held by the same people. Although empirical research is important in demonstrating the subtleties of jury

equity, even when all of the evidence has been collected an important value judgment remains.

If the jury, however, is to perform a function different from that of the prosecutor in exercising his discretion to charge and the judge in exercising his discretion on sentencing, it would appear essential that the jury be representative of the community so that the breadth of community values be represented on the jury. Indeed if the juries were truly representative of the community, perhaps many of the present prejudices that influence the jury would be removed from their deliberations. In this regard, it is interesting that at present a heated battle is being fought over whether the jury should be reduced from the traditional twelve members to six (Note 2). If the jury is reduced in size, then the case for retaining it because of the injection into the legal process of community values would appear to be greatly weakened.

(b) *Morgentaler, Smoling and Scott* v. *The Queen*†

[DICKSON C.J. and Lamer J.:]

. . . . .

Defence Counsel's Address to the Jury

In his concluding remarks to the jury at the trial of the appellants, defence counsel asserted:

> The judge will tell you what the law is. He will tell you about the ingredient of the offence, what the Crown has to prove, what the defences may be or may not be, and you must take the law from him. But I submit to you that it is up to you and you alone to apply the law to this evidence and you have a right to say it shouldn't be applied.

The burden of his argument was that the jury should not apply s. 251 if they thought that it was a bad law, and that, in refusing to apply the law, they could send a signal to Parliament that the law should be changed. Although my disposition of the appeal makes it unnecessary, strictly speaking, to

review Mr. Manning's argument before the jury, I find the argument so troubling that I feel compelled to comment.

It has long been settled in Anglo-Canadian criminal law that in a trial before judge and jury, the judge's role is to state the law and the jury's role is to apply that law to the facts of the case. In *Joshua v. The Queen*, [1955] A.C. 121 at p. 130 (P.C.), Lord Oaksey enunciated the principle succinctly:

> It is a general principle of British law that on a trial by jury it is for the judge to direct the jury on the law and in so far as he thinks necessary on the facts, but the jury, whilst they must take the law from the judge, are the sole judges on the facts.

The jury is one of the great protectors of the citizen because it is composed of 12 persons who collectively express the common sense of the community. But the jury members are not expert in the law, and for that reason they must be guided by the judge on questions of law.

† [1988] 1 S.C.R. 30, 44 D.L.R. 4th. 385 at 417–19.

The contrary principle contended for by Mr. Manning, that a jury may be encouraged to ignore a law it does not like, could lead to gross inequities. One accused could be convicted by a jury who supported the existing law, while another person indicted for the same offence could be acquitted by a jury who, with reformist zeal, wished to express disapproval of the same law. Moreover, a jury could decide that although the law pointed to a conviction, the jury would simply refuse to apply the law to an accused for whom it had sympathy. Alternatively, a jury who feels antipathy towards an accused might convict despite a law which points to acquittal. To give a harsh but I think telling example, a jury fueled by the passions of racism could be told that they need not apply the law against murder to a white man who had killed a black man. Such a possibility need only be stated to reveal the potentially frightening implications of Mr. Manning's assertions. The dangerous argument that a jury may be encouraged to disregard the law was castigated as long ago as 1784 by Lord Mansfield in a criminal libel case, *R. v. Shipley* (1784), 4 Dougl. 73 at pp. 170–1, 99 E.R. 774 at p. 824:

> So the jury who usurp the judicature of law, though they happen to be right, are themselves wrong, because they are right by chance only, and have not taken the constitutional way of deciding the question. It is the duty of the Judge, in all cases of general justice, to tell the jury how to do right, though they have it in their power to do wrong, which is a matter entirely between God and their own consciences.
>
> To be free is to live under a government by law.... Miserable is the condition of individuals, dangerous is the condition of the State, if there is no certain law, or, which is the same thing, no certain administration of law, to protect individuals, or to guard the State.
>
> ...
>
> In opposition to this, what is contended for? — That the law shall be, in every particular cause, what any twelve men, who shall happen to be the jury, shall be inclined to think; liable to no review, and subject to no control, under all the prejudices of the popular cry of the day, and under all the bias of interest in this town, where thousands, more or less, are concerned in the publication of newspapers, paragraphs, and pamphlets. Under such an administration of law, no man could tell, no counsel could advise, whether a paper was or was not punishable.

I can only add my support to that eloquent statement of principle.

It is no doubt true that juries have a *de facto* power to disregard the law as stated to the jury by the judge. We cannot enter the jury room. The jury is never called upon to explain the reasons which lie behind a verdict. It may even be true that in some limited circumstances the private decision of a jury to refuse to apply the law will constitute, in the words of a Law Reform Commission of Canada working paper, "the citizen's ultimate protection against oppressive laws and the oppressive enforcement of the law" (Law Reform Commission of Canada, Working Paper 27, *The Jury in Criminal Trials* (1980)). But recognizing this reality is a far cry from suggesting that counsel may encourage a jury to ignore a law they do not support or to tell a jury that it has a *right* to do so. The difference between accepting the reality of *de facto* discretion in applying the law and elevating such discretion to the level of a right was stated clearly by the United States Court of Appeals, District of Columbia Circuit, in *U.S. v. Dougherty*, 473 F. 2d 1113 (1972), *per* Leventhal J., at p. 1134:

> The jury system has worked out reasonably well overall, providing "play in the joints" that imparts flexibility and avoid[s] undue rigidity. An equilibrium has evolved—an often marvelous balance—with the jury acting as a "safety valve" for exceptional cases, without being a wildcat or runaway institution. There is reason to believe that the simultaneous achievement of modest jury equity and avoidance of intolerable caprice depends on formal instructions that do not expressly delineate a jury charter to carve out its own rules of law.

To accept Mr. Manning's argument that defence counsel should be able to encourage juries to ignore the law would be to disturb the "marvelous balance" of our system of criminal trials before a judge and jury. Such a disturbance would be irresponsible. I agree with the trial judge and with the Court of Appeal that Mr. Manning was quite simply wrong to say to the jury that if they did not like the law they need not enforce it. He should not have done so.

Conclusion

Section [251] of the *Criminal Code* infringes the right to security of the person of many pregnant women. The procedures and administrative structures established in the section to provide for therapeutic abortions do not comply with the principles of fundamental justice. Section 7 of the Charter is infringed and that infringement cannot be saved under s. 1.

(c) *R. v. Williams*†

[McLACHLIN J. for the Court:]

INTRODUCTION

[1] Victor Daniel Williams, an aboriginal, was charged with the robbery of a Victoria pizza parlour in October, 1993. Mr. Williams pleaded not guilty and elected a trial by judge and jury. His defence was that the robbery had been committed by someone else, not him. The issue on this appeal is whether Mr. Williams has the right to question (challenge for cause) potential jurors to determine whether they possess prejudice against aboriginals which might impair their impartiality.

[2] The *Criminal Code*, R.S.C. 1985, c. C-46, s. 638, provides that "an accused is entitled to any number of challenges on the ground that ... a juror is not indifferent between the Queen and the accused," The section confers discretion on the trial judge to permit challenges for cause. The judge should do so where there is a realistic potential of juror partiality. The evidence in this case established widespread racial prejudice against aboriginals. I conclude that in the circumstances of this case, that prejudice established a realistic potential of partiality and that the trial judge should have exercised his discretion to allow the challenge for cause.

HISTORY OF THE PROCEEDINGS

The First Trial

[3] At his first trial, Williams applied to question potential jurors for racial bias under s. 638 of the Code. In support of his application, he filed materials alleging widespread racism against aboriginal people in Canadian society and an affidavit which stated, in part, "[I] hope that the 12 people that try me are not Indian haters." Hutchison J. ruled that Williams had met the threshold test and allowed potential jurors to be asked two questions:

1. Would your ability to judge the evidence in the case without bias, prejudice or partiality be affected by the fact that the person charged is an Indian?

2. Would your ability to judge the evidence in the case without bias, prejudice, or partiality be affected by the fact that the person charged is an Indian and the complainant is white?

On a number of occasions, Hutchison J. allowed additional questions to clarify responses to the first two questions. Forty-three panel members were questioned and 12 were dismissed for risk of bias. The Crown applied for a mistrial on the basis of procedural errors, including use of the same two jurors on all the challenges, coupled with "unfortunate publicity" of the jury selection process. The accused objected, arguing that the Crown was seeking a new trial in order to obtain reversal of the challenge for cause ruling. The trial judge replied that he doubted this would happen, given the case law, and granted the Crown's application for a mistrial.

. . . .

Statutory and Constitutional Provisions

[8] *Criminal Code*, R.S.C., 1985 c. C-46

> **638.**(1) A prosecutor or an accused is entitled to any number of challenges on the ground that
>
> ...
>
> (b) a juror is not indifferent between the Queen and the accused;
>
> ...
>
> (2) No challenge for cause shall be allowed on a ground not mentioned in subsection (1).

Canadian Charter of Rights and Freedoms

> **7.** Everyone has the right to life, liberty and security of the person and the right not to be deprived thereof except in accordance with the principles of fundamental justice.
>
> **11.** Any person charged with an offence has the right
>
> ...
>
> (d) to be presumed innocent until proven guilty according to law in a fair and public hearing by an independent and impartial tribunal;
>
> **15.**(1) Every individual is equal before and under the law and has the right to the equal protection and equal benefit of the law without discrimina-

---

† [1998] 1 S.C.R. 1128 at paras. 1–3, 8–13, 15–22, 25, 28–30, 36, 40–42, 52, 55, 58–60.

tion and, in particular, without discrimination based on race, national or ethnic origin, colour, religion, sex, age or mental or physical disability.

ANALYSIS

What Is the Rule?

The Prevailing Canadian Approach to Jury Challenges for Lack of Indifference between the Crown and the Accused

[9] The prosecution and the defence are entitled to challenge potential jurors for cause on the ground that "a juror is not indifferent between the Queen and the accused." Lack of "indifference" may be translated as "partiality," the term used by the Courts below. "Lack of indifference" or "partiality," in turn, refer to the possibility that a juror's knowledge or beliefs may affect the way he or she discharges the jury function in a way that is improper or unfair to the accused. A juror who is partial or "not indifferent" is a juror who is inclined to a certain party or a certain conclusion. The synonyms for "partial" in Burton's Legal Thesaurus (2nd ed. 1992), at p. 374, illustrate the attitudes that may serve to disqualify a juror:

> bigoted, ... discriminatory, favorably disposed, inclined, influenced, ... interested, jaundiced, narrow-minded, one-sided, partisan, predisposed, prejudiced, prepossessed, prone, restricted, ... subjective, swayed, unbalanced, unequal, uneven, unfair, unjust, unjustified, unreasonable.

[10] The predisposed state of mind caught by the term "partial" may arise from a variety of sources. Four classes of potential juror prejudice have been identified — interest, specific, generic and conformity: see Neil Vidmar, "Pretrial prejudice in Canada: a comparative perspective on the criminal jury" (1996), 79 Jud. 249, at p. 252. Interest prejudice arises when jurors may have a direct stake in the trial due to their relationship to the defendant, the victim, witnesses or outcome. Specific prejudice involves attitudes and beliefs about the particular case that may render the juror incapable of deciding guilt or innocence with an impartial mind. These attitudes and beliefs may arise from personal knowledge of the case, publicity through mass media, or public discussion and rumour in the community. Generic prejudice, the class of prejudice at issue on this appeal, arises from stereotypical attitudes about the defendant, victims, witnesses or the nature of the crime itself. Bias against a racial or ethnic group or against persons charged with sex abuse are examples

of generic prejudice. Finally, conformity prejudice arises when the case is of significant interest to the community causing a juror to perceive that there is strong community feeling about a case coupled with an expectation as to the outcome.

[11] Knowledge or bias may affect the trial in different ways. It may incline a juror to believe that the accused is likely to have committed the crime alleged. It may incline a juror to reject or put less weight on the evidence of the accused. Or it may, in a general way, predispose the juror to the Crown, perceived as representative of the "white" majority against the minority-member accused, inclining the juror, for example, to resolve doubts about aspects of the Crown's case more readily: see Sheri Lynn Johnson, "Black Innocence and the White Jury" (1985), 83 Mich. L. Rev. 1611. When these things occur, a juror, however well intentioned, is not indifferent between the Crown and the accused. The juror's own deliberations and the deliberations of other jurors who may be influenced by the juror, risk a verdict that reflects, not the evidence and the law, but juror preconceptions and prejudices. The aim of s. 638 of the Code is to prevent effects like these from contaminating the jury's deliberations and hence the trial: see *R. v. Hubbert* (1975), 29 C.C.C. (2d) 279 (Ont. C.A.). The aim, to put it succinctly, is to ensure a fair trial.

[12] The practical problem is how to ascertain when a potential juror may be partial or "not indifferent" between the Crown and the accused. There are two approaches to this problem. The first approach is that prevailing in the United States. On this approach, every jury panel is suspect. Every candidate for jury duty may be challenged and questioned as to preconceptions and prejudices on any sort of trial. As a result, lengthy trials of jurors before the trial of the accused are routine.

[13] Canada has taken a different approach. In this country, candidates for jury duty are presumed to be indifferent or impartial. Before the Crown or the accused can challenge and question them, they must raise concerns which displace that presumption. Usually this is done by the party seeking the challenge calling evidence substantiating the basis of the concern. Alternatively, where the basis of the concern is "notorious" in the sense of being widely known and accepted, the law of evidence may permit a judge to take judicial notice of it. This might happen, for example, where the basis of the concern is widespread publicity of which the judge and everyone else in the community is aware. The judge has a

wide discretion in controlling the challenge process, to prevent its abuse, to ensure it is fair to the prospective juror as well as the accused, and to prevent the trial from being unnecessarily delayed by unfounded challenges for cause: see Hubbert, *supra*.

.   .   .   .

Identifying Evidentiary Threshold

.   .   .

(1) The Assumption that Prejudice Will Be Judicially Cleansed

[20] Underlying the Crown's submissions (as well as the judgments of Esson C.J. and the Court of Appeal) is the assumption that generally jurors will be able to identify and set aside racial prejudice. Only in exceptional cases is there a danger that racial prejudice will affect a juror's impartiality. In contrast, the defence says that jurors may not be able to set aside racial prejudices that fall short of extreme prejudice. Is it correct to assume that jurors who harbour racial prejudices falling short of extreme prejudice will set them aside when asked to serve on a jury? A consideration of the nature of racial prejudice and how it may affect the decision-making process suggests that it is not.

[21] To suggest that all persons who possess racial prejudices will erase those prejudices from the mind when serving as jurors is to underestimate the insidious nature of racial prejudice and the stereotyping that underlies it. As Vidmar, *supra*, points out, racial prejudice interfering with jurors' impartiality is a form of discrimination. It involves making distinctions on the basis of class or category without regard to individual merit. It rests on preconceptions and unchallenged assumptions that unconsciously shape the daily behaviour of individuals. Buried deep in the human psyche, these preconceptions cannot be easily and effectively identified and set aside, even if one wishes to do so. For this reason, it cannot be assumed that judicial directions to act impartially will always effectively counter racial prejudice: see Johnson, *supra*. Doherty J.A. recognized this in *Parks*, *supra*, at p. 371:

> In deciding whether the post-jury selection safeguards against partiality provide a reliable antidote to racial bias, the nature of that bias must be emphasized. For some people, anti-black biases rest on unstated and unchallenged assumptions learned over a lifetime. Those assumptions shape the daily behaviour of individuals, often without any conscious reference to them. In my

opinion, attitudes which are engrained in an individual's subconscious, and reflected in both individual and institutional conduct within the community, will prove more resistant to judicial cleansing than will opinions based on yesterday's news and referable to a specific person or event.

[22] Racial prejudice and its effects are as invasive and elusive as they are corrosive. We should not assume that instructions from the judge or other safeguards will eliminate biases that may be deeply ingrained in the subconscious psyches of jurors. Rather, we should acknowledge the destructive potential of subconscious racial prejudice by recognizing that the post-jury selection safeguards may not suffice. Where doubts are raised, the better policy is to err on the side of caution and permit prejudices to be examined. Only then can we know with any certainty whether they exist and whether they can be set aside or not. It is better to risk allowing what are in fact unnecessary challenges, than to risk prohibiting challenges which are necessary: see *Aldridge* v. *United States*, 283 U.S. 308 (1931), at p. 314, and *Parks*, *supra*.

.   .   .   .

[25] This Court rejected the argument that prejudice based on pre-trial publicity could be cured by the safeguards in the trial process in *Sherratt*, *supra*, at p. 532, per L'Heureux-Dubé J.:

> While it is no doubt true that trial judges have a wide discretion in these matters and that jurors will usually behave in accordance with their oaths, these two principles cannot supersede the right of every accused person to a fair trial, which necessarily includes the empanelling of an impartial jury.

The same may be said of many forms of prejudice based on racial stereotypes. The expectation that jurors usually behave in accordance with their oaths does not obviate the need to permit challenges for cause in circumstances such as the case at bar, where it is established that the community suffers from widespread prejudice against people of the accused's race.

(2) Insistence on the Necessity of a Link Between the Racist Attitude and the Potential for Juror Partiality

.   .   .   .

[28] Racial prejudice against the accused may be detrimental to an accused in a variety of ways. The

link between prejudice and verdict is clearest where there is an "interracial element" to the crime or a perceived link between those of the accused's race and the particular crime. But racial prejudice may play a role in other, less obvious ways. Racist stereotypes may affect how jurors assess the credibility of the accused. Bias can shape the information received during the course of the trial to conform with the bias: see *Parks, supra,* at p. 372. Jurors harbouring racial prejudices may consider those of the accused's race less worthy or perceive a link between those of the accused's race and crime in general. In this manner, subconscious racism may make it easier to conclude that a black or aboriginal accused engaged in the crime regardless of the race of the complainant: see Kent Roach, "Challenges for Cause and Racial Discrimination" (1995), 37 Crim. L.Q. 410, at p. 421.

[29] Again, a prejudiced juror might see the Crown as non-aboriginal or non-black and hence to be favoured over an aboriginal or black accused. The contest at the trial is between the accused and the Crown. Only in a subsidiary sense is it between the accused and another aboriginal. A prejudiced juror might be inclined to favour non-aboriginal Crown witnesses against aboriginal accused. Or a racially prejudiced juror might simply tend to side with the Crown because, consciously or unconsciously, the juror sees the Crown as a defender of majoritarian interests against the minority he or she fears or disfavours. Such feeling might incline the juror to resolve any doubts against the accused.

[30] Ultimately, it is within the discretion of the trial judge to determine whether widespread racial prejudice in the community, absent specific "links" to the trial, is sufficient to give an "air of reality" to the challenge in the particular circumstances of each case. The following excerpt from *Parks, supra,* at pp. 378–79, per Doherty J.A., states the law correctly:

> I am satisfied that in at least some cases involving a black accused there is a realistic possibility that one or more jurors will discriminate against that accused because of his or her colour. In my view, a trial judge, in the proper exercise of his or her discretion, could permit counsel to put the question posed in this case, in any trial held in Metropolitan Toronto involving a black accused. I would go further and hold that it would be the better course to permit that question in all such cases where the accused requests the inquiry.
>
> There will be circumstances in addition to the colour of the accused which will increase the possibility of racially prejudiced verdicts. It is

impossible to provide an exhaustive catalogue of those circumstances. Where they exist, the trial judge must allow counsel to put the question suggested in this case.

. . . .

(4) Impossibility of Proving That Racism in Society Will Lead to Juror Partiality

. . . .

[36] "Concrete" evidence as to whether potential jurors can or cannot set aside their racial prejudices can be obtained only by questioning a juror. If the Canadian system permitted jurors to be questioned after trials as to how and why they made the decisions they did, there might be a prospect of obtaining empirical information on whether racially prejudiced jurors can set aside their prejudices. But s. 649 of the Code forbids this. So, imperfect as it is, the only way we have to test whether racially prejudiced jurors will be able to set aside their prejudices and judge impartially between the Crown and the accused, is by questioning prospective jurors on challenges for cause. In many cases, we can infer from the nature of widespread racial prejudice, that some jurors at least may be influenced by those prejudices in their deliberations. Whether or not this risk will materialize must be left to the triers of impartiality on the challenge for cause. To make it a condition of the right to challenge [for] cause is to require the defence to prove the impossible and to accept that some jurors may be partial.

. . . .

(5) Failure to Read s. 638(1)(b) Purposively

. . . .

[40] This raises the question of what evidentiary standard is appropriate on applications to challenge for cause based on racial prejudice. The appellant appears to accept the standard of widespread racial prejudice in the community. Interveners, however, urge a lower standard. One suggestion is that all aboriginal accused should have the right to challenge for cause. Another is that any accused who is a member of a disadvantaged group under s. 15 of the *Charter* should have the right to challenge for cause. Also possible is a rule which permits challenge for cause whenever there is bias against the accused's

race in the community, even if that bias is not general or widespread.

[41] A rule that accords an automatic right to challenge for cause on the basis that the accused is an aboriginal or member of a group that encounters discrimination conflicts from a methodological point of view with the approach in *Sherratt, supra*, that an accused may challenge for cause only upon establishing that there is a realistic potential for juror partiality. For example, it is difficult to see why women should have an automatic right to challenge for cause merely because they have been held to constitute a disadvantaged group under s. 15 of the *Charter*. Moreover, it is not correct to assume that membership in an aboriginal or minority group always implies a realistic potential for partiality. The relevant community for purposes of the rule is the community from which the jury pool is drawn. That community may or may not harbour prejudices against aboriginals. It likely would not, for example, in a community where aboriginals are in a majority position. That said, absent evidence to the contrary, where widespread prejudice against people of the accused's race is demonstrated at a national or provincial level, it will often be reasonable to infer that such prejudice is replicated at the community level.

[42] On the understanding that the jury pool is representative, one may safely insist that the accused demonstrate widespread or general prejudice against his or her race in the community as a condition of bringing a challenge for cause. It is at this point that bigoted or prejudiced people have the capacity to affect the impartiality of the jury.

. . . .

(7) The Slippery Slope Argument

. . . .

[52] In my view, the rule enunciated by this Court in *Sherratt, supra*, suffices to maintain the right to a fair and impartial trial, without adopting the United States model or a variant on it. Sherratt starts from the presumption that members of the jury pool are capable of serving as impartial jurors. This means that there can be no automatic right to challenge for cause. In order to establish such a right, the accused must show that there is a realistic potential that some members of the jury pool may be biased in a way that may impact negatively on the accused. A realistic potential of racial prejudice can often be demonstrated by establishing widespread prejudice in

the community against people of the accused's race. As long as this requirement is in place, the Canadian rule will be much more restrictive than the rule in the United States.

[53] In addition, procedures on challenges for cause can and should be tailored to protect the accused's right to a fair trial by an impartial jury, while also protecting the privacy interests of prospective jurors and avoiding lengthening trials or increasing their cost.

. . . .

[55] At the stage of the actual challenge for cause, the procedure is similarly likely to be summary. The trial judge has a wide discretion in controlling the process to prevent its abuse, to ensure that it is fair to the prospective juror as well as to the accused, and to avoid the trial's being unnecessarily prolonged by challenges for cause: see Hubbert, *supra*. In the case at bar, Hutchison J. at the first trial confined the challenge to two questions, subject to a few tightly controlled subsidiary questions. This is a practice to be emulated. The fear that trials will be lengthened and rendered more costly by upholding the right to challenge for cause where widespread racial prejudice is established is belied by the experience in Ontario since the ruling in *Parks, supra*. The Criminal Lawyers' Association (Ontario), an intervener, advised that in those cases where the matter arises, an average of 35–45 minutes is consumed. The Attorney General for Ontario did not contradict this statement and supports the appellant's position.

. . . .

CONCLUSION

[58] Although they acknowledged the existence of widespread bias against aboriginals, both Esson C.J. and the British Columbia Court of Appeal held that the evidence did not demonstrate a reasonable possibility that prospective jurors would be partial. In my view, there was ample evidence that this widespread prejudice included elements that could have affected the impartiality of jurors. Racism against aboriginals includes stereotypes that relate to credibility, worthiness and criminal propensity. As the Canadian Bar Association stated in Locking up Natives in Canada: A Report of the Committee of the Canadian Bar Association on Imprisonment and Release (1988), at p. 5:

> Put at its baldest, there is an equation of being drunk, Indian and in prison. Like many stereo-

types, this one has a dark underside. It reflects a view of native people as uncivilized and without a coherent social or moral order. The stereotype prevents us from seeing native people as equals.

.   .   .   .

[59] In these circumstances, the trial judge should have allowed the accused to challenge prospective jurors for cause. Notwithstanding the accused's defence that another aboriginal person committed the robbery, juror prejudice could have affected the trial in many other ways. Consequently, there was a realistic potential that some of the jurors might not have been indifferent between the Crown and the accused. The potential for prejudice was increased by the failure of the trial judge to instruct the jury to set aside any racial prejudices that they might have against aboriginals. It cannot be said that the accused had the fair trial by an impartial jury to which he was entitled.

[60] I would allow the appeal and direct a new trial.

(a)   Embracing Change: How NJI Adapts to the Changing Role of the Judge†

Honourable Justice C. Adèle Kent

With the election of President Obama in the United States, everyone is talking about change in the future. The idea of change led me to think about the work of a trial judge in the 15 years that I have sat on the Court of Queen's Bench of Alberta. When I was appointed, the work of a trial judge involved predominantly trials. When a decision had to be made, that is all the judge did. Reasons? Maybe. Other than trial work, from time to time, there was a week of motions court and, every so often, there were some pre-trial conferences — perfunctory meetings to make sure the lawyers were ready for trial. And, unlike today, there were almost always lawyers! On the darker side, judges could say almost anything they wanted to, regardless of whether it was relevant to the issue before them, or how it might affect the sensibilities of those involved in the case.

Today, trials make up a much smaller portion of my work — but how those trials have changed! Jury charges are more complex, and they happen not only at the end of trial, but throughout the trial. Sentencing has become a longer, more involved process. The extent of scientific evidence presented has expanded and requires a careful analysis of its quality. Although the cases we do are structured in the context of an adversarial system, the emphasis is more on settlement than trial. In fact, the demand

for judicial dispute resolution is higher than for trials. And, as for lawyers, much of their work — particularly in the area of family law — is now done with self-represented litigants. Judging today occurs in a more diverse society — one that demands respect from those who judge, not just from those who are being judged.

That is the context within which I think of the National Judicial institute (NJI). The NJI has not only changed dramatically over the past 15 years, but has, in my view, accepted that change is an important principle in creating worthwhile education programs for judges. There are good reasons for this. First, the leaders of the NJI have all been willing to experiment, to consult with judges, and to accept new ideas about the art and craft of judging. Naming names is always dangerous for fear of omitting someone, but the people who have embodied the idea of change include the Executive Directors who have been at the NJI during my judicial career — Dolores M. Hansen, George Thomson, Lynn Smith and Brian Lennox — the Academic and Education Directors, Brettel Dawson and Susan Lightstone, and the many senior advisors with whom I have worked.

The second reason that the NJI has so effectively adapted over the years to the changing role of the judge is because the organization conducts its programs across Canada. Unlike other countries,

---

where judges are sent to the capital city for training at a judicial education institute, when the NJI was established, the model adopted was to take the seminars out to the judges. This allows judges to travel to different parts of the country for seminars, itself a valuable way to learn. It also allows the NJI and, therefore, the judges to make use of the valuable resources available all across the country. For example, as part of the science seminar, *Neuroscience in the Courtroom: What Judges Need to Know*, scheduled to take place in Halifax in 2010, we are organizing a visit to the Brain Repair Centre in Halifax, which studies the brain and recovery of brain function.

So, for all the reasons that judges need to know about the brain — with respect to pain, end of life, memory and so on — leading experts in the field are available within the context of their work. For seminars where it is so important to have input from community leaders, whether it be from the native community, or those involved in addressing domestic violence or poverty, for example, being in the community itself makes the experience authentic. I would suggest that having judicial education seminars move around the country — instead of having a static model — was a brilliant idea. That movement itself encourages change.

The third reason for the effectiveness of the NJI in both leading and embracing change also stems from the way in which programs are developed. I have been fortunate to work on a number of NJI programs, some of which have been a staple of judicial education for years, such as the *Civil Law Seminar*, and some of which are new and developing, like the science programs. One of the fundamental principles of NJI course design is the involvement of judges. Not only does it ensure that the courses are relevant to what the judges are doing, but it also means that judges from across the country and from all levels of court can discuss their work in the context of a particular course. Trends and changes can be more readily identified and incorporated into the courses.

The ability of the NJI to adapt to the changing role of the judge has meant that the array of courses available to judges continues to expand. Two courses come to mind as illustrating not only how broad the range of courses is, but how central they are to effective judging. *Emerging Issues: Judging in the Context of Diverse Faiths and Cultures* was the first in a series of seminars that addressed judging in a diverse society. In addition to featuring compelling lectures on religion and law in Canada by judges and academics, community members addressed the issues that arise as a result of the interface between our legal system and cultures that developed within the context of other legal and cultural systems. At the end of the seminar, it was not hard to see how what we learned would be useful in the courtroom.

As an aside, this seminar is part of the continuing commitment of the NJI to provide courses in contextual judging. When I was appointed, the process of developing judicial education on social context was just beginning. There was significant resistance at that time, in large part, I think, because judges did not understand what social context education entailed. Now, I believe that judges not only accept, but expect to understand the context in which they judge. From time to time, judges may not immediately see how useful this kind of education is, but they understand why it is there.

The second example was the NJI's seminar on sentencing, *Criminal Law Seminar: The Ins and Outs of Sentencing*, which took place a few years ago. As with the course on *Emerging Issues: Judging in the Context of Diverse Faiths and Cultures*, substantive law was presented and applied through small group work. There was more, however. Judges saw the process through the eyes of a victim and through the work of a risk assessment expert.

I began this essay talking about the change that has occurred in the job of judging during my 15 years on the bench. Judging was perhaps simpler 15 years ago, when I was appointed to the bench, but the quality of justice was not of as high a quality as it is today. Despite the complexities that have been added to a judge's role — owing to changing economics, demographics and attitudes about resolving disputes — the fact that Canadian judges are so well equipped to handle those changes is, in large part, due to the effectiveness of the NJI. As I mentioned, I have been involved in the planning process of several NJI courses, which has meant working with many people at the NJI. I note continually the generosity, willingness to volunteer and, quite plainly, the cheerfulness of everyone I work with. That says so much about the organization.

(b)   The Meaning and Scope of Judicial Independence†

Bora Laskin

... I hope I do not abuse this privilege if I strike a serious note in this address. It would please me better if I could banter and amuse, which I may assure you is not beyond my capacity. But special reasons, to which I will come shortly, impel me to speak more soberly on a subject of fundamental importance to the judicial office. That subject is the meaning and scope of judicial independence. I would have thought that its meaning would have been well understood over the years in which the Judges have exercised their judicial roles. I would have thought that there was a clear public understanding that Judges cannot be measured in the same way as other holders of public office or any members of the public. In my understanding, and in that of most of the members of the legal profession and members of the Bench, Judges are expected to abstain from participation in political controversy. Obviously, considering the storm that has brewed early this year on the Berger affair, I was somewhat mistaken. The limited public role of the Judge, one perfectly clear to me, seems to have been misunderstood or forgotten, even by lawyers, let alone by members of the press and of the public.

A fundamental principle has pervaded the judicial role since it took root in the reign of Queen Anne. It was established — not without fits and starts — that Judges would no longer hold office at the pleasure of the Crown, at the pleasure of the government. They would have the security of tenure, once assigned to their position, and would hold office during good behaviour to the age of retirement. Their duration in judicial office would no longer depend on governmental whim, and they could be removed only for judicial misbehaviour.

What this imported, as it evolved over the years, was the separation of the executive and the judiciary; no admixture of the one with the other; no mixture of the judiciary in politics or political controversy; correspondingly, no intermeddling of the executive with the judiciary; each branch was to be independent of the other, left alone to carry on its separate duties. For the Judges, they had utmost freedom of

speech in the discharge of their judicial functions. Unbelievably, some members of the press and some in public office in this country, seem to think that freedom of speech for the Judges gave them the full scope of participation and comment on current political controversies, on current social and political issues. Was there ever such ignorance of history and of principle?

A Judge, upon appointment — and I am speaking here of appointments which cover all members of our provincial and federal superior courts as well as the Supreme Court of Canada — takes a prescribed oath of office. It is a short oath which is common to all superior court Judges, being as follows:

> I do solemnly and sincerely promise and swear that I will duly and faithfully, and to the best of my skill and knowledge, execute the powers and trust reposed in me as ...
>
> So help me God.

But it is invested with all the authority and surrounded by all the limitations that are imported by the principle of judicial independence and that are spelled out in the *Judges Act*, the federal statute which defines the judicial office.

What does the *Judges Act* say about the judicial office? It says quite clearly that a Judge may not, directly or indirectly, engage in any occupation or business other than his judicial duties. There is a limited exception for him or her to act as commissioner or arbitrator or adjudicator or referee or conciliator or mediator, if so appointed in respect of a federal matter by the federal Government; and similarly, if so appointed by the provincial government in respect of a provincial matter. These are short-term, temporary assignments not intended to give a Judge a regular assignment to carry out a non-judicial role. Two recent illustrations of the distinction may be mentioned. A few years ago, the Government of Canada wished to appoint a Judge as Deputy Minister of an executive department. He was unwilling to accept unless he retained his security as Judge.

---

† An address to the Annual Meeting of the Canadian Bar Association, September 2, 1982, reprinted in F.L. Morton, ed., *Law, Politics and the Judicial Process in Canada* (Calgary: University of Calgary Press, 1985) at 115–20. Reproduced with permission.

The Government was prepared to go along. I felt it my duty as Chief Justice to protest and did so vigorously, pointing out that it was either the one position or the other, but not both.

A Judge who wishes to accept an executive appointment could not remain a Judge at the same time. In the case I mentioned, the Judge put more store on his judicial position than on the proposed executive position. The matter was accordingly dropped. The same thing happened a little later in Ontario when the provincial government wished to appoint an Ontario Supreme Court Judge as Chairman of the provincial Workman's Compensation Board. Again, I protested; if the Judge wished to accept the provincial appointment, he should resign from the Bench; he could not be both Judge and non-judicial or executive functionary. The principle was accepted and the matter was abandoned.

These instances concerned permanent appointments to governmental positions. The authorized exceptions to allow governments to appoint Judges to special assignments as, for example, by order-in-council or by a limited inquiry, do not involve Judges in executive government or in governmental operations. They are asked to perform a particular service, with generally a short-term duration, although some inquiries like the MacKenzie Valley Pipeline and the McDonald Inquiry into the R.C.M.P. did go on for some years.

I am myself not a great supporter of the use of Judges to carry out short-term assignments at the behest of a government, federal or provincial. Apart from anything else, it is not always convenient to spare a particular Judge, given the ever increasing workload of all Courts. Moreover, there is always the likelihood that the Judge will be required to pass on policy, which is not within the scope of the regular judicial function. But I recognize that governments will continue to ask Judges (generally with the consent of their Chief Justice) to perform these limited tasks. The important thing to remember is that these short-term assignments are not intended to establish a career for the Judge in the work he or she carried out. The Judge is expected to make his or her report to the particular government and to regard the assignment as completed without any supplementary comment. Any comment or action is for the government; the Judge himself or herself is *functus*, done with the matter. This has been the general behaviour of Judges who have accepted and carried out special or particular government assignments. Whatever has been the value of the inquiry must rest in what it says — the Judge is certainly not intended to be a protagonist, however enamored he or she may become of the work. Nor is the Judge intended to make a career of the special assignment.

There has been a large increase in the number of federally-appointed Judges in the last decade. Indeed, there are now 466 superior court Judges throughout Canada and 232 county and district court Judges. I do not take account of provincial court Judges who are appointed by provincial governments. The increase in the number of federally-appointed Judges increased the burden of judicial administration, the need to monitor complaints (which are inevitable, even if in most cases misconceived) and the need also to provide outlets for judicial conferences. It was beyond the capacity of Parliament to provide for these matters and they also raised sensitive matters engaging the independent position of the Judges.

In 1971, a new policy was introduced by Parliament to govern supervision of judicial behaviour or, I should say, alleged misbehaviour....

... The Canadian Judicial Council came into being in October, 1971 and has had a considerable amount of business in the past decade. It has exercised its powers of inquiry and investigation with great care, seeking on the one hand to satisfy complaints against alleged judicial misbehaviour and on the other hand to protect the reputation of the Judge against unfounded allegations. The most common type of complaint received against Judges has to do with objections to their judgments. Laymen have misconceived the role of the Council: it is not a court of appeal to rectify decisions alleged to be in error; for that there are established appeal courts, and the Council repeatedly has to tell complainants that the recourse is an appeal, not an invocation of the powers of the Canadian Judicial Council.

Since the Canadian Judicial Council has a statutory mandate to conduct inquiries into alleged judicial misbehaviour, it can hardly ignore a responsible complaint. In the Berger case, the complaint was made by a long-serving superior court Judge. Was the Canadian Judicial Council to ignore it? At least, it had the obligation to consider whether the complaint merited investigation, that it was not merely frivolous. Those members of the press who became engaged with the complaint in Justice Berger's support seemed entirely ignorant of the mandate of the Canadian Judicial Council. They appeared to be of the view that a Judge's behaviour was for him to measure, that it was not open to the Canadian Judicial Council to investigate, let alone admonish a Judge in respect of a complaint against objectionable behaviour. This was clearly wrong and could have been established by some modest inquiry.

My mention of the Berger case is not to reopen an issue which is closed. It is only to set the record straight on the statutory function and duty of the Canadian Judicial Council, whoever be the subject of a complaint to it. In view of the obvious misunderstanding to which the Berger incident gave rise, it seemed important to me that I, as Chairman, should underline the role and duty of the Canadian Judicial Council, however distasteful it may seem to be to assess the behaviour of a fellow Judge. I would have welcomed, as I always do, the balance provided by the media, by the press, and I regret that it was unfortunate that they did not discharge that responsibility on this occasion.

There was one respect in which members of the press, and indeed some public "bodies" and members of Parliament, showed their ignorance of judicial propriety. It was said that pursuit of the complaint against Justice Berger was an interference with his freedom of speech. Plain nonsense! A Judge has no freedom of speech to address political issues which have nothing to do with his judicial duties. His abstention from political involvement is one of the guarantees of his impartiality, his integrity, his independence. Does it matter that his political intervention supports what many, including the press, think is a desirable stance? Would the same support be offered to a Judge who intervenes in a political matter in an opposite way? Surely there must be one standard, and that is absolute abstention, except possibly where the role of a Court is itself brought into question. Otherwise, a Judge who feels so strongly on political issues that he must speak out is best advised to resign from the Bench. He cannot be allowed to speak from the shelter of a Judgeship.

In the Berger case, the Judge's intervention was on critical political and constitutional issues then under examination by the entire Canadian ministerial establishment. No Judge had a warrant to interfere, in a public way, and his conviction, however well intended, could not justify political intervention simply because he felt himself impelled to speak. To a large degree, Judge Berger was reactivating his McKenzie Valley Pipeline inquiry, a matter which was years behind him and should properly be left dormant for a political decision, if any, and not for his initiative in the midst of a sensitive political controversy.

The Canadian Judicial Council — one member of Parliament accused us of being engaged in a witch hunt — was badly served by those who, obviously, did no homework on the Council's role and on its obligation. There was another matter which seemed rather shabby, also the result of failure to do any homework. It was indicated, quite explicitly in some news quarters, that the Canadian Judicial Council acted because the Prime Minister had complained of the Judge's intrusion into the political sphere when the Prime Minister was giving a press interview in Vancouver. The record on this matter is quite clear. The written complaint against Judge Berger was addressed to me under dates of November 18 and 19, 1981, and delivered to me, from Ottawa, on those days. The next day, November 20, 1981, I sent a memorandum to the Executive Secretary of Council asking that the complaints — there were two successive ones — be referred for consideration by the Executive Committee. So far as the Canadian Judicial Council was concerned, the complaint had become part of our agenda. The interview of the Prime Minister did not take place until November 24, 1981. It is therefore mere mischief making to suggest that the Canadian Judicial Council was moved to action by the Prime Minister.

The Berger inquiry, as I have said, is behind us, and I regret that I found it necessary to say as much as I did about it. However, the Canadian Judicial Council, which does not and cannot reach out publicly to the media, deserves to have its record cleared. This would not have been necessary if we had been better served by the press throughout the whole affair. A matter like the Berger case is not likely to recur; the Canadian Judicial Council has signalled the danger of recommended removal from office if it should recur. As it was, the Council took a placating view and administered an admonishment in the following terms:

1. The Judicial Council is of the opinion that it was an indiscretion on the part of Mr. Justice Berger to express his views as to matters of a political nature, when such matters were in controversy.

2. While the Judicial Council is of the opinion that Mr. Justice Berger's actions were indiscreet, they constitute no basis for a recommendation that he be removed from office.

3. The Judicial Council is of the opinion that members of the judiciary should avoid taking part in controversial political discussions except only in respect of matters that directly affect the operation of the Courts.

In view of the obfuscation that surrounded the Berger case, there are a number of propositions that must be plainly stated. First, however personally compelled a Judge may feel to speak on a political issue, however knowledgeable the Judge may be or

505

think he or she be on such an issue, it is forbidden territory. The Judge must remain and be seen to remain impartial. Compromise which would impair judicial independence and integrity is out, if the Judge is to remain in judicial office. Second, no federally-appointed Judge can claim immunity from examination by the Canadian Judicial Council of complaints (unless obviously frivolous) lodged against the Judge; nor against the decision of the Canadian Judicial Council to investigate the complaints through a formal inquiry. Third, the Canadian Judicial Council is not limited to recommending removal or dismissal; it may attach a reprimand or admonishment without either recommending removal or abandoning the complaint. Only if it gets to removal does it become necessary, in the case of a superior court Judge, to engage the Minister of Justice and Parliament, whose approval on a recommended removal must be sought. Fourth, Judges who are objects or subjects of a complaint are entitled to a fair hearing, to appear before the Council or before an appointed committee or to refuse to appear (as Justice Berger did refuse). Refusal to appear does not paralyse the Council, and did not in the Case under discussion....

(c) Antonio Lamer: Should Judges Hold Their Tongues?†

Antonio Lamer

The Chief Justice worries that, by keeping silent, judges are helping misconceptions to spread

From my vantage point as Chief Justice of Canada, it strikes me that the place of the judiciary in our constitutional democracy has been a matter of considerable public debate and controversy, particularly over the past year. I see this in the editorials I read, the coverage that is given to judgments of my court and other courts and, indeed, in the public statements and debates of members of Parliament, senators and members of provincial legislatures.

And all that is fine.... It is natural, indeed desirable, for the roles of our various public institutions, including the courts, to be the subject of lively debate. There is only one aspect of the current discussion I wish to comment on.

Let me begin by reminding you of something you all know. The enactment in 1982 of a constitutionally entrenched Charter of Rights and Freedoms changed the *kind* of constitutional cases the courts have been faced with and, in that sense, changed their role. It did not really create a new *function* for the judiciary, since Canadian courts have always had the power to tell elected officials when they have gone too far. What has happened is that the basis on which the courts can, indeed must, do this has broadened considerably. There is no doubt that the judiciary was drawn into the political arena to a degree unknown prior to 1982.

Since 1982, judges as a whole have been subject to increasing criticism, especially of course in respect of controversial decisions made under the Charter. By no means would I ever suggest that this kind of criticism should be stifled. Of course not. It is valuable and healthy to our democracy. But, because of other factors I will come to in a moment, it causes me to wonder whether we now have to rethink another aspect of the attitude to be taken by the judiciary. In particular, I wonder whether judges, or maybe through their Chief Justices, should be rolling up the sleeves of their judicial robes and involving themselves in these public discussions more directly.

I am not saying that the judiciary should or should not be participating in public debates. I merely wish to raise the question for your consideration, perhaps over the next year....

† From *The Globe and Mail* (25 August 1998) A17. (Quoted from remarks made on Sunday by Antonio Lamer, Chief Justice of the Supreme Court of Canada, to the Canadian Bar Association in St. John's, August 23, 1998.) Reproduced by permission of the Hon. Daniele Tremblay-Lamer.

I am sure it seems peculiar to the public that the judges simply make their decisions and then remain mute while the rest of society reacts to them. The public hardly ever hears any reaction from the judges. From the judges' point of view, it is certainly frustrating sometimes to stand by when there are errors made, whether innocent or deliberate, by those who write about or comment on judicial decisions. But our judicial tradition has been that judges generally do not comment on judgments or, for that matter, on any issue in the public domain touching them.

I confess that there have been times when I felt a particularly strong urge to comment publicly about a judgment of my court, for example, such as when the inconvenience of the requirement to obtain a warrant is described without any mention of the existence of telewarrants, which are available over the phone in a few minutes. There have been other times when I wished I could say something, in the public interest, about a piece of legislation before Parliament, such as a bill affecting judicial salaries and benefits. But our tradition, and it is a strong one, is one of silence on such matters. I have always thought that this was proper — that the judiciary should keep silent lest it sacrifice its independence or, at least, the perception of impartiality.

But lately I have begun to wonder whether that tradition of silence continues to be appropriate. And my main concern is not for the judges who are criticized in the press or by public figures. Rather, it seems to me that judicial silence sometimes means that the public misses out on a full understanding of what the courts are doing and why. Public debate on issues that come before the courts and, indeed, on the role of the judiciary itself is not as full as it

should be because the perspective of the judiciary is usually absent.

It used to be the case that, while judges themselves were silent, the judicial perspective was supplied by the law officers of the Crown and by the bar. Accordingly, the tradition of judicial silence was paired with an equally strong tradition of support from other quarters. The purpose, of course, was not to defend every decision made by a judge but to explain, where necessary, the issues before the court, the basis on which the judge made the decision and any other necessary concepts to aid public understanding of the judicial role.

It appears to me, however, that the latter tradition of support for the judiciary has faded somewhat, which leads me to wonder whether the tradition of judicial silence itself should be revisited. I do not blame anyone for this state of affairs. It strikes me that it may be another inevitable by-product of the Charter. Perhaps as judicial decisions have become more entwined with political issues, the more difficult it has become for public figures and lawyers themselves to speak up. There is a political risk in their doing so. But the consequence is that the judiciary has no voice and no champion. In turn, public understanding of such fundamental concepts as judicial review under the Constitution and judicial independence is, I fear, fast eroding.

I admit that I do not have a clear solution to offer. I would be certainly reluctant to see judges enter the political fray. There would be enormous risks in this. On the other hand, I worry that there is also a risk in having judges hold their tongues. Perhaps there is some other solution....

I hope that you will agree with me that it is, at least, a matter worthy of discussion in the public interest.

(d) Will Women Judges Really Make a Difference?†

Justice Bertha Wilson

When I was appointed to the Supreme Court of Canada in the Spring of 1982 a great many women from all across the country telephoned, cabled or

wrote to me rejoicing in my appointment. "Now", they said, "we are represented on Canada's highest court. This is the beginning of a new era for

† From The Fourth Annual Barbara Betcherman Memorial Lecture, Osgoode Hall Law School, February 8, 1990. Reproduced by permission of the Estate of Hon. Madam Justice Bertha Wilson. [Notes and/or references omitted.]

women." So why was I not rejoicing? Why did I not share the tremendous confidence of these women? The reasons form the theme of my lecture this evening.

First of all, of course, came the realization that no-one could live up to the expectations of my well-wishers. I had the sense of being doomed to failure, not because of any excess of humility on my part or any desire to shirk the responsibility of the office, but because I knew from hard experience that the law does not work that way. Change in the law comes slowly and incrementally; that is its nature. It responds to changes in society; it seldom initiates them. And while I was prepared — and, indeed, as a woman judge anxious — to respond to these changes, I wondered to what extent I would be constrained in my attempts to do so by the nature of judicial office itself.

In the literature which is required reading for every newly appointed judge it is repeatedly stated that judges must be both independent and impartial, that these qualities are basic to the proper administration of justice and fundamental to the legitimacy of the judicial role. The judge must not approach his or her task with pre-conceived notions about law or policy, with personal prejudice against parties or issues, or with bias toward a particular outcome of a case. Socrates defined the essential qualities of a judge in the following manner. "Four things belong to a judge; to hear courteously; to answer wisely; to consider soberly and to decide impartially."[1]

In Winters' *Handbook for Judges*,[2] there is a section devoted to the essential qualities of a judge and these are defined as integrity and independence, impartiality, flexibility, creativity, responsibility and common sense. The late Justice Frankfurter was quoted as stating:

> To practise the requisite detachment and to achieve sufficient objectivity no doubt demands of judges the habit of self-discipline and self-criticism, incertitude that one's own views are incontestable and alert tolerance toward views not shared. But these are precisely the presuppositions of our judicial process. They are precisely the qualities society has a right to expect from those entrusted with ... judicial power.[3]

In an article entitled "The Virtue of Impartiality" the late Judge Shientag of the Appellate Division of the New York Supreme Court discusses the difficulty in attaining impartiality and states that the term implies an appreciation and understanding of the differing attitudes and viewpoints of those involved in a controversy.[4] He quotes Lord MacMillan's description of the difficulty judges face in this regard:

> The judicial oath of office imposes on the judge a lofty duty of impartiality. But impartiality is not easy of attainment. For a judge does not shed the attributes of common humanity when he assumes the ermine. The ordinary human mind is a mass of prepossessions inherited and acquired, often none the less dangerous because unrecognized by their possessor. Few minds are as neutral as a sheet of plate glass, and indeed a mind of that quality may actually fail in judicial efficiency, for the warmer tints of imagination and sympathy are needed to temper the cold light of reason if human justice is to be done.[5]

And later Lord MacMillan issues the following warning:

> [The judge] must purge his mind not only of partiality to persons, but of partiality to arguments, a much more subtle matter, for every legal mind is apt to have an innate susceptibility to particular classes of arguments.[6]

Many have criticized as totally unreal the concept that judges are somehow super-human, neutral, above politics and unbiased, and are able to completely separate themselves from their personal opinions and pre-dispositions when exercising their judicial function. For example, Lord Justice Scrutton doubted that complete impartiality was possible. He said:

> This is rather difficult to attain in any system. I am not speaking of conscious impartiality; but the habits you are trained in, the people with whom you mix, lead to your having a certain class of ideas of such a nature that, when you have to deal with other ideas, you do not give as sound and accurate judgments as you would wish. This is one of the great difficulties at present with Labour. Labour says: "Where are your impartial Judges? They all move in the same circle as the employers, and they are all educated and nursed in the same ideas as the employers. How can a labour man or a trade unionist get impartial justice?" It is very difficult sometimes to be sure that you have put yourself into a thoroughly impartial position between two disputants, one of your own class and one not of your class. Even in matters outside trade-unionist cases ... it is sometimes difficult to be sure, hard as you have tried, that you have put yourself in a perfectly impartial position between the two litigants.[7]

In his text on *The Politics of the Judiciary*,[8] Professor Griffith caused a furore in legal and judicial circles in the United Kingdom when he questioned whether the English judiciary were capable of impartiality. He stated that for a judge to be completely impartial he or she would have to be like a political, economic and social eunuch and have no interests in the world outside the court. Because this is impossible, Griffith concludes that impartiality is an ideal incapable of realization.[9] He says of the English judiciary:

> These judges have by their education and training and the pursuit of their profession as barristers acquired a strikingly homogeneous collection of attitudes, beliefs, and principles which to them represents the public interest.[19]

The public interest, in other words, is perceived from the viewpoint of their own class. Chief Justice Nemetz has suggested that the views of Professor Griffith may have some validity in Canada too, more particularly, Professor Griffith's view that judicial attitudes towards political and social issues reflect the lack of a proper understanding of the views of labour unions, minorities and the under-privileged.[11]

Judge Rosalie Abella, Chair of the Ontario Law Reform Commission, also doubts that judicial impartiality is a realistic requirement. She emphasizes in her article "The Dynamic Nature of Equality" that "every decision-maker who walks into a court room to hear a case is armed not only with the relevant legal texts but with a set of values, experiences and assumptions that are thoroughly embedded."[12]

Judge Shientag refers to the fact that many judges believe that they have acted with the cold neutrality of an impartial judge when in fact they have completely failed to examine their prejudices and biases. He points out that the partiality and prejudice with which we are concerned is not overt, not something tangible on which the judge can put his or her finger. Yet many judges by failing to appreciate this are lulled into a false sense of security.[13] Judge Shientag emphasizes that progress will only be made when judges recognize this condition as part of the weakness of human nature and then "[h]aving admitted the liability to prejudice, unconscious for the most part, subtle and nebulous at times, the next step is to determine what the judge, with his trained mind, can do to neutralize the incessant play of these obscure yet potent influences."[14] Judge Shientag concludes that "the judge who realizes, before listening to a case, that all men have a natural bias of mind and that thought is apt to be coloured by predilection, is more likely to make a conscientious effort at impartiality and dispassionateness than one who believes that his elevation to the bench makes him at once the dehumanized instrument of infallible logical truth."[15]

But what, you may be asking, has all this got to do with my subject: "Will women judges really make a difference?" Well, I think it has a great deal to do with it and whether you agree with me or not will probably depend on your perception of the degree to which the existing law reflects the judicial neutrality or impartiality we have been discussing. If the existing law can be viewed as the product of judicial neutrality or impartiality, [...] although the judiciary has been very substantially male, then you may conclude that the advent of increased numbers of women judges should make no difference, assuming, that is, that these women judges will bring to bear the same neutrality and impartiality. However, if you conclude that the existing law, in some areas at least, cannot be viewed as the product of judicial neutrality, then your answer may be very different.

Two law professors at New York University, Professor John Johnston and Professor Charles Knapp, have concluded, as a result of their studies of judicial attitudes reflected in the decisions of judges in the United States, that United States judges have succeeded in their conscious efforts to free themselves from habits of stereotypical thought with regard to discrimination based on colour.[16] However, they were unable to reach a similar conclusion with respect to discrimination based on sex and found that American judges had failed to bring to sex discrimination the judicial virtues of detachment, reflection and critical analysis which had served them so well with respect to other areas of discrimination. They state:

> "Sexism" — the making of unjustified (or at least unsupported) assumptions about individual capabilities, interests, goals and social roles solely on the basis of sex differences — is as easily discernible in contemporary judicial opinions as racism ever was.[17]

Professor Norma Wikler, a sociologist at the University of California, has reviewed a number of other studies of judicial attitudes by legal researchers and social scientists and states that these confirm that male judges tend to adhere to traditional values and beliefs about the "natures" of men and women and their proper roles in society. They have found overwhelming evidence that gender-based myths, biases and stereotypes are deeply embedded in the attitudes of many male judges as well as in the law itself. They have concluded that particularly in areas of tort law, criminal law and family law, gender difference has been a significant factor in judicial decision-making. Many have concluded that sexism is the unarticulated underlying premise of many judgments in these areas and that this is not really surprising having regard to the nature of the society in which the judges themselves have been socialized.[18]

A number of strategies have been tried in the United States for the elimination of gender bias from the courts — legislative reform, enhanced legal representation of women litigants, increased numbers of women lawyers and judges. These measures have been accompanied by an intensive educational program aimed at judges right across the country. Women judges and women lawyers in the United States played a very active role in the creation of this program. They were able to persuade substantial numbers of their male peers that gender bias, like all other forms of bias they had worked so hard to eradicate, violated the core principle of judicial impartiality and neutrality and posed an increasing threat in the seventies and eighties to the maintenance of public confidence in the judiciary.

As might be anticipated, a direct frontal attack on gender bias in the courts and especially the institution of an educational program for judges on this subject[] was highly controversial and would probably have died on the vine but for the support of a substantial number of the country's leading male judges and educators who recognized the profound changes that were taking place in the society[,] including a major redefinition of the roles of men and women.

Professor Wikler has been one of the moving forces behind the United States program to sensitize judges to the problem of gender bias. She reports some modest indicators of success of the program, although she acknowledges that it is too early to assess the long term effects. She reports that requests for speakers and material generated from courses and workshops indicate a growing interest as does also the positive evaluation by judges themselves of the courses presented. Even more gratifying, attorneys practising in States where the program has been actively promoted report a noticeable increase in judicial sensitivity to gender bias. Program materials have been cited in the courts and quoted in the judgments. Judicial Conduct Commissions are disciplining judges for gender biased behaviour such as sexist remarks to women lawyers and litigants and inappropriate comments in rape cases. Professor Wikler concludes that one very important goal has been achieved: gender bias is now a subject which judges and judicial educators think and care about.[19]

Another development in the United States has been the establishment of judicially appointed Task Forces to investigate the extent to which gender bias

exists in the judiciary. The first of these Task Forces was created in New Jersey in 1982 and, as stated by Chief Justice Wilentz, was mandated to "investigate the extent to which gender bias exists in the New Jersey judicial branch, and to develop an educational program to eliminate any such bias".[20] Since 1982 over twenty other States have created Task Forces. Lynn Hecht Schafran, in her article "The Success of the American Program", reports that the Task Forces have significantly enhanced judicial education programs and have created a level of public awareness that generates its own pressures for reform.[21]

Schafran identifies four reasons why a judicially appointed Task Force is important as opposed to other groups outside the court system focussing on particular concerns. The first is that a gender bias Task Force is able to look at a broad range of issues and demonstrate a pattern of gender bias that manifests itself throughout the judicial system. The second reason is credibility. She explains this critical reason in the following manner:

> When a coalition of rape crisis counsellors asserts that rape victims are ill-treated in court, or a women's bar association claims that women attorneys are denied a fair share of appointments to challenging and lucrative civil and criminal cases, these charges are heard as the claims of special interest groups. When a blue ribbon panel appointed by a state's chief justice makes these same charges, people listen. There was little in what the New Jersey and New York Task Forces reported that numerous women's rights organizations and feminists' legal commentators have not been saying for years, but the task force reports twice made the front page of the New York Times.[22]

The third reason relates to the administration of the Task Force. The Chief Justice of the State is in a position to authorize funds, compel co-operation, endorse and propose reforms and ensure their implementation, and support judicial education on the subject. A final reason in favour of the Task Force route to reform is that such a task force brings together judges, lawyers, law professors, and community activists to study an issue which many of them do not initially appreciate is an issue at all. Schafran reports that Task Force members from New Jersey and New York "who start out with no knowledge of gender bias in the courts, or even a conviction that the idea is nonsense, emerge from the data collection process convinced that the problem is real and has deeply serious implications for the administration of justice."[23]

(d) Will Women Judges Really Make a Difference?

So, where do we stand in Canada on this matter? Well, as you might expect, feminist scholars in Canada have over the past two decades produced a vast quantity of literature on the subject, some of it, in my view, very insightful, very balanced and very useful, and some of it very radical, quite provocative and probably less useful as a result. But all of it, it seems to me, is premised, at least as far as judicial decision-making is concerned, on two basic propositions, one that women view the world and what goes on in it from a different perspective from men, and two that women judges, by bringing to bear that perspective on the cases on which they sit, can play a major role in introducing judicial neutrality and impartiality into the justice system.

Let me say right away from my own experience as a judge of fourteen years' standing, working closely with my male colleagues on the bench, that in my view there are probably whole areas of the law on which there is no uniquely feminine perspective. This is not to say that the development of the law in these areas has not been influenced by the fact that the lawyers and the judges have all been men. But rather that the principles and the underlying premises are so firmly entrenched and, in my opinion, so fundamentally sound that no good would be achieved by attempting to re-invent the wheel, even if the revised version did have a few more spokes in it. I have in mind areas such as the law of contract, the law of real property and the law applicable to corporations. In some other areas of the law, however, I think that a distinctly male perspective is clearly discernible and has resulted in legal principles that are not fundamentally sound and should be revisited as and when the opportunity presents itself. Canadian feminist scholarship has, in my view, done an excellent job of identifying those areas and making suggestions for reform. Some aspects of the criminal law in particular cry out for change since they are based on presuppositions about the nature of women and women's sexuality that in this day and age are little short of ludicrous.

But how do we handle the problem that women judges, just as much as their male counterparts, are subject to the duty of impartiality? As we said at the outset, judges must not approach their task with pre-conceived notions about law and policy. They must approach it with detachment and, as Lord MacMillan said, purge their minds "not only of partiality to persons but of partiality to arguments."[24] Does this then foreclose any kind of "judicial affirmative action" to counteract the influence of the dominant male perspective of the past and establish

judicial neutrality through a countervailing female perspective? Is Karen Selick, writing recently in the Lawyers Weekly, correct when she argues that offsetting male bias with female bias would only be compounding the injustice?[25] Does the nature of the judicial process itself present an insuperable hurdle so that the legislatures rather than the courts must be looked to for any significant legal change?

I think in part this may be so. Certainly, the legislature is the more effective instrument for rapid or radical change. But I see no reason why the judiciary cannot exercise some modest degree of creativity in areas where modern insights and life's experience have indicated that the law has gone awry. However, and I think this is extremely important, it will be a Pyrrhic victory for women and for the justice system as a whole if changes in the law come only through the efforts of women lawyers and women judges. The Americans were smart to realize that courses and workshops on gender bias for judges male and female are an essential follow-up to scholarly research and learned writing. In Canada we are just beginning to touch the fringes.

The first national, interdisciplinary conference on the relationship between judicial neutrality and gender equality was held in Banff, Alberta, in May of 1986. At the conference judges, academics, practising lawyers and experts in anthropology, political science, sociology and social welfare examined judicial behaviour in equality related matters. The judicial acceptance of traditional stereotypes concerning women was noted as well as its impact in Canada on important areas of constitutional equality litigation, family law, criminal law, tort law and human rights.[26]

Mr. Justice Rothman of the Quebec Court of Appeal, one of the speakers at the conference, endorsed the approach adopted in the United States to counteract gender bias through nation-wide educational programs for judges and the creation of judicial task forces. In his perception, women face the same kind of discrimination in Canada as they do in the United States and we should be working to change the old attitudes *now*. He suggested that conferences and seminars for newly appointed judges would be a good place to start but, in addition, courses on gender bias should be part of the continuing education programs for judges at all stages of their careers. Justice Rothman added that it is not, however, going to be enough to sensitize judges to equality issues if lawyers are not sensitized to them as well![27]

The Canadian Judicial Council and the Canadian Judicial Centre have both recognized the need

511

for judicial education in this area and will include gender issues in their summer seminars for judges this year. I understand that the Centre hopes to subsequently present the program in a number of locations across the country and the course materials will be available to all Canadian judges. I heartily endorse this initiative. It is, in my view, a significant first step towards the achievement of true judicial neutrality. But it is only a first step and there is a long way to go.

Coming back then to the question whether the appointment of more women judges will make a difference. Because the entry of women into the judiciary is so recent, few studies have been done on the subject. Current statistics, however, show that just over nine percent of federally appointed judges are women[28] and it is reasonable to assume that more and more women will be appointed to the Bench as more and more women become licensed to practise law. Will this growing number of women judges by itself make a difference?

The expectation is that it will; that the mere presence of women on the bench will make a difference. In an article entitled "The Gender of Judges", Suzanna Sherry, an Associate Law Professor at the University of Minnesota, suggests that the mere fact that women are judges serves an educative function and helps to shatter stereotypes about the role of women in society that are held by male judges and lawyers as well as by litigants, jurors and witnesses.[29]

Judge Gladys Kessler, former President of the National Association of Women Judges in the United States, defends the search for competent women appointees to the bench. She says:

> But the ultimate justification for deliberately seeking judges of both sexes and all colors and backgrounds is to keep the public's trust. The public must perceive its judges as fair, impartial and representative of the diversity of those who are being judged.[30]

Justice Wald has expressed similar sentiments. She believes that women judges are indispensable to the public's confidence in the ability of the courts to respond to the legal problems of all classes of citizens.[31]

Diane Martin, a criminal lawyer writing in the Lawyers Weekly, sees another way in which the presence of women on the bench is helpful and constructive. It is easier, she says, for women lawyers to appear as counsel before a woman judge. She says the "difference is that you are 'normal' — you and the judge have certain shared experiences and a shared reality that removes, to a certain extent, the

need to 'translate' your submissions into 'man talk' or a context that a male judge will understand."[32] The woman judge does not see you as "out of place" or having "something to prove by appearing in a courtroom arguing a case before her."[33]

For women counsel, appearing in front of a woman judge also decreases the risk of sexist comments and inappropriate efforts at humour. The courtroom treatment of women litigants, witnesses and lawyers was examined by the New Jersey and New York task forces. The New York Task Force found that "[w]omen uniquely, disproportionately, and with unacceptable frequency must endure a climate of condescension, indifference, and hostility".[34] The New Jersey Task Force found strong evidence that women are often treated differently in courtrooms, in judges' chambers and at professional gatherings.[35] As Justice Rothman pointed out at the Banff conference, there is no excuse for a judge allowing himself or anyone else in his courtroom to make unprofessional or inappropriate references to gender. He saw as a possible solution the appointment of more women judges and more courteous and sensitive male judges![36]

Some feminist writers are persuaded that the appointment of more women judges will have an impact on the process of judicial decision-making itself and on the development of the substantive law. As I mentioned earlier, this flows from the belief that women view the world and what goes on in it from a different perspective from men. Some define the difference in perspective solely in terms that women do not accept male perceptions and interpretations of events as the norm or as objective reality. Carol Gilligan, a Professor of Education at Harvard University, sees the difference as going much deeper than that. In her view women think differently from men, particularly in responding to moral dilemmas. They have, she says, different ways of thinking about themselves and their relationships to others.[37]

In her book, *In a Different Voice*,[38] Gilligan analyses data she collected in the form of responses from male and female participants in a number of different studies. These responses, she submits, support her central thesis that women see themselves as essentially connected to others and as members of a community while men see themselves as essentially autonomous and independent of others. Gilligan makes no claim about the origins of the differences she describes. She does, however, use the psychoanalytical work of Dr. Nancy Chodorow as a starting point.[39] Chodorow postulates that gender differences arise from the fact that women do the mothering of children. Because the gender identity of male children is not the same as their mothers, they tend to distance and separate themselves from their mothers' female characteristics in order to develop their masculinity. Female children, on the other hand, define themselves through attachment to their mothers.[40] Masculinity is therefore, according to Gilligan, defined through separation and individualism while femininity is defined through attachment and the formation of relationships. The gender identity of the male, she submits, is threatened by relationships while the gender identity of the female is threatened by separation.[41]

Gilligan's work on conceptions of morality among adults suggests that women's ethical sense is significantly different from men's. Men see moral problems as arising from competing rights; the adversarial process comes easily to them. Women see moral problems as arising from competing obligations, the one to the other, because the important thing is to preserve relationships, to develop an ethic of caring. The goal, according to women's ethical sense, is not seen in terms of winning or losing but rather in terms of achieving an optimum outcome for all individuals involved in the moral dilemma.[42] It is not difficult to see how this contrast in thinking might form the basis of different perceptions of justice.

I think there is merit in Gilligan's analysis. I think it may in part explain the traditional reluctance of courts to get too deeply into the circumstances of a case, their anxiety to reduce the context of the dispute to its bare bones through a complex system of exclusionary evidentiary rules. This is, it seems to me, one of the characteristic features of the adversarial process. We are all familiar with the witness on cross-examination who wants to explain his or her answer, who feels that a simple yes or no is not an adequate response, and who is frustrated and angry at being cut off with a half truth. It is so much easier to come up with a black and white answer if you are unencumbered by a broader context which might prompt you, in Lord MacMillan's words, to temper the cold light of reason with the warmer tints of imagination and sympathy.[43]

It may explain also the hostility of some male judges to permitting intervenors in human rights cases. The main purpose of having intervenors is to broaden the context of the dispute, to show the issue in a larger perspective or as impacting on other groups not directly involved in the litigation at all. But it certainly does complicate the issues to have them presented in polycentric terms.

Professor Patricia Cain of the University of Texas in an article entitled "Good and Bad Bias: A Comment on Feminist Theory and Judging" says:

> What we want, it seems to me, are lawyers who can tell their client's story, lawyers who can help judges to see the parties as human beings, and who can help remove the separation between judge and litigant. And, then, what we want from our judges is a special ability to listen with connection before engaging in the separation that accompanies judgment.[44]

Obviously, this is not an easy role for the judge — to enter into the skin of the litigant and make his or her experience part of your experience and only when you have done that, to judge. But I think we have to do it; or at least make an earnest attempt to do it. Whether the criticism of the justice system comes to us through Royal Commissions, through the media or just through our own personal friends, we cannot escape the conclusion that in some respects our existing system of justice has been found wanting. And as Mr. Justice Rothman says — the time to do something about it is *now*.

One of the important conclusions emerging from the Council of Europe's Seminar on Equality between Men and Women held in Strasbourg last November is that the universalist doctrine of Human Rights must include a realistic concept of masculine and feminine humanity regarded as a whole, that human kind *is* dual and must be represented in its dual form if the trap of an asexual abstraction in which "human being" is always declined in the masculine is to be avoided.[45] If women lawyers and women judges through their differing perspectives on life can bring a new humanity to bear on the decision-making process, perhaps they *will* make a difference. Perhaps they will succeed in infusing the law with an understanding of what it means to be fully human.

(e) *R. v. S. (R.D.)*†

[GONTHIER J. and La Forest J.:]

[26] I have had the benefit of the reasons of Justice Cory, the joint reasons of Justices L'Heureux-Dubé and McLachlin and the reasons of Justice Major. I agree with Cory J. and L'Heureux-Dubé and McLachlin JJ. as to the disposition of the appeal and with their exposition of the law on bias and impartiality and the relevance of context. However, I am in agreement with and adopt the joint reasons of L'Heureux-Dubé and McLachlin JJ in their treatment of social context and the manner in which it may appropriately enter the decision-making process as well as their assessment of the trial judge's reasons and comments in the present case.

[L'HEUREUX-DUBÉ and McLACHLIN JJ.:]

I. INTRODUCTION

[27] We have read the reasons of our colleague, Justice Cory, and while we agree that this appeal must be allowed, we differ substantially from him in how we reach that outcome. As a result, we find it necessary to write brief concurring reasons.

[28] We endorse Cory J.'s comments on judging in a multicultural society, the importance of perspective and social context in judicial decision-making, and the presumption of judicial integrity. However, we approach the test for reasonable apprehension of bias and its application to the case at bar somewhat differently from our colleague.

[29] In our view, the test for reasonable apprehension of bias established in the jurisprudence is reflective of the reality that while judges can never be neutral, in the sense of purely objective, they can and must strive for impartiality. It therefore recognizes as inevitable and appropriate that the differing experiences of judges assist them in their decision-making process and will be reflected in their judgments, so long as those experiences are relevant to the cases, are not based on inappropriate stereotypes, and do not prevent a fair and just determination of the cases based on the facts in evidence.

[30] We find that on the basis of these principles, there is no reasonable apprehension of bias in the case at bar. Like Cory J. we would, therefore, overturn the findings by the Nova Scotia Supreme Court (Trial Division) and the majority of the Nova Scotia Court of Appeal that a reasonable apprehension of bias arises in this case, and restore the acquittal of R.D.S. This said, we disagree with Cory J.'s position that the comments of Judge Sparks were unfortunate, unnecessary, or close to the line. Rather, we find them to reflect an entirely appropriate recognition of the facts in evidence in this case and of the context within which this case arose — a context known to Judge Sparks and to any well-informed member of the community.

II. THE TEST FOR REASONABLE APPREHENSION OF BIAS

[31] The test for reasonable apprehension of bias is that set out by de Grandpré J. in *Committee for Justice and Liberty* v. *National Energy Board*, [1978] 1 S.C.R. 369. Though he wrote dissenting reasons, de Grandpré J.'s articulation of the test for bias was adopted by the majority of the Court, and has been consistently endorsed by this Court in the intervening two decades: see, for example, *Valente* v. *The Queen*, [1985] 2 S.C.R. 673; *R.* v. *Lippé*, [1991] 2 S.C.R. 114; *Ruffo* v. *Conseil de la magistrature*, [1995] 4 S.C.R. 267. De Grandpré J. stated, at pp. 394–95:

> ... the apprehension of bias must be a reasonable one, held by reasonable and right-minded persons, applying themselves to the question and obtaining thereon the required information.... [T]hat test is "what would an informed person, viewing the matter realistically and practically — and having thought the matter through — conclude. Would he think that it is more likely than not that [the decision-maker], whether consciously or unconsciously, would not decide fairly."
>
> The grounds for this apprehension must, however, be substantial and I ... refus[e] to accept the suggestion that the test be related to the "very sensitive or scrupulous conscience".

† [1997] 3 S.C.R. 484 at paras. 60, aff'g (1995) 145 N.S.R. (2d) 284, 418 A.P.R. 284, 102 C.C.C. (3d) 233, 45 C.R. (4th) 361, aff'g [1995] N.S.J. No. 184 (QL).

[32] As Cory J. notes at para. 92, the scope and stringency of the duty of fairness articulated by de Grandpré depends largely on the role and function of the tribunal in question. Although judicial proceedings will generally be bound by the requirements of natural justice to a greater degree than will hearings before administrative tribunals, judicial decision-makers, by virtue of their positions, have nonetheless been granted considerable deference by appellate courts inquiring into the apprehension of bias. This is because judges "are assumed to be [people] of conscience and intellectual discipline, capable of judging a particular controversy fairly on the basis of its own circumstances": *United States* v. *Morgan*, 313 U.S. 409 (1941), at p. 421. The presumption of impartiality carries considerable weight, for as Blackstone opined at p. 361 in Commentaries on the Laws of England, Book III, cited at footnote 49 in Richard F. Devlin, "We Can't Go On Together with Suspicious Minds: Judicial Bias and Racialized Perspective in R. v. R.D.S." (1995), 18 Dalhousie L.J. 408, at p. 417, "the law will not suppose a possibility of bias or favour in a judge, who is already sworn to administer impartial justice, and whose authority greatly depends upon that presumption and idea". Thus, reviewing courts have been hesitant to make a finding of bias or to perceive a reasonable apprehension of bias on the part of a judge, in the absence of convincing evidence to that effect: *R.* v. *Smith & Whiteway Fisheries Ltd.* (1994), 133 N.S.R. (2d) 50 (C.A.), at pp. 60–61.

[33] Notwithstanding the strong presumption of impartiality that applies to judges, they will nevertheless be held to certain stringent standards regarding bias — "a reasonable apprehension that the judge might not act in an entirely impartial manner is ground for disqualification": *Blanchette* v. *C.I.S. Ltd.*, [1973] S.C.R. 833, at pp. 842–43.

[34] In order to apply this test, it is necessary to distinguish between the impartiality which is required of all judges, and the concept of judicial neutrality. The distinction we would draw is that reflected in the insightful words of Benjamin N. Cardozo in The Nature of the Judicial Process (1921), at pp. 12–13 and 167, where he affirmed the importance of impartiality, while at the same time recognizing the fallacy of judicial neutrality:

> There is in each of us a stream of tendency, whether you choose to call it philosophy or not, which gives coherence and direction to thought and action. Judges cannot escape that current any more than other mortals. All their lives, forces which they do not recognize and cannot name, have been tugging at them — inherited instincts, traditional beliefs, acquired convictions; and the resultant is an outlook on life, a conception of social needs.... In this mental background every problem finds its setting. We may try to see things as objectively as we please. None the less, we can never see them with any eyes except our own.
>
> ...
>
> Deep below consciousness are other forces, the likes and the dislikes, the predilections and the prejudices, the complex of instincts and emotions and habits and convictions, which make the [person], whether he [or she] be litigant or judge.

[35] Cardozo recognized that objectivity was an impossibility because judges, like all other humans, operate from their own perspectives. As the Canadian Judicial Council noted in Commentaries on Judicial Conduct (1991), at p. 12, "[t]here is no human being who is not the product of every social experience, every process of education, and every human contact". What is possible and desirable, they note, is impartiality:

> ... the wisdom required of a judge is to recognize, consciously allow for, and perhaps to question, all the baggage of past attitudes and sympathies that fellow citizens are free to carry, untested, to the grave.
>
> True impartiality does not require that the judge have no sympathies or opinions; it requires that the judge nevertheless be free to entertain and act upon different points of view with an open mind.

III.   THE REASONABLE PERSON

[36] The presence or absence of an apprehension of bias is evaluated through the eyes of the reasonable, informed, practical and realistic person who considers the matter in some detail (Committee for Justice and Liberty, supra.) The person postulated is not a "very sensitive or scrupulous" person, but rather a right-minded person familiar with the circumstances of the case.

[37] It follows that one must consider the reasonable person's knowledge and understanding of the judicial process and the nature of judging as well as of the community in which the alleged crime occurred.

A.   The Nature of Judging

[38] As discussed above, judges in a bilingual, multiracial and multicultural society will undoubtedly approach the task of judging from their varied perspectives. They will certainly have been shaped by,

and have gained insight from, their different experiences, and cannot be expected to divorce themselves from these experiences on the occasion of their appointment to the bench. In fact, such a transformation would deny society the benefit of the valuable knowledge gained by the judiciary while they were members of the Bar. As well, it would preclude the achievement of a diversity of backgrounds in the judiciary. The reasonable person does not expect that judges will function as neutral ciphers; however, the reasonable person does demand that judges achieve impartiality in their judging.

[39] It is apparent, and a reasonable person would expect, that triers of fact will be properly influenced in their deliberations by their individual perspectives on the world in which the events in dispute in the courtroom took place. Indeed, judges must rely on their background knowledge in fulfilling their adjudicative function. As David M. Paciocco and Lee Stuesser write in their book The Law of Evidence (1996), at p. 277:

> In general, the trier of fact is entitled simply to apply common sense and human experience in determining whether evidence is credible and in deciding what use, if any, to make of it in coming to its finding of fact. [Emphasis in original.]

[40] At the same time, where the matter is one of identifying and applying the law to the findings of fact, it must be the law that governs and not a judge's individual beliefs that may conflict with the law. Further, notwithstanding that their own insights into human nature will properly play a role in making findings of credibility or factual determinations, judges must make those determinations only after being equally open to, and considering the views of, all parties before them. The reasonable person, through whose eyes the apprehension of bias is assessed, expects judges to undertake an open-minded, carefully considered, and dispassionately deliberate investigation of the complicated reality of each case before them.

[41] It is axiomatic that all cases litigated before judges are, to a greater or lesser degree, complex. There is more to a case than who did what to whom, and the questions of fact and law to be determined in any given case do not arise in a vacuum. Rather, they are the consequence of numerous factors, influenced by the innumerable forces which impact on them in a particular context. Judges, acting as finders of fact, must inquire into those forces. In short, they must be aware of the context in which the alleged crime occurred.

[42] Judicial inquiry into the factual, social and psychological context within which litigation arises is not unusual. Rather, a conscious, contextual inquiry has become an accepted step towards judicial impartiality. In that regard, Professor Jennifer Nedelsky's "Embodied Diversity and the Challenges to Law" (1997), 42 McGill L.J. 91, at p. 107, offers the following comment:

> What makes it possible for us to genuinely judge, to move beyond our private idiosyncracies and preferences, is our capacity to achieve an "enlargement of mind". We do this by taking different perspectives into account. This is the path out of the blindness of our subjective private conditions. The more views we are able to take into account, the less likely we are to be locked into one perspective.... It is the capacity for "enlargement of mind" that makes autonomous, impartial judgment possible.

[43] Judicial inquiry into context provides the requisite background for the interpretation and the application of the law. For example, in a case involving alleged police misconduct in denying an accused's right to counsel, this Court inquired not simply into whether the accused had been read their *Charter* rights, but also used a contextual approach to ensure that the purpose of the constitutionally protected right was fulfilled: *R. v. Bartle*, [1994] 3 S.C.R. 173. The Court, placing itself in the position of the accused, asked how the accused would have experienced and responded to arrest and detention. Against this background, the Court went on to determine what was required to make the right to counsel truly meaningful. This inquiry provided the Court with a larger picture, which was in turn conducive to a more just determination of the case.

[44] An understanding of the context or background essential to judging may be gained from testimony from expert witnesses in order to put the case in context: *R. v. Lavallee*, [1990] 1 S.C.R. 852, *R. v. Parks* (1993), 15 O.R. (3d) 324 (C.A.), and *Moge v. Moge*, [1992] 3 S.C.R. 813, from academic studies properly placed before the Court; and from the judge's personal understanding and experience of the society in which the judge lives and works. This process of enlargement is not only consistent with impartiality; it may also be seen as its essential precondition.

[45] A reasonable person far from being troubled by this process, would see it as an important aid to judicial impartiality.

B. The Nature of the Community

[46] The reasonable person, identified by de Grandpré J. in Committee for Justice and Liberty, supra, is an informed and right-minded member of the community, a community which, in Canada, supports the fundamental principles entrenched in the Constitution by the Canadian Charter of Rights and Freedoms. Those fundamental principles include the principles of equality set out in s. 15 of the Charter and endorsed in nation-wide quasi-constitutional provincial and federal human rights legislation. The reasonable person must be taken to be aware of the history of discrimination faced by disadvantaged groups in Canadian society protected by the Charter's equality provisions. These are matters of which judicial notice may be taken. In Parks, supra, at p. 342, Doherty J.A., did just this, stating:

> Racism, and in particular anti-black racism, is a part of our community's psyche. A significant segment of our community holds overtly racist views. A much larger segment subconsciously operates on the basis of negative racial stereotypes. Furthermore, our institutions, including the criminal justice system, reflect and perpetuate those negative stereotypes.

[47] The reasonable person is not only a member of the Canadian community, but also, more specifically, is a member of the local communities in which the case at issue arose (in this case, the Nova Scotian and Halifax communities). Such a person must be taken to possess knowledge of the local population and its racial dynamics, including the existence in the community of a history of widespread and systemic discrimination against black and aboriginal people, and high profile clashes between the police and the visible minority population over policing issues: Royal Commission on the Donald Marshall Jr. Prosecution (1989); *R. v. Smith* (1991), 109 N.S.R. (2d) 394 (Co. Ct.). The reasonable person must thus be deemed to be cognizant of the existence of racism in Halifax, Nova Scotia. It follows that judges may take notice of actual racism known to exist in a particular society. Judges have done so with respect to racism in Nova Scotia. In *Nova Scotia (Minister of Community Services) v. S.M.S.* (1992), 110 N.S.R. (2d) 91 (Fam Ct.), it was stated at p. 108:

> [Racism] is a pernicious reality. The issue of racism existing in Nova Scotia has been well documented in the Marshall Inquiry Report (sub. nom. Royal Commission on the Donald Marshall, Jr., Prosecution). A person would have to be stupid, complacent or ignorant not to acknowledge its presence, not only individually, but also systemically and institutionally.

[48] We conclude that the reasonable person contemplated by de Grandpré J., and endorsed by Canadian courts is a person who approaches the question of whether there exists a reasonable apprehension of bias with a complex and contextualized understanding of the issues in the case. The reasonable person understands the impossibility of judicial neutrality, but demands judicial impartiality. The reasonable person is cognizant of the racial dynamics in the local community, and, as a member of the Canadian community, is supportive of the principles of equality.

[49] Before concluding that there exists a reasonable apprehension of bias in the conduct of a judge, the reasonable person would require some clear evidence that the judge in question had improperly used his or her perspective in the decision-making process; this flows from the presumption of impartiality of the judiciary. There must be some indication that the judge was not approaching the case with an open mind fair to all parties. Awareness of the context within which a case occurred would not constitute such evidence; on the contrary, such awareness is consistent with the highest tradition of judicial impartiality.

IV. APPLICATION OF THE TEST TO THE FACTS

[50] In assessing whether a reasonable person would perceive the comments of Judge Sparks to give rise to a reasonable apprehension of bias, it is important to bear in mind that the impugned reasons were delivered orally. As Professor Devlin puts it in "We Can't Go On Together with Suspicious Minds: Judicial Bias and Racialized Perspective in R. v. R.D.S.", supra, at p. 414:

> Trial judges have a heavy workload that allows little time for meticulously thought-through reasoning. This is particularly true when decisions are delivered orally immediately after counsel have finished their arguments.

(See also *R. v. Burns*, [1994] 1 S.C.R. 656, at p. 664.)

It follows that for the purposes of this appeal, the oral reasons issued by judge Sparks should be read in their entirety, and the impugned passages should be construed in light of the whole of the trial proceedings and in light of all other portions of the judgment.

[51] Judge Sparks was faced with contradictory testimony from the only two witnesses, the appellant R.D.S., and Constable Stienburg. Both testified as to the events that occurred and were subjected to cross-examination. As trier of fact, Judge Sparks was required to assess their testimony, and to determine whether or not, on the evidence before her, she had a reasonable doubt as to the guilt of the appellant R.D.S. It is evident in the transcript that Judge Sparks proceeded to do just that.

[52] Judge Sparks briefly summarized the contradictory evidence offered by the two witnesses, and then made several observations about credibility. She noted that R.D.S. testified quite candidly, and with considerable detail. She remarked that contrary to the testimony of Constable Stienburg, it was the evidence of R.D.S. that when he arrived on the scene on his bike, his cousin was handcuffed and not struggling in any way. She found the level of detail that R.D.S. provided to have "a ring of truth", and found him to be "a rather honest young boy". In the end, while Judge Sparks specifically noted that she did not accept all the evidence given by R.D.S., she nevertheless found him to have raised a reasonable doubt by raising queries in her mind as to what actually occurred.

[53] It is important to note that having already found R.D.S. to be credible, and having accepted a sufficient portion of his evidence to leave her with a reasonable doubt as to his guilt, Judge Sparks necessarily disbelieved at least a portion of the conflicting evidence of Constable Stienburg. At that point, Judge Sparks made reference to the submissions of the Crown that "there's absolutely no reason to attack the credibility of the officer", and then addressed herself to why there might, in fact, be a reason to attack the credibility of the officer in this case. It is in this context that Judge Sparks made the statements which have prompted this appeal:

> The Crown says, well, why would the officer say that events occurred the way in which he has relayed them to the Court this morning. I am not saying that the Constable has misled the court, although police officers have been known to do that in the past. I am not saying that the officer overreacted, but certainly police officers do overreact, particularly when they are dealing with non-white groups. That to me indicates a state of mind right there that is questionable. I believe that probably the situation in this particular case is the case of a young police officer who overreacted. I do accept the evidence of [R.D.S.] that he was told to shut up or he would

> be under arrest. It seems to be in keeping with the prevalent attitude of the day.
>
> At any rate, based upon my comments and based upon all the evidence before the court I have no other choice but to acquit.

[54] These remarks do not support the conclusion that Judge Sparks found Constable Stienburg to have lied. In fact, Judge Sparks did quite the opposite. She noted firstly, that she was not saying Constable Stienburg had misled the court, although that could be an explanation for his evidence. She then went on to remark that she was not saying that Constable Stienburg had overreacted, though she was alive to that possibility given that it had happened with police officers in the past, and in particular, it had happened when police officers were dealing with non-white groups. Finally, Judge Sparks concluded that, though she was not willing to say that Constable Stienburg did overreact, it was her belief that he probably overreacted. And, in support of that finding, she noted that she accepted the evidence of R.D.S. that "he was told to shut up or he would be under arrest".

[55] At no time did Judge Sparks rule that the probable overreaction by Stienburg was motivated by racism. Rather, she tied her finding of probable overreaction to the evidence that Constable Stienburg had threatened to arrest the appellant R.D.S. for speaking to his cousin. At the same time, there was evidence capable of supporting a finding of racially motivated overreaction. At an earlier point in the proceedings, she had accepted the evidence that the other youth arrested that day[] was handcuffed and thus secured when R.D.S. approached. This constitutes evidence which could lead one to question why it was necessary for both boys to be placed in choke holds by Constable Stienburg, purportedly to secure them. In the face of such evidence, we respectfully disagree with the views of our colleagues Cory and Major JJ. that there was no evidence on which Judge Sparks could have found "racially motivated" overreaction by the police officer.

[56] While it seems clear that Judge Sparks did not in fact relate the officer's probable overreaction to the race of the appellant R.D.S., it should be noted that if Judge Sparks had chosen to attribute the behaviour of Constable Stienburg to the racial dynamics of the situation, she would not necessarily have erred. As a member of the community, it was open to her to take into account the well-known presence of racism in that community and to evalu-

ate the evidence as to what occurred against that background.

[57] That Judge Sparks recognized that police officers sometimes overreact when dealing with non-white groups simply demonstrates that in making her determination in this case, she was alive to the well-known racial dynamics that may exist in interactions between police officers and visible minorities. As found by Freeman J.A. in his dissenting judgment at the Court of Appeal (1995), 145 N.S.R. (2d) 284, at p. 294:

> The case was racially charged, a classic confrontation between a white police officer representing the power of the state and a black youth charged with an offence. Judge Sparks was under a duty to be sensitive to the nuances and implications, and to rely on her own common sense which is necessarily informed by her own experience and understanding.

[58] Given these facts, the question is whether a reasonable and right-minded person, informed of the circumstances of this case, and knowledgeable about the local community and about Canadian Charter values, would perceive that the reasons of Judge Sparks would give rise to a reasonable apprehension of bias. In our view, they would not. The

clear evidence of prejudgment required to sustain a reasonable apprehension of bias is nowhere to be found.

[59] Judge Sparks' oral reasons show that she approached the case with an open mind, used her experience and knowledge of the community to achieve an understanding of the reality of the case, and applied the fundamental principle of proof beyond a reasonable doubt. Her comments were based entirely on the case before her, were made after a consideration of the conflicting testimony of the two witnesses and in response to the Crown's submissions, and were entirely supported by the evidence. In alerting herself to the racial dynamic in the case, she was simply engaging in the process of contextualized judging which, in our view, was entirely proper and conducive to a fair and just resolution of the case before her.

V. CONCLUSION

[60] In the result, we agree with Cory J. as to the disposition of this case. We would allow the appeal, overturn the findings of the Nova Scotia Supreme Court (Trial Division) and the majority of the Nova Scotia Court of Appeal, and restore the acquittal of the appellant R.D.S.

(f) Gavels, Microphones Don't Mix†

The Globe and Mail Editorial

Judicial decisions may be political, but judges don't need to act like politicians

Astutely, the Chief Justice of the Supreme Court of Canada has identified the next big political flashpoint on the fall horizon.

Populists in the Reform Party and in Premier Ralph Klein's Alberta are spoiling for battle against "judicial activism" — the perceived encroachment of judges on political decisions in Canada. Chief Justice Antonio Lamer is appropriately alert to the challenge.

But less wisely, Chief Justice Lamer has mused about a way to respond to this looming showdown

between populists and judges. So you think the Supreme Court has too loud a voice in politics? Curiously, the Chief Justice believes that the solution may lie in further amplifying and broadcasting that voice.

"I wonder whether judges, or maybe through their chief justices, should be rolling up the sleeves of their judicial robes and involving themselves in these public discussions more directly," he said Sunday in a speech to the Canadian Bar Association's annual conference.

It is a strange proposition indeed to suggest that people would want more of the Supreme Court's

---

† From "Editorial", *The Globe and Mail* (26 August 1998) A14. Reproduced with permission from The Globe and Mail.

thinking lobbed into the political arena in Canada. Critics of the court's power have not been asking to hear more from the judges in politics, but less.

Chief Justice Lamer wonders whether someone should be speaking on the court's behalf, if the August judiciary is going to be kicked around by the Reform Party, editorial writers and court critics. "The judiciary has no voice and no champion," he said, lamenting the loss of vocal support from lawyers and "law officers of the Crown."

Although we can admire the Chief Justice's understandable desire to defend his institution, we urge caution. When the fortress is under siege, it's foolhardy to mount the defence by dragging your leaders out from behind the walls.

The walls in this case are the walls of silence, the code that prevents judges from publicly discussing their rulings after they are released. These walls exist to ensure that the Supreme Court speaks through its rulings, not its individual personalities. If Chief Justice Lamer and his colleagues truly believe that the Supreme Court is in danger of being misunderstood in its increasingly activist role, there are other solutions.

Most obviously, they can do their best to explain their rulings better. Chief Justice Lamer should note that the uprising against the court's power rests largely on the rulings, not on the individual judges. Clearly, the current Supreme Court is up to the challenge of explaining itself more fully — in print. The recent ruling on Quebec's secession rights, for example, was deft in execution and accessible in style.

The rulings, let's not forget, represent the collected wisdom and opinions of the judges. Once a judge starts venturing out to do a "just-what-was-meant" on the ruling, whether on television or in speeches, it's almost inevitable that two things will happen: (1) he will start treading into questions not covered by the ruling; and (2) the judge will start speaking for himself instead of the court as a whole.

If Chief Justice Lamer and his eight colleagues truly believe that Canadians need to hear more from them, the time for their views to be aired is before their rulings — not after the fact — with more open selection processes for judges. The last thing Canada needs is nine more unelected political voices crowding to be heard around a microphone.

(g) *Re Conduct of Honourable Paul Cosgrove of the Ontario Superior Court of Justice*†

Canadian Judicial Council

IN THE MATTER OF

Section 65 of the *Judges Act*, R.S., 1985, c. J-1, and of the Inquiry Committee convened by the Canadian Judicial Council to review the conduct of the Honourable Paul Cosgrove of the Ontario Superior Court of Justice:

REPORT OF THE
CANADIAN JUDICIAL COUNCIL
TO THE MINISTER OF JUSTICE

Pursuant to its mandate under the *Judges Act*, and after inquiring into the conduct of Justice Cosgrove, the Canadian Judicial Council hereby recommends to the Minister of Justice, pursuant to section 65 of the *Judges Act*, that the Honourable Paul Cosgrove be removed from office, for the reasons outlined in this Report.

Presented in Ottawa, 30 March 2009

---

† From Report of the Canadian Judicial Council to the Minister of Justice, presented in Ottawa, March 30, 2009. Reproduced with permission. [Notes and/or references omitted.]

INTRODUCTION

[1] Public confidence in the judiciary is essential in maintaining the rule of law and preserving the strength of our democratic institutions. All judges have both a personal and collective duty to maintain this confidence by upholding the highest standards of conduct. After inquiring into the conduct of the Honourable Paul Cosgrove, we find that he has failed in the due execution of his office to such an extent that public confidence in his ability to properly discharge his judicial duties in the future cannot be restored. In the result, we conclude that a recommendation be made to the Minister of Justice that Justice Cosgrove be removed from office.

BACKGROUND

[2] On 27 November 2008, we received the *Report to the Canadian Judicial Council of the Inquiry Committee Appointed to Conduct an Investigation Into the Conduct of Mr. Justice Paul Cosgrove, a Justice of the Ontario Superior Court of Justice* (the "Inquiry Committee Report"). This inquiry resulted from the request made by the Attorney General of Ontario on 22 April 2004 pursuant to subsection 63(1) of the *Judges Act*.

[3] From 1997 to 1999, Justice Cosgrove presided over the murder trial of Julia Elliott. A stay of proceedings was granted on 7 September 1999 after Justice Cosgrove concluded that there had been over 150 violations of Ms Elliott's rights under the *Canadian Charter of Rights and Freedoms*. On appeal, the stay of proceedings was set aside, and a new trial was ordered. The Court of Appeal remarked (*R. v. Elliott* (2003), 179 O.A.C. 219, at paragraph 166):

> We conclude this part of our reasons as we began. The evidence does not support most of the findings of Charter breaches by the trial judge. The few Charter breaches that were made out, such as non-disclosure of certain items, were remedied before the trial proper would have commenced had the trial judge not entered the stay of proceedings. The trial judge made numerous legal errors as to the application of the Charter. He made findings of misconduct against Crown counsel and police officers that were unwarranted and unsubstantiated. He misused his powers of contempt and allowed investigations into areas that were extraneous to the real issues in the case.

[4] Following a challenge to the constitutionality of subsection 63(1) of the *Judges Act* by Justice Cosgrove, and subsequent appeals, the Inquiry Com-

mittee proceedings resumed on 2 September 2008. The full procedural history of the complaint, the Inquiry, and the related proceedings, is set out in the Inquiry Committee Report at paragraphs 3 to 26.

[5] In its review of the judge's conduct, the Inquiry Committee adopted the reasoning of the Supreme Court of Canada in *Moreau-Bérubé v. New Brunswick (Judicial Council)*, [2002] 1 S.C.R. 249 (paragraph 58):

> In some cases, however, the actions and expressions of an individual judge trigger concerns about the integrity of the judicial function itself. When a disciplinary process is launched to look at the conduct of an individual judge, it is alleged that an abuse of judicial independence by a judge has threatened the integrity of the judiciary as a whole. The harm alleged is not curable by the appeal process.

[6] The Inquiry Committee found that the judge's conduct included: an inappropriate aligning of the judge with defence counsel giving rise to an apprehension of bias; an abuse of judicial powers by a deliberate, repeated and unwarranted interference in the presentation of the Crown's case; the abuse of judicial powers by inappropriate interference with RCMP activities; the misuse of judicial powers by repeated inappropriate threats of citations for contempt or arrest without foundation; the use of rude, abusive or intemperate language; and the arbitrary quashing of a federal immigration warrant.

[7] The members of the Inquiry Committee then agreed unanimously as follows (paragraph 167):

> In our opinion, the evidence we have characterized as lack of restraint, abuse of judicial independence, or abuse of judicial powers fully warrants a recommendation for removal from office, subject to whatever effect may be given to the judge's statement [of apology] of 10 September 2008.

[8] After considering the judge's statement and the submissions, four out of the five members of the Inquiry Committee concluded as follows (paragraph 189):

> For the reasons given above, the words used and the conduct engaged in by Justice Cosgrove, over a prolonged period of time, constitute a failure in the due exercise of his office by abusing his powers as a judge. They give rise to a reasonable and irremediable apprehension of bias. Regrettably, his statement is insufficient to offset the serious harm done to public confidence in the concept of the judicial role, as described in

the Marshall test. He has rendered himself incapable of executing the judicial office.

[9] Chief Justice Allan Wachowich, a member of the Inquiry Committee, indicated in dissenting reasons that while he agreed with the conclusion of the Committee as quoted at paragraph 7 of these reasons, he accepted the view of Independent Counsel, following Justice Cosgrove's apology, that the judge could be strongly admonished and not removed from office.

[10] In accordance with section 9 of the *Canadian Judicial Council Inquiries and Investigations By-Laws*, Justice Cosgrove advised Council that he wished to appear in person to make an oral statement about the Report of the Inquiry Committee. Justice Cosgrove and Independent Counsel provided written submissions for Council's consideration.

[11] At the Council meeting held on 6 March 2009 to consider the Inquiry Committee Report and the response of Council to it, both Justice Cosgrove and his Counsel, Mr Chris Paliare, spoke.

[12] In his statement to Council, Justice Cosgrove confirmed that his personal statement of 10 September 2008 to the Inquiry Committee was intended to be an unqualified recognition of his judicial misconduct and an unqualified apology. He repeated these sentiments in his statement before us. Justice Cosgrove asked that Council, in assessing its recommendation to the Minister of Justice in this matter, take into account his entire judicial career and that the conclusion of the majority of the Inquiry Committee be rejected.

[13] In his submissions on behalf of Justice Cosgrove, Mr Paliare confirmed that the Committee findings of judicial misconduct were not disputed, but asked that Council not recommend to the Minister of Justice that Justice Cosgrove be removed from office. In his submission, the letters of support filed in support of Justice Cosgrove, the opinion expressed by Independent Counsel that a strong admonition was an appropriate sanction, the fact that Justice Cosgrove had sat effectively without incident for 4½ years after the events at issue and, finally, his statement to the Inquiry Committee and his remarks to Council, should lead to the application of a lesser sanction than removal.

[14] Independent Counsel, Mr Earl Cherniak, also spoke. He reiterated his view that "significant weight can be placed on the apology made by Justice Cosgrove" so that a strong admonition was an appropriate outcome in the circumstances, but also noted that both conclusions (removal or a lesser sanction) were open on the evidence. He emphasized that, in the end, the decision was for Council to make and not Independent Counsel.

ISSUES

[15] In discharging our duties pursuant to subsection 65(2) of the *Judges Act*, we must follow a two-stage process, as described in the *Majority Reasons of the Canadian Judicial Council In the Matter of an Inquiry into the Conduct Of the Honourable P. Theodore Matlow, 3 December 2008* (see, in particular, paragraph 166). First, we must decide whether or not the judge is "incapacitated or disabled from the due execution of the office of judge" within the meaning of subsection 65(2) of the *Judges Act*. If this question is answered in the affirmative, we must then proceed to the second stage and determine if a recommendation for removal is warranted.

[16] Counsel for Justice Cosgrove, in his written submission, acknowledges that the judge engaged in judicial misconduct and that "it falls within paragraph 65(2)(b) of the *Judges Act*." He also repeated, in relation to the judge's apology, that it "was, and was intended to be, a sincere admission of judicial misconduct."

> Submissions of the Honourable Paul Cosgrove, 26 January 2009, paragraph 107.

[17] Independent Counsel shares this view. He agrees (at paragraph 32 of his written submission) that the misconduct as found by the Inquiry Committee would certainly warrant removal in the absence of a genuine apology: "Independent Counsel was, and is, of the view that, absent Justice Cosgrove's apology, the facts presented to and found by the Inquiry Committee were capable [of] supporting a recommendation for removal to the Minister of Justice."

[18] Given the thorough and cogent analysis of the extensive evidence before the Inquiry Committee, we have no difficulty in agreeing and adopting as our own the conclusions reached by the Committee as expressed in paragraph 167 of its Report. There can be no doubt that Justice Cosgrove engaged in serious judicial misconduct, within the meaning of the *Judges Act*.

[19] Accordingly, it remains for Council to proceed to the second stage and determine if public confidence in the judge's ability to discharge the duties of his office has been undermined to such an extent that a recommendation for removal is warranted. In

this regard, we adopt the standard identified by Council in the *Marshall* matter and widely applied in other cases since then:

> Is the conduct alleged so manifestly and profoundly destructive of the concept of the impartiality, integrity, and independence of the judicial role, that public confidence would be sufficiently undermined to render the judge incapable of executing the judicial office?

[20] In order to assess the judge's conduct in relation to this standard, we must answer the following three questions:

1. What is the effect of Justice Cosgrove's statements of apology made before the Inquiry Committee and again before the Council?
2. What is the effect of the views expressed by Independent Counsel regarding removal?
3. What is the effect of taking into account the judge's entire judicial career, character and abilities, as described in the letters of support and submissions from counsel?

[21] We will address each question in turn.

The Apologies

[22] As noted, Justice Cosgrove apologized in person before both the Inquiry Committee and the Canadian Judicial Council. We wish to highlight some key passages from the transcripts of the lengthy hearing before the Inquiry Committee:

> ... I approached each decision I made with an open mind, and I never acted in bad faith, but I now realize that **I made a series of significant errors** that affected the proceedings. ...
>
> ... I made many findings against the Ministry of the Attorney General and its senior representatives, Crown counsel, police officers and public officials that were set aside by the Court of Appeal. **I erred in so doing and I regret those errors**. I regret the effect of my findings on them. ...
>
> ... For the **significant errors** that I have described, I sincerely and unreservedly apologize ...
>
> Finally, I would like to apologize to the family of the victim of this crime who, as a result of **my legal errors**, experienced a significant delay in achieving the closure arrived at by having a criminal prosecution reach its substantive conclusion.
>
> *Transcript of the proceedings before the Inquiry Committee, 10 September 2008, pages 1660 to 1665 — emphasis added*

[23] We also highlight the following passages from the hearing before Council:

> I understood, and I accepted that judgement. Nevertheless, I was sustained by my view that **notwithstanding the errors I had clearly made, those errors had been made in good faith** and what was now obviously a misguided attempt to achieve justice in the case. ...
>
> ... Moreover, I would like [to] apologize, again, to the family of the victim of the crime who, **as a result of my errors**, have experienced a significant delay in achieving the closure arrived at by having the criminal prosecution reach its substantive conclusion.
>
> *Transcript of proceedings before the Canadian Judicial Council, 6 March 2009, pages 8 and 11-12 — emphasis added*

[24] We note that the focus of the apologies appears to be directed more to the "errors" made during the *Elliott* trial and less on a recognition that many of these "errors" were caused by, or constituted in and of themselves, serious misconduct that was damaging both to the administration of justice and the public's confidence in the judiciary. These errors went far beyond the types of errors that can be readily corrected by appellate courts.

[25] As found by the Inquiry Committee, the judge's conduct included: giving rise to an apprehension of bias; repeated and unwarranted interference in the presentation of the Crown's case; inappropriate interference with RCMP activities; inappropriate threats of citations for contempt or arrest without foundation; the use of rude, abusive or intemperate language; and the arbitrary quashing of a federal immigration warrant. These are not mere judicial errors.

[26] Justice Cosgrove made these additional comments before us:

> The last thing that I would hope for would be to bring disrespect to this office. I realize that by my actions and my judicial misconduct, I may have done that. I deeply and acutely regret the prospect that my actions may have done damage to this office.

[27] Counsel for Justice Cosgrove argues that the judge's apology was:

> ... a sincere, complete, and abject apology for acts of judicial misconduct and other acts which may not even amount to judicial misconduct but nevertheless had a significant and troubling effect on the lives of public servants and citizens. It was a promise to do better in the future, which

was informed and infused by reference to the canonical works of the CJC.

Submissions on behalf of
the Honourable Paul Cosgrove, 26 January 2009,
paragraph 100.

[28] Independent Counsel's view is that:

> The recognition of errors made by Justice Cosgrove, his apparent understanding and recognition of the impact of his conduct, and the set of full and unreserved apologies he provided led Independent Counsel to the opinion that, in his view, it is unlikely that this conduct will happen again, such that public confidence in the administration of justice could be restored by a pointed and strong admonition.
>
> *Submissions of Independent Counsel,*
> *February 2009, paragraph 41.*

[29] We agree that an apology is an important factor for Council to consider in assessing the future conduct of a judge and, specifically, whether the judge recognizes that they have engaged in misconduct and, further, whether there is a reasonable prospect that the judge will sincerely strive to avoid inappropriate conduct in future.

[30] Justice Cosgrove's apology in this case addresses both of these aspects. Even accepting that the judge's apology was sincere, we must consider an additional — more important — aspect in deciding whether a recommendation for removal is warranted: the effect upon public confidence of the actions of the judge in light of the nature and seriousness of the misconduct.

[31] For Council, therefore, the key question is whether the apology is sufficient to restore public confidence. Even a heartfelt and sincere apology may not be sufficient to alleviate the harm done to public confidence by reason of serious and sustained judicial misconduct. The Supreme Court of Canada in *Moreau-Bérubé* considered the factors that must be considered by a Judicial Council in such circumstances:

> [72] The comments of judge Moreau-Bérubé, as well as her apology, are a matter of record. In deciding whether the comments created a reasonable apprehension of bias, the Council applied an objective test, and attempted to ascertain the degree of apprehension that might exist in an ordinary, reasonable person.... In discharging its function, the Council must be acutely sensitive to the requirements of judicial independence, and it must ensure never to kill the expression of unpopular, honestly held views in the context of court proceedings. It must also be

equally sensitive to the reasonable expectations of an informed dispassionate public that holders of judicial office will remain at all times worthy of trust, confidence and respect.

[32] Although the New Brunswick Judicial Council in the *Moreau-Bérubé* matter noted that a timely apology had been made, three days after the misconduct, the Supreme Court of Canada did not disturb the decision of the New Brunswick Judicial Council that, in light of the severity of the judge's misconduct, the application of the identified objective test required the removal of the judge despite the judge's apology.

[33] The Inquiry Committee Report, in Part III, reviews and quotes in some detail the uncontested testimony of four witnesses on the severe effects on them of Justice Cosgrove's conduct in the *Elliott* case (paragraphs 109 to 120). In accepting the uncontradicted evidence as reliable, the Inquiry Committee noted "the credibility of the witnesses was beyond question and they gave compelling evidence" (paragraph 108). We agree.

[34] In this case, it is our conclusion that the misconduct by Justice Cosgrove was so serious and so destructive of public confidence that no apology, no matter its sincerity, can restore public confidence in the judge's future ability to impartially carry out his judicial duties in accordance with the high standards expected of all judges. This was not a single instance of misconduct but, rather, misconduct that was pervasive in both scope and duration.

[35] We endorse the majority's conclusion in regard to the judge's apology (paragraph 187):

> Given the judge's serious misconduct over an extended period of time, this statement, even viewed in its most positive light, cannot serve to restore public confidence in the judge, or in the administration of justice.

[36] In our opinion, the statement made before us by Justice Cosgrove did not add to, or change, the nature and effect of his earlier apology.

[37] It is significant to note that Justice Cosgrove acknowledges that public confidence in his ability to preside [over] certain cases has been seriously shaken. He explains:

> However, under the circumstances, in the event I am assigned to hear cases in the future, it would be inappropriate for me to sit in cases involving the Attorney General of Canada or Her Majesty The Queen in Right of Canada, or the Attorney General of Ontario or Her Majesty The Queen

in Right of Ontario, and I would take steps to ensure that that would not occur.

> *Transcript of proceedings before*
> *the Inquiry Committee, 10 September 2008,*
> *page 1667.*

[38] The Inquiry Committee pointed out (at paragraph 188 of its report): "One may well ask what such a direction would say about the ability of the judge to execute his office." We agree. It seems to us that this concession is a tacit acknowledgement that a significant segment of those persons involved in litigation before the court, including federal and provincial Crown attorneys, may not have confidence in the judge's ability to judge impartially.

Timing of the apology of September 2008

[39] Much has been said about the timing of the apology. At paragraph 113 of his written submission, counsel for Justice Cosgrove argues that "it is difficult to see how Justice Cosgrove's statement could have been given prior to the inquiry. There is no process to do so. Moreover, his statement did not halt the work of the Inquiry Committee, which elected to receive all of the evidence marshal[l]ed by Independent Counsel in order to complete their mandate." Independent Counsel, in his oral submission to the Inquiry Committee, appears to suggest that Justice Cosgrove could not apologize earlier, given his challenge to the constitutionality of the process.

[40] While it is not strictly necessary to address this issue, given the decision just made, we make the following points. It was open to Justice Cosgrove to offer, at any time, an apology about his conduct but he did not. It appears that the judge did not, for years after the fact, appreciate that he had engaged in serious misconduct.

[41] Justice Cosgrove acknowledged his late realization:

> Recently, I began to prepare for the current hearing. My preparation has profoundly affected my appreciation of the circumstance of this case. Both on my own and with my counsel, I have spent literally weeks reviewing the record of the trial proceedings and even reviewing the bench books of the time.

> Finally, I have spent days in this room hearing independent counsel reading passages of the evidence from the proceedings.

All of these steps have caused me to relive the trial, but, for the first time, from an entirely different perspective.

> *Transcript of proceedings before*
> *the Inquiry Committee, 10 September 2008,*
> *page 1666.*

[42] The tardiness of the judge's apology reveals both his lack of insight and his lack of appreciation of the impact of his egregious misconduct on public confidence in the judiciary.

[43] It must also be emphasized that the apology was not made any time soon after the constitutional issue was resolved against Justice Cosgrove. In fact, it was only on the seventh day of the eight days of the hearings before the Inquiry Committee that Justice Cosgrove finally tendered his apology. It's not surprising that the Inquiry Committee, after considering all the relevant circumstances, including the timing of Justice Cosgrove's statement, found the apology insufficient to restore public confidence. We agree fully with this conclusion.

Timing of the Attorney General's Request for an Inquiry

[44] Justice Cosgrove's counsel commented on the fact that the Attorney General did not request the commencement of an inquiry until 4 years had passed since the verdict in the *Elliott* matter. In his presentation before us, he argued:

> So if, in fact, there was a concern by the Attorney General about whether or not public confidence could be maintained with respect to Justice Cosgrove sitting, in my respectful view, there was no reason for him not to have written that letter sooner. These two processes could have gone on in parallel, and I simply put that forward to you as yet another factor which demonstrates clearly that Justice Cosgrove can and does have the confidence of the public to continue to sit as a judge.

> *Transcript of Council hearing, 6 March 2009,*
> *page 55.*

[45] This interpretation does not take into account the many duties of an Attorney General. Attorneys General have an overall responsibility to administer justice in the public interest. In regard to judicial conduct, Justice Sharlow, in *Attorney General of Canada v. Cosgrove* 2007 FCA 103, commented as follows:

> [35] An important aspect of the traditional constitutional role of the Attorney General of England is to protect the public interest in the

administration of justice. In Canada, that role is now shared by all Attorneys General — the provincial Attorneys General within their respective provinces, and the Attorney General of Canada in federal matters.

[36] The public interest in an appropriate procedure for the review of the conduct of judges is an aspect of the public interest in the administration of justice. Therefore, it seems to me to be consistent with Canadian constitutional principles for provincial Attorneys General to play a part in the review of the conduct of judges of the superior courts of their respective provinces.

[46] However, Attorneys General are also responsible for the prosecution of crimes. In discharging this duty, it is well established that Attorneys General must act with the highest standards of fairness. The *Crown Policy Manual* of the Attorney General of Ontario emphasizes that:

> Public confidence in the administration of criminal justice is bolstered by a system where Crown counsel are not only strong and effective advocates for the prosecution, but also Ministers of Justice with a duty to ensure that the criminal justice system operates fairly to all: the accused, victims of crime, and the public.
>
> *"Crown Policy Manual,"*
> *Ministry of the Attorney General of Ontario, 2005*

[47] Given an Attorney General's role and duties, it is understandable that the Attorney General of Ontario at the time did not request that Council commence an inquiry into the conduct of Justice Cosgrove, since the matter giving rise to the complaint was the subject of an appeal by his own Crown counsel. For that reason, we place little weight on the fact that there was a delay between the time of the events in the *Elliott* trial and the time of the request of the Attorney General.

[48] In fact, the Attorney General acted less than 2 months after the appeal period in regard to the decision of the Court of Appeal in *Elliott* lapsed. We find that this timing does not suggest, in any way, that the Attorney General's actions can be characterized as an indication of confidence in the abilities of Justice Cosgrove to properly discharge the duties of his office.

[49] Counsel for Justice Cosgrove also argues that no complaints were made by anyone during the 4½ years in question and that this, therefore, demonstrates continued confidence in Justice Cosgrove. However, the public would not have known of the existence or extent of the judicial misconduct until the time of the decision of the Court of Appeal in

Elliott. The fact that there was no evidence presented to the Inquiry Committee about subsequent complaints does not lead to the conclusion advanced by Counsel for Justice Cosgrove.

The Views of Independent Counsel Regarding Removal

[50] Counsel for Justice Cosgrove argued that deference should be accorded to the views expressed by Independent Counsel in regard to removal.

[51] Independent Counsel did express his view, in his written submission to Council, that "public confidence in the administration of justice could be restored by a pointed and strong admonition."

[52] However, immediately after Justice Cosgrove made his statement to the Inquiry Committee on 10 September 2008, Independent Counsel had stated:

> I wish to say at the outset that nothing that I am about to say is intended to in any way fetter or interfere with the discretion that this panel has to find, conclude and recommend as you see fit should you see the case differently than I am about to tell you I see it.
>
> As I stated in my opening, my view is that judicial accountability is a matter entirely for the Canadian Judicial Council, including this panel, and not any other body, least of all independent counsel. In my view, that is the constitutional imperative of judicial independence.
>
> *Transcript of proceedings before*
> *the Inquiry Committee, 10 September 2008,*
> *page 1668.*

[53] At the hearing before us, Independent Counsel emphasized again that it was open to the Inquiry Committee to come to its own view and that both the majority and minority views regarding the judge's removal were defensible.

[54] The mandate of Independent Counsel, it must be remembered, is not that of a lawyer retained to achieve a certain result. His view is but one view, albeit a very important one, arrived at after considering all issues. It cannot be the case that the members of the Inquiry Committee are in a lesser position than Independent Counsel in coming to their own conclusion. Four of the five members of the Inquiry Committee were of the view that public confidence in the judge's ability to discharge his duties impartially could not be restored. We agree. Recommending that the judge be removed from office is a grave duty and, given the principle of

judicial independence, one that must ultimately rest with Council.

The Judge's Career, Character and Abilities

[55] Counsel for Justice Cosgrove referred to the many letters of support which in his view are evidence of the judge's character and integrity. As Council stated in its Report to the Minister in the Matlow matter in regard to comparable evidence:

> While the weight to be given to this evidence is admittedly for the inquiry committee, and while an inquiry committee may elect to give it little weight, still it is an error in principle to simply ignore this kind of evidence for all purposes. In particular, the evidence is relevant to the sanction phase of the proceedings and ought to have been considered in that context.
> *"Majority Reasons of the Canadian Judicial Council In the Matter of an Inquiry into the Conduct Of the Honourable P. Theodore Matlow,"*
> *3 December 2008, Paragraph 150*

[56] However, it is clear that the Inquiry Committee considered the letters of support but elected to give them no weight, given that there were unique circumstances before the Inquiry Committee not present in the *Matlow* matter (paragraph 38):

> We mention here also that we are not giving weight to the letters submitted to us on behalf of Justice Cosgrove in our determination of whether his conduct in *Elliott* should lead to a recommendation for removal. One element in some of the letters was that what Justice Cosgrove did in *Elliott* was isolated conduct. The two Court of Appeal decisions, *Perry* and *Lovelace*, might have suggested otherwise. We are leaving both the letters and the two decisions to the side and, as we said, confining our analysis to what happened in *Elliott*.

[57] We are of the view that the opinions of individuals, be they judicial colleagues or otherwise, who do not have the benefit of the evidentiary record and a complete knowledge and appreciation of the issues before Council, will generally be of little assistance in determining whether public confidence has been undermined to such an extent as to render a judge incapable of discharging the duties of their office. In this particular instance, we accord little weight to the letters of support. They may provide insight into the judge's character and work ethic, but they do not address the decisive issue before us, namely the damage done to public confidence by virtue of the judge's judicial misconduct. This is an issue that

rightly rests with the Inquiry Committee and Council itself.

THE ISSUE OF INCOMPETENCE

[58] While not required to do so, we wish to make some observations about the issue of incompetence.

[59] The Inquiry Committee expressed the view that some of Justice Cosgrove's conduct demonstrated incompetence. They also expressed the view (at paragraph 151) that "such pervasive incompetence is of grave concern and is bound to undermine public confidence in the administration of justice." We agree.

[60] However, the Inquiry Committee was ultimately of the opinion that (paragraph 152):

> ... [W]e consider that the public interest concern against removal for incompetence as expressed by Professor Shetreet should be given primacy. Protecting the judicial independence of all judges is more important than sanctioning the troubling incompetence of one.

[61] This perspective would appear to be based on the idea that since judicial independence protects a judge, after the fact, from having to justify or explain their decision, there should be no scrutiny of the judge's competence in arriving at a particular decision. However, we note the countervailing view, as indicated by Professor Shetreet, that incompetence could be grounds for removal in certain serious cases.

[62] In light of our earlier conclusion, we need not address whether incompetence could justify removal from office. The *Judges Act* refers in section 65 to a judge who "has become incapacitated or disabled" (in the French version *"est inapte"*). We are of the view that whether incompetence can be a ground for removal from office, in any given case, would best be dealt with another day, when the issue is more directly raised.

DECISION

[63] We agree with the conclusions reached by the majority of the members of the Inquiry Committee, as outlined in paragraph 189 of their report, which we now repeat:

> For the reasons given above, the words used and the conduct engaged in by Justice Cosgrove, over a prolonged period of time, constitute a failure in the due exercise of his office by abusing his powers as a judge. They give rise to a reason-

able and irremediable apprehension of bias. Regrettably, his statement is insufficient to offset the serious harm done to public confidence in the concept of the judicial role, as described in the Marshall test. He has rendered himself incapable of executing the judicial office.

[64] We find that Justice Cosgrove has failed in the execution of the duties of his judicial office and that public confidence in his ability to discharge those duties in future has been irrevocably lost. We find that there is no alternative measure to removal that would be sufficient to restore public confidence in the judge in this case. Therefore, we hereby recommend to the Minister of Justice, in accordance with section 65 of the *Judges Act*, that Justice Cosgrove be removed from office.

(h) Stupid Judge Tricks†

Sandra Martin

Why do our upholders of justice go off the rails? Incompetence, prejudice, ignorance and declining mental faculties are a few obvious explanations. But most often they trip up when they venture into the treacherous territory of social commentary.

Judges are people, like the rest of us, until they don their judicial robes and enter courtrooms. Then they are expected to rise above human frailties and become impartial triers of facts and arbiters of disputes. Mostly, but not always, they succeed.

When they fail, we are outraged. Martin Friedland, author of a 1995 report on judicial independence and accountability for the Canadian Judicial Council, says that's because we put them on a pedestal and expect them to operate with great integrity instead of seeing them as "real people who sometimes get drunk or do stupid things."

The passing of the Charter of Rights and Freedoms in 1982 gave judges both more visibility and more power to make rulings that have wide applications in social and public policy. Some of those decisions have sparked controversy — not only in academic debates but in the media and on political platforms. Psychiatrist Vivian Rakoff says judges are caught in a curious sort of contradiction. "They are given an elevated position in which they must express themselves with regard to the law," he says, "but they also think that gives them permission to talk about anything."

So why do judges sometimes go off the rails? Incompetence, prejudice, ignorance and declining mental faculties are a few obvious explanations. Typically, though, they tend to trip up when they veer from a strict interpretation of the law and venture into the treacherous territory of social and cultural commentary. Lest you thought for a second that the recent boner by Mr. Justice John McClung of the Alberta Court of Appeal was an isolated incident, herewith a lineup of gaffes from the past:

1. Mr. Justice Jean Bienvenue of the Quebec Superior Court berated a Trois-Rivières jury in 1995 for being "idiotic and incompetent" for finding a woman guilty of only second-degree murder after she had killed her husband by slashing his throat with a razor. Then he delivered full-bore invective against the defendant in pronouncing sentence: "When women ascend the scale of virtues, they reach higher than men; and I have always believed this. But it is also said, and this, too, I believe, that when they decide to degrade themselves, they sink to depths to which even the vilest man could not sink."

He continued: "Alas, you are indeed the image of these women so famous in history: the Delilahs, the Salomes, Charlotte Corday, Mata Hari and how many others who have been a sad part of our history and have debased the profile of women. You are one of them, and you are the clearest living example of them that I have seen." But he didn't stop there: "At the Auschwitz-Birkenau concentration camp in Poland, which I once visited, horror-stricken, even the Nazis did not eliminate millions of Jews in a painful or bloody manner. ... They died in the gas chambers, without suffering."

† From *The Globe and Mail* (12 March 1999) D2. Reproduced with permission of The Globe and Mail.

Judge Bienvenue also commented on the short skirt worn by a reporter covering the trial and asked the bailiff for a bottle of vodka while the jury was deliberating.

2. Judge Jocelyn Moreau-Bérubé told a court in Tracadie-Sheila, N.B., in 1998, that there were few "honest people" in the province's francophone Acadian peninsula. She also wondered aloud whether she was surrounded by crooks in her neighbourhood.

3. Judge Monique Dubreuil angered the Haitian community in Montreal in 1998 when she sentenced two men, whom she said were "immature" and not a threat to society, to an 18-month suspended sentence for sexual assault. She explained her leniency by saying that the victim was not a juvenile and that the men, who were of Haitian origin, came from a culture where rape is accepted. "The absence of regret of the two accused seems to be related more to the cultural context, particularly with regard to relations with women than a veritable problem of a sexual nature," she said in her ruling.

4. In a 1997 wrongful-dismissal suit against the owners of a McDonald's franchise in Milton, Ont., Mr. Justice Casimir Herold of the Ontario Court's General Division criticized "the goop that they put on Big Macs, the patented stuff," on the grounds that it "makes you sleepy, especially if you are a bookkeeper or an area manager." He impugned the defence lawyer's credibility by saying that some of his responses should be filed under the heading "the moon is made out of green cheese," and suggested he had either shredded some pertinent documents or had put them in "somebody's hamburger."

5. Criticizing the complainant in the Ewanchuk case because she "did not present herself [to the defendant] in a bonnet and crinolines" is not the first time that Judge McClung's rash judicial pen has gotten him into trouble. In 1996, he wrote the Alberta Court of Appeal judgment in a majority decision reversing a lower court ruling that the government should change the Individual Rights Protection Act to prohibit discrimination based on sexual orientation. "Rightly or wrongly, the electors of the province of Alberta, speaking through their parliamentary representatives, have declared that homosexuality ... is not to be included in the protected categories of the IRPA," he wrote in determining that a private Christian college had the right to fire Delwin Vriend from his job as a lab assistant because he is gay.

By ignoring the issue of sexual orientation in its human-rights legislation, the province was neither encouraging nor condoning discrimination, Judge McClung argued and therefore was not violating the Charter of Rights and Freedoms. "When they choose silence, provincial legislatures need not march to the Charter drum."

6. Mr. Justice Marcel Joyal of the Federal Court criticized his employer — Parliament — when he was presiding over a 1998 Toronto hearing in which Ted Weatherill, then head of the Canada Labour Relations Board, was seeking an injunction to prevent the federal cabinet from firing him. Mr. Weatherill had spent close to $150,000 on food and travel during his eight years at the CLRB. When then labour minister Lawrence MacAulay told the House of Commons that Mr. Weatherill would be fired for his extravagance, MPs stood up and applauded. In the subsequent hearing, Judge Joyal compared Parliament's treatment of Mr. Weatherill to the cheering crowds gathered at the guillotine during the French Revolution. "I don't know if I have the right to intervene. But it left a bad taste in my mouth," he said.

7. Martha and Joseph Sorger, both Holocaust survivors living in Toronto, sued the Bank of Nova Scotia, one of its branch managers and a lawyer acting for the bank for failing to perform their fiduciary duties. Halfway through the 1996 trial, the lawyer for the plaintiffs tried to obtain a mistrial because Mr. Justice Joseph Potts of the Ontario Court's General Division frequently interrupted testimony, gave the impression that he had made up his mind before hearing testimony, was rude and anti-Semitic. At one point, he allegedly interrupted Mrs. Sorger's evidence by saying: "Jesus Christ, it's like pulling hen's teeth." When the Sorgers' lawyer asked for an adjournment so they could observe the High Holidays, Judge Potts replied: "You're one of those, too?"

8. Mr. Justice Kerr Twaddle of the Manitoba Court of Appeal lessened the sentence of a man convicted of having sex with a 13-year-old girl from nine months in prison to a curfew and community service on these grounds: "She was apparently more sophisticated than many her age and was performing many household tasks, including babysitting the accused's children." Judge Twaddle described the relationship with the accused as "entirely inappropriate and criminal," but he argued that the victim was not coerced. "The girl, of course, could not consent in the legal sense, but nonetheless was a willing participant," he concluded.

9. In 1996, Mr. Justice Allyre Sirois of the Saskatchewan Court of Queen's Bench observed during a bail hearing for a man who beat his former girlfriend unconscious after she asked him to turn down the television set that "it takes two to tango." In 1993, at a dangerous-offender hearing, Judge Sirois referred to a prostitute who had been assaulted at knifepoint as belonging to "a different caste"; the year before, he told a woman who had been assaulted at the age of 12 that she had to accept some responsibility for the event.

10. During the 1987 trial of a Sri Lankan man accused of soliciting sexual services from a female police officer posing as a prostitute, Ontario Judge J.S. Climans advised the accused to "write back to Sri Lanka and get yourself a girlfriend. All she needs is a boat and she can come in."

11. Quebec Judge Denys Dionne observed during a trial in 1989 in Longeuil that: "Rules are like a woman, they are made to be violated."

12. Quebec Judge Raymonde Verreault cited "extenuating circumstances" when she handed down a 23-month sentence in 1994 to a man who had repeatedly sodomized his stepdaughter from the time she was 9 until 11. The victim did not have any "permanent scars" from the sexual assaults, according to Judge Verreault, because the attacker had respected the values of her Muslim faith and had "spared her virginity" by not engaging in vaginal intercourse. Besides, the girl may have encouraged the accused because she "harboured hatred" against her mother.

13. Quebec Judge René Crochetière ruled in 1993 that there was not enough evidence to bring a man to trial for threatening to kill his live-in lover. On leaving the crowded courtroom, the alleged victim said to the judge: "If I get killed, it will be your fault." To which he replied: "I would like to tell everyone here that, if ever this man kills this woman, it won't stop me from sleeping and I won't die — don't worry, I won't get depressed, either. It isn't my responsibility."

14. Manitoba Judge Frank Allen offered the following advice in 1989 to a 19-year-old man accused of beating a female acquaintance: "There isn't any woman worth the trouble you got yourself into." In a 1984 sexual-assault trial, the same judge observed: "You would have to be living in a vacuum, totally without wordly experience at all, not to know in many cases women are first to resist and later give in to persuasion and sometimes their own instinct."

(a)   Plural Policing: A Comparative Perspective — Canada†

George S. Rigakos and Cherie Leung

This chapter deals with the structure of contemporary Canadian policing by examining the variable roles of both public-sector and commercial security provision in the last three decades. It covers core municipal, provincial, and federal public policing as well as other quasi-public and ancillary state regulatory inspectorates and the rapid growth of private policing bodies especially in large metropolitan areas. The general approach is to provide a concise overview of the state of contemporary Canadian policy and to identify current large-scale demographic trends that are indicative of the future direction of public and private security provision in this country.

STATE POLICING

One of Canada's unique features is its identification with its federal police as a national symbol of sovereignty. The Royal Canadian Mounted Police (RCMP), affectionately known as the 'Mounties,' are perhaps internationally the most widely recognized police agency in their unique red tunic, Strathcona boots, and wide-brimmed hats. The RCMP's 'great march west,' their storied civilizing effect during the Klondike gold rush, and their reputation for 'always getting their man' is an embedded part of the Canadian national identity (e.g. Horrall 1973; Macleod 1976). While the RCMP are a federal, centralized, quasi-military constabulary, they are also responsible for local municipal and provincial policing through contractual relationships with regional municipalities,

provinces, and federal territories except in Québec and Ontario (who maintain their own provincial services: the Ontario Provincial Police and Sûreté du Québec). Of course, the RCMP still maintain primary responsibility for federal issues such as co-ordinating with Interpol, maintaining a centralized national police criminal database, national security and terrorism, co-ordinating efforts in drug trafficking, organized crime, and security for major international events.

When one includes specialized aboriginal policing, there are generally four levels of public policing in Canada: municipal, provincial, federal, and First Nations. The five largest Canadian police forces, the RCMP, Metropolitan Toronto Police, OPP, Sûreté du Québec, and the Montréal Urban Community Police, are thus alternately federal, municipal or provincial and account for over 60 percent of all Canadian police officers. First Nations policing is governed by an assortment of direct policing agreements between aboriginal communities across Canada and the RCMP, the OPP, or the Sûreté du Québec.[1] In certain instances, stand-alone First Nations police services have responsibility for policing their own communities and in others the community uses tribal police or band constables pursuant to the Indian Act. The latter band constables may enforce band bylaws but are not fully sworn constables. Bayley (1985: 57) adeptly describes the existing configuration of Canadian public policing as a *decentralized–co-ordinated–multiple* system because 'in any

---

† From Trevor Jones and Time Newburn (eds.), Plural Policing: A Comparative Perspective (New York: Routledge, 2006) 126–38. Reproduced with permission of Taylor & Francis Books UK. [Notes and/or references omitted.]

one place policing is overwhelmingly the responsibility of a single force — though that force may be variously national, provincial, or municipal.' When a contracted provincial force (or the RCMP) is removed, another fills its place with limited jurisdictional overlap. There is thus a great degree of variation across Canada when one looks at the number of police officers employed in the 581 Canadian municipal police services. For example, as of 1997, 196 municipal forces were RCMP contracts and 36 others were OPP contracts (Swol 1999: 13) while Canada's three federal territories (Yukon, Northwest, and Nunavut) had no municipal police whatsoever.

Municipal police services, therefore, vary greatly in size and operating expenditures — from Canada's largest municipal force, the Metropolitan Toronto Police Service with an annual operating budget of over $635 million to RCMP detachments such as Qualicum Beach, British Columbia at $389,689. The RCMP is thus a federal service but more than half of its officers provide policing services to provinces, territories or municipalities under contract to these levels of government. Overall, in 2001, total policing expenditures in Canada totaled $7.3 billion which represents an increase of 6.9 percent from 2000.

In constant dollars, expenditures are up 4.2 percent, the fifth year in a row that costs have increased (Canadian Center for Justice Statistics 2002:57). While costs have been rising, public police demographics suggest that there has been an overall decrease in the number of uniformed public police officers relative to the Canadian population since the 1950s. It is difficult, indeed, to get an accurate count of state-sponsored policing given the wide host of other public servants who conduct regulatory and enforcement functions (Jones and Newburn 1999) (such as social housing special constables, railway and other transit police, wildlife, game and park wardens, Competition Bureau investigators, etc.,) but the statistics compiled by the federal government focus on the defensible barometer of uniformed public police officers per the defensible barometer of uniformed public police officers at the provincial, federal, and municipal levels. The largest rise in police officers per population took place after the 1960s. In 1960 there were fewer than 145 police officers per 100,000 population but by the mid-1970s this had risen to 200 police per 100,000 population, peaking in 1991 at 203. By 2000, however that number had dropped to 182 police per 100,000 population (Canadian Center for Justice Statistics 2001: 40–1) reflecting the recent belief that public policing has not kept pace with the Canadian population. The cost of public policing has thus risen while the number of uni-

formed police officers per capita has been declining in recent years, creating an emerging perception that the Canadian public is paying more for less. Between the 1988–89 fiscal year and the 1994–5 fiscal year, the cost for public police services per Canadian rose from $163 to $198 while controlling for inflation (Rigakos 2000b: 176).

The increased cost of public policing has long been considered to be a key factor behind the expansion of private security (Spitzer and Scull 1977) although, in the Canadian context, there has been no direct empirical support to substantiate this claim (Rigakos 2000b). This issue, among others, will be explored in a more substantive manner when considering private security later in this chapter. Canadian public police unionization since the late 1970s has surely contributed to higher wages through nationally coordinated collective bargaining teams. In addition, it is important to reflect on two recent developments that bear directly on the increasing per capita cost of public police: the drive toward regionalization, and state investment in policing in the aftermath of the terrorist attacks in New York City on 11 September 2001.

Given Canada's contract-based policing arrangements between municipalities and either provincial services or the RCMP, it is not surprising to see a movement towards the amalgamation of smaller forces as a third option. One of the most significant developments in Canadian policing over the last three decades has been a general move towards larger regional or provincially contracted detachments in lieu of smaller local policing units. This process accelerated in the 1990s as the conservative provincial government in Ontario, in keeping with their wide-ranging neo-liberal initiatives, passed legislation that amended the Police Services Act in favor of 'equitable police financing.' Whereas the provincial government historically subsidized smaller town policing, amendments pursuant to Bill 105 created new regional authorities that were responsible for the full costs of their own policing. The process of regionalization was already under way: from 1962 to 1996, 153 police services were amalgamated into 11 regional police services providing policing to over 60 percent of Ontario's population. After legislative changes introduced by the Conservative government, the Ontario Provincial Police went from providing 35 police service contracts in 1998 to 92 contracts with full cost recovery in 2002. The OPP managed to cut the number of subsidized contracts in the same period from 576 to 199. The provincial government also made it possible for municipalities to contract from more than one service in any given jurisdiction.

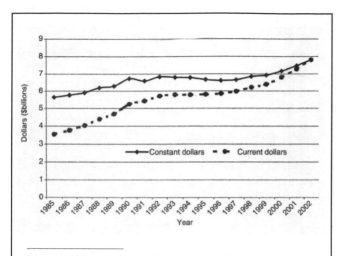

Figure 7.1: Current and constant dollar spending on policing, Canada, 1985–2002.
Source: Police Administration Survey, Canadian Centre for Justice Statistics

The main benefactors seem to be the OPP who contracted their specialized services such as emergency dispatch and detective work on top of local regional or municipal police patrol. Thus, as of 2003, the OPP was servicing 54 specialized contracts and providing quotes for an additional 24 municipalities (OPP 2003). This development lends itself to the possible long-term displacement of the dominant single-jurisdiction, single-police service model in Canada. In fact, the Quinte West police transition board entertained bids from private security companies for tertiary policing responsibilities to supplement the eventual creation of a regional police service (Rigakos 2002).

The federal government has for some time adopted a similar service delivery philosophy for the RCMP. From 1928 to 1966, the Solicitor General paid for 60 percent of local or provincial policing contracted with the RCMP. This federal share dropped slowly to 30 percent by 1990 and the long-term goal of the RCMP contract policing unit is 100 percent cost recovery. Thus, all expansions must be cost-neutral to the federal government. So, while the RCMP increased by five the number of its municipal contracts in British Columbia between 1997 to 2002, the municipal share of police expenditures also rose from 82.4 percent to 87.2 percent in the same five-year period (Canadian Center for Justice Statistics 1998: 18; Canadian Centre for Justice Statistics 2003: 23).

For both federal and provincial governments, the monetary incentive to divest policing responsibility to local regions and municipalities is rather transparent. But the move toward regional police services was also seen as essential for 'effective and efficient' policing. Despite this rationalization rhetoric there is actually contrary empirical evidence suggesting larger regional forces are no better or more effective than smaller, local police services based on measures such as clearance rates, and cost per officer (Lithopoulos and Rigakos forthcoming).

In the five years after 2005 federal expenditures on policing can be expected to increase due to the federal government's investment in the national security of Canadians following the terrorist attack in the United States on September 11, 2001. An immediate $280 million Anti-Terrorism Plan was announced in October 2001. Two months later, a new federal budget allocated $7.7 billion over five years for initiatives aimed at terrorism, including $1.6 billion for strengthened intelligence and policing. The funds are slated to enhance information-sharing capabilities among policing services and intelligence and national security agencies, as well as increase the number of police and intelligence officers and better equip them for response and prevention to terrorist activity (Canadian Center for Justice Statistics 2002: 21). By the time these initiatives are fully implemented they may have some effect on public police employment and expenditure statistics in Canada, including the police–citizen ratio.

OTHER STATE AND QUASI-STATE POLICING BODIES

There are myriad regulatory personnel involved in policing functions on behalf of Canada's three levels of government. These range from Canada's 400-plus park wardens, to tax investigators, to campus security, to military police, and the quasi-public Corps of Commissionaires, Canada's railway police, special constables who guard legislative assemblies, etc. Indeed, it would be impossible to cover even a representative minority of all of these various regulatory organizations. Instead, in this section we examine more closely three selected policing organizations that are of particular interest, playing as they do a prominent role in quasi-public policing in Canada.

The Corps of Commissionaires

The Corps of Commissionaires can trace their roots to 1859 and to Captain Edward Walter, who was concerned with the difficult transition of war veterans back into civilian life after the Crimean war. In 1915, the Governor General suggested that an organization similar to the British Corps of Commissionaires be formed in Canada after World War I. In 1925, the Canadian Corps of Commissionaires came into existence through a Federal Charter under a Letters Patent issued by the government.

Today, the Corps of Commissionaires is a private not-for-profit organization employing over 18,000 former members of the Armed Forces, the RCMP, and other organizations.[2] Some divisions of the Corps also recruit graduates with recognized law and security college qualifications, which has been somewhat controversial among executives in the private security industry. The Corps offers security services to businesses, industries, homeowners and provincial governments but its main client is the federal government through its role of guarding federal facilities and buildings. In 1945, the Corps of Commissionaires approached the Secretary of the Treasury Board for special dispensation. They argued that after the Second World War the number of security contracts filled by the Corps had been decreasing while the number of veterans available for work had increased. This resulted in the rather unique Treasury Board position that all federal departments, boards and commissions give first consideration to the Corps for all security service contracts. This has come to be known as the *right of first refusal* which means that all federal government security contracts are offered first to the Corps of Commissionaires. The Corps may choose to accept or reject contracts based on the availability of personnel. The right of first refusal was re-examined in 1996 and reinstated for another five years. In 2000, the Auditor General of Canada examined the policy and the right of first refusal was reinstated for another five years.

The Corps of Commissionaires is therefore in a rather ambiguous market position. Executives from security companies believe that the right of first refusal stunts competition and drives down market prices because members of the Corps are subsidized by their own federal and/or military pension plans. This allows the Corps of Commissionaires to accept contracts at very low rates. Indeed, the Corps of Commissionaires has more than doubled in size since 1961, from 5,211 officers gradually increasing to 11,217 officers in 1998 (see Figure 7.2). Proponents of the Corps argue that the agency fulfills a very important public function by providing employment to veterans. Moreover, the availability of the Corps allows the federal government to keep its security costs down all the while employing well-trained and certified security personnel who are also military pensioners. As it stands, the Corps of Commissionaires accepts about 80 percent of the right of first

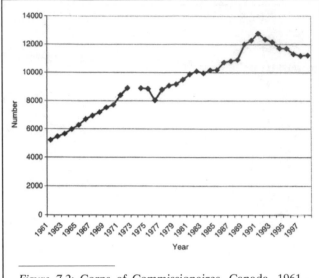

Figure 7.2: Corps of Commissionaires, Canada, 1961–1999.
Source: Compiled b George S. Rigakos, Minutes of Meeting (Annual)

refusal contracts it is offered by the federal government. The Corps of Commissionaires is also typically the security service of preference by other jurisdictions such as small municipalities that contract with it for municipal bylaw enforcement. Another source of discontent among some security executives is that the Corps of Commissionaires has started an ancillary branch known as 'Corps 2' that competes alongside other private-contract security providers and employs non-veteran staff. The Corps' right of first refusal is once again under review by the Treasury Board. The federal government is a major employer of contract security services and a change of policy would have serious implications for the configuration of private security provision in Canada.

The Canadian Air Transport Security Authority (CATSA)

Unlike the Corps of Commissionaires, the Canadian Air Transport Security Authority (CATSA) has a very recent history, being established on 1 April 2002 in response to the terrorist attacks of 11 September 2001.[3] The new federal authority is also a not-for-profit Crown corporation but is responsible for key aviation issues pursuant to the new Canadian Air Transport Security Authority Act. CATSA is part of a $2.2 billion federal initiative for aviation security.

CATSA officers, in their distinct security uniforms, are deployed in airports across Canada. They are responsible for screening passengers and baggage, patrolling restricted areas, enforcing pass systems and overseeing the program of RCMP officers on board aircraft. To most Canadians, CATSA would appear to be a large, federal, uniformed security agency and this is intended. The 'common look and feel, including the new CATSA logo and uniform worn by screening officers' conveys the image of 'consistent service to travelers' and is aimed at contributing to 'a greater sense of professionalism among screening officers' (CATSA 2004: 21). In terms of who actually services the public, however, very little has changed. While CATSA sets minimum standards and requirements for screening officers, this task is still contracted out to private security providers. Whereas the mish-mash of uniforms that dominated airports across Canada (Rigakos 2000a: 145) seems to have become more homogenized, CATSA screening officers are nonetheless contracted security personnel from a variety of competing regional providers. In many cases, screening officers simply switched their company uniforms for CATSA uniforms. CATSA has, however, improved working conditions for screening officers by introducing minimum wages, the latest in screening technology, and improved training and the potential for career development which has purportedly resulted in lower turnover rates (CATSA 2004: 36). Alongside CATSA personnel, the Corps of Commissionaires still patrols airport parking lots and entranceways, issuing parking notices and enforcing municipal bylaws.

BIAs and Paid Duty Policing

The proliferation of Business Improvement Areas or Associations (BIAs) across North America has had particular effects on policing. BIAs concern themselves with improving the area around storefronts including lighting, pedestrian walkways, general beautification and promotional activities for merchants. A BIA allows local businesses to join together and organize, finance and carry out physical improvements and promote economic development in their district. The BIA reports to the local municipality which approves the budget of the association. According to the Ontario Business Improvement Association there are over 230 BIAs operating in the province.[4] In British Columbia there are another 53 BIAs in operation.[5] Canadian police researchers have pointed out how these BIAs have used private security to patrol high-traffic public areas and act as 'ambassadors' to shoppers and tour-

ists (Murphy and Clarke 2002). The use of private security to patrol public streets is becoming increasingly common in Canada. In Halifax, the Spring Garden merchant district is patrolled by private security alongside the local municipal Halifax Police. In Gastown and the west end of Vancouver, BIAs employ uniformed ambassadors to direct tourists, issue parking notices, and move along undesirables. The Downtown Vancouver Business Improvement Association (DVBIA) meets regularly with the Vancouver public police to co-ordinate security efforts with its private security officers. Indeed, the DVBIA is perhaps the first Canadian BIA to have a full-time Crime Prevention Officer on its Board of Directors.

While the DVBIA utilizes private security guards to patrol public streets, the Yonge-Dundas BIA (YDBIA) in the heart of Toronto's merchant district employs paid duty Metropolitan Toronto Police officers. The YDBIA had difficulty with the high turnover of extra-duty police officers who patrolled the large downtown tract that includes over 1,400 businesses. In order to make sure its concerns were being met, the YDBIA Operations Manager insisted that police officers would file reports and conduct targeted runs on their patrols by visiting local merchants and asking them if there are any crime problems. This is probably the first instance in which public police officers are required to file shift reports summarizing their activities with a private client. The occurrence reports contain directions for officers including what stores they are to visit and a notification that failure to submit the reports will mean that they will not get paid. It is perhaps fitting that this development should take place in the heart of Toronto, where Shearing and Stenning first identified the rise of 'mass private property' (Shearing and Stenning 1983). Whereas the large tracts of feudal-like policing arrangements described by Shearing and Stenning increased the privatization of indoor spaces[6] such as large retail malls, thereby squeezing out the public police, here we have the mall literally being turned inside out in the same neighborhood and the police themselves being privatized.[7] In order to solidify their status to make arrests on behalf of merchants that line the YDBIA, the Metropolitan Toronto Police required that merchants fill out a Trespass to Property Act consent form allowing them to act as agents of the property owner for enforcing trespass-related issues. That downtown merchants would pool their resources together and insist that public police officers patrol their public storefronts and report in their association directly is truly revolutionary in the history of Canadian policing, albeit now common course for private security.

The interchangeability, overlapping jurisdiction, and cross-fertilization of public and private policing is thus perhaps most evident in the recent evolution of BIAs in Canada.

PRIVATE SECURITY

Ascertaining the relative size of the private security industry is no easy task in most national contexts (de Waard 1999; Jones and Newburn 1995). The generally accepted (conservative) estimate of the ratio of private security agents to public police officers in Canada is 2:1 (Swol 1999) despite more recent statistics that grossly under-count the industry based on national labor force estimates (Sanders 2003). It appears that the private security industry in Canada began to overtake the public police somewhere in the late sixties to early seventies (Rigakos 2000b) and that with the gradual decline of public police officers per 100,000 population, the private security industry has continued to increase the gap (see Figure 7.3). As might be imagined, the breadth of private security provision in this country is vast. Companies offer services ranging from forensic investigations to bodyguard services and access control. Although mass private property — especially with the development of large retail spaces — has dramatically affected delivery of security, Canada has not experienced the rapid growth of gated residential communities seen in the United States (Blakely and Snyder 1997).

Current oversight structures for the private security industry are in the hands of provincial registrars.

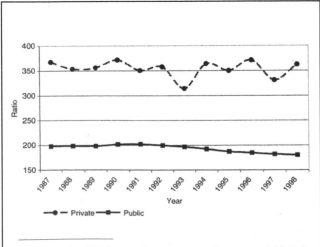

Figure 7.3: Public and private police per 100,000 population, Canada, 1987–1999.
Sources: Swol, 1999; CCJS, 2000.

With the exception of British Columbia and Newfoundland, there are no minimum training standards for security guards across Canada. Moreover, only contract private security personnel are required by law to pass background criminal history checks and the proprietary security sector is entirely unregulated. There has been a recent whirlwind of activity in Canada around regulating the private security industry including national radio documentaries, television specials, an international conference, and an imminent Report to Parliament on the relationship between public police and private security by the Law Commission of Canada. In the province of Ontario, a recent coroner's inquest into the death of Patrick Shand (a black shoplifter who died while being handcuffed and arrested by security agents in a Toronto Mall) resulted in recommendations that the private security industry be regulated, minimum training standards be set, and that the in-house security sector be brought into account. Given academic and policy concerns about the rise of the private security sector it would appear that changes are on the horizon, albeit 30 years overdue.

There is some comparative demographic information about the public police and private security industry in Canada. Women seem to be better represented in the private security industry on the whole depending on the type of work and company. Sanders (2003) reports that between 1991 to 2000 approximately 20 percent of security employees in Canada were female. In 1993, Erickson found that 34 percent of security guards in Toronto were women (Erickson 1993). However, in Rigakos' study of a private 'law enforcement company' that engaged in high-risk 'parapolicing' he found that only 8 percent of the workforce were women (Rigakos 2002: 85). There have been concerted efforts to increase recruitment and retention of female constables. Services such as day care and targeted recruiting have resulted in the gradual increase of women from 0.6 percent in 1962 to 12.2 percent in 1998 in public police services (Swol 1999: 8).

The percentage of Canadian-born security officers employed by contract firms has been reported at 57 percent in Ontario for 1980 (Shearing *et al.* 1980: 141), 44 percent in Toronto for 1993 (Erickson 1993: 15), and 23 percent for Rigakos' parapolic in 2002 (Rigakos 2002: 85). Comparatively, in 1998 only 7.6 percent of uniformed Metropolitan Toronto Police officers were members of visible minority groups (Rigakos 2002: 94). According to Statistics Canada, as of 1999, visible minorities accounted for 10 percent of the Canadian labor force, but only 3 percent of Canadian police officers. Aboriginal persons were

2 percent of the Canadian labor force but accounted for 3 percent of police officers (Swol 1999: 9).

CONCLUSIONS: PUBLIC AND PRIVATE POLICING IN CANADA AT THE CROSSROADS

The state of Canadian public and private policing is at a crossroads. The state was becoming increasingly involved in the use, management, and possible regulation of the private security sector even before the terrorist attack on New York City on 11 September 2001. Moreover, the interchangeable use of private security or paid duty public policing on public streets on behalf of BIAs is creating an atmosphere of increased competition and commodification (Loader 1999; Rigakos 2002) both between public police services, as in the case of regionalization and municipal sub-contracting, as well as between private security agencies and the public police. When the Yonge–Dundas BIA insisted that paid duty police officers report directly to the operations manager through shift reports it was under the auspices of a threat to move to private security. When the police transition board in Quinte West entertained bids for the policing contract under a new regional governance structure forced upon it by provincial neoliberal policies, the board listened to proposals from local town police, proposed regional forces, the Ontario Provin-

cial Police, and even private security companies to perform 'tertiary policing' duties.

Radical proposals have been floated that would allow current regional Police Service Boards to contract with and license special constabularies and private security companies to perform ancillary policing tasks (CAPB, 2002). These newly constituted boards would be in charge of public security and have a dedicated budget aside from funds earmarked for the public regional or municipal force aimed at subsidized local initiatives for securing communities. As a mechanism for recovering 'the public good' (Loader and Walker 2001) in Canadian private policing, proposals from all quarters including academics, policy-makers, police associations, and security executives themselves have called for an oversight system that includes civilians on provincial licensing, regulatory, and enforcement commissions.

This chapter has only highlighted a few areas where the confluence and confusion about public and private policing in Canada are apparent. In the next few years many of the proposals alluded to above may be either ignored or acted upon by provincial and federal policy-makers. It remains to be seen whether or not market principles alone will dictate the future of security provision in this country or whether the state will reimpose itself to reclaim policing as public good.

(b) Police Investigating Police — Executive Summary†

Commission for Public Complaints Against the RCMP

The RCMP currently investigates its own members for statutory offences. At issue is whether or not an organization whose members' actions have resulted in serious injury or death should be the very same organization then charged with the responsibility to investigate the incident (with the prospect of laying criminal charges).

Investigations of RCMP members resulting from a number of high profile cases including that of Ian Bush, who was shot and killed by an RCMP member

in 2005, to the 2007 death of Robert Dziekanski at the Vancouver International Airport (following the RCMP use of the conducted energy weapon), have brought the issue of police investigating police to front of mind domestically and internationally.

These cases raise a fundamental question. Can the current process of the RCMP investigating itself legitimately engender confidence in the transparency, impartiality and integrity of the criminal investigation and its outcome?

† Source "Executive Summary", *Police Investigating Police: Final Report*, pages iii–xvi, Commission for Public Complaints Against the RCMP, August 11, 2009. Reproduced with the permission of the Minister of Public Works and Government Services, 2010. [Notes and/or references omitted.]

The Chair of the Commission for Public Complaints Against the RCMP (CPC) set out to answer this and other questions by launching a public interest investigation on November 28, 2007, to assess the adequacy of how the RCMP investigates its own members, specifically in cases where member action resulted in serious injury or death.[1]

WHAT IS CURRENTLY GUIDING RCMP MEMBER INVESTIGATIONS?

An important part of the CPC assessment involved determining exactly how the RCMP is currently managing its own member investigations. To develop this baseline knowledge, the CPC looked at all legislation, policies and procedures currently guiding member investigations at the national and divisional (provincial)[2] level.

No specific requirements exist under the Criminal Code regarding how an investigation into police officers should be handled. And while specific reference to how police should investigate police is also absent from the *Royal Canadian Mounted Police Act (RCMP Act)*, there are a number of features of the *RCMP Act* that warrant special attention.

The first is section 37 of the *RCMP Act* which outlines eight guidelines for the appropriate behaviour expected of RCMP members at all times. This section legislates the imperative need for members, as representatives of the RCMP, to act respectfully, dutifully and free from conflict of interest, specifically requiring members to "avoid any actual, apparent or potential conflict of interests" (s. 37(d)). A second legislative feature is the Commissioner's Standing Orders (Public Complaints) (s. 9), which states: "A member shall not investigate a complaint where that member may be in a conflict of interest situation." Of particular concern is the fact that the term "conflict of interest" is not defined further in either the *RCMP Act* or the Commissioner's Standing Orders. Public and stakeholder criticism remains largely focused on the very issue that the nature of police investigating police creates a significant conflict of interest, or at the least the perception of one (particularly in cases of serious injury or death).

Of additional concern is subsection I.2.b of the Commissioner's Standing Orders, which states: "If, as a result of an investigation, a member is believed to have committed a statutory offence: 1. it is within RCMP primary jurisdiction, <u>take the same action as you would for any other person</u>." This passage is also found in the RCMP's *National Investigation*

Guidelines (F.1.a) and repeated further in some divisional policies.

While the intention of the RCMP requesting that member investigations[3] be handled like any other investigation may be an honourable one (meaning without bias), the very nature of an investigation by one police officer into another is fundamentally different from the police investigating a member of the public for the exact same crime. Police are held to higher account by the very nature of the work they do. Like other professions that directly impact the safety and welfare of those they serve, there is a public expectation requiring that a higher standard of behaviour be upheld. By exposing the police thinking that investigations into its own members should be handled like any other investigation, we begin to identify the root philosophy guiding individual member behaviour.

It is therefore the CPC's contention that criminal investigations into RCMP members should **not** be treated the same as any other criminal investigation.

Given the absence of direction prescribed in legislation regarding how members should investigate other members, the adequacy of RCMP policy to ensure impartiality, transparency and rigour in the process becomes all the more paramount. Results of the CPC's policy analysis revealed inconsistencies in content and application across RCMP divisions. While the RCMP has developed a number of policies relating to how criminal investigations should be undertaken generally, very few policies address the issue of RCMP member-committed offences specifically. This is a serious concern.

The sheer volume and variety of RCMP policies with implications for the issue of police investigating police is overwhelmingly large (e.g. hundreds of pages of policy relevant to the PIP were reviewed for this report alone). This policy "overload" poses a great threat to the RCMP's operational effectiveness. The very nature of front-line policing requires that direction be provided in a format that is clear, concise and easy to access. As previously stated in other CPC reports, law drives policy, which drives training, which directly influences member behaviour.

Inconsistencies across divisions demonstrate the absence of clear guidance on the issue. In some policies at both the national and divisional level, involvement of an independent investigator or an external police force is mandatory; in others, it is left to the discretion of the officer in charge. Only three RCMP divisions currently have memoranda of agreement in place with the involvement of external police forces for the purpose of member investigations in specific cases. Similarly, only three divisional policies dictate the appointment of an independent investigator in cases of member-committed offences. Some divisional policies do not address the issue of officer-committed violations and the pursuant investigations at all. The scope of policy varies as well — while most national policies are limited to cases of serious injury or death, many divisional policies encompass all statutory violations.

While a new proposed RCMP national policy, *External Investigations or Review*, takes active steps towards providing consolidated guidance in relation to member investigations, the content remains vague and far too much discretion remains with the divisions (divisional Commanding Officers, Officers in Charge or Criminal Operations Officers) to determine an appropriate response.

CPC ASSESSMENT OF THE HANDLING OF RCMP MEMBER INVESTIGATIONS

With this baseline understanding of the current handling and procedures guiding member investigations, the CPC then requested that the RCMP divisions identify all files related to criminal investigations of RCMP members by other RCMP members between April 1, 2002 and March 31, 2007 involving assault causing bodily harm; sexual assault; and death, including death caused by operating a personal motor vehicle (PMV).

The retrieval of member investigation cases from the RCMP revealed critical issues in the RCMP's administrative handling and management of these types of investigations. RCMP national and divisional headquarters do not have any centralized tracking or monitoring capacity for member investigations. As such, most divisions generated relevant files for the CPC public interest investigation by searching through divisional records housed at their respective headquarters using key word searches. Some divisions were better able to narrow the scope of their search to fit the parameters of the review through effective record-keeping processes making for easier retrieval, while other divisions did not have the same capacity. Overall, the lack of national and divisional data collection — or monitoring capacity — for member investigations (combined with varied divisional RCMP record-keeping and retrieval methods on this issue) demonstrates a lack of attention being placed on member investigations.

Bearing these challenges in mind, the CPC reviewed all RCMP files received in order to determine which ones were relevant to the parameters of the public interest investigation. Approximately 150 of the 600 RCMP cases provided were deemed relevant to the parameters of the public interest investigation. Recognizing that it would be prohibitive to review *all* relevant cases, they were further reduced to a sample size of 28 cases representative of each of the three categories (14 assault causing bodily harm cases; eight sexual assault cases; and six death cases).

It is important to note that, as per the map outlined in the *CPC Data at a Glance* section, the RCMP's Central Region was not represented in the random sample because no cases were identified by Quebec (C) Division; Ontario (O) Division; and HQ (A) Division that fit the parameters of the Chair-initiated complaint. Furthermore, no files were identified by Nova Scotia (H) Division, and Prince Edward Island (L) Division. And while a small number of files were initially identified by the RCMP for New Brunswick (J) Division and Yukon Territory (M) Division, these files did not meet the CPC criteria and were therefore excluded. Of concern to the CPC is the absence of any cases identified by the bulk of the Maritime Provinces given the RCMP's contract policing role there.

With all relevant material identified, the CPC Review Team investigators analyzed all files and written material provided by the RCMP to assess the appropriate handling of each case against the established CPC criteria and terms of reference (specifically: line management, level of response, timeliness, member conduct, and compliance with policy). After completing a comprehensive file review of the 28 cases, the CPC Review Team investigators then recommended that full-field reviews be undertaken for a select number of cases. Overall, eight cases were selected for full-field review. Field interviews were conducted in various divisions and detachments. In total, 31 members were interviewed regarding the files selected for in-depth review. Thirteen civilians were asked to be interviewed for the purposes of this report but refused or did not respond to our request for an interview. One comment from a family member associated to one file stated: "It won't do any good. [The RCMP members involved] have all been promoted and transferred out."

CPC ASSESSMENT OF RCMP HANDLING OF MEMBER INVESTIGATIONS

The criteria used to assess each of the 28 cases and the resultant findings are outlined in detail in chapter 5 of this report. Below are some highlights of the CPC findings.

As per the complaint parameters, the CPC investigators assessed 28 cases in order to determine how appropriately each RCMP member investigation was handled against five key criteria: conduct, policy compliance, timeliness, line management and level of response.

Overall, **RCMP member conduct was deemed highly appropriate in 100% of the cases reviewed.** The CPC found that the RCMP investigators charged with the task of investigating another member acted professionally and free from bias.

The CPC investigators also concluded that **RCMP member policy compliance was appropriate in 93% of the cases. Only two minor policy violations were found.** It is important to note that this criterion sought only to determine how well members followed policy in place at the time of each investigation, and did not seek to assess the adequacy of these policies (this issue was assessed separately, as outlined previously).

The timeliness of member investigations was also deemed overall appropriate 82% of the time. Of the 28 cases reviewed, 60% were completed in six months or less. However, 19% of these cases took over one year to complete, thereby potentially excluding members from internal disciplinary processes, if required. Specific concerns were also raised around the handling of historical cases which took considerably longer to investigate (one historical case still remained ongoing after 28 months at the time of publication).

The two criteria the CPC investigators found of greatest concern were the RCMP's handling of the investigations in relation to **line management (which looked at any actual/perceived conflict of interest[,] appropriate management structure and reporting relationships)** and **level of response (which looked at how appropriate and proportionate the RCMP response was to the gravity of the incident).** Given the fact that these two criteria specifically relate to the process of *how* member investigations are handled, this analysis further helps to illustrate the fact that **CPC concerns relate largely to the current RCMP process (which is flawed) and not individual RCMP member action.**

Of particular concern to the CPC is the RCMP's line management, which was deemed to be appropriate in only 32% of the cases. Sixty-eight percent of the cases reviewed were deemed to be handled either partially or entirely inappropriately. Of particular concern was the fact that **25% of primary investigators identified themselves as per-**

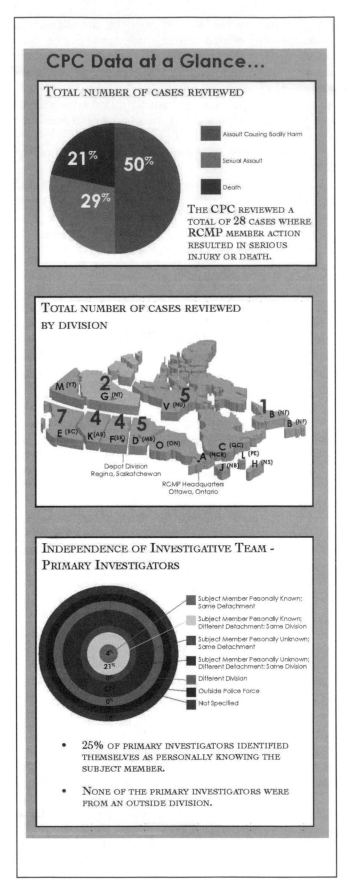

sonally knowing the subject member. Another critical concern is the fact that **in 60% of the cases reviewed, a single investigator was assigned** to investigate another member, thereby placing the integrity of the investigation at risk for potential conflict of interest or perception of bias.

Further, **in 32% of the cases, the primary investigator assigned was of the same or lower rank as the subject member**, thereby creating the potential for intimidation. Recommendations to address these concerns are outlined in greater detail in chapter 7, *CPC Recommended Model for RCMP Member Investigations*.

Of equal concern to the CPC is the 68% of cases deemed to be partially or entirely inappropriate for level of response. Of particular concern was the fact that **interviews with subject members and witness officers were conducted by a lone investigator in 17 of the 28 cases**, again creating the potential for intimidation or a conflict of interest.

It is important to note that while no specific conflicts of interest were noted in these particular cases, the practice of single-member interviews was deemed to be inappropriate.

CPC investigators also found a significant disparity in the qualifications of the investigators (including primary investigators) assigned to member investigations.

In addition, the complete **absence of reassignment of duties or adjustment of workload** for members assigned to investigators undertaking member investigations was also noted as a serious concern impacting the integrity and timeliness of member investigations undertaken. The call for an administrative review of member investigations was also found to be inconsistently applied across the country (an administrative review was only called for in four of the 28 cases).

Recommendations to address these concerns are outlined in greater detail in chapter 7, *CPC Recommended Model for RCMP Member Investigations*.

WHAT WE CAN LEARN FROM OTHER MODELS

Overall, an analysis of 14 different domestic and international police review agencies[4] was undertaken in an effort to determine how other jurisdictions handle allegations of police misconduct. Three types of models were identified based on the level of civilian involvement in the investigation: (1) Dependent Model, (2) Interdependent Model and (3) Independent Model.

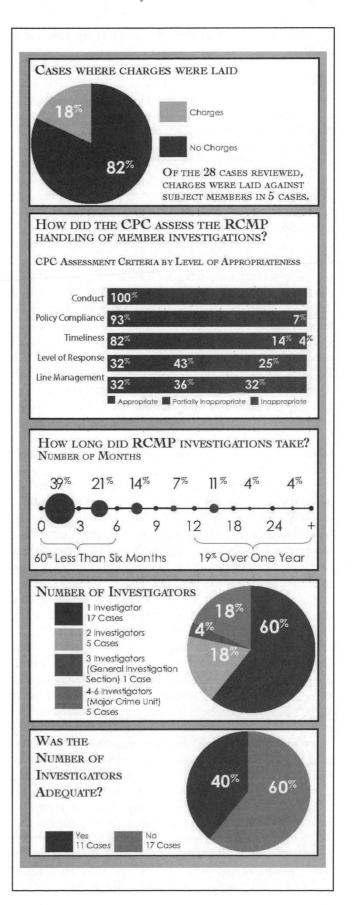

CASES WHERE CHARGES WERE LAID

Charges

No Charges

OF THE 28 CASES REVIEWED, CHARGES WERE LAID AGAINST SUBJECT MEMBERS IN 5 CASES.

HOW DID THE CPC ASSESS THE RCMP HANDLING OF MEMBER INVESTIGATIONS?

CPC ASSESSMENT CRITERIA BY LEVEL OF APPROPRIATENESS

Conduct 100%
Policy Compliance 93% 7%
Timeliness 82% 14% 4%
Level of Response 32% 43% 25%
Line Management 32% 36% 32%

■ Appropriate ■ Partially Inappropriate ■ Inappropriate

HOW LONG DID RCMP INVESTIGATIONS TAKE? NUMBER OF MONTHS

39% 21% 14% 7% 11% 4% 4%

0 3 6 9 12 18 24 +

60% Less Than Six Months   19% Over One Year

NUMBER OF INVESTIGATORS

1 Investigator 17 Cases
2 Investigators 5 Cases
3 Investigators (General Investigation Section) 1 Case
4-6 Investigators (Major Crime Unit) 5 Cases

18% 4% 18% 60%

WAS THE NUMBER OF INVESTIGATORS ADEQUATE?

40% 60%

Yes 11 Cases   No 17 Cases

The **dependent model** essentially represents more traditional "police investigation of police." There is no civilian involvement in the criminal investigation and, therefore, there is a total dependence on the police for the handling of criminal investigations. There are two subcategories to this model: (1.1) police investigating police and (1.2) police investigating another police force.

In the police investigating police subcategory, the police service is fully responsible for the criminal investigation and administration of public complaints alleging criminal offences. The review body in question does not conduct criminal investigations, but it may recognize complaints regarding service, internal discipline or public trust.

The second sub-category involves "police investigating *another* police force" in specific cases so that the police service does not investigate its own members in instances of serious injury or death. In three selected Canadian provinces, formal memoranda of agreement exist between the local police and the RCMP that allow an outside police force to handle the investigations of the RCMP member(s).

The **interdependent model** introduces civilian involvement into the criminal investigation to varying degrees. There are also two sub-types to this model: (2.1) civilian observation and (2.2) hybrid investigation.

In the first sub-type of the interdependent model, a civilian observer is assigned to the police investigation to ensure that the latter is conducted with impartiality. The hybrid investigation comprises mostly of a civilian review body whose involvement in the investigation goes beyond the role of mere overseer. In this model, the police force may be engaged in some form of collaboration with the review body, although the latter may have the ability to conduct the investigation entirely on its own.

Examples of the interdependent model, which introduces civilian involvement into the police criminal investigation, are found in British Columbia, Saskatchewan, Alberta, Yukon, New Zealand, United Kingdom and South Australia.

The **independent model** is embodied by a totally independent criminal investigation with no police involvement. The review body composed of civilians undertakes independent criminal investigation and may have the authority to make binding findings and lay charges. Ontario's Special Investigations Unit, the Independent Police Review Authority in Chicago and the Police Ombudsman for Northern Ireland are representative of this model. The key advantage of an independent review body is that it offers an appearance of total independence and objectivity.

For Canada, there is no single model that can be applied in its current form and expected to function effectively without taking into account the particular characteristics of our country and the size and scope (municipal, provincial, federal, territorial and First Nations) of the policing activities undertaken by the RCMP. The size of the territory and sheer vastness of the country, coupled with budget realities, must be considered. Valuable lessons were learned from our domestic and foreign counterparts in the development of the CPC's approach for the RCMP in the Canadian context, outlined next.

CPC'S RECOMMENDED MODEL FOR HANDLING OF RCMP MEMBER INVESTIGATIONS

The CPC's recommended option underlines the importance of police in the process (as part of the solution), while also recognizing that an enhanced degree of civilian engagement in the criminal investigation process is fundamental to ensure its impartiality and integrity. To that end, the CPC recommends shifting from the current "dependent model" towards the "interdependent model."

The recommended "interdependent model" rests between the basic dependent model and the full-featured interdependent model:

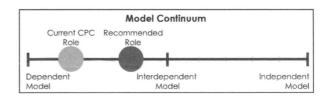

Overall, the CPC believes that a criminal investigation resulting from member conduct is unlike *any other* criminal investigation and accordingly must be handled procedurally very differently. Therefore, to help transition the RCMP from its current "dependent (police investigating police) model" to the "interdependent model" (involving an enhanced CPC role in the context of RCMP member investigations), a number of legislative, structural, and policy changes are recommended.

RECOMMENDED LEGISLATIVE CHANGES

To effectively enhance review capacity, legislative changes should be considered to provide the new RCMP Review Body the authority to:

- **Refer an RCMP member investigation** to another police force or to another criminal investigative body in Canada.

- Grant the RCMP Review Body the authority to **monitor any criminal investigation** relating to a member of the RCMP, where it deems it appropriate to do so. This would therefore extend the RCMP Review Body's ability to deploy the observer to an RCMP member investigation being undertaken by an external police service and/ or provincial criminal investigative body. While permission from the investigating body would be required to embed the observer, the authority would at least provide the RCMP Review Body with the power where granted permission to observe.

- **Undertake joint investigations** with like-mandated bodies. The amendment could allow the new RCMP Review Body to "conduct a joint investigation, review, inquiry, audit or hearing with another body in Canada that has powers, duties and functions that are similar to the RCMP Review Body's, including provincial criminal investigative bodies." This would allow the new RCMP Review Body to undertake investigations with new criminal investigative bodies (like the Alberta Serious Incident Response Team) as they emerge across the country.

Other recommended legislative changes should include:

- The RCMP Commissioner revise the current version of his Standing Orders to direct handling of member investigations, as per the recommendations herein (specify that member investigations are not to be handled like any other criminal investigation and a better definition of the term "conflict of interest" should be included).

RECOMMENDED STRUCTURAL CHANGES FOR THE RCMP

- Create the position of National RCMP Member Investigation Registrar to manage, track, train, promote and advise on all issues related to member investigations. The National Registrar would be responsible to:
  - Create an RCMP National Registry for all police investigating police data (especially for serious injury, sexual assault, and death cases) with timely sharing of data with the CPC.

- Create and manage an RCMP Police Investigating Police Advisory Group to help determine actions to be taken in sensitive cases.
- Monitor effective compliance with policy and enforce compliance where necessary (e.g. consultation with Crown re: laying of charges mandatory).
- Create and oversee a specialized unit with expertise on the handling of RCMP historical cases to be consulted — or deployed — where necessary.
- Create a mobile critical incident member investigation team (with a CPC civilian observer embedded) that can be deployed where both the RCMP National Registrar and the CPC Chair jointly determined it necessary to do so (a pool of qualified senior investigators placed on standby that can be deployed quickly).

RECOMMENDED RCMP POLICY AND PROCEDURAL CHANGES

There are certain instances where the RCMP should *not* investigate itself. Below is a chart that delineates that as the seriousness of the member-involved offence increases, a corresponding degree of independence and impartiality in that member investigation is required. The chart below highlights the CPC's contention that as the seriousness of the offence alleged against a member rises, the discretion for the RCMP to respond as it deems appropriate must be removed and **mandatory** requirements inserted in its place. [See Chart on next page.]

RECOMMENDED POLICY CHANGES FOR THE RCMP

The CPC's policy analysis revealed that RCMP policies, while voluminous, are inconsistent and do not adequately address the handling of member investigations. Criminal investigations into members should not be treated the same as any other criminal investigation. To address the current void in effective and consistent policies and procedures related to the handling of member investigations, the CPC recommends the following key changes:

- Criminal investigations of RCMP members into allegations of serious injury, sexual assault or death in hardship or remote postings must be consistent with all other member investigation protocols, no exception.
- An administrative review is mandatory for all member investigations.

543

Recommended RCMP Response to Member Investigations

Type of offence defined	Member offence *(by level of seriousness)*	Current RCMP handling	Recommended RCMP handling of member investigation
MANDATORY RCMP ACTION WITH CPC ROLE			
Indictable offences[5] An offence which, in Canada, is more serious than those which can proceed by summary conviction. In many regards, this is the Canadian equivalent to the USA felony. Murder and treason are examples of crimes committed in Canada which would be indictable offences. These crimes are usually tried by federally-appointed judges and carry heavy sentences.	**Death** Criminal Negligence causing Death (s. 220 CCC)	Discretionary at RCMP Division level	**RCMP Mandatory Action:** • CPC to refer all death cases to external police service or provincial criminal investigative body (no RCMP member involvement) • Divisional MOUs activated • CPC Observer embedded
	Serious Injury & Sexual Assault Assault with Weapon or Assault Causing Bodily Harm (s. 267 CCC) Sexual Assault (s. 272 CCC)	Discretionary at RCMP Division level	**RCMP Mandatory Action:** CPC and National Registrar to determine appropriate response from options below for serious injury/sexual assault cases: • Referral to external police service or to provincial investigative body through MOU[6] • Deployment of RCMP HQ mobile critical incident member investigation team • CPC Observer embedded
DISCRETION RETAINED BY THE RCMP			
Hybrid Offences Dual Procedure Offences which Crown can elect to proceed with an indictable offence or a summary conviction.	**Assault** (s. 265 CCC)	Discretionary at RCMP Division level	**RCMP HQ National Registrar retains discretion to determine appropriate response.**
Summary Conviction In Canada, a less serious offence than indictable offences for which both the procedure and punishment tends to be less onerous.	**Example:** Theft under $5,000	Discretionary at RCMP Division level	**RCMP HQ National Registrar retains discretion to determine appropriate response.** • Recommended CPC standard policies and procedures are followed (outlined next).

MANDATORY / DISCRETIONARY

- **The RCMP establish formalized MOUs for *every* RCMP division to ensure the mandatory referral of member investigations to an external police service is consistent and documented.** At present, only New Brunswick (J) Division, Nova Scotia (H) Division and Newfoundland (B) Division have formalized MOUs in place. These existing MOUs should be revised as per the CPC's recommendations to reflect new processes.

Where it is deemed appropriate for the RCMP to handle its own member investigation or where an RCMP member forms part of the investigative team (led by an external police force), the following policy recommendations would apply.

- **Create an RCMP integrated manual** to specifically address procedures for investigations undertaken by the RCMP into one of its own members. This integrated manual should have links to any additional relevant policies for ease of reference. Key features to be included in the integrated manual: CPC recommended investigative team structure:
- Qualified primary investigator at least one rank higher than that of subject member;
  - A minimum of two members required for every member [investigation] (including for subject and witness officer interviews);
  - Minimum mandatory qualifications of investigative team;
  - Workload of members assigned to member investigations reassigned or adjusted to prioritize member investigation accordingly;
  - Timely completion of investigation preferably six months and not recommended to exceed one year;
  - Assign liaison position to member of investigative team to ensure timely and effective communication with public, family and subject member;
  - Self-identification of knowledge of subject member mandatory;
  - Use of the probe[7] in lower-end investigations.

CPC OVERALL CONCLUSION

To answer the question raised at the outset, *"Can the current process of the RCMP investigating itself legitimately engender confidence in the transparency and integrity of the criminal investigation and its outcome?"* The informed CPC answer is that it cannot. To address this, the CPC has recommended legislative, policy, procedural and structural proposals for changes, including an enhanced civilian presence during the investigative process to protect against any real or perceived conflicts of interest involving RCMP member investigations. It is important to note that the RCMP recommendations specifically related to structure, procedure and policy do not rely on any legislative enhancements and can be implemented immediately.

(c) *Doe v. Metropolitan Toronto (Municipality) Commissioners of Police*†

[MacFARLAND J.:]

[1] Jane Doe was raped and otherwise sexually assaulted at knifepoint in her own bed in the early morning hours of August 24, 1986 by a stranger subsequently identified as Paul Douglas Callow. Ms. Doe then lived in a second-floor apartment at 88 Wellesley Street East, in the City of Toronto; her apartment had a balcony which was used by the rapist to gain access to her premises. At the time, Ms. Doe was the fifth known victim of Callow who would become known as "the balcony rapist".

[2] Ms. Doe brings a suit against the Metropolitan Toronto Police Force (hereafter referred to as MTPF) on two bases; firstly she suggests that the MTPF conducted a negligent investigation in relation to the balcony rapist and failed to warn women whom they knew to be potential targets of Callow of the fact that they were at risk. She says, as the result of such conduct, Callow was not apprehended as early as he might otherwise have been and she was denied the opportunity, had she known the risk she faced, to take any specific measures to protect herself from attack. Secondly, she said that the MTPF being a public body having the statutory duty to protect the public from criminal activity, must exercise that duty in accordance with the *Canadian Charter of Rights and Freedoms* and may not act in a way that is discriminatory because of gender. She says the police must act constitutionally, they did not do so in this case and as the result, her rights under ss. 15 and 7 of the *Charter* have been breached. She seeks damages against the MTPF under both heads of her claim.

[3] The trial of this action took place over approximately eight weeks; some 30 witnesses were called and voluminous documentary evidence filed. Counsel have filed lengthy written argument and had two days in which to give an oral outline of their written submissions.

· · · ·

CONCLUSIONS
Competency of the Investigation

[137] It is suggested that the investigation into the balcony rapist was slipshod and incompetent. The plaintiff has criticized the documentary productions of the defendant and suggested they are incomplete. Professor Hodgson testified that every step in an investigation should be recorded on supplementary occurrence reports. In this way he said anyone picking up the file could be reasonably informed on the status of the investigation. While that may be the ideal I accept that it is not the reality. Often steps taken and information gathered were recorded on supplementary reports but often they were not. Officers differ in their manner and method of note and record-keeping. I accept that there were numerous documents created in relation to this investigation which unfortunately were destroyed before the litigation was commenced.

---

† 39 O.R. (3d) 487, [1998] O.J. No. 2681 (Ont. Ct. (General Division)) at paras. 1–3, 137–79, 214–20, 253–55.

[138] I am not persuaded on the evidence that Callow would have been identified and apprehended any earlier because of documentary deficiencies.

[139] I am satisfied that the officers ultimately assigned to this investigation had too many other urgent assignments ongoing at the same time which prevented them from devoting the necessary attention which this investigation required. At the critical time much of their energy and attention was directed to other matters — often for days at a time. They had no back-up, no one else directly responsible for this investigation when they were otherwise engaged.

[140] While it is true that there was no evidence called in relation to what other demands there may have been on the MTPF for manpower at this time, one must bear in mind that it is the evidence of the police that sexual assault is a very serious crime second only to homicide and then consider the resources made available in the Annex Rapist investigation in his same division only a month or two before.

[141] While the plaintiff submits that I must infer that Callow would have been apprehended sooner had greater resources been devoted to this investigation earlier on the theory — the sooner a job is started the sooner it is finished — I cannot agree with. While one may say in that event Callow might have been apprehended sooner, it is to my mind equally probable that he might not have been.

[142] I am compelled, however, to conclude that the only difference between the Annex Rapist investigation and this investigation was the level of violence in addition to the rape itself. Dawson Davidson also physically beat many of his victims in addition to sexually assaulting them.

[143] As this is the only real distinguishing factor between the two investigations I must conclude that it was this factor — the lack of additional violence — which resulted in this investigation being essentially on the back burner in so far as resources were concerned. The sense of urgency which drove the Dawson Davidson investigation was markedly absent from this investigation. I can only conclude because Callow's victims were "merely raped" by a "gentleman rapist" — according to the Oliver Zink Rape Cookbook definition — this case did not have the urgency of the other.

Decision Not to Warn

[144] As I have said, Sgts. Cameron and Derry determined that this investigation would be "low

key" compared to the investigation conducted into the "Annex Rapist" and no warning would be given to the women they knew to be at risk for fear of displacing the rapist leaving him free to re-offend elsewhere undetected.

[145] I am not persuaded that their professed reason for not warning women is the real reason no warning was issued.

[146] Firstly, there is evidence that the Annex Rapist, Dawson Davidson, did not flee to Vancouver because of the media attention paid to his crimes and/or the obvious increased police presence in the neighbourhood. Indeed, much of the coverage occurred after Davidson had already left Toronto.

[147] Additionally P.C. Gary Ellis, who had assisted in the Dawson Davidson investigation at one point, actually telephoned Callow's ex-wife directly when he learned of Callow's existence and record from probation officer Alton. Police Constable Ellis worked out of the same 52 Division as Sgts. Cameron and Derry and would have, presumably, been aware of any discussions in relation to the fear of displacing Callow — by media attention or knocking on his door for the purpose of giving a warning about sexual assaults — yet he phoned directly to Callow's wife without even hesitating it seems.

[148] There was, I find, no "policy" not to issue warnings to potential victims in these cases — clearly warnings had been given in the Dawson Davidson Annex Rapist investigation — warnings [...] which incidentally all defence expert witnesses agreed were appropriate in the circumstances.

[149] I find that the real reason a warning was not given in the circumstances of this case was because Sgts. Cameron and Derry believed that women living in the area would become hysterical and panic and their investigation would thereby be jeopardized. In addition, they were not motivated by any sense of urgency because Callow's attacks were not seen as "violent" as Dawson Davidson's by comparison had been.

[150] I am satisfied on the evidence that a meaningful warning could and should have been given to the women who were at particular risk. That warning could have been by way of a canvass of their apartments, by a media blitz — by holding widely publicized public meetings or any one or combination of these methods. Such warning should have alerted the particular women at risk, and advised them of suggested precautions they might take to protect themselves. The defence experts, with the exception of

Mr. Piers, agreed that a warning could have been given without compromising the investigation on the facts of the case.

[151] Even the experienced defence expert witnesses Det. Inspector Kevin Rossmo and former FBI special agent McCrary agreed that as Det. Inspector Rossmo said:

> The police have a responsibility to release a balanced volume of information to protect the community. ... where that balance is will depend on the particular facts of the case.

[152] In my view it has been conceded in this case clearly and unequivocally by the Chief of Police at the time, Jack Marks, that no warning was given in this case and one ought to have been. His public response to the proposals of the group known as Women against Violence against Women in the aftermath of this investigation presented to the Board of Commissioners of Police could not in my view be any clearer when he said:

> I would concede that for a variety of reasons unique to the Church/Wellesley investigation, no press release in the nature of a general warning was issued and acknowledged that one should have been. This is not only a matter for concern and regret, but action has already been taken to prevent a similar breakdown from occurring in the future. Specifically, the Sexual Assault Coordinator who monitors all of these offences has been directed to ensure that members of the public are informed about such matters which may affect their safety. These warnings will be directed toward all potential victims with special attention given to members of the public who have been identified as most at risk, e.g. as in the case at hand, women living in high-rise buildings in the downtown area would be targeted as a high risk group and requiring extra efforts to bring the potential risk to their attention.

[153] I accept and agree entirely with these remarks.

[154] I must confess I was taken aback at the suggestion of Det. Sgt. Robin Breen who authored these remarks for the Chief when he suggested, I think, that in effect what it says is not what it says. The remarks were not intended to mean that the police felt a warning ought to have been given but rather were merely an invitation to get this group — known as WAVAW — to the discussion table.

[155] His evidence was pure double-talk as far as I am concerned and simply made no sense.

[156] It seems the MTPF has been trying to back away from these words of their then Chief ever since they were stated. The Chief's statement was an appropriate one in the circumstances and it is to his credit in my view, that he made the statement when and as he did.

[157] There are three other factors which have influenced my decision that a warning ought to have been given.

• the fact that Sgts. Cameron and Derry thought it appropriate to warn S.G. and M.L., that they may be potential targets of the balcony rapist after they reported break-ins to their apartments in their absence.
• the fact that Dawson Davidson had been arrested in July 1986 received considerable publicity. Women living in the general vicinity may have felt some relief knowing that a serial rapist had been apprehended and let down their guard somewhat completely unaware that another serial rapist was on the loose in their neighbourhood.
• the fact that Sgt. Hughes in his memo to his superior Staff Sgt. Hein — both of 52 Division — dated July 29, 1986 thought that building superintendents should have been contacted and told to advise "trusted tenants" especially single women to be aware of the occurrences and to advise police of any person they felt may be suspect.

[158] I am satisfied on Ms. Doe's evidence that if she had been aware a serial rapist was in her neighbourhood raping women whose apartments he accessed via their balconies she would have taken steps to protect herself and that most probably those steps would have prevented her from being raped.

[159] Section 57 of the *Police Act*, R.S.O. 1980, c. 381 (the governing statute at the time these events occurred), provides:

> 57. ... members of police forces ... are charged with the duty of preserving the peace, preventing robberies and other crimes ...

[160] The police are statutorily obligated to prevent crime and at common law they owe a duty to protect life and property. As Schroeder J.A. stated in *Schacht v. R.*, [1973] 1 O.R. 221 at pp. 231–32, 30 D.L.R. (3d) 641:

> The duties which I would lay upon them stem not only from the relevant statutes to which reference has been made, but from the common law, which recognizes the existence of a broad conventional or customary duty in the established

constabulary as an arm of the State to protect the life, limb and property of the subject.

[161] In my view, the police failed utterly in their duty to protect these women and the plaintiff in particular from the serial rapist the police knew to be in their midst by failing to warn so that they may have had the opportunity to take steps to protect themselves.

[162] It is no answer for the police to say women are always at risk and as an urban adult living in downtown Toronto they have an obligation to look out for themselves. Women generally do, every day of their lives, conduct themselves and their lives in such a way as to avoid the general pervasive threat of male violence which exists in our society. Here police were aware of a specific threat or risk to a specific group of women and they did nothing to warn those women of the danger they were in, nor did they take any measures to protect them.

Discrimination

[163] The plaintiff's argument is not simply that she has been discriminated against, because she is a woman, by individual officers in the investigation of her specific complaint, but that systemic discrimination existed within the MTPF in 1986 which impacted adversely on all women and, specifically, those who were survivors of sexual assault who came into contact with the MTPF — a class of persons of which the plaintiff was one. She says, in effect, the sexist stereotypical views held by the MTPF informed the investigation of this serial rapist and caused that investigation to be conducted incompetently and in such a way that the plaintiff has been denied the equal protection and equal benefit of law guaranteed to her by s. 15(1) of the *Charter*.

[164] The MTPF has since at least 1975 been aware of the problems it has in relation to the investigation of sexual assaults.

[165] Among those problems:

- survivors of sexual assault are not treated sensitively;
- lack of effective training for officers engaged in the investigation of sexual assault including a lack of understanding of rape trauma syndrome and the needs of survivors;
- lack of co-ordination of sexual assault investigations;
- some officers not suited by personality/attitude to investigation of sexual assault;

- too many investigators coming into contact with victims;
- lack of experienced investigators investigating sexual assault;
- lack of supervision of those conducting sexual assault investigations.

[166] The force has conceded in public documents as well as in internal documents at least since 1975, that it has difficulties in these areas, that it will take immediate steps to remedy these shortcomings — yet the problems continued through to 1987 and beyond.

[167] It seemed in that period that the public and persons who had brought their concerns in these areas to the attention of police were being publicly assured the problems would be eliminated, yet within the force the status quo remained pretty much as it had always been.

[168] Every police officer who testified agreed that sexual assault is a serious crime, second only to homicide. Yet, I cannot help but ask rhetorically — do they really believe that especially when one reviews their record in this area? It seems to me it was, as the plaintiff suggests, largely an effort in impression management rather than an indication of any genuine commitment for change.

[169] Former Chief of Police, Jack Marks, said that he would not have stood for problems like those outlined above continuing in the homicide squad for example. He said, assuming he were aware of the problems, that he would "root them out" and "correct" them — yet these problems were allowed to continue over at least the better part of two decades in relation to the investigation of sexual assaults. Although the MTPF say they took the crime of sexual assault seriously in 1985–86 I must conclude, on the evidence before me, that they did not.

[170] The rape trauma syndrome was clearly not understood by too many officers who were charged with the responsibility of investigating sexual assaults — others, including even some who had taken the sexual assault investigators course, adhered to rape myths. Examples can clearly be seen in this investigation — for example, Sgt. Duggan's occurrence reports in relation to the B.K. investigation — clearly "slanted toward disbelieving the victim", to quote Margo Pulford. It is obvious to anyone that Sgt. Duggan was strongly influenced by the fact that a bowl of potato chips on the bed where the rape occurred apparently remained undisturbed. He concluded there had been no struggle and hence no forced sexual intercourse. His denial in this regard is

simply incredible in the face of his own written record. Other examples are set out above as quoted from Det. Sgt. Boyd's report and her comment that these problems existed in every station in every division in the force.

[171] The protocol established by the force, AP No. 22, as it was designated, for the investigation of sexual assaults was often not followed and when it was not there is no evidence that any senior officer or supervisor followed up.

[172] The problems continued and because among adults, women are overwhelmingly the victims of sexual assault, they are and were disproportionately impacted by the resulting poor quality of investigation. The result is that women are discriminated against and their right to equal protection and benefit of the law is thereby compromised as the result.

[173] In my view the conduct of this investigation and the failure to warn in particular, was motivated and informed by the adherence to rape myths as well as sexist stereotypical reasoning about rape, about women and about women who are raped. The plaintiff therefore has been discriminated against by reason of her gender and as the result the plaintiff's rights to equal protection and equal benefit of the law were compromised.

Security of the Person

[174] I am satisfied that the defendants deprived the plaintiff of her right to security of the person by subjecting her to the very real risk of attack by a serial rapist — a risk of which they were aware but about which they quite deliberately failed to inform the plaintiff or any women living in the Church/Wellesley area at the time save only S.G. and M.L. and where in the face of that knowledge and their belief that the rapist would certainly attack again, they additionally failed to take any steps to protect the plaintiff or other women like her. Clearly the rape of the plaintiff constituted a deprivation of her security of the person. As Madam Justice Wilson stated in *Singh v. Canada (Minister of Employment & Immigration)*, [1985] 1 S.C.R. 177 at p. 207, 17 D.L.R. (4th) 422:

> ... "security of the person" must encompass freedom from the threat of physical punishment or suffering as well as freedom from such punishment itself.

[175] As I have indicated, because the defendants exercised their discretion in the investigation of this case in a discriminatory and negligent way as I have detailed above, their exercise of discretion was thereby contrary to the principle of fundamental justice.

[176] Section 1 of the *Charter* has no application in circumstances because the conduct of police in issue here is not "prescribed by law" within the meaning the jurisprudence has ascribed to that phrase.

[177] Here the plaintiff's *Charter* rights have been infringed by police conduct — not a legislative enactment or a common law rule.

[178] In any event the defendants made no effort in evidence to satisfy the requirements of s. 1 and demonstrate a s. 1 defence — they simply denied the plaintiff's rights which were infringed. I have found differently.

[179] In view of my findings the plaintiff is entitled under s. 24 to a remedy.

. . . .

Damages

[214] Ms. Doe precisely detailed the events of the early morning hours of August 24, 1986 in her evidence. It was obvious to everyone that giving this evidence was a difficult and painful process for her. Her attacker was armed with a knife and had concealed his identity with a mask he had fashioned and wore. The attack was terrifying and she feared for her life.

[215] Following her call to 911 a number of police officers arrived at her apartment and over the next hours she was obliged to repeat the details of her attack to a number of officers.

[216] She was taken to hospital for forensic testing by ambulance — an intrusive and painful process.

[217] This attack by a stranger in her own bed in her home has had a profound and lasting effect on Ms. Doe as she stated in her evidence:

> ... my life was shattered as a result of the rape, and I experienced it literally as being shattered for at least two to three years ...

[218] Some of the complaints include:

- difficulty sleeping;
- recurrent intrusive nightmares;
- panic attacks and nausea;
- lack of self-confidence;
- emotional detachment from friends;

- inability to socialize where strangers may be present;
- fear of men in general which impacted on everyday life, *i.e.*, stopped using TTC at night;
- no enjoyment of life.

[219] Although Ms. Doe had suffered from depression prior to August 24, 1986, this condition was greatly exacerbated as the result of the rape.

[220] On the evidence there can be no question but that the plaintiff suffered serious post-traumatic stress immediately following the rape and she continues to this day to exhibit symptoms which are consistent in post-traumatic stress disorder — at the time of trial some 11 years after her attack.

. . . .

Special Damages

. . . .

[253] I should add that the Chief of Police is responsible to see the members of his force carry out their duties properly and will be vicariously liable when they fail to do so as will the Board of Commissioners of Police which is charged with the overall responsibility of policing and maintaining law and order within the Municipality of Metropolitan Toronto (as it then was).

[241] In conclusion the plaintiff shall have judgment against the defendants in the following amounts:

General Damages	$175,000.00
Special Damages to date	$ 37,301.58
Future Costs	$ 8,062.74
Total	$220,364.32

together with an amount which represents the present value of a sum required to produce $2,000 annually for a period of 15 years and a declaration that the defendants did in 1986 violate Ms. Doe's s. 7 and s. 15(1) rights under the *Canadian Charter of Rights and Freedoms*.

[252] Matters of prejudgment interest and costs to be addressed at a future date to be agreed upon among counsel and the court and arranged through the trial co-ordinator's office.

Judgment accordingly.

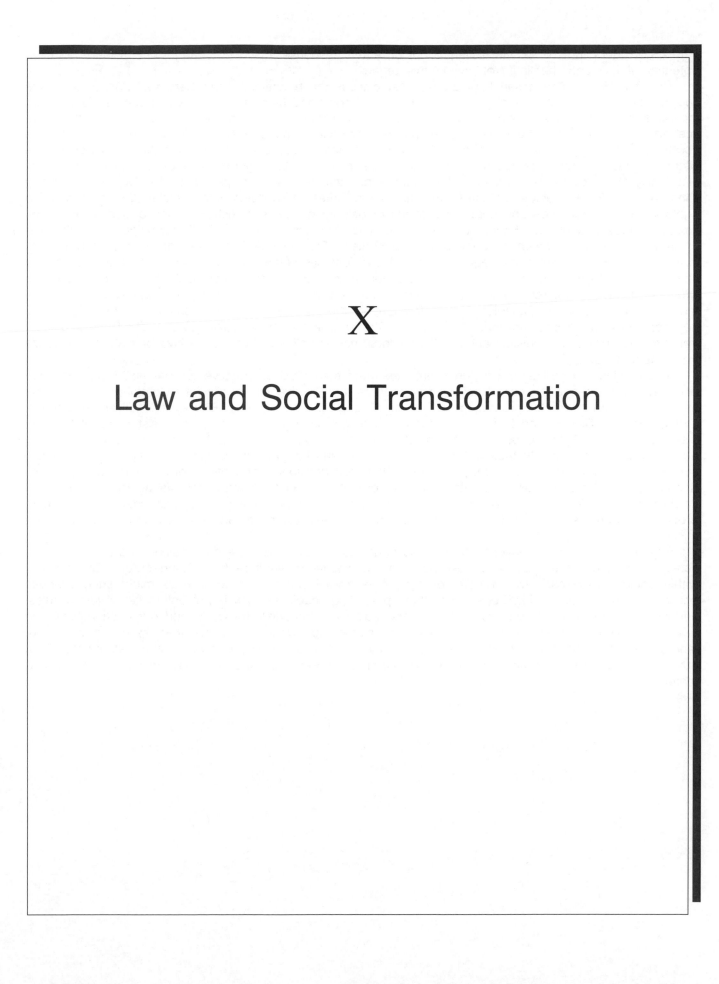

X

Law and Social Transformation

Part X considers the role of law as an agent of, and a response to, social change. It considers both the potential of law and the limits of law in this regard.

Chapter 26 includes a series of articles that discuss the potential for the *Canadian Charter of Rights and Freedoms* to act as a catalyst of social change. Knopff and Morton present a critique that focuses on the ways in which the *Charter* enhances the policy-making role of judges at the expense of legislators. Justice Abella counters that the legislators themselves entrenched the *Charter* and in so doing entrusted the courts with the role of protecting the public interest. When judges strike down legislation that violates the *Charter*, judges reinforce democracy rather than undermine it. B.S. Wray's article then considers the impact of equality rights discourse examining the portrayal of same-sex relationships adopted in both documentary films and litigation strategies in Canada and the United States. In so doing, she identifies the ways in which rights discourses reinforce dominant conceptions of belonging and relationships to the exclusion of others. Finally, Louise Arbour and Fannie Lafontaine consider the achievements of *Charter* litigation in the first 25 years since entrenchment in an international context. They identify a number of ways to improve the interaction between international legal norms and our domestic human rights system; they also identify key challenges for rights protection in Canada. As you read these different perspectives, consider how you would evaluate the impact of the *Charter*. Has it changed the values or behaviour of Canadians or, even, the way we identify as Canadians? Has it changed the way government operates, or the relationship between government and individuals? Does the *Charter* give too much power to judges? Does it distract from or does it provoke political action? On balance, has the *Charter* been a positive or negative influence on Canadian society?

The articles in Chapter 27 provide a broader, more theoretical perspective on the relationship between law and social change. Nathalie DesRosiers discusses the effectiveness of the Law Commission of Canada in its role as an agent for promoting law reform. The articles by Stephen Brickey and Elizabeth Comack and by Samuel Bowles and Herbert Gintis again highlight some of the internal inconsistencies of law and discuss the potential to harness law as a mechanism for not only resisting but, more important, *challenging* dominant social interests. In their article, Dennis Sullivan and Larry Tift investigate the ways in which native conceptions of restorative justice may effectively challenge traditional conceptions of law and justice. Finally, Rosemary Nagy critically examines how lawsuits brought by South African plaintiffs against multinational corporations for aiding and abetting apartheid may be understood as a part of a broader nation-building process through resolution of the "unfinished business" of the South African Truth and Reconciliation Commission.

The articles in this final section further challenge readers to rethink the composition and role of law; to see law as much more than a narrow instrument to secure or stabilize an existing order — or orders — within society. How can law promote, or even stifle, social change? In what ways might such changes occur given that — as we have seen throughout preceding chapters — law is not only a set of formal rules, and not only an extensive framework for understanding and ordering the world and our relationships with others, but also a critical part of our identity (e.g., citizenship). One might argue that law can never disentangle itself from the question of social transformation because it is, at its core, a basic statement about how society *ought* to be both now and in the future. Is law then inescapably a discourse of social transformation?

26 The Charter of Rights and Social Change

(a) Ardour in the Court†

Rainer Knopff and F.L. Morton

The Charter has done less to enhance your rights than to increase the policy-making power of judges

In 1992, former chief justice Antonio Lamer described the adoption of the Charter of Rights as "a revolution on the scale of the introduction of the metric system, the great medical discoveries of Louis Pasteur, and the invention of penicillin and the laser." Five years later, Mr. Lamer thanked "God for the Charter," adding that people "just don't have these rights." Life without the Charter, presumably, would be as bad as life before antibiotics.

We agree that the Charter has wrought a revolution but, contrary to the penicillin analogy, its effect hasn't been akin to saving and improving the lives of untold millions. Can anyone who remembers pre-1982 Canada seriously believe that the Charter has enriched and improved our lives to that extent?

Do we have dramatically improved freedom of speech? Well, okay, we are freer to collect kiddie porn.

Is freedom of religion much better protected? Maybe, but mainly in the sense of more freedom from religion, especially Christianity, which is increasingly seen as disqualifying any policy position with which it is associated.

Are we significantly less likely to convict the innocent? Probably not, though we may be more likely to let the guilty go free.

Are we more equal? Not if one is to believe equality rights advocates, who never tire of pointing out growing disparities.

The pre-Charter world was far from perfect, but it was hardly the Dark Age implied by Mr. Lamer's revolutionary rhetoric. Nor is the post-Charter world remarkably better. There have been changes, but inflationary "rights talk" notwithstanding, they have mainly been shifts in the policy balance on matters of ongoing reasonable disagreement.

The Charter's main revolutionary effect has not been to improve society but to enhance the political and policy influence of judges, to give them more power over the matters of reasonable disagreement that legislatures used to settle.

The judges themselves have admitted as much. Mr. Lamer, for example, has "no doubt" that the judiciary has been "drawn into the political arena to a degree unknown prior to 1982," and that it is often called upon "to make what used to be a political call." Similarly, the late Justice John Sopinka admitted that in "deciding a Charter case, the court is in a sense legislating." When York University's Ian Greene and several colleagues interviewed many of Canada's appellate court judges, virtually all of them admitted to a new lawmaking role. Earlier this week, Chief Justice Beverley McLachlin associated a "litigation explosion" with the advent of the Charter of Rights, indicating just how extensive the new policymaking role has become.

When so-called "court bashers" challenge this transfer of political power to unelected officials, the judges often reverse course insisting that there is no revolution after all. Judges have always enjoyed a degree of policymaking discretion, they contend, and

† From *The Globe and Mail* (April 7, 2000) A17. Reproduced with permission of the authors.

have exercised that discretion in applying the constitutional law of federalism. The Charter, far from effecting a revolutionary change, now appears as just a minor extension of well-established practice.

Unfortunately, this dodge doesn't work. While it is certainly true that federalism jurisprudence also involves judicial policymaking, deciding under the Charter whether government as such may (or must) do something goes far beyond deciding which government may do it. As Ian Hunter has aptly put it, "It may be true that elephants and chipmunks are both mammals, but to fail to acknowledge the difference between them is wilful deception."

Another response to the court bashers is to claim that judges are merely discharging duties imposed on them by the Canadian people when the Charter was democratically adopted. They are simply applying the Charter. However, this legalistic view of judging cannot be reconciled with whatever meaning the judges choose. "We have lots of discretion," Justice Claire L'Heureux-Dubé told the Canadian Bar Association last August. "So put yourself in where there is nothing else to go on." In other words, judges drive the Charter, not vice versa.

Judges do not drive the Charter alone, however. When Justice L'Heureux-Dubé admits to putting herself into the Charter, she is following the lead of countless activist commentators who insist, for example, that "the shaping of the Charter will be an intensely political process, far more responsive to public pressure than to constitutional law," or that litigating "law reform is part of an ideological battle." Groups such as LEAF (the Legal Education and Action Fund) have mounted fully self-conscious campaigns of "influencing the influencers," by "flooding the law reviews" with advice on just how judges should put themselves into the Charter.

Without the constant barrage of such activist scholarship, Justice L'Heureux-Dubé's unabashed put-yourself-in statement would be inconceivable, as would her remark in another speech that she is an "equality person" who will "do any thing I can to achieve it [equality]." Anything? Judges from earlier eras would never have so blatantly treated law as the vehicle for a political agenda.

Like the Charter itself, in other words, judges are as much a means as a cause of the Charter revolution. While judges are in the vanguard of the revolution, they are being pushed as much as they lead. They are being pushed by what we call the "Court Party," a loose constellation of interests that assiduously promote judicial power because they stand to benefit from it.

Today's Court Party, we contend, is a party of elites. It is dominated by the chattering classes. The Charter revolution it promotes is a revolution from the top, part of what Christopher Lasch — turning Ortega y Gassett on his head — has christened the "revolt of the elites."

Despite the rhetorical evasions, the revolution in judicial power is now widely conceded — even, as we have seen, by judges in their more candid moments. The Charter itself, however, is not so much the cause of the revolution as the means through which it is carried out. The Declaration of Independence did not cause the American Revolution, nor the Declaration of the Rights of Man the French Revolution. A revolution cannot occur without leaders and the support of interested classes. The Charter Revolution and the Court Party explains the political economy and sociology of the Charter revolution.

(b)   The Case for a Strong Court[†]

Judge Rosalie Abella

The judiciary is accountable to the public interest, not public opinion, says Judge Rosalie Abella

Democracy is not — and never was — just about the wishes of the majority. What pumps oxygen no less forcefully through vibrant democratic veins is the protection of rights, through the courts, notwithstand-

† From *The Globe and Mail* (April 13, 2000) A15. Adapted from the keynote address at the Constitutional Law Conference on April 7, 2000 at Osgoode Hall Law School. Reproduced with permission.

ing the wishes of the majority. It is this second, crucial aspect of democratic values that has been submerged by the [recent] swirling discourse [about the role of judges in enforcing rights].

I think it is fair to say that until 1981, when the Charter was donated to the British North America Act by the federal government, no one ever accused the Canadian judiciary of aggressive rights protection. In fact, many of us, reared on the constitutional diet of division-of-powers jurisprudence, looked wistfully at the wide selection on the constitutional menu available to American judges. With rare exceptions, the Canadian Supreme Court not only shared the apparent inhibitions of its American and British counterparts about welcoming rights into the judicial fold, they remained reluctant at least a generation longer.

By the time I graduated from law school in 1970, the perception was that the Supreme Court was the place that decided constitutional issues such as whether Persons in the British North [America] Act included women and whether egg marketing boards were a provincial or a federal undertaking.

Then, in 1978, just before we got a Charter, the Supreme Court in Rathwell v. Rathwell reversed a decision it had made only five years earlier in Murdoch v. Murdoch, thereby rewriting the archaic matrimonial property regime we had been subject to for over 100 years. No longer equitable, said the court. Time to adjust to a new appreciation about the role played by husbands and wives in a marriage. Time, in short, to create a new social contract. The public cheered. The media cheered. Within months, practically every province had amended its family property laws accordingly.

Then we got the Charter of Rights and Freedoms. To the Constitution's division of powers, it added rights: civil rights, such as the freedoms of religion, association and expression; the right to counsel; and the right to security of a person. And human rights, such as equality, linguistic rights, aboriginal rights and multiculturalism. What Canada got with the Charter was a dramatic package of guaranteed rights, subject only to those reasonable limits that were demonstrably justified in a free and democratic society; a package assembled by the legislature, which in turn, it bears repeating, assigned to the courts the duty to decide whether its laws, policies or practices met the constitutional standards set out in the Charter.

In the first decade of Charter adjudication, the Supreme Court was energetic. It struck down Sabbatarian and sign laws, said equality meant more than treating people the same, and decriminalized abortion. It ventured fearlessly into the overgrown

fields of the law and cut a wide path for other courts to follow. Again the public cheered. Even the media cheered. It was clear that the 1960s and 1970s had generated a public thirst for rights protection, and Charter adjudication in the Supreme Court in the 1980s was beginning to quench that thirst.

With the arrival of the 1990s, a few abrupt voices were heard to challenge the Supreme Court, voices in large part belonging to those whose psychological security or territorial hegemony were at risk from the Charter's reach. As the decade advanced, so did the courage and insistence of these New Inhibitors, most of whom appeared to congregate at one end of the ideological spectrum. While their articulated target was the Supreme Court of Canada, their real target was the way the Charter was transforming their traditional expectations and entitlements.

They made their arguments skillfully. In essence, they turned the good news of constitutionalized rights, the mark of a secure and mature democracy, into the bad news of judicial autocracy, the mark of a debilitated and devalued legislature. They called minorities seeking the right to be free from discrimination "special interest groups seeking to jump the queue." They called efforts to reverse discrimination "reverse discrimination."

They pretended that concepts or words in the Charter such as freedom, equality and justice had no pre-existing political aspect and bemoaned the politicization of the judiciary. They trumpeted the rights of the majority and ignored the fact that minorities are people who want rights, too. They said courts should only interpret, not make law, thereby ignoring the entire history of common law. They called advocates for equality, human rights, and the Charter "biased" and defenders of the status quo "impartial." They urged the courts to defer to legislation, unless, ironically, they disagreed with the legislation. They said judges are not accountable because they are not elected, yet held them to negative account for every expanded right. They claimed a monopoly on truth, frequently used invectives to assert it, then accused their detractors of personalizing the debate.

The essence of their message was that there is an anti-democratic, socially hazardous turbulence in the air, most notably during judicial flights. And while it is a message that has every right to be heard, it is not the whole story. The whole story is that the Charter does not represent heterodoxy about democracy, but rather its finest manifestation. People elect legislators who enact the laws they think the majority of their constituents want them to enact, and appoint judges who are expected to be independent from those legislators and impartial in determining whether the legislature's actions meet constitutional standards.

When legislatures elected by majorities enact laws such as the Charter, the majority is presumed to agree with that legislature's decision to entrench rights and extend a constitutionally guaranteed invitation to the courts to intervene when legislative conduct is not demonstrably justified in a democratic society.

In enforcing the Charter, therefore, the courts are not trespassing on legislative authority, they are fulfilling their assigned democratic duty to prevent legislative trespass on constitutional rights.

While all branches of government are responsible for the delivery of justice, they respond to different imperatives. Legislators, our elected proxies, consult constituents, fellow parliamentarians, and available research until the public's opinions are sufficiently digestible to be swallowed by a parliamentary majority. And if they cannot be made sufficiently palatable, they are starved for want of political nourishment.

This is the dilemma all legislators face — they are elected to implement the public will, the public will is often difficult to ascertain or implement, and they are therefore left to implement only those constituency concerns that can survive the gauntlet of the prevailing partisan ideology. At the end of any given parliamentary session, many public concerns [lie] scattered of necessity on the cutting-room floor, awaiting either wider public endorsement or a newly elected partisan ideology.

The judiciary has a different relationship with the public. It is accountable less to the public's opinions and more to the public interest. It discharges that accountability by being principled, independent,

and impartial. Of all the public institutions responsible for delivering justice, the judiciary is the only one for whom justice is the exclusive mandate. This means that while legislatures respond of necessity to the urgings of the public, however we define it, judges, on the other hand, serve only justice. As Lillian Hellman once said: "I will not cut my conscience to fit this year's fashions."

This means that the occasional judgment will collide with some public expectations, which will, inevitably, create controversy. But judgments that are controversial are not thereby illegitimate or undemocratic; they are, in fact, democracy at work.

This defence of constitutional rights does not mean that there are no outstanding issues. There are several to discuss: public information about who judges are and how they are appointed; the interrelationship between courts and legislatures, including the reminder that the notwithstanding clause gives legislatures the final say; when to read in corrective words to effect constitutional compliance and when to leave corrective compliance to the legislature; the tension between those who think the rights stage is overpopulated and those who are in the wings waiting to join the cast; whether labels such as progressive, conservative, activist, restraint, or politicization really contribute to a thoughtful analysis of judicial behaviour; whether the search for consensus is replacing compassion and courage as the defining justice objective and, as a corollary, whether the proposition that entitlement should be a matter of timing can ever be consistent with the fact that rights are guaranteed now.

All of these are issues that we are, and should be, talking about. It is a conversation I hope we will keep constructive, rigorous, and continuous.

(c) Screening Desire: Same-Sex-Marriage Documentaries, Citizenship, and the Law†

B.J. Wray

> Behind the documentary film from the first was a purpose, and it was the educational purpose with which we have been dealing. It was developed as a movement, and deliberately, to "bring alive" to the citizen the world in which his [*sic*] citizenship lay, to "bridge the gap" between the citizen and his community.
>
> — John Grierson[1]

† (2009) 24:1 C.J.L.S. 1 at 1–8, 16–20. Reproduced with permission of Canadian Journal of Law and Society/Revue Canadienne Droit et Societe. www.utpjournals.com. [Notes and/or references omitted.]

The legal struggle for the recognition of same-sex-marriage equality rights in Canada and the United States has not been confined to courts of law. While legal briefs, oral arguments, and constitutional interpretation may take centre stage in the same-sex-marriage trials, arguably it is the cultural matrix in which these legal discourses are embedded that is the real battleground of rights recognition. The courts may grant or deny state-sanctioned legitimacy to same-sex relationships, but every good human-rights litigator knows that the legal judgment itself is neither the beginning nor the end of any rights struggle; it is simply one moment in an ongoing conversation about the relationship of citizens to one another.

Two of the more recent North American documentaries on same-sex marriage work to situate legal discourses within this wider conversation about national belonging and relationships between citizens. *Tying the Knot: The Union That's Dividing America* (USA, 2004) and *The End of Second Class* (Canada, 2006) document American and Canadian debates on same-sex marriage from the perspective of the litigants and the lawyers involved in making these equality claims.[2] *Tying the Knot* makes its case for same-sex marriage by interweaving the personal stories of several same-sex couples with commentary on same-sex marriage from gay and lesbian activists, historians, and lawyers as well as from politicians and religious leaders on both sides of the issue. In addition to highlighting same-sex-marriage litigation in the United States, *Tying the Knot* also documents debates around the Defense of Marriage Act and the proposed Federal Marriage Amendment.[3] *Tying the Knot* is a call to arms for advocates of same-sex marriage, as the film showcases the very real and very traumatic consequences of America's refusal to legitimize same-sex relationships.

By contrast, *The End of Second Class* is a celebratory film that focuses exclusively on recent Canadian legal triumphs for same-sex couples. The film narrates the stories of several of the couples involved in same-sex-marriage litigation in British Columbia,[4] Ontario,[5] and Quebec.[6] The lawyers involved in those cases take centre stage in *The End of Second Class* as they describe their winning litigation strategies. Like *Tying the Knot*, *The End of Second Class* includes footage of prominent leaders of the religious right making their case against same-sex marriage, as well as clips of debates in the House of Commons over Bill C-38,[7] the federal act amending the definition of marriage to include same-sex couples. The film ends with a montage of Canadian same-sex wedding celebrations, including footage from Toronto's 2003 Pride Parade in which spectators wildly cheer and applaud the newlyweds.

My interest in these films lies in *how* they represent the legal challenges to their audiences. It is axiomatic that documentary representations are not simply unfiltered portrayals of "what really happened" but, instead, are highly mediated versions of the events they record. Like the litigation itself, each of these documentaries is built upon representational strategies that are intended to have the maximum impact on their audiences. In fact, *Tying the Knot* and *The End of Second Class* replicate the legal arguments and litigation strategies used by advocates of same-sex marriage. In doing so, both films also replicate the inherent limitations of these tactics, especially the normalizing impulses that characterize claims to equality rights.

My paper focuses on the ways in which these documentaries bring forward the discourse of sexuality equality rights from the legal arena into filmic representation. Just as the legal arguments for and against same-sex marriage are necessarily enmeshed in dominant narratives of relationships, so, too, *Tying the Knot* and *The End of Second Class* are caught up in the discursive demands of rights recognition. Equality-rights claims must be made intelligible through an existing legal framework that circumscribes the kinds of arguments that can be made. Similarly, filmic representations of these claims tend to reinforce the representational demands of equality-rights law in that they adhere to a model of equality rights that *a priori* delineates the types of arguments that can be made and the types of subjects who are appropriate to make those arguments. Each film represents the case for same-sex marriage through an appeal to three markers of equality-rights discourses: rights evolve over time; rights are comparative; rights are indicators of national belonging. *Tying the Knot* and *The End of Second Class* do not simply "bring alive to the citizen the world in which his citizenship [lies]"; instead, they actively participate in the ongoing process of delineating the connections among national belonging, same-sex relationships, and the law.

As I discuss below, *Tying the Knot* and *The End of Second Class* legitimize same-sex marriage by articulating the issues at stake through the familiarity of equality-rights discourses and discourses of national belonging that, in turn, reinforce dominant conceptions of conjugal relationships. Seen through these familiar lenses, same-sex marriage becomes intelligible as a human-rights goal. This is not to say that all viewers will suddenly embrace the cause of same-sex marriage; rather, it means that the debate around same-sex marriage will take place within these discursive boundaries. This discursive delineation matters because it forecloses any understandings of same-sex marriage that do not fit into either the pro- or the anti-same-sex-marriage camp. The narrative structures of *Tying the Knot* and *The End of Second Class* actively discourage viewers from thinking about same-sex relationships outside these oppositional camps.

DOCUMENTARY AS ACTIVISM

From its inception, documentary filmmaking has recognized its potential to intervene in social and political conversations. In his article on the political impact of documentary films, David Whiteman notes that "[t]he making of a documentary film is essentially an intervention into an ongoing social and political process, and the production may act as a catalyst in many different ways."[8] He goes on to observe that "social movements continually struggle to create public space for discussion of the issues they think are important and films can become a crucial part of that struggle."[9] *Tying the Knot* and *The End of Second Class* create a public space for the discussion of same-sex marriage in the form of high-quality 90-minute productions that bring the basic issues of this debate to a wide-ranging audience. The directors of these films assemble several years of complex same-sex-marriage litigation and political debate into viewer-friendly products, complete with sympathetic characters, dramatic arcs, and poignant endings.

Tying the Knot and *The End of Second Class* also fulfil an educative mandate in that they present the contours of the debate, the history of marriage, and the lives of same-sex couples to audiences who may not be familiar with the issue. These films contextualize complicated constitutional issues within the realm of the everyday by showing the impact that the denial of benefits and obligations has on same-sex couples. In this respect, *Tying the Knot* is particularly effective because the narrative trajectory of the film follows two individuals struggling with the legal, financial, and emotional consequences of the deaths of their long-term same-sex partners. The abstract notion of marital benefits and obligations is concretized through the filmmaker's depiction of the heart-wrenching circumstances of these surviving partners.

The stories of two couples, Sam and Earl and Mickie and Lois, humanize same-sex marriage and force audience members to grapple with their pain and suffering. The story of Earl and Sam takes place in rural Oklahoma. Sam is interviewed in 2003, not long after Earl's death. They lived together for 25 years and raised Sam's two sons from a previous marriage. In his will, Earl left Sam the house they built together. The house was in Earl's name because it stood on property Earl inherited from his parents. The film documents the challenge to Earl's will that is mounted by a band of his cousins. Alleging a technical error in the will (there was only one notary signature, instead of the required two), the cousins claimed that they, not Sam, should inherit the property. The Oklahoma courts agreed, and the cousins evicted Sam from his home. He moved to a rundown shack, which the cousins are currently trying to take from him as well, claiming that he owes back taxes.

The story of Lois and Mickie is similarly tragic. Lois and Mickie met as officers in the Tampa Police Force and had a commitment ceremony in 1991. Lois was killed in the line of duty in 2001, shortly after they had celebrated their tenth anniversary. *Tying the Knot* follows Mickie's attempt to claim a survivor's pension benefit from the Tampa Police. Saddled with the household debt they had incurred together, Mickie requested the benefit from the Tampa Police Pension Board in 2001. She was denied. Her appeal to the board in 2002 was also denied, and the board granted Lois's pension benefit to her family. Mickie filed a lawsuit against the city in 2002, and the Hillsborough County Circuit Court ruled in 2004 that she was not entitled to the pension. The city then sued Mickie to pay for their legal fees.

By narrating, through these couples, the consequences of denying same-sex partners the right to marry, *Tying the Knot* vividly illustrates what is at stake in same-sex-marriage litigation and activism. Audience education occurs not just through a discussion of the legal rights denied to same-sex couples (although this discussion is also a prominent feature of both films) but through the empathetic linkage of citizens to fellow citizens. As I discuss below, the similarities between heterosexual married couples and same-sex partnerships are clearly articulated in these films as one of the strategic tools used to foster a sense of equivalence between gay and straight relationships. Perhaps Sam expresses this most clearly when he is asked to describe the differences between being married to a woman and being married to a man: "Besides the sex, not a damn thing."

As activist projects, both films succeed in situating same-sex marriage solidly within the framework of human rights and equality discourses. This placement is a key element in the ability of these films to change the minds of sceptical viewers and to continue the project of inspiring advocates of same-sex marriage to battle for legal recognition. *Tying the Knot*, as a pre-same-sex-marriage-rights documentary, is particularly adept at mobilizing advocates to rally for this cause because it successfully foregrounds the injustice and indignity of the denial of same-sex marriage rights. In fact, the film itself gives viewers the opportunity to become activists by encouraging them to give monetary donations to both Sam and Mickie so that they can pay their debts and continue their fight for equality. The film's Web site provides regular updates on the lives of both Sam and Mickie, and similarly encourages visitors to the site to send in financial contributions.[10]

Tying the Knot and *The End of Second Class* do not confine their representations of same-sex marriage to its impact on individual couples and their rights claims. Each film goes beyond the importance of same-sex marriage in terms of ordering the private relations between individuals to suggest that same-sex marriage has a vital role to play in reordering the public realm. In particular, same-sex marriage in these films becomes a marker of nation-ness, and its recognition (or lack thereof) is construed as a commentary on the state of the nation. *Tying the Knot* uses same-sex marriage to offer a critique of national identity by juxtaposing American political responses to the issue with the actions of the Netherlands and Canada. The film travels to Amsterdam in 2001 to interview one of the first Dutch couples married under the Netherlands' newly passed same-sex-marriage law. Ton and Louis tell viewers that "in Holland we have a saying — 'you can judge a country by how it treats its minorities' — and if it treats them well, then it's a civilized country." By implication, America becomes an "uncivilized" country whose refusal to grant these rights is indicative of its national character. *Tying the Knot* also travels to the Toronto Pride Parade in 2003, shortly after the Ontario Court of Appeal legalized same-sex marriage and declared that Ontario must begin solemnizing same-sex marriages immediately. From a shot of Niagara Falls, complete with a colourful rainbow appearing in the mist of the falls and the soft strains of "O Canada" playing in the background, the film cuts to the parade route, where an unseen interviewer solicits a comment from Michael Leshner, one of the litigants in the Ontario case. Leshner kisses his partner, grins at the camera, and says, "You can't do that in America *yet*. But I'll be there." Once again, America is depicted as falling behind the advancements of other countries; the film suggests, however, that with a little help from its Canadian neighbours, the American nation might just be able to redeem itself.

The End of Second Class uses same-sex marriage to showcase the progressiveness of the Canadian state and to further the image of Canada as a diverse and tolerant nation. These central myths of Canadian nation-ness are reinforced not only through the triumphant storyline of Canadian same-sex-marriage litigation but also through the filmmaker's repeated deployment of national iconography, including the Parliament Buildings and the Canadian flag. *The End of Second Class* opens with images of historic and contemporary gay and lesbian protests in Canada, inter-cut with pithy clips from same-sex-marriage lawyers and law professors explaining what is at stake in this debate. The film shifts to Toronto's Metropolitan Community Church (MCC), where the MCC choir joyfully sings, "By your love, let the walls fall down." As this rousing same-sex-marriage anthem plays in the background, the film cuts to a shot of Canada's Parliament Buildings. The camera pans across Parliament Hill, and we see an unending row of Canadian flags flapping in the breeze in the foreground. The camera continues to pan skyward, up the Peace Tower, where it finally comes to rest on the Canadian flag that is permanently perched atop the tower. We continue to hear MCC's same-sex anthem (a new national anthem?) in the background, and as the camera reaches the apex of its shot, the film's title, *The End of Second Class*, is superimposed across the screen. This metaphoric rise to the top of the Canadian nation — to the end of second class — becomes the structuring theme of the film. Within minutes, *The End of Second Class* has not only situated same-sex marriage within an equality-rights discourse but also ensured that same-sex marriage is a marker of national pride and an indicator of the expansiveness of Canadian nation-ness. In these films, what is at stake in the same-sex-marriage debate is nothing less than the future of the nation and its place on the world stage of human rights.

With such a lofty project at stake, it is understandably difficult to represent a nuanced or complicated understanding of same-sex marriage in these films. In fact, their powerful impact stems from the narration of same-sex marriage within the familiar terrain of national identity. In *Tying the Knot*, audience members must grapple with the question of how to live in a nation where some citizens are less equal than others, while *The End of Second Class* gives audience members the opportunity to celebrate the tolerance of the Canadian nation, especially in relation to its American counterpart.

Ever the spoiler, I remain wary of the costs associated with these representational strategies, and particularly of the drive to normalcy that characterizes the narrative content and the narrative structure of *Tying the Knot* and *The End of Second Class*. The section below seeks to illuminate these costs. As activist projects, these films are squarely situated within an equality-rights-based agenda of relationship recognition. This agenda tends to aspire to inclusion within existing state-recognized paradigms of relationships rather than suggesting alternative forms of recognition. The costs associated with this approach — homogenization, normalization, "good" versus "bad" relationships, the triumph of sameness — merit consideration, if for no other reason than to present possible future directions for same-sex-relationship activism once recognition of same-sex marriage has been achieved. Contrary to what these films suggest, the legal recognition of same-sex marriage is not the culmination of the struggle but only the beginning of the much larger project of rethinking the way in which the state grants benefits and obligations.[11] We must be prepared to ask whether achieving recognition for same-sex marriage outweighs the risk of reinforcing the normalcy of conjugal relationships. Answering this question in the affirmative is merely the first step in what should be a lengthy consideration of precisely *how* the case for same-sex marriage should be made, both in the courtroom and on the screen. The legal and representational strategies employed within the same-sex-marriage debate generally do not call into question the benefits of a rights-based discourse, nor do they expose their investment in heteronormalizing arguments and representations.

RIGHTS DISCOURSES: LAW MEETS DOCUMENTARY

In his article on the use of documentary films by gay and lesbian activists in Oregon's 1992 Anti-Gay Ballot Measure, Ronald Gregg articulates the most pressing problem with pro-gay-rights documentaries: "[these documentaries] fail to represent the complexity of gay and lesbian identities, communities, and sexual behaviors ... [they] fail to represent any specific aspects of the gay subculture that might mark it as different from the mainstream; iconographies, histories, and literature remain unexplored."[12] This drive toward sameness results in the "mainstreaming" of gay and lesbian identity and the "sanitization" of queer citizens.[13] A similar normalizing impulse is readily discernible in *Tying the Knot* and *The End of Second Class*.[14] These films make the case for same-sex marriage from within a framework of equality rights. As they mimic the arguments made in the litigation on same-sex marriage, *Tying the Knot* and *The End of Second Class* also replicate the limitations of these arguments.

In particular, these films fail to move beyond an appeal for inclusion within existing state-based structures of relationship recognition and, in the process, leave viewers with a sense that inclusion within the institution of marriage is the "natural" aspiration of all couples, regardless of their sexuality. Rights theorist Carl Stychin astutely describes the impact that such arguments have in the legal context: "In attempting to appropriate a state benefit for same sex couples, the resulting judicial discourse leaves virtually no space for the articulation of a critique of the institutions upon which a system of compulsory heterosexuality is founded."[15] Similarly, in both films, the desirability of marriage is not only linked to the importance of equal benefits and obligations — that goal could be achieved through alternative forms of relationship recognition — but characterized as the "natural" impulse of all long-term couples and, indeed, all citizens. In other words, making the case for same-sex marriage in these films, and in the litigation, cannot be separated from the culturally pervasive ideal of conjugality. Indeed, the case for same-sex marriage is *predicated upon* sustaining and reinforcing this ideal as the ultimate marker of full and equal national belonging for gay and lesbian citizens.

Arguably, the structure of equality-rights discourses has determined *a priori* same-sex marriage litigation strategies and their subsequent representations in *Tying the Knot* and *The End of Second Class*. By iterating same-sex marriage within the familiar narratives of rights recognition, these films place same-sex marriage within the ambit of imagined possibilities. At the beginning of this article, I noted that three markers of equality-rights discourses tend to recur in the films and in the litigation: rights evolve over time; rights are comparative; rights are indicators of national belonging. By appealing to these markers, *Tying the Knot* and *The End of Second Class* mimic the litigators' attempts to situate same-sex marriage within a generally accepted framework for achieving minority rights in North America.

. . . .

Same-sex marriage and heterosexual analogies

While racial analogies are the most prominent of the narrative strategies employed in same-sex-marriage litigation and cultural representations, these comparisons are intimately linked to the myriad heterosexual analogies used in the litigation and in the films. The proliferation of "sameness" arguments with respect to the character of same-sex relationships is, like the racial analogies, part of the strategic representation of same-sex marriage within familiar cultural narratives. Same-sex relationships, in these arguments, are represented through the everyday norms of heterosexuality, such as monogamy, domesticity, childrearing, and commitment. The narration of these norms further serves to place same-sex relationships within the realm of legal and cultural intelligibility.

Many of the legal factums and oral arguments in the same-sex-marriage cases showcase the similarities between heterosexual and same-sex couples by invoking the same type of "paralleling" strategy that is used in relation to race-based analogies. Invariably, advocates assert that "[t]he plaintiffs in this case seek to marry for the same mix of reasons as heterosexual couples who choose to marry."[40] This assertion is typically backed by a highly strategic narration of the factual background of each couple involved in the litigation. The complaint filed by the couples in *Kerrigan* presents the story of each couple through the conventions associated with heterosexual relationships. The complaint includes a veritable litany of domesticity: the couples have been together for *x* years (usually at least 10) and intend to remain together forever; they have joint bank accounts and mortgages; they celebrate anniversaries with friends and families; they have nursed each other through bouts of ill health and are caring for elderly parents; they are raising children together and their co-workers threw baby showers for them; they changed their last names to reflect their commitment to each other; and so forth.[41] Each of these characteristics makes same-sex marriage recognizable to the Court within an already familiar narrative of heterosexual marriage. Like the racial analogies, these comparisons work to reassure the Court that the institution of marriage will not be altered by the addition of same-sex couples.

When effective, this strategy can actually become part of the Court's own narration of what is at stake in the recognition of same-sex marriage. For instance, in *Halpern*, Chief Justice McMurtry (as he then was) tells the story of these same-sex couples from within the heteronormative understanding of marriage that the couples themselves had advocated in their factums:

> Seven gay and lesbian couples [...] want to celebrate their love and commitment to each other by getting married in civil ceremonies. In this respect, they share the same goal as countless other Canadian couples. Their reasons for wanting to engage in a formal civil ceremony of marriage *are the same as the reasons of heterosexual couples*.[42]

McMurtry C.J. goes on to cite directly from the affidavits of three of the couples, in which they express their desire to obtain the recognition and validation accorded heterosexual couples. The essence of these affidavits is that their already existing relationships are unintelligible to the wider social community and that inclusion in the institution of marriage will remedy this inequality:

> We want our families, relatives, friends, and larger society to know and understand our relationship for what it is, a loving committed relationship between two people. A traditional marriage would allow us the opportunity to enter into such a commitment.[43]

Another couple states,

> We love one another and are happy to be married. We highly value the love and commitment to our relationship that marriage implies. Our parents were married for over 40 and 50 years respectively, and we value the tradition of marriage as seriously as did our parents.[44]

The tacit assumption in these statements is that relationships outside the ambit of marriage are second-class relationships that the couples view as undesirable. The couples thus play to the third marker of equality-rights discourses: rights signify full and equal national belonging. In the words of GLAD, "[t]o deny individuals the right to seek personal fulfillment through marriage is, at the most basic level, a denial of equal citizenship to gay and lesbian people."[45]

Like the litigation, *Tying the Knot* and *The End of Second Class* also use the dominant tropes of heterosexual relationships to justify inclusion within the institution of marriage. Each film represents the equivalence between heterosexual and homosexual relationships by framing the personal stories of same-sex couples within heteronormative relationship ideals. The banality of couplehood becomes a marker of "normal" relationships. *Tying the Knot* and *The End of Second Class* use myriad devices to showcase these norms: home videos by the couples depict significant moments in their relationships; long-term couples who live together are the only couples featured; several of the couples are raising children; interviews are conducted in the couples' homes, and the couples are shown tending gardens, grocery shopping, feeding livestock, and eating with family and friends. In short, there is nothing remarkable about these scenes, and that is precisely what brings these couples into the realm of normative heterosexuality. Any images that might threaten this idyllic portrayal of same-sex relationships are banished from the screen. These images are the visual equivalent of rights-based legal arguments: they foreground same-ness and foreclose difference to make the case that same-sex relationships deserve to be included within the scope of marriage.

One of the legal and cultural hurdles discussed in both *Tying the Knot* and *The End of Second Class* is the oppositional argument that marriage just *is* heterosexual. This view is encapsulated by Pearce Lacy, retired bishop of Toronto, in his speech to an anti-same-sex-marriage rally:

> Since the beginning of humanity, there has existed a natural institution composed of men and women, serving the needs of society by producing new citizens and educating them. They existed before all governments, before all societies, before the courts, before the *Charter*, before all laws.

Attempts to establish the unchanging and natural status of marriage as a heterosexual institution are explicitly countered, in both films, through a point/counterpoint narrative structure in which opposing arguments are immediately followed by direct rebuttals from advocates of same-sex marriage. The limitation of this representational style is that arguments for same-sex marriage are inevitably structured by the terms of the opposition. Substantial portions of both films are devoted to the presentation of gay and lesbian expert counter-opinion. For example, marriage historian E.J. Graff takes to task what she calls "the big lie of the family values debate — the idea that marriage has ever been some solid, static thing, and that it has stayed that way for 6000 years." The structure and the content of the debate become mired in a narrative logic in which pro-arguments are substituted for anti-arguments without actually questioning the terms of the debate itself.

Tying the Knot and *The End of Second Class* also use the personal stories of same-sex couples to debunk the aforementioned essentialist understandings of marriage. The significance of the quotidian images of domestic life discussed above is that they call into question the innate heterosexuality of marriage by depicting the everyday lives of same-sex couples as equivalent to those of straight couples. Just as they use racial analogies, both films use the dominant tropes of heterosexual relationships to argue that the inclusion of same-sex couples in the institution of marriage does not threaten either its structure or its centrality in discourses of nation-ness. This is a move designed to bring gays and lesbians into the fold of marriage while concurrently allaying fears of a queer transformation of marriage. In other words, while marriage may not be essentially heterosexual, in these films it remains essentially heteronormative.

PRODUCING "GOOD" SEXUAL CITIZENS AND BEYOND

The cumulative effect of the use of equality-rights discourses in these films and in the litigation is the normalization of same-sex relationships. One of the dangers of this representational reiteration of normalcy is that it has the potential to encourage the *internal* policing of group membership. The mantra of sameness that accompanies calls for inclusion ensures that couples who embrace non-normative configurations of relationships become the new second-class citizens. As Cathy Cohen notes,

> [c]entral [...] to this strategy is the manipulation and privileging of certain characteristics and behaviors within marginal communities as groups prove themselves worthy of inclusion. For as groups vie for the label of legitimate, normal, and citizen, they confront the requirement that they regulate and control the public behavior and image of all group members, especially those perceived as non-conformist.[46]

By rendering same-sex relationships legitimate within an established ideology of conjugality, these films and legal arguments unwittingly participate in the containment of excessive sexuality. The careful representation of same-sex couples through the longstanding relationship tropes of monogamous love and commitment aids in the process of "sanitizing" same-sex couplehood for inclusion in the normative categories of "spousal," "family," "conjugal," and "national."

The rights-based approach to equality represented in these films and in the litigation produces a particular kind of gay and lesbian subject whose aims and aspirations map onto those of the more powerful. Cohen observes that a rights framework "promises that if gays and lesbians present themselves as legitimate and deserving citizens, then equal status will be bestowed on all those deemed 'virtually normal.'"[47] Similarly, Michael Warner describes the far-reaching consequences of these legal and representational strategies:

> The campaign for gay marriage is not so much a campaign for marriage as a campaign about the constituency and vocabulary of the gay and lesbian public. The normalizing interpretation of marriage is increasingly established as the self-understanding of the national gay public. Whether marriage is normalizing or not for the individuals who marry, the debate about marriage has done much to normalize the gay movement, and thus the context in which marriage becomes a meaningful option.[48]

Significantly, when these queer critiques of same-sex marriage are raised in *The End of Second Class*, they are summarily dismissed, and, ironically, same-sex married couples are held up as the epitome of "queerness." barbara findlay,[49] one of the lawyers in the BC case, discusses two of the queer arguments raised against same-sex marriage: the argument against creating a class of "good" queers and the argument against homogenization; she abruptly dismisses these critiques and says that they make her angry. findlay's comments are immediately followed by an interview with Jane and Joy, litigants in the BC case. After describing how hurt they were by these critiques of same-sex marriage, Jane states that she thinks "it is more revolutionary to be queer and married in Surrey than to be queer and unmarried in the West End of Vancouver." Her comments unwittingly lend credence to the queer argument that a potential consequence of same-sex marriage may be the institution of a hierarchical understanding of gay relationships, in which married gays are the queerest of all. Jane's and Joy's comments, and the images of domesticity that accompany them, make heteronormativity the new marker of queerness.

But while these films and legal arguments represent gay and lesbian subjects as good (hetero)sexual citizens who are living out the American and Canadian dreams of conjugality, they also do something else: they highlight the tensions that are present in gay and lesbian and queer communities across these two countries. For some, same-sex marriage is the ultimate symbol of acceptance and validation after generations of struggle, violence, and heartbreak. For others, it is the "M-word" whose ubiquitous presence in the headlines and on the front lines has taken energy and resources away from queers at risk and queers in need. And for some of us, living with these two extremes held in abeyance is what we do every day, because neither position encapsulates how we feel or think about same-sex marriage. That space between has not yet been articulated in either legal or filmic representations of same-sex marriage, nor in the oppositional discourses that emanate from within the queer community. I would suggest that the space between is where the really hard thinking about same-sex marriage and its relationship to heteronomativity could take place. Without the constraints of normalizing or anti-normalizing relationship narratives, this space between has the potential to get at the complex feelings that I suspect most of us have about the form of our relationships, whatever that form may be.

Equality-rights discourses, however, are notoriously resistant to non-binarized stories — you are either for us or against us. So, too, the queer theory that was supposed to move us away from such polarizations has spent the last decade dividing gay and lesbian subjects into those who resist normalcy and those who fall into its clutches. What is to be made of those of us who watch these films and follow developments in same-sex marriage law with an unrelenting critique of their heteronormative tendencies and yet, at the same time, propose to our partners and cry at the sight of a gay or lesbian couple on their wedding day? Can these complicated stories be told from within the frameworks of either rights-based discourses or the anti-normalizing narratives of queer commentary? These are the tales that are still waiting to be represented.

(d) Beyond Self-congratulation: The *Charter* at 25 in an International Perspective†

Louise Arbour and Fannie Lafontaine

I. INTRODUCTION

[1] When celebrating the coming into force of an instrument aimed at protecting fundamental human rights, we are unavoidably torn between the desire to rejoice at the immense progress made because of the instrument and the disturbing awareness of the extent of the efforts required for what has yet to be accomplished. This is exactly as it should be. For anniversaries to be meaningful, one must be able to

† (2007) 45 Osgoode Hall L.J. 239–75 at paras. 1–25, 47–70. Reproduced with permission. [Notes and/or references omitted.]

both take note of the successes of the past and commit to meeting the challenges of the future.

[2] There is little room for progress while indulging in selfrighteousness and self-congratulation, an endearing tendency Canadians seem to have when nurturing their national self-image as humanitarian, pro-human rights, and internationalist.

[3] On this important occasion — the 25th Anniversary of the *Canadian Charter of Rights and Freedoms*[1] — this article will situate the Canadian human rights evolution in an international context. There, it should be noted that in 2008 we celebrate the 60th anniversary of the *Universal Declaration of Human Rights*,[2] a fundamental document which marked the international community's commitment to a new relationship between the state and the individual. The *Universal Declaration* sparked the steady and accelerating development of the field relating to persons as new subjects of international law.

[4] We will reflect on the influence that the "rights revolution"[3] at the international level continues to have on the *Charter*. In an era of globalization, how has the *Charter* contributed to the integration of universal values in Canada? How has the *Charter* accompanied the changing self-identification process of an internationalized Canada, strongly influenced socially, economically, and politically by its position in the global arena and increasingly identifying itself as a people of peoples, a people whose unity is built on recognizing the distinct identity not only of its founding peoples, but also of its first peoples and of its new members of various origins? We propose to look first at the context of the *Charter*'s adoption and the characteristics that make it an agent of positive social change. Second, we will discuss three areas where interaction between international legal values and our domestic human rights system can be rendered more effective. We will conclude by discussing briefly two key challenges for ensuring meaningful rights protection in Canada.

II. THE *CHARTER*: A DOMESTIC INSTRUMENT WITH AN INTERNATIONAL PURPOSE AND STATURE

A. 1982: Impetus for an Entrenched *Charter* of Rights: The Rise of Rights and the Rise of Law

[5] The *Charter* is situated in a post-war momentum at the international level that saw a proliferation of national and international rights-protection instruments, starting with the *Universal Declaration*. In powerful and somewhat symbolic language, the *Universal Declaration* expresses its repulsion at the excesses and barbarity of war, genocide, and fascism. Meanwhile, national contexts saw the emergence of new democracies, which functioned with a new understanding of the relationship between the state and the individual, and which were characterized by the establishment of structures for effective rights protection.[4]

[6] Through legislation such as the *Canadian Bill of Rights*[5] and provincial human rights codes, Canada was part of the post-Second World War move for rights development even before the enactment of the *Charter*; however, the evolution of human rights law had become stagnant. In many areas, notably in the field of equality rights, we were at a standstill. The establishment of the *Charter* marked a significant move from parliamentary to constitutional democracy and a desire to prevent, by empowering disadvantaged and minority groups, a possible rupture of the country's fabric and unity — a threat which, two years after Quebec's first referendum on sovereignty-association in 1980, deeply influenced the political climate in Canada. While the text is distinctive in ways that characterize Canada's particular historical and political features, the drafting of the *Charter* was heavily influenced by international rights-protection instruments. One of its primary purposes was to bring Canada into compliance with international law.[6]

[7] The connection between domestic efforts worldwide to move to new rights-based democracies and similar developments at the supranational level sparked the will and the need to draw on international human rights instruments, as well as to undertake comparative research in other jurisdictions. Canada drew from others' experiences, as others drew from ours. This trend illustrates the progressively more porous boundaries between domestic constitutional law, foreign law, and international human rights law, as well as the globalization of human rights and of jurisprudence. In a world where countries are increasingly linked by commonly agreed standards, the "rights practice and interpretation in one country rapidly spread to another," as Michael Ignatieff has put it.[7] Canada has become an exporter of its homemade human rights system and solutions, and a growing importer of international and foreign human rights experiences and standards. As Ignatieff rightly points out, "the world is interested in us because we have the world's problems — how to make a multi-cultural, multi-ethnic, multi-national,

multi-lingual state cohere in an age of rights."[8] For the same reasons, we should therefore be interested in the world.

[8] The adoption of the *Charter* also took place in a period of sharp increase in the use of legislation to effect social changes.[9] Notably coinciding with the development of human rights law at the international level, post-Second World War legislation focused on the needs of groups previously not protected or outrightly disadvantaged by law, and was designed to "promote social change on behalf of the 'have-nots.'"[10] Many parallel developments in Canada affirmed the positive role of the law in the accomplishment of social change. In the 1970s, the establishment of law reform commissions in Canada showed the importance of the process of reform through the legal system and the possibility of using the law to affect positively the lives of ordinary citizens. Arguably, the pre-*Charter* law-based initiatives aimed at social change — such as the law reform commissions — as well as the development of federal and provincial human rights legislation and specialized agencies and tribunals — including the *Canadian Bill of Rights* and its disappointing performance — contributed significantly to a political climate open to an entrenched rights document and, later, to a judicial climate receptive to generous interpretations of the *Charter* guarantees.[11]

[9] The *Charter* is thus Canada's response to various trends that developed worldwide after the Second World War. Fundamentally, it is an internationally oriented document that found its own ways to respond to the country's specificities. Let us now see how (or whether) the *Charter* has been a catalyst for positive social change in the country and which of its features allowed it to play that role.

B. The *Charter* as a Catalyst for Positive Social Change in Canada: The Rise of Democracy and of Judicial Review

[10] If the patriation of the *Constitution*[12] represented for some an expression of self-determination by the country, the *Charter* represented a broader agreement as a statement of the fundamental values that the country would endeavour to defend.[13] These include the right to participate in the democratic process, freedom of expression, freedom of religion, liberty, equality, linguistic rights, Aboriginal rights, and more. In the twenty-five years since its adoption, we have seen a growing resolve from citizens and civil society organizations to meet the challenge of

building a more just, more democratic, and more humane country, and world, according to the principles of the *Charter*. The *Charter* represented a local translation of internationally recognized minimal common denominators. It permitted rights-holders to assert ownership of these rights and it allowed those tasked to protect or interpret these rights to consider them as our homemade response to discrimination, unfairness, or abuse.

[11] The *Charter* has clearly been a catalyst for positive social change in Canada, in line with similar developments at the international level triggered by the post-war rights revolution. At the same time, some features of the *Charter* mark a distinctively Canadian approach, and have contributed greatly to the social change it has stimulated in the last twenty-five years. Indeed, although the normative content is very much in line with international standards — with some notable exceptions such as the absence of property rights — the implementation structure of the *Charter* is truly imaginative, and has contributed greatly to its early and lasting impact.

[12] Strikingly, the *Charter* begins by articulating the framework for the outer limits of the exercise of rights. Section 1 was the result of difficult compromises that led to a political agreement on a constitutionally entrenched rights document. The early jurisprudential development of the section 1 limitations framework proved critical in the evolution of the broader rights jurisprudence. Hesitance and false starts at that stage could have paralyzed the generous expression of substantive rights. Moreover, section 33, also the result of compromise, was a sort of political trump card negotiated in as a safety net. Though it has proven to be a more theoretical than real impediment to rights protection, it has preserved a notional preference for the tyranny of the majority over the potential tyranny of the judiciary.

[13] The three-year moratorium on equality rights also proved farsighted. It allowed judges to flex their intellectual muscles and express a newfound boldness in the familiar terrain of criminal procedure and fair trial standards, a field in which they had always been somewhat willing to stand up to parliaments for the protection of the vulnerable. Those early but easier decisions enabled them to tackle the more challenging section 15 issues that involved the kind of social engineering that judges were traditionally hesitant to embark upon. On the strength of this work on legal rights and section 1, truly progressive development of human rights law became possible. It is far from certain that we would be where we are today if the first

Charter challenges had called on courts to expand the enumerated list in section 15 or had impeached formal equality. The notable contributions of the Court Challenges Program, as well as those of the Women's Legal Education and Action Fund (LEAF) and others, led the way for the evolution of the *Charter* as a solid instrument of social progress in Canada.

[14] Apart from these features of the *Charter*'s structure and the particularities of its early implementation, we can safely say that the driving force of the development of human rights law in Canada has been judicial review. Many early landmark cases became solid pillars for meaningful judicial development of substantive human rights. In that regard, none was probably more significant, then and now, than the *B.C. Motor Vehicle Reference*,[14] for moving the courts from procedural to substantive rights. But we should not disregard process altogether. In fact, the criminal procedure and evidence litigation, like judicial review on federalism grounds, was a common feature of our pre-*Charter* legal system, and a proxy for a true "rights" debate.[15]

[15] The *Charter* has expanded the field and depth of judicial intervention, thereby opening the door to an appearance of activism or increased politicization. In reality, however, the *Charter* has not fundamentally altered the methods used for judicial review. The constitutional power of the courts, criticized by some as undemocratic, represents in our view a fundamentally democratic choice: that of articulating the constraints under which the majority can impose its will and the limits to its potential override of protected interests. Judicial review is therefore a democratic choice to be governed by the rule of law.[16] That choice effectively provides a megaphone to the voices of those who may not or cannot be heard in the other democratic institutions. Lacking a broad political base and faced with a lack of good faith or will by governments to negotiate on sensitive issues, many groups have chosen the courts as a forum of choice for the advancement of their rights. The land claims of indigenous peoples and the quest for equality for sexual minorities are good examples.

[16] Our understanding of democracy has evolved, again in line with similar developments at the international level since the Second World War.[17] The constitutionalization of rights has accompanied this evolving conception of democracy, and so has the legitimate demand on courts to check, against the fundamental rights on which we founded our democracy, the inevitable inclinations of the majority to

exclude the unpopular or the uninvited. Of course, the judiciary's influence on the development of the law has not taken place in isolation. The particularities of the *Charter*, notably its limitation and override clauses, call for the active role of the other branches of the government and allow for the aptly named "dialogue" between the judges and the legislatures.[18] The *Charter* has also contributed to the development of a rights consciousness at the administrative level; while some see this as a layer of protection for legislation to comply with *Charter* rights,[19] others claim that it legalizes politics and grants unprecedented powers to lawyers within the governance structure.[20]

[17] This article does not discuss the interaction between the various branches of government for effective rights protection in Canada. Rather, it will contrast the advances made possible by the adjudicative power of our courts with the non-adjudicative international framework. A mere quarter century has assured the irreversible impact of human rights in Canada; similar progress in the non-coercive international setting has taken some sixty years.

[18] The structure established by the *Charter* highlights the essential nature of judicial review as a feature of effective rights protection, a feature that is missing in many countries that work under the same substantive standards, but with less successful implementation. The same is true of the international arena. Indeed, the development of international human rights law is somewhat limited by the absence of binding jurisprudence. The reporting system to the treaty bodies[21] has proved to be a useful mechanism for the improvement of states' compliance with international standards. If nothing else, this mechanism stimulates discussion and requires states to justify their human rights performance or lack thereof. Decisions on individual complaints have also proved valuable and have allowed for increased dialogue between states and the international bodies, though the individual complaints mechanism remains underutilized.[22] However, it is clear that the binding nature of decisions by domestic courts, or by regional human rights courts such as the European Court of Human Rights[23] and the InterAmerican Court of Human Rights,[24] allows for a more sustained and rigorous development of the law.[25]

[19] That said, the dialogue provoked by the reporting process at the international level is very useful. In addition to a government's own report, the treaty bodies may receive information on that country's human rights situation from other sources, includ-

ing non-governmental organizations (NGOs), United Nations agencies, other intergovernmental organizations, academic institutions, and the press. Even accounting for generous intervention access, this inclusive process is very different from the judicial model, where the court must decide specific issues relating generally to the situation of only one group or individual, despite the broader impact of the resulting judgement. The international process, with its more consensual and consultative nature, may have contributed to the development of certain rights at the international level that have suffered from a lack of judicial recognition in domestic courts. Economic, social, and cultural rights, for example, are significantly more advanced at the international level than in Canada.[26]

[20] The *Charter* and the considerable impact of judicial review on the development of human rights law may have obscured the relevance and usefulness of parallel processes of consultation and dialogue on human rights issues, like the ones that the Law Reform Commission of Canada (LRCC) had successfully conducted in the past. In this regard, it is noteworthy that much of the LRCC's reform agenda became law, not through Parliament, but through the courts. Though some issues advanced via the *Charter*, many rights-related issues would have arisen in the courts regardless. Developments in the law of evidence were strongly influenced by the LRCC, including common law developments on the inadmissibility of illegally obtained evidence, which was evolving rapidly before section 24(2) of the *Charter* provided a constitutional remedy.

[21] Though the *Charter* has raised rights consciousness, Canada still lacks an entity tasked to evaluate human rights compliance. The federal human rights commission has a limited mandate, and Senate and Parliament standing committees, as well as administrative sensitivity, can only fulfill part of this task. Commissions of inquiry exist somewhere between courts and other oversight mechanisms, and have played a crucial role on many important human rights issues, but they remain ad hoc initiatives. Countries such as Australia, New Zealand, and the United Kingdom — where courts cannot invalidate legislation for violation of human rights — usually, perhaps consequentially, have effective mechanisms to ensure that bills conform to rights guarantees.[27] However, there is no reason not to have strong judicial oversight and strong institutional mechanisms to ensure legislative compliance. Improving those mechanisms would bring Canada to a privileged position for the advancement of human rights.

III. IMPLEMENTATION OF UNIVERSAL VALUES AND INVOLVEMENT IN REGIONAL AND INTERNATIONAL PROTECTION SYSTEMS

[22] Of course, Canada is not isolated from the phenomenon of globalization, and this cannot but impact on how we take into account and integrate international norms in our response to domestic challenges. More than a decade ago, Justice La Forest put it aptly in stating that human rights principles "are applied consistently, with an international vision and on the basis of international experience. Thus our courts — and many other national courts — are truly becoming international courts in many areas involving the rule of law."[28] Courts are increasingly opening themselves to the persuasion of international law in shaping Canadian domestic law. Professor William Schabas has noted that the *Charter* forced courts to open up to international law and, in doing so, to set an example for other constitutional courts. In 2000, he predicted: "A quarter century from now, we may speak of this as the dawn of judicial globalization."[29] It is unquestionable that the judicial globalization process is well in motion, and from a Canadian perspective it was sparked by a quarter century of *Charter* jurisprudence.[30]

[23] This reality is not restricted to Canadian courts, but has impregnated various layers of society. For instance, Parliamentary and Senate Committees discuss international human rights law and apply it to issues before them. Canadian NGOs dedicate significant time and resources to influence international human rights law, as well as domestic law, with the help of the international standards, both in Canada and in multilateral forums. Individuals also frequently use international remedies available to them, the most popular being the use of "communications" to the UN Human Rights Committee, but also to the UN Committee Against Torture and, though underutilized, to the Inter-American Commission on Human Rights for breaches of the *American Declaration of the Rights and Duties of Man*.[31]

[24] This dynamism and internationalism is beneficial both for Canada, which receives the by-products of the creativity it engenders, as well as for the community of states, which profits from Canada's vibrant experience of rights protection in a diverse environment. This demonstrates that true universality can accommodate domestic specificities and the uniqueness of each different system and culture.

[25] This irreversible internationalization process influences and guides the way human rights evolve in Canada. Let us briefly touch upon three different areas where this is particularly the case: a) the use of international law in defining the content and possible limitations of *Charter* rights; b) the increased necessity for a better implementation of international human rights obligations and interaction with international bodies; and c) the appropriateness of Canada's full integration to the Americas' human rights system.

. . . .

IV. LIVING UP TO THE PROMISE OF THE "LIVING TREE" METAPHOR: SOME CRITICAL CHALLENGES AHEAD FOR RIGHTS PROTECTION IN CANADA

Legal historians tend to concentrate on change and innovation. They wish to explain why an innovation occurred when it did. But to understand law and society one must also explain why a legal change did not occur when society changed, or when perceptions about the quality of the law changed.[82]

[47] Alan Watson's comments highlight the complexity of the relationship between law and social change. While we are quick to explain how the *Charter* has made our society evolve (we think readily of progressive changes with respect to the rights of same-sex partners, or of linguistic minorities, or in checking the abuse of police powers, for instance), we are hesitant to identify how and why the *Charter* has failed to prompt social change where it arguably should have. We can celebrate the social achievements of the *Charter* and still acknowledge that it has not yet brought Canada where it committed itself to be, in critical areas such as the protection of economic and social rights and access to justice for all. The protection of other human rights is far from fully secured, and these are but two of the numerous challenges ahead. We should not be complacent about the rights of vulnerable groups or decrease our efforts to ensure their effective protection and promotion, particularly as concerning the rights of women, of Aboriginal peoples, and of visible minorities. Any step backwards in the protection of these rights, and others, would be a blow to the credibility of the *Charter*.

[48] Let us further note that the *Charter* cannot be the sole legal tool for social change. Legislative

action in many fields is essential to attain various societal goals and achieve social justice. However, it is our view that the *Charter* is equipped to protect broader interests and values than the purely "negative" rights designed to protect individuals from state interference. The current individual-rights focus given to the *Charter* has limited communal or collective gains. The *Charter* is, and must be able, to offer effective tools for redressing social injustice.

A. Poverty, and Economic, Social, and Cultural Rights Generally

[49] As was emphasised with particular vigour on International Human Rights Day in December 2006,[83] dedicated to the fight against poverty, poverty is frequently both a cause and a consequence of human rights violations. All human rights — freedom of speech and the right to vote, but also to food, work, housing, and health — are jeopardized for the poor, because destitution and exclusion are intertwined with discrimination and unequal access to resources and opportunities. However, poverty is often perceived as a regrettable but accidental condition, or as an inevitable consequence of decisions and events occurring elsewhere, or even as the sole responsibility of those who suffer it. Various factors compound these misconceptions, including the fact that governments often see claims by the poor as stemming more from necessity alone than from enforceable legal entitlements. In addition, there is an overemphasis on civil and political rights, notably in western countries, to the detriment of economic, cultural, and social rights, which the west perceives as "second tier" rights. These "second tier" entitlements are seen as mere privileges, which can be claimed only after fundamental freedoms and civil and political rights have been established and secured, and when countries are strong enough, economically, to address these issues. We agree with Professor Lucie Lamarche that the effects of globalization on vulnerable groups in industrialized economies can be countered by reclaiming international economic rights as human rights in local struggles linked to the deleterious effects of globalization.[84]

[50] In Canada, social and economic rights have failed to be appropriately recognized as rights, and continue, in our view, to be inadequately protected. This accounts for poverty and inequities that are incompatible with the level of social justice that is within our reach. We do not intend here to argue the entire case for economic and social rights to be fully protected as rights in Canada. The High Com-

missioner has discussed this failure,[85] and frequently stated, at the international level, that human rights are indivisible, and that the western countries' historical hesitation to provide equal protection to economic and social rights is unjustified.[86] International monitoring bodies have often criticized Canada on its economic and social rights record,[87] and have noted, among other things, that, sadly, "poverty rates remain very high among disadvantaged and marginalized individuals and groups such as Aboriginal peoples, African Canadians, immigrants, persons with disabilities, youth, low-income women and single mothers."[88]

[51] As Ignatieff correctly points out, it is a major limitation of the rights discourse in Canada — as in other western countries — that it has focused on justice for ethnic, linguistic, and cultural minorities, and for women and persons with disabilities, without sufficient concern for the economic and social inequality resulting from capitalism. Indeed, Ignatieff suggests that the prevailing rights discourse diverts political attention from these inequalities.[89]

[52] While the current rights discourse in Canada does not adequately recognize social, economic, and cultural rights, a lack of capacity is not the problem. Rather, this reflects a choice, one that should be reversed. In fact, if courts and parliaments have been hesitant to recognize economic and social rights, it is not for a lack of discussion on these issues or a shortage of such claims being brought forward.[90] The "rights talk" in Canada is slowly but steadily putting economic and social rights at the forefront and advocating to have them recognized both by parliaments and by courts.

[53] Economic and social rights are arguably better protected elsewhere than in the *Charter* — for instance in provincial human rights legislation. The *Quebec Charter of Rights and Freedoms*[91] guarantees a whole range of economic, social, and cultural rights and prohibits discrimination based on social condition; the New Brunswick Human Rights Act[92] also prohibits discrimination based on social condition.[93] However, in addition to the Supreme Court's narrow view of the *Charter* protections of equality, life, and security, *Gosselin v. Quebec*[94] showed the limitations of internationally-protected rights that are not given the constitutional (or quasi-constitutional) status that allows courts to strike down laws that conflict with them. Chief Justice McLachlin, speaking for the majority, had this to say on the inherent value of these rights in the *Quebec Charter*:

These may be symbolic, in that they cannot ground the invalidation of other laws or an action in damages. But there is a remedy for breaches of the social and economic rights set out in Chapter IV of the *Quebec Charter*: where these rights are violated, a court of competent jurisdiction can declare that this is so.[95]

[54] Justice Bastarache (dissenting), with whom Justice Arbour (as she then was) agreed on this issue, said:

[E]ven though the section does not provide for financial redress from the government in this case, the section is not without value. Indeed it is not uncommon for governments to outline non-judiciable rights in human rights Charters. Courts are not the only institutions mandated to enforce constitutional documents. Legislatures also have a duty to uphold them. If, in this case, the court cannot force the government to change the law by virtue of s. 45, the *Quebec Charter* still has moral and political force.[96]

In separate dissenting reasons, Justice Arbour added:

The right that is provided for in s. 45, while not enforceable here, stands nevertheless as a strong political and moral benchmark in Quebec society and a reminder of the most fundamental requirements of that province's social compact. In that sense, its symbolic and political force cannot be underestimated.[97]

[55] While all of this is indeed correct legally, it highlights that the "symbolic," "moral," and "political" force of rights that are not truly enforceable does not give, in many instances, concrete remedies to the aggrieved right-holder. This shows the potential of judicial review as a driving force for the evolution of law in a democratic rights-based society. The Commission des droits de la personne et des droits de la jeunesse du Québec[98] and others have strongly argued, notably on the occasion of the 25th anniversary of the *Quebec Charter*, for a revision that would raise economic and social rights to the same level of protection as that afforded to other rights. This initiative should be supported.

[56] For several years now, many have argued that "social condition" should be added to the prohibited grounds of discrimination in the federal *Canadian Human Rights Act*.[99] Such a change was recommended, inter alia, by the *Canadian Human Rights Act* Review Panel in its June 2000 report,[100] as well as by the CESCR, notably in its December 1998 concluding observations on Canada's Third Report under the *ICESCR*.[101] Poverty has long been recog-

nized as a contributing factor in the discrimination suffered by disadvantaged social groups. Regardless of such an addition in the federal legislation, it is striking that the courts have been somewhat daring in recognizing nonenumerated "analogous" grounds under section 15 of the Charter on certain issues, such as sexual orientation, but timid and even cold-footed on others, such as poverty or social condition. In our view, this reflects an unjustified belief that social and economic rights are values dependent on the market or on governmental policy, not legal rights worthy of constitutional protection.

[57] Whichever avenue Canada takes to ensure full protection of economic and social rights, whether through a constitutional amendment, a more progressive interpretation of the current *Charter* text, a modification of other (federal and provincial) human rights instruments, or otherwise, this is the next step which must be taken if Canada wants to ensure that the most disadvantaged members of society will truly benefit from the immense promise of the *Charter*. As one author put it five years ago, on the 20th anniversary of the *Charter* — and we believe it more acutely now — social and economic rights are the "next frontier" of *Charter* rights protection.[102]

[58] It is high time to guarantee claimants access to the courts to articulate the full scope of these rights and secure their enforcement, in the same way that the contours of the civil and political rights took shape in the early years of the *Charter*. Rights are not just about protection against abusive or unjustified interference by the state. The role of the state has evolved and it has become central for human dignity and security to be fulfilled through a system of public policy and legislation aimed at protecting the individual and his or her family from want and need. This is indeed what is suggested by the *Universal Declaration*: a state both respectful of individual freedoms and responsible through positive action for the preservation of human dignity and legitimate expectations of social justice. The duality of roles for the state that is mandated by international human rights law needs to be integrated into our understanding of the *Charter*.

[59] Many modern constitutions have strived to attain that balance. The South African Constitution is one of the most progressive and modern constitutions in the world, with one of the most comprehensive bills of rights. It contains rights of access to housing, health care, social assistance, and education.[103] Some of these social and economic rights are qualified in that they require the state to take rea-

sonable steps, according to its available resources, to realize the rights progressively. Even so, the Constitutional Court has handed down some groundbreaking decisions in which, for instance, it declared the government's housing policy invalid,[104] and found that the state was not fulfilling its constitutional duty to provide access to health care because it had failed to take adequate steps to prevent the mother to child transmission of HIV.[105] Other high courts in many other countries, including India and Argentina, have taken progressive stances on economic and social rights.

[60] Meanwhile, it is incongruous for Canada to afford constitutional protection to some rights and allow others to be claimed only as reasonable limits to the exercise of other rights. Section 1 is indeed often said to set out collective values, including social justice, against which individual rights are to be balanced. Courts in Canada have looked at international human rights instruments for indications as to the criteria that may be invoked in section 1 analyses,[106] including the rights contained in the *ICESCR*.[107] Nevertheless, to selectively recognize and ensure the protection of some rights while not affording the same protection to others is at odds with the principles of international human rights law that embrace all human rights, be they civil, social, economic, cultural, or political in nature. There is no valid reason to claim that economic and social rights can be adequately addressed by deference to government's policy concerning social justice at the justification stage, rather than to recognize these rights as justiciable.

[61] At the international level, there is encouraging movement towards the adoption of a protocol to permit individual petitions alleging violations of the *ICESCR*,[108] which could have great, and positive, domestic impact in Canada. If and when ratified by Canada, this new instrument would provide Canadians with a forum of choice to claim their internationally-protected economic, social, and cultural rights, a particularly valuable remedy considering the unavailability of any such domestic legal avenues.

B. Access to Justice

[62] As was noted above, perhaps the most enduring impact of the *Charter* on our society and legal system is how it has been at the vanguard of social change in the country, aided in that by the vigorous judicial review it has prompted.

[63] Individuals and groups have turned to the courts to remedy violations of their rights or to artic-

ulate those rights. This could not have happened unless those who had succeeded had access to the courts. Though the "rights revolution" would not have happened without rightsholders' access to justice, there is no constitutionally protected general right to access to justice. The Supreme Court recently held that there is no general right to be represented by a lawyer in court or tribunal proceedings where a person's legal rights and obligations are at stake.[109]

[64] The *Charter* may not have always translated to concrete and substantive improvements in the lives of the most disadvantaged. Yet, the *Charter* has created a culture of expectations, perhaps even of entitlements. Individuals and groups turn to the *Charter*, and thus to the courts, to challenge discriminatory practices and other violations of their rights. In that context, the Canadian Bar Association's position that "access to justice is the biggest challenge facing our justice system at this time" is particularly acute.[110] Chief Justice McLachlin has also highlighted on numerous occasions the importance of access to justice for all Canadians. To protect the integrity of our legal system, and of the constitution that supports it, it is essential that everyone in Canada have access to the courts.

[65] Cuts in financial support to legal aid services across the country prevent, in many cases, the exercise of rights protected by the *Charter*, and lead to situations where poor people, in particular poor single women, who are denied benefits and services to which they are entitled under law, cannot access the available remedies.[111] Furthermore, the cancellation of the Court Challenges Program,[112] a program that had proved a significant ally to equality in the country and been hailed as uniquely Canadian, was a hard blow for access to justice. Many had identified the program as central to the rights revolution that occurred in the country.

[66] Critics of the program and of the power of judicial review more generally are quick to condemn the "interest group litigation"[113] that the *Charter* might have prompted. There is some truth to the myth that rights-advancing litigation has evolved with the *Charter*.[114] However, we must remember that the very people some discount as merely selfindulgent "interest groups" are called "human rights defenders" at the international level, and benefit from international protection.[115] We should be very careful about dismissing those who strive to advance human rights causes through legally available means.

[67] With the winding up of the Court Challenges Program, the serious obstacles facing legal aid programs, and the high bar imposed on litigants for obtaining interim costs in *Charter* litigation,[116] it may be a good time for the legal profession to unite on the issue of access to justice. Given the economic deterrent inherent in the current litigation system and the lack of access to funding, it is essential to find ways to ensure that the *Charter* is still seen as, and made to be, accessible to all.

[68] It is through the ingenuity of litigants that the protection of human rights in Canada has progressed this far. There is no reason to disempower them in the face of the challenges that lie ahead, be it on environmental issues, minority protection, the reach of equality, or the ever-present security concerns.

V.   CONCLUSION

[69] Central to the position of the *Charter* in Canadian federalism is the idea, perhaps counterintuitive, that the greatest protection for individual rights and freedoms comes in large, pluralistic environments. Conversely, the greater danger comes from small, homogeneous communities that lack the imagination and the means to deal effectively with the competing individual claims from within, specially the claims that question the apparent homogeneity.

[70] This also speaks loudly in favour of strong regional and international human rights protection systems, as they serve to push back narrow national horizons to put in full view the claims and aspirations of the whole of the human race.

Critical Perspectives on the Role of Law As an Agent of Change

(a)   In Memoriam: The Law Commission of Canada, 1997– 2006†

Nathalie Des Rosiers

INTRODUCTION: WEAVING THEORY AND PRACTICE

In the first part of this article, I explained how the Law Commission of Canada (LCC) developed a law reform model that sought to respond more effectively to the gap between law and reality and to democratize the process of law reform itself. The Law Commission situated its work directly at the interstice between law and action and experimented with different ideas about democratizing its research agenda, its networks of partners and its output. The LCC decided to firmly engage with interdisciplinary and community-based scholarship in the definition of its plan of action (from legal categories to dynamic social facts), in its research process (from legal expertise to social sciences and humanities and to action-based research) and its product (from legislative responses to mechanisms of empowerment). In my view, the mandate of the Law Commission in 1997, clearly spelled out in its empowering statute, was to break away from tradition. I suggest that the mandate was to move beyond what I describe as an "endogenous" or introvert mode of law reform, law reform constructed from within the legal system. In this part, I will examine the effects of the choice to go beyond this endogenous model and the methodological and ethical challenges that it brought about.

I have organized this part around four themes: first, that a democratized law reform project requires a *process of "translation"* between different audiences; second, that it necessarily implies a painful exercise of *destabilization* of the intellectual status quo; third, that it must support the *empowerment* and capacity building of the different social actors to embrace and demand change and fourth, that it must do so with *care*. I illustrate each idea with testimonies and case studies derived from my souvenirs, mementos and notes from the work of the LCC. This part is written in a more narrative style because it relates the story of the LCC from my perspective.[1] It includes many excerpts from my notes taken throughout the time that I have spent at the Commission.

A TRANSLATION PROCESS

In order for a research idea to get implemented, the new concept must be understood. Its potential must be assessed, debated and criticized. Its benefits must be discussed to become evident or at least recognized. In short, the idea or concept must become part of the language of civil society, of decision-makers and problem-solvers and not just of researchers. It must be translated from an academic framework to a citizens' perspective.

Three types of translation issues arose from the work of the LCC: translation between disciplines, translation from an academic perspective to a policy

† (2007) 22:2 C.J.L.S. 145 at 162–74 (Part II). Reproduced with permission of Canadian Journal of Law and Society/Revue Canadienne Droit et Societe. www.utpjournals.com. [Notes and/or references omitted.]

one and translation to a public engagement format. I will not discuss here the enrichment that came from the plurilingual nature of the work done by the LCC except to note that all three intellectual translations mentioned require additional adaptation so that ideas reach French, English and Aboriginal speakers.[2] The process of finding the right word in French, in English or in Cree involves a creative process of constantly reframing and reformulating one's thoughts to achieve the real meaning. I cannot overemphasize how this discipline is helpful to achieve clarity in expression.

Translation Between Disciplines

The *Law Commission of Canada Act*[3] is clear that the LCC was to engage in multidisciplinary research. The difficulties of the translation processes involved in this endeavour are well documented: concepts mean different things in different disciplines, methodological reflexes are different, [assessments] of quality stem from different viewpoints, and there are differences in presentation styles, footnoting and organization of ideas. Like other multidisciplinary organisations, the LCC was stimulated by the role of bringing together researchers from different disciplines to approach a similar problem. The use of study panels provided the main mechanism to explore which disciplines (or subdisciplines) should be invited to participate. It also generated the recognition of the much needed expertise of "intellectual animators" who are able to rephrase other peoples' thoughts in ways that create linkages between participants. It was indeed one of the marginal benefits of the Commission to build the expertise and networks within Canadian academic circles to better interact among themselves and with governments and the public.

I am pretty excited about the *Close Personal Adult Relationships Project*.[4] It seems to me that this project is the quintessential law reform project: a challenge to a fundamental organisational concept of law. Why do we only think of conjugality when we think of personal relationships? What are the characteristics of the conjugal bond that [make] it so special for the legal enterprise? Why do we care so much? The regulation of "interdependence" is what seems to come up from the consultations. However, some married couples are not as interdependent as they used to be — other relationships (same-sex couples among them) claim interdependence but in a less hierarchical way. Maybe the key concept should be interdependence?[5]

Had an interesting conversation today regarding *Close Personal Adult Relationships Project*. I was explaining the project to MC, a biologist — pretty sceptical about the project. I agreed that the title should be changed. I explained to him that interdependent relationships were good for society because statistics show that people in relationships are healthier than people who are alone. He laughed: "You read the statistics all wrong — it is because healthy people have relationships and sick people don't — that is the proper reading of [your] statistics and it is a fact of nature."[6]

Every project of the Law Commission involved at least two disciplines. For example, in the *Beyond Conjugality — Recognizing and Supporting Close Personal Adult Relationships Project*,[7] the idea of supporting interdependency generally as opposed to supporting only interdependency within conjugal or sexually intimate relationships required the input of many disciplines: psychology (Why do people stay together?), sociology (How have family groupings changed?), law (what type of distinctions could be acceptable within an equality framework?), history (How were caring relationships supported in the past? How was the regulation of marriage related to the distinction between State and religion?). Many domains of law and different experts were asked to contribute: legal historians, tax experts, family law specialists, bankruptcy experts and unemployment insurance advocates. The Commission also required a civil law and a common law analysis: the study of whether the list of dependents under the *Marine Liability Act*[8] ought to be framed in general language (*en droit civil*) or in specific language (*à la common law*) provided a good case study of ways in which each system manages the risk of an ever expanding list of related victims.

The LCC had to integrate the wisdom of all disciplines, and academics had to be prepared to engage with their colleagues in debating ideas in order for the work to advance. At a minimum, the co-operation that occurred, the methodological challenges that were confronted within the *Beyond Conjugality* project and others, prepared the ground for further interdisciplinary projects that many participating scholars undertook outside the Commission.

Translation from Research to Policy-Makers

The process of "translation" from research to policy is not without difficulty. To move an idea or a concept from academic circles to policy spheres, the idea must acquire a resonance for policy makers. It must respond to the problems as they see them, or at least challenge their understanding of the problem. Therefore, the translation process requires an ability to speak and understand the implications of concepts from the decision-maker's perspective as well as from an academic perspective. It meant using data that is familiar to decision-makers or [to] challenge the data currently used. It often meant doing "more" research to adequately respond to the imperatives of policy-makers.

> Part time work is supplementary or transition type income — it is either a youth going to high school or college who earns money to buy video games or it is the wife (pardon me, the "second earner") who works so the couple can buy a large TV or other consumer goods. This is not a real issue at this point for government.[9]

The *Vulnerable Workers Project* had to challenge this perception of the irrelevance of part-time work by acquiring data on the meaning of part time work for many Canadians and on the changing demographics of the part timer workers: workers who cumulate part time work arrangements and do not have enough hours to make ends meet. It also had to challenge the very idea that because workers earn supplementary incomes or were in transition between stages of their lives, they could have fewer rights. The debate was to reframe the way in which some people saw the problem. This became a main aspect of many projects:

> It was interesting to meet with the people responsible for Old Age pensions. Their perspective was fascinating: the program is really challenged by the shorter length and increasing number of sequential marriages because they have to keep track of more ex-spouses. It was interesting to explore whether they could (and how much it would cost) [...] rethink the category of "spouse". It might very well be that the costs of administering the benefits will eventually exceed the amounts disbursed — this could be an opportunity for change and to abandon the concept of conjugality.[10]

Often, the very way in which "success" was measured prevented the consideration of new policies. Again to use the *Beyond conjugality* example, if social policy is defined by the number of married people in a society, policies designed to support other types of interdependent relationships are bound to encounter resistance or to be missed altogether. Defining new and more appropriate measures of success is often a critical part of new conceptualizations.

> Strange that we only started to gather data about same sex couples so recently — it makes it difficult to discuss the issue meaningfully.

> The idea of letting go of the word "spouse" is meeting with resistance: since statistics are collected on spouses, it is hard to imagine that other relationships exist: we are captured by the way in which we count — relationships that are counted are the relationships that matter.[11]

Translation from Research to Public Engagement

The *LCCA* mandates that the work of the Commission be accessible.[12] The efforts made by the Commission to respond to this aspect of this mandate are well known.[13] Certainly, the idea was to design consultation strategies adapted to the audience. But who is the audience for a specific project? A law reform agency must reflect on how its understanding of who will be affected and who will benefit from the reform is often stereotypical and ill informed. We approach research questions with certain predispositions — we may try to think broadly about the affected interests, but may miss the mark. We are, to a certain extent, dependent on the way in which data has been collected before. Our understanding of social problems is often framed by the statistical information which has been collected and by the way the questions were asked before. For example, in our *Participatory Justice Project*,[14] the success of restorative justice programs may have been assessed in the past on the basis of certain criteria: the rate of recidivism or the cost of the program per offender. One must ask who is missing in the picture: has data been collected on the basis of the impact of the program on the community, on witnesses, on victims?

> I am not sure about restorative justice. The only statistics I have seen are about recidivism and offenders' rehabilitation[.] Yes, there are surveys showing that victims are satisfied as well, but that it is immediately after the process — what happens five years after? Do they still feel that they got justice?[15]

The danger in reforming the law is to not know enough about how law is lived and to ask the wrong questions. A democratic framework for law reform must be particularly sensitive to the question of who is missing because the poor and the vulnerable are not the ones whose stories are well-known, whose voices are heard regularly or whose data is collected. They are often stereotyped and their views are often ignored and misunderstood. It is a danger to assume homogeneity within a group. Who is missing from the data? This is a serious issue in designing the consultation strategy.

> There are not really any groups representing relationships that are absent from the policy radar screen. This is interesting. Is it because it is not a problem? But we are receiving comments from individual Canadians who have been affected by the over emphasis on conjugality: told to get divorced to get out of a tax problem, or prevented from accessing benefits to protect their loved ones.
>
> I like the example of the woman moving in with a man who is immediately presumed to be "sharing" the wealth, but if she moves with a woman, it depends solely on the level of their intimacy. If she moves in with her mother, she is presumed not to receive a cent from her mother. Who is more likely to share? Is this an example that resonates? It is often difficult when people write to know whether it is true, generalized or a simple bureaucratic error.[16]

The design of relevant and engaging consultation strategies presents constant challenges to law reformers. The consultations acquire a particular meaning when the project develops and it is seen as "trouble". No longer is the question who should participate but how to engage citizens and groups who want to derail, change, influence or abort the law reform project because it disturbs their way of seeing the world.

DESTABILIZING A STATUS QUO

Research often leads to new conceptualizations of problems and hence encounters resistance from specialists whose knowledge and expertise is embedded in a certain conception of the world. In a sense, it is a painful process to accept that one's vision of the world and of good policy is erroneous or outdated. Changes in policy often require an acceptance of the failures of past policies or, at least, a recognition of their inability to continue to provide satisfactory outcomes. In this section I address three aspects of the inevitable struggle to destabilize the status quo: (a) the attempt to put an issue on the agenda, (b) the challenge to the use of words and concepts, and (c) the management of fears about change.

The Power over the Agenda

> I don't understand why the government does not respond to these reports: they were done in conjunction with the Commercial Strategy of Uniform Law Conference of Canada, they are

hardly controversial, they remove uncertainty, they build the infrastructure necessary for productivity, innovation in our economy. They are probably good for business! Why are they remaining on a shelf? What is the problem?[17]

Governments control the legislative agenda. Many law reform institutions complain of their inability to access the legislative agenda to enact measures to see their work materialize. It is one of the challenges of law reform that even uncontroversial subjects get delayed until there is a crisis or until a spokesperson insists that a politician makes it her agenda to move on the issue. Often, law reform, with the well known exception of criminal law, does not have sufficient public appeal to motivate political ownership of the issue, even if it is needed and constitutes an enabling aspect for a society based on the rule of law. The destabilization of a legislative [status quo] is part of the challenge of a law reform body.

However, even interest from the government does not guarantee that the formal legislative or political reform will take place: many governments may entertain the idea of reform to eventually shy away from it if it proves unpopular finally or too dangerous for their constituencies. The Report which followed the Ministerial reference in *Restoring Dignity* was well received by the government but its recommendations were not implemented promptly (some are still not implemented).

The electoral reform project was even more interesting in this respect. While governments, provincial and federal, were lamenting the democratic deficit, the lack of citizen's participation in elections, the lack of representation of women in electoral politics, their appetite for engaging fully in the reform was lukewarm. It may be too early to say whether electoral reform is a viable or a preferred option for Canadians and their political aspirations, but it is interesting to note the ambivalent treatment of the issue by political parties, although citizen groups continue to want real debates of these issues.

> We want to participate — it is time that we get better information. I like your kit for a "Tupperware" party on electoral reform. This is a complex subject but the debate is happening in every province. We really need easily accessible documentation. The time is ripe — it is a good thing that someone tackles this issue. Good work.[18]

The Control over Concepts

Ideas get implemented because enough people are convinced of their merits and because the impetus for change overcomes the resistance to it. Understanding the "resistance" is therefore fundamental to the process of implementation: why are people resisting the idea? Are decision-makers paralysed because of conflicting points of view? Are they unable to imagine the potential of an idea because of their institutional biases? Because of their inability to access proper data? Because they have invested too much in a definition of the problem and are unable to abandon older conceptual models? Our law is often organized and shaped by words and concepts that are used and even "owned" by certain groups. The very idea of changing the word or concept is often viewed as a threat.

> My sense is that there is resistance on the use of the word "policing" in the discussion paper[19] — it regroups more people than just police officers. There is a sense of loss for them. There is a lot of anxiety around the control over the word (as much as around the word marriage?).[20] The police unions are upset that the very mentioning of private security gives the private sector legitimacy and raises its profile. It seems that the construction of the identity of police officers is built on this special sense of responsibility for public order and the pursuit of the public interest — anything that speaks to others partaking in this enterprise is experienced as a loss to them.[21]

The law reform journey is marked by attempts to diminish such resistance. It may be about overcoming institutional biases, acquiring new data, critically examining current conceptual frameworks, and about dispelling myths.

> This project reveals many hidden aspects of our social organizations: there are so many invisible interactions between the private and public sectors in this area and the consequences are important: from the [teenagers] who are "banned for life" from shopping malls to the police officers who control entry to boxes at hockey games, from university security guards who effect a gate keeping function on complaints to the police to the white collar crimes mostly handled by private forensic accounting companies. We cannot shy away from looking at the issue.[22]

It is important to understand the reluctance of all actors. Many groups are interested in social change: political parties, NGOs, citizens groups, business groups. However, not every social actor can engage with the discussion at the same level. Often NGOs' abilities to engage in the discussion vary. Their power varies, their perception of the urgency of a problem varies and their strategy may be at odds with the very questions that the law reform body wants to explore. It often leads to rethinking

the way in which the discussion is framed. Witness one intervener on the *What is a Crime* Project:[23]

> You have it all wrong: it is not decriminalization that we need, it is criminalization of different crimes: crimes against the environment, crimes of greed, crimes of exploitation of workers. The problem is not what is a crime, but who is a criminal.[24]

For an idea to become translated into reality, efforts must be directed at understanding the blockages. Who is afraid of the idea and why?

Fears of Change

Fears must be addressed. It may require gathering new data which initially appeared irrelevant but is crucial to diminishing certain groups' reluctance. Many new ideas, from restorative justice to looking beyond conjugality, to use the Law Commission's examples, evoke powerful fears. Fears of disorder and fears of expenses are often at the root of this opposition. In *In Search of Security*, the unions were worried about undermining their ability to secure good working conditions for their members and the potential for a contracting out policy to create a category of underpaid people who would perform bad "policing". We had to address all the aspects of their fears.

In *Participatory justice*, fears about the inability of communities to honour their role in conflict resolution were often repeated. It was helpful that the debate could engage on the concrete difficulties that were envisaged so that safeguards could be designed or evaluations be directed more particularly to address the concerns.

> Why do you ask me to choose between restorative justice and the traditional system? This is not a choice for me. I worry that my community would not take sexual assault seriously and would ostracize the victims who complained, but taking the stand to testify to send another of our men [to] jail is not a solution either.[25]

Ultimately, however, the journey from research to policy is not only a question of understanding the language of decision-makers, the blockages emerging from institutional players, the fears of different social actors, it must be about engaging the public in the change.

BUILDING CAPACITY

The public lives with the consequences of the implementation of reforms. It is also the general public who elects, writes to and influences politicians. More importantly, reform often occurs at the margins by the recognition of unfairness and by an openness to new ways of thinking and new ways of acting. Whether [it is] smoking or recycling, real changes occur with a combination of incentives and powerful social messages. Most policy changes require the co-operation of different actors. Successful implementation demands change in attitudes in the general public as much as it requires convincing powerful decision-makers. I explore here two aspects of the objective to build capacity for change: first, the duty to create space for discussion and reflection and second, the necessity to build the capacity to know and to act.

Space to Discuss and Reflect

A law reform is an institutional space to engage in critical discussion about law within society. The ability with which it can build an architecture that is inviting to all and allows for fruitful discussions and consensus building is what makes it more or less successful. There must be room to exchange and to explore. The vehicles for this are many: conferences, workshops, listserv discussions, video conferencing.

At times, raising the issue or creating the space for the discussion to take place may be sufficient to spark action. Private actors (probably fearing increased governmental regulation) may almost immediately start to invest in better training, and may demand regulation to eliminate the "bad apples" among them and ensure fair competition. This was the case, for example, with the project *In Search of Security* dealing with the privatisation of security arrangements. Raising the profile of an issue is in itself a public service.

It is not enough to raise the profile — there must be capacity within the public to seize the moment and engage with the issue. It is in this context that there must be a commitment to building the capacity within different groups, even the less powerful, to engage and be heard.

Capacity to Know and Act

One of the participants described an equivalent to a star system (it was called the three roses) program for seniors' residences. The local group visits the different places and then publishes its assessment of the residential places: one rose, two roses or three. It is the Michelin Guide to seniors living. What do you think? We could wait for the government to strengthen the health

regulation but we are fed up and decided to do something. It would be nice to have help to do a good job on this evaluation program.[26]

There is no doubt that the multidisciplinary strategies developed by the LCC built capacity within academia to interact with each other in an interdisciplinary manner. The efforts to create occasions for English speaking and French speaking scholars to exchange is in itself a service to Canada where the academic institutions continue to often operate in silos. In addition, the support to networks of researchers and community groups was also a service. However, the most important aspect is to attempt to give voice and power to citizens who don't have them. In small ways, the process of participating in webcasts on the organisation of personal relationships, the walk in the shopping malls on *Does Age matter?*, the video conferencing of small businesses on *Leveraging Knowledge Assets*, the high school contests on *Global citizenship*, were all attempts at building the capacity of citizens to engage in law reform. The objective was not only to give voice but also to recognize that positive actions are possible and can have a triggering effect, as the three roses initiative demonstrates. Many ideas came from these exchanges — they certainly reflected the neo-liberal governance model of the day as it situated power for action not only at the government level but elsewhere, in communities and within the private sector. It is not that government was exempted from reacting but the project was to recognize that change and law reform had to occur at various sites and that many people had the power to make it happen.

ETHIC OF CARE

Traditional law reform responds to the strong ethical standards of government and of public service: competence, transparency, integrity, independence, political neutrality and strict obedience to its mandate. My suggestion here is that the translation, destabilization and empowerment mandate imposed additional ethical standards. First, a consultation ethics had to be developed with honesty, timeliness, and accessibility as its key features, as well as a concern for the absent voices.

I would argue that an "ethic of care"[27] model also had to be adopted: people who participate in consultations should be treated with respect and concern, a duty of explanation is owed to them as well as a duty to share the knowledge and the results. In a way, the extrovert law commission has an ongoing responsibility toward the subjects (and not the objects) of its research and toward their on-going needs.

Recognizing the Subject of the Research

Why don't you just put a bracelet around my wrist like they do for birds? You could encrypt all the information that researchers have collected over the years on our community and on me. And, I would not have to repeat it and could move on. Here you are again: you come, you interview, you "report" and nothing changes.[28]

The Governance of Health Research Involving Human Subjects was one of the first governance projects of the LCC — it made very helpful recommendations with respect to ethical reviews within the research industry. To me, it also suggested a fundamental shift in the way in which research had to be approached. Consultation, explanation and sharing of results were no longer optional in the conduct of the research enterprise; they became central to its development, to its meaning and legitimacy. It seems to me that it created an obligation to view the citizen, his or her action and potential as the central feature of the work. It meant a certain collapse of the distinction between research on one hand and consultations on the other. Research and engagement became interrelated as a process of creation and advancement [of] law reform.

Needs and Expectations

XX called today. He was wondering what was happening with the report on institutional [child] abuse.[29] He participated in the discussions. Did I remember him? He still cannot find any help: no lawyer and no therapist. There are very few in the Maritimes. Has the government responded? What are we going to do to make it respond? Can I put him in touch with a good lawyer? Other survivors? Anybody? Can I do anything for him — other than milk his story?[30]

Engaging Canadians in law reform creates expectations among them that their participation will not be futile. The development of relationships that occur between the institution and its partners, interlocutors or callers is an interdependent one: the LCC needed to maintain its access to a network of Canadians who were interested in law reform and in the process, became cognizant of their immediate needs. Since law reform rarely provides immediate answers, the only recourse was to continue the work,

maintain the public profile of the issue, and support the continuing network of actors. *Restoring Dignity*, which was the first report of the LCC, was a particularly good example of the type of tensions that can exist. The report was not the "final" report.[31] This was because [...] the needs expressed by the members of the Study panels and other participants required on-going attention. The Commission continued to develop projects to help in the implementation of the report. In particular, it funded an economic analysis of the costs of child abuse which aimed at detailing the "costs of doing nothing," and co-operated in the creation of a video for Aboriginal survivors. Nevertheless the needs of survivors throughout Canada had been exposed and help was slow in materializing. The Commission could not become an advocate and had to "protect" its future relationships with other subjects of research by remaining within its mandate and [pursuing] it with integrity. For commissioners, the very process of highlighting the report and maintaining its profile had been moderately helpful in keeping the public's attention on the needs of survivors. However, how many resources could or should be dedicated to the pursuit of a sequel?[32] Could the Commission adopt a more traditional position and maintain a more passive role? If it continued to support the project, how long should this support last? Ultimately, the ethics of supporting relationships with the subjects of research must be addressed. It continued to be an on-going struggle for me.

CONCLUSION

The Law [Commission] of Canada had a legislative mandate to innovate. It is beyond the scope of this paper, and certainly beyond my intentions, to speculate as to whether the innovation mandate was the cause of its demise or whether its closing stemmed from a particular political antipathy toward independent research bodies.[33] Nevertheless, *In Memoriam* was an attempt to present an assessment of the experiment in transforming law reform. My purpose, in Part I, was to examine some key strategies of the LCC: the reframing of its research agenda beyond legal categories, its commitment to multidisciplinary and citizen led research participation and its decision to frame recommendations beyond governmental actors. In Part II, I have discussed several consequences of the new models: the necessary investment in "translation" between audiences (translation between disciplines, from academic research to policy frameworks and to [citizens'] engagement), the inevitable pain of destabilizing an intellectual status quo, the duty to imagine the process as capacity building for the citizenry and finally the ethical implications of engaging citizens in a process of change that one cannot control.

The way in which law reform should occur, whether there are institutions that should be charged

with stimulating reflection on this score or not, [and] the challenges of the enterprise warrant continuing discussions in Canada. It could be that other forms of institutional law reform will emerge from the memory of the Law Commission of Canada. Only time will tell. *À la prochaine.*

(b) The Role of Law in Social Transformation: Is a Jurisprudence of Insurgency Possible?†

Stephen Brickey and Elizabeth Comack

Contemporary Marxist theorizing on law has produced a number of different ways of conceptualizing the class character of law within a capitalist society. The main focus of these approaches has largely been on the role of law in maintaining and reproducing an unequal, exploitative system. As a consequence, the issue, even the possibility of using law as a mechanism for securing substantial social change has been downplayed and, in some cases, precluded.

The purpose of this paper is to argue for a rethinking of law, especially in terms of its potential as an agent for social transformation. The discussion will be divided into two main sections. The first involves theoretical considerations. Problems encountered with existing approaches to law *vis-à-vis* their implications for change will be examined and the direction in which a theoretical reformulation might proceed will be outlined. The second involves practical considerations. Here the focus will be on the kinds of legal strategies and particular forms and conditions of law that could be extended or developed in order to move in the direction of a socialist society.

.   .   .   .

Toward a Theoretical Reformulation

It is not our intention to deny the insights to be gained from current Marxist theorizing on law. Much has been accomplished, for example, in the way of clarifying the class character of law under

capitalism. Nor is it our intention to deny the significance of law as a mechanism of class domination. In this regard, we would agree with writers like Picciotto that the rule of law — to the extent that it has bourgeois limitations and characteristics — must and should be transcended. The question remains, however, as to *how* that is to be accomplished. Neither instrumentalism nor structuralism offers much hope for law as a mechanism for social transformation. Even those writers who are sensitive to the changing forms of state and law under advanced capitalism offer little guidance in the way of concrete strategies or proposals for bringing about substantive change.[20] As a result, we are left with the uneasy feeling that social transformation must await the 'revolution,' but are given no real indication as to how that will be possible.

In contrast, we would argue that law offers an important (although by no means the sole) source for realizing substantive social change. Implicit in this position is a particular conception of law. As opposed to instrumentalism, we take law to have a distinctly social character; that is, more than just a 'tool' or an external set of rules imposed on individuals, law emerges out of distinct social and historical conditions. In contrast to the structuralist tendency toward 'overdetermination,' we would suggest that emphasis be placed on the role of social actors in the constitution and reproduction of legal order. Following this, the legal sphere can be viewed as an arena of struggle which engages individuals of different classes and political positions.

† (1987) 2 C.J.L.S. 97 at 97, 102–14. Reproduced with permission of Canadian Journal of Law and Society/Revue Canadienne Droit et Societe. www.utpjournals.com. [Notes and/or references omitted.]

We would also argue that there are some very good reasons for not abandoning the law. First, if we turn our backs on law, then, as Young suggests, we are left in a position whereby we are denied *any* of the protections afforded by the law — however limited they may be.[21]

Second, although several writers have objected to the discourse of rights as an inappropriate form for generating liberating practices,[22] the fact remains that the very terms of political argument and debate in advanced capitalist societies are unavoidably legalistic. As Hunt remarks:

> All political issues involve, usually quite directly, appeals to rights; whether it be the 'right to work' or 'the right to a fair profit,' 'a woman's right to choose' or 'the right to life,' politics and political demands invoke appeals to rights, or to the analogous language of 'freedom.' So persistent is this appeal to rights that it makes little or no sense to dismiss this reality as some on the left seek to do, by arguing that "rights" are merely ideological masks disguising naked interests.[23]

In this respect, despite its 'bourgeois character,' rights discourse at the very least offers the potential of facilitating the mobilization of political action among subordinate groups.

Third, the tendency for those on the left to deny the possibility of 'legal justice' has left the door wide open for other interpretations. As a result, the right has been given relatively free [rein] in defining the terms and parameters of 'law and order' issues. The increasing prominence of right wing law and order campaigns, coupled with the emergence of the new law and order state,[24] with its reduction of welfare services and legal encroachments on civil liberties and legal rights, only showcases the need to mount a defense and extension of existing rights and liberties.[25] Indeed, if (as the structuralists suggest) 'crime control' and related issues are an important source of legitimation for the status quo, then there is all the more reason to formulate a Marxist dialectical position which justifies the defense of legal rights and civil liberties.

Finally, to view the law as irrelevant in the attempt to secure social transformation denies the significance of the rights struggles of women, Natives, youth, prisoners and other subordinated segments of society. It promotes a narrow conception of class struggle in that, as Sumner notes, it excises the class character of these conflicts and reduces the struggle of the working class to the economic claims of an urban, white, male labour aristocracy.[26] In effect, it amounts to the 'colonization' of subordinate fractions of the working class by a dominant fraction. Not to give significance to these types of rights struggles also suggests that social transformation may result in a classless society, but it would still be sexist, racist and ageist.[27]

The question remains, then, as [in] what direction theoretical reformulation should proceed in order to fashion an approach which incorporates, rather than abandons, law as a potential agent for social transformation?

If the law is too narrowly conceived as simply a mechanism of class rule, then it can be easily dismissed as a 'fraud'; as an empty set of guarantees of equity and fairness that have somehow been sold to an unwitting public. Such a narrow conception of law misses some important considerations, not the least of which is that justice *is* often seen to be done. In order to maintain the appearance of equity and fairness, the law must live up to its own claims. As Thompson notes:

> If the law is evidently partial and unjust, then it will mask nothing, legitimate nothing, contribute nothing to any class's hegemony. The essential precondition for the effectiveness of law, in its function as ideology, is that it shall display an independence from gross manipulation and shall seem to be just. It cannot seem to be so without upholding its own logic and criteria of equity; indeed, on occasion, by actually *being* just.[28]

Mandel offers further clarification in the distinction he makes between two opposing senses of the rule of law. The first, which he labels 'democratic,' is essentially the one invoked by Thompson. It "stresses the inhibitions placed on official power ... by clear rules strictly adhered to ... [rules which] contribute in content to real equality and freedom."[29] The second, which Mandel labels the "juridical," is best described by Pashukanis's analysis of the legal form under capitalism.[30] It "stresses those characteristic features which work to strengthen the *status quo* of unequal social power...."[31] One of the main insights to be gained from this distinction is that there is an inherent *tension* built into the law. This tension is further reflected in the fact that law is *both* a means of coercive and ideological domination; of force *and* consent. As an ideological form, the law acts as a legitimizer of capitalist social relations — it presents those relations in a certain light. Yet, at one and the same time, it too must be legitimized. The law requires an ideological base without which it is simply 'naked power.'[32]

In order to win the consent of the dominated classes to the capitalist order — in order to mediate class relations — the law has to take into account interests other than those of the dominant class. In this sense, "law is not simply imposed upon people, but is also a *product* and *object of* and provides an arena which circumscribes class (and other types of) struggle."[33] Indeed, the rights enshrined in law (universal suffrage, right to form a union, right to strike and so on) were not simply handed down by a benevolent state, but were the outcome of progressive struggles by the subordinate classes.

Thus, as Thompson and others have shown, if the law is to be a legitimizer of capitalist social relations, then the rhetoric and rules of law must be more than 'sham.' Law must provide some protection against the arbitrary use of state power. It must live up to its own claims of equity and fairness. While one need not go so far as to suggest, as Thompson does,[34] that the rule of law is an 'unqualified good' that should be defended at all costs (especially given its 'juridical' sense), the recognition of the tension built into law does open up a number of theoretical possibilities concerning its implications for social transformation. Specifically, law is no longer viewed exclusively as a weapon of class rule, as an abstract, homogeneous entity whose functions can be generalized across different historical periods and circumstances. Instead, the function of law can differ, depending upon the relative strength of social forces that struggle around and within the legal order. Such an assertion involves working at a different level of abstraction than most structuralist accounts.

As Hall and Scraton note, if we rely on Marx's writings in *Capital*, which discuss the 'laws of motion' of a capitalist economy at a very high and abstract level (generalizing these laws across historical periods and societies), then law will be assigned a more 'fixed' and determined role within capitalism.[35] If, however, we rely on the more historical writings of Marx, in which he takes account of the whole social formation — including its political, legal and ideological aspects — then the role of law is treated more problematically.[36] This latter viewpoint allows us to break with the notion of a 'necessary' or 'functional' fit between law and the economic interests of capital. Instead we are left with a very contradictory picture. To quote Hall and Scraton:

> There is no historical guarantee that capital must prevail, and no certainty that it can prevail on its own terms, outside the limits imposed by contestation and struggle. The outcomes of particular struggles, sometimes waged within and about the law, sometimes against it, will have real and pertinent effects on how particular historical struggles develop. Law, in this sense, is

constitutive of (i.e., it creates) the very conditions of historical development and struggle, and does not merely reflect them.[37]

What we would advocate, therefore, is a theoretical approach to law that moves beyond both a narrow conception of the relations between base and superstructure, and the more fixed and deterministic view of law as operating to the permanent advantage of capital. Such an approach must be materialist and dialectical. It must also be sensitive to the historically specific and contradictory nature of the bourgeois legal form and the system in which it operates.

An appropriate starting point for such an approach is the Marxist conception of social formation. 'Social formation' connotes that certain elements and forms of politics, culture and law are organic to a particular mode of production at a given phase of its development. Without their establishment and maintenance, such a mode of production cannot survive.[38] Once established, however, a capitalist mode of production generates its own internal contradictions. These contradictions will be expressed not only in the economic form (at the point of production), but also in the forms of politics, culture and law which correspond to it. Moreover, these internal contradictions will generate particular legal forms of resistance, which will emerge alongside economic, political and cultural forms. To quote Sumner: "Like feudalism, capitalism must breed its successor in legal forms ... before it leaves the scene."[39] As such, the task — both theoretical and practical — is to determine what forms and principles of law we should develop and extend *now* as a precondition for a socialist transformation.

A general strategy for realizing this task is the development of what Tigar and Levy refer to as a "jurisprudence of insurgency."[40] Jurisprudence can be defined as a "process by which legal ideology is created and elaborated." Following this, "jurisprudence of insurgency" can be used to refer to "a certain kind of jurisprudential activity in which a group challenging the prevailing system of social relations no longer seeks to reform it but rather to overthrow it and replace it with another."[41]

If capitalist legality contains the seeds of a socialist legality, then one step toward the development of a jurisprudence of insurgency would be to explore the limits of the dominant legal ideology in order to gauge how much can be accomplished within those limits.[42] This would involve, as Tigar and Levy note, the use of the assumptions of the governing class to one's own advantage. In short, given the tension built into law, the aim would be to grasp the contradictions inherent in the bourgeois legal form — to work *through* law — in order to alter the very nature of that legal form. Rather than dismissing the rule of law, therefore, we need to consider what effect pushing the 'democratic' sense of the rule of law to its full limit and extent would have on undermining the social relations of capitalism. It is this kind of strategy that we will explore in the remainder of this paper.

PRACTICAL CONSIDERATIONS

In approaching the task of assessing the role of law in social transformation, we start from the premise, documented in Tigar and Levy's analysis of European society between the eleventh and nineteenth centuries, that legal change did not simply go through a single stage of transformation in the movement from feudalism to capitalism. Rather, the process was one of an increasing number of small, incremental legal changes that gave increasing power and legitimacy to the fledgling capitalist class. Consistent with this premise, we do not expect law to be either the vanguard or the consequence of the transformation from capitalist to socialist society. We would argue, instead, that it will be one of many strategic areas where existing tension within the system can be used to push the contradictions that result from the structure of capitalism.

Before delineating those legal activities that best represent a jurisprudence of insurgency, we readily admit the difficulty in attempting to predict what will be the most 'progressive' avenues of legal reform. The advantage of retrospective analysis — like that conducted by Tigar and Levy — is that one can discern the significance of small legal changes over historical periods by examining the diverse consequences these changes had over time. When trying to forecast how current legal changes may facilitate future substantive changes in society, one is blind to all of the potential consequences these changes may produce. If, however, historical analysis has any value, it is in the extent to which it enables us to make prescriptive statements, even tentative ones, on how to transform the existing system.

The central issue to be addressed is one of specifying the criteria by which legal reforms are to be evaluated. More specifically, what kinds of legal reform could be defined as insurgent in terms of their orientation or consequence? How do we distinguish, for example, between reforms which aim only for a greater participation of individuals within the capitalist order (i.e., demanding a "bigger share" of the capitalist pie) from those which aim to transform the very basis of that order?[43]

Structuralists have premised their scepticism about law on the observation that equality is limited to the legal sphere (i.e., it does not extend to the economic sphere of capitalist society). It is in this respect that principles like "equality of all before the law" or "blind justice" are viewed as a major source of legitimation for the system of structured or economic inequality. However, several writers have argued that this position with its ritual invocation of the Anatole France quote, lets the law off too lightly since the law is applied in anything but an equal manner.[44] This recognition of the inequalities in the legal order has led to a number of suggestions for reform.

Mandel, for example, in his analysis of Canadian sentencing law, notes that a central feature of sentencing practices is the recognition of varying punishment according to the offender's 'character,' in particular, the offender's relation to the productive apparatus.[45] By taking into account such factors as educational attainment, employment record and one's "good standing in the community" in the determination of sentence, the law operates to the advantage of one class over another. High status offenders, by virtue of their class position, are perceived as requiring (even deserving) less punishment to ensure their continued conformity. Hence, by varying punishment according to class, the law has the net effect of preserving the status quo of inequality, dominance and subordination. In light of this analysis, Mandel suggests that if sentencing was based solely on the utilitarian principle of general deterrence, that is, the protection of individuals from the harmful effects of crime at the least social cost, punishment would then be based entirely on the conduct sought to be prevented, and not on the "character" (i.e., class) of the offender.

What would be the effect of such a reform? Mandel suggests that it would represent a move in the direction of the 'neutral' state which liberals claim exists in modern democratic societies, that is, the system would be more 'just' in the sense that punishment would no longer vary by class. In this respect, such a reform strategy is laudable to the extent that it would mitigate the unequal treatment to which members of the subordinate classes are subjected by the legal system.

Yet, what of the structuralist argument that equality in sentencing practices would only reinforce the system of economic inequality and hence further legitimate that system? On the one hand, removing the class-based nature of punishment (i.e., viewing dominant class members as 'deserving' of lesser punishment) would eliminate one of the means by which class relations are strengthened and reinforced by the legal order. On the other hand, not taking class differences into account could be viewed as a way of ignoring and/or denying the class differences that do exist.[46] Although punishment would no longer vary by class, crime would continue to vary by class. In this respect Mandel's reform proposal has its advantages, but it is limited.[47] It would only take us part way toward the development of a 'jurisprudence of insurgency.' Such a reform is not insurgent to the extent that it fails to call into question class relations.

Other writers have focused their attention on the content of law.[48] While the criminal law defines certain acts as 'socially injurious' or 'harmful,' it does not tend to define other acts — which are potentially more serious and harmful — as criminal and hence worthy of severe sanctions. For instance, violence against individuals occurs regularly in the workplace of capitalist societies. This typically takes the form of unsafe or hazardous working conditions, exposure to carcinogenic substances and the like. The result has been the loss of life and health for a substantial number of workers. Yet, while such occurrences meet the requirements normally associated with crime (for example, the intentional failure to provide safety equipment or the flagrant violation of safety regulations by owners in order to cut costs and increase profits), they are seldom defined or sanctioned as such. Reiman, therefore, has suggested that the criminal law be redrawn to more accurately reflect the real dangers that individuals pose to society:

> Avoidable acts where the actor had reason to know that his or her acts were likely to lead to someone's death should be counted as forms of murder. Avoidable acts where the actor had reason to believe that his or her acts were likely to lead to someone's injury should be counted as forms of assault and battery. Acts that illegitimately deprive people of their money or possessions should be treated as forms of theft regardless of the color of the thief's collar. Crime in the suites should be prosecuted and punished as vigorously as crime in the streets.[49]

Glasbeek and Rowland have taken this issue one step further.[50] They suggest that there already exist provisions in the criminal law which, although not initially designed for the purpose, could be applied to employer violations of workplace health and safety.[51] This approach is essentially one which advocates the use of criminal law as a vehicle for

highlighting the class conflicts inherent in the productive process. By criminalizing employer practices which result in worker injury and death, the severity of the problem would be reinforced. In effect, the strategy proposed by Glasbeek and Rowland is one which aims at using the assumptions of the governing class to the advantage of the working class. To quote the authors:

> Because of the assumptions of the liberal state, the ideology of law requires it to claim that it punishes behaviour which has been judged unacceptable by society no matter who the perpetrator of the offensive behaviour is. It will be interesting to see how the administrators of the legal justice system respond when it is argued that entrepreneurs offend against the criminal process in much the same way as do robbers of private property and people.[52]

In this respect, such a reform strategy would advance the development of a jurisprudence of insurgency in that it endeavours to push the rule of law to its full limit and extent. Defining the violence which occurs in the workplace of capitalist societies as criminal would have the potential of not only holding employers more accountable for their actions but raising the consciousness of workers as well.

On another level a jurisprudence of insurgency must also be capable of addressing the *manner* in which legal issues are handled by the courts. To elaborate, the law adheres to the principle of 'blind justice.' In so doing, it responds not to the "why" of an act, but to whether or not the act was committed. The race, class or sex of the accused is deemed irrelevant, as the primary criterion for judging cases is the empirical question of whether a formally proscribed act was committed. In short, the issue becomes a matter of "legally relevant facts" and, in the process of resolving this issue, the case is both *individualized* and *depoliticized*. As Grau explains:

> Cases are tried only between legal parties with defined legal interests that conflict over narrowly drawn legal issues. Collective needs are denied. The specificity of the rights and the narrowness of the legal issues combine to preclude the introduction of broader, though relevant, social questions. This restriction effectively depoliticizes the case.[53]

This feature of the legal order contributes to one of the main legitimizing effects of the rule of law, that is, the idea that society is composed, almost exclusively, of individuals and not groups, aggregates or classes. Equally significant is the related belief that legal struggles and political struggles are separate and distinct activities. We would argue, therefore, that a jurisprudence of insurgency must alter this artificial distinction between legal and political issues. This will encompass a two-sided dialectical process. The one side involves attempting to bring the collective nature of the problem into the legal arena while the other side involves broadening the definition of the situation to encompass the political nature of the problem.

"Collectivizing" and "Politicizing" Legal Battles

One way in which the law is being pushed to deal with problems that are more than individual concerns is the strategic use of law by groups to address collective problems. Historically, the labour movement was one of the first to view the problems of workers as a condition common to all individuals whose work placed them in a subordinated position to capital. Because of the blatant nature of this subordination and the fact that workers could readily interact with other co-workers who were experiencing the same consequences of subordination, craft workers were quicker than other groups to approach their problems as collective in nature.

Before describing how some collectivities are currently attempting to use the law and assessing the insurgent nature of these efforts, it is important to note the dynamic interplay that appears to exist between groups defining their problems as collective problems and the concomitant recognition of the political nature of their problems. The consistency with which groups redefine their problems as political issues suggests that politicization is a typical — if not inevitable — consequence of recognizing the collective nature of the problem. By the very act of sharing their problem with others in a similar condition, people come to realize that approaching the problem as a narrow legal issue is unrealistic and often ineffective.

Of greater significance, however, is the tendency for groups not to rely solely on the courts to resolve their problems. By recognizing the political nature of their problems, activist groups also attempt to put pressure directly on the state by engaging in legislative and lobbying activities, which has traditionally been the almost exclusive domain of the major economic interests in society. The use of lobbying by farmworkers, tenants, environmental groups, women, Indians, the handicapped and the elderly is an indication of the extent to which collectivities are broadening the scope of their struggles beyond the traditional locus of the courts.

Although the lobbying efforts of the above groups may not be successful, they are an indication of how the groups view their difficulties as political problems and not simply legal problems. Billings describes this difference in her assessment on the use of advocacy by women's organizations:

> More and more, therefore, lobbying ... has become a familiar tool of the women's movement. Although largely unproductive in proportion to the amount of energy [expended], *lobbying has at least familiarized women with the corridors of power*, created networks across the country and ... created lengthy policy agendas that are agreed to nation-wide as the action priorities.[54]

Although we will argue that the strategies utilized by some groups are more "insurgent" than other strategies, it is important to recognize that the very act of subordinate groups approaching the law as a collective is of value to the extent that it results in politicizing the manner in which the problem is defined.

Collectivities Using the Law

There appears to be a growing awareness among activist groups of the limitations and constraints of approaching the law as individuals. One way in which groups have attempted to increase their power in using the law is to develop strategies that increase the chances that cases heard before the courts represent the collective interests of the group (given the structural limitation that these collective interests must be fought on an individual basis since collectivities are not recognized as legal actors). Some of these strategies continue to use the courts as the arena for battle but expand the techniques by which groups gain access to the courts. The methods used include class action suits, test cases, judicial reviews, standing as *amicus curiae* and private prosecutions.[55]

There are a number of current examples of individuals in Canada forming groups with the sole purpose of fighting legal issues from a collective rather than an individual base. One of the most recent examples of this is the organization of women fighting for a range of issues that address the many consequences of the systemic subordination of women in capitalist society. These issues include affirmative action, equal pay for work of equal value, the handling of sexual offenses by the criminal justice system and the way in which wife battering is dealt with by the police and the courts. One of the consequences of women defining the legal battle as a collective battle is the shift in strategies that will increase the ability of women to influence the types of cases that should be emphasized in the legal arena. A report by the Canadian Advisory Council on the Status of Women, for example, suggests taking a systematic approach to litigation that would further the collective interests of women. The approach would involve the following four steps:

1. defining a goal in terms of the desired principle of law to be established;
2. plotting how the principle of law can be established from case to case in incremental, logical and clear steps;
3. selecting winnable cases suitable for each stage taken to achieve the goal;
4. consolidating wins at each stage by bringing similar cases to create a cluster of cases in support of the principle established.[56]

It is true that some of the above issues (such as affirmative action) simply strive for women to gain a larger piece of the pie within the existing system. Nonetheless, their importance is in the fact that the state is being asked to recognize that it is *not* the problem of a few individuals but a condition of a large segment of the population that has been adversely affected by the economic system. This demand for the recognition of problems as more than individual problems is also evident in the development of anti-poverty organizations, Indian groups fighting for aboriginal land claims and victims' groups demanding greater participation in the criminal justice system. The presumption that legal battles, particularly those in the area of civil law, are exclusively conflicts between individuals and the state or individuals against corporations is becoming less and less tenable.

Although the above strategies used by groups in approaching the law have a number of advantages over traditional approaches, the fact that the law forces these groups to fight their battles through cases of specific individuals in court limits the ability to use the law to redress collective problems. As long as the state is allowed to approach problems of inequality on an individual, case by case basis, there is little likelihood of the law being an effective tool for redressing the collective problems of subordinate groups.

Collective Rights

We would argue that one way in which the law could be used to promote substantive change is to have collectivities recognized as legal actors in society. In other words, to establish the legal principle that, in addition to individual rights in law, there are or should be collective rights that would acknowledge the existence of subordinate groups and provide them, analogically, with the same rights and freedoms that individuals currently have, in principle if not in practice. The recognition of collective rights enables groups to move away from the narrowly defined manner in which current legal ideology defines conflicts in society.

One subject which immediately comes to mind when discussing collective rights is the *Canadian Charter of Rights and Freedoms*. The passage of the *Constitution Act, 1982* has been lauded by some commentators as a means of providing the legal rights and guarantees that would mitigate against the discrimination of minorities in Canada. However, as Rush[57] has argued, while the *Charter* protects individual rights, collective rights are either ill-protected or disregarded altogether.[58] Rush suggests two ways in which collective rights can be perceived constitutionally:

> First, collective rights are those rights which accrue to individuals because of their placement or membership in an identifiable group. In this sense, the realization of the right for each individual depends on its realisation for everyone in the group. These are the rights of cultural communities, ethnic and minority groups.... Second, collective rights are also rights which accrue to groups as groups. These include: the right of Indian people to title to and jurisdiction over their aboriginal land; and the right of women to affirmative action programmes in the workplace.[59]

Following this, Rush notes that "working class rights," full aboriginal rights and the rights of women have not been recognized.[60] In this regard, we would argue, alongside Rush, that continued pressure from working people, women, and ethnic and minority groups for greater recognition of collective rights in the *Charter* is needed.

It should be noted that not every instance of the demand for, or recognition of, collective rights represents explicit insurgent activity. For example, the current legislation in Canada regarding hate literature gives groups the legal ability to prohibit the broadcast or publication of material that has the express purpose of producing hatred toward the group. It is the collective analogy to the law of libel that affords an individual the right to protection from malicious material. While this law recognizes the existence of groups as legal actors, there is nothing within the law that directly addresses the relationship of groups to the state or to the economic base of the system. Similarly, what has historically been recognized as the collective right of management to determine the conditions of work, rates of productivity and the like would obviously fall outside the boundaries of a jurisprudence of insurgency. What this highlights is the need to question "collective right to what?" and establish the criteria and principles on which collective rights should be based.

Legal Recognition of Structural Inequality

To what extent is the demand for collective rights and the politicization of collectivities in their legal struggles indicative of a jurisprudence of insurgency? We would argue that, in addition to the obvious value of individuals no longer viewing their problems as isolated, non-political problems, there has been limited success by collectivities in demanding that the legal system *not* approach all citizens as equals. That is, groups are contending that it is unjust to start from the premise that all individuals are equal legally.

The current emphasis on affirmative action programs by the government could be interpreted as a recognition by the state that there is *structural* and *systemic* inequality in capitalist society. Women, minority groups, the handicapped and other groups who have been at the economic margins have been successful in getting the state at least to acknowledge the problem (even if the remedies to the problem have not been forthcoming). In a similar manner, the current efforts to establish the principle of equal-pay-for-work-of-equal-value is an attempt to pressure the government to acknowledge the structural inequality that has resulted from a segmented labour market.

Both affirmative action and the principle of equal-pay-for-work-of-equal-value are *potentially* insurgent because they use a contradiction within legal ideology to push the law and the state past the limits established by the legal system. By groups bringing public attention to the inconsistency that the law is premised on all citizens being equal, yet large segments of the society have been placed in a position of structural inequality, the state is placed in a position of either admitting that all citizens are not equal or making adjustments to provide greater equality. Although the state may attempt to coopt movement toward greater equality, the public focus on the contradiction requires that the state take some form of ameliorative action.

CONCLUSION

The purpose of this paper has been to open up debate on and interest in the role of law in social transformation. If one accepts that a socialist society is not going to emerge in a full-blown manner, then one must assess how the existing system — including law — can be used to push capitalist society along the path toward socialism. The jurisprudence of insurgency is based on the idea that to abandon law as an agent of change is to negate one method that can be used to challenge the present system. The insurgent role of law is to identify the existing contradictions within legal ideology and to use those contradictions to pit that ideology against itself.

Although it has been argued in this paper that the area of collective rights is one avenue that has the potential of bringing the issue of systemic inequality to the forefront, it must also be admitted that the demand for collective rights has the potential of producing divisions within the working class. These divisions are most likely to occur where some segments of the working class perceive a threat from the collective rights won by other segments of that class. A current example of this is affirmative action policy and the negative reaction to this initiative by individuals who do not fit into one of the target groups identified in the policy. The nature of this conflict is often expressed in the form of collective rights versus individual rights. While there will undoubtedly be instances where collective and individual rights will come into conflict, one should also note that capitalists have in the past facilitated this view of the inherent incompatibility of collective rights and individual rights to suit their own interests.[61]

It must also be admitted that there is a danger in groups using the law in the attempt to achieve their aims. Chief among these dangers is the likelihood that groups will start to define their struggles as ones to be fought exclusively within the legal arena. The consequence of this is that a loss in the courts is seen as the end of the struggle.[62] Several authors have written on the difficulties encountered when a group places all of its energies in legal struggles. In fact, Glasbeek has taken the position that groups should avoid using the *Charter* as a political tool.[63] While recognizing the difficulties in using law in a progressive manner, we would continue to argue, for the reasons stated earlier, that the law should not be abandoned as an arena for social struggle.[64]

Finally, a jurisprudence of insurgency has implications for the role that social scientists and legal practitioners play in legal struggles. For the social scientist, perhaps the most important role is to perform the task originally explicated by C. Wright Mills: to demonstrate the linkage between private troubles and public issues.[65] Applying Mills's dictum to the area of law, the task of the social scientist is to show the commonality of individuals' legal problems and the commonality of interests individuals have in collectively addressing these problems.

For the legal practitioner, the traditional approach to the practice of law and the lawyer-client relationship would be inadequate in developing collective struggles in law. In an article written on the subject of poverty law, Wexler describes the inadequacies of approaching social problems from a narrow legal perspective and suggests that conventional legal training does not equip lawyers for the problems that are systemic in nature:

> Traditional practice hurts poor people by isolating them from each other, and fails to meet their need for a lawyer by completely misunder-

standing that need. Poor people have few individual legal problems in the traditional sense; their problems are the product of poverty, and are common to all poor people.... In this setting the object of practicing poverty law must be to organize poor people, rather than to solve their legal problems. The proper job for a poor people's lawyer is helping poor people to organize themselves to change things so that either no one is poor or (less radically) so that poverty does not entail misery.[66]

By defining legal problems in a larger economic and social context, the lawyer is more likely to adopt an approach to litigation and other legal activities that would best benefit the group. Just as importantly, a lawyer who views the problem in the above manner will, one hopes, also see the value of other kinds of insurgent activities that fall outside of the traditional boundaries of adversarial law, such as confrontations, rent strikes, boycotts and other actions that, while not always legal, can produce effective results for economically subordinate groups.

(c) Structure: The Mosaic of Dominion†

Samuel Bowles and Herbert Gintis

Power may be wielded in numerous ways. Historically, armed force has been a central pillar of power, as liberal theory rightly stresses. But the arsenal of domination goes beyond the gun. Control of the tools with which we produce our livelihood and the words that give our lives and loyalties their meanings have been no less central to the exercise of power.

Debates among Marxian and liberal theorists concerning the roots of domination have tended to adopt an impoverished conception of power. The liberal concern with the despotic state is matched in its narrowness by the Marxian concern with class domination. Each ignores the undeniable insights of the other; both give scant theoretical attention to forms of power that cannot be reduced to either state despotism and class. The most ubiquitous of these excluded forms of power is the domination of women by men.

Equally important, the grand debates between the liberal and Marxian political traditions skirt a central concern of democratic theory, the relationship between power and freedom. Democracy promises the collective accountability of power, but it promises another, more constructive concept as well; namely, the ability of people to effectively carry out their individual and common projects unencumbered by arbitrary constraint. For the liberal, this positive side of power — agency — is rendered minimally, as political liberty and the freedom to contract with whomever one pleases. Both of these liberal forms of freedom represent the absence of constraint rather than personal or collective empowerment. They are, in [Isaiah] Berlin's apt terminology, "negative freedoms." For the classical Marxist, agency is the ability of an emerging class to carry out a historic project dictated by the onward march of the productive forces of society. Neither the liberal nor the Marxian definition encompasses the vision of people and of a people free to be the architects of their own personal and social histories.

We will address the problems raised for democratic theory by these partial conceptions of power in this chapter and in chapter 5, which considers the question of the individual and agency. Here we will develop a conception of power, the structures of social domination, and the resistance to domination capable of understanding the historical dynamics of diverse forms of power — patriarchal, state, class, or other. We will analyze the reproduction of patriarchal domination both as a central issue of democracy in its own right and as an illustration of our approach.

. . . .

The underlying logic of our argument contrasts in two important ways with dominant conceptions in social theory. First, though we affirm that historical change is structured, systematic, and hence understandable in more than simply empirical terms, we reject the notion that either stability or change obeys a single logic, whether of enlightenment, modernization, or the advance of productive capacities. Underlying this denial is our second fundamental commitment, a rejection of the concept of power as unitary; it is the notion that power emanates from a single source in society that provides the bedrock of what might be called the unitary conception of history.

We believe that an alternative conception of power, social structure, and history can make better sense of the historical clash of rights in liberal democratic capitalism and the political nature of the economy. The next two sections develop such a conception of power, in terms of the following five propositions.

First, power is heterogeneous, wielding a variety of weapons, yielding to a host of counterpressures, and obeying no single logic. Here we focus on the distinct forms of domination and solidarity based on class, state, and gender.

Second, power is not an amorphous constraint on action but rather a structure of rules empowering and restraining actors in varying degrees. These distinct sets of rules may be embodied in concrete institutions (for example, the World Bank), in linguistic convention (as in the generic term *man*), in unwritten custom (for example, primogeniture), in legal practice (as in the formal recognition of collective

bargaining for wages), and, as we have seen, in more general conceptions of property and personal rights.

Third, the perpetuation of any power structure is generally problematic. Further, a structure of power is secured or toppled not only by history-making collective struggles, but more prosaically by a complex society-wide web of everyday individual action and compliance.

Fourth, distinct structures of power — be they the liberal democratic state, the patriarchal family, the capitalist economy, or other — are not merely juxtaposed, they are bound together in a common process of social reproduction. Each one may contribute to the survival of another; or they may foster mutually corrosive and subversive impulses.

And fifth, because people's lives are generally governed by more than one distinct power structure — for example one may be a worker, a wife, and a citizen — we experience power as heterogeneous, and are often able to bring the experiences within one system of power to bear in the pursuit of our projects within another. The clash of rights, based on impressive ability of elites and democratic movements alike to extend rights from one sphere of society to others, is the most important historical example of this transportation of practices from one social realm to another.

We refer to our approach as a historical-structural model of power. As we deny the usefulness of a general theory of power and its reproduction, we will seek to develop these five propositions in a particular historical setting; that is, the liberal capitalist nations of Europe and North America over the past two centuries.[1]

A POLITICAL CONCEPTION OF FAMILY, STATE, AND ECONOMY

It has become fashionable, in reacting against the traditional unitary conception of power, to profess a richly textured alternative notion — an idea of power as likely to be illuminated by the study of words and symbols as of armaments and property. Michel Foucault, for instance, writes:

> The analysis made in terms of power, must not assume that the sovereignty of the state, the form of the law or the overall unity of a domination are given at the outset.... Power is everywhere....[2]

This acute and welcome sensitivity to the ubiquity of power, however, can easily slip into treating power *per se* as domination, and replacing a critique of domination with a diffuse critique of authority of no particular use to democratic social movements. Thus Thomas Wartenberg notes, in a perceptive analysis of Foucault's attempt at deconstructing power, that

> at the political level, this problem asserts itself in Foucault's failure to distinguish different types of repressive societies.... Though all social systems do exist by means of a structuring of human beings to meet the needs of that system, we need to have a way to talk about how much pain such structuring inflicts upon the creatures for whom it exists.[3]

We also need, we might add, a way to talk about the *structure* of power in order to assess its *accountability.*

Our conception of power is at once a theory of domination and a theory of structural change flowing from collective resistance to domination. It is at the same time a structural theory and a theory of social action. Marx, in criticizing Ludwig Feuerbach, lamented the fact that materialist thought tended to denigrate action in favor of structure: "Hence it happened that the active side, in contradistinction to materialism, was developed by the idealism."[4] Analogously, structural theories of power often support a conception either of unquestioned, monolithic, uncontested domination or of the mechanistic inevitability of the collapse of domination.* The commonplace observation that structures do not reproduce or destroy themselves but are perpetuated or overturned by *what people do* finds no place in most structural theories. The active side of power is more fully developed by theories of choice.

Theories of choice, however — for reasons we will address in the next chapter — generally fail to provide an adequate account of the forms of collective action central to an active and historical conception of power. By developing the relationship between domination and solidarity, we seek to avoid both the individualism of choice theories and the presumption of a pregiven logic of either stability or crisis in structural theories. More positively, we will embrace the fundamental tenet of structural theories — that individual action is highly regulated — in a framework that insists that the historical dynamics of the structures regulating choice are themselves the result, however indirect and unintended, of individual action.

Vertical relationships of superior to subordinate, of employer to worker, of man to woman, of despot to subject, of white to black, provide the raw materials with which people construct the corresponding horizontal structures of social bonding — class consciousness, democratic nationalism, racial unity, and the like. (This rudimentary statement of the conditions of collective action simply generalizes Marx's insight that the structure of exploitation might provide the conditions for the unification of the exploited. We will turn to this issue in some detail in chapter 6.) These structures of social bonding allow people to forge from their individual experiences of oppression (and those of other people) an ensemble of cultural and organizational tools upon which collective action may be based.

The active side of power surely includes the exercise of domination by the powerful and the complicity of the oppressed in their oppression. But it also includes revolutionary collective action: forging communicative and organizational tools of bonding from the cacophony of discourses to which the mosaic of domination gives rise, and putting these tools to use in transforming structures of power. The clash of rights in liberal democratic capitalism, in particular, has seen both the collective action of the dispossessed in pitting personal rights against the privileges of wealth, race, and gender as well as the counterstrategies of the privileged in shoring up patriarchal rights, property rights, and "skin privilege."

Recognition of the heterogeneity of power invites a more searching analysis of the way in which distinct spheres of social life regulate social action in such a manner as to produce systems of domination *and* the possibility of their elimination.

Power is the capacity to render social action effective. It is coextensive with neither the state, nor with physical force, nor with face-to-face command.[5] Power may be exercised through the ability to overcome the resistance of others — as in Max Weber's conception — but it may equally be exercised through the ability to avoid resistance, either through control over which issues become contestable or through influence over others' wants, sentiments, desires, or, more generally, objectives.[6]

. . . .

We focus on three general forms of the asymmetrical exercise of power: domination through the monopoly of the means of coercion, through the exercise of property rights, and through the operation of gender-based privilege. These are certainly not the only forms of domination observed in modern society. Race, ethnicity, religion, language, and region, among others, have served as major bases of social oppression and *loci* of bitter conflict. We focus on these three forms of domination not because other forms are less general, affecting particular liberal democratic capitalist societies in widely differing degrees and in quite distinct manners.*

Each of these three forms of domination may be considered to be a means of regulating social action. Thus, in three distinct ways, action is structured by a specific set of rules of the game: (a) the forms and

rewards of participation of individuals in a practice are socially regulated; (b) the range of feasible alternative forms of practice are socially delimited; and (c) the potential effectiveness of distinct types of practice are socially mediated.

(d)   Introduction: The Healing Dimension of Restorative Justice — A one-world body[†]

Dennis Sullivan and Larry Tifft

THE ESSENCE OF RESTORATIVE JUSTICE

When members of the Navajo Nation try to explain why people harm others, they say that a person who does harm to another 'acts as if he [sic] has no relatives' (Yazzie 1998: 126; see Kaplan and Johnson 1964: 216–17). That is, the offending person has become so disconnected from the world around him, so disengaged from the world around him, so disengaged from the people he lives and works with each day, that his acts no longer have a personal foundation.

To remedy harm situations when they do occur, to help those affected by a harm to begin upon the path of healing, historically the Navajo have taken steps that are consistent with their views on the 'causes' of harm. They call upon the relatives of the person responsible for the harm (as well as those of the person harmed) to come forth and help their kin re-connect with the community they live in or, as happens in the case of some, become connected to that community for the very first time.

The Navajo call this process of connection and re-connection 'peacemaking'. It is a form of restorative justice an essential part of which is community members assembling to 'talk things out' so that harmony might be restored to relationships that have been set on end. It is the same kind of process that South Africans embraced with their Truth and Reconciliation Commission in 1995 in an effort to heal

from the human rights violations that occurred during apartheid (Skelton and Frank 2001).

On the best of days these processes, and all other forms of restorative justice, enable those responsible for a harm-done to work through their twisted logic and excuses — what Robert Yazzie (1998), former Chief Justice of the Navaho Nation Court, used to refer to in good Navajo vernacular as 'fuzzy thinking' (125; see also Zion 1997). The hope is that those responsible for a harm will be able to acknowledge to the community and perhaps to the person(s) they harmed what they did and in some way make amends, to 'make things right.' As anyone who has begun to familiarize him- or herself with the meaning of restorative justice knows, those affected by the harm in question seek to reach an agreement whereby the needs of the person(s) harmed, the victims/survivors, are taken into account to the fullest extent possible.

The Navajo peacemaking process is a quintessential form of restorative justice because it involves the community in restoring people and groups to well-being in a needs-meeting way: that is, the needs of everyone in the healing process are of paramount concern (Sullivan and Tifft 2005). Such a perspective or way of thinking derives from long-held indigenous customs in which kin, members of an immediate family, community, or nation seek to meet the needs of all involved in a harm situation. They know that, if a wrong is not righted in ways that take into account the needs of those who have been affected, the community will eat away at itself (Sather 2004).

---

† From Dennis Sullivan and Larry Tifft (eds.), *Handbook of Restorative Justice: A Global Perspective* (Oxon, U.K.: Routledge, 2006) 1 at 1–6. Reproduced with permission of Taylor & Francis Books UK. [Notes and/or references omitted.]

Such an ethic is strange to so many of us in our post-modern world because it harkens back to a time when people saw their lives 'bound up together in ... one common life. The members of one kindred looked on themselves as one living whole, a single animated mass of blood, flesh, and bones, of which no member could be touched without all the members suffering' (Smith 1907: 273–4). In other words, when one person suffers a harm, all suffer from the harm to one degree or other. And all are responsible for making things right in such situations because all are in some way responsible for that harm occurring in the first place, being a co-creator (whether actively or passively, directly or indirectly) of that 'single animated mass of blood, flesh, and bones.'

This is very powerful medicine and in part explains why restorative justice is at its core a form of insurgency and subversive in nature. That is, it is a process that competes with the state's way of doing business not only in ways to respond to harm (nonviolently, restoratively) but also in defining what harms we need to give attention to in the first place. Restorative justice sees the pain and suffering of all as worthy of our collective attention while the state discriminates between those worthy of the community's attention and those not. It is easy to see how such differing views contain the seeds of ideological and administrative dissension and why restorative justice is seen by the state as subversive, as an act of insurgency that must be put down, contained, co-opted, or modified in some other way to meet the state's ideological and administrative requirements.

With respect to the process of 'making things right,' the greatest hope of restorative justice advocates is that those who have been traumatized by a harm will want to participate in the process by telling their story as well as by listening to the story of the person who has harmed them so as to gain a better sense of who that person is (Mike *et al.* 2003). In this way the person harmed and their kin are more likely to develop some degree of compassion and empathy for the harming person and those who care for her/him, and are more likely to set aside feelings of anger, vengeance, and loss. We know, however, that this cannot be anything other than a voluntary process for those who have been harmed (Achilles 2004: 72), for sometimes their greatest need and that of their family is to keep as much distance between themselves and those responsible for the harm. So victim needs/wishes are paramount and must be respected at all times (Achilles 2004: 70; Amstutz 2004; Strang 2004).

While persons harmed may be receptive to participating in a victim–offender encounter and to

accepting a genuine apology when offered, and occasionally come to forgive the person who harmed them, they should always receive, before deciding whether to participate in a restorative process, direct assurances from the community that they will not be re-victimized and that steps will be taken to ensure that other members of the community will be less likely to suffer as they have (McCold 2003: 96). Therefore, as members of this community, we must rally to support those harmed by providing the short- and long-term care they require even in cases when no one has been identified as the offending person (Achilles 2004: 71). Such support might come in the form of emergency medical, legal, counselling, victim compensation, and financial recovery services but it also might come in the form of challenge to the structural inequalities in our communities that prevent us from attending to the needs of those harmed in the way they expressed them (Thomson 2004).

What is distinctive about restorative justice as a response to harm, then, is that it is a process that belongs to relatives, to the community at large (Mika 2002) and that, when they become involved in the healing process, they develop greater competency not only in resolving community conflicts themselves but also in defining those acts they wish to pay especial attention to (Johnstone 2002; Bush and Folger 1994). As might be expected, the development of such competencies does not occur *sua sponte* but requires conscious and deliberate reflection on the part of people about what kind of restorative justice encounter — be it a conference or circle experience — will best meet the needs of all involved (Bush and Folger 1994). By fostering such active participation, restorative justice empowers people in a world in which globalization increasingly excludes them from the definition and correction of what ails them (Garland 2001). And understandably so, for once community members commit themselves to developing competencies based in restorative principles, they are more likely to engage in effecting cultural and social change so as to prevent structural harms from occurring in the first place.

BARRIERS TO RESTORATIVE JUSTICE PROCESSES

As might be imagined, there are all sorts of ideological, political, social, and psychological barriers that can insert themselves into the restorative justice venture at any point (Zehr and Toews 2004). Indeed, one of the glaring ironies of restorative justice is that its wide array of programs are dependent upon the state for their funding, development, assessment, and continuation. As a result, many restorative programs quickly find themselves narrowed in focus and scope, soon evolving into little more than correctional alternatives such as probation and other forms of community supervision. Indeed, we see in such cases the restorative process become overwhelmingly 'offender-centered' with the 'offender's' liability becoming the event around which the justice system convenes to deliberate (Roche 2003: 143). Why, when this is the focus of justice, would anyone desire to work toward developing restorative, community competencies and toward fostering greater access to supportive 're-integrative' resources [since] the justice process is all about the state being harmed and state officials exacting retribution for the collective (Zehr and Mika 1998)?

But those who seek to encourage and/or regain interpersonal harmony restoratively know that it is not the state that has been physically harmed when interpersonal violence takes place, but persons; it is not the law that needs to be restored, but people's lives (Zehr 1990). We cannot call any correctional process restorative, therefore, if, in its defense of the state, it helps re-establish or reaffirms power-based, hierarchical, non-participatory, need-depriving relationships (Tifft and Sullivan 1980: 57). One of the competencies that restorative justice fosters is learning which questions to ask about the value or morality of social arrangements that manufacture and maintain structural inequities in societies, that are the root of most interpersonal crime, and that compete with restorative processes as an appropriate (healing) response to such crime (Lemonne 2003; Pavlich 2004).

When we look at the many ways that we might opt to relate to young people who grow up within non-participatory, needs-denying arrangements, restorative justice continually presents us with difficult moral choices (see Paul Goodman 1961; Sullivan 1982). For example, do we wish that young persons who harm others be deterred from undertaking 'irrational,' unlawful actions and treated/rehabilitated so they might be adjusted to the exploited, development-thwarted life-positions in the social hierarchies they come from? Or perhaps we wish that these young persons be shamed and reintegrated into structurally and spiritually violent life conditions and strife-torn, dead neighbourhoods and 'communities'? In other words, is it our wish that these young people become designated surrogates for the state's usurped responsibility for moral condemnation?

These are not rhetorical questions without consequence for, when we respond to them affirma-

tively, we insult those who have been harmed. We not only re-victimize them by not taking their suffering and needs into account but also lose an opportunity to commit ourselves to the restorative justice directive to create a more civil, participatory society (Braithwaite and Strang 2001), one with more competent individuals and communities. Lost is the opportunity that restorative justice offers as a philosophy of justice to facilitate a more inclusive society, one in which our prevailing concern is meeting everyone's needs (Sullivan and Tifft 2004, 2001, 2005; Tifft and Sullivan 2005), developing their talents and gifts, and thus greatly decreasing all forms of social harms and non-responsiveness (Pepinsky 1991). Also lost is 'the potential of restorative justice to transform entire legal systems, our family lives, our conduct in the workplace, our practice of politics' (Braithwaite 2003: 1; also see Sullivan and Tifft 2004 and the discussion in Johnstone 2004). When we set forth this larger, transformative vision of restorative justice, it is not surprising that many of its advocates come to see the restorative justice they practice (oftentimes begrudgingly) as the functional equivalent of an individual-offender-focused accountability process (see Bazemore 1996 regarding these paradigms). When we assess the needs of the young people we mentioned earlier within such a framework, restorative justice processes become 'programs' that fail to take these young persons seriously and to provide them with an environment for positive moral growth, a vocation, a connection to their relatives (Bazemore 1996).

RESTORATIVE JUSTICE AND COMMUNITY

The Navajo peacemaking process, though it might not meet all of the desired dimensions of the full restorative/transformative processes we alluded to, is a quintessential form of restorative justice because it involves the community in restoring persons and groups of people to well-being in a needs-meeting way. That is, the needs of everyone involved are of paramount concern (Sullivan and Tifft 2005). Such a perspective or way of thinking derives from long-held, pre-state, indigenous customs in which kin, members of an immediate family, community, or nation of people collaborate to meet the needs of all in daily life including in situations when someone was harmed. These relationships are of a continuous nature and, if not attended to, jeopardize the health and well-being of the community, even its collective survival. That is, if essential needs are not met, and if a 'wrong' is not righted in ways that take into account the needs of those who have been affected, the community loses its competencies to evolve successfully (Sather 2004; Piercy 1976; Kropotkin 1913).

In other forums and venues we have written extensively about the relationship between this needs-based perspective and personal and collective restoration (Sullivan and Tifft 2005). It is a perspective that repeatedly calls attention to our connectedness as relatives. In terms of needs it says that, when someone's essential needs are not met or when someone violates another's needs causing harm, all suffer from this harm to one degree or other (Gil 1999). And all have a responsibility to ensure that a restorative response is made, for all are additionally harmed when this situation is not addressed and things 'made right.' Again, 'made right,' especially in repetitive harm situations, requires social change, requires attention to how social life is organized, for clearly some persons' needs and freedoms have been thwarted. In such situations we recognize that we are all responsible for creating the contexts in which some persons' needs are (oftentimes with regularity) not met. And it is with this insight that we acknowledge that we are all responsible for making things right because we are all the co-creators of how we organize our collective social life and relate with one another. This perspective or re-conceptualization of restorative justice is one of immense human compassion and accountability. Making such a restorative response, a response that is simultaneously concerned with the personal empowerment and growth of each and the collective well-being of all, is powerful medicine. It explains why restorative justice is at its core subversive and a form of insurgency.

RESTORATIVE JUSTICE AS INSURGENCY

Restorative justice is a form of insurgency because it 'competes with' the state (and power-based social arrangements generally) in how it responds to interpersonal or intergroup conflicts and how it defines what harms the human community should give restorative attention to in the first place. But restorative justice is also subversive because it challenges, both conceptually and in practice, social arrangements and processes that thwart human development and prevent human needs from being met. As we mentioned earlier, it reflects a vision of social life that sees the pain and suffering of all as worthy of the community's attention while the state and power-based institutions discriminate between those worthy

of attention and those not. In its transformative dimensions restorative justice exposes the nature of power-based orders (disorders) as they manifest themselves in the home, the school, the workplace, and in societies throughout the world. And the measure restorative justice advocates use to assess the quality or value of social institutions in our globalizing world order is the extent to which they foster the full development of each and every person's human potential, meet each and every person's essential needs (Chomsky 2003). Are they organized to foster human development and meet the needs of all or of some at the expense and exclusion of others? Here we are introduced to the economics or political economy of restorative justice which many advocates of the process refuse to acknowledge as relevant to both its practices and theory (Sullivan and Tifft 1998).

But once we acknowledge the importance of understanding the political economy of restorative justice — how human relationships work and are enhanced or diminished — we find ourselves squarely situated in the realms of social and distributive justice, of visions of what kind of world we wish to live in, or must have, if we are to become a one-world (self-restoring) body. In puzzlement we have asked over and over how scholars and practitioners of restorative justice can speak of its various practices as responses to interpersonal harm without asking at the same time about the nature of the social conditions which the participants in a conference or circle come from and to which they return after the conference. Imagine for a moment holding a conference to address an instance or pattern of physical wife-battering. Would we call a restorative justice encounter successful that concluded with the persons involved returning home to resume a relationship in which one person was perceived as an object, an inferior, to be used in meeting the needs and desires of the other? That is, a relationship in which one person's life plan or existence is perceived as more important than the others, in which the more powerful person relies on tyrannical decision-making patterns to uphold his power and his needs-meeting while the voice of his 'partner' was silenced? Clearly such an encounter would not be considered successful for these are not social conditions for relating as intimates (relatives). They not only stimulate harms such as battering but themselves constitute structural battering or violence (Tifft 1993).

Imagine as well holding a conference to address an instance of physical battery/robbery between two strangers — a young man throwing an elderly man to the ground and taking his wallet and watch at a bus stop. Would we call a restorative justice conference successful that concluded with these persons returning to their neighborhoods that are without the resources to meet their respective needs? Of course not. Such 'killed neighborhoods,' as Nils Christie (1993) has described them, do not have the resources to help the elderly man ease his trauma or meet his need to have his trust in others revitalized, nor to help him physically recover from bodily injuries while paying his medical expenses. Such neighborhoods are without the resources to help the young man deal with his on-going trauma of being perceived as one of an economically produced 'army of superfluous workers,' with his need to belong to a real community where he is respected and acknowledged as being human: that is, viewed as worthy of attention in the first place going unrecognized. In such neighborhoods he will not be offered an opportunity to develop his human competencies and gifts, to channel his energy in ways that open him up to others, and to receive a livable wage. Yet these are the social conditions within which far too many young men and women grow up and suffer throughout their formative years and even later, the social conditions of having no 'relatives.'

Finally, imagine holding a series of truth and reconciliation hearings to acknowledge a pattern of gross human rights violations and attempting to make things right through a public airing and discussion of the impact of the harms on people's lives and the society as a whole (Walgrave 2003). Would such hearings be considered successful if they concluded with the persons involved returning home in largely segregated neighborhoods or in separate geographic regions of a nation-state to continue to relate as they had, with ethnic, tribal, or inter-nation-state hatred and gross stratification arrangements remaining intact, if only in less institutionalized and legal forms? Would such a series of processes be considered restorative if few acknowledgements were generated, if no reparations were forthcoming, or if a new nation-state administration instituted only slightly different modes of stratification and retribution? Restorative justice is a form of insurgency because it demands that we explore how the groups or nation-states involved are able to deny their responsibilities for such atrocities or, if they do acknowledge them, can go on without making things right, without reparation of a nature that supports those harmed [to] recover their dignity and cultural autonomy (Friedrichs 2002; Friedrichs and Friedrichs 2002).

(e) Postapartheid Justice: Can Cosmopolitanism and Nation-Building Be Reconciled?[†]

Rosemary Nagy

. . . .

In an action that seeks "justice without borders," South African plaintiffs have filed suit in the United States against numerous multinational corporations for aiding and abetting apartheid's crimes against humanity. The plaintiffs rely upon the Alien Tort Claims Act (ATCA), which grants universal jurisdiction over "any civil action by an alien for a tort only, committed in violation of the law of nations or a treaty of the United States" (28 U.S.C. sec. 1350 [1789]). The South African government has steadfastly opposed the litigation on the grounds of national sovereignty and, in particular, that foreign courts "bear no responsibility for the well-being of our country and ... our constitution[al] ... promotion of national reconciliation" (Mbeki 2003: n.p.). Although nation-building in postconflict societies arguably might take place only *within* the nation, this also provokes the question, "what is a nation?" in an era of economic globalization, legal and moral cosmopolitanism, and transnational violence and

† (2006) 40:3 Law & Soc'y Rev. 623 at 623–28, 641–49. Reproduced with permission of Wiley Blackwell, Oxford, UK. Copyright c2006 by Rosemary Nagy. Reproduced with permission of Blackwell Publishing Ltd. [Notes and/or references omitted.]

injustice. The politics surrounding *Re South African Apartheid Litigation* (2004) bring this question to the forefront of a long-standing debate between cosmopolitanism and nationhood, which typically presumes an inherent conflict between the two.

Contemporary cosmopolitanisms, theorized under the cluster of phenomena known as globalization, draw upon ancient Stoic ideas of world citizenship and Kantian principles of cosmopolitan or universal right. Cosmopolitanism in general upholds the moral dignity and equity of all human beings as individuals, regardless of their culture, nationality, or citizenship. Cosmopolitanism rejects ethnonationalism or unreflective patriotism and urges engagement with the world. It speaks of moral obligations beyond borders and of enforcing minimal standards of decency with borders.

This runs counter to the statist view of international relations. According to the statist view, nation-states are the ultimate source of legal or moral authority, and their integrity is guaranteed by principles of non-intervention and national self-determination (see Fine 2003: 452–3). These two principles must be respected for the sake of international peace and because they protect different ways of life amongst nations.[1] Nationalists argue that the nation provides the best context in which trust, reciprocity, right, obligation, and political self-determination can take place (see Tan 2002; 435–9). This is because co-nations have historic, political, and territorial ties; shared values and loyalties; and a common identity. A citizen of the world, in contrast, is in fact a citizen of nowhere (see Bowden 2003). Solidarity in the name of general humanity is too abstract to be meaningful. And, critics further charge, the promotion of cosmopolitan university is inevitably the imposition of somebody else's values.

The principles of non-intervention and national self-determination are both evident in the South African government's opposition to the apartheid litigation. First, in accordance with the statist view of international relations, the South African government objects to the intervention of a foreign court in its supposedly sovereign affairs. On this view, international law ought to recognize only states as legal subjects, whereas cosmopolitan law also recognizes individuals and groups in civil society as legal persons (see Fine 2003: 452–3). The ATCA decenters the state. It permits extraterritorial legal action for human rights crimes, and it recognizes individuals and multinational corporations as legal subjects. Moreover, the South African government sees the ATCA as threatening to override domestic constitutional law. This concern leads to the second principle

of objection, which is the focus of this article: the fear that external interference will jeopardize South Africa's chosen path toward national unity and reconciliation. Through democratic and constitutional means, South Africa established the Truth and Reconciliation Commission (TRC) and other policies to deal with its apartheid past. The "new" South Africa, so the argument goes, is based on values of reconciliation, reconstruction, and goodwill — and not on the antagonistic, alienating, and retributive values of litigation.

Thus, the fear is that the use of a cosmopolitan law from outside South Africa will undermine nation-building within the country. This fear can be mapped onto larger theoretical debates, which run something like this: if cosmopolitanism's moral allegiance to all human beings is seen as an antidote to the divisive, marginalizing, and sometimes violent politics of race, ethnicity, or nation, the dark side of cosmopolitanism is false universalism, colonialism, and violent imperialism (see Anderson 1998; Lu 2000). Even a relatively benign cosmopolitanism, critics accuse, casts aside the morally meaningful connections and affiliations that constitute human life. To put it in the context of postconflict transitions to democracy, it may indeed be inappropriate and unfeasible for outsiders to attempt to resolve the unique complexities of local or regional violence. Universal jurisdiction may have little bearing on domestic values of peace, justice, and reconciliation,[2] or it may jeopardize delicate peace arrangements.[3] In the case of the apartheid litigation, the claim is that a foreign court cannot promote national reconciliation, develop civic unity, or effectively reduce the ravages of apartheid because it is abstracted from South Africa's politics of a negotiated transition to democracy.

I argue, in contrast, that if we closely examine South Africa's transitional path toward "national unity and reconciliation,"[4] which is largely exemplified in the TRC, the apartheid litigation instead emerges as a cosmopolitan quest by victims for national belonging. The broader theoretical claim is that the apartheid litigation provides an illustration of cosmopolitanism as a rooted or differentiated concept, or what is sometimes called the "new cosmopolitanism" (e.g. Fine 2003; Hollinger 2002). The challenge of the new cosmopolitanism is to reconcile abstract universalism with concrete particulars. In this case, although the plaintiffs' claims are based on universal right, their claims call attention to connections and affiliations rather than stripping them away. What the apartheid litigation shows is that cosmopolitanism and nation-building can be reconciled to at least some degree.

Specially, I propose to bridge the apparent divide between cosmopolitanism and nation-building with the concept of victimhood. Insofar as nation-building in South Africa is seen to depend upon the restoration of victims, so too is cosmopolitanism victim-centered in its commitment to prevent harm and suffering. This argument develops a particular strand of cosmopolitanism[5] as a moral injunction to protect victims of injustice and cruelty (following Shklar 1989, 1990; Lu 2000). Its legal counterparts are human rights, international harms-based conventions and declarations, and universal jurisdiction (see Linklater 2002). While universal in scope, this cosmopolitanism also necessarily requires contextualized roots and concrete solidarities. For violence operates by denying victims their humanity *and* by stripping them of their place and belonging in the world. The prevention of cruelty — "never again" — thus depends in part upon recognizing those who had been excluded, marginalized, or silenced under the previous regime, affirming not only their humanity but also their belonging as equal citizens. The apartheid litigation enacts this duality: the South African plaintiffs press for justice on the basis of cosmopolitan right, yet they do so in part because of their continued marginalization within the "new" nation with respect to issues of "truth" and reparation. It is a cosmopolitan *re-membering* of the nation. The plaintiffs challenge closed-off constructions of historic violence and national reconciliation in an implicit demand for belonging as citizens whose lives matter.

Thus, the main argument is that cosmopolitan justice can intersect with national memory and belonging. These need not be antithetical to one another, either conceptually or in practice. In the first section, I develop the theoretical connections between cosmopolitanism, victimhood, and nation. The ATCA likely affords an especially strong claim about the intersection of these three concepts because it permits victims to take matters into their own hands by lodging civil claims, rather than being dependent upon foreign governments to indict international criminals. Nevertheless, generalizable questions regarding transitional justice[6] and globalization are raised: How do constructions of violence, victimhood, and responsibility fit into the meaning of the "new" nation? How does the supposed binary between "inside" and "outside" become complicated by international financing and transnational conflict economies in arms, diamonds, and oil? How extensively can we think past this same binary with respect to bringing cosmopolitan values "home" through the exercise of universal jurisdiction in hybrid tribunals, the International Criminal Court, and transnational prosecutions? Although I cannot respond to these questions due to space constraints, I raise them here to more broadly situate the analysis.

In the course of illustrating the theoretical argument through discussion of the apartheid litigation, secondary themes emerge that are more specific to the South African case. In the following sections, I outline how the contours of South Africa's negotiated settlement have shaped the trajectory of nation-building and also bring into question the government's claim of national sovereignty against the apartheid litigation. Although South African transition to democracy and the TRC in particular have been exemplary in many respects, the pursuit of reparation through outside courts presents a cautionary tale to those who embrace the notion of reconciliation too easily, or to those who celebrate South Africa's success without acknowledging its domestic frictions. Furthermore, the reparations debate in South Africa (and the outward movement of this debate) exposes various issues in what has been, until recently, a fairly neglected dimension of transitional justice, despite reparation being the only form of justice directed specifically toward victims. These issues include what, if anything, constitutes adequate reparation, and who should grant reparation and to whom. Although, in the end, civil remedy is not the same as reparation, this is not to dismiss the significance of a cosmopolitan push from outside South Africa's borders. Rather, as I explore in the concluding section, it raises the potential for the building of a more cosmopolitan nation.

Re South African Apartheid Litigation is under appeal after being dismissed on November 29, 2004 for lack of subject matter jurisdiction.[7] For my purposes, the moral and political symbolism of the litigation is just as significant as the unsettled question of legal culpability. Even successful alien tort claims rarely collect damages; they are usually filed with goals of affording victims a measure of recognition and respect, of publicly shaming those responsible for human rights violations, and of perhaps instigating change outside the courtroom. Certainly, a verdict of legal liability might strengthen these goals, but the publicity, political damage, or out-of-court settlements generated by the mere processing of a lawsuit should not be underestimated. Of interest here are the politics surrounding the apartheid litigation and how they have affected constructions of the "new" nation.

. . . .

COSMOPOLITAN RE-MEMBERING OF THE NATION

Reparation has taken on multiple meanings in South Africa, ranging from symbolic and compensatory measures for individual victims of torture and killing to more development-oriented programs for specific communities that were targeted by terror and for the general victims of basic apartheid. Likewise, the apartheid lawsuits encompass different interests and purposes among plaintiffs and supporters, including a greater corporate social responsibility, the expansion of global human rights and social justice, a challenge to South African domestic policy, an according of beneficiary complicity, the vindication of individual and collective victims, and broad-based or individual relief. Some of these dimensions of the litigation intersect with national memory and belonging. This is not an all-encompassing claim; certainly there are extrinsic considerations at stake. But there are a number of ways in which the litigation can be seen as an effort to bring cosmopolitan values home such that the recognition of victims and injustice is central to constructions of the "new" South Africa.

The litigation is "new cosmopolitan" because it wields international human rights law in order to reassert the language of accountability as a pointed counter to domestic developments. The plaintiffs challenge beneficiary denial of responsibility — both then and now — by arguing that profiting from and sustaining a system deemed a crime against humanity was not just moral abdication but also a violation of legal norms and UN sanctions. Even if the argument ultimately fails in the American courts — and at this point, *Re South African Apartheid Litigation* (2004) has failed due to interpretations of ATCA jurisdiction, and not on the substantive allegations — the publicity surrounding the lawsuits and the ATCA more generally contributes to the growing trend to establish human rights obligations for corporations. Increasingly, the global debate is not whether such obligations exist but whether they are enforceable or, as corporations who fight against the ATCA would like to see, voluntary (Shamir 2004). But the South African government appears to have side-stepped this debate with its conciliatory approach toward business's role in nation-building.

It is a popular sentiment in South Africa that the African National Congress (ANG) government has "sold out" to corporate interests, that indeed beneficiaries will "get off free." Corporate pledges to the Business Trust, an initiative of firms that supports social and economic reconstruction, have reportedly been made in explicit exchange for the South African government's support to quash the ATCA claims (C. Terreblanche 2003a). Moreover, contributions are given on condition that they are called *nation-building* rather than *reparation*, thereby avoiding issues of historic injustice and responsibility for it (C. Terreblanche 2003b). In the TRC's view, the amount in the Business Trust is "paltry" (TRC 2003: Vol. 6, sec. 2, ch. 5, para. 9). But former Minister of Justice and Constitutional Development Penuell Maduna, in his affidavit to the U.S. court asking for the apartheid lawsuits to be dismissed, points to the fund as a "meaningful contribution to the broad national goal of rehabilitating the lives of those affected by apartheid" (Maduna 2003: Para. 9). Citing the cabinet's belief that the lawsuits would jeopardize the government's policy of reconciliation, Maduna brandishes the right of the national sovereignty in order to denounce the plaintiffs' actions. Notably, the crux of Maduna's assertion of national sovereignty is economic.[25]

He takes umbrage with the lawsuits' insinuation that the government has done little to address the damages of apartheid. This is not surprising; as a preeminent democratic success story, South Africa is not a rogue nation such as those typically implicated in ATCA actions. Furthermore, from the government's perspective, supporting the apartheid litigation is tantamount to acknowledging that their plans for social and economic development are not working (see Hamber 2004: 19 and following.). Maduna points to the ANG's numerous advances in "social upliftment" and notes that it has been twice elected on a platform of socioeconomic transformation. An underlying argument, perhaps, is that development should be distinguished as a general right of citizenship whereas reparation is more specifically tied to historic wrongdoing. But this position of course depends upon one's characterization of wrongdoing, and it leaves the matter of community-based reparations hanging. In addition, there is an overwhelming lack of electoral alternatives for the majority of South Africans.[26] Voting for the ANC does not necessarily mean a wholesale endorsement of its policies, nor does it preclude the voicing of dissent in a healthy democracy (and the government certainly does recognize the right of victims to launch suit).

Domestic contention over South Africa's social and economic development policy underlies the debate about beneficiary reparations and the meaning of national reconciliation. Earlier, I noted that corporations had some influence in setting the terms of the transition to democracy including through scenario-planning exercises. While in 1990, Nelson Mandela had assured the nationalization of banks, mining and monopoly industries, progressive taxation, and redistribution, from 1992 onward, the ANC, partly through the influence of its negotiating partners, moved toward the virtues of market forces, foreign investment, and economic growth (see Bond 2000; Marais 2001). This shift is exemplified in the 1996 macroeconomic policy document, *Growth, Employment and Redistribution* (GEAR) (Republic of South Africa 1996), which is generally condemned on the left as an embrace of neoliberalism that has worsened rather than redressed poverty and inequality.

My purpose is not to assess GEAR per se but, rather, to point out that the policy shift occurred within *globalized* considerations. In short, the new South Africa — and subsequent claims of sovereignty — did not develop in a vacuum. The "organic" crisis facing the apartheid state in the late 1980s was in large part a consequence of structural limits on the growth of domestic demand, of severe skilled labor shortage, and of foreign sanctions and disinvestment. There was general recognition of the need to reinsert South Africa into the global economy. Elite consensus on the manner of global reintegration developed within overarching international trends, including the collapse of the (ANG's standby) Soviet model and the ascendancy of neoliberal doctrine. The main platforms of GEAR were first outlined in a 1993 letter of intent signed by the Transitional Executive Council, which included the ANG, to secure an $850 million IMF loan to help the country with balance of payment difficulties (Marais 2001: 104, 134).

Today, the primacy of this model over other modes of (re)distribution emerges in Maduna's affidavit as *the* path to nation-building. He writes:

> One of the structural features of the South Africa economy, and one of the terrible legacies of apartheid, is its high level of unemployment and its by-product, crime. Foreign direct investment is essential to address both these issues. If this litigation proceeds, far from promoting economic growth and employment and thus advantaging the previously disadvantaged, the litigation, by deterring foreign direct investment and undermining economic stability will do exactly the opposite of what it ostensibly sets out to do (Maduna 2003: Para. 12).

He cites GEAR as a key strategy in promoting "reconciliation with and business investment by all firms, foreign and South African". And faster economic growth, he argues, offers *"the only way* out of poverty, inequality and unemployment (Maduna 2003: Para. 8.1; emphasis added).

However, this (neoliberal) prescription is not necessarily the only way. Rumblings of dissent run through the Tripartite Alliance (ANG, South African Communist Party, Congress of South African Trade Unions [COSATU]) and from deep within South African civil society.[27] Furthermore, the claim of sovereignty is rather ironic. In Maduna's prescription, we see that the nation, ostensibly impervious to intrusion, is in fact dependent upon porous borders in a globalized economy. In these respects, the apartheid litigation is very much about the meaning of home in an increasingly globalized world. For some South Africans, the ANC appears to be a willing participant in, rather than a victim of, neoliberal globalization. Moreover, in rejecting the litigation, the government is seen to be colluding with the very oppressors whom it once struggled against. Thus, it appears to those who call for beneficiary responsibility [that] business and nation are neatly nestled together in a "co-operative and voluntary partnership" (Mbeki 2003: n.p.), embarking forward on a path of reconciliation that leaves little room for backward-looking obligations. On this view, beneficiaries need only continue with self-congratulatory acts, such as those articulated during the TRC business hearings, in order to contribute to the democratic evolution of South Africa.[28]

It is difficult to see how bonds of recognition that secure the commitment to prevent injustice can develop when this approach glosses over the very failure of beneficiaries to attend to cries of injustice. This approach is reinforced by the socioeconomic compromises of transition that enable continuities of privilege while allowing beneficiaries to claim a break with the past by merely condemning gross abuses committed by others. It is also reinforced by narratives of "healing the nation" that rely upon the stories of individual victims of torture and killing. The apartheid litigation, in contrast, insists that beneficiaries be held to account for their role in apartheid's violence, both everyday and extraordinary.

This advances a cosmopolitan re-membering of the nation. By cosmopolitan re-membering I mean, first, that the complaints function as an historical indictment, reiterating the findings of responsibility made by the TRC in its codicil report and with greater analytical detail.[29] In so doing, they confront insular views of the past, such as the story that only starts in the 1980s with businesses pressuring for the reform of apartheid. By pointing out the transnational nature of apartheid violence, which violated cosmopolitan rights and international principles, they urge the amendment of national memory.

Second, the litigation calls attention to neglected dimensions of victimhood. It challenges predominant conceptions of injustice by confronting the language of voluntary contributions toward nation-building, which implies that being black and poor is a misfortune rather than [recognizing that it is] tied at least in part to a history of racialized oppression and benefit. The class-action suits represent the millions of persons who suffered damages as a result of apartheid — in particular, its unfair and discriminatory labor practices.[30] Underlying these lawsuits is an insistence that reconciliation requires the involvement of apartheid's general victims (mostly black & Ntsebeza 2003: 349). Khulumani's Complaint, which narrows on individual victims of gross human rights violations, also spends considerable time outlining the systemic injustices of apartheid. It often implies that plaintiffs were injured in the course of resisting pass laws, forced removals, Bantu education, influx control, and poverty (Khulumani Statement of Complaint 2002: Paras. 174–223). On this accounting, gross abuses are the consequence of the crime of apartheid (whereas the TRC treats apartheid as merely the context). The crime of apartheid cannot be separated from the criminal means used to sustain it, and both, it is asserted, are violations of international law.

Going outside the nation to make these claims need not be seen as a foreign or alien intervention. It is, rather, a retrieval of an alternative account of national reconciliation that emphasizes reparative obligation based on historic wrongdoing rather than voluntary contributions in the name of a new patriotism. The alternative account secures the commitment to prevent injustice by explicitly acknowledging and repairing broken bonds, whereas the latter risks superficial reconciliation (see Nagy 2004b) because it elides notions of victimhood and responsibility altogether. We can only speculate whether the litigation would have been launched had businesses better responded to the TRC or had the government implemented all the TRC recommendations or embraced socioeconomic policy other than GEAR. What we do know is that the plaintiffs have made their claims as cosmopolitan citizens, with the support of a globalized civil society, from within the context of South African politics of reconciliation. The apartheid litigation is not simply a claim based on abstract right. It is rooted in and militates against a particular denial of injustice and how that denial has shaped the nation.

The third way that the apartheid litigation functions as a cosmopolitan re-membering of the nation pertains specifically to Khulumani's action. With avenues of satisfactory reparation seemingly cut off at home, the symbolic message of the lawsuit is that victims of gross abuses have had to turn outward for recognition and redress. The civil suit functions as a sharp rejoinder to a nation that has largely left victims to fend for themselves, despite their having been told otherwise during the TRC hearings. The claim for damages responds to basic needs, which, as noted above, Khulumani says will not be met by the once-off payment. Significantly, the Khulumani Support Group is itself a plaintiff, along with 85 individual victims of gross abuse. Khulumani positions its claim of injury on the basis of the marginalization of victims within the South African nation. It has borne the burden of providing direct medical assistance, psychological counselling, equipment such as wheelchairs, and educational assistance to its 32,700 members, many of whom were not identified by the TRC (Khulumani Statement of Complaint 2002: Para. 682). Khulumani's Complaint tells South Africans that the meaning of nation — and of equal belonging to that nation — rests, at minimum, upon the ability to properly attend to those who were often the most victimized under apartheid, those who are symbolic of apartheid's excesses and are the triumph of the "new" South Africa.

CONCLUSION: TOWARD A MORE COSMOPOLITAN NATION?

To a fair extent, then, cosmopolitanism and nation-building can be reconciled. By going outside the nation, plaintiffs remind South Africans of the spirit of the constitutional promises of truth, reparation, and reconciliation. The commitment to prevent cruelty — "never again" — is enacted through a call to acknowledge the victims of apartheid and to repair broken bonds of legal and moral responsibility. Victims seek to be recognized as human beings and, albeit more implicitly, as citizens whose lives matter. The class-action suits draw attention to the everyday violence of apartheid and invoke a conception of reconciliation that involves general victims and beneficiaries. Khulumani's suit makes clear that egregious abuses cannot be separated from systemic apartheid, and it functions to criticize the instrumental use of individual victims in "healing the nation." Themes of victims' exclusion and belonging arise in the indirect challenges of an economic policy that is seen as favoring beneficiaries and in indirect challenges to a reparations policy that is seen as treating victims of gross abuse like "third-class citizens" ("Apartheid victims 'treated like third-class citizens,'" *Mail & Guardian*, 1 Dec. 2003, n.p.).

The publicity and impact of the apartheid litigation in South Africa, while not necessarily as progressive as plaintiffs might hope, have succeeded in keeping salient the issues of reparation, beneficiary responsibility, and national reconciliation. Some, notably Anglican Archbishop Njongonkulu Ndungane and, to a lesser degree the government, have interpreted the litigation as a formal mechanism for lodging a grievance that ought to impel "national dialogue" ("Govt opposed to Apartheid Lawsuits," *Mail & Guardian*, 27 Aug. 2003; "Settle Reparations Claims with Dialogue, Anglicans says," *Mail & Guardian*, 10 April 2003, n.p.). In addition to solid media coverage, the lawsuits have spurred a large conference on reparation to which civil society, government, and business were invited (Civil Society Conference on Reparation, August 27, 2003, Randburg, South Africa; business representatives did not attend). Ndungane has attempted to organize roundtable talks between victims' groups and corporations, and he has urged South Africans to contribute to a national reparation fund. In the Brief of Amici Curiae that supports the appeal, Tutu and other TRC members state, "[b]y giving voice to those harmed by multinational corporations aiding and abetting apartheid, [the lawsuit] assists the healing and reconciliation process" (2005: 15–6).

The apartheid litigation, in other words, has from "outside" pushed the nation to better attend to victims. Not all extraterritorial legal action brought on behalf or of by victims will necessarily be new cosmopolitan in this sense, not unless they exhibit the rootedness or duality of the apartheid claims. Note also that there are some limits to the argument based on the South African case. Even if the appeals succeed and there is an official finding of beneficiary accountability for human rights violations, civil awards are not exactly the same as reparation. The forcible extraction of funds represents defendants' (continuing) denial. Civil damages may fulfill the compensatory and rehabilitative functions of reparation, but they do not satisfy the symbolic criteria of acknowledgment or apology.[31] Money without acknowledgment rings hollow, as seen in victims' and supporters' reactions to calling voluntary contributions *nation-building* rather than *reparation*. And to date there has been steadfast refusal of corporate beneficiaries to acknowledge responsibility, in part perhaps because this would now be an admission of liability. So in this symbolic regard, the alien tort claims may be counterproductive within South Africa. Then again, the lawsuits could contribute to the growing global culture of corporate accountability such that future collaboration in human rights violations is prohibitive. I suggest that in this respect the apartheid lawsuits offer South Africa an additional manner of bringing home cosmopolitan values.

There is some irony in Judge John E. Sprizzo's dismissal of the apartheid lawsuits. Part of his reasoning is that the International Convention on the Suppression and Punishment of the Crime of Apartheid is not binding international law because the United States, Great Britain, Germany, France, Canada, and Japan did not ratify it (*Re South African Apartheid Litigation* 2004: 29). So international complicity in the crime of apartheid in 1973 has a lasting effect some 30 years later. Judge Sprizzo's decision also places considerable weight on Maduna's affidavit. But the South African government, in avoiding the language of responsibility, misses an opportunity both to bring home and to send out a message that human rights violators will be held responsible for their actions. Acquiescing to the term *nation-building* rather than *reparations* not only risks superficial reconciliation. It also does little to arrest corporate complicity in human rights violations elsewhere in the world. Rather than taking a stance against corporate impunity, rather than taking a more cosmopolitan approach within the nation, it shows South Africa to be yet another safe haven.

In conclusion, the duality of cosmopolitanism is that all human beings matter morally, but the injunction to put cruelty first is grounded and realized in specific contexts. By attending to victims' cries of injustice, cosmopolitan re-membering affirms their equal belonging in concrete relationships of responsibility. While the commitment to never again repeat the past generally coincides with national processes, the new cosmopolitanism also claims that the bounds of belonging are reflexive constructions. The insistence denies that fact of transnational violence and benefit. It also undermines the "new" South Africa's commitment to human rights — a commitment, I might add, that bears international significance due to South Africa's prominence as a beacon of hope and model of stable transition. All in all, the cosmopolitan message of the apartheid litigation is that nation-building entails a commitment to acknowledging, redressing, and preventing injustice, which, for all its particularities, does not take place in a moral, territorial, or historical vacuum.